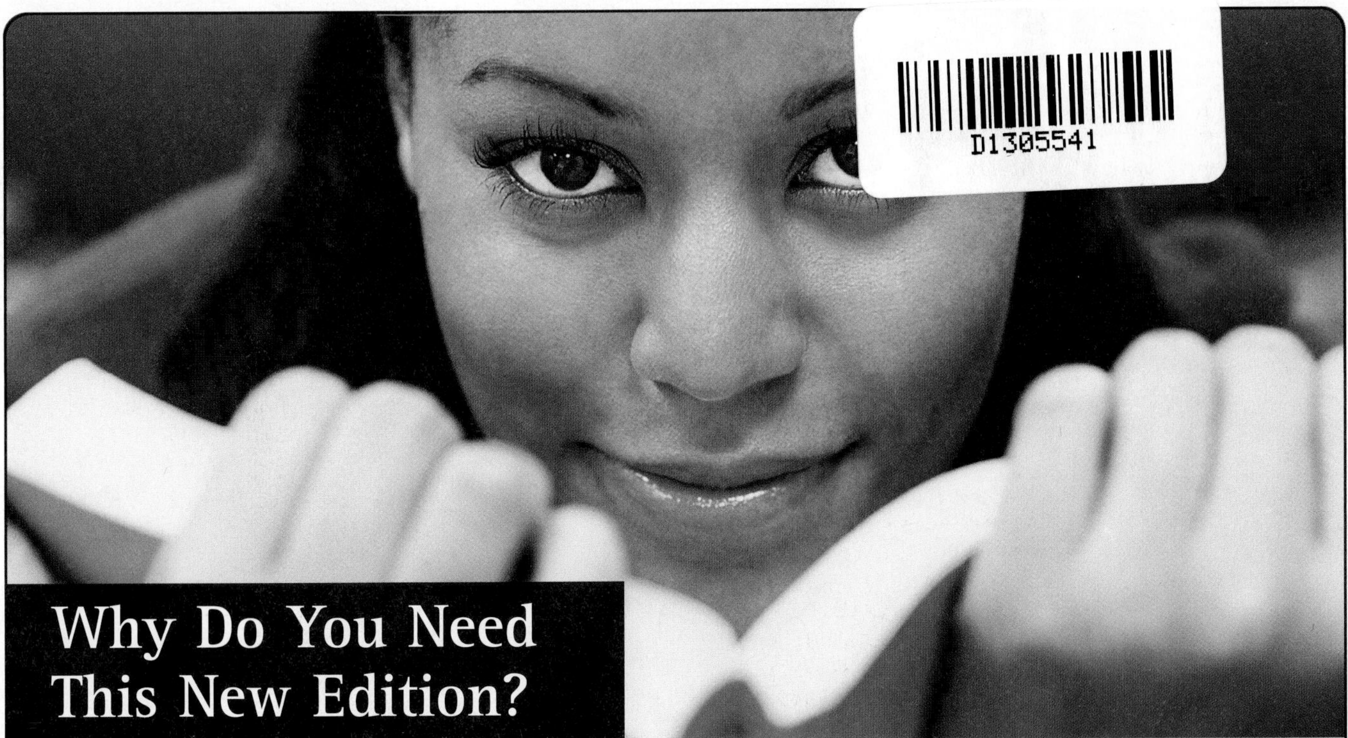

Why Do You Need This New Edition?

If you're wondering why you should buy this new edition of *Social Problems,* here are 9 good reasons!

1. **A major theme of this fourth edition** is "Constructing the Problem and Defining the Solution." You will discover how the claims people make about what issues should be defined as social problems and what policies should be applied as solutions reflect people's political attitudes.
2. **NEW! "Defining the Solution" end-of-chapter photo essays** provide real-life examples of how your political views guide you in finding solutions to social problems.
3. **NEW! An annotations program** written by the author appears on every page and provides useful student-oriented tips for "Making the Grade," "Seeing Social Problems in Everyday Life," and "Getting Involved."
4. **NEW! Key terms and definitions** appear at the top of the pages for easy review.
5. **NEW! Balloon annotations** have been added to figures and maps, offering quick, on-the-spot analysis of the data presented.
6. **Up to date!** More than 400 new research citations mean that this new edition has the latest statistical data and research findings.
7. **Current events integrated thoughout:** In-depth analysis of the recent recession and the greater government involvement in the economy under the Obama administration; updated coverage of health issues, including the AIDS epidemic, costs of health care, and proposals to extend health insurance to the U.S. population; analysis of the 2008 election results highlighting the increasing political power of women, the greater participation of young people, and the significance of the election of Barack Obama as this country's first African American president; updates on the rapidly changing status of same-sex marriage; discussion of the Madoff swindle and other financial scandals that helped trigger the recent economic crisis; focus on school choice and the results of the No Child Left Behind policy; updates on global warming, destruction of rain forests, recycling, and the growing strength of the environmental movement; and a new look at issues of war and terrorism in the world today.
8. **MySocLab** This interactive online solution for social problems combines multimedia, tutorials, video, audio, tests, and quizzes to enhance learning.
9. The inclusion of data from the 2010 Census throughout brings this edition thoroughly up-to-date.

SOCIAL PROBLEMS

Census Edition

Most of the readers of this book are among the world's privileged people—those who have enough to eat, a comfortable place to sleep, and who have the special opportunity to study the human condition. I offer this book in the hope that it will stimulate thinking about the state of our world as well as action toward making it a better place.

John J. Macionis

fourth edition

SOCIAL PROBLEMS

Census edition

JOHN J. MACIONIS

Kenyon College

Prentice Hall

Boston Columbus Indianapolis New York San Francisco Upper Saddle River
Amsterdam Cape Town Dubai London Madrid Milan Munich Paris Montreal Toronto
Delhi Mexico City Sao Paulo Sydney Hong Kong Seoul Singapore Taipei Tokyo

Editorial Director: Craig Campanella
Editor in Chief: Dickson Musslewhite
Publisher: Karen Hanson
Editorial Assistant: Christine Dore
Director of Marketing: Brandy Dawson
Executive Marketing Manager: Kelly May
Marketing Assistant: Janeli Bitor
Managing Editor: Maureen Richardson
Production Editor: Barbara Reilly and Patrick Cash-Peterson
Copy Editor: Bruce Emmer
Proofreaders: Donna Mulder, Louise Rothman
Supplements Edito: Mayda Bosco
Text Permissions Research: Margaret Gorenstein
Senior Operations Specialist: Sherry Lewis
Operations Specialist: Christina Amato
AV Production Project Manager: Maria Piper
Manager of Design Development: John Christiana
Art Director: Kathy Mrozek
Designer: Kenny Beck
Manager, Visual Research: Beth Brenzel
Photo Researcher: Rachel Lucas
Manager, Rights and Permissions: Zina Arabia
Image Permission Coordinator: Debra Hewitson
Manager, Cover Visual Research & Permissions: Karen Sanatar
Cover Art: Age Fotostock/SuperStock; Jim West/Alamy; Daymon Hartley/Alamy; Jeff Greenberg/Alamy
Media Director: Karen Scott
Senior Media Editor: Melanie MacFarlane
Lead Media Project Manager: Diane Lombardo
Composition: Nesbitt Graphics, Inc.
Printer/Binder: Courier Companies, Inc.
Cover Printer: Phoenix Color Corp.
Text Font: 10/12 Minion

Credits and acknowledgments borrowed from other sources and reproduced, with permission, in this textbook appear on appropriate page within text (or on pages 500–501).

Catalog-in-Publishing data unavailable at press time

10 9 8 7 6 5 4 3 2 1

Prentice Hall
is an imprint of

www.pearsonhighered.com

Student edition ISBN 10: 0-205-16491-9
ISBN 13: 978-0-205-16491-2

Brief Contents

Contents

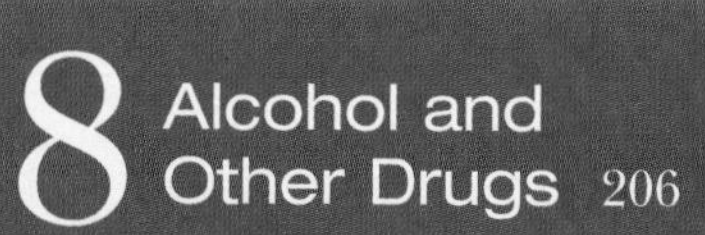

9 Physical and Mental Health 234

PART IV
Problems of Social Institutions

10 Economy and Politics 262

PART V
Global Problems

Maps

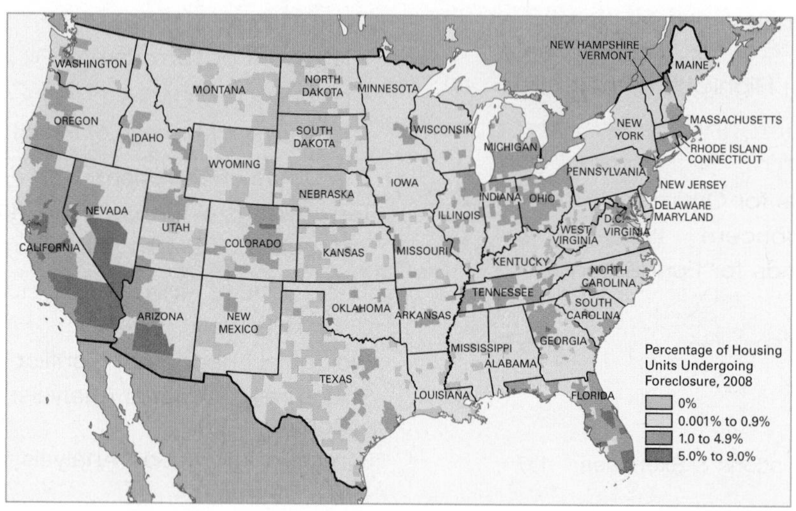

A Nation of Diversity

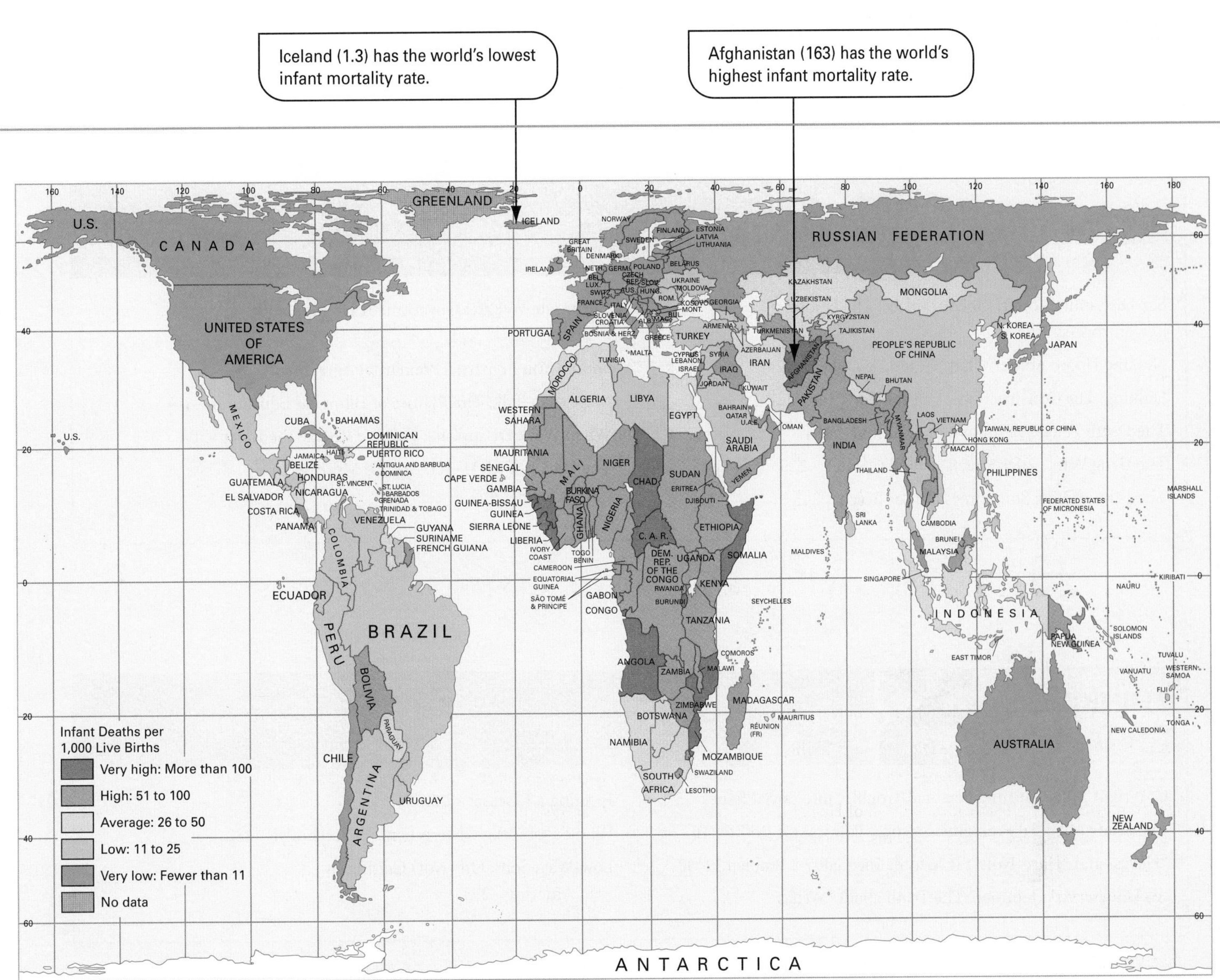

Iceland (1.3) has the world's lowest infant mortality rate.
Afghanistan (163) has the world's highest infant mortality rate.
Infant Deaths per 1,000 Live Births
Very high: More than 100
High: 51 to 100
Average: 26 to 50
Low: 11 to 25
Very low: Fewer than 11
No data
GREENLAND
ICELAND
CANADA
UNITED STATES OF AMERICA
MEXICO
BRAZIL
RUSSIAN FEDERATION
MONGOLIA
PEOPLE'S REPUBLIC OF CHINA
INDIA
AUSTRALIA
INDONESIA
ANTARCTICA

A World of Differences

Boxes

SOCIAL POLICY

THINKING CRITICALLY

DIVERSITY: RACE, CLASS, & GENDER

SOCIAL PROBLEMS IN GLOBAL PERSPECTIVE

PERSONAL STORIES

Preface

Are we living in the best of times or the worst of times? Certainly, compared to what people in the United States knew three or four generations ago, life has improved—we're living longer and, in many ways, better lives. At the same time, our nation slid into recession back in 2008, which put millions out of work and shook everyone's confidence in our economic system. In addition, economic inequality is at historically high levels and our country remains engaged in several military conflicts in a world where the number of nations with nuclear weapons continues to increase.

No wonder most people living in the United States say that our society is facing a lot of problems. Just as important, people claim that we are not doing enough to solve them. A majority of U.S. adults say we need to do more to not only improve the economy, but to control crime, deal with drug addiction, improve our schools, protect our health, make child care more widely available, and also to protect the planet's environment (NORC, 2008).

Dealing with these challenges is not just the job of our political leaders; it is the responsibility of all of us as citizens. It is also one of the central concerns of the discipline of sociology. This fourth edition of *Social Problems* is all about what the problems are and what should be done about them. This book makes all of today's issues and controversies come alive to students on campuses of colleges and universities across the country—only half of whom are registered to vote—but all of whom have a huge stake in the future of this country.

Connecting to Politics

One goal of this book is to connect readers with the political issues in the world around us. This is an important goal because *politics matters.* The candidates running for office in national elections represent a wide range of political positions—conservative and liberal and even radical positions—each of which envisions a distinctive type of society. Our responsibility as citizens is to learn more about political issues so that we can decide which vision is worthy of our support. Then we can become engaged in the political process by speaking out, volunteering in a campaign, offering financial support and, above all, voting.

Social Problems, Fourth Edition, helps readers become politically active citizens. But it does even more: *It explains what politics is all about.* Beginning with Chapter 1 ("Sociology: Studying Social Problems"), this text helps students understand the attitudes and values that define the conservative, liberal, radical left, and radical right positions on the political spectrum. In every chapter that follows, various political points of view are applied to dozens of issues—from wealth and poverty in the United States to terrorism and war around the world—empowering students to engage in politics and giving them the information and concepts to analyze tomorrow's issues on their own.

Politics involves several points of view. Just as there is no "up" without "down" and no "near" without "far," there is no "liberal" without "conservative" and no "middle of the road" without "radical." Throughout, this text presents multiple political positions. It is politically inclusive for four reasons.

1. **The text mirrors reality.** All political views—conservative and liberal, centrist and radical—are part of the political debate that plays out in cities and towns throughout the United States every day.
2. **Conviction comes from contrasts.** No one can formulate personal political beliefs with any conviction without understanding the arguments of those who disagree. In other words, to be, say, a good liberal, you need to understand not just liberal arguments but the conservative and radical positions as well.
3. **Politics is complex.** Anyone is likely to favor one position over others, but each position has something to teach us. A thoughtful person finds value in many political positions and may form attitudes that draw from them all, being more liberal on some issues and more conservative on others.
4. **Inclusiveness improves the classroom.** Finally, by presenting various political positions, this text invites all students to share their ideas and opinions, giving voice to all points of view and encouraging lively class discussion.

The Social-Constructionist Approach

When teaching the social problems course, the most important reason to use a text that "puts the politics in the problems" is that politics is the process by which society defines both social problems and their solutions. By including politics as well as sociological theory in every chapter, this text differs from all the others in a basic and exciting way. Other texts use a single point of view (whether explicit or implicit) that defines a list of "problems" and a list of "solutions," as if everyone agreed on what they are. By contrast, *Social Problems, Fourth Edition,* employs a multiperspective *social-constructionist approach.*

With this approach, *Social Problems* focuses attention on how and why certain issues come to be defined as problems in the first place. The text traces the emergence of social movements that led people to define issues such as gender inequality and domestic violence as social problems. The book also explains how specific events, such as the recent economic recession, can quickly push a new problem to the top of our national concerns.

One key benefit of the social-constructionist approach is that it helps students understand that there may be some issues that a society does not define as problems *even though they cause great harm*. For example, Chapter 8 ("Alcohol and Other Drugs") points out that the annual toll in the United States from cigarette smoking exceeds four hundred thousand deaths, a loss of life in a single year fifty times greater than caused by the September 11th terrorist attacks and Hurricane Katrina combined. Yet our society has not yet defined cigarette smoking as a serious social problem.

We see the same pattern in our nation's history. As Chapter 4 ("Gender Inequality") explains, a century ago, women had few rights and opportunities and lived as second-class citizens. But back then, few people considered women as equal to men. As a result, gender inequality was not widely defined as a social problem. Today, by contrast, our society has far greater gender equality. Yet because most people now believe that women and men should have the same rights and opportunities, the inequalities that remain (although much smaller) are widely defined as a problem in need of a solution.

Both in terms of competing claims today and changes in public attitudes over time, a social-constructionist approach is an effective strategy to teach students the importance of politics in the analysis of social problems.

Facts—and Theory, Too

Politics is not all there is to social problems. This fourth edition of *Social Problems* includes all the latest facts and complete theoretical analysis of today's issues and controversies.

In Chapter 2 ("Poverty and Wealth"), the analysis of poverty begins with the latest statistics: How many poor people are there? What categories of the population are at greatest risk of poverty? What do public opinion surveys reveal about attitudes toward poor people in the United States? A similar careful analysis of the latest facts and figures is found in every chapter of the text.

In addition, all chapters in *Social Problems* contain *theoretical analysis*, guided by the structural-functional, symbolic-interaction, and social-conflict approaches. Theoretical analysis helps students understand the society's role in creating and responding to poverty, gender inequality, crime, and other controversial issues. Including theory also allows this text to be used as an effective tool to teach introductory sociology.

This Text and MySocLab

This text offers many ways to learn because it is the heart of a complete learning package. Accompanying the textbook is a content-rich MySocLab that provides powerful support for learning and is provided at no additional cost to the student when packaged with a new text. MySocLab helps students to save time and improve results.

The textbook and MySocLab work together to make learning come alive. We invite you to make thorough use of them both. Visit www.mysoclab.com for more information.

The Organization of *Social Problems*

Part I of this book, **"Sociology's Basic Approach,"** introduces students to the discipline of sociology and to the study of social problems. **Chapter 1 ("Sociology: Studying Social Problems")** defines social problems and applies sociology's distinctive perspective to their study. It also presents sociology's commonly used methods for gathering facts and information and explains how to apply sociology's major theoretical approaches. In addition, this chapter explains the social construction of problems and solutions, highlighting the process of "claims making." The chapter explains the role of politics in this process, describes the political spectrum, and reveals what share of U.S. adults expresses support for each position.

Part II, "Problems of Social Inequality," examines issues linked to social stratification based on class, race, gender, and age. **Chapter 2 ("Poverty and Wealth")** explores the distribution of poverty and wealth in the United States, provides the latest data about economic inequality, profiles the rich and the poor, highlights the challenges faced by low-income people, and examines the welfare system, past and present. As in every chapter, conservative, liberal, and radical perspectives on economic inequality are included.

Chapter 3 ("Racial and Ethnic Inequality") tackles two other dimensions of inequality—race and ethnicity. This chapter explains how societies construct racial and ethnic categories, explains the concept of "minority" status, surveys the social standing of various racial and ethnic categories of the U.S. population, and investigates the causes and consequences of prejudice and discrimination.

Chapter 4 ("Gender Inequality") explains how societies construct gender; how gender guides the operation of the economy, the family, and other social institutions; the importance of gender as a dimension of social stratification; and the feminist movement in the United States, and it invites students to voice their opinions about all the political controversies involving gender.

Chapter 5 ("Aging and Inequality") spotlights inequality at different stages of life, explains how societies construct old age, examines the increasing share of older people in the United States, and provides both theoretical and political analyses of numerous issues linked to growing old, including social isolation, ageism, crime, poverty, poor housing, inadequate medical care, and facing up to the reality of death.

Part III, "Problems of Deviance, Conformity, and Well-Being," begins with **Chapter 6 ("Crime, Violence, and Criminal Justice")**, which explains how and why societies construct criminal law, how certain acts come to be defined as criminal, why some violence is defined as a problem and other violence is not, what official criminal statistics tell us (and don't tell us) about the extent of crime and violence, and who the "street criminals" are. The chapter analyzes various types of crime, including juvenile delinquency, hate crime, white-collar crime, corporate crime, organized crime, and victimless crime, and concludes by surveying the operation of the police, courts, and system of corrections. As always, analysis is built on both sociological theory and various political perspectives.

Chapter 7 ("Sexuality") explores sexuality as a biological process and, more importantly, as a vital element of human culture. The chapter then tackles political controversies surrounding sexual orientation, pornography, sexual harassment, prostitution, teenage pregnancy, abortion, and sexually transmitted diseases.

Chapter 8 ("Alcohol and Other Drugs") begins by defining the concept of "drugs" and examines how and why U.S. society endorses the use of some drugs while outlawing the use of others. The chapter surveys the extent of alcohol and other drug use; discusses the link between drug abuse and family life, homelessness, health, crime, and poverty; and concludes with theoretical and political analyses of drug abuse and policy responses.

Chapter 9 ("Physical and Mental Health") begins with a global survey of human health and health care policies, highlighting how societies define being healthy and how they fund health care. The chapter investigates the U.S. health care system with an eye toward who has care and who does not, surveys the challenges and policies relating to physical disabilities, and provides a brief overview of mental health and mental illness.

Part IV, "Problems of Social Institutions," begins with **Chapter 10 ("Economy and Politics")**, which investigates the economic and political systems by which societies distribute wealth and power. The chapter highlights the operation of corporations, examines the power of money to direct political life, covers the historic 2008 election, and offers theoretical and political analyses of the U.S. political economy.

Chapter 11 ("Work and the Workplace") explores how the economy has been changed by the Information Revolution, deindustrialization, and globalization. The chapter also identifies various workplace hazards, tracks unemployment during the recent economic downturn, and explores the experience of alienation and the rise of low-skill "McJobs" and temporary work. The chapter also discusses workplace barriers faced by women and other minorities and the decline of labor unions. As always, all the issues are given both theoretical and political analysis.

Chapter 12 ("Family Life") begins with a look at the changing definitions of what constitutes a family and then highlights all the current family trends and controversies, including cohabitation, delayed marriage, single parenting, work and family conflicts, child care, divorce, remarriage, gay and lesbian families, and new reproductive technology.

Chapter 13 ("Education") describes the development of formal schooling in the United States and surveys today's educational inequality. The chapter's theoretical and political analysis highlights the performance of U.S. schools, dropping out, illiteracy, racial segregation, unequal funding, tracking, violence, schooling people with disabilities, and challenges of schooling an increasingly diverse student population.

Chapter 14 ("Urban Life") begins by surveying the challenges faced by urbanites over the course of U.S. history and then tackles current issues, including fiscal problems of today's cities, urban sprawl, urban poverty, inadequate housing, urban homelessness, and the uneven growth of Snowbelt and Sunbelt cities.

Part V, "Global Problems," begins with **Chapter 15 ("Population and Global Inequality")**, which charts trends in fertility and mortality around the world and explains causes of the planet's continuing population increase. The chapter then explores global poverty and hunger, with a special focus on women and children, and documents the continued existence of slavery. Various theoretical and political perspectives assess the likely future of global inequality.

Chapter 16 ("Technology and the Environment") explores the emergence of the environment as a social problem. The chapter explains how technological advances, particular cultural values, and levels of consumption have created environmental challenges involving solid waste, inadequate fresh water, and air pollution and have diminished the rain forests and spurred global warming.

Finally, **Chapter 17 ("War and Terrorism")** presents causes and consequences of war, explores the changing nature of warfare over time, tracks the spread of nuclear weapons, discusses the use of children as soldiers around the world, and examines strategies for peace. The chapter provides theoretical and political analyses of terrorism as a new form of warfare.

What's New in the Fourth Edition

The fourth edition of *Social Problems* represents a major revision of the book and features numerous changes and additions. The most significant changes are listed here.

Rewriting for Clarity and Interest This revision has not simply been updated here and there. From front to back, it has been rewritten in order to make the material as clear as possible, to provide the newest examples and the latest data, and to boost reader interest.

A New Look *Social Problems* not only reads better but also looks better. Our design team has created a new look for the book that is more inviting than ever. Design is more than a matter of looks: The new design has been created to make reading easier and to encourage learning.

A Trimmer Text Do you want authors and publishers to look for ways to hold down the price? I hear you! This new edition of *Social Problems* is fifty pages shorter than last time around—without sacrificing content.

New Student Annotations On every page of each chapter, the author draws on his forty-year teaching experience to add notes to students to enhance their learning. These new annotations are of three types: ***Social Problems in Everyday Life*** notes help students see how issues affect their own lives; ***Getting Involved*** notes focus on activism and encourage students to think about ways they can become involved in today's political debates; ***Making the Grade*** notes help students assess their own understanding, point out sources of possible confusion, and highlight issues likely to be covered on exams.

New Instructor Annotations The text now includes additional teaching notes for instructors in the Annotated Instructor Edition. These notes include recent survey data, additional material highlighting diversity issues, insightful and sometimes humorous quotations, and suggestions for class discussion and exercises. Although these notes will be most widely use by new instructors, they are written to be enrich the classes of even the most seasoned teachers.

New "Defining the Solution" Photo Essays Each chapter in the new edition includes a photo essay that shows students at least two different ways to define solutions to social problems. Reflecting different points on the political spectrum, these photo essays encourage critical thinking about what values should guide our efforts to make our society a better place. In addition, four "Getting Involved: Applications & Exercises" suggest ways students can extend the learning beyond the chapter and beyond the classroom.

The Latest Statistical Data The fourth edition has been thoroughly updated from cover to cover. All the statistical data are new, and they are the latest available at the time of publication, including data for 2008 and 2009. Also included are all the results of the 2008 national elections.

The Latest Research Most instructors simply do not have the time to read all the sociological journals. By using *Social Problems, Fourth Edition,* students benefit from the latest research and developments in the field. This revision contains more than four hundred new research citations; a majority of the citations found in the text represent work published since 2005.

Updating in Every Chapter Finally, every chapter has new material. Here is a chapter-by-chapter listing of what's new in *Social Problems, Fourth Edition.*

Chapter 1: Sociology: Studying Social Problems A new chapter opening highlights the economic recession that got worse in 2008; updated discussion examples include the Madoff swindle and the plan to close the Guantanamo Bay detention facility by the Obama administration; there are new data on everything from the most serious social problems of 2008 to laws about drivers using handheld cell phones; the chapter has new student annotations, new instructor annotations, and a new end-of-chapter "defining solutions" photo essay that suggests various "solutions" to the current economic recession.

Chapter 2: Poverty and Wealth A new chapter opening uses the scandal over taxpayer-funded bonuses going to AIG executives to raise the larger question of the fairness of economic rewards in U.S. society; all the latest income and wealth data are found here, including the latest trends in economic inequality and the Obama administration changes in tax policy; numerous discussions include the recession that began in 2008 and its effects on poverty and unemployment; the chapter has the new student annotations, the new instructor annotations, and a new end-of-chapter "defining solutions" photo essay asks students to consider various "solutions" to our society's high level of economic inequality.

Chapter 3: Racial and Ethnic Inequality In the new chapter opening, a former president comments on our nation's history of racial inequality, leading to questions about the state of race relations today; all the data about the social standing of various racial and ethnic categories of the U.S. population have been updated to the latest available statistics; learn the latest about the English-only movement; a number of discussions include consideration of the significance of the election of Barack Obama as this country's first African American president; the chapter has the new student annotations, the new instructor annotations, and a new end-of-chapter "defining solutions" photo essay that focuses on how people respond to the current high level of immigration to the United States.

Chapter 4: Gender Inequality All the data in the chapter—including income and labor force participation—have been updated and are the latest available; the results of the 2008 national elections demonstrate the increasing political power of women in the United States; many discussions in the revised chapter have been rewritten not only for greater currency, but for great simplicity and clarity; the chapter has the new student annotations, the new instructor annotations, and a new end-of-chapter "defining solutions" photo essay that focuses on gender equality in college athletics.

Chapter 5: Aging and Inequality This chapter benefits from extensive rewriting to raise student interest; data on many topics and issues—from income to cases of abuse—have been updated with the latest statistics available; a new Defining Moment box highlights the creation of hospice by Cecily Saunders; the chapter has the new student annotations, the new instructor annotations, and a new end-of-chapter "defining solutions" photo essay that asks who should support us in our old age.

Chapter 6: Crime, Violence, and Criminal Justice A new chapter opening describes deadly violence in a Binghamton, New York, classroom for immigrants in 2009; there are new data throughout the chapter, including crime rates, profiling offenders, trends in hate crimes, and documenting the frequency of violence; this new combined chapter efficiently integrates the material that was in two separate chapters, helping to make this revision more than fifty pages shorter. Also, the chapter has the new student annotations, the new instructor annotations, and a new end-of-chapter "defining solutions" photo essay that considers various approaches to keeping crime in check.

Chapter 7: Sexuality The discussion of cultural variation in sexuality is expanded by describing the transsexual muxes (moo-shay) of central Mexico; the revised chapter contains the latest in the rapidly changing state of same-sex marriage; there is a new Constructing Problems & Defining Solutions box on Sweden's unique prostitution laws; public opinion data on issues such as pornography and abortion are now the latest available; the chapter has the new student annotations, the new instructor annotations, and a new end-of-chapter "defining solutions" photo essay that explores various ways to address sexual activity among young people.

Chapter 8: Alcohol and Other Drugs A new chapter opening describes the widespread use of drugs at a recent music concert, raising the point that drugs can be both a "solution" and a "problem"; there are statistical updates on the use and abuse of all the major categories of drugs and the latest on the steroids controversy in professional sports; included in the discussion of federal drug policy are changes by the Obama administration; there is new discussion of the sharp increase in drug-related violence in Mexico; the chapter has the new student annotations, the new instructor annotations, and a new end-of-chapter "defining solutions" photo essay that explores various policies on "soft drugs."

Chapter 9: Physical and Mental Health All the data on health issues are new or updated, including the AIDS epidemic, the costs of health care in the United States, and the plans by the Obama administration to extend health insurance to the U.S. population; the chapter has the new student annotations, the new instructor annotations, and a new end-of-chapter "defining solutions" photo essay on policy approaches to health care.

Chapter 10: Economy and Politics A new chapter opening asks students to consider what the election of Barack Obama suggests about how democratic the nation's political system is; the chapter includes discussion of the recent economic downturn as well as the greater government involvement in the U.S. economy under the Obama administration; the chapter has the new student annotations, the new instructor annotations, and a new end-of-chapter "defining solutions" photo essay on how the economy can best meet people's needs.

Chapter 11: Work and the Workplace The revised chapter updates all the latest statistics on employment and unemployment (most for 2009), reflecting the recession that began in 2008; there is a revised and expanded discussion of labor unions, including the "card check" controversy; the chapter has the new student annotations, the new instructor annotations, and a new end-of-chapter "defining solutions" photo essay that assesses the value of unions for workers.

Chapter 12: Family Life A new chapter-opening story tells of the recent divorce of an eight-year-old girl from her fifty-year-old husband in Saudi Arabia; data on all family forms and trends are updated to the latest available; the latest on the rapidly changing laws regarding same-sex marriage is included; the chapter has the new student annotations, the new instructor annotations, and a new "defining solutions" photo essay that examines how the mass media portray U.S. families.

Chapter 13: Education There is expanded discussion of the debate involving bilingual versus English-only schooling; all the statistics on education, including achievement scores, rates of dropping out, and patterns involving race, class, and gender have been updated; there is updated expanded discussion on school choice and the results of the No Child Left Behind policy; the chapter has the new student annotations, the new instructor annotations, and a new end-of-chapter "defining solutions" photo essay on how to improve public schools.

Chapter 14: Urban Life A new chapter opening describes how the recent economic recession threatens millions of people with the loss of their homes; there is more in the revised chapter on both housing and the economic downturn, including a new National Map showing the rate of housing foreclosures in counties across the country; the chapter now has the latest data on housing patterns, city populations, and homelessness; the chapter has the new student annotations, the new instructor annotations, and a new end-of-chapter "defining solutions" photo essay on urban renewal.

Chapter 15: Population and Global Inequality All the latest demographic trends in fertility, mortality, and population increase are included in the revised chapter; in addition, new data guide discussion of global stratification; there is a new figure showing the distribution of both global income and global wealth; the chapter has the new student annotations, the new instructor annotations, and a new end-of-chapter "defining solutions" photo essay that questions whether government should control a society's population size.

Chapter 16: Technology and the Environment The revised chapter has updates on all the data dealing with global warming, destruction of the rain forests, recycling, and the strength of the environmental movement; the chapter has the new student annotations, the new instructor annotations, and a new end-of-chapter "defining solutions" photo essay that explores whether new technology will "save" the planet's natural environment.

Chapter 17: War and Terrorism A new chapter opening highlights the importance of war and terrorism in today's political debates; a new discussion describes how the responsibility of military service falls heavily on working-class people; there is also a new section on the importance of the mass media in armed conflict and how they frame the events they report; the chapter has the new student annotations, the new instructor annotations, and a new end-of-chapter "defining solutions" photo essay on how young people might respond to military conflict in the world.

Established Features of *Social Problems*

Now in its fourth edition, *Social Problems* has become the most popular text of its kind. The book has achieved remarkable success based on a combination of features found in no other textbook:

A Writing Style Students Say They Love This text excites students, motivating them to *read the book*—even beyond their assignments. The best evidence of this comes from the students themselves. Here are recent e-mail comments from students and teachers about the author's texts:

> *Social Problems* is the best textbook that I have ever experienced. The students have commented that it reads like a *People* Magazine!
>
> You "made my day" with your speedy response and I will be sharing your comments with my class next session! It is such an honor to connect with someone who is really making such a contribution to education.
>
> I have just completed a class at my Georgia college using the book *Social Problems*. It is an incredibly written book. I enjoyed the various points of view you included within the chapters.
>
> I am using your *Social Problems* textbook for my sociology course. I have never had a better book. It's so easy to follow. The stories and extra highlights are very interesting and I love to read them. It's a great book!
>
> I'm a college student in California, and my sociology class used your book. It was by far the best textbook I have ever used. I actually liked to read it for pleasure as well as to study; anyway, I just wanted to say it was great.
>
> Thanks for writing such a brilliant book. It has sparked my sociological imagination. This was the first textbook that I have ever read completely and enjoyed. From the moment that I picked the book up, I started reading nonstop.
>
> I am a sociology major, and my department and I live by your textbook. I just wanted to tell you that writing it was definitely a stroke of genius. You did a great job. I appreciate the time and effort you put into the book, and I just wanted to let you know that you have touched a student across the United States.
>
> I have read four chapters ahead; it's like a good novel I can't put down! I just wanted to say thank you.
>
> I have been in college for three years now, and I have not found a book as remarkable and thought-provoking as your text.
>
> Your book is extremely well written and very interesting. I find myself reading it for pleasure, something I have never done with college texts. It is going to be the only collegiate textbook that I ever keep simply to read on my own. I am also thinking of picking up sociology as my minor due to the fact that I have enjoyed the class as well as the text so much. Your writing has my highest praise and utmost appreciation.
>
> I am taking a sociology class using your book, and I have told my professor it is the best textbook that I have ever seen, bar none. I've told her as well that I will be more than happy to take more sociology classes as long as there is a Macionis text to go with them.
>
> As an instructor, I can report that my students absolutely loved the *Social Problems* text. It is so readable, so clear, so colorful, so inviting. Their feedback made me glad I spent so much time choosing the best book for the course.
>
> Mr. Macionis, it meant the whole world to me that you personally wrote back. I don't know exactly how to tell you how much your work and love have put passion in my heart that I never knew was there. I have been completely overwhelmed by

> the power of your words and educational standards. Thank you once again for doing what you do and being who you are.
>
> I just want to tell you this is the best text I have ever used.
>
> I want to thank you for providing us with such a comprehensive, easy-to-read, and engaging book. . . . In fact, my instructor thought it was so interesting and well done, she read the book from cover to cover. Your work has been a great service to us all. My sociology book is the only textbook that I currently own that I actually enjoy reading.
>
> My sociology class used your book, and it was by far the best textbook I have ever used. I actually liked to read it for pleasure as well as to study. I just want to say it was great.
>
> I am fascinated by the contents of this textbook. In contrast to texts in my other classes, I actually enjoy the reading. Thank you for such a thought-provoking, well-written textbook.
>
> I am a student of nursing in Arizona. Once I began reading, I was enthralled. . . . You write in a way that conveys perfectly your excitement about the subject to us, the students. I wish you could be my instructor. Thank you for your work!
>
> Dude, your book *rocks!*

The Politics of Problems: The Social-Constructionist Approach Politics is the process by which a society debates and defines certain conditions as social problems and enacts specific policies as solutions. This text "puts the politics in the problems" by explaining the types of issues that people at various positions on the political spectrum are likely to view as problems and what policies they are likely to support as solutions.

Politics discussions are found in every chapter in a major section called "Politics: Constructing Problems and Defining Solutions." This section of each chapter applies the political perspectives of radicals, liberals, and conservatives to the topic at hand. Using multiple political perspectives is realistic and inclusive, adding breadth as well as depth to student understanding. By including multiple political perspectives, all students are encouraged to become part of the debate, developing their own positions and helping others to do the same. Each political analysis discussion ends with a "Left to Right" table that summarizes the way the various political perspectives construct problems and define solutions.

Theoretical Analysis of Problems in Every Chapter Just as the world of politics involves different ways of looking at issues and events, so the discipline of sociology uses different theoretical approaches to gain various insights about social arrangements. The chapters in *Social Problems, Fourth Edition,* apply three major theoretical approaches—the social-conflict, symbolic-interaction, and structural-functional approaches—to all the issues. Each theoretical analysis ends with an "Applying Theory" table that summarizes what each theoretical approach teaches us about the issues at hand.

Critical Thinking Made Easy As students learn to think about issues in different ways—both politically and theoretically—they engage in critical thinking. In addition, this text uses a number of teaching features to enhance critical-thinking skills. Right after each theoretical discussion, the text includes a "Critical Review" section that points up important contributions and limitations of each approach. In addition, all of the various theme boxes end with three "What Do You Think?" questions that encourage students to think through the issues in greater depth.

Finally, the captions that accompany many photographs and maps include questions that challenge students to actively engage the issues.

A Focus on Policy *Social Problems, Fourth Edition*, focuses on not only problems but also *solutions*. Therefore, a large part of every chapter of the text is devoted to social policy. In addition, the politics sections that conclude every chapter present and critically assess the policy approaches favored by liberals, radicals, and conservatives. Finally, a series of eleven "Social Policy" boxes provides multiple perspectives on many of today's important issues and controversies.

A National and Global Focus *Social Problems, Fourth Edition,* has a national focus but also places our society in global perspective. The reason for the national focus is that most instructors wish to make U.S. society the heart of the social problems course. The reason for placing our society in a global context is that looking internationally suggests other ways to define problems and solutions. For example, most other high-income countries consider poverty a more significant problem than we do here in the United States. Other nations also do more in terms of government policy to reduce economic inequality. Similarly, in the United States, prostitutes are subject to arrest; in Sweden, it is the "Johns" who pay for sex who face arrest. Making comparisons between countries sparks questions about why these differences exist and stimulates students to think about how a condition or policy many people in this country take for granted is defined very differently by people living someplace else.

An additional reason to include a global focus is that many issues are simply global in scope. Population increase, hunger, the state of the natural environment, war, and terrorism are issues that must be studied in a global context and that demand global responses.

Readers of this text will find information about not only the United States but also other countries in every chapter of this book. In addition, to help students learn more about the rest of the world, the chapters of this text contain "Social Problems in Global Perspective" theme boxes, "World of Differences" global maps, and "Dimensions of Difference" figures comparing the United States with other nations.

National and Global Maps *Social Problems, Fourth Edition,* includes thirty-two specially selected sociological maps that engage students as they convey important information. Seventeen "Nation of Diversity" national maps highlight the diversity of the United States with regard to the poverty rate, the geographic distribution of African American, Asian American, Hispanic American, and Arab American people, death row inmates, concealed weapon laws, cigarette smoking, voter apathy, teen pregnancy, risk of violent crime, divorce, air quality, housing foreclosures, and other issues of interest.

In addition, fifteen "World of Differences" global maps illustrate the planet's diversity with regard to the death penalty, life expectancy, infant mortality, Internet use, illiteracy, energy consumption, population growth, economic development, current military conflicts, and other issues of interest.

Boxes Highlighting Themes of the Text *Social Problems* includes fifty-one boxes (about three per chapter) that highlight important themes. These include "Thinking Critically" boxes, which help students assess arguments and form their own opinions; "Social Policy" boxes, which focus on controversial laws and public policies from different points of view; "Personal Stories" boxes, which describe social issues in terms of the personal life experiences of individuals; "Diversity: Race, Class & Gender" boxes, which highlight the importance of these dimensions of social stratification in various problems; and "Social Problems in Global Perspective" boxes, which offer international comparisons of important issues. In addition, the book features a series of "Defining Moment" boxes—one in each chapter—that highlights people and events that changed the way we look at specific social issues.

A Celebration of Social Diversity In its photographs, maps, boxes, and coverage of issues, this text reflects the social diversity of the United States and the larger world. The author has made a special effort to include the voices of all people—women and men, old and young, African American, Asian American, and those of Latino American, Arab American, and European heritage—and, of course, various political points of view. In addition, while recognizing that some categories of the U.S. population face many more challenges than others, this text is careful to avoid treating minority populations as "problems" in and of themselves.

Engaging Features That Enhance Learning This text provides a number of features that raise student interest and enhance learning. "Constructing the Problem" on the chapter-opening spread presents three facts about the subject in a catchy question/answer format illustrated by a photo. A chapter-opening vignette at the start of each chapter presents a real-world situation that generates interest and illustrates a major chapter theme. Questions and activities accompany every box in the text (other than "Defining Moment" boxes). At the end of each chapter are a number of helpful tools. "Making the Grade" contains a visual summary that highlights key arguments and helps students see the flow of the chapter material; accompanying this summary is a list of key concepts with clear definitions and page numbers (a full listing of these concepts appears in the Glossary at the end of the book). Sample test questions—in both multiple-choice and essay form—are included for each chapter in a special section at the end of the book. These questions are all written by the author and are similar to the questions found in the author-written Test Item File that is available to instructors. "Getting Involved: Applications & Exercises" includes four suggestions for applying the material found in the chapter, including easy and worthwhile learning projects.

Recent Research and the Latest Data All Macionis texts make this promise: You and your students will have the most up-to-date content possible. Current events that are familiar to students are used to illustrate important ideas throughout the book. All the statistical data are the most recent available. The author reviews dozens of scholarly journals, the popular press, as well as government publications and Web pages to ensure that this book stands at the cutting edge of current scholarship and political debate.

"Making the Grade" At the end of each chapter is the improved learning assessment tool "Making the Grade." First, a visual summary provides a clear overview of the chapter content and the flow of ideas in an engaging graphic presentation. Along with this, all the key concepts are listed with their definitions. In addition, in a new special section at the end of the text, students will find sample test questions, including multiple-choice questions (with answers) and essay questions.

A Word about Language

The commitment of this text to representing the social diversity of the United States and the world carries with it the responsibility to use language thoughtfully. In most cases, we prefer the terms *African American* and *person of color* to the word *black*. We use the terms *Latino* and *Hispanic* to refer to people of Spanish descent. Most tables and figures in the text refer to "Hispanics" because this is the term the U.S. Census Bureau uses when collecting statistical data about our population. Students should realize, however, that many individuals do not describe themselves using these terms. Although the terms "Hispanic," the masculine form "Latino," and the feminine form "Latina" are widely heard throughout the country, many people of Spanish descent identify more strongly with a particular ancestral nation, whether it be Argentina, Mexico, some other South or Central American country, or Spain or Portugal in Europe.

The same holds for Asian Americans and Arab Americans. Although these terms are a useful shorthand in sociological analysis, most people of Asian descent think of themselves in terms of a specific country of origin (say, Japan, the Philippines, Taiwan, or Vietnam), and most Arab Americans likewise identify with a specific nation (such as Libya, Egypt, Lebanon, or Syria).

In this text, the term "Native American" refers to all the inhabitants of the Americas (including the Hawaiian Islands) whose ancestors lived here prior to the arrival of Europeans. Here again, however, most people in this broad category identify with their historical society (for example, Cherokee, Hopi, or Zuni). The term "American Indian" designates only those Native Americans who live in the continental United States, not including Native peoples living in Alaska or Hawaii.

Learning to think globally also leads us to use language carefully. This text avoids the word "American"—which literally designates two continents—to refer to just the United States. For example, referring to this country, the term "U.S. economy" is more correct than "American economy." This convention may seem a small point, but it implies the significant recognition that we in this country represent only one society (albeit a very important one) in the Americas.

2010 Census Update Edition—Features fully updated data throughout the text–including all charts and graphs–to reflect the results of the 2010 Census.

A Short Introduction to the U.S. Census—A brief seven-chapter overview of the Census, including important information about the Constitutional mandate, research methods, who is affected by the Census, and how data is used. Additionally, the primer explores key contemporary topics such as race and ethnicity, the family, and poverty. The primer can be packaged at no additional cost, and is also available online in MySeachLab, as a part of MySocLab.

A Short Introduction to the U.S. Census Instructor's Manual with Test Bank—Includes explanations of what has been updated, in-class activities, homework activities, discussion questions for the primer, and test questions related to the primer.

MySocLab 2010 Census Update gives students the opportunity to explore 2010 Census methods and data and apply Census results in a dynamic interactive online environment. It includes a series of activities using 2010 Census results , video clips explaining and exploring the Census , primary source readings relevant to the Census, and an online version of *A Short Introduction to the U.S. Census*

Supplements

Instructor's Resource Manual (ISBN 020575970X) Revised by Naima Prince of Santa Fe College, this supplement offers resources that reinforce the focal point of the text—constructing social problems through the political spectrum and delivering solutions. Each chapter in the manual includes the following elements: What's New to This Chapter in the Fourth Edition; Chapter Outline; Teaching Objectives; Teaching Suggestions, Discussion Questions, Class Exercises/Demonstrations, and Student Projects; Essay Questions; Web Links; and a Video/Film List. Designed to make your lectures more effective and to save you preparation time, this extensive resource gathers together the most effective activities and strategies for teaching your Social Problems course.

Test Bank (ISBN 0205759688) Revised by John Macionis, this test bank includes approximately two thousand multiple-choice, short-answer, true/false, and essay questions. The test bank also includes a ready-made ten-item quiz for each chapter with an answer key for immediate use in class.

MyTest (ISBN 020575998X) This computerized software allows instructors to create their own personalized exams, to edit any or all of the existing test questions and to add new questions. Other special features of this program include random generation of test questions, creation of alternate versions of the same test, scrambling question sequence, and test preview before printing. For easy access, this software is available within the instructor section of the MySocLab for *Social Problems, Fourth Edition*, or at www.pearsonhighered.com.

PowerPoint Presentations (ISBN 0205759696) Informed by instructional and design theory, the PowerPoint presentations for *Social Problems, Fourth Edition,* will bring your class alive. You have the option in every chapter of choosing from any of the following types of slides: Lecture, Line Art, Clicker Response System, and/or Special Topics PowerPoints. The Lecture PowerPoint slides follow the chapter outline and feature images from the textbook integrated with the text. The Line Art PowerPoints feature all of the art, organized by chapter, available in a PowerPoint-ready format. The Clicker Response System allows you to get immediate feedback from your students regardless of class size. The Special Topics PowerPoint slides allow you to integrate rich supplementary material into your course with minimal preparation time. Additionally, all of the PowerPoints are uniquely designed to present concepts in a clear and succinct way. They are available to adopters at www.pearsonhighered.com.

Combining an e-book, video, audio, research support, practice tests, exams and more, MySocLab is a state-of-the-art interactive and instructive solution for the Social Problems course.

In Appreciation

Many talented and hardworking women and men have had a hand in this revision. At the top of the list are members of the Prentice Hall editorial, production, and marketing teams, including Yolanda de Rooy, division president; Dickson Musslewhite, editor-in-chief, and Karen Hanson, publisher in sociology. My thanks to you all for the many ways you have supported this book and ensured its high quality.

I offer thanks to Kathy Mrozek and Kenny Beck for providing the design of the book and to Maria Piper for drafting the line art. Photo research was provided by Rachel Lucas. Thanks are also due to Bruce Emmer for his skillful copyediting of the manuscript. Barbara Reilly, production editor, made an enormous contribution to this project, untangling language, checking facts, and helping make this book so attractive to the eye. She works with both care and enthusiasm. Special thanks to Kimberlee Klesner; we have worked together at Kenyon a long time, and now she has added her remarkable talents and energy to securing the very latest data for the text.

Kelly May, marketing manager, leads the marketing efforts for this book. Thank you, Kelly. And to all the sales managers and the sales representatives across the country, thank you for your faith in the book.

A Personal Note

This fourth edition of *Social Problems* has been written in the hope that it will stimulate a spirit of community and compassion that exists within each of us. Most of us are quite privileged. The greatest danger of privilege is that it makes us feel distant from those who have less than we do, as if the suffering of others takes nothing away from our own lives. We are all members of a single human community, just as we share membership in one universe struggling to find the moral direction that some people think of as God and others conceive in terms of Justice. Either way, the suffering of any one of us diminishes each one of us. Likewise, any thought or action that helps lift up another raises us up as well. Four centuries ago, the English poet and priest John Donne (1573–1631) beautifully expressed this idea when he wrote:

> No man is an island, entire of itself;
>
> Every man is a piece of the continent,
>
> A part of the main. . . .
>
> Any man's death diminishes me,
>
> Because I am involved in mankind.
>
> And therefore never send to know
>
> For whom the bell tolls;
>
> It tolls for thee.

A course in social problems is an invitation to become involved in the effort to make society better, a process that begins by recognizing that all of us—throughout the United States and around the world—are connected. Looking at others, we see reflections of ourselves; when we think of ourselves, we need to learn to take account of others. It is my sincere hope that this text will make a difference by encouraging readers to think about their connections to others, nudging people toward an ethic of service. Serving others is the most important and most worthy activity for any human being. It is a choice that can be made by anyone and everyone. In a sermon he gave in 1968, the Reverend Martin Luther King, Jr. put it this way:

> Everybody can be great, because everybody can serve. You don't have to have a college degree to serve. You don't have to make your subject and your verb agree to serve. You don't have to know about Plato and Aristotle to serve. You don't have to know Einstein's theory of relativity to serve. You don't have to know the second theory of thermal dynamics in physics to serve. You only need a heart full of grace, a soul generated by love, and you can be that servant.

With love for all and in the hope that each of us can make a difference,

John J. Macionis

Kenyon College, 2009

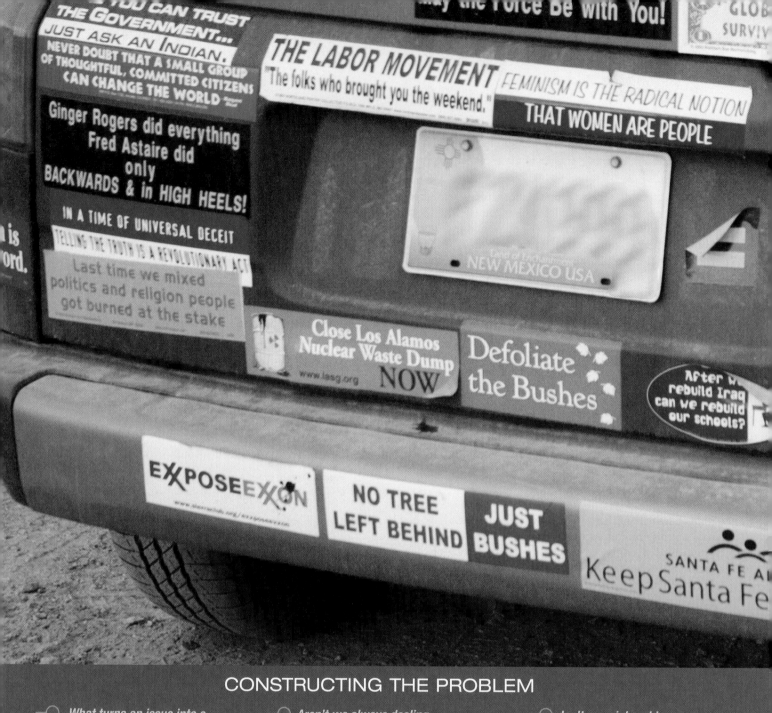

CONSTRUCTING THE PROBLEM

What turns an issue into a social problem?

Social problems come into being as people define an issue as harmful and in need of change.

Aren't we always dealing with the same problems?

Most of today's problems are not those that concerned the public several generations ago.

Isn't a social problem any condition that is harmful?

Many conditions harmful to thousands of people are never defined as social problems.

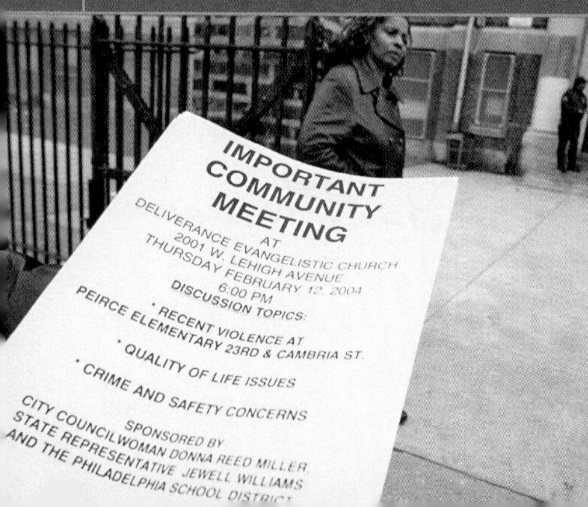

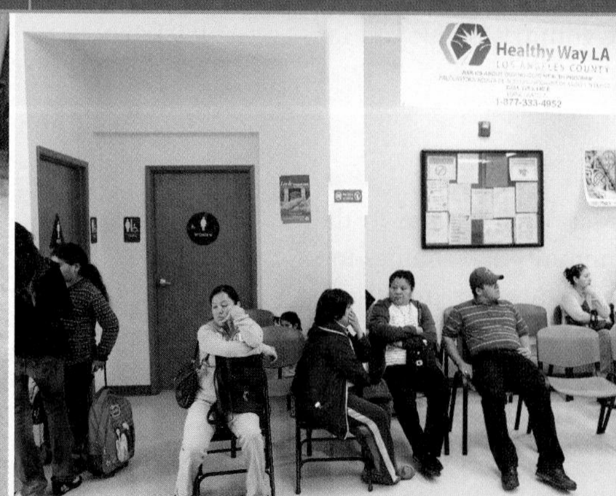

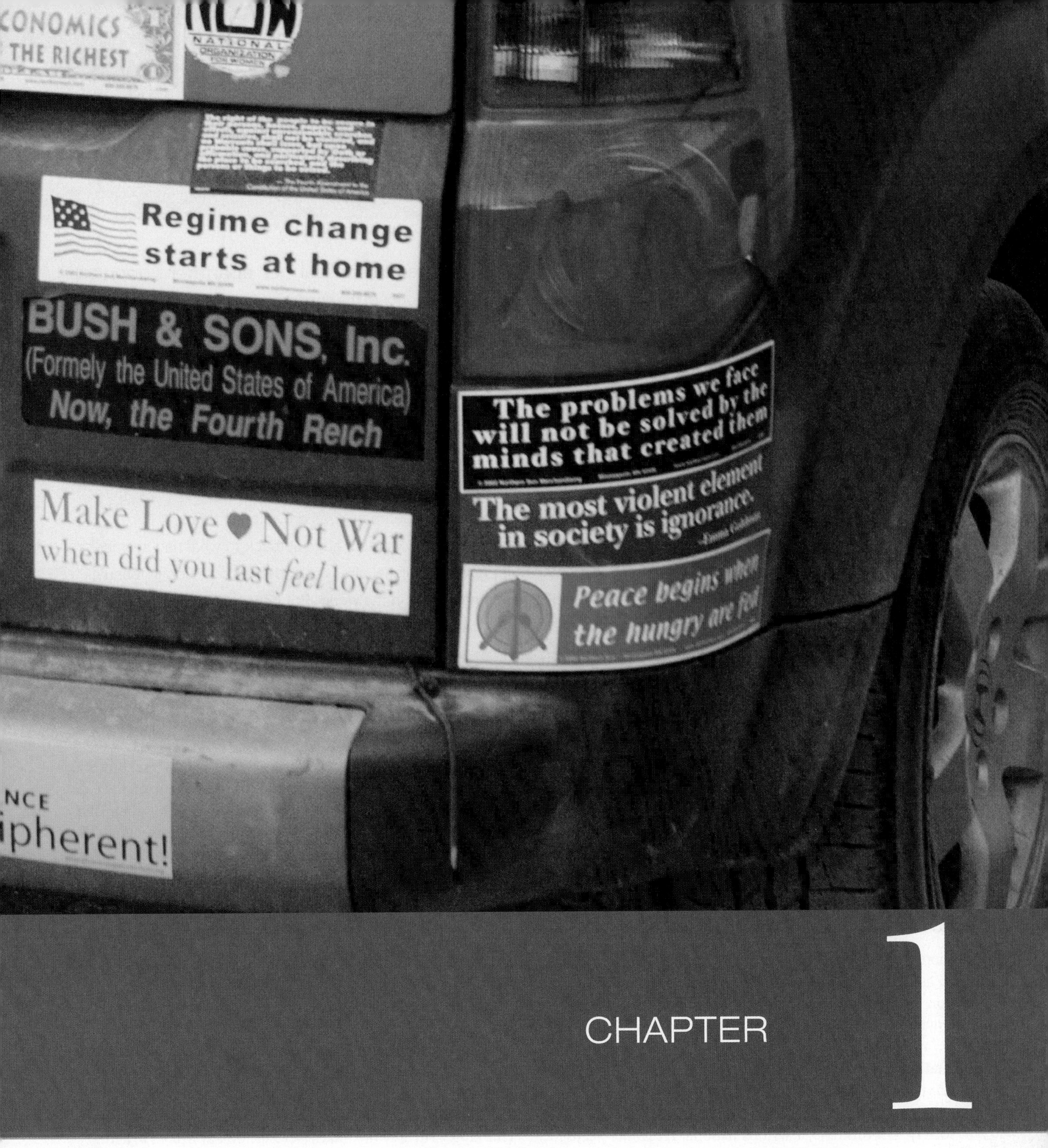

CHAPTER 1

Sociology: Studying Social Problems

CHAPTER OVERVIEW

THIS CHAPTER INTRODUCES THE STUDY of social problems by defining the sociological imagination, explaining sociology's theoretical approaches, and presenting sociological methods of research. You will learn how the claims people make about what issues should be defined as social problems and what policies should be applied as solutions reflect people's political attitudes. You will gain the ability to both describe and apply various positions on the political spectrum.

Michelle Jordan was already late as she rushed out her apartment door. She ran down the stairs and pulled open the old wooden door of the apartment building with her right arm, carrying her briefcase in her left hand. She glanced up the street. What luck! The bus was just half a block away. Catching her breath, Michelle climbed aboard as the door closed behind her and the bus slid back into the heavy rush hour traffic.

On the open seat was a copy of the *Times,* and Michelle began reading the front page. In an instant her heart stopped as she scanned the headline: *Lehman Brothers—her employer—was bankrupt!* Somehow, over the weekend, everything had come crashing down. One of the largest investment companies in the world had filed for bankruptcy protection. Citing losses resulting from its involvement in subprime housing mortgages, the company was drowning in debt.

Within a week, Michelle Jordan was out of a job. It was a huge setback to what had seemed like a success story. Within months of completing college, she had landed a dream job in Manhattan, at one of the largest and oldest investment firms in the world. But now, three years later, all that had changed. To make matters worse, no other banks or investment companies in New York (or elsewhere, for that matter) were hiring.

This story could be told millions of times, because millions of people—in jobs up and down Main Street across the country as well as on New York's Wall Street—lost their jobs during the recession that worsened throughout 2008 and into 2009.

Seeing Patterns: The Sociological Imagination

Common sense might lead us to think of one woman's losing her job as simple bad luck. Or perhaps we might think that the situation resulted from her choice to go into the sometimes unpredictable world of finance rather than finding a "secure" job as, say, a teacher. However, when we apply the **sociological imagination,** *a point of view that highlights how society affects the experiences we have and the choices we make,* the picture changes. Using the sociological imagination, we see that the operation of U.S. society—in this case, a serious national recession—caused the loss of millions of jobs. This event, which changed the lives of millions of people, can hardly be said to be a matter of bad personal choices; even less is it simply a matter of bad luck.

Sociology is *the systematic study of human societies.* **Society** refers to *people who live within some territory and share many patterns of behavior.* As sociologists study society, they pay attention to **culture,** *a way of life including widespread values (about what is good and bad), beliefs (about what is true), and behavior (what people do every day).*

Cultural patterns in the United States are diverse, but one widely shared value is the importance of individualism, the idea that for better or worse, people are responsible for their own lives. In the case of Michelle Jordan, it is easy to say, "Well, she lost her job because she got into the dangerous world of Wall Street; she really brought it on herself." In other words, our common sense often defines personal problems—even when the problems affect millions of people—as matters of *personal choice.* Without denying that individuals are sometimes lucky or unlucky and that people do make choices, sociologists point to ways in which society shapes our lives. Thinking sociologically, we see that widespread unemployment is not just a personal problem but also a *social issue.*

Sociology's key insight is that *many of the troubles people face have their roots in the operation of society.* As the U.S. sociologist C. Wright Mills (1916–1963) explained, using the sociological imagination helps us see how and why this is true. The Thinking Critically box takes a closer look at Mills's insight.

By asking us to look at the world in a new way, the sociological imagination gives us power to bring about change. But a sociological viewpoint can also be disturbing. A course in social problems asks us to face the fact that many people in our communities lose their jobs, become victims of crime, and go to bed hungry through no fault of their own. When the economy collapses, as it did in 2008, millions of people suddenly find that they are out of work. In this richest of nations—even during "good times"—tens of millions of people (especially women

society people who live within some territory and share many patterns of behavior

culture a way of life including widespread values (about what is good and bad), beliefs (about what is true), and behavior (what people do every day

sociology the systematic study of human societies

sociological imagination a point of view that highlights how society affects the experiences we have and the choices we make

THINKING CRITICALLY

C. Wright Mills: Turning Personal Troubles into Social Issues

All of us struggle with our own problems, which might include unemployment, falling into debt, marital conflict, drug or alcohol abuse, poor health, or even prostitution. We experience these problems; we *feel* them, sometimes on a gut-wrenching level. They are personal. But C. Wright Mills (1959) believed that the roots of such "personal" problems lie in society itself, often involving the ways our economic and political systems work. After all, the normal operation of our society favors some categories of people over others: the rich over the poor, white people over people of color, middle-aged people over the very young and the very old. When people see their problems as personal, they are likely to deal with their troubles individually. Doing this keeps them from seeing the bigger picture of how society operates. In the end, as Mills explained, people feel that "their lives are a series of traps. They sense that within their everyday worlds, they cannot overcome their troubles" (1959:3). Because we live in an individualistic culture, we are quick to conclude that the troubles we experience are simply our own fault.

A more accurate and more effective approach is to understand that it is society that shapes our lives. Using the sociological imagination transforms personal troubles into social issues by showing that these issues affect not only us but also countless people *like* us. This knowledge gives us power, because joining with others, we can improve our lives—and break free of our traps—as we set out to change society.

WHAT DO YOU THINK?

1. Provide three examples of personal problems that Mills would define as social issues.
2. To what extent do you think people in the United States think that problems such as unemployment result from bad personal choices or bad luck? Did this change during the recent recession? Explain.
3. Have you ever taken part in a movement seeking change? What was the movement trying to do? What were your reasons for joining?

and children) are poor. The study of social problems helps us see these truths more clearly. It also encourages us to play a part in shaping the future of our nation and the world.

Social Problems: The Basics

A **social problem** is *a condition that undermines the well-being of some or all members of a society and is usually a matter of public controversy*. According to this definition, "condition" refers to any situation that at least some people define as troublesome, such as having no job, lacking enough money, fearing crime, being overweight, or worrying about the effects of toxic wastes buried in the ground.

A condition that "undermines well-being" hurts people, either by causing them immediate harm or, perhaps, by limiting their choices. For example, poverty not only deprives people of nutritious food and safe housing but also takes away their dignity, leaving them passive and powerless.

Because any issue affects various segments of our population differently, a particular social problem is rarely harmful to *everyone*. As the economy slid in recent years, some executives ended up with huge bonuses and shared in government "bailout" money; some corporations (such as Wal-Mart, which sells at very low prices) actually did pretty well. Even war that brings death to young soldiers brings wealth to the companies that make and sell weapons and brings greater power to the military leaders who head our country's armed forces. As a result, the full consequences of any particular social problem are rarely simple or easy to understand.

Social problems spark public controversy. Sometimes a social problem (such as the suffering of tens of thousands of people—especially those with low incomes—in the aftermath of Hurricane Katrina) disturbs a significant number of people. In other cases (such as the outbreak of swine flu in Mexico and other regions of the world), a small number of significant people (researchers, public health officials, and government leaders) point out the problem and take action that affects the larger society (by, say, stockpiling vaccine and restricting travel to areas where infections have been reported).

Social Problems over Time

What are our country's most serious social problems? The answer depends on when you ask. As shown in Table 1–1 on page 4, the public's view of problems changes over time. A survey of U.S. adults in 1935 identified the ten biggest problems facing the country back then (Gallup, 1935), which we can compare to a similar survey completed in 2008 (Gallup, 2008). The Great Depression was the major concern in the mid-1930s because as much as 25 percent of U.S. adults were out of work. Not surprisingly, unemployment topped the list of problems that year. By the end of 2008, the worsening recession had pushed the Iraq War out of the number one spot to become the country's most serious social

social problem (p. 3) a condition that undermines the well-being of some or all members of a society and is usually a matter of public controversy

social-constructionist approach the assertion that social problems arise as people define conditions as undesirable and in need of change → **claims making** the process of convincing the public and important public officials that a particular issue or situation should be defined as a social problem

Table 1–1 Serious Social Problems, 1935 and 2008

1935	2008
1. Unemployment and a poor economy	1. The economy
2. Inefficient government	2. Unemployment
3. Danger of war	3. War in Iraq
4. High taxes	4. Lack of money
5. Government overinvolvement in business	5. Politicians, lack of leadership, and/or health care
6. Labor conflict	6. Ethical, moral, and religious decline
7. Poor farm conditions	7. Quality and cost of health care
8. Inadequate pensions for the elderly	8. Terrorism
9. High concentration of wealth	9. High federal budget deficit
10. Drinking alcohol	10. Environment and pollution

Sources: Gallup (1935, 2008).

problem. Notice that several of the other social problems named in 2008 as most serious also reflect the weak economy.

Comparing the two lists in the table, we find three issues on both: the economy, war, and bad government. But most of the issues are different, showing that social problems change over time. Of course, public opinion changes all the time: Between 2007 and the end of 2008, the Iraq War, illegal immigration, the rising price of gasoline, and the bad economy all topped the list of the nation's most serious social problems.

The Social-Constructionist Approach

The fact that people at different times define different issues as social problems points to the importance of the **social-constructionist approach,** *the assertion that social problems arise as people define conditions as undesirable and in need of change.* This approach states that social problems have a subjective foundation, reflecting people's judgments about their world. For example, even though health officials say that most adults in the United States are overweight, the public has yet to include obesity on the list of serious social problems. This is true despite the objective fact that illness brought on by obesity costs the lives of hundreds of thousands of people in our country each year, which is many times the number of our soldiers who have been killed in Iraq or Afghanistan.

Figure 1–1 explains the subjective and objective foundations of social problems. Box A includes issues—such as homicide—that are objectively very harmful (about 17,000 people are murdered each year in the United States) and cause widespread concern (polls show that a majority of U.S. adults worry about this kind of violent crime) (NORC, 2007). Box B includes issues—such as the use of automobiles—that, objectively speaking, cause even greater harm (about 40,000 people in the United States die each year in auto accidents), and yet hardly anyone sees them as a social problems. Of course, one reason people overlook the high death toll on our highways is that we think of automobiles as necessary to our way of life. Box C represents issues—such as school shootings—that, objectively speaking, cause relatively limited harm (only a few dozen people have died from such incidents, which is actually fewer than the number of people who die each year from bee stings), but these issues are widely viewed as serious problems all the same (Federal Bureau of Investigation, 2008; National Highway Traffic Safety Administration 2009). Finally, Box D includes the use of iPods and other issues that are not thought to be harmful and also are not considered a problem.

An issue can move from one box to another over time. For example, studies say that the use of cell phones by people driving automobiles causes more than 1 million accidents a year and costs several thousand lives (Cohen & Graham, 2003). For years, few claims were made that using cell phones while driving is a social problem (placing it in Box B). By 2009, however, six states (California, Connecticut, New Jersey, New York, Washington, and Oregon) had banned the practice, and more are considering such laws (suggesting a move to Box A) (Governors Highway Safety Association, 2009).

Other issues that are not considered a problem now may be viewed quite differently at some point in the future. For example, we may discover decades from now that the iPods so popular among young people will end up resulting in hearing loss (and perhaps high rates of auto accidents) among millions of people. Perhaps, too, we may come to see that iPods socially isolate people from their surroundings in ways that are harmful to them and to us all. Keep in mind that even potentially catastrophic trends such as global warming are now defined as a serious social problem by only a tiny share of the world's people.

Recognizing that the subjective and objective importance of social issues may not be the same opens the door for a deeper understanding of social change. Consider this curious pattern: A century ago, it was objectively true that the social standing of women was far below that of men. In 1900, nine out of ten adult men worked for income, and nine out of ten adult women stayed home doing housework and raising children. Women didn't even have the right to vote.

Although some people condemned what they saw as blatant inequality, most people did not define this situation as a problem. Why not? Most people believed that because women and men have some obvious biological differences, the two sexes must have different abilities. Thinking this way, it seemed natural for men to go out to earn a living while women—

SOCIAL PROBLEMS in Everyday Life

Looking at the 2008 column in Table 1–1, do you agree that these are the most serious social problems facing our nation? Are there problems you would add to this list? Are there any you would remove? Explain.

SOCIAL PROBLEMS in Everyday Life

Can you explain why even though the divorce rate is about ten times higher than it was a century ago, people are less likely to consider divorce a "problem"?

thought back then to be the "weaker sex"—stayed behind to manage the home. Objectively, gender inequality was huge; subjectively, however, it was rarely defined as a social problem.

Today, women and men are far closer to being socially equal than they were in 1900. Yet awareness of a "gender problem" in the United States has actually become greater. Why? Our cultural standards have changed, to the point that people now see the two sexes as mostly the same, and so we *expect* women and men to be socially equal. As a result, we perceive even small instances of gender inequality as a problem.

When we investigate social issues, it is important to consider both objective facts and subjective perceptions. Both play a part in the social construction of social problems.

Does it objectively cause serious harm to thousands of people?	Is it subjectively considered a very serious problem? Yes	No
Yes	A Homicide	B Use of automobiles
No	C School shootings	D Use of iPods

FIGURE 1–1 The Objective and Subjective Assessment of Social Issues

This figure shows that some issues (such as homicide) are both objectively harmful and widely seen as problems. But many issues that are objectively harmful (the use of automobiles results in more than 40,000 deaths each year) are not perceived as serious social problems. Likewise, some issues that are viewed as serious social problems (school shootings, for example) actually harm very few people. Many other issues (such as using iPods) do not now appear to be harmful, although this may change at some point in the future.

Claims Making

Back in 1981, the Centers for Disease Control and Prevention began to receive reports of a strange disease that was killing people. The victims were mostly homosexual men. The disease came to be known as AIDS (acquired immune deficiency syndrome). For several years, even as the numbers of cases in the United States climbed into the thousands, there was limited media coverage and little public outcry. By 1985, however, the public had become concerned about AIDS, and this disease was defined as a serious social problem.

What made this happen? For any condition to be defined as a social problem, people—usually a small number at first—make claims that the issue should be defined this way. In the case of AIDS, the gay community in large cities (notably San Francisco and New York) mobilized to spread information about the dangers posed by this deadly disease.

Claims making is *the process of convincing the public and important public officials that a particular issue or situation should be defined as a social problem.* Claims begin when people reject the status quo (Latin words meaning "the situation as it is"). The first step in claims making is to create controversy, beginning the process of change by convincing others that the existing situation is not acceptable. Claims making continues as people explain exactly *what* changes are needed and *why* they are needed.

Ordinary people can make claims more effectively by joining together. In 1980, women who had lost children in auto accidents caused by drunk drivers joined together to form MADD, Mothers Against Drunk Driving. This organization campaigned for tougher laws against drinking and driving in order to make the roads safer. In recent decades, students on college campuses have claimed that many women are victims of violence, trying to raise awareness by encouraging victims to speak out. This effort has been assisted by national organizations such as Take Back the Night.

The mass media are important to the process of claims making. Television, radio, newspapers, and the Internet can convey information to tens of millions of people and help mobilize individuals to form groups actively seeking change. The greater the media coverage of a topic and the more media stories argue for change, the more likely the issue in question is to develop into a social problem.

Success in claims making can occur quickly. After the economy went into a tailspin in 2008, government officials and the public quickly came to see the collapsing banking system and the rising unemployment rate as serious social problems. In other cases, the process may take years. As noted earlier, although experts estimate that driving while talking on handheld cellular telephones causes several thousand deaths every year, only six states have passed laws banning this practice (Governors Highway Safety Association, 2009).

As claims making gains public attention, it is likely to prompt counterclaims from opponents. In other words, most controversial issues involve claims making from at least two different positions. Take the abortion controversy, for example. One side of the debate claims that abortion is the wrongful killing of unborn babies. The other side claims that abortion is

social movement an organized effort at claims making that tries to shape the way people think about an issue in order to encourage or discourage social change

SOCIAL PROBLEMS in Everyday Life

What three social movements do you think have shaped our society the most? Explain your choices.

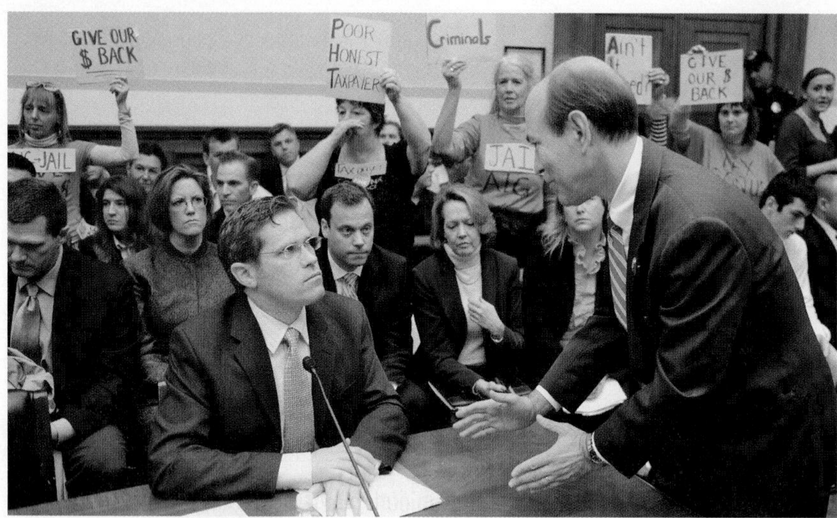

Claims making is the process of defining certain issues as social problems. After the federal government spent billions to bail out a number of financial corporations, many top executives paid themselves huge bonuses, stating at public meetings that the money was an incentive to keep talented people in their jobs. Many ordinary people who attended the meetings disagreed.

a woman's right, a reproductive choice that should be made only by the woman herself. Politics—how power plays out in a society—is usually a matter of claims and counterclaims about what should and should not be defined as social problems.

Success in claims making is often marked by the passing of a law. This act is a clear statement that some behavior is wrong, and it also enlists the power of government to oppose it. In recent decades, the passage of laws against stalking and sexual harassment clearly defined these behaviors as problems and allowed the criminal justice system to act against offenders (Welch, Dawson, & Nierobisz, 2002).

Problems and Social Movements

The process of claims making that turns a condition into a social problem almost always involves the efforts of many people working together. A **social movement** is *an organized effort at claims making that tries to shape the way people think about an issue in order to encourage or discourage social change.* Over the past several decades, social movements have played a key part in the construction of numerous social problems, including the AIDS epidemic, sexual harassment, family violence, and the Iraq War.

Stages in Social Movements

Typically, social movements progress through four distinct stages, shown in Figure 1–2, in their efforts to define a condition as a social problem (Blumer, 1969; Mauss, 1975; Tilly, 1978):

1. **Emergence.** The emergence of a movement occurs when people (initially just a few) come together sharing their concern about the status quo and begin to make claims about the need for change. In the 1960s, for example, environmental activists alerted the public to the fact that our way of life was harming the natural environment.
2. **Coalescence.** The coalescence of a movement occurs as a new organization begins holding rallies and demonstrations, making public its beliefs, and engaging in political lobbying. A major step in the environmental movement occurred in 1970 as people across the United States joined in celebrating the first Earth Day.
3. **Formalization.** Social movements become formalized as they become established players on the political scene. Although social movements usually begin with only volunteers, at this stage the organization is likely to include a trained and salaried staff. The environmental movement became formalized when the government created the Environmental Protection Agency (EPA) in 1970 to monitor compliance with new environmental laws.
4. **Decline.** Becoming established is no guarantee of continuing success. Social movements may decline because they run out of money, because their claims fail to catch on with the public, or because opposing organizations are more convincing than they are. In addition, organizations that succeed in reaching one goal often adopt additional goals and continue to operate. The feminist movement began with the goal of getting women the right to vote and moved on to improving the standing of women in the workplace and elsewhere. More recently, MADD has shifted its attention from combating drunken driving to the goal of opposing the movement that seeks to lower the drinking age from twenty-one to eighteen.

Social Problems: Eight Assertions

To complete our discussion of the basics about social problems, we need to say something about how sociologists define and analyze everyday issues. The following eight assertions describe how sociologists approach social problems. These statements sum up much of what has already been presented in this chapter, and they form the foundation for everything that follows in this text.

MAKING THE GRADE

Because problems are viewed subjectively, one person's problem may be another's solution. The discussion of politics (beginning on page 19) explains why this is the case.

GETTING INVOLVED

Can you think of an issue that you see differently than someone else in your family? Explain.

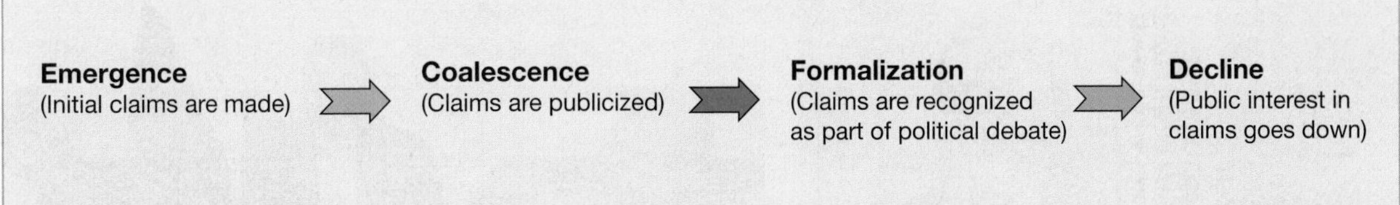

FIGURE 1–2 **Four Stages in the Life Course of a Social Movement**
Social movements typically pass through these four stages over time. How quickly this process unfolds varies from movement to movement.

1. **Social problems result from the ways in which society operates.** Society shapes the lives of each and every one of us. Because U.S. culture stresses individualism, we tend to think that people are responsible for their own lives. As C. Wright Mills (1959) pointed out, however, a sociological perspective shows us that social problems are caused less by personal failings than by the operation of society itself. For example, a problem such as poverty results less from the fact that some people may lack skills or may not try hard to get ahead than it does from the fact that our society distributes income very unequally and millions of people can find only low-paying jobs or no jobs at all. In other words, problems such as poverty have their roots in the way our economic and political systems operate. For this reason, correcting social problems requires change to society itself.
2. **Social problems are not caused by bad people.** This is the flipside of the first assertion. Especially when some individual harms a lot of innocent people—as when Bernard Madoff swindled investors, including charities, out of some $65 billion—we think of the problem in terms of bad actions by evil people. The law holds us individuals accountable for our actions.

   But in general, pointing to "bad people" does not go very far toward explaining social problems. It is true that, say, some people commit serious crimes that hurt others. But whether the crime rate is high or low depends not on individuals but on how society itself is organized. As Chapter 6 ("Crime, Violence, and the Criminal Justice System") explains, whether the economy is strong or not and whether all categories of people have access to good jobs or not go a long way toward explaining whether the crime rate is low or high.
3. **Problems are socially constructed as people define a condition as harmful and in need of change.** Whatever the objective facts of any situation, people must come to see the condition as a serious social problem. Claims making is the process of defining a condition as a social problem.
4. **People see problems differently.** Some issues, such as the soaring unemployment rate during 2009, are widely regarded as serious problems. But most issues are matters of controversy. For example, the Bush administration claimed that operating the detention facility at Guantánamo Bay in Cuba was important in controlling "enemy combatants" who are a threat to the United States. The Obama administration, however, is in the process of closing this facility, claiming that harsh treatment of prisoners violates our country's moral principles and only serves to encourage hostility toward the United States. As this example suggests, one person's "solution" may be another's "problem."
5. **Definitions of problems change over time.** The public's views on what constitutes a serious problem change as time goes on. A century ago, the United States was a much poorer nation where no one was surprised to find many people living in shacks in rural areas and many people living on the streets of large cities. But as living standards rose, members of our society began to think of safe housing as a basic right, and so bad housing and homelessness emerged as social problems. Going in the other direction, some problems of the past have largely gone away, not because the situations don't exist but because people no longer think of them as problems. For example, fifty years ago, most people defined interracial marriage as a social problem; this practice, however, raises far fewer eyebrows today.
6. **Problems involve subjective values as well as objective facts.** Today, more than three out of ten marriages end in divorce. But does this mean that there is a "divorce problem"? Facts are important, but so are subjective perceptions about any issue. People who value traditional families are likely to view a high divorce rate as a serious problem. But others who think family responsibilities limit the opportunities of individuals, especially women, may disagree.

GETTING INVOLVED

Can you list several social problems that have been solved? What about problems that you think may never be solved?

GETTING INVOLVED

Have you lived or traveled in another country? How does this experience help you better understand social problems, either abroad or at home?

Compared with women fifty years ago, women today are much more equal to men in terms of rights and opportunities. Yet today's women are more likely to see gender inequality as a problem. Can you explain this apparent contradiction?

7. **Many—but not all—social problems can be solved.** One good reason to study social problems is to improve society. Sociologists believe that many social problems can be reduced, if not eliminated entirely. Back in 1960, for example, 35 percent of elderly men and women in the United States lived below the poverty line. Since then, rising Social Security benefits and better employer pensions have reduced the poverty rate among seniors to less than one-third of what it used to be.

   But sociologists do not expect that every social problem will be solved. As already noted, situations that are problems for some people are advantageous to others, and sometimes those who benefit are powerful enough to slow the pace of change or to prevent change entirely.

   For example, in mid-2009, the United States remains the only industrial nation without a tax-funded system that helps pay for everyone's medical care. Although 46 million people lack health insurance, political opposition to government-funded universal health care by organizations representing physicians and insurance companies has been a powerful barrier to change.

   Even problems that everyone wants to solve sometimes defy solution. For instance, just about everyone hopes that we will find for a cure for AIDS. But the research breakthrough that finally cures this disease may lie years in the future.

8. **Various social problems are related.** Because social problems are rooted in the operation of society, many social problems are related to one another. This means that addressing one problem—say, reducing the number of children growing up in poverty—may in turn help solve other problems, such as the high rate of high school dropouts, drug abuse, and crime.

   It is also true that solving one problem may create a new problem that we did not expect. For example, the invention of the automobile in the late 1800s helped people move about more easily, but as decades went by automobiles were polluting the air and causing tens of thousands of traffic deaths (about 40,000 in 2008) every year.

These eight assertions will help you gain a sociological understanding of social problems. In the next section, we turn to another important idea: that addressing many social problems requires the use of a global perspective.

Beyond Our Borders: A Global Perspective

Many beginning students of sociology find it hard to imagine just how serious such problems as poverty and hunger are in poor regions of the world. To help you understand the seriousness of global problems, the Social Problems in Global Perspective box asks you to imagine the entire world as a village of 1,000 people.

Adopting a *global perspective* shows us, first, that some social problems cross national boundaries. For example, Chapter 15 ("Population and Global Inequality") explains that the problem of Earth's increasing human population threatens the well-being of everyone on the planet. Chapter 16

theory a statement of how and why specific facts are related

structural-functional approach a theoretical framework that sees society as a system of many interrelated parts

social institutions major spheres of social life, or societal subsystems, organized to meet a basic human need

MAKING THE GRADE

Sociology has three major theoretical approaches. Each gives its own view of what the "problems" are.

SOCIAL PROBLEMS IN GLOBAL PERSPECTIVE

The Global Village: Problems around the World

To see just how desperate the lives of many of the world's 6.7 billion people really are, imagine the entire planet reduced to the size of a "global village" of 1,000 people. The global village contains 604 Asians (including 198 citizens of the People's Republic of China), 145 Africans, 109 Europeans, 86 Latin Americans, 5 residents of Australia and the South Pacific, and 50 North Americans, 45 of them from the United States.

The village is a very rich place with a vast array of goods and services. Yet anything beyond the basics is too expensive for almost everyone. This is because of economic inequality: The richest 200 villagers (20 percent) earn 75 percent of all the income. By contrast, the worst-off 200 villagers (20 percent), earn just 3 percent of all income, which means that they *together* have less money than the richest *person* in the village. These people are hungry every day and lack even safe drinking water. Because of their deprivation, the poorest villagers have little energy to work and fall victim to life-threatening diseases.

Villagers boast of their fine schools, yet only 50 people (5 percent) have a college degree, and one-fifth of the village's adult population cannot read or write.

Many troubling issues such as health, illiteracy, and poverty are much worse elsewhere in the world than in a rich nation such as the United States. In fact, half the world's people have a standard of living far below what we in the United States consider "poor." This harsh reality of suffering—detailed in Chapter 15 ("Population and Global Inequality")—is one good reason to take a global perspective in our study of social problems.

WHAT DO YOU THINK?

1. Do any of the facts presented in this box surprise you? Which ones? Why?
2. As a person living in a rich nation, do you think you have a responsibility to help solve problems in poor nations? Why or why not?
3. Can you see ways that you, personally, benefit from the economic inequality of our world? Can you point to ways that you are harmed by inequality? Explain.

Sources: Calculations based on data from World Bank (2008), United Nations Development Programme (2008), and U.S. Census Bureau (2008).

("Technology and the Environment") offers another example, showing how people living in rich countries are consuming the planet's resources very quickly and polluting the planet's air and water.

Second, a global perspective shows that many dimensions of life—and many of lifes's challenges—may be quite different elsewhere. Global Map 1–1 on page 10 shows us that in rich countries such as the United States, the typical woman has one or two children. But in a poorer country such as India, three children is the norm. In even poorer nations, the number goes even higher: In Guatemala, four children is common, in Ethiopia, it's five, in Yemen, about six, and Niger, it's seven.

Analyzing Social Problems: Sociological Theory

Sociologists weave various facts into meaning using **theory,** *a statement of how and why specific facts are related.* Building a theory, in turn, depends on a **theoretical approach,** *a basic image of society that guides theory and research.* Using a particular theoretical approach leads sociologists to ask certain questions. The following sections present the discipline's three most widely used theoretical models: the structural-functional, social-conflict, and symbolic-interaction approaches.

The Structural-Functional Approach

The **structural-functional approach** is *a theoretical framework that sees society as a system of many interrelated parts.* Sociologists describe the main parts of this system as **social institutions,** *major spheres of social life, or societal subsystems, organized to meet a basic human need.* For example, the structural-functional approach might explore how the family is a system to ensure the care and raising of children, how schools provide young people with the skills they need for adult life, how the economy produces and distributes material goods, how the political system sets national goals and priorities, and how religion gives our lives purpose and meaning.

Early Functional Theory: Problems as Social Pathology

A century ago, the structural-functional approach looked on society as if it were a living organism. This view led to a *social pathology theory,* a model that treats social problems as a disruption in society's normal operation, in the same way that a disease upsets the operation of the human body. Crime, truancy, and premarital sex were all seen as pathologies (from a Greek word meaning "disease") that threatened the health of society.

What caused society to break down? Because early functionalists saw society as good and healthy, many were quick to

Cindy Rucker, 29 years old, recently took time off from her job in the New Orleans public school system to have her first child.

Although she is only 28 years old, Baktnizar Kahn has six children, a common pattern in Afghanistan.

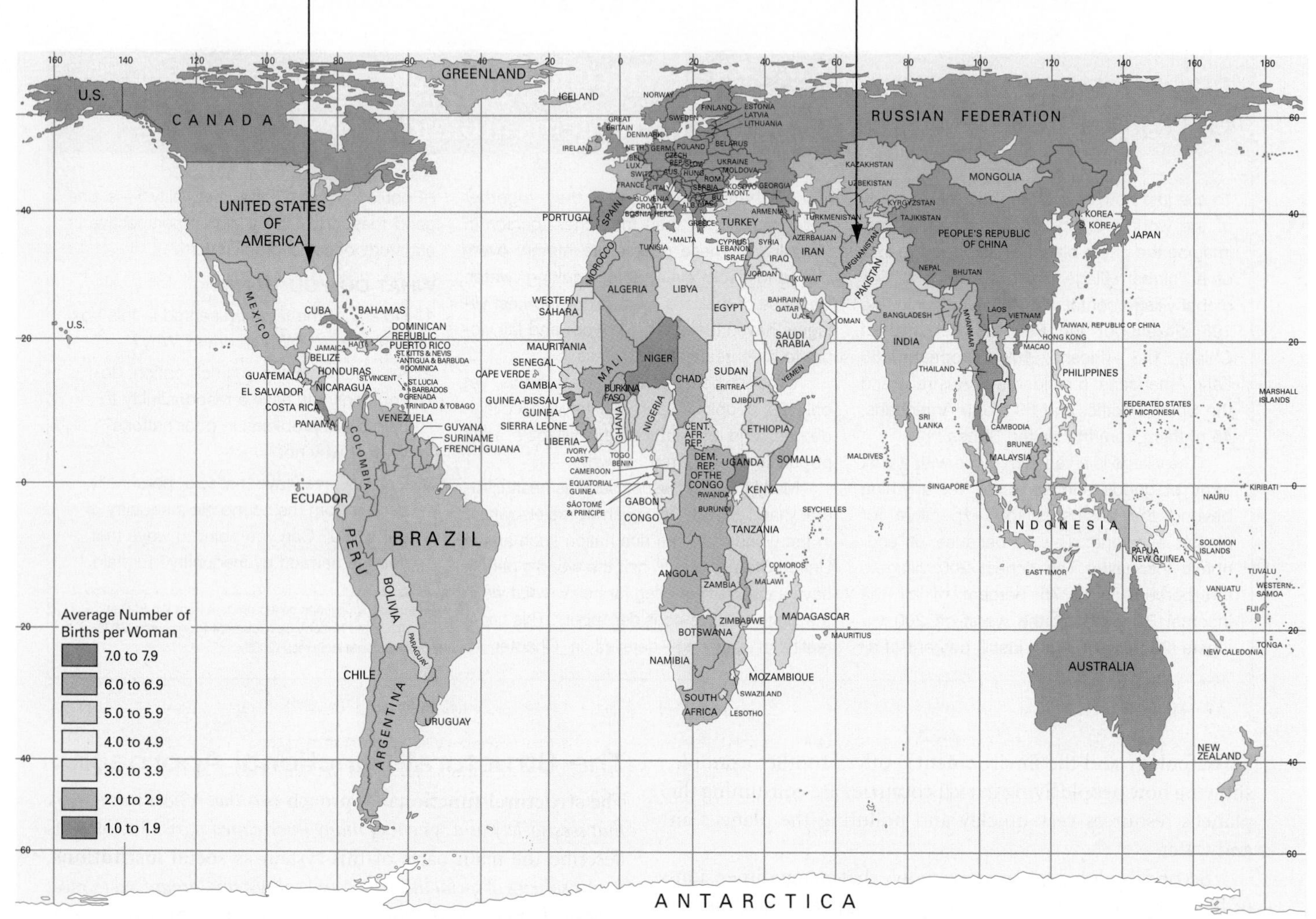

A World of Differences

GLOBAL MAP 1–1 Women's Childbearing around the World

How people live, and the challenges they face, differ dramatically around the world. If you are a woman living in a high-income nation, the chances are that you will have one or two children during your lifetme. But had you been born in one of the low-income nations of Africa, five, six, or even seven children would be the rule. Can you point to several reasons for this global disparity?

Source: Data from Martin et al. (2007). Population Reference Bureau (2007), United Nations Development Programme (2007). and Central Intelligence Agency (2008). Map projection from Peters Atlas of the Worrld (1990).

assume that pathologies must be caused by bad or weak people. The English sociologist Herbert Spencer (1820–1903) made the claim that the problem of poverty was the result of people's lacking the ability and personal discipline to work. Spencer based his thinking on the ideas of the biologist Charles Darwin, who published a groundbreaking theory of evolution in 1859. Spencer's "social Darwinism" viewed the rich as society's most successful members and the poor as those who could not keep up. To Spencer, the harsh competition of the marketplace was good for society because it guaranteed the "survival of the fittest." For this reason, Spencer opposed social welfare programs as harmful to society because they transfer wealth from the people he considered the most able to the ones he regarded as the weakest.

There is no surprise in the fact that Spencer was very popular among the rich factory owners of his day. But sociologists

Do you think society should be competitive, as Herbert Spencer claimed? Why or why not?

social-conflict approach is a theoretical framework that sees society as divided by inequality and conflict

gradually turned against Spencer because there is no scientific evidence that the rich and powerful are any more worthy than others or that a competitive economy benefits everyone. Social Darwinism has little support among sociologists today, although lots of people, including many politicians, still think this way.

The Chicago School: Problems as Disorganization

A second type of structural-functional theory—often called the Chicago School because it originated at the University of Chicago, home of the first sociology department in the United States—linked problems not to deficient people but to social "disorganization" (Park & Burgess, 1970, orig. 1921). *Social disorganization theory* holds that problems arise when society breaks down due to social change that occurs too rapidly.

A century ago, evidence of disorganization was easy to find as industrial cities grew rapidly with the arrival of millions of immigrants. Traditional neighborhoods and family patterns were both breaking down. Schools were filled to overflowing, there was not enough housing for everyone, and crime seemed to be rising out of control.

In response to such problems, many Chicago sociologists in the 1920s and 1930s became active reformers. They supported local settlement houses, set up programs to teach English to immigrants, and in a few cases even ran for public office (Faris, 1967).

More Recent Functionalism: Problems as Dysfunctions

By about 1950, the structural-functional approach had changed its emphasis from activism to scientific analysis. Sociologists then began to study both the positive functions (or *eufunctions*) of patterns like sports, pointing out functions that are intended and widely recognized (the *manifest functions*), and others that are unintended and less well known (called *latent functions*). A manifest function of sports is improving physical fitness; a latent function of sports is strengthening the cultural values of individual effort and personal achievement. Sociologists noted that social patterns also have negative functions (called *dysfunctions*). For example, one dysfunction of sports on the campus is leaving thousands of college athletes with little time for their studies. From this point of view, social problems can be thought of as the dysfunctions of various social patterns.

These sociologists also pointed out that just as "good" things such as sports can have some bad consequences, "bad" things such as terrorism can sometimes do some good. For example, the terrorist attacks of September 11, 2001, cost thousands of lives but also had the effect of uniting the country behind the effort to combat terrorism. Similarly, one good thing to come out of the recent recession is reminding people that most of us can live with less.

CRITICAL REVIEW Although the structural-functional approach has been influential for more than a century, its importance has declined in recent decades. For one thing, many of today's sociologists have a renewed interest in activism and shy away from a "hands-off" approach that they think defends the status quo. For another, by viewing society as a smoothly functioning system, the structural-functional approach pays little attention to social divisions based on race, class, and gender. Since the 1960s, more attention has been paid to a second theoretical framework: the social-conflict approach.

The Social-Conflict Approach

The **social-conflict approach** is *a theoretical framework that sees society as divided by inequality and conflict.* In general, conflict theories claim that social problems arise from the fact that our society is divided into "haves" and "have-nots."

Marxism: Problems and Class Conflict

Class conflict theory is an explanation of social problems guided by Karl Marx's theory of class struggle. Marx (1818–1883), a German-born thinker and social activist, was awed by how much the new industrial factories could produce. Yet Marx criticized society for concentrating most of this wealth in the hands of a few. How, he wondered, could a society so rich contain so many people who were so poor?

Marx devoted his life to analyzing *capitalism,* an economic system in which businesses are privately owned by people called *capitalists* who operate them for profit. The industrial technology of modern societies produces enough to meet everyone's needs; modern society therefore has the capacity to end human suffering. Yet, Marx observed, allowing this technology to operate under a capitalist economy means that only a few will benefit from the high productivity. Capitalism is not a system intended to meet human needs; it is a system that seeks profit—for the small share of the people who own factories and other productive property. As a result, the normal operation of the capitalist system creates social problems such as poverty.

Marx was critical of modern society, but he was also optimistic about the future. He predicted that capitalism would bring about its own destruction. Under this economic system, Marx concluded, the rich would become richer and richer, while the poor would have less and less. Industrial workers, whom he called *proletarians,* performed hard labor in factories for low wages while facing the threat that machines would take away their jobs.

MAKING THE GRADE

Marxism, multiculturalism, and feminism are all specific theories using a conflct approach.

feminism a political movement that seeks the social equality of women and men

The structural-functional approach points to the contribution that young people working in factories in Indonesia make to their families' income. The social-conflict approach provides a different insight: Many of the products popular in the United States are made by young people in sweatshops that pay pennies an hour to workers.

Marx was certain that with little hope for the future, workers would rise up, join together, and end this oppressive system.

As Chapter 2 ("Poverty and Wealth") explains, however, such a revolution has not yet happened, at least not in industrial-capitalist nations. But followers of Marx still support a radical restructuring of society as the best means to address most social problems.

Multiculturalism: Problems of Racial and Ethnic Inequality

Sociologists see conflict based not only on class but also on color and culture. Societies attach importance to skin color and cultural background in the process of ranking people in a hierarchy. *Multicultural theory* explains social problems in terms of racial and ethnic inequality.

The great social diversity of the United States and the rest of the Western Hemisphere is the result of centuries of immigration. Every person who lives anywhere in the Americas, from the northern reaches of Canada to the southern tip of Chile, either migrated here from someplace else or has an ancestor who did. Here in the United States, some categories of people (especially white Anglo-Saxon Protestants, or WASPs) have enjoyed higher social standing than others (especially people of color).

In 1865, the United States ended centuries of slavery, an important step in the process of giving people more equal standing before the law. Yet as Chapter 3 ("Racial and Ethnic Inequality") points out, minorities remain disadvantaged today, at higher risk of poverty, poor health, street violence, and numerous other social problems. In addition, racial and ethnic prejudice is great enough on the part of some people that they see the very presence of minorities in their communities as a social problem.

Feminism: Problems and Gender Conflict

Feminism is *a political movement that seeks the social equality of women and men.* Feminists claim that women suffer more from poverty and many other social problems because society places men in positions of power over women. *Gender conflict theory* explains social problems in terms of men's dominance over women.

Chapter 4 ("Gender Inequality") points out that although the social standing of women and men has become more equal during the past century, women working full time still earn just 77 percent as much as men do (U.S. Census Bureau, 2010). In recent decades, a rising share of the poor are women (especially single women) and their children. Just as important, from childhood to old age, women are subject to violence at the hands of men.

CRITICAL REVIEW Offering a striking contrast to the structural-functional view of society as a well-integrated system, various social-conflict approaches now dominate the study of social problems. But taking a social-conflict approach also has limitations.

Critics fault this approach for overstating the significance of social divisions. They point out that because members of our society have enjoyed a rising standard of living, few show interest in Marxist class revolution. Although there is still much to be done, progress has been real: Women, African Americans, and other minorities have far more opportunities than they did in the past.

A second criticism is that social-conflict analysis rejects scientific objectivity in favor of political activism, which calls into question the truth of some of its claims. Conflict theorists respond that their work is certainly political, but as they see it, so is any theoretical approach, including structural-functionalism. They add that functionalism escapes the criticism of being biased only because it supports the status quo.

A final criticism, which applies to both the structural-functional and social-conflict approaches, is that these macro-level approaches make use of broad generalities that

symbolic-interaction approach a theoretical framework that sees society as the product of individuals interacting with one another

MAKING THE GRADE

Both the structural-functional and social-conflict approaches have a macro-level focus on social structure. The symbolic-interaction approach has a micro-level focus on individuals in specific situations.

seem removed from how individuals actually experience their world. This concern has led to the development of a third theoretical model: the symbolic-interaction approach.

The Symbolic-Interaction Approach

The goal of describing society more in terms of how people experience the world underlies the **symbolic-interaction approach,** *a theoretical framework that sees society as the product of individuals interacting with one another.* We can apply this approach to social problems by asking two questions: How do people become involved in problematic behavior? And more generally, how do people come to define issues as social problems in the first place?

Learning Theory: Problems and the Social Environment

Why do young people in one neighborhood get into more trouble than those who live in another neighborhood? *Learning theory* claims that people learn troublesome attitudes and behaviors from others around them. The point here is that no one sets out to become a burglar, a Wall Street swindler, a drug abuser, or an industrial polluter; rather, people gradually engage in such behavior as they learn skills and attitudes from others.

A learning approach guided Nanette Davis (1980, 2000) in her study of thirty women working as prostitutes. Interviewing these women, Davis discovered that no one simply decides to sell sex. A woman might turn to such a life for any number of reasons, perhaps as a way to cope with loneliness or as a means of economic survival. Whatever the reason, Davis found, the women she studied gradually "drifted" toward prostitution, usually taking years to learn the skills, norms, and attitudes that characterize the professional sex worker. In short, people learn such roles a little at a time, eventually reaching the point where the role becomes their livelihood as well as part of their social identity.

Labeling Theory: Problems and Social Definitions

The symbolic-interaction approach also explores how people socially construct reality. *Labeling theory* states that the reality of any particular situation depends on how people define it. For example, the spirited consumption of alcohol that young people view as normal partying may be labeled by college officials as dangerous binge drinking.

The distinction between a "social drinker" and a "problem drinker" often depends on which audience is watching (do parents view drinking the same way that friends do?), who the actor is (do we view men who drink the same as we view women who do?), where the action takes place (is drinking in a park the same as drinking at a bar?), and when the action occurs (is drinking on Saturday night more acceptable than drinking on Sunday morning?). Obviously, many factors come into play as a people socially define a given situation.

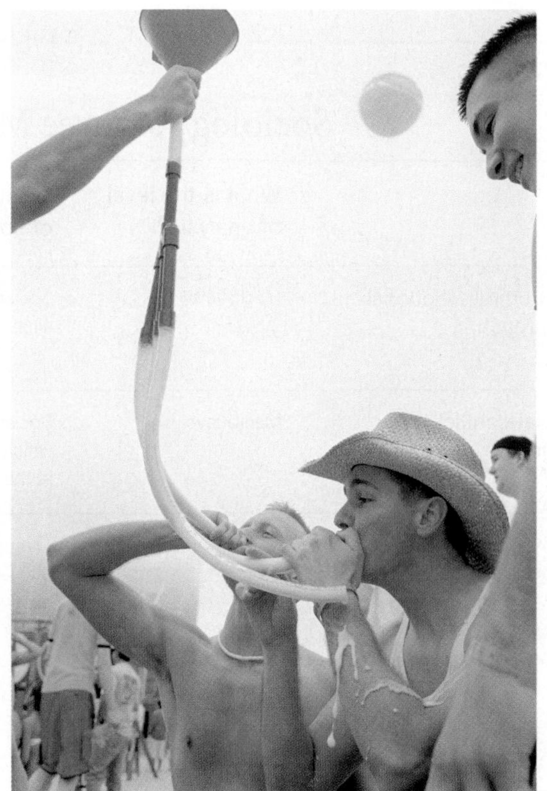

Reality is often less a matter of what people do than of how they define their own behavior. Studies show that many college students consume large amounts of alcohol on a regular basis. To these students, drinking heavily may just be "partying." College officials, however, may define such behavior as "binge drinking" or "alcohol abuse," which can result in serious penalties.

CRITICAL REVIEW The symbolic-interaction approach adds a micro-level or "real-world" view of social problems. But by highlighting how individuals differ in their perceptions, this approach overlooks the extent to which social structure, including class and race, shapes people's lives. In other words, pointing out that prostitution involves both learning and labeling is worthwhile, but we don't want to forget the broader issue that men dominate society and cast women into sexual roles in the first place.

This completes the introduction to the three basic theoretical approaches, summarized in the Applying Theory table on page 14. But not only do sociologists use theory to analyze social problems, they also engage in research to gather relevant facts. We turn next to the ways in which sociologists conduct research.

MAKING THE GRADE

Applying Theory tables let you review theory and assess your understanding.

GETTING INVOLVED

Are there places or activities in your life that you might be able to understand better by doing a survey or field study? What are they?

APPLYING THEORY

Sociology's Three Major Theoretical Approaches

	What is the level of analysis?	What is the basic image of society?	How do we understand problems?
Structural-functional approach	Macro-level	Society is a system of interrelated parts, all of which contribute to its operation.	Society is basically good; problems are the result of deficient people, too rapid change, or dysfunctional consequences.
Social-conflict approach	Macro-level	Society is a system of social inequality in which some categories of people benefit at the expense of others.	Problems result from inequality in terms of class (Marxism), race (multiculturalism), or gender (feminism).
Symbolic-interaction approach	Micro-level	Through social interaction, we construct the variable and changing reality we experience.	People learn attitudes and behavior for all patterns of behavior; this approach explores how people may or may not define situations as problems.

Finding the Facts: Sociological Research

Many sociologists devote their lives to investigating the nature and causes of social problems in the hope of making the world a better place. Barbara Ehrenreich (2001), for example, spent weeks working alongside low-wage workers in Florida, Maine, and Minnesota, documenting the many challenges faced by this country's "working poor." The willingness to work hard, she found, is sometimes not enough to escape poverty, as millions of people throughout the United States know all too well.

The sociologist Lois Benjamin (1991) investigated the problem of racial prejudice. Is prejudice directed only at poor people, or are successful people also victimized in this way? After interviewing 100 of the most successful African American men and women in the United States, Benjamin concluded that success provides no escape from prejudice. Even black people at the top of their fields encounter racial hostility in their daily lives.

William Julius Wilson (1996a) conducted interviews and examined available data in a major study of poor people living in Chicago. He found that people who have lived in poverty for many years contend with a host of social problems, including joblessness, unstable families, and perhaps worst of all, a loss of hope. Wilson found that the major reason for this poverty is the disappearance of good jobs from Chicago's inner city.

These are just a few examples of the research being done by thousands of sociologists across the country. The following sections provide a brief description of the research methods used by Ehrenreich, Benjamin, Wilson, and many others to study social problems—and to make the world a better place.

Research Methods

Sociologists use four major research methods in their investigation of social problems: surveys, field research, experimental research, and secondary analysis.

Survey Research: Asking Questions

The most widely used research procedure is the **survey**, *a research method in which subjects respond to items on a questionnaire or in an interview.* A *questionnaire* is a series of items a researcher presents to subjects for their response. Researchers may deliver questionnaires in person, send them through the mail, or use e-mail.

However you contact the subjects, the success of a project often depends on your ability to locate the people you want to survey. If you are studying, say, homeless people, identifying and tracking down subjects may be difficult because many have no stable addresses. Alternatively, it would not be hard for researchers studying the medical system from the patient's point of view to find sick people in hospitals, but gaining access to them and getting them to complete a questionnaire may be challenging.

Research Methods

survey a research method in which subjects respond to items on a questionnaire or in an interview

field research (participant observation) a research method for observing people while joining them in their everyday activities

experiment a research method for investigating cause-and-effect relationships under tightly controlled conditions

secondary analysis a research method that makes use of data originally collected by others

The *interview* is a more personal survey technique in which a researcher meets face to face with respondents to discuss some issue. This interactive format allows an investigator to probe people's opinions with follow-up questions. Interviews take a lot of time, of course, which usually limits the number of people one can survey in this way. A good way to think about surveys is this: Questionnaires offer the chance for greater *breadth* of opinion, and interviews can provide greater *depth* of understanding.

Whether you use a questionnaire or an interview format, the key to a successful survey is selecting a sample of people that represents the larger population of interest. For example, researchers try to reach conclusions about all the police officers in a city by studying only a small number of them. To make a sample representative of the larger population, researchers typically use various techniques to select subjects randomly.

Sometimes, researchers pursue a *case study,* in which they focus on a single case: a person (say, a divorced mother), an organization (a college or a gambling casino), or an event (a rock concert or a hurricane). The advantage of this approach is that focusing on a single case allows greater detail and depth of understanding. However, because this strategy involves a single case, the researchers are not able to generalize their results.

Field Research: Joining In

Have you ever walked through an unfamiliar neighborhood and observed the people who lived there? If so, you have some experience with **field research** (also called **participant observation**), *a research method for observing people while joining them in their everyday activities.* Field research might mean investigating a particular community to understand the problems and hopes of the people who live there. Elijah Anderson (1999) did this when he studied families in some of Philadelphia's poor African American neighborhoods. Anderson discovered that although most people in these neighborhoods had "decent" values, some had come to accept what Anderson calls the "code of the streets." Such people were likely to have weak family ties, to use drugs, and especially if they were males, to engage in episodes of violence in an effort to defend themselves and to maintain the respect of others.

Field studies involve a number of challenges. For example, the researcher benefits from observing people in their natural surroundings, but as Anderson's work suggests, fieldwork can be dangerous, especially to a researcher working alone. In addition, although this method makes sense for researchers with little money, it requires a lot of time, often a year or more. Finally, field researchers often have to balance the demands of being a *participant,* who is personally involved in the setting, with those of an *observer,* who adopts a more detached role in order to assess a setting or situation more objectively.

Experimental Research: Looking for Causes

Why are this country's prisons so violent? Philip Zimbardo and his colleagues investigated this question using an **experiment,** *a research method for investigating cause-and-effect relationships under tightly controlled conditions.* Unlike field research, which takes place almost anywhere in the "real world," most experiments are carried out in a specially designed laboratory. There, researchers change one variable while keeping the others the same. Comparing results allows them to identify specific causes of certain patterns of behavior.

To investigate the causes of jailhouse violence, Zimbardo built an artificial prison in a basement at Stanford University. He recruited male volunteers from among the university's students and then assigned the most physically and mentally healthy subjects to the roles of inmates and guards. After the "prison" had been in operation for just a few days, Zimbardo was alarmed to see that on both sides of the bars, people performing their assigned roles were becoming hostile and violent. In fact, the aggression was so great that Zimbardo had to end the research for fear that someone would get seriously hurt.

Zimbardo's research highlights the responsibility researchers have for the safety and well-being of their subjects. His study also points to a fascinating conclusion: The prison system itself—not any personal problems on the part of inmates or guards—can trigger prison violence (Zimbardo, 1972; Haney, Banks, & Zimbardo, 1973).

Secondary Analysis: Using Available Data

Sometimes all that is needed to study social problems is a trip to the local library. Easier still is going online, where a vast amount of sociological information can be found. **Secondary analysis** is *a research method that makes use of data originally collected by others.* In simple terms, why go to the trouble and expense of collecting information for yourself if suitable data already exist?

Just because data are easy to find does not mean that the data are accurate. Much information that is readily available on the Internet, for example, is misleading, and some of it is just plain wrong. Always look carefully to learn as much as you can about the source: Is it a reputable organization? Does the organization have a political bias? Asking these types of questions and using more than one source will improve the quality of the data you find.

The federal government is a good source of data about almost all aspects of U.S. society. The Census Bureau continuously updates a statistical picture of the U.S. population, counting people, tracking immigration, assessing patterns of health, and reporting levels of employment, income, education, and much more. Other government agencies also collect specific information; for example, the Federal Bureau of Investigation publishes detailed statistics on crime in the United States.

SOCIAL PROBLEMS in Everyday Life

In terms of the discussion below, what does it mean to call a statement "politically correct"?

THINKING CRITICALLY 

The Study of Social Problems: Science? Politics? Or Both?

How should sociologists tackle important and controversial issues such as poverty, family violence, and abortion? Should we simply try to discover the "facts"—reporting what is happening and perhaps why—and leave the political decisions about what the problems and solutions are to others? Or should we take a stand and actively try to change society for the better?

Sociologists have long debated how to square science and politics. No one wrestled more with this question than the German sociologist Max Weber (1864–1920), who urged his colleagues to focus on the facts in an effort to make research *value-free.* Weber knew that personal values lead people to choose one topic over another. But, Weber insisted, once a topic is selected and research is under way, social scientists should keep a professional objectivity in their work. This means that as much as possible, researchers should hold their personal politics in check to avoid distorting the results. In practice, for example, a researcher who personally supports the death penalty must be willing to accept any and all results—even those that show that capital punishment has little or no effect on the murder rate. For Weber, the sociologist's main goal should be discovering truth rather than engaging in politics and promoting change.

In recent decades, however, an increasing number of sociologists have taken an opposing view. Many believe that sociologists have a responsibility not just to learn about the world but also to help improve the lives of people who suffer from poverty and prejudice. This might seem like taking sides—and it is. In defense of this value commitment, many sociologists (especially those using the social-conflict approach) argue that "objective" research is impossible because whatever theory we use or whatever we may say (or not say) about the world, we end up taking some position (even if by remaining silent). If this is so, then all knowledge is political, and trying to be neutral is itself a political position that ends up favoring the status quo. In the end, critics of Weber's view say, all sociologists must take one side or another on any issue they study. This activist orientation was the hallmark of Karl Marx, who summed up his view of this controversy in words placed on his tombstone: "The philosophers have only interpreted the world in various ways; the point, however, is to change it."

WHAT DO YOU THINK?

1. Do you think researchers can be objective? Give reasons for your position.
2. Is all knowledge political? Or is there such a thing as "truth"? How does the claim of "political correctness" on campus play into this debate?
3. What about teaching? Should professors try to remain objective in front of a class (as Max Weber insisted), or should they express their personal political values (as Karl Marx might have urged)? Ask several professors for their views.

Secondary analysis is often quick and easy, but this approach has its own problems. For one thing, a researcher who has not collected the data personally may be unaware of any bias or errors. Fortunately, however, the quality of most government data is high, and enough material is available to satisfy almost any researcher.

Truth, Science, and Politics

Once sociologists have data in hand, they must decide what to do with them. Sociologists turn to science in order to gather their data, but science cannot solve problems for us. Science can help us learn, say, *how many* U.S. families are poor and even yield some insights as to *why* they are poor, but science cannot tell us *what we should do* about poverty.

When we confront a social problem, we may use science to gather facts, which represent one kind of truth. But deciding how to respond to the problem always involves another kind of truth: our political values. The Thinking Critically box looks more closely at the relationship between facts and values in the study of social problems.

Truth and Statistics

Finally, a brief word about *statistics,* the numerical results that researchers often include when they report their findings. Statistics are easy ways to characterize a large number of subjects, as when a professor announces that members of a class had an average grade of 90 on a midterm examination.

Many of us have been brought up to think of statistics as "facts." How often have we been told that "numbers don't lie"? But numbers may not always be so truthful, for two reasons.

First, like all research findings, numbers must be interpreted. A class exam average may be 90, but does that mean the students studied hard or that the exam was fairly easy? Similarly, one person can point out that the U.S. unemployment rate rose above 9 percent in 2009 and interpret this as bad news because this is almost double what the rate was two years ago. Another may see this as good news because there have been times (such as during the Great Depression) when the rate was three times higher.

Second, organizations, politicians, and even sociologists often present statistics that support some preferred conclusion. How are we to know whether the statistics we read are pre-

SOCIAL PROBLEMS in Everyday Life

Can you point to recent news stories that "spin" data to encourage a particular view of some issue?

social policy formal strategies that affect how society operates

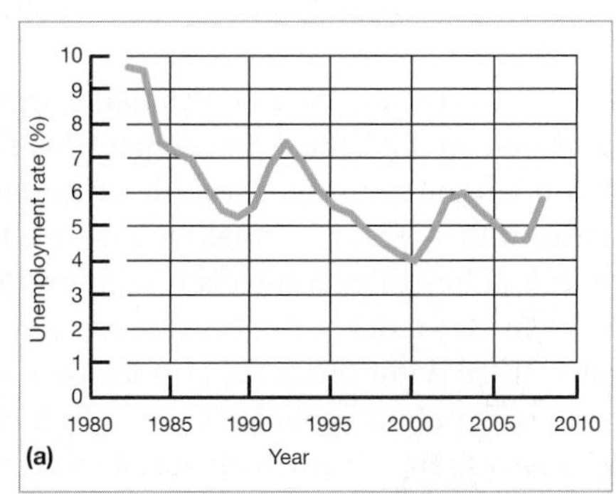

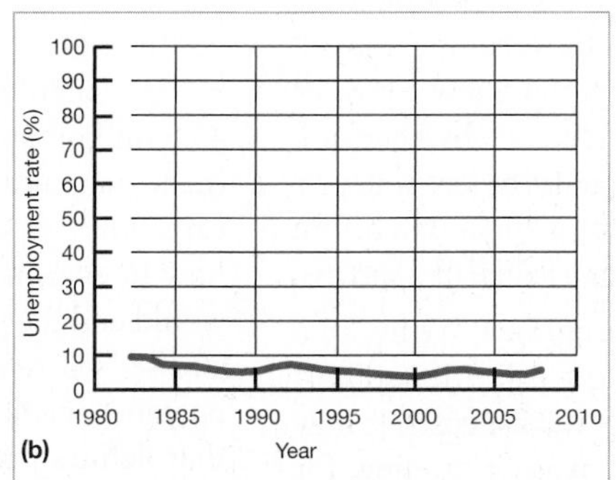

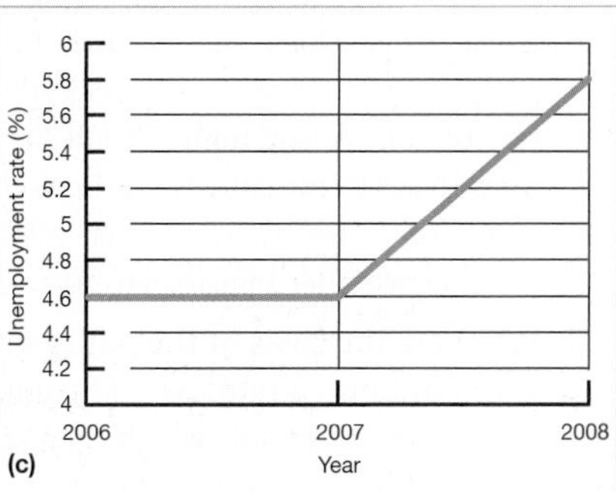

FIGURE 1–3 Do Statistics Lie?

Analysts, including sociologists, can "spin" their data to encourage readers to reach various conclusions. These three graphs are based on the same factual data. Yet the way we construct each graph suggests a different reality. The scale used in graph (a) gives the impression that over time, unemployment has gone down. Graph (b) changes the scale to flatten the line, thus giving the impression that the unemployment rate has changed little. Graph (c) presents data only for the years 2006 through 2008, giving the impression that the unemployment rate is going up.

Source: Data from U.S. Department of Labor (2009).

sented in a misleading way? There is no easy answer, but here are three tips to make you a more critical reader:

1. **Check how researchers define their terms.** How people define terms affects the results. Even the most careful counts of the poor will vary widely, depending on how each researcher defines poverty.
2. **Remember that research is never perfect.** Even if we agree on how to define the poor, actually counting millions of poor women, men, and children is a very difficult task. This is especially true of those who are homeless and therefore difficult to contact. In most cases, researchers end up undercounting the poor and especially the homeless.
3. **Researchers may "spin" their statistics.** What does a "steep decrease" in the homicide rate really mean? "Low unemployment" means low in relation to what? There are countless ways to select and present statistics, and researchers often present their findings in a way that advances the argument they wish to make.

Use special care when reading tables and graphs. Figure 1–3 illustrates the problem with three graphs showing changes in the U.S. rate. All are drawn from the same government data. Graph (a) might be titled "Unemployment Declines!" because it has an expanded scale that makes the decline look big. Graph (b) uses a smaller scale to make change seem smaller; one might label this figure "Unemployment Holds Steady!" Graph (c) uses just three years to show a recent rise in unemployment. Here we can announce "Unemployment on Rise!"

Ideally, sociologists strive for accuracy, clarity, and fairness in their work and use statistical data with the intent to convey information rather than to mislead readers. But because researchers have to make choices about how to present their numbers, you should always think critically about statistical information, whether it appears in textbooks or anywhere else. Never assume that statistics are the absolute truth.

Responding to Social Problems: Social Policy

How does a society respond to social problems? This question brings us to the topic of **social policy,** *formal strategies that affect how society operates.* Organizations, including governments and colleges, create social policy to get their work done and to address social problems. Sociologists play an important role in developing social policy. Over the years, sociologists have helped direct our nation's policy in dealing with racially segregated schools, poverty, pornography, health care, gun regulations, homelessness, racial discrimination, problems of family life, sexual harassment, and many other issues.

Policy Evaluation

How do we know whether a policy works? To evaluate any policy, we must answer the following, often difficult questions:

1. **How do we measure "success"?** There is more than one way to measure the success of any policy or program. Take, for

SOCIAL PROBLEMS in Everyday Life

Can you tihnk of policies or programs that might make society better but seem too expensive? Explain.

GETTING INVOLVED

How would you describe yourself in terms of the political spectrum?

example, a rehabilitation program for young people who abuse drugs. Does "success" mean that those completing the program stay "clean" for a year? Five years? Show a greater rate of completing high school? Or finding a job? There are many ways to measure the success or failure of any policy or program, so researchers must look at more than one before deciding whether a particular program is a failure or a success.

2. **What are the costs of the policy or program?** We live in a world of limited budgets and competing priorities, so policy evaluation means weighing results against costs. It may be possible to improve schools by increasing funding, for example, but a local community may not support raising property taxes.

   The costs of any program involve not just money but ethics as well. For example, installing surveillance cameras on public streets may reduce crime or at least drive criminal activity elsewhere. Yet many citizens object to having their movements—including which stores they visit and with whom they strike up a conversation—recorded on videotape by public officials. In short, street surveillance may be "successful" in reducing crime but may involve an unacceptable cost by taking away people's privacy.

3. **Who should get the help?** In assessing a social policy, another key question is whom the policy should target for assistance. To combat poverty, should agencies work with adults who need jobs? Provide a good breakfast to poor children in school? Provide prenatal care to pregnant women? All of these things may be helpful, but limited budgets require agencies to make choices about whom to target.

   One guideline for making such decisions is Benjamin Franklin's old saying, "An ounce of prevention is worth a pound of cure." Generally, the earlier the intervention, the more successful a policy is and the lower the costs. For example, helping boys before they get into trouble costs less—and accomplishes more—than putting them in jail later on.

   Sherry Deane of the National Black Child Development Institute says that too many programs kick in too late: "We spend so much more money after the problem has occurred—after a baby is born at low birth weight, after a child begins to fail in school, after a child is in trouble with the law—instead of making an early investment in the child with prenatal care, preventive health care, early education" (Goldman, 1991:5).

Policy and Culture

Social policy is also shaped by cultural values. That is, societies respond to a social problem in a particular way not necessarily because that approach is cheapest or works best but because a particular response seems, according to the society's culture, to be "the right thing to do."

As Chapter 2 ("Poverty and Wealth") explains, there are 43.6 million poor people in the United States, many living with inadequate nutrition, unsafe housing, and little or no medical care. Poverty persists in this country not because no one knows how to eliminate it; a policy to guarantee a minimum income would end the problem very quickly. But because our way of life stresses self-reliance, there is not much support for what would be widely criticized as "handout" policies. Guided by a culture that defines people as responsible for their social standing, we tend to see the poor as "undeserving" of assistance. As the next chapter describes in detail, such cultural values were at work when Congress and the White House in 1996 acted with widespread public support to change public assistance programs so that fewer people were dependent on government support.

Policy and Politics

The kinds of policies people favor depend on their political outlook. People with a politically conservative outlook usually try to limit the scope of societal change. If the existing society is viewed as good, then when problems arise, they must be caused by bad individuals. This is why conservatives favor policies that treat problems as shortcomings of particular individuals rather than as shortcomings of society. If the problem is unemployment, for example, conservatives might suggest helping jobless people get more schooling or learn new skills in order to make them more attractive to employers. In taking this more individualistic approach, conservatives are also saying that society is basically good the way it is and end up supporting the status quo.

By contrast, people with more liberal views see problems in the organization of society itself and favor greater social change. Unemployment, for example, is a reflection of the economy. Therefore, to combat unemployment, liberals seek societal reforms, such as strengthening antidiscrimination laws, expanding the power of labor unions, or calling for government to create enough jobs to provide work for the people who need it.

People with radical-left views seek policies that go beyond the reforms suggested by liberals. From their point of view, social problems are evidence that the entire system is flawed in some basic way. For example, Marxists claim that replacing the capitalist economy is the only real answer to unemployment. Because radical policies are, by definition, outside the political mainstream, they usually spark strong opposition.

We conclude this chapter—and each of the remaining chapters—with a discussion of how political attitudes lead people to define certain situations as problems in the first place and to define certain kinds of policies and programs as solutions to those problems.

political spectrum a continuum representing a range of political attitudes, from "left" to "right"

social issues (p. 20) political debates involving moral judgments about how people should live

economic issues (p. 20) political debates about how a society should distribute material resources

Table 1–2 The Political Spectrum: A National Survey, 2008

Survey Question: "We hear a lot of talk these days about liberals and conservatives. I'm going to show you a seven-point scale on which the political views people might hold are arranged from extremely liberal—point 1—to extremely conservative—point 7. Where would you place yourself on this scale?"

1	2	3	4	5	6	7
Extremely liberal	**Liberal**	**Slightly liberal**	**Middle of the road**	**Slightly conservative**	**Conservative**	**Extremely conservative**
3.4%	11.9%	10.9%	36.6%	13.2%	16.2%	3.4%

[*Don't know/no answer* 2.3%]

Source: *General Social Surveys, 1972–2008: Cumulative Codebook* (Chicago: National Opinion Research Center, 2009).

POLITICS

Constructing Problems and Defining Solutions

The social-construction approach described earlier is useful for exploring how political views guide people as they define social problems and devise solutions. Let us begin with a look at the political spectrum.

The Political Spectrum

We become part of the political process as we form attitudes about various issues. Social scientists measure people's opinions using a model called the **political spectrum,** *a continuum representing a range of political attitudes, from "left" to "right."* As shown in Table 1–2, attitudes on the political spectrum range from the far left at one extreme through "middle of the road" views at the center to the far right at the other extreme.

The data in Table 1–2 show that 26.2 percent of people consider themselves liberal to some degree (adding the numbers at points 1, 2, and 3 together), 36.6 percent say they are moderates (in the middle at point 4), and 32.8 percent say that they are conservative (adding the numbers at points 5, 6, and 7 together). Notice that just a small percentage describe themselves as being either extremely liberal (radicals who are far to the left) or extremely conservative (radicals who are far to the right) (NORC, 2009).

Over time, political attitudes may shift to the left (as they did in the 1960s) or to the right (as they did in the 1980s). The election of Barack Obama marked a shift to the left again in 2008. But at any time, there is always wide variation in people's political thinking. Some of this variation is regional: Massachusetts and Minnesota almost always elect liberal candidates, just as Mississippi and Texas usually elect conservatives. Similarly, some ethnic categories, such as African Americans and Jews, historically have favored liberal positions; others, such as Asian Americans, tend to be more conservative.

Conservatives, Liberals, and Radicals

What do labels such as "conservative, "liberal," and "radical" really mean? Here is a brief statement to get us going. The deeper meaning of these three concepts will become clear as you read through the chapters that follow, applying each point of view to various issues.

Conservatives look to the past for guidance on how to live. They believe that the past is a store of wisdom developed by countless generations who have already faced many of the same questions and issues that we face today. A "good" society, from the conservative point of view, is respectful of traditions and tries to conserve what has been learned in the past. Conservatives have a special interest in the family and religion—the social institutions that transmit our moral traditions.

Liberals have a different view of the world. In simple terms, *liberals* (from a Latin word for "free") think people should be free from the past to decide, on their own, questions about how to live. A "good" society, from a liberal point of view, is one in which people are able to make choices for themselves. This requires that the society be both tolerant and respectful of individual rights. It also requires that categories of people be more or less equal in terms of basic rights and opportunities. Therefore, liberals have a special interest in the economy and politics, because these are the social institutions that distribute wealth and power.

Although liberals and conservatives differ in some important ways, both accept the existing political system, at least in most respects. In contrast, people with more extreme views seek more basic change in society. Such attitudes are *radical* (from

SOCIAL PROBLEMS in Everyday Life

As you read these pages, see if you can link political views to the Republican Party ("leaning right") and the Democratic Party ("leaning left").

GETTING INVOLVED

What social issues that have been in the news recently are of concern to you? What about economic issues?

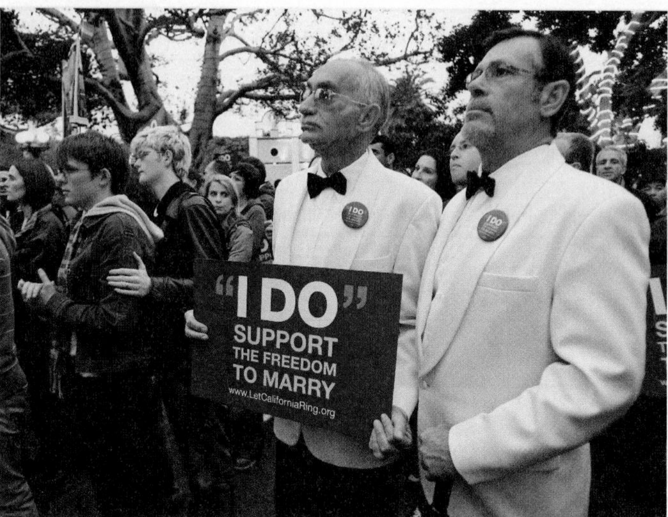

Lower-income people tend to be very concerned about economic issues, for the simple reason that they lack economic security. Members of the United Auto Workers recently engaged in this action against the auto companies to protest layoffs. Higher-income people, by contrast, take economic security for granted. They are likely to be most concerned about social issues, such as legalizing same-sex marriage.

Latin meaning "of the root") because they hold that the system must be changed right down to its roots. Radicals find some basic flaw in society that is responsible for any number of social problems. For people on the far right, the growth of big government is the basic flaw, leading some who hold such views to withdraw from society into remote places where they live as "survivalists." Radicals also include people on the far left. For Marxists, the basic flaw is the capitalist economic system that creates social classes; for radical feminists, the basic flaw is the concept of gender that gives rise to patriarchy, the power of men over women.

Can we sum this up in a single sentence? It would go something like this: Conservatives talk about the importance of traditions; liberals talk about the need for reforms; radicals talk about organizing society in a completely new way.

Social Issues

Regardless of their political positions, people hold political attitudes on two kinds of issues: social issues and economic issues. **Social issues** are *political debates involving moral judgments about how people should live.* Some of today's leading social issues include feminism, abortion, immigration, same-sex marriage, and the use of the death penalty.

Leaning Left

People who lean to the left on social issues are called *social liberals.* In general, social liberals think that people should be free to shape their lifestyles for themselves. Social liberals are broadly tolerant of various "alternative" lifestyles, favor expanding opportunities for women, support the "pro-choice" side of the abortion controversy, look favorably on immigrants coming to the United States, and support legal marriage for gay and lesbian people. Similarly, social liberals oppose the death penalty partly because in the past, states have been more likely to execute African Americans than whites and the poor rather than the rich, even when convicted of the same crimes.

Leaning Right

People who lean to the right on social issues are called *social conservatives.* Social conservatives are respectful of traditional values and want to conserve them. Conservatives criticize what they see as too much individualism in today's society. Social conservatives favor the "pro-life" side of the abortion controversy, are more concerned about controlling this country's borders to protect our cultural traditions, and support the traditional family in which women and men have different roles and responsibilities. Social conservatives also endorse the death penalty as a proper moral response to brutal criminal acts.

Economic Issues

The second type of issues involves economics. **Economic issues** are *political debates about how a society should distribute material resources.* These debates often focus on the degree to which the government should control the economy and reduce income disparity (Chapter 10, "Economy and Politics," explores these issues).

GETTING INVOLVED

How liberal or conservative are you on social issues? What about economic issues?

GETTING INVOLVED

Are you registered to vote?

Leaning Left

In general, *economic liberals* (leaning to the left on economic issues) favor government regulation of the economy in order to reduce inequality. A free-market system, they claim, too often works to the advantage of a select few and harms everyone else. For this reason, economic liberals support government action raising the minimum wage as well as setting high taxes, especially on the rich, to pay for social service programs that help the poor.

Leaning Right

By contrast, *economic conservatives* (who lean to the right on economic issues) call for a smaller role for government in the economy. From their point of view, the market—not government officials—should set wage levels. Economic conservatives support lower tax rates in the belief that people should be able to keep more of their own earnings as they take responsibility for their own well-being.

Who Thinks What?

What types of people are likely to fall on each side of the political spectrum? Social standing is a good predictor, but it turns out that most people are actually liberal on one kind of issue and conservative on the other.

People of high social position, with lots of schooling and above-average wealth, tend to be liberal on social issues but may be conservative on economic issues. That is, highly educated people tend to be tolerant of lifestyle diversity (the liberal view), but many also seek to protect their wealth (the conservative position).

People with less education and wealth show the opposite pattern, taking a conservative stand on social issues and a liberal stand on economic issues. With a limited education, they tend to see moral issues more as clear-cut choices that are right or wrong, which is the socially conservative view. At the same time, poor people support government-enacted economic programs that may benefit them, which makes them economically liberal.

Most of us hold some combination of liberal and conservative attitudes. This inconsistency helps explain why so many people call themselves "moderates," "centrists," or "middle-of-the-roaders."

A Word about Gender

Finally, what about any differences between women and men? Research suggests that if they are of the same social class, women and men hold roughly the same political attitudes. Even on abortion, which is often called a "woman's issue," men are as likely as women to support the liberal pro-choice position (NORC, 2007). However, political analysts have documented a "gender gap" in voting patterns: Women are somewhat more likely to vote for Democratic candidates, and men are more likely to favor Republicans. In the 2008 presidential election, for example, 56 percent of women but only 49 percent of men voted for the Democratic candidate, Barack Obama. In general, men express greater concerns about strong national security (more a Republican issue), and women express greater concerns about keeping an adequate social "safety net" to help those in need (typically a Democratic issue).

Going On from Here

This chapter has presented the groundwork you will need for understanding the rest of the book. Each chapter that follows presents research findings related to the issue at hand. In addition, each chapter also applies sociology's major theoretical approaches—the structural-functional, social-conflict, and symbolic-interaction approaches—to the issues.

Always keep in mind this fact: *Social problems are socially constructed.* Political attitudes guide what we define as a problem and what policies we are likely to favor as solutions. Recognizing and respecting the diversity of political attitudes in the United States, this text does not assume that everyone will agree about what the problems are or what the best solutions might be. On the contrary, what we assume is that there will be disagreement. Therefore, the remaining chapters present the various ideas that conservatives, liberals, and radicals have about exactly what the problems are and what we ought to do about them. You will soon see for yourself that one person's solution often turns out to be another's problem.

What should you expect by the time you have finished this book? You will have learned a great deal about many social problems—in the United States and around the world—that command the attention of government officials and the public. You will also become familiar with sociology's three theoretical approaches so that you can apply them to new issues as they arise. Finally, you will gain a firm grasp of the conservative, liberal, and radical views of society so that as you encounter new issues in the future, you will be able to analyze them from each of these political perspectives. As you succeed in doing this, you will become an active participant in the nation's political process.

Finally, the remainder of this text serves as an invitation to get involved in political debates and political action. "Constructing Social Problems: A Defining Moment" provides an account of how easy—and how important—it is to become involved in the political life of our nation. Each of the chapters that follows provides a profile of a "defining moment" in the history of our country or our world, a time when an individual—often an "ordinary" person like you or me—decided to take some action in a way that made a difference. Such examples provide inspiration to us all.

GETTING INVOLVED

Can you remember the first time you thought about our society having a "problem"? What was it?

CONSTRUCTING SOCIAL PROBLEMS

A DEFINING MOMENT

A Call to Action: The Message of Martin Luther King Jr.

Martin Luther King Jr. (1929–1968) was born in Atlanta at a time when black people and white people were kept apart by a strict system of racial segregation. King was taught in segregated classrooms and graduated from high school at the age of fifteen. Then, like his father and grandfather, he earned a bachelor's degree from Morehouse College, a traditionally black institution.

Also like his father and grandfather, King set out to become a preacher. He enrolled at the Crozer Theological Seminary in Pennsylvania, where his mostly white classmates elected him president of the senior class. He received his theology degree in 1951. King continued his studies at Boston University, which awarded him a doctorate in 1955.

In 1954, King was appointed pastor at the Dexter Avenue Baptist Church in Montgomery, Alabama. He quickly became a community leader, heading up not only his church but also the local chapter of the National Association for the Advancement of Colored People (NAACP). The city of Montgomery—like the rest of the South—was still racially segregated, and people of color were restricted to their own businesses and neighborhoods and required to sit in separate sections at the rear of city buses. King opposed racial segregation as morally wrong and decided to take action to challenge the status quo. In December 1955, he led a nonviolent social movement that came to be known as the Montgomery bus boycott. Thousands of people refused to ride the buses until the city allowed equal access to seats on public transportation. The boycott continued for more than a year, ending only after the U.S. Supreme Court declared that the racial segregation of public transportation was unconstitutional.

King had won a great victory, but his life was not easy. He continued to struggle for racial equality, often facing hostility from both the police and members of the public. He was arrested dozens of times, his home was attacked, and some opponents made threats against his life. But he held firm in his beliefs. In 1957, he was elected president of the Southern Christian Leadership Conference, emerging as the leader of the national civil rights movement. His activism continued for another decade, culminating in a civil rights march in Washington, D.C., that included more than 250,000 people who gathered to hear him deliver his famous "I Have a Dream" speech.

King was a great national and international leader, and he stands among a handful of people in the United States honored with a national holiday each year (celebrated on the third Monday in January, near King's birthday). But the power of his message is not that great people can accomplish great things but that the ability to make a difference is within the reach of all of us. Here are King's words:

> Everybody can be great, because everybody can serve. You don't have to have a college degree to serve. You don't have to make your subject and your verb agree to serve. You don't have to know about Plato and Aristotle to serve. You don't have to know Einstein's theory of relativity to serve. You don't have to know the second theory of thermal dynamics in physics to serve. You only need a heart full of grace, a soul generated with love, and you can be that servant.

This message is an invitation to us to learn more about our society and to recognize that as human beings, our lives are bound up with the lives of everyone else around the corner and around the world. Following King's example, look for a way in which you can make a positive difference in the life of at least one other person. Get involved!

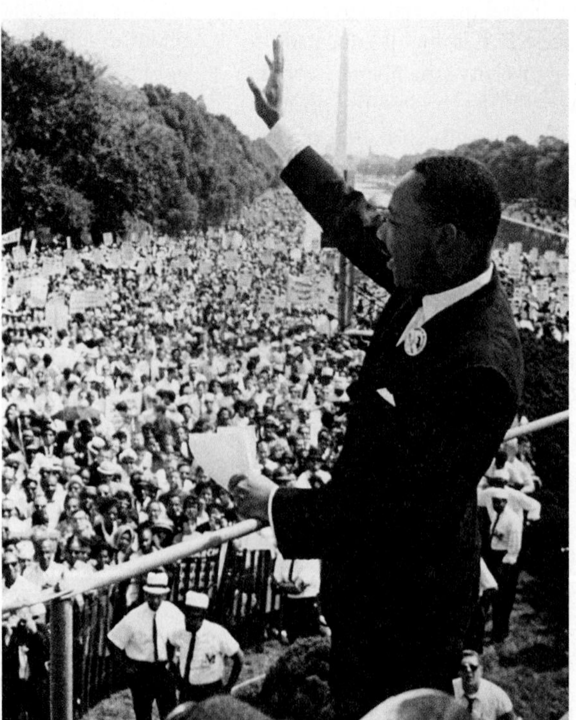

Dr. Martin Luther King Jr. is one of only four people in the history of our country whose birthday has become a national holiday (George Washington, Abraham Lincoln, and Christopher Columbus are the others). When we celebrate King's life, we are recognizing that our society has grappled with the issue of racial inequality for centuries and that this problem is still not solved.

DEFINING SOLUTIONS

Whose problem is it?

This chapter has explained that different political attitudes lead people to disagree about what the problems are. And even when we do agree about the problems, we are likely to define different courses of action as solutions. Today, most people in the United States agree that a major problem is the weak economy. Look at the two photos to see two different approaches to fixing the problem

HINT

In 2008, the conservative Bush administration started a limited government bailout program in an attempt to stabilize the failing economy. In 2009, the more liberal Obama administration extended government regulation (of the banking industry) and ownership of struggling corporations (including auto companies). Generally, liberals see government acting in the public interest and they distrust "big business" as favoring the rich. Conservatives tend to support the free market and they distrust "big government" as a threat to personal freedom. As for personal responsibility, liberals believe that because many problems are rooted in society, individuals cannot solve them on their own; conservatives claim people must learn to take responsibility for their own lives.

The more we favor the right side of the political spectrum, the more we expect people to solve economic problems like unemployment by themselves. What arguments might conservatives make in support of personal responsibility?

The more we favor the left side of the political spectrum, the more we look to government to manage the economy. In 2009, the "Cash for Clunkers" program was enacted to jump start the auto industry and give a boost to the entire economy. What other government programs did the Obama administration enact?

Getting Involved: Applications & Exercises

1. Explain how the following slogans from bumper stickers are examples of claims making: (a) "Guns Don't Kill People; People Kill People"; (b) "It's a Child, Not a Choice"; (c) "God is not spelled G.O.P."; and (d) "No War for Oil."
2. What kinds of questions might you ask about, say, poverty, using the structural-functional, symbolic-interaction, and social-conflict approaches?
3. Identify several national politicians—try to include your own members of Congress—who fall on the conservative and liberal sides of the political spectrum. What are their views on social issues such as gay rights and on economic issues such as using tax money to stabilize the economy and raising taxes to reduce income inequality? Are there any radical politicians in Congress?
4. Explain how people's political attitudes affect the kinds of isses they are likely to define as social problems. For example, do conservatives or liberals see the "breakdown of the traditional family" as a social problem? Why? Are conservatives or liberals more concerned about gender inequality? Explain.

MAKING THE GRADE

A DEFINING MOMENT
A Call to Action: The Message of Martin Luther King Jr. p. 22

CHAPTER 1 Sociology: Studying Social Problems

Seeing Patterns: The Sociological Imagination

- **SOCIOLOGY** is the systematic study of human societies.
- Sociologist C. Wright Mills coined the expression "the sociological imagination" to encourage people to view their own personal problems as connected to the workings of society.

p. 2

sociological imagination (p. 2) a point of view that highlights how society affects the experiences we have and the choices we make

sociology (p. 2) the systematic study of human societies

society (p. 2) people who live within some territory and share many patterns of behavior

culture (p. 2) a way of life including widespread values (about what is good and bad), beliefs (about what is true), and behavior (what people do every day)

Social Problems: The Basics

A **SOCIAL PROBLEM** is a condition that undermines the well-being of some or all members of a society and is usually controversial.

- A social-constructionist approach holds that a social problem is created as society defines some condition as undesirable and in need of change.
- The specific conditions defined as social problems change over time.
- At any particular time, the objective facts and the subjective perception of any social issue may or may not be the same.

pp. 3–8

CLAIMS MAKING is the process by which members of a social movement try to convince the public and public officials that a condition should be defined as a social problem. Claims made by one group of people typically prompt counterclaims by other groups.

pp. 5–6

SOCIAL MOVEMENTS typically go through four stages:

- emergence
- coalescence
- formalization
- decline

p. 6

✓ *Sociologists view social problems as the result of the operation of society rather than simply the actions of bad people. They point out that many social problems are related. (pp. 7–8)*

✓ *A global perspective is important because many social problems cross national boundaries. In addition, many problems are more serious elsewhere in the world than in the United States. (pp. 8–9)*

social problem (p. 3) a condition that undermines the well-being of some or all members of a society and is usually a matter of public controversy

social-constructionist approach (p. 4) the assertion that social problems arise as people define conditions as undesirable and in need of change

claims making (p. 5) the process of convincing the public and important public officials that a particular issue or situation should be defined as a social problem

social movement (p. 6) an organized effort at claims making that tries to shape the way people think about an issue in order to encourage or discourage social change

Analyzing Social Problems: Sociological Theory

Sociologists use **THEORETICAL APPROACHES** to guide their research and theory building. The major theoretical approaches—structural-functional, social-conflict, and symbolic-interaction—all provide insights into various social problems.

pp. 9–13

macro-level

The **STRUCTURAL-FUNCTIONAL APPROACH** sees society as a complex system of many different parts.

- Early *social pathology theory* viewed problems as disruptions in society's normal operation.
- Later, *social disorganization theory* linked social problems to rapid change.
- More recently, functionalism views social problems in terms of the dysfunctions of various social patterns.

pp. 9–11

The **SOCIAL-CONFLICT APPROACH** highlights social inequality.

- *Class conflict theory,* based on the ideas of Karl Marx, links social problems to the operation of a capitalist economic system.
- *Multicultural theory* spotlights problems arising from inequality between people in various racial and ethnic categories.
- *Feminist theory* links social problems to men's domination of women.

pp. 11–13

micro-level

The **SYMBOLIC-INTERACTION APPROACH** helps us understand how people experience social problems in their routine, everyday interactions.

- The learning approach links social problems to the learning of undesirable skills and attitudes from others.
- The labeling approach investigates how and why people come to define certain behaviors as problematic and others as normal.

p. 13

theory (p. 9) a statement of how and why specific facts are related

theoretical approach (p. 9) a basic image of society that guides theory and research

structural-functional approach (p. 9) a theoretical framework that sees society as a system of many interrelated parts

social institution (p. 9) a major sphere of social life, or a societal subsystem, organized to meet a basic human need

social-conflict approach (p. 11) a theoretical framework that sees society as divided by inequality and conflict

feminism (p. 12) a political movement that seeks the social equality of women and men

symbolic-interaction approach (p. 15) a theoretical framework that sees society as the product of individuals interacting with one another

 See the **Applying Theory** table on page 14.

Finding the Facts: Sociological Research

Sociologists use a variety of methods to investigate social problems:

SURVEY RESEARCH can take different forms:
- A *questionnaire* is a series of items a researcher presents to subjects for their response.
- An *interview* is a more personal survey technique in which a researcher meets face to face with respondents to discuss some issue.
- A *case study* focuses on a single person, organization, or event.

pp. 14–15

FIELD RESEARCH allows a researcher to observe people over a long period of time while joining them in their everyday activities.

p. 15

EXPERIMENTAL RESEARCH is carried out in a specially designed laboratory. Researchers change one variable while keeping the others the same in order to identify specific causes of certain patterns of behavior.

p. 15

SECONDARY ANALYSIS OF EXISTING DATA can be a quick and easy research method, but a researcher must be careful not to rely on data that may be incorrect or may contain a political bias.

pp. 15–16

✓ *Do not assume all statistical data are the same as "truth": Pay attention to how researchers define concepts and how they choose to present their data. (pp. 16–17)*

survey (p. 14) a research method by which subjects respond to items on a questionnaire or in an interview

field research (participant observation) (p. 15) a research method for observing people while joining them in their everyday activities

experiment (p. 15) a research method for investigating cause-and-effect relationships under tightly controlled conditions

secondary analysis (p. 15) a research method that makes use of data originally collected by others

Responding to Social Problems: Social Policy

SOCIAL POLICY refers to strategies that societies use to address problems.
- A society evaluates a social policy based on its success, its cost, and whether the population it targets represents the best solution to a social problem.
- Societies favor social policy that reflects important cultural values.
- The kinds of policies individual people favor depends on their political attitudes.

pp. 17–18

social policy (p. 17) formal strategies that affect how society operates

Politics: Constructing Problems and Defining Solutions

The **POLITICAL SPECTRUM** is a model representing people's attitudes about social issues and economic issues.

p. 19

On the **RADICAL LEFT**, Marxists claim that social problems result from the operation of the capitalist economic system.
- From this point of view, the solution to social problems requires radical change to our society's institutions, beginning with the economy.

pp. 19–20

LIBERALS claim that social problems arise from the operation of society, including patterns of social inequality that prevent categories of people from having equal opportunity.
- Liberals seek reform rather than radical change in social institutions.

pp. 19–20

CONSERVATIVES claim that social problems arise from the short-comings of particular individuals or the bad choices people make about how to live.
- Conservatives see the family and religion as important social institutions transmitting the moral traditions that guide people to live good lives.

pp. 19–20

The **RADICAL RIGHT** claims that the most serious problem our society faces is the growth of big government, which threatens individual freedoms.
- Some people on the radical right withdraw from society altogether to live as survivalists in remote areas.

pp. 19–20

political spectrum (p. 19) a continuum representing a range of political attitudes from "left" to "right"

social issues (p. 20) political debates involving moral judgments about how people should live

economic issues (p. 20) political debates about how a society should distribute material resources

✓ *Generally, people of high social position (highly educated and wealthy) are liberal on social issues and conservative on economic issues. (pp. 20–21)*

✓ *People of low social position (with less schooling and little wealth) tend to be conservative on social issues and liberal on economic issues. (pp. 20–21)*

CONSTRUCTING THE PROBLEM

How much economic inequality is fair?

The richest 20 percent of U.S. families earn almost as much as the remaining 80 percent combined; the richest 5 percent of families own about half of all privately held property.

Do you think U.S. society is becoming more equal?

In recent decades, income inequality in the United States has increased.

Is there poverty in the United States?

In 2009, 43.6 million people were poor, the highest poverty rate since 1994.

Chapter 2

Poverty and Wealth

CHAPTER OVERVIEW

HOW UNEQUAL IS U.S. SOCIETY in terms of income and wealth? This chapter documents the extent of economic inequality and describes the contrasting lives of this country's rich and poor. You will analyze a range of problems—including poor health, unsafe housing, and political alienation—that are linked to poverty. You will learn how our society has assisted the poor over our history. Finally, you will carry out theoretical analysis of social inequality and learn how political attitudes guide people to construct certain "problems" and favor certain "solutions."

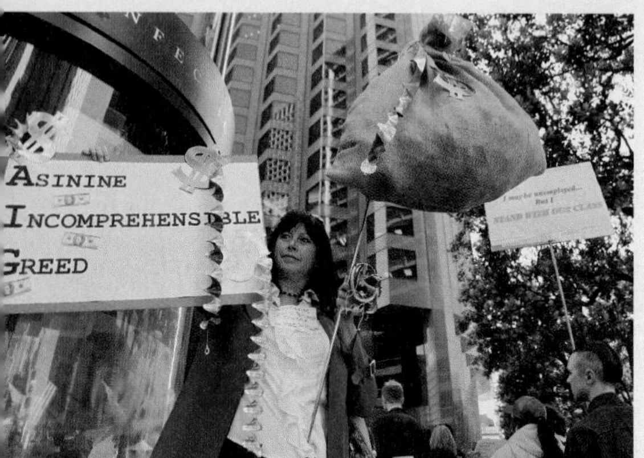

In simple terms, people across the country were getting pretty angry. The economic recession was getting worse, and in an effort to stabilize the economy, Congress had acted to bail out major banks in danger of going bankrupt. American International Group, Inc. (AIG), a large insurance and financial services company, received more than $180 billion in taxpayer money.

Not everyone thinks the government should be in the business of propping up failed corporations. Probably most people are not quite sure what the "subprime mortgage crisis" is really all about and can only hope somebody comes up with a way to turn the economy around.

But almost everybody was angry to learn that after receiving so much government money, AIG executives had paid themselves large bonuses. According to documents provided by the company, seventy-three executives received bonuses of $1 million or more and five executives received more than $4 million. In all, more than $218 million of the government bailout funds went right into the pockets of AIG managers—the very people who had run the company into the ground.

With public anger over the huge bonuses growing by the day, more than a dozen AIG executives said publicly that they would give the bonus money they had received back to the government. But Congress had already begun to enact legislation to create special taxes that would take back almost all the bonus money paid to executives at AIG, as well as other companies receiving large amounts of bailout funds (Freifeld, 2009; Lepro, 2009; Marshall, 2009; Saporito, 2009).

But however this matter is resolved, a larger question—and the issue on the minds of many people across the country—remains: Does U.S. society distribute income fairly? Most people think workers should be paid what they are worth, but the AIG bonus scandal is only the most recent chapter in a long story of top executives getting huge salaries and bonuses—even when it seems clear that they have done their jobs very badly.

Is U.S. society "fair" when it comes to how much money people receive? How unequal are we? Is our society becoming more or less equal as time goes on? How many people in this rich country are poor? And what should be done about poverty? This chapter examines poverty and wealth in the United States and provides answers to these questions. We begin by establishing some basic facts about the unequal distribution of economic resources in the United States.

Economic Inequality in the United States

It doesn't take a sociologist to point out that some people have much more money than others. The evidence of economic inequality is everywhere: Large, fancy houses with swimming pools and workout rooms in one neighborhood stand in striking contrast to small homes in need of repair across town. Some children dress in the latest styles, eat nutritious meals, have regular checkups at the doctor, and go on vacations to destinations around the world. But others wear hand-me-downs, eat poorly, go the emergency room when they are injured or sick, and rarely travel anywhere.

These patterns are just some of the consequences of **social stratification,** *society's system of ranking categories of people in a hierarchy.* Stratification produces **social classes,** *categories of people who have similar access to resources and opportunities.* Being born into a particular social class affects people's *life chances,* including how much schooling they receive, the kind of work they will do (or their chances of not finding a job), and even how long they will live. Social stratification is a powerful system, and few people realize just how economically unequal people in the United States really are. We begin, then, with some important economic indicators.

social stratification society's system of ranking categories of people in a hierarchy

social classes categories of people who have similar access to resources and opportunities

income salary or wages from a job plus earnings from investments and other sources

wealth the value of all the economic assets owned by a person or family, minus any debts

Dimensions of Difference

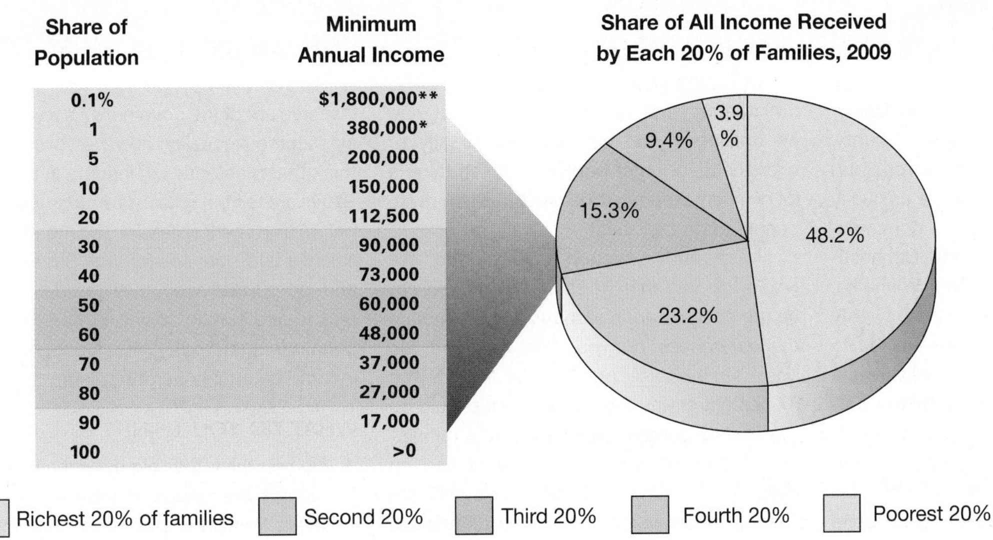

Share of Population	Minimum Annual Income
0.1%	$1,800,000**
1	380,000*
5	200,000
10	150,000
20	112,500
30	90,000
40	73,000
50	60,000
60	48,000
70	37,000
80	27,000
90	17,000
100	>0

FIGURE 2–1 Distribution of Income in the United States

Income is unequally distributed, with the highest-earning one-fifth of U.S. families receiving 48.2 percent of all income. This is twelve times as much as the 3.9 percent of income earned by the bottom one-fifth of U.S. families.

Source: U.S. Census Bureau (2010).

Inequality of Income and Wealth

Any discussion of problems such as poverty must begin with a look at inequality in **income**, *salary or wages from a job plus earnings from investments and other sources.* According to the U.S. government, in 2009, the *median* family income—that is, the middle case of all families when ranked by income—was $60,088.

As the pie chart on the right in Figure 2–1 shows, the highest-earning 20 percent of U.S. families (with income of at least $112,500 a year and with a mean or average of $189,500) received 48.2 percent of all income. At the other end of the hierarchy, the lowest-paid 20 percent (with income below $27,000 a year and averaging $15,000) received just 3.9 percent of all income. Comparing these categories, we see that the high-income families earn twelve times as much as the low-income families. From another angle, the highest-earning 20 percent of families earn nearly almost as much as the remaining 80 percent of families combined (U.S. Census Bureau, 2010).

The table at the left in Figure 2–1 gives a more detailed look at the U.S. income distribution. Families in the top 10 percent earn at least $150,000 annually, those in the top 5 percent earn at least $200,000, and families in the top 1 percent receive almost $400,000 each year. At the very top, the highest-paid tenth of 1 percent of families earn at least $1.8 million each year. This means that a very small share of families earns as much money in a single year as a typical family earns in an entire lifetime.

Since about 1980, income inequality among U.S. families has been increasing. Between 1980 and 2009, the annual income of the highest-paid 20 percent of U.S. families (these are not necessarily the same actual families over the entire period) increased by 55 percent (from $122,000, on average, to $189,500). During this period, people in the middle of the income distribution typically saw gains of about 16 percent. The lowest-paid 20 percent of U.S. families—those with incomes below $27,000 annually, actually had their incomes decrease by 3.8 percent. In other words, as the rich have gotten richer, the poor have become poorer, making income inequality in the United States greater than at any time in the last fifty years (U.S. Census Bureau, 2010). What do people think of this trend? The Thinking Critically box on page 30 provides some answers.

In the United States, economic inequality is even greater when it comes to **wealth,** *the value of all the economic assets owned by a person or family, minus any debts.* Wealth is made up of more than money earned; it also includes the value of homes, automobiles, stocks, bonds, real estate, and businesses. Figure 2–2 on page 31 shows that the wealthiest 20 percent of U.S. families own about 85 percent of all privately held wealth. Near the top,

SOCIAL PROBLEMS in Everyday Life

The United States has more economic inequality than every other high-income country. What about our national culture helps explain this fact?

progressive taxation a policy that raises tax rates as income increases

THINKING CRITICALLY

"Haves" and "Have-Nots": Is Income Inequality a Problem?

In the poorest communities in the United States—such as rural Loup County, Nebraska; Chemung County, New York; and Bighorn County, Wyoming—people are lucky to clear $10,000 a year. In rich communities—such as urban Greenwich, Connecticut; Palm Beach, Florida; and Winnetka, Illinois—most people earn ten to twenty times that much. Some people—including the highest-paid executives on Wall Street—make $25 million or even $100 million in a single year. Should one person earn so much more than another? Is marked income inequality a problem? In the most recent survey of a representative sample of U.S. adults (taken before the recent economic recession), the National Opinion Research Center (NORC) asked about income inequality.

One item stated, "*Some people earn a lot of money, while others do not earn very much. In order to get people to work hard, do you think large differences in pay are necessary?*" In response, 67 percent of U.S. adults stated that large differences are necessary in order to get people to work hard; 27 percent disagreed, saying that such differences are not needed (the remaining 6 percent had no opinion or did not answer). Rightly or wrongly, then, most people seem to think a lot of income inequality is needed to motivate people to do their best.

A second question asked, "*On the whole, do you think it should or should not be the government's responsibility to reduce the differences between the rich and the poor?*" In this case, opinion was divided, with 37 percent saying the government should do this and 42 percent disagreeing (the remaining 21 percent were undecided or had no opinion). This item suggests that a significant share of people do think income differences are a problem.

A third item asked subjects to agree or disagree with the statement "*Differences in income in America are too large.*" In this case, 63 percent agreed, 20 percent said they neither agreed nor disagreed, and 16 percent disagreed (the remaining 1 percent had no opinion or did not respond).

The responses to these survey questions suggest that people do not think that income inequality is a major problem and that people disagree about the government's role in reducing income inequality; however, two-thirds do think that differences in income in the United States are too big. These questions were asked before the recent recession, a time when huge salaries and bonuses for Wall Street bankers and corporate executives made headlines and fueled public anger. In seems safe to conclude that today, most people do see income inequality as a problem.

WHAT DO YOU THINK?

1. Do you think that big differences in income are needed to motivate people to work hard? Explain your answer.
2. What about some of the multimillion-dollar salaries and bonuses paid to Wall Street executives in recent years? Are such payments fair? Why or why not?
3. Through taxes (higher on the rich than the poor) and social programs for people in need, government does lessen economic inequality. Should government do more? What should be done?

Source: NORC (2009).

the very rich—those in the top 5 percent—own 62 percent of all wealth, and the super-rich, in the top 1 percent, control 35 percent of all private assets. Recent reductions in taxes on income and on inheritance are likely to make inequality of wealth even greater in years to come (Keister, 2000; Keister & Moller, 2000; Federal Reserve Board, 2009; Wolff, 2010).

The second 20 percent of U.S. families owns about 11 percent of all wealth, which includes some stocks and bonds but is mostly in the form of homes, automobiles, and other consumer goods. For about half of all U.S. families, however, wealth hardly exists at all. In other words, most ordinary families own a home and other property, but the value of these assets is roughly balanced by what they owe. This fact means that most families live from paycheck to paycheck and lack cash reserves to carry them through an emergency. In a world in which illness or unemployment can strike unexpectedly, many families are only a paycheck or two away from poverty.

Taxation

There is an old saying that the only certainties in life are death and taxes. The government taxes what we earn and what we buy for three major reasons. First, taxes provide the government with the money it needs to operate, paying the salaries of government employees, including members of the military, and also carrying out projects that benefit the public, such as building roads, bridges, and schools. Second, the government uses taxes to discourage certain types of behavior; for example, the high taxation placed on cigarettes discourages smoking by making it more expensive. Third, and most important to this discussion, taxation is a means of reducing economic inequality.

The government reduces economic inequality through **progressive taxation,** *a policy that raises tax rates as income increases.* The idea is a modern-day version of the story of Robin Hood, with government taking more from the rich in taxes and giving more to the poor in assistance programs. As

GETTING INVOLVED

Do you think that the Obama administration's tax policies will succeed in redistributing wealth from rich to poor families? What is your opinion of using taxation to create greater economic equality?

MAKING THE GRADE

Compare Figures 2-2 and 2-1: Wealth is more unequally distributed than income.

shown in Table 2–1, people with very high incomes, of $2 million or more, paid 22 percent of their incomes in federal taxes (state, local, and sales taxes are not included). Families with large incomes in the $100,000 to $150,000 range pay about 19 percent of their earnings in federal taxes (state, local, and sales taxes are not included). Families with lower incomes of $32,000 or less annually pay just 3 percent of their earnings in federal taxes. In general, families with lower incomes pay at a lower rate and receive more financial benefits from the government, and those with high incomes pay at a higher rate and receive fewer benefits (Internal Revenue Service, 2008).

Looking at dollars rather than rates, families with incomes from $389,000 to $2 million a year pay an average of about $170,000 in federal income tax. Lower-income families earning less than $32,000 pay an average of about $450. This means that these rich families together earn almost 50 times more than all the poor families put together but contribute almost 400 times more in income tax revenues. In other words, the rich are taxed eight times more heavily—showing the progressive principle at work in the process of reducing income inequality. To the extent that the Obama administration raises the top tax rates, the dollar amounts and the share of taxes paid by high-income families will increase.

At the very top of the income pyramid, people earning $2 million or more per year (who average more than $6 million) typically pay about $1,475,000 in federal income taxes (Internal Revenue Service, 2008). The top 1 percent of families in terms of income actually pay about one-third of all income taxes collected by the federal government, and the bottom half of all U.S. families pay only about 3 percent of all such taxes. This contrast helps us see that tax cuts or tax increases typically have the biggest effect on high-income families.

High-income families have strategies to lower their income taxes. For example, they may ask companies to defer their income until a later time, or they may make charitable contributions that can be deducted from taxable income. Because members of high-income families must also pay a share of any inheritance that passes from one generation to the next, they make use of strategies such as annual gifts and trust funds to reduce these taxes (Johnston, 2005; Moore & Anderson, 2005).

Dimensions of Difference

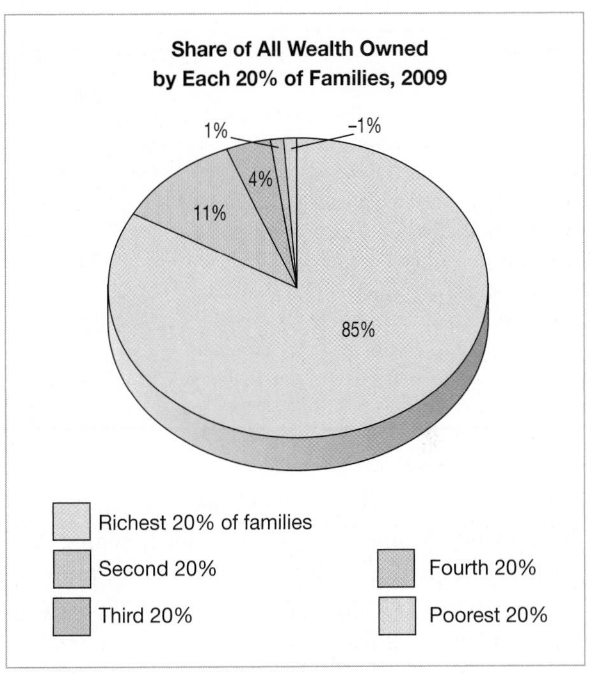

FIGURE 2–2 Distribution of Wealth in the United States
Wealth is distributed much more unequally than income is. The richest one-fifth of U.S. families control 85 percent of all privately owned wealth; the poorest one-fifth of families are in debt.
Source: Estimates based on Federal Reserve Board (2009), and Wolff (2010).

Not all taxes are progressive. The tax on gasoline, for example, works the other way around. The gas tax is *regressive* because although the tax per gallon is the same for everyone, rich and poor, it takes a bigger bite out of lower-income

Table 2–1 Progressive Tax on Income, 2006

Share of Population	Adjusted Gross Income	Number of Tax Returns	Average Tax Rate	Share of Total Income Tax
Top 0.1%	$2,044,689 or more	135,719	22%	20%
Top 5%	153,542 or more	6,785,958	21	60
Top 10%	108,904 or more	13,571,916	19	71
Top 25%	64,702 or more	33,929,790	16	86
Top 50%	31,987 or more	67,859,580	14	97
Bottom 50%	31,986 or less	67,859,580	3	3

Source: Internal Revenue Service (2008).

MAKING THE GRADE

The government does set a "poverty line," but there is no official standard that defines being rich.

SOCIAL PROBLEMS in Everyday Life

Do you see the rich as part of the problem of economic inequality or part of the solution? Explain your view.

Table 2–2 U.S. Government Poverty Threshold, by Family Type, 2009

Family Size	Annual Household Income
One person	$10,956
Two persons	13,991
Three persons	17,098
Four persons	21,954
Five persons	25,991
Six persons	29,405
Seven persons	33,372
Eight persons	37,252
Nine or more persons	44,366

Source: U.S. Census Bureau (2010).

budgets. Overall, our national tax policy is progressive (especially taxes on income and inheritance), lessening income inequality to some extent, depending on the tax rates. In the end, however, taxes change this country's economic inequality only a small amount.

The Rich and the Poor: A Social Profile

Many families in the United States have roughly average income and wealth. But to sharpen your understanding of the extent of economic inequality in U.S. society, we now take a brief look at the two extremes: the rich and the poor.

The Rich

There is no standard definition of what it means to be "rich." But it seems reasonable to define this category of the population as people with family income in the top 10 percent of the distribution. This means that a rich family has an income of at least $150,000, with an average of about $250,000 per year. Many men and women with high incomes are successful in business; others are distinguished physicians, lawyers, and college presidents (although rarely college professors). Over their working lives, a good portion of the rich will become millionaires—about 6.7 million people in this country have $1 million or more of wealth in the form of investments. The number of millionaires is several times higher if you count the value of their homes (Frank, 2009).

Typically, well-off people live in large, expensive homes, wear expensive clothes, and are regarded by people around them as highly successful. Many in this category are important decision makers, sitting on the boards of businesses and community organizations. High up in this elite category, we find a number of familiar names, such as Oprah Winfrey, one of the highest-paid people on television and a highly successful businesswoman. President Obama (with income of about $4 million in 2008) may earn far less than Oprah Winfrey ($200 million), but he lives in a bigger house and has more power to shape the world.

An estimate for 2008 placed the wealth of the ten richest individuals in the United States at more than $285 billion, which is as much as more than 10 million average people, or the entire populations of Vermont, Alaska, North Dakota, South Dakota, Wyoming, Montana, Iowa, Kansas, and the District of Columbia combined. The richest of the rich is Bill Gates, a founder of Microsoft Corporation and its largest shareholder, who has more money than 2 million "ordinary" people, equal in number to the entire population of New Mexico (Miller & Greenberg, 2008).

What categories of people are most likely to be rich? In general, older people have more wealth because earnings rise through middle age and savings grow over time. Men have more wealth than women do, as detailed in Chapter 4 ("Gender Inequality") because, on average, men earn almost 30 percent more than women. Married couples generally do better than single people because most benefit from double incomes and share their living expenses. Finally, white people in the United States fare better than people of color. The Census Bureau (2010) reports that 65 percent of white families earn more than $50,000 annually, compared with just 39 percent of African American and Hispanic families.

Should we define the rich as a social problem? On one hand, the rich are successful people who are living out the "American dream," and many people see this as good. On the other hand, a society that distributes opportunity and wealth so unequally also leaves others behind: the poor.

The Poor

In this nation of great wealth, millions of people scratch out a living in cities and rural areas on too little income. Every day across the United States, millions of families struggle to get the food they need, to pay the monthly rent, and to stay healthy. Some poor families experience the same daily struggle that is common in low-income countries in Latin America, Africa, and Asia. (A full discussion of global poverty and hunger is found in Chapter 15, "Population and Global Inequality.")

The Poverty Line

How many people in the United States are poor? Back in 1964, when the federal government launched a "war on poverty," offi-

poverty line an income level set by the U.S. government for the purpose of counting the poor

GETTING INVOLVED

Have you ever lived below the poverty line? Do you know people who have? If so, what can you add to the box below?

PERSONAL STORIES

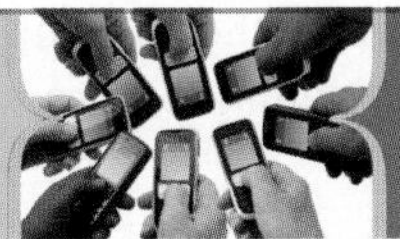

The Reality of Poverty: Living on the Edge

Zach Perkins, who lives in Richmond, Indiana, knows how hard it is to live at the poverty line. Zach had worked for seven years building school buses in a nearby factory before he was laid off eighteen months ago. He now looks after seven-year-old twins Michael and Sonya while Sandy Perkins, his wife, works in a fast-food restaurant. Sandy barely earns the minimum wage—she averages $7.50 an hour—for forty-eight hours each week, year round, for an annual income of $18,720. Zach earns another $300 per month doing part-time work, which boosts the family's total annual earnings to about $22,000, just above the official poverty line for a family of four, which in 2007 was $21,203.

To buy food, the Perkinses budget $6,000, almost one-third of their income, which amounts to $16 per day. For this amount to provide three meals for four people, the family can spend just $1.25 per meal. "You know," says Sandy with a look of pain, "that's not even enough to eat in the Burger King where I work." Although it is enough to buy low-cost foods (such as spaghetti, beans, and eggs), it is not enough to buy meals with wholesome meat and fresh vegetables.

If the Perkinses manage to stay within their annual food budget, they will have to meet all their other expenses for the year with $15,000, or about $1,250 per month. The monthly rent on a simple but adequate mobile home is $600 (they were lucky to find a rental unit well below the national average rent level of about $750). But they also have to pay for utilities, including gas, electricity, and water, and these add another $200 monthly. Sandy also needs a car to get to work, and the gasoline, insurance, and repair for their old Honda add another $200 to their monthly total. So far, total expenses come to $1,000, leaving the Perkins family with $250 (about $8 per day) to cover the cost of clothes for the entire family; everyone's medical and dental care; repairs on the washing machine, television, and other home appliances; school supplies and toys for the children; and other household items.

At this income level, the family has little money for entertainment, child care, or music lessons for the children. Zach and Sandy were glad to see the price of gas come down during the past year, but with the economy doing so badly, Zach has more trouble finding work, and Sandy is fearful that she could lose her job. Even if their income stays at the current level, they realize that sending a child to college or someday owning their home seems out of the question. "I have to be very careful with my clothes," jokes Zach. "By the time I can afford new ones, these will probably be back in style."

Zach knows how hard it is to make ends meet. But he adds firmly, "This family will *never* ask for a handout." Seated across the room, Sandy nods in agreement. Like everyone else, the poor are proud, even if they are barely able to pay their bills.

Can a family in the United States survive at the poverty level? Barely. Getting by month to month demands careful attention to every dollar spent. It also requires a bit of luck: The family must avoid unplanned expenses, which means everyone must manage to stay healthy. "Am I sure we can get by?" Zach wonders, looking down at the floor. "I guess not. But I do know one thing: We have to try."

WHAT DO YOU THINK?

1. Can a family survive on an income near the poverty line? Why or why not?
2. In what ways does growing up in a poor family limit the chances of children to succeed as adults?
3. Would you support policies or programs to assist a family like this? What should be done?

cials devised what they called the **poverty line**, *an income level set by the U.S. government for the purpose of counting the poor.* The poverty line represents a dollar amount of annual income below which a person or family is defined as poor and may therefore become eligible for government assistance. In 2009, some 44 million people out of a total 307 million—giving a *poverty rate* of 14.3 percent of the U.S. population—lived in a household with income below the official poverty line (not counting the value of benefits such as food stamps, Medicaid, and public housing).

The U.S Department of Agriculture set the poverty line to represent an annual income three times what a family has to spend in order to eat a basic, nutritious diet. Every year, government officials adjust this dollar amount to reflect the changing cost of living. In 2009, the poverty line for a nonfarm family of four was $21,954; poverty thresholds by family size are shown in Table 2–2.

How easily can a family live on poverty line income? Many analysts claim it is difficult. In the real world, they suggest, a U.S. family would need an income at least 25 percent higher to be economically secure. For this reason, critics say the poverty line should be raised. As they see it, the government sets the poverty line low to make the poverty problem seem smaller (Ehrenreich, 2001; Lichter & Crowley, 2002). The Personal Stories box lets you see for yourself to what extent a family can meet basic needs on income at the poverty line.

poverty gap the difference between the actual income of the typical poor household and the official poverty line

feminization of poverty the trend of women making up an increasing share of the poor

Dimensions of Difference

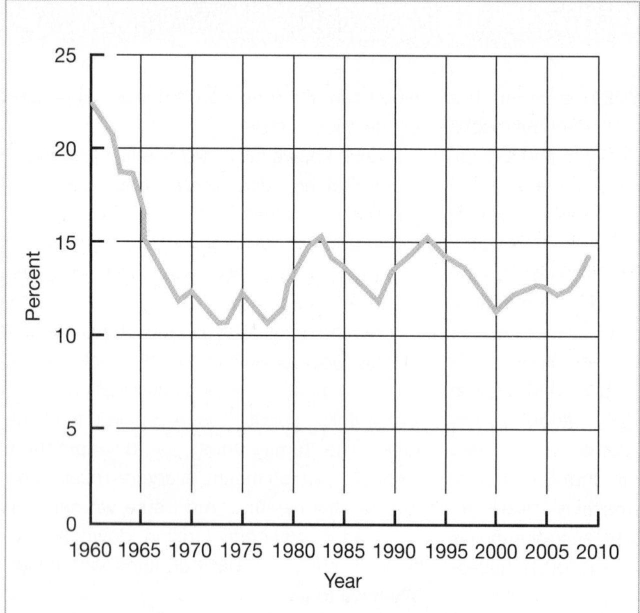

FIGURE 2–3 **The Poverty Rate in the United States, 1960–2009**

The poverty rate declined sharply in the 1960s, rising and falling since then but always staying above 10 percent of the U.S. population.

Source: U.S. Census Bureau (2010).

The Poverty Gap

Most poor families in the United States live on much less than poverty line income. The **poverty gap** is *the difference between the actual income of the typical poor household and the official poverty line.* The poverty gap has been growing in recent years.

As the story of the Perkins family in the Personal Stories box suggests, it is hard enough to live on poverty line income. But in 2009, the average poor family in the United States had an income of about $11,000, which is a poverty gap of more than $11,000 (U.S. Census Bureau, 2010). In human terms, the greater the poverty gap, the greater the hardship caused by poverty.

The Poor: A Closer Look

In 2009, the federal government counted 43.5 million men, women, and children—14.3 percent of the U.S. population—as poor. As shown in Figure 2–3, the poverty rate was 22 percent in 1960, fell to about 12 percent by the mid-1970s, and has risen and fallen since then. Economic downturns, like the one that began in 2008, increase unemployment and raise the poverty rate.

As you might expect, the categories of people at risk of being poor are quite different from those likely to be rich. We can profile the poor in the United States according to age, race, gender, family patterns, and residence.

Age

The age category at greatest risk of poverty is children, who make up 36 percent of the U.S. poor. In 2009, 15.5 million (21 percent) of young people under the age of eighteen were living in poor households. More seriously, almost half of these children live in families with incomes no more than *half* the poverty line ($11,000 or less). A generation ago, the elderly were most likely to be poor. Today, however, poverty wears a youthful face, as the Diversity: Race, Class, & Gender box explains.

Race

Many people in the United States link being poor with being African American or Hispanic. But far more white people than black people are poor, and more non-Hispanic than Hispanic people live in poverty.

It is true that the *percentage* of minority people who are poor is higher than that of whites. In 2009, some 25.8 percent of African Americans (9.9 million people), 25.3 percent of Hispanics (12.4 million people), and 12.5 percent of Asian and Pacific Islanders (1.75 million) were poor, compared to 9.4 percent of non-Hispanic whites (18.5 million people). African Americans, Hispanics, and Asian Americans are at higher risk of being poor than whites. This is why more than half of all poor people in the United States fall into these disadvantaged categories (U.S. Census Bureau, 2010).

Gender

Women, too, are at greater risk of poverty: Fifty-eight percent of all U.S. adults who are poor are women, and 42 percent are men. The gender gap has become so large that sociologists speak of the **feminization of poverty** to refer to *the trend of women making up an increasing share of the poor.* In 1960, most poor families contained both men and women; today, by contrast, 51 percent of poor families are headed by a woman with no husband present, and just 11 percent are headed by a single man (U.S. Census Bureau, 2010).

Family Patterns

Being married helps build income and wealth and greatly reduces the risk of being poor. The poverty rate for married people is 5.8% (all married) married with no children is 3.9%, compared to 20.0 percent for single men and 24.0 percent for single women (Zagorsky, 2006; U.S. Census Bureau, 2010).

Single women with children are at even higher risk of poverty because many stay at home to care for their children or cannot afford the child care they need to go to work. For all sin-

MAKING THE GRADE

Be sure you understand how age, race, gender, family patterns, and religion are linked to the risk of poverty.

SOCIAL PROBLEMS in Everyday Life

There has been a lot of talk about immigration to the United States lately. Close to 2 million people come to the United States each year. Does that support the conclusion that the American dream is alive and well? Explain.

DIVERSITY: RACE, CLASS, & GENDER

The United States: A Land of Poor Children

The United States is the richest country in the world. Even so, more than one child in six under the age of eighteen—15 million boys and girls—is poor. Since the "war on poverty" began in 1964, the nation has managed to cut poverty among senior citizens by more than half. Yet the rate of child poverty is about the same today as it was then.

What is your mental picture of poor children? The common stereotype is of African American children living in an inner city with a teenage mother who is on welfare. But in truth, two-thirds of poor children are white, and more than half live not in inner cities but in other urban, suburban, and rural areas.

Why are there so many poor children? Liberals point to the loss of good-paying jobs in the United States. In inner cities, where factories have closed, and in declining rural communities, many people simply cannot find good jobs. Conservatives note the role of family breakdown in the rising tide of poverty. They point out that 60 percent of poor children live with a single parent, and 75 percent of these households have no adult working full time (U.S. Census Bureau, 2010).

Everyone agrees that children, wherever they live, are not to blame for their own poverty. Why, then, do we continue to tolerate their suffering? Isn't reducing the crushing experience of child poverty easier and less costly than dealing with the problems that come later, such as unemployment, drug use, and crime?

WHAT DO YOU THINK?

1. Of the liberal and conservative explanations for the high rate of child poverty, which makes more sense to you? Why?
2. Few people think children themselves are responsible for being poor. Why, then, isn't there more popular support for increasing assistance to poor families with children?
3. As the unemployment rate has doubled in the past few years, what do you think has happened to the rate of child poverty? Why?

gle mothers, the poverty rate in 2009 was 38.5 percent. Single African American or Hispanic mothers bear an added risk: About 45 percent have incomes below the poverty line. If the mother is also young and has not completed high school, poverty is almost a certainty (U.S. Census Bureau, 2010).

It is easy to see why divorce raises the odds of poverty for adults and, especially, children. One study found that within a year, one in eight children of divorcing parents had slipped below the poverty line. It is also true that most poor children live with their mothers in families that are likely to remain poor (Furstenberg & Cherlin, 1991).

Region

The official poverty rate varies from state to state, from a low of 7.8 percent in New Hampshire and 8.4 percent in Connecticut to a high of 21.2 percent in Arizona and 23.1 percent in Mississippi. By region, the South (15.7 percent) and the West (14.8 percent) have higher poverty rates, followed by the Midwest (13.3 percent) and the Northeast (12.2 percent) (U.S. Census Bureau, 2010).

Many people link poverty with the inner city. Most poor people—just like most affluent people—do live in urban areas. But as National Map 2–1 on page 36 shows, rural areas have a greater share of the population living below the poverty level than do urban areas. Poverty is widespread across Appalachia (including West Virginia and Kentucky), along the Texas border with Mexico (where many new immigrants live), and in parts of the Great Plains and the Southwest (especially on American Indian lands). In 2009, some 16.6 percent of the rural population was poor, compared with 13.9 percent for people in urban areas or, looking more closely, 18.7 percent of people in central cities and 11.0 percent of people in suburbs (U.S. Census Bureau, 2010). Why do suburban areas show an advantage when it comes to income? By and large, poverty is lowest in areas that offer more jobs and more educational opportunity.

Working Families: Working Harder

Economic struggle is not limited to the poor. In recent decades, the American dream—the belief that with hard work, people can have a secure and improving way of life—has been shaken by some disturbing facts. Beginning about 1970, many U.S. families found themselves working harder than ever yet feeling that they were falling behind (C. Russell, 1995; Ehrenreich, 2001).

What's going on? For some families, of course, times have never been better. But for a large share of workers, income has nearly stalled. The earnings of a typical fifty-year-old man working full time jumped 65 percent between 1958 and 1974 in dollars controlled for inflation. Between 1974 and 2009, however, this same worker's income actually decreased by 7 percent, so he had to work more hours to meet the rising costs of groceries, housing, college tuition, and medical care. Wage

Anna Mae Peters lives in Nitta Yuma, Mississippi. Almost everyone she knows lives below the government's poverty line.

Julie Garland lives in Greenwich, Connecticut, where people have very high income and there is little evidence of poverty.

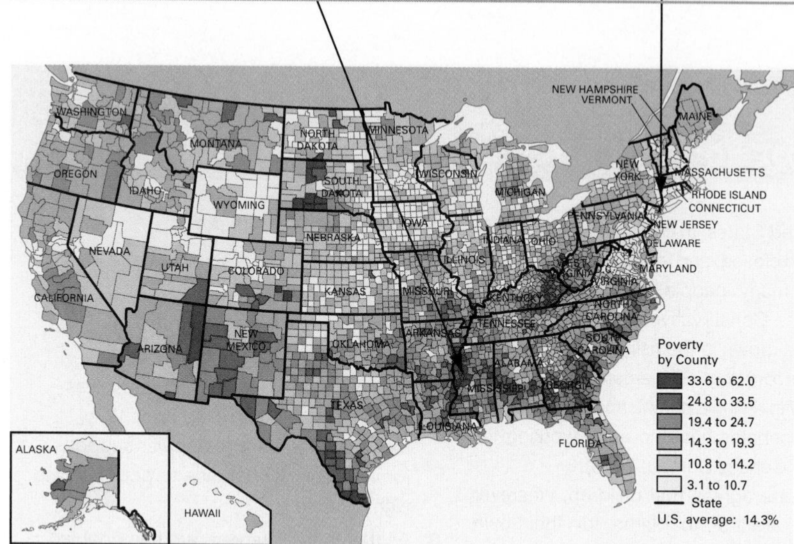

A Nation of Diversity

NATIONAL MAP 2–1

Poverty across the United States

This map shows that the poorest counties in the United States—where the poverty rate is more than twice the national average—are in Appalachia, spread across the Deep South, along the border with Mexico, near the Four Corners region of the Southwest, and in the Dakotas. Can you suggest some reasons for this pattern?

Source: U.S. Census Bureau (2010).

increases for younger workers have been very small over the past twenty years. This is the major reason that half of women and men between the ages of eighteen and twenty-four are living with their parents (U.S. Census Bureau, 2010).

Underlying this pattern of stalled earnings are changes in the economy detailed in Chapter 11 ("Work and the Workplace"). Through much of the twentieth century, the U.S. economy created jobs with *higher* pay; for example, low-paying farm jobs were replaced with higher-paying factory work. More recently, however, most new jobs have been in the service sector, including sales positions, computer data entry, and food service jobs that pay *less* than the factory jobs they are replacing.

The Working Poor

Barbara Ehrenreich, whom you met in Chapter 1, wanted to see for herself what it is like to be a low-wage worker, so she left her comfortable life as a writer to spend several months in Florida, Maine, and Minnesota, pretending to be in need of work, taking whatever jobs she could find, and trying to live on what she earned. Ehrenreich found that it was not easy. At the end of her journey, she explained (2001:220):

> I grew up hearing over and over . . . that hard work was the secret of success. "Work hard and you'll get ahead" or "It's hard work that got us where we are." No one ever said that you could work hard—harder than you ever thought possible—and still find yourself sinking ever deeper into debt and poverty.

In 2009, according to the government, 15 percent of the heads of poor families worked full time, at least fifty weeks during the year, yet remained below the poverty line. The reason is that low-wage work—Ehrenreich worked as a waitress, motel room cleaner, and sales clerk at a discount store—rarely pays much more than the (2009) federal minimum hourly wage of $7.25 per hour. At this wage level, even full-time, year-round work yields just $15,000, about $7,000 below the poverty line for a nonfarm family of four (U.S. Census Bureau, 2010).

The Nonworking Poor

Many poor families do not have a steady income from work. Government data show that in 2009, 54 percent of the heads of poor families did not work at all; another 32 percent remained poor while doing part-time work (U.S. Census Bureau, 2010).

There are many reasons for not working. Some people have health problems; others lack the skills or self-confidence needed to hold a steady job. Some parents cannot afford to pay for child care because it costs more than they can earn at a low-wage job. For many others, the problem is a lack of available work. Most inner-city areas in the United States offer few jobs. Similarly, many rural areas and small towns are in decline, with stores and factories that have closed their doors. The recent recession has sent the unemployment rate in many communities to 15 and even 20 percent, which means a big increase in the number of nonworking poor. Elkhart, Indiana, the town that makes most of the nation's recreational vehicles, is a case in point. As the bad economy has hurt the sales of RVs, one in five adults in this town is out of work and cannot find a job (W. J. Wilson, 1996a; O'Hare, 2002; Martin, 2009).

The Underclass

Poverty is most severe among the **underclass**, *poor people who live in areas with high concentrations of poverty and limited opportunities for schooling or work.* The largest concentration of

underclass poor people who live in areas with high concentrations of poverty and limited opportunities for schooling or work

SOCIAL PROBLEMS in Everyday Life

What policies or programs would help poor people who do not have the skills they need to earn a good living in today's economy?

people in the underclass live in inner cities in a condition sociologists call *hypersegregation,* cut off from the larger society and having no access to either good schools or good-paying jobs. Under such conditions, children grow up poor, and most remain poor as adults (Massey & Denton, 1989; E. Anderson, 1999).

Hypersegregation is found in rural areas as well, which can be just as isolated from the larger world as the inner cities. Across the United States, the underclass includes perhaps one in seven poor people, or 1 to 2 percent of the total U.S. population.

For people who are part of the underclass, the reality of everyday life is *persistent poverty.* But most people in the United States who are poor are not part of the underclass. For the society as a whole, *temporary poverty* is more the rule. Over ten years, about one-fourth of the U.S. population falls below the poverty line, usually because of unemployment, illness, or divorce. When this happens, the typical pattern is for a household to remain poor for perhaps a year or two.

Whether poverty is a short-term or long-term experience, it is rarely a problem that exists all by itself. On the contrary, poverty brings with it a wide range of additional challenges, which we shall now examine.

One way that we know that poverty is a social problem rather than simply an individual problem is by looking at poverty rates, which are very high in certain regions of the country. Economic opportunity is all but gone from a number of rural areas, especially in the Great Plains; as a result, entire communities suffer.

Problems Linked to Poverty

Without the income needed for a safe and secure life, the poor suffer in many ways. The following sections take a closer look at six problems linked to poverty: poor health, substandard housing, homelessness, limited schooling, crime, and political alienation.

Poor Health

There is a strong link between income and health. In fact, there is a good deal of truth in the claim that "wealth means health." Poverty, disease, and illness often go together.

Good nutrition is the foundation of a healthy life. Yet many poor people cannot afford nutritious foods. In 2007, about 11 percent of U.S. households (and 37 percent of poor households) experienced "food insecurity." But the challenges of living poor go beyond having enough healthful food. In addition, poverty breeds stress, increasing the use of tobacco and alcohol and raising the risk of drug abuse and violence. Just as important, when illness or injury strikes, poor people have fewer resources to fight back. About one-third lack health insurance, so they simply cannot afford medical care. As a result, poor people may not seek medical care right away. A common pattern is for poor people to show up at an emergency room with a serious condition that could have been cured easily had the person been treated much earlier (Center on Hunger and Poverty, 2000; Nord, Andrews, & Carlson, 2002; U.S. Census Bureau, 2010).

Poverty affects health throughout the life course. Among the poor, *infant mortality,* the risk of death during the first year of life, is twice the national average. Among the very poor, the death rate among newborns rises to about four times the national average, which is on the same level as we commonly find in low-income countries such as Nigeria and Vietnam.

Income continues to shape health into adulthood. When asked to rate their personal health, 80 percent of adults living in families with incomes over $75,000 replied "excellent" or "very good." But only 54 percent of people whose families had incomes of $35,000 or less could say the same (Adams et al., 2010).

Finally, for people who are poor, life can be short. Low-income men and women are more likely to die young from infectious diseases, from violence, and even from natural disasters—almost all of the people who died in Hurricane Katrina were poor. By contrast, most rich people die of cancer and heart disease, diseases that typically take their toll in old age. For this reason, life expectancy for affluent people is almost five years greater than for low-income people, and this "health gap" has doubled in the years since 1980 (Miniño, Heron, & Smith, 2006; Congressional Budget Office, 2008).

homelessness the plight of poor people who lack shelter and live primarily on the streets

MAKING THE GRADE

Notice below how explanations of the causes of homelessness reflect political attitudes.

Substandard Housing

In the United States, better housing is available to those who can pay for it. For this reason, poor people take what is left: crowded homes containing dangerous lead-based paint, faulty plumbing, inadequate heating, and even collapsing walls and crumbling ceilings. The poor in New Orleans who were ravaged by Hurricane Katrina, for example, were twice as likely as average people to lack good plumbing or some other basic system in their homes (Bass, 2005).

Recent years have seen a steady decline in the number of low-rent apartments in the United States. As a result, many poor families are forced to spend most of what they earn for housing, leaving too little for food, clothing, and other needs. Not surprisingly, in large cities across the United States, tens of thousands of poor people are on waiting lists for programs that will help them secure better housing (Adler & Malone, 1996; Ehrenreich, 2001).

Homelessness

In recent decades, the problem of **homelessness,** *the plight of poor people who lack shelter and live primarily on the streets,* has received a lot of attention. Researchers estimate that 500,000 people are homeless in the United States on any given night, and as many as 3.5 million people are homeless at some point during a year (L. Kaufman, 2004; U.S. Department of Housing and Urban Development, 2007).

There are many causes of homelessness, and how much emphasis is given to any particular cause depends on one's political outlook. Conservatives point to personal problems, noting that one-fourth of homeless people suffer from mental disorders, and many abuse alcohol and other drugs. Liberals counter that homelessness has less to do with personal shortcomings than with poverty, and they point to low-wage jobs and a lack of affordable housing as major causes.

About half of homeless people do not work, almost half work part time, and a few work full time. Average income for homeless individuals is low—just $350 per month; for families, the figure is about $475. Such income is simply not enough to pay for housing (U.S. Department of Housing and Urban Development, 1999).

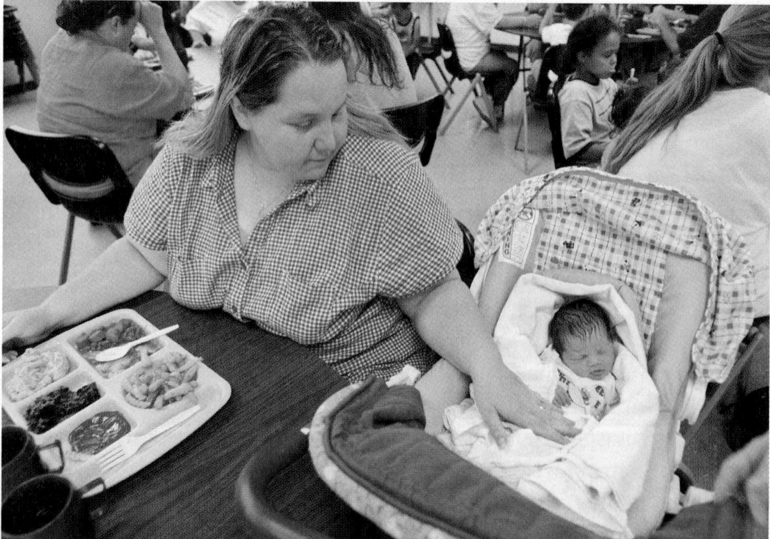

Homeless shelters provide necessary housing to hundreds of thousands of people across the United States. But the larger question is why do so many people lack affordable housing in the first place?

Limited Schooling

Poor children are less likely than rich children to complete high school. Therefore, the odds of going to college are low, and the chances of completing an advanced degree are smaller still. Too often, underperforming public schools transform low-income children into low-achieving students who grow up to be low-income adults. The public school systems in many of the largest cities in the United States fail to graduate half of all young people who enroll in the schools. Under these conditions, it is easy to see how poor schooling can help pass poverty from one generation to the next.

Even for those who stay in school, rich and poor children typically have different experiences. Many schools use some form of *tracking,* by which the schools divide children into college-bound ("academic") and job-oriented ("vocational") coursework tracks. The stated goal of tracking is to teach children according to their academic abilities. But research suggests that school officials often label children as less able just because they are poor and see privileged children as more talented. The result is that many poor children are taught in crowded classrooms with fewer computers, older books, and the weakest teachers (Hallinan & Williams, 1989; Kilgore, 1991; Kozol, 1991; Thornburgh, 2006).

Crime and Punishment

If you watch police "reality" shows on TV, you are bound to think that most criminals are poor people. Assault, robbery, burglary, auto theft—these "street crimes" get most of the public's attention and are featured most in the mass media. As Chapter 6 ("Crime, Violence, and the Criminal Justice System")

social welfare programs organized efforts by government, private organizations, or individuals to assist needy people considered worthy of assistance

SOCIAL PROBLEMS in Everyday Life

Our welfare system is not based on what "works" to end poverty, but on what is consistent with our cultural values and beliefs. Can you explain how?

explains, when it comes to street crimes, poor people are involved more often than affluent people—both as offenders and as victims. The public pays less attention to the types of crimes commonly committed by wealthy people, including tax evasion, stock fraud, false advertising, bribery, and environmental pollution, even though such offenses almost certainly cause greater harm to society as a whole.

The greater public attention given to street crime means that it is the poor who are most likely to be arrested, go to trial, and face a prison sentence. Poor people who enter the criminal justice system must also rely on public defenders or court-appointed attorneys, typically lawyers who are underpaid and overworked. Wealthy people in trouble—including the Wall Street executives widely thought to have contributed to the collapse of the country's banking system in 2008—can afford to enlist the help of private lawyers who in turn employ other specialists to support their claims in court. Such an advantage does not always get people off the hook, but it does lower the chances of being charged with a crime or, if they are charged, of being convicted.

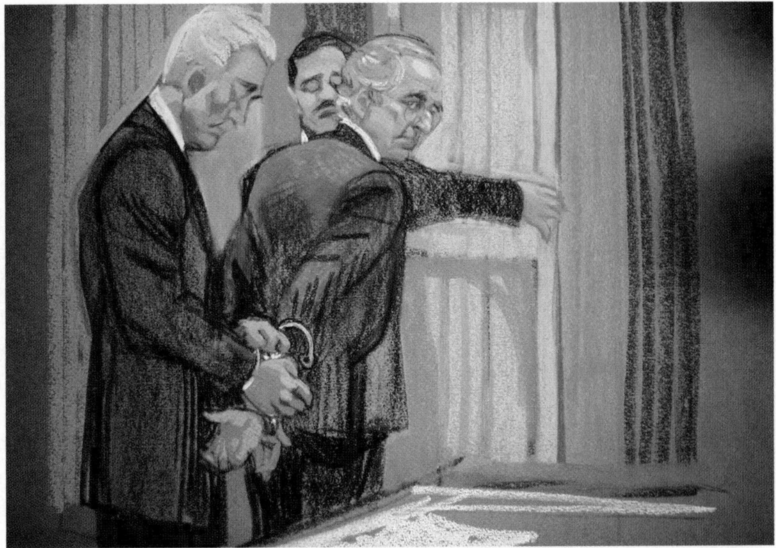

The common view is that the poor are the most likely to commit crimes. But recent corporate scandals have gone a long way toward changing that view. In 2009, mega-swindler Bernard Madoff was sentenced to 150 years in prison for carrying off what was probably the largest investment fraud in history.

Finally, going to jail means that later on, it will be hard to find a good job. Just as poverty raises the risk of getting into trouble with the law, being convicted of a crime raises the odds that a low-income person will end up staying poor (Western, 2002).

Political Alienation

Given how hard the poor have to struggle to get by, you might expect that they would be politically active and eager to bring about change. Sometimes poor people do organize politically, but many do not even bother to vote. In the 2008 presidential election, about 80 percent of people earning $100,000 or more voted; just under half of people earning less than $10,000 did the same. This pattern suggests that many poor people feel alienated from a system that they think does not serve their interests (Samuelson, 2003; U.S. Census Bureau, 2009).

Responding to Poverty: The Welfare System

To address the problem of poverty, all high-income countries rely on various kinds of **social welfare programs,** *organized efforts by government, private organizations, or individuals to assist needy people considered worthy of assistance.* Social welfare takes many forms, including government unemployment insurance for workers, Red Cross benefits for flood victims, or simply people lending a hand to their neighbors after a disaster. But the largest welfare programs, run by the government, have three characteristics:

1. **Social welfare programs benefit people or activities defined as worthy.** The public and its leaders debate and decide which categories of people or activities are most worthy of support. The categories of people who benefit from social welfare programs change along with the level of available resources and swings in the political mood of the country.
2. **Social welfare programs benefit most people.** Welfare programs include not only assistance to poor families but also price supports for farmers, the oil depletion allowance to petroleum companies, the homeowner's tax deduction for home mortgage interest, pensions paid to the elderly, benefits for veterans, and low-interest loans for students. The government bailout of AIG and other financial corporations in 2008 and 2009 was also an example of massive social welfare assistance.
3. **Overall, social welfare programs change income inequality only a little.** Some government programs take from the rich (in taxes) and others give to the poor (in benefits), which has the effect of reducing economic inequality. But many programs, such as the recent corporate bailouts, benefit wealthier individuals and families. Even among "ordinary"

SOCIAL PROBLEMS in Everyday Life

Reading the pages below, how conservative or liberal was our nation's view of poverty across our history? Explain.

Who gets government welfare? In 2009, the government's billion-dollar bailout of General Motors helped that corporation go through a short bankruptcy and reorganize in the hope of becoming a stronger company in the future. The government action meant that hundreds of thousands of autoworkers (who now own a share of the company) still have their jobs.

people, the tax deduction on home mortgage interest costs the government about $491 billion annually, and most of this benefit goes to affluent people who own larger homes. The home mortgage deduction is worth ten times as much as what the government spends to provide food assistance to low-income people (U.S. Census Bureau, 2010).

The ongoing welfare debate points up a hard truth: People in this country like to think they are compassionate, but our cultural emphasis on personal responsibility makes many people uneasy with giving assistance to the poor. The Thinking Critically box evaluates six common assumptions about public assistance.

A Brief History of Welfare

Social welfare has a long and controversial history in the United States. The following discussion surveys welfare policies in three historical periods—the colonial era, the early industrial era, and the modern era after the Great Depression—and then highlights the 1996 welfare reforms (Trattner, 1980; Katz, 1990, 1996).

The Colonial Era

During the 1600s and 1700s, early immigrants who came to the United States settled in small communities where families living in a strange and uncertain world struggled to survive. Because almost everyone was poor, family members and neighbors were quick to help one another.

Even so, some colonists, including the early Puritans in New England, looked down on the very poor, seeing poverty as a sign of moral weakness. Throughout the colonies, free people looked down on slaves as personally inferior and therefore morally undeserving. During this period, there was hardly any government at all, and "welfare" was limited to acts of personal kindness between kin and neighbors.

The Early Industrial Era

As the Industrial Revolution began in the early 1800s, U.S. cities swelled with immigrants. The new industrial capitalist economy encouraged a spirit of individualism and self-reliance. The idea that people were responsible for their own social position made attitudes toward the poor more negative. In addition, the public criticized charity as a policy that would only reduce people's need to work and end up making them lazy. Organizations such as the Salvation Army (founded in 1865) that did offer food and shelter to the poor included moral instruction reinforcing the belief that the poor were weak and of bad character.

But not everyone shared this harsh view of the poor. In the 1870s, the *scientific charity movement* (really an early form of sociology) began studying who were poor, why they were poor, and what could be done to help them. Researchers soon learned that most poor people were not lazy but were men and women without jobs, children without parents, women without husbands, victims of factory accidents, and working people earning too little to support a family. In short, scientific charity claimed that most poverty was not the fault of the poor themselves but the result of how society operates.

This new thinking helped guide the *settlement house movement.* Settlement houses were buildings located in the worst slums of a city, where a staff of social scientists and reform-minded activists helped new immigrants get settled in their new surroundings. This social movement also tried to influence public opinion with the goal of making the public more compassionate toward the poor.

The Twentieth Century

By 1900, the millions of immigrants streaming into the United States were fueling hostility toward the poor. World War I

MAKING THE GRADE

A closer look at Roosevelt's "New Deal" is found on page 42.

SOCIAL PROBLEMS in Everyday Life

In general, Democratic presidents have been more likely to use government power to address poverty. How have Republican presidents tried to reduce poverty?

THINKING CRITICALLY

An Undeserved Handout? The Truth about "Welfare"

Are welfare assistance checks and food stamps just handouts for people too lazy to work? What are the facts? Let's evaluate six widespread assumptions about public assistance.

1. **"Most welfare goes to the poor."** Not true. If we look at *all* government income programs, we find hundreds that offer financial benefits—cash transfers or reduced taxes—to many categories of people. For example, almost all of the government "bailout" money given to banks in 2008 and 2009 ended up going to rich people. Overall, no more than half of all government benefits go to poor people.
2. **"Most income assistance goes to able-bodied people."** Not true. Most low-income people who benefit from government assistance are too old or too young to work. Some programs do assist poor parents who do not work. But these funds are primarily for support of children, and the assistance is provided only for a limited time.
3. **"Once on welfare, always on welfare."** Before the welfare reforms of 1996, there was some truth to this. Back then, half of families who ever enrolled in Aid for Families with Dependent Children received public assistance for four years or more. But because of limits in the current program (including a lifetime benefit limit of five years), this is no longer the case.
4. **"Most welfare benefits go to African Americans and other minorities."** True, but just barely. Non-Hispanic whites receive 43 percent of all food stamps; African Americans receive 33 percent, and Hispanics receive 20 percent. So the two minority categories added together receive 53 percent all these benefits. Minorities are more likely than whites to receive income assistance because, as we have already explained, these categories of the population are at higher risk for being poor.
5. **"Welfare encourages single women to have children."** Not true. The average number of children among women without husbands is the same whether or not families receive welfare support. The case has also been made that welfare assistance enabled some women to support children without marrying. This may be so, but the trend toward more single parenting is found among people of all income levels and in all high-income nations.
6. **"Welfare fraud is a serious national problem."** Not really. Social service agency employees will tell you that a few people do take advantage of the system, but they will also confirm that the vast majority of benefits go to people who are truly needy.

WHAT DO YOU THINK?

1. Did any of the facts presented in this box surprise you? Which ones? Why?
2. Do you think the election of President Obama has brought about changes in attitudes or policy toward the poor? If so, what changes?
3. Has the recent economic recession affected how people think about poverty and welfare assistance? Explain your answer.

(1914–18) made matters worse by raising fear and suspicion of "foreigners." There was little public support for welfare programs of any kind.

Then, in 1929, the Great Depression rolled across the United States. As many as one-fourth of all working people lost their jobs, sending millions of families into poverty. Banks closed, wiping out people's life savings, and families in debt lost their farms or their homes. Under such conditions, it became impossible to see poverty as caused by people who were lazy or "different." It was then that U.S. society began to define poverty as a *social* problem.

Franklin Roosevelt became president in 1933 and proposed a program he called the New Deal to help the millions made poor by the Depression. Throughout the 1930s, the federal government enacted many new programs to fight poverty, the most important of which was Social Security. Today, this program provides monthly income to 45 million people, most of whom are elderly.

Roosevelt's reforms eased the suffering, and World War II (1939–45) spurred the economy, ending the Depression and also directing public attention to other issues. Later, in the 1960s, researchers "rediscovered" poverty in both cities and the rural countryside (Harrington, 1962), prompting President Lyndon Johnson in 1964 to launch his War on Poverty. The Defining Moment box on page 42 takes a closer look at U.S. society facing up to the continuing reality of poverty.

A glance back at Figure 2–3 shows that the War on Poverty actually worked. The official poverty rate, which was about 22 percent in 1960, fell to about 11 percent by the early 1970s. But by the 1980s, the mood of the country again turned against social welfare programs. Beginning with the Reagan administration, the federal government scaled back assistance programs, claiming (like critics a century earlier) that welfare programs were discouraging personal initiative and creating "dependency."

MAKING THE GRADE

Notice how the box below describes the social construction of the problem of poverty.

CONSTRUCTING SOCIAL PROBLEMS

A DEFINING MOMENT

U.S. Society "Discovers" Poverty

During the first centuries of our country's history, many people lived with so little that we can barely imagine such poverty today. Back then, most poor people accepted their situation because when they looked around, everyone else was living pretty much the same way.

When the Industrial Revolution came along, dramatically raising living standards for the majority of the population, the gap between rich and poor became bigger. Still, the poverty of those left behind—in urban neighborhoods and rural communities—provoked little public concern, probably because many of the poor were seen as "different" (as immigrants or "hillbillies") by those who were better off.

Then came the Great Depression in 1929, when people in all social classes lost much of the security they had previously taken for granted. Suddenly, people started to talk about poverty as a serious social problem. This process was encouraged by Franklin D. Roosevelt, elected president in 1932, who pointed out the problem of "one-third of a nation ill-clothed, ill-housed, and ill-fed." The economic programs that came to be known as the New Deal—most importantly, the Works Progress Administration (WPA) employment projects and Social Security—addressed the problem of poverty by providing a social "safety net" for the U.S. population.

By the end of World War II, the Depression had given way to a period of economic prosperity. But despite the fact that the United States had become a very rich nation, a large underclass of poor people continued to live in both urban and rural areas. Lyndon B. Johnson, president from 1963 until 1968, mobilized the country once again to define poverty as a problem when he declared that the government would wage a "war on poverty." He pushed the government to "strike at the causes, not the consequences" of poverty, and Congress reacted by passing programs such as Title I federal funding for public schools in low-income districts, Head Start for preschool children, and the Job Corps training program for adults.

Together, Presidents Roosevelt and Johnson did more than any other U.S. leaders to define poverty as a social problem. Just as important, they directed the power of the government toward creating a solution.

Franklin Delano Roosevelt, who was president from 1933 until 1945, established Social Security and other programs that provide a social "safety net" to the U.S. population. A generation later, Lyndon Baines Johnson, who was president from 1963 until 1968, declared a national "war on poverty" that succeeded in reducing the poverty rate.

GETTING INVOLVED

Have you or someone you know ever been on welfare? If so, can you add anything to the discussion below?

culture of poverty cultural patterns that make poverty a way of life

meritocracy a system of social inequality in which social standing corresponds to personal ability and effort

social disorganization a breakdown in social order caused by rapid social change

The 1996 Welfare Reform

In the early 1990s, about 8 million poor households in the United States were receiving public assistance totaling some $40 billion annually, for an average of about $5,000 per family. The most important assistance program was Aid to Families with Dependent Children (AFDC), which provided income to poor mothers with children.

Changes in the welfare system began to take shape in 1992, when President Bill Clinton pledged to "end welfare as we know it." In 1994, the Democratic president and a Republican Congress joined forces to produce the most sweeping welfare reform since the Roosevelt era. The purpose of the reform was suggested by its formal title: the 1996 Personal Responsibility and Work Opportunity Reconciliation Act. First, responsibility for helping the poor shifted from the federal government to the states. The old federal program, AFDC, was ended in favor of a state-level program called Temporary Assistance for Needy Families (TANF). The new rules were intended to increase the "personal responsibility" of the poor by requiring able-bodied people seeking benefits to find a job or enroll in job training. In addition, the program limits the period of time that families can receive benefits to two consecutive years, with a lifetime cap of five years.

Supporters of welfare reform (mainly conservatives) call the policy a success. They point to the fact that the nation's welfare rolls have fallen by half. In addition, half of those who have left welfare now have jobs, and most of the remainder are attending school or enrolled in training programs. But critics (mostly liberals) counter that most people who have left welfare for work now have low-wage jobs that leave them struggling to make ends meet. They claim that reform has reduced welfare assistance, but it has not done much to reduce *poverty* (Lichter & Crowley, 2002; Lichter & Jayakody, 2002).

Theoretical Analysis: Understanding Poverty

Why does poverty exist in the first place? Some answers can be found by applying sociology's major theoretical approaches to the issue of poverty.

Structural-Functional Analysis: Some Poverty Is Inevitable

Chapter 1 ("Sociology: Studying Social Problems") identified a number of structural-functional approaches to social problems. Each has something to say about why poverty exists.

Social Pathology Theories: Personal Deficiency

Some early sociologists argued in favor of a "bad apple" theory that claimed that poverty was the result of personal flaws. For example, Herbert Spencer (1820–1903) developed an analysis, called *social Darwinism,* that viewed society as a competitive arena where the most able became rich and the least able fell into poverty. Spencer described the operation of society as the "survival of the fittest."

The social pathology approach is also found in the work of the anthropologist Oscar Lewis (1961, 1966). Lewis studied poor communities in San Juan (Puerto Rico), Mexico City, and New York City, asking why some neighborhoods remained poor from generation to generation. His conclusion: They contain a **culture of poverty,** *cultural patterns that make poverty a way of life.* Lewis claimed that people *adapt* to poverty, accepting their plight and giving up hope that life can improve. Thinking this way, Lewis continued, people may turn to alcohol or drugs, become violent, neglect their families, and end up living just for the moment. Doing so, they pass on the culture of poverty from one generation to the next.

A more recent social pathology theory is the "bell curve" thesis of Richard J. Herrnstein and Charles Murray (1994). Over the course of the twentieth century, they argue, the United States became more of a **meritocracy,** *a system of social inequality in which social standing corresponds to personal ability and effort.* In today's information age, intelligence matters more than ever. Therefore, the argument goes, the ranks of the rich are increasingly filled by people who are very smart, leaving behind the poor who are more and more likely to be people with limited intelligence. For this reason, Herrnstein and Murray conclude, government programs can do only so much to improve the plight of the poor: As Herbert Spencer said a century earlier, they are capable of little more.

Social Disorganization Theory: Too Much Change

In the 1920s and 1930s, sociologists at the University of Chicago linked poverty to **social disorganization,** *a breakdown in social order caused by rapid social change.* Industrial factories drew tens of millions of people—rural midwesterners, men and women from towns in Appalachia, African Americans from the South's Cotton Belt, and immigrants from Europe—to the rapidly growing cities of the North and Midwest.

People arrived too fast for a city's neighborhoods, schools, and factories to absorb them. The result was overcrowded apartment buildings, overflowing classrooms, and too many people for the number of available jobs. The overall result was poverty and related social problems. Only with time could we expect local communities to respond to these imbalances reducing the poverty problem.

blaming the victim finding the cause of a social problem in the behavior of people who suffer from it

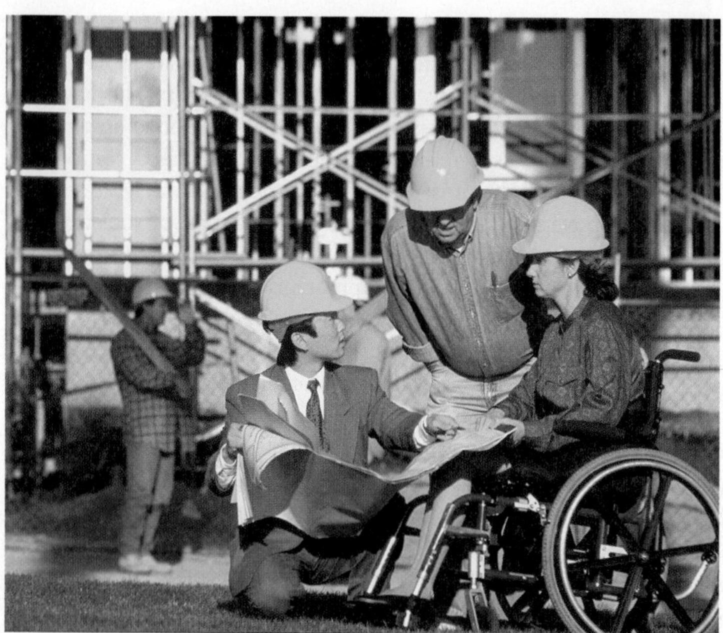

Engineers and architects are among the higher-paid workers in the U.S. labor force. From a structural-functional point of view, our society rewards work that requires rare skills and expensive education. As you read on, try to develop a critical response to this position based on social-conflict theory.

In recent years, the high rate of immigration to the United States, especially from Latin America, has contributed to high poverty rates in many regions of the Southwest and West, where many new arrivals struggle to find housing and work. In time, according to the social disorganization approach, we would expect most of these families to improve their situation.

Modern Functional Theory: Inequality Is Useful

In 1945, Kingsley Davis and Wilbert Moore asked, "Why does inequality exist everywhere?" Their answer was that inequality—specifically, differences in the rewards given to people who perform various jobs—is useful for the operation of society. Davis and Moore explained that some jobs (say, as a security guard) are not very important and can be performed by just about anyone. But other positions (for example, that of a surgeon) require rare talents and extensive training. How can society motivate people to develop their abilities and gain the schooling they need to do important jobs? Only by providing greater rewards, such as higher income, increased power, and more prestige. Linking rewards to the importance of various jobs is useful and creates social stratification, with some people having more resources than others.

Davis and Moore point out that any society could reward everyone equally, but only if it makes no difference who does what job or how well the job is done. A society with no differences in rewards, they claim, would not be very productive because it would give people little incentive to work hard or to improve their skills. In sum, inequality actually helps society be productive.

Another sociologist, Herbert Gans (1971), offers a different take, pointing out that inequality is useful only to *affluent* people. The function of inequality, Gans claims, is to ensure that there is a supply of poor people willing to do almost any job, no matter how unpleasant. Other than poor people (who have few choices in their lives), he asks, who would want to perform farm labor, pick up garbage, or clean other people's homes? In addition, the poor also buy things no one else wants, including rundown housing, old cars, rebuilt appliances, and secondhand clothing. In short, Gans suggests, poverty exists because many people benefit from it.

CRITICAL REVIEW All structural-functional theories share a key argument: At least some poverty is a natural, expected part of life that has some useful consequences. Critics, especially people who are more liberal, take issue with these theories, especially the idea that poor people are somehow inferior. As they see it, poverty is not something that people bring on themselves, nor is it inevitable. Rather, poverty has economic causes, including unemployment and low wage levels that leave even full-time workers poor.

Why, then, have such theories been popular? Perhaps because locating the causes of poverty in poor people themselves justifies the status quo and turns attention away from flaws in society itself, which we look at next.

Symbolic-Interaction Analysis: Defining the Problem

Symbolic-interaction theory highlights the social construction of problems and solutions. This approach explores how members of a society view the poor and how those views lead to particular understandings of the causes of poverty.

For instance, there's the view of poor people as lazy, lacking intelligence, or in some other way personally flawed, a notion mentioned earlier in connection with the structural-functional approach. Given our society's individualistic culture, it's not surprising that many people are quick to construct poverty as a problem caused by the poor, whom they view as responsible for their own condition.

William Ryan (1976) describes how this can happen. He calls this process **blaming the victim,** *finding the cause of a*

GETTING INVOLVED

Do you think Ryan's "blaming the victim" theory is conservative or liberal? Why?

cultural capital skills, values, attitudes, and schooling that increase a person's chances of success

social problem in the behavior of people who suffer from it. He explains that blaming the victim involves four simple steps:

1. **Pick a social problem.** Almost any will do; here, our focus is poverty.
2. **Decide how people who suffer from the problem differ from everyone else.** It is easy to see that poor people don't dress as well as others; many also don't speak English very well. Many have little schooling. They live in rundown housing. They sometimes get into trouble with the police. The list goes on and on.
3. **Define these differences as the cause of the problem.** Claim, "*Of course* those people are poor! Just look at them! Listen to them speak! See where they live! Who is surprised that people like that are poor? They *deserve* to be where they are."
4. **Respond to the problem by trying to change the victims, not the larger society.** Think to yourself that people would not be poor if only they would dress better, speak better, live in better neighborhoods—in short, be more like those who are well off.

However, if one sees the poor as people who are no different from anyone else, the picture changes. Poor people become individuals who are struggling—often heroically—against disadvantages that exist through no fault of their own. When the poor are viewed this way, it is society, not any personal failings of poor people themselves, that is to blame for poverty.

Ryan suggests that instead of shaking our heads at the rundown houses where poor people live, we should ask why U.S. society provides such housing for some of its people. Instead of pointing out how little schooling someone has, we should ask why our schools fail to meet the needs of so many students.

CRITICAL REVIEW Symbolic-interaction analysis is useful in showing that poverty is not simply an issue of money; it is also a matter of meanings, or how we view the poor. Although this approach points to society as the cause of poverty, it says little about exactly how society makes some people poor. This issue brings us to the social-conflict approach.

Social-Conflict Analysis: Poverty Can Be Eliminated

Social-conflict theory takes the view that poverty is in no way inevitable or natural, and it is certainly not a good thing. This analysis also rejects the idea that poverty results from flaws in people. On the contrary, this approach claims that poverty is caused by flaws in society itself.

Marxist Theory: Poverty and Capitalism

Karl Marx could see how much the Industrial Revolution had increased economic production. But Marx objected to the fact that all the wealth it generated remained in the hands of so few people.

Marx pointed to what he called an *internal contradiction* in the capitalist economy: A system that produced so much ended up making so many people poor. From this observation, Marx went on to encourage workers to join together to overthrow this system (for details about how capitalism works, see Chapter 10, "Economy and Politics").

In the century and a quarter since Marx's death, the United States and other high-income nations have seen living standards rise for all categories of people, a fact that helps explain why the workers' revolution that Marx predicted has not taken place, at least not yet. Even so, as noted earlier in this chapter, most income and wealth still go to a very small share of the people. Just as important, economic inequality has been increasing in recent years. Following Marx's thinking, although U.S. society has managed to avoid a workers' revolution, the problem of poverty remains very real.

More than Money: Cultural Capital

More recent conflict theories have explained that social inequality involves not only income and wealth but also **cultural capital,**

What makes these well-to-do children different from those who are less affluent? On the face of it, the answer is that their families have more wealth. In addition, however, they benefit from a richer cultural capital—the skills, values, and attitudes that come with privilege.

intersection theory the investigation of the interplay of race, class, and gender often resulting in multiple dimensions of disadvantage

The basic insight of intersection theory is that various dimensions of social stratification—including race and gender—can add up to great disadvantages for some categories of people. Just as African Americans earn less than whites, women earn less than men. Thus African American women face a "double disadvantage," earning just 61 cents for every dollar earned by non-Hispanic white men. How would you explain the fact that some categories of people are much more likely to end up in low-paying jobs like this one?

skills, values, attitudes, and schooling that increase a person's chances of success. Pierre Bourdieu and Jean-Claude Passeron (1977) argue that young people born into affluent families benefit from a rich cultural environment, both at home and at school, that all but ensures their success. On the other hand, those born to low-income families have few such advantages, so they are impoverished in more ways than one.

Feminist Theory: Poverty and Patriarchy

Feminist theory adds to our understanding by highlighting the importance of gender. This theory begins with the fact that women of all racial and ethnic categories are at high risk of poverty. This is especially true of single mothers, who are more than six times as likely (51 percent) as single fathers (8 percent) to be poor (U.S. Census Bureau, 2008).

The link between gender and poverty is actually stronger than it was several generations ago. In 1960, just one in four poor families was headed by a woman; in 2009, more than half were. What explains this *feminization of poverty*? As feminists see it, the reason is simply that even as more and more women enter the labor force, U.S. society continues to provide more income, wealth, power, and prestige to men than to women. As Chapter 4 ("Gender Inequality") explains, our culture defines most high-paying jobs (as doctors, airline pilots, and college presidents) as "men's work" while expecting that lower-paying positions (as nurses, flight attendants, and clerical workers) will be filled by women.

Multicultural Theory: Poverty, Race, and Ethnicity

The multicultural perspective highlights how poverty is linked to race and ethnicity. For example, the 2009 median income for non-Hispanic white families was $67,341. For African American families, it was $38,401, or 57 percent as much as white families. The figure for Hispanic families was $39,730, or 59 percent of the white income level. As noted earlier, both African Americans (25.8 percent) and Hispanics (25.3 percent) have almost three times the risk of poverty as non-Hispanic whites (9.4 percent). Asian American and Pacific Islander families have above-average income ($75,027 in 2009) and a poverty rate (12.5 percent) somewhat above that of non-Hispanic whites. Chapter 3 ("Racial and Ethnic Inequality") presents a full discussion of this issue.

Intersection Theory: Multiple Disadvantage

If African Americans and Hispanics are disadvantaged and women are also disadvantaged, are African American or Hispanic women doubly disadvantaged? This question is the focus of **intersection theory,** *the investigation of the interplay of race, class, and gender often resulting in multiple dimensions of disadvantage.*

To see how this works, let's start by noting the inequalities linked to race and ethnicity: The 2009 median income of non-Hispanic white men working full time was $52,469; African American men typically earned just $39,362, which is 75 percent as much; Hispanic men earned $31,638, or 60 percent as much.

Now add in gender. Compared with African American men, African American women (again, comparing just full-time workers) earned $32,470, or 83 percent as much. Hispanic women earned an average of $27,883, or 88 percent as much as Hispanic men. These disparities are linked to gender.

Now combine the two dimensions. Compared with non-Hispanic white men, African American women earned just 62 percent as much; Hispanic women earned only 53 percent as much. By comparing all these numbers, we see that race or ethnicity and gender not only operate alone but also combine so

MAKING THE GRADE

Be sure you understand the differences between feminist, multicultural, and intersection theories of poverty. All use the social-conflict approach.

GETTING INVOLVED

How much do you think personal choices figure into the risk of poverty? Explain.

APPLYING THEORY

Poverty

	What is the level of analysis?	What is the view of poverty?
Structural-functional approach	Macro-level	Early social pathology theory and the later culture of poverty theory see personal flaws and the culture of poor communities as the causes of poverty. Social disorganization theory links poverty and other social problems to rapid social change. The Davis and Moore theory explains that a system of unequal rewards draws talent to important work and encourages effort, in the process creating social stratification. Gans points out that inequality is useful primarily to richer people.
Symbolic-interaction approach	Micro-level	Symbolic-interaction theory highlights the meanings people attach to the poor. Ryan describes a common view of the poor as "blaming the victim," which is finding the causes of poverty in the attitudes or behavior of the poor themselves. Viewing the poor as no different from anyone else encourages the view that society, rather than the poor themselves, is responsible for poverty.
Social-conflict approach	Macro-level	Marx claimed that poverty results from the operation of capitalism. Poor people suffer from less cultural capital, as well as less money. Feminist theory points to patriarchy as placing women and their children at high risk of poverty. Multicultural theory notes the high poverty rates of African Americans and Latinos. Intersection theory explains that class, gender, and race combine to produce disadvantage.

that certain categories of people are doubly disadvantaged (Saint Jean & Feagin, 1998; U.S. Census Bureau, 2010).

CRITICAL REVIEW Beginning with Karl Marx's claim that the most important inequality in a class society involves struggle between the owners and workers in the capitalist economy, more recent conflict theorists have extended this analysis to cultural capital as well as inequality involving race, ethnicity, and gender.

Marx argued that poverty is a normal part of society, at least one with a capitalist economy. Yet people further to the political right are likely to point out that Marx did not foresee ways that capitalist societies would improve living standards for working people and greatly reduce the extent of poverty.

More conservative critics might also ask, doesn't being rich or poor at least partly reflect the choices people make or the talents they have as individuals? If we take away all of people's responsibility for their situation, we end up being little more than passive victims of society. Critics of the conflict approach also claim that there is more meritocracy—the ability to rise or fall based on individual talent and effort—in today's society than ever before.

Finally, multicultural and feminist theories, as well as intersection theory, point up how our society puts racial and ethnic minorities and all women at high risk for poverty. But more conservative critics say that these approaches ignore how opportunities for women and minorities have improved in the past hundred years. Back then, the segregation of African Americans was a matter of law and women could not even vote; these blatant examples of inequality simply no longer exist.

The Applying Theory table summarizes what each theoretical approach teaches us about poverty.

MAKING THE GRADE

Notice how conservatives distinguish between relative and absolute poverty. Why do liberals and radicals not share this focus?

GETTING INVOLVED

To what extent do you support each of the three political views described below? Explain.

 POLITICS AND POVERTY

Constructing Problems and Defining Solutions

What are we to make of the fact that 44 million people in one of the richest nations on earth are poor? Like every other issue we deal with in this book, poverty and wealth are controversial. Some people consider income inequality as inevitable and even good for society. Others are highly critical of income inequality and define poverty as a pressing national problem that can be reduced. Let us now examine how conservatives, liberals, and radicals construct the poverty problem and how they define solutions.

Conservatives: Personal Responsibility

Conservatives (more to the right on the political spectrum) point out that almost all the poverty in the United States is *relative* poverty. That is, only a small percentage of the people that the government defines as poor live anywhere close to *absolute* poverty, where day-to-day survival is at stake. Rather, U.S. families are poor relative to what government officials claim people living in our rich society *ought to have*. In fact, about one-third of the "official" poor own their homes, two-thirds have at least one car, and almost all have a television set and a personal computer (Gallagher, 1999; U.S. Census Bureau, 2010). If we keep in mind that living standards have risen dramatically over the past century, conservatives argue, it seems reasonable to conclude that our society is working pretty well.

Conservatives value self-reliance and support the idea that people should take responsibility for their personal well-being. They claim that U.S. society offers plenty of opportunity to anyone who is willing to take advantage of it. Our way of life rewards both talent and effort, with the result that even though a few inherit great wealth, most successful people—and even most rich people—are men and women who spend long years in school and who work hard at their jobs (Stanley & Danko, 1996).

Speaking for conservatives, the retired general and former U.S. Secretary of State Colin Powell recalls that as a young boy, he began his working life pushing a broom. He explains that he always worked hard, doing his best and learning whatever he could from the job he had. As soon as he mastered one task, he asked for another one. He credits discipline and determination—learned from his parents—as the key to his success, helping him to rise to a top position in the U.S. military and become one of this country's political leaders. In short, Powell argues, the most effective way to prevent poverty may well be to teach children to value personal responsibility and hard work (Powell & Persico, 1995).

Conservatives see individual effort within a market system as the key to the good life. Is there a role for government in all this—especially in the fight against poverty? Because conservatives believe people are responsible for their own social standing, they want to limit the size of government and keep taxes low. Most conservatives support welfare programs that provide assistance to people who are poor through no fault of their own—those with disabilities, the elderly, and children. Most also think that the government should provide a helping hand to veterans who have sacrificed for their country and to make available short-term help to anyone thrown out of work. But government should never replace personal responsibility; in fact, conservatives claim, welfare programs can make poverty worse by fostering dependency. For this reason, most conservatives supported the 1996 welfare reform (C. Murray, 1984; Bennett, 1995; Connerly, 2000; Bork, 2008).

Liberals: Societal Responsibility

Conservatives claim that promoting personal responsibility is the best solution to the problem of poverty. But liberals think that helping the poor is a job for everybody. From a liberal point of view, poverty is more societal than individual. Most people become poor not because they are lazy or because they make bad choices but because of the way society operates. As Chapter 11 ("Work and the Workplace") explains, most unemployment is caused by economic recession, corporate mergers, downsizing, or outsourcing of work overseas that reduces the number of available jobs.

The societal causes of poverty are also evident in the fact that specific categories of people are at high risk of poverty. For example, because women are given fewer opportunities than men to work for income and because our society pays women less when they do work, women are at higher risk of being poor.

Because they define poverty as a societal problem, liberals look for societal solutions. They reject the conservative arguments that individuals must take full responsibility for themselves. According to the liberal viewpoint, the U.S. economy is highly productive, but it distributes income very unequally. In addition, many people are disadvantaged by racism and other forms of discrimination that prevent them from ever getting good jobs. Part of the liberal solution to poverty, then, is active enforcement of laws banning discrimination in education and the workplace.

In addition, liberals support government assistance programs that offer some measure of financial security to everyone—

a "social safety net." Dismissing conservative worries about creating dependency, liberals view assistance programs as needed by millions of people—especially children—who are poor through no fault of their own. Liberals also support higher taxes, especially on the rich, to pay for such programs and also to reduce economic inequality. For this reason, liberals opposed the Bush administration tax cuts favored by conservatives and support President Obama's plan to raise taxes on high-income families.

Liberals would direct the money raised through taxation to social welfare programs that would lift millions of poor families above the poverty line. Currently, public assistance benefits are so small—the typical "welfare family" receives only about $400 per month—that people cannot improve their lives. For example, more generous assistance might enable a poor working mother to commute to a better job in a nearby suburb, to purchase better medical care so that she loses fewer days each year to illness, or to finish a high school diploma by taking night courses.

Finally, liberals point out that millions of poor people never even apply for welfare benefits. Why not? In a culture that stresses personal responsibility, asking for help is regarded as an admission of personal failure and a source of shame (W. J. Wilson, 1996a; Mouw, 2000; H. Murray, 2000).

The Radical Left: Change the System

Radicals on the left agree with liberals that poverty is a societal issue and that we cannot expect poor people to improve their situation on their own. But they differ by claiming that the problem of poverty is built in to a capitalist society (Liazos, 1982). In other words, the normal operation of a capitalist economic system creates such extremes of wealth and poverty that the welfare programs supported by liberals are little more than a bandage applied to the body of a person with a terminal disease.

Karl Marx pointed to widespread poverty as one of the internal contradictions of capitalism. By this, he meant that industrial capitalism produces great wealth, but production is controlled by the capitalist elite for their own benefit at the expense of working people. Thus a very rich society can contain millions of people who are desperately poor.

Radicals claim that the way to solve the problem of poverty is to replace capitalism with a more humane economic system that will greatly reduce economic inequality. The goal of such a system would be not to increase private profits but to meet the needs of everyone. In this way, radicals offer yet another distinctive definition of the problem and a particular solution.

Conservatives claim that we should all take personal responsibility for our social standing; reducing poverty, then, depends on the choices and actions of the poor themselves. Liberals claim that poverty is mostly a matter of how society operates; according to this view, government should act to reduce poverty. Radicals on the left claim that ending poverty depends on replacing capitalism. Which view is closest to your own? Why?

The Left to Right table on page 50 sums up the views of all three political approaches. To understand each of the political positions, it is necessary to look closely at them all.

Going On from Here

This chapter describes the inequality of income and wealth that defines the rich and poor in the United States. It points out that certain categories of people—women, children, and people of color—are at high risk of being poor and that all people who are economically disadvantaged contend with poor health, substandard housing, too little schooling, too few jobs, and a higher rate of crime and violence.

GETTING INVOLVED

Ask members of your sociology class which of the positions below they support. Has reading this chapter changed anyone's mind?

LEFT TO RIGHT

The Politics of Income Inequality

	RADICAL-LEFT VIEW	LIBERAL VIEW	CONSERVATIVE VIEW
WHAT IS THE PROBLEM?	The capitalist economic system concentrates most of the country's wealth in the hands of a small share of the population.	Millions of men, women, and children have too little income and need assistance.	Some "worthy" people are poor and should be helped, but social welfare programs can discourage people's desire to work and may foster dependency.
WHAT IS THE SOLUTION?	The capitalist economic system must undergo fundamental changes.	Use higher taxes to expand government assistance programs and raise the income of the poor.	Provide short-term help to those who really need it; strengthen families and promote personal responsibility.

JOIN THE DEBATE

1. Using the radical-left, liberal, and conservative points of view, in turn, assess the 1996 welfare reforms. From each political position, has the reform been helpful or harmful? To whom? Why?
2. During the 2008 presidential campaign, Democrats called for higher taxes on wealthy people to fund expanded social programs, primarily to assist low-income families. Republicans defended the Bush administration tax cuts intended to create jobs and give people more money to spend and invest. What arguments can you make for and against each position? What would be a radical-left response to this debate?
3. Which of the three political analyses of income inequality included here do you find the most convincing? Why?

What can we expect in the future? Keep in mind that some trends are positive. Between 1960 and 2009, the official poverty rate fell by more than one-third, from 22 percent to 14.3 percent. Among the elderly, the poverty rate dropped by three-quarters, from 33 percent to 8 percent (U.S. Census Bureau, 2010). It is all but certain, however, that the recent recession has pushed the poverty rate up for all categories of people.

Looking back in time, as shown in Figure 2–3, most of the decrease in poverty in the United States occurred between 1960 and the early 1970s. Since then, the overall trend has been slightly upward. Even more troubling, the age category at greatest risk of poverty is now children: Overall, 21 percent of U.S. children are poor, with much higher rates among African American (36 percent) and Hispanic American (33 percent) youngsters. Perhaps the most pressing question for the future is what to do about the "new poverty" in the United States involving households composed of women and children. The dramatic decline in the poverty rate among the elderly shows that this nation can reduce poverty when the public supports doing so. The question is whether we will do as much for our children as we have done for seniors.

Wealth and poverty in the United States have always been controversial, and debate will surely continue. Conservatives focus on the need for personal responsibility and the importance of strong families, pointing out that that not having a job or having children without being married raises the odds of being poor for both adults and their children. Liberals call for raising the minimum wage, expanding child care and job training programs, and combating workplace discrimination that harms women and people of color. Radical-left voices claim that a capitalist economic system always leaves many people behind. Whatever political position one favors, a focus of national attention in the decades to come will be the striking degree of economic inequality in the United States.

DEFINING SOLUTIONS

Is social inequality a problem?

And whose problem is it? This chapter has explained that how people understand social inequality depends on their political attitudes. What people say we ought to do about poverty and wealth also depends on politics. Look at the two photos below to see two different ways to respond to poverty and wealth.

HINT

Liberals tend to see social structure (including class, gender, and race) as giving privileges to some people and putting others at a disadvantage. From this point of view, a young homeless woman needs assistance. A gift of money would be an act of kindness; but because the problem of inequality is based on the way society is organized, the real solution requires changes to society itself. Conservatives tend to see people as responsible for their own situations. Again, a gift of money might be kind, but as long as this young person is able-bodied and healthy, she should really take care of herself (and a handout only encourages more panhandling). As for the issue of taxation, conservatives typically see wealth as a product of personal talent and a lot of hard work; people are entitled to what they can earn. Liberals, on the other hand, see wealth and poverty as twin products of a free market that should be regulated by government, which should tax the rich (progressive taxation) to provide more for the poor (in government benefits).

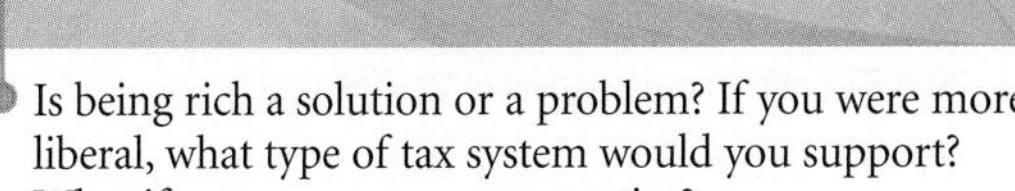

Is being rich a solution or a problem? If you were more liberal, what type of tax system would you support? What if you were more conservative?

How would you react to confronting this young woman on a New York City street? If your politics were more liberal, what would say is the problem here? What would you think should be done about it? What if you were more conservative?

Getting Involved: Applications & Exercises

1. We hear many people refer to the United States as a "middle-class society." Based on what you now know about social inequality in this country, to what extent is this description accurate? Offer specific evidence to support your position.
2. Find out more about the extent of poverty in your local area. U.S. Census Bureau reports are available from the local library, and you can find census data on the Internet at http://www.census.gov/datamap/www or by visiting a local social service agency.
3. Have you ever had a low-wage job? If not, this is one good way to begin to understand what it means to be working but poor. Many low-wage jobs are available on or around campus. Whether you actually take such a job or not, work out a monthly household budget for a family of three, and see how far a minimum-wage job ($7.25 hourly in 2009) takes you toward supporting a family.
4. Do you tend to favor the Democratic or the Republican party? Whichever you prefer, go to its national Web site (http://www.dnc.org or http://www.rnc.org) to learn about the party's policies toward poverty and related issues such as welfare reform and taxes.

MAKING THE GRADE

A DEFINING MOMENT
U.S. Society Discovers Poverty p. 42

CHAPTER 2 Poverty and Wealth

Economic Inequality in the United States

INCOME is distributed unequally in the United States, with the richest 20% of families earning 48.2% of all income, more than twelve times as much as the lowest-paid 20% of families.

pp. 29–30

WEALTH is even more unequally distributed, with the richest 20% of families controlling 85% of all privately owned wealth, while the poorest 20% of families are actually in debt.

pp. 29–30

✓ *Progressive taxation lessens U.S. income inequality, but only slightly. (pp. 30–32)*

social stratification (p. 28) society's system of ranking categories of people in a hierarchy

social classes (p. 28) categories of people who have similar access to resources and opportunities

income (p. 29) salary or wages from a job plus earnings from investments and other sources

wealth (p. 29) the value of all the economic assets owned by a person or family, minus any debts

progressive taxation (p. 30) a policy that raises tax rates as income increases

The Rich and the Poor: A Social Profile

- Rich families have incomes that average about $200,000 (with some ten times this much or more). Older people, white people, and men are overly represented among the rich.
- The government defines "poverty" as families living with income below a poverty line roughly equal to three times the cost of food. The 2009 **POVERTY LINE** was $21,954 for a nonfarm family of four.
- Income for the average poor family in the United States is about $11,000 less than the poverty line, a difference called the **"POVERTY GAP."**
- At greatest risk of poverty are children, women who head households, and racial and ethnic minorities.
- The child poverty rate in the United States is high and now stands at 21%.
- What sociologists call the **"FEMINIZATION OF POVERTY"** means that over time, women have made up a rising share (now 58%) of the poor.
- The **UNDERCLASS** represents a small share of the poor, cut off from the larger society, who live in rural areas or inner cities where poverty is widespread.

pp. 32–37

poverty line (p. 33) an income level set by the U.S. government for the purpose of counting the poor

poverty gap (p. 34) the difference between the actual income of the typical poor household and the official poverty line

feminization of poverty (p. 34) the trend of women making up an increasing share of the poor

underclass (p. 36) poor people who live in areas with high concentrations of poverty and limited opportunities for schooling or work

Problems Linked to Poverty

POVERTY affects every aspect of life. The poor

- endure more illness
- receive less schooling
- experience more unemployment and crime
- are more likely to live in inadequate housing or to be homeless

pp. 37–39

homelessness (p. 38) the plight of poor people who lack shelter and live primarily on the streets

Responding to Poverty: The Welfare System

Public attitudes toward the poor and support for **SOCIAL WELFARE PROGRAMS** have varied over the course of this nation's history.

- The settlement house movement in the late 1800s offered a helping hand to poor immigrants and tried to make the public more compassionate toward the poor.
- President Franklin Roosevelt's New Deal in the 1930s was the first of many government poverty programs, the most important of which was Social Security.
- In 1964, President Lyndon Johnson declared the War on Poverty to address the growing underclass of poor people in the United States.
- In 1996, welfare reform pushed people off welfare rolls and toward work and schooling. This reform decreased the number of people receiving benefits but did little to lower the poverty rate.

pp. 39–43

social welfare programs (p. 39) organized efforts by government, private organizations, or individuals to assist needy people considered worthy of assistance

Theoretical Analysis: Understanding Poverty

Structural-Functional Analysis: Some Poverty Is Inevitable

SOCIAL PATHOLOGY THEORIES (including Spencer's social Darwinism, Lewis's *culture of poverty thesis*, and Herrnstein and Murray's *bell curve thesis*) view poverty mostly as the result of shortcomings on the part of the poor themselves.

p. 43

SOCIAL DISORGANIZATION THEORY views poverty as the result of rapid social change, which makes society unable to meet the needs of all its members.

pp. 43–44

- More recent functionalism includes the *Davis and Moore thesis*, which argues that society uses unequal rewards to attract talent to the most important jobs.
- Herbert Gans states that the poor serve the needs of the nonpoor in various ways, including doing work that no one else wants to do.

p. 44

Symbolic-Interaction Analysis: Defining the Problem

The **SYMBOLIC-INTERACTION APPROACH** highlights our socially constructed understandings of poverty. One common view is **"blaming the victim,"** which claims that poverty results from traits of the poor themselves.

pp. 44–45

Social-Conflict Analysis: Poverty Can Be Eliminated

Karl Marx claimed that poverty follows from the operation of a capitalist economy. He believed the increasing misery of the working class would eventually lead people to overthrow the capitalist system.

p. 45

More recent conflict theory explains that inequality involves not just money but cultural capital—advantages in skills, attitudes, and schooling—that are not available to people born into poverty.

pp. 45–46

FEMINIST THEORY links the higher poverty rate among women to the fact that men dominate women in our society.

p. 46

MULTICULTURAL THEORY highlights how African Americans and people in other disadvantaged racial and ethnic categories are at higher risk of poverty.

p. 46

INTERSECTION THEORY highlights the fact that inequality based on race, class, and gender combine, resulting in greater disadvantage.

pp. 46–47

See the Applying Theory table on page 47.

culture of poverty (p. 43) cultural patterns that make poverty a way of life

meritocracy (p. 43) a system of social inequality in which social standing corresponds to personal ability and effort

social disorganization (p. 43) a breakdown in social order caused by rapid social change

blaming the victim (p. 44) finding the cause of a social problem in the behavior of people who suffer from it

cultural capital (p. 45) skills, values, attitudes, and schooling that increase a person's chances of success

intersection theory (p. 46) the investigation of the interplay of race, class, and gender, often resulting in multiple dimensions of disadvantage

Politics and Poverty: Constructing Problems and Defining Solutions

The Radical Left: Change the System

- **RADICALS ON THE LEFT** claim that poverty results from the normal operation of the capitalist economy, which benefits the capitalist elite.
- Radicals on the left argue that solving the poverty problem requires fundamental change to the economy so that production meets social needs rather than increases private profits.

p. 49

Liberals: Societal Responsibility

- **LIBERALS** believe that poverty is a societal problem, stemming mostly from a lack of good jobs.
- Liberals consider poverty a societal responsibility; they support government social programs that benefit the needy.

pp. 48–49

Conservatives: Personal Responsibility

- **CONSERVATIVES** believe that social standing is a matter of personal responsibility; people can escape poverty by taking advantage of the opportunities U.S. society offers.
- Conservatives claim that government social welfare programs often make the poverty problem worse by fostering dependency.

p. 48

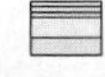
See the Left to Right table on page 50.

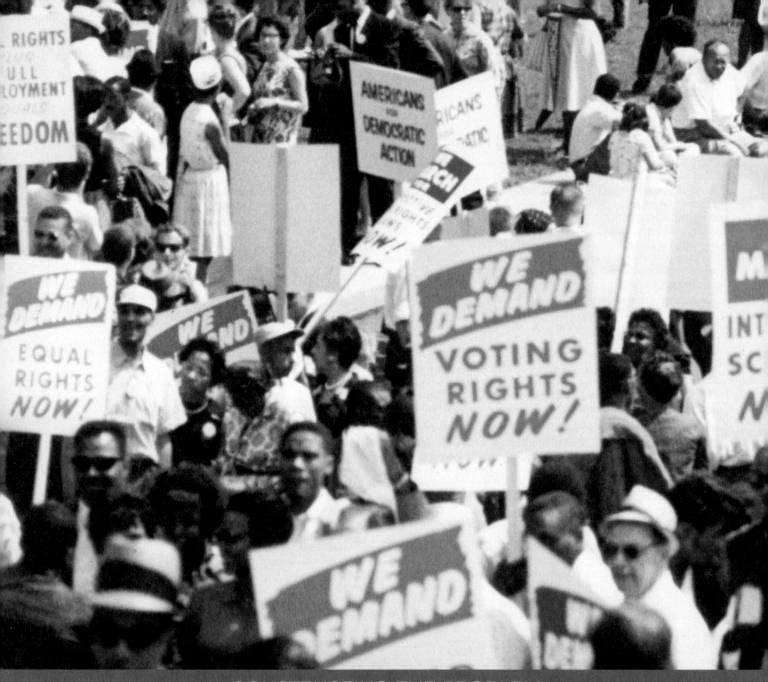

CONSTRUCTING THE PROBLEM

What is race? Is it only about skin color?

Race involves socially constructed categories that often give people advantages over others.

What are minorities? Are they just categories of people with small numbers?

Being a minority is mainly about power. Societies construct minority categories as they give more power and privileges to some than to others.

Is prejudice simply about what people think?

Prejudice and discrimination do involve individual attitudes, but both are also built into the operation of society.

CHAPTER 3

Racial and Ethnic Inequality

CHAPTER OVERVIEW

WHAT IS RACE AND ETHNICITY? How are they related to social inequality? This chapter explores the social standing of various racial and ethnic categories of the U.S. population and describes examples of genocide, segregation, assimilation, and pluralism in our nation's history. You will carry out theoretical analysis of racial and ethnic inequality and learn how "problems" and "solutions" involving diversity reflect people's political attitudes.

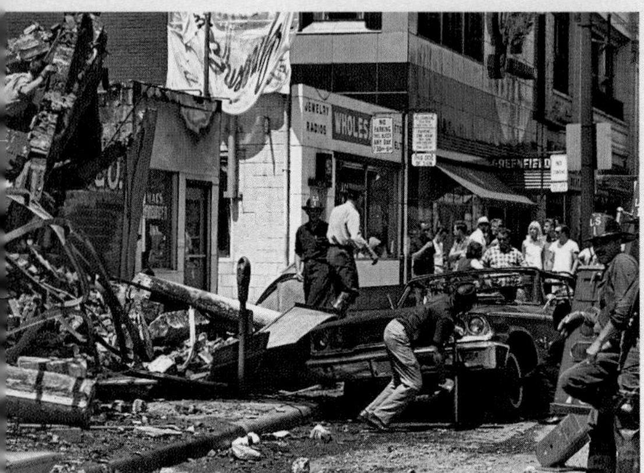

On a winter morning in 2008, a former president of the United States joined a panel at a conference hosted by a major university in Philadelphia to discuss the state of racial and ethnic relations in the United States. Bill Clinton began by recalling how, back in 1967, the city of Detroit had exploded in violence on a hot July day, unleashing a riot that lasted for almost a week. When the violence finally came to an end, 2,000 buildings had been burned across 14 square miles of the city, hundreds of people were injured, and forty-six men and women were dead.

Making sense of this tragic event, a 1968 government commission concluded that the basic cause of the rioting was white racism and warned that "our nation is moving toward two societies, one black, one white—separate and unequal." President Clinton then reminded the audience that just a few weeks after the release of the Kerner Commission report, Dr. Martin Luther King Jr. was shot and killed in Memphis, which sparked rioting in 100 more cities across the country.

Clinton then stated, "We should not have to have a riot to do the right things." The generation of people who came of age in the 1960s has grown up and is now nearing retirement age. The children and grandchildren of the '60s generation are now taking their places at the center of U.S. society. Over past decades, how much has changed in the United States in terms of race relations? President Clinton was quick to offer some positive comments: "The general acceptance of people from other races and religions into our political life is something of enormous significance—inconceivable when I grew up in the segregated South" (cited in Popp, 2008:19).

As this chapter explains, racial and ethnic inequality is still with us today. In some respects, the inequality has decreased—for example, no one back in 1967 could have imagined electing an African American to be president of the United States. Yet in other respects, the gaps remain almost as wide as they were back then.

Race and ethnicity are the foundation for many issues that people come to define as social problems. To understand why this is the case, we need to answer some basic questions: What is "race"? How do race and ethnicity affect our everyday lives? How do they figure into problems of social inequality? This chapter will also explore a range of related issues, including prejudice, discrimination, segregation, multiculturalism, and affirmative action. We start with a look at the central concepts of race and ethnicity.

Race and Ethnicity

In the United States and other countries, race and ethnicity are important aspects of social identity, just as they are major dimensions of social inequality. Yet many people are not quite sure what race and ethnicity are all about. Our first step is to clarify the meanings of the concepts.

Race

Race is *a socially constructed category of people who share biologically transmitted traits that members of a society define as important.* For hundreds of years, societies have divided humanity into categories based on skin color, hair texture, facial features, and body shape.

Race has nothing to do with being human. All people everywhere belong to a single biological species, *Homo sapiens* (Latin words meaning "thinking person"), that first emerged in Africa some 250,000 years ago. But societies may attach importance to physical differences that developed over thousands of generations among people living in different regions of the world. In tropical areas, humans living in the hot sun developed darker skin from a natural pigment called melanin; in cooler regions, humans developed lighter skin.

If people had never moved from the place where they were born, everyone in any given geographic area of the world would

race a socially constructed category of people who share biologically transmitted traits that members of a society define as important

ethnicity (p. 58) a shared cultural heritage, which typically involves common ancestors, language, and religion

GETTING INVOLVED

How important is race in the dating patterns on your campus?

look pretty much the same. But throughout history, people have migrated from place to place, and this movement has spread the physical traits carried in our genes the world over.

This is especially true among people living in the world's "crossroads" regions, such as the Middle East, who display a great deal of physical diversity. On the other hand, historically isolated people have many physical traits in common. For example, almost all Japanese people have black hair.

The fact that race is a socially constructed category means that any distinctive physical traits may be used to assign people to a racial category. In the early decades of the twentieth century, public opinion turned against European immigrants as their numbers grew. For a time, many southern Europeans—such as Italians—were "racialized" and defined as nonwhite.

When Was Race Invented?

Centuries ago, global trade brought the world's people into greater contact, raising awareness of human diversity. By the late 1500s, Europeans began using the term *race.* By about 1800, European scientists came up with three broad classifications for humanity. They coined the term *Caucasian* (meaning European and Western Asian) to designate people with light skin and fine hair; *Negroid* (derived from Latin meaning "black") to refer to people with dark skin and the coarse, curly hair typical of people living in sub-Saharan Africa; and *Mongoloid* (referring to the Mongolian region of Asia) to refer to people with yellow or brown skin and distinctive folds on the eyelids.

Are Races Real?

Sociologists are quick to point out that at best, racial categories are misleading and at worst, they are a harmful way to divide humanity. First, there is no biologically pure race. Because human beings have migrated and reproduced throughout the world, we find physical diversity everywhere. For example, Caucasian people can have very light skin (common in Scandinavia) or very dark skin (common in southern India). Similarly, Negroid people can be dark-skinned (common in Africa) or light-skinned (the Australian Aborigines).

Other physical traits often linked to race do not always line up the same way. For example, people with dark skin can have kinky hair (common in Africa) or straight hair (common in India). Biologists tell us that people in various racial categories differ in only about 6 percent of their genes, which is less than the genetic variation that we find within each racial category. What this means is that from a scientific standpoint, physical variation is real, but racial categories simply do not describe that reality very well (Boza, 2002; Harris & Sim, 2002).

Should Races Exist at All?

If racial categories are not real, why do they exist? Some sociologists argue that dividing humanity into racial categories is simply a strategy to allow some people to dominate others (Bonilla-Silva, 1999; Johnson, Rush, & Feagin, 2000; Zuberi, 2001). That is, Europeans attached cultural traits to skin color—constructing the "honest and rational" European versus the "beastlike" African and the "devious" Asian—in order to make themselves seem better than the peoples they wanted to control. In this way, European colonists justified oppressing people all over the world. North Americans did much the same thing, defining native peoples in less than human terms—as "red savages"—to justify killing them and taking their land. Similarly, when people of English ancestry needed Irish and Italian immigrants to work for low pay, they defined them as racially different (Ignatiev, 1995; Camara, 2000; Brodkin, 2007).

Well into the twentieth century, many southern states legally defined as "colored" anyone having as little as 1/32 African ancestry (that is, one African American great-great-great-grandparent). By 1970, such "one drop of blood" laws had been overturned by the courts, allowing parents to declare the race of their child as they wish (usually on the birth certificate). Even today, however, most people still consider racial identity important.

Multiracial People

Today, more people in this country than ever before identify themselves as multiracial. In a recent government survey, almost

GETTING INVOLVED

Describe yourself using the categories in Table 3–1. Is this an accurate picture of you? Explain.

MAKING THE GRADE

Be sure you understand the difference between race and ethnicity.

Table 3–1 Racial and Ethnic Categories in the United States, 2009

Racial or Ethnic Classification	Approximate U.S. Population	Percentage of Total Pop
Hispanic Descent	**48,419,324**	**15.8%**
Mexican	31,689,879	10.3%
Puerto Rican	4,426,738	1.4%
Cuban	1,696,141	0.6%
Other Hispanic	10,606,566	3.5%
African Descent	**39,641,060**	**12.9%**
Nigerian	254,794	0.1%
Ethiopian	186,679	0.1%
Somalian	103,117	<
Other African	39,096,470	12.7%
Native American Descent	**2,457,552**	**0.8%**
American Indian	1,998,949	0.7%
Alaska Native Tribes	108,763	<
Other Native American	349,840	0.1%
Asian or Pacific Island Descent	**14,592,307**	**4.8%**
Chinese	3,204,379	1.0%
Asian Indian	2,602,676	0.8%
Filipino	2,475,794	0.8%
Vietnamese	1,481,513	0.5%
Korean	1,335,973	0.4%
Japanese	766,875	0.2%
Cambodian	241,520	0.1%
Other Asian or Pacific Islander	2,483,577	0.8%
West Indian descent	**2,572,415**	**0.8%**
Arab descent	**1,706,629**	**0.6%**
Non-Hispanic European descent	**199,851,240**	**65.1%**
German	50,709,194	16.5%
Irish	36,915,325	12.0%
English	27,658,720	9.0%
Italian	18,086,617	5.9%
Polish	10,091,056	3.3%
French	9,411,910	3.1%
Scottish	5,847,063	1.9%
Dutch	5,024,309	1.6%
Norwegian	4,642,526	1.5%
Other non-Hispanic European	**31,464,520**	**10.2%**
Two or more races	**7,505,173**	**2.4%**

*People of Hispanic descent may be of any race. Many people also identify with more than one ethnic category. Figures therefore total more than 100 percent.

<indicates less than 1/10 of 1 percent.

Source: U.S. Census Bureau (2010).

7.5 million people in the United States described themselves as multiracial, identifying with more than one racial category (U.S. Census Bureau, 2010).

Marriage between people of different racial categories is becoming more common and now accounts for 7.4 percent of all marriages in the United States. One predictable result is that the official number of multiracial births has tripled over the past twenty years and represents about 4 percent of all births (U.S. Census Bureau, 2010). As time goes on, fewer members of our society will see one another in terms of rigid racial categories.

Ethnicity

Race revolves around biological traits, but ethnicity is a matter of culture. **Ethnicity** is *a shared cultural heritage, which typically involves common ancestors, language, and religion.* Just as U.S. society is racially diverse, so the population contains hundreds of distinctive ethnic categories. Table 3–1 shows the breadth of this nation's racial and ethnic diversity.

Although race and ethnicity are different, the two may go together. For example, Korean Americans, Native Americans, and people of Italian or Nigerian descent share not only certain physical traits but ethnic traits as well.

Immigration

This country's remarkable racial and ethnic diversity is a product of immigration. Everyone living in North America is descended from people who lived elsewhere. Immigration may be a key reason our society is here at all, but immigration is also a source of difference causing conflict. This conflict is nothing new, as you will soon see.

The "Great Immigration"

What historians call the "Great Immigration" started with the end of the Civil War in 1865 and lasted until World War I, which began in 1914. New industrial factories offered many jobs, and East Coast cities were transformed as ships brought some 25 million people across the Atlantic Ocean in search of economic opportunity. In 1900, fully 80 percent of the people living in New York City either had been born abroad or had parents who were (Glaab & Brown, 1967).

Nativists and the Quota System

Many people extended a welcome to the newcomers, but others—called *nativists*—opposed the high level of immigration, fearing that it would endanger this country's mostly English culture. Nativist attitudes were especially common after 1900 when most immigrants came from southern and eastern Europe, where people had darker skin, spoke languages other than English, and were Catholic, Orthodox, or Jewish rather than Protestant.

Pressured by nativists, Congress acted during the 1920s to pass laws, including the Immigration Act of 1924, that cut immigration by creating a quota system for admitting people from various countries. These laws—and the economic depression that began in 1929—reduced immigration to a trickle, and the numbers stayed low until the mid-1960s.

minority any category of people, identified by physical or cultural traits, that a society subjects to disadvantages

GETTING INVOLVED

Do you think all people of color, regardless of whether they are rich or poor, should be considered minorities? Why or why not?

The End of the Quota System

In 1965, Congress ended the quota system, leading to another wave of mass immigration. Again, the arrival of immigrants—this time mostly from Mexico and other nations in Latin America, as well as the Philippines, South Korea, and other Asian countries—became controversial. Congress enacted the 1986 Immigrant Control and Reform Act in another effort to reduce the number of immigrants coming to this country. This act outlawed the hiring of undocumented immigrants and threatened businesses with fines for doing so. The idea was that if immigrants could not get jobs, they would not come here. But many workers produced fraudulent documents and were able to find work. In addition, the 1986 law granted amnesty to almost 3 million illegal immigrants already in the country, which had the effect of encouraging even more people to cross the border (Gamboa, 2003; Tumulty, 2006).

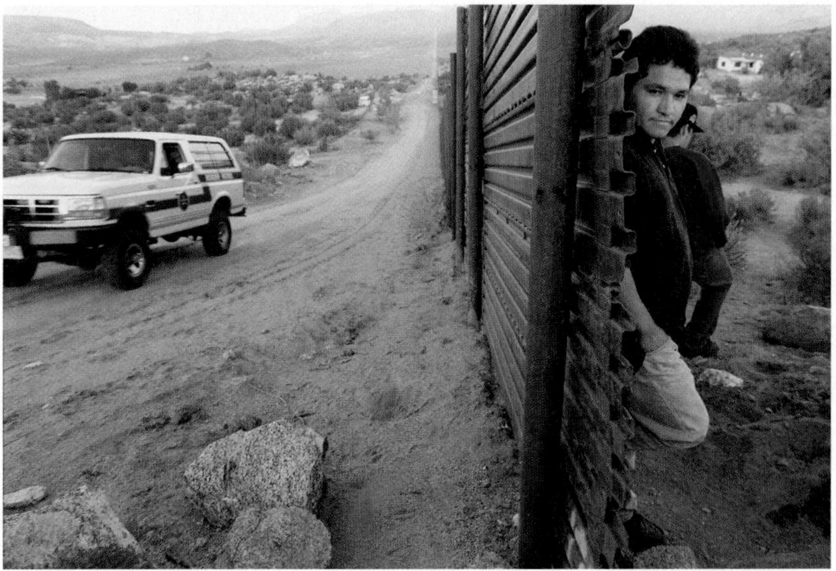

The United States has always been a nation of immigrants. But immigration has always been controversial, and in recent years the debate has sparked demonstrations across the country. Currently, about 500,000 people enter this country illegally by crossing the border from Mexico. Do you think that this flow of people is helpful or harmful to the United States? Why?

Nowhere is the immigration issue more important than in California, the state with the largest immigrant population and where 43 percent of the people speak a language other than English at home. In 1994, in reaction to the rising number of illegal immigrants, Californians enacted Proposition 187, which discouraged immigration by cutting off social service benefits, including schooling, health care, and food stamps, to immigrants who had entered the country illegally. This law did reduce illegal immigration, but it also hurt those people already in California.

The Current Immigration Controversy

As Congress continued to debate the immigration issue during the 1990s, about 1 million people entered the United States each year. This is actually a larger number than during the Great Immigration a century ago, although today's newcomers are joining a population five times larger. In 2009, the total U.S. population of about 307 million included about 38.5 million (12.5 percent) who are foreign-born. About twice as many people have at least one parent born abroad (U.S. Census Bureau, 2010).

In recent years, immigration has become a major issue across the United States. The focus of the debate is now illegal immigration. Although the numbers have fallen off with the weak economy, in recent years estimates suggest that at least 500,000 people have been crossing this country's southern border with Mexico illegally each year. Of these, only a small number have been caught by police. It is very difficult to control a border that extends for almost 2,000 miles, along the southern boundaries of California, Arizona, New Mexico, and Texas. Currently, most of the border has no fence or marking at all. Congress has debated various proposals in an effort to decide how to improve control of the border and how to deal with illegal immigrants already living and working in the United States. The Diversity: Race, Class, & Gender box on pages 60–61 takes a closer look at the current immigration issue.

Minorities

Most immigrants to the United States have found more opportunities than they had in their homelands. But many have also discovered that their race and ethnicity keep them at the margins of U.S. society. Social scientists use the term **minority** to refer to *any category of people, identified by physical or cultural traits, that a society subjects to disadvantages.*

Visibility

Minorities share a *distinctive identity,* which may be racial (based on physical traits, which are difficult to change) or ethnic (including dress or accent, which people can change). For example, many people of Japanese ancestry in the United States have little knowledge of their native language, and more than half have non-Japanese spouses. Thus Japanese Americans are becoming less of an ethnic category, and by marrying people of other backgrounds, they are becoming less distinctive as a racial

GETTING INVOLVED

Have you ever joined an organization, attended a rally, or written a letter about the immigration issue?

MAKING THE GRADE

All four patterns of majority-minority interaction are found in our society, although patterns have shifted in importance over our history.

DIVERSITY: RACE, CLASS, & GENDER

Let Them Stay or Make Them Go? The Debate over Illegal Immigration

So many immigrants now enter the United States across the border with Mexico that transportation departments have erected signs warning motorists to watch for people running across the roadways. The reason for this steady flow of people is economics. Wages in the United States average about nine times higher than in Mexico.

Every year, about 500,000 people enter this country legally from Mexico, but at least another 500,000 people cross the border illegally. About 61 percent of all those who enter the United States illegally are from Mexico, 22 percent are from other Latin American nations, 10 percent are from an Asian country, and the remaining 7 percent are from African countries and elsewhere.

So much immigration—especially illegal immigration—is troubling to most people in the United States. In 2006, in public opinion surveys, more than 80 percent of U.S. adults said that this country is not doing enough to control its borders, and 65 percent called illegal immigration a serious social problem (Tumulty, 2006). By 2009, the weak economy had reduced the number of people coming to the United States. But this country remains divided over how to handle more than 11 million illegal immigrants who are already here.

Conservatives point out that entering the country illegally is a crime, and many would like to declare illegal immigrants to be criminals subject to arrest and punishment or deportation. A bill that would have done this was passed by the House of Representatives in 2005 but never became law. But most people think that with many millions of illegal immigrants already here, this proposal is impractical—there are not enough jails to lock up everyone who might be arrested. But there is broad support for the conservative position that illegal immigrants should not be allowed to become citizens ahead of others who follow the law and apply officially to enter the country. And many people share conservatives' concerns that illegal immigrants overtax schools and social service programs in many communities. Some people also worry that immigrants' ethnic differences will bring dramatic changes to U.S. culture.

As social policy, conservatives support greater enforcement of border security and favor either returning illegal immigrants to their home country or allowing them to stay as guest workers if they pay a fine, pay back taxes on their earnings, learn English, and go to the end of the line among people seeking citizenship.

Liberals, too, support border control but are more accepting of undocumented immigrants already here. They point out that through their work, most illegal immigrants contribute to our economy, often doing jobs that others in our country do not want to do.

category as well. A minority's ability to blend in with others depends on the minority members' desire to hold on to their traditions and also on the willingness of other people to accept them. For instance, whites have shown a far greater willingness to marry people of Japanese ancestry than to marry people of African descent (U.S. Census Bureau, 2010).

Power

A second characteristic of minorities is *disadvantage.* Minorities have less schooling and lower-paying jobs, which means higher rates of poverty. Of course, not all people in any minority category are disadvantaged. In other words, despite the statistical averages, some people of African, Asian, or Latino ancestry have very high social standing. But even the most successful individuals know that their membership in a minority category reduces their standing in some people's eyes (Benjamin, 1991).

Numbers

More than one-third of the U.S. population falls into a racial or ethnic minority category. Minorities make up an increasing share of this nation's people. In fact, minorities have already become a majority in more than half of the 100 largest U.S. cities. A minority majority also exists in four states—Hawaii, California, New Mexico, and Texas—as well as the District of Columbia. Other states will be added to the list in years to come. Based on current trends, by about 2042, racial and ethnic minorities will become a majority of the U.S. population (U.S. Census Bureau, 2008, 2010).

We take up the question of whether women—of any race or ethnicity—should also be counted as a minority in Chapter 4 ("Gender Inequality").

Patterns of Majority-Minority Interaction

The way majority and minority populations interact can range from deadly to peaceful. In studying such patterns, sociologists use four models: genocide, segregation, assimilation, and pluralism.

Patterns of Majority-Minority Interaction

genocide the systematic killing of one category of people by another

segregation the physical and social separation of categories of people

assimilation (p. 63) the process by which minorities gradually adopt cultural patterns from the dominant majority population

pluralism (p. 63) a state in which people of all racial and ethnic categories have about the same overall social standing

Much low-wage labor on farms, at hotels and restaurants, and in private homes is performed by immigrants. Liberals also remind us that 1.6 million undocumented immigrants are children, and the children of illegal immigrants born on U.S. soil (as most were) are U.S. citizens under the law, even if their parents are not.

Liberals favor amnesty for illegal immigrants and giving those here illegally citizenship if they work and pay their taxes for a number of years. Liberals want to free millions of men, women, and children from "living in the shadows," with no chance to apply for a scholarship to go to a community college or even to get a driver's license. Most seriously, liberals point out, illegal immigrants must live in constant fear that they or another family member may be arrested.

What is the radical-left position on the immigration debate? Radicals on the left oppose walling off this country from the rest of the world and support legalization and citizenship for all immigrants already here. In addition, they claim, we must reduce the inequality that separates the United States from other countries. Until that happens, they continue, millions of people will keep coming to this country, many risking their lives in the process.

Finally, the immigration debate has political consequences. Allowing all immigrants to become citizens would create 10 million new voters. In the 2008 presidential election, about 65 percent of Hispanic or Latino voters supported Democratic candidates and 35 percent voted Republican. If all immigrants were able to vote, the Democratic candidate for president in 2012 would have a very good chance of winning the election. This is one reason liberals are willing to extend citizenship to Latinos. At the same time, conservatives must try to gain favor within what is now this country's largest minority population.

WHAT DO YOU THINK?

1. Do you think this country should reduce the number of people crossing the border illegally? Do you think this will happen? Explain your view.
2. Should public schools provide publicly funded education to the children of illegal immigrants? Should colleges and universities be able to extend scholarships to these young people? Why or why not?
3. Do you tend to agree more with conservatives, liberals, or radicals on this issue? Explain.

Sources: Campo-Flores (2006), LoScalzo (2006), Hoefer, Rytina, & Baker (2009), and U.S. Department of Labor (2009).

Genocide

Genocide is *the systematic killing of one category of people by another.* Genocide is mass murder; even so, it has taken place time and again in human history, often tolerated and sometimes even encouraged by governments and their people.

Beginning about 1500, the Spanish, Portuguese, English, French, and Dutch forcefully colonized North and South America, resulting in the deaths of thousands of native people. Although most native people died from diseases brought by Europeans to which they had no natural defenses, many were killed outright (Matthiessen, 1984; Sale, 1990).

In the 1930s and 1940s, Adolf Hitler and his Nazi government murdered more than 6 million "undesirables," including homosexuals, people with disabilities, and most of Europe's Jews. The Soviet dictator Josef Stalin slaughtered his country's people on an even greater scale, killing some 30 million people, all of whom he defined as enemies. Between 1975 and 1980, Cambodia's Communist regime butchered millions whom they saw as "Western" in their cultural patterns. More recently, Hutus massacred Tutsis in the African nation of Rwanda, Serbs systematically killed Croats in Eastern Europe, and several hundred thousand people have been killed in the Darfur region of Africa's Sudan.

Segregation

Segregation is *the physical and social separation of categories of people.* Sometimes minority populations decide that they wish to segregate themselves; this is the case with religious orders such as the Amish. Usually, though, the majority population segregates minorities by forcing them to the margins of society, where they have to "stay with their own."

Racial segregation in the United States began with slavery and later included legally separate hotels, restaurants, schools, buses, and trains for black and white people. A number of court cases have reduced *de jure* (Latin words meaning "by law") segregation in the United States. However, *de facto* ("in fact") segregation is still common because most neighborhoods, schools, hospitals, and even cemeteries still contain mostly people of

SOCIAL PROBLEMS in Everyday Life

Is racial segregation still an important issue in our society? Explain.

MAKING THE GRADE

Can you see how immigration is linked to language diversity in National Map 3-1?

CONSTRUCTING SOCIAL PROBLEMS

A DEFINING MOMENT

Rosa Parks: Saying No to Segregation

It began so routinely that no one would have known history was being made. On December 1, 1955, Rosa Parks, a young African American woman living in Montgomery, Alabama, had just finished a day of hard work as a seamstress. She was tired and eager to get home. She walked to the street and boarded a city bus. At that time, Montgomery city law required African Americans to ride in certain seats near the back of the bus, and Parks did exactly that. Slowly the bus filled with people. As the bus pulled to the curb to pick up some white passengers, the driver turned and asked four black people to give up their seats so that the white people could sit down. Three did as he asked. But Parks refused to move.

The driver pulled to the curb, left the bus, and returned with a police officer, who arrested Parks for breaking the city's segregation law. She appeared in court, was convicted by a judge, and was fined $14. The story of Parks's stand (or sitting) for justice quickly spread throughout the African American community. Activists printed and distributed thousands of handbills asking every Negro to stay off the buses Monday in protest of the arrest and trial. "You can afford to stay out of school for one day. If you work, take a cab, or walk. But please, children and grown-ups, don't ride the bus at all on Monday. Please stay off the buses Monday."

A social movement was under way. African Americans in Montgomery successfully boycotted city buses on that Monday and for 382 days after that. A year later, the city of Montgomery officially ended segregation on its buses, and within the decade, the U.S. Supreme Court had banned racial segregation in any public accommodation anywhere in the country.

Rosa Parks lived the rest of her life as a symbol of the quiet determination to achieve justice. When she died in 2005, her funeral was attended by national leaders including every living president. She will be remembered as a leader of the civil rights movement and as proof of the power of people—even one at a time—to change the world.

This photo shows Rosa Parks being fingerprinted by police in Montgomery, Alabama. At the time of her arrest, the law defined Parks as the problem. But the bus boycott that followed her arrest soon changed that, defining racial segregation as the problem.

one race. For example, the city of Detroit is 76 percent African American, and Livonia, Michigan, right next door, is 90 percent white (Emerson, Yancey, & Chai, 2001; Krysan, 2002; U.S. Census Bureau, 2010).

Intense segregation occurs in many inner-city areas. Douglas Massey and Nancy Denton (1989) documented the *hypersegregation* of African Americans who have little contact with people outside of their community. Hypersegregation affects just a few percent of poor white people, but it affects about one in five African Americans living in about twenty-five of the largest U.S. cities (Wilkes & Iceland, 2004).

Because minorities, by definition, have little power, challenging segregation is not easy and may even be dangerous. Sometimes, however, the actions of a single person do make a difference. The Defining Moment box describes the actions of Rosa Parks, who sparked a social movement to end segregation on buses and other forms of public transportation throughout the South.

Elvira Martinez lives in Zapata County, Texas, where about three-quarters of the people in her community speak Spanish at home.

Jeffrey Steen lives in Adams County, Ohio, where almost none of his neighbors speaks a language other than English.

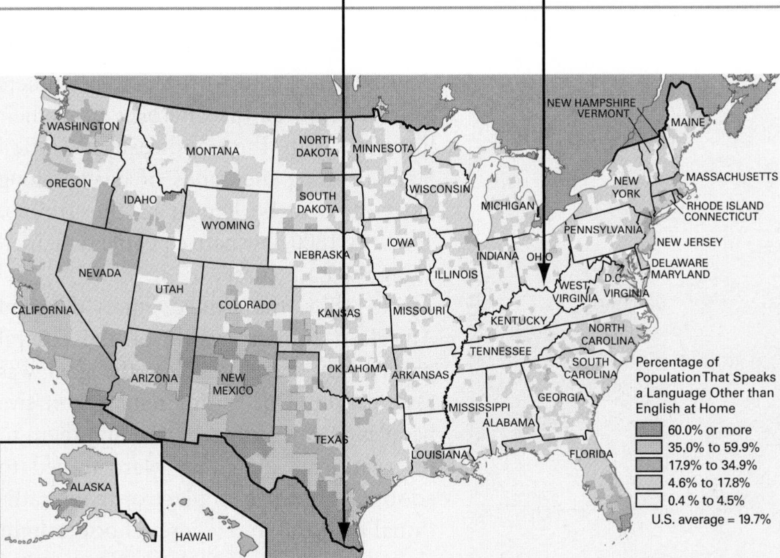

A Nation of Diversity

NATIONAL MAP 3–1

Language Diversity across the United States

Of more than 285 million people age five or older in the United States, the Census Bureau reports that 57 million (20 percent) speak a language other than English at home. Of these, 62 percent speak Spanish and 15 percent use an Asian language (the Census Bureau lists 29 languages, each of which is favored by more than 100,000 people). The map shows that non-English speakers are concentrated in certain regions of the country. Which ones? Can you explain this pattern?

Source: U.S. Census Bureau (2010).

Assimilation

Assimilation is *the process by which minorities gradually adopt cultural patterns from the dominant majority population.* When minorities—especially new immigrants—assimilate, they may change their styles of dress, language, cultural values, and even religion.

Many people think of the United States as a "melting pot" where the different ways of immigrants blend to produce one national lifestyle. There is some truth to this image, but our history shows that minorities are the ones who do most of the changing as they adopt the cultural patterns of more powerful people who have been here longer. In some cases, minorities imitate people they regard as their "betters" in order to escape hostility and to move up socially. In many cases, however, the majority population forces change on minorities. For example, by 2008, legislatures in thirty states had enacted laws making English the official language. National Map 3–1 shows the share of people in the United States who speak a language other than English at home.

The amount of assimilation on the part of minorities also depends on where they live. Latinos living in Ohio or New Hampshire (where they represent a small part of the population) are more likely to speak English than their counterparts living in south Texas along the Mexican border (where, in many communities, Spanish-speaking people are a numerical majority). Of course, wherever they live, some minorities assimilate more than others. Looking back over the decades, we also see that Germans and Irish have "melted" more than Italians, and Japanese have assimilated more than Chinese or Koreans.

Pluralism

Pluralism is *a state in which people of all racial and ethnic categories have about the same overall social standing.* Pluralism represents a situation in which no minority category is subject to disadvantage. The United States is pluralistic to the extent that—officially, at least—all people have equal standing under the law. But in reality, tolerance for diversity (majority tolerance for minorities and one minority population's tolerance for another) is limited. As just noted, for example, thirty states have passed laws designating English as their official language. In addition, the social standing of most minority populations is below that of the white, European-origin majority.

The Social Standing of U.S. Minorities

The United States is a nation of racial and ethnic diversity. It is important to know something of the history of the largest minorities in order to understand today's racial and ethnicity inequality.

Native Americans

Native Americans (many of whom now prefer to be called "American Indians") are descendants of the first people to come to North America across the Bering Strait from Asia. Over thousands of years, they spread throughout the hemisphere, forming hundreds of distinct societies, including the Aleuts and Eskimos of Alaska; a large number of North American Indian

MAKING THE GRADE

To what extent did genocide, segregation, assimilation, and pluralism play a part in the history of American Indians?

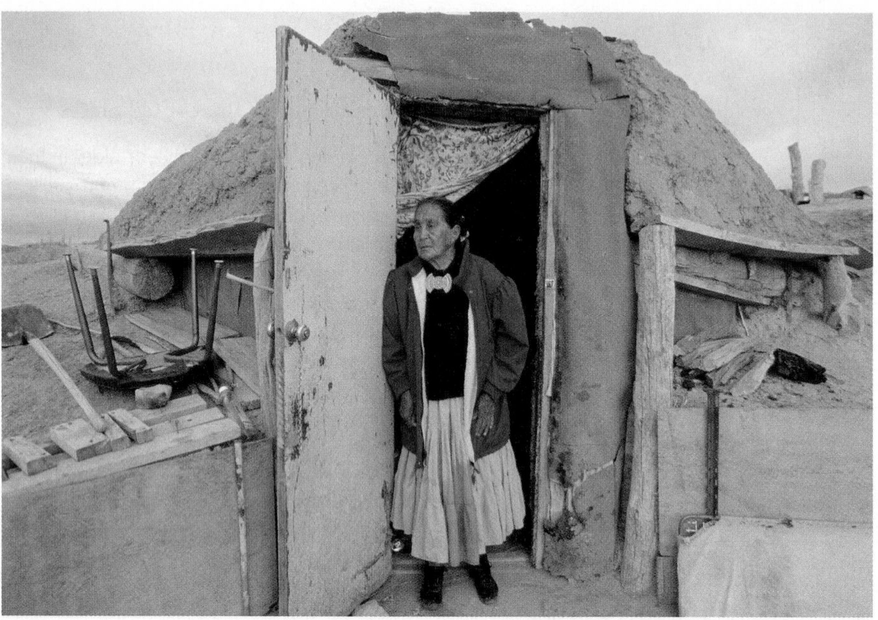

Despite media reports of the financial success that legal gambling on reservations has brought to some American Indians, the majority of Native people in the United States are greatly disadvantaged. Scenes such as this one from the Hopi reservation near Tuba City, Arizona, are more the rule than the exception.

societies, including the Cherokee, Zuni, Sioux, and Iroquois; the Aztec of Central America; and the Inca of South America.

By 1500, the arrival of European explorers and colonizers began centuries of conflict. What some Europeans called "bringing civilization to the New World" was for Native Americans the destruction of their ancient and thriving civilizations. From a population in the millions before Europeans arrived, the number of "vanishing Americans" fell to barely 250,000 by 1900 (Dobyns, 1966; Tyler, 1973).

At first, the U.S. government viewed native peoples as independent nations and tried to gain land from them through treaties. But the government was quick to use superior military power against any who resisted. Soldiers forcibly removed the Cherokee from their homelands in the southeastern United States, causing thousands of deaths along what came to be known as the Trail of Tears. By 1800, few native people remained along the East Coast.

In 1871, the United States declared American Indians wards of the federal government. At this point, the goal was assimilation. This meant remaking native peoples as "Americans" by moving them to reservations where they were forced to adopt Christianity in place of their traditional religions and where schools taught children English in place of ancestral tongues.

Since gaining full citizenship in 1924, many American Indians have assimilated, marrying people of other backgrounds. Yet many continue to live on reservations where poverty rates are very high. As Table 3–2 shows, American Indians remain disadvantaged, with below-average income, a high rate of poverty, and a low rate of college graduation.

In the past decade, American Indian organizations have received a large number of new membership applications, and many children are learning to speak native languages better than their parents (Nagel, 1996; Martin, 1997). Many American Indians operate a wide range of successful businesses, and some tribes have used the legal autonomy of reservations to build casinos. But the enormous profits from these casinos actually enrich only a few native people, with most profits going to non-Indian investors (Raymond, 2001; Bartlett & Steele, 2002). Overall, while some prosper, most American Indians remain severely disadvantaged and share a profound sense of historical injustice suffered at the hands of white people.

Table 3–2 The Social Standing of Native Americans, 2009

	Median Family Income	Percentage Living in Poverty	Percentage with Four or More Years of College (age 25 and over)
Entire U.S. population	$60,088	14.3%	29.9%
Native Americans	40,552	27.3	13.0

Source: U.S. Census Bureau (2010).

SOCIAL PROBLEMS in Everyday Life

Do you think that people living during the civil rights movement of the 1960s expected they would see an African American elected president?

African Americans

People of African ancestry arrived in the Americas along with the first European explorers. After 1619, however, when a Dutch trading ship delivered twenty Africans to Jamestown, Virginia, to work for whites, people came to see dark skin as a marker of subordination. In 1661, Virginia enacted the first slave law. By 1776, the year the United States declared its independence from Great Britain, slavery was legal in every state, and African Americans labored as slaves throughout the North as well as the South.

The demand for slaves was especially high in the South, where the plantation system required large numbers of people to work the cotton and tobacco fields. To meet this demand for labor, slave traders (including Arabs and Africans as well as Europeans and North Americans) legally transported human beings across the Atlantic Ocean, in chains and under horrific conditions. Before 1808, when the United States declared the slave trade illegal, 500,000 Africans were brought to the United States, and almost 10 million came to all of the Americas, North and South. Keep in mind that this was just half the number who left Africa—the other half died during the brutal journey (Tannenbaum, 1946; Franklin, 1967; Sowell, 1981).

The mass media played a powerful role in the civil rights movement of the 1950s and 1960s. Televised scenes such as this one in Birmingham, Alabama, in which police turned dogs and fire hoses on demonstrators, changed the mood of the nation in favor of the idea that all people should have equal opportunity and equal standing before the law.

Owners could force slaves to do just about anything and could discipline them in whatever way they wished. Slaves were not allowed to attend school, and owners routinely separated families as they traded men, women, and children for profit.

Not all people of African descent were slaves. Roughly 1 million free persons of color lived in the North and the South, most farming small parcels of farmland, working at skilled jobs in cities, or operating small businesses.

How could slavery exist in a society whose Declaration of Independence declared that "all men are created equal" and entitled to "life, liberty, and the pursuit of happiness"? Rather than making all people free, our society decided that African Americans were not really people. In the 1857 Dred Scott case, the U.S. Supreme Court stated that slaves were not citizens entitled to the rights and protections of U.S. law (Lach, 2002).

In the northern states, where slavery had less economic value, the practice had gradually come to an end. In the South, it took the Civil War to abolish slavery. As the guns roared, President Abraham Lincoln issued the Emancipation Proclamation on January 1, 1863, declaring slavery abolished in the breakaway southern Confederacy. When the fighting ended in 1865, Congress banned slavery everywhere in the country with the Thirteenth Amendment to the Constitution. In 1868, the Fourteenth Amendment reversed the Dred Scott decision, giving citizenship to all people, regardless of color, born in the United States.

But ending slavery did not mean ending racial discrimination. States soon enacted so-called Jim Crow laws, which barred black people from voting and sitting on juries and called for segregated trains, restaurants, hotels, and other public places (Woodward, 1974).

After World War I, when Congress closed the borders to further immigration, the need for labor in the booming factories sparked the "Great Migration," which drew tens of thousands of men and women of color from the rural South to the industrialized North. These were times of great achievements in African American life as, for example, the Harlem Renaissance (centered in the large African American community in New York City) produced writers such as Langston Hughes and musicians such as Duke Ellington and Louis Armstrong. Even so, racial segregation in neighborhoods, schools, and jobs was a way of life in most of the United States.

But change was coming. In 1948, President Harry Truman declared an end to segregation in the U.S. military. Black legal scholars, including Thurgood Marshall (1908–1993), who later served for thirty years on the U.S. Supreme Court, led an attack

SOCIAL PROBLEMS in Everyday Life

Notice that African American families have income below the national average. Make a list of factors that may explain this disparity.

SOCIAL PROBLEMS in Everyday Life

Although the United States was also at war with Germany, there was never any effort by the U.S. government to round up people of German ancestry. Why do you think the Japanese and the Germans in this country were viewed differently?

Table 3–3 The Social Standing of African Americans, 2009

	Median Family Income	Percentage Living in Poverty	Percentage with Four or More Years of College (age 25 and over)
Entire U.S. population	$60,088	14.3%	29.9%
African Americans	38,409	25.8	19.8

Source: U.S. Census Bureau (2010).

on school segregation, leading to the 1954 case of *Brown* v. *Board of Education of Topeka* (Kansas). In this landmark decision, the Supreme Court rejected the claim that black and white children could be taught in "separate but equal" schools.

A year later, the heroic action of Rosa Parks sparked the bus boycott that desegregated public transportation in Montgomery, Alabama. In the next decade, the federal government passed the Civil Rights Act of 1964 (prohibiting segregation in employment and public accommodations), the Voting Rights Act of 1965 (banning voting requirements that prevented African Americans from having a political voice), and the Civil Rights Act of 1968 (which outlawed discrimination in housing). Together, these laws brought an end to most legal discrimination in public life.

But African Americans' struggle for full participation in U.S. society is far from over. People of African descent are still disadvantaged, as shown in Table 3–3. African American families still have below-average income, and the black poverty rate is almost three times as high as the white poverty rate. Although about 84 percent of African Americans now complete high school, their college graduation rate is well below the national average.

By 2009, 41 percent of African American families earned more than $50,000 a year. But most black families remain in the working class, and many remain in poverty. On average, African American families earn 57 percent as much as white families—and this gap has changed little in the past forty years. One reason is that factory jobs, a key source of income for people living in central cities, have moved away from the United States to countries with lower labor costs. This is one reason that black unemployment is double the rate among white people; in some large cities, the rate is more than 40 percent (W. J. Wilson, 1996a; R. A. Smith, 2002; U.S. Department of Labor, 2008).

Asian Americans

Asian Americans include people with historical ties to any of several dozen Asian nations. The largest number have roots in China (3.2 million), India (2.6 million), the Philippines (2.5 million), Vietnam (1.5 million), South Korea (1.3 million), and Japan (767,000). In all, Asian Americans number more than 14 million, which is 4.6 percent of the total U.S. population. Other than Hispanics, Asian Americans are increasing in number faster than any other minority (U.S. Census Bureau, 2010).

The flow of immigrants from China and Japan to North America began when the Gold Rush of 1849 created a demand for laborers in California. Chinese men answered the call, numbering 100,000 within a generation, and they were joined by a small number of Japanese immigrants. As long as cheap labor was needed, whites welcomed them.

But when the economy slowed, these workers were seen as an economic threat by whites who labeled them the "Yellow Peril."

Table 3–4 The Social Standing of Asian Americans, 2009

	Median Family Income	Percentage Living in Poverty	Percentage with Four or More Years of College (age 25 and over)
Entire U.S. population	$60,088	14.3%	29.9%
All Asian Americans	75,027	12.5	52.4
Chinese Americans	82,129	12.7	51.9
Japanese Americans	88,129	7.8	47.4
Korean Americans	61,683	14.9	52.8

Source: U.S. Census Bureau (2010).

GETTING INVOLVED

After reading the section below, decide how much truth there is to the claim that Asians are a "model minority."

Legislatures and courts were pressured to bar Asians from certain work. In 1882, the federal government passed the Chinese Exclusion Act, which ended the flow of new immigrants from China. A similar action against Japan took place in 1908. After these laws were passed, the Asian population in the United States fell because almost all the people already here were men, and racial hostility prevented Asian men from marrying non-Asian women. Beginning in 1920, California and other states enacted laws banning interracial marriage outright.

Many Asians settled in urban neighborhoods where they could help one another. Chinatowns soon flourished in San Francisco, New York, and other large cities, with Chinese-owned restaurants, laundries, and other small businesses. Self-employment has been popular not only among the Chinese but also among all minorities who find few employers willing to hire them for good wages.

World War II brought important changes to both the Japanese American and Chinese American populations. The war in the Pacific began when Japan attacked Hawaii's Pearl Harbor naval base. The military strike stunned the United States, and many people wondered which side Japanese Americans would take in the conflict. Japanese Americans always remained loyal to the United States. But fear of Japan's industrial and military might, coupled with racial hostility, pushed President Franklin Roosevelt to issue Executive Order 9066, forcibly relocating all people of Japanese ancestry to military camps in remote areas away from the coast. The order forced more than 100,000 Japanese Americans to sell their businesses, homes, and farms for a fraction of their true value. Taken to camps, they lived under the watchful eyes of armed soldiers until 1944, when the U.S. Supreme Court declared the policy unconstitutional. In 1988, Congress admitted that this action was wrong and awarded a symbolic compensation of $20,000 to each surviving camp inmate (Ewers, 2008).

Because China joined the United States in the fight against Japan, in 1943 the federal government ended the 1882 ban on Chinese immigration and gave citizenship to Chinese Americans born abroad. The same offer was made after the war, in 1952, to foreign-born Japanese Americans.

After the war, many young people of Chinese and Japanese descent entered college, believing that more schooling was the key to success. By the 1980s, based on their cultural emphasis on study and hard work, Asian Americans were finding themselves described as the "model minority."

There is some truth to the "model minority" notion. As Table 3–4 shows, Chinese, Japanese, and Korean Americans now have above-average income and education. Poverty rates also are close to or below the national average. But this stereotype is misleading because many Asian families work long and hard in low-paying jobs. In addition, although the Chinatowns and Little Tokyos found in some large cities may offer social support, they may limit job opportunities by discouraging their residents from learning English (Kinkead, 1992; Gilbertson & Gurak, 1993).

From 1942 until 1944, more than 100,000 men, women, and children of Japanese ancestry were forced to live in military detention camps. This policy took away not just Japanese Americans' liberty but also most of their property as families were forced to sell homes and businesses for a small share of what they were really worth.

Today, more than one-third of all immigrants to the United States each year are from an Asian nation. Many Asian Americans, especially those with high social standing, have assimilated into the larger cultural mix. For example, few third- and fourth-generation Japanese Americans (the *Sansei* and *Yonsei*) live in segregated neighborhoods. Most people of Japanese ancestry marry someone of another racial and ethnic background.

Many Koreans and Indians, on the other hand, follow the example of immigrants a century ago and settle in ethnic neighborhoods, sometimes for protection from racial and ethnic hostility. Although Asian Americans have fared better than most minorities, anti-Asian prejudice remains strong (Chua-Eoan, 2000; Parrillo, 2003). Many Asian Americans remain socially marginal, living in two worlds and fully belonging to neither one.

MAKING THE GRADE

How do historical factors such as immigration account for patterns shown in the four maps below?

SOCIAL PROBLEMS in Everyday Life

In 2006, President Bush stated that people in this country should sing "The Star-Spangled Banner," our national anthem, only in English. Why do many people feel this way? Do you agree or not? Explain your position.

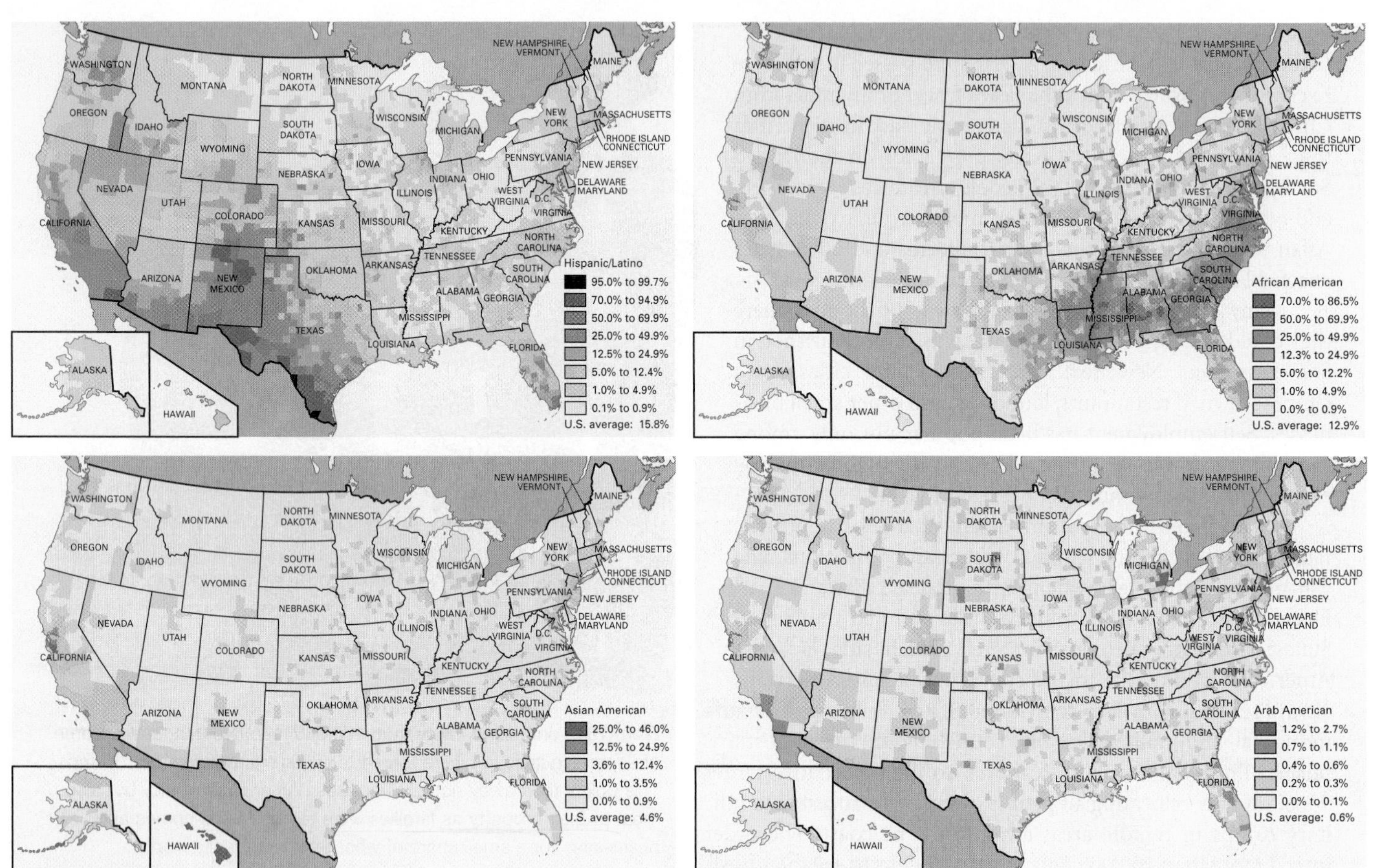

A Nation of Diversity

NATIONAL MAP 3–2

The Concentration of Hispanics/Latinos, African Americans, Asian Americans, and Arab Americans, by County

In 2010, Hispanic Americans represented 15.8 percent of the U.S. population, compared with 12.9 percent for African Americans, 4.6 percent for Asian Americans, and 0.6 percent for Arab Americans. These four maps show the geographic distribution of these categories of people in 2010 (2000 for Arab Americans). Comparing them, we see that the southern half of the United States is home to far more minorities than the northern half. But do the four concentrate in the same areas? What patterns do the maps reveal?

Source: U.S. Census Bureau (2010).

Hispanic Americans/Latinos

Hispanic Americans, also known as Latinos, are people with cultural roots in the nations of Central and South America, the Caribbean, and Spain. As a result, there are many Latino cultures. Racially, eight in ten Latinos consider themselves white, although these diverse people have a range of skin colors and physical features.

On Census Bureau forms, people of any race may identify themselves as being of Hispanic origin. In 2009, the official Hispanic population of the United States topped 48 million, making Hispanics the largest U.S. minority, with 15.8 percent of the population (exceeding African Americans at 39.6 million, or 12.9 percent).

National Map 3–2 shows the concentration of Latinos—as well as African Americans, Asian Americans, and Arab Americans—across the United States. Many Latinos reside in the Southwest because about two-thirds (almost 32 million) are of Mexican origin. Next in terms of numbers are Puerto Ricans (4.4 million) and Cuban Americans (1.7 million), with smaller

MAKING THE GRADE

Look ahead to pages 72-73 to see evidence of a relatively high level of prejudice against Arab Americans.

Table 3–5 The Social Standing of Hispanic Americans, 2009

	Median Family Income	Percentage Living in Poverty	Percentage with Four or More Years of College (age 25 and over)
Entire U.S. population	$60,088	14.3%	29.9%
All Hispanic Americans	39,730	25.3	13.9
Mexican Americans	39,754	25.1	9.0
Puerto Ricans	41,542	25.7	15.4
Cuban Americans	49,356	15.5	24.0

Source: U.S. Census Bureau (2010).

numbers from dozens of other countries. Overall, Latinos are so numerous and their cultural contributions so great that Spanish has become the unofficial second language of the United States.

Many Mexican Americans have lived for centuries on land that after the Mexican War (1846–1848) became what is now Texas, New Mexico, Arizona, Nevada, Utah, California, and Colorado. Others are new arrivals, drawn to the United States by a desire for greater economic opportunity. As already explained, a majority of people entering the United States illegally are from Mexico, where wages are typically far lower than in this country.

Puerto Rico, an island controlled by the Spanish for about 300 years, became a U.S. territory at the end of the Spanish-American War in 1898. Since 1917, all island residents have been U.S. citizens, although Puerto Rico is a commonwealth and not a state. The largest Puerto Rican community off the island is New York's Spanish Harlem, home to roughly 800,000 people. "Between 1990 and 2009, the Puerto Rican population of New York actually fell by more than 100,000." (U.S. Census Bureau, 2010) (Navarro, 2000).

Many Cubans fled to the United States after Fidel Castro gained control of Cuba in 1959. These men and women, numbering several hundred thousand, included affluent businesspeople and professionals. Most settled in Miami, Florida, where thay established a vibrant Cuban American community.

Table 3–5 shows that the social standing of Hispanic Americans is below the U.S. average. However, various categories of Latinos have very different rankings. The best-off are Cuban Americans, who have higher income and more schooling. Puerto Ricans occupy a middle position in terms of income, although those who are immigrants have a low rate of high school completion. Mexican Americans have the lowest relative ranking, with median family income at slightly less than two-thirds the national average. One reason for this disadvantage is that many Mexican Americans continue to speak only Spanish and not English, which can limit job opportunities.

More than one-third of Hispanic American families now earn more than $50,000 annually. But many challenges remain, including schools that do not do a very good job teaching students whose first language is Spanish. Chapter 13 ("Education") reports that 21 percent of Latinos between the ages of sixteen and twenty-four leave school without a high school diploma. In addition, their cultural differences—and dark skin—still spark hostility.

Arab Americans

Arab Americans are another U.S. minority that is increasing in size. Like Asian Americans and Latinos, these are people who trace their ancestry to one of several different nations around the world, in this case the nations of northern Africa or the Middle East. It is important to remember, however, that some of the people who live in one of the twenty-two nations that are considered part of the "Arab world" are not Arabs. For example, Morocco in northwestern Africa is home to the Berber people, just as Iraq in the Middle East is home to the Kurds.

Arab cultures are diverse but share use of the Arabic alphabet and language, and Islam is the dominant religion. But once again, the term "Arab" refers to an ethnic category, and the word "Muslim" refers to a follower of Islam. A majority of the people living in Arab countries are Muslims, but some Arabs are Christians or followers of other religions. To make matters more complex, most of the world's Muslims actually live in Asia rather than Africa or the Middle East and are not Arabs.

Immigration to the United States from many nations has created a culturally diverse population of Arab Americans. Some Arab Americans are Muslims and some are not; some

SOCIAL PROBLEMS in Everyday Life

Why do you think many people of Arab descent may not openly reveal their ancestry? Can you think of any other categories of people who might do likewise?

prejudice any rigid and unfounded generalization about an entire category of people

Table 3–6 The Social Standing of Arab Americans, 2009

	Median Family Income	Percentage Living in Poverty	Percentage with Four or More Years of College (age 25 and over)
Entire U.S. population	$60,088	14.3%	29.9%
Arab Americans	65,843	17.8	44.5

Source: U.S. Census Bureau (2010).

speak Arabic and some do not; some maintain the traditions of their homeland and some do not. As is the case with Latinos and Asian Americans, some are recent immigrants and some have lived in this country for decades or even generations.

Officially, the government counts 1.7 million Arab Americans, but because many people may choose not to declare their ethnic background, the actual number may well be twice that high. If so, Arab Americans represent 1 percent of the population. The largest populations of Arab Americans have ancestral ties to Lebanon (30 percent of all Arab Americans), Egypt (12 percent), and Syria (10 percent). Most Arab Americans (69 percent) report ancestral ties to one nation, but 31 percent report both Arab and non-Arab ancestry (U.S. Census Bureau, 2010). A look at National Map 3–2 shows the distribution of the Arab American population throughout the United States.

Arab Americans are diverse in terms of social class. Some are highly educated professionals who work as physicians, engineers, and professors; others are working-class people who perform various skilled jobs in factories or on construction sites; still others do service work in restaurants, hospitals, or other settings or work in small family businesses. Overall, as shown in Table 3–6, median family income for Arab Americans is slightly above the national average ($65,843 compared to a national median of $60,088 in 2009), but Arab Americans have a higher than average poverty rate (17.8 percent versus 14.3 percent for the population as a whole). Arab Americans are highly educated; 44.5 percent over age twenty-five have a college degree, compared to about 30 percent of the population as a whole (U.S. Census Bureau, 2010).

A number of large U.S. cities—including New York, Chicago, Los Angeles, Houston, and Dearborn (Michigan)—have large, visible Arab American communities. Even so, many Arab Americans choose to downplay their ethnicity as a way to avoid prejudice and discrimination. The fact that many of the terrorist attacks against the United States and other nations have been carried out by Arabs encourages some people to link being Arab (or Muslim) with being a terrorist. This attitude is unfair because it blames an entire category of people for the actions of a few individuals. But this attitude helps explain rising hostility toward Arabs and Arab Americans after 2001. It is also true that Arab Americans have been targets of an increasing number of hate crimes, and many feel that they are subject to "ethnic profiling" that threatens their privacy and civil liberties (Ali & Juarez, 2003; Ali, Lipper, & Mack, 2004; Hagopian, 2004).

Some people in the United States link being Arab American or Muslim with support for anti-American terrorism. Why is this so? What can you suggest to eliminate this stereotype?

Prejudice

As the preceding accounts show, minorities face the problem of **prejudice,** *any rigid and unfounded generalization about an entire category of people.* Prejudice is a prejudgment, an attitude one develops *before* interacting with the specific people in question. Because such attitudes are not based on direct experience, prejudices are not only wrong but also difficult to change.

GETTING INVOLVED

How does the box below demonstrate the value of sociological research in combating prejudice?

DIVERSITY: RACE, CLASS, & GENDER

Attitudes toward Race and Intelligence

Almost every year, as part of a national research project known as the General Social Survey, researchers ask a representative sample of U.S. adults to rank racial and ethnic categories with regard to overall intelligence. They ask people to use a seven-point scale that ranges from 1 (very low intelligence) to 7 (very high intelligence). The graph shows the average score respondents gave to each category of people.

Apparently, the U.S. public believes that some racial and ethnic categories are smarter than others. Whites, the majority category, rank themselves high in intelligence. Notice, however, that southern whites—who historically have had less education than those in other regions—get a lower rating. A common opinion is that most minorities are less bright. An exception is Jewish people, most of whom are white and nonsouthern and who have above-average education. Asian Americans also are ranked slightly above whites. The survey data place African Americans and Latinos farther down the scale.

Almost all scientists agree that some individuals are smarter than other individuals. But just a few researchers argue that entire categories of people are innately smarter than others. For example, Richard Herrnstein and Charles Murray reviewed research on intelligence and reported that the average intelligence quotient (IQ) of white people (of European ancestry) was about 100, the average IQ for people of East Asian ancestry was a bit higher at 103, and the IQ for people of African descent was somewhat lower at 90.

Most social scientists consider any such differences a reflection of environment and culture rather than innate intelligence. For example, Thomas Sowell found that early in the last century, immigrants from Poland, Lithuania, Italy, Greece, China, and Japan scored 10 to 15 points below the U.S. average on IQ tests. Today, people in these same categories have IQ scores that are average or above. Among Italian Americans, average IQ jumped almost 10 points in fifty years; among Polish and Chinese Americans, the rise was almost 20 points.

Sowell found a similar pattern among African Americans. On IQ tests, black people living in the North outscore black people living in the South by about 10 points, a difference that biology cannot explain. Similarly, African Americans who migrated from the South to the North after 1940 soon performed much better on IQ tests.

Sowell concludes that cultural patterns are the main cause of IQ differences between categories of people. Asians score higher on tests not because they are smarter but because their cultures value learning and encourage excellence. African Americans score lower because they carry a legacy of disadvantage that can undermine self-confidence and discourage achievement.

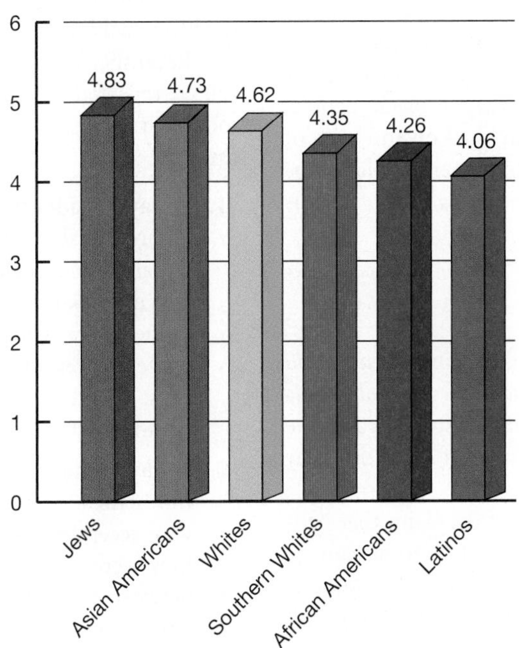

How U.S. Adults Link Intelligence to Race and Ethnicity

Survey research shows that people in the United States tend to view some racial and ethnic categories as more intelligent than others.

Source: NORC (2008).

WHAT DO YOU THINK?

1. Why do you think U.S. adults rank racial and ethnic categories differently with regard to intelligence?
2. Do you think what we call "intelligence" is real? Can it be measured fairly?
3. Why are IQ tests important? Do you think the use of IQ tests can fuel unfair prejudice? Why or why not?

Sources: Sowell (1994, 1995), Herrnstein & Murray (1994), and NORC (2008).

Prejudice can be both positive and negative. Positive prejudices lead us to assume that certain people (usually those like ourselves) are better or smarter. Negative prejudices lead us to see someone who differs from us as less worthy. Prejudices—both positive and negative—involve social class, gender, religion, age, and sexual or political orientation. But probably no dimensions of difference involve as many prejudices as race and ethnicity. The Diversity: Race, Class, & Gender box uses national survey data to reveal the extent of prejudice toward various racial and ethnic categories of people.

stereotype an exaggerated description applied to every person in some category

SOCIAL PROBLEMS in Everyday Life

Is the stereotype of Asian Americans as a "model minority" really positive or not? Explain.

Stereotypes

A concept closely linked to prejudice is **stereotype,** *an exaggerated description applied to every person in some category.* The word *stereo* comes from the Greek word for "hard" or "solid," suggesting a rigid belief, one that is largely at odds with reality. For just about every racial or ethnic category, our culture contains stereotypes, which typically describe a category of people in negative terms. What stereotypes are conveyed in phrases such as "Dutch treat," "French kiss," "Russian roulette," and "getting gypped" (a reference to Gypsies)?

We all form opinions about the world, identifying people as "good" or "bad" in various ways. Generalizations about specific people that are based on actual experience may be quite valid. But racial or ethnic stereotypes are more of a problem because they assume that an entire category of people shares particular traits, as when a white person thinks all African Americans are unwilling to work hard or a person of color thinks every white person is hostile toward black people. Forming a judgment about another individual on the basis of actual personal experience is one thing, but when we place others in a category before we have a chance to judge them as individuals, stereotypes dehumanize people.

Racism

The most serious example of prejudice is **racism,** *the assertion that people of one race are less worthy than or even biologically inferior to others.* Over the course of human history, people the world over have assumed they were superior to those they viewed as lesser human beings.

Why is racism so widespread? Because the claim that people are *biologically* inferior, although entirely wrong, can be used to justify making them *socially* inferior. For example, Europeans used racism to support the often brutal colonization of much of Latin America, Asia, and Africa. When Europeans spoke of the "white man's burden," they were claiming to be superior beings who had the obligation to help "inferior" beings become more like them.

Even today, hundreds of hate groups in the United States continue to claim that minorities are inferior. In addition, subtle forms of racism are common in everyday life.

Measuring Prejudice: The Social Distance Scale

Prejudice shapes everyday life as it draws us toward some categories of people and away from others. Early in the twentieth century, Emory Bogardus (1925) developed the *social distance scale* to measure prejudice among students at U.S. colleges and universities. Bogardus asked students how closely they were willing to interact with people in thirty racial and ethnic categories. Figure 3–1 shows the seven-point scale Bogardus used. At one extreme, people express very high social distance (high negative prejudice) when they say that some category of people should be barred from the country (point 7 in the figure). At the other extreme (little or no negative prejudice), people say they would accept members of some category into their family through marriage (Bogardus, 1925, 1967; Owen, Elsner, & McFaul, 1977).

Decades ago, Bogardus found that students, regardless of their own race and ethnicity, were most prejudiced against Latinos, African Americans, Asians, and Turks; they were willing to have these people as coworkers but not as neighbors, friends, or family members. At the other extreme, they were most accepting of the English, Scots, and Canadians, whom they were willing to have marry into their families.

Recently, Vincent Parrillo and Christopher Donoghue (2005) repeated the social distance study to see how students today felt about various minorities[1]. There were three major findings:

1. **Today's students are more accepting of all minorities.** Figure 3–1 shows that the average (mean) response on the social distance scale was 2.14 in 1925 and 1946, dropping to 2.08 in 1956, 1.92 in 1966, 1.93 in 1977, and just 1.44 in 2001. In the most recent study, students (81 percent of whom were white) expressed much more acceptance of African Americans: Placed near the bottom in 1925, this category was near the top in 2001.
2. **Today's students see less difference between the various minorities.** In the earliest studies, although students were very accepting of some people (scores between 1 and 2), they were not very accepting of other minorities (scores between 4 and 5). In the 2001 study, no minority received a score greater than 1.94.
3. **The terrorist attacks in 2001 probably increased prejudice against Arabs and Muslims.** The most recent study was done just weeks after the terrorist attacks of September 11, 2001. Perhaps the fact that the nineteen attackers were Arabs and Muslims helps explain why students expressed the greatest social distance toward these categories. Even so, not one student in the study said that Arabs or Muslims should be

[1]Parrillo and Donoghue dropped seven of Bogardus's original categories (Armenians, Czechs, Finns, Norwegians, Scots, Swedes, and Turks) because they are no longer visible minorities and added nine new categories (Africans, Arabs, Cubans, Dominicans, Haitians, Jamaicans, Muslims, Puerto Ricans, and Vietnamese). This change probably encouraged higher social distance scores, making the downward trend all the more significant.

racism the assertion that people of one race are less worthy than or even biologically inferior to others

institutional racism racism at work in the operation of social institutions, including the economy, schools, hospitals, the military, and the criminal justice system

GETTING INVOLVED

Do any of the results shown in Figure 3-1 below surprise you? Explain.

Dimensions of Difference

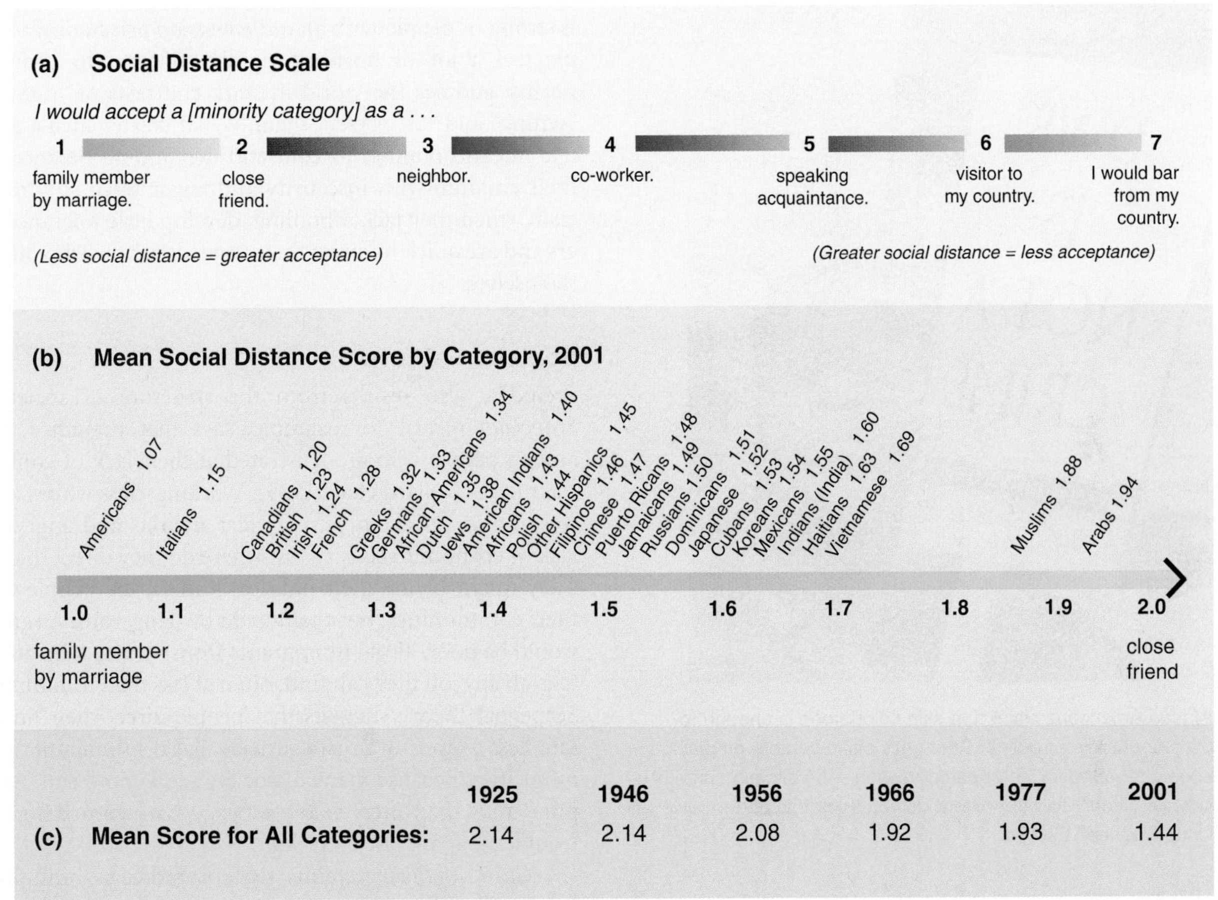

FIGURE 3–1 Bogardus Social Distance Scale

Using this seven-point scale, Emory Bogardus and others have shown that people feel much closer to some categories of people than they do to others. Between 1925, when the study was first carried out, and the most recent study in 2001, the average social distance response has dropped from 2.14 to 1.44, showing increasing tolerance of diversity.

Source: Parrillo & Donoghue (2005).

barred from the United States. Also, even the most prejudiced score by today's students (Arabs, with a mean score of 1.94) shows much more tolerance than students back in 1977 expressed toward eighteen of the thirty minority categories.

Institutional Racism: The Case of Racial Profiling

The studies we have just looked at involve prejudice in terms of individual attitudes. But if those attitudes are widespread, we should expect prejudice to be built into the operation of society itself. This idea underlies the work of Stokely Carmichael and Charles Hamilton (1967), who described **institutional racism** as *racism at work in the operation of social institutions, including the economy, schools, hospitals, the military, and the criminal justice system.* Whenever race plays a part in the operation of any of these social institutions, harming minorities, institutional racism is at work.

Racial profiling—in which police or others in power consider race or ethnicity to be, by itself, a sign of probable guilt—illustrates the operation of institutional racism. This is not a matter of one individual police officer being prejudiced and thinking that, say, all African Americans are potential criminals. Prejudice is institutional when such attitudes are part of the

SOCIAL PROBLEMS in Everyday Life

Many African Americans report having been pulled over by police for "driving while black." How is that a case of institutional prejudice?

multiculturalism educational programs designed to recognize cultural diversity in the United States and to promote respect for all cultural traditions

Eurocentrism the practice of using European (particularly English) cultural standards to judge everyone

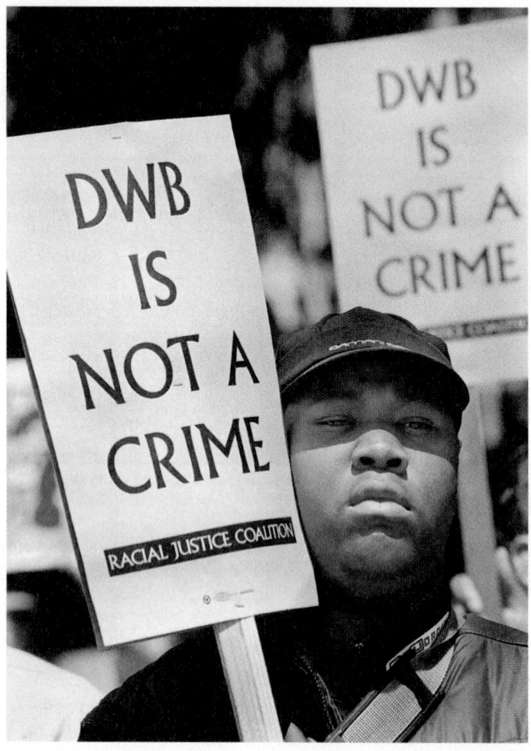

Many African Americans claim that skin color alone is enough to prompt a response from police. Often, this claim centers on black drivers being stopped for no apparent reason—the alleged crime of "driving while black." To what extent do you think this pattern exists in the United States? Explain.

society's culture—and also part of the culture of a police department—so that there is a widespread pattern of police automatically assuming that a black person who comes to their attention is engaged in wrongdoing. If police generally consider black persons more dangerous than whites, they may be quicker to draw their weapons on black people, perhaps with tragic results. In recent years, a number of African Americans who turned out to be neither armed nor guilty of any crime have been killed by police who may well have reacted partly or primarily to their skin color.

Challenging cases of institutionalized racism is difficult. Police departments are part of society's power structure and claim to serve the public interest. When institutional racism involves an organization with a lot of power, it is often ignored.

Causes of Prejudice

What causes people to become prejudiced in the first place? Researchers point to two key factors: the personality of individuals and the structure of society itself.

Personality Factors

T. W. Adorno and his colleagues (1950) claimed that prejudice is strong in people with an *authoritarian personality.* Such people feel a lot of hostility, rigidly conform to conventional norms, and see the world in stark contrasts of "right" versus "wrong" and "us" versus "them." What creates such a personality? Adorno pointed to cold and demanding parents who fill their children with insecurity and anger. Such children, especially when they lack schooling, develop little tolerance of others and are quick to direct their anger at people who differ from themselves.

Societal Factors

Prejudice also results from the structure of society itself. *Scapegoat theory,* for example, says that prejudice develops among people who are frustrated at their lack of control over their lives (Dollard et al., 1939). Working-class whites in southwest Texas, for example, may feel anxious and angry at their lack of economic security, but where do they direct their anger? They might blame their political leaders, the people who run their communities, but that would be dangerous. A safer target would be poor, illegal immigrants from Mexico who are willing to grab any job they can find, often at less than minimum wage. Scapegoat theory suggests that people direct their hostility at safe, less powerful targets such as illegal immigrants or other minorities. Because many of society's least powerful people are minorities, they often end up as scapegoats blamed for a host of troubles that are not their fault.

Cultural theory claims that prejudice is built into our culture. An illustration of this is the research using Emory Bogardus's social distance scale, described earlier in this chapter. Bogardus showed that most of us turn out to have the same kinds of prejudice, favoring certain categories of people and avoiding others. The fact that these attitudes are so widely shared suggests that prejudice is not a trait of deviant individuals as much as it is a normal part of our cultural system.

Multiculturalism

Is there a way to address prejudice deeply rooted in our culture? One strategy for change is **multiculturalism,** *educational programs designed to recognize cultural diversity in the United States and to promote respect for all cultural traditions.*

Multiculturalism claims, first, that U.S. society has long downplayed its cultural diversity. Schools have taught generations of children that the United States is a cultural "melting pot" that blends human diversity into a single culture we call "American." However, multiculturalism maintains that our diverse population has "melted" far less than most people think. More cor-

discrimination the unequal treatment of various categories of people

institutional discrimination discrimination that is built into the operation of social institutions, including the economy, schools, and the legal system

MAKING THE GRADE

Be sure you are clear as to how discrimination differs from prejudice.

rectly, race and ethnicity have formed a hierarchy. At the top, Europeans (especially the English) represent the cultural ideal of the well-informed, well-groomed, and well-behaved man and woman. What we call assimilation, then, is really a process of *Anglicization* as immigrants try to become more like the privileged white Anglo-Saxon Protestants (WASPs).

In addition, U.S. institutions—including schools, law, and the economy, as well as dominant religions and family forms—are all modeled along Western European lines. Multiculturalists describe this bias as **Eurocentrism,** *the practice of using European (particularly English) cultural standards to judge everyone.* To multiculturalists, U.S. culture is itself an expression of prejudice against people in this country who differ from the dominant model. Multiculturalism asks that we rethink our national heritage and recognize the accomplishments not just of the cultural elite but of people of every race and ethnicity.

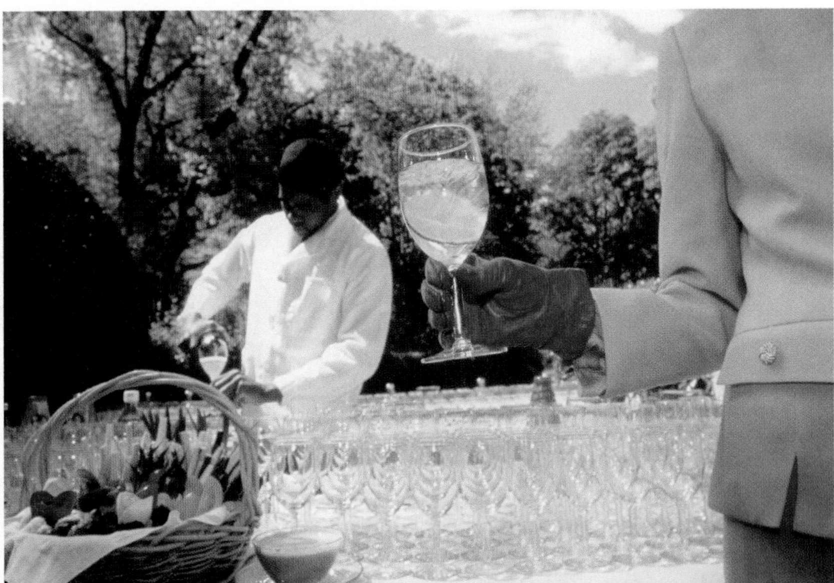

Wouldn't most people assume that the gloved hand holding the wine glass is white? Despite the outlawing of racial discrimination, there is still considerable social inequality beween white and black people in U.S. society. The widespread pattern of people of color providing personal service to members of the dominant white majority goes all the way back to the beginnings of slavery.

Although there is strong support for multiculturalism (especially among liberals) because it gives more visibility and power to minorities, others (especially conservatives) claim that this approach divides society by downplaying what we have in common. The Latin phrase that appears on all U.S. currency—*E pluribus unum*—literally means "out of many, one." Thus the controversy over multiculturalism is really about how much stress we should place on a single national identity and how much we should highlight differences.

Discrimination

Discrimination involves *the unequal treatment of various categories of people.* Prejudice is a matter of *attitudes*, but discrimination is a matter of *actions*. Like prejudice, discrimination can be positive or negative. We discriminate in a positive way when we single out people who do especially good work or when we provide special favors to family members or friends. We discriminate in a negative way when we put others down or avoid entire categories of people based on their race or ethnicity.

Few people would object to an employer who hires a job applicant with more schooling over one with less. But what if an employer favors one category of people (say, Christians) over another (say, Jews)? Unless a person's religion is directly related to the job (for example, if a church is hiring a priest), ruling out an entire category of people is wrongful discrimination, which violates the law.

Institutional Discrimination

As in the case of prejudice, some discrimination involves the actions of individuals. For example, a restaurant owner might refuse to serve students with dark skin. Almost everyone condemns discrimination of this kind, and in a public setting such as a restaurant, it is against the law.

Institutional discrimination is *discrimination that is built into the operation of social institutions, including the economy, schools, and the legal system.* A well-known example of institutional discrimination is this nation's history of treating black and white children differently by placing them in separate schools. As noted earlier, not until 1954 did civil rights activists succeed in overturning the legal doctrine of "separate but equal" schools, which the U.S. Supreme Court concluded was unconstitutional in the landmark case of *Brown* v. *Board of Education of Topeka*. But that did not end racial segregation in our country; more than half a century after the *Brown* decision, most children still sit in classrooms surrounded by students of the same race (Kozol, 2005).

affirmative action policies intended to improve the social standing of minorities subject to past prejudice and discrimination

GETTING INVOLVED

How do you suggest breaking the vicious circle of prejudice and discrimination?

Throughout much of the United States until the 1960s, public facilities, including bus and railroad stations, were segregated. But today—fifty years later—racial segregation is still commonly found. For example, Montgomery County High School in Mount Vernon, Georgia, still holds a white prom and a black prom that divide students by race.

Prejudice and Discrimination: A Vicious Circle

Prejudice and discrimination reinforce each other, maintaining social inequality over time. Let's begin with how prejudice can lead to discrimination: If prejudiced white police officers think that most African Americans are criminals, they may well engage in racial profiling, stopping a large number of black motorists and being quick to arrest black citizens on the street. Such discrimination, if it is widespread, will overly criminalize African Americans, reducing their chances of finding good jobs and raising their odds of living in neighborhoods marked by poverty, drug abuse, and crime. As people see minorities in such conditions, this discrimination unleashes a new round of prejudice. And so it goes, around and around, forming a vicious circle that harms minorities.

Affirmative Action: Reverse Discrimination or Cure for Prejudice?

One strategy aimed at breaking the vicious circle of prejudice and discrimination is **affirmative action,** *policies intended to improve the social standing of minorities subject to past prejudice and discrimination.* Affirmative action policies have changed over time, and they will continue to change in response to court rulings.

History of Affirmative Action

After World War II, the government assisted veterans by funding education under what was known as the GI Bill, and minorities who might not otherwise have gone to college were thus able to enter classrooms across the country. By 1960, almost 350,000 African Americans had used government help to earn a college degree, but many of these men and women were not getting the types of jobs for which they were qualified. The Kennedy administration concluded that education alone could not overcome deep-seated, institutionalized prejudice and discrimination against people of color, so it devised the policy of affirmative action, which required employers to "throw a wider net" to identify and hire qualified minority applicants. In the years that followed, employers hired thousands of African American women and men for good jobs, helping build the black middle class and reduce racial prejudice.

By the 1970s, affirmative action was extended to include college admissions, and many policies took the form of "quota

GETTING INVOLVED

To what extent do you support affirmative action based on race? Explain.

systems" in which employers or colleges set aside a certain number of places for minorities, which by then included women, Hispanics, veterans, and in some cases people with physical disabilities. In 1978, the Supreme Court heard the case of *University of California Regents* v. *Bakke,* brought by Allen Bakke, a white man who was denied admission to medical school at the University of California at Davis. The medical school had a policy of setting aside 16 places (out of 100 in each entering class) for African Americans, Asian Americans, Native Americans, and Hispanic Americans. Such rigid quotas were ruled to be illegal, but the Court did endorse the use of race and ethnicity as part of the overall process of admitting students or hiring employees in order to increase minority representation in settings from which minorities had historically been excluded.

By the mid-1990s, opposition to affirmative action programs had increased. In 1995, the University of California system declared it would no longer consider race and gender when making admission, hiring, and contract decisions. The following year, California voters passed Proposition 209, which required state agencies to operate without regard to race, ethnicity, or gender. A similar proposition passed in the state of Washington. Also in 1996, a federal district court declared (in *Hopwood* v. *Texas*) that race and gender could no longer be considered by public colleges and universities in Texas, Louisiana, and Mississippi.

Seeking a socially diverse student body, many colleges and universities have tried to find a way around the new regulations. In Texas, for example, public universities admit all students in the top 10 percent of their high school class, a policy that benefits students from predominantly African American and Latino schools.

In 2003, the U.S. Supreme Court once again addressed the issue of affirmative action. The case involved admission policies at the University of Michigan, a state university. In the undergraduate admissions process, applicants of underrepresented minorities had received a numerical bonus that was added to a total score, which also reflected grades and College Board scores. The Supreme Court struck down this point system as too similar to the racial quota systems rejected by the Court in the past. However, the Court did say that colleges and universities could continue to take account of applicants' race with the goal of creating a racially diverse student body. In this administrative process, rather than a rigid point system, race was treated as one of several variables used in giving each applicant individual consideration. In these decisions, the Court was affirming the national importance of allowing colleges and universities to create racially diverse campuses while at the same time stating that all applicants must be considered as individuals (Stout, 2003).

The United States continues to wrestle with the issue of affirmative action. Most people agree that society needs to give real opportunity to people in every racial and ethnic category. But disagreement remains as to whether affirmative action is part of the problem or part of the solution (Fineman & Lipper, 2003; Kantrowitz & Wingert, 2003; NORC, 2007).

Theoretical Analysis: Understanding Racial and Ethnic Inequality

Why do the various racial and ethnic categories of the U.S. population have unequal social standing? The following discussion draws answers from sociology's three major theoretical approaches: structural-functional, symbolic-interaction, and social-conflict analysis.

Structural-Functional Analysis: The Importance of Culture

Structural-functional theory places great importance on culture. To the extent that various racial and ethnic categories have different cultural orientations—for example, more or less emphasis on education or achievement—unequal social standing is the likely result.

The Culture of Poverty

Chapter 2 ("Poverty and Wealth") introduced the "culture of poverty" thesis of Oscar Lewis (1966). Lewis studied the low-income Puerto Rican population of San Juan and New York and found a widespread way of thinking that he called "fatalism." This outlook leads people to accept their situation and the assumption that life will never get better. Growing up poor and learning to accept that situation, young people develop low self-esteem and a sense of hopelessness. Over time, they grow into adults who are not likely to take advantage of the opportunities society offers them.

Joan Albon made a similar claim about American Indians, whose traditional cultures tend to be cooperative and "in direct opposition to the principles of the modern, competitive, capitalistic order" (1971:387). Some African American peer groups have also been described as having an "oppositional culture" that discourages members from excelling by defining school achievement as "acting white" (Fordham & Ogbu, 1992). In such an environment, adds Shelby Steele (1990), a successful man or woman of color risks the charge of not being a "real" African American.

MAKING THE GRADE

Remember that social-conflict theories can focus on class (Marx) and also race (multiculturalism).

CRITICAL REVIEW Although few people doubt that culture matters, critics claim that relying on this approach amounts to defining people as responsible for their own disadvantage—what Chapter 2 described as "blaming the victim." People who live in individualistic societies such as the United States find it easy to blame people for their own poverty. But do poor people really deserve to live as they do? If disadvantaged people lack some of the optimism and confidence found among people who are better off, critics suggest, this is more the *result* than the *cause* of low social standing.

The Applying Theory table summarizes the contributions of the structural-functional approach, as well as the social-interaction and social-conflict approaches, which follow.

Symbolic-Interaction Analysis: The Personal Meaning of Race

Forty years after the end of slavery in the United States, the pioneering sociologist W. E. B. Du Bois published *The Souls of Black Folk*, an analysis of the social standing of black people. As Du Bois saw it, even though slavery was gone, most African Americans were still living as second-class citizens.

Every time black people and white people met, said Du Bois, race hung in the air, defining each in the eyes of the other. From the African American perspective, race produces "a peculiar sensation, [a] double-consciousness, [a] sense of always looking at oneself through the eyes of others, of measuring one's soul by the tape of a world that looks on in amused contempt and pity" (2001:227, orig. 1903). In effect, Du Bois said, U.S. society makes whites the standard by which others (including African Americans) should be measured. In daily encounters, race operates as a *master status*, a trait that defines and devalues any person of color.

Today, more than a century later, race continues to shape the everyday lives of everyone, regardless of their color. Manning Marable sums it up this way: "As long as I can remember, the fundamentally defining feature of my life, and the lives of my family, was the stark reality of race" (1995:1).

CRITICAL REVIEW Symbolic-interaction analysis investigates how we use color (or in the case of ethnicity, cultural background) as we define ourselves and evaluate other people. In short, race and ethnicity are key building blocks of the reality we experience in everyday life.

At the same time, race involves more than personal understandings. Race is also an important structure of society, a dimension of social stratification. This insight brings us to the social-conflict approach.

Social-Conflict Analysis: The Structure of Inequality

Social-conflict analysis claims that the unequal standing of minorities reflects the organization of society itself. Class, race, and ethnicity operate together as important dimensions of social inequality.

The Importance of Class

Karl Marx traced the roots of social inequality to a society's economy. As explained in Chapter 2 ("Poverty and Wealth"), Marx criticized capitalism for concentrating wealth and power in the hands of a small elite. He explained that this capitalist elite, realizing that the strength of the working class lies in its greater numbers, tries to divide the workers by playing up racial and ethnic differences. Marx's colleague Friedrich Engels pointed to the racial and ethnic diversity of the United States as the main reason U.S. workers had not come together to form a socialist movement. "Immigration," Marx and Engels wrote,

> divides the workers into two groups: the native born and the foreigners, and the latter in turn into (1) the Irish, (2) the Germans, (3) the many small groups, each of which understands only itself: Czechs, Poles, Italians, Scandinavians, etc. And then the Negroes. To form a single party out of these requires unusually powerful incentives. (1959:458, orig. 1893)

Marx and Engels hoped that the increasing misery of workers would eventually provide the incentive for workers to unify themselves into a politically active class. To some degree, this has happened, and a number of unions and worker organizations have memberships that are black and white, Anglo and Latino. However, racial and ethnic differences still divide the U.S. workforce as they do workers around the world.

Multicultural Theory

Social-conflict theory also notes the importance of culture. A multicultural perspective claims that U.S. culture provides privileges to the European majority while pushing minorities to the margins of society.

Cultural bias against minorities colors accounts of U.S. history. When Christopher Columbus landed in the Bahamas in 1492, he encountered Native Americans who were, on the whole, peaceful. Tragically, this gentleness made it easy for the more competitive and aggressive Europeans to take advantage of them. Yet most of our historical accounts portray Europeans as heroic explorers and Native Americans as thieves and murderers (Matthiessen, 1984; Sale, 1990).

As W. E. B. Du Bois noted, bias involving race and ethnicity is still part of everyday life. Take the common case in which people assume that "classical music" refers only to European

MAKING THE GRADE

Use the table below to review the three theoretical approaches to racial and ethnic inequality.

APPLYING THEORY

Racial and Ethnic Inequality

	What is the level of analysis?	What do we learn about racial and ethnic inequality?	Are racial and ethnic differences helpful or harmful to society?
Structural-functional approach	Macro-level	The structural-functional approach highlights the importance of culture to social standing. Various categories of the population have differing cultural orientations that affect patterns of education and achievement. The "culture of poverty" thesis developed by Oscar Lewis is one example of a theory to explain why some low-income people have a fatalistic view of their situation.	Ethnic differences are cultural and a source of identity and pride for most people. At the same time, traditional or fatalistic cultural orientations can be a barrier to achievement for some categories of people.
Symbolic-interaction approach	Micro-level	The symbolic-interaction approach focuses on how people experience society in their everyday lives. Race and ethnicity affect the way we evaluate ourselves and others. W. E. B. Du Bois claimed that most people consider race a basic element of social identity, to the disadvantage of people of color.	To the extent that race or ethnicity becomes a master status that devalues people, these social structures take away from our common humanity.
Social-conflict approach	Macro-level	The social-conflict approach links race and ethnicity to class—all are elements of social stratification. Marx and Engels claimed that race and ethnicity divided the working class. Multicultural theory claims that our culture has a European bias that pushes minority ways of life to the margins of society.	As elements of social stratification, race and ethnicity serve the interests of elites and are harmful to the operation of society.

and not to Chinese, Indian, or Zulu compositions of a certain period. Cultural bias also leads people to apply the term "ethnic" to anyone not of English background or even to speak of "whites and blacks," placing the dominant category first (as we do for "husbands and wives").

CRITICAL REVIEW One criticism of social-conflict theory is that this approach downplays what people in the United States have in common. Whatever their color or cultural background, most people identify themselves as "Americans," and they have joined together over and over again to help each other in bad times and, in good times, to celebrate the principle of individual freedom that defines our way of life.

A second problem is that painting minorities as victims runs the risk of taking away people's responsibility for their own lives. It is true that minorities face serious barriers, but we need to remember that people also make choices about how to live and can act to raise their social standing and join together to improve their communities.

Third and finally, conflict theory all but ignores the significant strides this nation has made in dealing with its

GETTING INVOLVED

What do you think are the strongest point and the weakest point made by conservatives?

GETTING INVOLVED

What do you think are the strongest point and the weakest point made by liberals?

social diversity. Over time, U.S. society has moved closer to the ideals of political participation, public education, and equal standing before the law for everyone. As a result, the share of minorities who are well schooled, politically active, and affluent has steadily increased. Although much remains to be done, there is also reason for pride and optimism. The election of Barack Obama, an African American man, as president of the United States is surely a sign that race is no longer the barrier it once was (West, 2008).

POLITICS, RACE, AND ETHNICITY

Constructing Problems and Defining Solutions

Should racial and ethnic inequality be defined as a problem? If so, what should be done about it? Conservative, liberal, and radical-left viewpoints produce different answers.

Conservatives: Culture and Effort Matter

Conservatives support the idea that all people should have equal standing before the law and the chance to improve their lives. Believing that these things are mostly true in the United States, conservatives also believe that people are responsible for their own social standing.

If some racial and ethnic minorities are more successful than others, it is likely that cultural differences are at work. On average, people in various racial and ethnic categories place different emphasis on schooling, aspire to different kinds of jobs, and even attach different levels of importance to financial success. For instance, Italians have long worked in the building trades, the Irish lean toward public service occupations, Jews have long dominated the garment industry and are well represented in most professions, and many Koreans operate retail businesses (Keister, 2003). Such differences make no one "better" than anyone else. But as conservatives see it, they do produce social inequality.

According to the conservative view, social standing should reflect people's level of ambition, the importance they place on schooling, and their commitment to hard work. In a society such as ours, people are free but also unequal. Conservatives claim that any society in which government tries to engineer rigid social equality would almost certainly offer little personal freedom.

The defense of individual freedom is the reason conservatives typically oppose affirmative action policies. They argue that instead of being an effective way to give everyone an equal chance—a path toward the goal of a color-blind society—affirmative action is really a system of "group preferences." In practice, as they see it, such policies amount to "reverse discrimination" that favors people based not on their individual qualifications and performance but on their race, ethnicity, or gender. If treating people according to color was wrong in the past, how can it be right today?

Conservatives add that affirmative action harms minorities by calling into question their accomplishments: How would you feel, for example, if other people thought you had been admitted to college not because of your abilities but because of your skin color or ethnic background?

Finally, conservatives point out that affirmative action helps the minorities who need it least. Minorities on college campuses and in the corporate world are, by and large, already well off; affirmative action does less for the minority poor, who need help the most (Gilder, 1980; C. Murray, 1984; Sowell, 1987, 1990; Carter, 1991; Steele, 1990; B. L. Stone, 2000).

Liberals: Society and Government Matter

Liberals claim that prejudice and discrimination, and not cultural differences, are the main causes of social inequality. For this reason, liberals claim, it is simply not true that everyone has the same chance to get ahead. Prejudice and discrimination are still very much a part of our society's schools, military, corporate economy, criminal justice system, and other institutions.

Liberals acknowledge that there may be cultural differences between various categories of the population. But liberals see such differences as more the *result* than the *cause* of social inequality. That is, people who are shut out of opportunity—whether they are inner-city or rural residents—may develop a sense of hopelessness about their situation. But minorities themselves are not the problem; the responsibility for this situation lies in the structure of power and privilege in the larger society.

If inequality is so deeply rooted in our society, we cannot expect minorities acting as individuals to improve their situation. Therefore, liberals look to government as the solution, supporting policies—including antidiscrimination laws—that reduce racial and ethnic inequality.

This call for government action helps explain why liberals support affirmative action. As they see it, an affirmative action program is a necessary correction for historical prejudice and discrimination directed against minorities. African Americans today face the legacy of two centuries of slavery and an additional century and a half of racial segregation. In short, for most of its history, our nation has had a policy of *majority* preference, one reason the social standing of whites is higher than that of

GETTING INVOLVED

What do you think are the strongest point and the weakest point made by the radical left?

blacks and other minorities. For this reason, liberals think that minority preference is not only fair but also necessary as a step to help level the playing field.

Liberals claim that affirmative action has been good for the country. Where would minorities be today without the affirmative action that began in the 1960s? After all, major employers in government and corporate business began hiring large numbers of minorities and women only because of affirmative action, resulting in the growth of the African American middle class (Johnson, Rush, & Feagin, 2000; Kantrowitz & Wingert, 2003).

The Radical Left: Fundamental Changes Are Needed

Left radicals claim that much more than liberal reform is needed to end the problem of racial and ethnic inequality. Following Marx, radicals point out that as long as a capitalist society defines workers simply as a supply of labor, there is little reason to expect an end to exploitation and oppression, which is based on both class and race. Therefore, left radicals argue that the only way to reduce racial and ethnic inequality is to attack the source of *all* inequality: capitalism itself (Liazos, 1982).

A more recent addition to radical thinking about racial inequality focuses not on economics but on culture. Some of today's activist scholars conclude that to end racial inequality, a society must eliminate the concept of race entirely. As they see it, as long as a society continues to recognize race, it will divide people, giving advantages to some at the expense of others. Could we really leave behind the notion of race, which has been so basic to conventional ways of thinking? In time, perhaps. Doing so would certainly be a radical change because abolishing race will demand basic changes to the current white power structure. As one group of sociologists claims:

> A useful place to begin undoing racism is to address the social, economic, and political embeddedness of white racism within the foundation of the U.S. political system. . . . Thus, [we] call for a new constitutional convention, one that will represent fairly and equally, for the first time, all major groups of U.S. citizens. What might the social, political, and economic landscape of the United States look like if we started with a social system constructed to actually meet the needs of democracy and humanity rather than the goals of privilege-maintenance and racial hierarchy? (Johnson, Rush, & Feagin, 2000:101)

The Left to Right table on page 82 provides a summary of the three political perspectives applied to the issue of racial and ethnic inequality.

Conservatives tend to support restricting immigration laws not only out of respect for law but also to limit the rate of cultural change. Liberals endorse greater immigration out of respect for diversity and welcome cultural change. Radicals on the left claim that racial and ethnic inequality will persist as long as our capitalist economy continues.

Going On from Here

For most people living in the lower-income nations of the world, everyday life is guided by their kin group, tribe, or religion. In high-income countries, by contrast, people break free of traditional categories and are more likely to say that their lives should be guided by personal choices, talents, and efforts.

MAKING THE GRADE

Use the table below to review the three political approaches to racial and ethnic inequality.

LEFT TO RIGHT

The Politics of Racial and Ethnic Inequality

	RADICAL-LEFT VIEW	LIBERAL VIEW	CONSERVATIVE VIEW
WHAT IS THE PROBLEM?	Striking inequality and racism are built into the very institutions of U.S. society.	Social and economic inequality places minorities at the margins of U.S. society.	Some people are still prejudiced and discriminate against minorities; some minority communities need to improve their standing.
WHAT IS THE SOLUTION?	There must be fundamental change in economic, political, and other social institutions to eliminate racial hierarchy.	Government programs must attack prejudice and discrimination and provide assistance to minorities.	All people need to treat others as individuals. Some minorities must overcome cultural disadvantages through individual effort in order to realize higher achievement.

JOIN THE DEBATE

1. Consider the following statement: "Over the course of its history, the United States has moved closer to the ideal of being a color-blind society." Do you agree or disagree with this statement? Why? How would conservatives, liberals, and left radicals respond to this statement?
2. What does the election of Barack Obama, an African American, as this country's president suggest about the changing importance of race in our national life? Do you expect this event to encourage further change? Explain.
3. Which of the three political approaches regarding racial and ethnic inequality included here do you find most convincing? Why?

This is why most members of our society think that categorizing people on the basis of their skin color or cultural heritage is wrong. That is also why we define this type of race-based ranking as unfair prejudice and discrimination.

Social institutions in the United States have changed over time to reflect these new beliefs. Slavery was abolished (1865); soon after, African Americans gained citizenship (1868), followed by Native Americans (1924), Chinese immigrants (1943), and Japanese immigrants (1952).

But as this chapter has explained, racial and ethnic inequality continues today. Minorities still suffer the consequences of prejudice and discrimination. These harmful biases exist not only in the attitudes and actions of individuals but also in the operation of society itself. For this reason, the inequality described in this chapter is carried from generation to generation, as too many young Latinos, African Americans, and Native people grow up poor.

In 1903, W. E. B. Du Bois predicted that race would be the defining problem of the twentieth century. He was right. Could we say the same for the twenty-first century? What are the prospects for change over the next 100 years? What does the fact that our country has now elected an African American to the highest office in the land mean for our nation's future?

The conservative solution to problems of race amounts to adopting a set of "color-blind" attitudes: Treat people as individuals and demand that people take responsibility for their own social standing. Liberals also endorse the long-range "color-blind" goal, but they argue that to reach it, government action (including programs that take people's race and ethnicity into account) is needed to guarantee that all categories of people are full participants in society. Radicals on the left weigh in with a greater challenge: Racism is too deeply entrenched in U.S. institutions to expect well-meaning individuals or even government reform to level the playing field; therefore, institutions must undergo fundamental change to ensure equality for all.

Throughout its history, U.S. society has debated issues related to racial and ethnic inequality. Let us hope that by the end of this century, we find answers that satisfy all categories of people.

DEFINING SOLUTIONS

Is increased immigration to the United States a problem?

For many people, the answer to this question depends on whether the immigration is legal or illegal, and for everyone, it reflects political attitudes. What people say we ought to do about the current high level of immigration also depends on their political viewpoint. Look at the photos below, which show two responses to this issue.

HINT

Liberals see the United States as the product of immigration. In addition, they view ethnic and racial diversity as good, and they seek to promote tolerance of different ways of life. Immigration is also a source of talent as newcomers to the country bring their skills, work hard, and pay taxes. Conservatives recognize that we're all immigrants, but they see increasing numbers of immigrants as bringing too much cultural change—a concern that leads many conservatives to support making English our nation's official language. In addition, conservatives point to the importance of the rule of law and believe that we cannot allow hundreds of thousands of people to break the law by entering this country illegally. They also say that only immigrants with legal status should be eligible to receive government benefits such as education and health care.

Do you see increased immigration as a threat to our way of life or as a source of national strength? If you are more liberal, you might well support the approach of Rosendo Delgado, who teaches English to Mexican immigrants in his town near Detroit, Michigan. From this point of view, why does immigration strengthen the country?

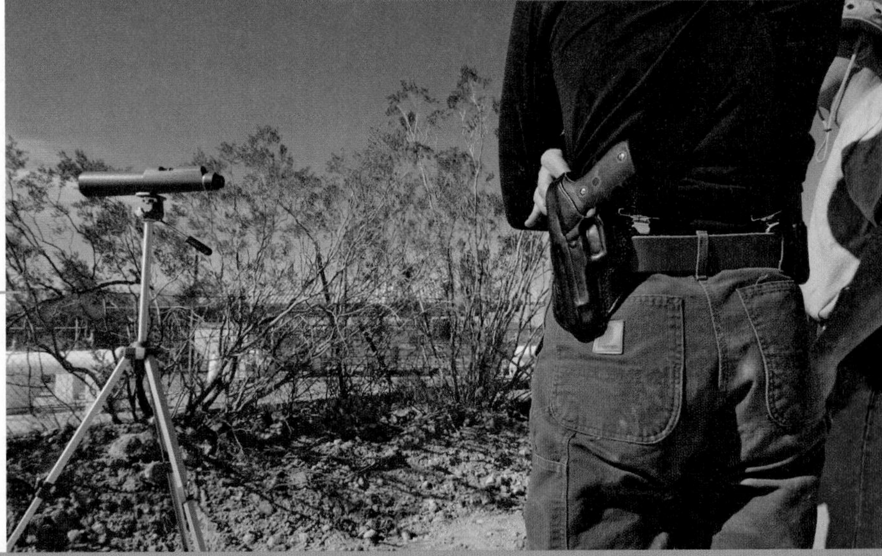

What about the idea that everyone should obey the law? If you are more conservative, you might have some sympathy for these volunteers who work for the Minuteman Project along the Arizona border with Mexico. This organization, with about 1,000 members, sets up observation points and reports illegal border crossings to the U.S. Border Patrol. From this point of view, what's wrong with a high level of immigration?

Getting Involved: Applications & Exercises

1. Use the campus library and the Internet to learn more about the history of a racial or ethnic category of interest to you. When did these people begin to come to the United States? What patterns of prejudice and discrimination have they faced? What are their special achievements? What is their social standing today?
2. An easy and interesting research project is to watch ten or twenty hours of television over the next week or two while taking notes on the race of TV actors and the kinds of characters they play. Although your sample may not be representative of all shows, it will get you thinking about racial stereotypes in the mass media.
3. The U.S. Census Bureau collects data on interracial marriage: Refer to the *Statistical Abstract* or other documents in the library, or go to http://www.census.gov. Since 1970, how has the percentage of interracial marriages changed? What other interesting patterns involving interracial marriage can you find?
4. Do an Internet search to learn the latest on the debate about developing a national policy on illegal immigrants. Try to identify both conservative and liberal approaches to this issue. Can you find radical proposals?

MAKING THE GRADE

A DEFINING MOMENT
Rosa Parks: Saying No to Segregation p. 62

CHAPTER 3 Racial and Ethnic Inequality

Race and Ethnicity

- **RACE** is a socially constructed category based on physical traits that members of a society define as important.
- **ETHNICITY** is a shared cultural heritage.
- Both race and ethnicity are important dimensions of inequality in the United States.

pp. 56–58

MINORITIES are categories of people that
- share a distinctive identity (which may be racial or ethnic)
- suffer disadvantages (such as poor schooling and low-paying jobs)

pp. 59–60

The great racial and ethnic diversity of the United States is a product of **IMMIGRATION** from other countries.
- The "Great Immigration" (1865–1914) brought 25 million people in search of economic opportunity.
- *Nativists*, fearing that high immigration would endanger this country's mostly English culture, pressured for a quota system, which Congress enacted in the 1920s.
- Congress ended the quota system in 1965, resulting in another large wave of immigration.
- Today, the issue of illegal immigration is a hotly debated topic.

pp. 58–59

race (p. 56) a socially constructed category of people who share biologically transmitted traits that a society defines as important

ethnicity (p. 58) a shared cultural heritage, which typically involves common ancestors, language, and religion

minority (p. 59) any category of people, identified by physical or cultural traits, that a society subjects to disadvantages

Patterns of Majority-Minority Interaction

GENOCIDE is the deliberate killing of a category of people. European colonization of the Americas resulted in the deaths of thousands of native people.

pp. 60–61

SEGREGATION is the physical and social separation of some category of a population. *De jure* racial segregation existed in the U.S. until the 1960s. *De facto* segregation continues today.

pp. 61–62

ASSIMILATION is a process (a "melting pot") by which minorities adopt styles of dress, the language, cultural values, and even the religion of the dominant majority.

p. 63

PLURALISM is a state in which racial and ethnic categories, though distinct, have equal social standing. In the U.S., all people have equal standing by law; however, social tolerance for diversity is limited.

p. 63

genocide (p. 61) the systematic killing of one category of people by another

segregation (p. 61) the physical and social separation of categories of people

assimilation (p. 63) the process by which minorities gradually adopt cultural patterns from the dominant majority population

pluralism (p. 63) a state in which people of all racial and ethnic categories have about the same overall social standing

The Social Standing of U.S. Minorities

Native Americans suffered greatly at the hands of Europeans over the course of five hundred years. Even today, Native Americans have relatively low social standing.

pp. 63–64

African Americans came to the United States as cargo transported by slave traders. Despite substantial gains, African Americans are still, on average, disadvantaged.

pp. 65–66

Asian Americans have lived in the United States for more than a century. Although their social standing is average or above average today, they still suffer from prejudice and discrimination.

pp. 66–67

Hispanic Americans or Latinos are a diverse people sharing a cultural heritage. Some categories, such as Puerto Ricans, have low social standing; others, such as Cuban Americans, are better off.

pp. 68–69

Arab Americans have ancestors in various nations. Like other categories of minorities, they are subject to both prejudice and discrimination.

pp. 69–70

Prejudice

PREJUDICE consists of rigid prejudgments about some category of people.
- A **STEREOTYPE** is an exaggerated and unfair description.
- The study of prejudice using the *social distance scale* shows a trend toward greater tolerance on the part of U.S. college students.
- **RACISM** is the assertion that people of one race are innately superior to people of another. Racism has been used throughout human history to justify the social inferiority of some category of people.
- Researchers have linked prejudice to individual traits (*authoritarian personality theory*) and to social structure (*scapegoat theory*) and patterns of belief (*culture theory*).

pp. 70–75

prejudice (p. 70) any rigid and unfounded generalization about an entire category of people

stereotype (p. 72) an exaggerated description applied to every person in some category

racism (p. 72) the assertion that people of one race are less worthy than or even biologically inferior to others

institutional racism (p. 73) racism at work in the operation of social institutions, including the economy, schools, hospitals, the military, and the criminal justice system

multiculturalism (p. 74) educational programs designed to recognize cultural diversity in the United States and to promote respect for all cultural traditions

Eurocentrism (p. 75) the practice of using European (particularly English) cultural standards to judge everyone

Discrimination

DISCRIMINATION consists of actions that treat various categories of a population differently.

- *Example:* An employer refuses to consider job applications from people with Arabic-sounding names.

p. 75

- **INSTITUTIONAL DISCRIMINATION** is bias built into the operation of the economy, legal system, or other social institution.
- *Example:* U.S. law prior to 1954 required black and white children to attend separate schools.

p. 75

✓ *Prejudice is a matter of attitudes; discrimination is a matter of actions. (p. 75)*
✓ *Prejudice and discrimination reinforce each other and form a vicious circle that harms minorities. (p. 76)*

AFFIRMATIVE ACTION policies allow employers and universities to consider factors such as race in hiring and admissions decisions.

- Liberals favor affirmative action in order to increase minority representation in settings from which minorities have been excluded in the past, but conservatives criticize such policies as reverse discrimination.

pp. 76–77

discrimination (p. 75) the unequal treatment of various categories of people

institutional discrimination (p. 75) discrimination that is built into the operation of social institutions, including the economy, schools, and the legal system

affirmative action (p. 76) policies intended to improve the social standing of minorities subject to past prejudice and discrimination

Theoretical Analysis: Understanding Racial and Ethnic Inequality

Structural-Functional Analysis: The Importance of Culture

The **STRUCTURAL-FUNCTIONAL APPROACH** explains racial and ethnic inequality in terms of cultural values.

- The *"culture of poverty" theory* developed by Oscar Lewis claims that minorities develop a fatalistic cultural outlook that leads to a sense of hopelessness and low self-esteem.

pp. 77–78

Symbolic-Interaction Analysis: The Personal Meaning of Race

The **SYMBOLIC-INTERACTION APPROACH** highlights how race often operates as a *master status* in everyday interaction.

- W. E. B. DuBois claimed that U.S. society makes whites the standard by which others should be measured and in so doing devalues any person of color.

p. 78

Social-Conflict Analysis: The Structure of Inequality

The **SOCIAL-CONFLICT APPROACH** highlights how racial and ethnic inequality is built into the structure of society.

- *Marxist theory* argues that elites encourage racial and ethnic divisions as a strategy to weaken the working class.
- More recently, *multicultural theory* notes ways in which much U.S. culture is biased against minorities.

pp. 78–80

See the **Applying Theory** table on page 79.

Politics, Race, and Ethnicity: Constructing Problems and Defining Solutions

The Radical Left: Fundamental Changes Are Needed

- **RADICALS ON THE LEFT** claim that capitalism is the root cause of racial and ethnic inequality.
- Radicals on the left call for basic change to all U.S. social institutions, including the capitalist economic system and the political system, so that they operate in the interests of all categories of people.

p. 81

Liberals: Society and Government Matter

- **LIBERALS** point to social structure, including institutional prejudice and discrimination, as the cause of racial and ethnic inequality.
- Liberals endorse government reforms to promote equality, including enforcement of antidiscrimination laws and affirmative action.

pp. 80–81

Conservatives: Culture and Effort Matter

- **CONSERVATIVES** point to cultural patterns, such as the importance given to education, as a cause of racial and ethnic inequality.
- Conservatives claim that individuals should be responsible for their social standing; they oppose government policies that treat categories of people differently.

p. 80

See the **Left to Right** table on page 82.

CONSTRUCTING THE PROBLEM

Are women and men equal in U.S. society?

Not in terms of income, with women on average earning 77 percent as much as men.

Can a woman be anything she wants to be?

Today's women have more choices, but many jobs are almost entirely done by one sex or the other.

Is beauty just about looking good?

Women who are very concerned about beauty give men power over them.

CHAPTER 4

Gender Inequality

CHAPTER OVERVIEW

WHAT IS GENDER? How is gender a dimension of social inequality that affects almost every aspect of everyday life? This chapter documents the different social standing of women and men. You will learn how income, housework, violence, and even ideas about beauty all reflect gender stratification. You will carry out theoretical analysis of gender inequality and learn how "problems" and "solutions" involving gender reflect people's political attitudes.

It was a great day for Janet Nore, who had come to the large campus of a historic university to see her daughter graduate from one of the world's most famous law schools. It had been three long years of hard work for her daughter, not to mention three difficult years for Janet and her husband, Tom, helping pay the high cost of their daughter's tuition. But as the proud parents watched their daughter march across the stage and receive her law degree, Janet squeezed Tom's hand and they turned to each other and smiled. They both knew it was all worth it.

Janet Nore is herself a lawyer, one of the very first women to have received a law degree from this university. As she and her husband drove home, Janet pointed out how much the law profession had changed in the forty years since her own graduation. Back then, there was only a handful of women in law schools in the United States, and she and the other women felt out of place in what was a very male world. Janet recalled that, during a class, one of her professors had looked at her—the only woman in the room—and asked her how she could justify accepting a job as a lawyer, knowing that she was taking work away from a man who needed the money to support his family.

Today, much has changed. The typical law school graduating class of 2010 has as many women as men. And these women are going on to legal jobs every bit as challenging and fulfilling as the jobs their male colleagues will take. But as this chapter explains, a great deal of inequality between women and men remains. In the world of law, only about 30 percent of full professors or deans in this country's law schools are women (Association of American Law Schools, 2008). Across all occupations in our country's labor force, women continue to earn much less than men. In addition, women still deal with unwanted sexual attention in the workplace as well as outright violence at home. To understand many of the issues facing women and men today, we begin by looking at the important part that gender plays in the way society operates.

What Is Gender?

In societies around the world, women and men lead lives that differ in important ways. Sociologists describe these differences using the concept of **gender,** *the personal traits and life chances that a society links to being female or male.* Gender is not the same as **sex,** *the biological distinction between females and males.* Sex is determined biologically as an embryo is conceived. As Chapter 7 ("Sexuality") explains, specific biological differences are what give women and men the capacity to reproduce. Gender is a societal construction that shapes the entire lives of women and men, affecting the amount of schooling they receive, the kind of work they do, and how much money they earn. All societies define men and women as different types of people, in the process creating gender inequality. **Gender stratification** is *the unequal distribution of wealth, power, and privilege between men and women.* Gender is an important dimension of social inequality just about everywhere.

Patriarchy

Around the world, we find various degrees of **patriarchy** (literally, "rule by fathers"), *a social pattern in which males dominate females.* **Matriarchy,** *a social pattern in which females dominate males,* is extremely rare. Two centuries ago, the North American Seneca (an American Indian nation) assigned to their women the job of providing most of the food, and they required men to obtain women's permission for any military campaign or other important decision. Today, the Musuo is a very small society in China's Yunnan province where women control most property, select their sexual partners, and make most decisions about everyday life (Arrighi, 2001; E. B. Freedman, 2002).

Global Map 4–1 on page 90 surveys women's power relative to that of men around the world. Looking at the map, look for a general pattern that women living in poor countries are more disadvantaged than those living in high-income nations.

gender the personal traits and life chances that a society links to being female or male

sex the biological distinction between females and males

sexism the belief that one sex is innately superior to the other

gender stratification the unequal distribution of wealth, power, and privilege between men and women

patriarchy a social pattern in which males dominate females

matriarchy a social pattern in which females dominate males

Explanations of Patriarchy

Is patriarchy just a matter of men's greater body size? On average, according to government health data, males are 9 percent taller, 18 percent heavier, and 20 percent stronger than females (McDowell et al., 2008). However, it is widely noted that women are catching up to men in almost every test of physical performance. Furthermore, to our cave-dwelling ancestors, physical strength may have made all the difference in survival, but muscles have little to do with how well people do in today's high-technology societies.

Nor does patriarchy reflect differences in brain power. On the SAT, young men outperform young women on the math test, but women do just as well as men on the verbal test. All in all, performance differences linked to sex are small, and scientists find no overall differences in intelligence between men and women of similar social background (Tavris & Wade, 2001; Lewin, 2008).

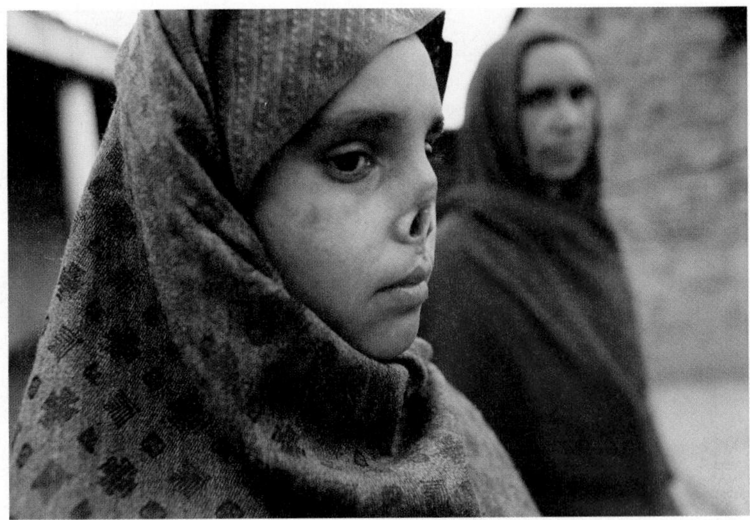

Patriarchy means that men have power to control the behavior of women. In some societies, this power can be almost absolute. This young Pakistani woman was mutilated by the men in her family, who declared that her behavior had dishonored them.

Another theory links patriarchy to greater aggressiveness in males based on their higher levels of sex hormones (Goldberg, 1974; Maccoby & Jacklin, 1974; Popenoe, 1993b; Udry, 2000, 2001). Chapter 6 ("Crime, Violence, and Criminal Justice") reports that most murders are the work of young males, who generally have high levels of testosterone. But not everyone agrees with the testosterone theory. Barbara Ehrenreich (1999) counters that the male hormone testosterone and the female hormone estrogen are found to varying degrees in both sexes, and scientists have yet to explain the precise connection between these hormones and aggressive behavior.

Most sociologists reject the idea that any behavior is "hardwired" into human biology. On the contrary, we believe that patriarchy and all the behaviors linked to gender are mostly creations of society. In short, whatever biological forces are at work, societies can and do shape the social differences between the sexes.

Prejudice and Discrimination

Like race and ethnicity, gender shapes the kinds of people we become. Familiar stereotypes cast women as dependent, sensitive, and emotional while portraying men as independent, rational, and competitive. Notice that gender stereotypes divide humanity by constructing femininity and masculinity in opposing terms.

Such stereotypes overlook the fact that most women and men exhibit a mixture of traits, being more "feminine" in some respects and more "masculine" in others. Also, does the capacity for showing emotions make anyone less rational? In truth, gender stereotypes do not describe real people very well.

Our culture also assigns more worth to what we call masculine than what we call feminine. For example, would anyone prefer being dependent to being independent? Being passive to being active? Being timid to being brave? Taken together, gender stereotypes amount to a form of prejudice against women.

In a society that devalues what is feminine, it is not surprising that discrimination against women is widespread. For centuries, U.S. society defined women as little more than the property of men. Women had to respect the authority of their fathers and, later, their husbands. To some degree, times have changed: A large majority of U.S. adults now say that they would support a qualified woman for president (NORC, 2007). In 2008, Hillary Clinton came close to winning her party's nomination for president, suggesting that a woman is likely to lead this country in the not-too-distant future. Still, of our country's forty-four presidents so far, all have been men.

The Problem of Sexism

Similar to racism, discussed in Chapter 3, **sexism** is *the belief that one sex is innately superior to the other.* Sexism supports patriarchy by claiming that men are "better" than women and therefore should have power over them.

Astrid Brügger, age 19, lives in Norway; like most girls growing up in high-income nations, she enjoys most of the rights and opportunities available to men.

Jendayi Gattuso, age 20, lives in Mozambique, a low-income nation that limits the rights and opportunities of women.

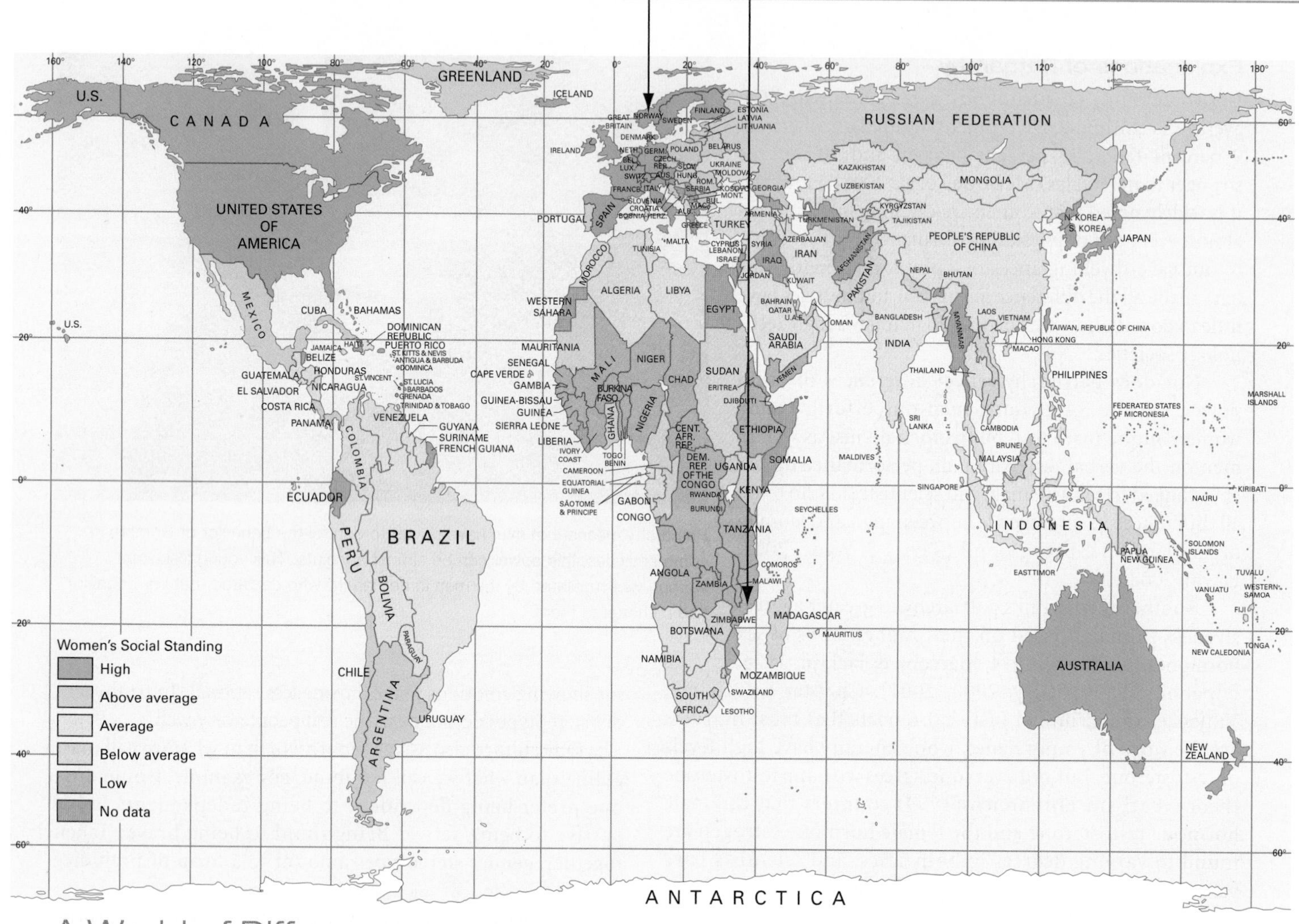

A World of Differences

GLOBAL MAP 4–1 Women's Power around the World

The social power of women in relation to that of men varies around the world. In general, women are closer to equality with men in high-income nations, and men have more control over women's lives in low-income nations. Where are women and men most equal? The answer is in Norway, Australia, and Iceland.

Source: Data from United Nations Development Programme (2008).

Sexism involves not just individual attitudes but also the operation of social institutions. As the following sections explain, male superiority is built into the operation of the workplace (with men running most companies and women performing most of the clerical support work), our political system (women may be more likely to vote, but most elected leaders are men), and even religious life (although women attend religious services more often, most religious leaders are men).

Gender and Social Institutions

Like class, race, and ethnicity, gender shapes just about every part of our lives. The importance of gender can be seen in the operation of all the social institutions, as the following survey explains. We begin with the family.

GETTING INVOLVED

Think of an example from your own life in which people assumed that you should think or act in a certain way based on your gender. Did you do what they expected? Explain.

GETTING INVOLVED

Did gender play a role in the classes you have chosen to take at college? How?

Gender and the Family

Do parents value boys more than girls? Traditionally, parents in the United States did value boys more, although this bias has weakened in recent decades. But in poor countries around the world, a pro-male bias is still strong. In rural areas of India, for example, families benefit from the earnings of a son, but they have to pay a dowry to marry off a daughter. As a result, many pregnant women pay for ultrasound examinations to find out the sex of the fetus, and many who learn they are carrying a female request an abortion. Sometimes families may even kill an unwelcome newborn girl, the practice of *female infanticide.*

In the United States, gender shapes our experience of marriage. As Jessie Bernard (1982) explained in her classic study of traditional marriage, men experience marriage as the responsibility to provide economic support for the family and the power to make key decisions. In the female version of marriage, women provide emotional support to husbands and raise the children, sometimes to the point that they have little identity of their own. If Bernard was right that most marriages are unequal partnerships that favor men, why does it seem that far more women than men are eager to marry? The Diversity: Race, Class, & Gender box on page 92 takes a closer look at this curious pattern.

In most sports played by both sexes, male athletes attract more fans and earn more money than female athletes. Fifty years ago, women who won championships earned only about one-third as much as men who did the same. Today, major tennis tournaments award equal prize money to women's and men's champions.

Gender and Education

By the time they begin school, children have learned a great deal about gender from books. Children's books used to be full of gender stereotypes, showing girls and women mostly in the home while boys and men did almost everything else outside the home. Newer children's books present the two sexes in a more balanced way, although some antifemale bias remains (Purcell & Stewart, 1990; F. Taylor, 2003).

And what of school itself? Today's primary and secondary schools do a pretty good job of providing equal education to both boys and girls. In addition, most college students are now women, with women earning 59 percent of all associate's and bachelor's degrees. Even so, gender stereotyping still steers women toward college majors in English, education, dance, drama, or sociology while pushing men toward physics, economics, mathematics, computer science, and architecture (U.S. Department of Education, 2009).

Women have also made gains in postgraduate education. In the United States in 2008, women earned 61 percent of all master's degrees and 50 percent of all doctorates (including 64 percent of all Ph.D.'s in sociology). Women are now well represented in many graduate fields that used to be almost all male. Back in 1970, for example, hardly any women earned a master's of business administration (M.B.A.) degree; in 2007, more than 66,000 women did so, accounting for 44 percent of all M.B.A. degrees (U.S. Department of Education, 2009).

But gender still matters. Men slightly outnumber women in some professional fields, receiving 51 percent of medical (M.D.) degrees, 52 percent of law (LL.B. and J.D.) degrees, and 55 percent of dental (D.D.S. and D.M.D.) degrees (U.S. Department of Education, 2009).

Gender and College Sports

Gender is at work on the playing fields as much as in the classroom. In decades past, extracurricular athletics was a male world, and females were expected to watch instead of play. In 1972, Congress passed Title IX, the Educational Amendment to the Civil Rights Act, banning sex discrimination in any educational program receiving federal funding. In recent years, colleges and universities have also tried to provide an equal number of sports for both women and men. Even so, men benefit from higher-paid coaches and enjoy larger crowds of spectators. In short, despite the federal policy outlawing gender bias, in few athletic programs is gender equality a reality.

SOCIAL PROBLEMS in Everyday Life

You are probably a television watcher. What patterns do you see in the characters portrayed by men and women?

SOCIAL PROBLEMS in Everyday Life

Examine how women and men are portrayed in magazine and newspaper advertising.

DIVERSITY: RACE, CLASS, & GENDER

Marriage: Life Gets Better—but for Whom?

At countless bridal showers, women celebrate a friend's upcoming marriage by showering her with gifts to help her keep house. But the scene is very different at bachelor parties, where men give their friend one last fling before he must settle down to the constraints and routines of married life. We find the same pattern among singles: Contrast the positive image of a carefree bachelor with the negative one of the lonely spinster.[1]

On the face of it, it seems that our society constructs marriage as a *solution* for women but a *problem* for men. But is this really the case? Research indicates that in general, marriage is good for men and women alike, not only raising levels of personal happiness but also improving health, enhancing sexual satisfaction, and boosting income (Waite & Gallagher, 2000; Ohlemacher, 2006).

But as Jessie Bernard (1982) sees it, to the extent that marriages follow the traditional pattern of giving men power over women, tying the knot is a better deal for men and may even be harmful to women. Bernard claims that there is no better prescription for a man to have a long, healthy, happy life than to have a wife devoted to caring for him and keeping an orderly home. Perhaps this is why divorced men are less happy than divorced women and are more eager to remarry.

But when marriage puts women under the control of men, Bernard continues, wives experience less happiness and may even be at risk for depression or other personality disorders. Why? Bernard explains that the problem is not marriage in general but the fact that conventional marriage places men in charge and saddles women with most of the housework.

In the past, most marriages were unequal relationships that put men in charge. So why have women always seemed so eager to marry? Bernard explains that when women were virtually shut out of the labor force, "landing a man" was the only way for a woman to gain economic security.

Today, however, women have both more economic opportunity and more choices about marriage. This is one reason that more couples are sharing responsibilities, including housework, more equally. As Bernard sees it, breaking away from conventional ideas about gender is making both women and men happier and healthier.

WHAT DO YOU THINK?

1. Throughout the past century, women moved into the labor force in ever greater numbers. In your opinion, what changes has this trend brought to marriage?
2. In your opinion, what elements of today's marriages might be called "gendered"? Why?
3. Evaluate marriages you or your parents have had with regard to (a) who makes decisions, (b) who earns income, and (c) who does the housework.

[1]The term "spinster" originally referred to a woman who worked spinning thread in a New England textile mill in the early nineteenth century. Most women who worked outside the home at that time were unmarried.

Gender and the Mass Media

With some 250 million television sets in the United States and people watching an average of three hours of TV each day (U.S. Department of Labor, 2008), who can doubt the importance of the mass media in shaping how we think and act? What messages about gender do we find on TV?

When television became popular in the 1950s, almost all the starring roles belonged to men. Only in recent decades have television shows featured women as central characters. But we still find fewer women than men cast as talented athletes, successful executives, brilliant detectives, and skilled surgeons. More often than not, women have supporting roles as wives, assistants, and secretaries. Music videos also come in for criticism: Most performing groups are all men, and when women do appear on stage, they are there for little more than their sex appeal. And today's song lyrics reinforce men's power over women.

What about advertising? In the early years of television, advertisers targeted women during the day because so many women were at-home wives. In fact, because most of the commercials advertised laundry and household products, daytime TV dramas became known as "soap operas." On television and in newspaper and magazine advertising, even today, most ads still use female models to sell products such as clothing, cosmetics, cleaning products, and food to women and male models to pitch products such as automobiles, banking services, travel, and alcoholic beverages to men. Ads have always been more likely to show men in offices or in rugged outdoor scenes and women in the home.

Gender bias in advertising is not always so obvious. Look closely at ads and you will see that they often present men as taller than women, and women (but never men) often lie on sofas and beds or sit on the floor like children. In addition, men's facial expressions suggest competence and authority, whereas women laugh, pout, or strike childlike poses. Finally, the men featured in advertising focus on the products they are promoting; women, as often as not, pay attention to men (Goffman, 1979; Cortese, 1999).

MAKING THE GRADE

A good learning exercise can be found at http://www.ltcconline.net/lukas/gender/background/howto.htm

SOCIAL PROBLEMS in Everyday Life

Do any of the facts in Table 4-1 below surprise you? Explain.

Gender and Politics

Patriarchy is about power. Because of patriarchy, women have played only a marginal role in the political history of our country. As Table 4–1 shows, the first woman to win election to the United States Congress joined the House of Representatives in 1917, after that body had existed for 128 years. In 1920, the country reached a political milestone with the passage of the Nineteenth Amendment to the U.S. Constitution, which permitted women to vote in national elections.

Winning the right to vote brought women only so far into the U.S. political mainstream. At the local level, thousands of women now serve as mayors of cities and towns and as members of other governing boards across the country. In 2009, about 24 percent of state legislators were women (up from just 4 percent in 1970), and eight of the fifty state governors were women (16 percent). National Map 4–1 on page 94 compares regions of the United States in terms of women's power in state government.

In national government, the picture is similar. In 2009, a total of 73 of 435 members of the House of Representatives (17 percent) and 17 of 100 senators (17 percent) were women (Center for American Women and Politics, 2009).

Around the world, the pattern is much the same: Women hold just 18 percent of seats in the world's 188 parliaments. In only fifteen countries (8 percent of all countries), among them Sweden and Norway, do women make up more than one-third of the members of parliament (Inter-Parliamentary Union, 2008).

Table 4–1 Political "Firsts" for U.S. Women

1869	Law allows women to vote in Wyoming Territory.
1872	First woman to run for the presidency (Victoria Woodhull) represents the Equal Rights party.
1917	First woman elected to the House of Representatives (Jeannette Rankin of Montana).
1924	First women elected state governors (Nellie Taylor Ross of Wyoming and Miriam "Ma" Ferguson of Texas); both followed their husbands into office. First woman to have her name placed in nomination for the vice-presidency at the convention of a major political party (Lena Jones Springs, a Democrat).
1931	First woman to serve in the Senate (Hattie Caraway of Arkansas); completed the term of her husband upon his death and won reelection in 1932.
1932	First woman appointed to the presidential cabinet (Frances Perkins, secretary of labor in the cabinet of President Franklin D. Roosevelt).
1964	First woman to have her name placed in nomination for the presidency at the convention of a major political party (Margaret Chase Smith, a Republican).
1972	First African American woman to have her name placed in nomination for the presidency at the convention of a major political party (Shirley Chisholm, a Democrat).
1981	First woman appointed to the U.S. Supreme Court (Sandra Day O'Connor).
1984	First woman to be successfully nominated for the vice-presidency (Geraldine Ferraro, a Democrat).
1988	First woman chief executive to be elected to a consecutive third term (Madeleine Kunin, governor of Vermont).
1992	A record number of women in the Senate (six) and the House (forty-eight), as well as (1) first African American woman to win election to U.S. Senate (Carol Moseley-Braun of Illinois), (2) first state (California) to be served by two women senators (Barbara Boxer and Dianne Feinstein), and (3) first woman of Puerto Rican descent elected to the House (Nydia Velazquez of New York).
1996	First woman appointed secretary of state (Madeleine Albright).
2000	First First Lady to win elected political office (Hillary Rodham Clinton, senator from New York).
2001	First woman to serve as national security adviser (Condoleezza Rice); first Asian American woman to serve in a presidential cabinet (Elaine Chao, secretary of labor).
2005	First African American woman appointed secretary of state (Condoleezza Rice).
2007	First woman speaker of the House (Nancy Pelosi); record number of women in the House (seventy) and the Senate (sixteen).
2008	For the first time, women make up the majority of a state legislature (New Hampshire).
2009	Another record for women in the House (seventy-three) and the Senate (seventeen).

Gender and Religion

What does religion teach us about gender? When people in a national sample of U.S. adults were asked whether they tend to think of God as "Mother" or "Father," 6 percent replied they envision God more as "Mother." Two-thirds—eleven times as many—favored "Father," with the remaining one-fourth imagining God equally in these terms (NORC, 2007).

The fact that most of us think of God as male is no surprise because societies give power and privilege to men. That's probably why all the Western religious traditions portray the divine being as male. The Qur'an (Koran), the sacred text of Islam, clearly endorses patriarchy with these words: "Men are in charge of women. . . . Hence good women are obedient. . . . As for those whose rebelliousness you fear, admonish them, banish them from your bed, and scourge them" (quoted in W. Kaufman, 1976:163). Paul, perhaps the most influential leader of the early Christian church, also supported the social dominance of men over women:

> A man . . . is the image and glory of God; but woman is the glory of man. For man was not made from woman, but woman from man. Neither was man created for woman, but woman for man. (1 Corinthians 11:7–9)

> Wives, be subject to your husbands, as to the Lord. For the husband is the head of the wife as Christ is the head of the church. . . . As the church is subject to Christ, so let wives also be subject in everything to their husbands. (Ephesians 5:22–24)

In general, the western states have a higher percentage of legislators who are women than the southern states.

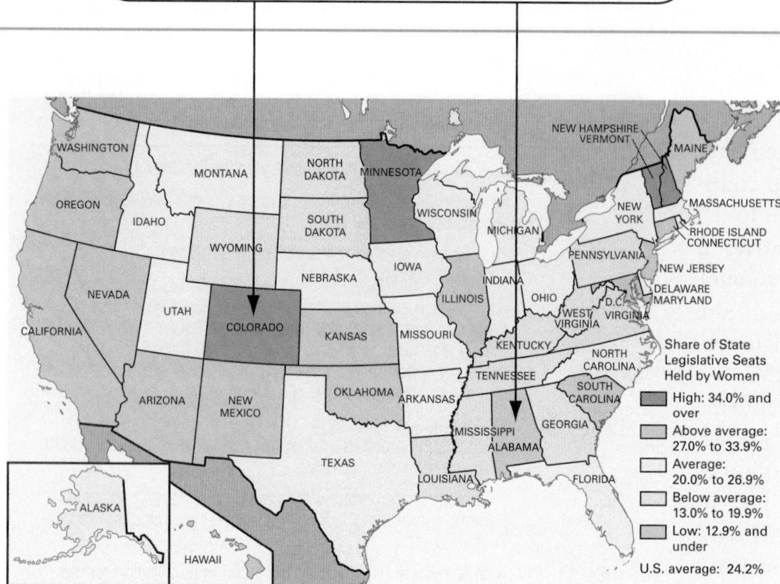

A Nation of Diversity

NATIONAL MAP 4–1

Women's Political Power across the United States

Women represent slightly more than half of U.S. adults. Even so, women hold just 24 percent of seats in the state legislatures across the country. The map provides the state-by-state percentages. Looking at the map, what pattern can you detect? What factors can you think of that might account for this pattern?

Source: Center for American Women and Politics (2009).

Judaism also has a long history of supporting the social power of men. A daily prayer among Orthodox Jewish men includes the following words:

> Blessed art thou, O Lord our God, King of the Universe, that I was not born a gentile.
> Blessed art thou, O Lord our God, King of the Universe, that I was not born a slave.
> Blessed art thou, O Lord our God, King of the Universe, that I was not born a woman.

In recent decades, more liberal denominations in the United States, including Episcopalians and Presbyterians, have moved toward greater gender equality. This liberal trend includes not only the revision of prayers, hymnals, and even the Bible to reduce sexist language but also the ordination of both women and men as priests and ministers. Not all religious organizations share in this spirit of change. Orthodox Judaism, Islam, and Roman Catholicism have retained traditional male leadership. But throughout the religious community, a lively debate surrounds the question of whether patriarchal traditions represent God's will or merely reflect patterns of the past.

Gender and the Military

Women have been part of the military since the Revolutionary War. During World War II, when the government officially opened the military to both sexes, women made up just 2 percent of the armed forces. By the Gulf War in 1991, that share had risen to almost 7 percent, and 5 of the 148 soldiers killed in that conflict were women. Women have made up 14 percent of the U.S. military force in Iraq. Between March 2003 and April 2009, the Iraq war claimed the lives of 102 women soldiers; another 14 died in Afghanistan (U.S. Department of Defense, 2009).

Today, almost all military assignments are open to women. But there is still resistance to expanding the role of women in the military. The traditional explanation for limiting women's opportunities is the claim that women are not as strong as men, although this argument makes much less sense in a high-technology military that depends less and less on muscle power. The real reason people oppose women in the military has to do with gender itself. Many people have difficulty with the idea of women—whom our culture defines as nurturers—being put in a position to kill and be killed.

Gender and Work

Many people still think of different kinds of jobs as either "men's work" or "women's work." A century ago in the United States, in fact, most people did not think women should work at all, at least not for pay. Back then, as the saying used to be, "a woman's place is in the home," and in 1900, just one woman in five worked for income. The most recent data, found in Figure 4–1, show this share has jumped to three in five (60 percent), even as the share of adult men in the labor force declined. Most (74 percent) of women in today's labor force work full time (U.S. Department of Labor, 2009).

What accounts for this dramatic rise in the share of working women? Many factors are involved. At the beginning of the twentieth century, most people lived in rural areas where few people had electric power. Back then, women typically spent long hours cooking, doing housework, and raising large families. Today's typical home has a host of appliances, including wash-

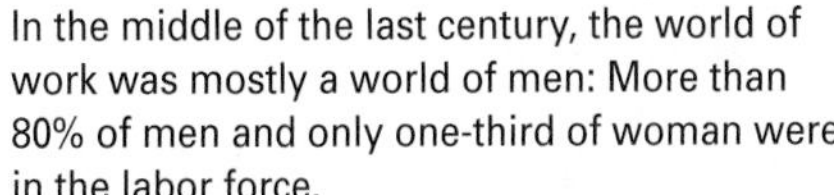

In the middle of the last century, the world of work was mostly a world of men: More than 80% of men and only one-third of woman were in the labor force.

Working for income is now part of adult life for both men and women.

Dimensions of Difference

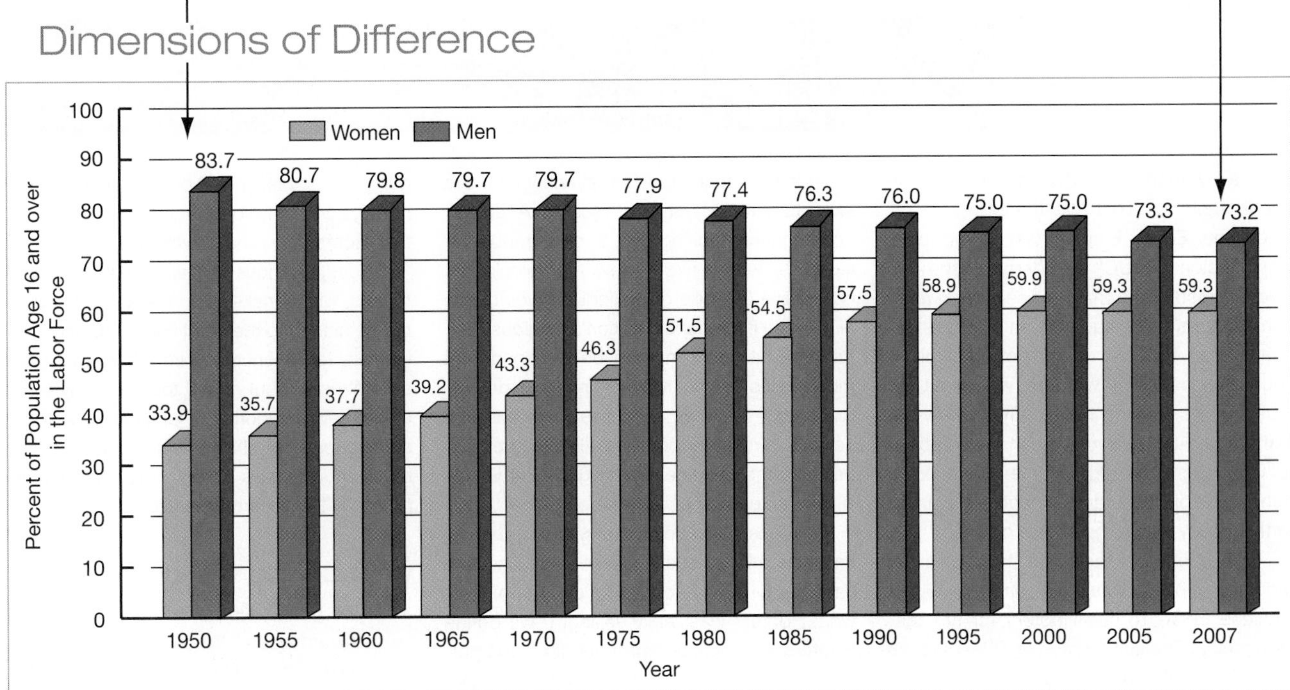

FIGURE 4–1 Women and Men in the U.S. Labor Force

Over the past half century, the share of men in the labor force has gone down (with men retiring earlier and living longer), while the share of women working for income has gone up rapidly.

Source: U.S. Department of Labor (2009).

ers, vacuums, and microwaves, that have dramatically reduced the time needed for housework so that women and men have more chance to work for income.

In addition, today's average woman has just two children, half the number that was typical a century ago. Having young children does not prevent most women from working: 60 percent of married women with children under age six work, as do 73 percent of married women with children six to seventeen years old. From another angle, more than half of today's married couples have both partners working for income (U.S. Department of Labor, 2008).

Even though more women now work for pay, the range of jobs open to them is still limited, and our society still labels most jobs as either feminine or masculine (Bellas & Coventry, 2001; van der Lippe & van Dijk, 2002). Work that our society has defined as "masculine" involves physical danger (such as firefighting and police work), strength and endurance (construction work and truck driving), and leadership roles (clergy, judges, and business executives). Work defined as "feminine" includes support positions (secretarial work or medical assisting) or occupations requiring nurturing skills (child care and teaching young children). A number of jobs that are defined as feminine are performed almost entirely by women even today, as shown in Table 4–2.

Table 4–2 Gender Segregation in the Workplace: Jobs Defined as "Feminine"

Occupation	Percentage of Women in the Occupation
1. Speech or language pathologist	98.1%
2. Dental hygienist	97.7
3. Preschool or kindergarten teacher	97.6
4. Dental assistant	96.3
5. Secretary or administrative assistant	96.1
6. Occupational therapist	95.9
7. Child care worker	95.6
8. Medical record and health information technician	95.0
9. Receptionist or information clerk	93.6
10. Licensed practical or licensed vocational nurse	93.3

Source: U.S. Department of Labor (2008).

SOCIAL PROBLEMS in Everyday Life

After reading the box below, can you point to other ways employers use women in a sexual way?

SOCIAL PROBLEMS in Everyday Life

Look to National Map 4-2 to see the gender gap in earnings in your state.

SOCIAL POLICY

Sex Discrimination in the Workplace: The Hooters Controversy

Does a company have the right to hire anyone it wants to? That was the issue in 1991 when the Equal Employment Opportunity Commission (EEOC) decided to sue the Hooters restaurant chain for sex discrimination. Hooters stands apart from other restaurant chains because of its policy of hiring young and buxom women, who wait on tables while dressed in form-fitting, low-cut T-shirts and tight shorts. When men applied to work there, officials of the restaurant—dubbed a "breastaurant" by critics—pointed to this policy and turned them down.

But some of the men turned away thought the policy was unfair, and they joined with the EEOC to sue Hooters for sex discrimination. The suit pointed to Title VII of the 1964 Civil Rights Act, which bans hiring discrimination on the basis of race, color, sex, religion, or national origin. Following the letter of this law, a company cannot just hire only women any more than it could decide to hire only white people. But the law does recognize exceptions to this rule, which involve what the law calls a "bona fide occupational qualification." This means that if a company can show that an applicant's sex is an important factor in doing the job that is being filled, hiring one category of people over another may be allowed.

It is easy to imagine situations where this exception makes obvious sense. A Jewish congregation looking for a new rabbi, for example, would hire a Jew and would not consider a Catholic or a Hindu. It would also hire a man if the denomination's religious doctrine permits only men to be ordained. But most cases are not this clear-cut. A department store in a largely white neighborhood cannot hire only white salespeople just because the management might think whites "fit in" better than people of color.

In a business like Hooters, is sex actually an occupational qualification? Deciding this case required the court to decide exactly what Hooters was really selling. If we define Hooters as simply a restaurant, its hiring policy would be a clear violation of the law. But Hooters claimed that customers come to their restaurants as much to see the women working as waitresses as they do to get a meal. For that reason, Hooters continued, hiring only women (and hiring only *certain* women) should be within the law.

When the case was settled in 1997, the court did not agree with Hooters' claims—at least not entirely—and something of a compromise resulted. Because Hooters had provided employment to only one sex and excluded the other, the court found the restaurant chain guilty of sex discrimination and fined the corporation $3.75 million. But the court also found that Hooters' business was not just food but "providing vicarious sexual recreation" to customers, which makes sex relevant to the company's hiring. So the court ended up permitting Hooters to continue to hire attractive women as waitresses, but only if the company would create new categories of jobs—such as hosts and bartenders—that would provide employment opportunities to both men and women (Reiland, 1998; Bernstein, 2001).

WHAT DO YOU THINK?

1. In the past, airlines hired only women as "stewardesses." When challenged, airline executives claimed that passengers liked having women rather than men serve them. Courts defined this practice as sex discrimination. Do you agree? Why or why not?
2. Should a college be allowed to refuse to hire a man to teach courses in women's studies or a woman to teach courses in men's studies? Why or why not?
3. Have you ever personally experienced sex discrimination? Explain what happened, and why it was a case of illegal discrimination.

Gender discrimination was outlawed by the federal Equal Pay Act of 1963 and Title VII of the Civil Rights Act of 1964. This means that employers cannot discriminate between men and women in hiring or when setting pay. But gender inequality is deeply rooted in U.S. society; officials investigate thousands of discrimination complaints every year, and few doubt that the real number of cases of discrimination is far higher. The Social Policy box takes a look at one well-known case.

Gender Stratification

As noted earlier, gender stratification is the unequal distribution of wealth, power, and privilege between men and women. Gender inequality is evident in the fact that compared to men, women have both less income and greater responsibility for housework. Women also contend with other disadvantages, including high risk of domestic violence and sexual harassment.

Income

Income is one important dimension of gender inequality. As you have learned, women and men perform different kinds of work, with women generally holding clerical and service jobs and men having most executive and professional positions. The predictable result is that women and men receive different levels of pay.

In 2009, the median pay for men working full time was $47,127; women working full time earned $36,278, or 77 percent as much. National Map 4–2 shows that there are considerable

Nancy Willis works as a waitress in Laramie, Wyoming, earning less than $20,000 a year.

Karen Sachs works on the staff of a member of Congress, earning more than $70,000 a year.

MAKING THE GRADE

The "glass ceiling" refers to subtle forms of gender discrimination.

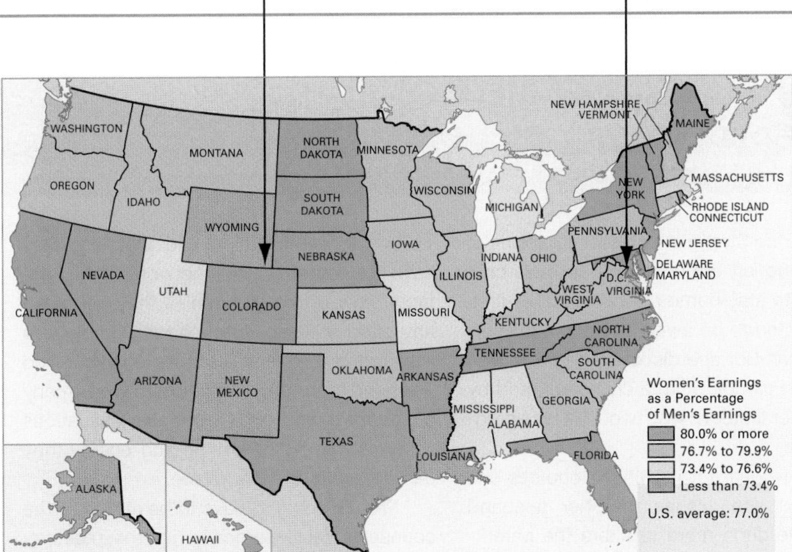

A Nation of Diversity

NATIONAL MAP 4–2

The Salary Gender Gap across the United States

Nationwide, women working full time earn about 77 percent as much as comparable men. In states with strong economies and younger populations (such as Florida and Texas), the gender gap is smaller; in states with weaker economies and older populations (such as Michigan and Wyoming), the gender gap is greater. Why do you think age plays a part in this pattern?

Source: U.S. Department of Labor (2008).

differences among the states with regard to the female-male pay difference, but in every state men earn considerably more than women.

The gender gap in earnings means that to a greater or lesser degree, women are more likely to be at the low end of the income scale. In 2009, 24 percent of full-time women workers earned less than $25,000, compared to 15 percent of men. The gender pattern is reversed for high-income people: More than twice as many men as women (23 percent versus 11 percent) earned more than $75,000 (U.S. Census Bureau, 2010).

Most women who share a household with a man depend on his earnings. For this reason, after separation, divorce, or the partner's death, a woman's income may fall dramatically. Especially if she has young children, the loss of a partner's income may cause financial problems and raises her risk of falling into poverty.

In the United States, why do men earn so much more than women? The first and biggest reason, noted earlier, is that men and women typically have different types of jobs. A second reason is that U.S. society assigns women most of the responsibility for raising children. Pregnancy, childbirth, and the task of raising small children limit women's careers more than men's. Because women devote more of their time to the home—sometimes taking extended periods of time away from work to raise young children—men end up with more workplace seniority and career advancement. In addition, some women with young children or aging parents choose jobs, even at lower pay, that do not tie up their evenings and weekends or require them to travel far from home. Still other mothers (but rarely fathers) choose a job because it is nearby, offers a flexible schedule, or provides child care facilities. The greater family focus means that during their twenties and thirties, women fall behind men in their careers. For example, a study of college professors found that women with at least one child were 22 percent less likely to have tenure than men in the same field (Shea, 2002). Such research reveals that the effect of family-based gender inequality is that *even if both sexes start out with exactly the same jobs*, women typically fall behind their male colleagues.

The greater family obligations that fall on women mean they spend more time out of the labor force during important career-building years. When the time comes to return to work, many women realize that simply getting back in the game is harder than they expected. The Personal Stories box on page 98 takes a closer look.

The third reason for gender inequality is that women suffer from gender discrimination. This means that many employers pay women less than men simply because they can get away with it. This practice is illegal, and equal opportunity laws have reduced the blatant discrimination that was common in the past. But more subtle discrimination continues, as in this case, in which one company

> frequently invited [men] to out-of-town business meetings and social functions from which [women] were excluded. These occasions were a source of information on business trends and store promotions and were a rich source of potentially important business contacts. When [one woman] asked why she had not been invited to these meetings and social gatherings, the response was that her employer thought it was "too dangerous for her to be driving out of town at night by herself." (Benokraitis & Feagin, 1995:85)

The Glass Ceiling

Today, when a company is looking to fill a top job, no one is likely to come right out and say, "Let's promote a man." But cultural bias

glass ceiling subtle discrimination that effectively blocks the movement of women into the highest positions in organizations

sexual harassment unwanted comments, gestures, or physical contact of a sexual nature

PERSONAL STORIES

After the Children: Getting Back in the Game

Catherine Strong shifted nervously in her chair as the woman behind the large desk in front of her read through the papers in her hands. Strong remembered how she used to sit behind a big desk like that during her many years as an investment officer with several high-profile banks in New York City. She thought about how she used to interview people seeking a promotion or eager to find a new job. That seemed a long time ago. Now it was her turn to be looking for work, and she had enlisted the help of a large search firm.

The search firm counselor completed the file, looked up, and with a serious expression, began to speak. She explained to Strong that she has a good education—a college degree from a well-known school and also an M.B.A. degree from a large university. The fact that she has worked for several large banks is also very impressive. But, the counselor continued, times are tight, with the weak economy, and jobs are much harder to find than they once were. Even more important, she continued, is the fact that Strong has not taken home a paycheck for almost fifteen years. In the very competitive world of high finance, the odds were slim that Strong would find anything even close to the jobs she once had.

Catherine Strong is one of the millions of women who left the workforce to have children and to stay home raising them. At first, she expected to be away from work for perhaps a year. But she discovered that raising a newborn can be quite a challenge, and by the time her firstborn was two, she was pregnant again.

Strong does not regret the choices she made. But she wishes that her husband could have done more to share the parenting. She is quick to point out that once she stopped working, his paycheck was all the family had to live on, and he worked harder than ever. But she always thought that once the kids got into their teenage years, she could go back to the job she had loved. Now that dream seems to be far out of reach.

The recent recession has made job-hunting hard for everyone. But women who have been out of the labor force (the polite expression is "having gaps in your résumé") have the toughest time of all. Their skills may be rusty or even completely out of date. Talking to people in the job search firm, Strong was startled to learn how much has changed in the financial field since she was last in the office. In addition, she and most other women in her situation find that that they have lost most of their networks and contacts. Few of the companies they left make any effort to keep in touch with employees like Strong who leave to raise children. And when the time comes to return to work, many of these women still face family obligations at home that limit the time and energy they can devote to the workplace.

"You're going to have to be realistic," the counselor says, summing up the meeting. "You are not going to find the type of job you left fifteen years ago. You'll need to take a big step down."

WHAT DO YOU THINK?

1. Should companies help women like Catherine Strong who are trying to return to work? How might they help?
2. What about fathers in all of this? Should they do more to share the work of parenting?
3. Have you or anyone you know ever been in Catherine Strong's position? What happened?

Source: Based on Chaker & Stout (2004).

against women affects many promotion decisions. Sociologists use the term **glass ceiling** to refer to *subtle discrimination that effectively blocks the movement of women into the highest positions in organizations.* According to one recent survey, just 24 of the 1,000 largest U.S. corporations (including Pearson Education, the publisher of this text) have a woman as their chief executive officer (Catalyst, 2009).

Housework

Just as patriarchy gives men control of the workplace, it also assigns women most of the housework. In Japan, probably the most patriarchal of all high-income nations, women do almost all the shopping, cooking, cleaning, and child care. In the United States, where two incomes is the norm among married couples, women still do most of the housework (or pay other women to do it). Figure 4–2 shows that the amount of housework people do depends on whether they are single or married and working for pay or staying at home. But in every one of these categories, women spend a lot more time doing housework than men—one reason that housework is sometimes called women's "second shift" (U.S Department of Labor, 2009).

Violence against Women

Perhaps the most serious problem linked to patriarchy is men's physical violence against women. Assault, rape, and even murder are common enough that many sociologists view them as a dimension of men's domination of women.

The U.S. government estimates that about 1.7 million physical assaults against women take place each year, with an additional 304,000 aggravated (serious) assaults and 237,000 sexual assaults, including rape and attempted rape (U.S. Department of Justice, 2008). On campus, in any academic year, the govern-

SOCIAL PROBLEMS in Everyday Life

Hooters restaurants, described in the box on page 96, was the target of lawsuits by women claiming that its work environment invited customers and employees to make unwanted, sexually suggestive comments to waitresses. These cases were settled without a clear court ruling. Do you think this situation is a case of sexual harassment or not? Explain.

ment estimates that 3 percent of female college students were victims of rape or attempted rape. Over a typical five-year college career, about 20 percent of all women experience such a crime (Karjane, Fisher, & Cullen, 2005).

Violence is a crime, but what makes it a gender issue? First, physical aggressiveness is part of our cultural definition of masculinity. Put simply, "real men" take control of a situation and do not allow themselves to be pushed around, one reason most violent crimes are committed by males (see Chapter 6, "Crime, Violence, and the Criminal Justice System"). Second, many people treat with contempt whatever a patriarchal society labels as "feminine" or less worthy (Goetting, 1999; Herman, 2001).

Gender violence ranges from annoying actions such as men whistling at a woman walking down a city street to unwanted physical contact such as "cornering" a woman against a wall in a dorm hallway to outright violence such as an angry punch in a suburban home. In all cases, these assaults are not so much sexual—as is commonly thought—as they are displays of male power over women. For this reason, sexual violence is a dimension of gender stratification.

Looking over the statistics, the most dangerous setting for women turns out not to be the dark alley but the well-lit home, the very place where people are supposed to find peace and support (Gelles & Cornell, 1990; Smolowe, 1994; Frias & Angel, 2007).

In a number of countries, including the United States, families use violence to control the behavior of women. The Social Problems in Global Perspective box on page 100 looks at the dramatic case of female genital mutilation.

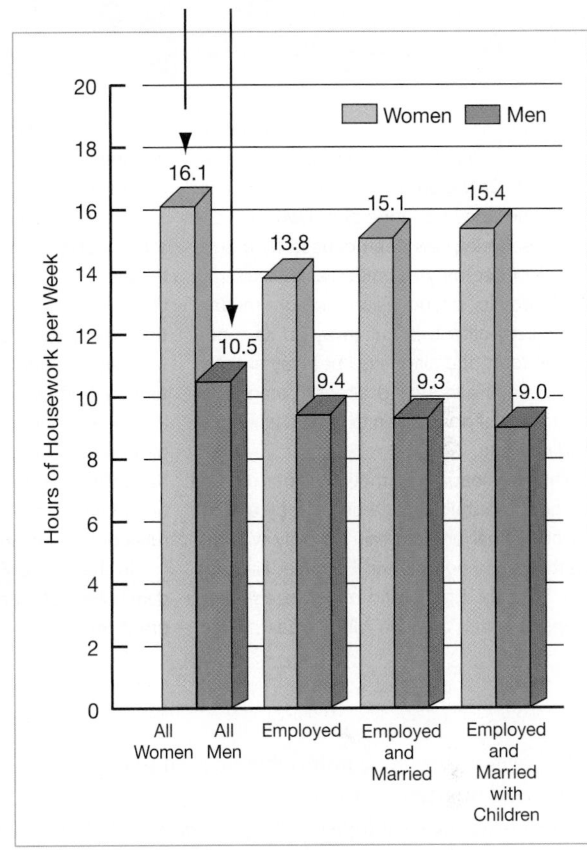

FIGURE 4–2 Gender and Housework
Regardless of employment or family status, women do more housework than men.
Source: Bureau of Labor Statistics (2009).

Sexual Harassment

Sexual harassment refers to *unwanted comments, gestures, or physical contact of a sexual nature.* Only in the 1980s did U.S. society begin to define sexual harassment as a social problem. This problem developed as more and more people objected to the traditional male practice of viewing women in sexual terms. Why? Because men who think of women in sexual terms are unlikely to accept women as equals in the workplace, on the campus, or anywhere else. Just as important, if sexual harassment is not defined as a problem, men in positions of power are free to coerce sex from women they supervise. Surveys show that about 50 percent of women claim they have received unwanted sexual attention (NORC, 2007).

Sexual harassment can be blatant and direct: A professor pressures a student for sex, threatening a poor grade if she refuses. This is a case of *quid pro quo* (the Latin words mean "one thing in return for another") sexual harassment, which the law defines as a violation of civil rights. But sexual harassment can involve subtle behavior—sexual teasing or off-color jokes—that someone may not even intend as harassment. Such behavior is still harmful if it has the effect of creating a *hostile environment* that prevents people from doing their work. In that case, the offender and the offended party may well interpret the behavior in question differently. For example, a man may view a compliment to a co-worker on some aspect of her appearance as simply a friendly gesture, but she may consider such comments intrusive and unprofessional.

Sexuality, Beauty, and Reproduction

A patriarchal culture teaches men to assess women not according to their abilities but on the basis of their sexual attractiveness. Women may also learn these lessons. Social norms encourage girls and women to wear figure-flattering clothing and shoes

SOCIAL PROBLEMS in Everyday Life

In the case of abortion, how do supporters and opponents construct the problem? How do they define the solution?

MAKING THE GRADE

The question of whether or not women are a minority illustrates how objective and subjective dimensions of a social issue may differ.

SOCIAL PROBLEMS IN GLOBAL PERSPECTIVE

Female Genital Mutilation: Using Violence to Control Women

In a poor home in the East African nation of Ethiopia, a little girl huddles in the corner of a small bed. Only eighteen months old, she is in pain and does not understand why.

Her suffering has been caused by a surgical clitoridectomy—sometimes mistakenly called female circumcision—which means the external clitoris is cut away. In its more extreme form, the clitoris is cut away entirely and the vagina is sewed almost completely shut, to be cut open again only on a woman's wedding night.

The procedure—sometimes performed by a doctor but usually carried out by a midwife or a tribal practitioner, typically without anesthesia—is common in Ethiopia, Nigeria, Togo, Somalia, Egypt, and three dozen other nations in Africa and the Middle East. More than 100 million girls worldwide have endured a clitoridectomy, now widely called female genital mutilation.

This so-called medical procedure is not about curing any illness or disorder; it is a means to control women. In highly patriarchal societies, men demand that the women they marry be virgins and that wives remain sexually faithful after that. Without the clitoris, a woman loses some or all of her ability to experience sexual pleasure. This procedure, some people believe, will make her unlikely to become sexually promiscuous or unfaithful and more likely to live by the rules of her society.

In the United States, although this procedure is illegal, thousands of young girls in immigrant families undergo clitoridectomy each year. In fact, some immigrant mothers believe that this procedure is even *more* necessary once they are living in the United States, where women have far more sexual freedom.

WHAT DO YOU THINK?

1. How is the practice of female genital mutilation used to control the behavior of women?
2. What steps should be taken—in the United States and elsewhere—to eliminate this practice?
3. Does female genital mutilation amount to child abuse? Explain your view.

Sources: Based on Crossette (1995) and Boyle, Songora, & Foss (2001).

(whether or not they are comfortable or even safe) and to flirt with men and be attentive to them.

In recent years, sociologists have pointed out that beauty is not simply about looking good; it is about power and inequality. The Diversity: Race, Class, & Gender box takes a closer look at what this means for women.

Our society has also debated who should control sexual reproduction. In the past, physicians and legislators, almost all of them men, restricted access to birth control technology. As late as the 1960s, state laws controlled even the sale of condoms and other birth control devices. We continue to debate who should make decisions about birth control: Should women have to consult a doctor to obtain birth control? Should women below a certain age have to obtain permission from parents?

Abortion is perhaps an even more controversial practice, dividing the country along political lines. Conservatives see abortion as a moral issue and stress the need to protect unborn children. Liberals—especially feminists—see abortion as an issue of power and choice. Restricting access to abortion puts the decision about whether to continue a pregnancy in the hands of men—fathers, husbands, physicians, and legislators—rather than with the women whose bodies and lives will be affected by the decision. In the liberal view, access to birth control and safe abortion expands women's choices about their lives, including their ability to work, and helps reduce gender inequality.

Women: A Majority Minority?

Chapter 3 ("Racial and Ethnic Inequality") defined a minority as any distinctive category of people who are socially disadvantaged. Are women a minority? Numerically, women are a slight majority (about 51 percent) of the U.S. population. Even so, in a patriarchal society, they meet the test of being physically distinctive and disadvantaged (U.S. Census Bureau, 2010).

Researchers have long noted that most women do not think of themselves as a minority (Hacker, 1951; Lengermann & Wallace, 1985). One reason that they do not is that many women assess their degree of privilege based on their race, ethnicity, and class position. Also, although women do not have the same power as men, our society teaches women to think that they *should* defer to men, defining a husband's career, for example, as more important than their own.

However women may feel about this matter, it is objectively the case that as a category of the population, women do have less income, wealth, and power than men. For this reason, it makes sense to define women as a minority.

Minority Women: Intersection Theory

If racial and ethnic minorities are disadvantaged, and women are, too, what about minority women? Are they doubly disadvantaged? Intersection theory claims that the answer is yes. **Intersection**

intersection theory analysis of how race, class, and gender interact, often creating multiple disadvantages for some categories of people

MAKING THE GRADE

Remember that a structural-functional approach asks how social patterns (in this case, gender) may be useful to society.

DIVERSITY: RACE, CLASS, & GENDER

Beauty: What's It Really About?

Beauty is about good looks—what could be more obvious? But beauty is also about gender and power.

Naomi Wolf (1990) claims that our culture's ideas about beauty put men in a position of power over women. Women, she says, learn to measure their personal importance in terms of their physical appearance, a practice that discourages other avenues of personal development. Furthermore, the standards by which society encourages women to judge themselves are those created by the multimillion-dollar fashion, cosmetics, and diet industries. These standards (in the form of the *Playboy* "playmate" or the 100-pound New York fashion model) have little to do with the reality of most women's bodies or lives.

In addition, a focus on beauty teaches women to try to please men. The pursuit of beauty makes women highly sensitive to how men react to them and encourages them to view other women not as allies but as competitors.

Taken together, our cultural ideas about beauty amount to an effective strategy to maintain patriarchy. Much advertising directed at women on television and in magazines and newspapers is not simply about what women should buy and use. Rather, it is about what women *should be*. This cultural "beauty myth," Wolf charges, is a form of gender bias that is harmful to women.

WHAT DO YOU THINK?

1. The Duchess of Windsor once said, "A woman cannot be too rich or too thin." Does this advice apply in the same way to men? Why or why not?
2. Chapter 9 ("Physical and Mental Health") explains that almost all people suffering from eating disorders are women. Why do you think this is the case?
3. After reading this box, would you encourage or discourage your own daughter from thinking about beauty in conventional terms? Why or why not?

theory is *analysis of how race, class, and gender interact, often creating multiple disadvantages for some categories of people.*

In 2009, the median income for non-Hispanic white women working full time was $39,010. But African American women earned $31,933, or 82 percent as much, and Hispanic women earned $27,268, or 70 percent as much. Among women, then, race and ethnicity are one source of disadvantage.

Then there is the second disadvantage based on gender. Within racial and ethnic categories, we see that in 2009, African American women earned 85 percent as much as African American men, and Hispanic women earned 86 percent as much as Hispanic men.

Combining these two dimensions of inequality, African American women earned 62 percent as much as non-Hispanic white men and Hispanic women earned 53 percent as much as white men (U.S. Census Bureau, 2010). Therefore, the intersection of gender with race and ethnicity does result in even greater disadvantages for some categories of the U.S. population.

Theoretical Analysis: Understanding Gender Inequality

Each of sociology's three major theoretical orientations—the structural-functional, social-conflict, and symbolic-interaction approaches—helps us understand gender inequality. As you have seen in earlier chapters, each approach highlights different facts and reaches different conclusions.

Structural-Functional Analysis: Gender and Complementarity

According to the functionalist approach, gender is society's recognition that women and men differ in some useful ways. In this approach, society defines gender in terms of *complementarity*, as if to say, "Differences between men and women help unite people into families, which ties together society as a whole."

Talcott Parsons: A Theory of Complementary Roles

The best-known theory of this kind was developed by Talcott Parsons (1942, 1951, 1954). To understand his ideas, it is helpful to begin with a historical look at gender.

Among early hunters and gatherers, biological differences between the sexes were very important. Our distant ancestors had no way to control reproduction, so women experienced frequent pregnancies and spent much of their adult lives caring for children. As a result, women in these societies were expected to build their lives around the home, gathering vegetation and raising the young. Men's greater size and strength placed them in charge of hunting and warfare, tasks that took them away from

MAKING THE GRADE

Parsons's claim that males are more instrumental and females are more expressive strikes many as a reflection of gender bias in our culture.

SOCIAL PROBLEMS in Everyday Life

Observe women and men sitting in public spaces around campus. Do you note any gender-linked patterns?

the home. Over many generations, this sex-based division of labor became *institutionalized*, meaning it was built into the culture and passed from generation to generation.

By the time of the Industrial Revolution, the division of labor based on gender had become less necessary. For one thing, societies had devised effective means of birth control. As Chapter 7 ("Sexuality") explains, rubber condoms, first made around 1850, were a fairly reliable method of contraception. Industrial technology also reduced the importance of physical strength in the labor force, opening more jobs to women.

Parsons claimed that gender differences are getting smaller because over the course of human history, the biological facts of sex—physical size and strength—matter less and less. Yet, Parsons suggested, modern societies still point to some gender differences because they serve to integrate people and help them work together. Specifically, society defines the two sexes in *complementary* ways, which ensures that men and women need each other and benefit from joining together as families. In the family, women still bear the children, of course, and they take more responsibility for the household. By contrast, men do more to link the family to the larger world through their greater participation in the labor force.

Given this pattern, society guides parents to raise their boys and girls differently. Masculinity, explains Parsons, involves an *instrumental* orientation, emphasizing rationality, competition, and a focus on goals. Femininity involves an opposing *expressive* orientation: emotional responsiveness, cooperation, and concern for other people and relationships.

Young people soon learn that looking or acting too differently from society's standards of masculinity or femininity can bring sharp disapproval from others. As they grow older, boys and girls also learn that failure to display the right gender patterns may result in loss of sexual appeal. In short, society teaches men to favor women who are feminine and women to favor men who are masculine. The end result is that men and women bring different elements to a relationship, and each needs the other.

CRITICAL REVIEW Structural-functional analysis of gender was quite influential fifty years ago but is far less so today. Why? Because the functionalist argument that "gender differences work" strikes researchers today as very conservative. Many of today's sociologists interpret what Parsons called "complementary roles" as little more than male domination.

There are other problems with this approach as well. First, by arguing that society benefits from conventional ideas about gender, the structural-functional approach ignores the fact that men and women can and do relate to one another in a variety of ways that do not fit any norm. We cannot assume that everyone will fit into either the "instrumental" or "expressive" category. Today, most people, male and female, have "instrumental" roles in the labor force.

A second problem cited by critics is that functional thinking glosses over personal strains and social conflicts produced by rigid gender patterns (Giele, 1988). They argue that in everyday life, we may experience gender as both helpful and harmful. How people actually experience gender in their lives brings us to symbolic-interaction analysis.

Symbolic-Interaction Analysis: Gender in Everyday Life

The symbolic-interaction approach provides a micro-level analysis of gender, which highlights how individuals experience gender in their everyday lives.

Personal Behavior

How does gender shape daily behavior? As we have seen, gender involves power; more powerful people have more choices about how to behave. In general, our society gives men greater freedom in personal behavior. For example, would you react the same way to a man who uses foul language as you would to a woman who does the same thing? Similarly, researchers have documented that men, in everyday conversation, have a tendency to interrupt others (especially women); women, by contrast, are more likely to listen politely, especially to men (Smith-Lovin & Brody, 1989; Henley, Hamilton, & Thorne, 1992; C. Johnson, 1994).

The same gender pattern is evident in facial expression. In addition to symbolizing pleasure, smiling shows respect and a desire to make peace. Not surprisingly, then, researchers note that women tend to smile more than men (Henley, Hamilton, & Thorne, 1992).

Use of Space

A general pattern is that people with more power use more space in their everyday activities. In the classroom, for example, the professor can pace around the room while speaking, but students are expected to stay in their seats. Because men have greater social power, they typically use more space than women, whether they are speaking in front of a group at work or relaxing on the sidelines at a sporting event. We judge masculinity by how much space a man uses (the standard of "turf"), and we judge femininity by how little space a woman uses (the standard of "daintiness").

In addition, men's greater power gives them the option of moving closer to others, even to the point of breaking into what we consider our personal space. Women have to be more

SOCIAL PROBLEMS in Everyday Life

Can you point out additional ways that our language gives greater value to what is masculine?

MAKING THE GRADE

The social-conflict analysis in this chapter includes both a class focus (Engels) and a gender focus (feminism).

careful in this regard because "moving in on a man" is likely to be treated as a sexual come-on (Henley, Hamilton, & Thorne, 1992).

Language

Finally, gender is at work in the language we use. When talking about proud possessions, many men use female pronouns, as when a young man shows off his new car, saying, "Isn't she a beauty?" Using a male pronoun in this case ("Isn't *he* a beauty?") seems wrong; this reflects the fact that in a patriarchal culture, men control women, not the other way around.

People's names show the same pattern. Among newlyweds, the conventional practice is for the woman to take her husband's last name. The opposite pattern—a man taking his wife's last name—is extremely rare. Although few people today would claim that this pattern means that the man actually owns the woman, it does suggest that men expect to have control over their wives.

Finally, notice how the English language tends to give what is masculine more value than what is feminine. Traditional titles associated with men—such as *king* and *lord*—have positive meanings, but the corresponding titles associated with women—such as *queen, madam*, and *dame*—are often negative.

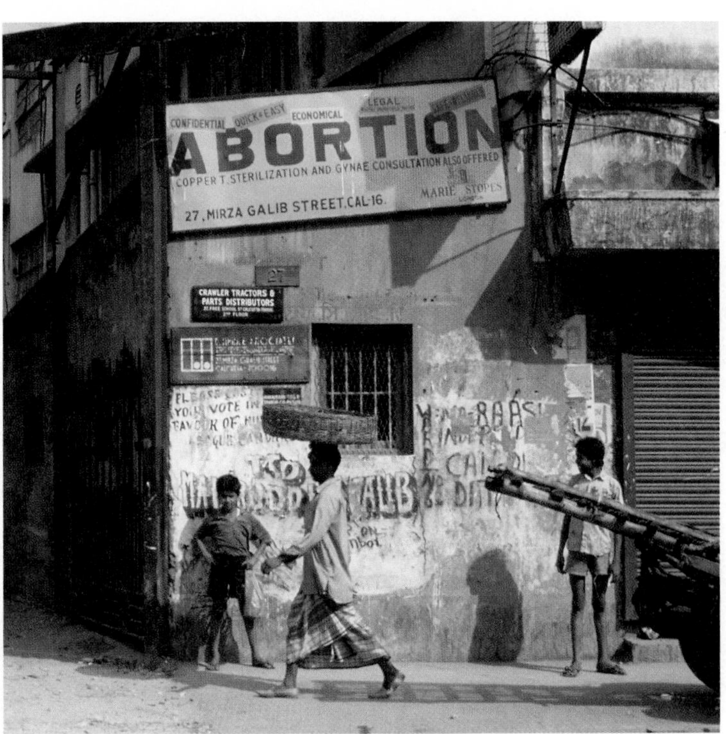

In low-income nations, boys have more economic value than girls because they can earn more money. Therefore, many poor families engage in sex-selective abortion to avoid giving birth to a daughter. In villages in India, clinics provide sonograms that usually reveal the sex of a fetus; they also provide abortions to women who choose to "try again" in the hopes of having a son.

CRITICAL REVIEW The strength of symbolic-interaction analysis lies in putting a human face on gender, showing how gender is at work in familiar dimensions of everyday life. This approach also shows that gender is an important building block of social reality.

At the same time, a limitation of this approach (and of all other microtheories) is that it overlooks gender as a structure of society. We now turn to social-conflict theory to examine broad issues of gender inequality and gender conflict.

Social-Conflict Analysis: Gender and Inequality

Social-conflict analysis switches the focus from functionalism's horizontal image of gender differences as complementary to a more vertical view of gender as a dimension of social inequality. Rather than promoting social integration, conflict theory argues, gender generates conflict between male "haves" and female "have-nots."

Friedrich Engels: The Rise of Patriarchy

Friedrich Engels (1820–1895), Karl Marx's lifelong friend and collaborator, extended Marx's thinking about class conflict to include gender (Engels, 1902, orig. 1884). Engels argued that the same process that allows a ruling class to dominate workers places men in a dominant position over women.

Early hunting and gathering societies assigned women and men different daily routines, but both sexes made vital contributions to daily life. That is, men may have done the hunting, but women collected the vegetation that provided most of the food.

Gaining the ability to raise animals and crops provided societies with a surplus—more than people needed just to survive. Typically, some families gained most of this surplus for themselves, and as this happened, social classes were born. Once some people had more than others, elites developed the idea of private property as a strategy to protect what they had. It was also at that time that men began controlling the behavior of women. Why? Because men with property are concerned about passing their wealth on to their heirs, and they need to be sure of who their offspring are. Therefore, wealthy men devised the family as a way to control the sexuality of women, who were to

MAKING THE GRADE

Use the table below to review the three theoretical approaches to gender.

feminism the study of gender with the goal of changing society to make women and men equal

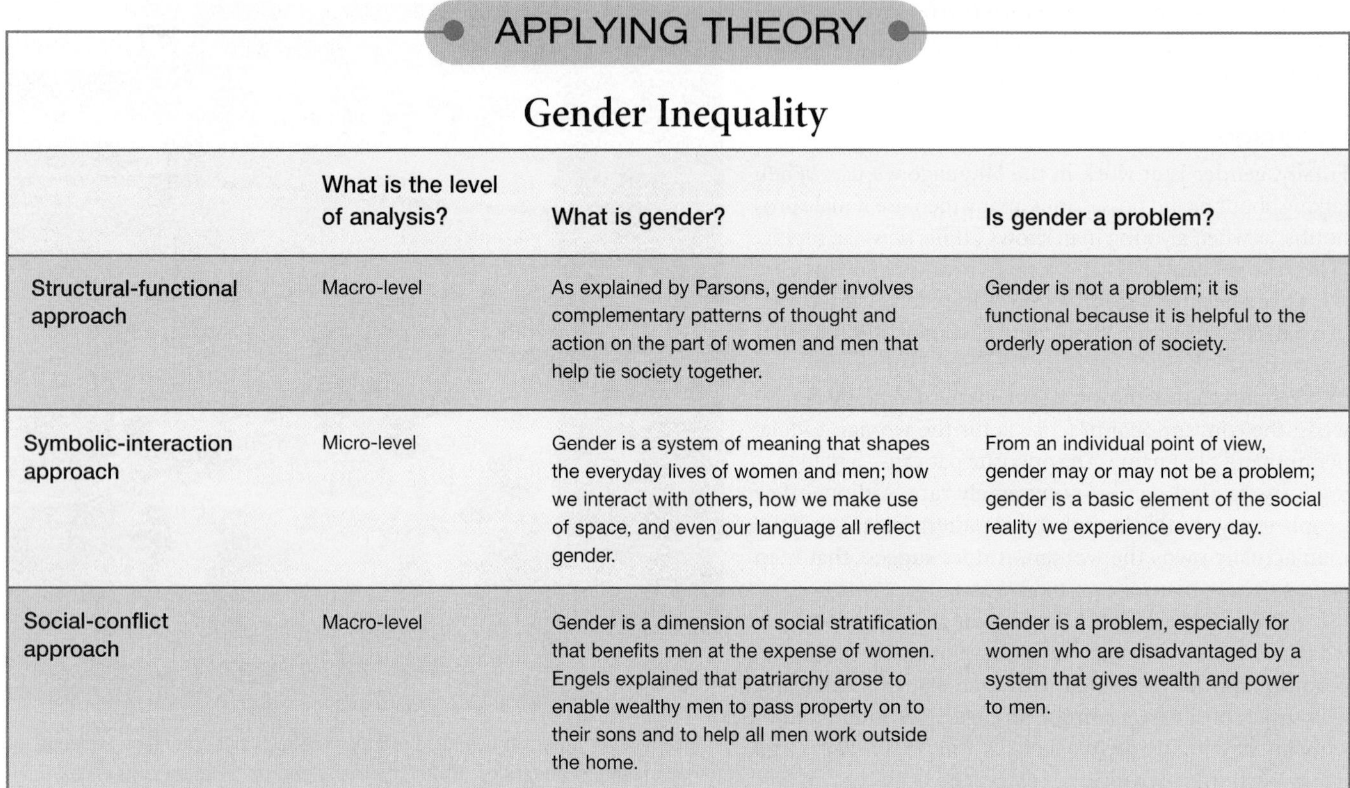

APPLYING THEORY

Gender Inequality

	What is the level of analysis?	What is gender?	Is gender a problem?
Structural-functional approach	Macro-level	As explained by Parsons, gender involves complementary patterns of thought and action on the part of women and men that help tie society together.	Gender is not a problem; it is functional because it is helpful to the orderly operation of society.
Symbolic-interaction approach	Micro-level	Gender is a system of meaning that shapes the everyday lives of women and men; how we interact with others, how we make use of space, and even our language all reflect gender.	From an individual point of view, gender may or may not be a problem; gender is a basic element of the social reality we experience every day.
Social-conflict approach	Macro-level	Gender is a dimension of social stratification that benefits men at the expense of women. Engels explained that patriarchy arose to enable wealthy men to pass property on to their sons and to help all men work outside the home.	Gender is a problem, especially for women who are disadvantaged by a system that gives wealth and power to men.

remain faithful and raise a man's children. In Engels's view, patriarchy is a system by which wealthy men pass property to their sons.

With the rise of capitalism, Engels continued, patriarchy became stronger than ever, taking the form of a male-dominated capitalist class. In addition, to ensure an ever-expanding market for capitalist production, society teaches women that personal happiness lies in marriage and the domestic role as a consumer of products and services. Finally, because capitalism forced most men to work long hours in factories, men expected their wives to do all the housework. To Engels, the double problem of capitalism lies in exploiting men in factories for low pay and exploiting women in the home for no pay at all (K. Barry, 1983; Jagger, 1983; L. Vogel, 1983).

CRITICAL REVIEW The social-conflict approach shows how gender became part of social stratification. Engels's work also highlights the close link between gender and class.

But conflict theory has its critics. First, families may be patriarchal, but they perform the vital task of raising children. Second, the lives of men and women may be different, but not everyone defines these differences as unjust. In other words, say critics, conflict theorists minimize the extent to which women and men live together cooperatively and, often enough, quite happily. Third, some challenge Engels's assertion that capitalism is at the heart of gender stratification. After all, patriarchy is also strong in socialist nations, including Cuba and the People's Republic of China.

The Applying Theory table summarizes what each approach teaches us about gender.

Feminism

Since the 1960s, feminism has gained great importance in sociology. Formally defined, **feminism** is *the study of gender with the goal of changing society to make women and men equal.* Feminism therefore involves both theory and action.

The history of feminism in the United States goes back more than 150 years. The movement's first wave began in the 1840s as a spinoff of efforts to abolish slavery. Back then, Lucretia Mott (1793–1880) and Elizabeth Cady Stanton (1815–1902) saw par-

MAKING THE GRADE

Be sure you understand the three types of feminism: liberal feminism, socialist feminism, and radical feminism.

MAKING THE GRADE

Can you state the words of the Equal Rights Amendment?

allels between whites oppressing people of color and men oppressing women. The Defining Moment box on page 106 takes a closer look.

Feminist Foundations

There is more than one version of feminism. But almost all feminists agree on the following six general points:

1. **The importance of gender.** Everyone, feminists claim, must recognize how gender shapes our lives as men or women. Men don't just choose to be competitive any more than women decide to be deferential; this kind of behavior has much to do with how our society defines masculine and feminine behavior.
2. **The importance of change.** Because U.S. society gives men both power and privilege, feminists oppose the status quo. Feminism seeks both to understand and to change the social world.

   Feminists claim that everyone—women and men—would benefit from gender equality. Obviously, patriarchy limits the development and opportunities of women, who make up half the population. But men also suffer from a system that drives them to seek control of others, a pattern that results in high risk of death from suicide, violence, accidents, heart attacks, and other diseases related to stress. To a large degree, what psychologists call the *Type A personality*—marked by impatience, driving ambition, and competitiveness, all of which increase the risk of heart disease—is the same behavior our culture defines as masculine (Ehrenreich, 1983).
3. **The importance of choice.** Feminists see gender as a cultural creation that imposes a narrow set of opportunities on both women and men. Only if we abandon conventional ideas about the kinds of lives women and men "ought" to lead will we all be free to decide for ourselves the direction of our own lives.
4. **Eliminating patriarchy.** Feminism opposes all forms of sexism and gender inequality. One important step in this process, as feminists see it, is for U.S. society to affirm that women and men have equal standing before the law. This is why, since its introduction in Congress in 1923, feminists have supported passage of the Equal Rights Amendment (ERA) to the U.S. Constitution. The ERA simply states, "Equality of rights under the law shall not be denied or abridged by the United States or any State on account of sex."
5. **Eliminating violence against women.** As noted earlier in this chapter, many sociologists see violence against women as a pressing social problem. Feminists claim that violence against women can end only when society places women and men on the same level.
6. **The importance of sexual autonomy.** Feminists claim that women have the right to control their sexuality. Feminists support the wide availability of birth control technology and oppose legal restrictions on abortion. Many feminists also support the gay rights movement. As some feminists see it, lesbians, even more than gay men, are targets of prejudice and discrimination because they violate both the norm of heterosexuality and the expectation that men should control the sexuality of women (Hadley, 1996; Jackson & Scott, 1996; Benokraitis, 1997; Herman, 2001).

Types of Feminism

All feminists agree on the general goals just noted, but they favor various paths to achieving them. Generally speaking, there are three feminist solutions to the problem of patriarchy: liberal feminism, socialist feminism, and radical feminism (Jagger, 1983; A. Phillips, 1987; Lindsay, 1994; Armstrong, 2002; E. B. Freedman, 2002).

Liberal Feminism

Liberal feminism seeks a society in which all people are treated as individuals so that both women and men can freely develop their talents and pursue their interests. Liberal feminism is a reform approach, meaning that it seeks change within existing social institutions. The goal of liberal feminism is for women to enjoy the same rights, opportunities, and rewards as men.

Passage of the Equal Rights Amendment is one objective. In addition, liberal feminists support laws to combat prejudice and discrimination against women. They also endorse policies such as maternity leave for women workers and child care facilities in the workplace so that women caring for young children can still hold a job.

Finally, liberal feminists do not expect that all women will have the same social standing. Individual talent and effort will always elevate some people above others. The liberal feminist position is that society should place no barriers in people's way simply because they are women or men; people should be treated as individuals.

Socialist Feminism

Further to the political left, other feminists doubt that existing social institutions will ever end patriarchy. Supporters of *socialist feminism* claim that Marxist class revolution is needed to secure equality for all people. Recall from our earlier discussion that Friedrich Engels pointed to the roots of patriarchy in capitalist

MAKING THE GRADE

The Latin root of "radical" means "root." Radical feminism seeks to eliminate the entire concept of gender.

CONSTRUCTING SOCIAL PROBLEMS

A DEFINING MOMENT

Elizabeth Cady Stanton: Claiming Women's Right to Equality

It may be hard to imagine, but just a few generations ago, women in the United States were legally second-class citizens. Women could not vote, own property, or enter into legal contracts. It was rare for women to earn income, and the few who did typically turned the money over to their husbands or fathers.

Many people who joined together to oppose the enslavement of African Americans soon began to wonder if women were the slaves of men. Elizabeth Cady Stanton understood the second-class standing of women and decided to do something about it. In 1848, Stanton and her friend Lucretia Mott began the process of change by organizing a meeting in Seneca Falls, New York.

Some 300 women gathered at Wesleyan Chapel in the small upstate New York town to hear more about "women's rights." Stanton led the meeting, asking why women did not have the same rights and opportunities as men, including the right to vote. Even many of those who thought women deserved something more were shocked by the suggestion that women should have a political voice equal to men's. Stanton's husband, Henry, muttering that his wife had gone too far, rode out of town in protest.

Stanton lived for another half century after her historic meeting without seeing her dream of women's equality come true. But she did make a difference. In 1920—eighteen years after Stanton's death—women did finally gain the right to vote. But even after this victory, many people realized that much work remained to be done. After all, the sexes remained unequal in so many other ways. As a result, a "second wave" of the feminist movement continues to this day, addressing issues such as equality in the workplace, domestic violence, and reproductive rights.

Here we see the beginnings of the feminist movement in the United States: Elizabeth Cady Stanton speaks to people who traveled great distances to attend the first women's rights convention in Seneca Falls, New York, in June, 1848.

private property. That is, capitalism oppresses women by forcing them to do housework (which Engels called "domestic slavery") and hold low-wage jobs. Without the ability to earn enough to support themselves, women are dependent on men for economic security.

From a socialist perspective, abolishing the capitalist class system means replacing private property (including the private household) with collective living arrangements in which people come together to share tasks such as cooking and child care. If work were shared in this way, there would be no classes, nor would men dominate women.

To sum up, socialist feminism sees class revolution as necessary for gender revolution. In other words, liberal feminism accepts the basic institutions of U.S. society; socialist feminism does not. From this point of view, women's liberation can be achieved only through elimination of the broader economic conditions that have historically oppressed all humanity.

Radical Feminism

A third strategy on the political left calls for the most basic change of all. *Radical feminism* argues that patriarchy is built into the

SOCIAL PROBLEMS in Everyday Life

In what specific ways would society change if the concept of gender did not exist? Think about work, family life, sports, and any other aspects of life that interest you.

MAKING THE GRADE

How revolutionary are each of the three types of feminism?

concept of gender itself, and so nothing short of ending gender will bring about equality. Why? Radical feminists begin with what may seem to be a surprising assertion: The roots of gender are the biological differences that allow women to bear children. In other words, the main reason women have always been unequal to men is *motherhood*. From this point of view, the family is not so much an economic relationship (as Engels and socialist feminists claim) as it is a form of institutionalized heterosexuality that limits women by demanding that they bear and raise children and carry out home responsibilities.

But if the problem of patriarchy is rooted in human biology, what hope is there for change? Until recently, radical feminists explain, there was none, because societies had little control over reproduction. But that is no longer true. With the latest scientific technology, we have far more control over reproduction, and people are able to reproduce outside of the conventional pattern of heterosexual parenting. For example, *in vitro* ("in glass") *fertilization*—surgically extracting a woman's ovum, fertilizing it manually in a glass dish, and then reinserting it into her body—has been a reality for decades, and the thousands of normal, healthy children produced in this way demonstrate that neither heterosexuality nor the traditional family is necessary to reproduce the human species (a more complete discussion of new reproductive technologies is found in Chapter 12, "Family Life").

The future imagined by radical feminism is more revolutionary than that imagined by socialists. Here we consider abolishing not only the traditional family but also all differences between women and men and perhaps even ending heterosexual relationships entirely.

Could this ever happen? If it did, social institutions would be very different from those we know today. The economy and political systems would have to evolve toward greater social equality. Families would take a new form, with collective responsibility for raising children. Some observers have suggested that in order for adults not to be defined by the task of parenting, children must gain greater rights and responsibilities for themselves (Jagger, 1983). Others, who see heterosexuality as part of the problem, claim that equality for women and men would require new thinking about sexuality itself. Andrea Dworkin (1987), for example, argued that an equal society would be one that gave up all sexual norms, including those that currently discourage masturbation, homosexuality, and sex outside marriage.

In the end, we can only imagine what a gender-free society would be like. But for many feminists, that is exactly the point. Whether or not one agrees with this view, radical feminism helps us see how deeply gender is woven into all aspects of our everyday lives.

CRITICAL REVIEW Because feminism has become a powerful social movement throughout the United States, it is a major force in sociology. The contributions of feminism lie in showing how gender affects almost every aspect of our lives and in bringing about change toward greater equality of women and men.

Like any successful social movement, feminism is controversial. Some critics claim that feminists focus too much attention on ways in which women remain unequal to men, ignoring the enormous progress women have made and the many opportunities they now enjoy (Sommers, 2003). Certainly, some men oppose feminism because this movement wants to take away their power and privileges. But there are also men—and women, too—who reject the idea that all differences between the sexes are unjust and oppressive. Some critics claim that differences between men and women, whether biological or cultural, provide useful ways to organize social life (this was the view of Talcott Parsons, noted earlier). Others suggest that even though women can earn income, their choice to remain at home makes a crucial contribution to the well-being of their children (Baydar & Brooks-Gunn, 1991; Popenoe, 1993a). Still others argue that feminism has wrongly sought to deny any differences between women and men; by contrast, we need to recognize the special strengths of women and build on them (Ehrenreich, 1999).

In the end, of course, the view one takes of feminism—or of any issue related to gender—is a matter of values and politics. We now explore how politics shapes what people define as the social problems and solutions related to gender.

POLITICS AND GENDER

Constructing Problems and Defining Solutions

According to the Declaration of Independence, "All men are created equal." Doesn't this statement seem to define gender inequality as a problem? Not if, as most historians claim, our founding fathers did not intend to include women in this statement. Remember that at the time, all of our country's political leaders were men, and women had no political voice. But the issue of gender inequality has sparked controversy ever since, and people's views of this issue vary according to their political positions.

The Left to Right table on page 109 summarizes what we learn by applying the three political perspectives to the issue of gender inequality.

MAKING THE GRADE

Be sure you understand how conservatives, liberals, and radicals construct the problem of gender and how each point of view defines the solution.

Conservatives: The Value of Families

Generally speaking, conservatives accept the wider social role of today's women. They realize that most families depend on the income of both wives and husbands, and an increasing number of leaders in both the Democratic and Republican parties are women.

But many conservatives define the trend toward gender equality as a problem to the extent that it weakens the family. In this view, many conservatives agree with Talcott Parsons, whose structural-functional analysis described gender as a pair of complementary roles that encourage men and women to depend on each other and form strong families. Since the 1960s, as women have entered college and the labor force in record numbers, the divorce rate has gone up and there are more people living alone (see Chapter 12, "Family Life").

A second important issue for conservatives involves child care. Now that most mothers have joined fathers in the workplace, who's minding the kids? Evidence suggests that today's children are getting less—some people say much too little—attention from adults. In an age of two-career couples, home life often involves weary men and women with little time and energy for their children. No one doubts that most parents do their best to raise their daughters and sons, but conservatives point out that popular ideas such as having a little "quality time" with the kids amount to excuses for fathers and mothers who do too little parenting. This retreat from parenting may be why important measures of well-being among children—including rates of poverty, arrest, and suicide—are up (Popenoe, 1993a; Blankenhorn, 1995; U.S. Census Bureau, 2010).

Although most conservatives are willing to support women in the workplace and also in positions of national leadership, most also support policies to strengthen traditional families. Conservatives continue to support policies that will raise the importance of families in our national life and encourage women and men to make their partners and children their highest priority. In sum, conservatives claim that—especially for parents—the choices people make about how to live should be guided by what is best for the entire family.

Conservatives argue that strong families and effective parenting depend on at least one parent spending much of the day in the home with young children. Liberals counter that most women want the chance to pursue careers just as men do. In your opinion, how should men and women share the responsibilities of work and parenting?

Liberals: The Pursuit of Equality

Liberals point out that at the time of the Declaration of Independence, the U.S. political system did not even define women (or African Americans and many other minorities) as full human beings. In a 2006 speech, President Barack Obama (a senator at the time) reported meeting a 105-year-old African American woman who was born before women had the right to vote, which was also a time when people of color never expected to see one of their own in the U.S. Senate, never mind as president. Liberals speak out in favor of the slow but steady progress this country has made to expand the rights and opportunities available to women and other minorities.

But liberals claim that there is still much work to do. As this chapter has shown, in the United States, most low-income jobs in this country are filled by women. In addition, almost ninety years after gaining the right to vote, only a small share of our national political leaders are women—14 percent of House members and 17 percent of senators in 2009. Looking at such numbers, liberals conclude that patriarchy is alive and well in the United States and gender inequality remains a serious social problem.

Liberals disagree with the conservative claim that the trend toward gender equality has weakened families. First, as liberals see it, conservatives have a nostalgic—and distorted—view of some "golden age" of family life built around visions drawn from the 1950s. Although television shows such as *Leave It to Beaver* celebrated the stay-at-home moms of that era, should we conclude that most women wanted to live that way? Furthermore, liberals believe that families have changed in recent decades largely

MAKING THE GRADE

Use the table below to review the three political approaches to gender.

LEFT TO RIGHT

The Politics of Gender Inequality

	RADICAL-LEFT VIEW	LIBERAL VIEW	CONSERVATIVE VIEW
WHAT IS THE PROBLEM?	Serious gender inequality is built into not only the institutions of U.S. society but also the biological task of childbearing.	Although U.S. society has made strides toward greater equality for women and men, women still have lower social standing.	The trend toward gender equality has boosted incomes but has weakened families and reduced the importance of parenting in people's eyes.
WHAT IS THE SOLUTION?	There must be fundamental change in economic, political, and family institutions in order to eliminate gender inequality. Some suggest that reproduction, too, must change to liberate women from childbearing.	Government programs (including passing the ERA) can combat prejudice and discrimination; affirmative action will open more doors to women; a comparable worth policy would reduce income differences between women and men.	Cultural values should encourage people to strengthen their commitment to marriage partners and children.

JOIN THE DEBATE

1. Can you identify areas on which the three political perspectives agree? What are they?
2. Do you think that a century from now, gender inequality will be greater, about the same, or less than it is now? Why?
3. Which of the three political analyses of gender inequality included here do you find most convincing? Why?

because most families *need* two working adults to make ends meet (Stacey, 1990).

Liberals claim they are profamily because they seek government support for the kinds of families that actually exist today. One pressing need is affordable child care. Liberals support the expansion of child care programs by both employers and government so that women can have the same career opportunities as men.

Second, liberals believe that men must take greater responsibility for the home and for children. Liberals respond to conservative claims that working women neglect their children by suggesting that working men should do more parenting—and also perform their fair share of housework.

Third, liberals place a high priority on policies that will raise the earning power of women. Enforcing laws to eliminate workplace discrimination against women is part of the solution. In addition, liberals support affirmative action (see Chapter 3, "Racial and Ethnic Inequality") as an effective strategy to increase the presence of women in workplace settings, such as executive positions, that have excluded them in the past.

In addition, the U.S. economy has long provided lower pay for some jobs simply because they are performed mostly by women. For example, laundry workers who wash clothes (typically women) are paid less than the laundry truck drivers (mostly men) who transport the laundry, showing that our culture values "women's work" less than "men's work" even when both types of work require about the same level of skill and effort.

To counter this form of institutionalized discrimination, some liberals support a policy of *comparable worth*, by which women and men would receive the same pay not just for doing the same work but for doing different work that has the same value. In other words, supporters of a comparable worth policy claim that it is possible to measure the worth of different jobs in objective terms, and they note that women currently earn about 25 percent less than men for work of equal value. Although courts have debated this policy, the United States—unlike Great Britain and Australia—has no comparable worth laws (England, 1992; Huffman, Velasco, & Bielby, 1996; England, Hermsen, & Cotter, 2000).

Liberals claim that all these efforts at increasing gender equality have the support of a majority of U.S. adults. Indeed, survey data show that most U.S. adults are committed, in principle, to equal rights for women and men (NORC, 2007).

SOCIAL PROBLEMS in Everyday Life

Make three predictions involving gender about our society fifty years from now.

In 2009, President Barack Obama signed the Lilly Ledbetter Fair Pay Act. Ledbetter was a production supervisor at an Alabama tire plant who sued her employer for sex discrimination. The act states that workers have 180 days from the time of their last paycheck (rather than from the time that their pay was first set) to file a discrimination case.

The Radical Left: Change the System

Most people who support feminism identify with its liberal form, seeking greater gender equality within the bounds of current social institutions. But as already noted, others believe that more basic change is needed before U.S. society will ever approach gender equality.

For some people, the target of basic change is the family. For example, Judith Stacey (1990:269–70) states, "'The family' is *not* 'here to stay.' Nor should we wish it were. On the contrary, I believe that all democratic people, whatever their kinship preferences, should work to hasten its demise." The reason, Stacey explains, is that families perpetuate traditional forms of inequality based on class, race, and gender.

How should families change? What are the alternatives? Most radicals argue that at a minimum, basic change must come to the economic and political systems. The socialist feminist solution to gender inequality, described earlier, begins with change from a capitalist economy toward a socialist system. This transformation would allow people to perform economic and domestic work collectively, making people more equal. The end result would be movement away from class inequality as well as the patriarchy that has subordinated women throughout history.

Radical feminism offers the even more far-reaching vision of the elimination of gender itself. From this point of view, complete equality between women and men depends on liberating women from their historical task of childbearing and nurture. And new reproductive technology makes such a vision theoretically possible.

Going On from Here

Imagine a woman living in the United States back in 1850—when the feminist movement began—stepping into a time machine and being transported to our society today. No doubt she would be startled to learn that most women work for pay, that women vote and hold elected office, and that women actually outnumber men on college campuses.

She might be pleased to learn that in the United States today, very few women die in childbirth, which was a common occurrence in her day. In fact, women live far healthier and longer lives than ever before—and live longer than men. Our visitor from the past, when electricity was unknown, would expect most women to spend all day doing housework. She would recall an average woman having about five children, compared to one or two now.

In light of such great changes, perhaps our visitor from the past would be surprised to find that the social standing of women is still controversial. One reason that gender continues to be a matter of controversy is that our expectations have changed. Almost no one today accepts the centuries-old belief that women should remain in the home. Yet in many important ways, women are still unequal to men.

Where are we likely to be 150 years from now? Will the controversies surrounding gender inequality continue? This seems all but certain. Although the gap has been slowly closing, women still earn less than men. This difference exists partly because many people still assume that men and women should do different types of work. In addition, many people think that family responsibilities fall more to women than to men. Given that such beliefs remain with us, it seems unlikely that, anytime soon, women will do the same work as men, earn as much as men, and share domestic chores equally with men. Keep in mind that gender equality has not yet been realized anywhere in the world.

At the same time, the worldwide trend is unmistakable. Women are moving closer to equality with men, and all indications are that the trend will continue.

DEFINING SOLUTIONS

Is gender inequality in college athletics a problem? If so, what is the solution?

Men have a dominant position in athletics at colleges and universities, just as they do in professional sports. Back in 1972, Title IX of the Civil Rights Act tried to eliminate gender inequality in college athletics by mandating equal opportunity for both sexes in sports programs. But almost forty years later, gender equality seems a distant goal—if it is a goal at all. Look at the photos below, which show the reality of inequality and suggest ways to define a solution.

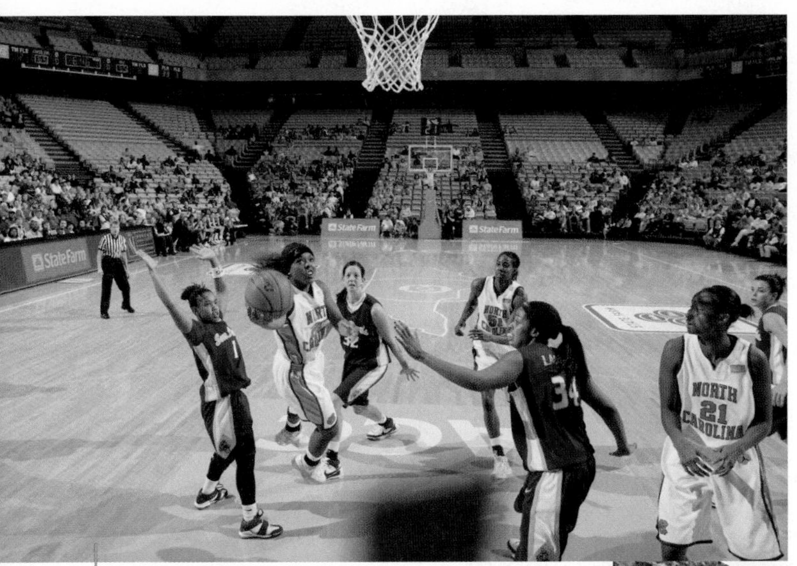

HINT

Across the country, an undisputed fact is that the biggest crowds are drawn to male athletics, especially football and basketball. These are also the sports that earn the most revenues and pay the highest salaries to coaches. For example, the Alabama football program earned more than $50 million in 2008 and the head football coach earns about $5 million a year. The more to the left you are, the more you would support government regulation that would make athletic opportunities the same for women and men. The more to the right you are, the greater your support for allowing the market, that is, people themselves, to decide what sports they wish to spend money to see; you would also point out that allowing universities to make tens of millions from men's basketball and football can and does provide the money to pay for other "non-revenue" sports, both women's and men's.

Here we see two Division I women's basketball teams recently facing off in a mostly empty arena. If you are more liberal, this is clear evidence of the heart of the problem—men get the attention (and their sports get the money) and women are left to be cheerleaders or to play in front of small crowds. Title IX may be a good start, but clearly more needs to be done. What additional steps would you suggest as a solution to this gender inequality?

When the football teams of Alabama and Tulane took to the field recently, the event drew close to 100,000 people and sold out the huge stadium. If you are more conservative, you probably think people should freely attend the events they wish, and if men's sports generate more interest and revenue, so be it. But how do you square this view with the demands of Title IX?

Getting Involved: Applications & Exercises

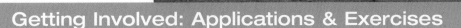

1. Walk around your campus with an eye toward gender. Identify spaces (buildings, rooms, activities) that are dominated by men or women. Which are the men's and women's spaces? Which sex controls more space?
2. Visit a magazine rack in your local bookstore or supermarket. Examine popular magazines aimed at women. What images are on the covers? What topics—stories, features, and photographs—do magazines consider "women's issues"?
3. Visit the offices of an organization in your community or campus that deals with violence against women. What are its goals and strategies to achieve them?
4. Does popular music contain bias against women? Listen to at least two kinds of music (rap, hip-hop, rock, country, and so on), and see what messages about the life goals and relative power of females and males you can find.

MAKING THE GRADE

A DEFINING MOMENT
Elizabeth Cady Stanton: Claiming Women's Right to Equality p. 106

CHAPTER 4 Gender Inequality

What Is Gender?

SEX is the biological distinction between females and males.

- Sex is determined at the moment when an embryo is conceived.

p. 88

GENDER refers to the personal traits and life chances that a society links to each sex, creating the cultural concepts of "feminine" and "masculine."

- Gender is a dimension of social stratification.

p. 88

PATRIARCHY is a social pattern in which males dominate females.

- Almost all societies display some degree of patriarchy.
- **GENDER STEREOTYPES** are one form of prejudice against women, which devalues what a society defines as feminine.
- **SEXISM** is the assertion that one sex is less worthy than or even innately inferior to the other.

pp. 88–90

gender (p. 88) the personal traits and life chances that a society links to being female or male

sex (p. 88) the biological distinction between females and males

gender stratification (p. 88) the unequal distribution of wealth, power, and privilege between men and women

patriarchy (p. 88) a social pattern in which males dominate females

matriarchy (p. 88) a social pattern in which females dominate males

sexism (p. 89) the belief that one sex is innately superior to the other

Gender and Social Institutions

FAMILY

- In poor countries the world over, parents value sons more than daughters, encouraging selective abortions and in some cases, female infanticide.
- In the United States, gender shapes people's experience of marriage, which is often an unequal partnership that favors the man.

p. 91

EDUCATION

- Gender stereotyping steers women away from fields of study (such as engineering and physics) considered masculine.
- Despite policies against gender bias in college sports, men's sports typically receive more funding and public attention.

p. 91

MASS MEDIA

- Historically, television and film have cast women mainly in supporting roles.
- Advertising reinforces gender stereotypes by pitching certain products (such as household cleansers) to women and others (such as cars and banking services) to men.

p. 92

RELIGION

- Traditional religions allow only men to be leaders.
- Many religious writings teach women to submit to the social dominance of men.

pp. 93–94

POLITICS

- Women hold only 18% of seats in the world's 185 parliaments.
- In the United States, until 1920 women were barred from voting in national elections.
- In 2008, a record number of women were elected to Congress.

p. 93

MILITARY

- Until recently, the claim that women are not as strong as men has allowed the military to bar women from certain assignments.
- Women represent 14% of the U.S. forces in the Iraq War.

p. 94

WORK

- Many people still think of certain jobs as "women's work" and others as "men's work."
- Although gender discrimination in the workplace is illegal, officials investigate thousands of discrimination complaints each year.

pp. 94–96

Gender Stratification

INCOME is an important dimension of gender inequality.

- In the United States, women working full time earn 77% as much as men.
- Child-rearing duties often cause women to fall behind their male colleagues in career advancement.

pp. 96–98

HOUSEWORK is still perfomed mainly by women, despite the fact that women have been entering the labor force in record numbers in recent years.

p. 98

VIOLENCE AGAINST WOMEN is a serious problem in the United States and throughout the world. U.S. government agencies receive 1.7 million reports of nonsexual assaults and 237,000 reports of sexual assaults against women each year.

pp. 98–99

SEXUAL HARASSMENT came to be defined as a social problem in the 1980s; about 50% of women surveyed claim to have received unwanted sexual attention in the workplace.

p. 99

Our **IDEAS ABOUT SEXUALITY AND BEAUTY** have consequences for giving men power over women. Reproduction is also an important issue because controlling reproduction gives women the freedom to work outside the home.

pp. 99–100

glass ceiling (p. 98) subtle discrimination that effectively blocks the movement of women into the highest positions in organizations

sexual harassment (p. 99) unwanted comments, gestures, or physical contact of a sexual nature

intersection theory (p. 100) analysis of how race, class, and gender interact, often creating multiple disadvantages for some categories of people

✓ *Because women have a subordinate position in relation to men, they should be considered a* ***MINORITY.*** *(p. 100)*

✓ ***INTERSECTION THEORY*** *points out that women who are also racial or ethnic minorities contend with multiple disadvantages. (pp. 100–101)*

Theoretical Analysis: Understanding Gender Inequality

Structural-Functional Analysis: Gender and Complementarity

The **STRUCTURAL-FUNCTIONAL APPROACH** views gender in terms of complementary roles that link men and women, building families and integrating society as a whole.

- In traditional societies, women bear children and are primarily responsible for the household; men link the family to the larger world by their participation in the workforce.
- With greater control over reproduction, modern societies have less gender specialization.

pp. 101–2

Symbolic-Interaction Analysis: Gender in Everyday Life

The **SYMBOLIC-INTERACTION APPROACH** highlights how gender influences people's actions in everyday situations.

- Gender involves social power: Our society gives men greater freedom in personal behavior and allows them to use more space than women do.
- Language also reflects the social dominance of males.

pp. 102–3

Social-Conflict Analysis: Gender and Inequality

The **SOCIAL-CONFLICT APPROACH** sees gender as a dimension of social inequality, with men having greater wealth, power, and privileges than women.

- Friedrich Engels linked gender stratification to men's desire to pass on property to their offspring.
- The rise of capitalism fostered patriarchy by forcing men to work long hours in factories; the burden of housework and child rearing fell to women.

pp. 103–4

See the **Applying Theory** table on page 104.

Feminism

FEMINISM is an important social-conflict approach in sociology.

- *Liberal feminism* seeks reform within existing institutional arrangements.
- *Socialist feminism* links gender equality to broader class revolution, following Marxist principles.
- *Radical feminism* calls for the elimination of gender itself, partly through the use of new reproductive technologies to liberate women from childbearing.

pp. 104–7

feminism (p. 104) the study of gender with the goal of changing society to make women and men equal

Politics and Gender: Constructing Problems and Defining Solutions

The Radical Left: Change the System

- **RADICALS ON THE LEFT** claim that gender stratification is deeply rooted in present social institutions.
- Radicals on the left believe that reaching the goal of gender equality requires basic change in the economy, political system, and family life. Socialism would allow women and men to work collectively for the benefit of everyone.

p. 110

Liberals: The Pursuit of Equality

- **LIBERALS** object to gender inequality that limits the earning power of women and discourages women from assuming leadership positions.
- Liberals look to government to raise the social standing of women by putting an end to gender discrimination and by increasing women's economic opportunities and providing affordable child care.

pp. 108–9

Conservatives: The Value of Families

- **CONSERVATIVES** place great importance on the traditional family.
- Conservatives see the trend toward gender equality as a problem. They say that this trend weakens families and reduces the importance of parenting, and they claim that children may suffer when both parents work outside the home.

p. 108

See the **Left to Right** table on page 109.

CONSTRUCTING THE PROBLEM

Do you know many elderly people?

The number of seniors is increasing so fast that by 2025, people aged sixty-five and older will outnumber young people aged thirteen to twenty-four.

Do older people get the respect they deserve?

Each year, at least 1 million elders in the United States suffer from some form of abuse; many are victimized by family members.

Is using medical technology to extend life a good thing?

It can be. But because most deaths in the United States come after a decision to halt medical treatment, people must face the difficult responsibility of deciding when life should end.

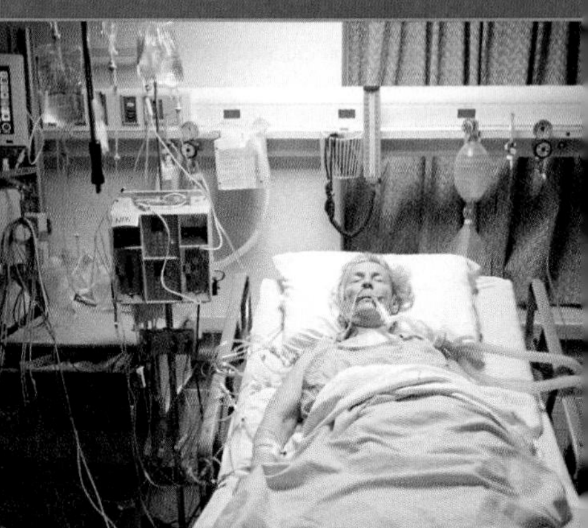

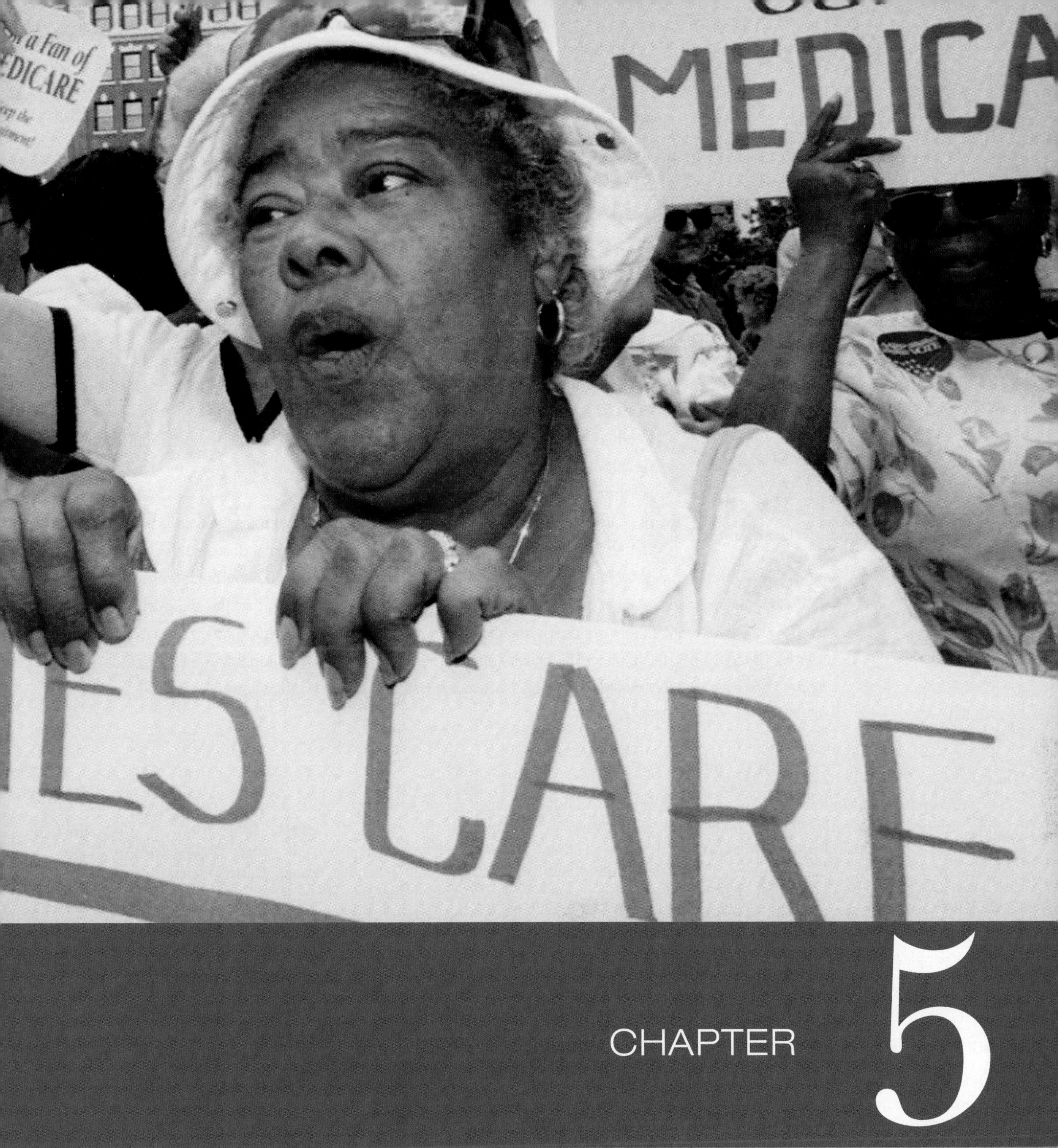

CHAPTER 5

Aging and Inequality

CHAPTER OVERVIEW

WHAT DOES IT MEAN TO GROW "OLD"? This chapter describes the increasing population over the age of sixty-five that is described as the "graying of the United States." You will learn about many of the challenges facing older people, from social isolation to poverty to outright abuse, and understand why aging is a dimension of social stratification. You will carry out theoretical analysis of age-related inequality and learn how "problems" and "solutions" involving old age reflect people's political attitudes.

Verona Vacca drives down the Maryland Freeway with three of her friends, She's the one behind the wheel, talking up a storm. It's Wednesday, and Vacca is driving three of her elderly friends to the shopping center to shop and buy groceries. "I'm the designated driver," she explains with a smile. "The others are not so comfortable driving any longer." The other three—all in their early eighties—are glad to have a ride to the store. The unexpected part of the story is that Vacca is a lot older than they are, having just celebrated her ninety-sixth birthday.

Verona Vacca tells all her friends that performing this "taxi service" three times a week helps keep her feeling young. And she is doing quite well for her age: Still in remarkably good health, she lives in a small, two-story house in a suburban community.

Sometimes people ask her how she stays so young. Her usual answer is that the secret to long life is that she never smoked, always drank only a little alcohol, and kept her weight under control. To hear her daughter, Carola, tell it, Vacca's longevity also comes from a positive attitude about life. "She has a light in her eyes that is very alive, alert, and interested," says Carola. "It radiates over her whole face" (Corliss & Lemonick, 2004:42).

More people in the United States are living well into their eighties, nineties, and beyond. Many of them—like Verona Vacca—are quite content with their lives. But growing old is not a happy time of life for everyone. As this chapter explains, the oldest members of our society face a number of challenges, including social isolation, prejudice and discrimination, a rising rate of poverty, and sometimes even outright violence. In addition, older people must face up to the fact that their lives are coming to an end.

Growing Old

Old age is the final stage in the **life course,** the *socially constructed stages that people pass through as they live out their lives.* In our culture, common stages of life include childhood, adolescence, adulthood, and old age. The last of these stages is the focus of **gerontology,** *the study of aging and the elderly.*

We tend to think of the gradual physical, mental, and social changes that occur during the first half of the life course as "growing up." By about age forty, however, members of our society begin to define the process of aging in more negative terms, as if people start "growing down." Physical strength declines, hair turns gray or falls out, and the skin becomes wrinkled. Among older men and women, injuries come more easily and take longer to heal, illness becomes more common, and the senses (sight, taste, hearing, and smell) are less sharp. There is truth to the idea that people "slow down" as they age. Compared with thirty-year-olds, people at age seventy-five have a bodily metabolism that has slowed by one-sixth; their heart and kidney functions are reduced by one-third; and their breathing capacity has fallen by half.

Older people can fall seriously ill with an infection such as the flu that a younger person would shake off in a day or two. Elderly people also suffer from more chronic (long-term) illnesses such as arthritis that, though not life-threatening, often cause pain and can make everyday activities difficult. Most seriously, the odds of a deadly disease, such as cancer, stroke, or heart disease, keep going up with advancing age.

In terms of health, elderly people differ in some important respects. The higher people's income level, the better their health usually is because they can spend more for safe housing, good nutrition, and high-quality health care. Well-being also reflects lifestyle and personal choices: Factors such as regular exercise, not smoking cigarettes, and limiting use of alcohol all contribute to good health at any age (Holmes & Holmes, 1995; Medina, 1996).

Industrialization and Aging

The life course is "socially constructed" because growing old is not just a matter of biological changes. How a culture defines

life course the socially constructed stages that people pass through as they live out their lives

life expectancy the average life span of a country's population

gerontology the study of aging and the elderly

gerontocracy a social system that gives a society's oldest members the most wealth, power, and prestige

GETTING INVOLVED

List the three best things about growing old. List the three worst things. On balance, do you perceive the aging process as positive or negative?

this stage of life makes a big difference in how people experience old age.

Preindustrial Societies: Elders as Social Elite

In traditional, rural societies where many people engage in farming, ways of life change slowly. The knowledge gained by the oldest members of society remains valuable, so younger people look up to elders as wise and deserving of respect. In addition, the oldest people (typically the oldest *men*) own most of the land, which gives them not only wisdom but also a great deal of power. For these reasons, preindustrial societies take the form of a **gerontocracy,** *a social system that gives a society's oldest members the most wealth, power, and prestige.*

In farming societies, seniors typically remain active, working and leading the family until they are physically unable to continue. At this point, elders can expect to be well cared for by their children for the rest of their lives. Even after death, in many societies, they remain objects of respect and devotion through the religious pattern of ancestor worship.

In traditional, agricultural communities, as in this rice-producing region of Japan, most wealth and power are held by older people, who typically continue working well into old age. Why does industrialization reduce the social standing of older people?

Industrial Societies: Elderly as Social Problem

The Industrial Revolution did much to raise everyone's living standards, but it also reduced the social power and prestige of older people. This is because industrial technology speeds up the rate of cultural change, which encourages us (especially young people) to view the knowledge and skill of seniors as "old-fashioned" and unimportant to our lives. This is why, in preindustrial societies, people use the word "elder" as a term of respect. In modern industrial societies, however, older people are referred to as "elderly," which has a more negative meaning. It is not far off the mark to say that in societies like our own, many younger people regard older people as something of a social problem.

Industrialization also changed family relationships, separating the generations. For centuries, family members worked together on the farm, the young learning from the old. In the nineteenth century, as factories sprang up, the lure of better pay drew younger workers from rural farming communities to the cities. In the new industrial economy, young people had less reason to look to their elders for work or for guidance. Just as important, as many younger men and women headed off for the growing cities and left their aging parents behind, the share of the elderly in poverty began to rise.

As the twentieth century got under way, the number of elderly people facing serious poverty was high, and some ended up in poorhouses that were hardly better than prisons. Fortunately, as the century moved ahead, the economic standing of older people in the United States started getting better. The poorhouses were closed, in part due to a social movement demanding better treatment for older people. A milestone was reached in 1935 when the federal government passed the Social Security Act, which provides a monthly pension to everyone over a certain age (currently sixty-five). In addition to providing needed income, this program makes the statement that older people are worthy of support. After about 1970, the average income and wealth of older people began to climb and poverty rates began to fall (Watkins, 1993; Powell, Branco, & Williamson, 1996; U.S. Census Bureau, 2010).

But money, as they say, isn't everything. Today's older people may be better off economically, but many feel devalued by today's "youth culture." The mass media focus on the lives, fashions, and attitudes of young people, making older people seem old-fashioned and of little value (Kosterlitz, 1997; Wise, 1997).

Not all industrial countries have been so hard on their oldest members. Japan stands out as a nation that still has some of its centuries-old respect for old people. But even in Japan, older people face challenges, as the Social Problems in Global Perspective box on page 118 explains.

Life Expectancy

Life expectancy is *the average life span of a country's population.* In the earliest hunting and gathering societies, most people died

GETTING INVOLVED

Estimate your own life expectancy at http://www.demko.com/deathcalculator.htm

MAKING THE GRADE

The median age of the population has more than doubled over the course of our nation's history.

SOCIAL PROBLEMS IN GLOBAL PERSPECTIVE

Will the Golden Years Lose Their Glow? Growing Old in Japan

Sixty-two-year-old Taizo Komurasaki grew up during the horrors of World War II, went to college, and found a job with a trading company, where he spent his whole career. At age sixty, he retired with a pension and looked forward to another fifteen or twenty years of financial security.

But his golden years have already lost some of their glow. Even before the current economic crisis, his pension was only $1,625 per month ($19,500 per year) in a country where the cost of living is among the highest in the world. To make matters worse, both corporations and government in Japan have been forced to reduce pensions during the long period of economic recession that began about 1990 and has recently become worse. Second, the share of Japan's population that is over the age of sixty-five is increasing faster than in any country in the world. In 2011, more than 20 percent of Japanese people were over age sixty-five (compared with 13 percent in the United States); in 2025, the Japanese figure will be about 29 percent (18 percent in the United States).

The main reason for the rapid increase in the elderly population is the low Japanese birth rate. The birth rate has fallen so low in Japan that in decades to come, the country's total population will actually go down. The predictable outcome? Fewer workers to pay into the system that provides pensions to the elderly who have retired.

It has long been a Japanese tradition that children (especially daughters) provide care for aging parents. But tough economic times have left most couples feeling they cannot afford to support aging parents. Also, most Japanese couples live in small apartments with little space for another person. Finally, as more Japanese women have joined the labor force, they have less time and energy to devote to elder care.

One sign of changing times is that the Japanese are now building what was once unknown in that nation: nursing homes. As elders live longer, as pensions run low, and as families find they have less to offer to aging parents, the cultural taboo against placing parents in nursing homes is breaking down.

WHAT DO YOU THINK?

1. In both Japan and the United States, the number of retired seniors drawing government funds is outpacing the number of younger workers paying into the system. What do you think should be done to head off a crisis?
2. What responsibilities should families have for their elder members?
3. Do you see ways in which the recent economic recession has affected the lives of older people here in the United States? Explain.

Source: Strom (2000) and U.S. Census Bureau (2011).

in childhood; someone who lived to thirty was considered to have reached a "ripe old age." As Global Map 5–1 shows, life expectancy in the world's poorest nations, most of which are in Africa, can be as low as forty years (Population Reference Bureau, 2009).

Life expectancy is much higher in high-income countries, which have better nutrition, sanitation, and medical care. Today, males born in the United States can expect to live seventy-six years and females eighty-one years (Kochanek et al., 2011).

Rising life expectancy is good, of course, but it also means that these societies must meet the needs of an increasing number of older people. This is especially true in the United States.

The Graying of the United States

When the United States won its independence in 1776, ours was a very young nation in more ways than one. Half the new country's population was under age sixteen, and it was rare for someone to live to the age of sixty. Despite the familiar image of gray-haired "founding fathers," the great leaders of that time were actually young by today's standards. When George Washington, who became our nation's first president, commanded the troops in the Revolutionary War, he was in his early forties, and when Thomas Jefferson wrote the Declaration of Independence, he was just thirty-three.

By 1900, about 3 million people were older than sixty-five, but they made up just 4 percent of the population. As shown in Figure 5–1 on page 120, that share doubled by 1950 and will double again by 2020, with an elderly population of about 55 million (U.S. Census Bureau, 2008). The trend is that the elderly population is increasing rapidly, while the number of young people is staying about the same. The result is what sociologists call the "graying of the United States." Figure 5–1 shows that the share of the U.S. population over age sixty-five is projected to reach 20 percent by about 2035.

Elders: A Diverse Population

Sociologists conduct research to help us understand the needs and problems of the elderly population of the United States. The evidence shows that elders are quite diverse socially.

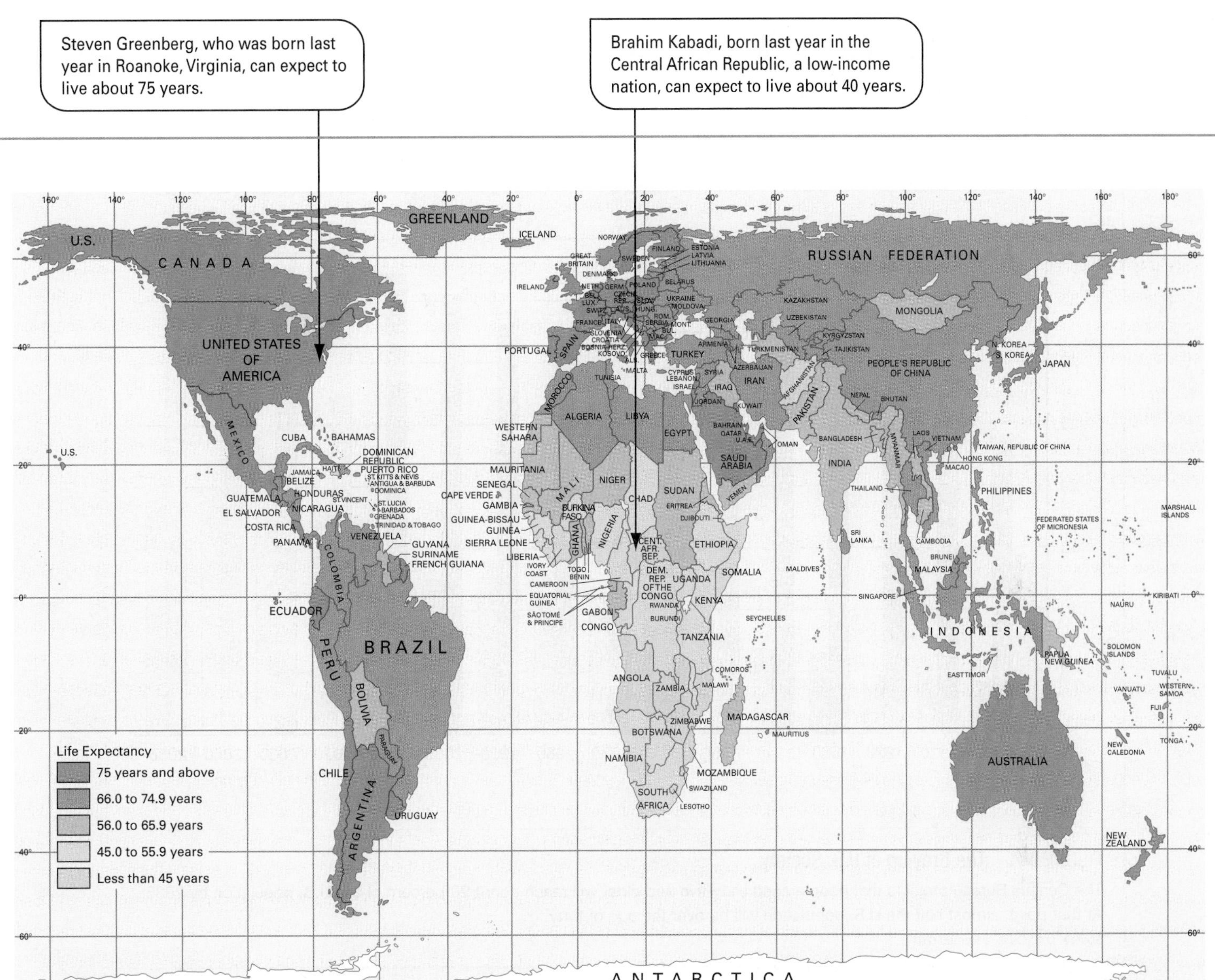

A World of Differences

GLOBAL MAP 5–1 Life Expectancy around the World

Life expectancy shot upward over the course of the twentieth century in high-income countries, including Canada, the United States, Japan, Australia, and the nations of Western Europe. A newborn in the United States can now expect to live about seventy-eight years, and our life expectancy would be greater still were it not for the high risk of death among infants born into poverty. Poverty cuts lives short in much of the world, especially in parts of Africa, where life expectancy may be less than forty years.

Source: Population Reference Bureau (2008).

Three Levels of "Old"

One way in which older people differ from one another is age in itself. Researchers divide the elderly into three categories. Most people sixty-five to seventy-four years of age—the "younger old"—enjoy good health and live independently. People aged seventy-five to eighty-four, who are more likely to need support services, might be called the "older old." Elders aged eighty-five and older, who need the most help, are the "oldest old." Of the three categories, the oldest old are increasing in number most rapidly. Just 0.1 percent of the U.S. population in 1900, they made up 1.8 percent in 2010, an eighteenfold increase (U.S. Census Bureau, 2011).

Class, Race, Ethnicity, and Gender

Social inequality shapes the lives of people of all ages. Older men and women who are well-off financially, especially the

MAKING THE GRADE

Note the trends: The share of elderly people and the median age of the U.S population are going up.

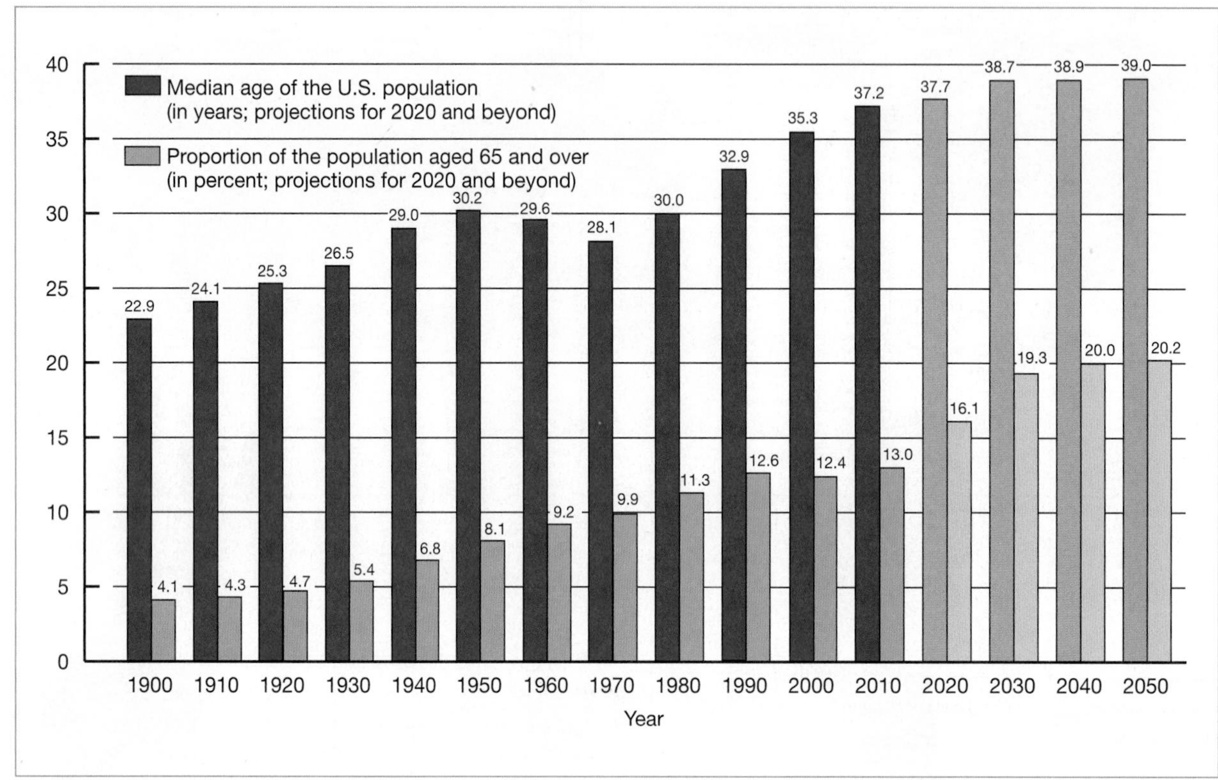

FIGURE 5–1 The Graying of U.S. Society

The Census Bureau projects that people aged sixty-five and older will reach about 20 percent of the U.S. population by 2035. At that point, almost half the U.S. population will be over the age of forty.

Source: U.S. Census Bureau (2011).

younger old, have lots of choices about where and how they want to live. For many of these fortunate women and men, travel provides both adventure and learning. Some well-off seniors retire to Florida, Arizona, or other Sunbelt states to enjoy the mild weather and reasonable cost of living.

But these are the exceptions, not the rule. Just one in twenty older people ends up making a move to the Sunbelt. Why? Many (especially those with health problems) want to stay close to family members. For most, however, the reason comes down to money: They simply cannot afford it.

The elderly are also racially and ethnically diverse, and the older minority population faces most of the challenges that all minorities face—lower incomes, on average, as well as prejudice and discrimination.

Keep in mind that the older population of the United States is not as diverse as the younger population. One reason is that, on average, minorities do not live as long. As noted in Chapter 3 ("Racial and Ethnic Inequality"), life expectancy among African Americans is four years less than for white people. In addition, much of our country's racial and ethnic diversity results from immigration, and most immigrants are young. About 48 percent of children under five years of age are minorities (including African, Asian, Latino, and Native Americans), but this is true of just 20 percent of those over age sixty-five (U.S. Census Bureau, 2010; Kochanek et al., 2011).

A final dimension of diversity among the elderly involves gender. Women tend to live longer than men. Therefore, although women are a slight majority of the total population (51 percent), they represent 57 percent of all people over the age of sixty-five. Among this country's 53,000 centenarians—people aged 100 years or older—83 percent are women (U.S. Census Bureau, 2011).

Problems of Aging

People face change at every stage of life. But most elderly say that the changes of old age present the greatest challenges they have ever faced. Although the physical health of seniors is, on

SOCIAL PROBLEMS in Everyday Life

As you read through the problems of aging, try to see these challenges in the lives of older people you know.

MAKING THE GRADE

Retirement is a fairly new idea that was constructed as societies industrialized.

the whole, better than stereotypes of "frail old people" suggest, most older women and men spend a lot of time and money dealing with their health. Many live with pain from various ailments. Just about everyone also has to learn a tough lesson: accepting the fact that they must depend on others during their everyday routines. In addition, as family and friends die, older people face loneliness and the knowledge that the end of their own lives is drawing near. We now take a closer look at problems common to society's oldest members.

A rising number of older women and men are in the paid labor force, a trend that increased during the recent economic downturn. How does ageism affect the types of jobs older people hold?

Social Isolation

At any age, being lonely can cause anxiety and depression. But among people at all the stages of life, older people are the most likely to experience social isolation. Retirement from work closes off an important source of social activity. As people age, declining health limits their ability to get around, and negative stereotypes of the elderly as sickly, old-fashioned, or "out of touch" may keep younger people away.

As friends, neighbors, and family members die, an older person's social world becomes smaller and smaller. Few human experiences are as painful and isolating as the death of a close friend and, especially, a spouse. One study of older men and women who had lost a spouse found that three-fourths cited loneliness as a serious problem. This experience of social isolation is surely why researchers have long documented the fact that in the months following the death of a spouse, the surviving partner is at high risk of death, sometimes by suicide (Benjamin & Wallis, 1963; Lund, 1989).

The problem of social isolation is more common among elderly women than men. Among people over sixty-five, 72 percent of men live with a wife, but only 42 percent of women live with a husband. From another angle, 19 percent of elderly men live alone, compared with 31 percent of older women (Federal Interagency Forum, 2008). Why? In part, because women typically outlive men. But it is also true that widowers are more likely to remarry than widows. Men have a better chance to find another partner because U.S. culture supports the pairing of older men and younger women much more than the pairing of older women with younger men.

Many elderly people look to community services provided by senior citizen centers as a source of social contact. But for most seniors, families are the main support system. Almost half of all elders have at least one adult child who lives no more than 20 minutes away. Caregivers are typically adult children (mostly women) who live with or near the older person (Rimer, 1998; AARP Public Policy Institute, 2005).

Retirement

Because industrialization makes societies more productive, not everyone has to work. Members of industrial societies commonly view child labor as wrong—although it is common in low-income nations around the world—and they expect young people to spend most of their daily lives in school. At the other end of the life course, it has become common for older people to retire from the labor force so that they can spend their remaining years doing what they wish.

Most younger people imagine that they will retire from paid work at about the age of sixty-five, and in recent decades, the median age for retirement actually has fallen from sixty-eight (in 1950) to sixty-two (in 2000). During the last few years, however, the economic recession has reversed this trend, forcing people who have faced pay cuts or who have lost some or all of their pensions or retirement funds to remain in the labor force. In a world of economic uncertainty, people are now more likely to be cautious about giving up paid work, perhaps retiring in small steps, a pattern called *staged retirement* (Gendell, 2002; Kadlec, 2002; U.S. Census Bureau, 2008).

Even if you are decades away from retirement, it is a good idea to do some planning for this transition. Obviously, saving enough to fund retirement is one important issue. But because work is also a source of personal satisfaction and social contact,

MAKING THE GRADE

Can you see how ageism is like sexism and racism?

ageism prejudice and discrimination against older people

THINKING CRITICALLY

Is Aging a Disease?

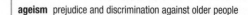

A seventy-five-year-old man who loved to square dance suddenly had a sharp pain in his left knee. He went to his doctor to find out what the trouble was. The doctor noted his age, gave his knee a fairly superficial examination, and said, "I can't find anything obviously wrong with your knee. It must be due to your age." The man asked the doctor to explain. The doctor launched into a discussion of various theories of aging and how they might explain his knee problem, and concluded, "Now do you understand?" The old man replied, "No, I don't, because my right knee is just as old as my left knee, and it's not giving me a bit of trouble!"

The medical sociologist Erdman Palmore (1998:29) tells this story to make a point about subtle forms of ageism. Had this patient been twenty-five years old, Palmore explains, the doctor would never have treated him this way. The doctor probably would have ordered an X-ray or some other procedure immediately to find out what was causing the pain. But with elderly patients, doctors sometimes engage in a subtle form of ageism by acting as if aging itself were the problem. This response is not good medical practice; it is actually a form of age-based prejudice.

WHAT DO YOU THINK?

1. If it is true that people suffer more illnesses as they age, what's wrong with treating aging as a disease?
2. Can you point out other subtle forms of ageism? What about age-related stereotypes?
3. What do you think is a good solution to the problem of age-based prejudice?

people must think about how they can replace work with other activities that provide the same personal benefits. Of course, there is no one formula for a satisfying retirement. Some people are eager to jump into entirely new activities, others are satisfied to spend much more time with children and grandchildren, and still others are content simply to sit back and relax. In nearly all cases, however, what people can and cannot do in retirement will depend on health and finances (Neugarten, 1996; Gall, Evans, & Howard, 1997; Pitt, 2009).

Employers can play a part in a successful retirement, easing this transition by allowing people to retire in steps. For example, colleges and universities may allow professors nearing retirement to "step down" their teaching load. Employers may also provide support for retired professors to conduct research and to attend professional meetings. Many colleges and universities also help older people by letting those who stop working keep some of their privileges. Most schools give retiring faculty members the title "emeritus professor" so that they keep their faculty standing, and many permit them to continue using an e-mail account, make use of the gym, and maybe even hold on to a campus parking space. But most employers are not so helpful. In today's age of corporate downsizing, some companies simply push older (and often higher-paid) workers out the door. Such forced retirement usually offers the greatest challenges.

What is the government's retirement policy? Back in the 1930s, the U.S. government set the retirement age at sixty-five, which was about how long people lived at that time. But today, on average, people live more than fifteen years beyond that. Recognizing increasing life expectancy, in 1987 Congress enacted legislation phasing out mandatory retirement policies by 1994. Rigid retirement policies remain for only a small number of occupations, such as airline pilots, who must retire at age sixty-five (Bosworth & Burtless, 1998; Wyatt, 2000).

Ageism

Whether older people are working or retired, they may find that others look down on them simply because of their age. **Ageism** is *prejudice and discrimination against older people* (Butler, 1975, 1994; E. Cohen, 2001). Like racism and sexism, ageism defines physical traits—in this case, graying hair, wrinkled skin, or any other signs of advancing age—as evidence of being less worthy as a person. Certainly, ageism helps explain the fact that many older people turn to medications such as Botox and Viagra and even undergo cosmetic surgery in order to lessen the effects of aging on their appearance and behavior.

Because women are more likely than men to be judged by their physical appearance, ageism is often a bigger issue for them. But whenever anyone portrays elders of either sex as if they were old-fashioned, narrow-minded, or even senile, they devalue them as human beings.

Age-Based Prejudice

Ageism involves prejudice: negative prejudgments about the elderly. Such prejudice can be blatant, as when college officials pass over a job application from an older person because they prefer hiring someone younger. Prejudice can also be subtle, as when a

SOCIAL PROBLEMS in Everyday Life

What do you think about aging people having cosmetic surgery to appear younger? Would this be as popular if our society were more accepting of growing old?

SOCIAL PROBLEMS in Everyday Life

Make a list of as many age-based stereotypes as you can. How many are positive, and how many are negative?

doctor assumes that an ailment is caused simply by a patient's age, as described in the Thinking Critically box.

Prejudice directed toward the elderly may take the form of stereotypes depicting older people as "sick, senile, useless, sexually impotent, ugly, isolated, poor, or miserable" (Palmore, 1998:30–31). Such stereotypes are wrong because most elderly people are none of these things: Eighty-nine percent of people age sixty-five and older live healthy and independent lives, and just 6 percent have health problems that force them to be institutionalized. Most seniors work as hard and as effectively as younger workers, and most employers rate older workers as more trustworthy and loyal. Just as important, most elderly men and women are quite capable of having satisfying sexual relationships (National Center for Health Statistics, 2007).

Age-Based Discrimination

Prejudiced thinking often leads to unfair treatment or discrimination. This is why, back in 1967, Congress passed the Age Discrimination in Employment Act, banning employers from discriminating against people because of their age. Because the average age of the U.S. workforce is going up—in 2008, more than 61 million workers (42 percent of the total) were age forty-five or older—the number of complaints of age-based discrimination is rising, and this trend is likely to continue in the years ahead. Age discrimination harms many people who think of themselves as middle-aged. Data show that the typical complaint of age discrimination now comes from workers in their forties, not their sixties (Elmer, 2009; U.S. Department of Labor, 2009).

Whatever the age of victims, age discrimination is illegal. But the law is difficult to enforce because many people who are turned down for a job never know exactly why. In addition, companies can legally lay off higher-salaried workers, even though this usually hurts older people the most (Palmore, 1998; Labaton, 2000).

Ageism in the Mass Media

Think about the older women and men you have seen on television and in films. When older people appear on screen, it is often in stereotypical roles. In the Oscar-winning film *Driving Miss Daisy,* for example, Jessica Tandy played an old, lonely woman unable to cope with change. By contrast, older men are seen on screen much more often—think of the many roles played by Harrison Ford, Sean Connery, and Clint Eastwood—and they usually appear (both on- and off-screen) in leading roles opposite women half their age. Twenty-nine-year-old actress Mary McCormack recalled her excitement playing opposite Clint Eastwood, who was more than twice her age:

> I only shot one scene with Clint, but I got to make out with him. He's sixty-eight and completely sexy. It's a man's world, because when I'm sixty-eight, there's not going to be a twenty-nine-year-old actor saying, "And then I got to make out with Mary McCormack." ("There's Something," 1998, p. 63)

Older people who do appear in the mass media are also likely to be white. African Americans in television and the movies are typically young people; minorities become increasingly invisible once they pass the age of age of sixty-five.

Victimization of the Elderly

Only in the 1980s, as the political power of older people was increasing, did our society began to define *elder abuse* as a social problem. Elder abuse ranges from passive neglect to active verbal, emotional, and physical mistreatment. Experts estimate that about 3 million people (about 10 percent of all

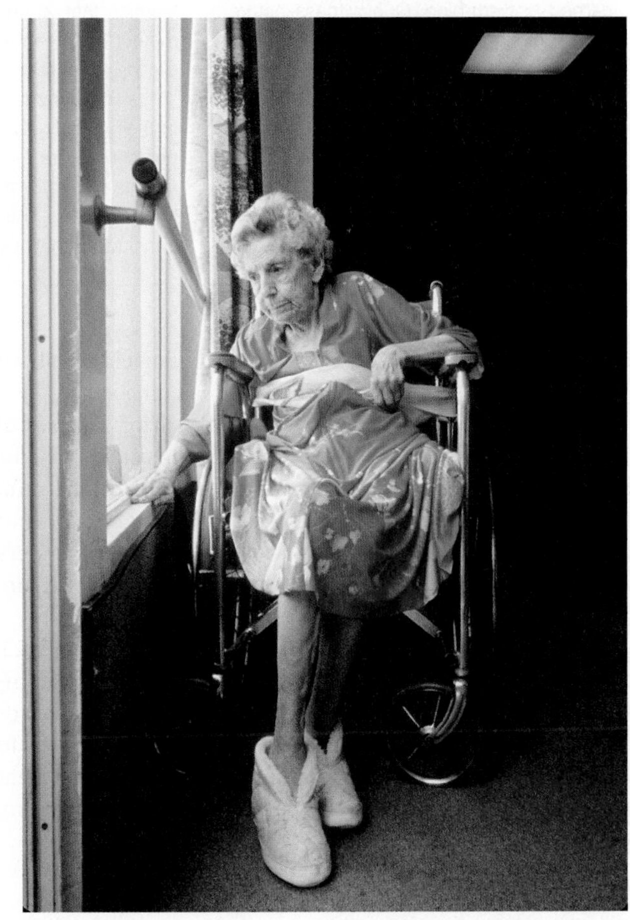

Perhaps 1 million elders in the United States are victims of serious abuse every year. Countless others suffer from neglect and from treatment that robs them of their dignity. What are some of the causes of this problem? What do you think should be done about it?

MAKING THE GRADE

The sections below make clear why growing old is not just a stage of life but also a dimension of social stratification.

MAKING THE GRADE

Although the poverty rate for children has risen over recent decades, the poverty rate for people over age sixty-five has gone down.

SOCIAL POLICY

Nursing Home Abuse: What Should Be Done?

Few people disagree with the idea that society's oldest members deserve at least their fair share of kindness. Yet investigations show more than 90 percent of nursing homes were cited for violations of federal health and safety standards in a recent year. About 17 percent of nursing homes had deficiencies that caused "actual harm or immediate jeopardy" to residents (Pear, 2008).

Most nursing facilities provide good care to their residents. But bad care is common enough to cause government officials and others to investigate. Some of what they learned is disturbing. One witness before a congressional committee was Leslie Olivia, who had been caring for her aging mother at home. When her mother's needs became greater than what Olivia could provide, she turned to a nursing home for help. Within months of her mother moving in, Olivia discovered that her mother suffered bruises, bedsores, and a broken pelvis. Sometimes attendants simply left a meal tray at the end of her bed, out of reach. Without adequate nutrition, her mother quickly lost weight. Olivia was so concerned that she moved her mother to another home. But problems continued, and her mother soon suffered from bedsores and severe dehydration. Olivia moved her mother yet again.

In the last of the homes, the staff called Olivia to report devastating news—her mother had choked to death on her food. In light of what had happened at the other nursing homes, Olivia did not believe them. She soon learned that at the time of her death, her mother had been attached to a feeding tube. Clearly, the facts pointed to abuse.

Is this disturbing story an isolated case? In their investigations, congressional officials heard many reports of this kind. Based on reports by family members and also nursing home workers, the congressional committee concluded that elder abuse occurs much more frequently than we like to think, and it is commonly covered up.

Available evidence suggests that elder abuse is especially likely to occur in facilities that are understaffed and where employees are underpaid and have little training. As a result, tens of thousands of our society's oldest members are suffering needlessly, and many are in danger.

WHAT DO YOU THINK?

1. Why isn't the public more concerned about the problem of abuse that is described here?
2. What changes in the operation of nursing homes might prevent cases like that of Leslie Olivia's mother?
3. What do you see as the solution to the problem described here? Explain.

Sources: Thompson (1998), U.S. House of Representatives (2001), and Pear (2008).

elders) suffer some abuse each year, and 1 million elders (about 3 percent) suffer serious and even life-threatening abuse.

According to the federal government, half of all cases of elder abuse involve neglect of older people who cannot care for themselves. The remaining half involve a range of harmful actions, including active physical or psychological abuse (but rarely sexual abuse), wrongfully taking an older person's money, or unfairly taking some other property (Thompson, 1998; National Center on Elder Abuse, 2006).

Like other forms of family violence (discussed in Chapter 12, "Family Life"), elder abuse often goes undetected because victims are afraid to speak out. Many worry that if they were to file a complaint, their abusers might harm them even more or might try to have them institutionalized. For this reason, only about 15 percent of all actual abuse cases are ever reported (Barnett, Miller-Perrin, & Perrin, 1997; National Center on Elder Abuse, 2006).

Causes of Elder Abuse

What would cause someone to neglect or abuse an older person? One important pattern is that many abusers are themselves victims of abuse. This vicious circle of abuse can be explained in simple terms: People who have experienced abuse in their own lives (often as children) are likely to re-create this pattern in response to the challenge of caring for an aging parent or other person (Greenberg, McKibben, & Raymond, 1990; Bendick, 1992; Barnett, Miller-Perrin, & Perrin, 1997).

People who abuse family members often have other issues. They may be addicted to alcohol or other drugs, they may have emotional problems, or they may suffer from unhealthy personal relationships. People who are poor often have a lot of stress in their lives, a fact that may make it hard to care for another needy person. But any younger person caught between the demands of working, caring for young children, and looking after an aging parent may feel out of control and slip into abusive behavior (Hinrichsen, Hernandez, & Pollack, 1992; Barnett, Miller-Perrin, & Perrin, 1997).

Abuse also occurs in institutional settings such as nursing facilities. Sometimes this problem results from efforts to cut costs. For example, nursing home owners may try to operate their businesses with fewer workers or replace nurses with less trained aides. As a result of such policies, overburdened staff end up neglecting patients (Manheimer, 1994). Like family members, in other words, staff members who face patient demands they cannot meet may reach a point of desperation

caregiving informal and unpaid care provided to a dependent person by family members, other relatives, or friends

age stratification social inequality among various age categories within a society

that triggers abuse. The Social Policy box describes a government investigation of nursing home abuse.

The Growing Need for Caregiving

The share of the U.S. population over age sixty-five is increasing. But less than half of our elders will ever live in a nursing home or care facility. Therefore, most of the care needed by the increasing number of seniors will come from other people in their lives. Understandably, then, sociologists are interested in **caregiving,** *informal and unpaid care provided to a dependent person by family members, other relatives, or friends* (Lund, 1993; Spillman, 2002).

In the United States and other high-income nations, today's middle-aged people are a "sandwich generation" who may well spend as much time caring for their aging parents as they did raising their young children. In most cases, care for an aging person is provided by one particular family member. Most caregivers are women, typically a wife, daughter, or daughter-in-law.

Most caregiving is the job of one individual, which means that the demands on personal time and energy can be great. Most caregivers have other family members to think about—and, of course, their own needs as well. In addition, half of caregivers have jobs. Typically, then, a caregiver provides help for several hours a day on top of what is already a full day's work (Himes, 2001; AARP Policy Institute, 2005).

All of us, as we grow older, will require care from others. How does being poor affect your options for receiving care?

Poverty

In 2009, some 8.9 percent of people over age sixty-five—about 3.4 million women and men—were living below the government's poverty line. Since then, the economic recession has pushed poverty rates up. But the long-term trend for poverty among seniors has been downward: Back in 1965, the elderly poverty rate was almost 30 percent (U.S. Census Bureau, 2010).

What accounts for this decline in elder poverty? The main reason is that seniors now receive better retirement benefits, especially Social Security payments with automatic cost-of-living adjustments. The reduction of poverty among the elderly is a success story that shows that social problems can be improved. But of course, there is still much to be done.

Keep in mind that government poverty statistics do not include elders who are institutionalized, most of whom are poor. Also worth noting is that the poverty line for an older person (in 2010, it was $10,458 for a single person over sixty-five) is below the line for everyone else ($11,344 for a single person below age sixty-five). For these reasons, the official poverty rate for elders probably presents a picture that is more positive than it should be (U.S. Census Bureau, 2011).

Age Stratification

Age stratification is *social inequality among various age categories within a society.* As explained earlier in the chapter, in preindustrial societies, elders have more wealth and power than younger people. In modern industrial societies, the opposite is true.

Figure 5–2 on page 126 shows the average income and the poverty rate for the U.S. population broken down by age. Notice that average income rises through middle age, peaking at about age fifty, and then falls as people enter old age. As we would expect, the poverty rate shows the inverse pattern, falling through middle age and staying low (although rising again after age seventy-five).

Intersection Theory: Age, Race, Ethnicity, and Gender

Sooner or later, the challenges of aging will affect everyone—at least those of us who are lucky enough live to an old age. However, some elderly people also deal with additional prejudice, based on race or gender. Intersection theory points out

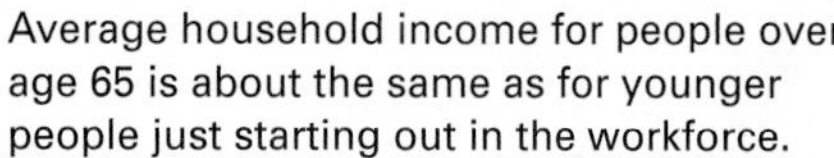

Average household income for people over age 65 is about the same as for younger people just starting out in the workforce.

A generation ago in the United States, it was the elderly who were at highest risk of poverty; today, it is children and young adults.

Dimensions of Difference

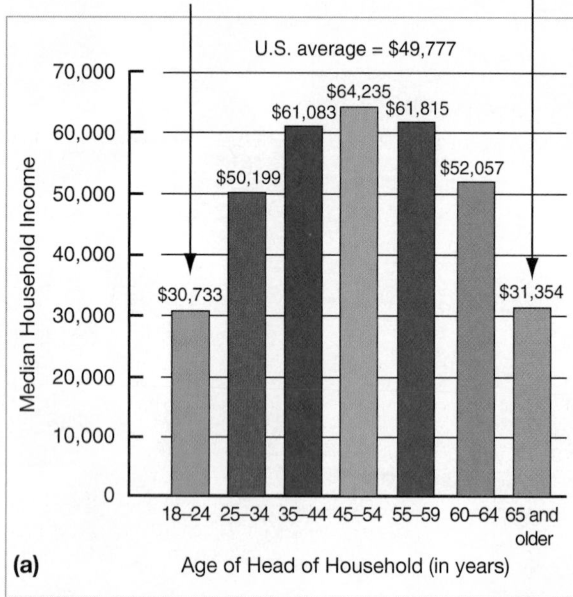

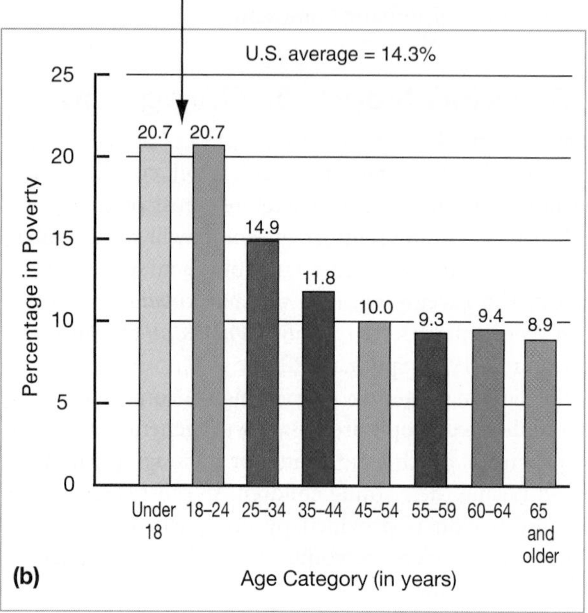

FIGURE 5–2 U.S. Household Income and Poverty Rate, by Age, 2009

In part (a), we see that median household income typically rises over the life course, peaking at around age fifty and falling as people enter old age. Part (b) shows that poverty rates are highest for people under the age of twenty-five. Although millions of seniors are poor, the poverty rate for older people is well below the national average.

Source: U.S. Census Bureau (2010).

that people with multiple minority standing—such as elderly people who are also African American or women—may experience even greater disadvantages.

Figure 5–3 contrasts the poverty rate for various categories of the elderly population in the United States. The poverty rate among elderly African Americans (for both sexes) is 19.5 percent, three times as high as the 6.6 percent rate among elderly non-Hispanic whites (U.S. Census Bureau, 2010). The lesson here is that with advancing age, the risk of poverty goes up for everyone. But among people over sixty-five, the highest poverty rates are for those categories of the population, including racial and ethnic minorities, who are more likely to be poor over the entire life course.

A closer look at the case of elderly women shows the interaction of age and gender stratification. First, gender stratification, which defines family responsibilities as women's work, makes it harder for women to join the paid labor force. Second, as Chapter 4 ("Gender Inequality") explains, women who do work full time earn, on average, just 77 percent as much as male full-time workers. Third—and here is where age stratification comes in—both these factors disadvantage older women more than younger women. Women twenty-five to forty-four years old earn 80 percent as much as men the same age, but women forty-five to sixty-four years old earn just 75 percent as much as men. What accounts for the age difference in earnings? Today's older women grew up at a time when social norms kept many women off the campus and out of the workplace. With less education and job seniority, these women now have lower earnings.

In the years ahead, as a larger share of women graduate from college and are employed throughout their lives, the income disparity between older women and older men will go down. But because women's wages will probably still lag behind men's and also because more women than men will work in jobs lacking pension benefits, we should expect gender inequality in old age to continue (Neugarten, 1996; U.S. Census Bureau, 2010).

Housing

Between 2010 and 2020, the U.S. elderly population will grow by almost 15 million, with an additional 1 million over the age of eighty-five. Yet according to policymakers and social service

SOCIAL PROBLEMS in Everyday Life

Walk around your dorm or apartment and try to imagine how an older person would make out living there.

MAKING THE GRADE

As Figure 5-3 suggests, the elderly are diverse, with some categories doing much better than others.

providers, there will not be enough suitable housing for them (U.S. Census Bureau, 2008).

In the United States, nearly everyone, young or old, views keeping a home as one key to an independent and happy life. About 90 percent of today's older men and 80 percent of older women live independently. About 80 percent of elders own their own homes, and most own them mortgage-free. Even so, older homeowners pay taxes, insurance, maintenance, and utility bills, leaving many elders "asset rich but income poor" (Kontos, 1998; Federal Interagency Forum, 2008; U.S. Census Bureau, 2010).

Most elders prefer to "age in place," staying in the homes where they lived while working and raising their children. But only 15 percent of elders live in housing specifically designed for older people. Physical changes that occur as we age—including loss of strength, a slowing of reaction time, and a weakening of eyesight—require safety modifications to a home such as grab bars near toilets and bathtubs or extra lighting. Stairways are a common challenge to many older people.

As you might expect, the houses owned by seniors tend to be older than average. Many of these homes need repairs, lack insulation, and require improvements to heating and air-conditioning systems. Such housing problems are especially common among categories of elders at higher risk of poverty: African Americans, women, and rural as well as inner-city people.

When housing is not up-to-date, the risk of accident or injury goes up. For example, a fall on dangerous stairs may cause a broken hip, landing an otherwise healthy person in a nursing facility. Trying to heat a drafty home with a space heater raises the risk of fire or death by asphyxiation. Government programs such as Medicare pay for some nonmedical equipment, such as safety seats for showers and tubs. But many elders are unaware of the federal programs that can help make their homes safer (Manheimer, 1994; U.S. Department of Housing and Urban Development, 2008).

Access to shopping and services is another issue important to seniors. Suburban communities have few buses and require the use of cars, yet some older people no longer drive. As a result, aging people may find stores, businesses, churches, and recreational facilities out of reach.

In a classic study of a declining neighborhood in southern California, Barbara Myerhoff (1979) found that elderly residents wanted, more than anything, to stay independent. But dressing, shopping, cooking, and cleaning an apartment are not easy for those challenged by arthritis or failing eyesight. Myerhoff found that the neighborhood had no large grocery store, forcing residents to take the bus, with high steps that were hard to climb and prevented older shoppers from taking a wheeled shopping cart. Night was another matter: Fear of crime kept older people behind locked doors.

Dimensions of Difference

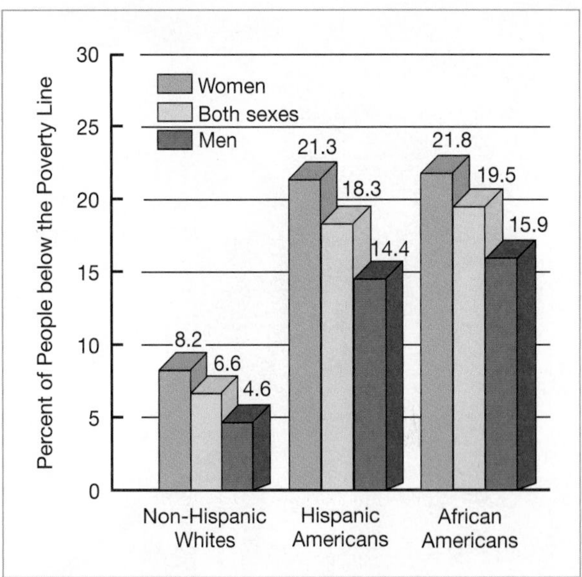

FIGURE 5–3 U.S. Poverty Rates by Race, Ethnicity, and Gender, Age 65 and Older, 2009

Among people over age sixty-five, Hispanic Americans and African Americans are more than twice as likely to be poor as non-Hispanic whites. In every category, older women are more likely to be poor than older men.

Source: U.S. Census Bureau (2010).

Housing Programs for Older People

Across the United States, there are thousands of retirement communities that offer comfortable, accessible apartments with on-site health care services and help with cleaning, meals, and transportation. But the costs are high, including entrance fees of as much as $250,000 plus thousands more a month for an apartment and meals, which puts this type of housing within reach of a very limited number of older people.

To make safe, accessible housing available to those with lower incomes, the federal government provides seniors with rental subsidies based on need. Elderly people occupy one-third of the 5 million public housing units. In 1990, Congress passed the National Affordable Housing Act, making additional money available for housing frail elders, a population that will increase quickly in the years to come as more seniors live past age eighty-five (Binstock, 1996; U.S. Department of Housing and Urban Development, 2000; U.S. Census Bureau, 2006).

Passage of the National Affordable Housing Act also made available so-called reverse mortgages, financial arrangements

SOCIAL PROBLEMS in Everyday Life

Is death a part of everyday life? One way to answer this is to ask another question: Have you ever seen a person die?

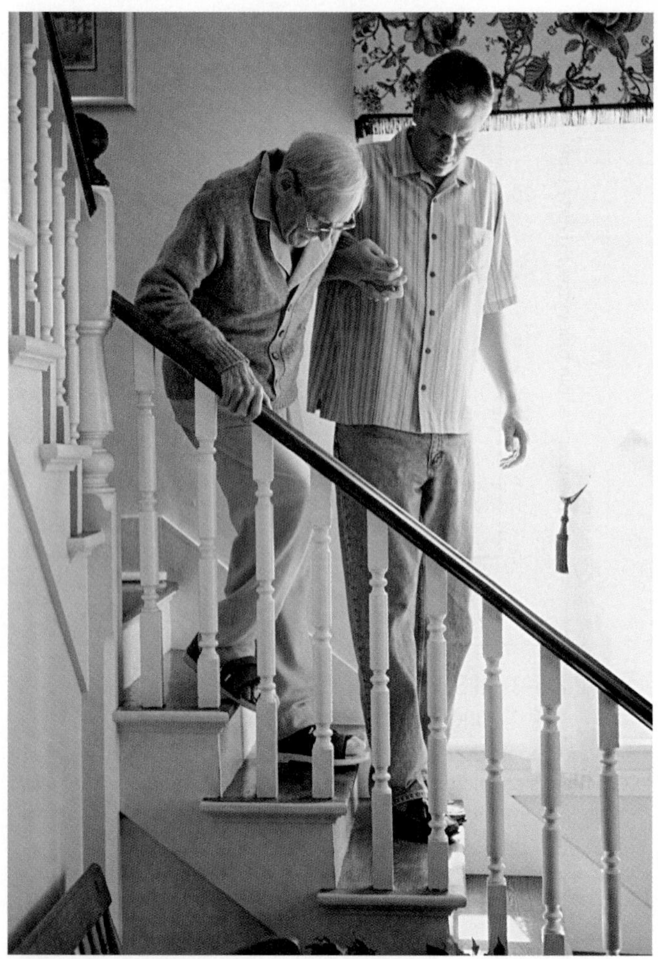

Many elderly people prefer to "age in place." But homes that were comfortable for middle-aged people can become challenging to those who are entering old age. Alterations to make a home suitable for an older person can be very expensive, and alternatives such as moving to a retirement community can be more expensive still. Do you think U.S. society should expect individuals to meet these challenges for themselves?

that allow qualified elders to borrow against their home equity without making any monthly payments. The cash can be used as they wish—say, for home repairs, medical care, or housekeeping services. Eventually, the loan is paid back from the proceeds of the sale of the house after the person dies or moves elsewhere. Many seniors are not comfortable borrowing against their most important financial asset, although gradually turning the value of a home into cash would certainly reduce the elder poverty rate (Kutty, 1998).

Finally, faced with the high cost of housing and declining income, many elders cut costs by sharing a home. About 10 percent of U.S. seniors live with a relative or an unrelated adult (U.S. Census Bureau, 2010).

Medical Care

People need much more medical care as they grow old. Since 1965, the federal government has provided benefits to seniors through Medicare, a program that pays for hospital care and 80 percent of other medical costs for people over age sixty-five. In 2003, Congress added prescription drug subsidies to the Medicare program.

The cost of medical care has been rising steadily in the United States. To help cover the expenses not covered by Medicare, about 60 percent of elders purchase private health insurance. When all the costs are added together, seniors typically spend about 15 percent of their annual income on health care. The Obama administration has set a goal of extending health care coverage to everyone in the United States. This may improve the state of health care for seniors in the years to come.

Costs skyrocket for people who move to a nursing facility. Although just 4 percent of U.S. elders live in a nursing facility at any given time, almost half will at some point. Here again, Medicare and insurance typically pay only some of the costs, and the rest can easily overwhelm many people (Fetto, 2003; Federal Interagency Forum, 2008; U.S. Census Bureau, 2010).

Death and Dying

Sooner or later, we all face the reality of death. One of the most important challenges of growing old is coming to terms with the end of this life.

How we think about death and dying begins with culture. In low-income nations, people learn to accept death as a common part of everyday life. Many infants die at birth, and accidents and illness take such a high toll that as many as half of those born die before reaching age ten. Because family members care for one another in times of illness, people in low-income nations die in the company of family and friends.

Modern societies, however, remove death and dying from everyday life. Have you ever seen a person die? For most of us, the answer is no because family members and friends approaching death are whisked away to die behind closed doors in the company of medical specialists. Even in hospitals, morgues are well out of sight for patients and visitors (Ariès, 1974; F. R. Lee, 2002).

In our society, preparing bodies for burial or cremation is work done not by family members but by professional morticians, and most of our rituals dealing with death take place not in family homes but in funeral homes.

euthanasia assisting in the death of a person suffering from an incurable disease

GETTING INVOLVED

Do you support physician-assisted suicide or not? Why?

In sum, U.S. culture treats death as a topic to avoid. However, a new social movement, with elders leading the way, is trying to bring death and dying out in the open, raising some important questions that we now examine.

Euthanasia and the Right to Die

Thanks to advances in medical technology, higher income, and better nutrition, people live far longer than in the past. Yet our modern ability to extend life also changes death from an event into a decision. In recent decades, a right-to-die movement has developed, advancing the idea that dying people—rather than doctors and hospital personnel—should decide when, where, and how people die (Morris, 1997; Ogden, 2001).

It may not be possible to escape death, but the right-to-die movement claims that people with terminal diseases should be allowed to guide the process of dying and, if they wish, to ask others for help in bringing about their deaths. This policy is called **euthanasia** (from Greek words meaning "a good death"), *assisting in the death of a person suffering from an incurable disease.*

Dr. Jack Kevorkian, who was convicted of murder and is currently serving a prison sentence, claims that people have a right to die with the assistance of a physician.

Euthanasia has two forms. *Passive euthanasia* involves doctors ending the treatment of a terminally ill person by, say, turning off respirators or other life-support machines. Passive euthanasia is generally accepted by lawmakers and is widely practiced by doctors. An increasing number of people expect to invoke passive euthanasia—today, about 30 percent of U.S. adults have a *living will* stating which treatments they do and do not want if they are facing death and are unable to speak for themselves (Pew Research Center, 2006)

Active euthanasia, by contrast, involves a physician or other person actively bringing about the death of a person. For example, a doctor might administer a lethal injection to a dying person to bring a painless end to life.

A middle ground between passive and active euthanasia is called *physician-assisted suicide.* In this case, a patient requests help in dying from a physician, who typically writes a prescription for lethal drugs. The doctor does nothing more; the patient is the one who decides if, when, and where to take the drugs.

Euthanasia in the Netherlands

Since 1981, the Netherlands has permitted active euthanasia under specific circumstances. More recently, Belgium, Luxembourg, and Switzerland have enacted similar laws. Under Dutch law, patients can request euthanasia if they are dying with no hope of recovery, are suffering, and understand all the medical options available. If they meet these conditions, they may request help in dying from a physician. The doctor, in turn, must consult with another physician before acting to end a life (Della Cava, 1997; Mauro, 1997; Tagliabue, 2008). Dutch authorities report that about 2,000 people a year die with a physician's help. Because many cases are never reported, the number may be twice as high.

Most people in the Netherlands support this policy. Yet there is evidence that doctors do not always follow the rules. Critics point out that Dutch doctors assist in the death of people who, due to their illness, cannot clearly state that they want to die. In such cases, doctors help bring about death believing that this is in the patient's best interest, and usually nothing is reported to the government (Gillon, 1999; Barr, 2004).

Euthanasia in the United States

The right-to-die debate continues in the United States, with people lining up to support or oppose active euthanasia. In 1997, the U.S. Supreme Court ruled (in *Vacco* v. *Quill* and *Washington* v. *Glucksberg*) that people have no legal right to die, a decision that slowed the right-to-die movement seeking legalization of active euthanasia and physician-assisted suicide. Yet a majority of voters in Oregon endorsed a "death with dignity" law that took effect in 1997, permitting physicians to assist people in dying if the patients are believed to have less than six

hospice homelike care that provides physical and emotional comfort to dying people and their families

GETTING INVOLVED

Do you have a living will?

months to live. The number of cases in Oregon has remained low—about 400 in eleven years. In 2008, Washington became the second state to permit physician-assisted suicide (Leff, 2008; State of Oregon, 2009).

The right-to-die movement remains controversial. Supporters claim that people would like to have a choice about when and how to die, and many people will welcome help from a doctor to bring about a "good death." Opponents counter that some patients may ask for a quick death not because of pain or even a terminal illness but because of sadness and depression. National surveys show that most people in the United States do support terminally ill people receiving help from doctors in bringing about a good death. But the public is concerned that doctors not cause death among people who are simply "tired of living" (NORC, 2007).

Critics of the right-to-die movement remain wary that the laws enacted in Oregon and Washington will create a "slippery slope" such that assisted suicide will become more and more common over time. How could we be sure, for example, that a request to end a life was not prompted by depression on the part of the patient? Isn't it likely that family members, who may be eager for an inheritance or fearful of high medical bills, will pressure an old or sick parent to die? How can we be sure that health insurance companies won't weigh in to encourage this practice, knowing that they will earn bigger profits if patients opt to end their lives rather than continuing with expensive treatments? Finally, what about the poor? Wouldn't doctors and hospitals treating poor patients or those without health insurance save a lot of money by "getting it over with"? In short, critics claim that it is difficult to set clear moral guidelines for euthanasia and even harder to prevent abuse (Kleinman, 1997).

So far, the small number of assisted suicide cases in Oregon does not confirm the fears of critics. But as the elder population of the country rapidly increases, the euthanasia debate is sure to continue.

Hospice

Another important development that affects patterns of death is the increasing use of **hospice,** *homelike care that provides physical and emotional comfort to dying people and their families.* The first hospice facility in the United States opened in 1974. The Defining Moment box describes the work of Cicely Saunders, who helped found the hospice movement.

Today, approximately 4,700 hospice organizations care for more than 1 million people each year. Unlike a hospital, where medical personnel work to save lives and restore health, a hospice staff helps people die in comfort and with dignity. Some hospice organizations operate homes where dying people go; more often, hospice workers go to the homes of dying people to assist them and their families.

The growth of hospice reflects the fact that many people want to avoid the impersonal and highly regimented environment of a hospital. Typically, hospice personnel work with a doctor and family members to be sure that the dying person is comfortable, using drugs as necessary to control pain but making no efforts to extend life unnaturally. The work of hospice is to help the patient and family members accept death in an environment that is as comfortable as possible. The Personal Stories box on page 132 profiles one hospice volunteer in a midwestern town.

Theoretical Analysis: Understanding Aging and Inequality

Sociological theory can help us better understand the many challenges related to aging. The following sections apply the structural-functional, social-conflict, and symbolic-interaction approaches to many of the issues raised in this chapter.

Structural-Functional Analysis: The Need to Disengage

The structural-functional approach highlights ways in which social patterns help societies operate smoothly. Faced with the reality that its people get old and eventually die, all societies must develop ways to replace old workers with young ones. A logical solution to the problem of people's physical decline is *disengaging* the elderly, transferring their workplace roles and other responsibilities to younger people. Disengagement is a strategy to ensure that the aging of the population does not disrupt the performance of important tasks.

Retirement is the main strategy for easing aging people out of productive roles when they near the point when they will not be capable of performing them. Retirement occurs in rapidly changing societies, where many older workers lack recent knowledge and many up-to-date skills; younger workers, by contrast, have the benefit of the latest training. Formally stated, **disengagement theory** is *the idea that modern societies operate in an orderly way by removing people from positions of responsibility as they reach old age.*

Disengagement is functional for society as a whole. But it also provides older people, who can look back on years of hard work, with the chance to rest, relax, and explore opportunities for travel or spending more time with family (Cumming & Henry, 1961; Voltz, 2000).

MAKING THE GRADE

Be sure you understand how hospice care differs from hospital care.

MAKING THE GRADE

The structural-functional approach has produced disengagement theory.

CONSTRUCTING SOCIAL PROBLEMS

A DEFINING MOMENT

A Good Death: Cicely Saunders and Hospice

Life in rapidly growing cities during the Industrial Revolution was not easy. Poverty was widespread, disease was common, and most people moved about in a world of strangers. With so many problems facing the living, would anyone take time to think about people who were dying?

Cicely Saunders (1918–2005) was a nurse and physician who grew up in London early in the last century. She had been challenged with illness during her own life and was motivated by a strong desire to help others. From her years of working with patients in hospitals, Saunders knew that illness was not just a medical or biological event; it was also a social experience. Therefore, she fashioned her job into what we might call a medical social worker.

In 1948, Saunders began work with a patient, a refugee who had fled Poland for London during World War II, and the two became very close. Their personal relationship was doomed by the fact that the man was dying of cancer. But from the time they spent together, Saunders took away the powerful idea that dying people do not get what they need from hospitals, which are facilities that try to cure illness. Once people are dying, she concluded, they have special needs that called for a new type of care center. This was to become hospice, a place where people will find the means to control their pain and the compassionate care that can make their final stage of life as comfortable and peaceful as possible. In addition, Saunders could see, dying people need help in addressing their fears and in bringing closure to their lives. The vision of hospice can be summed up as *palliative care,* which involves helpfully addressing a dying person's symptoms and physical, emotional, social, and spiritual needs.

As her ideas came together, Saunders also completed her medical training. Based on her vision of hospice care, Saunders in 1967 founded St. Christopher's Hospice, in London, the first facility devoted completely to the care of dying people. In the United States, the first hospice facilities were started in the 1970s. Today, more than 1 million people receive hospice care each year, which represents about one-fourth of people who die.

In 1979, Queen Elizabeth II recognized the efforts of Cicely Saunders by elevating her to the knighthood. Saunders received much praise and many awards during the remainder of her life, which helped change the way the medical profession—and the public—thinks about dying.

Cicely Saunders was a nurse and physician who believed that our medical system did not serve dying people very well. By founding St. Christopher's Hospice in London, she helped the world understand the meaning of a "good death."

CRITICAL REVIEW The eventual disengagement of elderly people may be necessary for society as a whole, but giving up a job or other responsibility is not always good news for older men and women. Many enjoy their work, and most look to their jobs for needed income. Therefore, a criticism of this approach is that disengagement of the elderly may carry important personal costs, including loss of income, loss of social standing in the eyes of others, and rising risk of social

disengagement theory (p. 130) the idea that modern societies operate in an orderly way by removing people from positions of responsibility as they reach old age

activity theory the idea that people enhance personal satisfaction in old age by keeping up a high level of social activity

PERSONAL STORIES  A Hospice Volunteer: "I Take Away More than I Give"

"No, I'm not afraid of death," says Kim as she talks about her work helping others die. "But then again," she adds, "it's not me who's dying." Kim is a middle-aged woman living in a small town in central Ohio. She works as a massage therapist and is a mother to a grown daughter. Several years ago, her husband was stricken with a terminal illness; for almost a year, she cared for him in their home, even though it kept her from working and consumed all her time and energy.

For more than eight years, Kim has been a hospice volunteer and has helped more than 150 people reach the end of life. Kim shares something of her experiences:

> The typical case begins when I get a call from the hospice volunteer director. She tells me they have matched me with a patient. I call the patient's home and we set up the first visit. I do a lot of things: I might give patients a bed bath, make lunch, maybe just give the spouse an hour or so break and a chance to get out of the house.
>
> In these situations, people get to know each other pretty fast. Something about dying strips away all the games and pretenses, and within a month or so, I get to be like one of the family. I don't mean to say this work is easy—it's not. Sometimes it's real tough. Some family members don't like a stranger in the house. Once I even had kids in the family stealing drugs from the mother who was dying.
>
> Things get pretty intense as the time of death gets near. The problem is that most people have never experienced death up close. They need someone to be there to tell them what to expect, how they can help. To tell them when it is time to let go.
>
> Letting go. That's kind of the main thing. Letting a loved one die is very hard for most people. The first thing people want to do is to fight death. But when it's going to happen soon, fighting it can also end up making death harder for themselves and for the person who is dying.
>
> Actually, the people who *really* fight death don't use hospice at all—they send the dying person to the hospital. Hospitals do all sorts of stuff to prevent death. And when there's no more to be done, hospitals make death antiseptic. They shoot you up with drugs to sedate you to the point that you will die smoothly and quickly. Very neat. It's also very expensive. The hospice approach is more natural. It's like letting the body just shut down on its own. We use drugs for pain, but that's all. This way, dying sometimes takes hours, and near the end, a dying person might go two or three minutes between each breath. I've been there when this went on for five or six hours! This is the point when the hospice worker—there is often a doctor or nurse there, too—is most helpful telling people what is happening. We are really just guides. When someone is close to death, we have a saying, "Don't just do something; stand there!" The most important thing is just being there with the family and the dying person, helping them understand and accept the coming death.
>
> I know everyone talks about the "right to die." We try to stay away from the debate over physician-assisted suicide. But you know what? In the real world, a doctor and family members usually talk about if and when to use a drug to bring the dying process to an end. Whether you are in a hospital, at a hospice facility, or in the patient's home, dying almost always involves a decision.
>
> I am glad I was able to be there with [my husband]. And I wish there had been someone like me available years ago when my own father died. I know I do good for people. But I always take away more than I give.

WHAT DO YOU THINK?

1. What do you see as the advantages of hospice care? Do you see any disadvantages?
2. Would you volunteer to do this kind of work? Why or why not?
3. To what extent is our society coming to terms with death as a natural stage in the journey of life? Do hospice volunteers such as Kim help in this process?

Source: Personal interviews (2003, 2006).

isolation. The need for people to remain active in old age points us to the symbolic-interaction approach.

Symbolic-Interaction Analysis: Staying Active

The symbolic-interaction approach focuses on the meaning people find in their everyday lives. As aging people withdraw from some activities, especially those that are physically challenging, most try to find new things to do. For example, many older people retire from paid work but expand their hobbies, do more traveling, and perform volunteer work. Finding new activities is especially important in light of the fact that people in the United States who reach age sixty-five typically look forward to another twenty years of life (Robinson, Werner, & Godbey, 1997; Smart, 2001; U.S. Census Bureau, 2008).

Researchers have found that personal satisfaction in old age depends on remaining socially active (Havinghurst,

MAKING THE GRADE

The symbolic-interaction approach to aging has produced activity theory, which opposes the idea of disengagement.

MAKING THE GRADE

The social-conflict approach applies a class conflict analysis that shows how elders are a disadvantaged minority.

Neugarten, & Tobin, 1968; Neugarten, 1996). **Activity theory** is *the idea that people enhance personal satisfaction in old age by keeping up a high level of social activity.* Activity theory also reminds us that older people, like people of any age, are diverse, with differing needs, abilities, and interests. For this reason, no single policy of disengagement is likely to fit everyone, nor should we expect seniors who choose to withdraw from work to agree on the kinds of activities they will enjoy most (Havinghurst, Neugarten, & Tobin, 1968; Palmore, 1979).

CRITICAL REVIEW Activity theory helps us keep in mind the diverse abilities, needs, and interests of older people. But it overlooks the fact that at least some older people are not physically able to maintain a busy schedule. Even healthy older people in some situations do not have a great deal of choice about their lives. In nursing facilities, for example, many elders would welcome the chance to be more active but find limited opportunities for recreation. Many elders with low incomes also face limited choices about how to live. In short, seniors who are disadvantaged in various ways may not be able to shape their lives as they may wish. This concern brings us to social-conflict theory.

Activity theory states that staying happy and healthy depends on maintaining an active life as we age. People on the Japanese island of Okinawa seem to support this claim. The active lifestyle of elder women and men there is linked to one of the highest percentages of people reaching the age of 100 in the world.

Social-Conflict Analysis: Age and Inequality

Social-conflict analysis focuses on age stratification, pointing to ways in which U.S. society limits the opportunities and resources available to older people. By and large, our society gives the most power and the greatest privileges to middle-aged people. As we have explained, modern societies tend to define elderly people in negative terms, a pattern that encourages both prejudice and discrimination against elders. The law bans age discrimination in the workplace, but all the same, companies usually prefer hiring younger workers. Similarly, the law forbids forcing most older workers to retire, but companies are often eager to replace older employees with younger, lower-paid employees as a strategy to keep their costs down. In short, some analysts conclude that capitalist societies turn older people into second-class citizens as a means of increasing profits (Atchley, 1982; Phillipson, 1982).

Social-conflict analysis also shows us that these disadvantages are greater for some categories of elders than for others. Social class, gender, and race all affect everyone's range of opportunities. Many low-income people, women, and people of color work in low-skill service jobs that rarely provide pensions and other benefits. The categories of people who earn lower wages early in life are also those that have the hardest time in retirement.

CRITICAL REVIEW Age is one important dimension of social stratification, one that combines with other dimensions of inequality including class, race, and gender. Yet by focusing on the relative disadvantages of some elders, the social-conflict approach misses the larger picture that, on average, recent decades have brought major economic gains to seniors. In the United States, the poverty rate for seniors is actually below the rate for the society as a whole. In addition, today's seniors have a lot of political clout because most of them vote. In 2008, 70.3 percent of people age sixty-five or older voted, compared to 48.5 percent of people between the ages of eighteen and twenty-four (U.S. Census Bureau, 2009). It is true that some elders live in poverty and that many encounter prejudice and discrimination. But critics of this approach also point out that the system seems to meet the needs of the aging population fairly well.

MAKING THE GRADE

Use the table below to review the three theoretical approaches to aging and inequality.

APPLYING THEORY

Aging and Inequality

	What is the level of analysis?	How do we understand aging?	Is aging a problem?
Structural-functional approach	Macro-level	The structural functional approach supports disengagement theory, which claims that modern societies operate smoothly by disengaging people from positions of responsibility as they reach old age. Aging, then, amounts to a loss of ability to perform important roles.	Aging is inevitable and causes people to lose their abilities sooner or later. Societies avoid the problem of older people not performing their responsibilities through disengagement of the elderly.
Symbolic-interaction approach	Micro-level	The symbolic-interaction approach supports activity theory, which links satisfaction in old age to keeping a high level of social activity. Aging is a time of transition during which people disengage from some activities and take on new ones.	The problems of aging can be minimized by remaining active, according to an individual's abilities, interests, and desires.
Social-conflict approach	Macro-level	The social-conflict approach focuses on age stratification. Society gives most power and privileges to people in midlife. In spite of age discrimination laws, most employers favor younger workers whom they can pay less.	Many of the problems of aging are caused by our society's profit orientation. In addition, problems of aging are greater for disadvantaged categories of the population who contend with more social problems throughout the life course.

The Applying Theory table sums up what we learn by applying sociology's three theoretical approaches to the issue of aging.

POLITICS AND AGING

Constructing Problems and Defining Solutions

As in other areas of social life, exactly how a person views the social problems of the elderly is guided by that person's political views. We turn now to examining how politics shapes our view of specific issues related to aging. The Left to Right table on page 136 summarizes how each political perspective—from conservative to radical right—defines age-related problems and solutions.

Conservatives: More Family Responsibility

As conservatives see it, a healthy society is built on strong families in which people care for one another. Conservatives also claim that our society's families have been getting weaker. In an age that celebrates individualism and independence, they say, the age-old system by which family members take care of their own is breaking down. And this is happening just when the elderly population is increasing and more caregiving than ever is needed. The result is a number of the social problems we have covered in this chapter, including poverty, social isolation, and elder abuse.

Women and men today are living longer and longer, which is good news, but it also means that many families are raising young children and caring for aging parents at the same time. Conservatives argue that to face these challenges, we must reject

MAKING THE GRADE

Notice that conservatives claim older people should rely on themselves or their families; liberals claim government should ensure the security of all.

MAKING THE GRADE

Can you see why the radical-left view seeks greater changes than the liberal view?

a "me first" culture that makes many younger people unwilling to take on family responsibilities. Conservatives also part ways with feminists on this issue, claiming that feminism encourages women to view the family as less important than the workplace (Sommers, 2003).

Another important conservative value is planning for the future. Conservatives argue that people of all ages should take responsibility for their own old age by planning ahead and saving. With a long-tem and disciplined savings plan, people will maximize the resources they have available for their old age.

All this is consistent with the conservative desire for limited government. Almost all conservatives support Social Security, although many have argued for allowing people to invest some of their money in private accounts in order to earn a larger return. Although Social Security reform has not yet been passed, both Republicans and Democrats did join together to support an extension of Medicare to help pay for prescription drugs. At the same time, conservatives claim that we need to control government spending for other social programs. One way to do this is to limit or even cut off government benefits to well-off seniors who do not need them, a proposal that also has support among some liberals. In the process, as the number of seniors rises in the years to come, more money will be available within Social Security for those who need it the most.

Liberals: More Government Assistance

As liberals see it, there are many serious problems related to aging in the United States. Liberals reject the conservative position, which basically asks individuals and families to solve these problems for themselves. Liberals point out that many older people—especially those who have faced prejudice and discrimination their whole lives—simply don't have the opportunity to earn the money they need to carry them through old age.

Liberals also remind us that especially these days, many of today's families depend on the earnings of both spouses just to meet their own needs. How, then, can we expect them also to support aging parents? In addition to the financial burdens, many younger adults (especially women) come home tired from a day of work. Stretched to the limit trying meet the needs of their children, they cannot easily provide the care needed by family elders.

Few older people want to depend on their children; indeed, the greatest fear of many older people is becoming a burden to their children. To help seniors remain independent, liberals conclude, the solution is not to limit social programs for the elderly but to expand them. Programs that extend medical care coverage to all, programs that make affordable housing available to more people, programs that make public transportation more widespread and friendly to older people—these are the "solutions" that would dramatically improve the quality of life for elders as well as their children.

The Radical Left: Capitalism and the Elderly

Radicals on the left have focused more on inequality based on class, race, and gender than on age stratification. But a radical analysis of aging was developed by Steven Spitzer (1980). Following Karl Marx, Spitzer argues that capitalist societies have an overriding focus on profits. For this reason, the culture of capitalism devalues any category of people that is economically less productive. To the extent that elderly people do not work—and to the extent that elders depend on pensions and other benefits—they are viewed as a costly burden. This is the reason so many people tend to view elderly people in negative terms and push them to the margins of society.

From the radical-left point of view, the solution to ageism and other problems of inequality is to take the radical step of replacing the capitalist economy with one that values and serves all people. In short, a socialist economy would lessen all dimensions of inequality, including age stratification.

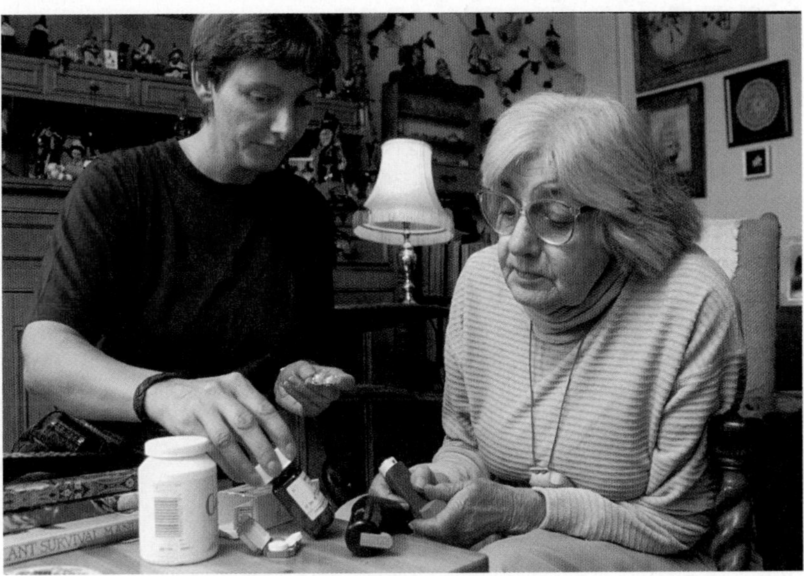

Conservatives believe that families should provide care as their members grow old. Liberals look to government to expand social programs that benefit seniors. Which political viewpoint do you think seniors themselves prefer? Why?

MAKING THE GRADE

Use the table below to review the three political approaches to understanding aging.

SOCIAL PROBLEMS in Everyday Life

Overall, do you think problems involving older people will be greater or less fifty years from now? Explain.

LEFT TO RIGHT

The Politics of Aging

	RADICAL-LEFT VIEW	LIBERAL VIEW	CONSERVATIVE VIEW
WHAT IS THE PROBLEM?	Age stratification is one dimension of the striking social inequality caused by the capitalist U.S. economy.	Elders face a higher risk of poverty, as well as prejudice and discrimination based on their age, sometimes in combination with disadvantages based on class, race, and gender.	Although some seniors are poor, in general, older people do not face a host of social problems. In the United States, elders are more prosperous and live longer than they did in the past.
WHAT IS THE SOLUTION?	Replacing the capitalist economy with a socialist system would end the practice of devaluing less productive people. Government must provide for the well-being of people of all ages.	Government programs (including Social Security and laws banning age discrimination) are crucial to meeting the needs of the rising elder population.	A culture of self-reliance will encourage most people to provide for their own old age; families should support elder members as necessary, and government programs should be a last resort.

JOIN THE DEBATE

1. To what extent, as radicals, liberals, and conservatives see it, are U.S. elders disadvantaged? What problems involving the elderly does each political position identify?
2. Compared to inequality based on gender, race, and class, how serious a problem do you think age-based inequality is? Provide specific facts to support your argument.
3. Of the three political analyses of aging and inequality included here, which do you find most convincing? Why?

Going On from Here

This chapter has explained that older people suffer from a number of problems, including prejudice and discrimination, social isolation, poverty, and inadequate housing. Historically, as industrial societies raised living standards for everyone, they reduced the social standing of their oldest members. Given this trend, what can we expect in the future?

Looking ahead, perhaps the most important fact to keep in mind is the steadily rising share of elders in the U.S. population. Perhaps even more than women, African Americans, and other disadvantaged categories, elders are well organized and very active politically: As noted earlier, people over age sixty-five are three times more likely to vote than those aged eighteen to twenty-four. It is no surprise, then, that most politicians listen to the concerns of older people.

The greatest test for the elderly of tomorrow is likely to be the Social Security system. It seems simple enough: Working people pay into the system, and retired people collect benefits. Yet the rapid increase in the elderly population of the United States is placing demands on Social Security as never before. In 1950, there were six workers for every retired person. By 2050, projections indicate that there will be just two workers for every retiree, and most analysts believe that the current system will be bankrupt before then. The strength of Social Security is especially important to African Americans and Latinos, who are more likely to depend on the system for income in old age than non-Hispanic whites. The challenge is to ensure the financial security of all older people without placing an unfair burden on the young (Riche, 2000; Gendell, 2002; Andrews, 2005).

As government officials debate the future of Social Security, some critics—especially conservatives—point to the many older people who are well-off. They see the solution as cutting future Social Security benefits to well-off people who do not need government help as well as letting people set up private investment accounts. Liberals claim that more tax revenues must flow into Social Security to keep the current system operating. Radicals argue that basic change must produce greater equality for everyone, regardless of age.

Most seniors are keenly interested in this debate. With their substantial political clout, today's seniors—and those of tomorrow—may have the power to bring about changes needed to improve their lives.

DEFINING SOLUTIONS

Whose responsibility is it to support you in your old age?

This chapter has explained people age sixty-five and older, on average, face declining income and rising risk of poverty. The solution to this problem, as always, reflects people's political attitudes. Look at the photos below, which show two general approaches to defining the solution.

HINT

Everyone who is lucky enough to live to old age will face the challenge of paying the costs of housing, food, and medical care. The question that our society wrestles with is how we should meet this challenge. In general, conservatives claim that individuals should take responsibility for themselves. From this point of view, people must ensure that they will have the resources they need—through working and a systematic plan to save for their retirement. Liberals claim that self-reliance is fine for well-off people, but what about those who have not been able to earn enough? From their point of view, a government-centered approach is best. How conservative or liberal you are on this issue may come down to this: To what extent do you think higher-income people should help provide economic security for lower-income people?

Back in 1935, our society decided that government should provide part of the solution to economic security in old age. When President Franklin Delano Roosevelt signed the Social Security Bill as a cornerstone of his "New Deal," he established old age pensions funded out of the earnings of younger workers. Today, however, as the ratio of older people (receiving benefits) to younger workers (paying into the system) keeps going up, the Social Security system needs more money—a problem that could be solved by raising Social Security taxes or by eliminating benefits to elderly people who are well-off. But the idea that the government should ensure everyone's basic economic security still has strong support from liberals.

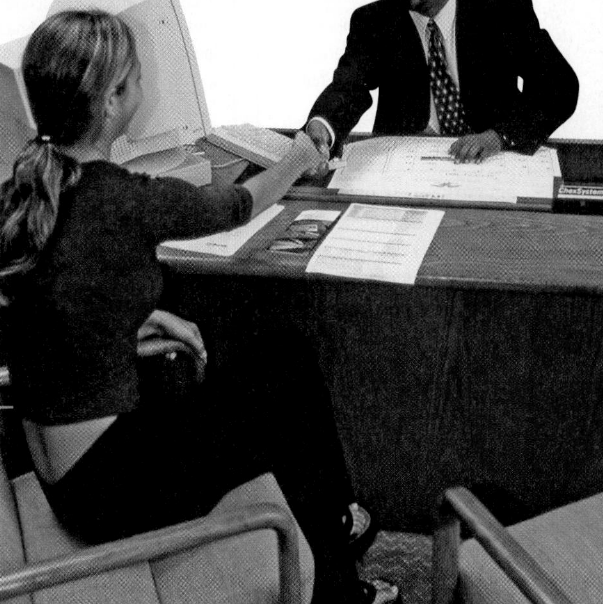

Shouldn't you take responsibility for yourself? If you are more conservative, you are likely to see meeting your needs in old age (or, for that matter, at any age) as mostly your own responsibility. We expect people to give and receive support from family members. But, from this point of view, the solution to economic security in old age lies in personal financial planning and disciplined savings, and the earlier you get started the better.

Getting Involved: Applications & Exercises

1. Talk to someone who grew up in a culture outside the United States. Ask how members of that culture view the life course, and note how childhood and old age differ from what we understand.
2. Visit a senior citizen center in your community or near your campus. Ask about the social problems common to older people in your community. Why not volunteer to help out at the center once a week? This is an excellent way to get to know older people. Your efforts can be an enriching experience for all involved.
3. Ask your grandparents or other older people you know about their own experiences with aging. What do they say are the joys and sorrows of aging? What can they teach you about the experience of retirement?
4. Although there is more attention to death and dying today, this issue is still something of a social taboo. Are there any courses on your campus that deal with death and dying? Is there any organization such as a hospice in your community? If so, contact the organization to discover the range of services it provides.

MAKING THE GRADE

A DEFINING MOMENT
A Good Death: Cicely Saunders and Hospice p. 131

VISUAL SUMMARY

CHAPTER 5 Aging and Inequality

Growing Old

The **LIFE COURSE** refers to the socially constructed stages that people pass through as they live out their lives. **GERONTOLOGY** is the study of old age, the final stage in the life course.

p. 116

AGING is a biological fact of life, but the experience of growing old—and how people define "old"—is shaped by society.

- Preindustrial societies give most wealth and power to elders.
- Industrial societies confer lower social standing on the elderly.

pp. 116–17

life course (p. 116) the socially constructed stages that people pass through as they live out their lives

gerontology (p. 116) the study of aging and the elderly

gerontocracy (p. 117) a social system that gives a society's oldest members the most wealth, power, and prestige

life expectancy (p. 117) the average life span of a country's population

The Graying of the United States

The **"GRAYING OF THE UNITED STATES"** refers to the increasing share of the U.S. population over age sixty-five.

- People sixty-five to seventy-four—the "younger old"—are typically active and in good health.
- "Older old" people—from seventy-five to eighty-four—experience more health-related problems and need more assistance.
- For the "oldest old"—people over eighty-five—staying healthy is the greatest problem.

pp. 118–20

Problems of Aging

SOCIAL ISOLATION often occurs after retirement or the death of a spouse.

- Social isolation is more common among elderly women, who typically outlive their husbands.

pp. 120–21

POVERTY among elderly people is less common than it was 50 years ago because of improved retirement benefits and Social Security.

- In 2009, 8.9% of people over age 65 were living below the government's poverty line.
- A reflection of age stratification in our society, average income rises through middle age, peaks around age 50, and falls as people enter old age.
- Intersection theory describes the increased risk of poverty for elderly women and minorities.

pp. 125–26

Safe, accessible, and affordable **HOUSING** is a concern for many seniors.

- The United States lacks enough suitable housing to meet the needs of this nation's surging elder population.

pp. 126–28

RETIREMENT is an option in industrialized societies because a productive economy means that not everyone has to work.

- Corporate downsizing often results in forced retirement of older, higher-paid workers.
- Less economic security in recent years has resulted in many people finding themselves financially unable to retire.

p. 121–22

The need for **CAREGIVING** is growing as the share of the U.S population over age 65 steadily increases.

- Today's middle-aged people are a "sandwich generation" who will spend as much time caring for aging parents as they did raising children.

p. 125

The rising cost of **MEDICAL CARE** is a growing concern for all categories of the U.S. population, but it is most pressing among older people.

- Government programs such as Medicare cover only some of the costs of medical care and nursing homes.

p. 128

AGEISM is prejudice and discrimination against older people.

- Ageism involves not just stereotypes but also discrimination in employment and housing.
- Ageism in the mass media casts older women and men in negative, stereotypical roles.

pp. 122–23

ELDER ABUSE, ranging from passive neglect to active verbal, emotional, and physical mistreatment, was recognized as a serious social problem only in the 1980s.

- An estimated 1 million elders suffer serious abuse each year, both from family members and from caretakers in institutional settings.

pp. 123–25

Facing the reality of **DEATH AND DYING** is a challenge of growing old.

- Advances in medical technology that extend life now make death a decision; the right of very ill people to decide when to die is at the heart of the debate over euthanasia and physician-assisted suicide.

pp. 128–30

ageism (p. 122) prejudice and discrimination against older people

caregiving (p. 125) informal and unpaid care provided to a dependent person by family members, other relatives, or friends

age stratification (p. 125) social inequality among various age categories within a society

euthanasia (p. 129) assisting in the death of a person suffering from an incurable disease

hospice (p. 130) homelike care that provides physical and emotional comfort to dying people and their families

Theoretical Analysis: Understanding Aging and Inequality

Structural-Functional Analysis: The Need to Disengage

The **STRUCTURAL-FUNCTIONAL APPROACH** highlights ways in which social patterns help societies operate smoothly.

- *Disengagement theory* argues that society must disengage elders from important roles, passing responsibilities from one generation to the next.

pp. 130–32

Symbolic-Interaction Analysis: Staying Active

The **SYMBOLIC-INTERACTION APPROACH** focuses on the meaning people find in their everyday lives.

- *Activity theory* states that elders who remain involved in many social activities have greater life satisfaction.

pp. 132–33

Social-Conflict Analysis: Age and Inequality

The **SOCIAL-CONFLICT APPROACH** highlights age as a dimension of social stratification.

- Modern societies define elderly people in negative terms, causing both prejudice and discrimination.
- Older women and other minorities, subject not only to ageism but also to sexism and racism, are much more disadvantaged.

p. 133

disengagement theory (p. 130) the idea that modern societies operate in an orderly way by removing people from positions of responsibility as they reach old age

activity theory (p. 133) the idea that people enhance personal satisfaction in old age by keeping up a high level of social activity

See the **Applying Theory** table on page 134.

Politics and Aging: Constructing Problems and Defining Solutions

The Radical Left: Capitalism and the Elderly

- **RADICALS ON THE LEFT** criticize capitalism's emphasis on efficiency and profit, claiming that this is why many look down on older people who are no longer economically productive.
- Radicals on the left believe the way to address poverty and other problems experienced by the elderly is to create a more equal society for the benefit of everyone.

p. 135

Liberals: More Government Assistance

- **LIBERALS** point to social structure, including institutional prejudice and discrimination, as the cause of racial and ethnic inequality.
- Liberals endorse government reforms to promote equality, including enforcement of antidiscrimination laws and affirmative action.

p. 135

Conservatives: More Family Responsibility

- **CONSERVATIVES** point to cultural patterns, such as the importance given to education, as a cause of racial and ethnic inequality.
- Conservatives claim that individuals should be responsible for their social standing; they oppose government policies that treat categories of people differently.

pp. 134–35

See the **Left to Right** table on page 136.

CONSTRUCTING THE PROBLEM

Are you safe from crime?

Despite a downward trend in crime rates, 11 million serious crimes are recorded each year in the United States, and the actual number may be three times that high.

Is violence always wrong?

Our society defines some violence as a problem, but we also rely on violence to solve some problems.

Does our criminal justice system guarantee everyone accused of a crime a fair trial?

About 95 percent of people charged with a crime never stand trial but are sentenced through a plea bargain.

CHAPTER 6

Crime, Violence, and Criminal Justice

CHAPTER OVERVIEW

WHAT ARE THE MOST SERIOUS TYPES OF CRIME? This chapter tracks trends in both violent and property crime. You will learn to profile "street criminals" and recognize how "street crime" differs from "organized crime" and "corporate crime." This chapter also explores the extent of violence in our society and explains when and why violence is defined as either harmful or useful. You wil carry out theoretical analysis of crime and violence and understand the major justifications for punishment. Finally, you will learn how "problems" and "solutions" involving crime and violence reflect people's political attitudes.

The classroom was filled with people who had come to this country full of dreams. But tragically, their hope was snuffed out by an act of unspeakable violence. It was Friday—the end of a long week—at the American Civic Association building in Binghamton, New York. But the people assembled in the classroom were excited to be learning the English language and other information that would allow them to become U.S. citizens. This was a citizenship class for new arrivals, and the students, ranging in age from twenty-two to fifty-seven, were immigrants from Haiti, Brazil, Iraq, Pakistan, the Philippines, and China.

The teacher, an elderly widow volunteering her time, was throwing out questions to the class: Who was the first U.S. president? How many stripes are on the U.S. flag? Suddenly, a forty-one-year-old man walked into the room carrying two handguns. He began shooting and methodically struck down each and every person there. In barely a minute, thirteen people were dead and four more lay wounded. Then the gunman turned a gun on himself.

In the days that followed the 2009 killings, the nation wondered why this man—an immigrant himself—would have cut short the lives of so many others. Looking back, he seemed to have lived a lonely and frustrated life; he had lost his job and may have wanted to have a moment of power and importance. As always in such cases, however, there are no easy answers. All that the family and friends of those who died could hope for was the strength to carry on. Two days later, at the first of the funerals, the minister looked at the solemn crowd and said softly, "Let the healing begin" (Bello & Hampson, 2009; Von Drehle, 2009).

This chapter examines the problem of crime in the United States, asking what crime is, how much takes place, and who the offenders are. Special attention is given to violence, including the violent crime that causes a great deal of fear among the public. Finally, we shall examine how our society responds to violations of the law through the criminal justice system, and we shall assess how good a solution this system is to the crime problem. Let us begin by defining several important terms.

Norms, Law, and Crime

All societies make rules defining what people should and should not do. **Norms** are *rules and expectations by which a society guides the behavior of its members.* Many everyday norms are informal and are enforced with just a verbal comment, a raised eyebrow, or some other nonverbal expression. A stricter type of norm is a **law**, a *norm formally created through a society's political system.* Most laws are enacted by a legislature (such as Congress), although laws also come into being through executive orders (by a local mayor, state governor, or national president) and through international treaties.

Law includes both civil and criminal statutes. *Civil law* defines the legal rights and relationships involving individuals and businesses. Civil law comes into play when, say, one person sues another after an automobile accident. *Criminal law* defines people's responsibilities to uphold public order. After an accident, for example, a driver who is found to be drunk is likely to face arrest for a criminal violation. So civil law involves harm or loss leading to a financial settlement, and violations of criminal law involve arrest and punishment.

Crime is *the violation of a criminal law enacted by the federal, state, or local government.* Federal laws apply everywhere in the United States, and state and local laws apply within limited areas or jurisdictions. There are two major categories of crimes. A **misdemeanor** is *a less serious crime punishable by less than one year in prison.* A **felony** is *a more serious crime punishable by at least one year in prison.*

In deciding whether a person has committed a crime, courts must establish not only what the person did but also the

norms rules and expectations by which a society guides the behavior of its members

law a norm formally created through a society's political system

crime the violation of a criminal law enacted by the federal, state, or local government

misdemeanor a less serious crime punishable by less than one year in prison

felony a more serious crime punishable by at least one year in prison

person's *intent*, that is, what the person meant to do. For example, a court can classify a killing in many ways, ranging from self-defense (in which someone acts with deadly force but with the intent to escape serious injury or death) to murder in the first degree (in which someone plans and carries out the killing of another person).

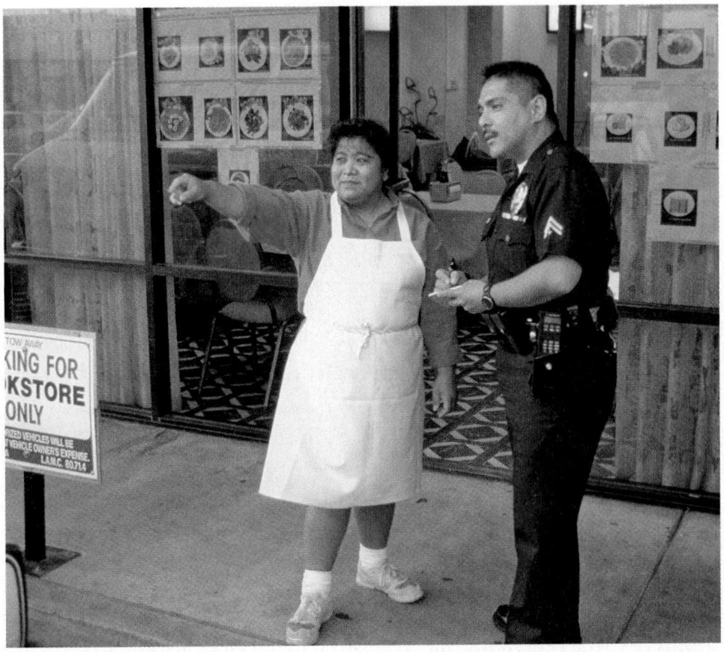

Crime represents a special category of wrongdoing—the breaking of formally enacted laws. The response to crime is also formal, typically involving citizen reports to police. Here a woman who witnessed a robbery gives information to a police officer.

Crime: The Extent of the Problem

Surveys show that most people in the United States consider crime to be a serious problem (NORC, 2007). Police record some 11 million serious crimes each year. At some time during our lives, most people living in the United States will be victimized by crime (Federal Bureau of Investigation, 2006). Because crime is common, as well as widely reported in the mass media, there is widespread fear of crime in this country. In fact, fear of crime is itself a social problem because it limits the things people do and the places they go. For example, more than one-third of U.S. adults say they are afraid to walk alone at night in their own communities (NORC, 2007).

Crime Statistics

Police departments across the country make regular reports to the Federal Bureau of Investigation (FBI), which compiles an annual book titled *Crime in the United States: Uniform Crime Reports* (UCR). This book includes data on felonies or serious crimes of two types. The first is **crime against property**, which is *crime that involves theft of property belonging to others.* Crimes against property include burglary, larceny-theft, motor vehicle theft, and arson. The second type is **crime against persons**, *crime that involves violence or the threat of violence against others.* Crimes against persons include murder and manslaughter, aggravated assault, forcible rape, and robbery. Table 6–1 on page 144 defines all of these serious crimes.

The UCR data are certainly useful, but there are two reasons to view these statistics with caution. First, the UCR includes only crimes known to the police. But how many crimes are not reported? To answer this question, the FBI conducts the annual National Crime Victimization Survey. Researchers ask a random sample of the U.S. population whether they have been victims of serious crime within the past year. A comparison of survey responses with official crime reports suggests that less than half of serious crimes are reported to the police. Realistically, then, a complete tally might show that as many as 25 million offenses actually occur each year (U.S. Department of Justice, 2009).

A second concern about the UCR is that it gathers statistics on "street crimes" but not more "elite crimes," which include business fraud, corruption, price fixing, and illegal dumping of toxic wastes, all likely to be committed by rich people and often at the direction of corporate executives. When we put these shortcomings together, we see that the UCR not only underestimates the actual extent of street crime but also gives a biased picture of the typical criminal based on only one kind of crime.

Violent Crime: Patterns and Trends

Violent crimes, that is, crimes against persons, account for just 12 percent of all serious offenses; crimes against property account for the remaining 88 percent. Put differently, the crime rate for property offenses is about seven times higher than that for violent crimes against persons (U.S. Department of Justice, 2008). Figure 6–1 on page 145 shows the rates (the number of reported crimes per 100,000 people) for both crimes against persons and crimes against property.

From 1960 until the early 1990s, the rate of violent crime rose quickly. After that, the trend turned downward. (The rate of property offenses also went up after 1960, with a downturn in the early 1980s and further decline through 2007.) What

crime against property (p. 143) crime that involves theft of property belonging to others

crime against persons (p. 143) crime that involves violence or the threat of violence against others

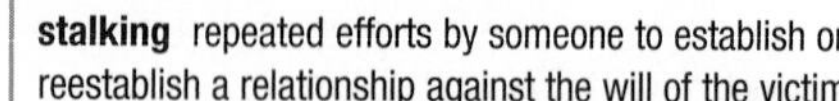

stalking repeated efforts by someone to establish or reestablish a relationship against the will of the victim

Table 6–1 Serious Crime in the *Uniform Crime Reports*

	Crimes Against Property
Burglary	The unlawful entry of a structure to commit a [serious crime] or theft
Larceny-theft	The unlawful taking, carrying, leading, or riding away of property from the possession . . . of another
Motor vehicle theft	The theft or attempted theft of a motor vehicle
Arson	Any willful or malicious burning or attempting to burn . . . the personal property of another
	Crimes Against Persons
Murder or nonnegligent manslaughter	The willful (nonnegligent) killing of one human being by another
Aggravated assault	An unlawful attack by one person upon another for the purpose of inflicting severe or aggravated bodily injury
Forcible rape	The carnal knowledge of a female forcibly and against her will
Robbery	The taking or attempting to take anything of value from the care, custody, or control of a person or persons by force or threat of force or violence and/or by putting the victim in fear

Source: U.S. Department of Justice (2008).

accounts for the drop in crime rates? Analysts point to a number of factors, including a strong economy during the 1990s; we should expect the economic recession that began in 2008 to push crime rates higher once again. In addition, the downward trend in crime reflects a drop in the use of crack cocaine, the hiring of more police, and tougher sentences for criminal convictions (Fagan, Zimring, & Kim, 1998; Witkin, 1998; K. Johnson, 2000). We now turn to take a closer look at trends for each offense covered by the UCR.

Murder

In 2007, police recorded 16,929 murders, which means that on average, across the United States, a murder took place every thirty-one minutes.[1] Looking back in time, however, the U.S. murder rate has been falling since 1993, and it now stands at about the same level as in it did back in 1960 (U.S. Department of Justice, 2008).

The FBI also tracks the percentage of murders that are "cleared," meaning that the police arrested someone for the crime, whether or not that person was later found to be guilty. In 2007, police made arrests in 61 percent of all reported murders (U.S. Department of Justice, 2008).

Most murder victims (78 percent in 2007) are males. African Americans (about 13 percent of the population) are at especially high risk: The FBI reports that 49 percent of murder victims are black, 47 percent are white, and the remainder are of other races. The statistics also show that murder is an intraracial crime, meaning that offenders and victims typically are of the same race. In 90 percent of cases involving an African American victim, the arrested suspect is of the same race; the same is true in 81 percent of cases involving a white victim (U.S. Department of Justice, 2008).

FBI data show that for murder cases in which the relationship of the victim to the offender could be determined, 76 percent of victims knew the offender. Furthermore, in 22 percent of the cases, victim and offender were actually related. A relationship between the victim and the offender is especially likely when the murder victim is a woman: 13 percent of female victims were slain by husbands or boyfriends, but just 4 percent of male victims were killed by wives or girlfriends (U.S. Department of Justice, 2008).

Many cases of homicide also include a history of the killer stalking the victim (Lowney & Best, 1995). **Stalking** is defined as *repeated efforts by someone to establish or reestablish a relationship against the will of the victim.* One study found that about 3.4 million people say they have been stalked during the past year, and in some cases the stalking went on for five years or more. About 80 percent of these victims are women. Men (in most cases, celebrities) are usually stalked by strangers, but women are almost always stalked by people they know—in most cases, by former husbands or boyfriends. Most stalkers threaten their victims, some vandalize property, some harm or kill pets, and a few end up engaging in deadly violence (U.S. Department of Justice, 2008). The Social Policy box on page 146 takes a closer look at how stalking came to be defined as a serious social problem.

One factor that plays a part in the high murder rate in the United States is the availability of firearms. Two-thirds of mur-

[1]Time data of this kind exaggerate the amount of crime. A murder occurs, on average, every thirty-one minutes, not in any one community but somewhere throughout the United States. The best way to use time data is to make comparisons to gain a sense of which crimes are more common than others and by how much.

GETTING INVOLVED

Does fear of crime affect choices you make or the way you live? How?

MAKING THE GRADE

Notice that property crimes are much more common than violent crimes.

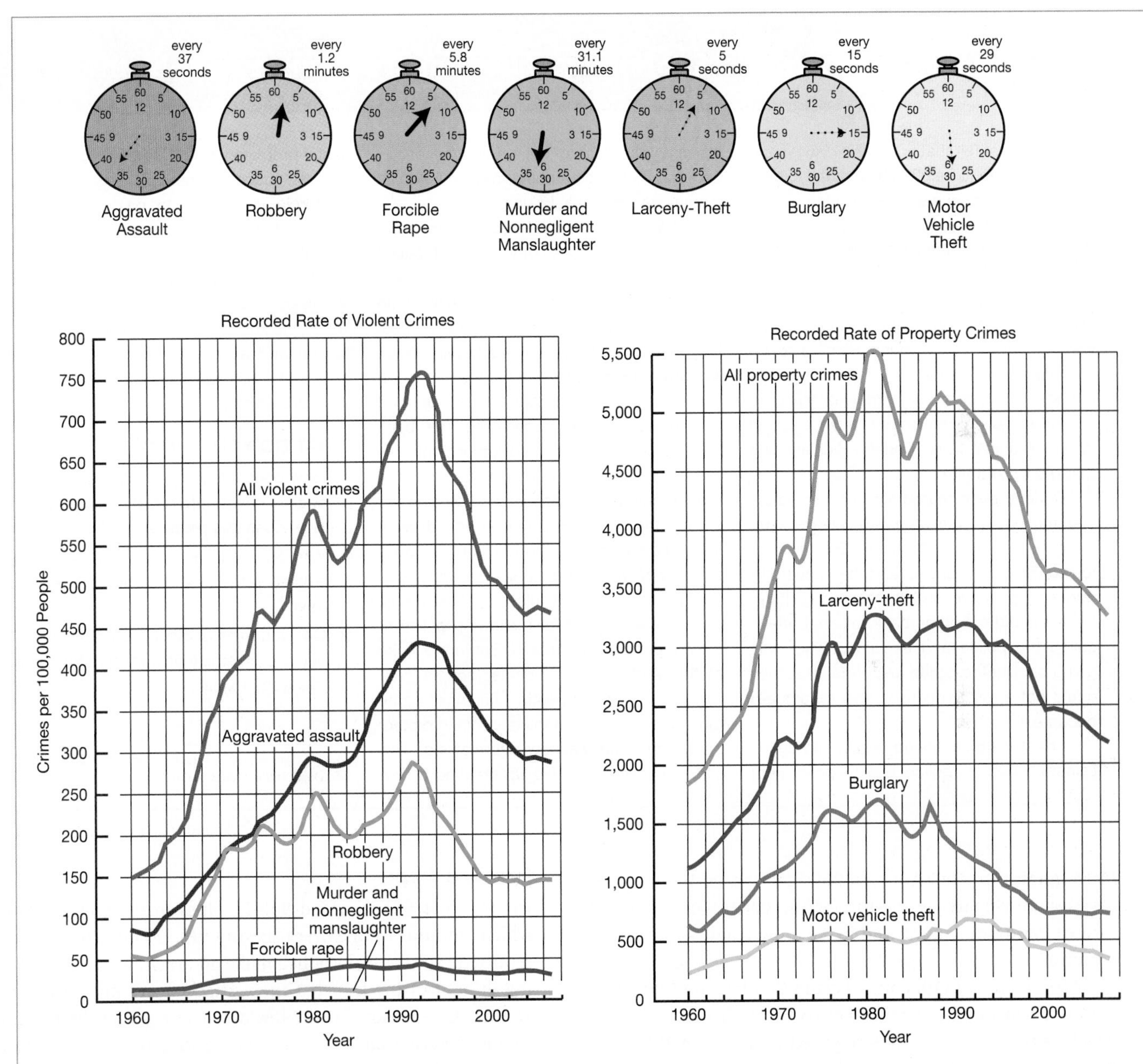

FIGURE 6–1 Crime Rates in the United States, 1960–2007

The graphs represent crime rates for various violent crimes and property crimes between 1960 and 2007. "Crime clocks," shown at the top of the figure, are another way of describing the frequency of crimes.

Source: Federal Bureau of Investigation (2008).

der victims die as a result of shootings. There are as many guns as adults in the United States—more than 200 million in all—40 percent of which are handguns, the typical weapon in these cases (Brady Campaign, 2008).

People who favor stricter government control of firearms argue that easy availability of handguns goes a long way toward making violence in the United States so deadly. For example, the man who carried out the classroom shootings

MAKING THE GRADE

The box below illustrates how a social problem is socially constructed as part of a social movement.

SOCIAL PROBLEMS in Everyday Life

Do you think the way our society defines masculinity encourages violence? Explain how violence may be a gender issue.

SOCIAL POLICY

Stalking: The Construction of a Problem

Have you ever felt that you are in danger and no one is there to help? That was the experience of a woman we will call Darlene. This is a story of crime and violence, and it is also the story of how our society came to define a social problem.

Darlene had been living with Richard for about two years. Their relationship started off well enough; Darlene found Richard to be charming and kind. But gradually he changed, and soon Richard was trying to control her every movement, often erupting in fits of anger when Darlene did anything that displeased him.

Darlene soon feared for her own safety and moved out, staying with relatives and trying to steer clear of Richard. But this only fueled Richard's anger, and he repeatedly tracked her down and threatened to harm her if she did not come back to him. Darlene called the police and explained what was going on. But the police responded that they could not arrest Richard unless he actually became violent.

The threats continued. Again and again, Darlene called the police. But the police kept insisting that Richard had not broken any law and that there was nothing they could do as long as he was "only talking."

As you can probably guess, the story ended violently. One day, Richard called Darlene to say he was leaving town and wanted to pick up some things from her. With a sense of relief, Darlene agreed to meet Richard in front of her aunt's house. When Richard arrived, she walked to the street and handed him a box. Suddenly, he exploded with rage. Darlene turned and ran back toward the house. Richard jumped into his van, drove up over the curb and across the lawn, running down Darlene and pinning her against the house. Her family looked on in horror as bricks from the front of the house tumbled down around her lifeless body.

This murder took place in the 1980s, when there were no laws allowing police to protect people like Darlene. But in the wake of this and similar incidents, people concerned about domestic violence came together, claiming that the law should protect victims of what we now call stalking. This social movement ended up creating a new social problem. In 1990, the movement had its first success when activists convinced California lawmakers to pass the nation's first antistalking law.

Efforts to define stalking as a social problem spread across the country. Within a few years, every state enacted a similar law. Today, victims of stalkers can get police protection and a court order demanding that people like Richard stay away from them or face arrest and jail.

WHAT DO YOU THINK?

1. How does this story illustrate the way society constructs social problems? How does this process usually work?
2. Why do you think no law of this kind existed in the United States before 1990?
3. Can you think of other examples of social problems that were constructed in this way? Explain.

Sources: Tjaden (1997), Tjaden & Thoennes (1998), and U.S. Department of Justice (2008).

in Binghamton, New York, in 2009 purchased the handguns he used at a nearby gun store (Hill, 2009). Greater regulation of handguns might well make these tragic shootings less common.

Opponents of gun control claim that law-abiding citizens who wish to buy guns willingly go through the background checks and waiting periods required by law (the 1993 Brady Bill), but such controls do little to keep weapons out of the hands of criminals, who typically get guns illegally. Some critics of gun control go further and argue that gun ownership actually reduces crime by making people who might be thinking about robbing a store or breaking into a home stop to think about whether someone inside might be armed. In any case, gun control is no magic bullet: The number of Californians killed each year by weapons other than guns is greater than the number of Canadians killed by all weapons (Currie, 1985; R. Wright, 1995; Lott, 2000; Statistics Canada, 2008; U.S. Department of Justice, 2008).

Forcible Rape

In 2007, the FBI recorded 90,427 rapes in the United States, which amounts to one every six minutes. In only 26 percent of reported rape cases do police make an arrest, which is surprising in light of the fact that most attackers are known to their victims. One reason for the low arrest rate is that the fear and shame experienced by some women discourages them from reporting the crime. Efforts by colleges and universities to educate women and men about "date rape"—sexual assault in which the offender and victim know one another—have encouraged more victims to come forward in recent years. Even so, across the country, only about 42 percent of women who are raped make a report to the police.

The FBI statistics do not include attempted rape, nor do they include sex with a minor (typically a person under eighteen) when no force is used, which is a crime known as *statutory rape*. In addition, rape statistics do not reflect attacks on males, even though some researchers have found that male rape victims suffer greater

SOCIAL PROBLEMS in Everyday Life

Do you think most rapes that occur on or near your campus are reported? Do you think most victims of rape who report this crime go to the police or to college authorities?

GETTING INVOLVED

Is there one or more guns in the home where you live? Explain why or why not.

physical injury than women (U.S. Department of Justice, 2008). The Personal Stories box on page 148 takes a closer look at the problem of rape in men's prisons.

Aggravated Assault

Aggravated assault is the most common crime against a person, accounting for nearly two-thirds of all reported violent crime. Despite a downward trend in the assault rate after 1991, police recorded 855,856 aggravated assaults in 2007, which works out to one every thirty-seven seconds. Police make arrests in 51 percent of reported cases. Aggravated assault is a very male crime: A large majority of both victims and offenders are young men (U.S. Department of Justice, 2008).

Robbery

Robbery involves both stealing and threatening another person, making this act both a property crime and a violent crime. In 2007, there were 445,125 robberies, with one occurring somewhere in the United States every minute. Since 1991, the general trend in the robbery rate has been downward.

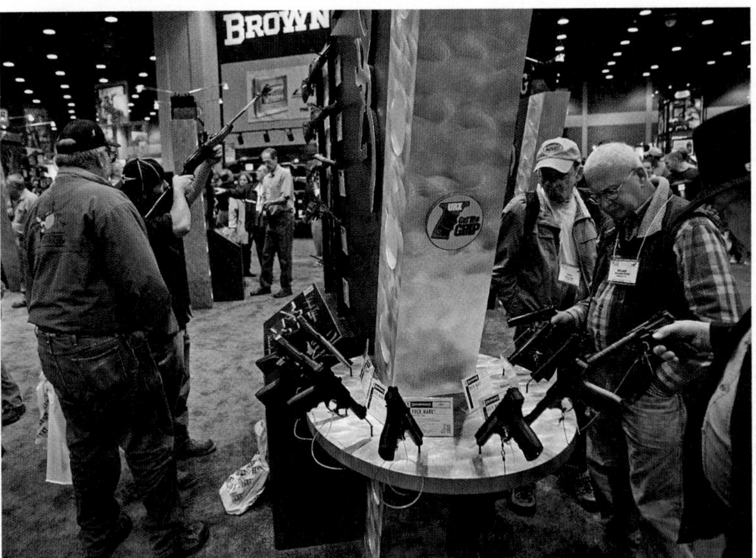

To what extent does the availability of firearms contribute to this country's high rate of violent crime? Especially since the election of President Obama, gun sales have been brisk, perhaps driven by a concern that tighter controls on firearms are coming. Supporters of the constitutional right to bear arms consider gun ownership to be a basic freedom. Critics, however, claim that being able to reach for a gun often turns violence deadly.

Because the victims usually do not know the robbers, this crime is the least likely of all violent offenses to result in an arrest: In 2007, police cleared just 29 percent of robberies. Again, almost all offenders are males, and most are under age twenty-five. Race is also a factor in robbery: In 2007, African Americans accounted for 57 percent of arrests, whites represented 42 percent, and the remaining 1 percent were classified in some other racial category (U.S. Department of Justice, 2008).

What are your chances of becoming a victim of a violent crime? National Map 6-1 on page 149 shows the risks of violent crime for people living in counties across the United States.

Property Crime: Patterns and Trends

In 2007, law enforcement agencies across the United States recorded 9.8 million property crimes, which is seven times the number of violent crimes. Nationwide, a property crime occurs every three seconds, with annual losses of $18 billion (U.S. Department of Justice, 2008).

In most property crimes, the victim never sees the offender. This is one reason that police make an arrest in only 16 percent of property crimes, compared to 42 percent of reported violent crimes (U.S. Department of Justice, 2008). The following sections provide a brief look at each property crime.

Burglary

Despite a decadelong decline in the burglary rate, there were more than 2 million burglaries in 2007. This translates to one crime every fifteen seconds and an annual total property loss of more than $4 billion (the average loss per burglary is about $2,000).

In 2007, police cleared just 11 percent of burglary cases. Of suspects arrested, 86 percent were male and 59 percent were under the age of twenty-five (U.S. Department of Justice, 2008).

Larceny-Theft

Larceny-theft includes familiar forms of stealing such as shoplifting, picking pockets, purse-snatching, taking property from a motor vehicle, and bicycle theft. Unlike burglary, such cases do not involve "breaking and entering," and offenders typically use no force or violence.

Larceny-theft is the most common of all the serious crimes tracked by the FBI and accounts for 67 percent of the total. In 2007, the FBI reported 6.7 million incidents of larceny-theft, which averages one such crime every five seconds. Even after a recent downward trend, the larceny-theft rate in 2007 was twice as high as it was in 1960. In 2007, the value of lost property from such crimes nationwide was $5.8 billion (an average loss of $886 per incident).

In 2007, law enforcement agencies cleared 18 percent of larceny-theft cases. Most of the suspects arrested were male (60 percent), with females making up the rest (40 percent) (U.S. Department of Justice, 2008).

SOCIAL PROBLEMS in Everyday Life

Were you aware of the problem of rape in prison? Do you think the public is concerned about this issue or not? Why?

MAKING THE GRADE

Using crime theories in this chapter, can you explain the fact that young people commit such a large share of serious crimes?

PERSONAL STORIES

Rape: Memories That Don't Go Away

David Pittman was eighteen the first time he went to jail for robbing a convenience store. A big man (6 feet 2 inches tall and 180 pounds), David entered prison thinking he could take care of himself. He was wrong. Within days of being jailed while awaiting his trial, David was repeatedly gang-raped. He felt ashamed and powerless and filled with rage. Eighteen years later—and back in jail again—he has joined a therapy group with others who have been through the same ordeal. The following account is based on the story he posted on the Internet in the hope that it might help others.

> Prison life is so negative and repressive that prisoners look anywhere to relieve loneliness and despair. Some guys decide it's better to be an abuser than a victim. To them, survival and dominance are everything. They get pleasure by dominating and humiliating others. But their victims are traumatized for life.
>
> When I got to jail, there were twenty guys in my "tank," which was split into two ten-man "pods." Each pod had five bunks with a day room between them. My first night in jail, three men approached me. Two were about my size; the third was 20 pounds lighter and 6 inches shorter. They asked what I was in for. I told them, and the biggest guy asked if I had ever been f—ed. I said, "No, and I'm not planning on it." He said, "We're gonna f—you." I was scared out of my mind. I swung at him, but he blocked my punch and his buddy knocked me down. They grabbed me by the hair and slammed my head into the floor, knocking me out.
>
> When I came to, I was on my stomach. They had pulled my pants off and spread my legs wide apart. One guy was sitting on each leg, and the biggest guy was lying on my back. He was slapping me in the face to wake me up. He said, "I want you to feel this." When I was fully conscious, he raped me. I never felt such pain in my life. I tried to get away, but it was no use. It seemed like he took forever. When he was finished, he switched places with another guy. When it was over, all three had raped me. When they were done, they held me in a head lock while they debated whether to kill me. They asked if I was going to snitch. I knew they'd kill me if I said yes, so I said, "No." They threatened to kill me if I said anything. I thought my life was over.
>
> I was completely numb inside. I didn't know what to do. My father always taught me to handle my own problems. Navy boot camp reinforced that lesson. I was from another state and didn't know a soul in California. I was terrified and filled with shame. I had no choice but to keep my mouth shut. I was paralyzed with fear.
>
> That night, the same three guys came to my bunk. I was their "punk" now, and fighting wouldn't do any good. They'd just beat me up worse than before. I was like a robot. I did exactly what they told me to do. I didn't think about it. I just did it. Going along was better than getting killed. After that, other guys started waking me up at night, demanding sex. It was established in the tank that I was a sex toy. I just did what I was told to avoid a beating. I figured I better make the best of things and try to endure it the best I could. Finally, I went to trial. I was found guilty and sent to prison.
>
> In prison, I'd fight anyone at the drop of a hat and got in a lot of trouble. After I got out of prison, I was just as bad on the street. I wasn't going to be anybody's punk again. Today I'm doing life for killing a guy who threatened me. I'm 6 feet 2 inches tall and weigh 250 pounds. I'm a power lifter, and I run with some of the meanest guys in the joint. None of my friends would believe I'd ever been a punk. It's been eighteen years since that experience in county jail.
>
> Rape is a horrible act, whether it's of a man or a woman. I know the helplessness, shame, guilt, self-doubt, self-blame, and terror. But for me, the greatest fear was that someone I knew would find out. In some ways, male rape is worse than female rape, because men have no one they can talk to. Even my wife laughed at me when I tried to tell her about my experiences. Most guys bottle everything up inside, where it just turns to rage. Male rape probably causes a lot of alcohol and drug abuse, and it's probably led to the murder of men who have threatened a male rape victim.

WHAT DO YOU THINK?

1. Why does our society do little to combat the problem of rape in prison?
2. What would you do to address the problem of prison rape? Explain why.
3. Do you think men inside prison walls rape for the same reason that men on the outside rape women? Explain your answer.

Source: Adapted from Pittman (2001) with permission of Stop Prisoner Rape, Inc.

Motor Vehicle Theft

Here again, the recent past shows a downward trend in this crime. Yet, despite the decline, the number of motor vehicle thefts—including stealing cars, trucks, buses, motorcycles, and snowmobiles—still exceeded 1 million in 2007. Nationally, one motor vehicle theft took place every twenty-nine seconds. The FBI estimated losses in 2007 at $7.4 billion (an average loss of $6,755).

Sam Pearson, who lives in Renville County, North Dakota, rarely locks his doors when he leaves the house.

Serge Shuman, who lives in Mecklenburg County, North Carolina, knows many people who have been victims of crime and avoids going out at night.

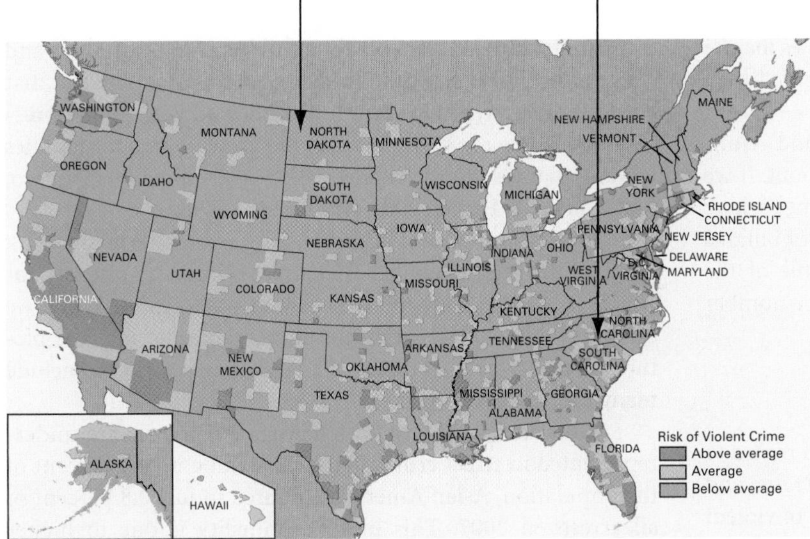

A Nation of Diversity

NATIONAL MAP 6–1

The Risk of Violent Crime across the United States

The map shows the risk of falling victim to violent crime—in this case including murder, rape, and robbery but not aggravated assault—for all counties across the United States. In most places, the risk is below the national average, suggesting that violent crime is concentrated in certain areas of the country. Can you explain the pattern?

Source: CAP Index, Inc. (2009).

In 2007, police cleared just 11 percent of motor vehicle thefts. More than 50 percent of those arrested were under age twenty-five, and 82 percent were males (U.S. Department of Justice, 2008).

Arson

Police and fire investigators determine whether a suspicious fire was caused by arson. The FBI does not have data on arson for the entire country, but some studies suggest that millions of cases of arson occur annually, a rate that has remained about the same in recent years. The FBI reports that the average loss in arson cases comes to about $17,000, typically a much greater loss than in other types of property crime.

In 2007, police cleared 27 percent of known cases of arson. Again, of suspects arrested, 84 percent were male, and 67 percent were under age twenty-five (U.S. Department of Justice, 2008).

"Street Crime": Who Are the Criminals?

Using FBI data, we can "profile" the typical street criminal in terms of age, gender, social class, race, and ethnicity. Keep in mind that this profile is based not on courtroom convictions but on arrest data.

Age

For all offenses, there is strong link between getting arrested and being young. Arrest rates for both violent crime and property crime are highest in the late teens and fall steadily among older people. In the United States, people aged fifteen to twenty-four make up just 14 percent of the population, but in 2007, they accounted for 41 percent of arrests for violent crimes and 47 percent of arrests for property crimes (U.S. Department of Justice, 2008).

Gender

Men make up about half of the general population, but in 2007, they accounted for 67 percent of arrests for property crimes. This means that police arrest men for property crimes more than twice as often as they arrest women. For violent crimes, gender is even more important: Men represent 82 percent of all arrests, almost five times as many as women.

Women show up more often in the arrest data for certain crimes, including larceny-theft (40 percent of arrests are of women), fraud (44 percent), embezzlement (52 percent), runaway youth (56 percent), and prostitution (68 percent). In addition, for all serious crimes, the gender gap is narrowing: From 1996 to 2007, the number of arrests of women *increased* 7 percent, while arrests of men *fell* by 6 percent (U.S. Department of Justice, 2008).

Social Class

Because there is no easy measure of someone's social class, the FBI does not track the class standing of people arrested for serious crime. But sociological research shows that people of lower social position are involved in most arrests for street crime (Thornberry & Farnsworth, 1982; Wolfgang, Thornberry, & Figlio, 1987; Reiman, 1998).

Crime and violence are serious problems in many low-income neighborhoods. But it is important to remember that most people who live in these neighborhoods obey the law. The sociologist Elijah Anderson (1994, 2002) conducted field research in Philadelphia and has found that inner-city neighborhood to

MAKING THE GRADE

Be sure to pay attention to the fact that whites represent 59 percent of all arrests for serious crimes.

juvenile delinquency violation of the law by young people

contain mostly decent, hardworking families. Crime rates may be high in such communities, but most crime is committed by a small number of repeat offenders.

Keep in mind also that the link between class and criminality depends on the type of crime we are talking about. If we consider not just street crime but the types of crimes where "investment advisers" like Bernard Madoff steal tens of billions of dollars from people and organizations, our profile of the "common criminal" suddenly includes a much larger number of rich people.

Race and Ethnicity

Both race and ethnicity are linked to crime rates. With regard to property crime, whites represent 68 percent of all arrests, and African Americans account for 30 percent. In the case of violent crime, whites represent 59 percent of arrests and African Americans 39 percent. In terms of actual numbers, then, most "street crime" arrests involve white suspects. But in proportion to their share of the population (about 13 percent), African Americans are more likely than whites to be arrested (U.S. Department of Justice, 2008).

African American men in the United States face a serious problem: Black males are five times more likely than white males to spend time in jail (U.S. Department of Justice, 2008). In fact, one study found that one-third of black men in their twenties were either in jail, on probation (sentenced to a period of time under court supervision), or on parole (under court supervision after being released from prison) (Mauer, 1999).

Why does race play such a large part in the crime picture? First and most important, African Americans have a high poverty rate. More than one-third of all black children grow up in poverty, compared with one in eight white children (U.S. Census Bureau, 2010). For some, a lack of hope for the future breeds hostility toward police and distrust of "the system." As a result, some young people adopt what Elijah Anderson calls the "code of the streets," which endorses crime and violence as a way to survive in a dangerous society.

The second reason for the high arrest rate among people of color is closely related to the first: More police patrols are found in poor neighborhoods, which have a high African American population. Prejudice based on race and class can prompt people to suspect blacks of criminal behavior simply on the basis of skin color (the practice of racial profiling discussed in Chapter 3, "Racial and Ethnic Inequality"). Research suggests that such biases lead police to be quicker to arrest African Americans than whites (Reiman, 1998; Chiricos, McEntire, & Gertz, 2001; Quillian & Pager, 2001).

A third factor linking race and arrest involves family patterns. Two-thirds of black children are born to single mothers, compared with one-third of white children. Single mothers and single fathers have less time to supervise children. The fact that single mothers typically earn less money adds to family pressures. For these reasons, children who grow up in poor families without fathers are at higher risk for criminality (Piquero, MacDonald, & Parker, 2002; Martin et al., 2009).

Once again, when considering all these patterns that link crime with race, remember that street crimes are offenses for which police are likely to arrest low-income people. When we examine white-collar, corporate, and organized crime, the picture of the typical criminal changes dramatically to include many more white people.

A final racial pattern is that Asian Americans are under-represented in street crime statistics. Making up 4.4 percent of the population, Asian Americans figured in just 0.8 percent of all arrests in 2007. This lower criminality is due to higher income levels and also a strong cultural emphasis on family, discipline, and honor, all of which tend to discourage criminal behavior.

Other Dimensions of the Crime Problem

Although street crimes command the greatest attention from the U.S. public, there are many additional types of crime. The following sections address problems of juvenile delinquency, hate crimes, white-collar crime, corporate crime, organized crime, and victimless crimes.

Juvenile Delinquency

Arrest rates make clear that young people play a big part in the U.S. crime problem. **Juvenile delinquency** is *violation of the law by young people* (the precise age of a "juvenile" varies from state to state, but it is generally someone under the age of eighteen). Any violation of criminal law can lead a court to declare a young person delinquent. In addition, some laws—such as curfews and truancy statutes that require school attendance—apply only to the young. Cases involving young people are heard in a *juvenile court,* where the focus is on helping children straighten out rather than simply punishing them.

Similarly, when punishment is applied in juvenile cases, the sentence is usually only until the legal age of adulthood (typically between eighteen and twenty-one), and incarceration takes place at a juvenile detention center rather than an adult prison. The assumption here is that young people are more likely than older offenders to be reformed. Thus the goal of the juvenile justice system is not just to protect the community but also to serve the best interests of youthful offenders.

hate crime a criminal offense against a person, property, or society motivated by the offender's bias against a race, religion, disability, sexual orientation, or ethnicity or national origin

white-collar crime illegal activities conducted by people of high social position during the course of their employment or regular business activities

corporate crime (p. 152) an illegal act committed by a corporation or by persons acting on its behalf

When a young person is charged with a serious offense, such as robbery or murder, however, officials may decide to file adult charges. This means that the suspect is tried in an adult court, sentenced as an adult, held in a juvenile detention center until the legal age of adulthood, and then transferred to an adult prison to serve out the rest of the sentence.

In the past, U.S. courts have also sentenced young people to death. But in 2005, the U.S. Supreme Court ruled that offenders who were under the age of eighteen when they committed their offenses cannot be sentenced to death, whatever their crime.

Larceny-theft—including shoplifting—is the most common of all serious crimes tracked by the FBI. In many cases, stealing is motivated by the "kicks" young people get if they are able to "beat the system." Because of the high-tech surveillance equipment used by stores today, the odds of getting caught are high. How do you think courts respond to offenders who claim that their actions were "only a game"?

Hate Crimes

What we call *hate crimes* were not defined until the mid-1980s, when civil rights groups successfully led campaigns for states to pass laws creating this new category of crime (Jenness & Grattet, 2001). By 2009, forty-five states and the federal government had passed statutes that mandate additional penalties for offenses if they also meet the criteria of a hate crime. According to the FBI, a **hate crime** is *a criminal offense against a person, property, or society motivated by the offender's bias against a race, religion, disability, sexual orientation, or ethnicity or national origin.*

In 1990, Congress passed the Hate Crime Statistics Act, directing the U.S. attorney general to collect data from law enforcement agencies about bias-motivated crimes. In 2007, the government recorded about 7,600 hate crimes. Figure 6–2 on page 152 shows that just over half of hate crimes on record (52.5 percent) involve racial bias (U.S. Department of Justice, 2008).

Many—perhaps even most—hate crimes are not reported. For one thing, some police organizations do not record or submit hate crime data. For another, many victims—particularly gay men and lesbians—are reluctant to report their victimization. For these reasons, the problem of hate crimes is surely greater than official statistics indicate.

The odds of becoming a victim of a hate crime are especially high for people with multiple disadvantages, such as gay men of color. Even so, hate crimes can victimize anyone: The government reports that in 2007, 18 percent of the hate crimes based on race targeted white people (U.S Department of Justice, 2008).

Hate crime laws remain controversial. Critics argue that because acts such as assault are already against the law, special hate crime laws are unnecessary. In addition, because such laws end up punishing people's attitudes toward others, critics view such laws as a step in the direction of government control over not just what we do but also how we think (A. Sullivan, 2002). Supporters of hate crime laws counter that the government must take extra steps to protect categories of people who are targets of hostility and violence. They argue that because hate crimes harm not just a single victim but entire communities, they should bring more severe penalties.

White-Collar Crime

If you watch police "reality" shows on television, it is easy to think that every person arrested for a crime is poor. But there is another side to crime that typically involves people who are much better off. **White-collar crime** refers to *illegal activities conducted by people of high social position during the course of their employment or regular business activities.* White-collar crime occurs in banks and corporations and often involves important members of a community. As compared with crime on the streets, then, white-collar crime is better described as "crime in the suites." The case of Bernard Madoff, convicted of numerous crimes after swindling investors out of at least $50 billion, provides a good example of white-collar crime.

Edwin Sutherland (1940), who pioneered the study of white-collar crime, noted that crimes ranging from fraud (obtaining money under false pretenses) to insider trading (using restricted company information as the basis for a decision to buy or sell stock) to embezzlement (taking money

MAKING THE GRADE

Be sure you understand the difference between white-collar crime and corporate crime.

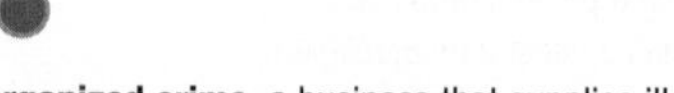

organized crime a business that supplies illegal goods and services

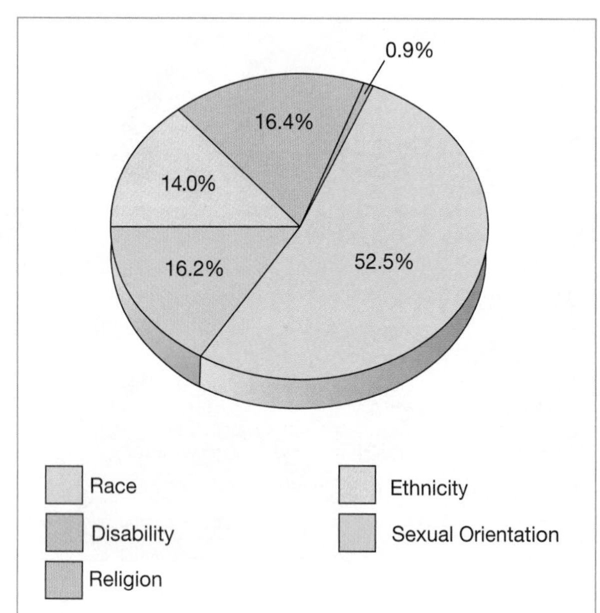

FIGURE 6–2 Bias-Motivated Offenses, 2007

Although the motivations for hate crimes vary, about half of all such crimes express racial bias.

Source: Federal Bureau of Investigation (2008).

illegally from one's employer) are far more common than people imagine.

Sutherland pointed out that the public often pays little attention to white-collar offenses. Historically, he explained, cases of white-collar crime were heard in a civil court rather than a criminal court. This means that the person accused may have to pay damages but is not labeled a criminal and will not go to prison. In today's world, we are all well aware of the Wall Street executives who do bad things—perhaps even breaking the law—but never face a judge or jury. Research confirms that white-collar offenders often get off easy, so that even those who are convicted in a criminal court often serve no jail time. For example, just half of embezzlers convicted in the U.S. District Court system received any jail time at all; the remainder were fined or placed on probation, requiring them to report regularly to a court official (U.S. Department of Justice, 2008). However, corporate scandals from the Enron collapse to the 2008 financial crisis have awakened the public to the dangers and harm of white-collar crime. In recent years, long jail terms have been handed down to dozens of corporate executives and investment company officials, including John Rigas (former CEO of Adelphia Communications, fifteen years) and Bernard Ebbers (former CEO of WorldCom, twenty-five years); Kenneth Lay, Jeffrey Skilling, and other Enron executives; and people running fraudulent investment schemes, including Bernard Madoff, who was sentenced to 150 years in prison in 2009.

Corporate Crime

Business crime can involve not only the actions of individuals working within a company but also the policies and actions of companies themselves. **Corporate crime** is *an illegal act committed by a corporation or by persons acting on its behalf.* One example of corporate crime is *gross negligence*: knowingly producing faulty or dangerous products. In one well-known case from the 1970s, Ford Motor Company continued to produce the subcompact Pinto automobile despite knowledge that a rear-end collision could cause its gas tank to explode. Even after deadly accidents took place, Ford refused to support a recall that would have saved lives, deciding it would be cheaper to pay the legal claims that would result from future accidents. Eventually, lawsuits and public demands forced the recall and brought an end to the Pinto (Kitman, 2003).

Sometimes the line between white-collar crime (acts by individuals) and corporate crime (policies carried out by entire companies) is not clear. This is especially likely when the white-collar crimes are committed by top leaders in a company. In the case of Enron, which misstated its profits and losses so that the company was forced to declare bankruptcy in 2001, nineteen former executives either pleaded guilty or were convicted of crimes. These convicted executives may be viewed as white-collar criminals, but the Enron collapse as a whole is also a case of corporate crime.

The losses due to corporate crime in the United States run into the hundreds of billions of dollars. The Enron case alone involved losses exceeding $50 billion, which is far less than the losses from the collapse of the banking system in 2008, leading to government "bailouts" of well over $1 trillion. Numbers this high are difficult to fully comprehend. But the simple fact is that the cost of white-collar and corporate crime is far greater than the costs of all the property crimes described earlier in this chapter. In terms of dollars, white-collar and corporate crime are the heart of this country's crime problem (Reiman, 1998; Lavella, 2002; CBS News, 2006).

Organized Crime

Organized crime is *a business that supplies illegal goods and services.* Such businesses profit from selling any number of goods and services that many people want—including gambling, sex, and drugs—in violation of the law.

Organized crime in the United States expanded greatly during Prohibition (1919–33), when the government outlawed the manufacture and sale of alcoholic beverages throughout the

victimless crimes offenses that directly harm only the person who commits them

GETTING INVOLVED

Do you engage in any victimless crimes? Do you think of this behavior as wrong or not? Why or why not?

SOCIAL PROBLEMS IN GLOBAL PERSPECTIVE

Organized Crime: All Over the World

Companies are "going global," everyone says, with large corporations operating as "multinationals," doing business all around the world. Organized crime, too, has gone global, raking in profits that the early gangsters who ran local businesses in Brooklyn, New York, or the South Side of Chicago could never have imagined.

Organized crime's most profitable business is drug trafficking, which generates enough money to make the leaders of the biggest drug gangs richer than some countries. Just the sale of cocaine in the United States generates about $25 billion to the drug cartels that are based in Colombia. And drugs are not organized crime's only business. Gangs also smuggle illegal immigrants, sell weapons, illegally copy and sell CDs and DVDs, kill people for profit, and even carry out acts of terrorism.

The Russian *mafiya* has a very profitable worldwide business in weapons sales, car theft, illegal drug sales, money laundering, identity theft, and human slavery. Since the collapse of the Soviet Union in 1991, Russian crime organizations have expanded and formed partnerships with other criminal organizations around the world.

China's Six Great Triads are centuries-old organizations that are, today, the world's largest criminal organizations, with more than 100,000 members. Based in Chinese communities in nations around the world, the Triads deal in drugs, weapons, and stolen cars. They smuggle illegal immigrants, pirate electronics and software, and profit from gambling, loan sharking, and prostitution. Japan, too, has a vast organization: The 60,000 member *Yakuza* engages in the same wide range of criminal activities.

All these organizations carry out their operations in the United States. In 2008 and 2009, drug-related violence in Mexico, which has claimed about 7,000 lives a year in that country, began spilling over into the United States. More broadly, just the illegal copying of books, software, videos, and CDs costs legitimate businesses in the United States billions of dollars in lost sales. Add to that the fact that great wealth gives organized crime the ability to bribe public officials. Put it all together and you can see why some analysts claim that global organized crime is a threat to the security of the United States.

WHAT DO YOU THINK?

1. Do criminal organizations simply meet a demand from the public, or are they a real threat to the United States? Why?
2. What actions, here and abroad, should the United States take to combat organized crime?
3. The U.S. government has stated that organized crime could possibly bring down the government in Mexico. Does our country have a legitimate interest in controlling the drug trade in that country? What could we do?

Sources: Valdez (1997) and Padgett (2009).

United States. The ban on alcohol gave the Mafia, also known as *La Cosa Nostra* (Italian for "our thing"), the opportunity to gain wealth and power by illegally making and distributing liquor to an eager public. With so much money to be made, criminal gangs—made up of people in just about every ethnic category—commonly used violence against members of opposing gangs as well as to frighten law enforcement officials.

Even after Prohibition was ended, organized crime continued to make huge profits, shifting their business from selling alcohol to selling illegal drugs. Mafia "families" became huge business enterprises, with profits rivaling those of legitimate corporations.

As the wealth and power of organized crime grew, Congress passed the Racketeer Influenced and Corrupt Organization Act (RICO) in 1970. This law gives police the authority to seize property such as cars, boats, or homes used in the commission of crimes involving gambling, prostitution, loan sharking, or illegal drugs.

In the decades since then, with the expansion of the global economy, organized crime has also become multinational in scale. The Social Problems in Global Perspective box takes a closer look.

Victimless Crime

Victimless crimes are *offenses that directly harm only the person who commits them.* Sometimes called *public order crimes*, victimless crime includes gambling, prostitution, public drunkenness, drug use, and vagrancy. These activities are against the law because they violate conventional norms and values, although people who engage in these things may not think of them as wrong. Still, victimless crimes can and do cause harm. For example, a large share of prostitutes fall victim to violence at the hands of clients or pimps. In the same way, many "johns" who visit prostitutes pick up sexually transmitted diseases that they pass on to their wives or others.

Laws regulating victimless crimes vary from place to place. Twelve states have gambling casinos; twenty-nine states have casinos on Indian reservations; in all other states, gambling is against the law (American Gaming Association, 2009). Prostitution is legal in parts of rural Nevada but nowhere else. Using marijuana is legal in only a few communities on the East and West Coasts. But in most places, the enforcement of victimless crime laws is not consistent, usually taking the form of occasional crackdowns.

violence is behavior that causes injury to people or damage to property

institutional violence violence carried out by government representatives under the law

anti-institutional violence violence directed against the government in violation of the law

SOCIAL PROBLEMS in Everyday Life

To what extent do you think the operation of our society depends on "official" violence? Explain.

Many examples of violence exist within our society. The crash of a football tackle is certainly violent, yet few people consider this to be a problem. Under what conditions is violence likely to be defined as a social problem?

Violence

Violence is *behavior that causes injury to people or damage to property.* This chapter has already described a number of cases of criminal violence—all the crimes against persons (homicide, rape, robbery, and aggravated assault) are examples of criminal violence.

But violence is also part of our everyday lives, without breaking any laws. Many of our favorite sports (such as football) involve violence, as do some forms of live entertainment (such as World Federation Wrestling), and many movies and video games present us with violent images.

Violence, then, may or may not be a crime, and people may or may not define violence as a social problem. Many people think that some acts of violence are normal and may even be desirable. Polls show, for example, that a majority of people in the United States have supported many wars as necessary, just as most people support the death penalty (itself an act of deadly violence) as justified punishment for people convicted of certain serious crimes. Certainly, there can be little doubt about the popularity of violent movies and violent sports.

Is Violence a Social Problem?

So when does violence become a social problem? The short answer is that violence becomes a social problem to the extent that people define it that way. In other words, whether violence is or is not a problem has less to do with the violent act itself and more to do with how the action is defined by some audience. In deciding what meaning lies in any violence, people consider several factors, including the following:

1. **What do the actors intend by their actions?** A car crash is violent, but in most cases, people assume that the event was an accident, thinking that the driver did not want the crash to happen. Unintended violence is often forgiven. On the other hand, a driver who intentionally runs down a pedestrian almost certainly would face a criminal prosecution.
2. **Does the violence conform to or violate social norms and values?** Many sports are violent without being seen as social problems. As the sociologist Harry Edwards (2000) explains, football is about as violent as hand-to-hand combat, causing personal harm including spinal cord injuries and brain damage. Even so, football fans crave the bone-crushing hits between rival teams. Why? Football, as Edwards explains, is a national ritual that upholds our cultural values of competitiveness, toughness, and masculinity.
3. **Does the violence support or threaten the social order?** Football may be violent, but it upholds our way of life and is also big business. Therefore, most people celebrate rather than condemn football. On the other hand, hazing incidents involving sororities and fraternities on campus usually do not cause serious injuries but they do break the rules and, if discovered by college authorities, are likely to result in disciplinary action.
4. **Is the violence committed by or against the government?** In general, people accept violence such as war, capital punishment, and the action of police SWAT teams because these are government-sanctioned actions that most of us assume are done for good reasons. In general, there is widespread support for **institutional violence,** *violence carried out by government representatives under the law.* In fact, most people believe that a certain amount of violence is actually necessary to keep society operating, whether it is used to oppose criminals or to defend against foreign enemies. This does not mean that violence on the part of police or military personnel is always lawful, as allegations of police brutality or U.S. soldiers intentionally killing Iraqi civilians remind us, but most people seem to accept a considerable amount of violence when carried out by "the system."

On the other hand, people are quick to condemn **anti-institutional violence,** *violence directed against the government in violation of the law.* The war on terrorism, which began after the 2001 attacks on the World Trade Center and the Pentagon, has clearly defined any violence directed against the U.S. government or its citizens as a serious prob-

mass murder the intentional, unlawful killing of four or more people at one time and place

serial murder the killing of several people by one offender over a period of time

MAKING THE GRADE

Mass murder and serial murder make headlines, but they account for a very small share of all killings each year.

lem. In the United States, most people were outraged by the anti-institutional violence of the nineteen September 11 terrorists yet supported the institutional violence of the United States' military response in Afghanistan and Iraq. Of course, the antiwar movement has tried to shift national opinion and has had considerable success in its efforts to define the wars in Iraq and Afghanistan as unjust violence against others.

Over time, then, members of a society debate the right and wrong use of violence, in the process coming to define new social problems. The Defining Moment box on page 156 explains how this country came to define one type of violence—what we now call child abuse—as a serious problem.

Serious Violence: Mass Murder and Serial Killings

Certain types of violence are almost always defined as serious social problems. Two examples of serious criminal violence are mass murder and serial killings.

Mass Murder

The story that opened this chapter—the 2009 classroom shootings that took the lives of thirteen recent immigrants who were learning English and looking forward to becoming U.S. citizens—is an example of **mass murder,** *the intentional, unlawful killing of four or more people at one time and place.*

This type of violent crime is tragically frequent in the United States, with fifty deaths taking place in mass murders across the country during the same month in 2009 as the Binghamton killings. The number of mass murders increased during the 1990s, with a number of deadly shootings occurring at a dozen public schools across the country. The worst was the killing of thirteen people at Columbine High School in Littleton, Colorado, in 1999. Mass murder occurs not only in schools but also in the workplace when disgruntled workers vent their rage against a number of people they feel have wronged them (Von Drehle, 2009).

Mass murder can also occur in the home. For example, in 2009, Graham Troyer's wife announced that she planned to divorce him. He responded by using a rifle to kill all five of his own children. He then searched for his wife but, unable to find her, turned the gun on himself.

Another type of mass murder involves terrorism. The September 11, 2001, attacks amounted to mass murder on a horrific scale, killing almost 3,000 people.

In most years, mass murder in the United States involves about fifty killings. This means that mass murder represents only about 0.3 percent of all the murders that take place in a year (in 2007, the total was 16,929 killings) (U.S. Department of Justice, 2008). But cases of mass murder are of great concern to the public because, for one thing, they receive extensive attention in the mass media. Just as important, most mass murders occur in schools, businesses, or homes, where people assume they are safe from violence.

What do mass murderers have in common? Almost all are men. School shootings typically involve young men—students or ex-students—who have experienced rejection by their peers. Mass murder in the workplace usually involves employees or ex-employees, many of whom abuse alcohol or other drugs. Mass murder in the home typically involves men who have been rejected by spouses or other family members and who are emotionally distraught. Mass murderers are people with access to guns, and many are gun collectors (R. M. Holmes & S. T. Holmes, 1993; Hill, 2009).

Serial Murder

Another type of killing that gets a great deal of public attention is **serial murder,** *the killing of several people by one offender over a period of time.* Typically, a serial killer commits a murder and then goes for weeks or months before doing so again. Over time, however, the death toll—along with public fear—builds. For example, Derrick Todd Lee was arrested and charged with the murder of five women in Louisiana. The killings had made women in the Baton Rouge area fearful for over a year (Deslatte, 2003).

A number of convicted serial killers have had even more victims. Ted Bundy killed as many as thirty women during the 1970s. He was not the first known serial killer, but it was his repeated crimes that prompted our society to define serial killing as a serious type of violence. Bundy was executed in 1989. John Wayne Gacy, convicted of killing thirty-three young men, was executed in 1994. Jeffrey Dahmer was convicted of fifteen murders and later died in a prison attack in 1994. In 2006, Robert Charles Browne, currently serving a life sentence in prison for one murder, confessed to forty-seven others. This total makes Browne the deadliest serial killer to date (Sarche, 2006).

Serial killers are probably the best known of all deadly offenders, and fictitious killers such as Hannibal "the Cannibal" Lecter have thrilled millions of moviegoers. Such cases grab the headlines, but keep in mind that serial killers represent only a tiny fraction of all murderers.

What do we know about serial killers? Almost all are men. Most are mentally ill, suffering from psychotic disorders that distort their sense of reality and make them unable to feel compassion for others. Some serial killers claim to hear voices or receive messages urging them to kill people in some specific category, such as women who are prostitutes or men who are gay. Others have an irresistible desire to control other people and feel great

MAKING THE GRADE

The box below describes how child abuse became a serious social problem back in the 1960s.

GETTING INVOLVED

What are your favorite television shows? How much violence do they contain?

CONSTRUCTING SOCIAL PROBLEMS

A DEFINING MOMENT

U.S. Society Discovers Child Abuse

In 1958, C. Henry Kempe was working as a physician in Denver's Colorado General Hospital. Every day, Kempe treated children for injuries including broken bones. After years working in the emergency room and examining thousands of X-rays, Kempe began to wonder if some children's injuries were really the "accidents" that the parents said they were. Kempe suspected that the real cause of some of these injuries was violence in the home.

At this time, the concept of "child abuse" did not exist. People assumed that parents had both the right and the duty to care for their children, including punishing children as they felt was necessary. What went on in the privacy of people's homes was a family matter, not a public issue.

Kempe decided that he would try to change that. To protect children from what he viewed as violence at home, Kempe set up the hospital's first "child protection team," a group of people trained to investigate and evaluate children's injuries, deciding which might be the result of violence. Three years later, he presented a paper reporting a surprisingly high level of violence against children, drawing the nation's attention to a new problem he defined as "battered child syndrome."

Family violence obviously harms children physically, he noted, but it also results in psychological harm—including poor self-image and depression—and makes it difficult for injured children to form trusting relationships.

Kempe's research helped U.S. society come to define violence against children as a social problem rather than a private family matter. By 1966, every state in the country had passed a law making child abuse a crime and requiring medical personnel to report suspected cases to authorities. As a result of these laws, about 3 millions cases are reported each year, and about 1 million turn out to be serious. Kempe not only made a difference in the lives of children, but he also set the stage for our society, in the years ahead, to define two other types of family violence as social problems: violence against women and violence against the elderly.

Sources: Kempe et al. (1962) and U.S. Department of Health and Human Services (2008).

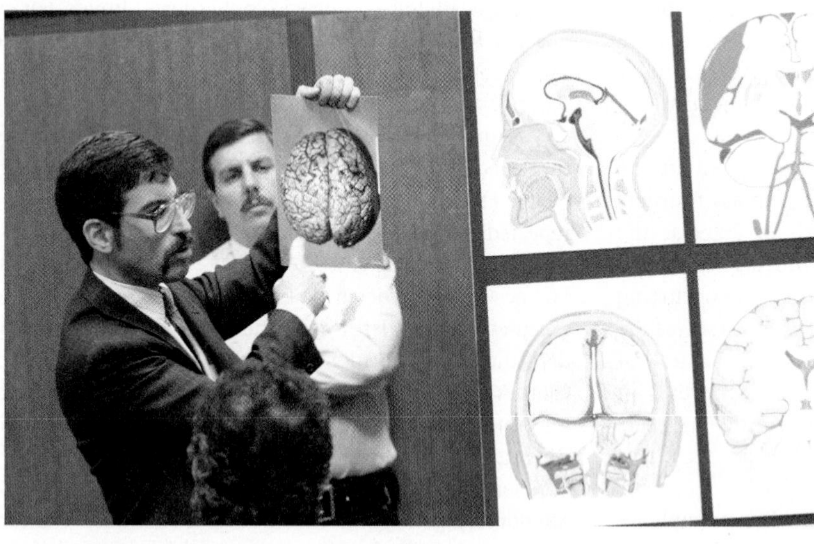

Thanks to Dr. Kempe, doctors today routinely review medical data with an eye toward identifying cases of child abuse. This physician is using autopsy charts to describe the brain damage suffered by an abused six-year-old.

pleasure when they put others in fear. Still others lack all compassion and strike out violently at anyone who might happen to get in their way. Finally, compared to those who commit single murders, most serial killers are somewhat older. These violent offenders are as likely to target men as women (P. Jenkins, 1994; R. M. Holmes & S. T. Holmes, 1998; Warf & Waddell, 2002).

The Mass Media and Violence

The mass media—radio, television, movies, and the Internet—have a huge influence on the way people, especially children, view the world around them. Violence has no one cause, but many people wonder if the mass media might be part of the problem.

GETTING INVOLVED

Do you have any personal experience with violent gangs? What can you add to the discussion below?

youth gangs groups of young people who identify with one another and with a particular territory

The reason for these concerns is the fact that there is a lot of violence in today's mass media. The typical young person in the United States watches about six and one-half hours of television each day, and many television shows, even cartoons, contain plenty of violence. Over the course of a year, estimates suggest that a typical child observes roughly 12,000 violent acts (Groves, 1997; Rideout, Roberts, & Foehr, 2005).

Movies, on average, are even more violent than television shows. The high level of violence in the movies prompted the American Medical Association (AMA; 1997) to declare that the mass media are hazardous to our health. The AMA reports that three-fourths of U.S. adults say they have either turned off a television program or walked out of a movie because of high and disturbing levels of violence.

In a statistical study of violence on television shows broadcast during the 2000–01 season, the Center for Media and Public Affairs (2002) counted an average of fifteen scenes involving serious violence (defined as murder, aggravated assault, rape, and kidnapping) per hour, and they observed the same level of violence in movies.

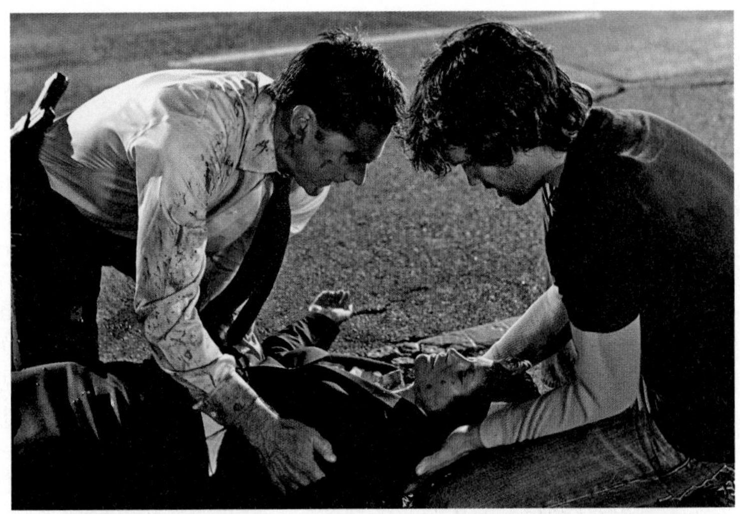

How much violence is presented on television? Researchers have concluded that most television shows contain at least some violence. Just as important, almost no shows contain antiviolence themes. At the very least, the high dose of violence that we receive from shows like *Criminal Minds* seems likely to reduce our reaction to violence, so we accept violence as an element of everyday life.

A violent scene every four minutes may seem high. But the researchers noted a modest decline in the rate of serious violence on television compared to a few years earlier. Perhaps, they suggested, criticism of TV violence is having some effect. They found no change in the level of violence in movies.

Does viewing violence make people commit violent acts? The answer may well be yes. Studies conclude that the more media violence children watch, the more they engage in rough play and the more likely they are to resort to violence when they become adults. In addition, some violent offenders claim that they were trying to act out behavior they saw in violent movies (Gibbs & Roche, 1999; Ritter, 2003; Federal Communication Commission, 2007).

Watching violence in the mass media, then, may actually encourage people to be more violent. But perhaps an even more serious concern is that the media may end up *desensitizing* us all to violence. Living in a media-violence culture, in other words, we become so used to violence that the idea of people deliberately hurting each other no longer bothers us (Sege & Dietz, 1994; Groves, 1997; Kromar & Valkenburg, 1999).

Poverty and Violence

Violence is also linked to poverty. Low-income people are disadvantaged by poor nutrition, limited schooling, substandard housing, and lack of job opportunities, and all these factors raise everyday levels of stress. For this reason, some analysts view poverty itself as a form of violence, one that harms tens of millions of people in the United States. It is not surprising, then, that low-income people are highly represented among both offenders and victims of violent crime (Reiman, 1998; Parler & Pruitt, 2000; Hannon, 2005).

Despite these facts, keep in mind that most poor families go about their daily lives without turning to either crime or violence. It is true that poor neighborhoods have higher rates of violent crime than rich communities, but most violent crime is the work of a small number of repeat offenders.

Youth Gangs and Violence

Another factor contributing to violence, especially in the poor neighborhoods of large U.S. cities, is **youth gangs,** *groups of young people who identify with one another and with a particular territory*. Not all gangs are violent, of course. In fact, not all groups of young people are even called "gangs." We have a tendency to call middle-class groups "clubs" while calling groups of poor young people "gangs," regardless of how their members act.

A recent government study surveyed 2,551 cities and identified more than 26,500 street gangs with 785,000 members (U.S. Department of Justice, 2008). These gangs range from nonviolent groups to groups that sometimes clash over turf to all-out criminal organizations that engage in drug dealing, robbery, extortion, and even murder.

Who is likely to join a violent gang? The typical member comes from a poor, single-parent family in a neighborhood

SOCIAL PROBLEMS in Everyday Life

What do you think about the idea that legalizing some drugs might reduce the level of violence in our society? Explain your view.

SOCIAL PROBLEMS in Everyday Life

In 2009, gun sales were very high. Does the public expect stricter laws regulating guns?

Across the United States, at least 785,000 young people are members of youth gangs, some of which routinely engage in violence. What are the reasons that many young people are drawn to gangs in the first place? What are some of the causes of gang violence?

with high rates of crime and drug abuse and few jobs. Many gang members have experienced violence in their own homes. Many young people look to gangs for protection and a positive self-image that they cannot find elsewhere (Zimring, 1998; Hixon, 1999).

Some low-income communities develop a "street culture" that teaches young people that the only way people will leave you alone is for you to be tough and quick to fight. In such a setting, young people—especially males—learn that violence can be a strategy to avoid becoming a victim (E. Anderson, 1994, 2002).

The level of gang violence dropped, along with the overall crime rate, during the 1990s. Within a decade, however, gang-related violence in large cities was again on the rise, with 1,334 gang-related killings in 2001. Two cities—Los Angeles and Chicago—accounted for more than half of the total. Some of the dead were innocent victims of stray bullets fired by people they never even saw (U.S. Office of Juvenile Justice and Delinquency Prevention, 2006).

Drugs and Violence

Violence is also fueled by the use of alcohol and other drugs. A government study found that more than 60 percent of people in prison for violent offenses say they were under the influence of drugs, alcohol, or both when they committed their crimes (U.S. Bureau of Justice Statistics, 2002). In addition, a number of studies show that alcohol and other drugs play a role in most cases of family violence (Gelles, 1997; Kantor & Jasinski, 1998).

Drugs encourage violence by distorting judgment and reducing inhibitions. When a person already inclined to violent behavior uses drugs, the odds of "losing it" go up (Gelles & Straus, 1988; Gelles, 1997). In addition, some drugs are addictive and cause cravings so strong that the search for the next high may cause some people to turn to violence. Drug abusers commonly neglect their children or even engage in outright abuse. In this way, drugs may create a cycle of violence that spills from one generation to another.

Guns and Violence

Finally, many people blame our society's high level of violent crime on the easy availability of guns. There is no doubt that guns are everywhere: About 35 percent of U.S. households have one or more guns, for a total of more than 280 million firearms, enough to arm everyone over age twelve. About one-third of these weapons are handguns (Brady Campaign, 2008).

Because many of these guns find their way into the hands of criminals and curious children, some people (especially liberals) define gun ownership itself as a serious social problem. From this point of view, we need tougher laws that make guns harder to get and mandatory devices such as trigger locks that make guns harder to use.

Supporters of gun control point to countries such as Canada, where the government sharply restricts gun ownership (Canada has just 1 million handguns, compared with more than 90 million in the United States). There is no easy way to assess cause and effect here, but Canada's rate of firearms deaths is one-seventh that of the United States (Burns, Francia, & Herrnson, 2000). In this country, as shown on National Map 6-2, most states allow citizens to get a permit to carry a concealed handgun.

Not everyone thinks guns are part of the problem. For some people (typically conservatives), when it comes to violent crime, guns may even be part of the solution. Gun owners point to the Second Amendment to the U.S. Constitution, which guarantees citizens the right to "keep and bear arms." From this point of view, government efforts to regulate gun ownership violate this basic right and threaten our freedom. In addition, supporters of gun ownership claim that the presence of guns in many U.S. households actually discourages violent crime (Lott, 2000). Don't criminals think twice about breaking into a home or trying to mug someone if they might end up facing a firearm? Taking guns out of the hands of law-abiding people does not take guns from the criminals, after all, so such a policy would end up making everyone more vulnerable to violent

criminal justice system society's use of due process, involving police, courts, and punishment, to enforce the law

GETTING INVOLVED

Are you surprised that most people in most states can carry a concealed weapon? Does that make you feel more or less safe? Why?

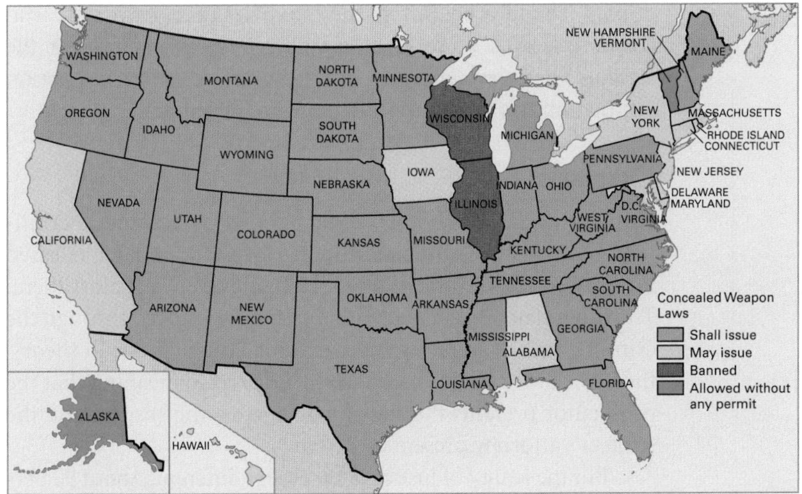

A Nation of Diversity

NATIONAL MAP 6–2

Who's Packin'? Concealed Weapon Laws across the United States

In only two states (Alaska and Vermont), any person can carry a concealed weapon without a permit. In just two states, no one can do so by law. Eleven states (identified as "may issue" states) issue concealed weapon permits in cases of demonstrated special need. But in most states ("shall issue" states)—thirty-five in all—permits are available to most people without special need. What regional pattern do you see? Can you explain this pattern?

Source: Brady Campaign (2008).

crime. As the popular bumper sticker puts it, "If guns are outlawed, only outlaws will have guns."

Figure 6–3 on page 160 shows that half of murder cases involve handguns. This fact suggests that controlling handguns might lower the rate of deadly violence. In other words, many fights that end up with someone being killed might not be fatal were no gun available. But the fact that almost half the murders in the United States do not involve handguns shows that deadly violence has many causes and reducing this problem requires complex solutions.

The Criminal Justice System

The **criminal justice system** is *society's use of due process, involving police, courts, and punishment, to enforce the law.* The following sections survey elements of the U.S. criminal justice system.

Due Process

The Constitution requires that our society respond to crime using *due process.* In simple terms, this means that the criminal justice system must operate within the bounds of law. No person, the Constitution states, can be "deprived of life, liberty, or property without due process of law." Therefore, people charged with a crime have a right to defend themselves and to confront their accusers; they have a right to legal counsel and a speedy, impartial, and public trial, with a jury if desired; they can refuse to testify against themselves; and they cannot be tried twice for the same crime. In addition, the Constitution gives all people protection against excessive bail as well as protection against cruel and unusual punishment if found guilty (Inciardi, 2000).

Police

The first official response to crime involves police. The United States has 669,850 police officers (U.S. Department of Justice, 2008). Still, even this many officers cannot keep track of more than 300 million people. Therefore, police must make decisions as to which situations are serious enough to require their attention. In a study of police discretion in five cities, Douglas Smith and Christy Visher (1981; D. A. Smith, 1987) noted six factors that guided police in deciding whether or not to make an arrest:

1. **How serious is the crime?** The more serious a situation seems, and the more it involves violence, the greater the odds that police will make an arrest.
2. **What does the victim want?** If a victim demands that an arrest be made, police are more likely to do so.
3. **Is the suspect cooperative?** Police are more likely to arrest an uncooperative suspect.
4. **Does the suspect have a record?** Police are more likely to arrest someone they know has been arrested before.
5. **Are bystanders watching?** Police are more likely to make an arrest when people are watching. This gives police more control of the situation by moving it off the street.
6. **What is the suspect's race?** Smith and Visher argue that, all other factors being equal, police are more likely to arrest African American and Hispanic suspects than whites.

Three recent changes in police work have contributed to the downturn in crime rates in U.S. cities. First, the practice of *community policing* makes police more visible to the public by moving some police officers from cars to riding bicycles or

MAKING THE GRADE

Notice that about half of all murders involve handguns.

plea bargaining a negotiation in which the state reduces a defendant's charge in exchange for a guilty plea

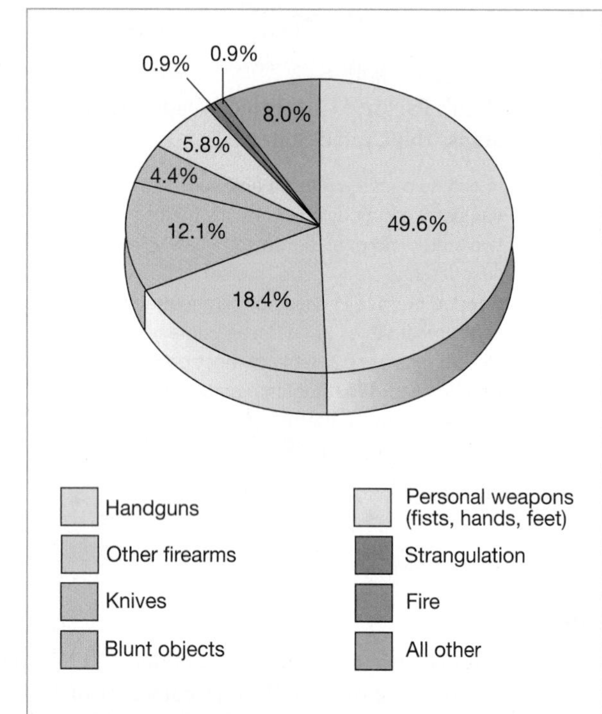

FIGURE 6–3 Murder: Type of Weapon Used

Firearms are used in two-thirds of all murders. Handguns are involved in as many killings as all other weapons combined.

Source: Federal Bureau of Investigation (2008).

patrolling on foot. The idea is for officers to get to know local neighborhoods and for neighbors to get to know them; police and community cooperation is a proven strategy to reduce crime.

A second innovation is a *zero-tolerance policy* under which police respond to any offense, no matter how minor. In recent years, for example, police in New York began ticketing or arresting people for minor offenses including jaywalking and jumping turnstiles to enter the city's subway system. This strategy, although effective, has attracted controversy. Critics claim that this policy encourages police to harass law-abiding people for minor infractions instead of concentrating on solving major crimes. But supporters counter that this policy deters crime because fewer people will risk carrying an illegal weapon, knowing that any minor infraction may cause police to stop and search them.

Third, a number of states have enacted tough sentencing laws. One example is "three strikes and you're out" laws that require a life sentence for a third felony conviction. Currently, twenty-six states have such laws. Another example is enacting laws requiring a mandatory prison sentence for specific serious crimes. The idea behind all these policies is to get people who commit serious crimes—especially repeat offenders—off the streets. These laws are one important reason that the prison population has grown rapidly in recent decades.

Courts

Being arrested does not mean that someone becomes a criminal. About half of suspects who are arrested are later released for various reasons, including a lack of evidence against them. The other half are charged with a crime and moved through the criminal justice system to be tried in a court of law. In theory, the U.S. court system is an *adversarial process*, meaning that the prosecutor presents the state's case against the suspect and the suspect's attorney presents a defense.

But the reality of justice often is very different. About 90 percent of cases are settled through **plea bargaining,** *a negotiation in which the state reduces a defendant's charge in exchange for a guilty plea.* Plea bargaining saves the time and expense of a trial, allowing courts to focus on the most serious cases. But a system that is efficient is not always just. This is especially true when dealing with low-income defendants. Under the law, the government must provide a public defender to all defendants who are unable to pay for a lawyer. Because public defenders are usually young lawyers with limited experience and are typically overworked and underpaid, they may be eager to settle a case quickly. As a result, low-income defendants often feel that they have no choice but to plea-bargain, also known as "copping a plea" (Novak, 1999). By relying so heavily on plea bargaining, our criminal justice system sometimes violates the ideal of due process by taking away a defendant's constitutional right to a trial in which the defendant is presumed innocent until proven guilty.

Punishment

In response to lawbreaking, the criminal justice system makes use of various forms of punishment, ranging from fines to jail time to death. In 2008, about 2.3 million people were incarcerated in the United States, five times the number behind bars back in 1980 (U.S. Department of Justice, 2008). As shown in Figure 6–4 on page 162, this country now imprisons a larger share of its population than any other nation.

But is the crime problem solved by prison and other forms of punishment? In principle, punishing convicted offenders reduces crime in four ways: through retribution, deterrence, rehabilitation, and societal protection.

Retribution

Looking back in history, the oldest reason to punish is to gain revenge. **Retribution** is *moral vengeance by which society inflicts*

Justifications for Punishment

retribution moral vengeance by which society inflicts suffering on an offender comparable to that caused by the offense

deterrence using punishment to discourage further crime

rehabilitation reforming an offender to prevent future offenses

societal protection protecting the public by preventing an offender from committing further offenses through incarceration or execution

suffering on an offender comparable to that caused by the offense. Retribution is based on the idea that society is a moral order that is upset by crime. But morality can be restored by declaring the offender guilty and exacting a punishment fitting the crime. The biblical saying "an eye for an eye, a tooth for a tooth" expresses this vision of justice.

Deterrence

A second reason to punish is **deterrence,** *using punishment to discourage further crime.* Deterrence is a more modern idea, emerging as the eighteenth-century Enlightenment came to view people as rational decision makers. If society makes sure that the pain of punishment outweighs the pleasure of the offense, people should realize that "crime does not pay" and behave themselves.

Punishment provides *specific deterrence* to the individual offender. At the same time, punishment provides *general deterrence* by teaching everyone what happens to people who break the law. For deterrence to work, of course, people must be rational; this is why punishment may not prevent "crimes of passion." In addition, deterrence requires that people think that most offenders will be caught, which, at least with respect to property crimes, is not the case in the United States today.

Police departments in many U.S. cities have adopted "zero tolerance" policies that permit officers to stop and investigate any minor offense in order to check individuals for weapons. Some people see this practice as a solution to the violence problem. Others claim it opens the door to racial profiling and subjects some categories of people to what amounts to harassment. What do you think?

Rehabilitation

A third reason to punish is **rehabilitation,** *reforming an offender to prevent future offenses.* The idea of rehabilitation emerged along with the social sciences in the nineteenth century. If the reason people turn to crime in the first place is a bad environment, then a new and better environment can reform them into law-abiding citizens.

Rehabilitation differs from retribution and deterrence in its positive character: helping people improve rather than making them suffer. Rehabilitation also differs in another way: Retribution and deterrence demand that the punishment fit the crime, but rehabilitation means tailoring treatment to the needs of a specific offender.

Societal Protection

The fourth reason for punishment is **societal protection,** *protecting the public by preventing an offender from committing further offenses through incarceration or execution.* In recent decades, the United States has been building prisons at the rate of a new 1,000-bed facility every week.

Does Punishment Work?

Is punishment a solution to the crime problem? Or does it cause problems of its own? The answers are far from clear. Retribution is based on the idea that responding to crime strengthens public morality. Yet some people argue that punishment—especially the death penalty—further brutalizes a society that already has too much violence.

Deterrence, too, is controversial. Although common sense suggests that punishment discourages crime, this country has a high rate of **criminal recidivism,** *later offenses by people previously convicted of crimes.* A government study reported that two-thirds of state prison inmates released from jail in 1994 were rearrested for a serious crime within three years (U.S. Bureau of Justice Statistics, 2002). A high rate of repeat offenders casts doubt on the idea that prison deters further crime. Some critics claim the opposite, saying that prison stigmatizes people and allows them to share their knowledge with one another, actually encouraging further crime (Petersilia, 1997; DeFina & Arvanites, 2002).

What about rehabilitation? Again, prison may help some offenders "straighten out." But the high recidivism rate suggests that successful rehabilitation is the exception rather than the rule.

Finally, punishment probably does result in societal protection. Few people doubt that in the short term, the growing number of people in prisons has played a part in bringing down the crime rate. But whether this pattern holds for the long criminal recidivism (p. 161) later offenses by people previously convicted of crimes

community-based corrections correctional programs that take place in society at large rather than behind prison walls

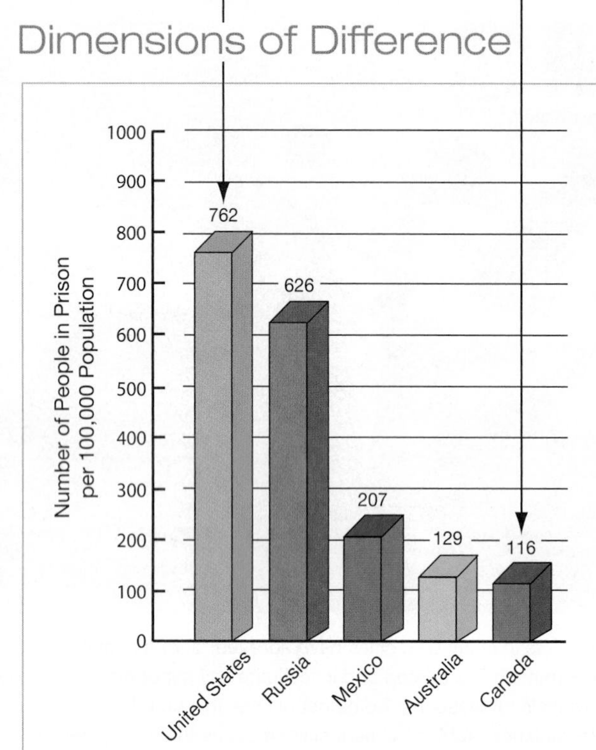

FIGURE 6–4 **Rates of Incarceration for Selected Countries**

The 2008 rate of incarceration for the United States was 762 people for every 100,000 in the population. Among all the nations of the world, this country has the highest share of its people in prison.

Source: U.S. Department of Justice (2008) and King's College School of Law (2009).

term—that is, as our large prison population is gradually released back into society—is less certain (K. Johnson, 2000).

In recent years, the greatest debate concerning punishment has centered on the death penalty. As Global Map 6–1 shows, the United States is one of the few high-income nations in the world that puts convicted offenders to death. The Social Policy box on page 164 takes a closer look at the controversy over the risk of innocent people being executed.

Community-Based Corrections

Prisons keep convicted criminals off the streets. But as we have already noted, prisons may do little to rehabilitate most offenders. In addition, prisons are expensive: The cost of jailing one inmate is about $30,000 per year (not including the cost of building the prison in the first place).

An alternative to prison is **community-based corrections,** *correctional programs that take place in society at large rather than behind prison walls.* Community-based corrections have several advantages, including lower cost, a reduction in prison overcrowding, and the ability to supervise a convicted offender without applying the stigma that comes from imprisonment. However, because this policy lets offenders remain in the community, it is generally applied only to those convicted of less serious crimes who seem likely to avoid future criminal violations (Inciardi, 2000).

Probation

One form of community-based corrections is *probation,* a policy of letting a convicted offender stay in the community with regular supervision and under conditions imposed by a court. These conditions might include going to counseling sessions, enrolling in a drug treatment program, keeping a steady job, and avoiding known criminals. Should the probationer miss regular meetings with the probation officer, fail to comply with other conditions set by the court, or commit another crime, the court may end probation and send the offender to prison.

Shock Probation

Another community-based corrections policy is *shock probation.* In this case, a judge sentences a convicted offender to prison for a substantial length of time but then orders that only part of the sentence will be served in prison and the rest will be served on probation. Shock probation mixes prison and probation with the goal of impressing the offender with the seriousness of the situation without requiring a long prison term. In some cases, the lock-up portion of shock probation takes place in a special "boot camp" facility where offenders might spend several months in a military-style setting intended to teach discipline and respect for authority (Cole & Smith, 2002).

Parole

Parole is a policy of releasing inmates from prison to serve the rest of their sentence under supervision in the local community. Most inmates become eligible for parole after serving a specified portion of a prison term. At that time, a parole board evaluates the offender's chances of staying out of trouble; if the board votes for parole, the inmate is released and the court tracks the offender's conduct until the sentence is completed. Should the offender not comply with conditions of parole or be arrested for another crime, the board can revoke parole and require the person to complete the sentence in prison. In some cases of serious crimes, courts may sentence an offender to prison for a specified time without possibility of parole.

Do Probation and Parole Work?

The evidence is mixed. Probation and parole cost much less than prison, and these policies do reduce prison overcrowding. It also makes sense to use prisons for people who commit seri-

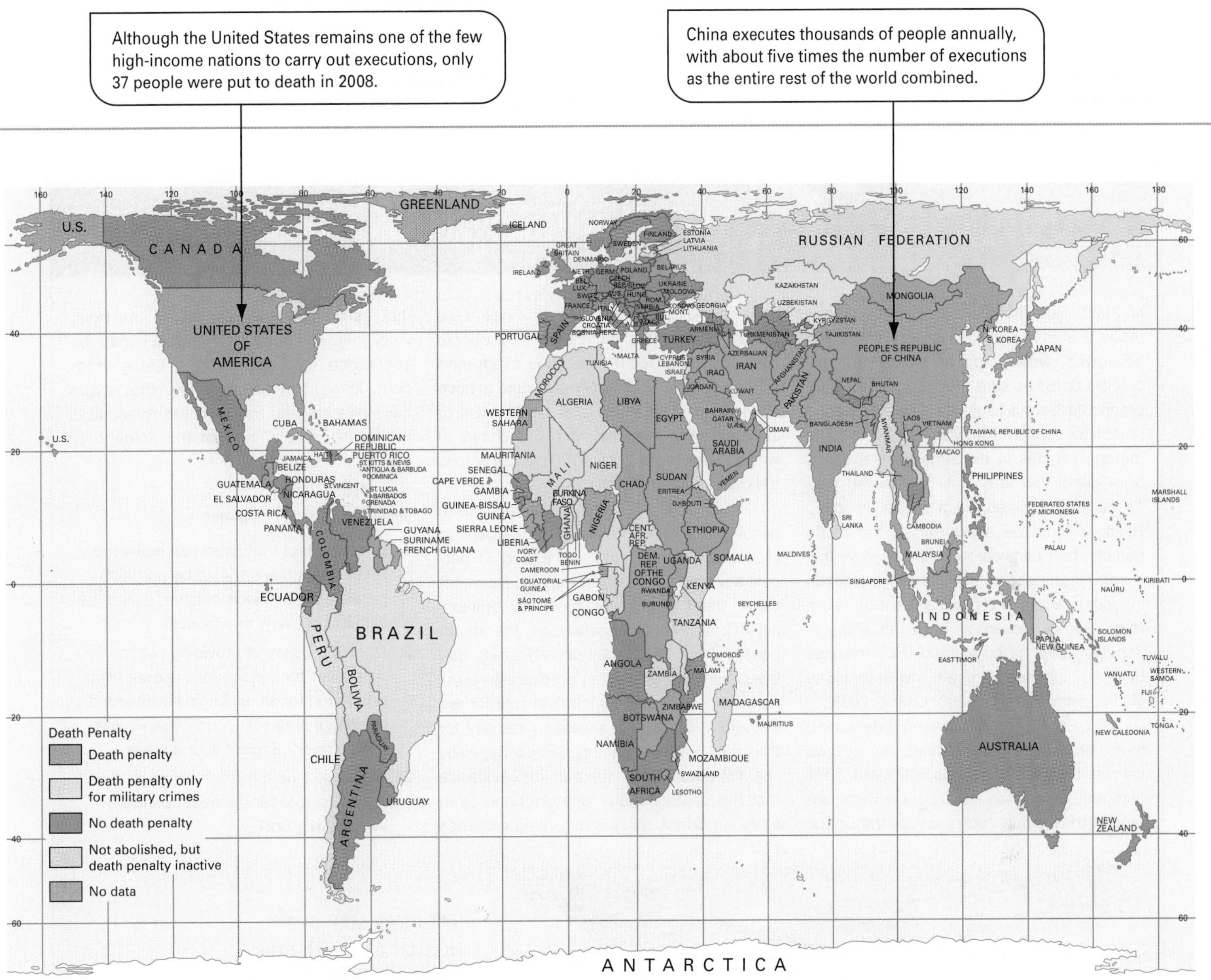

A World of Differences

GLOBAL MAP 6–1 Capital Punishment around the World

The map identifies fifty-nine countries and territories in which the law allows the death penalty for ordinary crimes; in ten more, the death penalty is reserved for special crimes under military law or during times of war. There is no death penalty in ninety-two countries and territories. In the remaining thirty-six countries, although the death penalty remains legal, no execution has taken place in more than ten years. Compare rich and poor nations: What general pattern do you see? In what way are the United States and Japan exceptions to this pattern?

Source: Amnesty International (2009).

ous crimes while monitoring those who commit less serious crimes in the community.

Probation and shock probation seem to be effective for some people. Parole is more controversial because of the fact that so many people released on parole are soon arrested for another crime. For this reason, some states have abandoned parole. Yet this policy remains popular with prison officials because the chance to be released encourages good behavior among inmates.

Explaining Crime: Biological and Psychological Theories

Having examined both property crime and violent crime, we now turn to a basic question: Why does crime exist at all? In the following sections, we first review biological and psychological theories and then turn to sociological explanations.

MAKING THE GRADE

Half of all prisoners on death row are in three states. Which states are they?

SOCIAL PROBLEMS in Everyday Life

Do you consider the death penalty more of a problem or more of a solution? Why?

SOCIAL POLICY

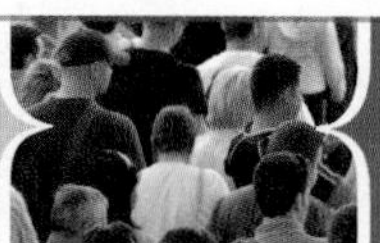

The Death Penalty: Problem or Solution?

In 2000, Governor George Ryan of Illinois made a startling announcement. His state, he vowed, would stop all executions until officials could be sure that no innocent people would be put to death. Ryan had good reason for concern: Between 1987 and 2000, thirteen inmates in his state were released from death row after courts reviewed their cases and declared them to be innocent. Ryan, a longtime supporter of the death penalty, had come around to the view that Illinois "had a shameful record of convicting innocent people and placing them on death row." Before Governor Ryan left office in January 2003, he commuted the sentences of all 167 inmates on death row in Illinois to life in prison (Babwin, 2003; Levine, 2003).

Since then, the controversy has spread to all thirty-six states with death penalty laws on the books. Nationwide, between 1977 and 2009, more than 7,000 people were sentenced to death in courts across the United States, and about 1,100 executions were carried out. At the same time, 131 people have had their death sentences overturned by the courts, including people found to have been innocent all along (U.S. Department of Justice, 2008). National Map 6-3 shows in which states more than 3,100 people across the country sit on death row.

When asked about using the death penalty in cases of murder, 63 percent of U.S. adults say they support it, and 31 percent say they do not (the remaining 6 percent either can't decide or have no opinion) (NORC, 2007). Supporters of the death penalty (typically conservatives) claim that this extreme punishment is used rarely—just 1 percent of people convicted of murder are executed—but it is a necessary penalty for the most serious cases. Critics (typically liberals) counter that there is little evidence that the death penalty deters crime. Even more important, there is mounting evidence that certain people—especially the poor, who rely on public defenders—may be sentenced to death despite being innocent. In light of the evidence that errors have been made, the question remains: Is the death penalty part of the solution or part of the problem?

WHAT DO YOU THINK?

1. Does the fact that juries can make mistakes mean there should be no death penalty, which, once inflicted, cannot be withdrawn? Why or why not?
2. Does the policy of providing public defenders for the accused ensure legal protection for all, as originally intended, or does it mean "second-class justice" for the poor? Explain your answer.
3. Would you, as a member of a jury, be willing to vote for the death penalty? Why or why not?

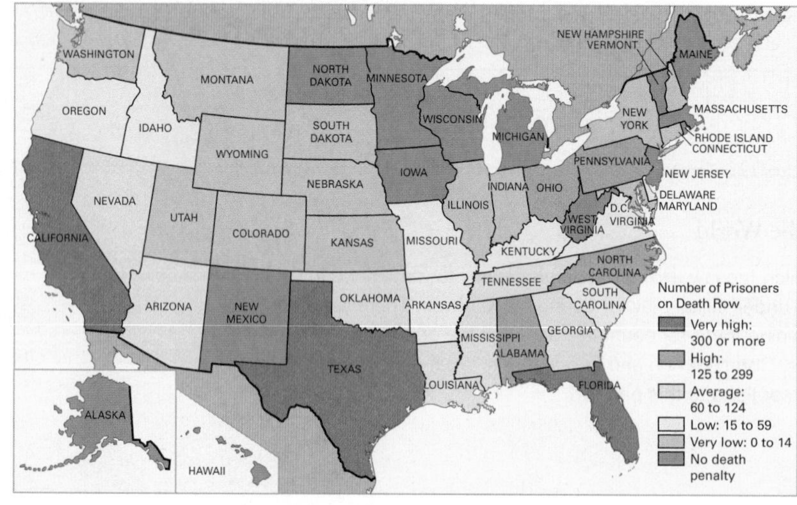

A Nation of Diversity

NATIONAL MAP 6–3

Inmates on Death Row across the United States

In the United States, thirty-six states have laws permitting the death penalty. But some states apply these laws frequently, and others do not. For this reason, almost half (45 percent) of all prisoners on death row are in just three states. What regional pattern do you see for states that have condemned the most people? Can you explain this pattern?

Source: U.S. Department of Justice (2008).

Biological Causes

In the nineteenth century, an Italian doctor named Cesare Lombroso (1911, orig. 1876) came up with the idea that criminals were physically different from law-abiding people. Studying the physical features of men in prison, Lombroso pointed to several distinctive traits the men seemed to share: low foreheads, prominent jaws and cheekbones, protruding ears, excessively hairy bodies, and unusually long arms. Putting these traits together, Lombroso concluded that criminals appeared apelike. But Lombroso's work was flawed. He

MAKING THE GRADE

The limitation of biological theories of crime is that most criminals are, biologically speaking, quite normal.

MAKING THE GRADE

What are two criticisms of psychological theories of crime?

failed to see that the physical traits he found among prisoners were just as likely to be found in the general population.

Decades later, William Sheldon (Sheldon, Hartl, & McDermott, 1949) examined the body types of hundreds of young men, some criminal, some not. Sheldon found that men with athletic builds (*mesomorphs*) were more likely to be criminals than fat, round people (*endomorphs*) or thin, wiry people (*ectomorphs*). This pattern was later confirmed by Sheldon and Eleanor Glueck (1950). But the Gluecks cautioned that a muscular build may not be the *cause* of criminal behavior. A more likely explanation, they thought, was that athletic boys become more independent. With more emotional distance from parents, perhaps muscular boys grow up less sensitive to others. The Gluecks also pointed out that people may expect muscular boys to act like bullies and treat them that way, creating a self-fulfilling prophecy that accounts for a higher rate of violence and criminal behavior.

By the 1960s, researchers began looking for a link between genetics and criminal behavior. An interesting finding is that men with an extra Y chromosome (XYY, a rare pattern compared with the normal XY pattern) may have a greater chance of criminal violence (L. Taylor, 1984; LaFree, 1998). But clear evidence linking criminality to any specific genetic trait has not yet been found.

CRITICAL REVIEW Biological theories have yet to explain criminality. What is more likely is that genes, together with social influences, will eventually explain some types of criminality. Some research suggests that genetic factors (such as a defective gene that produces too much of an enzyme) together with environmental factors (such as abuse in early childhood) are linked to adult crime and violence (Lemonick, 2003; Pinker, 2003). But the major problem with this approach is that most people convicted of crime turn out to be biologically just like the rest of us.

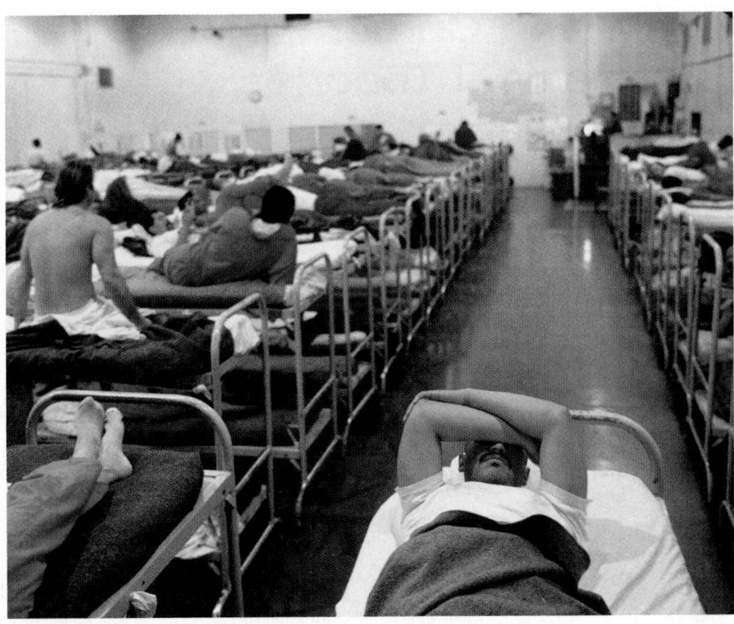

In recent years, the United States has imprisoned record numbers of people with the goal of controlling the crime problem. What arguments can you point to in support of this policy? On balance, do you think this policy works or not? Why?

Psychological Causes

Like biological research, psychological study of crime focuses on the individual traits of offenders—in this case, abnormal personalities. Walter Reckless and Simon Dinitz explain delinquency in terms of a boy's degree of moral conscience. These researchers began by asking teachers to identify twelve-year-old male students who were likely to get in trouble with the law and those who were not. Researchers then interviewed all the boys and their mothers, trying to assess the boys' personalities and how they related to others. They found that the boys whom the teachers had identified as nondelinquent had a more positive self-concept and a stronger conscience. In practice, the "good boys" held to conventional norms and values and could handle frustration without becoming angry or violent. By contrast, the "bad boys" had weak belief in conventional norms and values and reacted angrily when frustrated (Reckless, Dinitz, & Murray, 1956, 1957; Dinitz, Scarpitti, & Reckless, 1962; Reckless & Dinitz, 1972; Reckless, 1973).

CRITICAL REVIEW Social workers and law enforcement officers give much attention to psychological theories. Few people doubt that personality traits play a part in encouraging or discouraging criminality. Some violent crimes are committed by people who are considered psychopaths because they do not feel guilt or shame or show any fear of punishment (Herpertz & Sass, 2000). But one problem with this approach, as with biological theories, is that many serious crimes are committed by people who are quite normal (Vito & Holmes, 1994). A second problem is that psychological theories focus on the individual, ignoring why a society defines some people as rule breakers in the first place. In short, to understand crime, we need to turn to sociological theories.

MAKING THE GRADE

Durkheim argued that crime was necessary to the operation of society.

SOCIAL PROBLEMS in Everyday Life

Has some campus crime brought people together, as in the photo below? Explain.

Explaining Crime: Sociological Theories

According to the sociological approach, the organization of society itself gives rise to certain laws and certain patterns of criminality. The following discussions apply sociology's three major theoretical approaches to the issue of crime.

Structural-Functional Analysis: Why Society Creates Crime

The structural-functionalist approach highlights the importance of any social pattern to the operation of society as a system. This approach guides several important theories of crime, beginning with the classic work of Emile Durkheim.

Emile Durkheim: The Functions of Crime

Emile Durkheim (1964a, orig. 1895; 1964b, orig. 1893), one of the first great sociologists, began by pointing out that crime exists everywhere. If so, he reasoned, crime must somehow be useful to society. He went on to identify four functions of crime:

1. **Crime affirms a society's norms and values.** People cannot have a belief in what is good without having a corresponding belief in what is bad. In short, societies must recognize crime if they are to uphold a sense of morality.
2. **Recognizing crime helps everyone clarify the line between right and wrong.** When a college convicts a student of cheating, that community is educating everyone on campus about behavior that will not be tolerated.
3. **Reacting to crime brings people together.** When someone in a community is victimized by crime, others are likely to share a sense of outrage.
4. **Crime encourages social change.** Deviant members of a community act in ways that sugest alternatives to the status quo. What people condemn as wrong at one point in time (whether it is rock-and-roll music or use of a particular drug) may end up being the norm later on.

Notice that Durkheim's theory asks not why some *individual* would engage in crime but why *society* defines some behavior as criminal. This insight explains the pattern noted earlier, that most people who are defined as criminals are quite normal. Durkheim concluded that crime itself is a normal part of society.

Robert Merton: Strain Theory

Robert Merton (1938, 1968) agreed that crime is a product of society itself. His theory helps explain why rule breaking takes various forms. Merton begins by saying that our society defines "success" in terms of certain goals (such as financial security) but does not always provide everyone with the means (including schooling and good jobs) to reach these goals. Therefore, Merton continues, patterns of rule breaking depend on whether or not people accept society's goals and whether or not they have the opportunity to reach them. Merton identified five specific outcomes, shown in Figure 6–5.

Conformity is likely when people accept society's goals and also have the approved means to get there. But what if legitimate means to success are not available? Children growing up in poor rural communities of Appalachia, for example, may see rich people on television but find few good jobs available locally. As a result of the strain between cultural goals and limited means to achieve them, people may engage in what Merton calls *innovation,* the use of unconventional means to achieve a conventional goal. For example, to make a living, some poor people in the Appalachian region have turned to growing marijuana. Theft and other property crimes can also be explained in this way.

Another option for people who lack legitimate means to achieve success

According to Emile Durkheim, one of the key functions of crime is uniting people with a shared sense of outrage. These residents of Binghamton, New York, came together in 2009 to remember the people killed in the violent episode described in the opening to this chapter. Has any similar event taken place in your community? Explain.

MAKING THE GRADE

Can you give an example of each of Merton's categories in the figure below?

is *ritualism*, which Merton defined as living almost obsessively by the rules. Doing this does not bring great success, but it does offer some measure of respectability. A ritualist—for example, the local county clerk who never misses a day, takes exactly forty-five minutes for lunch, and never makes personal telephone calls at work—might never get rich but is proud to play by the rules.

Still another response to a lack of opportunity is *retreatism*, turning away from both approved goals and legitimate means. In effect, retreatists "drop out" of society. Retreatists include some alcoholics, drug addicts, street people, and backwoods survivalists.

Finally, *rebellion* involves not just rejecting conventional goals and means but also advocating some new system. Instead of dropping out of society the way retreatists do, rebels come up with a new system, playing out their ideas as members of religious cults or revolutionary political groups.

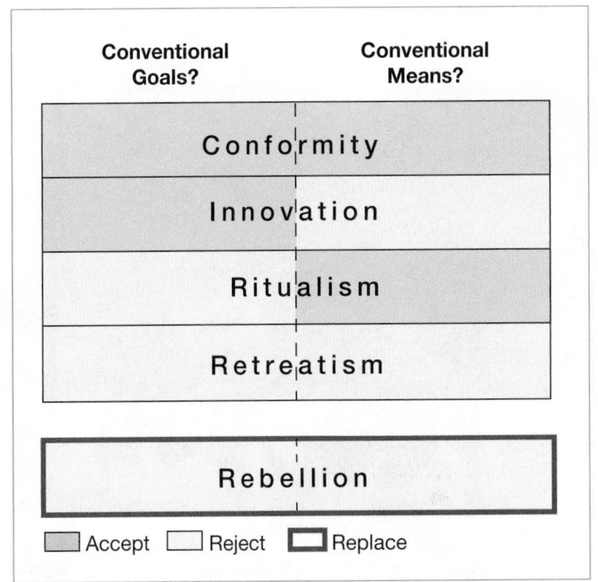

FIGURE 6–5 Merton's Strain Theory of Deviance

Source: Based on Merton (1968).

Richard Cloward and Lloyd Ohlin: Opportunity Structure

Richard Cloward and Lloyd Ohlin (1966) extended Merton's theory, arguing that whether or not one becomes a criminal depends not only on the lack of legitimate opportunity (such as schooling or jobs) but also on the presence of illegitimate opportunity (such as the chance to learn crime skills and carry out a crime). In other words, people cut off from conventional opportunity are likely to engage in crime only if they have the resources to do so. In short, patterns of conformity and criminality depend on what Cloward and Ohlin call people's *relative opportunity structure.*

Among people who have little legitimate opportunity to get to college but who do have illegitimate opportunity to make money through, say, prostitution or drug dealing, criminal activity is likely. People who are cut off from both legitimate and illegitimate opportunity may express their frustration through violence.

Travis Hirschi: Control Theory

Perhaps the best-known theory of crime is Travis Hirschi's *control theory*. Hirschi (1969) argues that what discourages people from committing crime is having strong social ties, being well integrated within the community. Hirschi points out four kinds of social ties that operate to control crime:

1. **Attachment to other people,** including parents, teachers, coaches, and friends
2. **Commitment to conformity,** a belief that playing by the rules usually pays off
3. **Involvement in conventional activities,** including team sports or religious groups
4. **A belief in the rightness of cultural norms and values** and seeing society as basically good

If these four kinds of social ties are strong, people are likely to resist the temptation of crime. To the extent that they are weak, the risk of criminality rises.

CRITICAL REVIEW The strength of structural-functional theories lies in showing, first, that the consequences of crime are good as well as bad. In addition, this approach explains that crime cannot be understood simply by looking at individuals but requires that we examine the organization of society itself.

At the same time, these theories have limitations. Durkheim may be right about crime being necessary, but how much crime is needed? Similarly, looking at Merton's theory, not everyone defines success in the same way or agrees about the right and wrong ways to get there. Cloward and Ohlin's theory seems unable to explain white-collar offenses committed by people who already have so much going for them. Finally, although Hirschi's theory is supported by other research (Langbein & Bess, 2002), it says little about how and why society defines some people who break the law as criminal while ignoring others. We turn now to the symbolic-interaction approach, which addresses exactly this issue.

MAKING THE GRADE

Labeling theory shifts our focus from what a person does to how others respond.

labeling theory the idea that crime and all other forms of rule breaking result not so much from what people do as from how others respond to those actions

stigma a powerful negative social label that radically changes a person's self-concept and social identity

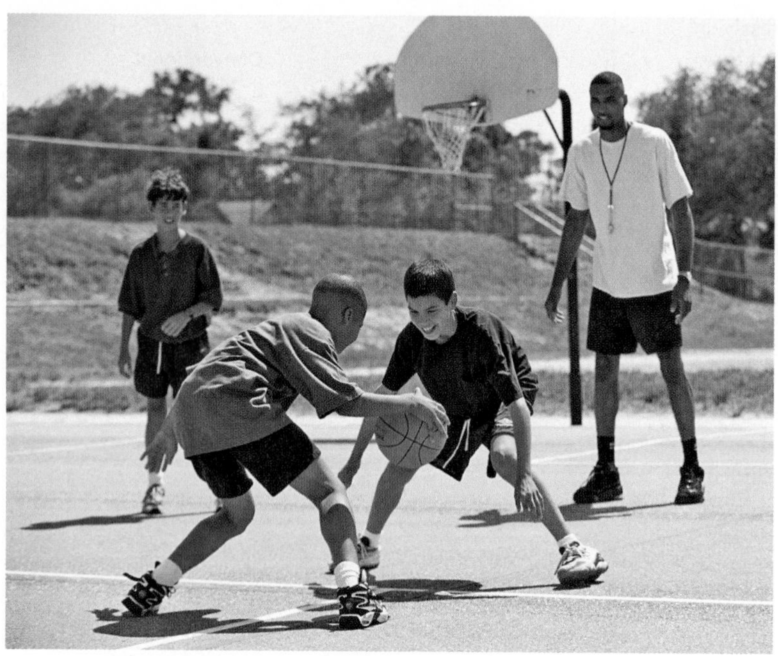

How might Travis Hirschi, who developed control theory, see something very important in this everyday scene on a community playground? Can you apply his theory to this situation?

Symbolic-Interaction Analysis: Socially Constructing Reality

Symbolic-interaction analysis examines how people construct reality in everyday interaction. From this point of view, people learn criminal or violent behavior as they learn everything else: from their surroundings. In addition, what becomes a crime and who becomes a criminal result from a process of social definition that may vary from time to time and from place to place.

Edwin Sutherland: Differential Association Theory

Edwin Sutherland (1940) pointed out that learning takes place in social groups. Therefore, he continued, whether a person moves toward conformity or deviance depends on the extent of association with others who encourage—versus those who discourage—conventional behavior. This is Sutherland's theory of *differential association*.

Researchers studying high school students have found a link between young people turning to drugs or becoming sexually active and the degree to which their peer groups encouraged such activity. In short, peer groups can be a powerful influence on young people, encouraging either conventional or delinquent behavior (Akers et al., 1979; Miller & Mathews, 2001; Little & Rankin, 2001).

Howard S. Becker: Labeling Theory

When does behavior "cross the line"? Howard S. Becker (1966:9) states that the only real definition of rule breaking is behavior that people label that way. **Labeling theory** is *the idea that crime and all other forms of rule breaking result not so much from what people do as from how others respond to those actions.* In other words, no action is right or wrong in any absolute sense. Consider the case of drinking alcohol: Is drinking likely to get a teenager into trouble? The answer depends on any number of factors, including whether anyone saw it; if so, how the observer defined it (taking into account *when* the drinking took place, *where* it took place, and *who* was doing the drinking); and whether the observer decided to do anything about it.

Labeling theory states that the "reality" of drinking, being sexually active, or taking something that belongs to someone else is a matter of how people label that behavior. Crime is simply one example of socially constructed reality, which is a highly variable process of detection, definition, and response. From Becker's point of view, the line separating crime from conformity is both thin and ever-changing.

Edwin Lemert: Primary and Secondary Deviance

Edwin Lemert (1951, 1972) explored how individuals can be changed by the labels others apply to them. To begin, many common norm violations—skipping school, underage drinking, experimenting with drugs—bring little reaction from others. Lemert refers to these incidents, which may have only passing significance, as *primary* acts of deviance.

But what if others define these minor norm violations as important? People might define a young man who tries an illegal drug as a "user" and keep their distance from him. Or a young woman who has a love affair might find herself being talked about as "easy" by others on campus. Such reactions often provoke confusion and anger and may have long-term consequences, such as the loss of friends. The person may then seek the company of people who are more accepting, perhaps those who have experienced rejection for the same behavior themselves. In this way, the reaction of others to primary deviance can provoke *secondary* deviance, in which the person begins to change, now basing choices on this deviant identity.

GETTING INVOLVED

To see the power of stigma, consider this: How do most people feel about someone they learn is an "ex-con"?

MAKING THE GRADE

Be sure you understand the difference between primary deviance and secondary deviance.

Erving Goffman: The Power of Stigma

Growing up, we hear people say, "Sticks and stones can break your bones, but names can never hurt you." Erving Goffman (1963), for one, disagreed. Calling someone a "criminal" can be a form of **stigma,** *a powerful negative social label that radically changes a person's self-concept and social identity.* Once stigmatized, a person may find that friends and legitimate opportunities begin to disappear. In some cases, being stigmatized by others may launch a person on what sociologists call a *deviant career,* marked by an increasingly deviant identity and deeper involvement in rule-breaking behavior.

Criminal prosecution is a powerful ritual that stigmatizes a person. In court, the person stands before the community as the prosecutor presents the evidence, and if found guilty, a judge or jury may well declare the person unfit to remain in society. The stigma attached by this "degradation ceremony" may be very hard to lose (Garfinkel, 1956).

CRITICAL REVIEW Symbolic-interaction theories help us understand how people may come to define certain criminal behavior in positive terms and how some people end up defined as "criminal" by others. In each case, the reality of crime is socially constructed.

Even so, there is little disagreement that some behavior—such as intentionally killing a person—is a serious crime. Therefore, labeling theory may best be applied to milder offenses such as drug use or prostitution. Another problem is that by making crime seem highly relative, symbolic-interaction theory misses the fact that some categories of people are always at higher risk of being called criminal. This concern brings us to the third theoretical approach, social-conflict theory.

Social-Conflict Analysis: Crime and Inequality

The social-conflict approach highlights how social inequality shapes who and what is defined as criminal. How laws are written, which neighborhoods police patrol, which categories of people end up being arrested—all these reflect who has power and who does not.

Karl Marx: Class and Crime

Karl Marx understood social problems in terms of class conflict. He believed that in a capitalist society, the legal system protects the property of the capitalist class. Capitalists gain wealth legally simply by "doing business"; ordinary people who threaten capitalists' wealth risk arrest as "common criminals" or "political revolutionaries." Furthermore, with little wealth of their own, members of the working class may turn to crime in order to survive (Spitzer, 1980).

From a Marxist point of view, then, the solution to the crime problem is to eliminate capitalism in favor of a more egalitarian system that serves the interests of everyone (McClellan, 1985; Vito & Holmes, 1994).

Feminist Theory: Gender and Crime

As Chapter 4 ("Gender Inequality") explains, gender stratification is the pattern by which men have more wealth, prestige, and power than women. Feminists argue that gender stratification is also evident in patterns of crime.

Feminists claim that U.S. society subordinates women to men. Therefore, as second-class citizens, many women look to crime, including fraud, drug dealing, and prostitution, to increase their opportunity to make a living. To support their position, feminists point out that when law enforcement officials combat crimes such as prostitution, they are far more likely to arrest women (working as prostitutes) than men (clients who also break the law) (Daly & Chesney-Lind, 1988; Simpson, 1989; Jenness, 1993). Some feminists—especially socialist feminists who support the ideas of Karl Marx—argue that capitalism exploits both men and women, who must turn to crime in their struggle to get by. Here again, the solution to the crime problem begins with eliminating capitalism.

CRITICAL REVIEW All social-conflict theories argue that the criminal justice system serves the interests of powerful segments of the population. But this approach has limitations. For one thing, it has little to say about why well-off people engage in white-collar, corporate crime, and organized crime—and sometimes land in jail for doing so. In addition, if capitalism is the cause of crime, why do socialist societies have so many prisons? And if feminist analysis is correct, why are men many times more likely than women to end up in prison?

The Applying Theory table on page 170 summarizes what each theoretical approach says about the crime problem.

 POLITICS AND CRIME

Constructing Problems and Defining Solutions

Crime has long been an issue of great public concern. But like so many social issues, how people see the crime problem and its solutions depends on their political viewpoints. We now examine the crime problem from the conservative, liberal, and radical-left perspectives.

MAKING THE GRADE

Use the table below to review the three theoretical approaches to crime.

MAKING THE GRADE

Based on the political analysis on pages 170–171, would you say that Hirschi's conrol theory is conservative, liberal, or radical? Why?

APPLYING THEORY

Crime and Criminal Justice

	What is the level of analysis?	What is crime?	Who commits crime?
Structural-functional approach	Macro-level	Durkheim said that as a society defines crime, it affirms norms and values, draws the line between right and wrong, brings people together, and encourages social change. Merton's strain theory linked types of rule breaking to a society's goals and the means available to attain them. Cloward and Ohlin's opportunity structure theory linked crime to legitimate and illegitimate opportunity. Hirschi's control theory states that strong social ties discourage crime.	Durkheim claimed that all societies create crime. Merton, Cloward and Ohlin, and Hirschi all point to conditions that make crime more or less likely.
Symbolic-interaction approach	Micro-level	Sutherland's differential association theory links crime and violence to patterns of learning. Labeling theory claims that rule breaking results from an audience defining some action in that way. Lemert explains how primary deviance can lead to secondary deviance and a deviant identity. Goffman pointed out that a deviant identity can be a powerful stigma.	This approach claims that anyone or anything can be defined as deviant. All deviance results from a highly variable process of social definition on the part of some audience.
Social-conflict approach	Macro-level	Marx viewed the legal system as a way for capitalists to protect their wealth; criminals are those who threaten capitalism. Feminism points to gender inequality as forcing poor women to engage in crime; male power is evident in the operation of the criminal justice system.	This approach claims that people with less social power—workers in relation to capitalists, women in relation to men—are at greater risk of criminal involvement.

Conservatives: Crime, Violence, and Morality

Conservatives believe that social controls are needed to keep people from engaging in violence or criminal behavior. The most effective control, as they see it, is conscience—a person's own sense of right and wrong. For this reason, conservatives emphasize the need for families, churches, schools, and local communities to teach moral values to young people. Young women and men who learn from their families respect for the law, who have strong religious values, and who are actively involved in their communities are unlikely to get into trouble.

Conservatives see the rise in crime rates beginning in the 1960s as the result of a growing permissiveness in society.

MAKING THE GRADE

Conservatives see crime as a moral issue; liberals and radicals see crime as an economic issue.

SOCIAL PROBLEMS in Everyday Life

Has the recent recession caused any rise in crime in your community?

Crime rates went up, they claim, because the share of two-parent families started going down, coupled to a weakening of religious values, tradition, and neighborhood ties. It is no surprise to conservatives, for example, that a majority of young people arrested for violent crimes do not have a father living at home.

If some families fail to raise children with proper values, conservatives continue, society must turn to tougher laws, more aggressive policing, and harsher penalties to keep crime and violence in check. But conservatives doubt that the criminal justice system, by itself, can ever solve the crime problem. The key to controlling crime always lies with parents who teach their children to make the right choices in a world filled with pressures to do the wrong thing.

Liberals: Crime, Violence, and Jobs

Liberals like to think that most people want to do the right thing, but many live in situations that pressure them to break the law. Thus, as liberals see it, crime and violence are caused by a harmful environment, especially lives twisted by poverty. Millions of U.S. children are born into poor families, pass through substandard schools, and find few jobs waiting for them. It should be no surprise that in such surroundings, some young people lose hope, adopt an "oppositional culture" that rejects authority figures, and end up joining criminal gangs (E. Anderson, 1994, 2002). In short, liberals agree with conservatives that crime and violence are serious social problems, but they disagree about the cause.

Liberals also disagree with conservatives about the solution to the crime problem. They claim that whole districts of our cities and many rural regions need economic renewal. If jobs are available, liberals argue, families will be stronger, youngsters will not lose hope, and fewer people will turn to crime. As evidence, liberals point to the strong economy of the 1990s as the main reason for the drop in crime rates throughout that decade. Likewise, they claim that the categories of people who suffer most from poverty are those who also suffer most from crime—both as offenders and as victims. Liberals worry that the economic recession that began in 2008 will push the crime rate higher in the years to come.

Finally, until our society can provide enough jobs for everyone, liberals see the criminal justice system as a revolving door: People leave prison only to return because they have little opportunity to make it through honest work.

The Radical Left: Crime and Inequality

The real crime in this society, from a radical-left perspective, is the great economic inequality, a vast gap that has increased in recent decades. The recent economic downturn, with people losing their jobs and some even losing their homes, is only the latest chapter in the story of an economic system that fails to meet the needs of tens of millions of people. Economic insecurity is the real violence that is carried out against people every day, and if some people resort to crime, it is because there may be no other way to get by.

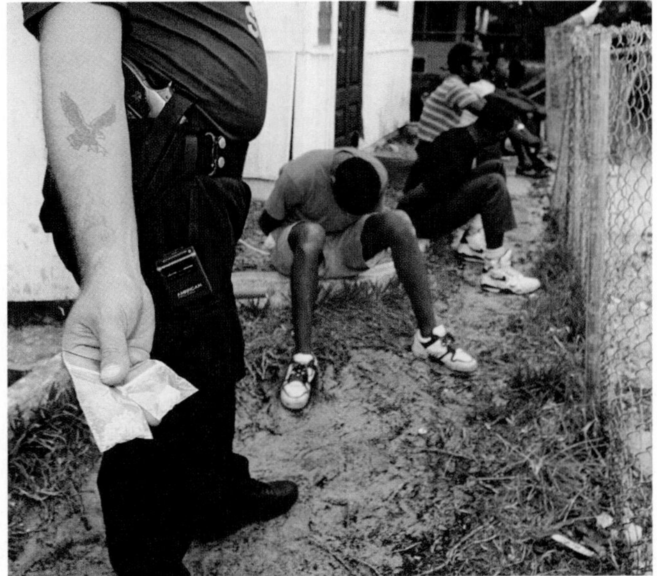

Young people growing up in low-income urban neighborhoods are at risk for getting into trouble with the law. Conservatives claim that the solution to crime lies in strong families, churches, and schools that teach moral values, including respect for the law. Liberals point to poverty caused by a lack of jobs that pressures people toward crime. Radicals on the left say that our capitalist society fails to support millions of people, forcing them to turn to crime to survive. Which view is closest to your own? Why?

Radicals on the left accuse conservatives of blaming the victims by pointing to single parents as the source of the crime problem. They criticize liberals for seeking mere reform measures and for not recognizing that economic inequality and a lack of jobs are built into the capitalist system. Radicals on the left see the "get tough" policies of the criminal justice system—including proposals to add to the numbers of police and to build more prisons—as simply one more way to oppress poor people and stabilize an inhuman system. The radical-left solution begins with restructuring the economic and political system toward an egalitarian social order that can make a real claim to justice.

The Left to Right table on page 172 sums up the various political views of the crime problem and its solutions.

MAKING THE GRADE

Use the table below to review the three political approaches to crime and violence.

LEFT TO RIGHT

The Politics of Crime, Violence, and Criminal Justice

	RADICAL-LEFT VIEW	LIBERAL VIEW	CONSERVATIVE VIEW
WHAT IS THE PROBLEM?	The great economic inequality of a capitalist society promotes criminal activity by the underclass, individuals unable to succeed by legitimate means; the criminal justice system is used to maintain order and protect the interests of capitalist elites.	A lack of jobs is the major factor that forces people to break the law, often as a means to survive and to support their families.	The moral order of society is breaking down; because of the decline of the two-parent family, weakening religious values, and so much violence in the mass media, children are not being taught to behave responsibly.
WHAT IS THE SOLUTION?	Crime and violence can never be controlled until class differences cease to exist. The real violence in our society is the oppression of capitalism. Therefore, the capitalist economy should be eliminated in favor of a more equitable system.	Government needs to use resources not to build more prisons but to expand economic opportunities in poor urban and rural areas where people are in desperate need of work.	The single most significant step toward reducing crime and violence is to strengthen families and increase the culture's emphasis on good parenting; tougher law enforcement is also necessary when crime has occurred.

JOIN THE DEBATE

1. About three-fourths of men in federal prisons grew up without a father present in the home. How would conservatives interpret this fact? How might liberals and radicals interpret it?
2. What trends in crime would people across the political spectrum expect to see in the coming decades? Provide reasons for your predictions.
3. Which of the three political analyses of crime and violence presented here do you find most convincing? Why?

Going On from Here

Crime has been part of the human story since people enacted the first laws thousands of years ago. Although some crime helps society operate, as Durkheim explained, few people deny that today's high crime rate is a serious social problem. Current debates over crime focus not only on street crimes (property crimes and violent crimes) but also on white-collar crime, corporate crime, and crime motivated by hate. In addition, organized crime now operates on a global scale.

What is the likely future of crime? As you have seen, a decline in drug use, adding more police, and building more prisons have pushed the rates down in recent years. In the short term, however, the recent economic recession is likely to push crime rates up.

Politics is also part of the crime debate. Conservatives point to the need to strengthen families, but exactly how to do that has never been very clear. Liberals point to the need for more jobs, yet even during good economic times, crime rates have been high. Radicals call for a complete overhaul of the economic system, although even countries with far more economic equality than we have in the United States still have high crime rates.

In the foreseeable future, the burden of crime control is likely to remain squarely on the shoulders of the criminal justice system. Without doubt, the most popular idea in the United States when it comes to solving the problem of crime is to "get tough," which means adding more police, more prisons, and tougher sentences for people convicted of serious crimes. So strong is this public opinion that no politician today can afford to be viewed as being "soft on crime." However, sociological research casts doubt on the idea that the criminal justice system can solve the crime problem on its own.

We can hope that the recent economic recession will come to an end soon so that the downward trend in the U.S. crime rate will continue. In addition, population experts tell us that the share of people in the "high-crime years" between the middle teens and middle twenties will fall in decades to come. Perhaps this trend will help control crime—at least until U.S. society develops a more effective solution.

DEFINING SOLUTIONS

What is the best way to keep crime in check?

As this chapter has explained, although the crime rate has declined in recent decades, crime and violence remain serious problems in much of the country. Look at the photos below to see two different ways of defining solutions to these problems.

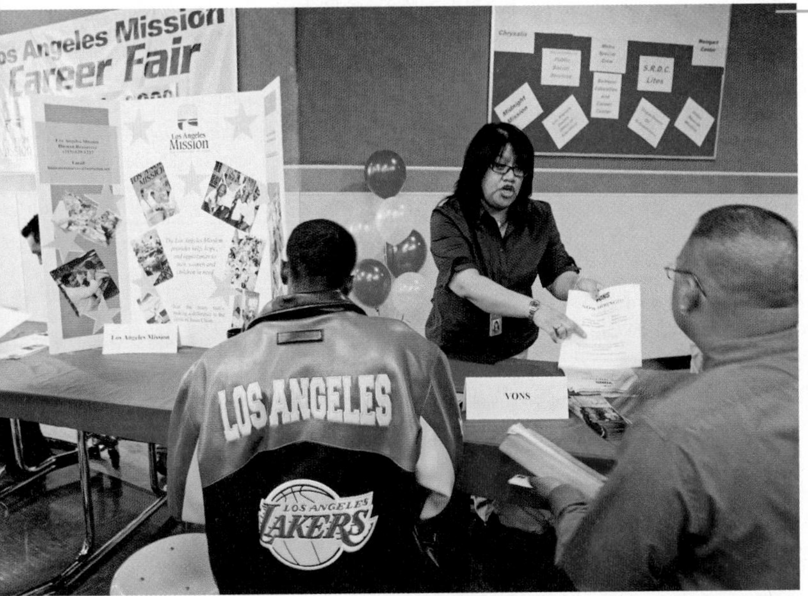

Liberals tend to see crime and violence as an economic issue, the result of too few jobs, which leads young people to feel hopeless about their chances of succeeding in an unjust world. The solution to these problems lies in providing economic opportunity, so that young people have plenty of "legitimate opportunity" to lead productive and law-abiding lives as adults. Liberals look to government to set economic policy that benefits the population as a whole, to provide job counseling to young people, and to ensure that everyone receives a sound education.

Conservatives tend to see crime and violence as caused by greed or perhaps even an aggressive human nature. The solution to these problems lies in society providing restraints. Parents should raise children to care about others and to respect the law, and all members of a community should look out for one another. Such thinking is embodied in the Guardian Angels, a nonprofit organization founded in New York City in 1979. Now active in a dozen cities and spreading around the world, the Guardian Angels are volunteers who patrol neighborhoods in their distinctive uniforms to get the message out that "someone is watching!"

HINT

Political attitudes guide how people view crime and violence and also lead them to prefer one solution over another. The conservative approach focuses on people themselves—the claim that individuals must make good choices—and supports solutions such as strong families and integrated communities. The liberal approach, and even more the approach of the radical left, focuses on the larger economic system as setting the stage for the opportunities we all have. From that point of view, a peaceful society must also be a just society, one in which there is equal opportunity for all. So which is it—a focus on individuals and the choices they make or a focus on structuring society in a equal way? Where do you fall on this important question?

Getting Involved: Applications & Exercises

1. Do some research about the developing problem of computer crime, including identity theft. How big a problem is identity theft now? What do analysts predict about the future? What new tactics will law enforcement need to control computer offenses?
2. See whether a local law enforcement agency (such as local or campus police) will let you accompany an officer on duty. Note how a police officer's view of crime and law enforcement may differ from your own.
3. Watch several episodes of the television show *COPS*. How does this show portray the typical offender? Does this portrayal seem fair to you in light of what you have learned in this chapter? Why or why not?
4. The psychologist Philip Zimbardo conducted a famous prison study at Stanford University (see Chapter 1, "Studying Social Problems"). Look at reports of this research: One report is on the Web at http://www.prisonexp.org. What conclusions about prison does this research suggest?

MAKING THE GRADE

A DEFINING MOMENT
U.S. Society Discovers Child Abuse p. 156

CHAPTER 6 Crime, Violence, and Criminal Justice

Norms, Law, and Crime

- Societies formally enact some **NORMS** in the form of **LAWS**.
- **CRIME**, which is the violation of criminal law, includes more serious felonies and less serious misdemeanors.

pp. 142–43

norms (p. 142) rules and expectations by which a society guides the behavior of its members

law (p. 142) a norm formally created through a society's political system

crime (p. 142) the violation of a criminal law enacted by federal, state, or local government

misdemeanor (p. 142) a less serious crime punishable by less than one year in prison

felony (p. 142) a more serious crime punishable by at least one year in prison

Crime: The Extent of the Problem

CRIMES AGAINST PERSONS (or **VIOLENT CRIME**), include murder, rape, aggravated assault, and robbery.

Arrests for Violent Crimes

- young people ages 15–24: 41% of all arrests
- males: 82% of all arrests
- whites: 59% of all arrests

pp. 143–47

CRIMES AGAINST PROPERTY include burglary, larceny-theft, motor vehicle theft, and arson.

Arrests for Property Crimes

- young people ages 15–24: 47% of all arrests
- males: 67% of all arrests
- whites: 68% of all arrests

pp. 147–49

crime against property (p. 143) crime that involves theft of property belonging to others

crime against persons (p. 143) crime that involves violence or the threat of violence against others

stalking (p. 144) repeated efforts by someone to establish or reestablish a relationship against the will of the victim

Other Dimensions of the Crime Problem

JUVENILE DELINQUENCY

- The juvenile justice system seeks to reform rather than simply to punish offenders.

pp. 150–51

HATE CRIME

- Forty-five states and the federal government have **HATE CRIME** laws that provide more severe penalties for such crimes.

p. 151

WHITE-COLLAR CRIME and **CORPORATE CRIME**

- Typically, such wrongdoing is handled in civil courts, but a recent trend is toward the filing of criminal charges.

pp. 151–52

ORGANIZED CRIME, which has a long history in the United States, also operates throughout most of the world.

pp. 152–53

VICTIMLESS CRIMES are offenses that directly harm only the offender.

p. 153

juvenile delinquency (p. 150) violation of the law by young people

hate crime (p. 151) a criminal offense against a person, property, or society motivated by the offender's bias against a race, religion, disability, sexual orientation, or ethnicity or national origin

white-collar crime (p. 151) illegal activities conducted by people of high social position during the course of their employment or regular business activities

corporate crime (p. 152) an illegal act committed by a corporation or by persons acting on its behalf

organized crime (p. 152) a business operation that supplies illegal goods and services

victimless crimes (p. 153) offenses that directly harm only the person who commits them

What Is Violence?

VIOLENCE is behavior that causes injury to people or damage to property. Whether people view violence as a problem depends on many factors, including

- the intentions of the actor
- whether the action conforms to cultural norms and values
- whether the action threatens the social order
- whether the actions are carried out by or against the government

pp. 154–55

Most **MURDERS** are committed by male offenders using guns. In many cases, offender and victim are of the same race.

- **Mass murder** usually occurs in homes, schools, or workplaces, where people expect to be safe.
- Most **serial killers** are considered mentally ill.

pp. 155–56

violence (p. 154) behavior that causes injury to people or damage to property

institutional violence (p. 154) violence carried out by government representatives under the law

anti-institutional violence (p. 154) violence directed against the government in violation of the law

mass murder (p. 155) the intentional, unlawful killing of four or more people at one time and place

serial murder (p. 155) the killing of several people by one offender over a period of time

Social Dimensions of Violence

Research suggests that violence in the **MASS MEDIA** raises the risk of deadly violence in some people, increases aggressiveness in many people, and desensitizes all of us to violence.

pp. 156–57

POVERTY is linked to violence. Poor nutrition, inadequate schooling, substandard housing, and lack of jobs all raise the stress of daily living.

p. 157

Government studies suggest there are more than 26,500 **YOUTH GANGS** in the United States.

pp. 157–58

60% of inmates imprisoned for violent offenses claim they were under the influence of illegal **DRUGS** when they committed their crime.

p. 158

There are some 280 million **GUNS** in the United States; 35% of U.S. households have at least one gun.

p. 193

youth gangs (p. 157) groups of young people who identify with one another and with a particular territory

The Criminal Justice System

POLICE are the most visible part of the criminal justice system. Police officers use discretion, evaluating situations before deciding whether or not to intervene.

pp. 159–60

COURTS determine the innocence or guilt of people charged with crimes. Although the U.S. court system is an adversarial process, most cases are settled through plea bargaining.

p. 160

PUNISHMENT of offenders is carried out for four reasons: retribution, deterrence, rehabilitation, and societal protection.

pp. 160–62

criminal justice system (p. 159) society's use of due process, police, courts, and punishment to enforce the law

plea bargaining (p. 160) a negotiation in which the state reduces a defendant's charge in exchange for a guilty plea

retribution (p. 160) moral vengeance by which society inflicts suffering on an offender comparable to that caused by the offense

deterrence (p. 161) using punishment to discourage further crime

rehabilitation (p. 161) reforming an offender to prevent future offenses

societal protection (p. 161) protecting the public by rendering an offender incapable of further offenses through incarceration or execution

criminal recidivism (p. 161) later offenses by people previously convicted of crimes

community-based corrections (p. 162) correctional programs that take place in society at large rather than behind prison walls

Explaining Crime: Sociological Theories

Structural-Functional Analysis: Why Society Creates Crime

- Durkheim argued that crime is a normal element of society's operation.
- Merton, Cloward, and Ohlin described the role of opportunity in explaining patterns of rule breaking.
- Hirschi's *control theory* argues that social ties are important in helping a person resist temptation to break the law.

pp. 166–67

Symbolic-Interaction Analysis: Socially Constructing Reality

- Sutherland's *differential association theory* states that people learn criminal or noncriminal attitudes from others in groups.
- *Labeling theory* argues that crime results less from what people do than from how others respond to the behavior.
- Goffman explained that being stigmatized as a rule breaker may deepen a person's deviant identity.

pp. 168–69

Social-Conflict Analysis: Crime and Social Inequality

- Marxist theory highlights how capitalism provides most wealth and power to a small elite who use the criminal justice system against those who challenge the system.
- Feminist theory points to male domination of society as limiting women's opportunity and forcing women into lives of crime.

p. 169

labeling theory (p. 168) the idea that crime and all other forms of rule breaking result not so much from what people do as from how others respond to those actions

stigma (p. 169) a powerful negative social label that radically changes a person's self-concept and social identity

See the **Applying Theory** table on page 170.

Politics and Crime: Constructing Problems and Defining Solutions

Radical Left: Crime and Inequality

RADICALS ON THE LEFT point to the injustice of economic inequality in capitalist societies as the reason for crime.

p. 171

Liberals: Crime and Jobs

LIBERALS see crime as caused by a harmful environment that is the result of poverty and a lack of jobs. People resort to crime because there is no opportunity to succeed in life through honest work.

p. 171

Conservatives: Crime and Morality

CONSERVATIVES blame the rise in crime rates on the growing permissiveness in society that has resulted from a decline in traditional values.

pp. 170–71

See the **Left to Right** table on page 172.

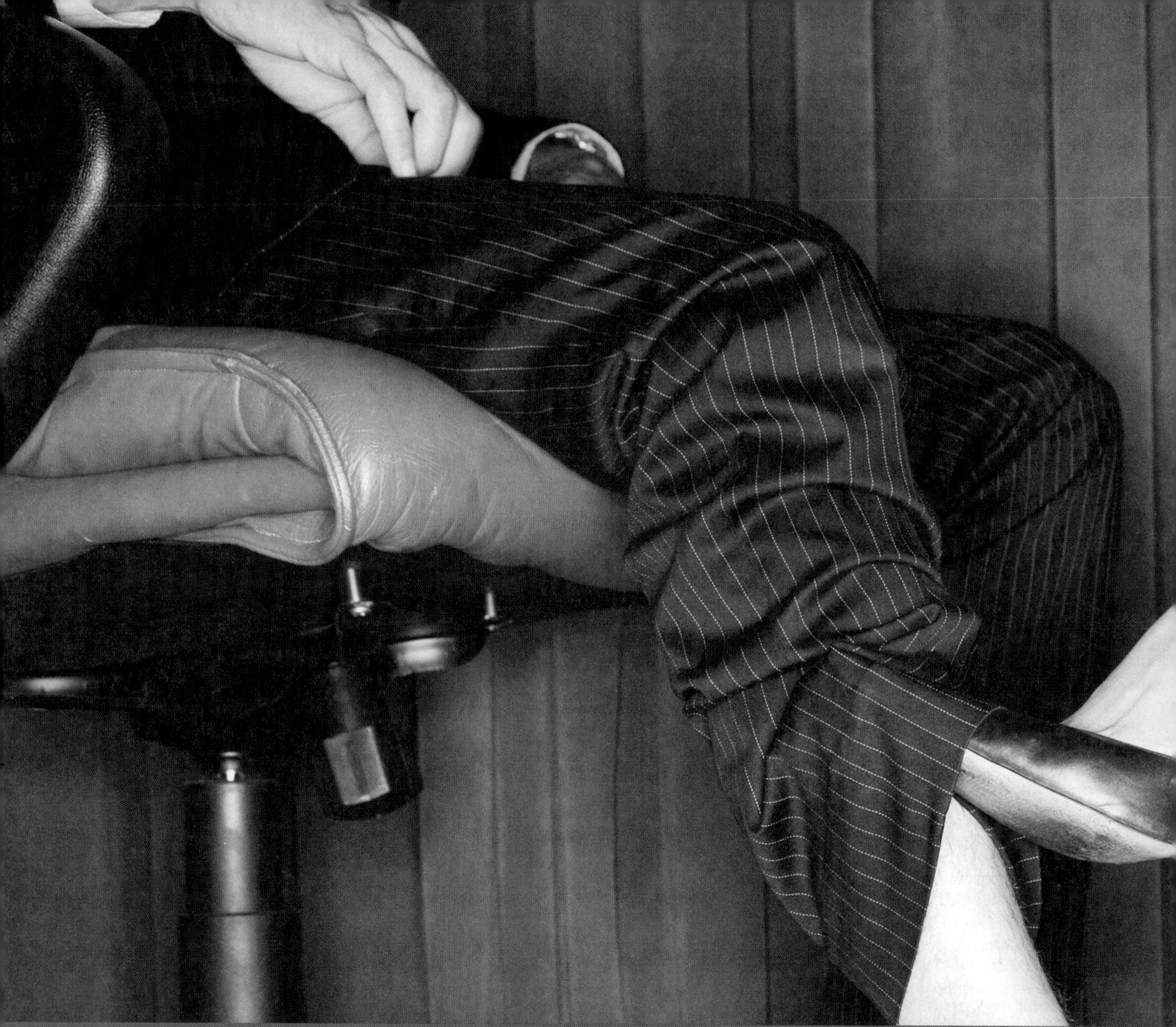

CONSTRUCTING THE PROBLEM

How can sex be the cause of social problems?

For most of our country's history, people didn't talk much about sex, and most people considered any sexual activity other than intercourse by married partners to be wrong.

Does the law decide how people can or cannot express their sexuality?

Yes. For example, during most of our country's history, homosexual activity was against the law; even today, same-sex couples are still denied the right to marry in most states.

Do you know all the dangers of sexual activity?

Sexual activity exposes people to the risk of infection by more than fifty diseases, including AIDS.

CHAPTER 7

Sexuality

CHAPTER OVERVIEW

WHAT IS SEX, and how is sex both a biological and a cultural issue? This chapter examines sexual attitudes and practices over the course of our nation's history, including the sexual revolution and society's increasing support of gay rights. It also explores controversial sexuality-related issues such as pornography, prostitution, and abortion. You will learn about the major types of sexually transmitted diseases and behaviors that put people at risk. You will carry out theoretical analysis of sexuality and learn how "problems" and "solutions" involving sexuality reflect people's political attitudes.

The biggest complaint among young people in Jefferson City, a small town in Missouri, is that there is "nothing to do." But Peter Bearman, a sociologist who studied the students at Jefferson High, discovered that there is one thing these young men and women often do: They have sex.

Interviews with 832 high school students revealed that 573 (69 percent) had been involved in one or more "sexual and romantic relationships" during the previous eighteen months. The research, which sought to learn about the spread of sexually transmitted diseases (STDs), tracked the sexual partners of each of the students who reported being sexually active. The result: Students were linked by common sexual partners to a greater degree than anyone might have expected. In fact, half of the sexually active students (288 in all; in the diagram, red dots represent females and blue dots represent males) were "chained together" through other sexual partners (Bearman, Moody, & Stovel, 2004).

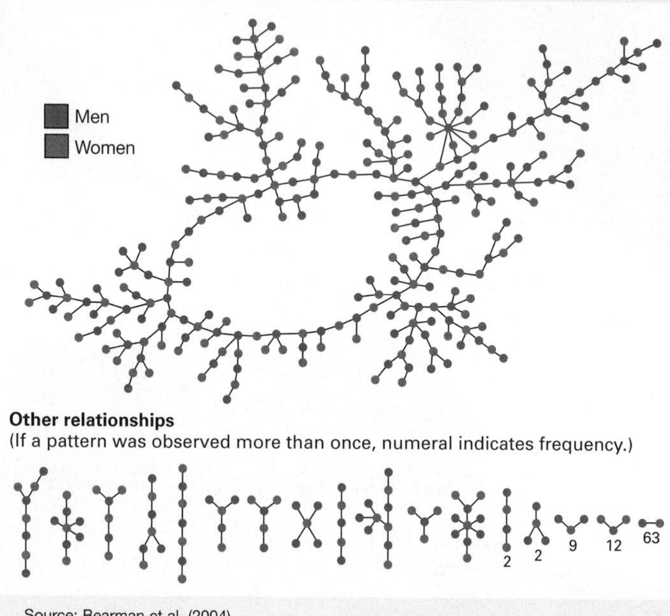

Source: Bearman et al. (2004).

Sexual networks like this represent pathways through which STDs can be transmitted and suggest how STDs can spread from one individual to a much larger population in a short period of time. This study also shows how sociological research can teach us about important social problems involving sexuality. This chapter explores many sexuality issues, including not only STDs but also gay marriage, prostitution, and pornography. We begin with some basic definitions.

What Is Sex?

Sex reflects the operation of both biology and culture. To better understand this concept, we need to examine sex from a biological and a cultural perspective.

Sex: A Biological Issue

Sex is *the biological distinction between females and males.* The two sexes have different organs used for reproduction, the *genitals,* which are also called *primary sex characteristics.* In addition, when people mature, they typically display different physical traits, called *secondary sex characteristics:* Females develop breasts and wider hips, and males develop more muscle and body hair.

The term **sex** also refers to *activity that leads to sexual gratification and possibly reproduction.* From a biological point of view, reproduction is vital to the survival of a species. Among humans, a female provides an ovum, or egg, which is fertilized by a male's sperm through sexual intercourse to form a fertilized embryo. The embryo contains twenty-three matching chromosomes, which are the biological codes that determine a child's sex and other physical traits.

Sex: A Cultural Issue

Sociologists point out that sex, like all behavior, is guided by culture. Because sex is cultural, sexual attitudes and practices vary from one place to another. In every society, some of the most important cultural norms influence the selection of sexual partners. These norms involve *age* (some societies accept sexual activity on the part of children, for example, but others define such behavior as a serious problem), *marital status* (some societies restrict sexual activity to married partners, but others are more permissive), and *sex of partner* (societies differ dramatically in their attitudes toward sexuality involving people of the same sex). In the United States, the historical norm for sexual activity has been adult, male-female married partners engaging in vaginal intercourse.

In reality, of course, much sexual behavior in our society does not conform to this model. People have sex within and outside marriage, sexual relationships involve both other-sex and same-sex partners, and sexual activity includes anal as well as vaginal intercourse, oral-genital contact, and masturbation alone or with a partner. In addition, some people by choice or by circumstance, engage in little or no sexual activity (Laumann et al., 1994).

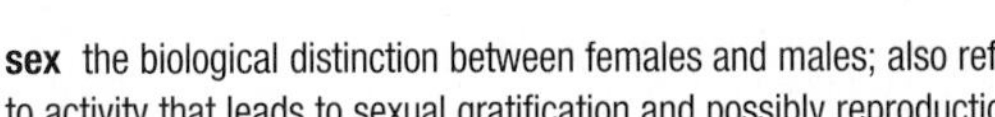

sex the biological distinction between females and males; also refers to activity that leads to sexual gratification and possibly reproduction

GETTING INVOLVED

Has the sexual revolution affected your life? If so, how?

Sexual Attitudes in the United States

How people think and act regarding sex has changed over the course of this nation's history. During the colonial era, the earliest European settlers had no effective means of birth control. Therefore, most communities had strict norms limiting sex to married couples and for the purpose of reproduction. For example, the New England Puritans condemned sex outside marriage and thought any sex (including masturbation) that was not intended to result in conception was sinful. Without strict rules to control people's behavior, they believed, the ever-present temptation of sex would lead to unwanted pregnancy and also prostitution.

Gradually, advances in technology gave people more control over reproduction and more choices about their sexual practices. Other factors played a part, too. After 1920, millions of people migrated from farms and small towns across the United States to industrial cities, where many young men and women lived on their own and worked together. The result was an increase in sexual freedom, which is one of the reasons that decade was dubbed the Roaring Twenties.

A landmark in the nation's changing view of sexuality came after World War II in the research of Alfred Kinsey (1894–1956). Perhaps the most remarkable thing about Kinsey was that he investigated sex, which had never been the focus of a major research project. The Defining Moment box on page 181 explains how Kinsey changed a whole nation's way of thinking.

The Sexual Revolution

From the growing sexual freedom of the Roaring Twenties to the Kinsey research of the 1940s and 1950s, sexual attitudes evolved throughout the twentieth century. But not until the late 1960s—when young people embraced a culture of freedom summed up in the cry "Sex, drugs, and rock-and-roll!"—did people start to talk of a "sexual revolution."

A major factor in the sexual revolution was the introduction in 1960 of the birth control pill. Unlike condoms and diaphragms, which had to be applied at the time of intercourse, "the pill" could be taken at a woman's convenience, and she could have sex anytime. This fact, combined with the pill's high effectiveness, dramatically reduced the historical connection between heterosexual intercourse and pregnancy.

Figure 7–1 on page 180 confirms that the U.S. population became more free and easy about sex in the 1960s. Among those born between 1933 and 1942, people now in their late sixties to late seventies and who reached the age of twenty before 1962, only 56 percent of men and 16 percent of women reported having had two or more sexual partners before they were twenty. But

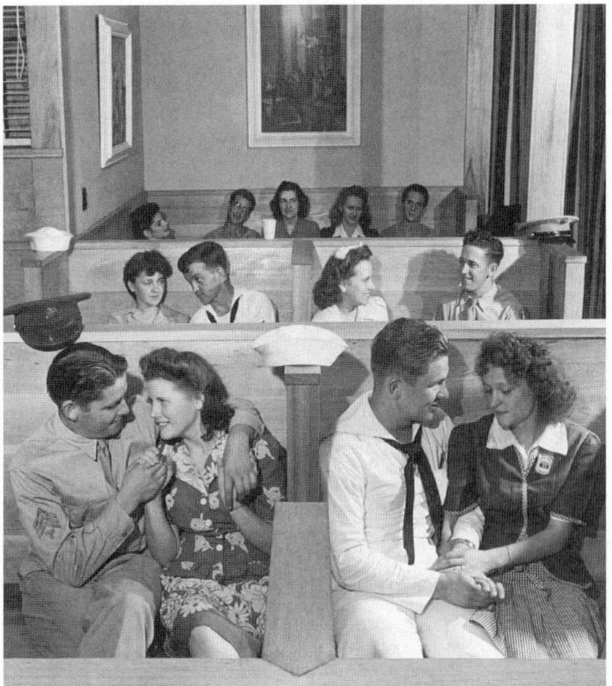

Before the sexual revolution, U.S. society tolerated little in the way of public displays of sexuality, as suggested by this visiting day for World War II military personnel.

one generation later, among people born between 1953 and 1962, 62 percent of men and 48 percent of women reported two or more sexual partners by age twenty (Laumann et al., 1994:198).

The Sexual Revolution and Gender

The smaller difference in male and female responses in the younger cohort also suggests that U.S. society was moving away from the traditional *double standard* by which men enjoyed sexual freedom while women were expected to delay sex until they were married and then forever remain faithful to their husbands. By the 1960s, women were organizing in opposition to long-standing domination by men. In fact, many feminists placed sexuality at the heart of male domination. Kate Millet (1970) summed up the argument, saying that sex is really about *power*: As long as men view women as mere sexual creatures and women accept this definition of themselves, men will dominate women. The word "sexism" became part of our society's vocabulary, thereby constructing a new social problem.

Feminists challenged male power by demanding equal pay for equal work, condemning pornography, and taking a stand against sexual violence, including rape and incest. In addition, women demanded access to contraception (which in the 1960s was still illegal in some states) and abortion (which was illegal

MAKING THE GRADE

Be sure you can explain the significance of both the sexual revolution and the sexual counterrevolution for our society.

SOCIAL PROBLEMS in Everyday Life

Can you point to some of the lasting effects of the sexual revolution in today's society?

Dimensions of Difference

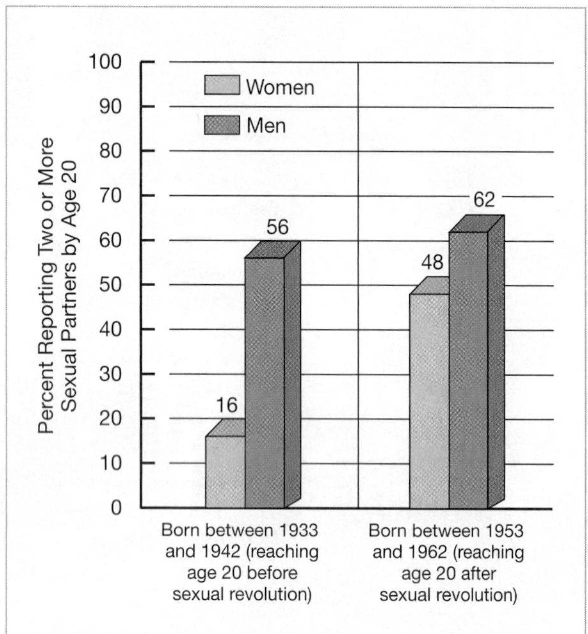

FIGURE 7–1 **The Sexual Revolution: Moving Away from the Double Standard**

Among people who came of age before the sexual revolution (shown on the left), a smaller share had two or more sexual partners by age 20 compared with people who came of age after the sexual revolution (shown on the right). The difference is especially marked among women.

Source: Laumann et al. (1994).

everywhere in the United States until 1973). In short, out of the sexual revolution emerged the claim that the only person with the right to control a woman's body is the woman herself.

The Sexual Counterrevolution

The movements toward freer sexuality and greater power for women found support among liberals but also sparked opposition. By the 1970s, a sexual counterrevolution was under way as conservatives called for a return to traditional "family values." As conservatives saw it, what people needed was not more freedom but stronger families and more personal responsibility.

The conservative response to the sexual revolution did not succeed in turning back the clock. Since the 1960s, most adults in the United States support the liberal idea that people should decide for themselves whether and with whom to have sex. In practice, such beliefs lead about half of young people—more than half among men and less than half among women—to have sexual intercourse by their senior year in high school (Wallis, 2005; Centers for Disease Control and Prevention, 2008). Yet many issues involving sexuality remain controversial, as later sections of this chapter will explain.

The Continuing Sexual Revolution: Older People

During the past decade, the men and women who began the sexual revolution of the 1960s—people who are now in their sixties and seventies—are carrying that movement into old age. The popular stereotype is that being sexually active and growing old simply don't go together. And for older men, there is some truth to this claim. "Trying to have sex at ninety," quipped the comedian George Burns, "is like trying to shoot pool with a rope."

But just as the birth control pill helped the '60s generation spark a sexual revolution, another pill—this time in the form of Viagra, Levitra, and Cialis—offers the promise that the baby boomers will keep love alive as they grow old. These drugs that treat "erectile dysfunction," or ED for short, help otherwise healthy males achieve and maintain an erection, making sexual activity possible.

Researchers have confirmed that more older people than ever before are having sex—a slight majority of seventy-year-old men and women report being sexually active, which is up from about one-third a generation ago. Among eighty-year-olds, about one-fourth of people say they are sexually active.

The pharmaceutical companies have a financial interest in defining erectile dysfunction as a new problem. As the number of older men who think they should be having sex rises, the sale of drugs to treat erectile dysfunction goes up just as fast. Doctors now issue almost 20 million prescriptions a year, earning the drug companies more than $1.5 billion.

The good news is that ED pills have extended sexual activity for millions of older people. The more sex, researchers find, the closer a couple's relationship and the more youthful people look and act. At the same time, critics point out that the "blue pill" is not a magic wand that erases the effects of age—no seventy-five-year-old male performs sexually like he did in his teens or twenties. In addition, like any other drug, these pills can cause side effects, which include headaches and even persistent and painful erections. Then, too, it is natural for hormone levels that encourage sexual activity to decline as people move into old age; this raises the question as to whether the medical and pharmaceutical establishment should try to artificially alter that fact.

But given the popularity of these male drugs, many older men seem quite happy with their effects. Given the amount of money being made, there is little surprise in the fact that drug companies are working hard to create a new "pink pill"—for older women (Kotz, 2008).

sexual orientation a person's romantic and emotional attraction to another person

heterosexuality sexual attraction to someone of the other sex

homosexuality sexual attraction to someone of the same sex

bisexuality sexual attraction to people of both sexes

asexuality the absence of sexual attraction to people of either sex

CONSTRUCTING SOCIAL PROBLEMS

A DEFINING MOMENT

Alfred Kinsey: Talking Openly about Sex

Alfred Kinsey asked people to talk about sex. From today's point of view, that may not seem very controversial. But in Kinsey's day—more than sixty years ago—most people did not think sex was a topic for polite conversation, much less scientific research.

Kinsey founded the Institute for Sex Research at Indiana University in 1942, and in the years that followed, he and a dozen research assistants interviewed more than 11,000 men and women about their sexual practices. His first book, *Sexual Behavior in the Human Male* (Kinsey, Pomeroy, & Martin, 1948), is a fairly dry, scientific work, yet it sold more than half a million copies. A second volume, *Sexual Behavior in the Human Female* (Kinsey et al., 1953), was even more popular. People in the United States had a greater interest in sex than they were willing to let on.

Some of Kinsey's findings made news headlines, especially his conclusion that people in the United States were far less conventional about sex than popularly believed. Kinsey's subjects confessed to breaking many cultural taboos of that time: Almost half of female subjects reported having sexual intercourse before marriage, and one-third of married men said that while married, they had a sexual relationship with someone other than their wives.

There were flaws in the way Kinsey conducted his research. In his eagerness to find people willing to talk about their sexual experiences, Kinsey ended up using far too many college students and people in prison while almost totally ignoring those who were older, rural, or poor. As a result, Kinsey's subjects were probably not representative of the U.S. population. But despite the shortcomings, Kinsey's research marked a defining moment in our nation's history. This researcher made a difference by bringing sex out of the closet and making it a topic of people's everyday conversation.

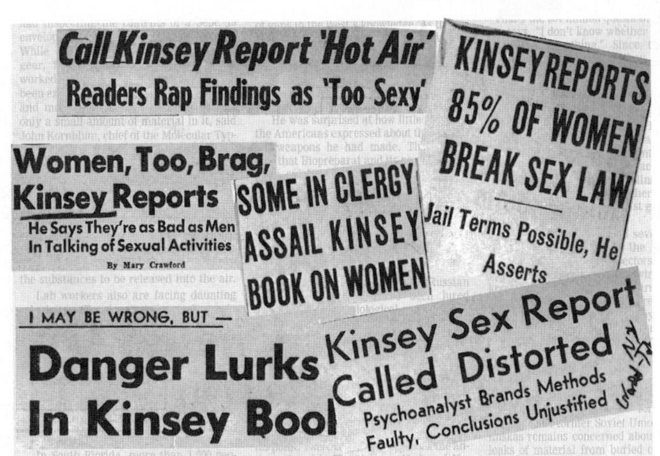

Reports of Alfred Kinsey's survey of human sexual practices caused a sensation in the news media in the mid-1900s.

Sexual Orientation

Sexual orientation refers to *a person's romantic and emotional attraction to another person.* People can be drawn to partners of the same sex, the other sex, both sexes, or neither sex.

The most common sexual orientation, approved by cultures the world over, is **heterosexuality** (*hetero* is Greek, meaning "other"), *sexual attraction to someone of the other sex.* In addition, in all societies, a small but significant share of people favor **homosexuality** (*homo* is Greek for "same"), which is *sexual attraction to someone of the same sex.*

Most people tend to think that heterosexuality and homosexuality are opposite patterns, with each of us falling neatly into one category or the other. But as Kinsey discovered, many people have varying degrees of both sexual orientations. Also, keep in mind that sexual *attraction* is not the same as sexual *behavior.* Although most people have experienced some attraction to a person of the same sex, far fewer have engaged in homosexual behavior. The fact that many people do not act on their attraction is due to cultural norms that discourage same-sex relationships.

Kinsey's finding that sexual orientation is often not clear-cut called attention to the existence of **bisexuality,** *sexual attraction to people of both sexes.* Some bisexual people experience equal attraction to females and males; others have a stronger attraction to one sex than to the other. There are also many cases of bisexuals who experience attraction to both sexes but limit their sexual behavior to partners of one sex.

Finally, not everyone experiences sexual attraction at all. **Asexuality** is *the absence of sexual attraction to people of either sex.* Throughout the population, the extent of asexuality increases gradually as people get older.

We now take a closer look at issues related to homosexuality.

GETTING INVOLVED

Do you think most people understand the four sexual orientations? What makes sexual orientation difficult for most people to understand?

SOCIAL PROBLEMS in Everyday Life

To what degree do you think gays and lesbians experience prejudice and discrimination on your campus? Point to whatever evidence you can.

Dimensions of Difference

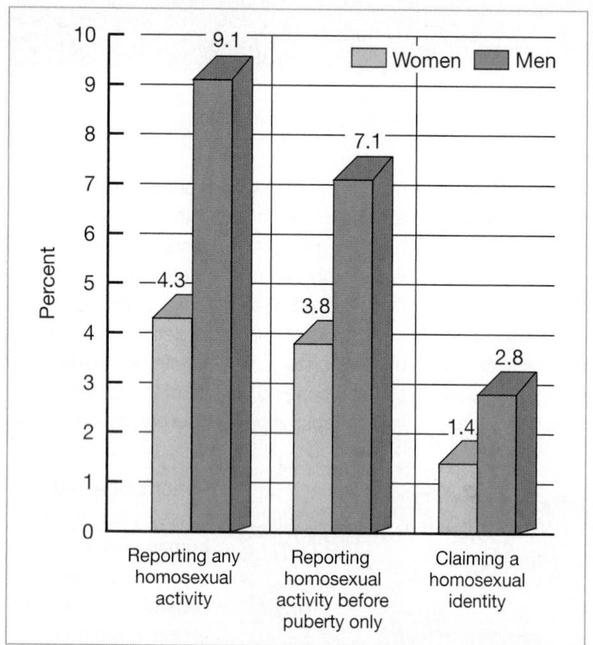

FIGURE 7–2 Measuring Homosexual Orientation

How one defines homosexual orientation affects the number of people considered to be homosexual.

Source: Laumann et al. (1994).

Homosexuality

Because heterosexuality is the cultural norm, homosexual people—gay men and lesbians—are pushed to the margins of society. Some people view homosexuality as a social problem because it conflicts with their moral standards. This attitude is the major reason that gay men and lesbians have long experienced prejudice and discrimination.

Today, as acceptance of homosexuality increases, states and the federal government have enacted laws banning discrimination in many areas—including jobs and housing—based on sexual orientation. But other forms of discrimination are within the law: The military can and does legally discharge homosexual men and women who are open about their sexual orientation, and many religious organizations refuse to ordain gay men or lesbians as leaders. In addition, although the movement supporting same-sex marriage has gained ground in recent years, in 2009 this practice was still illegal in all but six states: Massachusetts, Vermont, New Hampshire, Maine, Connecticut, and Iowa.

Prejudice against gay men and lesbians also exists on college campuses. One study found that one-third of gay and lesbian students reported that they had experienced harassment in the past year (Rankin, 2003).

Sometimes hostility toward gay men and lesbians leads to violence. The FBI (2008) records some 1,500 hate crimes against gays each year, and the true number is certainly far higher. Many of these violent acts—including assault and even murder—are directed at people simply because of their sexual orientation. According to the National Coalition of Anti-Violence Programs (2008), 40 percent of lesbians and gay men in the United States say they have been the victim of a hate crime, and almost all young lesbians and gay men say they have experienced at least verbal abuse.

The Extent of Homosexuality

What share of the U.S. population has a homosexual orientation? This is a hard question to answer because, as already noted, sexual orientation is not a matter of neat categories. The extent of homosexuality depends on exactly how you define the term.

Back in 1948, Alfred Kinsey reported that most women and men experience at least some same-sex attraction. Although most do not act on it, many do: Kinsey estimated that one-third of men and one-eighth of women engage in one or more homosexual acts at some point, often in adolescence. In addition, Kinsey estimated that 4 percent of men and 2 percent of women were exclusively homosexual in orientation, meaning they had *only* same-sex desires, engaged in *only* same-sex sexual activity, and thought of themselves as gay men or lesbians.

More recent research by Edward Laumann and his colleagues (1994) provides a more scientific estimate of homosexuality. Figure 7–2 shows that 9.1 percent of men and 4.3 percent of women (some 20 million people in all) reported at least some homosexual activity, typically in adolescence. Laumann concluded that 2.8 percent of men and 1.4 percent of women (about 6 million people) define themselves as homosexual or bisexual, and these statistics are confirmed by other surveys (NORC, 2008).

What Determines Sexual Orientation?

It is even harder to explain sexual orientation than it is to define it. Sexual orientation is the result of many factors, including genetics, brain structure, hormones, life experiences, and culture. Not surprisingly, experts point out that both culture and biology play a part in sexual orientation.

Cultural Factors

In the past, most people did not pay much attention to sexual orientation. The French social philosopher Michel Foucault (1990) notes that homosexuals were not thought of as a category until

SOCIAL PROBLEMS in Everyday Life

Does your campus have a gay and lesbian center? What are its goals?

SOCIAL PROBLEMS in Everyday Life

What evidence of transgendered living can you find in the mass media?

DIVERSITY: RACE, CLASS, & GENDER

Female, Male, or Both: The Muxes of Mexico

Alejandro Taledo, age sixteen, stands at the corner in Juchitán, a small town in the state of Oaxaca, in the middle of southern Mexico. Called Alex by her friends, she has finished a day of selling flowers with her mother and now waits for a bus to ride home for dinner.

As you already may have noticed, Alejandro is commonly a boy's name. In fact, this young Mexican was born a boy. But several years ago, Alex decided that, whatever her sex, she felt like she was a girl and she decided to live according to her own feelings.

In this community, she is not alone. Juchitán and the surrounding region is well known not only for beautiful black pottery and delicious local foods but also for the large number of gays and lesbians and transgendered people who live there. At first glance, this fact may surprise many people who think of Mexico as a traditional country, especially when it comes to gender and sexuality. In Mexico, the stereotype goes, men control the lives of women, especially when it comes to sex. But, as in the case of most stereotypes, this one is misses some important facts. Nationally, Mexico is becoming more tolerant in matters of sexual orientation, and same-sex domestic partnerships are now legal in Mexico City, the nation's capital. And nowhere is tolerance for many forms of sexual orientation as strong and widespread as it is in the region around Juchitán.

In this area of Mexico, transgendered people are called muxe (pronounced MOO-shay), which is based on the Spanish word mujer meaning "woman." This means that the local culture does not divide people neatly into men and women, but rather recognizes a third gender category as well. Some muxes wear women's clothing and act almost entirely in a feminine way. Others adopt a feminine look and behavior only on special occasions. One of the most popular events is the region's grand celebration, which happens every year in November, is attended by more than 2,000 muxes and their families, and includes a competition won by the "transvestite of the year."

Anthropologists tell us that the acceptance of transgendered people in central Mexico has its roots in the culture that existed centuries before the Spanish arrived. At that time, anyone with ambiguous gender was viewed as especially wise and talented. The region's history includes accounts of Aztec priests and Mayan gods who cross-dressed, or were considered to be both male and female. In the 16th century, the coming of the Spanish colonists and the influence of the Catholic Church did reduce much of this gender tolerance. But acceptance of mixed sex-identities continues to this day in Juchitán, a region where people hold so tight to their traditions that many speak only their ancient Zapotec language, rather than Spanish.

And so it is in Juchitán that muxes are respected, accepted, and even celebrated. Muxes are successful in business and take leadership roles in the church and in politics. Most important, they are commonly accepted by friends and family alike. Alejandro lives with her parents and five siblings, and helps her mother both at home and working on the street selling flowers. Her father, Victor Martinez Jimenez, is a local construction worker who speaks only Zapotec. He still refers to Alex as "him" but says, "It was God who sent him, and why would I reject him? He helps his mother very much. Why would I get mad?" Alex's mother, Rosa Taledo Vicente, adds, "Every family considers it a blessing to have one gay son. While daughters marry and leave home, a muxe cares for his parents in their old age."

WHAT DO YOU THINK?

1. Do you think that U.S. society is tolerant of people wishing to combine male and female dress and qualities? Why or why not?
2. Muxes are people who were born males. How do you think the local people in this story would feel about women who want to dress and act like men? Do you think there would be widespread support for this as well? Why or why not?
3. How do you personally feel about a third category of sexual identity? Explain your views.

Sources: Gave (2005), Lacey (2008), and Rosenberg (2008).

scientists began defining people that way in the late nineteenth century. This is not to say that people in earlier times did not have same-sex experiences; society simply took little note of it. But once societies socially constructed the categories of "heterosexual" and "homosexual," people who had homosexual experiences began to be set apart as "different" and also became targets of prejudice and discrimination. This historical change shows us that how we express and experience sexuality is shaped by culture.

Sexual behavior also varies from culture to culture. Among the Chukchee Eskimo of Siberia, a man may take on the role known as a *berdache*, dressing and acting like a woman, doing women's work, even marrying another man. Among the Sambia of New Guinea, most boys engage in a sexual ritual in which they perform oral sex on older men with the idea that ingesting semen will enhance their masculinity. In central Mexico, a region where religious traditions recognize gods who are both female and male, the local culture recognizes not only females and males but also *muxes* (pronounced "MOO-shays") as a third sexual category. *Muxes* are men who dress and act as women, some only on ritual occasions, some all the time. The Diversity: Race, Class, & Gender box takes a closer look. Such diversity of sexual expression around the world shows that sexual orientation has much to

MAKING THE GRADE

Most evidence points to sexual orientation as rooted in biology.

SOCIAL PROBLEMS in Everyday Life

Do you think same-sex marriage will become legal throughout the United States? If so, when?

do with society itself (Herdt, 1993; Blackwood & Wieringa, 1999; Gave, 2005; Lacey, 2008; Rosenberg, 2008).

Finally, a few sociological studies claim that sexual orientation reflects patterns of socialization. One recent study of opposite-sex twins found a higher likelihood of homosexual orientation among people raised in a gender-neutral environment than among those raised according to conventional ideas of masculine and feminine behavior (Bearman & Brückner, 2002).

Biological Factors

Culture may play a part in the way societies think about sexuality, but on the individual level, most evidence points to the conclusion that sexual orientation is rooted in human biology. Like being left- or right-handed, sexual orientation appears to be largely fixed at birth.

The neurobiologist Simon LeVay (1993) claims that the key to sexual orientation is found in the brain. LeVay studied the brains of homosexual men and heterosexual men and noted a difference in the hypothalamus, an organ of the brain that regulates the body's hormone levels. Biologists have established that hormone levels—especially testosterone levels in men—affect sexual orientation. They claim that small differences in the brain play a significant part in establishing a person's sexual orientation (Grady, 1992).

Genes, as well as hormones, may affect sexual orientation. In a study of forty-four pairs of brothers, all homosexual, researchers found that thirty-three of the pairs had a unique feature on the X chromosome (one of the genetic traits that affects human sexuality). Could this be evidence of a "gay gene"? Some researchers think so, noting that the gay brothers had an unexpectedly high number of gay male relatives on their mother's side, the source of the X chromosome (Hamer & Copeland, 1994).

CRITICAL REVIEW Scientists continue to debate the social and biological causes of sexual orientation. So far, the evidence supports the conclusion that biology plays a major part in how people experience sexual attraction (Weinrich, 1987; Isay, 1989; Angier, 1992; Gelman, 1992). But although biology may be the key to sexual orientation, keep in mind that many people do not fit into simple categories as being "gay" or "straight."

Does it really matter whether sexual orientation is caused by society or human biology? It does, for an important reason. If sexual orientation is biological, it is as much beyond our control as the color of our skin. Therefore, gay people are no more responsible for their sexual orientation than African American people are for their skin color, and both categories of people are entitled to the same legal protection from discrimination (Herek, 1991; Schmalz, 1993).

But a biological foundation of sexual orientation poses dangers, given the rapid pace of advancements in medical technology. For example, if someday parents are able to learn that their future child has a gay gene, they might decide to abort the fetus; another possibility is that doctors might try to develop surgical techniques in an effort to "correct" the brains of gay men and lesbians (Zicklin, 1992).

Homosexuality and Public Policy

Back in 1960, homosexuality was widely viewed as wrong almost everywhere in the United States. Many people also considered this sexual orientation to be a sickness; even the American Psychiatric Association included homosexuality in its list of mental disorders. Discrimination against gay men and lesbians was common as companies, schools, government agencies, and the military routinely refused to hire people thought to be homosexual. Just as important, employees found to be gay or lesbian were fired for no reason other than their sexual orientation. Given this hostile environment, it is easy to see why most lesbians and gay men stayed "in the closet," keeping their homosexuality secret from all but a few close friends.

Since then, attitudes toward homosexuality have become more tolerant (Loftus, 2001). In 1973, the American Psychiatric Association removed homosexuality from its list of mental disorders. Public attitudes, too, have become more accepting. As shown in Figure 7–3, the percentage of U.S. adults who claim that homosexuality is wrong was well over 70 percent twenty years ago; in 2007, the figure stood at 58 percent (NORC, 2007). Such surveys also show that a majority of people now believe that homosexual people should have the same job opportunities and basic civil rights as everyone else.

The growing acceptance of homosexuality appears to have been on the minds of the justices of the U.S. Supreme Court when in 2003 they handed down a landmark ruling (*Lawrence et al.* v. *Texas*) that struck down the Texas law banning sodomy ("unnatural sex, especially anal intercourse") between same-sex couples. This ruling ended similar laws that had been on the books in other states. There have also been legal changes in the case of gay marriage, to which we now turn.

Gay Marriage

In 2004, the supreme court of Massachusetts ruled that gay men and lesbians had the right to marry. Gay rights advocates were elated by the Massachusetts decision and, since then, four more states (Connecticut, Vermont, Iowa, and New Hampshire) and the District of Columbia have enacted laws permitting same-sex marriage. New Jersey, Washington, and California (which briefly legalized same-sex marriage in 2008) recognize same-sex unions

homophobia an aversion to or hostility toward people thought to be gay, lesbian, or bisexual

pornography words or images intended to cause sexual arousal

that are very similar to marriage. Many cities permit couples to register "domestic partnerships" that provide many of the rights of marriage, including family health care and inheritance rights (National Conference of State Legislatures, 2011).

The legal tide is turning in favor of same-sex marriage. At the same time, a majority of states have enacted laws that prohibit gay men and lesbians from marrying. A total of thirty-eight states have passed some law stating that they will not recognize gay marriages, even if they are performed in a state where they are legal. This position is in keeping with a federal law, called the Defense of Marriage Act, passed in 1996, which allows any state to ignore a same-sex marriage performed elsewhere.

Whether same-sex couples can marry or not, thousands of business corporations across the country—including a growing number of colleges and universities as well as the country's major automakers and the federal government—have extended to domestic partners the same employee benefits they give to married spouses.

Elsewhere in the world, the Netherlands, Belgium, Canada, South Africa, Spain, Norway, and Sweden recognize same-sex marriage. Another fifteen nations recognize same-sex partnerships or civil unions that extend to gays and lesbians many of the legal rights that married people have (Pew Research Center, 2009).

In the United States, same-sex marriage remains controversial. In general, liberals support extending the right to marry to same-sex couples everywhere. Many conservatives oppose this trend, claiming that the traditional idea of marriage in the United States has always been a union between a man and a woman (Thomas, 2003). But some people who support conservative "family values" *do* favor gay marriage—as well as the right of gay couples to adopt children—on the grounds that because families are good for people and good for society, we should encourage families for everyone, whether straight or gay (A. Sullivan, 2002).

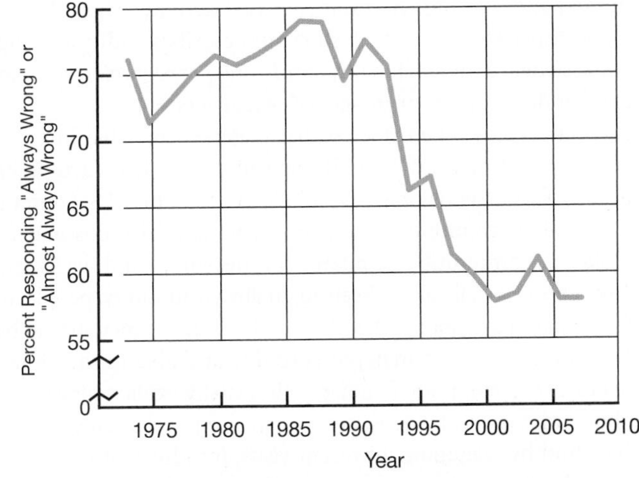

FIGURE 7–3 **U.S. Attitudes toward Homosexual Relations, 1973–2007**

Survey Question: "What about sexual relations between two adults of the same sex? Do you think it is always wrong, almost always wrong, wrong only sometimes, or not wrong at all?"

Source: NORC (2007).

The Gay Rights Movement

The recent social gains made by gay men and lesbians are the result of efforts over decades by people who have supported the gay rights movement. The first gay rights group was formed in Chicago in 1924, but the movement did not gain public attention until the 1950s (Chauncy, 1994). Like all social movements, the gay rights movement constructs the problem and defines the solution in a particular way. This movement rejects the conventional idea that homosexuality is a problem, instead claiming that the problem is prejudice and discrimination directed against gay people. The solution? Acceptance of homosexuality on equal terms with any other sexual orientation.

Acceptance is indeed increasing, but the pace of change has been slow. Back in the 1960s, despite the risks of being identified as homosexual, more and more lesbians and gay men stepped forward demanding acceptance. A turning point occurred on June 27, 1969, when police raided the Stonewall Inn, a bar in New York's Greenwich Village. At that time, New York police made a practice of raiding gay bars, arresting patrons, and recording their names, which often ended up in the newspaper. This time, however, the patrons of the Stonewall Inn openly resisted police harassment. Joined by people off the street, they battled the police for the better part of two days. This event, which came to be known as the Stonewall Riot, marked a new militancy in the gay rights movement.

Soon after the Stonewall Riot, the gay rights movement began using the term **homophobia** to describe *an aversion to or hostility toward people thought to be gay, lesbian, or bisexual.* This concept reinforced the idea that the problem was not homosexuality but people who would not accept others simply because of their sexual orientation. The success of the gay rights movement is evident in the increasingly widespread condemnation of homophobia as a social problem today.

Pornography

Pornography is defined as *words or images intended to cause sexual arousal.* But there is little agreement about precisely what is and what is not pornographic. For one thing, sexual material comes in many forms. *Erotica* includes the artistic portrayal of

GETTING INVOLVED

Can you think of any other issues where liberals and conservatives take a similar position but for different reasons?

nudity, although not necessarily sexual activity. Then there is *soft-core pornography*, which shows or describes nudity and suggests sexual activity. Finally, *hard-core pornography* contains explicit descriptions or images of sexual acts.

But exactly when does sexual material cross the line into *obscenity* and violate the law? Recognizing that what is acceptable in one place may be objectionable in another, the U.S. Supreme Court allows communities to ban sexual material as obscene if it violates "community standards of decency" and lacks any "redeeming social value." Even so, in any community, people are likely to disagree about what the standards of decency should be.

Sexually explicit material is readily available in the United States. Most people are familiar with sexually explicit magazines, books, movies, and videos; people can also purchase sexual conversation by telephone. In recent years, hundreds of thousands of Web sites have opened on the Internet that portray every imaginable type of sexual behavior. The sale of sex-oriented material is today a $5 billion-a-year industry, which is more than the total economic output of some countries.

Is Pornography a Social Problem?

Pornography is big business in the United States and throughout the world. But is the sale of sexually explicit material a social problem? There is nearly universal agreement that involving children under age eighteen in sexual situations is wrong; almost everywhere, police enforce federal and state laws against creating, selling, or possessing child pornography. There is also widespread concern about the effects of pornography on adults. Yet as you will see, various categories of people object to pornography for different reasons.

Conservatives: The Moral Issue

Conservatives treat sex as a moral issue; they define pornography as a social problem, claiming that it threatens conventional morality. Pornography encourages lustful behavior, they say, which can become an addiction, as it has for several million people in the United States. In addition, pornography weakens a society's moral virtue and may threaten the stability of marriage and family. About 60 percent of U.S. adults echo conservative concerns, claiming that "sexual material leads to a breakdown of morals" (NORC, 2008:300). In short, conservatives have public morality in mind as they define pornography as a social problem.

Liberals: Issues of Freedom and Power

Liberals are divided over whether to define pornography as a social problem. Some liberals believe that what material people choose to read or view is their own business. Therefore, without claiming that pornography is necessarily good, liberals defend freedom of expression and the individual's right to privacy. Liberals who share this position have been outspoken in defending government support of the arts, even including art that many people feel violates community standards of decency.

Although some liberals defend pornography on the grounds of protecting free speech, a growing number of feminist liberals object to pornography as demeaning to women. They see pornography as a power issue, noting that much sexually explicit material depicts women as the playthings of men (Dworkin, 1991; MacKinnon, 2001).

In sum, many liberals defend the right of free expression and the idea that people should be free to choose whatever entertainment they want. But opposition to pornography has increased across the political spectrum. In this case, conservatives (who object to sexually explicit material on moral grounds) have joined with feminist liberals (who object on political grounds) in their opposition to pornography.

Pornography is an unusual issue in that both liberals and conservatives oppose it, although for different reasons. Liberals condemn pornography as degrading to women, while conservatives condemn it as morally wrong, a violation of traditional codes of acceptable sexual conduct. Which political approach is shown here?

Pornography and Violence

Another widespread concern is that pornography promotes violence. Back in 1985, President Ronald Reagan appointed the Attorney General's Commission on Pornography (commonly called the Meese Commission, after Attorney General Edwin Meese) to investigate how people react to

sexual harassment unwanted comments, gestures, or physical contact of a sexual nature

SOCIAL PROBLEMS in Everyday Life

After reading the box below, point to other ways our culture links sex and violence.

DIVERSITY: RACE, CLASS, & GENDER

Sex and Violence: Linked by Culture

The sociologist Dianne Herman (2001) characterizes the United States as a "rape culture." By this, she means that our way of life links sex and violence. Can you see how?

First, think about language. Common slang phrases such as "Screw you!" have both sexual and aggressive meaning. Second, it is easy for most young men to imagine themselves in the roles of violent, sexually active mass-media characters, such as British superagent James Bond, who has appealed to generations of men. What is Bond's claim to being a "real man"? The answer, presumably, is the ease with which he "alternately whips out his revolver and his [penis]" (Griffin, 1971, cited in Herman, 2001:38). For James Bond, sex and violence are two sides of the same coin.

To the extent that this is a "rape culture," Herman concludes, we encourage the problem of sexual violence. And this problem is not caused by "weirdos" but rather by men who are well adjusted to a cultural system—one that that equates sex and violence. In short, when you combine males brought up to link sex and aggression with females raised to submit to males, you have a recipe for widespread sexual violence.

WHAT DO YOU THINK?

1. Do you agree with Herman that our culture links masculinity, sexuality, and violence? If so, can you think of ways other than those mentioned here? If not, why not?
2. How many slang terms can you think of that also imply violence? (Examples: "bang" or "slam")
3. Make a list of film characters whose behavior combines the traits of sex and violence.

sexually explicit materials. The commission (1986) concluded that exposure to pornography causes sexual arousal, increases people's sexual activity, and encourages men to be aggressive and more accepting of violent acts such as rape. In addition, concluded the researchers, pornography involving children encourages some men to desire sexual activity with them (a crime called *pedophilia*). Critics challenged some of these conclusions, but the report found widespread acceptance among both conservatives and liberals. National survey data confirm that about half of U.S. adults believe that pornography does encourage people to commit rape (NORC, 2008:300).

Sexual Harassment

As explained in Chapter 6 ("Crime, Violence, and Criminal Justice"), sexual violence—ranging from verbal abuse to forced sex—is a problem for both women and men. As the Diversity: Race, Class, & Gender box explains, some people claim that by linking sex with violence, our culture makes this problem much worse.

In recent years, people have come to recognize another type of sexual violence: **sexual harassment**, *unwanted comments, gestures, or physical contact of a sexual nature.* Fifty years ago, harassment of women on the job, the campus, and the street was routine. In fact, harassment was so much a part of our way of life that few men or women defined such behavior as a problem.

But the situation gradually changed with the rise of the women's movement in the 1960s. In 1964, Congress passed the Civil Rights Act with the goal of protecting African Americans from employment discrimination. The women's movement successfully lobbied to extend the bill to include people disadvantaged not just by their race but also by their sex. Thus Title VII of the Civil Rights Act prohibits discrimination in the terms, conditions, and privileges of employment on the basis of race and also sex. In 1972, Congress extended these protections to schools, colleges, and universities when it passed Title IX of the Higher Education Amendment, which banned sex discrimination in institutions receiving federal funds.

Congress then set up the Equal Employment Opportunity Commission (EEOC) to investigate complaints of racial or sexual discrimination. In 1976, in the case of *Williams* v. *Saxbe*, a federal court declared that sexual harassment is a type of illegal sex discrimination. This decision brought sexual harassment to public attention, and it was soon defined as a serious problem.

The EEOC recognizes two types of sexual harassment. The first is *quid pro quo* (Latin, meaning "one thing for another") *harassment*, in which a person directs sexual advances or requests for sexual favors to an employee or other subordinate as a condition of employment. In this case, a boss might demand or imply that sex is a condition for an employee's promotion. The second type of harassment is more subtle behavior, such as telling sexual jokes, displaying nude photos, offering compliments on someone's good looks, or engaging in unnecessary touching that the offender may not intend to be harassing. The law is concerned with *effects,* not just the offender's intent. It considers unlawful any behavior that has the effect of *creating a hostile environment,* regardless of what the offender's intentions might have been. The point of the law is to protect people who are trying to do their prostitution the selling of sexual services

Prostitution is another issue that brings together conservatives and liberals. From a conservative point of view, prostitution violates traditional moral standards. Many liberals, and especially feminists, object to prostitution as the exploitation of women. Which political approach is illustrated in this protest against the sex tourism industry in Kiev, Ukraine?

jobs from having unwanted sexuality imposed on them (U.S. Equal Employment Opportunity Commission, 2006).

Who Harasses Whom? A Court Case

Because men hold most positions of power in U.S. society, 84 percent of known harassers are men who harass women (U.S. Equal Employment Opportunity Commission, 2009). But not all harassment follows this pattern. In *Oncale* v. *Sundowner Offshore Services* (1998), the U.S. Supreme Court stated that a person can be sexually harassed by someone of either sex. In the *Oncale* case, after male co-workers threatened a married man with rape, he reported the incident to his supervisor. When the company did not respond to the situation, the man quit his job and filed a lawsuit against the company. This case shows us that in some circumstances, men sexually harass other men who do not display what harassers think of as typical "masculine" behavior. In this situation, sexual harassment was a form of control used by men to force others to conform to gender stereotypes (D. Lee, 2000).

Must Harassment Harm Victims? Other Court Cases

Does sexual harassment exist only when a victim suffers clear harm? The U.S. Supreme Court addressed this question twice in 1998. In the first case, *Ellerth* v. *Burlington Industries*, a woman complained that her supervisor made sexual advances in which he threatened that he could make her job easy or difficult, depending on whether she "loosened up." Although she resisted his advances, she did not report the behavior, and there was no evidence that her career was harmed. Soon after, however, she quit her job and then filed suit, claiming she had been the victim of sexual harassment.

In a second case, *Faragher* v. *City of Boca Raton*, three women who worked as lifeguards claimed they had endured a hostile environment for years, based on physical touching and sexual comments by their supervisors. Their employer, the city of Boca Raton, had a sexual harassment policy in place, but no one had informed the women of the policy. Subsequently, the women filed a lawsuit against the city, charging that they had been harassed on the job.

In considering the two cases, the Supreme Court ruled that employees can be harassed even if they were not obviously harmed by, say, losing out on a promotion. The court also stated that employers are responsible when a supervisor harasses another employee, even if the company was not aware of the behavior, unless the company can demonstrate that it had a well-publicized sexual harassment policy in place that the employee knew about but chose not to use.

Prostitution

The cultural ideal of sex involves companionship and intimacy between two people. Therefore, **prostitution,** or *the selling of sexual services,* may be "the world's oldest profession," but it has always been controversial. Both offering to provide and offering to buy the services of a prostitute are against the law everywhere in the United States except in parts of rural Nevada.

Legal or not, prostitution is common. There is no accurate count of the number of people who work as prostitutes in the United States, but national surveys reveal that about 16 percent of adult men (and just a very small share of women) say that they have paid someone for sex or have been paid for sex at least once (NORC, 2008:1876). In global perspective, prostitution is most common in low-income nations, where women's economic opportunities are most limited.

Prostitutes: A Profile

Most prostitutes—many prefer to call themselves sex workers—are women. But they are a diverse category, with better or worse working conditions, depending on their physical attractiveness, age, and social class position.

MAKING THE GRADE

The box below provides a good example of how different societies can "construct the problem" in different ways.

SOCIAL PROBLEMS IN GLOBAL PERSPECTIVE

Prostitutes and Johns in Sweden: Who Is Breaking the Law?

In the United States, it is against the law to sell sex. This means that when they work, prostitutes break the law. It is also against the law to buy sex. This means that when they solicit sex, "johns" also break the law. In reality, in about 90 percent of all arrests involving prostitution, police nab women working as prostitutes. Police tend to leave johns alone. This policy, in effect, defines the prostitution problem as *women selling sex*.

Sweden has taken a different approach to prostitution. For several decades, prostitution was legal in Sweden. Then, in 1999, that country passed a new law that kept it legal to *sell* sex but made it a crime to *buy* sex. As one of Sweden's police officials recently put it, "We don't have a problem with prostitutes. We have a problem with men who buy sex."

The government's policy is guided by feminist theory, claiming that prostitution is a form of male violence against women. In addition, the government reasons, equality between the sexes can only be achieved when men do not exploit women in sexual ways. As for women, the law ended criminal prosecution for selling sex and created a wide range of social services that were available to any woman who wanted to stop working as a prostitute.

What happened as a result of the new law? Critics claim that the law encourages men cruising for sex to get women into a car quickly, before the woman has a chance to assess any possible danger. In addition, most prostitution has been forced off the city streets and takes place out of town and out of sight, where women may be more vulnerable. But almost everyone agrees, the number of women working as prostitutes has fallen by as much as half. In Stockholm, the capital, estimates are that prostitution has been reduced by 80 percent. Just as important, before the law was enacted, thousands of women were brought into the country each year to work as prostitutes. Since the law has taken effect, the number of cases of sex trafficking has been reduced to a few hundred annually.

Overall, Swedes credit their new policy for successfully solving much of the problem of prostitution. Compared to the United States, where women working as prostitutes experience a "revolving door" of arrest followed by a return to working the streets, Sweden appears to have largely ended the problem by replacing a male viewpoint of the issue (arresting women for selling sex) with a female viewpoint of the issue (helping women get out of prostitution and arresting men who buy sex).

WHAT DO YOU THINK?

1. How does the Swedish policy on prostitution differ from that in the United States in terms of constructing the problem and defining the solution?
2. Do you think this country will adopt the Swedish policy? Why or why not?
3. Would you support such a change? Why or why not?

Sources: Ritter (2008) and Women's Justice Center (2009).

The most advantaged prostitutes are *call girls*, who arrange appointments with clients by telephone. Typically, these women are young, attractive, and well educated, and they are also highly paid. Most call girls work independently rather than for a manager. Many advertise their services in the classified ads of big-city papers, typically as "escorts," which is a polite way of saying they offer an evening of charming company, gracious conversation, and often, for an additional fee, sex.

Less well off are prostitutes who work in brothels or "massage parlors" or for large "escort services." These women are employees who must follow the direction of their superiors. In addition, most of these women turn over at least half their earnings to their employer.

The worst-off prostitutes—and the largest in number—are *streetwalkers*. These prostitutes work the streets, offering sex to people who drive by in cars. Streetwalkers are mostly lower-class women, and they earn the least money. Although some of these women work on their own, they typically give most of their earnings to managers, or *pimps*, who "look after them." With little control over who their customers are, streetwalkers are at high risk of violence and other abuse, as well as sexually transmitted diseases. Researchers estimate that the majority of streetwalkers have histories as victims of rape, incest, or other forms of sexual abuse, often going back to childhood (Estes, 2001; Williamson & Cluse-Tolar, 2002).

Prostitutes typically offer the sexual service that appeals to the client. Research suggests that the most common sexual act performed by prostitutes is oral sex, followed by sexual intercourse (Monto, 2001).

What about men who work as prostitutes? About 10 percent of prostitutes are men, and almost all sell sex to other men. They, too, are a diverse category, ranging from well-paid "escorts" to young runaways trying to survive from day to day on the streets (Boyer, 1989; Strong & DeVault, 1994).

Arrests for Prostitution

Although prostitution is against the law almost everywhere in the United States, law enforcement is selective. About two-thirds of the roughly 60,000 people arrested for prostitution in

SOCIAL PROBLEMS in Everyday Life

Do you think prostitution is a "victimless crime" (as described in Chapter 6)? Why or why not?

SOCIAL PROBLEMS in Everyday Life

Is the term "sex tourism" an attempt to spin reality? What other terms might one use for adults having sex with children?

SOCIAL PROBLEMS IN GLOBAL PERSPECTIVE

Children and Sex Tourism

"On this trip, I had sex with a fourteen-year-old girl in Mexico and a fifteen-year-old in Colombia. I am helping them financially. If they don't have sex with me, they may not have enough food."

These words were spoken by a retired U.S. schoolteacher who had just returned from a "vacation" in Latin America, where he was part of the global sex tourism business.

In the past fifty years, the number of people traveling all over the world has increased tenfold. But a dark side of this increased travel involves men from high-income countries who travel with one main goal: visiting lower-income nations to have sex with children.

Sex tourism is big business. Although there are no exact figures, it is likely that about 10 percent of the gross domestic product of several countries in Southeast Asia—including Malaysia, the Philippines, and Thailand—comes from sex tourism. In recent years, sex tourism has increased in Africa, Eastern Europe, and Latin America. Around the world, perhaps 1 million children are selling sex.

What accounts for the high level of sex tourism? One underlying cause is poverty. Sex tourism is most widespread in countries where the average person is very poor. With little economic opportunity, families are willing to allow their children to go to work, in many cases turning children over to "agents" who promise to find them jobs.

Gender stratification is also at work here. Most low-income countries are patriarchal, and boys get more schooling than girls do. This means that families who need money may have few alternatives to sending their daughters off to work in the sex trade.

A final factor that has increased sex tourism in recent years is the spread of the Internet. Not only do millions of men travel to have sex with children, but many of them share their experiences, posting detailed accounts on thousands of Web sites that support this industry. Such accounts only stimulate more men to travel for this purpose.

The plight of children working as prostitutes is shocking. Estimates suggest that most children have more than 100 clients a year, and some have as many as 1,500 (that would be almost five a day, working all year). Beyond being forced to have sex, these children face violence from clients and employers, deal with the constant fear of arrest by the police, and run a high risk of getting sexually transmitted diseases. Within months of going to work as prostitutes, most young children become depressed, lose their self-esteem, and view their situation as hopeless. Drug use and even suicide are common.

In response to increasing sex tourism, many national governments are calling for an end to child prostitution and a full-scale assault on the entire sex tourism industry. But given the severe poverty that is widespread in many countries, not to mention the added problem of police corruption, great change is unlikely any time soon.

WHAT DO YOU THINK?

1. Many men who take part in sex tourism make excuses for their behavior, as we read at the beginning of this box. Can you think of ways to discourage men from high-income countries from traveling to have sex with children?
2. Some travelers feel that the social norms we recognize at home do not apply in foreign lands, so sex with children is somehow OK. Do you think people everywhere should declare sex tourism a "universal wrong"? Why or why not?
3. Children also sell sex in the United States. Have you heard of this practice, which has been documented at truck stops as well as business conventions? How do you explain this happening in high-income countries like ours?

Source: Based on U.S. Department of Justice (2006).

2007 were women; the remaining one-third were men, including both male prostitutes and male clients (Federal Bureau of Investigation, 2008).

According to COYOTE (Call Off Your Old Tired Ethics, 2009), a sex workers' rights organization founded in 1973, fully 90 percent of women arrested for prostitution are streetwalkers from low-social-class backgrounds; very few are high-status call girls. Race also figures into the picture: COYOTE reports that although most prostitutes are white, most of those arrested are African Americans.

Should police and the courts get tougher in cases involving prostitution? Most people think that prostitution is wrong. In a recent survey, only 39.1 percent of respondents agreed with the statement "There is nothing inherently wrong with prostitution as long as the health risks can be minimized. If consenting adults agree to exchange money for sex, that is their business" (NORC, 2005:757). The health risks of prostitution include the danger of spreading sexually transmitted diseases, including AIDS. In addition, it is likely that even fewer people would approve of prostitution if they knew the extent of violence and drug abuse that often accompanies this way of life.

Finally, one country stands out as having a successful record of reducing prostitution. The surprising solution is simpler than you might expect, as the Social Problems in Global Perspective box on page 189 explains.

Child Prostitution

Few people defend prostitution when it involves children. Around the world, hundreds of thousands of children (mostly

SOCIAL PROBLEMS in Everyday Life

Why do you think the teen pregnancy rate is higher in the United States than in most other nations?

GETTING INVOLVED

Did you take sex education classes in school? If so, what effect did they have on you or others?

boys) live primarily on the streets, many selling sex to survive. Some of these children work to provide income for their families; others were orphaned by AIDS or war. Almost all are desperately poor (UNICEF, 2006).

In the Southeast Asian nation of Thailand, which has become a center for the global "sex tourism" industry, the number of prostitutes may be as high as 2 million. In countless brothels and sex shows on the streets of Bangkok, Thailand's capital city, half the women who are selling sex are not yet out of their teens.

Why are child prostitutes so popular? Customers favor young women in the belief that they pose less risk of spreading AIDS. But the fact is that about half of Bangkok's prostitutes are HIV-positive, so the risks of infection are high. Many of these girls and women also have other sexually transmitted diseases as well as conditions caused by years of neglect and abuse (Janus, 1996; U.S. Department of Justice, 2007). The Social Problems in Global Perspective box takes a closer look at sex tourism involving children.

Dimensions of Difference

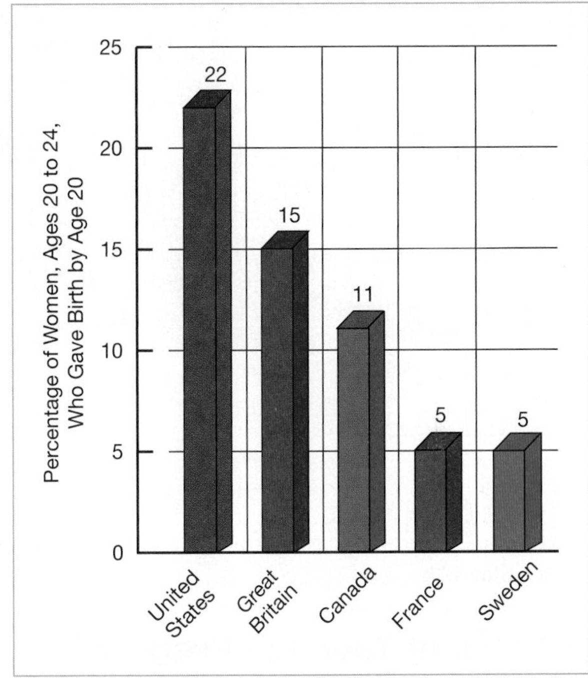

FIGURE 7–4 Births to Teenage Women

The rate of teenage pregnancy is higher in the United States than in other high-income countries.

Source: Population Reference Bureau (2009).

Teenage Pregnancy

In the United States, about 750,000 teenagers (out of a total of about 20 million) become pregnant each year. Most did not plan the pregnancy, and neither did the young men they were involved with. More seriously, most of these young people are unprepared to face the responsibilities of parenthood. As Figure 7–4 shows, the rate of teenage pregnancy is much higher in the United States than in other high-income nations.

The good news is that compared to fifty years ago, the share of teens who became pregnant is much lower. Back then, people married younger, and most teens who became pregnant were young wives who, with their husbands, were starting families. In the 1950s, there was widespread condemnation of having an "illegitimate" child, so unmarried couples who learned they were expecting a baby married quickly (the so-called shotgun marriage, often held at the insistence of the woman's father), or the woman quietly moved away and, after the birth, put the child up for adoption. In some cases, women obtained abortions, although this was against the law almost everywhere.

Today, most young women who become pregnant are not married. Among teens who become pregnant, few rush to get married. And few put their babies up for adoption. Research shows us this picture: Of all pregnant teens, 14 percent have miscarriages, 27 percent have abortions, and the majority (58 percent) keep their babies (Ventura at al., 2009; Alan Guttmacher Institute, 2010).

In recent decades, the pregnancy rate among girls in their teens has fallen substantially, despite the fact that at least half of teenage girls and boys are sexually active. The main reason for the decline is almost certainly increased use of contraceptives among sexually active teens.

The risk of unwanted pregnancy is greatest among girls who may be biologically mature but do not yet have a good understanding of how their reproductive systems work. Such girls are likely to be from poor families. Compared with those from richer families, these girls are also more likely to keep their babies. Why? Researchers point out that most poor girls and boys think that attending college and finding a good career is simply out of their reach. This is even more true in tough economic times, as we have seen in recent years. As a result, having a baby—being a parent—may seem to be the only way young people can claim to have reached adulthood. Single motherhood is particularly common among poor African Americans, who are doubly disadvantaged by poverty and racism. For all racial and ethnic categories, becoming an unmarried teenage mother makes it harder to finish school and find a good job, dramatically increasing the odds of remaining poor (Ventura et al, 2009; Guttmacher Institute, 2011).

In Tucson, Arizona, 18-year-old Ramona Ramirez was just given a baby shower by her high school classmates, many of whom are already married and have children.

In Bangor, Maine, Sandy Johnson, also 18, reports that only "one or two"girls in her high school have become pregnant.

MAKING THE GRADE

Can you explain why sex education is seen by some as the "problem" and by others as the "solution"?

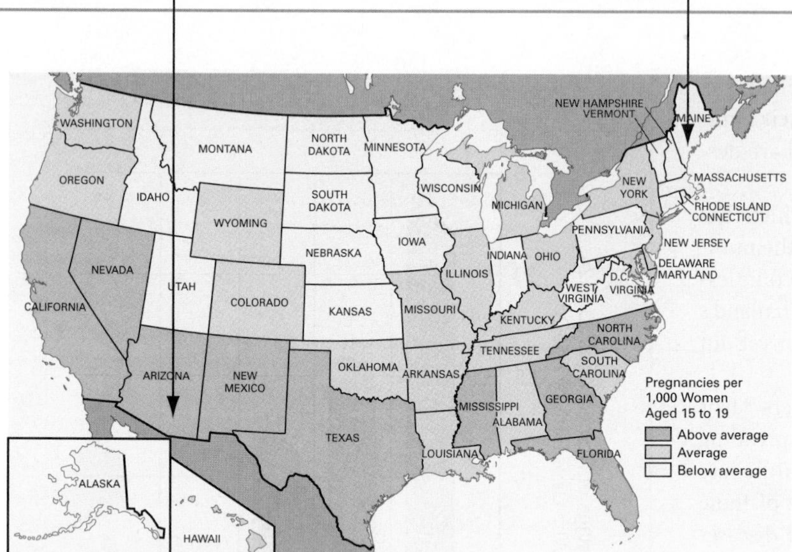

A Nation of Diversity

NATIONAL MAP 7–1

Teenage Pregnancy Rates across the United States

The map shows pregnancy rates for women aged fifteen to nineteen across the United States. What can you say about the regions of the country where rates are high? Where they are low? Can you explain these patterns?

Source: Alan Guttmacher Institute (2006).

National Map 7–1 shows the rate of teenage pregnancy across the United States.

The Costs of Teenage Pregnancy

At its best, parenthood brings people great joy. But for men and women who are young and poor, parenthood can be a nightmare of economic pressures that they simply cannot handle. They look to government for help, and the cost of income assistance, medical care, and other support for pregnant teenagers in the United States is probably about $10 billion each year (Hoffman, 2006).

The greatest burden of poverty, however, is borne by those who understand none of this—the babies. On average, infants born to poor teens have lower birthweight and higher risk of physical and developmental problems. Many such infants face a life of challenges that often accompany poverty, including poor nutrition, violence in the local neighborhood, little schooling, and inadequate health care. To make matters worse, most of these children face these hardships with little or no help from their fathers. Not surprisingly, perhaps, these children grow up at high risk for becoming single parents themselves.

Sex Education: A Solution?

What can society do to reduce the extent of unwanted teen pregnancy? One strategy looks to schools. Sex education programs teach young people how their bodies grow and change, present the biology of reproduction, and explain how to avoid pregnancy by using birth control or abstaining from sex.

Today, "sex ed" is offered in most public schools. But although it is an established part of the curriculum, it remains controversial. Critics (typically political conservatives) point out that as more schools have adopted sex education programs over the past two decades, the level of sexual activity among teenagers has gone up. Researchers tell us that about half of today's high school students have sexual intercourse. Although such data do not clearly show that sex education it what is causing this change, they do raise doubts about whether this program is (as conservatives tend to say) part of the problem or (as liberals claim) part of the solution.

Supporters of sex education say that the biggest cause of teenage pregnancy is ignorance. It makes sense, they say, to teach young people—many of whom are sexually active—about birth control methods and the risks of contracting sexually transmitted diseases. From this point of view, sex education is the main reason for the recent decline in unwanted teenage pregnancy.

Perhaps no sex education issue provokes more heated discussion than the policy of distributing condoms in school. Conservatives claim that this policy only encourages young people to rush headlong into sexual activity. Liberals respond that most young people will be sexually active one way or another; the point is to give them what they need to avoid pregnancy and sexually transmitted diseases (Alan Guttmacher Institute, 2002; Ventura et al., 2008).

Abortion

Of all the issues surrounding sexuality in the United States, surely the most controversial is **abortion**, *the deliberate termination of a pregnancy.* Each year, about 1.2 million abortions are performed in the United States, about one for every three live births. The typical woman receiving an abortion is in her

abortion the deliberate termination of a pregnancy

twenties and has never had one before; 81 percent of these women are unmarried, and 61 percent are white (Ventura et al., 2009; Alan Guttmacher Institute, 2011).

Abortion: A Look Back

Abortion goes far back in history; this practice was common among the ancient Egyptians, Romans, and Greeks (Luker, 1984; Tannahill, 1992). In the United States, from the colonial era until the mid-nineteenth century, early-term abortion was legal everywhere. The picture began to change in 1847, when the newly formed American Medical Association (AMA) pressed to outlaw the procedure. The AMA claimed that doctors were the best qualified to perform this procedure, but it is also clear that the AMA was trying to put midwives and other traditional healers who performed abortions out of business. Their efforts were successful. By the early twentieth century, every state in the country had enacted a law banning abortion (Luker, 1984).

These new laws did not end the practice of abortion, however. Women with money could find a doctor willing to perform a safe abortion. But for poor women, it was another story. They either endured an unwanted pregnancy or submitted to an inexpensive "back alley" procedure performed by an unlicensed practitioner, with sometimes deadly results.

By the 1960s, all across the United States, a social movement was under way to repeal laws banning abortion. In 1973, the movement succeeded when the U.S. Supreme Court issued decisions in the cases of *Roe* v. *Wade* and *Doe* v. *Bolton*, which struck down all state abortion laws. Ever since, "pro-choice" people (typically liberals) have fought to keep abortion available to women. "Antiabortion" people (typically conservatives) are working just as hard to reverse the High Court decision and once again make abortion illegal.

The Abortion Controversy Today

Since 1973, various laws and court decisions have limited women's access to abortion. In 1977, for example, Congress passed the Hyde Amendment prohibiting the use of Medicaid funds for abortions, except to save the life of the mother. In 1980, the U.S. Supreme Court ruled in *Harris* v. *McRae* that state and federal governments need not provide poor women with taxpayer-funded abortions. In 1989, the Supreme Court upheld a state law that banned public employees or public facilities from performing abortions, except to save the mother's life. In *Webster* v. *Reproductive Health Services* (1989), the Court also upheld state laws that require doctors, before performing an abortion, to conduct medical tests to see whether the fetus could survive outside the mother's body.

Table 7–1 U.S. Attitudes toward Abortion

Survey Question: It should be possible for a woman to obtain a *legal* abortion . . ."

	Percentage Answering Yes
". . . if the woman's own health is seriously endangered by the pregnancy."	84.8%
". . . if she becomes pregnant as a result of rape."	72.6
". . . if there is a strong chance of a serious defect in the baby."	70.4
". . . if she is married and does not want any more children."	42.8
". . . if she is not married and does not want to marry the man."	39.6
". . . if the family has a very low income and cannot afford any more children."	41.1
". . . for any reason."	40.7

Source: NORC (2009:329–31).

In 1992, the Court's decision in *Planned Parenthood of Southeastern Pennsylvania* v. *Casey* reaffirmed that states had wide latitude in setting abortion policy. Later in the 1990s, Congress twice proposed laws banning so-called partial-birth abortions performed in the third trimester of pregnancy, but President Clinton vetoed both bills. Finally, by 2009, twenty-four states have enacted laws requiring minors to obtain the consent of one or both parents before an abortion can be performed. The George W. Bush administration was less supportive of abortion rights than the Clinton administration, and in 2003, Congress again attempted to restrict late-term abortion. But no such law was ever passed, and after Democrats gained control of Congress in 2006, the chances of limiting access to abortion became very small. The Obama administration has taken a position in favor of abortion rights, so few analysts predict any basic change to current law in the next few years.

All the same, the public remains divided on this issue. Table 7–1 shows the proportion of U.S. adults who support abortion under various circumstances. Although a large majority (84.8 percent) support legal abortion if a woman's health is threatened by her pregnancy, less than half (40.7 percent) support legal abortion for any reason at all (NORC, 2009:329). Surprisingly, perhaps, support for abortion is almost the same among women (54 percent) and men (53 percent). Support for abortion is greater among Democrats (63 percent) than among Republicans (41 percent). In addition, attitudes toward abortion vary by race and ethnicity. For example, people of Arab and Italian descent are more conservative on this issue, with only sexually transmitted diseases (STDs) diseases spread by sexual contact

GETTING INVOLVED

Do you know the symptoms for common STDs?

29 percent supporting abortion for any reason. At the liberal end of the political spectrum, 62 percent of Jewish Americans support abortion for any reason (Zogby International, 2001; Pew Research Center, 2008).

Why is the abortion controversy so intense? Because from anyone's point of view, a lot is at stake. Antiabortion activists claim that abortion is nothing less than the killing of unborn children. On matters of life and death, many people will not compromise their beliefs. Yet pro-choice activists, too, have reason to stand firm. As they see it, legal access to abortion is the key to women's control over childbearing and therefore their whole lives. Only women who can avoid unwanted pregnancy have the opportunity to earn income and establish their independence from men. In short, without legal abortion, women are unlikely ever to achieve social equality with men (Simon, 2003).

Sexually Transmitted Diseases

Sexually transmitted diseases (STDs) are *diseases spread by sexual contact.* In all, there are more than fifty STDs. Rates of infection of most STDs—including gonorrhea, syphilis, and genital herpes—began to rise during the sexual revolution of the 1960s. By the 1980s, the rising danger of STDs played a part in encouraging the sexual counterrevolution, described earlier in this chapter. The following sections briefly describe several common STDs.

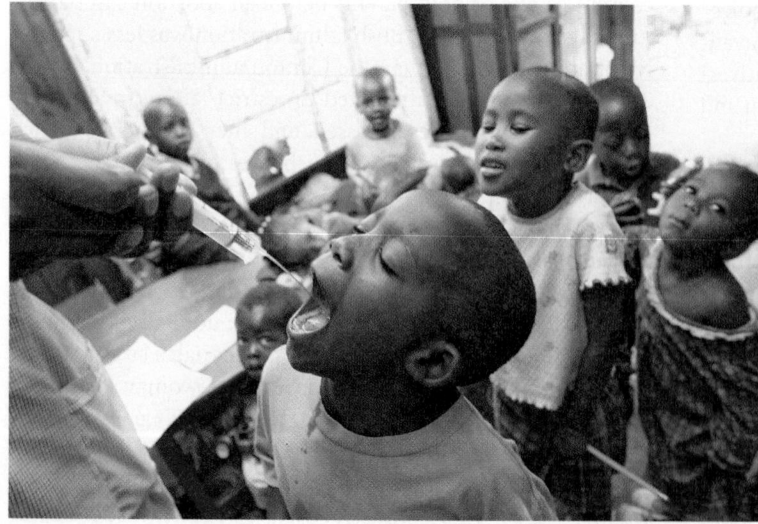

There are more than 2 million children with HIV in Africa. In this orphanage in Nairobi, Kenya, children with HIV receive liquid AZT, a medical treatment that extends their lives. But the high cost of such drugs—about $100 each month—means that only a small share of infected children can be helped.

Gonorrhea and Syphilis

Gonorrhea and syphilis, among the oldest diseases to afflict humans, result from microscopic organisms typically transmitted during sexual activity. Untreated, gonorrhea can cause sterility; syphilis can result in blindness, mental disorders, and even death.

In 2007, the official record shows 356,000 cases of gonorrhea and 11,500 cases of syphilis in the United States, although the actual totals are probably much higher. Official data show that most cases involve non-Hispanic African Americans (70 percent), with lower numbers reported among non-Hispanic whites (20 percent), Latinos (9 percent), and Asian Americans and Native Americans (under 1 percent) (Centers for Disease Control and Prevention, 2009).

Doctors treat gonorrhea and syphilis effectively with antibiotics, such as penicillin. For this reason, neither disease is considered a major U.S. health problem today.

Genital Herpes

Genital herpes is a virus that infects at least 45 million people, or one in five adults in the United States. Although herpes poses less danger than gonorrhea and syphilis, it has no cure. Some people with genital herpes have no symptoms at all; others experience periodic, painful blisters on the genitals accompanied by fever and headache.

One serious concern is that women with active genital herpes can transmit the disease to infants during a vaginal delivery, and it can be deadly to a newborn. Therefore, doctors usually advise infected women to give birth by cesarean section.

AIDS

The most serious of all sexually transmitted diseases is *acquired immune deficiency syndrome,* or *AIDS.* Soon after identifying this disease in 1981, doctors concluded that it is incurable and, if untreated, almost always fatal. AIDS is caused by the *human immunodeficiency virus,* or *HIV,* which destroys the body's immune system. AIDS itself does not kill; it makes a person unable to fight off a wide range of other diseases that eventually cause death.

Extent of the AIDS Problem

Government officials recorded 14,110 deaths due to AIDS in the United States in 2007. Officials also noted 35,962 new cases that year. The number of cases reported each year has been decreasing. But the official count of people who have contracted AIDS stands at

Parker Marsden goes to a small college in Minnesota; although aware of AIDS, he does not know anyone infected with HIV.

Mukoya Saarelma-Maunumaa lives in Namibia, where as many as half the people in some rural regions are infected with HIV; he has lost his father and two cousins to AIDS.

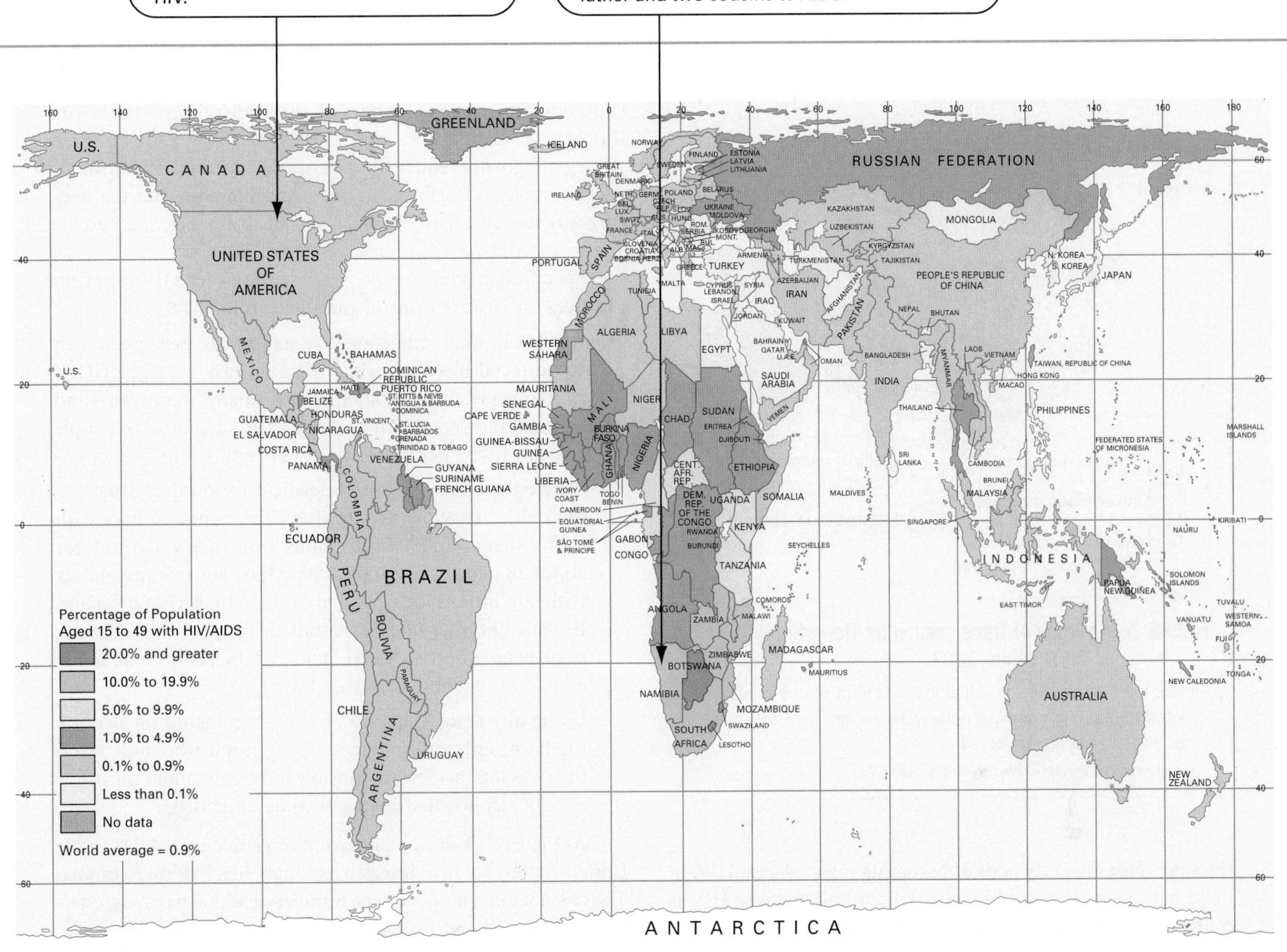

A World of Differences

GLOBAL MAP 7–1 HIV Infections around the World

The nations of sub-Saharan Africa contain two-thirds of the world's cases of HIV. Currently, however, it is Asia that shows the fastest increase in HIV infections, accounting for about 15 percent of global cases. Infection rates are fairly low in North and South America, which together account for 9 percent of global cases of HIV.

Sources: Population Reference Bureau (2009).

1,018,428. Of these, 562,793 have died (Centers for Disease Control and Prevention, 2009).

Non-Hispanic white people (66 percent of the population) account for 29 percent of patients with AIDS, and non-Hispanic African Americans (13 percent of the population) account for 49 percent of people with AIDS. Latinos also show high infection rates: They represent 15 percent of the total U.S. population, 19 percent of people with AIDS, and 15 percent of all women with AIDS. About 80 percent of women and children with the disease are African Americans or Latinos. Asian Americans and Native Americans (together almost 5 percent of the population) account for only about 1 percent of people with AIDS (Centers for Disease Control and Prevention, 2008).

In many regions of the world, AIDS is a medical catastrophe. Just how great is the global toll? Around the world, HIV infects some 33 million people, half under age twenty-five, and the number continues to rise. Global Map 7–1 shows that the countries with the highest rates of HIV infections are in sub-Saharan Africa, which accounts for 68 percent of the world's cases. According to the United Nations, in much of this region,

MAKING THE GRADE

Do you know where in the world the spread of HIV is the greatest?

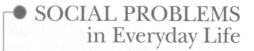

SOCIAL PROBLEMS in Everyday Life

Do you think most young people who are sexually active are as aware of sexually transmitted diseases as they ought to be? Explain your view.

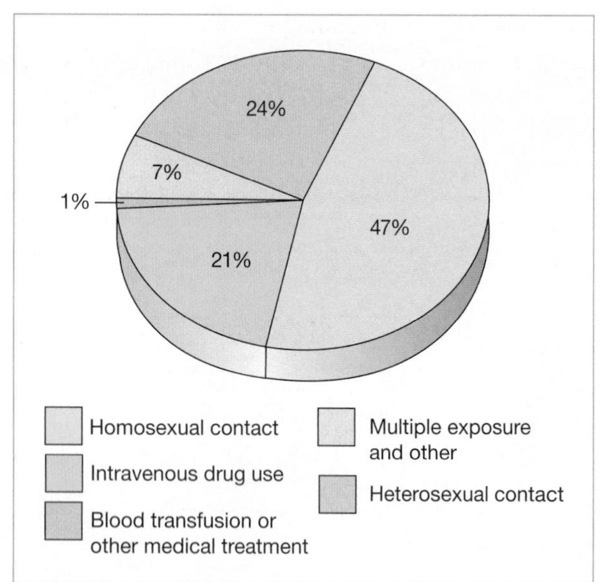

FIGURE 7–5 Types of Transmission for Reported U.S. AIDS Cases, 2007

Almost half the people with AIDS in the United States were infected through homosexual activity. However, there are many other ways to become infected.

Source: Centers for Disease Control and Prevention (2009).

teenagers face fifty-fifty odds of becoming infected with HIV. In these nations, girls are at higher risk than boys because HIV is more easily transmitted from males to females than the other way around.

Africa remains the center of the AIDS epidemic. But an increase in the infection rate in India and China, each with more than 1 billion people, is expected to cause a surge in the global population with AIDS in the coming decade (Whitelaw, 2003; UNAIDS, 2008).

The Spread of HIV

Because people who become infected with HIV display no symptoms for a year or even longer, most remain unaware of their condition and may unknowingly spread the disease. Within five years, one-third of infected people develop full-blown AIDS; half do so within ten years, and almost all become sick within twenty years.

Although HIV is infectious, it is not contagious. This means that HIV is transmitted from person to person in only a few, specific ways: through blood, semen, or breast milk. It is not transmitted through casual contact such as shaking hands, hugging, sharing towels or dishes, swimming together, or even coughing or sneezing. The risk of transmitting the virus through saliva (as in kissing) is extremely low. One effective strategy to greatly reduce the risk of transmitting HIV through sexual activity is for males to use a latex condom. But the only sure way to stay safe from HIV is sexual abstinence or an exclusive relationship with an uninfected person.

Specific behaviors put people at high risk for HIV infection (Centers for Disease Control and Prevention, 2008):

1. **Anal sex.** Anal intercourse is dangerous because it can cause rectal bleeding, which permits easy passage of HIV from one person to another. Because many homosexual and bisexual men engage in anal sex, these categories of people account for 51 percent of all cases diagnosed in 2007.
2. **Sharing needles.** Sharing a needle used to inject drugs is a high-risk behavior because users come into contact with each other's blood. Intravenous drug users account for about 28 percent of people with AIDS. For this reason, sex with an intravenous drug user is a high-risk behavior. Because the rate of intravenous drug use is high among poor people in the United States, AIDS has become a disease of the economically disadvantaged.
3. **Using any drug.** The use of any drug, including alcohol, can harm a person's judgment. Even people who understand the risks may act less responsibly if they are under the influence of alcohol, marijuana, or some other drug.

As Figure 7–5 shows, 24 percent of people with AIDS in the United States became infected through heterosexual contact. The risk goes up along with the number of sexual partners, especially if they fall into high-risk categories. Around the world, heterosexual activity accounts for two-thirds of all infections.

Combating AIDS

In the early 1980s, the gay community was the first to call attention to the problem of AIDS. The government was slow to respond, perhaps because it was gay men who were most affected by the epidemic. Activists pressed for greater government funding for AIDS research and more social services for people with AIDS. By the mid-1980s, when the epidemic had spread into the heterosexual population through infected blood used for transfusions, officials gave the problem greater attention and began screening the nation's blood supply for HIV.

As the death toll mounted, the gay and lesbian community came together to begin safer-sex outreach programs, spreading the word about what HIV is and how it is spread. These efforts succeeded as gay men began to reduce the number of sexual partners and avoid high-risk behaviors.

In recent years, new drug therapies have extended the lives of people with HIV. Prices have been coming down, but the

SOCIAL PROBLEMS in Everyday Life

How is characterizing a birth as "legitimate" a way of constructing a problem and defining a solution?

high cost of treatments—many of which are not covered by health insurance—is a burden many people simply cannot afford (Altman, 2006b).

Theoretical Analysis: Understanding Sexuality

Sociological theory can help us understand various social problems more completely. The following sections look at sexuality using sociology's three major approaches. The Applying Theory table on page 199 summarizes what we can learn about sexuality issues using each theoretical approach.

Structural-Functional Analysis: Controlling Sexuality

Perhaps the most important function of sexuality is human reproduction, to ensure that our species continues to exist. But controlling sexuality is also important to social organization, which is why society demands that people reproduce according to specific norms. To see why controlling sexuality is important, imagine for a moment that people reproduced again and again with just anybody. If this were to happen, the family as we know it would not exist, and people would have no sense of kinship. Without families, no one would have any particular relationship to anyone else, and society as we know it would largely collapse.

Incest and Legitimacy

One important norm guiding reproduction is the *incest taboo,* the norm that bans sex and reproduction between certain close family members. The incest taboo is found all over the world, although exactly which kin are included varies from society to society. Why is this norm important? Again, if close kin (other than husband and wife) were to reproduce, social relationships would soon become hopelessly confusing (if a father and a daughter reproduced and had a son, what would the boy's relationship be to each of them?).

In the same way, the traditional norms favoring *legitimate* offspring—meaning children born to married couples—is a strategy to ensure that children are cared for and also that they establish legal ties, including rights of inheritance, with their biological parents. In short, structural-functional analysis helps explain why inappropriate sexual relationships, including incest and childbearing out of wedlock, have been widely viewed as social problems in societies around the world.

The Functions of Prostitution

If certain sexual relationships cause social problems, it is also true that some sexual problems may not be entirely bad for everybody. Take the case of prostitution. As explained earlier in this chapter, most people view prostitution as a problem because it spreads disease and exploits women (NORC, 2007). But as Kingsley Davis (1971) pointed out many years ago, prostitution also performs a few useful, if less noticed, functions.

According to Davis, prostitution is one way to meet the sexual needs of those members of a society who do not have ready access to sex, including soldiers, travelers, and people who are not physically attractive or who are too poor to attract a marriage partner. In addition, some people may favor prostitution simply because they want sex without the commitment of a relationship. One analyst put it this way: "Men don't pay for sex; they pay so they can leave" (Miracle, Miracle, & Baumeister, 2003:421).

CRITICAL REVIEW The structural-functional approach shows that sexuality plays an important role in the organization of society and helps us understand why societies have always paid attention to who reproduces with whom. At the same time, now that modern technology has largely separated sex from reproduction, does society need to regulate sex as much as it once did?

Functional analysis sometimes ignores gender; when Kingsley Davis wrote of the benefits of prostitution for society,

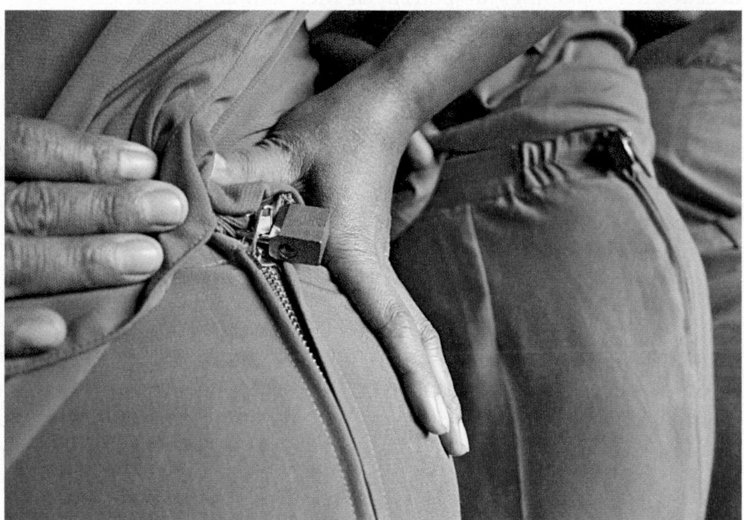

Are chastity belts a thing of the past? In a clear case of society controlling sexuality, these women who work in massage parlors in one Indonesian city are required to wear padlocked trousers to prevent prostitution. Whose interests do you think are served by such a practice?

MAKING THE GRADE

Can you explain the feminist view of sexuality?

he was really talking about benefits to some *men*. Another limitation of this approach is that it ignores the diversity of sexual norms in the United States as well as the fact that sexual patterns change over time. To appreciate the varied and changeable character of sexuality, we now turn to the symbolic-interaction approach.

Symbolic-Interaction Analysis: Defining Sexuality

The symbolic-interaction approach highlights the fact that members of a society socially construct sexuality just as they create all other aspects of reality. Thus the meanings people attach to sexuality can vary quite a bit. One good way to see the different ways people understand sex is to look back in history.

The Meaning of Virginity

A good example of the changing meanings attached to sex is the idea of *virginity*, that is, never having had sexual intercourse. Through most of this nation's history, strong cultural norms have demanded that people—or more precisely, women—remain virgins until marriage. Before modern methods of birth control were available, the norm of virginity was the only way men could be sure they were not marrying a woman who was carrying another man's child.

Once effective birth control was available, sexuality became separated from reproduction, so virginity did not matter nearly as much. One study shows that among people born in the decade after 1963, fully 84 percent of men and 80 percent of women reported that they were not virgins at first marriage. Fifty years ago, many people defined premarital sexual intercourse as a social problem; today, however, it is widely considered the norm (Laumann et al., 1994; NORC, 2007).

Learning Sexual Roles: The Case of Topless Dancers

The symbolic-interaction approach not only points out that sexual norms vary from time to time and place to place but also offers insights into how people learn and interpret their own sexual behavior. For example, how do women become topless dancers? How do women who do this work think of themselves?

In a study of forty topless dancers in a southwestern city, researchers found that women came to this kind of work gradually, step by step, just as people enter any other career (Thompson & Harrod, 1999). Most of the women explained that they first danced topless only briefly, in response to a dare from someone else, and only after having had a few drinks. The women reported receiving encouragement for their efforts, and more important, they soon realized that they could earn more money dancing than through other "straight" work.

At that point, they made the decision to earn some or all of their income doing something many people consider to be deviant. But most of the women insisted they were doing nothing wrong. Their clubs helped them think well of themselves by having strict "look but don't touch" policies, which allowed the women to consider themselves entertainers, not prostitutes. In addition, all the women used stage names so that customers knew nothing of their "real world" identities. Likewise, most women told only a few people beyond the club what their job actually was; to the rest, including parents, they were simply "in the nightclub business."

Finally, almost all the women working as topless dancers learned to see their work as useful, pointing out that they provided entertainment that did not hurt anyone and for which they were well paid. The women gradually built a world of meanings that both protected them and made them comfortable with their work (Thompson & Harrod, 1999).

CRITICAL REVIEW The symbolic-interaction approach highlights how people construct reality in their everyday lives, a process that applies to sexuality as it does to other forms of behavior. But although many aspects of sexuality vary over time and from place to place, some patterns are remarkably consistent, such as men's tendency to devalue women as sex objects. To understand this pattern, we turn to the social-conflict approach.

Social-Conflict Analysis: Feminist Theory and Queer Theory

The social-conflict approach highlights social inequality. Following this approach, feminist theory explains that sexuality involves inequality between women and men; similarly, queer theory highlights inequality between homosexuals and heterosexuals.

Feminist Theory: Women as Sexual Objects

Feminist theory points out that sexuality plays a part in men's domination of women. Pornography, prostitution, and even topless dancing degrade women, casting them in the role of sexual objects that exist only for men's pleasure. If men value women only for their looks and submissiveness, feminists ask, can the two sexes ever participate in society on equal terms? Probably not, which is the reason that the movement for gender equality has helped define sexuality in the workplace as a social problem, prompting governments and companies to enact anti-harassment policies.

MAKING THE GRADE

Use the table below to review the three theoretical approaches to sexuality.

queer theory a body of theory and research that challenges the heterosexual bias in U.S. society

APPLYING THEORY

Sexuality

	What is the level of analysis?	What is important about sexuality?	Is sexuality a problem?
Structural-functional approach	Macro-level	The structural-functional approach begins pointing to the importance of sexuality for human reproduction. But society must control sexuality—that is, must control who reproduces with whom—to maintain social order.	All societies make use of the incest taboo to regulate reproduction, preventing reproduction by closely related partners. To ensure that parents care for children and to ensure the right of offspring to inheritance, many societies also employ the idea of "legitimate" birth.
Symbolic-interaction approach	Micro-level	The symbolic-interaction approach explains that sexuality, like many social patterns, involves meanings that people attach to their behavior. Patterns of sexuality and the way people understand them vary from place to place and over time. Sexual roles, including engaging in controversial behavior such as topless dancing, is learned over time.	Meanings attached to sexual behavior change over time. Not being a virgin was defined as a problem in the past, especially for women, but virginity does not mean nearly as much today. To avoid the problem of negative labels, people who engage in controversial behavior involving sexuality, such as topless dancing, develop attitudes and behavior that protect their interests and self-esteem.
Social-conflict approach	Macro-level	All social-conflict approaches focus on how sexuality is linked to social inequality. Both feminist theory and queer theory are efforts to make society more equal with regard to gender and sexual orientation.	Feminist theory considers sexuality a problem to the extent that it allows men to dominate women. The problem of patriarchy contributes to other problems, such as prostitution and pornography, both of which involve men devaluing women. Queer theory opposes the hetero-sexism in our culture and seeks acceptance of homosexuality alongside heterosexuality.

Male domination involves not just inequality but also violence. As already explained, U.S. culture weaves sex and violence together, evident in expressions such as "hitting on" someone, a phrase that can refer to either sexuality or physical violence. For this reason, social-conflict theory—especially feminism—has been sharply critical of sexuality. A few feminists reject sexual relations with men entirely, claiming that women who sleep with men are like slaves having sexual relationships with their masters (Dworkin, 1987).

Queer Theory

A recent development in sociology is **queer theory,** *a body of theory and research that challenges the heterosexual bias in U.S. society.* Just as feminist theory seeks equal standing for women

heterosexism bias that treats heterosexuality as the norm while stigmatizing anyone who differs from this norm as "queer"

and men, queer theory seeks equal acceptance of homosexuality and heterosexuality.

Feminism characterizes U.S. society as *sexist.* Queer theory claims that our society is distorted by **heterosexism,** *bias that treats heterosexuality as the norm while stigmatizing anyone who differs from this norm as "queer."* The heterosexism of U.S. society condemns not only gay men and lesbians but also bisexual people, asexual people, and transgender individuals who alter their sex surgically. Heterosexist norms are common in everyday life, as when the mass media celebrate the "sex appeal" of popular movie stars, almost all of whom are portrayed as heterosexual. In 1998, the comedian and actress Ellen DeGeneres sparked controversy when she "came out" as a lesbian on her television show. Yet in recent years, popular shows like *Queer Eye for the Straight Guy* and *Will and Grace*, featuring openly gay characters, suggest that attitudes are changing.

Although discrimination against women and African Americans is illegal, bias against people who differ in their sexuality is both common and, in many cases, within the law. Organizations from the Boy Scouts to the U.S. military still exclude anyone who displays behavior considered "queer."

CRITICAL REVIEW Feminist theory and queer theory highlight how closely sexuality is tied to various dimensions of social inequality. But critics of the social-conflict approaches point out that not everyone thinks of sexuality as a power issue. Rather, most people find that sexuality strengthens their relationship to another person. In addition, the social-conflict approach gives little attention to the many steps U.S. society has taken to attack bias against women, gay men, and lesbians, including antidiscrimination policies and hate crime laws.

POLITICS AND SEXUALITY

Constructing Problems and Defining Solutions

In this chapter, once again, we see that how people construct problems and what strategies they define as solutions depend on their political values. This holds for sexuality as well. This section explores the issues raised in this chapter from the conservative, liberal, and radical-left points of view.

Conservatives: The Value of Traditional Morality

The basic principle that defines the conservative view of sexuality is that people should be guided not by selfish desires but by established moral principles of right and wrong. If society encourages the traditional behavior we associate with "gentlemen" and "ladies," conservatives argue, most of the problems noted in this chapter can be avoided (Sommers, 2003).

Many conservatives support the conventional norms that place sexuality within the traditional bonds of marriage. For this reason, conservatives view premarital sex and extramarital sex as social problems, behavior that may lead to other problems such as teenage pregnancy and sexually transmitted diseases. Conservatives also condemn prostitution and pornography not only because they violate traditional standards of decency but also because they can threaten marriages.

Conservatives oppose laws that permit abortion on demand because this policy gives one person the power to end the life of another who is innocent and helpless: the unborn child. Rather than ending 1.2 million unwanted pregnancies each year through abortion, conservatives advocate greater sexual responsibility so that fewer unwanted pregnancies occur in the first place.

Of course, not all conservatives agree on every issue. Homosexuality is a case in point. Some conservatives condemn homosexuality as an immoral lifestyle and oppose same-sex marriage as a violation of tradition and, in the case of religious conservatives, biblical Scripture. Other, more moderate conservatives believe that sexual orientation cannot be a moral issue because it is not a matter of choice; they support same-sex marriage as a means of bringing the benefits of family life to all people, gay and straight.

Overall, the conservative answer to social problems involving sexuality is to have strong social institutions—including churches, schools, and especially families. These institutions can teach young people to resist peer pressure and other temptations in the interest of doing what is right. Today, conservatives support a number of policies that promise to strengthen families, such as tougher child support laws, laws requiring parental notification whenever young women seek abortions, and policies giving parents time away from work to care for family members. Most of all, conservatives claim, U.S. society would greatly benefit from a national effort to ensure that as many children as possible are raised in a home with both a father and a mother.

Liberals: Sex and Individual Choice

Liberals emphasize not the traditional morality so important to conservatives but the importance of individual freedom. As liberals see it, all people should be free to choose how they express their sexuality. This makes the liberal attitude toward sexuality

MAKING THE GRADE

Conservatives tend to see sexuality in moral terms; lliberals see sexuality in terms of personal choice; radicals see sexuality in terms of inequality.

one of tolerance. In the case of sexual orientation, for example, liberals avoid making judgments that a particular behavior is always right or always wrong; they favor allowing individuals to decide for themselves how they wish to behave. In the same way, liberals are tolerant of premarital sex as long as the people involved have the maturity and the knowledge to make responsible choices.

The limits of liberal tolerance come when someone threatens another with harm. Liberals define sexual violence, AIDS, and teenage pregnancy as social problems for this reason. Similarly, although liberals defend freedom of expression, many are concerned that pornography and prostitution end up harming women.

Liberals look to government to address various social problems. Schools can take the lead in teaching young people what they need to know to make responsible choices about sex. Liberals expect the criminal justice system to protect women from domestic violence and rape. In their view, government agencies should monitor the workplace to be sure that companies protect employees from sexual harassment. Finally, only the vast resources available to the government are likely to bring an eventual end to the AIDS epidemic.

Believing that individuals should be responsible for their own behavior, liberals support making abortion available to all, based on a decision by the woman herself. Most liberals support government funding for abortions so that all pregnant women, regardless of their ability to pay, have choices.

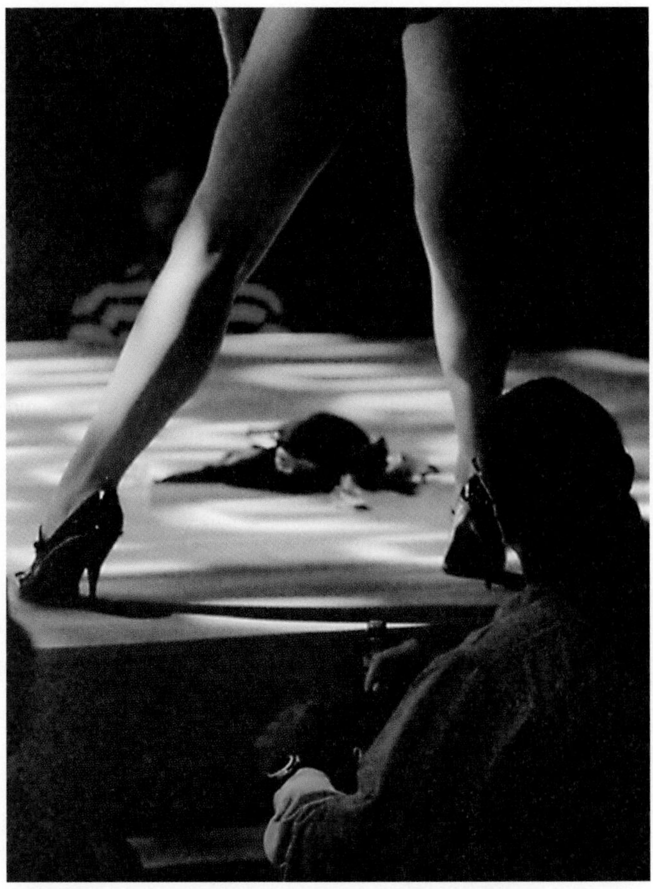

Are so-called gentlemen's clubs and strip joints a problem? Conservatives tend to oppose such establishments on moral grounds. Many liberals support the idea that adults should be free to behave as they wish as long as they do not harm others. But other liberals—and most radicals—condemn the selling of sex because it perpetuates traditional gender stereotypes that harm women.

The Radical Left: Go to the Root of the Problem

Radicals on the left see the issues raised in this chapter—including sexual orientation, pornography, sexual violence, and prostitution—as dimensions of social inequality. In their view, each problem comes about because some category of people has power over another.

Radical feminists explain that U.S. society is strongly patriarchal. Because male power runs deep into the structure of U.S. society, radical feminists doubt that efforts at reform will ever create a society in which women and men stand as equals. As a result, radical feminists seek the elimination of gender itself. As noted in Chapter 4 ("Gender Inequality"), many radical feminists believe that to do this, society must challenge the biological facts of reproduction. Perhaps, they suggest, new reproductive technologies will liberate women from their historical link to childbearing, which will open up the possibility of equal participation in social life.

In the short term, many radical feminists encourage women to work together to achieve political aims and to avoid dependency on men. Some even call for ending sexual ties to men, offering a strong voice on behalf of lesbians. It is lesbians, after all, who defy two basic structures of U.S. society: They challenge the heterosexual norm by being homosexual, and they challenge male power by choosing to live without men.

Queer theory argues that U.S. society privileges heterosexuality while dismissing anyone who differs from that norm as "queer." So deep is this heterosexual bias, queer theory claims, that nothing less than challenging the roots of our way of life can produce an egalitarian society in which all people are equal participants in social life.

The Left to Right table on page 202 summarizes issues related to sexuality as viewed from each of the three poitical perspectives.

MAKING THE GRADE

Use the table below to review the three political approaches to sexuality.

LEFT TO RIGHT

The Politics of Sexuality

	RADICAL-LEFT VIEW	LIBERAL VIEW	CONSERVATIVE VIEW
WHAT IS THE PROBLEM?	Men dominate women, just as heterosexuals dominate people with other sexual orientations.	Prostitution and pornography harm women, teen pregnancy is linked to poverty, and sexual harassment prevents people from doing their jobs.	Premarital sex, extramarital sex, and homosexuality violate traditional principles of right and wrong; abortion, too, is morally wrong.
WHAT IS THE SOLUTION?	Because sexism and heterosexism are deeply rooted in the existing system, radical feminism advocates change in the direction of a gender-free society. Similarly, queer theory argues that equality for people of all sexual orientations will require a basic change in our culture.	Government must combat prostitution and pornography, keep sexuality out of the workplace, ensure that abortion is available to all women, and pursue a cure for AIDS.	Families—preferably with two active, involved parents—must teach children traditional virtues, such as self-restraint in matters of sexuality. To the extent that they do, problems such as teen pregnancy and sexually transmitted diseases will decline.

JOIN THE DEBATE

1. In your opinion, which issues discussed in this chapter are the most serious social problems? Why?
2. Overall, do you think social problems involving sexuality are getting better or worse? Which problems? Why?
3. Which of the three political analyses of sexuality included here do you find most convincing? Why?

Going On from Here

If anything is sure to be around a century from now, it is sex. Societies may change in many ways, but sex seems to remain a steady element of human experience.

But is it? This chapter has traced some remarkable changes in sexual practices and attitudes in the United States. From the rigid "sex as reproduction" view held by the earliest European settlers on our shores to the open, "anything goes" views of the sexual revolution, ideas about sex have been anything but static.

Change is also evident in the definition of sexual problems. At the beginning of the twentieth century, homosexuality was treated as a serious problem: No one talked about it, many people saw it as a sin or a sickness, and homosexual behavior was against the law almost everywhere. As the gay rights movement gained strength, the idea of sexual diversity entered U.S. culture. Today, it is now possible to live an openly gay life, and millions of people do.

Several decades ago, few people considered sexual harassment to be a problem, accepting the idea that men should think of women primarily in sexual terms. As women have gained economic, political, and educational clout in the United States, such thinking has been replaced by the idea that women as well as men should be evaluated on the basis of their abilities rather than their looks. In the past decade, the widespread enactment of sexual harassment policies has sought to remove sexuality from workplace relationships.

Going on from here, what changes should we expect in the future? Although continued controversy is certain, the trend toward greater tolerance of homosexuality seems sure to continue. In the span of just a few years, six states have decided to allow gay men and lesbians to form legal marriages; other states are likely to follow suit. Likewise, efforts to bring an end to the AIDS epidemic are likely to intensify. With time, this disease, which has cost more than a million lives in the United States, will be tamed. But what about the poor nations of the world, where the death toll is expected to reach hundreds of millions? And back at home, what about the divisive issue of abortion? All that is certain is that this controversy will continue.

Sex may always be part of social life, but in this case, the more things stay the same, the more they change.

DEFINING SOLUTIONS

Is it OK for young people to be sexually active?

Just about everyone has an opinion about this issue, if only because sexual activity can lead to a number of problems, including pregnancy and sexually transmitted diseases. Look at the photos below to see two different approaches to defining a solution to these problems.

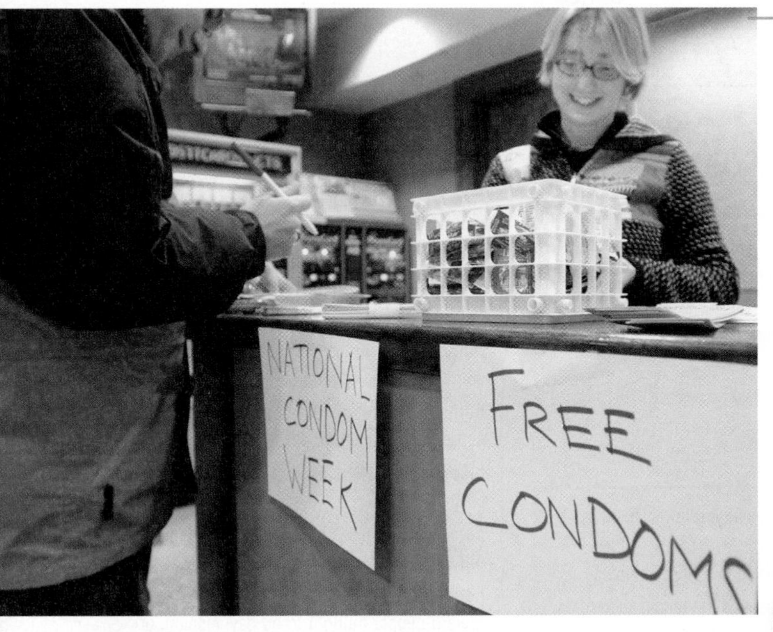

Liberals agree that unwanted pregnancy and sexually transmitted diseases are serious problems. But they claim that the problem is not sex itself, but a lack of understanding about how to have "safe sex." For that reason, liberals favor solutions such as sex education and also making condoms and other forms of birth control widely available. Here, a Wisconsin university student distributes free samples during "National Condom Week." What are the advantages and disadvantages of this approach?

Conservatives claim that our society has become too permissive with regard to sexual activity. Many favor the traditional idea that young people should delay sexual activity until marriage. If everyone followed this standard, they say, problems such as unwanted pregnancy and STDs would be very rare. The abstinence movement is one conservative solution that is asking young women to wear "chastity rings" that symbolize their pledge to abstain from sexual activity until marriage. What do you see as the "pros" and "cons" of this solution?

HINT

Both of these approaches will obviously "work" to some degree. At the same time, which one you would favor depends on your political attitudes. Conservatives take the position that traditional moral values, combined with personal responsibility, go a long way to solving problems. But what happens if young people are sexually active? The liberal approach assumes that young people will be sexually active; they say that availability of condoms or other birth control (as well as sex education) will help young people make safer choices. But this approach offers little guidance to help a young person know whether and when getting into a sexual relationship with someone is a good idea. Where do you stand on this issue?

Getting Involved: Applications & Exercises

1. Almost every campus has student organizations involved in sexual issues discussed in this chapter, including gay rights, sexual violence, and abortion. Find out which organizations operate on your campus. What are their goals? What changes do they seek? How would you characterize them politically?
2. Ask an official in your college's student services office about the extent of sexual violence on campus. See what you can learn about the percentage of crimes reported and the policies and procedures to assist and protect victims.
3. Do some research in the library and on the Internet to learn more about past and present laws in your state and local community regarding a sexuality-related issue of interest to you, such as prostitution, sodomy, sexual violence, stalking, or sexual harassment.
4. In recent years, "hooking up" has emerged as a pattern of sexual behavior on college campuses. Organize a class discussion that explores what people think "hooking up" means, why this pattern has emerged, and what problems it involves.

MAKING THE GRADE

A DEFINING MOMENT
Alfred Kinsey: Talking Openly about Sex p. 181

CHAPTER 7 Sexuality

What Is Sex?

Sex is a **BIOLOGICAL** issue.

- Females and males have different organs used for reproduction and also different physical traits.

p. 178

Sex is a **CULTURAL** issue.

- Sexual attitudes and practices vary from one place to another and over time.

p. 178

sex (p. 179) the biological distinction between females and males; also, activity that leads to physical gratification and possibly reproduction

Sexual Attitudes in the United States

Sexual attitudes have changed over the course of U.S. history:

- Early colonists viewed sex rigidly as intended solely for reproduction.
- In recent decades, sex has become more a matter of intimacy and personal pleasure.
- The **SEXUAL REVOLUTION** that began in the 1960s encouraged people to be freer and more open about sexuality.
- By the 1980s, a **SEXUAL COUNTERREVOLUTION** arose, reflecting the country's more conservative politics as well as fears about sexually transmitted diseases.
- The sexual revolution is continuing today among older people, sometimes making use of drugs that treat "erectile dysfunction."

pp. 179–80

Sexual Orientation

- Although the norm in all societies is heterosexuality, other sexual orientations—including homosexuality, bisexuality, and asexuality—are found as well.
- Although sexual orientation is partly a cultural issue, most evidence suggests that it is rooted in biology.
- The gay rights movement has been influential since the 1950s. A recent success was the legalization of same-sex marriage in several states.

pp. 181–85

sexual orientation (p. 181) a person's romantic and emotional attraction to another person

heterosexuality (p. 181) sexual attraction to someone of the other sex

homosexuality (p. 181) sexual attraction to someone of the same sex

bisexuality (p. 181) sexual attraction to people of both sexes

asexuality (p. 181) the absence of sexual attraction to people of either sex

homophobia (p. 185) an aversion to or hostility toward people thought to be gay, lesbian, or bisexual

Social Problems Related to Sexuality

PORNOGRAPHY

- Pornography consists of words or images that cause sexual arousal.
- Conservatives oppose pornography on moral grounds; many liberals object to it as demeaning to women.
- Some research links viewing pornography among males to higher aggression and greater acceptance of violence.

pp. 185–87

SEXUAL HARASSMENT

- In recent years, sexual harassment has been defined as a social problem.
- Today, laws protect people from sexual harassment, especially in the workplace.
- Most but not all cases of harassment involve men victimizing women.

pp. 187–88

PROSTITUTION

- Prostitution has long been widespread in the United States.
- Law enforcement usually targets female prostitutes rather than male clients and low-income streetwalkers rather than more affluent call girls.
- The extent of prostitution is even greater in Asia and many other poor regions of the world where "sex tourism" is widespread.

pp. 188–91

TEENAGE PREGNANCY

- About 750,000 U.S. teens become pregnant each year.
- Most teens who become pregnant are not married, and about half decide to keep their babies.
- Babies born to teens, especially young women who are poor, are at high risk for poverty as adults.

pp. 191–92

pornography (p. 185) words or images intended to cause sexual arousal

sexual harassment (p. 187) unwanted comments, gestures, or physical contact of a sexual nature

prostitution (p. 188) the selling of sexual services

abortion (p. 193) the deliberate termination of a pregnancy

sexually transmitted diseases (STDs) (p. 194) diseases spread by sexual contact

ABORTION

- Abortion is among the most divisive issues in the United States.
- The debate over abortion rights involves not just unintended pregnancy but also the social standing of women.

pp. 192–94

SEXUALLY TRANSMITTED DISEASES

- Unprotected sexual activity transmits some fifty diseases, including deadly AIDS.
- In global perspective, AIDS is becoming a medical catastrophe, especially in Africa.

pp. 194–97

Theoretical Analysis: Understanding Sexuality

Structural-Functional Analysis: Controlling Sexuality

The **STRUCTURAL-FUNCTIONAL APPROACH** emphasizes society's need to control sexuality.

- The incest taboo and social norms regarding "legitimate" offspring help clarify social relationships and obligations between members of families.
- Some sexual patterns that are widely regarded as deviant, such as prostitution, may also have positive functions, at least for men.

pp. 197–98

Symbolic-Interaction Analysis: Defining Sexuality

The **SYMBOLIC-INTERACTION APPROACH** highlights the fact that members of a society socially construct sexuality just as they create all reality.

- Sexual norms, such as those involving virginity, often change over time and also vary from place to place.
- People learn sexual behavior; the meaning they attach to sexuality affects how they think of themselves.

p. 198

Social-Conflict Analysis: Feminist Theory and Queer Theory

The **SOCIAL-CONFLICT APPROACH** focuses on social inequality.

- *Feminist theory* points out that many aspects of sexuality reflect men's social domination of women.
- *Queer theory* claims that the heterosexist bias in U.S. culture stigmatizes gay men and lesbians, bisexual people, asexual people, and transgender individuals.

pp. 198–200

queer theory (p. 199) a body of theory and research that challenges the heterosexual bias in U.S. society

heterosexism (p. 200) bias that treats heterosexuality as the norm while stigmatizing anyone who differs from this norm as "queer"

See the **Applying Theory** table on page 199.

Politics and Sexuality: Constructing Problems and Defining Solutions

The Radical Left: Go to the Root of the Problem

- **RADICALS ON THE LEFT** point out that the root of many social problems related to sexuality is inequality.
- Radical feminism and queer theory argue the need for basic changes in U.S. society in pursuit of equality for all, female and male, gay and straight.

p. 201

Liberals: Sex and Individual Choice

- **LIBERALS** emphasize the importance of individual freedoms. All people should be free to choose how they express their sexuality as long as their choices do not harm others.
- Liberals look to government to address social problems such as domestic violence and rape, sexual harassment, and the AIDS epidemic.

pp. 200–201

Conservatives: The Value of Traditional Morality

- **CONSERVATIVES** believe sexuality should be guided by traditional moral principles of right and wrong. They oppose abortion and premarital and extramarital sex, and many condemn homosexuality.
- Conservatives emphasize the importance of two-parent families in raising children with strong values and self-control.

p. 200

See the **Left to Right** table on page 202.

CONSTRUCTING THE PROBLEM

Why are some drugs legal and others illegal?

Many factors are involved, and standards of what is legal or illegal change over time. Until 1903, Coca-Cola was sold legally although it was made using cocaine; from 1920 until 1933, all alcoholic drinks were illegal throughout the United States.

Is drinking alcohol by students a problem?

Most college officials express concerns. A recent survey found that 40 percent of U.S. college students reported abusing alcohol in the past two weeks.

Isn't drug abuse really a victimless crime?

Each year, more people die as a result of using alcohol, tobacco, and other drugs than from gunshots, car accidents, and AIDS combined.

CHAPTER 8

Alcohol and Other Drugs

CHAPTER OVERVIEW

WHAT IS A DRUG? This chapter explains the major categories of drugs and why some drugs are legal and other are not. You will learn how drug abuse is related to issues such as homelessness, crime, and global poverty. You will assess various strategies our government has used to counter illegal drug use. You will carry out theoretical analysis of drug use and learn how "problems" and "solutions" involving drugs reflect people's political attitudes.

Sarah Markson, a patrol officer for the Hampton, Virginia, police department, put in plenty of overtime during the first weekend in March. The popular band Phish was playing at the Hampton Coliseum, and some 75,000 of the band's fans showed up for the concert. Markson, along with 200 other officers, worked the concert and was busy from the time the doors opened until the last fans filed out.

The biggest problem, according to Markson? Drugs. Police arrested 194 people, almost all for drug possession, use, or sale. By the end of the concert, the police had confiscated more than $1 million in illegal drugs and $68,000 in cash from those who were arrested on drug charges. To many of the Phish fans who were looking to unwind after a long week at work, drugs were part of the solution. But to Sarah Markson and her colleagues on the Hampton police force, drugs were definitely part of the problem ("Police Seize," 2009).

Drugs of all kinds are part of the culture in the United States. As this chapter explains, tens of thousands of young people throughout the nation smoke marijuana at music events, at home, and sometimes on the job. People of all ages abuse prescription drugs such as Vicodin and OxyContin, as well as dozens of drugs they buy over the counter. And alcohol is the most widely used—and abused—drug of all.

Alcohol and other drugs can be a source of pleasure and in appropriate doses can benefit both physical and mental health. Yet drugs also harm people of all ages, causing accidents, anxious trips to the emergency room, and even death. This chapter explains what drugs are, how they work, and the consequences of their use. We begin with a basic definition.

What Is a Drug?

Broadly defined, a **drug** is *any chemical substance other than food or water that affects the mind or body* (A. Goldstein, 1994). For millennia, people have used various natural substances to cause changes in the human body. In addition, thousands of synthetic substances have been added to the list of available drugs. In fact, most people use a number of drugs, from the caffeine in their morning coffee that helps them wake up to the aspirin that eases a headache at the end of the day.

Most of the time, drugs cause changes that people think of as good. But most people in the United States also point to "dangerous" drugs—substances such as crack cocaine and heroin—and define their use as a serious social problem (NORC, 2005:131). In the case of still other drugs, such as marijuana, some people see a problem while others see a harmless drug and still others see a helpful medical substance (Stein, 2002).

These differences in opinion raise a basic question: When and why are drugs defined as good or as harmful? To find the answer, we first need to explore the link between drugs and culture.

Drugs and Culture

How people view any particular drug varies from one society to the next. Europeans, for example, have enjoyed drinking alcohol for thousands of years. But Native Americans, who had never tasted wine or hard liquor until the arrival of European colonists in North America five centuries ago, had no customs to guide their use. As a result, many Native Americans drank too much, sometimes falling into a drunken stupor. For this reason, tribal leaders soon defined alcohol as a serious problem (Mancall, 1995; Unrau, 1996).

On the other hand, for centuries many Native people have used peyote as part of their religious rituals. When Europeans learned about peyote from American Indians, some of them began to use this drug. But having no experience with it, many became terrified by the hallucinations peyote produces and soon declared that peyote was a dangerous drug.

Cultural differences in the way people view drugs continue today. Coca, the plant used to make cocaine, has been grown for thousands of years in the South American nations of Bolivia, Peru, and Colombia, countries where it is legal

drug any chemical substance other than food or water that affects the mind or body

SOCIAL PROBLEMS in Everyday Life

Can you think of drugs we accept today that may well be viewed as dangerous and may even be outlawed at some point in the future?

today. In those nations, many local farmers (and some tourists) chew the plant or make tea from it in order to give themselves a "lift." But in the United States, the growing of coca and the sale or possession of cocaine are illegal, and most people view this drug as a cause of violence and crime (Léons & Sanabria, 1997).

Just as the definition of what is a drug changes from one society to another, it also changes over time. A century ago, almost no one in the United States talked about the country having a "cocaine problem," even though there was plenty of cocaine around: Famous people such as Sigmund Freud used cocaine openly, and anyone could stop by a corner drugstore to enjoy a glass of a popular "brain tonic" called Coca-Cola, which contained cocaine as one of its ingredients (Inciardi, 1996; Léons & Sanabria, 1997).

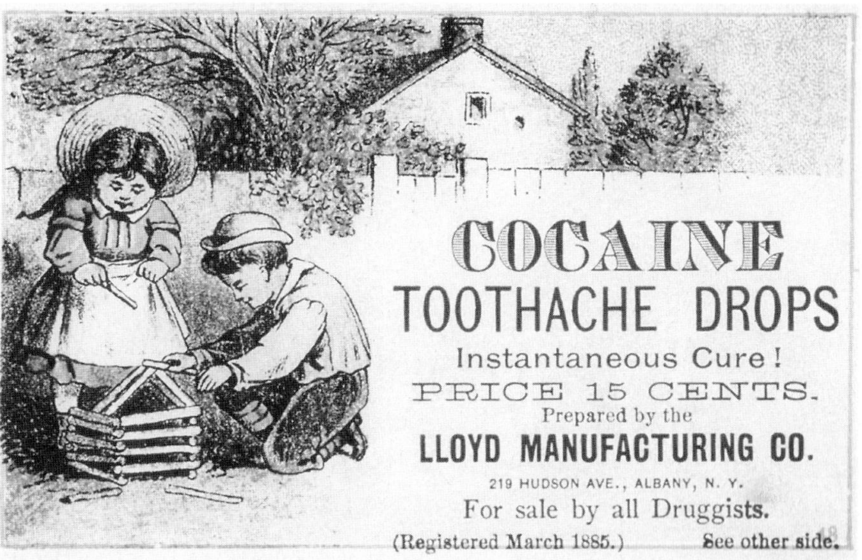

Whether a society defines a substance as a useful medication or a dangerous drug varies over time. It would surprise many people to learn that a century ago, cocaine was an ingredient in a number of readily available products, such as this remedy for toothaches.

Drugs, Race, and Ethnicity

People's attitudes toward various drugs also have much to do with which racial and ethnic categories they think may be using the drug. A century ago in the South, many white people feared that easily available cocaine would fall into the hands of African Americans, who might then commit crimes or become violent toward whites. Such fears were one reason that in 1903, the Coca-Cola Company stopped putting cocaine in its beverage. In the years that followed, state after state outlawed the use of cocaine (Goode, 1993; Bertram et al., 1996).

We find the same pattern in public opinion about other drugs. In the nineteenth century, as ever-increasing numbers of immigrants came to the United States, they brought not only their dreams but also their favored drugs. In the 1850s, for example, many Chinese immigrants in California smoked opium (a practice they learned from British colonists in China). Anti-Chinese feelings prompted public officials in eleven western states to ban opium. At the same time, in the East, where there were few Chinese people, getting your hands on opium was as easy as going to the corner store or picking up a Sears, Roebuck mail-order catalogue.

As the number of immigrants climbed, so did concern about drugs as a social problem. In 1914, Congress passed the Harrison Act, a national law restricting the sale of cocaine and heroin. By 1919, not even doctors could write prescriptions for these drugs. In 1920, the nation's attention turned to a much more widely used drug: alcohol.

Changing Views of Alcohol

Alcohol has a long history in the United States, and the story has much to do with ethnic diversity. At the outset, after Europeans first settled this land, alcohol (at least in moderation) was defined as a good drug. But in the nineteenth century, opinions began to turn negative as the tide of immigration increased. Why? Common stereotypes linked alcohol with immigrants—the Germans drank beer, the Irish drank whiskey, and the Italians drank wine. In short, to people who thought that a million immigrants entering the country each year was a million too many, immigrants drinking alcohol added up to a serious social problem (Pleck, 1987; Unrau, 1996).

As opposition to immigration increased (see Chapter 3, "Racial and Ethnic Inequality"), so did support for the *temperance movement*, a social movement that wanted to ban alcohol. In 1920, this social movement succeeded in reaching its goal when Congress passed the Eighteenth Amendment to the Constitution, which outlawed the manufacture and sale of alcohol throughout the United States.

Of course, many people, including those whose families had been in this country for centuries, liked to drink. Therefore, although Prohibition reduced alcohol consumption, it did not end it. In addition, by limiting the supply of alcoholic beverages, Prohibition pushed prices sharply higher. With so much money to be made selling booze illegally, people began smuggling liquor from Canada or distilling it themselves here at home. In the rural South, for example, the poor made "moonshine" in

MAKING THE GRADE

Be sure you understand the difference between use and abuse of drugs as well as the difference between addiction and dependency.

GETTING INVOLVED

Have you ever abused a drug? If so, was it a legal or an illegal drug? Why do you think of it as a case of abuse rather than use?

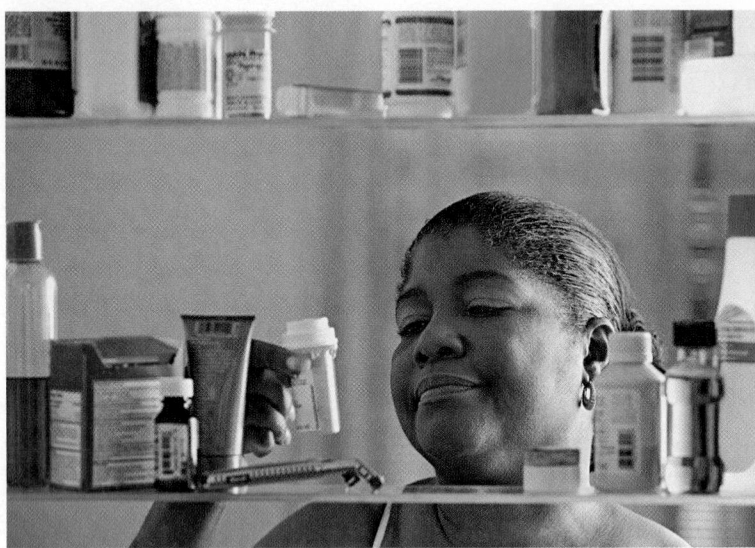

Drugs are part of our way of life, a fact that is evident in the collection of pills, capsules, and liquid medications found in most U.S. homes.

local stills hidden in the mountains. In the urban North, notorious gangsters such as Al Capone made fortunes smuggling and distributing liquor to secret "speakeasy" nightclubs.

As Prohibition tried to solve one problem, it created another—giving organized crime more power and money than ever before. As a result, the public gradually came to see that Prohibition was not a solution but more of a problem. In 1933, Congress passed the Twenty-First Amendment, repealing Prohibition and bringing an end to the failed "Great Experiment."

The Extent of Drug Use

What is the extent of drug use today? The answer depends on which drugs you are talking about. If we define drugs in a broad way to include aspirin and caffeine, almost everyone in the United States is a "user." Parents give analgesics to teething infants and Ritalin to overactive schoolchildren, college students take appetite suppressants to control their weight, adults reach for antidepressants and tranquilizers, and older people use pills to restore sexual functioning. Most people in the United States rely on drugs to help them go to sleep, wake up, relax, or ease aches and pains.

It is not far off the mark to say that we live in a "drug culture." At the same time, most people don't define this kind of drug use as a problem. The positive view of most drugs reflects not only how widespread use is but also the fact that many people think drugs make life better.

When most people in the United States think of a "drug problem," what comes to mind is the use of *illegal* drugs. In 2007, according to government surveys, nearly 20 million people—or about 8 percent of the population aged twelve and older—had used some illegal drug at least once in the past thirty days. Figure 8–1 traces the use of illegal drugs in recent decades, as well as the use of alcohol and cigarettes, both of which are legal but regulated. The use of all these drugs declined after 1980 and rose slightly after 2000. Notice that alcohol is widely used and is the only drug that a majority of people report using in the last thirty days. Tobacco is used by about 30 percent of adults. Among the illegal drugs, marijuana and hashish are used by a smaller share of the population (around 5 percent), and cocaine, hallucinogens (such as LSD), and heroin are used by only about 1 percent of people (U.S. Department of Health and Human Services, 2008).

Age is related to the likelihood of using an illegal drug. The share of the population reporting illegal drug use peaks among people in their late teens and early twenties, the time in life when people are experimenting with the limits of personal freedom. The use of illegal drugs declines as people get older and take on family and job responsibilities.

Why Do People Use Drugs?

People use drugs—both legal and illegal—for any number of reasons. The following are probably the most common uses.

1. **Therapeutic uses.** Some drugs have therapeutic uses, meaning that they offer medical benefits such as controlling seizures, lessening depression, or reducing pain.
2. **Recreational uses.** People use many drugs for recreational reasons; for example, consuming beer or wine with a meal can make people feel more relaxed and can even make foods taste better.
3. **Spiritual or psychological uses.** Because drugs can alter human consciousness, some people use them for spiritual or psychological reasons. Native American societies, for example, use peyote to change their awareness and deepen their spiritual experiences.
4. **Escape.** Especially when used often or in large dosages, some drugs offer a form of escape. Many people enduring serious trouble in their lives turn to alcohol or other drugs to dull the pain of living.
5. **Social conformity.** Finally, most people probably use drugs to conform—that is, to fit in socially. Peer pressure may lead young people to smoke cigarettes or older people to drink cocktails.

addiction a physical or psychological craving for a drug

dependency a state in which a person's body has adjusted to regular use of a drug

SOCIAL PROBLEMS in Everyday Life

Why do you think a dose of a drug is sometimes called a "fix"?

Often, of course, several of these factors operate at once. When dining at a restaurant with business associates, people may have a glass of wine with dinner to help them relax (recreational) and also because it is expected of them (social conformity). Whether they realize it or not, they may also be improving their health (therapeutic), because doctors report that consuming small amounts of red wine each day can reduce the risk of heart disease.

Use and Abuse

What is the difference between *using* drugs and *abusing* them? In simple terms, these two words mark a socially constructed boundary between acceptable and unacceptable behavior. Most people use the term "drug abuse" to refer to the use of any illegal substance or the use of a legal substance (such as a prescription drug) in a way that violates accepted medical practice (Abadinsky, 1989). In this case, the distinction between using and abusing a drug is based on law and other social norms.

A second way to distinguish use and abuse is to focus on the *effect* of a drug. From this point of view, people who *use* a drug may manage to function well in everyday life, but people who *abuse* a drug suffer physical, mental, or social harm (Weil & Rosen, 1983; J. M. White, 1991). This definition means that any drug—legal or illegal—can be used or abused. After all, many people smoke a little marijuana without harmful consequences, and even a few legal glasses of wine can have devastating consequences for a person who gets behind the wheel of a car (Goode, 1993).

Of course, it is not always easy to decide whether or not a drug causes harm. For example, a person who regularly uses marijuana may get through the day just fine and may be convinced that this practice poses no personal danger. Friends, however, may shake their heads, noting that this drug use—or from their point of view, *abuse*—is responsible for the person missing classes or failing to meet other daily obligations and at the very least raises the risk of trouble with the law.

Dimensions of Difference

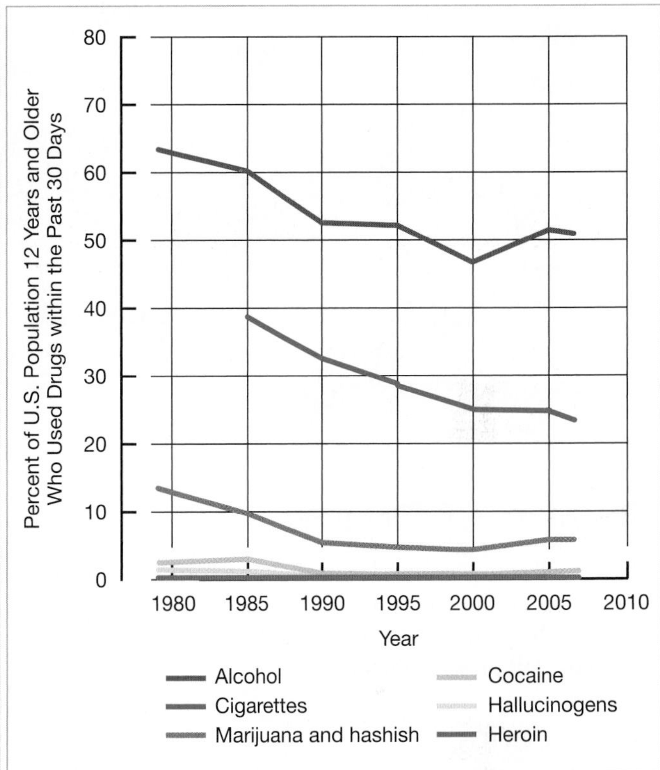

FIGURE 8–1 Use of Selected Drugs by the U.S. Population, 1979–2007

The most commonly used of the drugs listed here is alcohol, followed by cigarettes. The trend in overall drug use has been downward, with an upward turn in the last few years.

Source: U.S. Department of Health and Human Services (2008).

Addiction and Dependency

Another term that requires careful understanding is **addiction,** *a physical or psychological craving for a drug.* Doctors first began using this term back in the nineteenth century, and they considered people "addicted" if they suffered physical distress—sometimes called *withdrawal symptoms*—when they stopped using the drug. Withdrawal symptoms that accompany the use of drugs such as opium and cocaine include chills, fever, diarrhea, twitching, nausea, vomiting, cramps, and aches and pains. The only quick way to end such symptoms is to take more of the drug.

The point at which someone becomes addicted to a drug depends on a number of factors, including the dosage and how long the drug use has continued. Addiction also reflects the physical and mental health of the user. In recent years, researchers have focused on how addictive drugs affect the brain. Drug use raises levels of a substance called dopamine, which gives the user feelings of euphoria (Begley, 2001). Such research shows that different people may react differently to the same amount of a drug.

In recent decades, health professionals have linked addiction to **dependency,** *a state in which a person's body has adjusted to regular use of a drug.* People who have a drug dependency experience a need to continue using the drug in order to feel comfortable. This dependency is the reason that people sometimes talk about someone having a drug "habit." Today, the terms "addiction" and "dependency" are also used more loosely to refer to the use of just about any substance—including food—over which a person seems to have little or no control (Goode, 1993; Milkman & Sunderwirth, 1995).

Stan Querry lives near Salt Lake City, Utah, in a largely Mormon community where few people smoke cigarettes.

Charlene Wood lives in Carlisle, Kentucky, a low-income community where most adults smoke cigarettes.

stimulants drugs that increase alertness, altering a person's mood by increasing energy

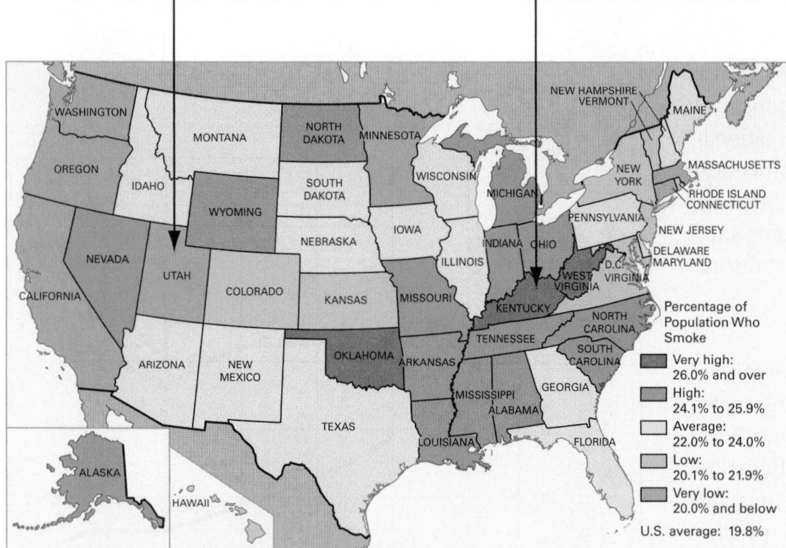

A Nation of Diversity

NATIONAL MAP 8–1

Cigarette Smoking across the United States

The highest percentage of smokers is found in Kentucky (28.3 percent), a tobacco-growing state and also a state where unemployment and poverty are serious problems. By contrast, Utah, with its high Mormon population, has the fewest smokers (11.7 percent) of all states. In general, what pattern can you see when it comes to smoking across the country? Hint: States with very few smokers generally have affluent populations who are concerned about health.

Source: Centers for Disease Control and Prevention (2008).

Types of Drugs

Drugs fall into various classifications according to the effects they have on the body and brain. Here we briefly examine six types of drugs: stimulants, depressants, hallucinogens, cannabis, steroids, and prescription drugs.

Stimulants

Stimulants are *drugs that increase alertness, altering a person's mood by increasing energy.* Because U.S. culture values action and achievement, stimulants are widely used in the United States.

Caffeine

Probably the single most popular drug in the United States is caffeine, which is available in many products, including coffee, tea, soft drinks, chocolate, and "stay alert" pills. Just about everybody—from long-distance truck drivers to college students facing an exam to anyone trying to wake up fully before getting to work—depends on caffeine for alertness.

Nicotine

Although nicotine is legal in this country and almost everywhere else in the world, this stimulant is both toxic and highly addictive. The most common way people ingest nicotine is through smoking cigarettes, a practice that became popular among men in the United States during World War I, when the army issued free cigarettes to soldiers. Within about twenty years, the health hazards of cigarette smoking were becoming clear, but the government did little to discourage cigarette smoking until the 1960s. By then, 45 percent of U.S. adults smoked, including almost the same share of women as men. Since that time, people have become aware of the health hazards of smoking, and the share of adults who smoke cigarettes has steadily declined. By 2007, just 24 percent were lighting up (Centers for Disease Control and Prevention, 2008). National Map 8–1 gives a state-by-state survey of smoking.

Worldwide, the share of adults who smoke is higher—about 30 percent—than it is in this country, and the global use of cigarettes is climbing in low-income nations (Stobbe, 2008). Figure 8–2 shows that in many other countries, a majority of men smoke, and many have little awareness of the harm this practice causes to the heart, lungs, and other organs of the body.

In the United States, cigarette smoking remains by far the single greatest preventable cause of death. Each year, more than 440,000 people die prematurely due to tobacco use, a death toll that far exceeds that caused by the use of alcohol and all illegal drugs combined (Centers for Disease Control and Prevention, 2008). In 1998, the U.S. tobacco companies reached a settlement with a number of states that had filed lawsuits seeking compensation for harm caused to people by smoking. In the settlement, cigarette manufacturers received protection from mounting lawsuits in exchange for paying billions of dollars that would be used for medical care for past smokers. The settlement also banned cigarette advertising directed at young people. Even so, thousands of young people start smoking every day, and unless they quit, smoking will harm them just as smoking places an enormous burden on our health care system. In 2009, in an effort to further discourage tobacco use, President Obama placed additional government restrictions on the tobacco industry.

There is a cure for the problems related to smoking: Quit. Although some researchers warn that smoking during adolescence can permanently damage the lungs, a decade after quitting, most ex-smokers have health as good as that of people who never lit up in the first place (Recer, 1999).

GETTING INVOLVED

How much use of Ritalin occurs on your campus? Do students use this as a "study drug"?

Ritalin

Ritalin, the brand name for methylphenidate hydrochloride, is a legal drug prescribed by doctors to treat children with attention deficit hyperactivity disorder (ADHD) or attention deficit disorder (ADD). These are disorders in which children are overactive, have trouble concentrating, or cannot focus attention on a teacher or another adult.

In recent years, the use of Ritalin has increased sharply in the United States: More than 10 percent of school-age boys and 5 percent of school-age girls (a total of about 6 million youngsters) take the drug. About 8 percent of college students, too, take the drug to treat a disorder. Many also obtain the substance illegally from others who have a doctor's prescription, using it to help them concentrate more effectively on their studies (U.S. Department of Health and Human Services, 2006; National Institute of Mental Health, 2007).

This widespread use of Ritalin has sparked controversy. Defenders of the drug, which include drug companies and many parents, claim that Ritalin helps children stay calm in school and focus on their work. Critics, though, reject the idea of using drugs to control children's behavior. Speaking against the widespread use of Ritalin, the pediatrician Lawrence Diller (1998) claims that U.S. children are being unnecessarily medicated by parents who are overworked or overly concerned with their children's level of achievement.

Rates of cigarette smoking have fallen in high-income nations such as the United States, but they are increasing in many lower-income countries, including Vietnam.

Dimensions of Difference

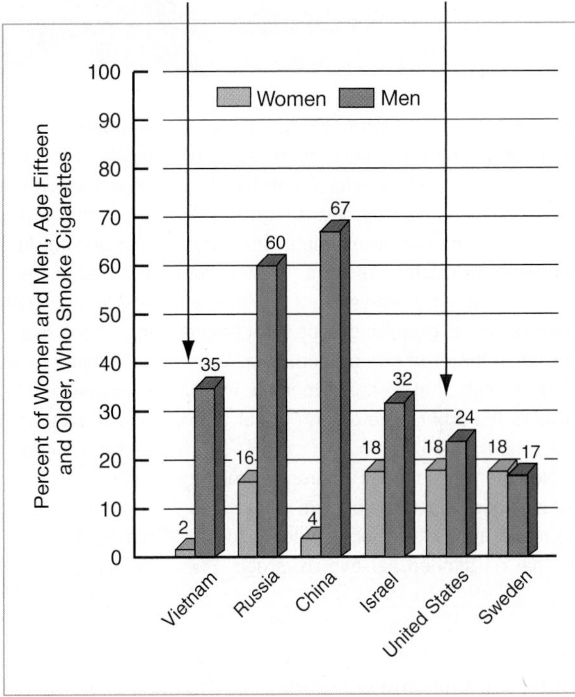

FIGURE 8–2 Cigarette Smoking in Selected Countries

In many of the world's low-income nations, cigarette smoking is more widespread among men than in the United States. At the same time, in these strongly patriarchal countries, gender norms limit the extent of smoking among women.

Sources: Centers for Disease Control and Prevention (2008) and World Bank (2008).

Cocaine and Crack

Cocaine and crack are powerful stimulants that heighten alertness as they raise blood pressure and pulse rate. These drugs keep people awake, reduce appetite, and cause some people to become agitated and perhaps even violent.

In 2006, about 3 percent of people over the age of twelve (or about 8 percent of high school seniors) had used cocaine in some form during the past year. In powder form, cocaine can be snorted (inhaled through the nose). Cocaine is very addictive, and it can be harmful—its use leads to about 3,500 deaths each year in the United States. Cocaine's popularity peaked in the 1980s, when it was the drug of choice among many young urban professionals ("yuppies"). Even though its popularity declined in the 1990s, the typical cocaine user is still well-to-do, a fact that challenges the stereotype of drug abusers as people who are "down and out" (U.S. Department of Health and Human Services, 2009).

Crack is a hardened form of cocaine usually smoked in a pipe. Although most people think crack is stronger than cocaine and more likely to provoke violence, research indicates that the effects of the two drugs are pretty similar (Wren, 1996; Gómez, 1997).

During the 1980s, crack became popular in large cities in the United States, pushing crime rates sharply higher. As with powdered cocaine, crack's popularity declined in the 1990s. However, experts estimate that about 1.5 million people use crack for some period of time each year. African Americans have been about twice as likely as whites to use crack (U.S. Department of Health and Human Services, 2009).

Amphetamines

Amphetamines were first developed for the medical treatment of personality disorders and also obesity. These drugs increase alertness, cause an excited sense of well-being, and reduce the desire to sleep and to eat. Because amphetamines are easy to make, many underground chemists operate highly profitable businesses selling drugs known on the street as "crank," "speed," "crystal," "go," "meth," or "ice." Surveys suggest that police officials regard methamphetamine use as the most serious drug problem not only because there are so many "meth labs" in operation but also because use of this drug can encourage people to engage in other serious crime (Hananel, 2006).

depressants drugs that slow the operation of the central nervous system

GETTING INVOLVED

Is alcohol abuse a problem on your campus? Have you taken any part in addressing this issue?

PERSONAL STORIES

"My Life Is Gone": A Crank User's Story

It is a warm Friday evening in Billings, Montana, and a bright moon shines overhead. But twenty-five-year-old Jennifer Smith hasn't a clue whether it is night or day. A regular user of "crank" or methamphetamine, Smith has been wide awake for five days. On Monday night, she left her three-year-old daughter at a friend's house, promising to be back before long. Then the drug ride started. Crank produces a high that keeps the user madly active to the point of forgetting about time, food, and even children.

Now Jennifer sits on a barstool, gulping shots of bourbon to help calm her nerves. She looks around for her boyfriend, forgetting that he ditched her two days ago. She wonders, too, what happened to her purse, in which she had a child support check she hoped would pay for more drugs.

Smith strikes up a conversation with a man she has known for several years. He can see that she is out of control. "Crank makes you lose everything," she stammers, reaching for the rest of her bourbon.

What has she lost? The list begins with her purse and her boyfriend and includes her good looks, her job, her hopes for the future, and most important, the child she calls her "little angel."

"I'm not afraid, though," she says, shaking her head. "I've cranked for seven years... I'm getting pretty used to losing everything."

WHAT DO YOU THINK?

1. Do you think there is much public sympathy for women like Jennifer Smith? Why or why not?
2. Do you consider Jennifer Smith "bad" or "sick?" What would you hope might happen to this woman?
3. Do you think of this situation as a personal problem or a social problem? Explain your view.

Source: Based on Kirn (1998).

After cocaine, amphetamines are the most popular illegal stimulants, and they are the only type of drug whose use by women is at almost as widespread as it is among men. Official statistics suggest that more than 13 million people (about 5 percent of adults) have tried amphetamines. Many become dependent on them, including patients who begin taking amphetamines under a doctor's supervision. When they stop taking this type of drug, users typically experience withdrawal symptoms such as apathy, depression, irritability, and disorientation (U.S. Department of Health and Human Services, 2008). More seriously, as usage increases, amphetamines carry more and more risk of agitation, fever, hallucinations, and convulsions that may even lead to death. The Personal Stories box provides a look at the tragic effects of the use of amphetamines in the life of one young woman.

Depressants

Depressants are *drugs that slow the operation of the central nervous system.* In short, depressants ("downers") have an effect opposite to stimulants ("uppers").

Analgesics

One class of depressants is analgesics, drugs that dull pain. The most widely used analgesics include familiar over-the-counter pain relievers such as aspirin, ibuprofen (Motrin and Advil), and acetaminophen (Tylenol). Although these drugs can be abused, they present little problem when used according to directions (Goode, 1993).

More problematic are naturally occurring narcotics, or *opiates*, such as opium and opium derivatives, including morphine, codeine, and heroin. All are highly addictive, and they are dangerous because they are capable of disrupting the lives of abusers.

Heroin is made from morphine, which comes from the seed pods of poppy plants. A synthetic form of the drug is merperidine (marketed as Demerol). Although most people have heard of heroin, only 0.1 percent of the U.S. population are current users (look back at Figure 8–1). When injected, sniffed, or smoked, this drug quickly causes euphoria and drowsiness. Because heroin is highly addictive, the law bans its use for any purpose. Addicts who stop using heroin experience strong cravings and severe withdrawal symptoms. Because users can never be sure how pure their heroin is, overdoses are common and can be fatal (Leinwand, 2001; U.S. Department of Health and Human Services, 2008).

Sedatives, Hypnotics, and Alcohol

Other depressants with a more wide-ranging effect on the central nervous system are sedatives and hypnotics. These drugs help people relax and at higher dosages cause drowsiness and sleep. Examples of sedatives and hypnotics include barbiturates, such as secobarbital (Seconal) and pentobarbital, and tranquilizers, including alprazolam (Xanax), diazepam (Valium), and

alcoholism addiction to alcohol

GETTING INVOLVED

To what extent do students on your campus engage in binge drinking? What programs are available to help students who drink too much?

triazolam (Halcion). Overuse of these drugs, available by prescription, is dangerous, and when combined with alcohol or other drugs, they can be fatal.

Alcohol is the most widely used depressant in the United States. As noted in Figure 8–1, about half the adult population aged twelve and over (and about one-third of teens) consumes alcohol regularly. For many adults who drink responsibly and in moderation, alcohol poses no problem. But more than four in ten people in this country have been affected directly or indirectly (through the struggle of a close friend or family member) by **alcoholism,** *addiction to alcohol.* Estimates place the number of U.S. adults who have a drinking problem at about 17 million (about 8 percent of the adult population); about 30 million people have such a problem at some point in their lives (about 14 percent) (U.S. Department of Health and Human Services, 2008).

Yet only 2.5 million people each year seek help for a problem related to alcohol. Many try to become sober, but many more continue to deal with the many problems of alcoholism. And even more people face the daily challenges of living or working with an alcoholic person.

With the exception of nicotine, alcohol is the most addictive drug available legally without a prescription. Analysts put the total cost of alcoholism in the United States (reflecting everything from accidents to lost days at work) at about $275 billion per year (National Council on Alcoholism and Drug Dependence, 2009).

Alcohol abuse is a serious problem at U.S. colleges and universities. A government study found that about 44 percent of college students said they had engaged in binge drinking—which the researchers defined as having at least five drinks in a row for men or four drinks for women—at least once in the past month. In addition, almost half of these students fell into the "extreme binge drinker" category, with five or more such drinking episodes in the past month. At the other extreme, about 36 percent of students reported drinking no alcohol in the past month (U.S. Department of Health and Human Services, 2008).

Researchers estimate that consuming alcohol—especially "drink till you drop" binge drinking—leads to 1,700 student deaths and 500,000 injuries each year. In addition, 474,000 students claim that after drinking alcohol, they had unprotected sex, which can lead to unwanted pregnancy as well as sexually transmitted diseases. Finally, by affecting people's judgment, alcohol also plays a part in about 100,000 cases of date rape each year (Hingson et al., 2005).

The use of alcohol is related to other crimes as well: In 2007, police made about 450,000 arrests for public drunkenness and disorderly conduct involving alcohol. More serious, another 1.1 million arrests are made each year for driving a motor vehicle while under the influence of alcohol. Police records also show that alcohol is involved in about 32 percent of the 40,000 motor vehicle deaths on U.S. roads each year. In addition, about 33 percent of convicted jail inmates report that they were under the influence of alcohol when they committed their crimes (Karberg & James, 2005; National Highway Traffic Safety Administration, 2008; U.S. Department of Justice, 2008).

Finally, although an occasional alcoholic beverage may provide some health benefits, heavy drinking is not good for you. For one thing, drinking provides many calories but no nutrition, causing weight gain, and, as consumption increases, harms the heart and the liver. Pregnant women who consume alcohol also put their unborn child's health at risk (U.S. Department of Health and Human Services, 2008).

Antipsychotics

Antipsychotics, including lithium and haloperidol (Haldol), are powerful drugs that doctors prescribe to people with serious personality disorders such as schizophrenia. Although these substances are dangerous if they are overused, they are effective in reducing psychotic symptoms such as paranoia, visual hallucinations, and hearing voices. Supervised use of antipsychotic drugs allows hundreds of thousands of people who might otherwise need hospitalization to live independently (Goode, 1993).

Hallucinogens

Hallucinogens are stimulants, generally taken in pill or capsule form, that cause hallucinations. In the United States, the most commonly used hallucinogens include LSD, peyote, mescaline, psilocybin, phencyclidine (PCP, "angel dust"), and methylenedimethamphetamine (MDMA, "ecstasy"). Estimates suggest that by the time they complete high school, about 6 percent of young people will have tried ecstasy (Johnston, 2008). Although about 14 percent of the U.S. population has tried a hallucinogenic drug at some point, only 1.5 percent of the U.S. population reports using one in the past year (U.S. Department of Health and Human Services, 2008).

Hallucinogens are nonaddictive but powerful. They can sharply raise pulse rates and blood pressure and alter perceptions of time and space. Their ability to produce vivid hallucinations is the main reason people use them. In some cases, people find taking hallucinogens very pleasurable; at best, people describe the experience as "consciousness-expanding." But these drugs can also trigger panic attacks, and many people find the experience terrifying. The fact is that you can never be sure what the experience will be and whether you will have a "good trip" or a "bad trip." Perhaps most seriously, hallucinogens can have long-term effects. People who use these drugs may experience

SOCIAL PROBLEMS in Everyday Life

What about the use of steroids? How common is this on your campus?

MAKING THE GRADE

Be sure you can provide arguments for and against legalizing cannabis.

In a small number of U.S. communities, people can legally use marijuana for medical purposes. (This drug is now available in a wide range of products.) Do you think this practice will spread throughout the country in years to come? Why or why not?

"flashbacks"—unexpected hallucinations—months or years later without having taken the drug again. For all these reasons, hallucinogens are dangerous. Overdoses can cause psychosis and even death.

In the United States, the use of hallucinogens peaked in the 1960s. Even so, the government reports that use of these drugs by teens rose in the 1990s. White people are twice as likely as African Americans to use hallucinogens (U.S. Department of Health and Human Services, 2008).

Cannabis

Marijuana and hashish are two types of cannabis that have been used for centuries in much of the world. During the 1960s, both drugs gained widespread popularity in the United States. Today, these two substances make up about 73 percent of this country's illegal drug use. Figure 8–1 puts the share of U.S. adults currently using marijuana or hashish at 6 percent, but almost half (some 100 million people) say they have used marijuana or hashish at some time in the past (U.S. Department of Health and Human Services, 2008).

People smoke marijuana and hashish or consume the drugs in food such as "magic" brownies or cookies. Both drugs produce a sense of euphoria, help people relax, and stimulate appetite. At higher dosages, however, these drugs can produce fatigue, disorientation, paranoia, and even serious personality disorders (U.S. Department of Health and Human Services, 2008).

For decades, a social movement has tried to legalize marijuana, claiming that this drug is not addictive and poses little danger to users. Opponents of legal marijuana counter that the drug's dangers are real, especially if users operate motor vehicles. At present, a handful of communities (mostly in Maine and California) permit the use of marijuana for medical purposes, under the supervision of a doctor. For example, many people undergoing chemotherapy for cancer or AIDS find that marijuana eases the nausea that is often a side effect of the treatment.

Public opinion is closely split on whether possession of small amounts of marijuana should be legal. In general, the public does not support making marijuana legal, but most people also don't think that marijuana smokers should go to jail (ABC News/Washington Post, 2009).

Steroids

The full name for this class of drugs is quite a mouthful: *androgenic* (promoting masculine characteristics) *anabolic* (building) *steroids.* Many professional and amateur athletes use steroids, although athletic programs ban their use. Typically, to avoid detection, athletes use steroids in cycles: a few weeks or months on, followed by a similar period off before a drug test.

Surveys suggest that about 2 percent of high school seniors have used steroids at some time in their lives. Although 90 percent of these students disapprove of steroid use, more than one-third of students say that steroids are easy to obtain (Johnston et al., 2008).

Allegations of steroid use among professional athletes are well known. In 2007, the U.S. Senate issued a report concluding that steroid use was widespread in professional baseball and that the problem was widely ignored. The report called for more frequent drug testing as well as enforcement of a no-tolerance policy (Nightengale, 2007).

The use of steroids can improve athletic performance. But these drugs also pose significant dangers, ranging from acne and fluid retention to high blood pressure and liver tumors. In addition, some men who take steroids experience baldness, infertility, and breast development. Women using steroids may stop menstruating, grow facial hair, and experience an enlargement of the clitoris and a deepening of the voice. Among young people, use of steroids may cause the body to stop growing too soon. Finally, people who inject steroids and share needles increase their risk of contracting a range of diseases, including hepatitis and HIV (U.S. Department of Health and Human Services, 2005).

codependency behavior on the part of others that helps a substance abuser continue the abuse

GETTING INVOLVED

Have you ever been in a codependency situation involving drug use or abuse? Explain.

Prescription Drugs

Physicians prescribe a wide range of drugs to patients, and almost everyone at some time has taken drugs as part of treatment for a physical injury or illness or a psychological condition. But prescription drugs are defined as part of the drug problem in the United States because as many as 16 million people use them in a nonmedical way. Unapproved use of prescription drugs includes taking a higher dosage than was prescribed, mixing drugs, or continuing to use a drug when the medical need no longer exists (U.S. Department of Health and Human Services, 2008).

Because prescription drugs are legal and because most prescription drugs (which are expensive) are used by relatively affluent people, it is easy to overlook abuse of these drugs. For this reason, the abuse of prescription medications is sometimes considered "the invisible part of the drug problem" (ABC News, 1997; Corliss, 2001).

Of all prescription drugs, the most often abused are painkillers (analgesics) such as codeine, diazepam (Valium), and among college students, oxycodone (Percodan) and hydrocodone (Vicodin). Not only are these drugs widely prescribed, but people build up tolerances to painkillers and gradually take higher and higher dosages. Prescriptions limit the number of pills available, but many patients increase their supply by seeing several doctors at one time, obtaining prescriptions from each for the same drug (U.S. Department of Health and Human Services, 2008).

This completes our brief survey of types of drugs. We now take a look at the role of drugs in various other social problems.

Drugs and Other Social Problems

Drugs play a part in many social problems, from crime to poverty. The government estimates that the cost of illegal drug use, in terms of medical care as well as time lost from work, exceeds $180 billion annually (U.S. Office of National Drug Control Policy, 2009). If we added in the losses from health issues related to the use of tobacco and alcohol, that number would be many times greater. We look first at the links between drugs and family life.

Problems of Family Life

Drugs play a part in many cases of child neglect and family violence, both as a cause and as a consequence. Although it is difficult to specify cause and effect here, drug abuse often makes the problems of family life worse. Why? Drugs reduce inhibitions and also affect judgment, raising the risk of abusive behavior (Gelles & Straus, 1988; Gelles, 1997). In extreme cases, like Jennifer Smith's crank abuse described on page 214, the craving for drugs can be so strong that parents harm or abandon their own children.

Codependency

The problem of drug abuse rarely affects only a single person. Typically, this problem involves not just an individual but also parents, brothers and sisters, partners, and children. Many people addicted to alcohol or other drugs spend their whole paychecks on the substances they crave; others cannot keep a job at all.

Such cases encourage a pattern called **codependency**, *behavior on the part of others that helps a substance abuser continue the abuse.* In simple terms, members of the family change their behavior to make up for the shortcomings of the drug abuser. Codependent family members may try to earn extra money, help with the housework, hide evidence of accidents, cover for an abuser who misses work, or even provide drugs to the abuser in an effort to keep the peace and just get through another day.

Jacqueline Wiseman (1991) studied the wives of alcoholics and found that these women commonly experienced problems ranging from income uncertainty to outright violence. Children who live in a household with a substance abuser may lose their ability to trust others because the abuser has let them down so many times. Such children often grow up too soon, taking over the tasks not performed by the older drug abuser and sacrificing their own wants and needs in the process. Not surprisingly, many of these young people drop out of school, get into trouble with the law, and may end up abusing drugs themselves. In this way, drugs begin a cycle of problems that spills over from one generation to another.

Homelessness

For many people, the use of drugs—especially alcohol—is part of the stereotype of the homeless man passed out on the street. Research confirms that there is some truth to this belief: About 60 percent of homeless men and women have had a serious drinking problem (U.S. Office of National Drug Control Policy, 2009).

Recall from Chapter 2 ("Poverty and Wealth") that much homelessness in the United States results from underemployment and a lack of affordable housing. Although U.S. culture encourages us to think that people are responsible for their social position, many individuals and families become homeless through no fault of their own. Certainly some people

MAKING THE GRADE

Notice that the link between homelessness and drug use is substantial, but it is far less clear which is cause and which is effect.

SOCIAL PROBLEMS in Everyday Life

Given the personal harm and enormous costs that result when pregnant women use drugs, do you think society should hold these women responsible or not? Should the women face criminal charges for giving drugs to a child or harming a child? Explain your position.

The use of drugs—especially alcohol—by people who are homeless is widespread. Do you think such drug use is more often the cause or the result of being desperately poor?

become homeless because they use drugs, but the opposite is often true: People who do not have work, who lose the support of neighbors, family, and friends, and who are forced to live on the streets may turn to alcohol or other drugs as a means of escape.

Drugs and homelessness interact in another way, too. With the development of antipsychotic drugs in the 1960s, many mental institutions began releasing patients to live on their own, with periodic visits to community mental health centers. But less than half of the planned mental health centers were ever built. In addition, many patients who were released did not take their medications and ended up being unable to find a job or affordable housing. As a result, a number of these mental patients became homeless, and some ended up abusing alcohol and other drugs (Weiss, Griffin, & Mirin, 1992; Baum & Burnes, 1993).

Health Problems

The use of drugs by people who are ill saves countless lives each year. At the same time, as many people die from the use of drugs (including tobacco and alcohol) as die from gun violence, accidents, and infectious diseases combined. Some drugs such as heroin harm people right away, damaging the brain or other vital organs. But many drugs harm people over the long haul: Years of alcohol abuse, for example, can lead to malnutrition and liver damage. Remember, too, that the distortion of judgment caused by drug use raises the risk of death or injury from accidents and from unsafe sex.

Prenatal Exposure to Drugs

Many people suffer from drug problems that began before they were born. Both physical and mental health problems can result from prenatal exposure to drugs, that is, the use of drugs by a pregnant woman. About 12 percent of all pregnant women put their babies at risk by drinking alcohol at some time during their pregnancy; about 5 percent of pregnant women use marijuana, cocaine, or some other drug. As a result, about half a million babies are born each year exposed to one or more harmful drugs (U.S. Department of Health and Human Services, 2008).

Many of the women who use drugs in this way do not know they are pregnant. This is especially true of women whose drug use is so heavy that it causes irregular menstrual cycles. Even when they do learn of their pregnancies, some women are unable to stop taking drugs. And even if they are able to stop, because an embryo's nervous system and major organs begin to develop within two months after conception, the damage may already be done (Gomby & Shiono, 1991; Gómez, 1997).

Drug exposure greatly increases the risk of premature delivery, low birthweight, and birth defects. Longer-term problems for the child include retarded growth, poor physical coordination, learning disabilities, and emotional problems. Each year, the cost of hospital care for children with prenatal exposure to drugs and alcohol approaches $3 billion (Centers for Disease Control and Prevention, 2009).

Sharing Needles and HIV Transmission

Many people who abuse drugs use syringes and hypodermic needles to inject drugs directly into a vein. Drugs introduced to the body in this way have an effect that is both immediate and intense. Intravenous (IV) drug users typically "shoot up" in groups, and some engage in the dangerous practice of sharing needles.

What makes sharing needles dangerous? Traces of blood retained in a needle can transmit the human immunodeficiency virus (HIV), which causes AIDS. To make matters worse, some women (who may or may not use needles themselves) trade sex

MAKING THE GRADE

Notice that more than half of all federal prisoners are people convicted of drug offenses.

SOCIAL PROBLEMS in Everyday Life

What would happen to the global economy if, somehow, all use of illegal drugs suddenly ceased?

for drugs, which risks further spread of HIV and other sexually transmitted diseases.

In 1994, officials at the Centers for Disease Control and Prevention proposed—as a solution to transmitting disease—a program of needle exchange: Local health centers would exchange used hypodermic needles for new ones. But this program never caught on because opponents view the policy not as a solution but as a problem, claiming that giving out needles encourages drug use. As an alternative, many local health departments provide instructions on how to clean a used needle with a bleach solution to kill HIV and other dangerous agents.

Crime

The manufacture, distribution, or possession of illegal drugs is a crime. And as already noted, both illegal substances such as cocaine and legal drugs such as alcohol are also linked to criminal behavior. Government officials report that about three-fourths of federal prison inmates have a history of substance abuse, and more than one-fourth say they were abusing drugs when they committed their crimes (U.S. Office of National Drug Control Policy, 2009). The Personal Stories box on page 220 explains how abusing alcohol landed one college student in jail—and put her on probation.

Not everyone agrees with the simple statement that drugs cause crime. Some people claim that the enforcement of our nation's drug laws actually makes the crime problem worse. For one thing, existing laws drive up drug prices. High prices in turn lead users to commit crimes such as prostitution or burglary to get money for drugs. Government research shows that almost one in five federal prison inmates reports committing a violent crime to obtain money to buy drugs (U.S. Department of Justice, 2008).

Because the high price of drugs generates large profits, the opportunity to earn a living from drug dealing may outweigh the risk of being sent to jail, especially among people with few other chances to get ahead. In addition, to protect their profits, drug dealers may turn to violence, often harming not only each other but also innocent people caught in the crossfire. In recent years, the level of violence related to drug dealing has increased sharply in Mexico, where more than 2,000 people died in 2008. Each year, Mexico spends about $7 billion fighting illegal drug activity, but the drug cartels take in about $25 billion, which also allows them to engage in bribery and even assassination of public officials. This drug-related violence now threatens to spill into the United States (Padgett & Grillo, 2008).

Currently, one-fifth of inmates in state and local prisons and more than half of all federal prison inmates are there for drug offenses (U.S. Office of National Drug Control Policy, 2009). To the extent that jail time stigmatizes people (as "convicts") and makes getting a good job upon release less likely, people who have "done time" may be more likely to commit later crimes.

If all of this is true, is legalization of some drugs a way to bring the crime rate down? No one knows for sure. It is possible that doing so would reduce street crime. At the same time, legalization might make other problems, such as accidents, child neglect, and drug addiction, worse.

Global Poverty

In the United States, illegal drug use and poverty are linked, although it is difficult to sort out which is cause and which is effect. In much the same way, drugs are linked to poverty throughout the world.

Drugs that are illegal in the United States represent a significant share of the global economy. Millions of people in poor nations of the world with few other economic opportunities grow the plants and manufacture the drugs that are smuggled into rich nations such as the United States. For example, opiates from Afghanistan and other low-income countries in Asia are

The global trade in illegal drugs has much to do with widespread poverty in lower-income nations. These children play soccer on a playground that is also used to dry coca leaves, which are later refined into cocaine. Cocaine production represents a bigger part of the national economy in Peru than wheat production is here in the United States.

GETTING INVOLVED

Have you ever had an experience similar to the one presented in the box below?

PERSONAL STORIES

"Hello, Dad? It's Me, and I'm in Jail . . ."

Jamie Powell will never forget those words she spoke late at night over the phone to her father several years ago. It was a night she thought could never happen—but it did, and it changed her life.

The episode began when Jamie (not her real name) left home and drove through a March thunderstorm up the interstate to Michigan State University, where she was a junior. She was eager to get back to campus for what promised to be a fun-filled evening with friends watching television coverage of the university basketball team play as it worked its way through the NCAA tournament.

In an hour or so, she arrived at her apartment complex and settled comfortably in front of the TV with Kelly Arnold, her roommate and best friend. Soon a dozen other students joined them. There was lots of noise, plenty of beer, and several bottles of liquor.

Jamie and Kelly were both under the age of twenty-one. Legally speaking, therefore, they were drinking underage, and their friends were guilty of furnishing alcohol to minors. But who ever thinks about things like that? As Jamie recalls, "You just get so into it that you kind of forget what's going on."

When their team won, hundreds of students poured out of the apartments into the streets, cheering, with drinks in hand and throwing empty beer cans. By this time, Jamie was pretty drunk, and she began to get rowdy. She and Kelly climbed onto the shoulders of two male friends, who carried them high above the heads of others in the crowd.

After neighbors complained about the noise, Kelly noticed several police officers working their way through the crowd, trying to calm people down and get the students to go back home. She climbed down and tugged at Jamie's leg, pointing to the apartment. Jamie, however, was flying high. Kelly explained what happened next: "I saw these two cops coming down the street, right toward us. I turned to Jamie to tell her to cool it. She had pulled up her shirt and was flashing everybody. Suddenly it wasn't fun anymore."

The police had seen enough. In a minute, a police officer grabbed Jamie, pulled her down, and placed her under arrest. As the one officer held her, another placed handcuffs on her wrists. Then the two officers led her away. Kelly walked back to the apartment alone, thinking, "She's not really going to jail. . . . Jail is for bad people!"

Jamie would spend the rest of the night at the Ingham County jail in a holding cell with concrete benches and a toilet in open view. At about 2 A.M., she was allowed to use the telephone and called her father. He did not take the news very well. Neither did her mother.

In the morning, Jamie's parents posted a bond, and by afternoon, she was released. Everyone was talking about 3,000 students being on the streets the night before in what was being called a "student riot." There was thousands of dollars in damage; fifteen people had been arrested.

When her court date came, Jamie pleaded not guilty to disorderly conduct and being a minor in possession of alcohol. She had no previous record and was represented by a privately hired lawyer. But the judge thought the evidence was clear and found her guilty, sentencing her to a year's probation and requiring her to remain in her apartment except to go to class unless she received special permission from her probation officer. The judge ordered that she not drink any alcohol, and she was required to blow into a Breathalyzer twice a day to prove it. Around the clock, she was required to wear an electronic ankle bracelet that monitored her location.

Jamie Powell had learned that college students are part of the real world and have to accept the consequences of their actions. She has spoken to students new to the campus to help them understand how the pressure to drink can lead to trouble. It is a message she wishes she had heard when she first came to college.

WHAT DO YOU THINK?

1. Do you think that most young students realize all the ways that drinking—especially to excess—puts them at risk? Explain.
2. Do you think that college students are treated more leniently under the law for incidents of this kind than other people would be? Why or why not?
3. To what extent do you think drinking alcohol is responsible for the type of "student riot" described here? Has any such incident ever taken place at your school?

Sources: Based on a personal interview with "Jamie Powell."

sold in the United States, Canada, the wealthy nations of Western Europe, and Australia. Hashish from the Middle East and western Africa moves readily to Western Europe, just as marijuana grown in Mexico, Cuba, and Central America is shipped to the United States. Finally, cocaine produced in mountainous regions of South America travels to both North America and Western Europe.

Each year, people in the United States spend more than $60 billion on illegal drugs, including, marijuana, hashish, cocaine, and heroin. This sum exceeds the total economic output of dozens of the world's countries. This enormous demand means that drugs can be a poor country's biggest export and the major source of economic opportunity for its people. In Bolivia, for example, cocaine production represents one-fourth of eco-

MAKING THE GRADE

Be sure you understand the four strategies to control drug use: interdiction, prosecution, education, and treatment.

SOCIAL PROBLEMS in Everyday Life

Which of the four treatment strategies do you favor? Why?

nomic output and three-fourths of all exports. Cocaine has enormous economic importance in Peru, as does marijuana in Mexico and hashish in Afghanistan (Ramo, 2001; U.S. Office of National Drug Control Policy, 2009).

Terrorism

Here in the United States, the Office of National Drug Control Policy links drug use and terrorism. Buying illegal drugs at home, officials argue, puts money in the hands of terrorists abroad. Worse still, terrorists may use this money to finance attacks on this country.

Since the September 11, 2001, attacks, the level of public concern about terrorism has remained high. But is the link between illegal drugs and terrorism real? Evidence suggests that about one-fourth of illegal drug trafficking organizations are linked to terrorist organizations. But this means that most of the illegal drug trade is not carried out by terrorists and that most terrorist funding does not come from drug sales. As critics see it, the federal government has overstated the link between terrorism and drugs in an effort to discourage illegal drug use among young people (Grimm, 2002; U.S. Office of National Drug Control Policy, 2009).

Social Policy: Responding to the Drug Problem

There is widespread agreement that the use of drugs is linked to a number of social problems. But there is far less agreement about what U.S. society should do to control the use of drugs.

Strategies to Control Drugs

The simple fact is that controlling the amount of illegal drugs in the United States is no easy task. For one thing, the country has lots of political freedoms, which limit the power of police to conduct searches and make arrests. For another, there is a high demand for illegal drugs, which draws a huge supply. In the following sections, we take a closer look at four control strategies: interdiction, prosecution, education, and treatment.

Interdiction

Interdiction means stopping the movement of drugs across this country's borders. Interdiction makes use of the Drug Enforcement Agency, the Customs Service, the Border Patrol, and the U.S. military.

But consider what these agencies are up against: The United States has 12,000 miles of coastline and 7,500 miles of land borders. Each year, some 200,000 boats and ships, 600,000 aircraft, 200 million cars, and 500 million people cross this nation's borders, and each could be carrying drugs. As long as this country does not strictly control the flow of people across the border, we will never control the flow of drugs.

Government agents manage to seize only a tiny portion of the drugs that enter the United States. No one doubts that the flow of illegal drugs would be greater without such efforts. But interdiction has had limited success in the war on drugs (Bertram et al., 1996).

Table 8–1 Federal Minimum Mandatory Sentencing Guidelines

Type of Drug	Five-Year Sentence without Parole	Ten-Year Sentence without Parole
LSD	1 gram	10 grams
Marijuana	100 plants or 100 kilograms	1,000 plants or 1,000 kilograms
Crack cocaine	5 grams	50 grams
Powder cocaine	500 grams	5 kilograms
Heroin	100 grams	1 kilogram
Methamphetamine	5 grams	50 grams
PCP ("angel dust")	10 grams	100 grams

Source: United States Code, Title 21, Sec. 841 (2008).

Prosecution

"Putting drug dealers where they belong: in jail" is a popular idea in the United States. But catching drug dealers is difficult. Perhaps even more important, giving police more power to stop and search people can threaten our basic freedoms.

In addition, the policy of prosecuting drug dealers often unfairly punishes the poor and minorities. The war on crack is one example. In the 1980s, Congress passed tough mandatory sentencing laws for drug-related crimes. Conservatives support such laws to discourage people from using drugs; liberals, however, claim that many of these laws have a bias that harms minorities.

Why? The federal minimum mandatory sentencing guidelines, shown in Table 8–1, dictate prison sentences according to type of drug and quantity. Under the law, you will be sent to jail for five years for possessing 500 grams of cocaine, but only 5 grams of crack gets you the same jail time. White people and middle-class people are more likely to use cocaine; black people and the poor are more likely to use crack. For this reason, critics claim, the sentencing law punishes one category of people more than another. Breaking with past administrations, the Obama White House has gone on record as seeking equal penalties for

SOCIAL PROBLEMS in Everyday Life

Do you think there should be a "war on drugs"? Is it possible to make peace with drugs? Explain your view.

people convicted of dealing crack and powdered cocaine (S. G. Freedman, 1998; Meyer, 2009).

Education

A third strategy for controlling drug use is education. Unlike prosecution, which is aimed at current drug users, educational programs try to discourage people from trying drugs in the first place. Typically, such programs operate in schools and target young people.

The most widespread drug education program, started in 1983, is Drug Abuse Resistance Education (DARE). This program, which operates in about 75 percent of elementary schools in the United States, has police officers instruct children on the dangers of drugs.

Police, school administrators, and parents all agree on the need to teach young people about drugs. However, research suggests that educational programs such as DARE don't make much of a difference in drug use among young people. In 2001, DARE officials acknowledged that their program is not having the effect they had hoped and began a new, more interactive program aimed at drawing older students, those in middle school and high school, into discussions about drug use (Glass, 1997; Zernike, 2001).

Treatment

Another drug control strategy is to help users, especially people struggling with addiction, kick the habit. Beginning in the early 1970s, the Nixon administration expanded drug treatment programs that offered methadone, a synthetic form of heroin, to treat heroin addicts. In practice, methadone programs replace one form of addiction with another. But there is a difference. For one thing, the government can be sure that methadone is pure; heroin bought on the street is of unknown strength and may be mixed with other chemicals. For another, by supplying methadone, the government reduces demand for heroin. Finally, programs offering methadone (and more recently, a drug called buprenorphine) have the added benefit of reducing a drug user's involvement in crime (Bowersox, 1995; Cloud, 1998; Hunt & Sun, 1998).

Treatment involves not only drugs but also counseling and group support (Cowley, 2001). No organization has done more to show the power of people to help those addicted to drugs than Alcoholics Anonymous. The Defining Moment box provides a look at Bill Wilson and the organization he founded.

The success of programs such as Alcoholics Anonymous confirms the importance of treatment in the efforts to control drug abuse. But treatment also has its limitations. For one thing, there are not enough treatment programs to help everybody who needs them. Just as important, programs may help people stop using drugs, but they do little to change the environment that pushed the people toward drugs in the first place. The risk of relapse (going back to drugs) is why Alcoholics Anonymous teaches its members that they will always be alcoholics who must actively control their addiction for the rest of their lives. A final problem is that although many people speak out in favor of treatment of people who abuse drugs, public opinion has always favored prosecution over treatment for those who break the law.

The War on Drugs

All the strategies just described—interdiction, prosecution, education, and treatment—have played some part in U.S. drug policy. But the main focus has always been on prosecution: targeting users and dealers with criminal penalties.

This emphasis emerged back in 1968, when President Richard Nixon claimed that illegal drugs were "public enemy number one." He backed up those words by creating the Drug Enforcement Agency (DEA), the federal antidrug organization that tries to keep other countries from producing illegal drugs and also works to keep drugs from entering the United States. The DEA has broad police powers to search private homes and seize illegal drugs (U.S. Bureau of Justice Statistics, 2002).

The next two presidents (Gerald Ford and Jimmy Carter) viewed illegal drugs as less of a problem and said relatively little about it. But the election of Ronald Reagan in 1980 brought renewed efforts to combat drugs. President Reagan declared drugs to be a major moral challenge, and he urged parents to teach their children the importance of resisting drugs, using the slogan "Just say no to drugs." During Reagan's two terms in the White House, the federal budget for fighting illegal drugs rose tenfold (U.S. Department of Justice, 1993). In addition, the federal government adopted a policy of mandatory prison sentences for convicted drug offenders (see Table 8–1 on page 221). As shown in Figure 8–3 on page 224, the result was a sharp increase in the number of people charged with federal drug crimes and sent to jail.

In addition, a new weapon was created to fight the war on drugs. Government officials knew that many drug dealers were using their wealth to avoid convictions and going to jail. In 1984, Congress enacted a law allowing police to seize drug dealers' property *before* they were convicted of any crime (Eldredge, 1998). Supporters of this law claim that seizing property is one effective way to put drug dealers out of business. But critics respond that such a law allows government agents to harm innocent people. The Social Policy box on page 225 takes a closer look.

When George H. W. Bush became president in 1989, he created the Office of National Drug Control Policy, headed by

SOCIAL PROBLEMS in Everyday Life

Like many of the people in our "Defining Moment" boxes, Bill Wilson did much more than he ever imagined to change the way we think about alcohol.

GETTING INVOLVED

Have you ever been to an AA meeting? If so, what can you say about how effective this strategy is?

CONSTRUCTING SOCIAL PROBLEMS

A DEFINING MOMENT

Bill Wilson: Alcoholics Can Learn to Be Sober

Bill Wilson was a successful stockbroker working in New York City. In some respects, he was living the good life. But he also had a serious drinking problem. He reached a point where alcohol had made his life unmanageable, and he needed a way out. In 1935, he devised a solution to his own problem by drawing on support from others with similar experiences and adopting a new set of personal values.

Wilson built his plan into a powerful program to help himself and others like him. He founded Alcoholics Anonymous (AA), and his idea spread quickly throughout the United States and abroad.

Today, AA is a global organization with some 2 million members. Not only has AA helped millions of people stop drinking, but it has changed the way the rest of us look at alcoholism. A century ago, most people viewed alcoholics as morally weak individuals who gave in to the temptation of drink and deserved little sympathy. AA redefined the problem of alcoholism as an illness—of the body and also of the mind and soul—that, like any other illness, can be treated and cured.

How does AA work? People who suffer from alcoholism join simply by showing up at regular meetings. There they realize that they are not alone, that alcoholism has made the lives of others unmanageable too. Often people who feel alone also feel powerless. In AA, people dealing with alcoholism gain strength from one another and begin to move on the path toward sobriety.

Although AA believes that alcoholics can learn to lead a sober life, it cautions that they will always remain alcoholics. Therefore, AA members never call themselves "ex-alcoholics"; rather, they say they are "recovering from" their addiction.

The AA philosophy has been adapted by a number of similar organizations, including Al-Anon Family Groups (for friends and family members of addicts), Alateen (for teenagers whose parents are alcoholics), Adult Children of Alcoholics (for adults who grew up in an alcoholic home), Narcotics Anonymous (for people addicted to drugs other than alcohol), Gamblers Anonymous, and numerous programs aimed at helping people with eating disorders.

At thousands of AA meetings like this one, people throughout the United States learn to confront their alcoholism and to live a sober life.

William Bennett, who became known as the "drug czar." Getting tough on drugs remained the order of the day. Public opinion surveys at that time showed that two-thirds of U.S. adults considered illegal drugs the most serious social problem facing the country (Bertram at al., 1996).

A change came when Bill Clinton entered the White House in 1993. Clinton pointed out that once released from jail, most drug users simply go back to their old habits. Therefore, he urged a step back from mandatory sentencing policies and pushed for treatment as a strategy to deal with illegal drugs.

SOCIAL PROBLEMS in Everyday Life

Do you see the increasing number of federal inmates as a "solution" or a "problem"?

decriminalization removing the current criminal penalties that punish the manufacturing, sale, and personal use of drugs

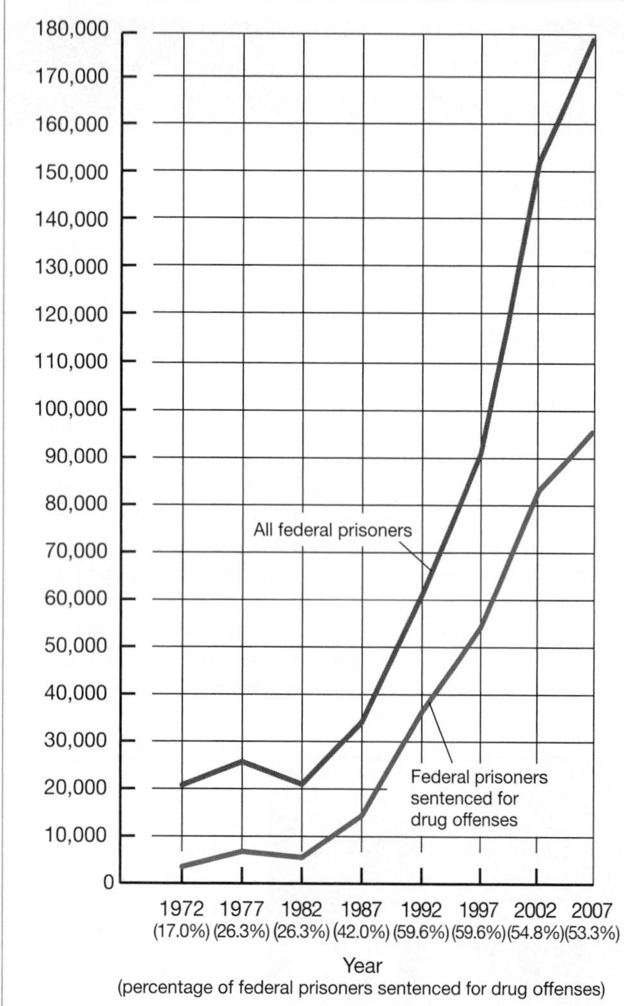

FIGURE 8–3 Total Federal Prison Population and Share of Drug Offenders, 1972–2007

The number of federal prisoners rose rapidly in the United States after 1982. (The total number of prisoners in federal, state, and local facilities is now about 2.3 million.) Increasing convictions for drug offenses has helped push up the total.

Source: U.S. Bureau of Justice Statistics (2008).

Conservatives charged that Clinton was "soft on drugs," a charge reinforced in the public's mind by the president's admission that he had smoked (but not inhaled) marijuana. When a top official in the Clinton administration suggested that perhaps government should consider legalizing some drugs, public reaction was quick and negative. Stung by this response, Clinton adopted a tougher line on drugs for the remainder of his presidency. Soon more than 1 million people a year were being arrested for drug offenses—almost twice as many as under the Reagan administration ten years earlier (U.S. Department of Justice, 2000).

After the September 11, 2001, terrorist attacks, George W. Bush did not make the control of illegal drugs a major focus of his presidency. But the Bush administration continued efforts to reduce the supply of drugs, especially the growing of coca (used to make cocaine) in Bolivia. The Bush administration also continued the country's reliance on prosecution as the main strategy to combat illegal drug use. During the Bush presidency, the United States spent more than $40 billion per year to seize illegal drugs at U.S. borders, to eliminate marijuana farms in California and elsewhere, and to prosecute and jail offenders (Alter, 2001; Roosevelt, 2001; Padgett, 2002).

The Obama administration is taking a different approach to illegal drug use. First, the federal government has started a review of drug policy with the goal of eliminating racial disparity in sentences for drug convictions. An important case in point is the greater sentences given for offenses involving crack (involving African American defendants) compared to offenses involving powdered cocaine (typically involving white defendants). In addition, the Obama administration appears to be shifting the focus of government efforts from reducing supply through controlling the borders to reducing demand through education and treatment programs (Meyer, 2009; Tierney, 2009).

Counterpoint: Decriminalization

From President Nixon to President Obama, the federal government has tried to reduce the use of illegal drugs. An alternative to this general approach is the policy of allowing these substances to be legally available. This is the policy called **decriminalization,** *removing the current criminal penalties that punish the manufacturing, sale, and personal use of drugs.* This policy is based on the idea that the only effective way to end the drug problem is simply to stop defining illegal drugs as a problem.

The degree of public support for decriminalization depends on the drug in question. Almost no one wants "hard" drugs such as heroin to be legally available. But one-third of U.S. adults support making the "soft" drug marijuana legal. Making marijuana legal for medical purposes (when prescribed by a physician) has the support of about 80 percent of U.S. adults (NORC, 2009:219).

In practice, legalizing a drug such as marijuana would mean treating it in much the same way we treat alcohol and tobacco, including the government's regulating quality and banning sales to children. Legalization, supporters argue, would have three benefits. First, by regulating the quality of drugs, the government could reduce the risk of injury or death from "bad" drugs. Second, the cost of the drug would go down, so users would have less need to commit crimes to get drug money, and

GETTING INVOLVED

Massachusetts recently decriminalized possession of small amounts of marijuana. Do you support this policy or not? Why?

SOCIAL POLICY  The Drug Wars: Safer Streets or Police State?

Federal agents seized the home of seventy-five-year-old Mary Miller. She has never used illegal drugs; in fact, she doesn't know a thing about them. But Mary Miller has a grandson who came to stay with her for a while, and during that time, he began selling drugs from the home. When federal agents were sure the young man was selling drugs, they applied a law passed by Congress in 1984 and seized the house where drugs had been sold.

Only by taking their money, cars, boats, and other property, say supporters of this law, can police put drug dealers out of business. But critics counter that the law permits police to take property from people who have not have been convicted in a court of law and should be presumed innocent until proven guilty.

Critics also point out that this law encourages police to investigate rich people for possible drug offenses and to act even with weak evidence of someone's guilt. A case in point involved Donald Scott, a wealthy sixty-one-year-old man living on a $5-million, 200-acre ranch in Malibu, California. In 1991, someone told the Los Angeles County Sheriff's Department that Scott was growing marijuana plants on his land. The tip was false; there were no illegal drugs anywhere at the ranch. But the sheriff's office sent a team to investigate. Early in the morning, thirty heavily armed officers surrounded the Scott ranch. They knocked and then forced open the door, rushing through the house. They confronted Scott, who, holding his wife, was armed with a gun. In the scuffle that followed, agents fired twice, killing Scott. Police found no drugs at the ranch. Later, an investigation of the tragic incident suggested that "the one purpose of this operation was to garner the proceeds expected from forfeiture of the $5 million ranch" (Blumenson, 1998:6).

WHAT DO YOU THINK?

1. How does the 1984 seizure law help the public? In what ways might it threaten basic freedoms?
2. Does this law seem likely to help people living in poor neighborhoods plagued by drug dealers? Why or why not?
3. Have a class discussion of this statement: "A society that provides extensive personal freedoms can never be drug-free."

drug dealer violence would disappear. Third, our society would no longer bear the cost of locking up as many as 1 million people convicted of violating drug laws.

On the other side of the argument, opponents of legalization respond that if drugs are widespread now, imagine how bad this problem would be if people were able to buy drugs the same way they buy, say, cigarettes at the corner drive-through. As they see it, legalizing drugs would send rates of poverty, homelessness, and family problems—not to mention automobile accidents—sky high. Such arguments lead a majority of adults in the United States to oppose the legalization of drugs, including marijuana (Inciardi & McBride, 1991; Goode, 1997).

What would happen if the use of many drugs were legalized? There is no easy answer, as can be seen by looking at the cases of two countries that have experimented with such a policy, with very different results.

Zurich: Decriminalization That Failed

In the 1970s, people began gathering in Zurich, Switzerland's capital city, to use illegal drugs. By the mid-1980s, the drug activity had become centered in one of the city's public greens, which soon became known as "Needle Park."

As the AIDS epidemic began, Zurich's leaders feared that drug users sharing needles might spark a health nightmare. A police crackdown on drug use would be counterproductive, they reasoned, serving only to spread drug users all over the city. What not let people use drugs legally, as long as they stay in the park? That way, health officials thought they would be able to monitor their behavior. This policy led to an experiment in decriminalization. City police stopped making drug arrests, and city health stations provided heroin and methadone along with clean needles and condoms to addicts in the hope of limiting the spread of AIDS.

But the program had an unexpected result, drawing drug users and dealers to the park from all over Switzerland and other European countries. By 1990, Zurich officials were handing out as many as 8,000 clean needles each day. It had become clear that the experiment had failed: The park was completely overrun with drug users, vandalism was out of control, and everyone else in the community was afraid to go anywhere near the area.

In February 1992, government officials gave up and closed the park. The city of Zurich continues to offer small dosages of heroin to hard-core addicts, but they must inject it at clinics rather than in public places. In 2008, voters in Switzerland passed a referendum continuing the free heroin program, but they also voted to keep the drug—and also marijuana—illegal (Huber, 1994; Nadelmann, 1995; Bruppacher, 2008).

SOCIAL PROBLEMS in Everyday Life

In 2006, the city council in West Hollywood voted to stop arresting adults for using marijuana. What consequences would you imagine if this policy were enacted by the entire state of California?

Would legalization make the drug problem worse or better? When the Swiss permitted drug use in the city of Zurich (*left*), problems increased and officials reversed course. In the Netherlands (*right*), by contrast, legalization of soft drugs had a different result, and the policy continues to this day.

The Netherlands: Decriminalization That Works

The second case is the Netherlands, another European nation, where decriminalization of some drugs has produced some positive results. In 1976, Dutch officials enacted a drug policy that permits coffee shops ("cannabis cafés") to sell up to 5 grams of "soft" drugs such as marijuana or hashish (but not "hard" drugs such as heroin). Customers can legally buy and use (but not sell) these drugs as long as they remain orderly. Since 2004, reflecting clean-air concerns, the customers who buy marijuana or hashish have to smoke it outside (Ministry of Health, Welfare and Sport, 1998; van den Hurk, 1999; Henderson, 2003).

To date, the Dutch policy seems to be working. There has been no surge in crime, and the crime rate in the Netherlands remains well below that of the United States. In addition, although many people come to the Netherlands to smoke marijuana, the level of marijuana use among Dutch teenagers is no higher than it is among teens in the United States. Perhaps most important, Dutch prisons are not filling with people convicted of drug offenses, as is the case in the United States (Common Sense for Drug Policy, 1999; MacCoun, 2001; Bruppacher, 2008).

Does the Dutch case show that decriminalization works? Not exactly. What it does show is that legalizing "soft" drugs did not create a host of social problems *in the Netherlands.* Whether such a policy would work as well in this country remains an open question. But the Dutch experience does suggest that the worst fears about making "soft" drugs legally available may be exaggerated.

Other nations have followed the Dutch example. Belgium has made the possession of marijuana for personal use legal, and citizens can also grow their own plants. In about half of European nations, criminal penalties for personal use of marijuana have either been eliminated or enforcement of laws has been greatly reduced (Hoge, 2002; Tandy, 2009).

Theoretical Analysis: Understanding Drug-Related Social Problems

Each of sociology's major theoretical approaches offers insights into social problems involving drugs. As in earlier chapters, each analysis highlights different facts and points toward a different conclusion.

Structural-Functional Analysis: Regulating Drug Use

The structural-functional approach focuses on the functions of drugs for the operation of society. Some drugs, such as alcohol, ease social interaction, as when new neighbors enjoy a drink together. Other drugs—including caffeine, diazepam (Valium), or methylphenidate hydrochloride (Ritalin)—help people cope with the day-to-day demands of modern life. Legal and illegal

SOCIAL PROBLEMS in Everyday Life

Do you feel that our country's drug policies have been "functional" or "dysfunctional"? Why?

GETTING INVOLVED

Do you think cigarettes should be regulated more severely or even banned? Explain your view.

drugs also are a major source of economic activity, providing jobs and income for hundreds of thousands of people.

Because most drugs are personally harmful or socially disruptive when used to excess, societies establish social controls to regulate their use. In general, the more disruptive a drug's effects, the stronger the efforts to control its use. Traditionally, the family, schools, and religion played a major part in regulating individual behavior. It may be the case that a weakening in these social institutions, which leaves people with less certainty and meaning in their lives, explains some of the rise in drug use over the past century. In any case, as families and religion have lost some of their power over individuals, the task of regulating drug use has fallen more and more to health care professionals and the criminal justice system.

CRITICAL REVIEW The structural-functional approach suggests that drugs can be both helpful and harmful to the orderly operation of society. Yet this approach is unclear about how one defines a particular drug as useful or not. In addition, the functional approach takes such a broad view that we learn little about the ways in which individuals understand drugs, which is the focus of the symbolic-interaction approach.

Symbolic-Interaction Analysis: The Meaning of Drug Use

The symbolic-interaction approach calls attention to the various meanings people attach to their surroundings and behavior. From this point of view, a drug that one society defines as a part of sacred, religious rituals another society may ban as a dangerous substance. Even within any one society, a drug (say, cocaine in the United States) may be legal at one point in time and outlawed later on. Conversely, a drug largely ignored may become popular (as with tobacco in the United States) or a drug once outlawed may become legal (as with cannabis in the Netherlands).

A second issue is how individuals make sense of drugs. People do not simply become drug users; they gain skills and attitudes through a learning process. In the case of marijuana smoking, for example, a novice smoker usually "turns on" in the presence of more experienced people, who explain how to smoke the drug, the proper behavior expected when doing so, and how to enjoy the experience of being "high" (Becker, 1966).

CRITICAL REVIEW The symbolic-interaction approach highlights the variable meanings people attach to all behavior, including drug use. Yet because of its situational focus, this approach runs the risk of missing broader patterns. One such pattern, which has to do with social power, is at the heart of the social-conflict approach.

Social-Conflict Analysis: Power and Drug Use

The social-conflict approach understands issues in terms of social inequality. Throughout our own history, officials have outlawed the drugs favored by powerless people, especially minorities and immigrants. In the mid-nineteenth century, whites on the West Coast outlawed the opium used mainly by Chinese immigrants; about 1900, southern whites who feared black violence succeeded in outlawing cocaine. By 1920, the tide of European immigration led to Prohibition, which banned alcohol until 1933. On the other hand, powerful corporate interests sell highly profitable drugs—including tobacco and alcohol—with full protection of the law, even though these two drugs are linked to more deaths annually than all the illegal drugs combined.

Social-conflict theory points out that the social standing of users also has much to do with how severely our society punishes illegal drug use. Earlier it was suggested that racial inequality has played a part in explaining the harsher sentences handed down for use of crack (a less expensive cocaine derivative favored by African Americans and the poor) compared with those for the use of cocaine (a middle-class drug favored by white people).

CRITICAL REVIEW The social-conflict approach links drug problems to social inequality, suggesting that the poor bear the greatest burden. Yet it fails to account for the fact that many harmful drugs—such as nicotine and alcohol—are widely used by rich and poor alike. Similarly, the harm caused by alcohol—say, in contributing to automobile accidents—is not limited to any one class of people.

The Applying Theory table on page 228 summarizes what we learn from each theoretical approach.

POLITICS AND DRUGS

Constructing Problems and Defining Solutions

Theory helps us understand social problems, but the position a person takes on drug-related issues is a matter of values and politics. The final section of this chapter explains how politics shapes views of drug-related problems and their solutions.

Conservatives: Just Say No

In their analysis of social problems, conservatives emphasize the importance of moral values in guiding individual behavior. Historically, the family, the church, and the local school were

MAKING THE GRADE

Use the table below to review the three theoretical approaches to understanding drugs.

APPLYING THEORY

Alcohol and Other Drugs

	What is the level of analysis?	What is the approach to drugs?	Are drugs a problem?
Structural-functional approach	Macro-level	The structural-functional approach directs attention to the societal consequences of using various drugs. Some drugs, including caffeine and alcohol, encourage social interaction and are viewed positively. Other drugs, including heroin and crack cocaine, are disruptive and are viewed negatively.	All drugs can threaten social order if they are abused, so society must regulate drug use. Law enforcement is an important strategy to control drug use. Yet families, religious organizations, and schools should help regulate individual behavior to minimize problems related to drug use.
Symbolic-interaction approach	Micro-level	The symbolic-interaction approach explains that various societies attach different meanings to drugs and their use. The use of drugs, like other forms of behavior, is learned by people in various social settings. This learning involves both skills in using the drug as well as attitudes toward a drug and its use.	Whether drug use is defined as a problem depends on any number of situational factors. More broadly, what one society bans as a dangerous substance, members of another society may use as a part of sacred ritual. Finally, any society's view of a particular drug is subject to change over time.
Social-conflict approach	Macro-level	A social-conflict approach links society's view of various drugs to issues of social power and social inequality. Drugs that are highly profitable to powerful corporations are sold more freely, while those that are not are subject to greater legal controls.	Drugs favored by minorities with less social power are more likely to be defined as a problem and outlawed. Similarly, people with low social standing often receive more severe penalties for drug use than people with high social standing.

the main sources of moral instruction. From a conservative point of view, young people who are raised by committed, involved parents and who are guided by religious beliefs and caring teachers are usually able to resist any temptation presented by drugs.

As noted in earlier chapters, conservatives argue that our society's teaching of moral virtue has declined since the 1960s. They see the rise of drug use since then as one indication that, morally speaking, society has lost its way. Parents spend less time parenting, religion plays a smaller role in our society, and schools no longer teach moral values as they once did. The mass media, which have filled much of this void in the lives of young people, are as likely to glamorize drug use as to criticize it. Overall, our way of life now offers fewer moral certainties and has replaced them with a culture of permissiveness and relativism in which "anything goes." The drug scene, as conservatives see it, amounts to a self-centered and pleasure-seeking way of life on the part of people who have little understanding or appreciation of higher virtues, such as duty, self-control, and respect for authority figures.

Conservatives define drug use as a serious social problem that is both the cause and the effect of weak families. Drug use also encourages crime, poverty, dropping out of school, and many other problem patterns. In responding to illegal drug sale, possession, and use, conservatives favor tough laws, aggressive enforcement, and severe penalties. In the end, however, conservatives warn that there is only so much that police and other government agencies can do to control drugs. The major

libertarians people who favor the greatest possible individual freedom

MAKING THE GRADE

Be sure you understand all four political approaches to drugs, including the libertarian approach.

responsibility will always lie with parents, who must raise their children to make good moral choices in a world full of temptation. Nancy Reagan, wife of President Ronald Reagan, summed up the conservative solution to the drug problem as teaching our children to "just say no."

Liberals: Reform Society

When it comes to how to live, liberals support a great deal of personal freedom. Liberals are uneasy with the moralistic tone of the conservative argument, which seems to force everyone into one traditional mold. Liberals claim that drug use is the product of too little economic opportunity and too much hopelessness. Therefore, the liberal solution to the drug problem is increasing economic opportunity and decreasing poverty so that fewer people would turn to drugs in the first place.

Because they value personal choice and personal freedom, liberals take a tolerant view of "soft" drugs, and some favor decriminalization, following the example of the Netherlands. Why, some liberals ask, should marijuana be against the law when it causes less harm than a legal drug such as tobacco?

Although they support law enforcement when it comes to "hard" drugs—especially for big-time dealers—liberals argue that our current policies criminalize hundreds of thousands of people who pose little harm to anyone and may not even be a danger to themselves. They call for less emphasis on police, courts, and prisons and more emphasis on programs of drug education for children and treatment programs for people struggling with drug addiction.

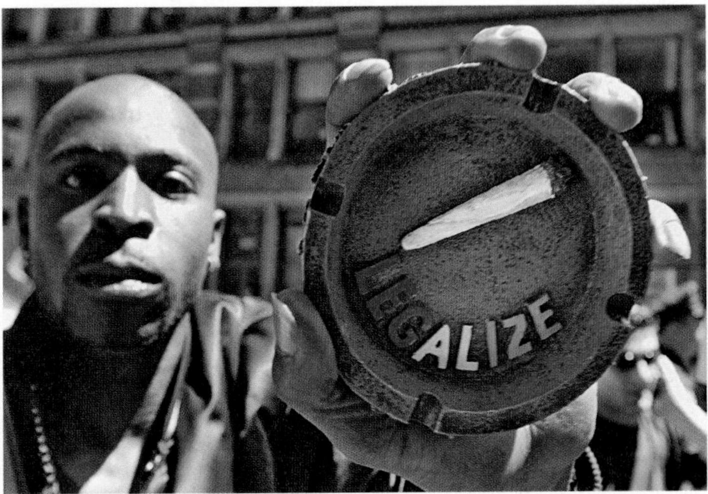

Conservatives claim that current drug laws are an effective tool to reduce the problem of illegal drugs. Liberals (and libertarians) argue that the main effect of our drug laws is putting people in jail. Do you favor enforcement or repeal of current drug laws? Why?

Radicals: Understanding Drugs from the Margins of Society

Both ends of the political spectrum figure into the national debate on drugs. First we look at the libertarian position on the far right; then we examine the socialist position on the far left.

The Radical Right: Libertarians

In political terms, **libertarians** are *people who favor the greatest possible individual freedom.* Although some people who call themselves libertarians fall close to the political mainstream on many issues, most libertarians see government as the biggest threat to their core value of individual liberty. What they seek, therefore, is the smallest government possible in order to have the largest degree of personal freedom.

Given this emphasis on personal freedom, libertarians oppose government efforts to regulate drugs (and almost anything else). As they see it, drug laws amount to a system that seeks to limit individual choice about how to live. Many libertarians believe that the government's war on drugs has already reduced our civil liberties, not only by limiting our choice about what to put in our own bodies but also by permitting widespread surveillance, searches, and seizure of property. In short, many libertarians see not a "drug problem" but a "government problem" that threatens everyone. Therefore, libertarians are at the forefront of the movement to legalize all drugs (Trebach & Inciardi, 1993).

The Radical Left: Socialists

Radicals on the far left of the political spectrum also oppose current drug laws, but for different reasons. From the point of view of socialists, drug laws (like all laws) reflect the interests of the rich and powerful members of society and target everyone else. Drug laws criminalize the poor—especially people of color—who now fill U.S. prisons in disproportionate numbers. In an effort to stabilize our society in crisis, the government has pushed the prisoner population to a level greater than at any time in our history. For this reason, the far left supports repeal of current drug laws.

But abolishing current drug laws is only a small part of the solution. From the radical left's point of view, society itself needs to be completely restructured. If a new society were created on the principles of equality and opportunities for all people, radicals claim, there would be far less demand for drugs in the first place. The Left to Right table on page 230 outlines the various political perspectives on drugs.

MAKING THE GRADE

Use the table below to review the four political approaches to drug use.

SOCIAL PROBLEMS in Everyday Life

What is the aging of U.S. society likely to do for the use of prescription drugs?

LEFT TO RIGHT

The Politics of the Drug Problem

	RADICAL-LEFT VIEW	LIBERAL VIEW	CONSERVATIVE VIEW	RADICAL-RIGHT (LIBERTARIAN) VIEW
WHAT IS THE PROBLEM?	Drug laws (like all laws) reflect the interests of the powerful and criminalize poor people and minorities.	Drug use is a symptom of the suffering of many people from various problems, such as poverty and powerlessness.	Drug use is a symptom of poor moral instruction to young people. Schools, churches, and especially families should raise children with the moral values that will give them the strength to resist the temptation to use drugs.	The government threatens civil liberties by using police power to make arrests, seize property, and monitor the lives of people suspected of using drugs.
WHAT IS THE SOLUTION?	A fundamental reorganization of society to spread wealth, power, and opportunity to all would go a long way toward reducing the conditions that lead people to sell and use drugs in the first place.	As economic opportunity and social equality increase, drug use should go down. Government should fund treatment programs for people with addictions.	Enforcement of drug laws is important, but active parenting is the first line of defense against the threat of drugs. Schools, houses of worship, and community organizations must play a part in educating children about the dangers of drugs.	Most drug laws—especially those regulating "soft" drugs—should be abolished as a step toward providing people with greater personal freedom.

JOIN THE DEBATE

1. If you were put in charge of a national drug commission, what new policies would you enact to address this problem?
2. Where on the political spectrum would you expect to find support for the various drug control strategies discussed in this chapter: interdiction, prosecution, education, and treatment?
3. Which of the four political analyses of the drug problem included here do you find most convincing? Why?

Going On from Here

Ever since people discovered the powers of certain plants, drugs have been part of human culture. Just as societies depend on the positive effects of some drugs, they define other drugs as problems that must be controlled.

There is little doubt that drugs, both illegal and legal, will remain controversial in the decades ahead. Drugs such as heroin and cocaine will continue to claim victims; the death toll from alcohol abuse—already at a much higher level—will almost certainly climb even more.

The debate over the causes of drug abuse will also go on, with various political camps making different claims. With its focus on moral values, conservatives will point to family breakdown; with its focus on economic inequality, liberals will point to a lack of jobs and poverty. Radical voices calling for freedom from government (the far right) and basic change to the economic system (the far left) will continue to be heard as well.

Will this debate change our national policies? Certainly, in some ways. But there is widespread support in the United States for aggressive use of the criminal justice system—including police, courts, and prisons—to combat drugs, and this view is likely to persist, even though it finds little support from sociological research. The Obama administration has signaled greater support for treatment, as opposed to prosecution, of people abusing drugs. How far the changes go will become clear in the next few years.

One hopeful sign: Research shows that illegal drug use declines with age (Wren, 1997). In the next few decades, the average age of people in the United States will continue to rise, raising the hope of a downward trend in illegal drug use. But in light of the uncertain economy, it is doubtful that aging alone will solve the drug problem in U.S. society.

DEFINING SOLUTIONS

Are you concerned about drugs?

From almost anyone's point of view, at least some drugs are harmful to people and are, therefore, the basis of a social problem. But what's the best way to create a solution to the many troubling issues surrounding the use of drugs? Look at the two photos below to see two different approaches to defining solutions.

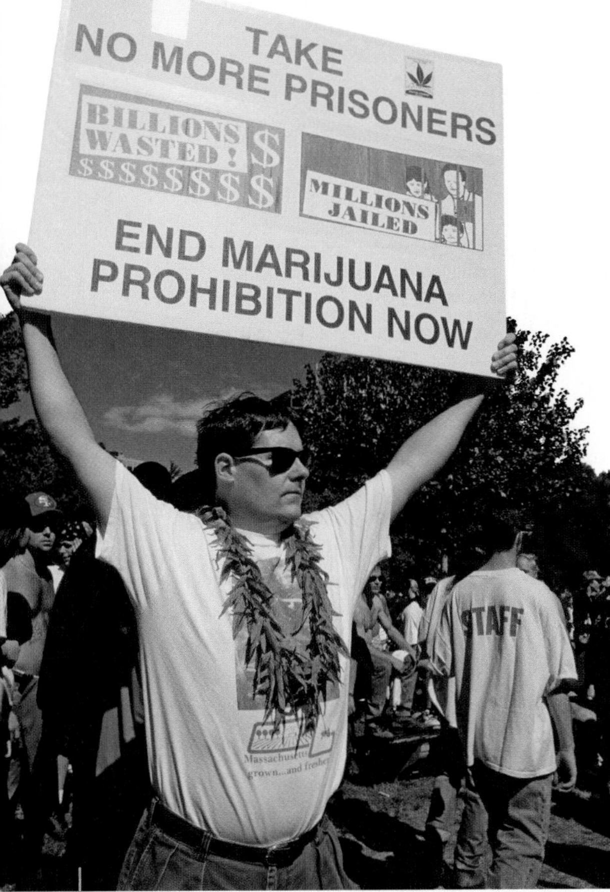

From the liberal point of view, soft drugs themselves are not nearly as dangerous as the nation's response to them—specifically, the policy of locking up a million people for drug offenses. Many liberals therefore support a policy of decriminalizing marijuana, as was recently done in Massachusetts. If soft drugs are not against the law, in other words, there is no more "soft-drug problem." What do you see as advantages and disadvantages of this approach?

HINT

As we have seen in earlier chapters, conservatives favor a solution based on personal responsibility ("Just say no!"), while liberals favor a solution based on making structural changes to our legal system. Decriminalizing marijuana would obviously reduce the number of drug offenses, but its effect on the rate of marijuana use remains unclear. Education programs such as D.A.R.E. are also controversial, partly because the effect of such programs on children has not been established. What about libertarians on the far right? From their point of view, maximum freedom is the goal and keeping government at arm's length is the way to do that. Which of these two approaches do you think libertarians (perhaps surprisingly) would support? Why?

From a conservative point of view, there is entirely too much illegal drug use in our society, and these drugs weaken individual judgment and undermine families and communities. Of course, law enforcement is the policy of last resort for conservatives, who would prefer to guide behavior through moral education. These students have just completed the D.A.R.E. anti-drug education program in their local school. What do you see as the strengths and shortcomings of this approach?

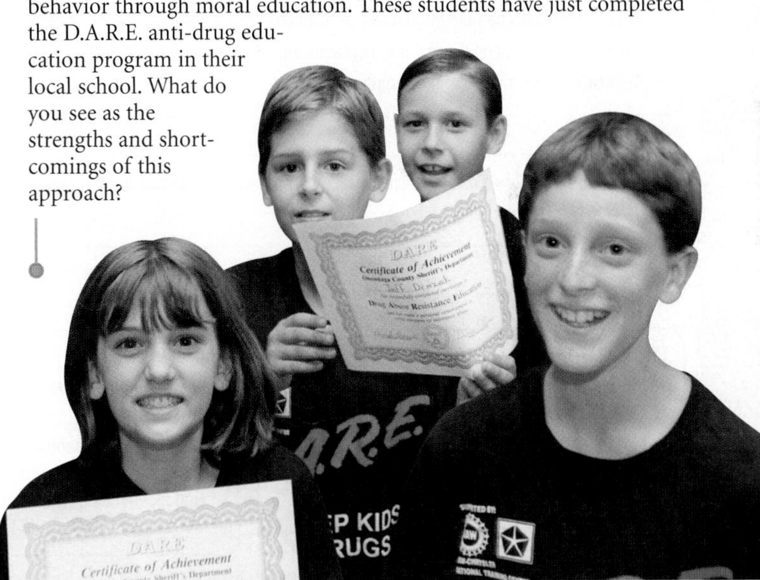

Getting Involved: Applications & Exercises

1. Take a walk around your campus with an eye toward drug use. What can you say about the places where people smoke cigarettes? Drink coffee? Drink alcohol? How are the places where each of these drugs is used different from one another? What does that tell you about the drugs?
2. A fascinating and easy research project is to visit a library, obtain copies of U.S. magazines from the 1920s and 1930s, and look at cigarette advertising. What, if any, statements are made by cigarette companies regarding the dangers of smoking tobacco? What claims are made about the benefits?
3. Most communities have Alcoholics Anonymous and Al-Anon Family Group meetings. Look up the number for AA in your local phone directory, and ask about the time and location of a meeting open to the public. Attend a meeting, and afterward, talk to people about how AA helps them recover from alcoholism or helps them cope with a family member's addiction.
4. Go to your local library and see what you can learn about the extent of illegal drug use in your state. In what region of the state (for example, rural versus urban) is the arrest rate for drug offenses higher? Can you discover why?

MAKING THE GRADE

A DEFINING MOMENT
Bill Wilson: Alcoholics Can Learn to be Sober p. 223

CHAPTER 8 Alcohol and Other Drugs

What Is a Drug?

DRUGS are substances other than food and water that affect the body or the mind.

- Drugs have been a part of society throughout human history.

p. 208

Drugs and **CULTURE**

- Which drugs people use and which substances they define as helpful and harmful vary from society to society and over time.

pp. 208–9

drug (p. 208) any chemical substance other than food or water that affects the mind or body

✓ *One factor shaping attitudes about drugs in the United States is controversy over immigration; in the past, government has outlawed drugs favored by various categories of immigrants. (pp. 209–10)*

The Extent of Drug Use

- About 8% of the U.S. population aged 12 and older currently uses at least one illegal drug. The trend in drug use in recent decades has been downward, with an upswing in the last few years.
- People use drugs for various reasons, including recreation, therapy, escape, spiritual or psychological stimulation, and social conformity.

pp. 210–11

addiction (p. 211) a physical or psychological craving for a drug

dependency (p. 211) a state in which a person's body has adjusted to regular use of a drug

Types of Drugs

Drugs fall into various categories according to their effect on the body and brain.

- **STIMULANTS** produce alertness and speed up activity (*examples:* caffeine, nicotine, cocaine, amphetamines).
- **DEPRESSANTS** slow activity and dull pain (*examples:* aspirin, Valium, alcohol).
- **HALLUCINOGENS** can distort sensory perceptions (*examples:* LSD, peyote, ecstasy).
- **CANNABIS** helps people relax and increases appetite (*examples:* marijuana, hashish).
- **STEROIDS** build muscle and strength.

pp. 212–16

stimulants (p. 212) drugs that increase alertness, changing a person's mood by increasing energy

depressants (p. 214) drugs that slow the operation of the central nervous system

alcoholism (p. 215) addiction to alcohol

✓ *Abuse of prescription drugs involving 116 million people, is part of the drug problem in the United States. (p. 217)*

Drugs and Other Social Problems

PROBLEMS OF FAMILY LIFE

- Drug use—and especially addiction—can lead to codependency among family members and friends.
- Parental addiction harms children, who are more likely to use drugs themselves, to drop out of school, and to get in trouble with the law.
- Drugs play a part in many cases of child neglect and family violence.

p. 217

HOMELESSNESS

- Drug and alcohol use is common among the homeless.
- Although some people become homeless because they abuse drugs, others turn to drugs and alcohol as a means of escape from the stresses of living on the streets.

pp. 217–18

codependency (p. 217) behavior on the part of others that helps a substance abuser continue the abuse

HEALTH PROBLEMS

- Drug abuse can damage the brain, liver, and other vital organs and lead to malnutrition.
- Among pregnant women, drug abuse increases the risk of premature delivery and birth defects.
- Drug users can transmit HIV by sharing needles.

pp. 218–19

CRIME

- Most violent offenders report being under the influence of alcohol or other drugs when they committed their crimes.
- Drug laws contribute to crime by driving prices up so that addicted users of crack, cocaine, and heroin turn to crime to support their habit.
- Drug dealers often use violence to protect their profits against competition from other dealers.

p. 219

GLOBAL POVERTY

- People in poor nations grow and manufacture illegal drugs as a needed source of income.
- The $60 billion that people in the United States spend each year on illegal drugs exceeds the total economic output of dozens of the world's countries.

p. 219–21

TERRORISM

- Terrorist organizations may engage in drug trafficking to raise money for terrorist activities.

p. 221

✓ *Research has shown that needle exchange programs reduce the transmission of HIV and other diseases, but critics claim that such programs encourage illegal drug use. (p. 219)*

Social Policy: Responding to the Drug Problem

Four **STRATEGIES** for controlling illegal drugs in the United States are
- interdiction
- prosecution
- education
- treatment

pp. 221–22

The **WAR ON DRUGS** has resulted in an increase in the number of people jailed for drug offenses in the United States. People convicted of drug offenses now represent about half of all people in prison.

pp. 222–24

DECRIMINALIZATION as a strategy to eliminate drug-related social problems has met with varied success in countries around the world.

pp. 224–26

decriminalization (p. 224) removing the current criminal penalties that punish the manufacturing, sale, and personal use of drugs

Theoretical Analysis: Understanding Drug-Related Social Problems

Structural-Functional Analysis: Regulating Drug Use

The **STRUCTURAL-FUNCTIONAL APPROACH** focuses on the functions of drugs for the normal operation of society.
- Societies rely on some drugs to ease social interaction and help people cope with the demands of modern living.
- Drugs are a source of economic activity, providing jobs and income for many people.
- Societies control drugs that have dangerous consequences.

pp. 226–27

Symbolic-Interaction Analysis: The Meaning of Drug Use

The **SYMBOLIC-INTERACTION APPROACH** highlights the various meanings people attach to drug use.
- A drug that one society defines as beneficial may be banned as dangerous in another society or at another time in history.
- People learn to use drugs in the same way that they learn other forms of behavior.

p. 227

Social-Conflict Analysis: Power and Drug Use

The **SOCIAL-CONFLICT APPROACH** focuses on how the issue of social power shapes our drug policies.
- The United States has historically banned drugs favored by immigrants and other minorities.
- The degree to which illegal drug use is punished reflects the social standing of the drug users.

p. 227

See the **Applying Theory** table on page 228.

Politics and Drugs: Constructing Problems and Defining Solutions

The Radical Left: Socialists

- **SOCIALISTS**, radicals on the far left, argue that current drug laws tend to criminalize the poor.
- Socialists call for basic change in the U.S. economy leading to a more egalitarian society, which they believe would be characterized by far less demand for drugs.

p. 229

Liberals: Reform Society

- **LIBERALS** claim that drug abuse is the product of too little economic opportunity, which creates hopelessness. They are generally tolerant of "soft" drug use.
- Liberals support expanded education and drug treatment programs.

p. 229

Conservatives: Just Say No

- **CONSERVATIVES** view illegal drug use as a serious social problem linked to the decline of traditional families and religion.
- Conservatives favor tough drug laws and urge parents to provide moral instruction to children.

pp. 227–29

The Radical Right: Libertarians

- **LIBERTARIANS**, radicals on the far right, believe that the government's war on drugs has reduced people's civil liberties.
- Libertarians oppose all drug laws in an effort to expand individual freedoms.

p. 229

libertarians (p. 229) people who favor the greatest individual freedom possible

See the **Left to Right** table on page 230.

CONSTRUCTING THE PROBLEM

Does this country do enough to help people pay for medical care?

The United States remains the only high-income nation with no government-based system to pay for everyone's health care.

Poverty hurts people, but can it kill?

In the world's poorest nations, half of all children die before they reach age ten.

Is mental illness unusual?

Nearly half of all adults in the United States have symptoms of mental disorders at some time in their lives.

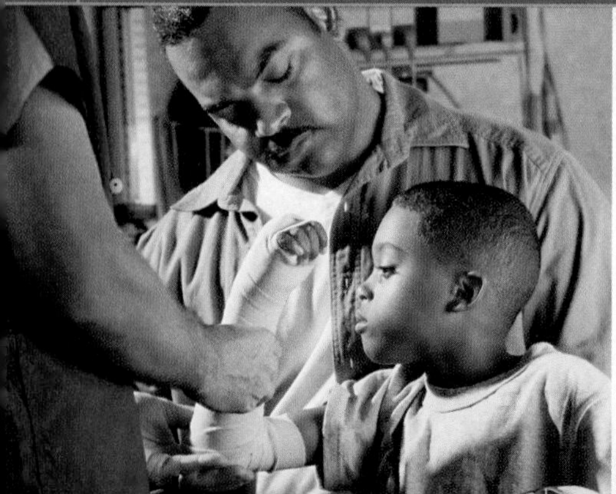

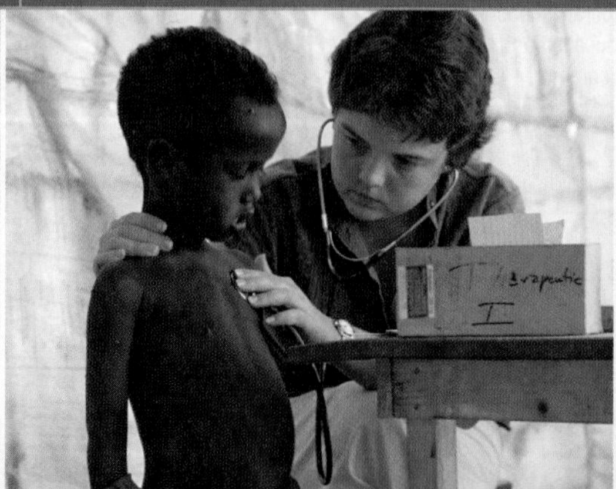

CHAPTER 9

Physical and Mental Health

CHAPTER OVERVIEW

WHAT DIFFERENCES IN HEALTH are found comparing high- and low-income nations? What about rich and poor people here in the United States? This chapter explores health and how people pay for health care in both national and global context. You will gain a better understanding of mental illness and various categories of disorders. You will carry out theoretical analysis of health issues and learn how "problems" and "solutions" involving health and illness reflect people's political attitudes.

Who are the most stigmatized people in the United States? What category of people are we most likely to avoid, to stereotype, and to fear? In the past, the answer might have been gays and lesbians, handicapped people, or perhaps members of various racial and ethnic minorities.

Today, there is increasing tolerance for many categories of people once pushed to the margins. But there is still very little acceptance of one category of people—men and women with mental illness. Undoubtedly, the mass media play a part; everyone remembers "crazy" and genuinely scary characters in films from *Psycho* to *Friday the 13th* to *Silence of the Lambs.* But such movies frighten us precisely because they play on fears that lie deep within U.S. culture. Almost 60 million people—about one-third of the adult population in the United States—suffer from a mental illness at some point in their lives. More than 10 percent of adults claimed that they had a serious mental problem in 2007 (U.S. Department of Health and Human Services, 2008). Given these high numbers, it is surprising that most people know very little about what mental illness is and what its causes are.

This chapter explores problems related to both mental and physical health. We begin by looking at problems of physical health in the United States. We will also take a look at health in low-income nations of the world, where illness caused by poverty kills half the people before they become adults. Then we survey health care systems, giving special attention to how people in various countries pay for care and why many people claim that the U.S. health care system is in crisis. Finally, we turn to mental health, explaining what mental illnesses are, what causes them, and why there is so little understanding of this widespread problem. Although health is partly a matter of biology and medicine, society guides how we define people as "healthy" or "sick" and allows some categories of people to enjoy excellent health while stacking the odds against others from the day they are born.

Health and Illness: A Global Perspective

Many of us think that being healthy simply means not being sick. However, the World Health Organization (1946:3) defines **health** as *a state of complete physical, mental, and social well-being.* In other words, just as there are degrees of illness, there are degrees of health. Looking around the world, we see that one major predictor of health is income. To put it succinctly, the global pattern is "health comes with wealth."

High-Income Nations

On average, people living in rich nations—in North America and Western Europe—are far healthier than those living in poor countries. One good measure of a society's health is the **infant mortality rate,** *the number of babies who die before their first birthday out of every 1,000 babies born.* In the world's rich nations, infant mortality rates are low, usually less than 10 deaths for every 1,000 babies born. That means that a baby has at least a 99.9 percent chance of surviving the first year, and so infant deaths are quite rare. When they do occur, people view them as both unexpected and tragic. Global Map 9–1 shows that the infant mortality rates for rich countries are quite low by world standards.

Another way to gauge global patterns of health is by calculating how long, on average, people live. **Life expectancy at birth** is *the number of years, on average, people in a society can expect to live.* In the United States, boys born in 2009 can expect to live seventy-six years, and girls born that year can expect to live eighty-one years. By contrast, in the world's poorest nations, life expectancy is less than fifty-five years (Population Reference Bureau, 2010; Kochanek et al., 2011).

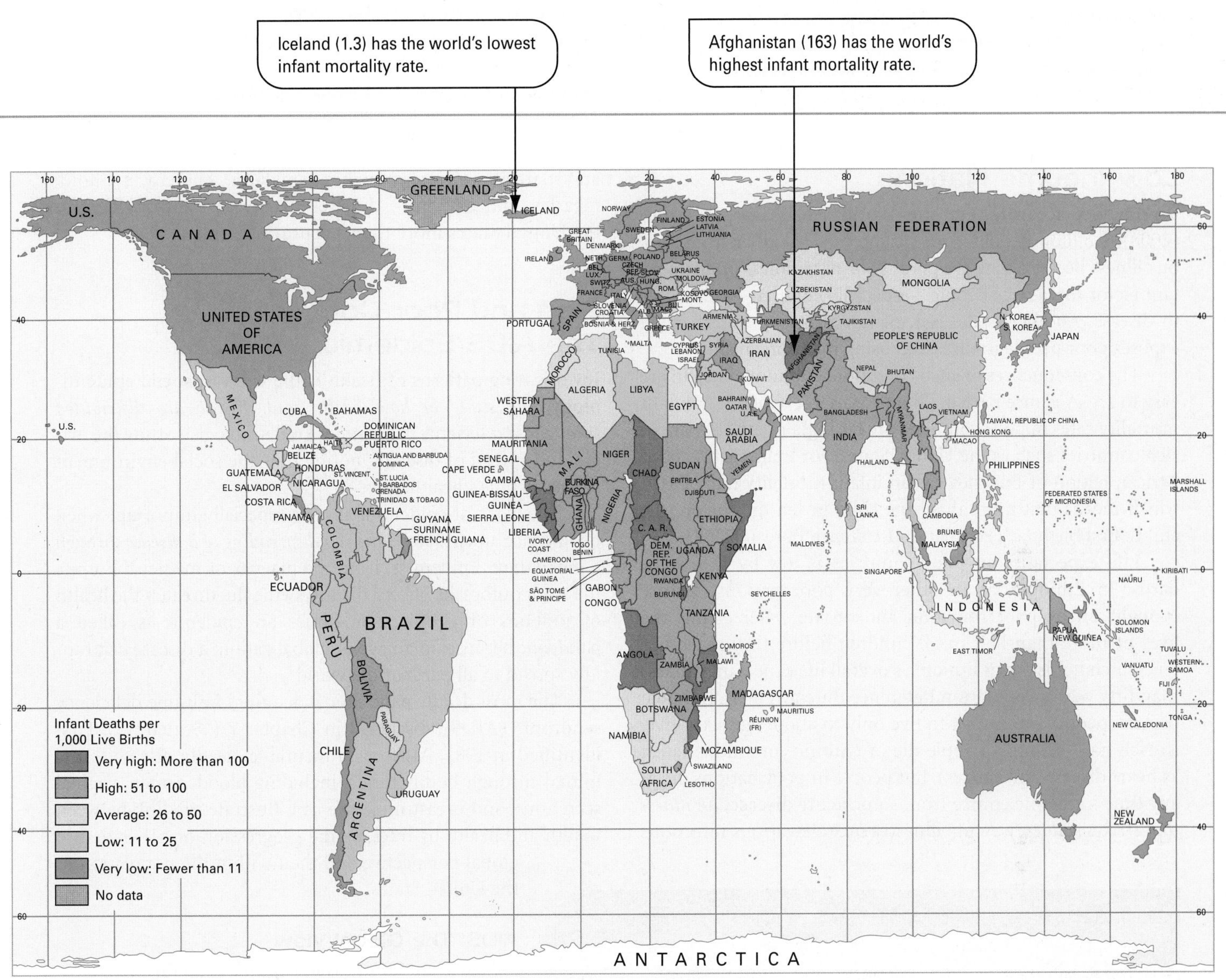

A World of Differences

GLOBAL MAP 9–1 Infant Mortality around the World

A good measure of health for any nation is the rate of infant mortality: death in the first year of life. In rich nations, infant deaths are generally less than 10 per 1,000 live births. In poor nations, by contrast, infant mortality is high, with rates exceeding 100 across much of Africa.

Source: Population Reference Bureau (2008).

A society's average level of income also has a lot to do with the types of health problems its people face. People who live in rich societies typically don't worry too much about health until they are past middle age. In most cases, they live long enough to die in old age—typically, after age seventy-five—of some **chronic disease,** *an illness that has a long-term development*. Chronic diseases include heart disease, cancer, and stroke.

In most respects, being affluent is a lot better for human health than being poor. But a higher standard of living does carry some health dangers of its own. For example, people in the United States eat a high-fat diet; in addition, many of us don't do very much physical work. Taken together, these factors help explain the fact that two-thirds of adults in the United States are overweight. Being too heavy sets the stage for a number of other health problems, which is why the leading cause of death in this country is heart disease and why cases of diabetes have increased more than 40 percent in the last ten years (Centers for Disease Control and Prevention, 2009; Heron et al., 2009).

health (p. 236) a state of complete physical, mental, and social well-being

infant mortality rate (p. 236) the number of babies who die before their first birthday out of every 1,000 babies born

life expectancy at birth (p. 236) the number of years, on average, people in a society can expect to live

chronic disease (p. 237) an illness that has a long-term development

acute disease an illness that strikes suddenly

social epidemiology the study of how health and disease are distributed throughout a society's population

epidemic the rapid spreading of a disease through a population

Low-Income Nations

Worldwide, according to the World Health Organization (2008), 1 billion people—one person in six—suffer from serious illness because they are poor. Poor nutrition is one important factor that leaves people—especially children—vulnerable to disease. Another is the lack of safe drinking water, which exposes poor people to disease-causing microorganisms.

The consequences of such conditions for human health are easy to see. A glance back at Global Map 9–1 shows that infant mortality rates in poor countries are far higher than they are in rich countries such as the United States. For example, the poor African nation of Burundi has an infant mortality rate of 107, which means that more than one child in ten dies before the child's first birthday (Population Reference Bureau, 2009).

Life expectancy in poor countries is low by U.S. standards. In Ethiopia, as in other very poor nations, disease brought on by poor nutrition and unsafe water claims the lives of more than half of all children before they reach age ten, which holds down Ethiopia's overall life expectancy to less than fifty years (Population Reference Bureau, 2008). In much of Asia, people can expect to live only to about age sixty-five. In rich nations, most people die of chronic conditions (such as heart disease and cancer), but people in poor nations die at any time in the life course from some **acute disease,** *an illness that strikes suddenly.* Acute illnesses include various infectious and parasitic diseases such as malaria, cholera, typhoid, measles, and diarrhea—diseases that were leading killers in the United States more than a century ago.

A strong predictor of any population's life expectancy is level of income: In simple terms, richer people typically live a long time and poorer people do not. This family lives on a vast garbage dump outside Guayaquil, Ecuador. What would you expect to be true about life expectancy for such people?

Rich and Poor Compared: The AIDS Epidemic

Investigating patterns of health is the work of **social epidemiology,** *the study of how health and disease are distributed throughout a society's population.* Epidemiologists study the origin and spread of diseases, noting how the social environment shapes people's health.

The work of epidemiologists is especially important when people face an **epidemic,** *the rapid spreading of a disease through a population.* Epidemics, from the plagues of medieval Europe to recent outbreaks of bird flu and swine flu, threaten the health of millions of people. Sometimes an epidemic is called a *pandemic* because, in an age of globalization, a disease can rapidly spread to all parts of the world.

The most deadly pandemic is acquired immune deficiency syndrome (AIDS), discussed in Chapter 7 ("Sexuality"). First identified in 1981, AIDS is an incurable, deadly disease transmitted through bodily fluids, including blood, semen, vaginal secretions, and breast milk. We can illustrate the link between wealth and health by tracking the progression of AIDS, first in global perspective and then within the population of the United States.

AIDS: The Global View

Global Map 7–1 on page 195, mapping the global distribution of roughly 33 million cases of HIV infection, shows that they are concentrated in low-income nations. Africa, the world's poorest continent, has 14 percent of the world's people but is home to 68 percent of the world's HIV-positive people.

Over the past decade, Presidents Clinton, Bush, and Obama have all stated that AIDS is a threat to the political and economic future of many African nations. The AIDS epidemic has already wiped out 20 million people in Africa, dramatically dropping life expectancy in much of central and southern Africa to about forty years. This epidemic has shattered these societies, overwhelming medical facilities, destroying families, and leaving huge numbers of orphaned children (Whitelaw, 2003; Altman, 2005; UNAIDS, 2008).

Why are many of the world's poorest nations so hard hit by AIDS? As already noted, poor people often have weakened health, so they are less resistant to

GETTING INVOLVED

Has HIV or AIDS affected your life in any way? Explain.

infection. In addition, poor countries have few resources for education and prevention programs (say, to provide condoms and teach people the importance of using them). But cultural patterns—especially those involving gender—also have an impact. The Social Problems in Global Perspective box on page 240 takes a closer look at the problem of AIDS in Central Africa.

AIDS in the United States

The AIDS epidemic is not as serious in the United States as it is in the nations of Central Africa. This country accounts for less than 5 percent of the world's cases. Still, the government recorded 14,110 deaths due to AIDS in 2007, and the numbers have been going down. But the total number of people who have contracted AIDS had reached 1,018,428 and, of these, 562,793 have died (Centers for Disease Control and Prevention, 2009).

But a death toll exceeding half a million makes AIDS a deadly serious social problem. AIDS education programs, which have been operating in this country since 1987, have reduced the incidence of high-risk sex, such as having multiple sex partners, especially without using a condom. At the same time, many health officials are concerned that a new generation of young people may not take this deadly threat seriously. The Obama administration has asked Congress to spend more than $25 billion annually to fight AIDS, including $19 billion at home and $6 billion around the world (Kaiser Family Foundation, 2009). Although researchers have yet to produce a cure for this deadly disease, they have developed drug treatments that delay the onset of full-blown AIDS among many people infected with HIV.

In the United States, as around the world, AIDS is primarily a disease of poor people. As Figure 9–1 shows, African Americans and Hispanics, who together make up one-fourth of the population, accounted for more than half of all AIDS deaths in recent years. From another angle, non-Hispanic African Americans are nine times more likely than non-Hispanic whites to become infected; Latinos are more than three times as likely. Because of the higher poverty rates among African Americans and Hispanics, fewer people who are infected receive treatment, which can cost up to $100,000 a year. Predictably, the death toll among minorities is consequently also higher (Centers for Disease Control and Prevention, 2009).

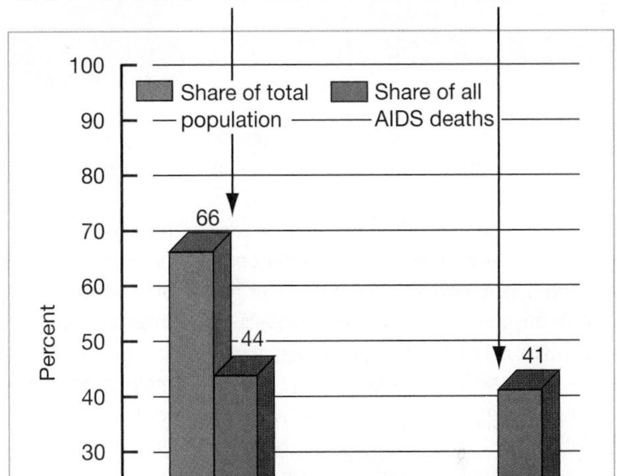

Whites have the largest share of AIDS deaths.

Share of total population

FIGURE 9–1 Deaths from AIDS in the United States

Death from AIDS among minorities is higher than population share would lead us to expect. Taken together, Hispanics and African Americans account for 27 percent of the U.S. population but 56 percent of all AIDS deaths.

Source: Centers for Disease Control and Prevention (2009).

Health Policy: Paying for Care

The expenses of health care can easily exceed what most people can afford. What policies should societies use to help cover the costs? Should a person's ability to pay determine the quality of health care available? Different countries provide different answers to these questions according to their political and economic systems.

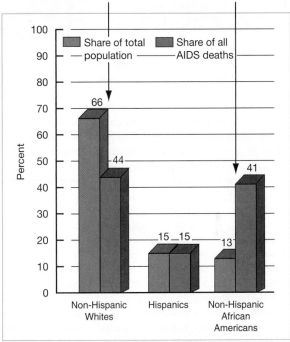

Socialist Systems

In societies with *socialist economies,* the government controls most economic activity. This means that government agencies provide medical services and operate hospitals and clinics; doctors and other medical professionals are state employees who receive salaries for their services. Examples of socialist systems are found in China and the Russian Federation.

The People's Republic of China

China is a middle-income country in the process of industrializing and is home to more than 1.3 billion people. In China, the government administers health care, operating hospitals and clinics in large population centers. In addition, China's famed "barefoot doctors" visit rural villages, providing basic health care to tens of millions of Chinese peasants.

SOCIAL PROBLEMS in Everyday Life

After reading the box below, can you explain why health and illness are social issues?

MAKING THE GRADE

Note one or two distinctive features about health care in each of the countries discussed below.

SOCIAL PROBLEMS IN GLOBAL PERSPECTIVE

The Social Roots of AIDS: Poverty, Culture, and Gender

Brigitte Syamaleuwe is a forty-year-old woman living in the African nation of Zambia. Several years ago, her life changed when she learned that she was HIV-positive. Like anyone else, her first question was, how could this have happened? Brigitte had never had sex with anyone other than her husband, so she quickly came to the conclusion that it was he who had infected her.

Angrily, she confronted him. He was visibly shaken, but he reacted by accusing *her* of infidelity. Only after several weeks was he willing to admit that he had been unfaithful, had become infected with HIV, and then infected his wife. They knew, at this point, that there was no cure. But they decided to devote the remainder of their lives to educating others about the dangers of HIV.

As explained in Chapter 4 ("Gender Inequality"), low-income countries are typically strongly patriarchal. Women in these nations have little say in what their husbands or boyfriends do. Many men have traditionally seen little wrong with having extramarital sex, often with prostitutes, even though they now know that this behavior places them, their wives, and perhaps other women at high risk for infection with HIV.

Another factor that contributes to the AIDS epidemic in Africa and elsewhere is that many men—sometimes even men who know they are infected with HIV—do not use condoms when they have sex. Some women may not insist that men use condoms, either because they don't know that their partners are being unfaithful or because the men threaten violence if they don't get their way.

To make matters worse, traditional laws make it easy for men to divorce their wives for being unfaithful, but women have a hard time doing the same thing. Even women who can get a divorce usually think twice about it because a court often ends up giving men control over family property. For women, in short, divorce often means falling into poverty.

In poor countries, becoming infected with HIV usually results in death within several years. In the United States, well-off people with HIV now rely on expensive drugs to prolong their lives for a decade or more. These drugs are becoming less expensive and therefore more available in poor countries. But they are still out of reach for most of the world's poor, who get little or no medical attention.

What strategies can be used to help the world's poor women protect themselves? One possible answer is the *female condom,* a plastic pouch that a woman inserts into her vagina before sexual intercourse that offers protection from HIV and other sexually transmitted diseases. Although the female condom is gaining popularity in Africa, many men object to it, and the cost is often too high.

The larger answer to the problem of AIDS lies in research to discover a cure for this deadly disease. In addition, the death toll would come down if societies could reduce patriarchy. Greater political and economic power would give women the ability to say no to sex, to insist on condom use, and even to demand that their men be faithful.

WHAT DO YOU THINK?

1. How does the spread of AIDS in Africa, which has already claimed 25 million victims, confirm that health is a social as well as a medical problem?
2. If AIDS continues to spread unchecked, what do you see as the likely future for African societies? What are the likely effects on the United States?
3. What might rich nations such as the United States do to respond to the AIDS epidemic?

Sources: Schoofs (1999), Singer (2001), and Altman (2005).

The Chinese approach combines modern scientific medicine with traditional healing arts, including acupuncture and medicinal herbs. In most regions, China's traditional sexual norms remain strong, which is one reason that much of this vast country (especially inland regions away from large cities on the coast) has so far escaped the AIDS epidemic that has ravaged other Asian nations to the south. On the other hand, 57 percent of Chinese men (but only 3 percent of Chinese women) smoke, which takes its toll in high rates of cancer and heart disease (World Health Organization, 2008).

The Russian Federation

Before the collapse of the Soviet Union in 1991, that nation had a government-controlled system of health care. Since then, the new Russian Federation—the largest former Soviet republic—has been changing its government-controlled, socialist economy in the direction of a market-based system. Yet health care is still mostly under government control, so as in China, people go to government-run clinics for treatment.

One consequence of state control is that physicians are paid much less for their work than their counterparts in the United States; many doctors in the Russian Federation earn little more than skilled factory workers. Also worth noting is the fact that about 75 percent of the Russian Federation's doctors are women, compared with 30 percent in the United States.

In the 1990s, the Russian Federation suffered an economic decline. One result was a sharp drop in the health of the popu-

socialized medicine a medical care system in which the government owns and operates most medical facilities and employs most physicians

MAKING THE GRADE

Point to both strengths and weaknesses of our health care system when compared to that of Canada.

lation. There has been a rebound in the past few years, but life expectancy (especially for men) has actually fallen in recent decades. This decline has further strained a bureaucratic system that has long provided standardized and impersonal care. Perhaps, as market reforms proceed, the quality of medical services will rise with living standards. For the moment, however, health and health care in the Russian Federation are serious problems (Zuckerman, 2006; U.S. Census Bureau, 2008).

Capitalist Systems

Societies with mostly *capitalist economies* make health care—like other goods and services—available through a market system. In practice, this means that people purchase health care according to their individual needs and resources. But the high cost of health care can easily exceed the reach of even fairly well-off people, so capitalist nations such as Sweden, Great Britain, Canada, and Japan have additional strategies to help people cover the expense.

Sweden

Although the Swedish economy is mostly market-based, for more than a century, Sweden has taken the socialist approach that health care is a basic right for all citizens. The country raises money to fund its government-run health care system by taxation, making Swedish taxes among the highest in the world. Most physicians are government employees who receive salaries rather than collecting fees from patients. Government officials also manage most of the country's hospitals.

Because this system resembles that found in socialist countries, it is often called **socialized medicine**, *a medical care system in which the government owns and operates most medical facilities and employs most physicians.* How well does this system perform? The United Nations calculates a life expectancy index for world nations, which is a good measure of the overall health of a population. As Figure 9–2 shows, the level of health in Sweden is high, and all Swedes receive much the same quality of care.

Great Britain

Since 1948, Great Britain, too, has had a system of socialized medicine. However, the British did not do away with private care; rather, they created a dual system with government and private medical services operating side by side. The government's National Health Service, funded by tax money, provides care to all British citizens and pays for a physician's services, hospital stays, and prescription drugs. At the same time, people who are able to pay for it can also obtain the services of private doctors and hospitals. Many British doctors work both sides of the system, splitting their time between the National Health Service and private practice.

The British system does a fairly good job of providing basic care to everyone. However, because only some people can afford the best private care, the British system is marked by a measure of inequality.

Canada

In Canada, the government has a major part in health care, but it does not control health care directly, as in Sweden or Britain. In Canada, the government operates rather like a large insurance company. In this "single-payer" system, the government pays physicians and hospitals, with the funding coming from taxes. Like Great Britain, however, Canada permits doctors to work outside the government-funded system, setting their own fees for patients who can purchase care privately.

Figure 9–2 shows that public health in Canada is very good. The Canadian system also provides care at a lower cost than the U.S. system. Supporters point to Canada's success in holding the line on doctors' fees and hospital costs. Critics, however, note that

Dimensions of Difference

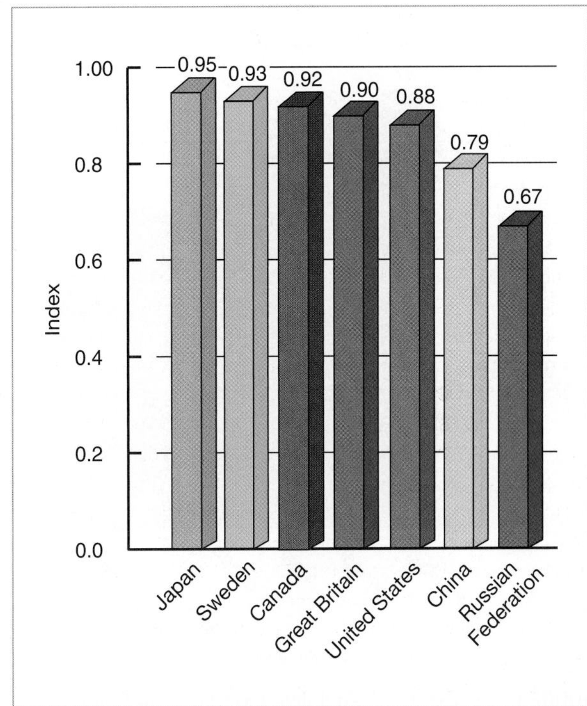

FIGURE 9–2 Life Expectancy Index for Selected Countries

Life expectancy in the United States is greater than what is typical of lower-income nations but less than that found in many other high-income nations.

Source: United Nations Development Programme (2008).

Where do you stand on the recent debate about national health care?

direct-fee system a medical care system in which patients or their insurers pay directly for the services of physicians and hospitals

Dimensions of Difference

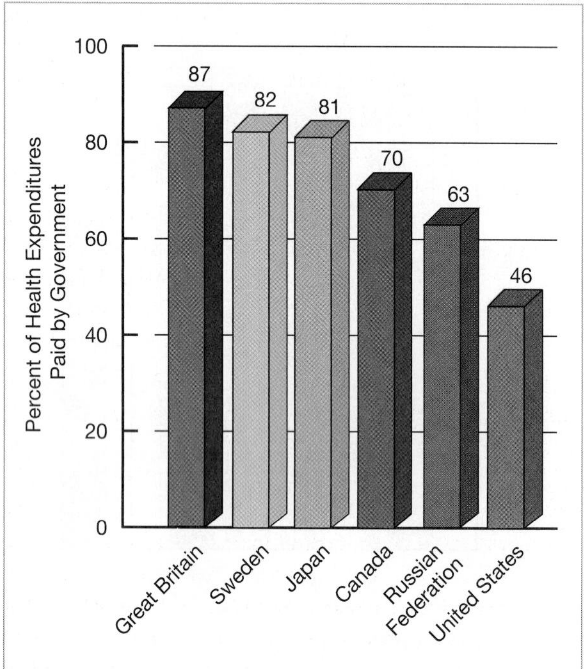

FIGURE 9–3 **Extent of Socialized Medicine in Selected Countries**

Compared with other high-income nations, government funding in the United States accounts for a far smaller share of health costs.

Source: World Bank (2009).

the lower costs reflect the fact that Canada uses less high-technology medicine, and the system is often slow to respond to people's needs. Often people must wait months to receive major surgery.

In short, Canada may not match the United States in providing the most cutting-edge procedures to some of its people, but it outperforms the United States in providing basic care to most of them (Rosenthal, 1991; United Nations Development Programme, 2005; Macionis & Gerber, 2008).

Japan

Physicians and hospitals in Japan operate privately in a market system. At the same time, a combination of government programs and private health insurance pays most medical costs. A glance back at Figure 9–2 shows that based on the life expectancy index, the Japanese get the highest mark for health of all the world's nations.

As Figure 9–3 shows, in Japan and the other countries we have surveyed, tax money is used by the government to pay most of the cost of medical care, which distributes the costs over the entire population, with people who earn more paying more in taxes. But one high-income nation stands out from the rest: the United States, which treats medical care not as a right but as a product to be purchased on the open market.

Health Care in the United States: A System in Crisis?

Beyond getting the economy back on track, if there is one thing the Obama administration promises to do in the next few years, it is overhaul the U.S. health care system. Why? One reason is that this country ranks below most other high-income nations when it comes to the health of the overall population. A second reason is that the United States spends more money per person for health care than any other country in the world.

Global comparisons show that the United States ranks only twenty-ninth in life expectancy (United Nations Development Programme, 2008). This places the United States below not only Canada and almost every country in Western Europe but also behind a number of less well-off nations, from Costa Rica in Latin America to Singapore in Asia. In addition, despite our country's unmatched wealth, the United States does not even make it onto the top twenty-five list of nations with the lowest infant mortality.

The U.S. health care system offers the best treatment in the world for people who can pay for it. But it does far less for the poor. What accounts for this mixed picture? The United States is the only high-income nation to rely on a **direct-fee system,** *a medical care system in which patients or their insurers pay directly for the services of physicians and hospitals.* In principle, people are free to shop for whatever health care they can afford, and hospitals and doctors compete with one another, offering various services and pricing.

According to some critics (typically, on the political left), the U.S. health care system is in a state of crisis. Two of the most pressing issues are soaring costs and access to heath care.

The Cost Problem

The cost of medical care in this country has soared in recent decades, from about $12 billion in 1950 to more than $2.5 trillion in 2010. Although the U.S. population has barely doubled in size since 1950, spending on health care has increased more than 200 times. Why has medical care become so expensive? There are six main reasons:

1. **The spread of private insurance.** Before World War II, most people in the United States paid for medical care out of their own pockets, so they went to doctors and hospitals only when

GETTING INVOLVED

How does the high cost of health care affect you and others in your family?

GETTING INVOLVED

Have you ever felt that you paid far too much for medical care? What was involved? Why do you think the costs were so high?

they had to. During World War II, companies began to offer health insurance to employees, partly as a way to attract new workers because wages were frozen by the government. After the war, in the 1950s and 1960s, the system of private insurance grew rapidly. More insurance meant that people received more medical care, but it also gave most people little reason to question the bills they received for prescription drugs, office visits, and hospital stays. Under these conditions, doctors and hospitals could benefit by pushing prices upward, and that's exactly what they did (P. Starr, 1982).

2. **More doctors who specialize.** With the growth of medical knowledge and advances in scientific technology, more doctors have chosen to specialize in limited areas of medicine, such as internal medicine, cancer treatment, or cosmetic surgery. Specialists also command higher fees, typically twice what a general practitioner receives. In a world of specialists, patients often end up seeing several physicians to treat a single problem and paying them all. Not surprisingly, the average income of physicians in the United States is now about $250,000 a year, more than twice the level it was in 1990 (Merritt Hawkins, 2008).
3. **More high technology**. The United States is a technology-oriented society. We favor high-tech medical treatments, such as computed axial tomography (CAT) scans to create images of internal organs and angioplasty to open clogged arteries. It is the advanced medical technologies that account for most of the rise in health care spending since 1950.

   With such a focus on high tech, we often overlook the value of everyday practices that promote good health, including changes in diet and exercise. This type of prevention costs little and is extremely effective in improving and maintaining well-being (Blank, 1997; Andrews, 2009).
4. **A lack of preventive care.** Many people, especially those with limited income, see doctors only when they face a medical crisis. People who go without preventive care, such as getting medication to control high blood pressure, often end up with a serious problem such as a stroke, which then requires a long and expensive hospital stay.
5. **An aging population.** As Chapter 5 ("Aging and Inequality") explains, the average age in the United States is on the rise. All the baby boomers—more than 75 million people born between 1945 and 1964—have entered middle age, so they are more concerned about their health just as they have more money to spend. Now that the boomers are starting to retire, they will surely face more medical problems and push medical spending ever higher.
6. **More lawsuits**. Many of us seem to believe that when accident or illness strikes, doctors and hospitals can always provide a cure. When treatment fails, patients or their families have become more and more likely to file a lawsuit, and this trend has driven up the cost of malpractice insurance, a cost that doctors pass along to patients. The fear of lawsuits raises costs in another way, too: Doctors who worry about being sued may order unnecessary tests and procedures just to protect themselves, a strategy of *defensive medicine* (Birenbaum, 1995).

Controlling Costs

In light of the rapidly rising costs of medical care in this country, both insurance companies and the public as a whole are looking for ways to keep a lid on medical costs. But what can be done?

A number of policies have been developed. One is *preadmission testing.* Doctors order blood work, X-rays, and other tests *before* deciding whether a patient needs to be admitted to a

One result of the high costs of prescription drugs in the United States is that more people are crossing our borders to shop in other countries. In the North, people make prescription "drug-runs" to Canada; this couple in the Southwest is traveling to visit a discount drug store in Mexico.

GETTING INVOLVED

Have you had a hospital stay in recent years? If so, what was the cost of the care?

MAKING THE GRADE

Notice below that most people in our society are covered by private health insurance.

hospital. There may be no reason to admit people to a hospital just to find out what the problem is.

A second policy is performing more *outpatient treatment*, meaning that the patient enters and leaves the hospital or clinic on the same day the procedure is performed. Minor procedures are routinely handled in this way, but many people also have surgery and cancer treatments on an outpatient basis.

A third practice is *regulating the length of hospitalization*. In this case, insurance companies limit the hospital stay for a particular condition. This gets patients home sooner, saving money. At the same time, limited hospital stays and outpatient treatment put a greater burden on families to care for people in the home.

What effect have these cost-containment measures had? Going by numbers alone, they have not brought about any reduction in this country's spending on medical care, an amount that continues to rise every year. But they have probably slowed the rate of increase.

Who Pays?

Every year, almost 35 million people in the United States enter the hospital, and they remain there, on average, for five days. The typical cost for this hospital care is about $8,000, plus several thousand more in doctors' fees (U.S. Census Bureau, 2010). Clearly, such medical costs are a financial burden few families can easily afford. Who ends up paying the bills?

As noted, in the United States, people are responsible for most of their own medical expenses. To cover the costs, most rely on various types of health insurance.

Private Insurance Programs

Private insurance companies, such as Blue Cross Blue Shield, sell policies to individuals and groups, usually through an employer. In 2009, some 195 million people (64 percent of the population) were covered by a private health insurance policy. Of that number, 87 percent received health insurance through an employer (their own or that of a family member); the remaining 13 percent bought policies on their own (U.S. Census Bureau, 2010).

Most employers require that people pay a share of the insurance premium. In addition, when people file claims, insurance companies rarely cover the entire bill. This means that insurance greatly reduces but does not eliminate the financial burden caused by a serious accident or illness.

Health Maintenance Organizations

Health maintenance organizations (HMOs) are *private insurance organizations that provide medical care to subscribers for a fixed fee.* In an effort to hold the line on costs, HMOs focus on disease prevention; they pay for weight-loss classes, immunizations, and treatments to help people quit smoking. But HMOs also limit patients' choices. As a type of *managed care,* HMOs require patients to choose their medical care providers from a list of participating professionals, which often forces people to use doctors they do not know. In addition, nonemergency care must be preapproved by a *primary care physician,* who diagnoses the patient, provides some treatment, and makes referrals to specialists.

In short, HMOs try to keep costs down through managed care—that is, by controlling the treatment process. In some cases, HMOs refuse to pay for a treatment altogether. For this reason, HMOs have become controversial.

Some 75 million individuals (25 percent of the U.S. population) are enrolled in HMOs (U.S. Census Bureau, 2010). Most have mixed feelings about their health plan, worrying that they will be denied needed treatment, and many fear that their doctors will select a course of treatment based on what the HMO will cover rather than what they really need. Many physicians confirm that HMO rules sometimes deny patients needed treatment. Such concerns have led some states to enact a patients' "bill of rights" that requires a health care provider to pay for a minimum level of care and to disclose all its policies regarding payment to consumers.

Thus the success of HMOs comes at a price. But most employers favor HMOs because they typically cost less than traditional private insurance programs (Hicks, 2006).

Government Insurance Programs

In the United States, the federal government pays much of the health costs for some categories of the population. In 1965, Congress enacted Medicare and Medicaid, tax-funded programs that pay part of the medical costs for the elderly, the poor, and the disabled.

Medicare is part of the Social Security system and serves people aged sixty-five or older as well as people of all ages who are totally and permanently disabled. In 2009, more than 43 million people (14 percent of the population) were enrolled in Medicare, more than 80 percent of them seniors over age sixty-five.

Medicaid serves poor people with special needs, including people who are blind, permanently disabled, pregnant, or aged or who live in families with dependent children. In 2009, some 48 million people (16 percent of the population) were enrolled in Medicaid. In addition, the nation's 12 million veterans (4 percent of the population) can obtain free care in government-operated hospitals (U.S. Census Bureau, 2010).

In all, about 31 percent of U.S. citizens receive medical benefits from the government. Yet these programs provide only limited benefits, which is why many people who are covered (especially by Medicare) purchase additional medical insurance from private companies. Those who rely entirely on govern-

GETTING INVOLVED

Do you have health insurance? Why do you think many young people do not have this protection?

SOCIAL PROBLEMS in Everyday Life

Which issue concerns you more—coverage or cost? Explain.

SOCIAL POLICY

The Price of Life: Sometimes Out of Reach

How would you feel about a government policy that says, "People who are rich will be healthy; people who are poor will not"? Does this sound fair to you? Elizabeth Hale does not think so. But as she sees it, this is how our medical system works.

Fifty-seven-year-old Elizabeth Hale has failing kidneys. As a result, three days a week, she must lie connected to a dialysis machine that cleans her blood, doing the work her kidneys no longer can. Because Hale has retired and has seen her savings and income decline in recent years, she relies on both Medicare (based on her disability) and Medicaid (because she is poor) to pay most of her medical bills.

To become healthy and end the dialysis, Hale needs a new kidney. But she will probably never get an organ transplant because she is too poor. Hospital officials explained that government assistance will pay for the surgery, but it covers just 80 percent of the cost of the antirejection drugs she would have to take for the rest of her life. According to hospital policy, Hale has to prove she can pay at least $1,500 toward the drugs before her name is even placed on the list to become an organ recipient. Hale shakes her head: "I have some money saved, but not that much. I am poor—who is going to lend me the money?"

Should being poor prevent people from receiving a needed organ transplant? Existing policy says it should. With donated organs in short supply, the argument goes, doctors and hospitals must restrict transplant surgery to "patients most likely to do well." They do not want to risk wasting an organ by transplanting it into a patient who may not be able to follow up with all the necessary treatment. That rules out someone who cannot afford the drugs needed after the operation.

Elizabeth Hale objects: "It doesn't seem right. If I had the money to pay for the drugs, they would give me the transplant." In simple terms, if she cannot get the kidney she needs, she will die too soon, simply because she is poor.

WHAT DO YOU THINK?

1. Do you think people without the means to pay for treatment, like Elizabeth Hale, should be kept off organ recipient lists? Why or why not?
2. Would you describe Hale's situation as discrimination against the poor or simply a sensible decision about using a limited resource?
3. Should a society provide medical care on the basis of need or ability to pay? Develop arguments for and against both positions.

Source: Adapted from Kaukas (1999).

ment programs may find that their coverage falls far short of their needs, as the Social Policy box explains.

The Coverage Problem

Most people who have medical insurance may be unable to pay all the costs when they are faced with a serious condition. But that's only part of the problem. More serious still is the fact that some 51 million people—about 17 percent of the population—have no medical coverage at all.

One reason for the large population without insurance is that employers have been cutting back on benefits provided to workers. Several decades ago, most jobs in the United States offered vacation pay, sick leave, a retirement program, and health insurance. Today, fewer jobs offer all these benefits, and more offer none at all. This trend leaves many workers to fend for themselves.

The larger question is whether the United States should remain the only high-income country in the world without a universal health care program. In 1994, the Clinton administration proposed a sweeping program of health care reform by which the government would ensure that everyone had medical insurance. The Clinton "managed competition" plan required employers to provide coverage to employees; employers could bargain with various providers to get the best plan. People not covered in this way (including those out of work) would be given insurance directly by the government.

Congress rejected the Clinton reforms, concluding that they would push medical spending even higher than it was already. In addition, critics objected to putting health under the control of a new government bureaucracy instead of doctors and patients.

After winning control of Congress in 2006, Democrats indicated a desire to move closer to universal coverage. With the 2008 election of President Barack Obama, who has made extending health care coverage to everyone a key priority, it seems likely that change will occur in the next year or two, with government having a larger role in health care and coverage extended to more people.

Health: Class, Ethnicity, and Race

The health of affluent people in the United States is among the best in the world. But many U.S. poor people are no better off than people who live in the world's low-income nations. For

GETTING INVOLVED

How have your class position and your race and ethnicity shaped your own patterns of health?

prenatal care health care for women during pregnancy

Very thin fashion models are commonplace in the mass media. In the belief that these images increase the rate of eating disorders among young women, several European countries have recently banned such displays. Would you support similar restrictions here in the United States? Why or why not?

example, life expectancy among the Oglala Sioux Indians of South Dakota—among the poorest people in the United States—is just sixty-six years for women and fifty-six years for men. By contrast, life expectancy in the low-income Asian nation of Sri Lanka is seventy-five years for women and sixty-seven years for men (Winslow, 1997; Population Reference Bureau, 2009).

Chapter 2 ("Poverty and Wealth") pointed out that roughly 44 million people in the United States—14.3 percent of the population—live below the poverty line. Most poor people cannot afford a healthful diet. Poor nutrition, in turn, leaves people (especially children) less able to fight off infectious diseases. But poverty harms health in other ways as well. Poor people are likely to live in a crowded and often unsafe environment marked by stress and violence. They may not have adequate heating and cooling, they may be exposed to poisoning from lead-based paint, and they suffer from a higher rate of accidents. National Map 9–1 presents a health assessment for people across the United States.

Research confirms the strong connection between class and health. When researchers asked people living in high-income families (those earning at least $75,000 annually) about their health, 80 percent reported it as "excellent" or "very good." By contrast, only 48 percent of low-income people (family income under $20,000) said the same (Adams et al., 2008).

This difference helps explain the fact that African Americans, who are three times as likely to be poor as white people, die an average of four years earlier than whites. Figure 9–4 on page 248 provides life expectancy data for black and white men and women born in 2009. Black men fare the worst of all because poverty is a cause of poor health and being male puts these men at greater risk of violence. This helps explain the fact that the leading cause of death among African American men between the ages of fifteen and thirty-four is homicide (Kochanek et al., 2011). To get a better sense of how serious a health problem violence is in the African American community, note that in 2007 alone, 2,905 African Americans were killed by others of their own race—seven times the number of black soldiers killed in the Iraq war (Federal Bureau of Investigation, 2008).

The harmful effects of poverty begin early in life, often before birth. Because African Americans suffer from both higher poverty and higher unemployment, these families have less access to health insurance. One result is that African American women are more than twice as likely as white women to go without **prenatal care,** *health care for women during pregnancy,* and to have low-birthweight infants at high risk of dying soon after birth (Martin et al., 2009).

Racial bias plays a part in patterns of health even for African Americans who are not poor. For example, research shows that people of color often receive less thorough medical treatment than whites. One study, which focused on men who complained to doctors about chest pain, found that doctors were 40 percent less likely to order advanced tests for African Americans than for white patients with exactly the same symptoms, a racial bias that contributes to higher death rates (J. E. White, 1999a).

Health: The Importance of Gender

The numbers say that women have a health advantage over men: Figure 9–4 shows that on average, women outlive men by at least five years. Notice that despite having a much higher level of poverty, African American women have a higher life expectancy than white men. Such facts highlight the importance of gender to human health.

Gender affects the health of both men and women. One important factor is the way U.S. culture defines masculinity. Our society encourages men to be more individualistic and aggressive, placing them at higher risk of accidents, violence, and suicide. Such factors help explain men's lower life expectancy.

Parker Jeeter lives in McCurtain County, Oklahoma, a low-income community, where health problems are common among his neighbors.

Marina Treleaven lives in an affluent neighborhood of Chester County, Pennsylvania, where health indicators are well above the national average.

disability a physical or mental condition that limits everyday activities

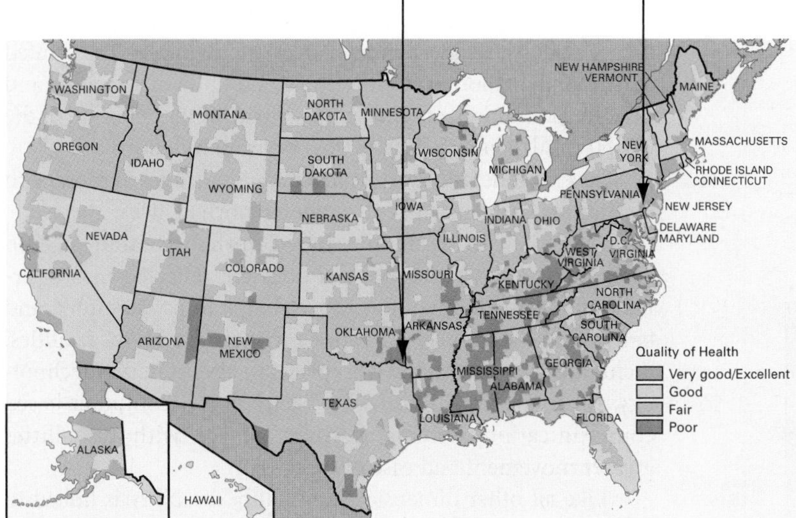

A Nation of Diversity

NATIONAL MAP 9–1

Health across the United States

Average health varies from place to place throughout the United States. This map shows the results of a survey that asked people across the country about their personal health, including their smoking habits, nutritional diet, and frequency of illness. Looking at the map, what pattern do you see? Can you explain it?

Source: American Demographics, October 2000, p. 50. Reprinted with permission from American Demographics. © 2004 by Crain Communications, Inc.

But gender works against women too. Because women have lower social standing than men, women have often been ignored by medical researchers. For years, most research on heart disease, smoking, and the effects of medications was conducted only on male subjects. The result is that doctors know far less about the needs of women and how women respond to many treatments. This is why in 1990, the National Institutes of Health (NIH) created the Office of Research on Women's Health, a government agency that directs attention to women's health issues (Hafner-Eaton, 1994).

Some old ways of thinking about gender, even among modern scientists, also distort medical treatment. Some critics claim that doctors turn normal life events, such as menopause, into medical "problems" that require long-term medication. In addition, they argue, women's health problems are sometimes not treated as aggressively as men's problems. For example, heart disease is the second leading killer (behind cancer) of women ages forty-five to seventy-four. According to the American Heart Association, however, doctors provide less care for women than for men with the same symptoms of heart disease.

Physicians also offer women less counseling about proper nutrition, exercise, and weight loss. Why? Perhaps because many doctors associate heart disease with men, they overlook potential problems in women. Today, 30 percent of physicians are women, and as the share continues to rise, doctors and hospitals should respond better to women's concerns (U.S. Department of Labor, 2008).

An Illustration: Eating Disorders

A good illustration of the power of gender in shaping health involves eating disorders. In the United States, as many as 10 million people suffer from eating disorders, and about 90 percent of them are female (National Institute of Mental Health, 2008).

Experts estimate that about 2 percent of teenage girls suffer from *anorexia*, a form of compulsive dieting that leads people to eat too little to maintain a healthy body weight. Another 3 percent suffer from *bulimia,* a disease that involves binge-purge cycles of eating large amounts of food at one sitting and then purging by taking laxatives or inducing vomiting in order to avoid gaining weight (Duffy, 1999; National Institute of Mental Health, 2008).

How is gender linked to eating disorders? The social roots of this disease lie in a culture that defines women's value in terms of physical attractiveness. In addition, girls grow up learning to judge their looks and their self-worth against an unrealistic, media-based image of thinness and beauty. Because these beliefs are so deeply held, eating disorders are difficult to cure and often end up causing serious health problems, including kidney damage, brittle bones, life-threatening infections, heart disease, and in extreme cases, death (Duffy, 1999; Lerner, 1999).

People with Disabilities

We have noted that people with lower social standing—women, minorities, and the poor—in the United States have greater health problems. Another category that struggles with the health care system is people with any **disability,** *a physical or mental condition that limits everyday activities.*

To medical professionals, a disability is some impairment to the functioning of the mind or body. For sociologists, the question is how people construct the reality of a disability, that is, how people react to having a disability and how others react

SOCIAL PROBLEMS in Everyday Life

How much does your college or university do to accommodate students with physical disabilities?

SOCIAL PROBLEMS in Everyday Life

Ask officials at your campus office that assists students with disabilities what share of students at your college claim to have learning disabilities.

Dimensions of Difference

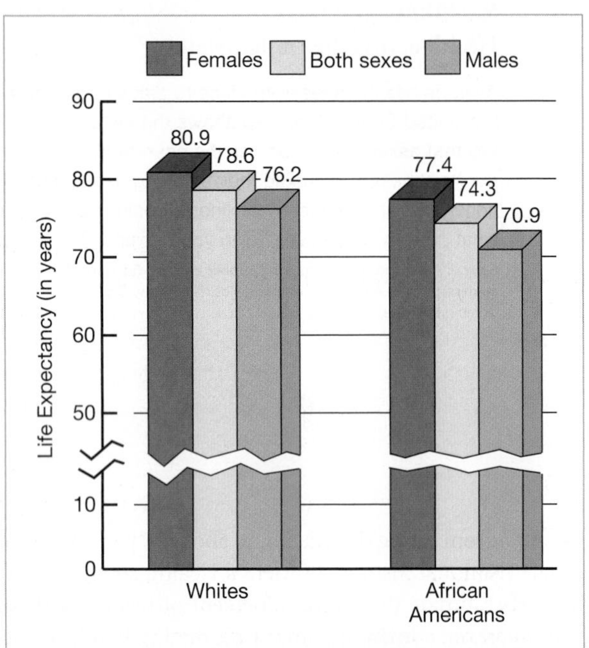

FIGURE 9–4 Life Expectancy for U.S. Children Born in 2009

On average, whites live longer than African Americans and women live longer than men.

Source: Kochanek et al. (2011)

to them. Therefore, sociologists investigate how physical barriers, prejudice, and discrimination affect the everyday lives of people with disabilities.

Sociologists note that physical disability often operates as a *master status*, meaning that other people may overlook a person's abilities and see only the disability. Thinking this way, people sometimes assume that those with physical disabilities must therefore have other limitations—such as low intelligence—and treat them accordingly.

Because there is no precise definition of disability, there is no exact count of people who are challenged in this way. One government tally estimates that about 4 percent of children, 10 percent of people aged eighteen to sixty-four, and 37 percent of the elderly suffer from some disability (U.S. Census Bureau, 2010). This number is rising, partly because medical advances now save infants with birth defects who would have died several decades ago. The same is true for adults who suffer serious accidents and soldiers wounded in battle—many more who have lost a limb or sustained other serious injury now survive but with a permanent disability. More generally, because people in the United States are living longer, more people end up with a chronic and disabling condition, ranging from arthritis (inflammation of the joints) to Alzheimer's disease (loss of brain function).

Several generations ago, most people considered those with disabilities to be incapable of living normal lives; therefore, most people with disabilities ended up housebound or even bedridden. Today's changed attitudes are reflected in barrier-free architecture—including wheelchair ramps, elevators, and bathrooms—that give everyone greater access to facilities, including schools and the workplace. In addition, new technology, ranging from motorized wheelchairs to computer-based communication systems, permits people with disabilities greater movement and ease of expression.

Like all other dimensions of health, disability is linked to income. People with a severe disability have a poverty rate (27 percent) that is three time the rate for people with no disability (9 percent) (Brault, 2008).

Disability Legislation

In 1990, the disability rights movement, a political organization seeking to expand the rights and opportunities of people with disabilities, was successful in convincing Congress to pass the Americans with Disabilities Act (ADA). This law outlawed discrimination against people with disabilities in employment and public accommodations, including hotels, theaters, restaurants, and stores.

Proponents call the ADA the most important civil rights legislation since the 1964 Civil Rights Act, which banned discrimination based on race and sex. When President George H. W. Bush signed the bill into law, he expressed his hope that the act would make most public places accessible to people with disabilities. But two decades later, there is still work to do, as many people with disabilities have trouble riding a bus, attending school, watching a sports event, or even eating in a restaurant.

In 1997, the federal government expanded the definition of "disability" beyond physical problems to include a host of conditions from mental illness to learning disabilities to fear of open places. As a result, schools, colleges, and employers are engaged in debates about how to diagnose these disabilities and other conditions and what proper accommodations may be. In 2000, the U.S. Supreme Court narrowed the definition of a disability to exclude impairments that can be corrected or do not substantially limit everyday activities (Fujiura, 2001).

The Nursing Shortage

An additional problem facing the U.S. medical care system is a shortage of nurses. In 2007, there were 2.5 million registered nurses (people with an R.N. degree) in the United States, with

mental disorder a condition involving thinking, mood, or behavior that causes distress and reduces a person's ability to function in everyday life

MAKING THE GRADE

Be sure you understand Thomas Szasz's theory and criticisms of it.

116,000 positions unfilled. This shortage is projected to double by 2020 (U.S. Department of Labor, 2008).

What accounts for the shortage? Part of the answer is that fewer people are choosing to become nurses. Although the number of people earning bachelor's degrees in nursing has been going up, many of these graduates do not end up making nursing their career. One reason is that the range of jobs open to women has greatly increased, so fewer women are drawn to the traditionally female occupation of nursing. In addition, many of today's nurses are unhappy with their jobs: Many cite heavy patient loads, required overtime, a stressful working environment, and a lack of respect from supervisors, physicians, and hospital managers. Most working nurses say they would not recommend nursing to others, and many are leaving the field for other jobs.

Given the high demand, salaries are increasing. Currently, general-duty nurses earn about $62,000 a year, and many nurses with specialized skills (such as nurse-anesthetists) are making $100,000 a year. Many hospitals and private practice physicians offer hiring bonuses to nurses. Finally, nursing programs are seeking to recruit more minorities as well as more men, who currently account for just 8 percent of R.N.'s (Marquez, 2006; American Association of Colleges of Nursing, 2008; U.S. Department of Labor, 2008).

Mental Health and Illness

A **mental disorder** is *a condition involving thinking, mood, or behavior that causes distress and reduces a person's ability to function in everyday life* (U.S. Department of Health and Human Services, 1999:vii). According to the American Psychiatric Association, there are more than 300 different mental disorders, including anxiety disorders, mood disorders, eating disorders, sleep disorders, personality disorders, and mental retardation.

About 58 million adults (roughly one in four) suffer from a diagnosable mental illness in any given year, and nearly half of U.S. adults (100 million people) do so at some point in their lives. Most of these disorders are of minor importance and do not threaten a person's long-term well-being. But one-third of U.S. adults have at least one serious mental problem, such as approaching a nervous breakdown. Keep in mind that our lack of understanding concerning mental illness probably discourages many people who are suffering from a mental disorder from seeking treatment (U.S. Department of Health and Human Services, 2008).

The experience of mental illness varies but may include extreme anxiety and fear, wild elation, mood swings, panic attacks, debilitating depression, or even hallucinations. Such symptoms are clearly troubling in themselves, but they also lead to other problems, ranging from strain in relationships to child neglect to outright violence.

For society as a whole, losses due to mental illness approach $200 billion annually, mostly in terms of lost workplace productivity. The government estimates that the cost to our society from mental illness is greater than that caused by all forms of cancer (U.S. Department of Health and Human Services, 2008).

As noted at the start of this chapter, mental illness provokes much confusion and fear. Why? Perhaps it is because some mental disorders prompt people to do the unexpected, which frightens or disorients us. It is also true that all of us—doctors included—know much less about mental illness than about physical ailments. As a result, although we might not stigmatize someone for having a broken leg or other physical ailment, people often do just that to those with mental disorders. We might label a person who experiences severe mood swings as "strange" or claim that someone who experiences hallucinations from time to time is "crazy." This type of stigma serves to socially isolate the person, which usually makes the problem worse.

Types of Mental Disorders

Effective treatment of any illness depends on accurate diagnosis. The most widely used classification of mental disorders, prepared by the American Psychiatric Association (2000), is the fourth edition of the *Diagnostic and Statistical Manual of Mental Disorders* (DSM-IV-TR). The DSM includes a wide range of disorders, as shown in Table 9–1 on page 250.

As noted in the table, some mental disorders, such as those resulting from drug use, have an immediate cause. But most have many causes, both biological and social. In other words, people are born with a higher or lower risk of certain mental disorders, but social experiences beginning in childhood also play an important part in shaping everyone's mental health.

Mental Illness: A Myth?

Because mental disorders and their many causes are not well understood, a few specialists in the field claim that they do not exist. The psychiatrist Thomas Szasz charges that people apply the label of "insanity" to behavior they find disturbing when in reality these patterns are only "different."

Consider a man who stands on a city street corner, shouting that God has told him that the end of the world is near. This action may be unusual, and if the man is jumping up and down, people standing nearby might even become a bit alarmed. But who is to say that the man is wrong? And whether he is right or not, is he mentally ill or just expressing his deep religious convictions?

GETTING INVOLVED

Have you ever done something "crazy" that really disturbed other people? What did they do about it? Have you responded to "craziness" on the part of others? Explain.

Notice in the discussion below how poverty and mental illness can form a vicious cycle.

Szasz argues that people are quick to condemn as "crazy" behavior that fails to conform to conventional norms, and he has spent his life arguing that we should give up the whole idea of mental illness (1961, 1970, 1994, 1995). As he sees it, an illness is real only if it affects the body in a way we can see. In the absence of some physical abnormality, then, mental "illness" is simply a myth.

Szasz's claim is controversial, and most of his colleagues in the field of psychiatry reject the notion that mental illness is fiction. Still, many mental health professionals hail his work for pointing out the danger of using medicine to promote conformity. From time to time, just about everyone behaves in ways that disturb others. But does this give others the right to force us to change? In addition, responding to "difference" with medical labels that stigmatize can do a great deal of harm—in the extreme, by defining those who are different as less than fully human.

Mental Illness: Class, Race, and Gender

The pattern found throughout this chapter—that disadvantaged categories of people are more likely to suffer from illness—applies to mental as well as physical health. Let's take a closer look at patterns of mental health linked to class, race, and gender.

Mental Health and Class

One of the earliest studies to document the link between class position and mental health dates to before World War II. Robert E. Faris and H. Warren Dunham (1939) traced 35,000 people living in Chicago who had received psychiatric care from private and public mental institutions and they found that most of the people with serious disorders lived in the worst slums. This link between poverty and mental illness has been confirmed again and again by research over the decades since then, both in the United States and in other countries (Hollingshead & Redlich, 1958; Srole et al., 1962; Rushing, 1969; Levy & Rowitz, 1973; Srole, 1975; Eaton, 1980; Mirowsky & Ross, 1983; Ross, Mirowsky, & Cockerham, 1983; Wiersma et al., 1983).

An interesting question to consider is whether mental illness causes poverty, or is it the other way around? It is easy to see that mental illness reduces people's ability to earn a living. But Faris and Dunham documented the power of poverty to cause mental illness. Poverty breeds stress and social isolation, they explained, which in turn increases the risk of mental disorders. As others have confirmed, the isolation and stigma associated with being poor in the United States may by itself be enough to harm the mental health of many people (Cockerham, 2007).

Table 9–1 Categories of Mental Disorders Listed in the *Diagnostic and Statistical Manual of Mental Disorders*

Disorders usually first diagnosed in infancy, childhood, or adolescence	Mental retardation, attention deficit hyperactivity disorder, dyslexia, stuttering, autism, Tourette syndrome, and bed-wetting
Cognitive disorders	Delirium and dementia: major changes in memory or the ability to think clearly, caused by brain damage or substance abuse
Mental disorders due to a medical condition that are not included in other categories	Symptoms such as delirium, dementia, amnesia, and sexual dysfunction that are a direct result of another medical condition
Substance-related disorders	Disorders such as intoxication, addiction, and withdrawal resulting from the use of alcohol or other drugs, such as heroin, cocaine, and amphetamines
Schizophrenia and other psychotic disorders	Disorders characterized by extreme paranoia, delusions, and hallucinations
Mood disorders	Major depression and bipolar disorder (manic depression)
Anxiety disorders	Obsessive-compulsive disorder and disorders characterized by extreme anxiety, panic, or phobia
Somatoform disorders	Disorders that manifest themselves as symptoms of physical disease, such as pain of an unidentifiable origin or hypochondria
Dissociative disorders	Disorders that involve a splitting or dissociation of normal consciousness, such as amnesia or multiple personality
Eating or sleeping disorders	Anorexia, bulimia, and insomnia
Sexual and gender identity disorders	An absence of sexual desire, the inability to function sexually, masochism, sadism, and gender identity disorders such as transsexualism
Impulse control disorders	Disorders that manifest themselves in symptoms such as kleptomania (theft), pyromania (setting fires), and pathological gambling
Personality disorders	Chronic, inflexible, and maladaptive personality traits that are resistant to treatment, such as excessive dependency, paranoia, and narcissism (the need for constant admiration and a lack of empathy)

Source: American Psychiatric Association (2000).

MAKING THE GRADE

Be sure you understand the effects of class, race, and gender on mental health.

SOCIAL PROBLEMS in Everyday Life

The discussion of various treatment strategies shows different ways of "defining the solution" to mental illness.

Mental Health and Race

Sociologists have documented the lack of jobs that weakens many inner-city communities in the United States. People who struggle economically and who are socially isolated by both low income and racial prejudice contend with high levels of stress and anxiety. This is the reality of life for many African Americans in the United States (W. J. Wilson, 1987; E. Anderson, 1994; Feagin & Sikes, 1994; Feagin & Hernán, 1995).

That said, research shows that race, by itself, does not seem to play a major part in patterns of mental health. When studies have compared people of roughly the same social class position, the findings showed that African Americans and whites have comparable levels of mental health (Williams, Takeuchi, & Adair, 1992; Kessler et al., 1994; Cockerham, 2007).

One interesting pattern is that people of Asian and also of Hispanic descent have a more favorable pattern of mental health. It is possible that cultural differences and language barriers discourage some Asians and Latinos from seeking treatment, so mental disorders may be underreported. But it is also true that even among people with low incomes, the strong family ties common in many Asian and Hispanic communities may help maintain mental health (U.S. Department of Health and Human Services, 2008).

Finally, American Indians have higher than average levels of alcoholism, suicide, and mental illness. Numerous social factors play a part in this pattern, including very high rates of unemployment and poverty, which account for a sense of despair that exists in many Native American communities (Cockerham, 2007).

Mental Health and Gender

Research shows that women and men have about the same rates of mental illness. However, members of our society are quicker to define women as mentally ill. Because women are a less powerful category of the population, when they violate conventional norms, they are at higher risk of being labeled as deviant. As the category with more power, men have more freedom to behave as they wish without people calling their mental health into question. Further, given the way society defines the lives of women and men, we should not be surprised to learn that women—who feel they must constantly worry about pleasing others—have higher rates of some mental disorders, notably anxiety and depression (Chesler, 1989; Schur, 1984).

At the same time, masculinity has some risks of its own. Because U.S. culture defines "real men" as independent, tough, unemotional, and always in control, some males endure considerable stress and social isolation, both of which contribute to poor mental health. When men try to contain their troubles (as "real men" are taught to do), the problems only become worse. Perhaps this is one reason that men have higher rates of certain personality disorders involving aggression and substance abuse (Aneshensel, Rutter, & Lachenbruch, 1991; Gupta, 1993; Kessler et al., 1994).

Treatment Strategies

Looking back to the Middle Ages in Europe, people commonly viewed individuals with the symptoms of mental illness as possessed by demons or suffering punishment by God. Therefore, while a few mentally ill people were tolerated as "village idiots," many more were burned as witches (Cockerham, 2005).

By about 1600, a new strategy arose for dealing with mentally ill people: locking them away in prisons with criminals and the poor. This era, sometimes called the Great Confinement, found people with mental disorders chained to walls or beds in dark, damp, rat-infested rooms, often without clothing or blankets, for years at a time (Foucault, 1965; Cockerham, 2005).

Reform came in the 1800s in large part because of the efforts of one woman, Dorothea Dix of the United States. The

We have all heard people call someone "crazy" for acting in a way that people find disturbing. Is such a label really an effort to discredit and control those who simply are different?

psychotherapy an approach to mental health in which patients talk with trained professionals to gain insight into the cause of their problems

deinstitutionalization the release of people from mental hospitals into local communities

SOCIAL PROBLEMS in Everyday Life

What resources to treat mental illness are found on your campus?

Defining Moment box takes a closer look at how Dix changed the way society viewed people with mental illness.

Dix popularized the idea that people with mental illnesses should receive caring treatment and not be shut away in prisons. Her efforts spread the concept of the asylum, a place of refuge and an early version of today's mental hospital. Unfortunately, the number of people who needed this kind of help was far greater than the number of facilities available. As a result, only a small share of people with mental illness received the humane care that Dix knew they all needed. Most were locked away in overcrowded prisons, out of sight and out of mind.

The twentieth century saw the development of several new treatment strategies. One important advance was **psychotherapy,** *an approach to mental health in which patients talk with trained professionals to gain insight into the cause of their problems.* The famous psychologist Sigmund Freud (1856–1939) played an important part in the rise of psychotherapy, and other practitioners have developed psychotherapy in various directions ever since.

Medical approaches also gained prominence during this time. One example is electroshock therapy, which was found to provide patients with temporary relief from severe depression. But the most important medical treatment was the development of *psychoactive drugs*, powerful substances that control symptoms of mental illness. Once these drugs came on the market in the 1950s, it was no longer necessary to confine people in institutions in order to control them. In 1963, Congress passed the Community Mental Health Centers Construction Act, a plan to move people out of big institutions and into communities where they could find outpatient treatment at local health centers.

This law set off a stampede of **deinstitutionalization,** *the release of people from mental hospitals into local communities.* In just a few years, hundreds of thousands of men and women were released from mental hospitals based on claims that they could get by on their own as long as they took their drugs. But not everyone did take their drugs. In addition, not enough community health centers were built. Within a few years, many former patients ended up back in mental hospitals, in prison, or living on the streets (Roche, 2000b). The Personal Stories box on page 255 describes an all-too-typical case.

Today, fewer than half of people suffering from mental disorders are receiving regular treatment (U.S. Department of Health and Human Services, 2008). Why is the percentage so low? There are too few community mental health centers, and too many people lack health insurance. In addition, many people who are struggling don't want to admit that they have a mental health problem.

One response by the government was the 1997 law that expanded the Americans with Disabilities Act to include mental disorders. The law requires employers to make reasonable efforts to accommodate workers who suffer from depression, anxiety, or other mental disorders. Although this is not always easy, our society is now more successful in supporting people with mild mental illness in their everyday lives.

Mental Illness on Campus

It is no surprise to college faculty that the number of students who suffer from mental health problems is increasing. According to the American College Health Association (2009), about 30 percent of college students in the United States report having been so depressed that they could not do their work; 87 percent admit to feeling overwhelmed from time to time. Across the country, colleges are seeing a sharp rise in student demand for counseling.

Most serious is the problem of suicide. Experts estimate that about 19 percent of students have thought seriously about suicide, and about 8 percent of students have attempted it, although the vast majority do not succeed (American College Health Association, 2009).

What accounts for the increase in mental health problems on campus? Everyone agrees that colleges are not the main cause of the trend. Experts point to a number of other factors, including high rates of children living in poverty, rising pressures on today's young people, and low levels of parental involvement in children's lives. In addition, psychoactive drugs make it possible for more young people with mental health problems to attend college. Once on campus, however, they may not take their medications properly or may find the demands of college work to be too great. Faced with an increasing challenge, colleges are trying to define their proper role in providing health care for their students (Fujiura, 2001; Kelly, 2001; Shea, 2002).

Theoretical Analysis: Understanding Health Problems

Each of sociology's major theoretical approaches helps us understand problems of physical and mental health. As you have seen in earlier chapters, each approach focuses on different aspects of the problems and points toward different conclusions.

Structural-Functional Analysis: Health and Social Roles

The structural-functional approach views our lives as a complex system of roles and responsibilities that, taken together,

sick role a pattern of behavior expected of people defined as ill

How did Dorothea Dix change our society's understanding of mental illness and its treatment?

CONSTRUCTING SOCIAL PROBLEMS

A DEFINING MOMENT

Dorothea Dix: Mentally Ill People Deserve Our Help

Dorothea Dix (1802–1887) was an extraordinary woman who made a difference. She began her career in an ordinary way, teaching at a girls' school. She rose to become head of the school, but at that point in her life, Dix's attention turned to prisons.

She was shocked to learn that the prison population included not only criminals but also people with mental illness—people who were sick and had broken no law. Dix was deeply concerned about the uncaring treatment given to these innocent people. She pledged to change the way society viewed people with mental illness and devoted the remainder of her life to writing, speaking, and lobbying government officials.

In 1840, when Dix began her crusade, the United States had only thirteen facilities that offered care to people with mental illness. Because of her efforts, twenty states passed laws creating what came to be known as the *asylum*: a place where troubled people could find shelter and peace. By 1885, near the end of Dix's life, she could boast that there were 125 asylums in the United States.

Dix is remembered today as the person, more than anyone else, who opened people's hearts to those with mental illness. Rather than locking these people away, she showed society that people with illnesses need help and compassion, whether their illness affects the body or the mind.

For centuries, people with mental illness were locked up in prisons with dangerous criminals. Dorothea Dix pioneered the building of asylums, where such people could find protection and treatment. Unfortunately, many asylums were no more than warehouses that did little to improve the condition of those locked within.

keep society running smoothly. Illness interferes with our ability to carry out our roles as workers and as members of families. Consequently, when we are sidelined by illness, society allows us to assume the **sick role**, *a pattern of behavior expected of people defined as ill.* In practice, the sick role means that people are *not* expected to carry out routine, day-to-day duties and responsibilities. As long as people are not to blame for their illness, explains Talcott Parsons (1951), the sick role excuses them from most everyday obligations. At the same time, the patient must try to get well by cooperating with medical personnel.

This theory helps explain why some members of U.S. society feel little sympathy for people with mental disorders

GETTING INVOLVED

Have you ever claimed being ill partly due to schoolwork or some other obligation you couldn't meet?

GETTING INVOLVED

Some researchers have noted the widening use of the term "depressed" (Horwitz & Wakefield, 2005). How often have you described yourself as "depressed"? Do you think you were clinically depressed or just feeling lonely or sad?

when these people are living on the streets. If people are sick, they deserve help, but if it seems that they do not want treatment—and some people see living on the streets as evidence of that—then they deserve no special assistance. Keep in mind, however, that people may be on the streets because they have no money to pay for treatment; similarly, refusing to cooperate with medical personnel might be one symptom of a mental illness.

The structural-functional approach also explains that social institutions are linked, with changes in one affecting others. From this point of view, problems of health often result from changes in other social institutions. For example, changes in the family include more people living alone and more single parenting. These trends mean that people have less access to caregiving, which can undermine health. In addition, when illness strikes, sick people are more likely to turn to health care professionals to meet their needs.

CRITICAL REVIEW Some illness is to be expected, and the sick role is a way society supports people while they recover from illness and also encourages them to seek medical treatment. However, taking on the sick role depends on a person's being able to afford to take time off work and to seek medical care.

Another limitation of the structural-functional approach is implying that doctors hold the key to good health. The trend toward prevention highlights the fact that people can make choices to improve their own health by, for example, eating a balanced diet, exercising, and avoiding dangerous behavior such as abusing alcohol and other drugs.

Finally, health is not a simple matter of being "sick" or "well." On the contrary, the reality of health is highly variable, a fact that brings us to the symbolic-interaction approach.

Symbolic-Interaction Analysis: The Meaning of Health

The symbolic-interaction approach highlights how people construct reality in their everyday lives. In many parts of the world, for example, poor families consider inadequate nutrition and hunger to be a normal part of life. On the other hand, people in rich nations have become much more accepting of obesity; in the United States, two-thirds of adults weigh more than they should (National Center for Health Statistics, 2005b). Obviously, what is considered "normal"—with regard to both physical and mental health—depends not only on medical fact but also on cultural standards that vary from place to place and time to time.

The variable reality of health and illness is also evident in constantly changing definitions used by medical professionals. For example, in the first half of the twentieth century, doctors defined homosexuality not as an illness but as a moral wrong, and the public followed their lead. In 1952, however, the first edition of the *Diagnostic and Statistical Manual of Mental Disorders* defined homosexuality as a "personality disorder," so homosexuality became a form of mental illness. In 1974, the definition changed again when the DSM dropped homosexuality from its list of disorders. It is now considered simply one sexual orientation (Conrad & Schneider, 1980; Livingston, 1999).

Finally, how people define any health situation may in fact affect how they feel physically. Doctors have long noted the existence of *psychosomatic* disorders, in which the mind seems to affect the body. When people believe they are sick or when they are convinced that they will get well, their belief often comes true.

CRITICAL REVIEW Because the symbolic-interaction approach highlights the variable meanings people attach to health and illness, it tends to ignore structural factors such as gender and wealth that play a major part in shaping the reality that people experience. For example, the importance of gender is shown in the fact that people stigmatize women more than men for having a sexually transmitted disease. Similarly, people tend to blame those with low incomes for having poor health, rather than asking why the U.S. medical care system does not provide more for poor people or why tens of millions of people in the United States are poor in the first place. Such issues bring us to the social-conflict approach.

Social-Conflict Analysis: Health and Inequality

The social-conflict approach links health to inequality. A basic pattern, found in the United States and around the world, is that people with more wealth have better health. Social-conflict analysis points to various ways in which social inequality shapes health and health care in the United States.

Perhaps the most basic issue is access to care. If good health is necessary to be a productive member of society, health care should be available to all. Yet as this chapter has explained, the United States stands alone among rich nations as having no system to guarantee care to everyone. In short, by linking care to the ability to pay, this country undermines the health of millions of people.

A second issue is that in a capitalist economy, medical practice is based on the profit motive. This fact goes a long way toward explaining why the United States overlooks the health of the poor, who, by definition, have little money to pay for it.

SOCIAL PROBLEMS in Everyday Life

What do you think of requiring people living on the street to get help at a mental health clinic? Explain.

SOCIAL PROBLEMS in Everyday Life

Do you think the health of our population is getting better than it was fifty years ago? Why? What has changed?

PERSONAL STORIES

Deinstitutionalization: When Good Intentions Have Bad Results

Mary Lee leans forward over the shopping cart that holds everything she owns. It is getting dark, and the fifty-nine-year-old woman pulls her coat tight against the cold, lowers her head, and pushes ahead into the icy wind. She is looking for a ventilation grate, where she can try to stay warm for the night without having to see anyone.

Mary Lee grew up in a poor farming family in Iowa. Her parents worked hard and were often impatient with their daughter, who could be disruptive in school. Unable to discipline her, the parents turned to a doctor for help. Mary recalls telling the doctor that as long as she could remember, she had "heard voices." The doctor decided that Mary was mentally ill and declared her to be suffering from paranoid schizophrenia, with symptoms including paranoia, anxiety, and hallucinations.

Her parents and the doctor agreed that Mary should be sent to a large state mental hospital, where she spent the next five years. Every day, the staff gave her chlorpromazine, a powerful psychoactive drug, to calm her. Mary recalls that the chlorpromazine stopped her fears and ended the hallucinations, but at a price: As she puts it, "I felt like a zombie."

Then came the deinstitutionalization movement. Mary first learned about the new policy when a member of the hospital staff told all the patients that they would be released. Mary did not understand why, but she was glad when a social worker promised to help her find an apartment and apply for food stamps and government disability payments. The social worker promised to visit her every week.

Mary left the asylum with a supply of her new drugs. For a few years, things worked out pretty well. But then her social worker started missing visits, and Mary began to skip her medication. It didn't take long for the "voices" to come back, and Mary was filled with panic. Driven by fear, she left the apartment and ended up on the street.

She spent her nights in an abandoned building or in a car. Within a week, she was arrested for stealing from a store. The court sent her back into the mental health care system, where she was assigned to a new social worker. She was given a new apartment and a new supply of medication. But after several months, she stopped taking the drugs again, got into a fight with her neighbors, and was evicted. And so the whole cycle has repeated itself, over and over.

Mary Lee's story shows us that good intentions sometimes have unexpected bad consequences. Supporters of deinstitutionalization were hopeful that the new psychoactive drugs would bring an end to the use of restraints in mental hospitals, allowing people with mental illness to live normal lives in the community. But budget cuts and bureaucratic indifference left too many people to fend for themselves, and many of them could not handle life on their own. Some people have been helped, but others have become part of the problem of homelessness.

WHAT DO YOU THINK?

1. Can you point to good and bad consequences of the policy of deinstitutionalization? On balance, how well do you think this policy worked?
2. Do you think it is society's responsibility to care for people like Mary Lee? Why or why not?
3. Should people who are thought to be mentally ill but do not want help from others have the right to live as they wish, even if it is on the street? Why or why not?

Source: Based on Gagné (1998).

From this point of view, the profit motive ends up not only denying care to the poor but also corrupting medical practice for everyone. Doctors are always keenly aware of their own interests when they make a diagnosis, decide on a treatment, or refer a patient to a hospital. Similarly, hospitals and insurance companies guide medical care with an eye on the bottom line, and pharmaceutical companies strive to convince doctors and the public as a whole that health depends not on how we live but on the pills we take (Pear & Eckholm, 1991; Cowley, 1995).

CRITICAL REVIEW The social-conflict approach reveals that the health of some people is better than that of others because of social inequality. Thus we can understand why people living in rich countries have relatively good health but also why the health of the poor in the United States is little better than that of people in many of the world's low-income nations.

With its focus on the failings of the U.S. health care system, the social-conflict approach overlooks the fact that the overall health of the U.S. population has improved dramatically over the course of the past century. Another criticism is that health care systems in countries with socialist economies—presumably with less social inequality—do not perform all that well, typically because they provide little incentive for people to develop new treatments and technology.

The Applying Theory table on page 256 summarizes the contribution of each theoretical approach to our understanding of health and health care.

MAKING THE GRADE

Use the table below to review the three theoretical approaches to health.

MAKING THE GRADE

Can you sum up in one sentence the conservative, liberal, and radical left view of health care?

APPLYING THEORY

Physical and Mental Health

	What is the level of analysis?	What does the approach say about health and illness?	How do we deal with illness as a social problem?
Structural-functional approach	Macro-level	The structural-functional approach states that health is necessary for people to perform their daily roles. Illness threatens to disrupt the operation of a society by making the individual unable to carry out daily responsibilities.	By allowing people to assume the sick role, society relieves people who are ill from daily responsibilities and encourages them to seek medical attention.
Symbolic-interaction approach	Micro-level	The symbolic-interaction approach explains that the meaning of both health and illness varies from one setting to another, depending on what people define as normal.	Because the reality of health and illness depends on situationally constructed meanings, illness (as well as health) is a social as well as medical issue, which may or may not be defined as a social problem.
Social-conflict approach	Macro-level	A social-conflict approach links patterns of health and illness to social inequality. In general, people with more wealth have better health. Economic inequality is the major cause of poor health for millions of people.	Under a capitalist economic system, the goal of the health care system is private profit rather than public well-being. To address the problem of illness, government would need to guarantee health care for all.

POLITICS AND HEALTH

Constructing Problems and Defining Solutions

What people see as right and wrong with the U.S. health care system is not just a matter of facts but also a reflection of politics. We turn now to how politics shapes what people across the political spectrum see as problems of health and the solutions they propose.

Conservatives: Free Markets Provide the Best Care

Whatever the issue, be it housing or health care, conservatives favor the policy of allowing individuals and companies to compete freely in a market system. Competition, they claim, improves value for consumers by encouraging doctors, hospitals, and other health care providers to keep quality high and prices low. In addition, they point out that companies would not be eager to develop new drugs or new technologies were it not for the promise of substantial profits (Bartlett, 2000). Conservatives boast that the U.S. free-market system offers the most advanced medical care in the world. Why else, they ask, do so many world leaders respond to illness by coming to the United States for treatment?

Another conservative value that applies to health is the importance of individual responsibility. As conservatives see it, personal health reflects the choices we make about how to live. Making good choices is important because doing so can prevent disease before it happens. For example, choosing to have multiple sexual partners raises the risk of sexually transmitted diseases; choosing not to do this reduces or eliminates this risk. Similarly, pregnant women who use or don't use drugs or who do or don't seek out prenatal care set their own risk of premature birth. In the same way, choosing to smoke cigarettes or not to use tobacco affects the risk of cancer, just as choosing what and how much to eat goes a long way toward setting a person's risk of having heart disease.

Given their support for free-market health care and their belief in taking personal responsibility for health, it is not surprising that conservatives endorse a limited role for government in this area. For the poorest people—especially the elderly or disabled—and for veterans who have served their country, the government should—and does—provide health care programs at little or no cost. But, conservatives claim, to put government in charge for *everyone* is likely to do the same for health care as it has for public schools: reduce the quality of care and give people little choice about who provides the service (Gingrich, 2009).

Liberals: Government Must Ensure Universal Care

Liberals believe that a fair and just society should strive to make everyone equal with regard to issues as basic as health care. As they see it, the rich fare well in a free-market system, but the poor are left out. The strongest evidence that the current system is broken is that 46 million people in the United States lack health insurance (Feder, 2009).

Many liberals accept the idea of doctors and hospitals operating for profit as long as government programs are expanded so that everyone receives care. One solution to this problem would be a national health care system similar to Great Britain's National Health Service or Canada's single-payer coverage.

Such a measure would certainly be expensive, at least in the short term. But the long-term benefit would be far better health for much of the population that is not well served now. If all mothers-to-be had prenatal care and all children had immunizations, regular checkups, and sound nutrition, this country's infant mortality rate would surely drop dramatically. Just as important, healthier people are more productive, leading to economic growth that would offset much of the cost of this kind of program.

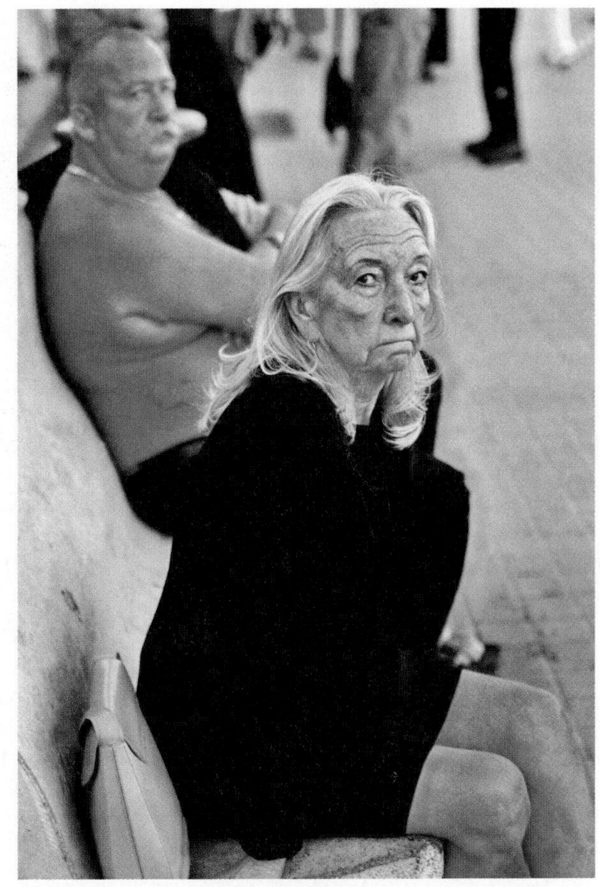

People who are poor not only endure more illness but also "get old before their time." What do conservatives, liberals, and radicals support as solutions to the poor health of millions of people in the United States?

The Radical Left: Capitalism Is Unhealthy

As we might expect, the strongest criticism of the U.S. health care system comes from the radical left. Seen from this point of view, the inequality in health care—both the gap between rich and poor in the United States and between the rich and poor nations of the world—is an injustice created by capitalism. When health is a commodity, people who have wealth end up living long and healthy lives, but those with little income cannot even be certain of survival. In effect, radicals on the left claim, the profit motive turns physicians, hospitals, and the entire health care system into a multibillion-dollar industry up for sale to the highest bidders.

From this perspective, the solution to the world's health care needs is to abandon capitalism—the source of the problem—in favor of an economic and political system that operates in the interests of the majority. The promise of such a socialist system lies in providing a range of benefits, from safe drinking water to basic medical attention, to everyone on the basis of need.

The Left to Right table on page 258 outlines the three political perspectives on health issues.

MAKING THE GRADE

Use the table below to review the three political approaches to health.

LEFT TO RIGHT

The Politics of Health

	RADICAL-LEFT VIEW	LIBERAL VIEW	CONSERVATIVE VIEW
WHAT IS THE PROBLEM?	The health of the rich is good, but the poor suffer. Not only is access to health care a problem, but also the medical establishment itself is distorted by the profit motive.	The average health of the U.S. population is good, but disadvantaged people are less healthy; 46 million people lack health insurance.	The health of the U.S. population has steadily improved and is very good by global standards. Individuals need to take greater responsibility for their own health.
WHAT IS THE SOLUTION?	High-quality health care should be the right of everyone. Only radical change toward an economic and political system that meets the needs of all will end the health inequalities in the U.S. population.	Government must extend access by putting in place a universal health care program so that prenatal care, nutrition, and appropriate medical treatment are available to all, regardless of their ability to pay.	Encouraging responsible behavior is key to illness prevention. Programs to extend health care coverage can help but should be provided by employers or paid for by individuals in a free-market system.

JOIN THE DEBATE

1. What have you heard about the Obama administration's approach to health care? What changes do you expect to see?
2. Why do liberals favor a national program of health insurance? Why do conservatives oppose expanding government's role in health care? Why do radicals on the left think that even a universal government care program does not go far enough?
3. Which of the three political analyses of health care included here do you find most convincing? Why?

Going On from Here

The central theme of this chapter is that health is not simply a medical matter; it is a reflection of how society operates. Improvements in human health are occurring in most regions of the world. Economic growth has resulted in higher living standards, including better nutrition and safer housing. These gains, coupled with better medical technology, have pushed life expectancy upward.

But enormous health problems still exist in countries where the problem of poverty is greatest. Around the world, about 1.4 billion people struggle to live with $1.25 a day in income, with little or no access to basic medical care. In these nations—especially in rural areas of Latin America, Africa, and Asia—illness and poverty form a vicious circle. Poverty breeds disease, which in turn reduces people's ability to work, and so they and their children remain poor.

The greatest health crisis is in Central Africa, where many of the world's poorest countries are found. Nations including Burundi, Rwanda, Uganda, Kenya, and Sudan face the problems of chronic hunger and unsafe drinking water, made worse in recent years by warfare.

Perhaps most serious of all is the AIDS epidemic, which has spread through many African villages and towns to infect 25 percent or more of young people. The challenge lies in the fact that the greatest medical care needs are found in precisely the countries with the least capable health care systems.

Compared with the desperate struggle in poor countries, the outlook for the United States, home to the world's most advanced medical technology, is far brighter. The problem this country faces now is that some 46 million people have no health insurance. As noted in this chapter, the United States falls behind many other nations—including those with much lower average incomes—on important health indicators. Where we stand in terms of health care a century from now will probably depend less on what happens in a high-tech laboratory than on the future extent of social inequality.

DEFINING SOLUTIONS

We all want a society in which people have good health, but what is the best way to reach that goal?

The path people favor as the solution to our need for health care reflects their political attitudes and also their social standing. Look at the two photos below to see two approaches to providing health care to our population.

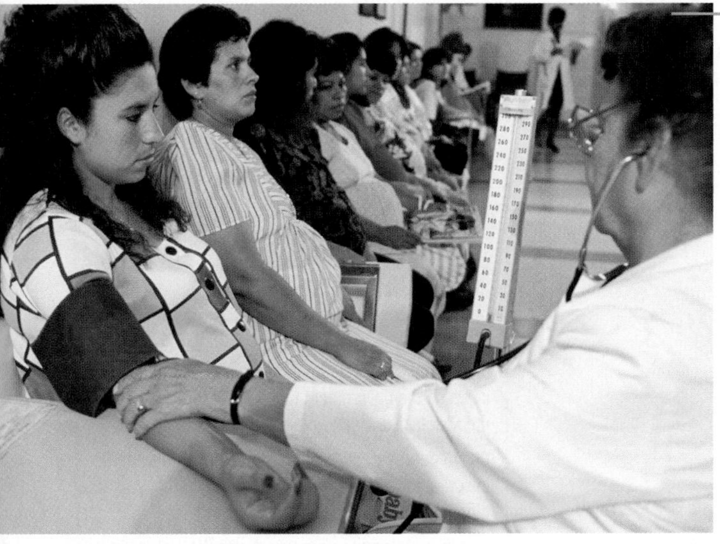

It may be that the United States offers the best care available anywhere in the world, but liberals point out that tens of millions of people make use of overcrowded and expensive emergency rooms like the one shown here, and others go without health care altogether because they lack health insurance. From this point of view, the core of the problem is the distribution of care. Striking inequality means that some people get little or no health care, which, in turn, is the reason that this country lags behind other high-income nations in measures of health. In the recent debate over our nation's health care, what solution do liberals support?

You already know that conservatives place great importance on individual responsibility for personal well-being. This means making good choices, including exercising regularly, eating nutritious food in moderation, and consulting regularly with medical professionals. From this point of view, this nation has the best medical care in the world, thanks largely to our free-market economy. The market economy makes good health care available to almost everyone, with government stepping in to give assistance to some categories of the population. In the recent debate over national health care, what solution do conservatives support?

HINT

The solution, as liberals see it, is to involve government to ensure that everyone has access to quality care. Whether government would operate clinics or simply pay for services, the goal is universal health care coverage. Conservatives are critical of extending government control into health care, believing that people should retain the right to select physicians and decide on treatment. Radicals on the left argue that basic changes to the economy are needed to eliminate the economic inequality that divides our population. Have you heard any radical-left voices in the recent health care debate?

Getting Involved: Applications & Exercises

1. Most communities have public health clinics run by the county health department. Make an appointment to visit a clinic and speak to officials. See what you can learn about the physical and mental health care available in your own community. How much emphasis is given to prevention? What categories of people are likely to rely on the public health clinic?
2. Visit a local library that has current copies of a variety of U.S. magazines. Look at the photographs of women in advertisements. What seems to be the ideal body shape for a woman? What effect do you think such images have on women? How might these images play a part in the problem of eating disorders?
3. Most communities have a shelter or soup kitchen for poor and homeless people. Visit such a facility in your area, and ask the director about the role, if any, of mental disabilities among the people they serve. What programs does the facility offer to help clients cope with their problems? Consider helping out as a volunteer.
4. Do research on the deinstitutionalization of people with mental illnesses that took place in the United States in the 1960s. See what you can learn about the causes of this movement and its consequences.

MAKING THE GRADE

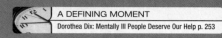

A DEFINING MOMENT

Dorothea Dix: Mentally Ill People Deserve Our Help p. 253

CHAPTER 9 Physical and Mental Health

Health and Illness: A Global Perspective

HEALTH is a state of complete mental, physical, and social well-being.

- The well-being of any population reflects the operation of society, including its level of technology and degree of social inequality.

pp. 236–39

HIGH-INCOME NATIONS:

- Low infant mortality
- High life expectancy
- Most people die after age 75 of chronic conditions such as heart disease or cancer.

pp. 236–37

LOW-INCOME NATIONS:

- High infant mortality
- Low life expectancy
- Most people die of acute diseases such as malaria, cholera, or measles, and as many as half of all children die before ten years of age.

p. 238

THE AIDS EPIDEMIC: Worldwide, some 33 million people are infected with HIV.

- The hardest-hit region is sub-Saharan Africa, with 67% of the world's AIDS cases.
- The United States accounts for less than 5% of global AIDS.

pp. 238–39

health (p. 236) a state of complete physical, mental, and social well-being

infant mortality rate (p. 236) the number of babies who die before their first birthday out of every 1,000 born

life expectancy at birth (p. 236) the number of years, on average, people in a society can expect to live

chronic disease (p. 237) an illness that has a long-term development

acute disease (p. 238) an illness that strikes suddenly

social epidemiology (p. 238) the study of how health and disease are distributed throughout a society's population

epidemic (p. 238) the rapid spread of a disease through a population

Health Policy: Paying for Care

SOCIALIST societies, in which governments own hospitals and employ doctors, treat health care as a basic right.

pp. 239–41

CAPITALIST societies, in which doctors and hospitals operate privately, treat health care as a product to be purchased on the open market.

pp. 241–42

✓ *Some mostly capitalist nations, such as Great Britain, have socialized medicine, in which government-run care is available to all. (p. 241)*

✓ *Of all high-income nations, only the United States lacks a universal coverage program to help pay the costs of everyone's medical care. (p. 242)*

socialized medicine (p. 241) a medical care system in which the government owns and operates most medical facilities and employs most physicians

direct-fee system (p. 242) a medical care system in which patients or their insurers pay directly for the services of physicians and hospitals

health maintenance organizations (HMOs) (p. 244) private insurance organizations that provide medical care to subscribers for a fixed fee

Health Care in the United States: A System in Crisis?

THE COST PROBLEM

- The United States has a direct-fee system in which most doctors and hospitals operate on a for-profit basis.
- Health care spending in the United States has increased steadily and topped $2.5 trillion in 2010.
- Factors pushing up health care spending include the system of private insurance, the trend toward doctors specializing, increasing use of high-technology treatment, the aging U.S. population, a lack of preventive care, and a rising number of malpractice lawsuits.

pp. 242–45

GENDER AND HEALTH

- On average, women outlive men by about five years. Even so, women's health concerns have often been treated less effectively and overlooked by researchers.
- Eating disorders, which are widespread among girls and women, illustrate the power of gender to harm health.

pp. 246–47

THE COVERAGE PROBLEM

- About 64% of the U.S. population have private health insurance.
- 25% have coverage from an HMO.
- 31% have some coverage from the government (categories overlap).
- 51 million people—17% of the population—lack any health care coverage.

pp. 244–45

POVERTY AND HEALTH

- Poverty means a lack of adequate nutrition, medical care, and safe housing; 44 million people in the United States live below the poverty line and most cannot afford a healthy diet.
- Poverty is also associated with violence, especially among men.
- Certain categories of poor people, including American Indians and African Americans, are at even greater risk of both physical and mental health problems.

pp. 245–46

PEOPLE WITH DISABILITIES

- Physical disability often operates as a *master status*, dominating other aspects of a person's identity.
- Despite the 1990 Americans with Disabilities Act, many public places remain inaccessible to people with disabilities.

pp. 247–48

THE NURSING SHORTAGE

- Many nurses are leaving the field, citing a stressful work environment and lack of respect from other hospital personnel.

pp. 248–49

prenatal care (p. 246) health care for women during pregnancy

disability (p. 247) a physical or mental condition that limits everyday activities

✓ *Despite the fact that this country spends more on health care than any other, the United States lags behind other rich nations in key indicators of health, including life expectancy and infant mortality. (p. 242)*

Mental Health and Illness

- Nearly half of all Americans have symptoms of a **MENTAL DISORDER** at some time in their lives, and one-third of the population suffers from a serious mental disorder at some point. Less than half of those with serious mental illness ever receive treatment.
- Poverty, which is linked to stress and social isolation, puts people at greater risk of mental illness.

pp. 249–51

mental disorder (p. 249) a condition involving thinking, mood, or behavior that causes distress and reduces a person's ability to function in everyday life

psychotherapy (p. 252) an approach to mental health in which patients talk with trained professionals to gain insight into the cause of their problems

deinstitutionalization (p. 252) the release of people from mental hospitals into local communities

Theoretical Analysis: Understanding Health Problems

Structural-Functional Analysis: Health and Social Roles

The **STRUCTURAL-FUNCTIONAL APPROACH** highlights the functions of health for the normal operation of society.

- Illness is a problem because it keeps people from fulfilling their social roles.
- People who become ill take on the sick role, which relieves them of most everyday social obligations as long as they make efforts to get well.

pp. 252–54

Symbolic-Interaction Analysis: The Meaning of Health

The **SYMBOLIC-INTERACTION APPROACH** focuses on the meanings people attach to health and illness.

- The meanings attached to various conditions change over time. Homosexuality has been viewed as a moral wrong, a mental illness, and finally, simply as a sexual orientation.
- The existence of *psychosomatic disorders* demonstrates that how people define any health situation may affect how they actually feel.

p. 254

Social-Conflict Analysis: Health and Inequality

The **SOCIAL-CONFLICT APPROACH** points out how social inequality shapes patterns of health.

- Both in the United States and throughout the world, poor people suffer from the most health problems.
- In a capitalist economy, medical practice is guided by the profit motive; many people in the United States lack health care because they cannot afford to pay for it.

p. 254–55

sick role (p. 253) a pattern of behavior expected of people defined as ill

See the **Applying Theory** table on page 256.

Politics and Health: Constructing Problems and Defining Solutions

The Radical Left: Capitalism Is Unhealthy

- **RADICALS ON THE LEFT** blame the profit motive for inequalities in health care in the United States.
- Radicals on the left call for a rejection of capitalism in favor of a socialist system that would provide equal health care for all.

p. 257

Liberals: Government Must Ensure Universal Care

- **LIBERALS** focus on inequalities in the health care received by rich and poor people.
- Liberals favor making government responsible for more of the health care system to ensure access for everyone.

p. 257

Conservatives: Free Markets Provide the Best Care

- **CONSERVATIVES** emphasize individual responsibility for health; they believe that good health results from wise decisions about how to live.
- Conservatives claim that competition in a free marketplace will result in high-quality, low-cost health care.

pp. 256–57

See the **Left to Right** table on page 258.

CONSTRUCTING THE PROBLEM

Most government money goes to the poor in the form of "welfare," doesn't it?

The recent bailouts of financial corporations and auto companies involved about fifty times as much money as poor families receive in government assistance.

Is our system of financing political campaigns fair?

If "money talks," then we might be concerned that U.S. corporations give more money to political campaigns than any other type of organization, including labor unions, civil rights groups, and women's organizations.

Is the United States a true democracy?

In the 2008 national elections, only about 63 percent of eligible voters went to the polls.

CHAPTER 10

Economy and Politics

CHAPTER OVERVIEW

WHAT ARE THE ADVANTAGES and disadvantages of capitalist and socialist economies? This chapter explains how the economy is linked to politics and the way power is used to make decisions and set policy. You will assess our society's system of campaign financing and understand various explanations of why so many people do not bother to vote. You will carry out theoretical analysis of our country's political economy and learn how "problems" and "solutions" involving the economy and other issues reflect people's political attitudes.

The tall, slim man walked up to the microphone, smiled first at his wife and two small children, and then gazed out over the vast crowd. In was late at night, but the dazzling lights made this scene in Chicago's Grant Park seem like midafternoon. About 100,000 people had come to hear the first public speech as the new leader declared victory in his campaign to become the president of the United States. His broad smile continued until the roar subsided. Then he began to speak: "If there is anyone out there who still doubts that America is a place where all things are possible, who still wonders if the dream of our Founders is alive in our time, who still questions the power of our democracy, tonight is your answer."

The man, of course, was Barack Obama—a relative newcomer to politics, an African American, a child of a single mother—who was soon to become the forty-fourth president of the United States. For millions of people, Obama's election to the highest office in the land signifies that "the system" works, that ordinary people in our democratic system can and do select their leaders. But new president or not, many people still have little trust in our government. As millions of others see it, our political system has long been rigged by the importance of money, giving power to "special interests" that usually get their way.

We all learn in school that the United States is a democracy in which the people rule and government officials play by the rules. But as this chapter explains, a lot of people in the United States are not so sure that this is the case. For one thing, many are concerned that the rich and powerful—including the people who run the Wall Street investment banks and the multinational corporations—have too much control over our political process. Then there are others who think that government has become far too big and that anything decided in Washington, D.C., is unlikely to meet the needs of ordinary women and men.

This chapter explores the operation of **politics,** *the social institution that guides a society's decision making about how to live.* As you will see, the political system has much to do with a country's **economy,** *the social institution that organizes the production, distribution, and consumption of goods and services.* By studying the operation of these two closely related social institutions, beginning with the economy and then turning to politics, we will learn more about many familiar problems that affect the lives of people across the United States.

Economic Systems: Defining Justice, Defining Problems

One way to think about the economy is in terms of justice. The operation of the economic system determines who gets what and also includes claims about what is fair. The operation of the economy has a lot to do with what issues end up being defined as social problems. We begin with a brief look at the two broad economic models, capitalism and socialism.

The Capitalist Model

Capitalism is *an economic system in which natural resources and the means of producing goods and services are privately owned.* In a capitalist system, individual men and women own the productive property, including investment banks, auto factories, large farms, and even hardwood forests. Capitalism also creates a special culture or way of thinking about the world. The culture of capitalism teaches people to think that everyone should behave according to their own self-interest. According to the Scottish economist Adam Smith (1723–1790), the pursuit of self-interest has widespread benefits, because guided by individual self-interest, an economy ends up producing the greatest good for the greatest number of people (1937:508, orig. 1776).

How does all this work? In theory, capitalism operates as a system of market competition in which people buy and sell goods and services with prices set by people themselves, what economists call the forces of supply and demand. In a free-market environment—sometimes described as *laissez-faire* (French words meaning "leave it alone")—both buyers and sellers compete with one another buying and selling goods and services to gain the most in return. From the sellers' side of the process, businesses that offer products of high value are likely to do well

politics the social institution that guides a society's decision making about how to live

economy the social institution that organizes the production, distribution, and consumption of goods and services

government a formal organization that directs the political life of a society

capitalism an economic system in which natural resources and the means of producing goods and services are privately owned

socialism an economic system in which natural resources and the means of producing goods and services are collectively owned

One way to "read" a nation's economic system is to examine housing in major cities. In the former East Berlin, socialist policies mandated similar, basic housing for almost everyone. In the Philippines' capital city, Manila, a capitalist system provides luxurious housing for some while others live in shanty settlements or on the street.

because they will have many buyers; companies that offer products of little value create little demand and soon fail. The overall result, explains Smith, is that the market system makes high-quality goods available to consumers at low prices.

According to Smith, a market economy based on a free exchange between buyers and sellers is highly efficient. He claimed that a market system is most productive when it operates without the interference of **government,** *a formal organization that directs the political life of a society.* Smith knew that countries need governments to perform some tasks, such as national defense. But he warned that when government interferes with market forces by telling people what to produce or what to buy, it not only limits people's freedom but also makes production inefficient, reduces value, and shortchanges consumers.

Mostly capitalist economies such as our own have been highly productive and have generated a high overall standard of living. At the same time, capitalism does create problems, at least for some people, when companies lay off workers in hard times or when producers find machines that do a job more cheaply than human labor. In other words, what is economically efficient is not always good for the local community or for the people losing their jobs.

In addition, as noted in Chapter 2 ("Poverty and Wealth"), a capitalist economy generates a high level of economic inequality. Finally, as we shall discuss later in this chapter, capitalism has a tendency to concentrate not only wealth but also power, which can weaken democracy. Global Map 10–1 on page 266 shows which nations have mostly capitalist economies.

The Socialist Model

In contrast to capitalism, **socialism** is *an economic system in which natural resources and the means of producing goods and services are collectively owned.* In a socialist economy, government limits the right of individuals to own productive property. Instead, the government owns and operates factories, offices, and farms, claiming to do so in the interest of the people as a whole. Socialism also develops its own culture: In contrast to capitalism's individualistic orientation, socialism has a collective orientation, teaching people to be motivated not by self-interest but by serving the common good.

The idea of a socialist economic system arose partly as a plan to solve the problems of capitalism. This plan was the work of Karl Marx (1964, orig. 1844; 1985, orig. 1847), who claimed that capitalism's private ownership of productive property is what creates unequal social classes. By putting the *means of production* (such as factories and other productive property) in private hands, the capitalist economy serves the interests of these owners. Marx envisioned socialism as an economic

We have all heard people describe capitalism as "natural." Why do many people think that? Do you think that is true or not? Why?

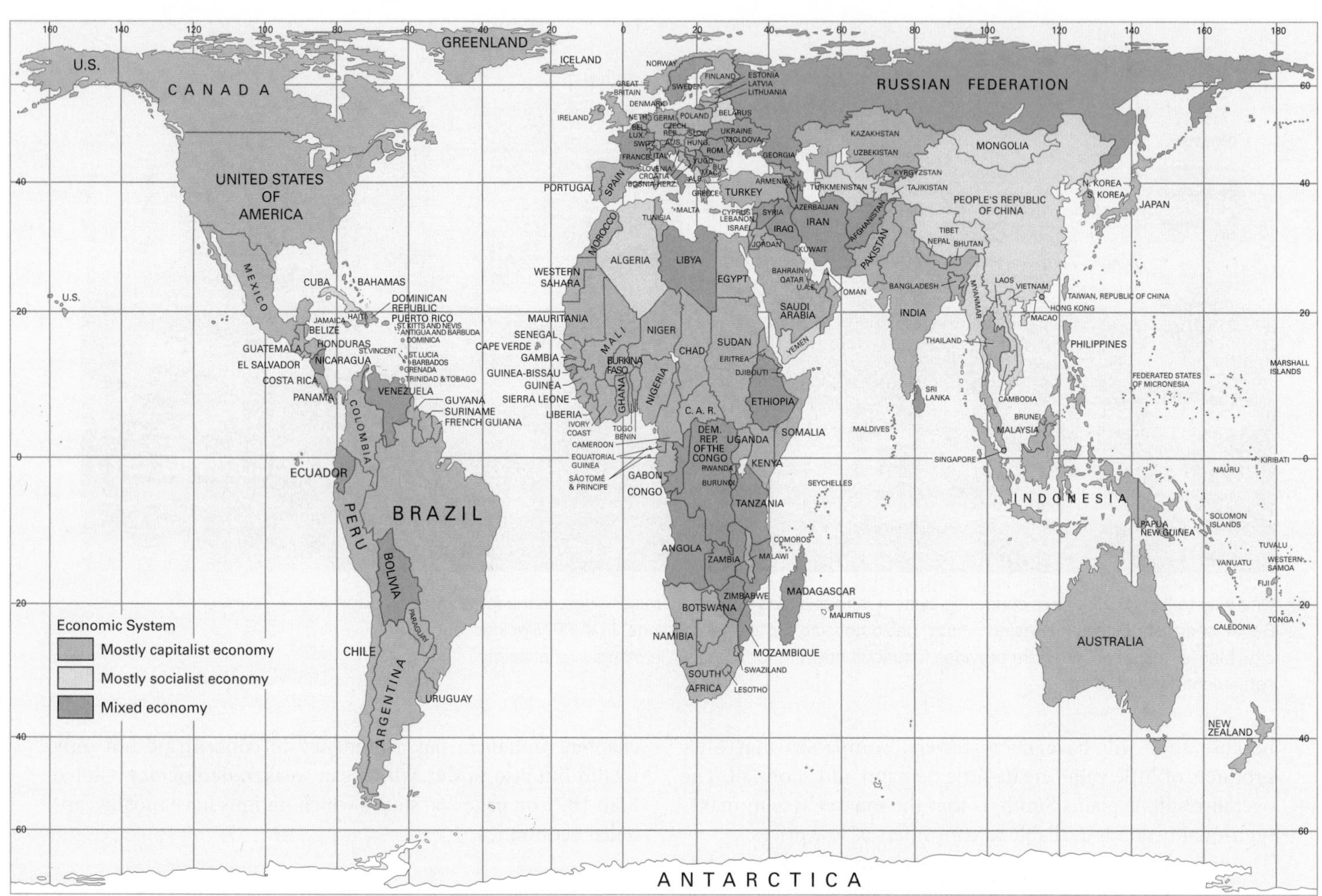

A World of Differences

GLOBAL MAP 10–1 Economic Systems around the World

The map organizes the world's 194 nations into three general categories: countries with mostly capitalist economies, countries with mostly socialist economies, and countries with more evenly mixed economies. What can you say about the nations that fall in each of the three categories?

Source: Based on data from Freedom House (2009) and Heritage Foundation (2009).

system that operates to meet the needs of everyone. The government, acting as an agent for all people, controls economic production. A socialist society expects everyone to work not out of self-interest but as a matter of social responsibility.

In practice, socialist nations such as China, Cuba, Laos, North Korea, and Vietnam have far less economic inequality than a capitalist society such as the United States. At the same time, socialist systems create problems of their own, including a relatively low standard of living. In addition, socialist societies have been criticized as highly regimented, with government limiting individual freedoms, including not only the chance to start a new business but also the freedom to speak out and to move about without restriction.

Mixed Systems

No nation in the world has an economy that is completely capitalist or completely socialist. As Global Map 10–1 shows, a

GETTING INVOLVED

What would you say are the best qualities of capitalist economic systems? Socialist economic systems? Which system would you rather live in? Why?

political economy the economic and political life of a nation or world region

majority of the world's nations are mostly capitalist, about fifteen are mostly socialist, and another two dozen nations have a fairly balanced mix of capitalism and socialism (Miller & Holmes, 2009).

In Asian countries, including Japan, South Korea, and Singapore, as well as in Middle Eastern nations such as Saudi Arabia and Kuwait, a mixed system known as *state capitalism* involves government working closely with large, privately owned companies. Although most property is privately owned, the government owns some large companies, such as automobile producers, telephone services, and airlines. In some cases, typically in Asia, this arrangement is intended to make big companies more efficient and more competitive in global markets. In others, such as Saudi Arabia, a large royal family owns most of the country's productive wealth.

Another mixed system, common in Western Europe, including Italy, France, and Sweden, is *welfare capitalism.* Here, too, most production is carried out by privately owned companies. What distinguishes welfare capitalist societies is extensive government welfare programs, funded by high taxes. These countries provide child care, housing, and medical care for the entire population. The goal here is to keep productivity high while keeping economic inequality in check.

The U.S. economy is a mix of private and government activity, but as Figure 10–1 shows, the United States has long been among the most capitalist of all nations. The U.S. government carries out only about 20 percent of the country's production, with 80 percent of production in the privately owned sector of the economy. As a strategy to pull the economy out of recession, the Obama administration has greatly expanded the role of government in the economy, for example, providing large loans of taxpayer money to the auto industry on the condition that these companies restructure themselves following government guidelines.

Is capitalism a problem or a solution? Your answer, of course, depends on politics—the more to the left you are, the more you are likely to see capitalism (or more specifically, the free market) as a problem because of the inequality it creates; the more to the right you are, the more you are likely to see capitalism as a solution because of how productive it is. Your view of the role of government is just the opposite. The more to the left you are, the bigger the part you would like government to have in the economy in the interest of economic equality. The more to the right you are, the smaller the part you would like government to have in the economy in the interest of individual freedom. Figure 10–2 on page 268 illustrates this pattern.

It is probably fair to say that most people don't spend much time thinking about what kind of economic system they prefer.

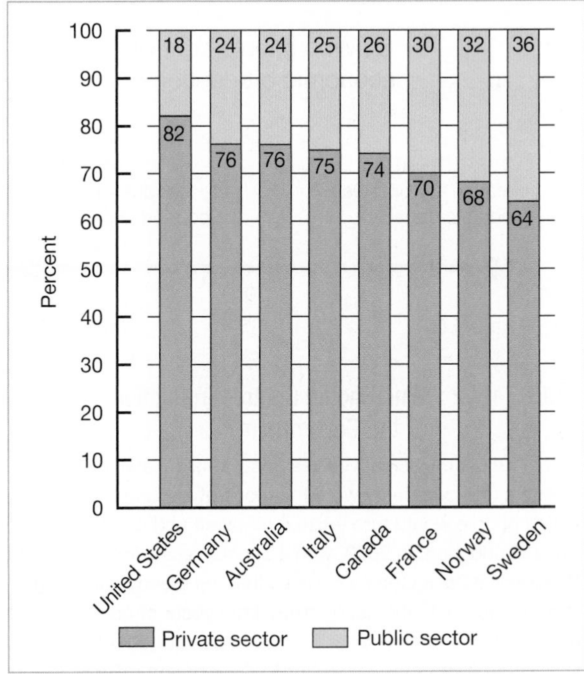

FIGURE 10–1 Percentage of Gross Domestic Product (GDP) in the Private Sector and the Public Sector

Compared with other high-income countries, the United States has a larger share of its economic productivity in the private sector, making this country more capitalist.

Source: World Bank (2008).

But over the past decade, the rapid growth of Wal-Mart has had the effect of making more people do just that. The Defining Moment box on page 269 explains how.

The Economy and Politics

How the economy operates says a lot about the way power is distributed throughout a society. For this reason, analysts talk about a society's **political economy**, *the economic and political life of a nation or world region.*

Supporters of capitalism claim that the limited role of government in a capitalist society provides people with lots of economic opportunity and extensive political freedoms (Rueschemeyer, Stephens, & Stephens, 1992; Lipset, 1994). Peter Berger (1986), a sociologist who has examined the political consequences of capitalism, points out that people living in capitalist societies enjoy not just the right to vote but also the

democracy a political system in which power is exercised by the people as a whole

authoritarianism a political system that denies popular participation in government

monarchy a political system in which a single family rules from generation to generation

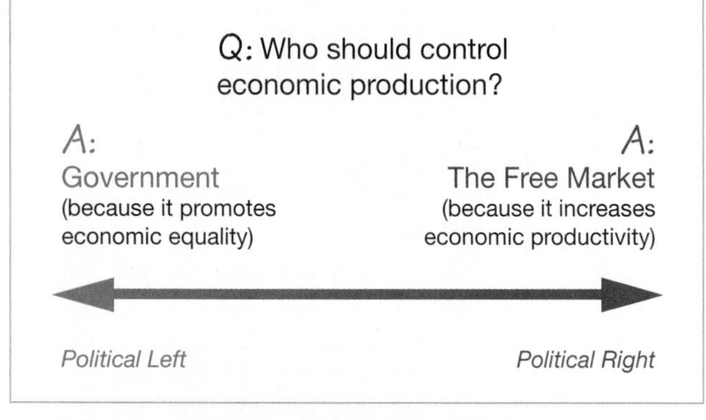

FIGURE 10–2 Who Should Control Production, the Market or the Government?

In the 1980s, conservative President Ronald Reagan claimed that freedom and prosperity were the result of a market economy in which people would turn loose their talent and creativity to produce abundance. In 2009, with a serious recession at hand, liberal President Barack Obama claimed that the steady hand of government could guide the nation away from years of greed, corruption, and rising economic inequality. How much control of the economy you would give to the market or to government reflects your position on the political spectrum.

right to work, travel, and speak according to their individual desires.

Supporters of socialism make other claims. Following the ideas of Karl Marx, they argue that capitalism actually reduces personal freedom, at least for most people (Domhoff, 1970; Bergsten, Horst, & Moran, 1978; Parenti, 1995). This is because capitalism concentrates wealth and power to such a degree that a small share of the population (Marx's "capitalist elite") has most of the wealth. In a capitalist society, the argument continues, money is power, which also allows the elite to dominate the political life of the society. For ordinary people to have a voice in shaping their own lives, at least rough economic equality is necessary, which is not the case in capitalist societies.

An important expression of political freedom is **democracy,** *a political system in which power is exercised by the people as a whole.* Most people in the United States claim that capitalist countries are democratic—because they allow people to vote—and that socialist countries are not because people cannot vote for their leaders. There is some truth to this view: In none of the socialist nations mentioned earlier (China, Cuba, Laos, North Korea, and Vietnam) can leaders be voted out of office by the people. In recent years, however, a number of Latin American nations (including Nicaragua, Bolivia, Venezuela, and Ecuador) have elected leaders who support socialism. At the same time, many countries in Africa, the Middle East, and Asia have mostly capitalist economies yet offer their people little voice in politics.

The opposite of democracy is **authoritarianism,** *a political system that denies popular participation in government.* Authoritarian countries can have various types of economies and power structures. Myanmar (Burma), in Southeast Asia, is an authoritarian society run by the military; Iran is another example, in this case run by a religious elite; Malaysia and Singapore in Southeast Asia are authoritarian nations that have elections but have long been controlled by a single political party.

Another example of authoritarian nations includes Saudi Arabia in the Middle East, where power takes the form of **monarchy,** *a political system in which a single family rules from generation to generation.* In this oil-rich country of 29 million people (about the population of Texas), most of the wealth is in the hands of an extended royal family containing several thousand people, who dominate economic and political life.

Saudi Arabia falls far short of the democratic ideal, which is a society in which all people have a political voice. But what about the United States? Is this country as democratic as many people like to think? We turn now to some of the economic and political problems in the "land of the free."

Problems of the U.S. Political Economy

The following sections investigate the political economy of the United States. First, we look at the great power of large corporations. Then we explore how well this nation lives up to its democratic ideals.

The Power of Corporations

In the United States, most goods and services are produced by **corporations,** *businesses with a legal existence, including rights and liabilities, separate from that of their members.* In the United States, 6 million businesses (of more than 32 million total) are incorporated. Of these, the largest 100 corporations are giants, each with more than $35 billion in assets. Together, these 100 businesses are responsible for most corporate production in the United States, and this share has been increasing in recent decades (U.S. Census Bureau, 2010).

The economic activity of corporations is far greater than that of government. Local, state, and federal governments in

corporations businesses with a legal existence, including rights and liabilities, separate from that of their members

GETTING INVOLVED

Have you ever spoken out either in favor of or against Wal-Mart? Explain.

CONSTRUCTING SOCIAL PROBLEMS

A DEFINING MOMENT

Store Wars: Is Wal-Mart the Problem or the Solution?

In March 2006, the voters of Saranac Lake came to the polls like never before. It was not a presidential election—not even a vote for a new senator. The issue was whether the local town council should let Wal-Mart build a new store in the small community in the Adirondack Mountains of upstate New York.

In 2008, Wal-Mart was the world's largest retailer, with more than 4,200 stores and 1.4 million employees in the United States. Another 3,615 stores operate around the world. What makes Wal-Mart so successful? The company developed a business plan that allows it to sell products more cheaply than just about anyone else. The appeal of Wal-Mart to shoppers is that you can find almost anything you might need in one store, and it will probably cost less than you expect. It is easy to think that Adam Smith—the architect of capitalism—would have loved a chance to go shopping at Wal-Mart. So many aisles full of goods of all kinds! So much choice! Such low prices! Wal-Mart could be on a poster promoting the benefits of capitalism.

In Saranac Lake, Linda Piro tells women in her beauty shop that she supports the idea of a Wal-Mart Supercenter in town. "Right now, local shoppers cannot find a lot of things they need," she explains. "If you want children's clothes or bed sheets, you have to drive an hour to buy them." Piro also thinks that Wal-Mart would be good for the local economy. "It will bring in people from the outside," she argues, "and while they're here, they will take a look at downtown."

But other people disagree. Mark Coleman, who runs a local music store, does not want a Wal-Mart in his town. "They take away from a community," he claims. "They don't add to it; they don't give anything back." Coleman and many other small business owners fear that once Wal-Mart has opened its doors, their stores in the old downtown area will not be able to compete, will lose customers, and will eventually have to close up.

Coleman and other critics also take issue with what they see as unfair business practices. The starting wage at Wal-Mart is about $7.25 an hour, and the company claims its average hourly wage for full-time workers is $10.83. But critics say that at this wage level, working full time does not generate enough income to support a family. Although some people who start in hourly jobs eventually earn higher salaries as managers, the critics claim that most of the Wal-Mart workforce is paid too little for people ever to reach the middle class.

Mike Smith sits on a street corner in Saranac Lake and smiles. He is more philosophical than most local residents. "Wal-Mart is a defining moment for us, as it is for every town. It forces you to decide who you are, what you want your town to be, what's important. Wal-Mart is pure capitalism—more stores, bigger buildings, more choice, lower prices—and the big guy usually wins. Lots of my friends all over the country shop at Wal-Mart for the simple reason that they feel they get more for their dollar. Like I said, it's pure capitalism. At one level, it works. But we need to ask ourselves whether more, bigger, and cheaper is necessarily better. It is better to save a couple of bucks on a car battery. But is it better if we end up losing many of our town's businesses? The ones that have supported our Little League for years and years? Is it better if all our family and neighbors end up having to work at Wal-Mart making nine or ten bucks an hour?"

Mike Smith asks some good questions. The coming of Wal-Mart to cities and towns across the United States has been a defining moment that has sparked critical discussion about the pros and cons of our economic system.

What happened in Saranac Lake? In the local election, voters elected officials who opposed giving Wal-Mart permission to build a store there. So for the present, there will be no Wal-Mart Supercenter in that community. But in Saranac Lake and elsewhere, questions about how our economy should work—what it is supposed to do and for whom—will continue.

Sources: Based on Wal-Mart (2009) and Rosenbloom & Barbaro (2009).

Does Wal-Mart help communities with its low prices or hurt communities with its low wages?

SOCIAL PROBLEMS in Everyday Life

Politically speaking, what categories of people talk about the problems of "big government"? What categories talk about the problems of "big corporations"?

monopoly the domination of an entire market by a single company

the United States do manage public resources, building highways, repairing bridges, running libraries and universities, and overseeing parks and beaches. In addition, the federal government operates the U.S. military. But as we would expect in a capitalist society, most economic production is in the private sector, which is dominated by huge corporations.

Government provides aid in the form of subsidies, price controls, and outright cash grants to businesses, especially when officials fear that a large industry might fail and cause damage to the overall economy. In the 1970s, for example, such fears led the federal government to provide financial assistance to bail out the Chrysler Corporation. Similarly, in the 1980s, the federal government provided $500 billion to head off a collapse of the savings and loan industry. In 2008 and 2009, the government provided more than $1 trillion to large financial corporations and major automakers to prevent their collapse (Calavita & Pontell, 1993; Drawbaugh, 2009).

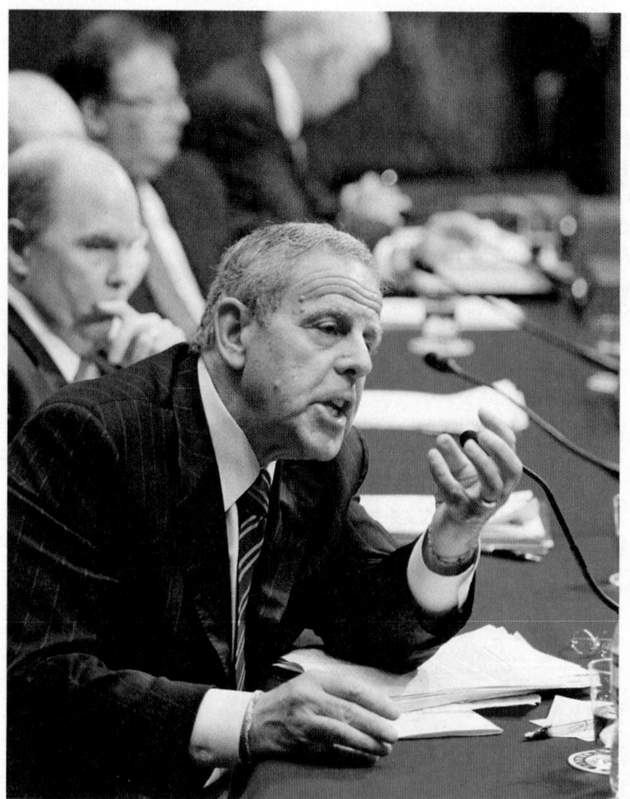

How much control should the government have over the operation of major corporations? The recent recession put the U.S. auto industry—already suffering a long-term decline in sales—on the ropes. After going through bankruptcy, both Chrysler and General Motors have had to accept government bailout money, and the government control that comes with it. In 2009, the CEOs of Chrysler and General Motors were in Washington to answer questions before a Congressional committee.

Government help goes to companies not just in times of economic crisis but all the time. For one thing, federal, state, and local governments are some of U.S. corporations' biggest customers. Especially in recent decades, corporations have also come to expect favors from government. As the Social Policy box explains, government handouts to corporations are common, with far more taxpayer money in the United States going to wealthy corporations than to poor families.

The U.S. government does shape economic life by regulating the workplace, monitoring foreign trade, protecting consumers, and setting interest rates. Since the Obama administration came to power, the government has taken a stake in some troubled corporations. But in this country, government ownership of corporations has always been the exception rather than the rule. Given the fact that private corporations generate most of the economic output of the United States, are corporations more powerful than even the government? If so, who really runs the country?

Monopoly and Oligopoly

In a mostly capitalist society, the very great power of business is not widely regarded as a social problem. But it is a problem if *any one company* comes to control a market, because that would defeat the market system.

Monopoly is *the domination of an entire market by a single company.* Monopolies arose in the final decades of the nineteenth century as one result of the Industrial Revolution. A small number of individuals—sometimes called "robber barons" because they engaged in ruthless business tactics and lived like royalty—built enormous corporations that ended up dominating entire new industries. For example, Andrew Carnegie (1835–1919) took control of the nation's steel industry, John D. Rockefeller (1839–1937) dominated oil production, and J. P. Morgan (1837–1913) took a leading role in banking. Not surprisingly, such men made enormous fortunes, earning tens of millions of dollars each year at a time when there was no income tax and the average worker earned about $600 annually.

In 1890, the federal government challenged the power of the giant monopolies when Congress passed the Sherman Antitrust Act. One result was that Rockefeller's Standard Oil Company was broken up into many smaller companies that would compete with one another. Almost a century later, the government broke up AT&T's monopoly in long-distance telephone service, creating the "Baby Bells" and setting the stage for MCI, Sprint, and dozens of other long-distance companies to compete and bring down the price of long-distance calling. In

oligopoly the domination of a market by a few companies

conglomerate a giant corporation composed of many smaller corporations

SOCIAL POLICY

Corporate Welfare: Government Handouts for Big Business

Who benefits most from "welfare" in the United States? If you are like most people, you would answer that most of the benefits go to needy people. In reality, however, government programs provide more benefits to corporations than to poor people.

Why do companies get such special treatment? With all their wealth, corporations have great power. In addition, many states and cities are eager to increase the number of available jobs; all a large company has to do is announce a willingness to relocate, and the offers from state and local governments—in the form of low-interest loans, tax relief, free utilities, and other benefits—come pouring in.

Some people call government aid to corporations "public-private partnerships." Such aid, they explain, creates jobs that may be needed by communities hard hit by business closings. Critics counter that handouts for big business amount to corporate welfare. Furthermore, the amounts provided are often far greater than any promise of new jobs justifies. In 1991, for example, Indiana offered a $451 million incentive package to United Airlines to build an aircraft maintenance facility in that state. United built the facility and created 6,300 new jobs. Some simple math shows that the cost of these new jobs came to a whopping $72,000 per person hired. In 1993, much the same happened when Alabama offered $253 million to lure Mercedes-Benz to build an automobile assembly plant in Tuscaloosa. The corporation created 1,500 new jobs, but at an average cost of $169,000 each. In 1997, Pennsylvania gave a $307 million incentive package to a Norwegian company to reopen part of Philadelphia's naval shipyard. Soon after, 950 people were hired, at a cost of $323,000 per new job. In 2002, Georgia spent $67,000 per job to close a deal on a new auto plant. In 2006, Indiana won the bidding for a new Honda plant near Indianapolis, spending $71,000 for each new job, and Nashville, Tennessee, closed a deal to bring a new Nissan plant to that city with an estimated 750 new jobs each costing $266,000 in incentives. Also in 2006, the state of New York approved $1.2 billion in tax reductions and other incentives to Advanced Microchip Devices to build a microchip factory creating 1,200 new jobs—at a cost of $1 million each.

Across the United States, even in good times, corporations benefit to the tune of tens of billions of dollars each year. In 2008 and 2009, government "bailouts" were far greater, totaling more than $1 trillion in an effort to bring an end to the most serious recession since the 1930s. This is about fifty times the amount that the government spends on welfare programs that benefit poor families.

WHAT DO YOU THINK?

1. If you were a public official in a state with high unemployment, would you support economic incentives to draw corporations to your state? Why or why not?
2. Why do you think welfare assistance to poor families has always been so controversial in the United States and yet few people object to the forms of corporate welfare described here?
3. Do you support the recent government bailouts to large financial corporations? What about the auto industry? Why or why not?

Sources: Bartlett & Steele (1998) and Sachs (2009).

2002, federal and state governments settled action against the Microsoft Corporation based on alleged violations of antimonopoly laws.

Such actions have trimmed the power of giant corporations, but only to a point. The law forbids corporations from operating as outright monopolies because a single producer dominating a market with no competition can push up prices and exploit consumers. But the law does not prevent **oligopoly,** *the domination of a market by a few companies.* Today, for example, the manufacture of breakfast cereal is dominated by Kellogg, General Mills, and Post, which together control about 90 percent of all sales. Similarly, General Electric, Phillips, and Sylvania dominate the market for electric lights; Goodyear, Bridgestone, and Michelin have a dominant position in the tire industry; Kodak, and Fuji are dominant producers of film; and Toyota, General Motors, Ford, and Honda dominate auto production.

Conglomerates and Other Linkages

Corporations, by themselves, are powerful. But as businesses grow and buy other businesses, they can become even larger and stronger. A **conglomerate** is *a giant corporation composed of many smaller corporations.* Examples of conglomerates include PepsiCo, the maker of Pepsi soft drinks, which also owns Taco Bell, KFC, and Pizza Hut restaurants as well as Frito-Lay and other snack and fast-food companies. Ford has recently sold the British auto company Aston Martin and is in the process of selling Swedish auto company Volvo, but Ford retains a share of

special-interest groups political alliances of people interested in some economic or social issue

lobbying the efforts of special-interest groups and their representatives to influence government officials.

political action committees (PACs) organizations formed by special-interest groups to raise and spend money in support of political goals

interlocking directorates social networks made up of people who serve as directors of several corporations at the same time

Mazda, a Japanese corporation. For their part, General Motors owns the German company Opel, the British company Vauxhall, and is seeking to sell its interest in the Swedish company, Saab, but still has partnerships with Suzuki, Isuzu, and Toyota in Japan. Pearson, a large British corporation, operates around the world, running newspapers (including London's *Financial Times*) and a number of publishing companies (including Prentice Hall, the publisher of this textbook).

Another way corporations work together is by sharing members of their boards of directors. **Interlocking directorates** are *social networks made up of people who serve as directors of several corporations at the same time.* A member of Kodak's board of directors, for example, might also serve on the boards of other film companies such as Fuji. The world's biggest corporations are linked to hundreds of other corporations through common board members.

Conglomerates and interlocking directorates are perfectly legal and don't necessarily do anything wrong. But they do increase the power of large corporations, and they may encourage oligopoly and illegal activities such as price fixing, in which various companies share information on pricing so they do not have to compete on price in the marketplace. Price fixing harms the public because consumers end up paying more than they would in a competitive economy.

Toward the end of the nineteenth century, the ever-increasing power of corporations reached the point at which the largest businesses had more power and money than the federal government. The government responded in 1890 by passing the Sherman Antitrust Act, which forbids single companies from controlling an entire market. In this cartoon from the early twentieth century, President Theodore Roosevelt plays Jack (from the fable "Jack and the Beanstalk"), out to slay the Wall Street giants who dominate the U.S. economy. Can you think of recent cases in which the government has charged that a particular corporation has gained control of an entire market?

The Power of Money

The enormous wealth of corporations brings us to the question of how money influences the political process. Corporations are not the only organizations with a voice in the political system. On the contrary, people across the United States join together to form many kinds of organizations that seek to advance various political goals. A notable feature of the U.S. political system is **special-interest groups,** *political alliances of people interested in some economic or social issue.*

We are all familiar with many special-interest groups such as AARP (formerly the American Association of Retired Persons), the National Rifle Association (NRA), and the American Civil Liberties Union (ACLU).

For both people and organizations, more money means more political influence. One way in which money buys political power is through **lobbying,** *the efforts of special-interest groups and their representatives to influence government officials.* AARP, the NRA, and the ACLU all employ lobbyists in Washington, D.C., and elsewhere who work full time pressuring members of Congress to pass legislation that advances their interests. Corporations, too, employ lobbyists—Wal-Mart, for example, has eight lobbyists working from its office in Washington, D.C. In all, almost 15,000 lobbyists work to influence the operation of the federal government (Federal Election Commission, 2008; Center for Responsive Politics, 2009).

Lobbying—explaining why to support a particular position on some issue—is perfectly legal. But many lobbyists offer more than information to our elected leaders. When elected leaders accept money or other valuable favors from lobbyists,

SOCIAL PROBLEMS in Everyday Life

Do you think lobbyists are democracy in action? Or do they undermine democracy? Why?

GETTING INVOLVED

Have you ever contributed to a political campaign?

both parties may well end up accused of committing a crime. Campaign contributions are perhaps the most controversial aspect of lobbying, as we now explain.

Campaign Financing

Concern about the power of money in politics involves not only the work of lobbyists but also the financing of political campaigns. A reality of political life in the United States is that running for office is very expensive. In the 2008 presidential elections, Barack Obama and John McCain together spent more than $1 billion on their campaigns. In the 2008 congressional races, candidates for seats in the House and the Senate also spent more than $1 billion (Pickler & Sidoti, 2008).

Where does all the money come from? Corporations provide more campaign contributions than all other types of groups, including labor unions, civil rights groups, and women's organizations. Political parties are another important source of money. In addition, candidates are free to spend as much of their own money as they wish. Very rich people have a huge advantage over "ordinary" people, although great wealth is no guarantee of success. For example, in 1996 and 2000, Steve Forbes spent $66 million of his own money to fund unsuccessful runs for the presidency.

Most candidates raise the vast sums needed to run a political campaign by appealing to individuals and organizations to make contributions. Candidates at all levels of government receive money from **political action committees (PACs),** *organizations formed by special-interest groups to raise and spend money in support of political goals.* There are currently about 5,200 PACs in the United States, representing a wide range of special-interest groups, including the pharmaceutical and tobacco industries, defense industries, labor unions, agribusinesses, religious organizations, senior citizens, and gun owners (Federal Election Commission, 2009).

As recently as 2000, campaign finance laws limited any PAC's contribution to a candidate to $5,000 in a primary election and an additional $5,000 in the general election. But PACs could solicit donations for candidates directly from donors and just pass along the money to the candidate. Such *bundling* of checks, along with high-priced fundraising dinners and other strategies that get around legal limits on campaign contributions, generated an almost unlimited amount of campaign contributions called *soft money.*

In addition, there was no limit on how much a PAC could spend to assist candidates as long as the PAC did not operate under the control of candidates or their campaign committees (Conway & Green, 1998). For this reason, many PACs focused their spending on particular issues that helped the candidates they favored. For example, raising money in support of abortion rights typically helps more liberal (usually Democratic) candidates, and raising money to oppose abortion typically helps the electoral campaigns of more conservative (usually Republican) candidates.

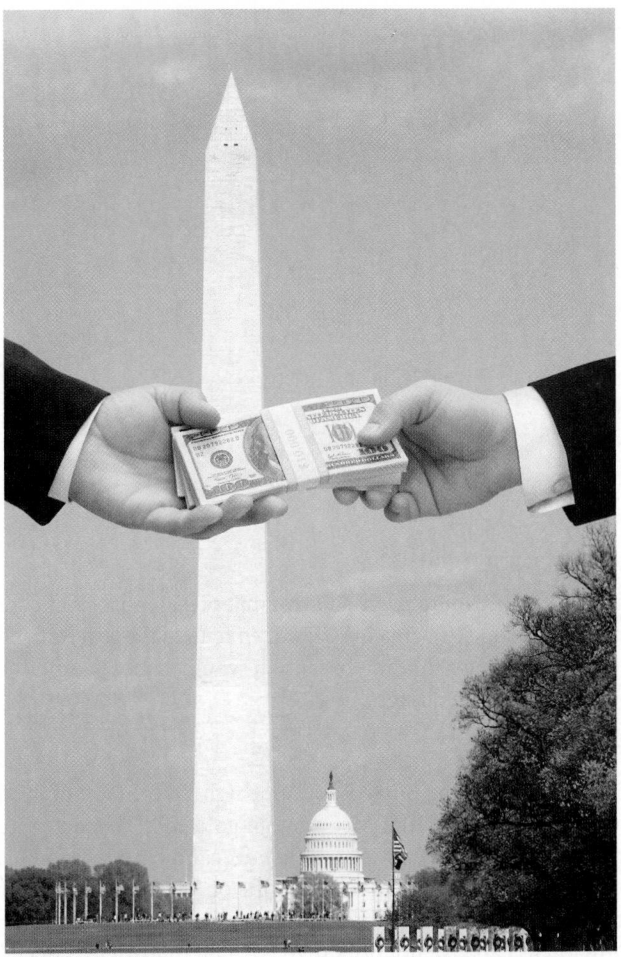

A number of major donors have access to this country's political leaders. To what extent is it true that wealthy people and powerful organizations shape the nation's political agenda?

Individuals, corporations, unions, and PACs were also able to donate larger sums of money to political parties. Although an individual could donate no more than $1,000 to any candidate in a specific political race, individuals were allowed to donate up to $20,000 per year to national parties and up to $5,000 to state parties (Herrnson, 1998). Federal law limited the amount an individual could contribute to all candidates for public office to $25,000 per year. Yet by combining the methods of support, many individuals easily spent much more. In fact, the available

Jake Lacona goes to a community college in Hawaii where few students are registered to vote.

Like most students on her Minnesota campus, Mae Prentice voted in the 2008 election.

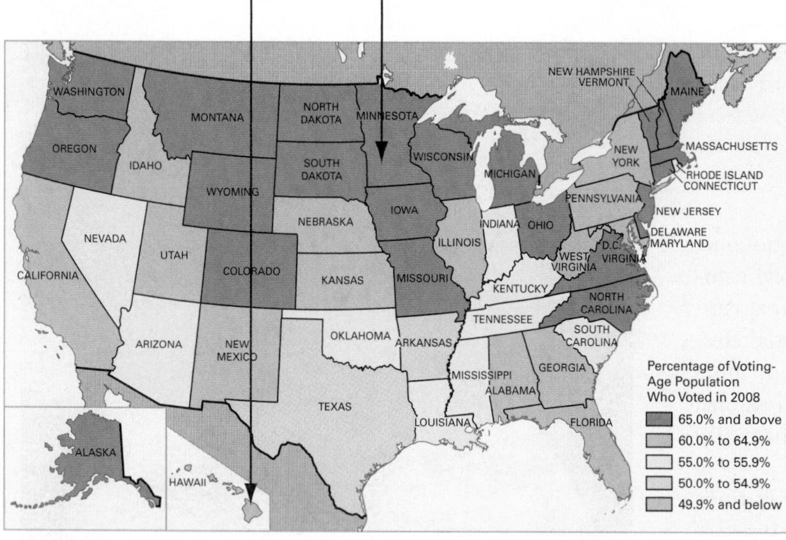

A Nation of Diversity

NATIONAL MAP 10–1

Voter Turnout across the United States

Overall, 63 percent of voting-age people went to the polls in the 2008 presidential election. By state, people in Minnesota were most likely to vote (76.1 percent) and people in Hawaii were least likely to do so (49.3 percent). What pattern do you see for the country as a whole? Can you explain the pattern?

Source: Center for the Study of the American Electorate (2009).

cash from contributors was so great that presidential candidates (including Barack Obama in 2008) often refused the government's offer of campaign funding because it would impose additional limits on their spending.

The 2002 Reforms

Congress passed the Bipartisan Campaign Reform Act of 2002, popularly known as the McCain-Feingold bill. This act states that soft money can no longer flow to candidates or political parties. Individuals are limited to gifts of $2,000 each to political candidates in any primary or general election. In addition, individuals can give no more than $95,000 in total gifts (a ceiling of $37,500 to all candidates and $57,500 to all political parties). PACs can now give no more than $5,000 to any one candidate and $15,000 to any one political party, with no overall limit. Under the new system, PACs have changed their strategy from collecting money and passing it along to candidates and parties to encouraging individuals to give money (under the limits noted earlier) directly to candidates and parties. In 2003, the U.S. Supreme Court (in a sharply divided five-to-four decision) upheld the key features of the campaign finance reform bill.

Why have so many people defined campaign financing as a serious problem? The simple answer is that the political contributions of $50 million and more made regularly by special-interest groups (such as organizations representing the real estate industry or lawyers) are given with the expectation that candidates who receive this money will support certain political goals. In other words, few political officials write a law or even cast a vote without thinking about the effects of their decisions on fundraising for their next campaign. In practice, say critics, our system of campaign financing puts the U.S. political system up for sale (A. Starr, 2003; Center for Responsive Politics, 2008; Federal Election Commission, 2008).

Voter Apathy

If money plays such a big part in U.S. politics, allowing special interests to dominate political events, perhaps we should not be surprised that many people do not bother to vote. The low rate of *voter turnout,* that is, the share of eligible people who vote, is cause for concern. In 2008, an election year that generated special excitement, only 63 percent of eligible voters went to the polls, up slightly from 61 percent in 2004 and 54 percent in 2000 (Center for the Study of the American Electorate, 2009).

Our country has a history of expanding voting rights, including the Fifteenth Amendment, which extended the vote to African American men in 1870; the Nineteenth Amendment, which gave women the vote in 1920; and the Twenty-Sixth Amendment, which lowered the voting age from twenty-one years to eighteen in 1971. Today, the only adult citizens in the United States without the right to vote are convicted felons. National Map 10–1 shows where in the United States people are most likely and least likely to vote.

In a society that has extended the right to vote to more and more people, why do so many of us not go to the polls? Conservatives suggest that the failure to vote is a sign of *indifference* on the part of people who are pretty much satisfied with the way things are. Liberals and radicals on the left take a different view, arguing that low voter turnout reflects widespread *alienation* from politics. As they see it, many people are

GETTING INVOLVED

Why do you think so many college-age people do not vote? Have you registered to vote?

dissatisfied with the way things are, but they doubt that voting will make any difference. Especially in recent decades, corporate fraud, scandals involving lobbyists in Congress, negative campaign advertising, and outright political corruption have caused a decline in public confidence in "the system," with the results shown in Figure 10–3. The bottom line seems to be that given the power of money in U.S. political life, many people doubt that "the little guy" makes much of a difference (Dye, 1999; U.S. Census Bureau, 2005).

Perhaps the United States should follow the lead of Australia, Belgium, Italy, and other nations that have enacted laws requiring people to vote. Another approach is to offer more choices. In other countries, higher turnouts are found where there are more political parties that represent a wider range of positions than are found in the United States. Here, as some people see it, the two major parties have much in common. The fact that Barack Obama attracted millions of new voters to the polls (as well as millions of small contributions) suggests that new faces and new policies may excite more voters.

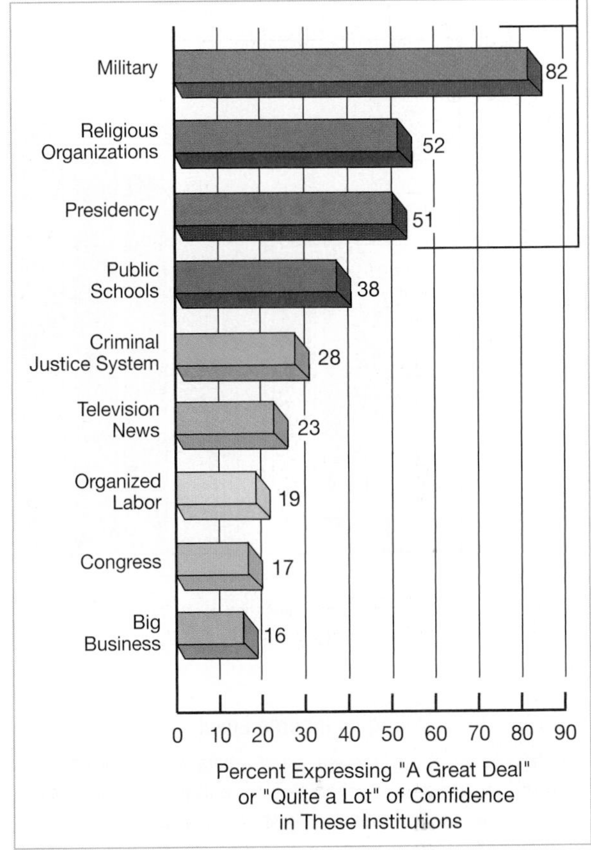

FIGURE 10–3 **Public Confidence in Selected Institutions, 2009**

Public confidence in important organizations has declined in recent decades. Why do you think public confidence in most of our institutions is so low?

Source: The Polling Report (2009).

Who Votes? Class, Age, Race, Ethnicity, and Gender

Low voter turnout not only weakens this country's democratic ideal but also reflects the fact that certain categories of people are especially likely to be left out of the political process.

Income

Income is one important factor. Most people with high incomes vote, but most people with low incomes do not. Figure 10–4 on page 276 shows that 80 percent of people earning more than $100,000 per year reported voting in the 2008 presidential election. By contrast, 49 percent of people earning less than $10,000 said that they had cast a vote (U.S. Census Bureau, 2009).

What explains this difference? Affluent people tend to be more highly educated, and college graduates are twice as likely to vote as high school dropouts. In addition, because income rises over the life course, affluent people, on average, are older. The older people are, the more likely they are to vote. People over the age of sixty-five are more likely to vote in presidential elections (70.3 percent did) than college-age adults (48.5 percent voted in 2008), many of whom have not even registered (U.S. Census Bureau, 2009).

Race

Historically, race has had much to do with voting. Until 1865, no person of color could vote in the United States. African American men gained the right to vote in 1870, as did women of any race in 1920. In 2008, African Americans were almost as likely to vote (65 percent of eligible people voted) as white people (66 percent). African Americans provide strong support for Democratic candidates; in 2008, more than 95 percent voted for Barack Obama (Kohut, 2008; U.S. Census Bureau, 2009).

Ethnicity

People of Hispanic descent are even less likely to vote (in 2008, just 50 percent of eligible voters did so). In part, this is because Hispanic Americans have a high rate of poverty. In addition, a sense of cultural marginality and less ability to speak English discourage many Latinas and Latinos from voting. The fact that the Hispanic population is increasing rapidly makes attracting this category of voters crucial to winning elections. The recent

gender gap the tendency for women and men to hold different opinions about certain issues and to support different candidates

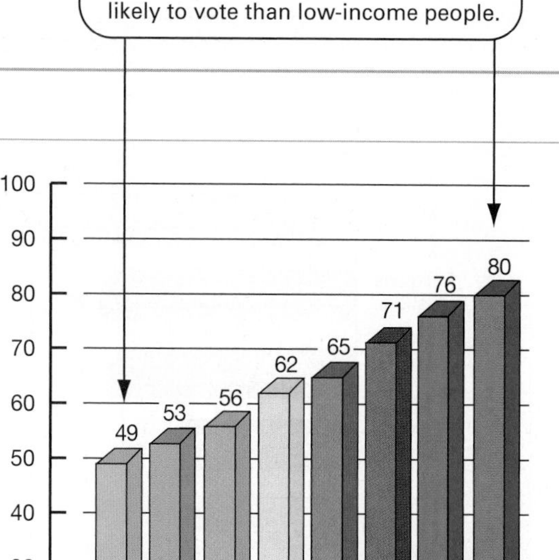

FIGURE 10–4 **Voting by Income Level**

The figure shows the percentage of adults who reported voting in the 2008 presidential election. A clear pattern is present. As income goes up, so does the likelihood of voting.

Source: U.S. Census Bureau (2009).

trend has been for Hispanics to favor Democratic candidates (Cisneros, 2009; Lopez & Taylor, 2009).

Gender

Gender matters in voting: In 2008, women (65.7 percent) were slightly more likely to vote than men (61.5 percent). In addition, women are more likely to support Democratic candidates. In 2008, women favored Obama over McCain by 56 percent to 43 percent. Men typically favor Republicans, although in 2008 they split close to even with 48 percent voting for McCain and 49 percent voting for Obama (*New York Times*, 2008).

The Gender Gap: Seeing Problems Differently

In political terms, the **gender gap** is *the tendency for women and men to hold different opinions about certain issues and to support different candidates.* Women and men tend to define the problems our country faces and what should be done about them in somewhat different ways. In general, women are more likely than men to support so-called compassion issues that seek to protect vulnerable members of society (including children, older people, and people with disabilities). In addition, women are more likely to support gun control and to oppose the death penalty. Men, by contrast, are more likely to favor a strong military, support the right to own a gun, and favor a tough response to crime, including use of the death penalty.

Such differences make women more likely to support Democrats and push men to favor Republicans. In recent presidential elections, a larger share of women have supported the Democratic candidate and, except in 2008, a larger share of men have voted Republican.

Voting Laws for Persons Convicted of Serious Crimes

The only category of people widely barred from voting in national elections are felons—people who have been convicted of committing serious crimes. Forty-eight of the fifty states (all except Vermont and Maine) have laws that bar people in prison from voting. Thirty states do not allow people on probation after conviction for a felony to vote. Eleven states ban voting by people who have completed their prison sentences, subject to various appeals to restore their right to vote. These laws take away the right to vote for more than 5 million people in the United States (Sentencing Project, 2008).

Should punishment include loss of the right to vote, even for people who have done their time in jail? That's what the law says in much of the country. But critics claim that this practice is politically motivated, because taking away the right to vote for convicted criminals has a predictable effect on the outcome of elections. Convicted felons, which include a high proportion of low-income people and racial and ethnic minorities, show better than a two-to-one preference for Democratic over Republican candidates. For this reason, it is likely that the Democratic political officials now in power may review this policy and act to change it.

Social Movements: How Much Change?

Donating money and voting are not the only ways for people to be politically active. Other options range from signing petitions to engaging in violent protest. Over the course of the twentieth century, political activism on the part of women, African Americans, gay men and lesbians, poor people, and workers led to important changes in social policy.

Early in the twentieth century, workers reacted to industrialization by demanding limited working hours and the rights to

GETTING INVOLVED

Have you taken part in a social movement seeking a political goal in the past year or so? If so, what movement? What was its goal? Was it successful?

pluralist model an analysis of the political system that sees power widely distributed among various groups and organizations in a society

form unions and to bargain collectively with employers. In the Great Depression of the 1930s and again in the 1960s, people successfully pressed for government programs to address problems such as poverty and homelessness.

In the 1950s and 1960s, African Americans joined together in the civil rights movement, demanding—and winning—an end to the segregation of schools and public facilities and protection from discrimination in employment, schooling, housing, and public accommodations. In the 1960s and 1970s, the women's movement gained similar protections from discrimination, guaranteeing women equal opportunities in schooling, athletics, employment, and the ability to obtain credit and greater opportunities in the military. Since then, in some states and cities, the gay and lesbian movement has achieved protection from discrimination in the workplace and in access to housing; in an increasing number of states (five by mid-2011), homosexual partners have gained the right to marry. Finally, throughout the past century, senior citizens have worked to improve retirement and health care benefits.

Elderly people in the United States have enormous political clout, based not just on their relative wealth but also on their high voter turnout. People over the age of sixty-five are much more likely to vote than young people in their late teens and twenties. How might the power of young people change if they, too, turned out to vote in large numbers?

No one can doubt that activism has been a powerful political force in the United States, resulting in changes in the law and, over time, in public attitudes. But it is also true that none of the movements mentioned has altered the U.S. political economy in any fundamental way. Over the course of the past century, there has been little change in the concentration of wealth. On the contrary, since 1980, the gap between the richest and poorest members of our society has increased. Nor has there been any notable reduction in the power of corporations in this country; rather, recent years witnessed less regulation, with the corporations (and the pay of corporate executives) growing ever bigger. Also keep in mind—as discussed in Chapter 2 ("Poverty and Wealth")—that during the 1990s, welfare reforms reduced the social safety net for the poor.

In sum, the question of who controls the political economy of the United States remains as important today as ever. Analysts offer varying views on this important question.

Theoretical Analysis: Understanding Economic and Political Problems

Sociology's two macro-level theoretical approaches offer insights into economic and political problems. Each approach highlights different facts and points to different conclusions.

Structural-Functional Analysis: Rule by the Many

The structural-functional approach views the economic system as a complex institution that operates to produce and distribute goods and services to the entire population. This approach has some similarity to the laissez-faire model that underlies capitalism because both share the idea that the economy serves the needs of individuals who make decisions about what to produce and what to consume. As Adam Smith argued, from individual decisions guided by self-interest the economy operates to produce the greatest good for the greatest number of people.

The structural-functional approach takes much the same view of politics. The theory most often linked to this approach is the pluralist model of Robert Dahl.

Robert Dahl: The Pluralist Model

The **pluralist model** is *an analysis of the political system that sees power widely distributed among various groups and organizations in a society.* This model, based largely on the work of Robert Dahl (1961, 1982), suggests that individuals and organizations

GETTING INVOLVED

Have you ever taken part in a march or demonstration? Why?

Throughout this country's history, people have banded together in an effort to gain power and change the system. In the 1950s and 1960s, African Americans mounted demonstrations, such as this march from Selma to Montgomery, Alabama, in an effort to gain a greater political voice. In your view, how much real change do such movements create?

compete in the political "marketplace" trying to win support from the people.

As Dahl sees it, some organizations have more clout than others, but none of the organizations is powerful enough to get its way all the time. This means that organizations achieve some of their goals, but most of the time, they operate as *veto groups*, working to keep their opponents from achieving all of *their* goals. In the pluralist model, various political organizations—including political parties, special-interest groups, and government agencies—not only compete for public support but also negotiate with one another, striking deals, forming alliances, and setting policy.

The pluralist model views society as an arena in which many organizations each appeal to some part of the population. In the same way that competition between businesses improves the economy, competition between parties and special-interest groups serves the public interest. Therefore, with so many organizations in operation, everyone has at least some political voice, and the United States ends up looking rather democratic (Rothman & Black, 1998).

CRITICAL REVIEW In a test of the pluralist model, Nelson Polsby (1959) examined how important decisions are made in a number of large cities in the United States. Polsby confirmed that power is widely distributed among many organizations. He found that any one group or organization in the city typically has some control over only a narrow range of issues (for example, the school board has influence in matters related to school policy but little else). Over the course of our history, the expansion of voting rights and the increase in the number of special-interest groups ensure that no one category of people has all the power and that just about everyone has some political voice.

But critics of the pluralist model claim that this view of U.S. society as highly democratic does not reflect political reality. Why is it, critics ask, that so many people in this country—especially the poor—see little reason to vote and many never even bother to register? Critics also point out that certain categories of people in this country clearly have more power than others (for example, the rich in relation to the poor), and certain organizations (say, large corporations compared with environmentalists) usually get their way. Such criticism that focuses on social inequality brings us to the social-conflict approach.

military-industrial complex, the close association of the federal government, the military, and the defense industries

power-elite model an analysis of the political system that sees power as concentrated among a small elite

Marxist political-economy model an analysis that sees the concentration of wealth and power in society as resulting from capitalism

Social-Conflict Analysis: Rule by the Few

The social-conflict approach sees the economic system as operating under the control of an elite. From this perspective, the economy of a capitalist country such as the United States operates to concentrate wealth in the hands of the few. The political system operates in much the same way, concentrating power. This conclusion challenges the pluralist claim that the United States is democratic. We briefly examine two social-conflict theories: the power-elite model of C. Wright Mills and the Marxist political economy model.

C. Wright Mills: The Power-Elite Model

In 1961, as he prepared to leave office after eight years as president, Dwight D. Eisenhower gave a farewell address in which he warned the country of the growing power of what he called the **military-industrial complex,** *the close association of the federal government, the military, and the defense industries.*

In giving this warning, Eisenhower might well have been thinking of what the sociologist C. Wright Mills (1956) called the **power-elite model,** *an analysis of the political system that sees power as concentrated among a small elite.* Who is this elite? According to Mills, the power elite is a small collection of individuals and their families that includes top military officials, the heads of major corporations, and top political leaders. In fact, many of the top military, corporate, and political officials are actually the same people because elites often move from one sector to another. For example, Eisenhower moved from a top spot in the military to a top spot in the world of politics. Likewise, many corporate leaders move into politics and return to corporate boardrooms after leaving office. Dick Cheney left a cabinet position to become a corporate CEO and later moved back into government as vice president only to return to the business world once again. Many power-elite families are socially connected, living in the same expensive communities, belonging to the same exclusive clubs, and sending their children to the same private schools.

Because they travel in the same social circles, Mills added, children of the power elite stand a good chance of marrying one another and passing along their privileges to another generation. Were he alive today, Mills would probably point out that all the candidates in recent presidential elections were well-connected millionaires.

Based on such observations, the power-elite model rejects the pluralist claim that power is widely spread throughout society, with organizations preventing one another from gaining too much power. On the contrary, this model leads to the conclusion that both wealth and power in U.S. society are highly concentrated so that the power elite pretty much run the country as they wish.

Karl Marx: Capitalist Political Economy

The **Marxist political-economy model** is *an analysis that sees the concentration of wealth and power in society as resulting from capitalism.* A Marxist approach accepts the power-elite model that U.S. society is far from democratic because it is dominated by an economic and political elite. But rather than focusing on the great power of certain individuals, the Marxist model takes a more radical approach and focuses on the institutional system that concentrates this wealth and power in the first place.

In Marx's view, the economy is the foundation that guides the way any society operates. Therefore, the concentration of wealth and power in the hands of a few results not from the ability and efforts of certain individuals but from the routine operation of the capitalist economy. From this point of view, as

Each year, the political leaders of the United States assemble for the president's State of the Union speech. The pluralist approach claims that these leaders represent a wide range of interests and organizations. The power-elite model sees them as a ruling elite, representing mainly their own interests. The political-economy model claims that the political process is guided by the capitalist economy.

MAKING THE GRADE

Use the table below to review two theoretical approaches to the economy and politics.

APPLYING THEORY

Economy and Politics

	What is the level of analysis?	How is power spread throughout U.S. society?	Is U.S. society democratic?
Structural-functional approach	Macro-level	The structural-functional approach sees power as spread throughout society. Dahl's pluralist theory states that many diverse organizations operate as veto groups and compete for support so that just about everyone has some political voice.	Yes, because most organizations deal with only limited numbers of issues and no one organization gets its way all the time. Power is dispersed widely enough that our society can fairly claim to be democratic.
Social-conflict approach	Macro-level	One important social-conflict theory is the power-elite model developed by C. Wright Mills. This theory states that our society is run by a power elite made up of leaders in government, the economy, and the military. This alliance, or military-industrial complex, controls the political life of the nation.	No, because power is concentrated within a small circle of families that make up the power elite. By controlling the government, the economy, and the military, these families effectively run the entire society.
		A more radical social-conflict theory is the political-economy model based on the ideas of Karl Marx. This approach claims that wealth and power are highly concentrated as a result of the operation of the capitalist economic system.	No, and power will always be highly concentrated as long as the United States has a capitalist economy. This means that radical change, not mere reform, is needed to make our society truly democratic.

long as the United States has a capitalist economy, the majority of people will be shut out of politics, just as they are exploited in the workplace.

CRITICAL REVIEW The social-conflict approach challenges the notion that U.S. society is democratic and highlights the extent of economic and political inequality. At the same time, this approach gives little attention to the progress U.S. society has made toward extending both economic and political opportunity over the course of its history. This greater opportunity is evident in the rapidly increasing number of minorities and women who hold political office. Furthermore, although a few U.S. presidents were born into the upper class (George W. Bush is one example), many more rose from humble origins (for example, Bill Clinton was born into a working-class family, and Barack Obama is the son of a single mother). Another criticism comes from the observation that elites also dominate the politics of nations with socialist economies such as China, Cuba, and North Korea, where leaders tolerate little opposition and many of the same people remain in power for decades.

The Applying Theory table summarizes what each approach teaches us about the economy and politics.

 POLITICS AND THE ECONOMY

Constructing Problems and Defining Solutions

Theory provides helpful ways to think about the economy and politics, but what the problems are and how to go about solving them are matters of political opinion. Here we explore conservative, liberal, and radical-left political positions on economic and political problems and solutions from each of these points of view.

GETTING INVOLVED

Many people consider themselves to be conservative on some issues and liberal or even radical on others. Do you have such mixed attitudes? Explain.

welfare state a range of policies and programs that transfer wealth from the rich to the poor and provide benefits to needy members of society

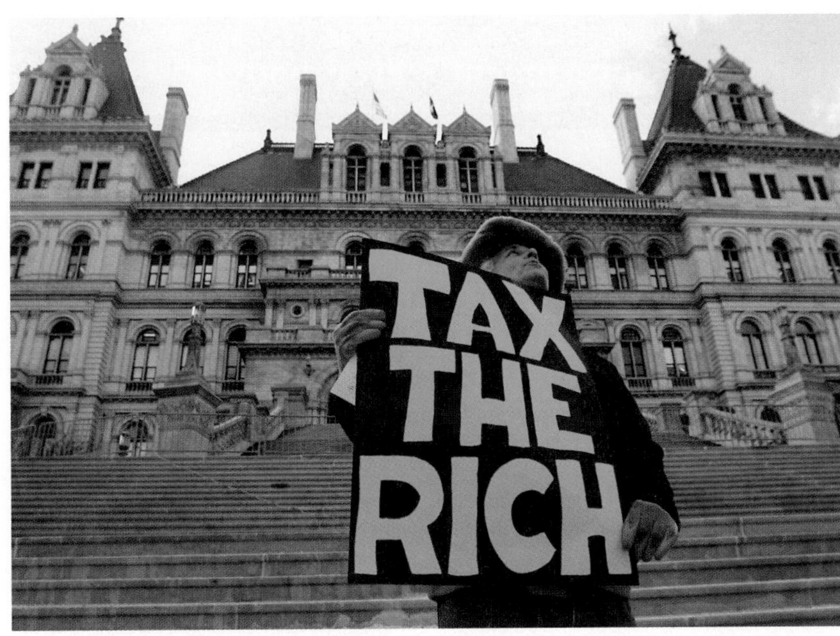

Conservatives claim that by providing everyone with a vote and by linking rewards to personal ability and effort, our economic and political systems serve the entire population fairly. Liberals support government reforms to better serve the most needy people and reduce inequality. Radicals on the left call for a government-run economy that would meet everyone's basic needs equally. Which view comes closest to your own? Why?

Conservatives: The System Is Working

Believing that free competition in the marketplace is good for society, conservatives favor limiting government involvement in the economy. Likewise, they hold that competition between political candidates for voter support, as well as competition between special-interest groups, is good for democracy.

Conservatives point out that our political system permits every adult citizen (except felons, in most states) to participate in the political process by voting—although it is up to the individual to register and cast a vote. In addition, people are free to join special-interest groups, contribute to campaigns, work for political parties, and participate in social movements and even join in political protests.

Most of these rights have been with us since the Constitution was ratified in 1788. In addition, ever since then, the United States has steadily extended the right to vote to almost every adult, and never have there been so many special-interest groups on the political scene as there are today. In short, all of us have many opportunities to express our views and to band together with others who share our positions.

As a result, conservatives claim that the current economic and political systems work pretty well. As the old saying goes, the economic and political systems in the United States may not be perfect, but they are better than anything else out there. In short, except for calling for smaller government in the interest of greater economic productivity, conservatives see few problems in the U.S. political economy.

What about the recent economic recession? Conservatives believe that letting markets operate on their own is the best way to serve the public interest. For this reason, they generally oppose efforts by the Obama administration to extend the arm of government into the operation of the economy (Klein, 2009).

Liberals: The Need for Reform

Liberals also favor a market economy, but only if it is regulated by the government. As they see it, a laissez-faire economy concentrates wealth in the hands of the few. Those with the greatest wealth, in turn, are able to gain control of the political process so that government action ends up mostly benefiting the rich and powerful interest groups such as large corporations.

To reduce the economic inequality produced by a market economy, liberals support a **welfare state,** *a range of policies and programs that transfer wealth from the rich to the poor and provide benefits to needy members of society.* Part of welfare state policy is progressive taxation, a policy that raises the tax rate as income goes up (take a glance back at Table 2–1 on page 31). In practice, those with higher incomes provide money in the form of taxes to pay for the programs that benefit people with lower incomes. The result of such income transfers from rich to poor is that government is able to

MAKING THE GRADE

Notice in the box below how both Republicans and Democrats support "big government" when it serves their interests.

THINKING CRITICALLY

Who Favors "Big Government"? Everybody!

A common assumption is that liberals (typically people who vote Democratic) support a larger government than conservatives (typically those who vote Republican). There is some truth to this statement. But more correctly, people on *both* sides of the political spectrum support the use of government power as long as it is in pursuit of the particular goals they consider important. After all, just as government has grown under (Democratic) President Obama, it grew as well under (Republican) President Bush.

The chart illustrates the politics of big government. Liberals typically define social problems in terms of social inequality. For example, liberals generally think that the rich have too much and the poor have too little. Therefore, liberals support progressive taxation, with the funds raised by taxes being used to pay for extensive social welfare programs. In addition, liberals support government activism to end discrimination against women and other minorities. To help all poor people, liberals would like the government to mandate a universal health care program. To reach these goals, government must get bigger.

But conservatives, too, support big government—except that they want government to do different things. Conservatives typically define social problems in moral terms. For example, conservatives see evil in the world that threatens the United States, and so they favor bigger government in the form of a larger military with more and better equipment. In the same way, many conservatives oppose abortion and gay marriage and would like the government to restrict access to abortion and to enact a constitutional ban on same-sex marriage.

In the end, liberals and conservatives do not differ drastically in their support for "big government." This is because government power is a very effective way to address many social problems. The recognition of the power of government is also the reason that government spending is high whether our leaders are mostly Republicans or Democrats. But identifying exactly what the problems are still depends on your point of view.

WHAT DO YOU THINK?

1. Make a list of three problems liberals want government to solve. Do the same for conservatives.
2. Why did government spending increase under Republican President Bush? Why has it increased again under Democratic President Obama?
3. How would radicals on the left respond to both the liberal and conservative positions?

"Are You in Favor of Big Government?"

On issues of:	*Liberals would say . . .*	*Conservatives would say . . .*
Inequality	YES! Government should actively reduce social inequality by enlarging social welfare programs, opposing discrimination, and supporting affirmative action.	NO! Government should keep taxes low and should not seek to expand social welfare programs that discourage personal effort and threaten freedom.
Morality	NO! Government should not try to legislate morality, because doing so weakens personal choice and threatens freedom.	YES! Government should actively promote national security (by enlarging military defense) and traditional morality (by opposing abortion and gay marriage).

reduce the economic inequality created by the market and assist the needy.

With regard to politics, liberals support social policies that would reduce the wealth of the nation's richest citizens. For example, most liberals opposed the tax cuts enacted by President Bush and support President Obama's plans to raise taxes on people with higher incomes and more earnings from investments.

Liberals also want to limit the political power of the corporate elites and other high-income people. To do this, liberals

MAKING THE GRADE

Use the table below to review the three political approaches to the political economy.

GETTING INVOLVED

How do you assess the work of President Obama and the Democrat-controlled Congress? Explain.

LEFT TO RIGHT

The Politics of the Political Economy

	RADICAL-LEFT VIEW	LIBERAL VIEW	CONSERVATIVE VIEW
WHAT IS THE PROBLEM?	The capitalist economy concentrates wealth in the hands of the few; the government serves the interests of the capitalist elite. Overall, U.S. society is neither economically just nor politically democratic.	The economy is productive, but some people fare much better than others; those with greater wealth have the most influence in the political system.	Politics and economics are not a problem. The economy is highly productive and responds to consumer demand; the political system is based on elections in which individuals vote and various organizations negotiate to form public policy.
WHAT IS THE SOLUTION?	Efforts to reform the capitalist political economy will have little effect. What is needed is fundamental change in the economic and political systems so that they reflect the interests and meet the needs of the majority.	Government social welfare programs should transfer wealth from rich to poor to lessen inequality. Political reforms are needed to reduce the role of corporate and individual wealth in the political process.	Market economics should be maintained because it provides the greatest good for the greatest number of people. The United States stands out among nations as a model of extensive rights and freedoms.

JOIN THE DEBATE

1. What, in your opinion, are the strengths and weaknesses of the U.S. economy? Provide specific facts to support your position.
2. To what degree do you think the United States can be described as a political democracy? What specific evidence can you present in support of your assessment?
3. Which of the three political analyses of political economy included here do you find most convincing? Why?

believe that encouraging people to vote is important but not enough. They want to empower people through policies such as raising the minimum wage, expanding child support programs, expanding access to higher education, and ensuring that health care is available to all. Liberals support a strong and activist government in the belief that only government, working for the interests of ordinary people, can effectively oppose the enormous power of special-interest groups such as large corporations.

In terms of the recent economic recession, liberals see the financial scandals that led to the collapse of the housing market and mortgage industry as evidence that more government regulation of the economy is needed. They generally support the Obama administration's efforts to give government greater control over the economy.

It is true that liberals generally support bigger government than conservatives do. But both liberals and conservatives at times favor using government power as a solution to what they define as social problems. The Thinking Critically box takes a closer look.

The Radical Left: A Call for Basic Change

Generally speaking, the further left you move, the more you want to replace a market system with government control of the economy. Radicals on the left (following Karl Marx) believe that the problem with a capitalist market system is that it concentrates wealth in the hands of the few. Government does little more than help the capitalist economy operate and works to protect the wealth of the rich. In a capitalist political economy, most people have little power or financial security.

From a radical-left perspective, the problem is not that a power elite has managed to seize control of the government, as liberals are inclined to say. Radicals believe that as long as a capitalist political economy exists in the United States, no small change—such as voters electing more liberal candidates or Congress passing campaign finance reform—will make much difference. For radicals, the only solution to capitalism's concentration of wealth and power is an end to capitalism itself. For a society to be truly democratic, all people must have

SOCIAL PROBLEMS in Everyday Life

Are you optimistic about our country's future? Are you pessimistic? Mixed feelings? Explain how you see our nation's future.

an equal say in politics; for that to happen, there must be equity in wealth.

Radicals on the left will certainly find the policies of the Obama administration preferable to those of its predecessor Bush administration. But they will claim that meaningful change demands not just extending government control of the market economy but eliminating the market and placing the economy entirely under government control. Only by ending private ownership of productive property will people share equally in everything our society produces (Eby, 2009).

The Left to Right table on page 283 views problems and issues of political economy from the various points of view.

Going On from Here

Over a century ago, during the Industrial Revolution, the emergence of huge corporations raised national concerns about the power of "big money." Congress enacted various laws to combat corporate monopoly and to limit the power of big business to control U.S. society. These laws had a modest effect, sharply reducing outright monopoly but permitting widespread oligopoly. For much of the twentieth century, few people doubted that corporations had enormous power in the halls of federal and state governments.

In the 1970s, Congress once again believed it was time to reduce corporate influence in U.S. politics. An important reform—the 1971 Federal Election Campaign Act—led to the creation of the political action committees we have discussed in this chapter. This law tried to level the playing field by placing limits on the political contributions of both rich individuals and large corporations.

The results of this bill fell short of its promise. For one thing, the costs of campaigning—now conducted primarily through paid advertising on television—have soared. Today's political candidates need more money than ever to get into office. Not surprisingly, in the past several decades, the number and influence of PACs have grown; PACs now provide more than four times as much money to members of Congress as they did in the 1970s. Although PACs represent a wide range of political interests, including labor unions, corporate PACs outnumber and give more money to candidates than any other type. This fact and recent lobbying scandals in Congress help explain why many people continue to link special-interest groups to political corruption.

Did the 2002 campaign finance reform law have much effect? As in the past, the intention was to limit the power of big money on the political process. Even under the new law, however, candidates continue to rely on contributions to finance expensive campaigns that reached a new height in the 2004 elections and again in 2008.

There can be little doubt that the operation of the U.S. economic and political systems will be debated for years to come. Many people see problems that they want solved, but most voices are calling for reform rather than revolution. Yet a troubling fact remains: Almost 40 percent of all U.S. citizens seem so turned off by the political process that they do not even bother to vote. Whether they really believe that the candidates and policy options presented offer no real choice (as radicals on the left tend to say) or whether they are basically satisfied with their lives (as conservatives to the right would have it) is hard to say. But the recent campaign finance reforms seem likely to have little effect on the low level of political participation in the United States. The prospect of change did draw millions of people into the political process in 2008, but the problem of apathy remains more or less as it was before.

In the end, perhaps we need to return to a basic question: What do we mean by "democracy"? Then we must face an even more difficult issue: how we as a nation will get there.

Is our country becoming more equal? At least in terms of popular culture, you might think so. Consider the fact that in the world of fashion, almost everyone—rich and poor alike—wears jeans. This type of pants was invented 150 years ago as tough, durable trousers for hard-working people, and the style has spread throughout the population. Does such a pattern say something about political attitudes?

DEFINING SOLUTIONS

What is the purpose of the economy?

The point of the economy is to provide goods and services to the people living in a society. That's easy enough, but the big question is how should the economy operate? All the great economic thinkers—including both Adam Smith on the right and Karl Marx on the left—understood that a key answer to this question is the balance between a market economy and a government-operated economy. Look at the photos below to see two distinct solutions to the question of how an economy should work.

From the point of view of the political left, the most important factor in the operation of the economy is the distribution of goods and services. The capitalist market economy, as Karl Marx explained, distributes everything unequally, thereby creating social classes. A market economy, as he saw it, was a problem rather than a solution. Only through government control of productive property, which allows an equal distribution of goods and services, can the needs of all people be met. Even capitalist countries such as the United States put government in control of building roadways and other public infrastructure.

HINT

Both Karl Marx and Adam Smith had it right, or at least partly right. The market economy is very productive, but it also generates considerable economic inequality. The question is where do you strike the balance between productivity and equality? Then there is the issue of freedom. Market systems provide extensive personal freedoms, but these freedoms mean less to the poor than to the rich. Government-run economies ensure freedom from want, but they attract criticism for limiting individual rights. In your opinion, where should the balance be struck?

From the point of view of the political right, the most important factor in the operation of the economy is its productivity. The market economy, as Adam Smith explained, generates the greatest good for the greatest number of people as long as it is allowed to operate with minimal government interference. Individuals should decide what to produce, and individuals also should decide what to consume.

Getting Involved: Applications & Exercises

1. Identify a small business in your area that is interesting to you; make an appointment for a brief interview with the owner or manager. Ask about the various laws and policies that regulate the business and the impact these policies have on workers and on the profitability of the business.
2. Go to a grocery store, and make a list of the brand names you find for breakfast cereal, canned soup, frozen dinners, spaghetti sauce, and potato chips. How many manufacturers produce each type of item?
3. Do you know who your representative in Congress is? Find out, and contact the person's office to see what you can learn about the costs of running campaigns and where this person's contributions come from. (By law, candidates must provide financial disclosure statements to all interested parties.)
4. Near your campus, find a local chapter of one of the following organizations: the National Organization for Women (NOW), AARP, the National Urban League, or the National Association for the Advancement of Colored People (NAACP). Explain your interest in the study of social problems, and ask about the organization's agenda, challenges, and success.

MAKING THE GRADE

A DEFINING MOMENT
Store Wars: Is Wal-Mart the Problem or the Solution? p. 269

CHAPTER 10 Economy and Politics

Economic Systems: Defining Justice, Defining Problems

- The **ECONOMY** is the social institution that organizes the production, distribution, and consumption of goods and services.
- **POLITICS** is the social institution that guides a society's decision making about how to live.
- **GOVERNMENT** is the formal organization that directs the political life of a society.

pp. 264–65

Two major economic models are **CAPITALISM** and **SOCIALISM**.

- Capitalism is based on the private ownership of productive property and a market system regulated by supply and demand.
- Socialism is based on collective ownership of productive property, with government control of the economy.

pp. 264–66

✓ *Nations differ in the degree to which their economies mix capitalism and socialism. (pp. 266–67)*

politics (p. 264) the social institution that guides a society's decision making about how to live

economy (p. 264) the social institution that organizes the production, distribution, and consumption of goods and services

capitalism (p. 264) an economic system in which natural resources and the means of producing goods and services are privately owned

government (p. 265) a formal organization that directs the political life of a society

socialism (p. 265) an economic system in which natural resources and the means of producing goods and services are collectively owned

The Economy and Politics

DEMOCRACY is a political system in which power is exercised by the people as a whole.

p. 268

AUTHORITARIAN political systems give people little voice in government.

p. 268

Are capitalist societies always democratic?

- Many conservatives and liberals point out that capitalism provides lots of personal freedom.
- Some liberals and people on the left counter that capitalism generates lots of economic inequality, which threatens democracy.

pp. 267–68

political economy (p. 267) the economic and political life of a nation or world region

democracy (p. 268) a political system in which power is exercised by the people as a whole

authoritarianism (p. 268) a political system that denies popular participation in government

monarchy (p. 268) a political system in which a single family rules from generation to generation

Problems of the U.S. Political Economy

CORPORATIONS stand at the center of the U.S. political economy.

- Government helps support corporations not only by buying corporate products but also with various incentives that critics call corporate welfare.

pp. 268–70

A century ago, some large corporations operated as **MONOPOLIES**, completely dominating a segment of the market.

- Today, government outlaws monopoly, but many large corporations operate as **OLIGOPOLIES**, in which a few giant corporations dominate a market.

pp. 270–71

Although **CONGLOMERATES** and **INTERLOCKING DIRECTORATES** are within the law, they can encourage illegal activities such as price fixing, and they certainly increase corporate wealth and power.

pp. 271–72

SPECIAL-INTEREST GROUPS raise money for political candidates and lobby government officials to advance particular interests.

- Raising campaign funds is a major concern of public officials, who seek money from individual donors, political parties, and political action committees (PACs).
- The importance of fundraising makes us ask whose interests government officials should serve.

pp. 272–74

VOTER APATHY is high in the United States, with only 63% of eligible people voting in the 2008 presidential election.

- Conservatives suggest that low voter turnout means that most people are content with their lives. Liberals and radicals counter that it means that people are dissatisfied but believe they have little power to bring about change.
- In general, voter apathy is greatest among the young, those with little education, and the poor.

pp. 274–76

SOCIAL MOVEMENTS offer us all the opportunity to be politically active.

- Various movements have changed U.S. society in important ways but have not brought fundamental change to our political economy.

pp. 276–77

corporations (p. 268) businesses with a legal existence, including rights and liabilities, separate from that of their members

monopoly (p. 270) the domination of an entire market by a single company

oligopoly (p. 271) the domination of a market by a few companies

conglomerate (p. 271) a giant corporation composed of many smaller corporations

interlocking directorates (p. 272) social networks made up of people who serve as directors of several corporations at the same time

special-interest groups (p. 272) political alliances of people interested in some economic or social issue

lobbying (p. 272) the efforts of special-interest groups and their representatives to influence government officials

political action committees (PACs) (p. 273) organizations formed by special-interest groups to raise and spend money in support of political goals

gender gap (p. 276) the tendency for women and men to hold different opinions about certain issues and to support different candidates

Theoretical Analysis: Understanding Economic and Political Problems

Structural-Functional Analysis: Rule by the Many

Guided by the structural-functional approach, the **PLURALIST MODEL** states that power is widely dispersed throughout U.S. society.

- Organizations compete for voter support and often operate as veto groups so that no single organization can dominate the political system.
- Just as economic competition results in the greatest good for the greatest number, competition between organizations and between candidates for popular support results in sound policy.

pp. 277–78

Social-Conflict Analysis: Rule by the Few

Guided by the social-conflict approach, the **POWER-ELITE MODEL** states that the U.S. political system is dominated by a power elite made up of the top leaders in this country's corporations, military, and government.

- A more radical social-conflict approach is the **MARXIST POLITICAL-ECONOMY MODEL**, which shifts the focus from elites to the capitalist system, which concentrates wealth and power in the hands of a few.

pp. 279–80

pluralist model (p. 277) an analysis of the political system that sees power widely distributed among various groups and organizations in a society

military-industrial complex (p. 279) the close association of the federal government, the military, and the defense industries

power-elite model (p. 279) an analysis of the political system that sees power as concentrated among a small elite

Marxist political-economy model (p. 279) an analysis that sees the concentration of wealth and power in society as resulting from capitalism

See the **Applying Theory** table on page 280.

Politics and the Economy: Constructing Problems and Defining Solutions

The Radical Left: A Call for Basic Change

- **RADICALS ON THE LEFT** believe that the root cause of political and economic problems in the United States is capitalism's concentration of wealth and power.
- Radicals on the left maintain that reform will not solve these problems; they call for elimination of the capitalist system.

pp. 283–84

Liberals: The Need for Reform

- **LIBERALS** point out that the U.S. economic and political systems produce significant social inequality.
- Liberals favor more government regulation of the economy and political system; they support social welfare programs funded by progressive taxation that redistribute income by providing various benefits to the poor.

pp. 281–83

Conservatives: The System Is Working

- **CONSERVATIVES** claim that the U.S. economic and political systems work well. Competition in the marketplace and in the political arena serves the public interest.
- Conservatives look to government to advance what they see as moral goals, such as national defense and restricting abortion and discouraging same-sex marriage.

p. 281

welfare state (p. 281) a range of policies and programs that transfer wealth from the rich to the poor and provide benefits to needy members of society

See the **Left to Right** table on page 283.

CONSTRUCTING THE PROBLEM

How can going to work become a problem?

Every year, more than 1 million U.S. workers suffer disabling accidents on the job; more seriously, almost 6,000 die as a result of workplace injuries.

Do U.S. workers have secure jobs?

About 30 percent of the U.S. labor force consists of temporary workers and part-timers. In bad economic times, just about everybody is at risk of a layoff.

Are all jobs open to everyone?

In the United States, almost 98 percent of dental hygienists—but just 27 percent of dentists—are women.

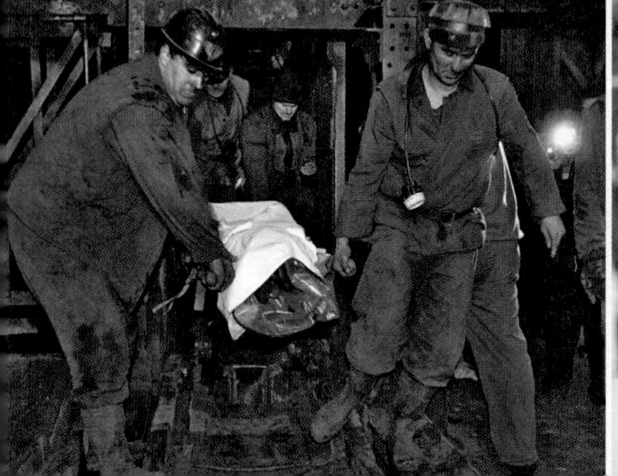

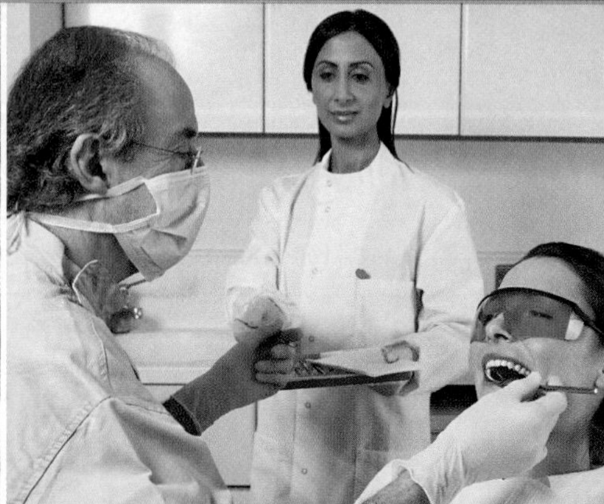

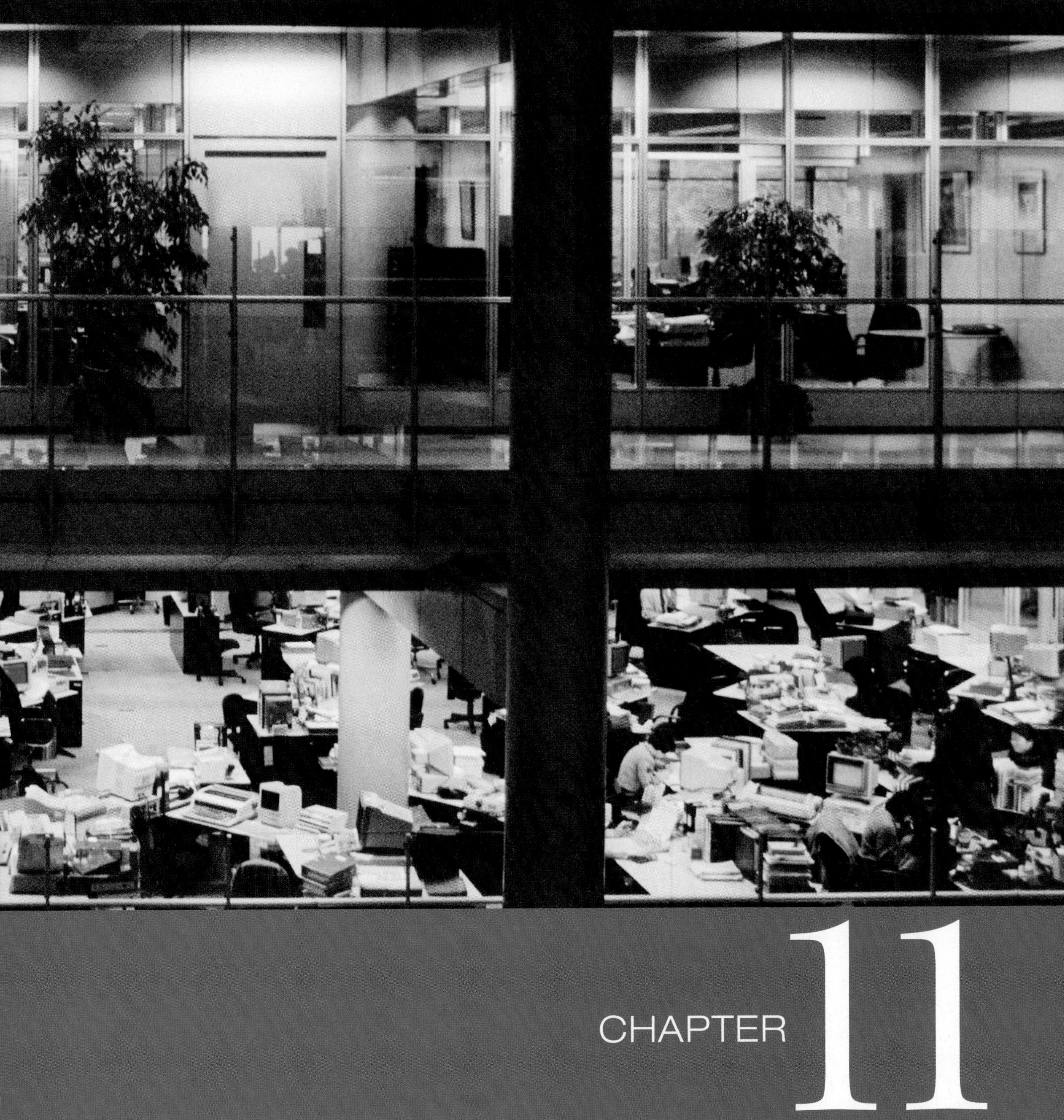

CHAPTER 11

Work and the Workplace

CHAPTER OVERVIEW

HOW DOES OUR ECONOMY shape people's jobs? This chapter looks at how the post-industrial economy and globalization affect each and every one of us. You will learn which types of jobs are likely to be more available in the future, which are the most dangerous, why many workers feel "alienation," who is at risk for unemployment, and what's happening to labor unions. You will carry out theoretical analysis of work and workplace issues and learn how "problems" and "solutions" involving work reflect people's political attitudes.

The blast rumbled like 1,000 freight trains, collapsing part of the Sago coal mine near Tallmansville, West Virginia. One man, who was working near the point of the explosion, was killed instantly. A dozen more were trapped 2 miles in, along the main shaft of the mine, more than half a mile below the surface.

As they had been trained to do, the men moved together into what they hoped would be a safe spot in the mine and pulled a large sheet of cloth across the shaft to block the flow of toxic gases from the explosion. On the surface, workers and emergency personnel launched a rescue operation. But the rescuers ran into high concentrations of deadly carbon monoxide gas, forcing them back out of the mine until they could vent the gas.

The progress was agonizingly slow. Families gathered at the Sago Baptist Church, fearing the worst but hoping that the men would make it out alive. For two long days, rescuers worked to clear the gas, move debris, secure the shaft, and finally, locate the men.

Despite an early report that twelve men had been found alive, by the time rescue workers reached the group of miners, only one was still breathing. Randal McCloy, the youngest of the men, lay clinging to life and would spend months in recovery. Later, McCloy reported that the men in the mine passed the long hours quietly sitting together, using as little of the available oxygen as possible. Right to the point that they could no longer breathe and lost consciousness, the men were convinced that help would come.

The 2006 Sago mine disaster points to the serious problems that surround the workplace. In recent years, this particular mine had been cited for hundreds of safety violations. Nor is this mining accident an isolated case: In 2008, more than 11,000 miners suffered a work-related illness or injury, and fifty-three miners lost their lives (Levin, Frank, & Overberg, 2006; Vanden Brook & Nichols, 2006; U.S. Department of Labor, 2008).

Illness, injury, and death are all a reality in the U.S. workplace—especially in high-risk occupations such as mining. As this chapter explains, despite a long-term decline in workplace casualties, the dangers remain very real. In addition, a host of other problems command our attention. In recent decades, millions of men and women in the United States lost their factory jobs as computers and robots replaced workers on assembly lines and old industrial plants shut down entirely. More recently, as corporations continue to "downsize," managers and other highly skilled people with office jobs have found that they, too, are at risk of unemployment. When the economy falls into recession, as it did in 2008, hardly anyone feels that a job is secure (Gumbel, 2009; McGeehan, 2009).

This chapter surveys all these social problems surrounding work and the workplace. We begin with a look at why work is important.

The Importance of Work

Most people in the United States count on their job to provide the income they need to live. But work is even more than that. A job gives many people a sense of pride and accomplishment, and for almost everyone, what one does for a living is an important source of identity and self-esteem. Most people think of themselves as doctors, firefighters, teachers, or carpenters, and they build their lives around the work they do every day.

Because work matters in so many ways, problems in the workplace take on special importance. To see the source of many workplace problems, we begin by looking at broader economic trends, which are beyond the control of ordinary people.

GETTING INVOLVED

A wide range of data about the U.S. economy can be found at the Web site of the U.S. Department of Labor: **http://www.dol.gov** Visit this site and check out the data available.

MAKING THE GRADE

Be sure you understand the changes made by the Industrial Revolution and the Information Revolution.

Structural Changes in the U.S. Economy

Many of the problems related to work in the United States have been brought on by changes in the economy. Over the history of this country, there have been two major structural changes. The first change, which began about 200 years ago, was the Industrial Revolution; the second change, which began in the 1950s and continues today, is the Information Revolution that has brought on deindustrialization and a globalization of the economy. As you will see, both revolutions transformed not just the economy but our entire way of life.

The Industrial Revolution

In the nineteenth century, most people lived in rural areas and small towns and worked in the *primary sector* of the economy, producing raw materials by farming, fishing, ranching, mining, or clearing forests. The nature of work changed as factories sprang up in cities and towns from New England to the new and rapidly growing cities of the Midwest. The Industrial Revolution pushed workers into the *secondary sector* of the economy, in which most transformed raw materials into finished products: For example, factory workers turned wood into furniture and steel into railroad tracks and, later, into automobiles.

Figure 11–1 shows that by 1900, as many people worked in industrial factories as remained on the farm. Factories drew millions of people from rural areas to live in or near large cities. Many people, especially those who stayed behind, saw this migration as a serious problem because it drained the population of small, rural communities, many of which became "ghost towns." From this point of view, the Industrial Revolution threatened a traditional, rural way of life that had existed in the United States since the colonial period.

The Industrial Revolution brought even more changes to the workplace by encouraging high levels of immigration. The new factories and rapidly growing cities attracted tens of millions of people from all over the world, mostly from Europe. These men and women came to the United States in search of work and a better life, but they were not always welcomed. As explained in Chapter 3 ("Racial and Ethnic Inequality"), public opinion in this country was critical of what was described as a flood of foreign immigrants who threatened this country's established culture.

Most who came to the new industrial cities to pursue their dreams found that life was far from easy. Many had no choice but to take poor housing, sometimes with little heat and no sanitation. Factories offered jobs, but the pay was low, the hours were long, and the work was backbreaking and often dangerous. Many jobs involved monotonous routines in settings filled with smoke and deafening noise. Supervisors closely monitored their workers and tolerated no complaints. By and large, companies treated workers—especially immigrants who spoke little English—as little more than muscle power. But immigrant families needed wages to live, and with little or no ability to organize to demand better working conditions, workers had little choice but to take whatever jobs they could find.

The challenges facing working people in the United States became worse in the 1930s with the start of the Great Depression. A major economic collapse put one-quarter of the labor force out of work. Hunger and hardship became widespread across the country. Not until World War II, a decade later, did the U.S. economy rebound and living standards start to improve.

In the 1950s and 1960s, the economy boomed. Many—perhaps most—working people in the United States enjoyed rising wages and a better standard of living. As Chapter 14 ("Urban Life") explains, many industrial workers earned enough to afford a modest house in a new subdivision outside

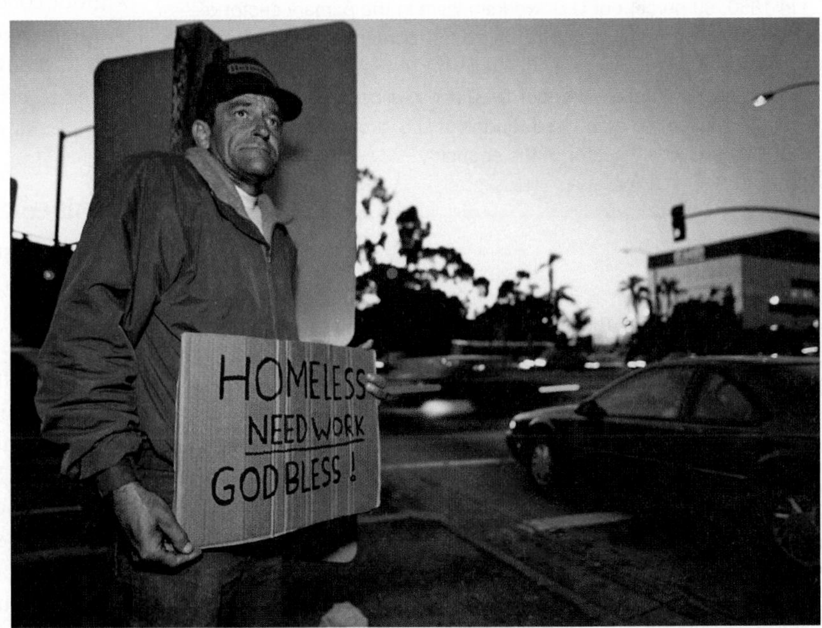

Work is more than a source of income. A job also provides prestige, identity, and—under favorable circumstances—a sense of satisfaction. With this in mind, how do you think most people feel about being unemployed?

SOCIAL PROBLEMS in Everyday Life

What effect do differences in wage levels between Mexico and the United States have on the flow of immigrants into this country?

deindustrialization the decline of industrial production that occurred in the United States after about 1950

globalization the expansion of economic activity around the world with little regard for national borders

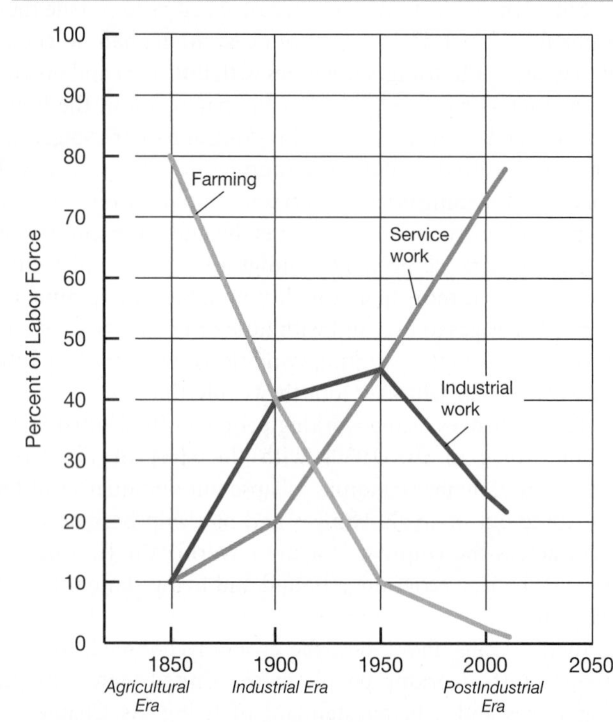

Figure 11–1 The Changing Nature of Work in the United States, 1850–2008

In 1850, 80 percent of U.S. workers were in the primary sector of the economy (farming); today, only a few percent of people in the labor force do such work. Industrial work in the secondary sector of the economy peaked about 1950 and has been in decline since then. Today, more than three-fourths of U.S. workers have service jobs in the tertiary sector of the economy.

Source: Based on U.S. Department of Labor (2009).

the city limits, and the population pushed outward from the central cities into the growing suburbs.

The Information Revolution

Figure 11–1 shows that by 1950, the economy was changing again. By that time, the share of the labor force in industrial jobs was matched by the rising share of workers in the *tertiary* (third) *sector* of the economy. Today, most people in the labor force work not in factories but in offices, where they perform *service work* in sales, consulting, law, advertising, and other fields. One important reason for this economic transformation is the invention of the computer and the spread of computer technology into almost every aspect of life.

The Information Revolution brought a shift from older, blue-collar industrial jobs toward newer, white-collar service work. Established professionals—including doctors, lawyers, and college professors—had long enjoyed good-paying service jobs. In addition, the ranks of new professionals—in advertising, consulting, and computer programming—increased, giving more people good pay and high regard. But the Information Revolution was not good news for all workers. Many of the new office jobs—especially those typically held by women—were low-paying and offered little chance for advancement.

Deindustrialization

The Information Revolution also signaled the onset of **deindustrialization**, *the decline of industrial production that occurred in the United States after about 1950.* As the economy created new service jobs, it lost old industrial jobs. Many former assembly-line workers and machine operators found their plants closing down, forcing them out and onto the job market, where many ended up taking jobs as clerical workers, delivery personnel, maintenance workers, and fast-food employees. Almost all of these new jobs paid much less than industrial jobs do, and often the new jobs included fewer benefits. By the end of the twentieth century, as a glance back at Figure 11–1 shows, far more workers were employed in service jobs than in industrial jobs. For this reason, many workers—especially those with industrial skills but without college degrees—have found the last several decades to be tough economic times. Tens of thousands of skilled workers who have lost their jobs in the auto industry in the recent economic recession have little hope of finding work that will offer them the same rewards.

Globalization

The deindustrialization of the United States is tied up with economic globalization. With regard to the economy, **globalization** is *the expansion of economic activity around the world with little regard for national borders.* Today, the largest corporations produce and sell products in many countries, and more and more products move from country to country.

A century ago, more industrial production took place in the United States than in any other country in the world. Today, however, lower wage levels in other nations have encouraged the "outsourcing" of industrial jobs. Consider, for example, that the average industrial worker in Mexico earns $2.88 an hour, far less than wages of more than $24 an hour in the United States. Just how much lower are wages in other countries? As Figure 11–2 shows, industrial workers in Mexico, Taiwan, and South Korea make only a fraction of what industrial workers in the United States earn. Such comparisons help

primary labor market jobs that provide good pay and extensive benefits to workers

secondary labor market jobs that provide low pay and few benefits to workers

explain why, in recent years, our economy has lost both factory jobs and also millions of white-collar jobs to Mexico, India, and other lower-wage countries (U.S Department of Labor, 2009).

Low wages make building factories and office buildings abroad profitable. In addition, new information technology, including computers and satellite communications, helps corporations stay in instant communication with their facilities in countries all over the world.

In sum, global expansion of the economy has been good for most corporations, raising profits for stockholders. At the same time, the loss of jobs here has been bad for many working families here in the United States.

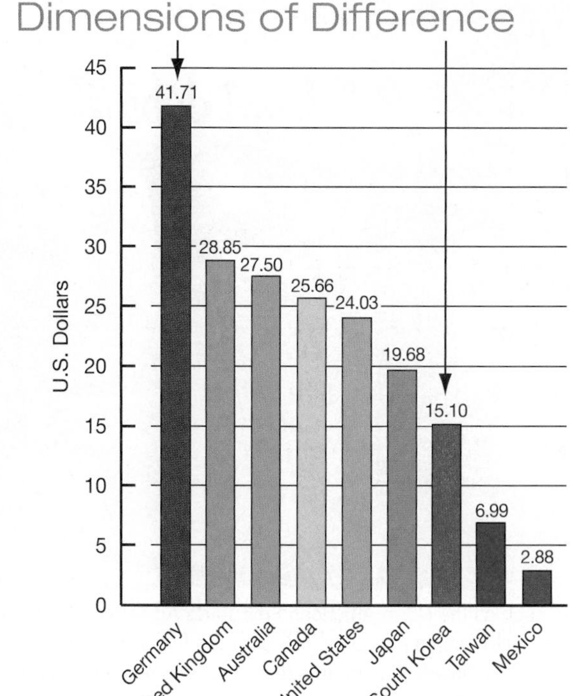

FIGURE 11–2 Average Hourly Wages for Workers in Manufacturing, 2009

Workers in countries such as Taiwan and Mexico are paid far less than their counterparts in the United States. This disparity is a key reason that the United States has been losing industrial jobs to these nations.

Source: U.S. Department of Labor (2009).

Other Problems of the U.S. Workplace

Going to work is a daily fact of life for many people in the United States. In addition to the job losses resulting from globalization of the economy, the workplace involves any number of problems, including low pay, alienation, discrimination, and the threat of unemployment, physical injury, violence, and even death. Although the workplace provides many benefits and great satisfaction to some people, it offers far less to others. So great are differences in workplace experiences that sociologists have distinguished two broad categories of work.

The Dual Labor Market

Today's labor market involves two broad categories of jobs that differ in terms of what they offer to workers. The **primary labor market** includes *jobs that provide good pay and extensive benefits to workers.* Jobs in the primary labor market are challenging and rewarding; they pay well and include extensive benefits such as pensions and health insurance. In addition, this type of work is secure and provides people with a good chance to move ahead. These are the jobs people perform with satisfaction and think of as *careers.*

At the top of the primary labor market are the *professions,* white-collar occupations, such as physician, lawyer, and college professor, that require extensive schooling and offer good pay and lots of prestige. Also included in the primary labor market are positions as business managers and executives, airline pilots, accountants, newspaper editors, electrical engineers, and the few good jobs in factories left in the United States.

Other work in the U.S. economy is in the **secondary labor market,** *jobs that provide low pay and few benefits to workers.* Examples of this type of work include many service jobs, such as restaurant work, retail sales, telemarketing, and building maintenance. This type of work is low-paying, provides limited benefits, carries a high risk of layoffs, and offers little opportunity for advancement. Workers in the secondary labor market are economically insecure, knowing that they have limited income today and not knowing if they will have a job tomorrow. Typically, people who work in the secondary labor market are women and men with less schooling and fewer skills—in short, those who have fewer options. The Thinking Critically box on page 295 takes a closer look at work in the secondary labor market.

Danger to Workers

A century ago, at the height of the industrial era, it was common for people to work in steel mills and deep within coal

GETTING INVOLVED

Have you ever known anyone who worked in farming? What about mining or fishing?

Policies such as the North American Free Trade Agreement (NAFTA) are intended to strengthen economic ties between the United States and other nations. Critics, however, point to a loss of jobs at home caused by more use of low-wage labor in poor countries.

mines—places that exposed them to serious danger every day. Back then, employers and the government paid much less attention to worker safety. Mining disasters, like the one described in the opening to this chapter, were almost daily events. In 1907, for example, 3,242 U.S. workers lost their lives in coal mines. Accidents were common not just in mines and factories but also on farms across rural America, where people use tractors, combines, and other powered machinery (Mine Safety and Health Administration, 2009).

In the decades since then, workplace accidents have become less common, mostly because of the change from industrial work to service jobs. But government has also played a role in today's better safety record. In 1970, the federal government established the Occupational Safety and Health Administration (OSHA) to regulate workplace health and safety. In addition, the government created the National Institute for Occupational Safety and Health (NIOSH) to conduct research on workplace hazards, ranging from toxic chemicals to ailments that result from repetitive motion or heavy lifting.

In 1976, Congress passed the Toxic Substances Control Act, which set guidelines for handling dangerous substances in the workplace. With ever-increasing use of chemicals in the production of food, clothing, automobiles, and other goods, federal agencies face the challenge of not only regulating the use of substances known to be dangerous but also testing new substances to protect workers from those that may be harmful.

Despite these efforts, on-the-job accidents and injuries are still a serious social problem in the United States. In 2007, about 1.2 million workers suffered disabling accidents that required they take time off from work. More seriously, each year, almost 6,000 workers lose their lives in workplace accidents. As Figure 11–3 on page 296 shows, mining and agriculture carry the greatest risks of death (U.S. Department of Labor, 2008).

Mining

As suggested by the opening to this chapter, mining has long been one of the most deadly jobs a person can do. Mine workers labor with heavy machinery deep underground, facing the ever-present dangers of cave-ins, explosions, fire, and poisonous fumes.

Events like the 2006 Sago coal mine disaster make headlines in the mass media. But even more deadly is something we rarely read about—the coal dust that miners breathe every day. Over many years, coal dust builds up in the lungs and causes a number of respiratory diseases, which eventually take their toll on retired miners. As one man described working in the mines, "You die quick or you die slow but—either way—you're just as dead" (Gup, 1991:55).

Farming

Farm machinery is now far safer than it once was, but farming still poses risks to workers. One reason is that today's farmers work with more toxic chemicals. Just as important, U.S. laws that ban child labor do not apply to farming. Therefore, agricultural work places children at especially high risk of injury or death.

Toxic Substances and Radiation

Human hazards are not limited to mines and farms. Toxic substances used in countless workplaces pose a hazard to workers. Nearly every factory or production facility in operation today contains at least some chemicals known to be hazardous to human health.

Radiation is another occupational hazard that places workers at risk of leukemia and other forms of cancer. The risk of being exposed to radiation exists at the 103 nuclear power plants across the United States and also at dozens of factories that produce nuclear materials. The precise hazards are difficult to document because the effects of human exposure to radiation take many years to show up.

But sometimes workers take action. In 1999, fourteen former employees of Kentucky's Paducah Gaseous Diffusion Plant filed a

GETTING INVOLVED

Have you ever held a low-wage job? How do your experiences compare to the description of these jobs in the box below?

MAKING THE GRADE

Why are women at special risk of violence in the workplace?

THINKING CRITICALLY

Low-Wage Jobs: On (Not) Getting By in America

What is it like to work on the floor at Wal-Mart, to clean rooms at a motel, or to wait tables at a small diner? Low-pay jobs may seem easy—but are they? Can you live on the $8 or $9 an hour you earn?

Barbara Ehrenreich, a gifted writer who holds a Ph.D., has made her living for years working behind a desk writing about social issues, including poverty and problems of the workplace. Sharing lunch in New York City with a magazine editor, she was kicking around the idea of writing about low-wage jobs. Without thinking, she said, "Somebody ought to do the old-fashioned kind [of research]—you know, go out there and try it for themselves." Her editor suddenly sat up and smiled, offering the simple reply: "*You!*"

So it was that in the spring of 1998, Ehrenreich left behind her comfortable life to join the millions of people in the United States who work at low-income jobs. Her plan was simple but challenging: She would not fall back on her writing skills; she would take the best job she could find and do it as well as she could. She would try to live on what she earned, finding the cheapest housing available, as long as it was safe.

Ehrenreich began her adventure in Key West, Florida, by replying to twenty want ads in the local paper. She eventually landed a job waitressing on the 2 P.M. to 10 P.M. shift at a small restaurant connected to a motel. Her pay was $2.43 per hour plus tips. Her first day on the job, she learned an important lesson: *Working as a waitress is much harder than most people think.* Ehrenreich (2001:17) explains, "As a server, I am beset by requests as if by bees: more iced tea here, catsup over there, a to-go box for table 14, and where are the high-chairs, anyway?" She also had to master a touch screen ordering system that did not always work well. And then there was the work she never expected, including "sweeping, scrubbing, slicing, refilling, and restocking." All this while being constantly watched by the assistant manager for any signs of drug use, stealing, or simply slowing down to catch her breath.

When the tips were collected (and shared with the kitchen staff), Ehrenreich earned $6 to $10 per hour, which totaled about $1,200 for a month of hard work. The cheapest housing she could find was a half-size trailer home fifteen minutes from town that cost $675 per month, leaving her with $525, which was less than $20 a day for food, clothing, transportation, telephone, health needs, and everything else.

In the months that followed, Ehrenreich performed low-wage work in Florida, Maine, and Minnesota. She swept hotel rooms, cleaned private homes, worked as an aide in a nursing home, and signed on as a sales associate at Wal-Mart. She found that all these jobs, like the waitressing, require many skills and demand long hours of hard labor. By the time her adventure came to an end, Ehrenreich had learned another important lesson: *Low-wage jobs do not pay enough to live on.* To have any kind of life, you need to work two of these jobs at the same time. And that—if you can do it—is no life at all.

WHAT DO YOU THINK?

1. Do you agree with Barbara Ehrenreich that low-wage work is much harder than most people think? Why or why not?
2. Should people who work full time have to live below the poverty line? Explain your position.
3. Would you support a higher minimum wage? Why or why not?

$10 billion lawsuit, alleging that hazardous radiation existed at the plant and that the firm concealed this fact from workers and from the general public. A government investigation documented that the workers had reason for concern: They found potential radiation leaks at the plant and some 37,000 uranium-containing cylinders stored outdoors (Carroll, 1999a, 1999b).

Workplace Violence

Not all job-related hazards involve accidents or illness; another hazard in the workplace is violence. In 2007, across the United States, workplace murder claimed the lives of 628 people, with some falling victim to robbers and others killed by fellow workers. Another 196 died from self-inflicted violence (U.S. Department of Labor, 2008). Although men hold most of the jobs in hazardous occupations such as mining and farming, women hold most clerical and other service jobs dealing with the public. When a violent person enters a business, the first people at risk are women. This is the reason that of all causes of job-related deaths for women workers, homicide ranks second, behind only auto accidents.

Workplace Alienation

Especially in the secondary labor market, workers have little control over what they do and how they do it. Therefore, for many workers, the main on-the-job experience is powerlessness. Different views of this problem were provided by Karl Marx and Max Weber.

Alienation: Marx's View

Well over a century ago, Karl Marx (1818–1883) characterized this problem as **alienation,** *powerlessness in the workplace resulting in the experience of isolation and misery.* For Marx, the problem

alienation (Marx) powerlessness in the workplace resulting in the experience of isolation and misery

alienation (Weber) a rational focus on efficiency, which causes depersonalization throughout society, including the workplace

rationalization of society the historical change from tradition to rationality and efficiency as the typical way people think about the world

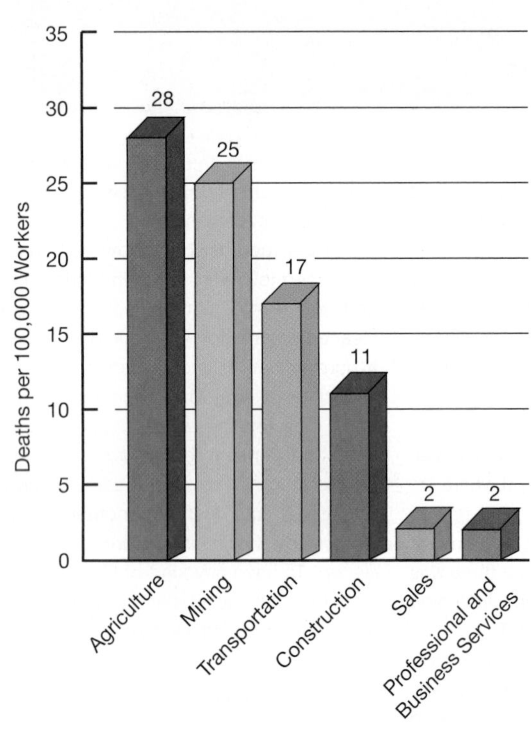

FIGURE 11–3 **Workplace Deaths by Type of Job, 2007**

Of all categories of work, agriculture and mining have the highest rates of on-the-job fatalities.

Source: U.S. Department of Labor (2009).

was not work itself. He believed work to be a natural human act, ideally a satisfying activity by which people meet their needs and develop their creative potential. Marx claimed that the problem of alienation stems from work shaped by the capitalist economic system.

How does capitalism produce worker alienation? Consider the job of making a coat. Traditionally, coats were made by highly skilled people who were responsible for the entire production of the garment and who could sell the final product, keeping whatever they could earn. Under the capitalist system, however, coat making falls under the control of mill owners, who break the work down into various low-skill tasks—some workers spin wool into yarn, others weave the yarn into cloth, others cut the cloth into patterns, and still others stitch the pieces together into the final coat. Under this system, work becomes a series of simple, repetitive tasks that allows no creativity and requires little skill. When the work is done, the coat is owned and then sold by the mill owner, who keeps whatever profit it brings. Under this system, workers have no say in what to make and how to produce it. Nor can they take any pride in the finished product.

With few skills, workers are easily replaced and have little job security. As a result, they end up competing with one another for work. In the end, Marx concluded, capitalism alienates workers in four ways: capitalism alienates them from their jobs, it alienates them from the products they make, it alienates them from each other, and it alienates them from their human potential. No wonder, Marx observed, that workers in a capitalist economy find so little satisfaction in their jobs and look for pleasure only in their leisure time. The Personal Stories box on page 298 describes the experience of Marxist alienation.

Alienation: Weber's View

Max Weber (1864–1920) agreed with Marx that the modern workplace causes worker alienation, but he understood the problem a bit differently. To Weber, **alienation** is *a rational focus on efficiency, which causes depersonalization throughout society, including the workplace.* For Weber, then, the cause of alienation is not capitalism, as it was for Marx, but something broader. The problem lies in the rationality—the impersonal focus on efficiency—that is a trait of all modern social life.

To Weber, the Industrial Revolution was one result of the **rationalization of society,** *the historical change from tradition to rationality and efficiency as the typical way people think about the world.* In the Middle Ages, tradition guided people's lives, so the "right" way to do something was simply the way it had been done in the past. Such an emphasis on tradition did little for efficient production, but it did make for strong families and tightly knit communities, which gave workers a sense of belonging and purpose.

The modern world's emphasis on rationality is different, guiding individuals and organizations to make decisions not with an eye to the past but on the basis of cool-headed calculations of the consequences of various courses of action. In this way, the goal of efficiency dictates how the workplace operates with little concern for the human costs of any policy or practice. Bank tellers, like Janice Moran in the Personal Stories box, are simply told to process transactions without taking time to get to know the people they serve. And her job will be at risk if the downtown office determines it can be done faster or cheaper by an automated teller machine (ATM). The result of such rationality may well be higher productivity; however, Weber feared that a focus on rationality strips us of our basic humanity.

McDonaldization and "McJobs"

Although Marx and Weber found different causes of alienation, they agreed that many people today find their work unsatisfying. Marx defined the problem as capitalist owners of production

McDonaldization defining work in terms of the principles of efficiency, predictability, uniformity, and automation

GETTING INVOLVED

Have you ever worked for McDonald's or in some other "McJob"? If so, what did you think about this type of work?

exploiting working people. Weber defined the problem as rationality, which makes production highly efficient but strips away concern for our humanity. Both points of view help us understand the spread of the low-paying yet productive workplace system typical of McDonald's fast-food restaurants.

According to George Ritzer (1993, 1998), the concept of **McDonaldization** refers to *defining work in terms of the principles of efficiency, predictability, uniformity, and automation:*

Efficiency: McDonald's tries to serve food quickly and easily.

Predictability: McDonald's prepares all food the same way each time using set formulas.

Uniformity: McDonald's serves meals that look and taste exactly the same in all of its restaurants.

Automation: By automating all tasks, McDonald's is able to precisely control the production process, minimizing human decision making.

Most people find it easy to agree that many Information Age jobs generate worker alienation, meaning that workers find little to like in their work. Can you explain, from Marx's point of view, how this setting might alienate workers? What about from Weber's point of view?

Ritzer points out that that these four principles are found not only in fast-food companies; they guide people's work throughout the low-skill service sector of the U.S. economy. The result is that people now perform "McJobs" by doing a series of simple tasks (often involving pushing buttons on a computer or other machine) that the worker repeats over and over. Not surprisingly, workers find little satisfaction in such jobs, and worker turnover rates are high.

McDonald's is a highly successful multinational corporation serving meals to hundreds of millions of people all over the world. In addition, McDonald's (and similar companies) offer entry-level work experience to countless people—Ritzer estimates that one of every fifteen U.S. workers first went to work at McDonald's, and one of every eight U.S. adults has worked at a McDonald's at some point in their lives. But McJobs do not encourage employees to think, nor do they stimulate human creativity and imagination. It would not be too far off the mark to suggest that such jobs turn workers into robots for eight hours a day.

The Temping of the Workplace

After World War II, the U.S. economy was booming. Across Europe and in much of Japan, the war had destroyed most factories, and many people had lost their homes and all of their possessions. The United States was one of the few countries that could supply the goods demanded in war-torn nations as well as here at home. In the strong postwar economy, most jobs paid pretty well, and employers and employees alike assumed that people who worked hard could count on keeping their jobs for life.

Today, the rules have changed. The deindustrialization of the United States—the closing of factories and the loss of white-collar jobs to foreign countries—means that more and more work in the U.S. economy is temporary. The economic downturns we have experienced in the past decade—especially the recession beginning in 2008—has made jobs less secure than ever. Many people, commonly called "temps," now hold jobs that are formally defined as temporary. These jobs typically pay low wages, give workers little say about their job, and provide no guarantees that their job will be there next year or even next month.

Every day, temp agencies such as Manpower and Kelly Services send 1.2 million people to work in temporary jobs. If we add in all part-timers and people contracted by companies from any outside agency, 30 percent of the U.S. labor force works without some of the benefits other workers count on, including retirement plans, sick leave, health insurance, and job security (U.S. Department of Labor, 2009).

Where can temps be found? Almost everywhere. Even universities use adjunct faculty, who work year to year or even semester to semester, to fill about one-third of all teaching

GETTING INVOLVED

How has unemployment affected the lives of your family members and friends?

PERSONAL STORIES 

"You Can't Take Pride in Your Job Anymore"

If you were to travel across the country asking people about their work, the results might surprise you. Many people have a lot to say, and much of it is not good.

Take the case of Mark Grannis, a thirty-seven-year-old steelworker. Grannis describes the experience of workplace alienation in these words:

> There aren't many like me left. I work—I mean *really* work. I am a laborer. A steel puller. All day long, I pick up steel, move it from here to there, there to here. You know how much I move in a day? Maybe forty or fifty thousand pounds. Real work. I am one of the last to do this kind of thing.
>
> The pay is not that bad. So what's my biggest complaint? You can't take pride in your job. It used to be that a man could point to a house he'd built with his own hands. Me? I move steel, load it on a truck going who knows where? I never see what other guys build with that steel. Just once I would like to see a building or something made with the steel I moved. Somebody should put a plaque on the side of all the big skyscrapers in Chicago and Los Angeles with the names of all the people whose sweat made the building in the first place—every electrician, every engineer, every stone cutter, every plumber, every guy like me. That way a worker could say to his kids, "See, that's me, I helped build this building." Everyone should have something to point to. Otherwise you work all day and no one ever knows.

Janice Moran is a twenty-eight-year-old bank teller, a job she has had for eight years. Like Mark Grannis, she finds little satisfaction in her work.

> My job? I'm a teller in the local bank. What do I do? Well, people walk up to my window, and I have to say, "Good morning, may I help you?" Then I transact their business: I take money from them and put it into their account, or I give them money out of their account. Take it out, put it in. Put it in, take it out. It's pretty simple, really, as long as you make sure the right amount goes to the right place. Then I have to say, "Thank you and have a nice day," or something like that. That's what my work is. I think they call it a service job.
>
> The bank has a time clock, and every day you punch in and punch out. I have to be there at 8:45. If I am even a few minutes late, the supervisor yells and screams about it. After punching in, I go to my vault, take out my cash, set up my booth, get my stamps and ink pad set up, and turn on my computer. Then I talk to the other tellers for a few minutes until the bank opens at nine. I get to talk to people on my breaks and at lunch—that's the best part of my job.
>
> I would really like to be able to strike up a conversation with customers, you know, to make my job more interesting. But don't let the supervisor find out—he says my job is to get people in and out of the bank as quickly as possible. The bank tracks our work on its computers. The people downtown know who's the fastest and who is slow. They know if you make a mistake. If you're too slow or you screw up, they'll fire you. It's as simple as that.

WHAT DO YOU THINK?

1. In what ways are these two workers powerless over their jobs? What changes to the workplace would give them more power and satisfaction?
2. Why is Mark Grannis disappointed that he never sees the buildings that are made using the steel he moves? Can you offer a similar personal experience based on your own work?
3. Based on these two accounts, list several differences and several similarities between older industrial work and newer service work. On balance, do you think the two types of jobs are more different or more alike? Why?

Source: Inspired by characters in Terkel (1974).

positions (Department of Education, 2009). Although all categories of the population are included in the ranks of temporary workers, women and other minorities are most likely to have such work, and they are overrepresented in the least desirable jobs (K. Hudson, 1999).

Not everyone finds temporary work to be a problem. Some people are glad to move from job to job. They may be looking for short-term employment—say, over the summer while they are out of school or perhaps an extra weekend job to help with unexpected expenses. Others may be seeking experience, trying out a line of work, and still others do not want the commitment of a permanent position. But overall, temporary work is a better deal for employers than it is for workers. By relying on temps, employers save the costs of training, health and retirement benefits, sick leave, and vacation time (K. Hudson, 1999).

Unemployment

If many people are not getting all they need on the job, others have no work at all. At the start of 2008, just as the U.S. economy was falling into recession, the unemployment rate was 5.8 percent of the civilian labor force. That means that about 8 million people over the age of sixteen were without work. By

MAKING THE GRADE

Be sure you understand why unemployment is a societal issue and not just a personal experience.

MAKING THE GRADE

Note below that minorities face the greatest challenge of unemployment.

the end of that year, however, another 5 million people had lost their jobs, so by mid-2009, the unemployment rate had soared to more than 9 percent with 14.5 million people out of work (U.S. Department of Labor, 2009).

But the official unemployment rate does not accurately describe the extent of the problem. To be counted among the ranks of the unemployed, a person must register with an unemployment office and actively seek work. Yet many people who are looking for jobs never register. Others become *discouraged workers* who initially look for work but give up without finding a job, at which point they are dropped from the official unemployment statistics. For these reasons, the true unemployment rate is quite a bit higher than the government figure.

Reasons for Unemployment

Some unemployment occurs in every society for a number of reasons. Some people have been laid off, others are new to the labor force and looking for work, and still others are between jobs. This is why analysts often describe an unemployment rate between 4 and 5 percent to be normal, "full" employment.

Other analysts—especially on the far left—claim that a capitalist economy actually creates unemployment as a strategy to lower labor costs and increase profits. How? The economy keeps some people out of work to create a reserve pool of unemployed labor. Having people eager to work means that employers can fill their positions paying as little as possible; after all, if one person won't work for a low wage, there is almost certainly someone else who will. Another benefit of having plenty of people without work is that there will always be someone willing to do even the least desirable work.

When the economy has a downturn, as it did beginning in 2008, the unemployment rate goes up. Most of the people out of work turn to unemployment benefits or welfare to get by. Frances Fox Piven and Richard Cloward (1971) argue that when the economy is weak, the government has little choice but to expand welfare assistance if only to keep people from rising up against the system. On the other hand, when times get better and demand for workers is high, as was the case in the mid-1990s, the government is likely to cut welfare programs to force more people into the labor force. The welfare reform of 1996 seems to provide support for Piven and Cloward's theory. Back then, government reacted to a strong economy by making cuts in welfare programs, as detailed in Chapter 2 ("Poverty and Wealth").

Unemployment can be a very challenging experience. As noted at the beginning of this chapter, work is important not only as a source of income but also as a basic element of social identity and self-esteem. To be out of work robs people of all these things. In addition, in the individualistic and competitive culture of the United States, being out of work often carries the stigma of personal failure, which might be considered a "hidden injury" of unemployment.

Dimensions of Difference

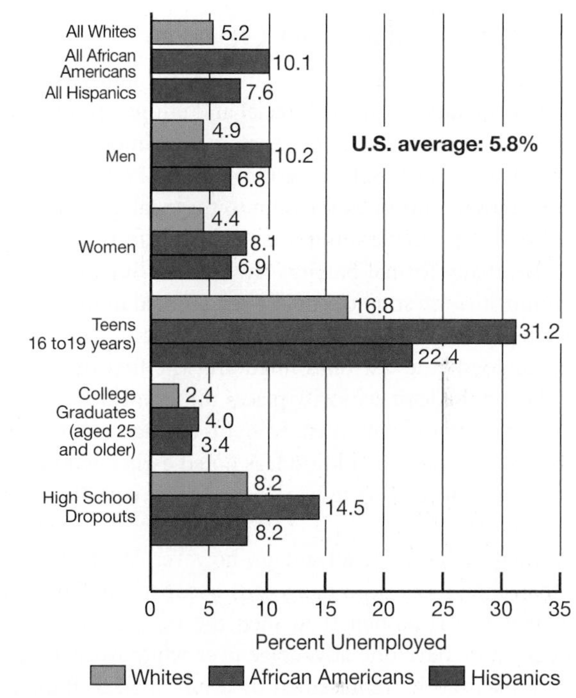

Figure 11–4 Unemployment Rates for Various Categories of the U.S. Population, 2008

Many factors affect the unemployment rate; among all categories of people, however, unemployment affects African Americans most, followed by Hispanic Americans.

Source: U.S. Department of Labor (2009).

Who Is at Risk for Unemployment?

In the U.S. population, some categories of people are at higher risk of unemployment than others. Figure 11–4 shows that in 2008, the unemployment rates were about the same for women and men. But look at race and ethnicity: The unemployment rates for African Americans (10.1 percent) and Hispanic Americans (7.6 percent) were well above the rate for non-Hispanic whites (5.2 percent).

Education also plays an important part for people in all racial and ethnic categories. According to government statistics, high school dropouts had an unemployment rate more than

SOCIAL PROBLEMS in Everyday Life

Are there still "women's jobs" and "minority jobs"? Explain and provide examples.

MAKING THE GRADE

Do you understand how institutional discrimination differs from individual acts of discrimination?

three times higher than that of college graduates (U.S. Department of Labor, 2008).

Race, Ethnicity, and Gender

As Chapter 3, "Racial and Ethnic Inequality," and Chapter 4, "Gender Inequality," explained, racial and ethnic minorities, as well as all women, were legally barred from most good jobs throughout most of U.S. history. Only in the 1950s and 1960s did social movements open the door to these categories of people for broader participation in the paid labor force.

Today, many formal barriers have fallen. But women and other minorities are still not equally represented in many of the better jobs. Often enough, women and other minorities are, as the saying goes, "the last ones hired and the first ones fired." Why? Having the least seniority places these workers at higher risk for layoffs than white men, who, on average, have been in the labor force longer. In addition, as noted earlier, women and minorities are more likely to work as temps or part-timers and in low-skill "McJobs."

Women do have one advantage, however: Women are less likely than men to work in dangerous occupations. This is the reason that fewer women than men die on the job. African Americans, too, have one advantage over white workers: They are more likely to be represented by a union (U.S. Bureau of Labor Statistics, 2008). The reason is simply that minorities are more likely to work in jobs where unionization is common.

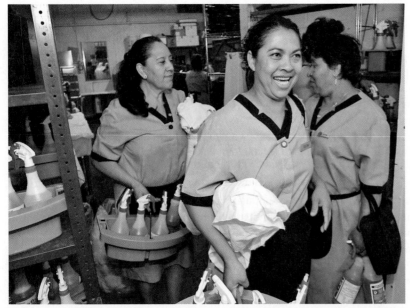

In most workplace settings across the United States, minorities are disproportionately found in the jobs that provide the lowest pay and prestige. Based on your own observations in hospitals, hotels, or office buildings, do you think this pattern holds?

Institutional Discrimination

Why is it still true that women and other minorities are concentrated in the secondary labor market? Some analysts see this pattern as evidence of *institutional discrimination,* discussed in Chapters 3 and 4. Institutional discrimination refers to bias that is built into the operation of the economy, education, or other social institutions.

Institutional discrimination does not depend on people setting out to treat others unfairly, but it is often the result of unfair treatment in the past. For example, through most of the twentieth century, the campus was considered a place for men, and women were underrepresented at colleges and universities not only as students but also as professors and as administrators. Today, most colleges and universities desire presidents with distinguished records of scholarly publications and lots of experience in academic leadership. But given that women were missing from the campus for so long, the number of very highly qualified female applicants is low. This fact helps explain why 77 percent of college and university presidents are men. Similarly, people of color account for only 14 percent of college and university presidents (Chronicle of Higher Education, 2007). In short, the fact that some categories of the U.S. population are less likely to rise to the highest positions in the workplace reflects long-term patterns that can be described as institutional discrimination.

The Glass Ceiling

In the past, women and other minorities were often banned outright from some work settings. Today, such blatant discrimination is against the law and has become rare. But more subtle forms of discrimination are still widely practiced.

For example, most employers have ideas about what type of person is most suitable for various jobs. When hiring a secretary, a company almost always selects a woman. When hiring an executive, by contrast, a company almost always hires a white person, usually a man.

Of course, no corporation or other organization is likely to admit to blatant prejudice and discrimination. But as noted in Chapter 4, many workplaces have a *glass ceiling,* a barrier—often involving institutional discrimination—that prevents women and other minorities from moving upward in the workplace.

Workplace Segregation

Consider the following jobs, which people in the United States rank at the bottom of the occupa-

GETTING INVOLVED

On your campus, what jobs are almost always held by men? Which ones are almost always held by women?

Dimensions of Difference

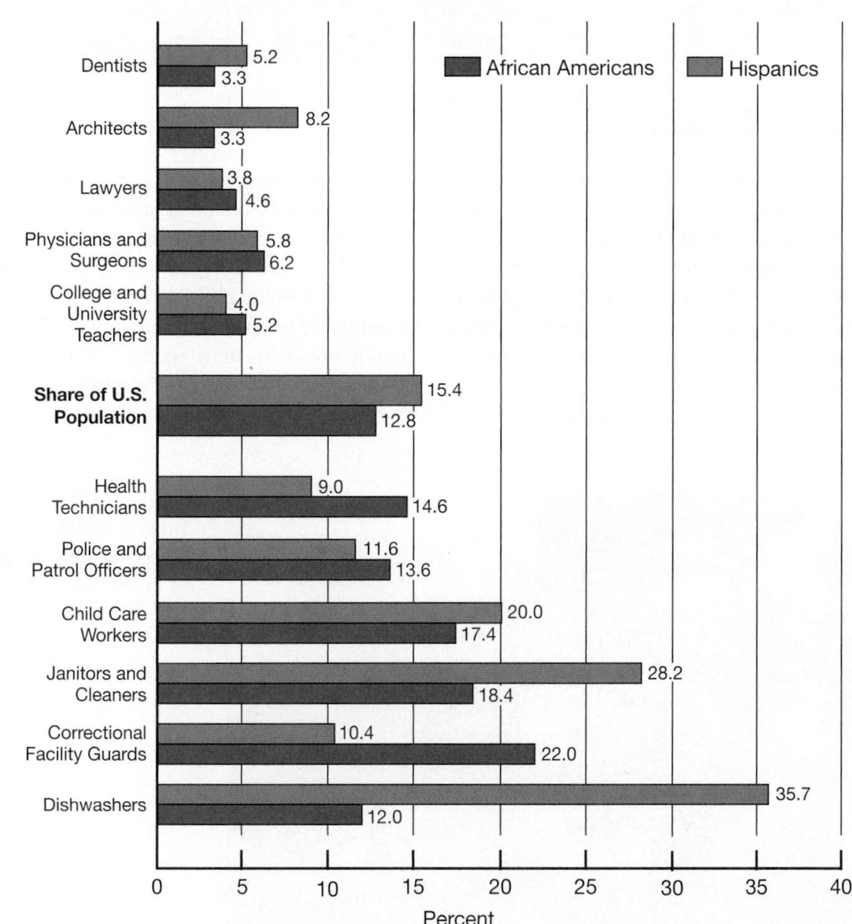

FIGURE 11–5 Percentage of Various U.S. Occupations Held by African Americans and by Hispanics, 2008

Minorities, including Hispanic Americans and African Americans, are underrepresented in jobs that provide high income and prestige and overrepresented in jobs that offer lower income and prestige.

Source: U.S. Department of Labor (2009).

tional ladder: shoe shiner, janitor, bellhop, and home health aide. Now try to imagine the race and ethnicity of most people who perform these jobs. What do you think is the case? Or consider positions near the very top rung of the job ladder: physician, lawyer, judge, architect, and university professor. What are the race and ethnicity of most people who hold these jobs? Are most of these people women or men?

It is easy to link gender and race to various occupations because the workplace is actually highly segregated. Minorities are concentrated in the least desirable jobs, and white men predominate in the most desirable jobs. Figure 11–5 shows the racial and ethnic composition of various occupations in the United States. These data show that African Americans and Hispanic Americans are overrepresented in lower-paying jobs (such as child care) and underrepresented in higher-paying jobs (such as physicians and dentists). Such differences in work are a major reason for disparities in income between the different racial and ethnic categories of the U.S. population. Among full-time workers in 2009, median income for whites ($51,699 for men and $39,010 for

SOCIAL PROBLEMS in Everyday Life

Have you ever taken part in a strike or other work-related action? If so, explain what happened.

CONSTRUCTING SOCIAL PROBLEMS

A DEFINING MOMENT

Eugene Debs: Standing Up for the Union

At the height of the Industrial Revolution, working conditions in the United States were a far cry from what they are today. People worked ten, twelve, or more hours per day, usually six days a week, earning 15 to 20 cents an hour. Work near blast furnaces in steel mills or high atop towering buildings was dangerous. But with so many people eager to take any available job, many employers gave little thought to worker safety.

Eugene Victor Debs (1855–1926) was raised in Indiana and attended school until age fourteen, when he went to work as a painter for the railroad. The longer Debs worked, the more he saw that workers were barely able to survive. But how could he bring about change? The company had the power, and there were no laws protecting workers. Standing alone, Debs realized, workers had no voice. But standing together, they could meet the bosses head on.

And so it was that Debs took a new job, working for the Brotherhood of Locomotive Firemen, an early labor union. By the late 1880s, Debs had become the editor of the union's national magazine; he also played a part in the creation of a number of other railroad unions. He was a skillful writer and a powerful speaker; coupled with his passion for building the union, these skills soon earned Debs a national reputation.

But opposition to unions was strong, and being an agent of change pushed Debs into a life of controversy. He led bitter strikes against the railroad companies, faced arrest, and spent years in jail. The controversy grew more intense in the final decades of his life, when Debs spoke openly about the need for radical change in the United States and was a five-time presidential candidate representing the Socialist party (he ran his last campaign for the presidency from inside the federal prison in Atlanta, Georgia).

Debs did not succeed in bringing about socialism. But he did bring about real change. As a result of his efforts, people accepted the idea that workers deserved a living wage, were entitled to safe working conditions, and had a legal right to organize and form unions. Today, Debs's home in Terre Haute, Indiana, is a National Historic Landmark—a museum documenting the struggle of early industrial workers.

Eugene Debs was a dynamic speaker who stirred the workers of his time to organize in pursuit of better lives.

women) was well above that for African Americans ($37,755 and $31,933) and Hispanic Americans ($31,554 and $27,268) (U.S. Census Bureau, 2010).

Compared with African Americans and Hispanics, women make out somewhat better in the U.S. labor market, with greater representation in many more desirable jobs. This is because minorities are overrepresented among the poor and among families just one generation removed from being poor, but women are found at all social class levels.

When it comes to leadership positions, such as business executives, clergy, judges, all the way up to national presidents, men dominate. At the same time, women are overrepresented in low-status positions in the business world, such as secretaries and other office workers, and in caring for the young, as child care workers and teachers.

Other notable examples of this male-female difference can be found in the health care field: 73 percent of dentists are men, but 98 percent of dental hygienists are women; 69 percent

labor unions worker organizations that seek to improve wages and working conditions through various strategies, including negotiations and strikes

MAKING THE GRADE

The general trend in recent years has been a decline in union strength.

of physicians and surgeons are men, and 92 percent of nurses are women. Of course, such differences in work lead to sharp gender differences in income. Among full-time workers in 2009, median income for men was $47,127, compared with $36,278 (77 percent as much) for women (U.S. Census Bureau, 2010).

Finally, women are less likely than men to be in the paid labor force in any position at all. Women make up about 51 percent of the U.S. adult population but only 42 percent of the full-time labor force (46 percent of workers if we count not just full-time workers but part-timers as well) (U.S. Department of Labor, 2008).

Labor Union Decline

Faced with many problems in the workplace, can workers improve their situation? One of the most effective strategies for working people has been to join together to form **labor unions,** *worker organizations that seek to improve wages and working conditions through various strategies, including negotiations and strikes.*

The history of labor unions in the United States extends back more than a century, with the first large-scale organizations beginning during the 1880s. Working conditions at that time were tough at best: People labored for long hours, faced many dangers, earned low wages, and had almost no job security. Factory owners had little reason to offer more because a steady stream of immigrants entering the United States provided plenty of people who were eager to work.

Under the laws of that time, company officials could fire workers for trying to form a union, and if employees did go out on strike, owners were often successful in getting a court to order workers back to the job. In short, a century ago, employers held all the high cards.

Despite the challenges, a number of people devoted their lives to promoting unions as a way to improve the lives of working people. The Defining Moment box explains how Eugene Debs advanced the cause of unions in the United States.

With the coming of the Great Depression in the 1930s, workers' organizations made important gains. The collapse of the economy put one-fourth of the U.S. labor force out of work at one point, and government took notice of the plight of working people. Congress passed several new laws (the Railway Labor Act, the Norris-LaGuardia Act, the National Labor Relations Act) that guaranteed the right of workers to organize and form labor unions.

Millions of working people responded to the union call. Throughout the 1930s, union membership increased sharply, and workers found strength in numbers. By 1950, unions claimed one-third of the entire U.S. nonfarm labor force. In terms of absolute numbers, union membership peaked in the 1970s at about 25 million people.

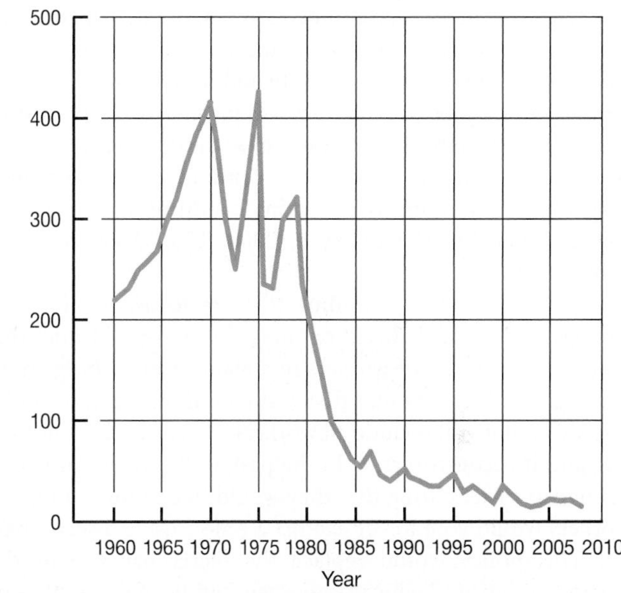

FIGURE 11–6 Number of Labor Strikes in the United States, 1960–2008

One indication of the declining power of unions in the U.S. workplace is the small number of labor strikes in recent decades.

Source: U.S. Department of Labor (2009).

But union strength was not to last. One reason was falling support for unions at the highest level of government. In 1981, air traffic controllers, who are federal employees, went on strike. President Ronald Reagan responded by ordering them back to work. When they refused, Reagan fired them all, and replacements were hired. This incident was a major defeat for labor unions and dramatized the weakening of the labor movement.

But an even bigger problem for labor unions was structural change in the U.S. economy. As already noted, the number of factory jobs—work that is heavily unionized—declined after 1950. Since then, most new jobs have been in the service sector of the economy, and this work is not likely to be unionized. Therefore, in 2008, just 12 percent of nonfarm workers (16 million men and women) were members of labor unions—quite a drop from 33 percent in 1950 (U.S. Department of Labor, 2009). Another measure of the declining strength of the labor movement is the decreasing number of strikes in the United States in recent decades, as shown in Figure 11–6.

SOCIAL PROBLEMS in Everyday Life

What advantages and disadvantages do you see in "working from home"?

telecommuting linking employees to a central office using information technology, including telephones, computers, and the Internet

But these downward trends may be turning around. In the past few years, unions have gained ground. About 37 percent of workers in the public sector of the economy—government employees—are now unionized. In addition, because many of today's service jobs provide low pay and few benefits (just as most industrial jobs did a century or so ago), more workers in the service sector are looking to unions to increase their bargaining power, improve working conditions, and increase pay and benefits (Greenhouse, 2000; U.S. Department of Labor, 2009).

Efforts to increase unionization are focusing on a new strategy, called "card check" or "majority sign-up." Under this policy, if a majority of workers in a plant or other bargaining unit sign cards saying that they want a union, a union will be formed, and it will include all workers. "Card check" is not yet law, and it is controversial. In the past, if 30 percent of workers signed cards stating that they would like to form a union, workers would vote for or against a union using a secret ballot. This policy would replace the secret ballot with the "majority sign-up," which is an open, public effort. Critics of the change claim that union activists would be likely to intimidate workers into signing a card; they see the secret ballot as a fundamental right and necessary to ensure that all workers have a true voice. Supporters of the change believe that this policy would make it easier for workers to organize, leading to higher wages and improved working conditions (Dalmia, 2008; Allen, 2009).

New Information Technology: The Brave New Workplace

Just as the Industrial Revolution brought sweeping changes to the workplace in the 1800s, the Information Revolution is transforming the workplace today. As Global Map 11–1 shows, access to the Internet is far better in the United States and other high-income nations than in low-income regions of the world.

Perhaps the biggest difference in the workplace of the twenty-first century is the types of skills that work demands. A century ago, people had to develop the industrial skills needed for making *things;* today, people in the postindustrial economy must develop literacy skills needed to create and manipulate *symbols* (words, ideas, music, and computer code).

The Information Revolution is changing not only the character of work but also how and where we do it. As the following sections explain, many people experience these changes as positive. Others, however, face new challenges every bit as serious as those faced by industrial workers a century ago.

Working at home can allow people with young children to manage both their careers and their family responsibilities. At the same time, what problems do you see in holding a job that requires you to work from home?

Telecommuting

In the centuries before the Industrial Revolution, most people worked in or near their homes. The development of industrial machinery changed this pattern, so that workers left home in the morning and traveled to factories. In this way, the Industrial Revolution *centralized* work. Today, however, the trend is in the opposite direction. With computers, instant messaging, cellular telephones, and other information technology at hand, "offices" can operate just about anywhere. One of the options gaining in popularity is for people armed with this new technology to work from home.

Telecommuting refers to *linking employees to a central office using information technology, including telephones, computers, and the Internet.* Only a small share of the U.S. labor force works exclusively in the home, but as many as one in five workers spends at least some work time at home during the week. Telecommuting has some obvious benefits, such as the time and expense workers save by not commuting to and from the office. Telecommuting also has

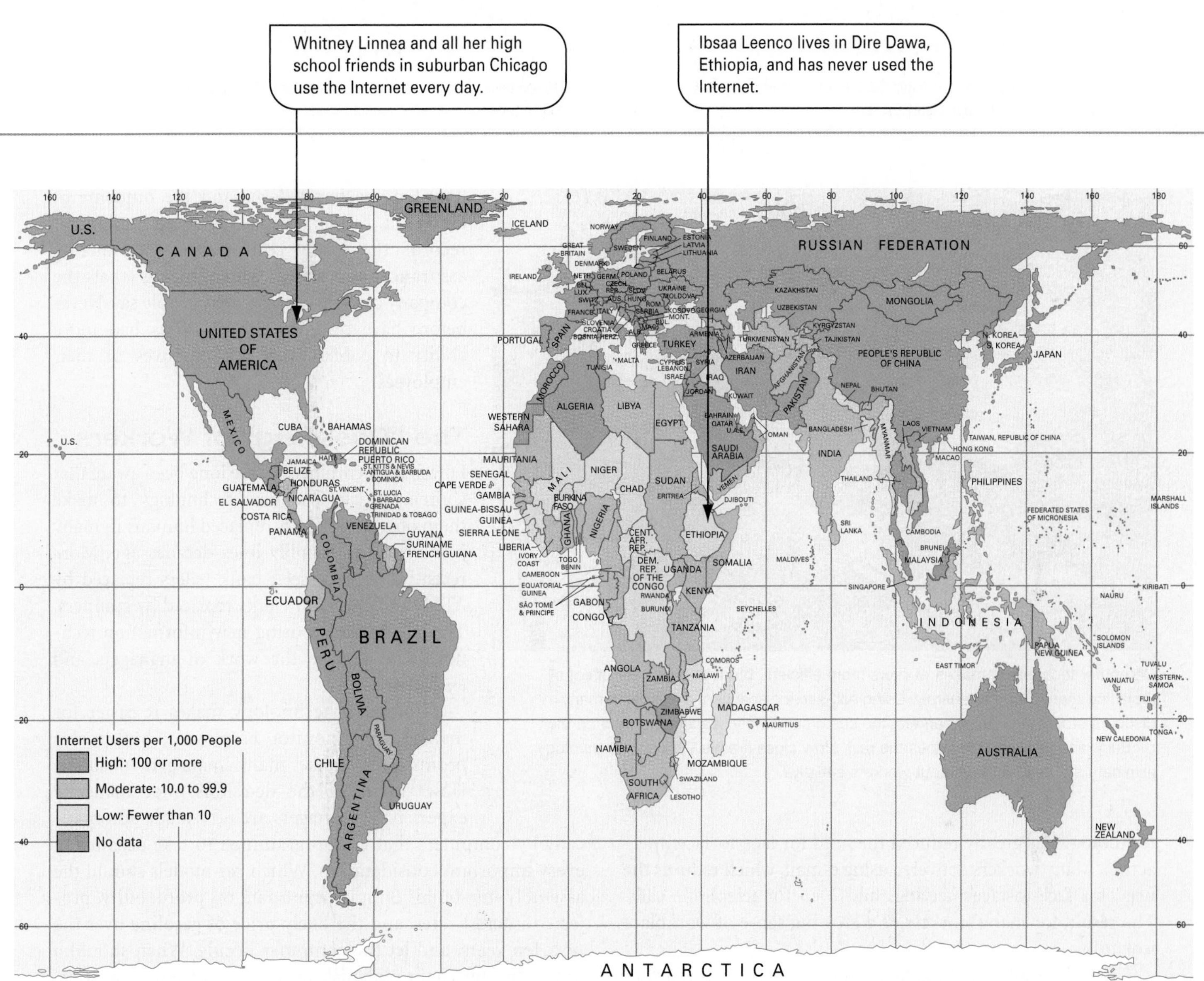

A World of Differences

GLOBAL MAP 11–1 Internet Users around the World

This map shows the state of the Information Revolution for countries around the world. In most high-income nations, at least one-third of the population uses the Internet. By contrast, only a small share of people in low-income nations does so. What effect does this lack of Internet access have for the future in terms of global inequality?

Sources: United Nations Development Programme (2008) and International Telecommunication Union (2009).

special appeal to people who want to hold a job but need to care for small children or aging parents. For many people, telecommuting offers flexibility to balance career goals and family obligations.

Telecommuting solves some problems, but it creates others. This pattern blurs the line between home and work, so that the pressures of work—which used to stay in the office—now fill the home. In addition, workers who stay at home risk becoming isolated, left out of key decisions, and overlooked for promotion. In addition, because telecommuting is more popular with women (who have greater family responsibilities), this pattern has the potential to perpetuate gender inequality in the workplace.

Workplace Isolation

Even people who travel to the office the old-fashioned way find that the Information Revolution is changing how they work. By connecting people in information networks, computer

SOCIAL PROBLEMS in Everyday Life

How has computer technology changed the lives of students? Do you think it links people or isolates them? Explain.

SOCIAL PROBLEMS in Everyday Life

Can you think of any ways in which computer technology can increase worker power or give workers more freedom?

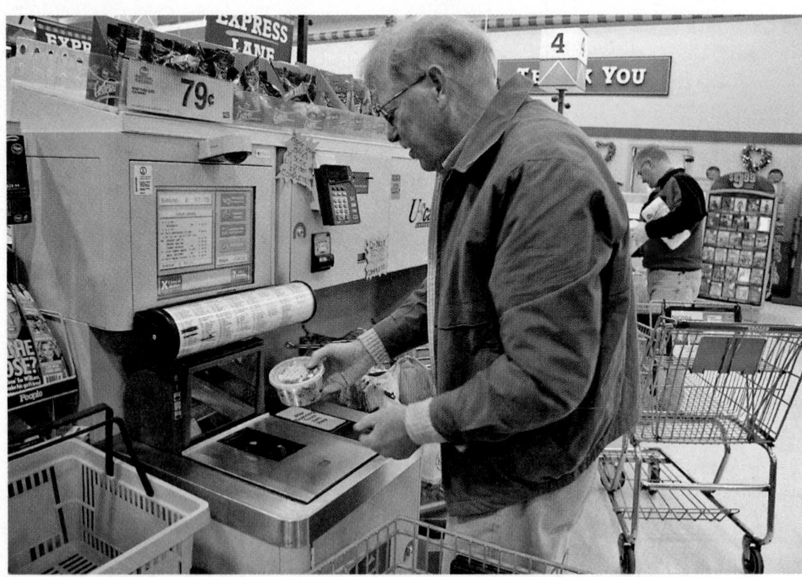

Computer technology makes workers more efficient, but it also has the effect of replacing many workers entirely. Using self-service scanners available in many discount stores and supermarkets, the customer simply scans a barcode on the product, and the computer does the rest. How close are we to seeing technology eliminate the need for checkout workers entirely?

technology has greatly reduced the need for face-to-face interaction. Many workers converse using e-mail, which reduces the need for face-to-face meetings and even for telephone calls. The result, for many workers, is a growing sense of workplace isolation.

In today's office setting, this pattern is easy to see. Many of today's office employees perform most of their work in small cubicles facing computer screens, having little contact with anyone else. Similarly, today's bank officials receive loan applications online, use computer programs to review the information, and make decisions as to whether to approve or reject customers they may never meet.

Workplace Supervision

Computer technology makes collecting and processing information easier than ever. Sometimes the information being compiled lets employers keep an eye on workers' behavior and productivity.

For example, telemarketing companies routinely use computers to monitor the work of their employees who sell products and services over the phone. Especially after the creation of the national "Do Not Call" list in 2003 greatly slowed their business, these companies have tried to increase productivity by tracking how many calls their workers make each day, how long each call lasts, and the outcome of every call. In many cases, high-tech equipment records the actual conversation "for quality assurance purposes," which means that the company can listen in on what people say. Never before have business organizations had more ability to control the working lives of their employees.

The "Deskilling" of Workers

Lower-level employees have long been aware that companies can use new technology to make them obsolete. Robots replaced humans in many jobs on auto assembly lines decades ago. More recently, we have seen bank tellers replaced by ATMs and checkout clerks replaced by scanners. The latest trend is using new information technology to replace the work of managers and executives.

Computer technology makes it easier for managers to monitor employees, but it also promises to make many managers obsolete. How? Many of the decisions once made by experienced managers are now made automatically by computers that are programmed to take account of every important consideration. Which car models should the assembly line build? Simply input data on profitability, projected interest rates, and the likely price of gasoline over the next ten years, and let the computer decide. When should a movie theater chain replenish its supplies of popcorn, soda, and candy? Computers monitor sales and automatically process orders for additional products. Given the proper input, computers are able to make more and more decisions without human assistance, which has the effect of *deskilling* managers and threatening their jobs. The final result is a decline in job security even for workers in the primary labor market.

Are computers capable of doing a better job of making business decisions than people? The answer to this question is unclear. Looking back at the collapse of so many financial companies and mortgage lenders during the last few years, perhaps there will be a trend away from allowing computers to manage risk, putting responsibility for business decisions back in the hands of people (Kivant, 2008). In any case, the increasing reliance on computers in business reminds us that new technology is never socially neutral. It changes the relationships between people in the workplace, shapes the way we work, and often alters the balance of power between employers and employees.

SOCIAL PROBLEMS in Everyday Life

One way to see shifts in our economy over generations is to ask parents and grandparents about the work they have done.

Theoretical Analysis: Understanding Work-Related Problems

Each of sociology's major theoretical approaches helps us understand work-related problems. Each approach highlights different facts and points to different conclusions.

Structural-Functional Analysis: Finding a New Equilibrium

A basic principle of the structural-functional approach is that the various social institutions are interrelated, so that change in one institution leads to adjustments in all the others. This chapter (and Chapter 10, "Economy and Politics") explains that changes in the economy and the workforce can cause hardship for people who lose their jobs. But the structural-functional approach suggests that the disruption of past economic patterns eventually brings a new social order. This means that although the decline of industry caused the elimination of millions of factory jobs, other institutions—especially education—responded by developing new courses of study to prepare workers for new types of work.

The structural-functional approach also deepens our understanding of how technological change reshapes the economy. The Industrial Revolution was the driving force behind the economy of the twentieth century. In much the same way, the Information Revolution has set the stage for the economy of the twenty-first century.

The changes now under way, like those in the past, will cause disruption in established ways of life. But we can expect other social institutions to respond to these changes, addressing what we experience as short-term problems, to help us redirect our lives. In the long term, new technology is likely to make our society more productive, which will be good for almost everyone.

Even economic setbacks, although painful in the short term, may help bring about greater long-term stability. Many analysts, for example, see the rapid economic expansion that began after 1980 as having pushed up housing prices too much and too quickly. At the same time, the typical household began to spend more of its income and to save less. The recession that began in 2008 may well bring such patterns back to a more sustainable level (K. Anderson, 2009).

CRITICAL REVIEW The biggest criticism of the structural-functional approach is that it is ends up being too optimistic. It takes a very positive view of society and its ability to rebound from the disruptions caused by structural changes in the workplace. It downplays the human suffering caused by these disruptions, describing them as temporary, and makes the case that technological change and even economic recession are likely to strengthen society in the long run. Some of this will likely turn out to be true, but this approach presents only one side of the story.

In addition, by treating society as a broad system, this macro-level approach provides little understanding about how real people who face everyday workplace problems feel about their jobs and themselves. To better understand how workplace issues are experienced by individuals, we turn to the symbolic-interaction approach.

Symbolic-Interaction Analysis: The Meaning of Work

The symbolic-interaction approach highlights the ways in which people attach meaning to the surrounding world, constructing the reality of their everyday lives. In the case of work, this approach leads us to focus on the meaning people attach to the jobs they hold and the work they perform.

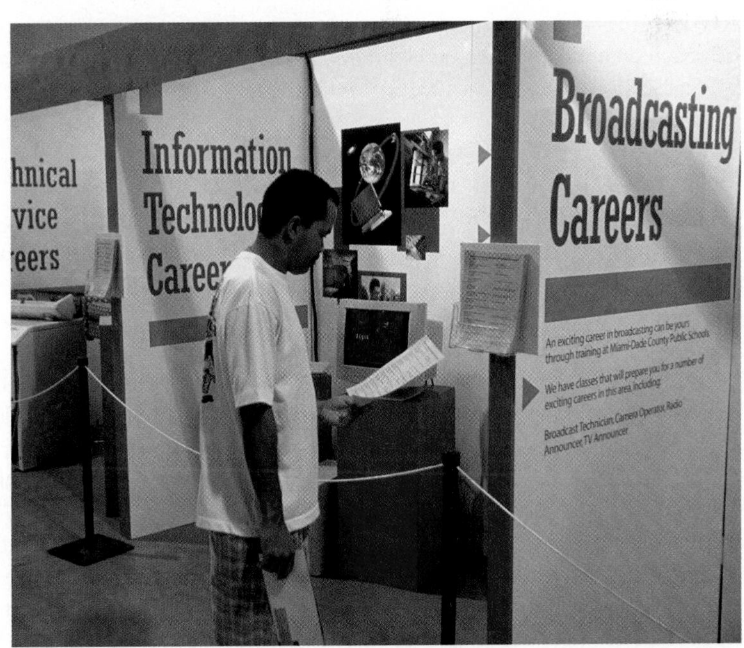

A society's economy changes as new technology creates new products and new types of work. One result of these shifts is that we can no longer assume that we will do only one type of job throughout our lives. A common experience for today's workers is retraining for a new career.

SOCIAL PROBLEMS in Everyday Life

In which sector of the labor market—primary or secondary—do you think workers are more likely to "watch the clock"? Why?

MAKING THE GRADE

Use the table below to review the three theoretical approaches to work and the workplace.

APPLYING THEORY

Work and the Workplace

	What is the level of analysis?	What does the approach say about the workplace?	How do we understand workplace problems?
Structural-functional approach	Macro-level	The structural-functional approach sees the workplace as linked to other aspects of society. Technology is crucial in shaping the workplace. The Industrial Revolution shaped the workplace of the twentieth century, just as the Information Revolution is shaping the workplace of the twenty-first century.	Rapid change can disrupt the social order, causing problems. For example, new technology has caused the loss of many traditional types of jobs. But other social institutions such as education respond, preparing workers for new types of jobs.
Symbolic-interaction approach	Micro-level	The symbolic-interaction approach focuses on the meanings people attach to the world around them. With regard to work, people who work in the primary labor market generally define their work in positive terms and think that the work reflects well on them. People who work in the secondary labor market find little positive meaning in their work, seeing the job mostly as a source of income.	The main problem is that workers with jobs in the secondary labor market are not able to find much positive meaning in their work. As a result, they must look for satisfaction outside of the workplace.
Social-conflict approach	Macro-level	The social-conflict approach links the workplace to social inequality. Marx explained that the capitalist elite does no work at all yet gains the profit from the work done by others. As long as the workplace operates according to the rules of a capitalist economy, work is the exploitation of the many by the few.	According to Marx, capitalism creates wealth for the few and alienation for the working majority. Weber agreed that alienation is a workplace problem, although he pointed to rationality in the modern world as the cause.

Many professionals and others in the primary labor market look forward to going to work every day and are motivated to advance; they think of their work as a *career.* Not only do such people attach positive meaning to their work, but they also believe that their work reflects well on them. Even after retiring from active work, teachers, doctors, and architects still hold on to the positive identity their work offered them. This fact helps explain why, for example, those who retire from teaching at colleges and universities are happy to enjoy a new status as professor *emeritus* (Latin, meaning "fully earned").

At the same time, people doing unskilled, repetitive jobs—whether in factories or office buildings—usually find far less positive meaning in their work. These people are likely to go to work each day mostly because they have no choice. Hour to hour, they listen to the radio and may even watch the clock, looking forward to quitting time when they can do something else. Such work rarely provides a chance for advancement and positive identity. People with secondary labor market jobs talk little about their work to others, and the value of their job lies mainly in the paycheck it provides.

CRITICAL REVIEW The symbolic-interaction approach highlights the different meanings people attach to their work, helping us understand why some people look

MAKING THE GRADE

Pay attention to differences in the ways Weber and Marx understood problems of work.

forward to going to work while others only look forward to "punching out."

Although the meaning people attach to work varies from person to person, the reality of work has much to do with people's social standing. To understand more about how and why work is linked to inequality, we turn to the social-conflict approach.

Social-Conflict Analysis: Work and Inequality

The defining feature of the social-conflict approach is its emphasis on social inequality. In the case of work, this approach highlights how the opportunities and the benefits provided by work are very different for advantaged and disadvantaged categories of people.

Following the ideas of Karl Marx, the operation of a capitalist economy serves to concentrate wealth and power in the hands of a small elite. From this point of view, this tiny share of the labor force does not actually work at all; rather, these people *own* everything. This capitalist elite benefits from the economic system for the simple reason that it has total control over it. By contrast, the majority of workers receive low wages and have little power in the production process. For most people, therefore, work is far from satisfying and produces only alienation.

As noted earlier, Max Weber took a different tack, arguing that capitalism was only one dimension of the larger pattern of increasing rationality, which defines modern society. A rational, matter-of-fact worldview stresses efficiency at the expense of meeting human needs and transforms the workplace into a highly regulated setting in which people have come to resemble machines. Weber would not have been surprised at the number of McJobs that are found in today's world.

Both Weber and Marx agreed that for most people, work is alienating rather than satisfying. For Marx, the root of the problem is the capitalist system and its effects on the working majority. For Weber, it is the historical trend toward greater rationality, which affects everybody. Differences aside, notice that both these theories reject the structural-functional claim that workplace problems result from temporary disruptions in the economy.

Perhaps both Weber and Marx would have expected to see the recent trend by which the share of jobs in the primary labor market has gone down and the share in the secondary market has gone up. The goal of rational efficiency (as Weber would put it) or of maximizing profit (as Marx might have said) encourages employers to exert more and more control over workers and, when possible, to replace them with machines. No one should be surprised that an ever-greater number of workers are forced to settle for McJobs and that more of us worry whether, at some point in the future, we will have any work at all.

CRITICAL REVIEW The social-conflict approach helps us see how the operation of the economy and major economic changes such as the Information Revolution affect various levels of our society differently. That is, the burden of workplace problems falls mostly on families of lower social status.

At the same time, one limitation of this approach is that it downplays the real gains in living standards realized by average people over the course of the twentieth century. Today, average workers earn about five times as much as they did back in 1900 after controlling for inflation. In terms of standard of living, the typical U.S. family owns a house with air conditioning, cable television, and at least one automobile parked in a garage—all of which was beyond the imagination of working families a century ago. Inequality is real, but in an absolute sense, just about everyone lives much better today than people did in the past.

The Applying Theory table summarizes what each theoretical approach teaches us about problems of the workplace.

POLITICS AND THE WORKPLACE

Constructing Problems and Defining Solutions

Theory provides helpful ways to think about work, but exactly what workplace problems are and what should be done about them is a matter of politics. Here we apply the conservative, liberal, and radical-left perspectives to topics involving work and the workplace.

Conservatives: Look to the Market

As noted in Chapter 10 ("Economy and Politics"), conservatives favor limited government regulation of the economy, believing that free competition is best for society. The conservative claim is that free-market economics—with minimal regulation from government—generates the greatest good for the greatest number of people.

Like everyone else, conservatives recognize that economic downturns occur and recessions can push up the unemployment rate for several years. They also know that technological change such as the Information Revolution causes problems for some people as old jobs disappear or move to other countries. But from this point of view, such dislocations turn out to be

SOCIAL PROBLEMS in Everyday Life

How would conservatives, liberals, and left radicals define solutions to our recent economic recession?

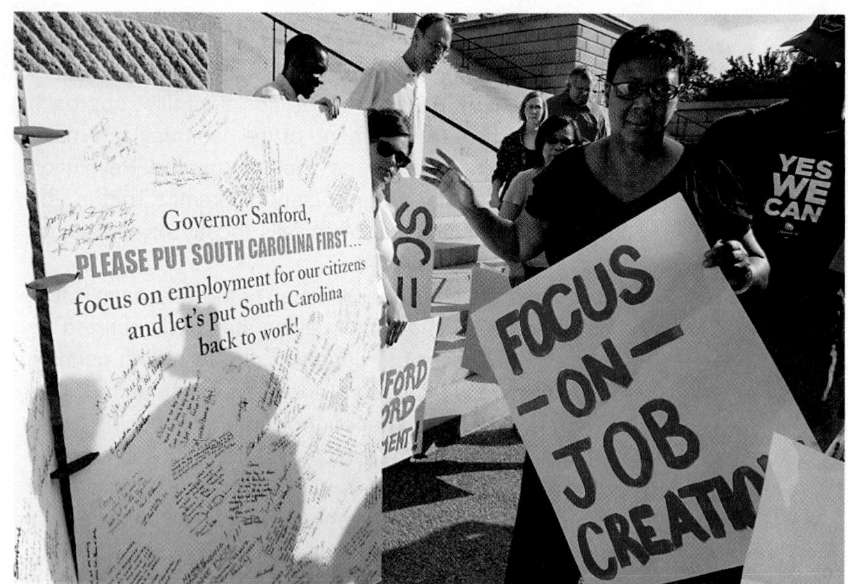

Conservatives believe that the capitalist market system offers people a wide range of job opportunities. Liberals, by contrast, maintain that because the market system favors some people more than others, government action is needed to ensure that everyone has access to work. Radicals claim that the market system serves only the rich and the powerful; as they see it, we must devise a more egalitarian economic and political system before the interests of all will be served.

temporary problems because market forces will gradually provide solutions.

For example, a steep recession began in 2008. But households responded by spending less and saving more, which is good for families and for the economy as a whole. Similarly, the drop in prices to more realistic levels will eventually stabilize the housing market. Perhaps we will all learn that it is possible—and maybe even preferable—to live with a little less.

Conservatives also claim that the housing crisis and the recession was caused not by free-market greed but by government intervention in the market. For example, mortgage giants Fannie Mae and Freddie Mac were operated under government-mandated policies that encouraged them and other banks to lend more money for housing than people could afford to repay. In the long run, conservatives believe, the operation of the market, rather than government, provides the best foundation for banks, the auto industry, and all other businesses (Horwitz, 2008; Andersen, 2009; White, 2009).

There is no doubt that the loss of "old" industries such as manufacturing appliances and televisions in the United States has closed factories and thrown millions of people out of work. But gradually, the labor force will be retrained for the types of jobs in sales and services that today's economy is creating. Eventually, most people who lost their jobs will find work in newer, more technologically advanced companies. In the end, as the economy stabilizes, everyone in the society benefit.

Another important conservative principle is individual responsibility. From this point of view, every able-bodied person should work, even at a low-paying job if that is all that is available. In general, conservatives claim that the market offers lots of opportunity and that it is up to individuals to prepare themselves to take advantage of it. For workers with limited skills, this may mean starting out at an entry-level job—perhaps even at McDonald's—with the expectation that over time, gaining skills and developing good work habits will lead to advancement. Government may be able to help people in the short term by providing training or encouraging the construction of new businesses in a particular area, but people should never expect government to do for them what they are not willing to do for themselves.

Such thinking helps explain conservative support for the 1996 welfare reforms, discussed in Chapter 2 ("Poverty and Wealth"), which moved millions of people capable of working from depending on government handouts to receiving paychecks from employers. Similarly, most conservatives oppose raising the legal minimum wage, in part because it is a form of government regulation but also because artificially setting wages above what employers are willing to pay some workers ends up increasing unemployment. In short, conservatives see the operation of a free market not as a problem but as a solution.

Liberals: Look to Government

Liberals also support a market-based economy as highly productive, but they believe that the market operating on its own creates a number of workplace problems. Therefore, liberals see a need for government regulation to protect the interests of everyone, especially low-income people, immigrants, and others who are vulnerable.

Liberals claim that without regulation, a market system would leave most people at the mercy of the rich, resulting in problems such as low wages, loss of pensions and other benefits, and a host of workplace dangers. After all, liberals continue, these problems were found everywhere in the United States

MAKING THE GRADE

Can you summarize each of the three political approaches in a sentence?

before the 1930s, when government took a larger hand in regulating the economy and improving the lives of working people. Similarly, liberals see the recession that began in 2008 as mostly caused by runaway greed on the part of a few, and they look to greater government regulation as the way to protect the public (Pierson, 2008).

There is an old saying that the market provides "rough justice," meaning that a free market gives greater rewards to those who work harder and especially to people with valuable and rare talents that create value. But liberals look to the government to smooth the rough edges of market justice to ensure that all workers are treated fairly. For this reason, liberals support a wide range of government policies, including minimum-wage laws (most liberals consider the current minimum wage of $7.25 per hour to be too low), laws protecting people from workplace hazards (so that workers are not harmed by, say, toxic chemicals), and laws protecting workers' right to join unions (so that they can bargain for higher wages and better working conditions). Liberals also support government efforts to reduce prejudice and discrimination based on race and ethnicity because when workers are divided in this way, they lose power against management. To sum up, liberals see an important role for both the marketplace and the government in the operation of an economy that truly serves the interest of all.

The sharpest disagreement between liberals and conservatives is on the role of government in economic life. In the 2008 election campaign, for example, John McCain and other Republicans claimed that people, rather than government, make the U.S. economy strong. From this point of view, government should get out of the way and let people make the economy grow. Barack Obama and other Democrats claimed that most people—especially those in need—look to government to ensure their economic well-being. From this point of view, government must both regulate the economy and provide programs such as educational benefits and health care that everyone needs. Since winning the election, President Obama and the Democratic Congress have expanded government along a more liberal path.

The Radical Left: Basic Change Is Needed

The further to the left people move on the political spectrum, the greater they believe the role of government should be in the operation of the economy. On the far left, people take a radical position that seeks to eliminate private enterprise completely, placing the entire economic system under the control of government.

From the radical-left point of view, the free market causes many serious problems. How? For one thing, by placing the economy in private hands so that individuals own factories and other businesses as their personal property, the economy operates to benefit the few rather than the many. Companies driven only by the goal of private profit will pay the lowest possible wages and show the least concern for worker well-being and workplace safety. Therefore, low wages, workplace hazards, and unemployment are predictable results of the operation of a privately owned, capitalist economy.

With this negative view of the market, radicals on the left clearly reject the conservative claim that the free market provides "the greatest good for the greatest number." And they also do not think that liberals' demands for government regulation of the market is an effective solution. The radical left goes to what it sees as the real root of the problem, calling for the replacement of the capitalist economy with a political and economic system that makes people rather than profits its highest priority.

How will such a change occur? Karl Marx claimed that working people, pushed to action by their misery, would join together in opposition to the capitalists who oppress them and eventually overthrow the capitalist system itself. As Marx put it, capitalism fails to meet the needs of the majority of people and in this way sows the seeds of its own destruction. Only when workers own and direct the workplace will they derive the rewards they should from a day's labor.

The Left to Right table on page 312 outlines the three political perspectives on work and the workplace.

Going On from Here

In the early twentieth century, the black smoke that streamed from factory chimneys in the large cities of the Northeast and Midwest signaled that the United States was becoming the world's most economically powerful nation.

The owners of this new industrial empire lived in mansions that rivaled the great castles of European monarchs. But all was not well with the majority of working people. Wages were low, thousands of workers were injured and killed in factories and mines each year, and there was little opportunity for workers to organize to better their working conditions.

In the 1930s, the Great Depression forced factories to close, and farmers who were unable to pay their mortgages lost their land. Back then, it must have seemed as if the problems of unemployment and poverty could not get any worse. Driven by such serious suffering, political support for radically changing the capitalist system was on the rise.

MAKING THE GRADE

Use the table below to review the three political approaches to work and the workplace.

LEFT TO RIGHT

The Politics of Work and the Workplace

	RADICAL-LEFT VIEW	LIBERAL VIEW	CONSERVATIVE VIEW
WHAT IS THE PROBLEM?	The capitalist market system gives rise to a host of related problems, including low wages, workplace hazards, and unemployment. Capitalism fails to meet most people's economic needs by placing profits ahead of people.	The market system is productive but does not ensure the welfare of all. Low wages, unemployment, and discrimination based on gender, race, and ethnicity are all problems in the U.S. workplace.	The market system operates efficiently and is highly productive. Government regulation reduces the productivity of the market. Therefore, government should regulate the economy as little as possible.
WHAT IS THE SOLUTION?	Workers should own and control the means of economic production. Government acting in the interest of the population as a whole should be responsible for economic policy.	While allowing market forces to operate, government agencies must regulate the economy to ensure that workers receive a living wage and that the workplace is safe and free from discrimination.	The greatest number of people will benefit most if market forces are allowed to operate freely. The economy does a good job of regulating itself and moving workers from older industries to newer kinds of work.

JOIN THE DEBATE

1. How would people at each of the political positions understand the economic recession that began in 2008? What would they suggest as a solution to this problem?
2. Do you think that on balance, the state of work in the United States improved over the course of the twentieth century? Why or why not? What new problems do workers face in the twenty-first century?
3. Which of the three political analyses of work and the workplace included here do you find most convincing? Why?

But that all changed with the start of World War II in 1939, when the nation's attention turned to international problems. The war also provided a huge boost to the struggling economy so that with the return to peace in 1945, this country entered a period of great economic prosperity.

There have been ups and downs in the economy since then. But the overall record of the U.S. economy has been impressive. Despite the recent economic downturn, the historical tend is that the economic productivity of this nation has never been greater; nor have so many of us ever lived so well. But without denying that many have prospered, many others have been left behind. As noted in Chapter 2 ("Poverty and Wealth"), the incomes of those already doing well have increased substantially in recent years, but tens of millions of working families have made little or no gains. Furthermore, millions of jobs—both blue-collar jobs in factories and white-collar jobs in offices—have been lost. Most of the new service jobs being created provide low pay, few benefits, and no union representation. Most families now depend on the incomes of at least two people. With unemployment rising, economic insecurity—and for some families, even the loss of homes—remains a concern throughout the United States.

In the foreseeable future, it seems highly likely that the nation will continue to rely on a market economy because this system has generated so much wealth. The challenge will be whether the U.S. political and economic systems can be made to operate so that all, rather than just some, of the population can achieve economic security. For the next several years, we are likely to see the Obama administration seek greater government involvement in the market, in terms of "bailouts," regulation, and extended health care and other benefits.

This chapter has focused on the United States. But we should remember that the problems of want are far worse in other countries. As Chapter 15 ("Population and Global Inequality") explains, a billion people around the world are in a desperate struggle every day simply to survive. In the long run, the stability and security of the entire planet—including the United States—may well depend on humanity's ability to provide for the needs of everyone.

CHAPTER 11 Work and the Workplace

DEFINING SOLUTIONS

Are unions necessary for workers to have good jobs?

As this chapter has explained, unions have been facing tough times, with union membership down as the economy has shifted from factory jobs (which were highly unionized) to service work (which is typically not unionized). Can unions make a comeback? Would that be good for this country's workers? Look at the photos below to see two approaches to answering such questions.

Some jobs are highly unionized. Most government workers, and almost all public school teachers, are members of labor unions. From the union point of view—which is shared by most teachers—workers acting collectively can improve their pay and working conditions in ways that individuals acting alone almost never can. If you had a choice at your place of work, would you want to join a union?

HINT

In today's service economy, many corporations—Wal-Mart among them—are strongly opposed to unions organizing their workers. What about workers themselves? There have been efforts to organize Wal-Mart employees, but so far, there is no groundswell of interest by workers in joining a union. Perhaps (as the company claims) this is because workers are getting pretty much what they want, perhaps (as unions claim) it is because workers fear losing their jobs if they try to organize. What most people can agree on is that the key to union success in today's service economy lies in being able to organize workers in "big-box" stores such as Wal-Mart.

As Wal-Mart sees it, this giant corporation is doing pretty well by its workers. Wal-Mart has created 1.5 million jobs and pays almost $300 billion in earnings each year. Wages for sales associates, according to the company, average more than $10 an hour. Wal-Mart claims that its workers have a lot to be happy about and have little to gain from joining a union. As part of their effort to keep employees smiling, managers at each of more than 5,000 company stores lead their workers through the Wal-Mart cheer each morning. Do you expect to see stores like these with a unionized workforce?

Getting Involved: Applications & Exercises

1. Contact the human resource department at your college or university, and ask about faculty pay and benefits such as health insurance, retirement pension, vacation time, and sick leave. Compare these with the pay and benefits offered to low-skill service workers, such as those in the campus food service.
2. Using your college catalogue, Web page, or information available from college officials, try to calculate the share of campus faculty who have adjunct or visiting positions. Ask several administrators and several visiting faculty why universities hire so many short-term teachers. How do visitors compare with regular faculty in terms of pay and benefits?
3. Observe the race and gender of faculty, secretarial staff, grounds workers, janitors, and cleaners on your campus. What patterns can you see?
4. Do some fieldwork at a local discount store such as Wal-Mart or Kmart. Look at various products—electronics, cameras, housewares, and clothing—and note in which countries various products are made. Does your research support the idea that the United States has deindustrialized?

VISUAL SUMMARY

MAKING THE GRADE

A DEFINING MOMENT
Eugene Debs: Standing Up for the Union p. 302

CHAPTER 11 Work and the Workplace

Structural Changes in the U.S. Economy

By 1800, the **INDUSTRIAL REVOLUTION** began changing the nature of work, moving people from *primary sector* jobs producing raw materials to *secondary sector* jobs turning raw materials into finished products.
pp. 291–92

After 1950, the **INFORMATION REVOLUTION** again changed the nature of work, this time through a process of deindustrialization as it moved people into service jobs in the *tertiary sector* of the economy.
p. 292

deindustrialization (p. 292) the decline of industrial production that occurred in the United States after about 1950

DEINDUSTRIALIZATION resulted in the closing of many industrial factories. Many people whose factory jobs disappeared ended up with service jobs offering lower pay and fewer benefits.
p. 292

Today's **GLOBAL ECONOMY** is linked to deindustrialization in the United States:

- Many U.S. corporations moved manufacturing plants abroad, where they could pay lower wages. In recent years, white-collar jobs, too, have moved to lower-income countries.

pp. 292–93

Other Problems of the U.S. Workplace

THE DUAL LABOR MARKET
The **PRIMARY LABOR MARKET** offers jobs with good pay and many benefits; jobs in the **SECONDARY LABOR MARKET** do not.

- Most of the new jobs created by today's service economy are in the secondary labor market.

p. 293

DANGERS TO HEALTH AND WELL-BEING exist in the workplace, especially in mining, agriculture, and construction work.

- Although the rate of U.S. workplace fatalities fell over the past century, each year 6,000 workers die on the job.

pp. 293–95

ALIENATION is a common workplace experience. Marx linked alienation to the powerlessness of workers in a capitalist economy. Weber linked alienation to modern rationality, which makes the workplace impersonal by emphasizing efficiency above all else.
pp. 295–96

MCDONALDIZATION defines work in terms of efficiency, predictability, uniformity, and control of workers through automation. The simplified, repetitive occupations that result can be described as "McJobs," which resemble the low-skill factory jobs common a century ago.
pp. 296–97

TEMP WORK
Counting temporary workers, contract employees, and part-timers, 25% of the U.S. labor force lack job security and have few benefits, such as employer-sponsored health insurance. This pattern benefits employers by reducing what they pay for wages and benefits.
pp. 297–98

Some **UNEMPLOYMENT** is normal as people enter the labor force or change jobs. Yet unemployment is also produced by the economy itself.

- The official U.S. unemployment rate in 2009 was above 9% of the labor force (about 14.5 million people).

pp. 298–300

RACE, ETHNICITY, AND GENDER
Although a wider range of jobs is open to women and other minorities, minorities remain concentrated in lower-paying work.

- *Institutional prejudice and discrimination* generate workplace segregation and limit the advancement of minorities; informal and often invisible barriers of this kind are called the "glass ceiling."

pp. 300–303

UNION DECLINE

- Labor unions gained strength along with the industrial economy in the twentieth century and, by 1950, claimed one-third of all U.S. nonfarm workers.
- Union membership has fallen due to deindustrialization and the expansion of service work. Today, just 12% of U.S. workers are union members.

pp. 303–4

globalization (p. 292) the expansion of economic activity around the world with little regard for national borders

primary labor market (p. 293) jobs that provide good pay and extensive benefits to workers

secondary labor market (p. 293) jobs that provide low pay and few benefits to workers

alienation (Marx) (p. 295) powerlessness in the workplace resulting in the experience of isolation and misery

alienation (Weber) (p. 296) a rational focus on efficiency, which causes depersonalization throughout society, including the workplace

rationalization of society (Weber) (p. 296) the historical change from tradition to rationality and efficiency as the typical way people think about the world

McDonaldization (p. 297) defining work in terms of the principles of efficiency, predictability, uniformity, and automation

labor unions (p. 303) worker organizations that seek to improve wages and working conditions through various strategies, including negotiations and strikes

New Information Technology: The Brave New Workplace

Computers and other new information technology are redefining work in the United States:

- **TELECOMMUTING** has increased as more people work away from the office.
- Computer technology can isolate workers and give employers greater ability to control worker activity.
- Computer technology also contributes to the "deskilling" of many jobs, including the work of managers.

pp. 304–6

telecommuting (p. 304) linking employees to the office using information technology, including telephones, computers, and the Internet

Theoretical Analysis: Understanding Work-Related Problems

Structural-Functional Analysis: Finding a New Equilibrium

The **STRUCTURAL-FUNCTIONAL APPROACH** looks at the importance of work for the operation of the economy.

- Changes (especially those brought on by new technology) can disrupt established patterns of work, causing problems such as unemployment.
- But other institutions, such as education, gradually retrain workers for new kinds of jobs, helping restore society's balance.

p. 307

Symbolic-Interaction Analysis: The Meaning of Work

The **SYMBOLIC-INTERACTION APPROACH** highlights the meaning people attach to work.

- In general, people in the primary labor market attach positive meaning to their work; their jobs are an important part of their social identity.
- People in the secondary labor market find less positive meaning in their work and value a job only for the income it provides.

pp. 307–9

Social-Conflict Analysis: Work and Inequality

The **SOCIAL-CONFLICT APPROACH** focuses on how wealth and power shape the workplace.

- A Marxist analysis argues that because factories and other productive property are privately owned, most people are powerless and find work alienating.
- Max Weber adds that modern rationality makes efficiency an all-important goal so that the workplace becomes impersonal, with workers coming to resemble machines.

p. 309

See the **Applying Theory** table on page 308.

Politics and the Workplace: Constructing Problems and Defining Solutions

The Radical Left: Basic Change Is Needed

- **RADICALS ON THE LEFT** see the free-market system as a source of problems. From this point of view, capitalism is concerned only with profits rather than the welfare of people.
- Radicals on the left believe that mere reform will not solve this problem; the capitalist system must be replaced with an economic system that operates in the interests of all workers.

p. 311

Liberals: Look to Government

- **LIBERALS** point out that a free-market economy, although productive, does not meet the needs of everyone. Rather, market systems cause problems, including dangerous working conditions, unemployment, and low wages.
- Liberals support government regulation of the economy and the workplace to enhance the well-being of all.

pp. 310–11

Conservatives: Look to the Market

- **CONSERVATIVES** hold that a free-market economy, with minimal government regulation, produces the greatest good for the greatest number of people.
- Conservatives believe that although new technology and downturns in the economy cause temporary disruptions, the market solves these problems over time, in the end creating a highly productive economy.

pp. 309–10

See the **Left to Right** table on page 312.

CONSTRUCTING THE PROBLEM

Is living together a good way to test a relationship?

Many people do, but research shows that living together without being married increases the chances of divorce later on.

Does marriage last "till death us do part"?

About three out of ten of today's marriages will end in divorce.

How strong are the family ties of U.S. children?

Half of U.S. children will live with just one of their parents at some time before reaching age eighteen.

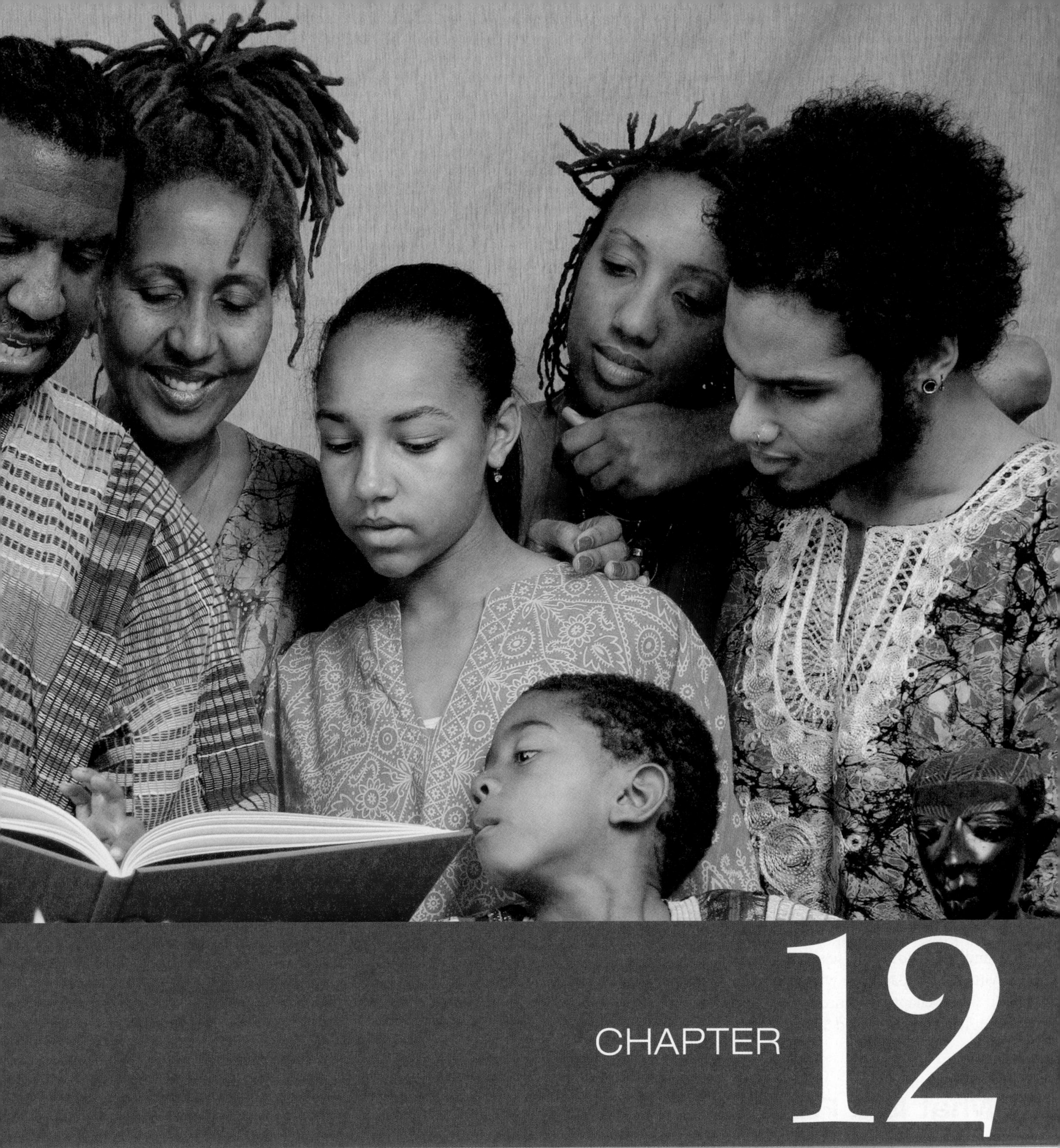

CHAPTER 12

Family Life

CHAPTER OVERVIEW

WHAT IS A FAMILY? How have families changed in recent decades? This chapter will explain why the family is important to society and explore many controversies involving families. You will learn about various family forms and assess their advantages and disadvantages. You will become familiar with recent legal changes expanding same-sex marriage. You will carry out theoretical analysis of family issues and learn how "problems" and "solutions" involving families and family life reflect people's political attitudes.

The judges returned to the courtroom, and as the crowd of people, including members of the press, sat quietly, they announced their verdict: The petition for divorce was hereby granted. A buzz of excitement swept through the room as the judges finished reading their statement, and reporters rushed to the door to file their stories.

What was so special about this divorce? It was unusual because the bride was only eight years old. The young girl lives in Saudi Arabia, where almost a year before, she had been given in marriage by her father to a fifty-year-old man for about $13,000. Arranged marriages are common in much of the world, and Saudi Arabia currently has no law setting a minimum age for marriage.

The decision to allow the divorce was hailed by liberals in that nation as a step forward for both women and children in a society that limits the rights of both. Conservatives, however, support arranged marriages—even when girls are this young—as a tradition that allows the family to control their own children and also as a strategy to ensure that girls do not engage in "illicit" relationships as they grow older (Al-Shalchi, 2009).

There is debate in Saudi Arabia about many aspects of marriage and family life, and change is taking place. In the same way, patterns involving marriage and family are changing here in the United States as well. The U.S. government issued a statement condemning child marriage in Saudi Arabia. At the same time, it is worth noting that divorce is many times more common in this country than it is there.

When it comes to marriage and families, the rules are changing almost everywhere. In our society, more people are living alone, more people are having children without being married, more families include same-sex couples, and more children are living with a single parent or with two moms or two dads.

This chapter explores the trends, issues, and problems of family life in the United States. We begin by defining some basic terms.

What Is a Family?

The **family** is *a social institution that unites individuals into cooperative groups that care for one another, including any children.* **Kinship,** a related concept, is *a social bond, based on common ancestry, marriage, or adoption, that joins individuals into families.*

Families have existed since at least the beginning of recorded history, but the forms families take have varied over time as they do from place to place today. In modern, high-income societies such as the United States, most people think in terms of the **nuclear family,** *one or two parents and their children.* In lower-income nations around the world, however, people typically recognize the **extended family,** *parents and children and also grandparents, aunts, uncles, and cousins who often live close to one another and operate as a family unit.*

Whatever the specific form, families are built around **marriage,** *a lawful relationship usually involving economic cooperation, sexual activity, and childbearing.* In the United States and throughout the world, people link marriage to having children, which explains why the word *matrimony* comes from the Latin word meaning "motherhood." This traditional link between marriage and having children is the reason a child born to an unwed mother was sometimes defined as "illegitimate," although as single parenting becomes more common in the United States and in other countries, this pattern is far less likely to be defined as a problem.

Debate over Definitions

With families changing so much, we should not be surprised to find that people disagree about what a "family" ought to be. In the United States, the traditional view of a family is a married couple and their children. Fifty years ago, most U.S. families fit

family a social institution that unites individuals into cooperative groups that care for one another, including any children

kinship a social bond, based on common ancestry, marriage, or adoption, that joins individuals into families

nuclear family one or two parents and their children

extended family parents and children and also grandparents, aunts, uncles, and cousins who often live close to one another and operate as a family unit

marriage a lawful relationship usually involving economic cooperation, sexual activity, and childbearing

families of affinity people with or without legal or blood ties who feel they belong together and define themselves as a family

cohabitation the sharing of a household by an unmarried couple

this form. Today, however, less than one in four does. More people now favor recognizing a wide range of **families of affinity,** *people with or without legal or blood ties who feel they belong together and define themselves as a family.*

Does it matter how we define families? The answer is yes because this question involves concerns about which types of relationships are defined as morally right or wrong. In addition, there are practical concerns, including whether all people who wish to marry or adopt children have the legal right to do so. The remainder of this chapter explores these issues.

A Sociological Approach to Family Problems

When most people speak about "family problems" or "problems at home," they usually have in mind conflicts between individuals or perhaps a situation involving a family member who is struggling with alcohol or some other drug.

The sociological perspective looks at not just the behavior of individuals but more broadly at how society supports certain types of families and at the many challenges of family life. For example, members of our society debate whether people should use advancing genetic technology to select the physical traits of unborn children. Similarly, in a society where most women as well as men now work for income, we struggle to balance work and family responsibilities and to find good, affordable child care.

How do the mass media portray families? Almost all major characters on today's popular television are unmarried, and most place their work ahead of their personal relationships. Certainly that is the case in *House*, among the most popular shows of 2009, in which no major character is married and most do not have a positive relationship with parents.

Controversies over Family Life

What are some of the ways in which U.S. families are changing? The trends include a rising number of people living together without being married, people marrying later, an increase in the share of children born to single mothers, more mothers joining fathers in the labor force so that more young children spend the day in care programs, a divorce rate much higher than it was fifty years ago, an increase in the number of blended families following remarriage, gains by gay men and lesbians in their pursuit of legal marriage, and new medical technology that offers amazing new possibilities for reproduction. All these trends have sparked both praise and criticism. In the following sections, we examine all the trends in turn.

Living Together: Do We Need to Marry?

Fifty years ago, most people took it for granted that couples married before moving in together. But a recent trend favors **cohabitation,** *the sharing of a household by an unmarried couple.* The number of cohabiting couples in the United States has risen from about 500,000 in 1970 to more than 6.2 million (5.5 million heterosexual couples and 700,000 gay or lesbian couples). In all, cohabiting people represent 5.5 percent of all households (U.S. Census Bureau, 2010).

In some countries, especially Sweden and other Scandinavian nations, cohabitation is very common, even for couples with children. This practice is rare in more traditional (and Roman Catholic) nations such as Italy. In the United States, about half of people between twenty-five and forty-four years of age cohabit at some point in their lives. Almost 40 percent of these couples include at least one child under eighteen (Raley, 1996; U.S. Census Bureau, 2010).

Critics of cohabiting, typically political conservatives, claim that marriage is better than cohabitation because marriage pro-

GETTING INVOLVED

Make a list of the people you would include as part of your "family." Do you tend to define the term narrowly (nuclear family) or broadly (extended family)? Why?

GETTING INVOLVED

In general, do you think cohabiting is a good idea? What about for couples having children? Why or why not?

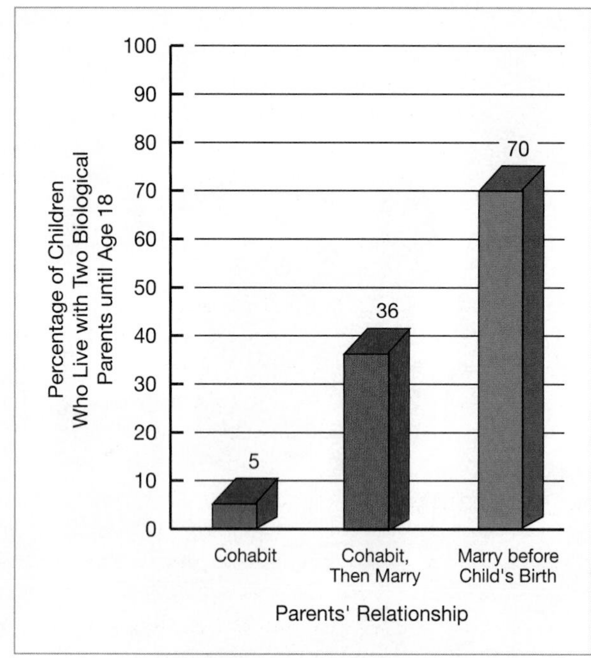

FIGURE 12–1 Chances of a Child Living with Both Biological Parents to Age Eighteen, by Type of Parental Relationship

Seventy percent of children born to married parents live with them until age eighteen, compared with just 5 percent of children born to cohabiting parents.

Source: M. Phillips (2001).

vides a more stable setting in which to raise children. As shown in Figure 12–1, just 5 percent of children born to cohabiting parents go on to live with both parents until age eighteen, compared with 70 percent of children born to married parents. One reason for this difference, say the critics, is that unmarried men more easily walk out on women and children. But cohabitation carries risks for men, too: When informal unions break up, men run the risk of losing legal rights to raise their children. Research shows that 61 percent of cohabiting couples eventually split up. In addition, researchers caution that living together can weaken marriage later on. Why? Because partners get used to relationships with less commitment (Popenoe & Whitehead, 1999; U.S. Department of Health and Human Services, 2011).

Supporters of cohabitation, typically liberals, argue that decisions about sexual relationships are private matters that should be left to individuals. In addition, there is little reason to expect that one relational form—monogamous marriage—will meet the needs of everyone in a large and diverse population. On the contrary, some argue that cohabitation better reflects U.S. cultural values of choice and freedom and typically encourages a more equal relationship between a woman and a man. What about the well-being of children? Supporters of cohabiting argue that all parents who separate, whether married or not, must take responsibility for the support and care of their children (Brines & Joyner, 1999; Scommegna, 2002).

Postponing Marriage

The trend toward cohabitation is linked to another pattern: On average, people in the United States are delaying marriage. In 1950, the median age at first marriage in the United States was 20.3 years for women and 22.8 years for men. By 2009, these figures had jumped about six years to 26.1 years for women and 28.2 years for men (U.S. Census Bureau, 2010).

Why are people marrying later? One important reason is that a larger share of young people are attending college and graduate school. Another is that after graduation, a rising share of women are entering the labor force. In addition, economic insecurity makes it hard for many young people to live on their own; today, more than half of young people between eighteen and twenty-four are still living with their parents. Finally, improvements in birth control technology and the availability of legal abortion also play a part because, facing an unexpected pregnancy, couples are not likely to feel forced to marry as they might have back in the 1950s.

Is this trend toward delaying marriage itself a problem? Not necessarily, but it does have some important consequences. For one thing, men and, especially, women who marry later in life have lower odds of being able to have children. If they do, of course, they will be "older" parents, who may not match the energy level of parents who are ten to twenty years younger. On the plus side, older parents typically have more time and knowledge to offer their children, and they earn much more money (Chandler, Kamo, & Werbel, 1994).

Delayed marriage is also linked to a drop in overall childbearing: A U.S. woman's average number of children dropped from 3.0 in 1976 to 2.0 in 2009. Other patterns linked to delayed marriage include a rising share of women who have no children (up from 9 percent in 1970 to 19 percent in 2010) and a rising share of the population that remains single (up from 11 percent in 1950 to 27 percent in 2010) (U.S. Census Bureau, 2010). In later life, remaining single is more likely for women than for men because U.S. culture encourages men—but not women—to marry a younger partner.

Another consequence of delayed marriage is that by the time that people consider getting married, they are more independent of their parents. With less parental input into the choice of partner, people are freer to form relationships that might have been discouraged in the past, such as same-sex or interracial unions.

SOCIAL PROBLEMS in Everyday Life

In general, young people in rural areas are likely to marry earlier than people in urban areas. Why do you think this is true?

GETTING INVOLVED

Have you or anyone you know ever lived in a single-parent family, either as a parent or as a child? If so, what challenges and what advantages does this type of family have?

Parenting: Is One Parent Enough?

In 2010, about one in three families with children under eighteen years of age had just one parent in the household, a share that has doubled since 1970. Half of U.S. children will live with a single parent at some point before reaching age eighteen.

There is no doubt that most children raised by a single parent turn out just fine; similarly, having two parents in the home is no guarantee of a child's well-being. Still, evidence is mounting that growing up in a one-parent family does put children at a disadvantage. Some studies indicate that a father and a mother each make a distinctive contribution to a child's social development, so either parent alone cannot do as complete a job as two working together. In addition, it stands to reason that all else being equal, two parents can provide greater attention to children than one.

But the biggest problem confronting one-parent families—especially in the 79 percent of all cases where the single parent is a woman—is poverty. Children in one-parent families begin with more than a one-in-three chance of being poor and, on average, end up with less education and lower incomes. Such disadvantages often develop into a vicious circle as boys and girls raised by single parents become single parents themselves (Popenoe, 1993a; Kantrowitz & Wingert, 2001; Pew Research Center, 2007; U.S. Census Bureau, 2010).

Families, Race, and Poverty

There are many reasons that children live with a single parent. Among white families, divorce is the most common reason; among African American families, most single women who have children have never married. Although the risk of being poor goes up in both situations, the problem of poverty is especially high for African American children. In the United States, about 23 percent of families headed by white women are poor, but 37 percent of families headed by African American women are poor, which contributes to the fact that one-third of all African American youngsters grow up in poverty (U.S. Census Bureau, 2010).

The Moynihan Report

Back in 1965, U.S. Senator Daniel Patrick Moynihan (who was trained as a social scientist) sounded an alarm that the African American family was in crisis because of the growing number of absent fathers who leave single mothers to raise children on their own. In Moynihan's view, single motherhood threatened the African American community with a cycle of poverty spilling from mothers to children.

When Moynihan issued his warning, 20 percent of African American children were born to single mothers; since then, the figure has climbed steadily upward to 73 percent (Martin et al., 2010). Not everyone agreed with Moynihan. Critics claimed that his concern reflected a traditional view of the two-parent family, rejecting anything different as "dysfunctional." There is no problem with a female-headed household, critics continued, at least nothing that adequate income cannot solve (Norton, 1985; Angelo, 1989).

Liberal critics concluded that for African Americans, single-parent families and poverty are not so much *family* problems as they are *economic* and *race prejudice* problems. Eleanor Holmes Norton (1985) argues that the "breakdown" of the African American family is the result of long-term racism, which results in discrimination in jobs, education, and housing. The sociologist William Julius Wilson (1987, 1996a) adds that African Americans who fall within a disadvantaged urban "underclass" find that there are simply not enough jobs to allow men and women to support a family. To claim that African Americans choose their family patterns (much less choose to be poor) amounts to blaming the victim (Hewlett & West, 1998).

African American Families: A Closer Look

There are plenty of stereotypes about African American families. For years, the image of the average "welfare mother" was an unmarried African American woman. But this stereotype is not accurate. As Chapter 2 ("Poverty and Wealth") explains, most

One of the strengths of African American families is the tendency to form multigenerational households. Why do you think this pattern is more common among African Americans than among whites?

GETTING INVOLVED

Describe conflicts you have experienced between work and family life.

DIVERSITY: RACE, CLASS, & GENDER

Reality Check: Five False Stereotypes about African American Families

In the United States, many people hold incorrect and stereotypical views of African American families. Here we do a reality check on five widespread stereotypes about African American families.

Stereotype 1. African Americans do not form strong families.

Historical studies show that even under slavery, most African Americans lived in families with a father and a mother. This pattern continued well into the twentieth century. After about 1960, a combination of racial segregation (which trapped many African Americans in inner cities) and industrial decline (which meant that many inner-city communities lost a lot of jobs) resulted in a declining rate of marriage among African Americans and a rising rate of children born to single mothers. But even against these odds, almost half of African American families still have both husband and wife in the home.

Stereotype 2. African American men do not make good husbands and fathers.

This stereotype is based on the fact that a larger share of African American families (44 percent) have no husband present than is the case with Latino families (27 percent), white families (13 percent), or Asian families (13 percent). This stereotype assumes that the lack of a husband in the home reflects people's choices rather than the fact that many African American communities do not provide the jobs men need to support a family (W. J. Wilson, 1996b).

Stereotype 3. The African American family is a matriarchy: Women dominate family life.

History shows that African American men have played vital leadership roles both in individual families and in larger communities. It is also important to recognize that men or men and women together head a majority (56 percent) of African American families.

Stereotype 4. African American women have more children, often in order to increase welfare benefits.

Regardless of race, poor women receiving income assistance do have more children than women who are not receiving public assistance. But this pattern holds for both black and white women. The birth rate for black women is just 17 percent higher than for non-Hispanic white women.

Stereotype 5. Today, African Americans have the same opportunities as everyone else.

Many white people believe, or want to believe, that racial prejudice and discrimination are things of the past. However, the evidence suggests that African American men and women—whether poor, middle-class, or rich—continue to face barriers based on race.

WHAT DO YOU THINK?

1. Why do you think stereotypes about African American families are widespread? Can you think of stereotypes other than those presented here?
2. How does sociology play a part in responding to stereotypes such as these?
3. What policies might the Obama administration follow to support African American families? Explain.

Sources: Concept adapted from Benokraitis (1999); data from U.S. Census Bureau (2010).

people who receive public assistance are white. The Diversity: Race, Class, & Gender box presents five common but false stereotypes about African American families.

African American families take many forms, and no single description accurately portrays them. In the United States, families—black and white, rich and poor—are much more diverse than most people realize.

Strengths of African American Families

There is little doubt that African American families face more challenges—including low income, racial prejudice, and discrimination—than white families do. Research shows that African American families, especially those struggling with poverty, have real strengths. These families adapt to their situation in a number of ways, building strong kinship bonds, drawing strength from traditional religious beliefs, and using the resources of grandparents (especially grandmothers) to form three-generation households. In addition, many poor households band together in networks of mutual assistance that help everyone get by (Stack, 1975; Littlejohn-Blake & Darling, 1993; Clemetson, 2000).

Conflict between Work and Family Life

For much of U.S. history, and for people of any race, work and family life occurred together because families lived and labored on farms. After the Industrial Revolution, people (mostly the men) went off to work in factories, which separated the home from the workplace.

Starting in the 1950s, with the rapid entry of women into the labor force, people began to feel greater tension between work and family life. Today, a majority of U.S. families, even those with young children, have both parents working for income. Typically, women now work for pay and also perform almost another full-time job when they are at home doing housework (Lewin, 2000; England, 2001; U.S. Census Bureau, 2010). This "double duty"

SOCIAL PROBLEMS in Everyday Life

Most women — including most married women with young children— are in the labor force.

GETTING INVOLVED

Have you ever been involved in an effort to expand child care for working parents? If so, explain.

means that many women are tired and overworked as they try to juggle their many responsibilities.

As Chapter 11 ("Work and the Workplace") explains, the Information Revolution has changed the nature of work, and one-fifth of people in the labor force now spend some time each week working at home. In some ways, working at home can help reduce work-family tensions. At the same time, however, as more people work at home or maintain home offices, workplace activities and concerns spill more and more into family life (Macionis, 2001).

Child Care

A century ago, most families considered child care the job of the mother, who worked in the home. Today, with 59 percent of U.S. women in the labor force working for income, most mothers are working mothers—53 percent of married women with infants, 60 percent of married women with preschoolers, and 74 percent of married women with school-age children work for pay outside the home. The figures are a little higher for single women with children and higher still for widowed, divorced, or separated women with children (U.S. Department of Labor, 2009).

With so many women and men working, our society began to define child care as an important issue. Who provides the care for the children of mothers in the labor force? Figure 12–2 answers this question. Half of all children (52 percent) receive care from family—from a parent (20 percent) or from a grandparent or other relative (32 percent). An additional 23 percent of children go to a day care program or attend preschool, 10 percent receive care in a nonrelative's home, 4 percent receive care in their own home, and 11 percent have no regular arrangement (U.S. Census Bureau, 2010).

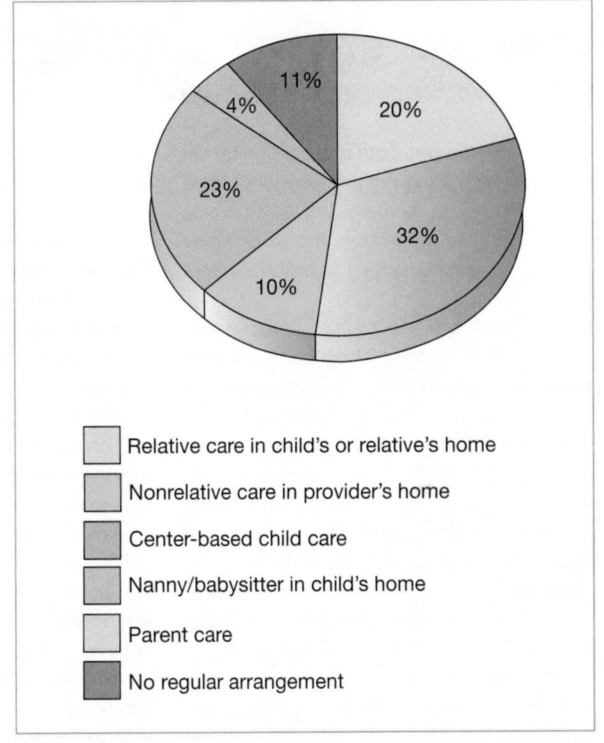

FIGURE 12–2 Child Care Arrangements for Working Mothers

Half of the young children of working mothers receive care from a parent, grandparent, or other relative.

Source: U.S. Census Bureau (2010).

Which option a family chooses has a lot to do with income. Parents with higher incomes can afford to send their children to care programs that emphasize learning and early childhood development. By contrast, those with lower incomes turn to relatives or friends, piece together a patchwork of babysitters, or send their children to less costly care centers where the staff does not have much training and gives less attention to each child.

Older children, of course, spend most of the day at school. But after school, about 5.3 million youngsters (14 percent of five- to fourteen-year-olds) are "latchkey kids" who fend for themselves until a parent returns from work (U.S. Census Bureau, 2010). Some children adapt well to being alone after school, becoming more independent and self-reliant. But especially in poor neighborhoods, unsupervised children are at high risk for several problems, including getting involved in drugs, crime, or sexual exploitation.

What role, if any, should the government play in ensuring that child care needs are met? In most high-income nations other than the United States, the government uses tax money to operate child care centers. In our country, government helps working parents indirectly by letting them deduct child care costs on income tax returns. In addition, states provide some financial assistance to poor families who need child care. Because of our country's cultural emphasis on self-sufficiency, the United States has yet to offer free or subsidized child care programs on a large scale.

Those who favor expanded government child care programs point out that many low-income families would welcome the assistance and more children could be well served. In addition, most existing child care centers operate only during business hours from Monday to Friday, which does not meet the needs of parents who work night shifts or "swing" shifts that change from week to week.

Today, more employers offer on-site child care programs. In most cases, employees pay for this care, but some employers provide this service as a workplace benefit. Such programs are usually of good quality and have two added advantages:

SOCIAL PROBLEMS in Everyday Life

Is a divorced person at all deviant to you? What about someone who has divorced twice? Three times?

SOCIAL PROBLEMS in Everyday Life

Is divorce best understood as a problem or as a solution? Can it be both? Explain.

PERSONAL STORIES

Dying for Foster Care

Terrell Peterson was born into a world he did not make and would never have chosen to live in. Born to a mother addicted to crack, Terrell lived like a candle in the wind, never getting the care he needed or knowing where to turn to get it.

He lived with his mother and her two other children, each of whom had a different father. Soon after his birth, the state of Georgia put Terrell on a "watch list," fearing that he would be neglected. Child welfare officials collected data for five years before they concluded that Terrell was in danger in his present home, at which point they took him from his mother and placed him in foster care. Because no blood relative was available to provide care, the boy ended up in the home of the grandmother of one of his half-siblings.

Pharina Peterson was probably the last person who should have been given a child to care for. Looking back, it is clear she did not want the child; apparently, she took him in just to get the monthly child support check. As Georgia officials now know, Terrell was terribly abused. Evidence suggests that he was starved, tied to a stairway, and beaten.

Within a year, Terrell Peterson was dead. At the time of his death, the six-year-old boy weighed only 29 pounds; his body showed so many injuries that the medical examiner could not list them all.

The police entered the picture, and Pharina Peterson was charged with murder. But it is easy to think that some of the responsibility for this boy's death lies with the system of foster care. The goal of foster care is to protect children, but it clearly failed in this case. The terrible truth is that Terrell Peterson is not the only child to have fallen through the cracks of a system that some critics claim is in crisis. One study found that 513 foster care children died over a three-year period just in the state of Georgia.

Across the country, more than half a million children are in foster care, twice the number a decade ago. The cost of foster care is about $5 billion a year, or roughly $10,000 per child. In a majority of cases, children are better off in foster care than they were before. But the foster care system cannot guarantee the safety of every child. Most analysts agree that the rate of neglect and abuse among foster children is far higher than among children living with biological parents. The exact number of abused foster children is a matter of guesswork: Each year, there are about 2,000 reported cases of abuse, but the real total could easily be twice as high. Not knowing what is happening to foster care children is at the heart of the problem. Too often government agencies place boys and girls in foster homes only to lose track of them as the years pass. "These systems should be a national scandal," claims Marcia Robinson Lowry, head of Children's Rights, Inc., a children's advocacy group. "In virtually every state there is no accountability" (Roche, 2000b:75).

WHAT DO YOU THINK?

1. Should the public consider foster care an important issue? Why or why not?
2. What can our society do to reduce the number of children in foster care who are not well cared for?
3. Do you think children should be placed with nonrelatives if there is doubt about the quality of care a relative would provide? Explain your position.

Sources: Roche (2000b), Polgreen & Worth (2003), and U.S. Department of Health and Human Services (2008).

Parents have a chance to visit their children during breaks throughout the day, and companies that provide workplace child care have the edge in attracting and retaining the best employees.

A final child care issue involves children whose parents cannot or will not care for them. Our society tries to assist these children through the foster care system. But as the Personal Stories box explains, sometimes this system fails the children it was created to serve.

Divorce

When they marry, many people vow that they will stay together "till death us do part." But the reality today is that divorce, not death, ends many marriages. In the United States, about three in ten of today's marriages will end in divorce (among African Americans, the rate is about half). Overall, about 10 percent of U.S. adults over age fifteen are divorced.

Today's divorce rate is four times what it was a century ago. Back then, family members (especially the half of U.S. families who lived and worked on farms) looked to one another to get by, and this economic dependency kept married people together. In addition, because women had yet to enter the labor force in large numbers, unless a woman could turn to relatives for support, divorce often meant a life of poverty. Finally, the more traditional culture of that time defined divorce as sinful and a sign of personal failure, so moral pressure also helped keep couples together, whether they were happily married or not.

During the twentieth century, the share of women working for income went up, and the average number of children per woman went down. These trends made divorce a more realistic

SOCIAL PROBLEMS in Everyday Life

Do you think no-fault divorce is better than the old "blame your spouse" system or not? Why?

SOCIAL PROBLEMS in Everyday Life

Looking at Figure 12–3, point to events or changes in our society that explain changes in the divorce rate.

option, and gradually, public attitudes became more accepting of divorce (Etzioni, 1993; Schoen at al., 2002).

As Figure 12–3 shows, the divorce rate soared for several years during World War II because the war forced millions of couples to live apart; it experienced another steady climb from about 1960 to 1980. Since then, the divorce rate has eased downward. National Map 12–1 on page 326 shows the percentage of the population that is divorced throughout the United States.

No-Fault Divorce

If increasing economic independence gave women more opportunity to move on from an unhappy marriage, changes in the law helped make divorces easier to get. In 1969, California became the first state to enact a policy of no-fault divorce. By 1985, every state in the country had done the same.

What is no-fault divorce? Perhaps the best way to answer this question is to explain that before this policy was in force, a couple could divorce only if one or both partners claimed in court that the other was at fault for *ruining* the marriage—typically, through abandonment, adultery, or physical or emotional injury. Divorce was a moral issue; someone had to have done something *very wrong.* And much was at stake because the courts took fault into account when dividing the couple's property and assigning custody of children. The "bad" person usually lost out.

No-fault divorce laws did away with this whole process. No longer does anyone have to be blamed for a failed marriage. Instead, couples simply declare that their marriage is over due to "irreconcilable differences." The court divides property fairly and places children where they seem best off. In addition, the court assigns *child support* according to the need of the custodial parent, the noncustodial parent's ability to pay, and the ability of both parents to work. Rarely does no-fault divorce involve *alimony,* regular payments from one ex-spouse to the other.

By greatly reducing the payment of alimony, no-fault divorce ended the longstanding idea that men ought to take care of women. But this new thinking does not mean that women are always better off. Researchers have found that after divorce, the living standard of men goes up, but the living standard of women and their children goes down (Weitzman, 1985, 1996; Faludi, 1991; Holden & Smock, 1991). Why is this so? Allen Parkman (1992) explains that no-fault divorce harms women because it ignores *cultural capital,* which includes skills and schooling that increase a person's earning power. In a traditional marriage, a wife may put little or no time into paid work, often devoting herself to helping her husband develop his career. Her focus on her husband makes sense only as long as she assumes that she will stay married and that her husband's success will benefit her as well. After divorce, the husband still has his job, but in most cases, the stay-at-home wife has few

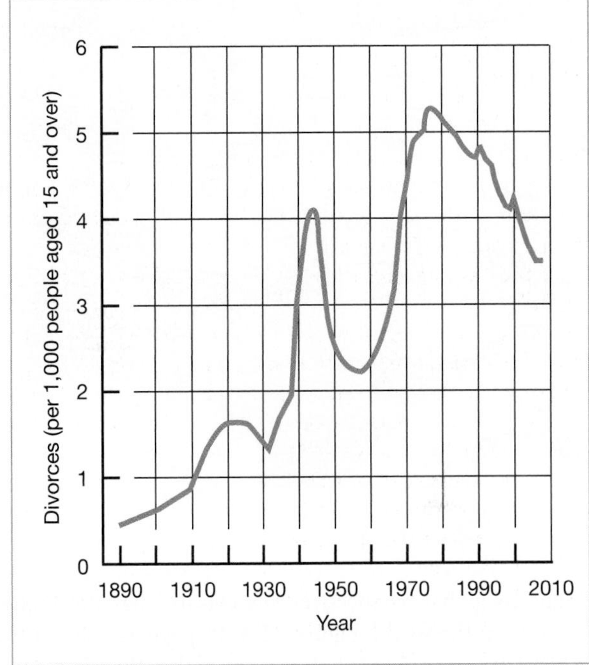

FIGURE 12–3 The U.S. Divorce Rate, 1890–2009

After 1890, the U.S. divorce rate climbed rapidly, especially during World War II (1939–1945). After falling in the 1950s, the rate rose again through the late 1970s and has since been on the decline.

Source: U.S. Census Bureau (2009) and National Center for Health Statistics (2011).

workplace skills to fall back on and also faces the expense of caring for the children.

Many people support no-fault divorce as a solution to the problem of unhappy marriages. In addition, supporters claim that this policy treats men and women as equals, reflecting the fact that a majority of both sexes now work for income. But some people see no-fault divorce as a problem, claiming that it is harmful to women. Pointing to the fact that men still earn more money than women, critics say that we should bring back the system of alimony so that the person with the greater earning power (usually the man) helps support the ex-partner who stayed at home (usually the woman).

Finally, if divorce is always a possibility, should couples prepare for it? Many couples try to spell out the terms of any future divorce by writing a premarital agreement. The Social Policy box on page 327 takes a closer look.

Too Much Divorce?

Just about everyone recognizes that divorce may be better than staying in an unhappy relationship. But is today's divorce rate

Marcia Ekberg grew up in rural Minnesota, where divorce was rare. She now lives in San Diego, California, where many of her friends have been divorced.

SOCIAL PROBLEMS in Everyday Life

Why do you think covenant marriage, described below, has not been more popular?

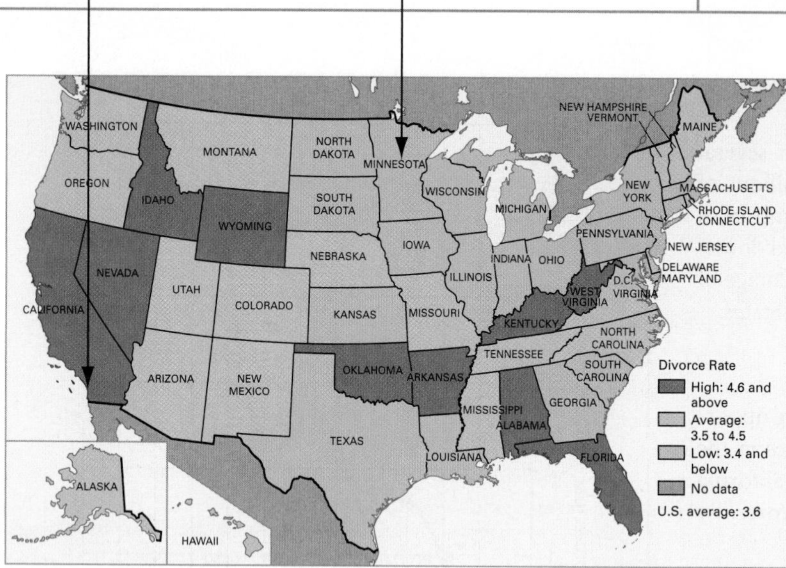

A Nation of Diversity

NATIONAL MAP 12–1

Divorce across the United States

The map shows the divorce rate (the number of divorces per 1,000 population), by state, for 2007. Divorce is far more common near the West Coast (and especially in Nevada, a state with very liberal divorce laws), somewhat less common in the East, and much less common in the middle of the country. Research suggests that divorce is more likely among people who are younger, who have weaker religious ties, and who move away from their parents' hometown. Can you apply these facts to make sense of this map?

Source: National Center for Health Statistics (2008).

too high? In global perspective, this country has the highest divorce rate in the world. Figure 12–4 on page 328 shows that the U.S. divorce rate is about 50 percent higher than in Canada and more than four times higher than "low-divorce" nations such as Italy and Ireland (European Union, 2009).

In the United States, liberals generally do not see divorce as a problem. They tend to favor easy divorce as a means by which women can free themselves from unhappy or abusive relationships. Conservatives are generally critical of a high divorce rate, claiming that it signifies a "me first" attitude that places individual needs and desires over obligations to others (Whitehead, 1997; Popenoe, 1999).

Then there is the effect of divorce on children. Again, the costs and benefits vary from case to case, but the evidence suggests that many divorces end up being difficult for the children involved (Amato & Sobolewski, 2001).

So is our present divorce rate a problem or not? The public is divided on the issue, but about half are concerned. When asked in a national survey whether divorce is too easy to get these days, 23 percent of U.S. adults say they are satisfied with the system as it is, 27 percent think divorce is still too hard to get, and 46 percent say that divorce is too easy to get, with the remaining 4 percent expressing no opinion (NORC, 2009).

In recent years, three states—Arkansas, Arizona, and Louisiana—have responded to high divorce rates by enacting *covenant marriage* laws. These laws allow couples, when they marry, to choose a conventional marriage or a covenant marriage, which is harder to dissolve. Couples who choose a covenant marriage agree, first, to seek marital counseling if problems develop during the marriage. They agree to seek divorce only for limited reasons, including adultery, conviction for a serious felony, abandonment for at least one year or living separately for at least two years, habitual drug or alcohol abuse, or physical or sexual abuse of the spouse or a child. Covenant marriage rejects the idea that people ought to be able to divorce simply because one of them no longer wants to stay married (Nock, Wright, & Sanchez, 1999; National Conference of State Legislatures, 2008).

In a dozen states, legislatures have considered enacting covenant marriage laws. In most cases, lawmakers have decided to pass a law or a resolution encouraging premarital counseling. In the three states that have such laws, only a small share of people have chosen to enter into a covenant marriage. Therefore, it seems safe to conclude that covenant marriage has not been widely viewed as a solution to the high divorce rate.

Child Support

After parents divorce, many children do not receive adequate financial support. The failure of a noncustodial parent (that is, the parent who does not have primary custody of a child) to make child support payments is one cause of high poverty rates among U.S. children.

After a separation or divorce, courts typically order noncustodial parents to help support their children. Such court orders are issued for 54 percent of the children of divorcing parents. Yet of the children who should receive this money, 54 percent receive only partial payments or no payments at all (U.S. Census Bureau, 2010).

When parents divorce, courts usually award custody of children to mothers. For this reason, most parents who fail to support their children are men, which explains the national

SOCIAL PROBLEMS in Everyday Life

Why do you think so many noncustodial parents fail to make court-ordered payments to their ex-spouse in support of children?

GETTING INVOLVED

What are the laws in your state that apply to nonsupport of children? Go online to find out.

SOCIAL POLICY

Should You Prepare a Premarital Agreement?

Any couple considering marriage today needs to face up to the fact that there are three-in-ten odds that at some point in the future, the relationship will end in divorce. Therefore, lawyers and others counsel that it makes good sense to prepare a premarital (prenuptial) agreement.

What should be included in such an agreement? The answer depends on the individuals involved and on how much property each person has going into the marriage.

1. **Property.** Start by making a list of each of your assets and liabilities. Will you retain separate ownership of existing property—including homes, furniture, jewelry, cash, cars, and investments—or combine it as joint property? Will you keep your own savings and checking accounts or create new joint accounts? Will you be responsible for each other's existing debts, such as loans for college tuition or car payments? What about property that you accumulate during the marriage? In the event of divorce or death of one partner, what will happen to all property? What about medical coverage? If either of you enters the marriage with children, what property rights do the children have?
2. **Income.** Do you know your partner's income as well as your own? How will these incomes be applied to household expenses, savings and investments, and future purchases such as a new home? Who will be responsible for paying bills? For supporting children?
3. **Children.** Do you have children? Do you plan on having children together? How will you divide responsibility for child care? What are each partner's attitudes about disciplining children? Is it important to give children a religious upbringing? Will children from a previous relationship have the same inheritance rights as any children you have with your new partner?
4. **Housework.** How much housework needs to be done? To answer this question, consider the likely size of your family and the size of your home. How will you divide responsibility for housework?
5. **In case of divorce.** Should your marriage end in divorce, how will you divide property? What marital property will be sold? What about assets (a house or investments) that go up in value during the marriage? What about custody and care of any children? What share of either person's income would be reasonable as child support? Will you both take responsibility for paying for college? Do you or your partner expect to receive alimony? If so, how much and for how long?

Raising questions such as these may seem too businesslike when people are deeply in love. This fact leads some people to wonder whether a couple isn't inviting conflict by preparing a premarital agreement. Perhaps. But discussion and even written statements of expectations for the marriage will probably reduce the chances for conflict later on and may even increase the chances of a happy marriage.

Finally, are there things you should *not* put in a "prenup"? In recent years, more couples have been adding lifestyle agreements, such as a woman who agrees to have sex with her new husband only if he manages to lose 25 pounds or a man who has his new wife promise to never again smoke cigarettes. Agreements of this type do express issues that are important to people. But what happens if the one person doesn't live up to the agreement? Then, as one lawyer put it, "You either live with it or you divorce" (Andrews, 2009:58).

WHAT DO YOU THINK?

1. Have you ever prepared a prenuptial agreement? How smooth was the process?
2. On balance, are prenuptial agreements a good or bad idea? Why?
3. Do you think most people who marry consider the odds of eventually divorcing?

attention given to the problem of "deadbeat dads." However, noncustodial mothers are actually less likely than fathers to make child support payments, probably because single women have lower incomes (U.S. Census Bureau, 2010).

What can be done about parents who do not support their children? As this issue became defined as a social problem, states passed laws requiring an employer to withhold money from the earnings of a parent who fails to pay up. Even so, some parents manage to duck their responsibilities by moving or switching jobs. In 1998, as a result, Congress passed the Deadbeat Parents Punishment Act, making it a serious crime to refuse to provide support payments to a child residing in another state or to move to another state in order to avoid making such payments. In addition, many states have begun publishing "Wanted" posters of delinquent parents on billboards or in newspapers in the hope that such publicity will shame them into paying up.

Remarriage: Problems of Blended Families

Because divorce is common in the United States, our society also has a lot of remarriage. In fact, three out of four people who divorce remarry, and most do so within four years.

blended families families in which children have some combination of biological parents and stepparents

Dimensions of Difference

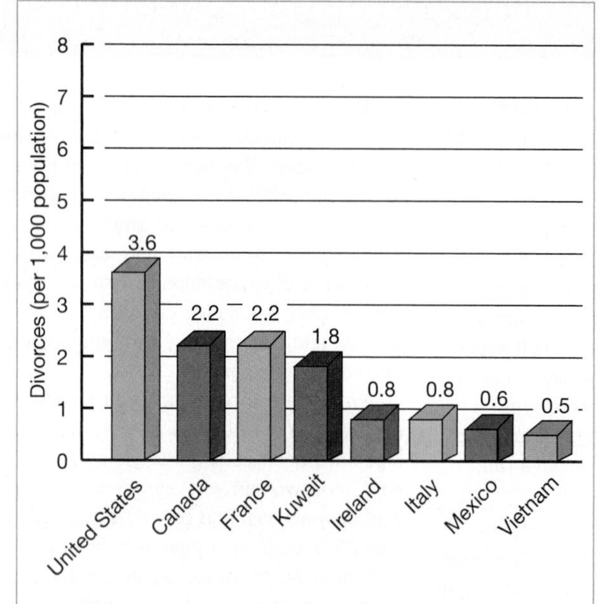

FIGURE 12–4 Divorce in Selected Countries

The odds of a marriage ending in divorce are higher in the United States than in other countries.

Source: European Union (2009).

Nationwide, more than one-fourth of all marriages are remarriages for at least one partner (Kreider and Ellis, 2011).

When partners with children from a previous relationship marry, they create **blended families,** *families in which children have some combination of biological parents and stepparents.* In the United States, one-fifth of all white and one-third of all African American married-couple households are blended families.

Blended families face a number of special challenges. For one thing, children who become part of a blended family must learn new household rules and routines and build relationships with new siblings. Stepparents, too, must make adjustments, establishing new relationships with children as well as a spouse. Most couples also have to maintain a relationship with a child's other biological parent and perhaps that person's new partner.

Most blended families manage to cope with these challenges. But research shows that members of blended families carry some special risks. For children, stepparent families have a high rate of physical and sexual abuse. For spouses, the likelihood of divorce, especially among people who remarry at a younger age, is higher than for those in first marriages (Fleming, Mullen, & Bammer, 1997; McLanahan, 2002).

Gay and Lesbian Families

Not all couples even have the choice of marrying. In 2004, Massachusetts became the first state to recognize same-sex marriage. The Defining Moment box takes a closer look at the Massachusetts decision.

Since the Massachusetts decision, Connecticut, Vermont, Iowa, New Hampshire, and the District of Columbia have also changed their laws to recognize same-sex marriage. In several other states, including New Jersey, Hawaii, and Illinois, civil unions grant same-sex couples most or all the rights of marriage.

At the same time, a majority of states have enacted laws that ban same-sex marriage and also prevent recognizing same-sex marriages performed elsewhere. Even so, across the United States, about 700,000 gay couples have formed committed partnerships, and almost 30 percent of these couples are parents raising children. Typically, these children are offspring from a previous heterosexual relationship, although many gay couples adopt children of their own (National Conference of State Legislatures, 2010; U.S. Census Bureau, 2010).

Many people, both homosexuals and heterosexuals, view the right to legally marry someone of the same sex as an important measure of society's acceptance of a same-sex orientation. Beyond symbolic importance, gay marriage has practical value because marriage extends benefits to legal spouses, ranging from hospital visitation rights to health insurance to child custody.

The first nation to permit registered partnerships with all the legal benefits of marriage for same-sex couples was Denmark in 1989. Since then, another fifteen nations have followed suit. But only seven countries have extended marriage, in name as well as in practice, to same-sex couples: the Netherlands (2001), Belgium (2003), Canada (2005), Spain (2005), South Africa (2005), Norway (2008), and Sweden (2009).

The same-sex marriage debate brings us again to the question of how to define a family. In general, conservatives argue that same-sex marriage undermines the definition of families that has guided societies for thousands of years and does not offer the best setting in which to raise children (Knight, 1998). Most liberals think of families as people—straight or gay—who share their lives and want that relationship to be recognized, leading them to support gay marriage. However, the political lines are not clearly drawn in this debate: Some conservatives who believe in the importance of "family values" also support same-sex marriage, claiming that all people, whatever their sexual orientation, benefit from being married.

Gay Parenting

As many as 250,000 gay couples in the United States are currently raising young children. Therefore, the diversity of U.S. families includes not only one-parent and two-parent families

GETTING INVOLVED

Have you ever been involved in a social movement either for or against same-sex marriage? If so, explain what you did and why.

SOCIAL PROBLEMS in Everyday Life

How many states do you think will permit same-sex marriage ten years from now? Fifty years from now?

CONSTRUCTING SOCIAL PROBLEMS

A DEFINING MOMENT

Same-Sex Marriage: The Massachusetts Decision

Hillary and Julie Goodridge had a wish. It had been three years since their daughter, Annie, asked her two mommies why they were not married. In response, the two women decided to take their case to the courts with the goal of obtaining the right to marry. The court supported their claim. The women's wish came true on May 17, 2004, as they became legally wedded spouses.

The Massachusetts case seeking same-sex marriage was brought by the Goodridges and six other couples. The couples' lawsuit came down to a simple question: Why should having a same-sex orientation be grounds for denying people the right others have to marry? In the case of *Goodridge et al.* v. *Department of Public Health,* the Massachusetts supreme court ruled in a four-to-three decision that there was no good reason to discriminate in this way against lesbians and gay men. The court's decision stated:

> Barred access to the protections, benefits, and obligations of civil marriage, a person who enters into an intimate, exclusive union with another of the same sex is arbitrarily deprived of membership in one of our community's most rewarding and cherished institutions. That exclusion is incompatible with the constitutional principles of respect for individual autonomy and equality under law.

The decision put to rest the contest over whether Massachusetts would allow same-sex marriage. But it did not end the debate. Polls at that time showed that a majority of people in Massachusetts did not support same-sex marriage. In light of this fact, there was much criticism of "activist judges" who, as critics saw it, were imposing their liberal politics on everyone. President Bush spoke out against the decision, describing marriage as "a sacred institution between a man and a woman" and pledging that the federal government would "protect the sanctity of marriage."

The significance of any state's decision to enact a gay marriage law is great because according to the "full faith and credit" clause of the U.S. Constitution, a contract (including marriage) performed in one state must be recognized in all states. For this reason, in 1996 congressional opponents of gay marriage passed the Defense of Marriage Act, which states that marriage must involve one man and one woman and that no state or other jurisdiction has to recognize a same-sex marriage law enacted by any other state or jurisdiction. By 2009, thirty-eight states had passed some law restricting marriage to one man and one woman or preventing the recognition of same-sex marriages performed elsewhere.

But gay rights activists have worked hard to change the marriage laws in other states. As of 2011, Connecticut, Vermont, Iowa, New Hampshire, and the District of Columbia also recognize same-sex marriage.

How many other states eventually follow the lead of Massachusetts remains to be seen. But the 2004 decision introducing legal same-sex marriage to the United States was a defining moment in the way our society views marriage and family life.

Hillary and Julie Goodridge, with their daughter Annie, applied for a marriage license in 2004 and became the first same-sex couple to legally marry in the United States.

How do you feel about parents using genetic techniques to select the traits of their children?

in vitro fertilization uniting egg and sperm in a laboratory

surrogate motherhood an arrangement by which one woman carries and bears a child for another woman

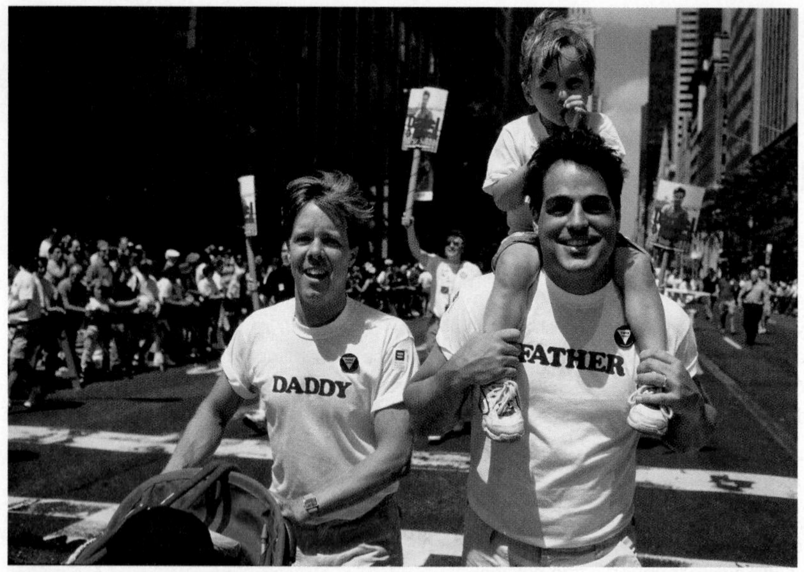

By 2011, five states changed their laws to give legal support to same-sex marriage. As a result, this type of family life is now less likely to be viewed as a problem and is more likely to be defined as a happy solution for the partners involved.

but also families in which children have two moms or two dads. Gay parenting is a controversial issue: There are no federal or state laws that ban this practice, but in custody disputes, courts may decide that children are better off with heterosexual parents.

Public opinion is divided on whether gay parenting is in the best interest of children. Some people fear that children living with homosexual parents are at higher risk of sexual abuse; however, research offers no support for such fears. Quite the opposite: Research shows that gay and lesbian parents provide the same supportive and effective parenting as heterosexual couples. Nor is there any evidence that children raised by homosexual parents are any more likely to be gay themselves. In short, gay and lesbian families face problems, but the problems come more from the stigma society attaches to homosexuality than from the family form itself (Peterson, 1992; Gates et al., 2007).

Brave New Families: High-Tech Reproduction

In 1978, Louise Brown became the world's first "test-tube baby." She was conceived not in the usual way but in a laboratory in England, where doctors fertilized a human ovum from her mother with a sperm cell from her father in a glass dish and implanted the embryo in her mother's womb. The importance of test-tube babies is not just that they are conceived in a different way but that scientists can use medical screening to "design" their genetic makeup, which opens the door to parents "ordering" a child with specific features or hair color. Advancing reproductive technology has created new choices for families and sparked new controversies as well.

In Vitro Fertilization

So-called test-tube babies result from the process of **in vitro fertilization,** which involves *uniting egg and sperm in a laboratory* (*in vitro* is Latin for "in glass"). Once a fertilized embryo is produced, doctors may implant it in a woman's body, or they can freeze it for use at a later time.

In vitro fertilization offers the 3 million couples in the United States who are unable to conceive children in the normal way an opportunity to become parents. However, the procedure is very expensive, so only 134,000 couples a year actually go through the process, resulting in about 52,000 births annually (Centers for Disease Control and Prevention, 2008). Those who are finally able to have the child they want view this procedure as nothing short of miraculous. But critics point out that the cost places this procedure out of reach of most people. In addition, because new reproductive technology permits parents to select the physical and perhaps even mental traits of their children, we must face the troubling possibility of the creation of a "super-race" of genetically designed children.

Surrogate Motherhood

One of the controversies arising from new reproductive technology is the issue of **surrogate motherhood,** *an arrangement by which one woman carries and bears a child for another woman.*

In 1986, the case known as "Baby M" brought surrogate motherhood to the nation's attention. In that case, William Stern, whose wife was unable to bear children, agreed to pay Mary Beth Whitehead to bear a child conceived with his sperm via artificial insemination. Although Whitehead would be the baby's biological mother, she agreed to give up all claims to the child.

The pregnancy went according to plan, and Whitehead gave birth to a healthy child. But by that time, Whitehead had changed her mind and wanted to keep her baby. The Sterns reacted by filing a court case seeking custody of the baby and pointing to the signed agreement. In 1988, the New Jersey supreme court declared surrogacy contracts of this kind illegal in that state; furthermore, the court declared, the natural mother (in this case, Whitehead) should have custody of a child

SOCIAL PROBLEMS in Everyday Life

Do you view new reproductive technology as solving problems or creating them? Explain your answer.

GETTING INVOLVED

How much was your father involved in raising you?

born from such an arrangement. Other states, however, have permitted such contracts, so there is no consistent policy across the United States, and in recent years, the issue has attracted relatively little attention.

Cases of surrogate parenthood also raise questions about responsibility for child support. In California, John and Luanne Buzzanca, a married couple unable to have children, enlisted a woman to serve as a surrogate mother. In this case, both the egg and sperm came from unknown donors. In 1995, the surrogate mother gave birth to a baby who had no biological ties to either her or the Buzzancas. A month before the child's birth, however, John Buzzanca filed for divorce from his wife. Luanne Buzzanca took custody of the child and sought child support from her ex-husband. But John refused, claiming he was not the child's father.

In the court suit that followed, a California judge ruled that although they were not the child's biological parents, both John and Luanne Buzzanca were the child's "intended parents." Therefore, the court ruled, both parties who engage a surrogate mother are responsible for any child born in this way. In the end, Luanne Buzzanca received custody of the baby, and her ex-husband was ordered to pay monthly child support.

Cases such as these show that although new reproductive technology has obvious benefits for some couples, our society has yet to work out clear rules to guide its use.

This is a good example of a pattern sociologists call *cultural lag,* when scientific discoveries advance more quickly than our ideas about the acceptable ways to use them. The result is procedures that are scientifically possible but may or may not be considered morally right.

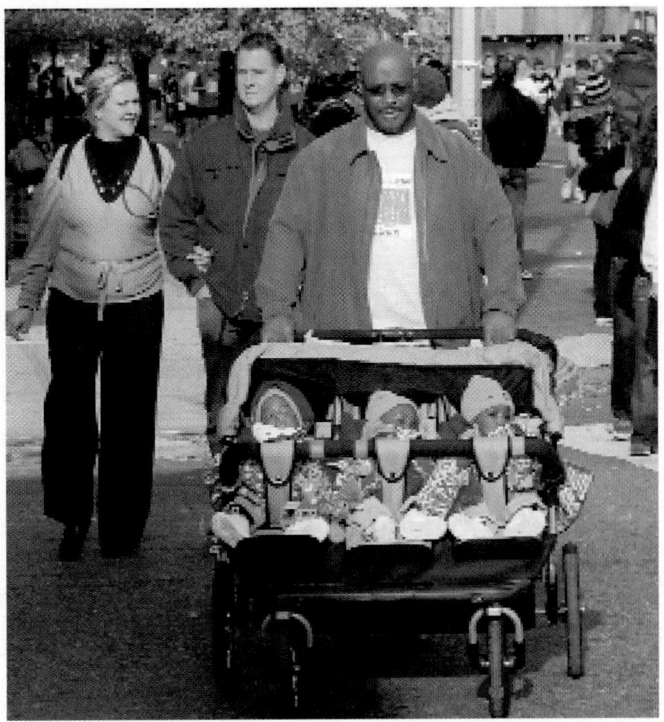

One of the consequences of using fertility drugs and in vitro fertilization is a higher rate of multiple births. How would your life change if, all of a sudden, you were the mother or father of triplets?

Theoretical Analysis: Understanding Family Problems

We can increase our understanding of issues surrounding the family by applying sociology's three theoretical approaches: structural-functional analysis, symbolic-interaction analysis, and social-conflict analysis. The following discussions are summarized in the Applying Theory table on page 332.

Structural-Functional Analysis: Family as Foundation

The structural-functional approach views the family as the most important unit of social organization. George Murdock (1949) claims that families exist everywhere in the world because they perform four major tasks essential for the operation of society.

First, as explained in Chapter 7 ("Sexuality"), families are the way in which society regulates reproduction, encouraging the birth of children to parents who have made a public commitment to one another. Second, families create a stable and caring environment for children. Third, families are units of economic cooperation between spouses as well as other kin. Fourth and finally, family members look to one another for emotional support in a world that can be uncaring and sometimes dangerous.

Because these functions are so important, structural-functional analysis claims that families operate as the foundation of a healthy society. If so, then any threat to family life is likely to be defined as a social problem. A structural-functional approach views many of the trends discussed in this chapter—including living together, single parenting, and high divorce rates—as threats to the stability of U.S. society.

CRITICAL REVIEW There is little doubt that families do matter: Research shows us that children who grow up in single-parent households complete less schooling and

MAKING THE GRADE

Use the table below to review the three theoretical approaches to family life.

MAKING THE GRADE

Be sure you understand how macro-level and micro-level approaches to family life differ.

APPLYING THEORY

Family Life

	What is the level of analysis?	What is the importance of the family to society?	What are the problems involving families?
Structural-functional approach	Macro-level	The structural-functional approach views the family as the foundation of society because it has several important functions, including regulating sexuality and providing a committed parental relationship as the setting for raising children. Families also provide their members with economic and emotional support.	Because of the importance of families to the operation of society, anything that threatens the strength or stability of families—the rise in divorce or the increase in single parenting—is likely to be defined as a social problem.
Symbolic-interaction approach	Micro-level	The symbolic-interaction approach focuses on the patterns of interaction by which people construct family life. For example, children raised with love and steady guidance are likely to develop a positive self-image. Gender can operate as a script in married life, with the effect of reducing a couple's intimacy.	This approach highlights how individuals experience family life. Individuals experience the family in their own ways, subjectively defining their situation—whatever it may be in objective terms—as a problem or not. Therefore, we cannot make broad generalizations about family problems.
Social-conflict approach	Macro-level	The social-conflict approach focuses on social inequality. Engels explained that the family is a system that allows men to know who their offspring are so that wealthy men can pass their wealth on to their sons.	From this point of view, the main problem is social inequality, and families contribute to this problem. The family is a system that helps maintain classes, reproducing inequality in each new generation. The family also allows men to control women.

are at higher risk of poverty than those from two-parent households. In addition, it is difficult to see how other social institutions could step in to perform the various functions that families perform now.

At the same time, the structural-functional approach is criticized for overlooking the extent of conflict and violence in families (discussed in Chapter 6, "Crime, Violence, and Criminal Justice"). Critics also point out that today's families also contribute to social inequality, typically supporting the dominance of men over women and perpetuating class inequality as parents pass along wealth and privileges to children.

Finally, the structural-functional approach takes a macro-level view of the family as a system, saying little about how individuals experience the family as part of everyday life. This concern brings us to the symbolic-interaction approach.

Symbolic-Interaction Analysis: Family and Learning

The symbolic-interaction approach views the family less as a societal institution and more as the ongoing interaction of individuals. Following this approach, we see that family life has a lot to do with the ways children learn to think about themselves. Children raised with love and steady parental guidance develop a positive self-image and are likely to make decisions confidently as they move through life. By contrast, children who experience a steady stream of criticism from parents may end up developing a paralyzing level of self-doubt.

A symbolic-interaction approach also highlights how people understand themselves and their partners. Ideally, marriage helps a couple build a relationship that is *intimate* (a word with Latin roots meaning "free from fear"), in which each partner finds comfort and support in the presence of the other. But the same marital ties that offer the promise of intimacy can work in the opposite direction to script the behavior of men (who then act "just like men") and women (who are constrained to act in "feminine" ways), with the result that the two sexes can have trouble expressing their personal feelings to one another (Macionis, 1978). The importance of gender in our everyday lives helps explain why women and men often have very different perceptions of the same marriage (Bernard, 1982).

Finally, the symbolic-interaction approach reminds us that the experience of family life differs over time and also from person to person. Whatever the state of a family, objectively speaking, the subjective reality is likely to vary according to the individual.

A functional analysis points to ways in which families unite individuals and provide a stable environment for raising children. A symbolic-interaction analysis might point to ways in which parents and children understand family life in different ways. A social-conflict analysis might point out ways in which family life gives unequal power and other resources to men and women. What insights into the family life shown here do you gain from each of these approaches?

CRITICAL REVIEW The symbolic-interaction approach shows the varied ways in which individuals understand family life. A husband, wife, and child typically perceive the same family quite differently, and all these experiences change over time and can vary from place to place.

A limitation of this approach is that although family life is variable, a number of patterns are common. Gender stratification, for example, is built into almost all families. The social-conflict approach offers a look at how the family is linked to gender inequality and other dimensions of social inequality.

Social-Conflict Analysis: Family and Inequality

As a macro-level approach, social-conflict analysis shares with structural-functional analysis the idea that the family plays an important part in the operation of society. But rather than highlighting ways in which family life benefits everyone, social-conflict analysis points to how the family operates to benefit some and disadvantage others. As in earlier chapters, this feminist approach focuses on social inequality, in this case showing how families *reproduce* social inequality in each new generation.

An early social-conflict theory of family life comes from Friedrich Engels (1902, orig. 1884). As Engels saw it, the family actually came into being among the wealthy mostly so that men, who wanted to pass their property from father to son, could be reasonably sure who their offspring were. Engels claimed that the family operates alongside the legal system to protect inheritance. Families also ensure that the class structure stays much the same from one generation to another.

Reproducing classes is only one way in which the family supports inequality. In addition, Engels explained, by making men the heads of households, the family gives men power over women. To know who their offspring are, as explained earlier, men must control female sexuality. This fact goes a long way toward explaining the traditional concern that women be virgins before they marry and faithful wives afterward. In addition, men have long expected women to care for their home and children while they work or do other things outside of the home. For Engels, the bottom line on the family is that this social institution turns women into the sexual and economic property of men.

CRITICAL REVIEW A social-conflict approach suggests that the path toward an egalitarian society is to eliminate the family, at least in its current form. However, this approach overlooks the fact that a large majority of people in the United States claim a great deal of satisfaction from family life (NORC, 2007). It may be possible for a society to eliminate the family as a strategy to increase social equality, but it is far from clear how important tasks such as raising children would be accomplished.

GETTING INVOLVED

What do you think of the idea that couples with young children limit their working week to sixty hours? What are the benefits and costs of such a decision?

POLITICS AND FAMILY LIFE

Constructing Problems and Defining Solutions

Theory provides helpful ways to think about families, but exactly what people define as family problems and what they think we ought to do about them are a matter of politics. We conclude this chapter by applying the conservative, liberal, and radical-left perspectives to issues surrounding families and family life.

Conservatives: Traditional "Family Values"

Conservatives see values as the core of a society because beliefs bind people together and define a way of life. The family is the most important social institution because it does the most to instill basic values. For this reason, conservatives support what they call "family values" by emphasizing the importance of raising children well, which in turn depends on people getting married, being committed to their spouses, and looking with disfavor on divorce.

In addition, conservatives point to evidence that marriage is good for adults as well as children. Compared with unmarried people, married spouses are better off financially, claim to be happier, and even report having more sex (Waite & Gallagher, 2000; R. W. Simon, 2002).

From a conservative point of view, whatever threatens the family is likely to be defined as a social problem. One example is the rise in cohabitation, which conservatives claim spells trouble for U.S. society. Many conservatives do not approve of living together because such a relationship lacks the commitment of legal marriage. According to conservatives, the popularity of cohabitation signals the rise of "me first" values by which people favor individualism over commitment. The greatest losers in this culture shift are often children, who have a greater chance of ending up in a single-parent family, raising their risk of poverty right away and pushing up their future risk of divorce (Popenoe & Whitehead, 1999; Glenn & Sylvester, 2005).

Conservatives also see the high rate of divorce since the 1960s as a serious problem. Many conservatives oppose the policy of no-fault divorce, claiming that this policy makes divorces too easy to obtain. More broadly, conservatives urge a change in our way of thinking from an individualistic culture favoring cohabitation and easy divorce to a culture favoring commitment and marriage. Favoring commitment over independence, they claim, gives men and women better mental health, strengthens families financially through greater earning power, and provides children with more stability during this important stage of life.

Supporting "family values" also means parents spending more time with children. Conservatives criticize the popular idea that parents spend a little "quality time" with children as an excuse for not making children a priority. Conservatives recognize that many households depend on the earnings of both mothers and fathers, but they suggest that couples with young children consider limiting their combined workweek to, say, sixty hours so that they may be sure to meet the needs of their children (Broude, 1996; Whitehead, 1997; Popenoe, 1988, 1993a, 1999).

Liberals: Many Kinds of Families

Because liberals celebrate individual freedom, their take on today's families and family problems is very different from that of conservatives. Liberals claim that conservatives recognize only one type of family as best for everyone. But as liberals see it, this is not the case; different people favor different kinds of families—or even no families at all. Liberals point out that a wide range of families has existed throughout U.S. history, and this family diversity continues today (Kain, 1990; Koontz, 1992).

Supporting family diversity, liberals say that people should have the right to choose from a wide range of family forms, including cohabitation, single-parent families, blended families, same-sex marriage, and singlehood. To liberals, and especially to feminists, these family patterns are not a problem (as they are to conservatives) but rather they are a solution. On the contrary, they say, locking people in "traditional families" is likely to limit the opportunities of women to earn a living and trap some women in abusive relationships. Therefore, liberals define the most serious family problems as poverty and domestic violence.

From a liberal perspective, then, the greater diversity in family forms is actually a solution to the historical problem of women remaining in the home under the control of men (Stacey, 1990, 1993). But what do liberals say about the fact that single-mother families have a higher risk of poverty? The liberal solution to this problem is to increase child care programs so that more women can work and to combat gender discrimination so that working women are paid as much as working men. More broadly, a liberal "profamily" agenda would include raising the minimum wage and perhaps even setting a guaranteed minimum income as policies that would strengthen U.S. families.

GETTING INVOLVED

Which of the family patterns just mentioned do you support? Which do you oppose? Why?

MAKING THE GRADE

How do conservatives and liberals differ on what we should call "family values"?

The Radical Left: Replace the Family

The radical-left view begins with the close link between the family and social inequality. From a radical-left perspective, the family—at least in its current form—perpetuates social inequality in at least three ways.

First, recall the analysis of Friedrich Engels, who claimed that the family creates and maintains class stratification. Through the family, individuals pass private property from one generation to another. This process reproduces the class structure over time.

Second, Engels also explained that the family helps perpetuate gender stratification. Men must control the sexuality of women in order to know who their heirs are. In addition, so that men can leave home for the workplace, women must perform unpaid work as homemakers and mothers.

Conservatives think that U.S. society should support the traditional family because families headed by both a father and a mother are good for individuals and good for society as a whole. Liberals support the expanding range of family forms, recognizing that no single family form is likely to be right for everyone. Radicals condemn traditional families for perpetuating social inequality and favor collective living arrangements that promote social equality.

Third, although there has been significant change in recent years, legal marriage is still restricted to partners of the opposite sex in all but six states. Therefore, by and large, the current family system does not accept homosexual couples, instead pushing them to the margins of society. This means that the family also perpetuates stratification based on sexual orientation.

Taken together, these arguments lead radicals on the left to support an end to the family as we know it in the interest of greater social equality. But what is their solution to the "problem" of the family? To eliminate class inequality, society would have to treat all children in the same manner by making child care a collective enterprise. In the same way, to eliminate gender inequality, society would have to redefine marriage as a partnership with shared responsibility for housework as well as earning income. Finally, as noted in Chapter 4 ("Gender Inequality"), radical feminists envision a future in which new reproductive technology allows women to break the bonds of biology that now require them to carry children.

The Left to Right table on page 336 views family problems and solutions from the three political perspectives.

Going On from Here

The past century has been a time of remarkable change for families in the United States. In 1900, women had, on average, five children, no jobs, and no right to vote. By and large, women were dependent on men. Today, women have, on average, just two children, and childbearing is much more a matter of choice. Women are working at an ever-wider range of jobs, they have increasing political power, and they live far more independently of men.

In the decades ahead, families will continue to change. We expect the share of women working for income to continue to rise and the birth rate to edge downward. These trends will make the lives of women and men more alike, which is a key reason that conventional ideas about marriage and family life are giving way to a greater diversity in relationships.

Even if the divorce rate continues its recent downward trend, it seems likely that for many people, marriage will not be a lifetime commitment. Rather, many family patterns—conventional marriage, living together, living alone, blended families, and raising children outside marriage—will all remain a part of U.S. society.

One issue that is likely to remain a topic of controversy is the large share of U.S. children living in poverty. Both conservatives and liberals define this as a problem, although they support different solutions. As conservatives see it, the solution to

MAKING THE GRADE

Use the table below to review the three political approaches to family life.

LEFT TO RIGHT

The Politics of Family Life

	RADICAL-LEFT VIEW	LIBERAL VIEW	CONSERVATIVE VIEW
WHAT IS THE PROBLEM?	Family life is bound up with inequality: Families support inequality based on class, gender, and sexual orientation, all of which is unjust.	There is not enough tolerance for the broad range of family life in today's society; efforts to impose any model of an "ideal family" limit people's choices; poverty among women and children is a serious problem.	Conventional families are breaking down: Divorce, single parenting, and living together without marriage are symptoms of a "me first" culture that weakens society and places children at risk.
WHAT IS THE SOLUTION?	Increasing social equality is possible only by radically restructuring the family as it exists today; society should consider collective arrangements for performing housework and child care.	Encourage tolerance for various kinds of families, including gay marriage. Increasing women's economic opportunities will benefit children. Enforce all antidiscrimination laws, and expand affordable child care programs.	Encourage the spread of a "culture of marriage": Make covenant marriage more widely available, abolish no-fault divorce laws, and discourage couples from living together in low-commitment relationships.

JOIN THE DEBATE

1. In the case of families, one person's problem is often another person's solution. Illustrate this idea using several issues examined in this chapter.
2. How do people who favor each of the three political perspectives define a "family"? Highlight areas of agreement and disagreement.
3. Which of the three political analyses of U.S. families included here do you find most convincing? Why?

child poverty is a return to a more traditional two-parent family. As liberals see it, the solution to child poverty lies in policies that increase wages for low-income workers and expand women's economic opportunities.

A second important issue is the pace of change in giving gay men and lesbians access to legal marriage. The fact that same-sex marriage is now legal in five states is a major victory for those supporting equal marriage rights for all citizens regardless of sexual orientation. At the same time, other states have yet to follow suit, and a majority of states have taken measures to prevent recognition of same-sex marriage. Although polls continue to show a slight majority of adults in the United States opposed to same-sex marriage, the long-term trend in public opinion is in favor of permitting all people, regardless of sexual orientation, to marry.

Third and finally, the possibilities raised by new reproductive technology are sure to expand. The challenge here is to ensure that we understand the consequences of using technology such as genetic engineering. In short, it is essential that ethical evaluation keep pace with scientific advancement.

For all these reasons, the debate over problems of family life and their solutions is sure to continue. A century from now, people may still be lining up on different sides as they try to answer the question "What is a family?"

DEFINING SOLUTIONS

Do the mass media present families from a conservative or a liberal point of view?

Or maybe the better question is does the media realistically portray the diversity of families in the United States today? Look at the two photos below to gain some insights about family life as seen through the mass media.

HINT

The Huxtable family may not be statistically realistic—certainly Bill Cosby knows that most African American families (or white families, for that matter) don't live like the Huxtables. But *The Cosby Show* is a rare case in the mass media of a "traditional" family that is a source of strength to its members. Typical? Maybe not. But, Cosby seems to tell us, something worth aspiring to all the same. Most TV shows are more like *Sex and the City,* in which characters do not live in traditional family settings. At the same time, these shows teach us that there are many ways to build relationships.

Bill Cosby is known as an advocate of strong families. Especially to African American audiences, Cosby has spoken out on the benefits of children being raised by two married parents. *The Cosby Show,* which was one of the most popular television shows in the country during the 1980s and early 1990s (and is still shown in re-reruns) presented the Huxtable family—an affluent African American family, with father (Cliff) and mother (Claire) living together and raising their children. This show makes a statement that the traditional family is a solution to the many challenges people face, a view widely endorsed by conservatives. Is this show realistic? Do you support the way it presents family life?

Sex and the City is more typical of television's portrayal of family life as seen from the liberal point of view, which is to say that families come in many different forms. This cable show was popular from 1998 until 2004 and has inspired a more recent feature film. Samantha Jones, a character played by actress Kim Cattrall, is a strong, independent woman, enjoying the single life in New York City. From her point of view, and that of most of her thirty-something friends, marriage may not be exactly a problem but it also is not necessary for a fulfilling life.

Getting Involved: Applications & Exercises

1. Call a nearby office of the Department of Health and Human Services or another local social services agency, and set up an appointment to talk about the range of services the organization offers to assist families. How can you become involved in helping local families?
2. Just about everyone has friends who live in blended families. Ask several people about the rewards and challenges of living with stepparents and stepsiblings.
3. Family life plays a part in almost every political campaign. Pay attention to the speeches and statements from candidates for national office, and note their views on family issues. What do Democrats see as family problems? What about Republicans? How are their solutions different?
4. Ethnicity affects people's view of family life. Identify people whose culture differs from your own, and learn what you can about how they see many of the issues raised in this chapter.

MAKING THE GRADE

A DEFINING MOMENT
Same-Sex Marriage: The Massachusetts Decision p. 329

CHAPTER 12 Family Life

What Is a Family?

- The **FAMILY** is a social institution that unites individuals into cooperative groups that care for members, regulate sexual relations, and oversee the raising of children.
- **KINSHIP** is a social bond, typically based on blood, marriage, or adoption, that joins individuals into families.

p. 318

- In high-income countries including the United States, people's lives revolve around **NUCLEAR FAMILIES.**
- In the world's low-income nations, most people live in **EXTENDED FAMILIES.**

p. 318

✓ *A traditional definition of family is a married couple with children. In recent decades, however, more people have taken a broader definition of families, even including **FAMILIES OF AFFINITY** made up of individuals who simply think of themselves as a family. (pp. 318–19)*

family (p. 318) a social institution that unites individuals into cooperative groups that care for one another, including any children

kinship (p. 318) a social bond, based on common ancestry, marriage, or adoption, that joins individuals into families

nuclear family (p. 318) one or two parents and their children

extended family (p. 318) parents and children, and also grandparents, aunts, uncles, and cousins, who often live close to one another and operate as a family unit

marriage (p. 318) a lawful relationship usually involving economic cooperation, sexual activity, and childbearing

families of affinity (p. 319) people with or without legal or blood ties who feel they belong together and define themselves as a family

Controversies over Family Life

LIVING TOGETHER

Some 6.2 (5.5 million opposite-sex plus 700,000 same-sex) million U.S. couples (7% of the total) cohabit.

- Many young people see cohabiting as a sensible way to try out a relationship.
- Evidence suggests that cohabitation discourages marriage and raises the rate of single parenting.

pp. 319–20

POSTPONING MARRIAGE

A trend since 1950 has been for first marriages to occur later in life; currently, the age at first marriage is about 26 years for women and 28 years for men.

p. 320

SINGLE PARENTING

- About half of children live with one parent at some point before they reach age 18.
- Children raised in single-parent homes are at high risk of being poor and of being single parents themselves.

p. 321

RACE AND POVERTY

- Among white families, single-parent families typically result from divorce; among African American families, 73% of children are born to unmarried mothers.
- Research suggests that a lack of available jobs is the major reason for the high proportion of single-parent households in poor African American communities.
- African American families have a number of distinctive strengths: building strong kinship bonds, drawing on religious faith, and having grandparents who help in child rearing.

pp. 321–22

cohabitation (p. 319) the sharing of a household by an unmarried couple

blended families (p. 328) families in which children have some combination of biological parents and stepparents

in vitro fertilization (p. 330) uniting eggs and sperm in a laboratory

surrogate motherhood (p. 330) an arrangement by which one woman carries and bears a child for another woman

CONFLICTS WITH WORK

Because most women and men work for income, the demands of work and family life often conflict, especially for women, who bear more responsibility for housework and child care.

pp. 322–23

CHILD CARE

Securing affordable child care is a serious problem for millions of families, especially those with low income.

pp. 323–24

DIVORCE

- About one-third of today's marriages will end in divorce, four times the rate of a century ago.
- Women's increasing financial independence from men, as well as no-fault divorce laws, have made divorce easier.

pp. 324–26

CHILD SUPPORT

Courts order a parent to provide financial support to 54% of young children after parental divorce. Yet in 53% of all such cases, these children receive only partial payments or no payments at all.

pp. 326–27

REMARRIAGE

- Because three out of four people who divorce remarry, one-fourth of all of today's marriages are remarriages for at least one partner.
- Remarriage creates **BLENDED FAMILIES**, which present some special challenges, such as forming new relationships with stepparents and stepsiblings.

pp. 327–28

GAY AND LESBIAN FAMILIES

Most states and other nations of the world prohibit same-sex couples from legally marrying. Still, in this country there are as many as 700,000 committed partnerships among gay men and lesbians, and these couples are steadily winning greater legal rights and social acceptance.

pp. 328–29

IN VITRO FERTILIZATION and other **NEW REPRODUCTIVE TECHNOLOGIES** help many infertile couples have children. But new reproductive technology also raises ethical questions about creating "designer" children.

pp. 329–30

Theoretical Analysis: Understanding Family Problems

Structural-Functional Analysis: Family as Foundation

The **STRUCTURAL-FUNCTIONAL APPROACH** points out the role that the family plays in the smooth operation of society.

- Families make a vital contribution to society's functioning by regulating sexual activity, overseeing the socialization of the young, fostering economic cooperation, and generating emotional support among kin.
- From this perspective, threats to family stability are defined as social problems.

pp. 330–32

Symbolic-Interaction Analysis: Family and Learning

The **SYMBOLIC-INTERACTION APPROACH** views family life as the interaction of individuals.

- The self-image of children and the degree of intimacy shared by couples are not fixed but variable outcomes of ongoing interactions.
- The experience of family life differs over time and from person to person.

pp. 332–33

Social-Conflict Analysis: Family and Inequality

The **SOCIAL-CONFLICT APPROACH** highlights the link between families and social inequality.

- Friedrich Engels viewed the rise of families as a strategy by which men could pass property from one generation to another, thus maintaining the class structure.
- By making men the heads of households, the family gives men power over women.

p. 333

See the **Applying Theory** table on page 332.

Politics and Family Life: Constructing Problems and Defining Solutions

The Radical Left: Replace the Family

- **RADICALS ON THE LEFT** claim that conventional families support inequality based on class, gender, and sexual orientation.
- Radicals on the left support the abolition of the family as we know it. Child care should be a collective enterprise, and marriage should be a partnership with shared responsibility for housework and earning income.

p. 335

Liberals: Many Kinds of Families

- **LIBERALS** define family diversity as positive and therefore support personal choice of family form.
- Liberals fear that locking people in "traditional families" will limit the ability of women to earn a living and trap some women in abusive relationships.

p. 334

Conservatives: Traditional "Family Values"

- **CONSERVATIVES** define the traditional family as the foundation of a healthy society and therefore define cohabitation, a high divorce rate, and single parenting as social problems.
- Conservatives support a return to traditional "family values" that rate commitment as more important than individualism. They urge parents to spend more time with their children.

p. 334

See the **Left to Right** table on page 336.

CONSTRUCTING THE PROBLEM

Can you imagine getting through the day without knowing how to read and write?

Around the world, almost 800 million women and men are illiterate.

Does the United States provide equal opportunity for schooling?

The poorest public school districts spend about $8,000 per year on each student; the richest spend more than $17,500.

Does social standing affect a child's school experience?

Children from the poorest 25 percent of U.S. families are five times more likely to drop out of school than those from the richest 25 percent of families.

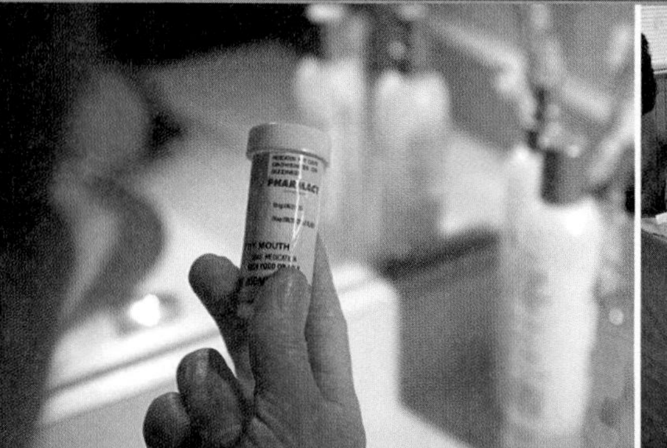

CHAPTER 13

Education

CHAPTER OVERVIEW

HOW HAS OUR SOCIETY made dramatic changes in schooling over the last century? This chapter explains all the trends. You will learn about many controversies involving schooling, including the academic performance of U.S. schools, dropping out, racial segregation, school funding, and how best to educate young immigrants. You will carry out theoretical analysis of schooling issues and learn how "problems" and "solutions" involving education reflect people's political attitudes.

May 17, 1954, was a day that promised to change the United States forever. It was on that day, now more than fifty-five years ago, that the U.S. Supreme Court handed down its landmark decision in *Brown* v. *Board of Education of Topeka.* With this decision, the Court declared that racially segregated schools, common in the United States at that time, violated the principles of the U.S. Constitution and could no longer be lawful.

Outside the Supreme Court building, a tall man in a dark suit stood on the steps. Thurgood Marshall had been the lead lawyer for the National Association for the Advancement of Colored People (NAACP), the organization that helped bring the lawsuit to the Supreme Court. After the decision was handed down, Marshall, who would later become a Supreme Court justice himself, spoke to reporters and to the entire nation from the steps of this famous landmark. He conceded that no statement from the Court would bring the needed change right away. On the contrary, he cautioned, there was still much work to be done in our nation's schools. But he assured the country that thanks to the Supreme Court's decision, racial segregation in U.S. schools would be gone within five years (A. Cohen, 2004).

That was more than half a century ago, and schools in the United States are almost as segregated today as they were back then. As this chapter explains, white children still attend schools with mostly white children, and black children still attend schools with mostly black children. Latino kids? The same holds—they go to schools with mostly Latino children.

Racial segregation is only one problem in today's schools. Other issues include unequal funding that favors some schools and disadvantages others, poor teaching in many classrooms, high dropout rates, and violence in the school buildings.

All of these problems relate to **education,** *the social institution by which a society transmits knowledge—including basic facts and job skills, as well as cultural norms and values—to its members.* This chapter begins with a brief survey of education around the world and then assesses how well schools in the United States meet their goals of preparing young people for productive lives as adults.

Problems of Education: A Global Perspective

Everywhere in the world, parents and others in local communities join together to teach young people important knowledge and skills. One important type of education is **schooling,** *formal instruction carried out by specially trained teachers.* Education occurs everywhere; schooling is more widely available to young people living in high-income parts of the world than to those living in low-income regions.

Low-Income Countries: Too Little Schooling

Schooling is not available to some children living in the world's poorest countries. In the lowest-income nations in Central Africa and western Asia, about one-fourth of all youngsters never set foot in a classroom. However, a majority of the world's children receive primary schooling—the first five or six grade levels. Secondary education is less common. In much of Africa and in parts of Latin America and Asia, as many as half of all children receive no secondary education (World Bank, 2009).

Why is schooling so limited in poor regions of the world? Low-income countries have largely agrarian (farming) economies, and about half the people live in rural communities. In this traditional setting, parents take most of the responsibility for teaching children the knowledge and skills needed for everyday life. There is also an economic benefit of keeping children at home, where they can work to help support their families.

To encourage the economic growth that comes with replacing farming with industry and service work, governments in poor nations are trying to expand **literacy,** *the ability to read and write.* Literacy skills are needed for people to work in factories and offices. A literate workforce also helps countries attract foreign investment, which in turn creates more jobs.

Miguel Milicchio, age 17, lives in Buenos Aires, Argentina's capital city, and expects to attend college next year.

Shreela Deeble, age 14, lives 4 miles from her school in Mwanza, Tanzania, and is the first member of her family to learn to read and write.

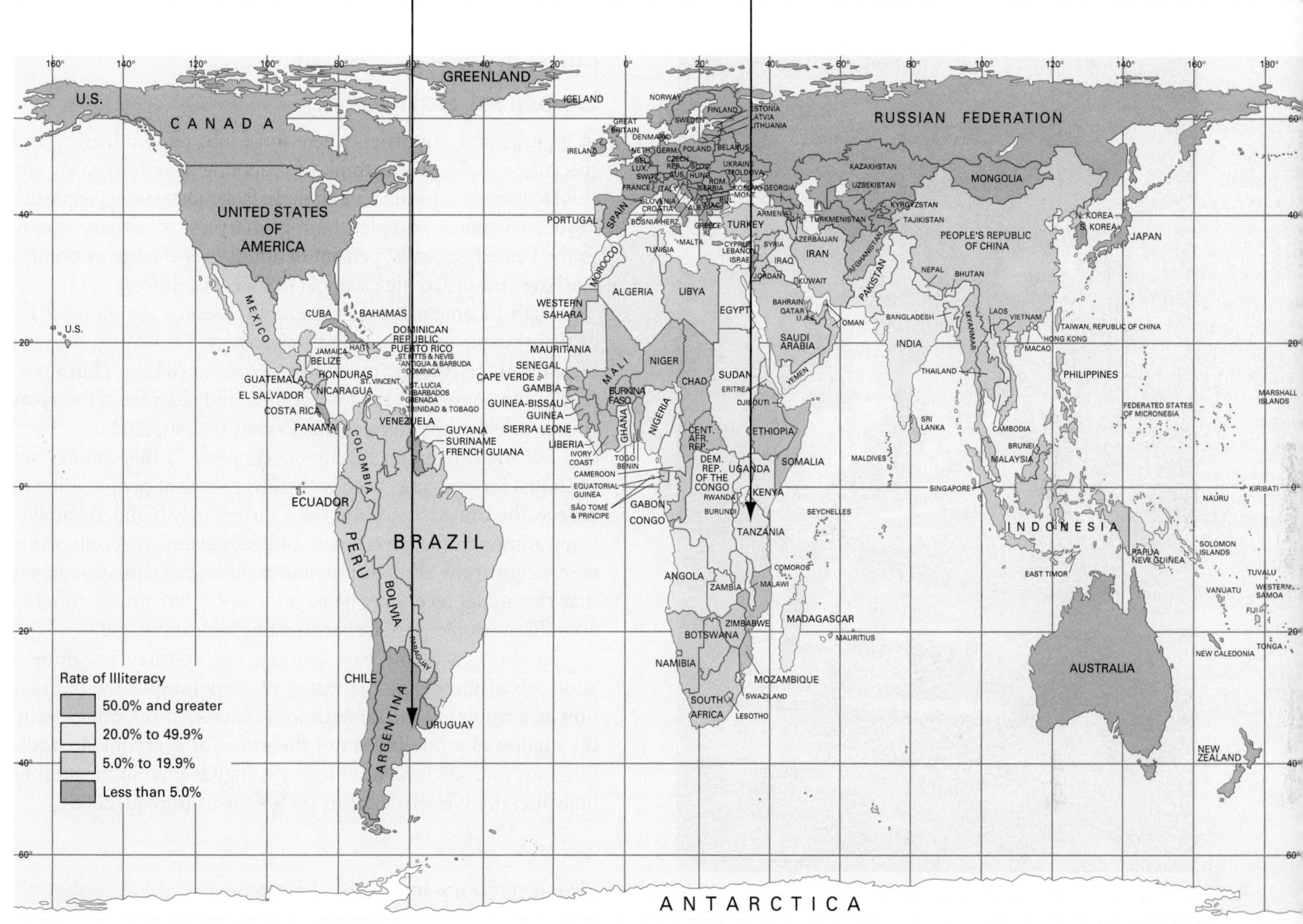

A World Of Differences

GLOBAL MAP 13–1 Illiteracy around the World

Illiteracy exists in the United States and other high-income nations, typically among the very poor. But in some of the world's lowest-income countries, half or more of the people cannot read and write.

Source: UNESCO (2009).

But expanding literacy is not easy. Countries struggling to feed their people don't have a great deal of money to spend on schooling. This is the main reason that almost 800 million of the world's adults (about one in five) are still illiterate (Population Reference Bureau, 2009). Global Map 13–1 shows that illiteracy rates are high—often more than 50 percent—in poor regions of the world.

Gender also plays an important part in patterns of global literacy. In the poorest countries, females are far less likely than males to be literate. For example, in Nepal, a poor Asian nation, fewer than half of all women can read, compared with nearly three-fourths of the men (UNESCO, 2008).

This gender disparity reflects the fact that in patriarchal societies, parents are more likely to send boys to school. Poor countries are typically not just patriarchal (men have power over women) but also patrilocal (a newly married couple lives with the husband's parents). Because a new bride leaves her parents to live with her husband's family, the parents of girls view sending their daughters to school as a poor investment of their resources. Sons remain close to home after they grow up

education (p. 342) the social institution by which a society transmits knowledge—including basic facts and job skills, as well as cultural norms and values—to its members

schooling (p. 342) formal instruction carried out by specially trained teachers

literacy (p. 342) the ability to read and write

Why did Thomas Jefferson believe education was vital to the future of this country?

This young girl working in a clothing factory in Thailand is evidence of a pattern common in low-income nations: Parents are more likely to send boys to school while girls go to work to earn income. Can you explain this double standard?

and marry, so parents are more willing to invest in their schooling. Parents get what they can from a daughter while she is young and living at home, typically by making her work for wages. These facts explain why most child labor in the world is performed by girls ("Why Girls," 1999; UNESCO, 2009).

High illiteracy rates mean a low quality of life for hundreds of millions of the world's women. But a lack of schooling also contributes to other problems. Without the ability to read, mothers have difficulty providing nutrition and health care to their young children and have few opportunities to work in higher-income jobs. Women who lack economic opportunity also end up having more children, adding to the burden of a poor nation already struggling to feed its people. Not only does this pattern hurt the women themselves, but it also slows economic development for the entire country.

High-Income Countries: Unequal Schooling

In high-income countries, where most jobs require literacy and specialized skills, people think of schooling as necessary for any child to become a productive adult. In fact, most young people living in rich nations complete both primary and secondary school. In the United States, 87 percent of adults over the age of twenty-five have completed high school (U.S. Census Bureau, 2011).

High-income nations are also able to send a significant share of their people to colleges and universities. The United States is second only to Norway in sending people to college: Thirty percent of the population aged twenty-five and older has a four-year college or university degree (U.S. Census Bureau, 2011).

But the extent and quality of schooling in this country are not equal for everyone. Even with a large share of people going to college, the United States also has a surprisingly high level of illiteracy. Although the government officially claims that only a tiny percentage of the adult population is illiterate, estimates suggest that the actual level may be as high as 15 percent, or roughly 30 million people (U.S. Department of Education, 2007).

In short, over the past century, our country has done a good job of increasing the extent of schooling for the population as a whole. At the same time, as later sections will explain, the quality of schooling is not the same for everyone. In addition, our nation's level of illiteracy is higher than in most other high-income Western nations (U.S. Census Bureau, 2008).

Education in U.S. History

Early national leaders, including Thomas Jefferson, recognized that literacy was the key to making the United States a political democracy. At that time, the new nation was both rural and poor, and most people were illiterate.

Illiteracy was not widely defined as a social problem, however, especially among certain segments of the population. For example, most people saw no reason to school women, who, they thought, belonged in the home. The same was true of African Americans, most of whom lived as slaves and received no schooling at all for fear that literacy would encourage organization and rebellion. Only after the Civil War, with the abolition of slavery, did school doors in the United States open to African Americans. In almost all cases, however, these schools were separate from and inferior to those enrolling white people.

It was only after the Industrial Revolution was well under way in the late 1800s that our society started to define illiteracy as a social problem. For one thing, operating the complex machinery used in factories required workers to have basic skills in reading, writing, and arithmetic. Another concern was that about 1

GETTING INVOLVED

Before reading the following section of the text, make a list of what you see as the most serious problems involving education in the United States. After finishing the section, come back and see whether your ideas have changed.

GETTING INVOLVED

How would you evaluate the public schools in the community in which you grew up?

million immigrants were entering the country each year. Our society looked to public schools to give these newcomers not only the skills they needed to work but also the cultural lessons—especially mastery of the English language—that would help them become "Americanized."

Therefore, by the beginning of the last century, states were extending schooling to more people. Most people supported public education as a solution to the problems already noted. Yet some immigrants did not want to send their children to public schools. Catholic immigrants, in particular, were concerned about losing their traditions and their faith in a mostly Protestant country. Catholics responded by forming church-sponsored *parochial schools,* which still operate throughout the country.

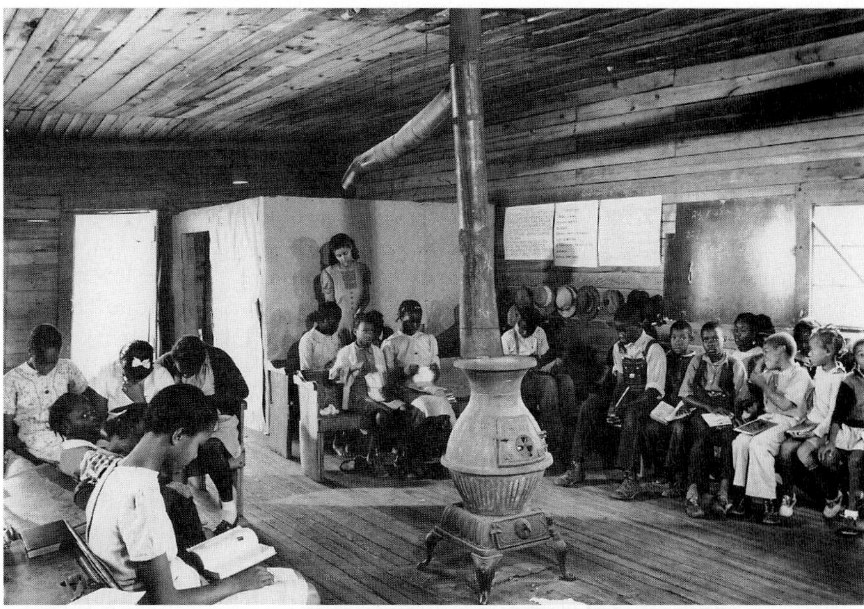

Over the course of U.S. history, the doors of schools have opened wider for white people than for African Americans. The school pictured here might seem to be from the nineteenth century, but the photograph was taken in Georgia in 1941.

By 1918, every state had enacted a mandatory education law requiring children to attend school until age sixteen or the completion of the eighth grade. Since then, as shown in Figure 13–1 on page 346, the extent of schooling for the U.S. population has increased steadily. In 1920, just 16.4 percent of people age twenty-five or older had completed high school; a college degree was even more rare, held by only 3.3 percent of adults. By 2010, as already noted, 87 percent of adults were high school graduates, and 30 percent had earned a college degree (U.S. Census Bureau, 2011).

The twentieth century was an era of dramatic change in terms of schooling in the United States. We now *expect* young people to attend school. But although formal education is part of everyday life, today's schools face a number of serious problems. In fact, many people think that public education in the United States is in a state of crisis.

Problems with U.S. Education

To understand what schools are up against, consider the scope of their task. Across the country, almost 55 million students, who speak more than 100 different languages, are enrolled in nearly 130,000 public, parochial, and private schools (U.S Department of Education, 2009).

The budget for the country's public schools, which enroll 90 percent of all students, is more than $520 billion. Yet many people across the country are unsatisfied with public schools. Surveys show that almost half of U.S. adults give their local schools a grade of A or B, but just as many give them a grade of C or below (Bushaw & Gallup, 2008). In the following pages, we survey the performance of U.S. schools and then consider a number of other problems and controversies surrounding schooling in the United States.

The Academic Performance of U.S. Schools

In only one nation of the world (Norway) does a larger share of the population earn a college degree than in the United States. But in terms of basic literacy in reading, mathematics, and science, the United States ranks below Japan, the United Kingdom, Canada, the Czech Republic, and about thirty other nations (Organization for Economic Cooperation and Development, 2008).

Another well-known measure of academic performance is the college entrance examination taken by U.S. high school students. The Scholastic Assessment Test (SAT), which measures both verbal and mathematical achievement, shows little change over the past forty years. In 1967, average scores for U.S. students were 516 (out of a possible 800) on the mathematical test and 543 on the verbal test. By 2008, the average score in math had dropped one point to 515 and the average verbal score had fallen to 502 (College Board, 2009).

SOCIAL PROBLEMS in Everyday Life

Looking at the figure below, do you see evidence of educational success or failure? Explain.

SOCIAL PROBLEMS in Everyday Life

How might we explain the fact that, on average, students from high-income families outperform those from low-income families on the SAT?

Dimensions of Difference

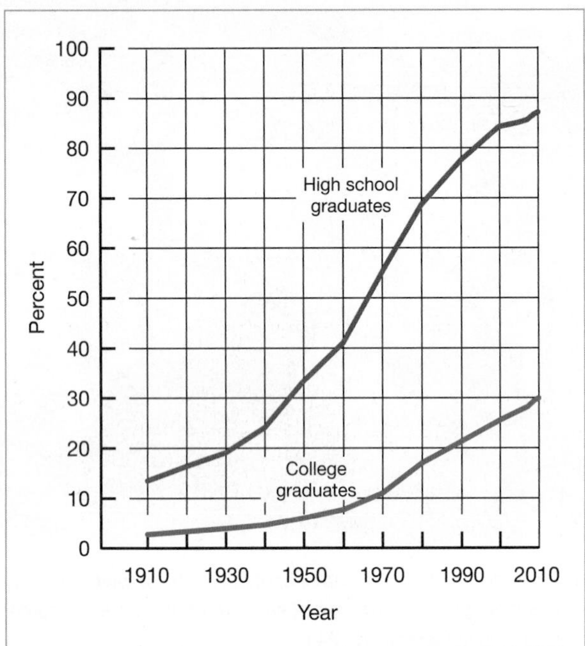

FIGURE 13–1 Schooling in the United States, 1910–2010

Today, the share of U.S. adults who complete college is more than twice as high as the share finishing high school back in 1910.

Source: U.S. Census Bureau (2011).

The Effects of Race, Ethnicity, and Class on Academic Performance

If the *average* performance of U.S. students has dropped a bit, the achievement of socially disadvantaged students remains a serious problem. There is evidence that our schools have failed whole segments of the U.S. population.

Although Asian American students average about the same as white students on the SAT, Latinos trail non-Latino whites by an average of about 200 points altogether, and African Americans score about 300 points below white students (College Board, 2009).

What accounts for these differences? A number of factors are at work. African American youngsters are more likely to live with a single parent and typically have less access to books, museums, travel, and other sources of learning. In addition, young people of color have to deal with racial stereotypes that call into question their academic ability, sometimes to the point that they begin to doubt themselves (NORC, 2007).

Many Latino youngsters begin school with little ability to speak English. If your only language is English, imagine how you might perform if you attended a school where Spanish was spoken and almost everyone was a native Spanish speaker. Although most Native Americans enter school speaking English, many view schools as representing an alien culture. Latino and Native Americans are the categories of the population least likely to complete a college education—only about 13 percent do (U.S. Census Bureau, 2011).

For all categories of people, the higher the risk of poverty, the lower the educational achievement. The poverty rates for Latino children (33 percent), African American children (36 percent), and Native American children (35 percent) are far greater than for non-Hispanic white children (12 percent) (U.S. Census Bureau, 2010). One important way average income affects quality of schooling involves funding. Schools enrolling well-off students spend much more money per student than schools in low-income communities. This means that children from richer families have access to better teachers, smaller classes, and more educational materials. Not surprisingly, students from higher-income families end up performing better on achievement tests. On average, high school students from families earning more than $200,000 per year score 350 points higher on the combined SAT than those from families with incomes below $20,000 per year (College Board, 2009).

The Effects of Home and School

Children from low-income families face a double burden of fewer educational advantages at home and also at school. A recent study helps us understand how these two factors affect the learning performance of U.S. schoolchildren.

A research team led by Doug Downey calculated that students—who attend school six or seven hours a day, five days a week, with summers and vacation time off—spend only about 13 percent of their waking hours in school. For that reason, the researchers concluded, we should realize the great importance of the home environment, where students spend the vast majority of their time (Downey, von Hippel, & Broh, 2004).

The research team then examined how quickly high- and low-income children gained skills in reading and mathematics. Collecting data on school performance throughout the year, they confirmed that there are large differences in academic performance between children from high-income homes and those from low-income homes. Looking more closely, they noted that during the school year, high-income children learn somewhat faster than low-income children. But during the summer months, when children spend the most time in their home environment, the gap in learning between high- and low-income children is greatest. This pattern points to the conclusion that schools matter, but the home environment matters

SOCIAL PROBLEMS in Everyday Life

In cases such as Cleveland, where one-third of students do not graduate, what new policies might raise the graduation rate?

more. Another way to say this is that schools close some of the learning gap that is created in the home community, but schools do not "level the playing field" between rich and poor children the way we sometimes like to think they do.

Dropping Out

Whatever the benefits of schooling to young people in the United States, the fact is that some of them are not in school at all. *Dropping out*—quitting school before earning a high school diploma—is a serious problem in this country.

How widespread is dropping out? Official government statistics show that 8.7 percent of the U.S. population aged sixteen to twenty-four (more than 3 million people) have left school without graduating. The good news is that in recent decades, dropping out of school has become less common: In 1960, the rate was 14 percent. But dropping out is still all too frequent among certain segments of the U.S. population. Figure 13–2 shows that the dropout rate is 5.3 percent for non-Hispanic whites, 8.4 percent among non-Hispanic African Americans, 21.4 percent among Latinos, and 14 percent among Native Americans (U.S. Department of Education, 2009).

Differences in income underlie much of this pattern. The dropout rate for young people from families with incomes $100,000 and above is less than 5 percent; for those from families with incomes below $25,000, the dropout rate is more than 15 percent (U.S. Department of Education, 2009).

Culture also plays a part in the decision to drop out of school. For people whose native language is not English, including many recent immigrants, dropout rates are especially high. The same is true for people—including many Native Americans—who have traditionally been uncomfortable sending their children to schools run by "outsiders."

In addition, the decision to leave school may be prompted by an unexpected pregnancy, a family's financial problems that require someone to go to work, or simple boredom with campus life. The decision to leave school is rarely simple, but the facts show that the problem of dropping out is greatest among people who face the greatest challenges—minorities and the poor (Hodkinson & Bloomer, 2001; Roscigno & Crowley, 2001). The Diversity: Race, Class, & Gender box on page 348 takes a closer look at one struggling school in Nebraska.

It is easy to think of dropping out of school as a choice made by students themselves. But especially in some school districts, something bigger is going on. Take the case of Cleveland, Ohio. In that city, of all children who begin high school, only 62 percent graduate four years later (Ohio Department of Education, 2008). If more than one-third of a city's public school students do not graduate, it seems to make more sense to point to the school system itself as part of the problem. In Cleveland and a number of other large U.S. cities, it is quite possible that the schools are failing the students.

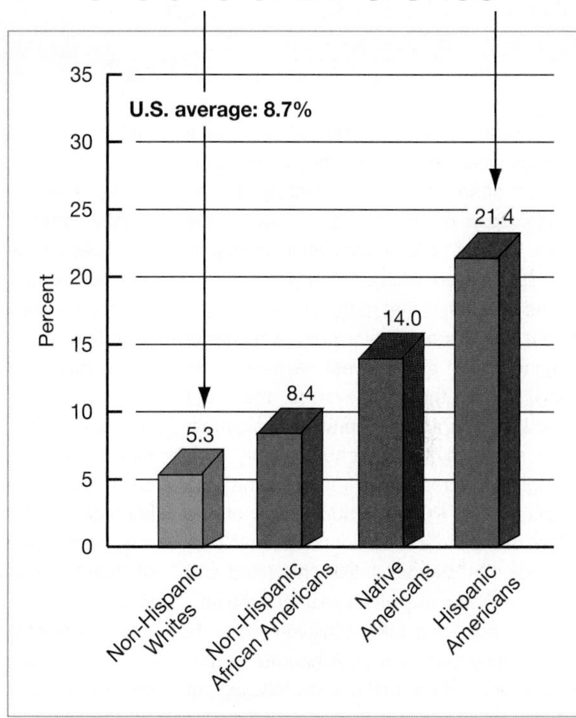

Figure 13–2 Percentage of Dropouts among Categories of the U.S. Population, Ages 16 to 24

Dropping out of school is a problem for all categories of people. But the rates are especially high among Hispanics and Native Americans.

Source: National Center for Education Statistics (2009).

Whatever its causes, dropping out has some serious consequences. Failing to finish school raises the risk of unemployment, poverty, drug abuse, and arrest later on as adults. For example, school dropouts account for more than half of all people receiving welfare assistance and 80 percent of this country's prison population (Christle, Jolivette, & Nelson, 2007). Thus a lack of schooling can become part of a multigenerational cycle in which children who grow up in a disadvantaged setting with too little schooling go on become disadvantaged adults who pass on their situation to their own children.

Functional Illiteracy

The poor performance of many schools helps explain the fact that as much as 15 percent of the U.S. adult population (about 30 million men and women) lacks literacy skills. This is the problem

MAKING THE GRADE

Be sure you know the importance of these two court cases: *Plessy* v. *Ferguson* and *Brown* v. *Board of Education of Topeka.*

DIVERSITY: RACE, CLASS, & GENDER

Dropping Out: Sometimes an Epidemic

Todd Chessmore knew that he was taking on a challenge when he accepted the job as superintendent of schools in Macy, Nebraska. One important part of his work is to oversee the Omaha Nation Public School, where almost all of the students are Native Americans.

The problem is that many of the students are not in school. Truancy is widespread throughout the school year, especially in spring. Once the sun warms the cold Nebraska plains and temperatures rise, most of the students at the school simply stop coming. One predictable result is that the Omaha Nation Public School ranks at the bottom of the state in student academic performance. Chessmore shakes his head and points out that in any given year, half the students do not even take achievement tests because they skip school. A handful of students at the school make it to college, but half of all students never even graduate. Nationwide, the rate of dropping out among Native Americans—one in three—is only slightly better.

Chessmore worked hard to improve attendance at the Omaha Nation Public School. He started by improving the physical condition of the building—crews washed floors, painted walls, and replaced hundreds of burned-out light bulbs. He hired more Native American teachers and provided cultural sensitivity classes to non-Indian teachers to help them understand the students' heritage and current problems. To these carrots, he added a stick, hiring several truancy officers to track down students who are not in school and, if necessary, to threaten legal action against their families.

Chessmore did one more thing: He decided to cancel both Christmas vacation and spring break so that there are more school days before the warm weather comes. His actions have helped reduce truancy. But so far, there has been little change in the dropout rate.

WHAT DO YOU THINK?

1. Why is the dropout rate so high among American Indians?
2. What policies can you suggest to address this problem? How well do you think they might work?
3. Is the situation described in this box a matter of students failing the school or the school failing the students? Why? Explain your answer.

Sources: Based on Belluck (2000) and other news reports.

of **functional illiteracy,** *the inability to read and write or do basic arithmetic well enough to carry out daily responsibilities.*

Being functionally illiterate in the modern world turns many everyday activities into real challenges. Reading food labels, paying bills, understanding letters children bring home from teachers at school, reading a newspaper, and making sense of the tables and graphs found in a textbook are all beyond the abilities of people who are functionally illiterate (National Center for Education Statistics, 2008).

To the women and men who suffer from this problem, functional illiteracy means more than not being able to cope. It is also a source of embarrassment and shame. More important, in a world that demands more and more literacy skills with each passing year, functional illiteracy stands as a barrier to getting a good job, locking people into low-wage work or unemployment and often poverty. The fact that a sizable share of our national workforce cannot read or write well also wastes talent and brain power and reduces this country's ability to compete in a global marketplace.

School Segregation and Busing

Before the Civil War, few African Americans attended school. With the end of the war and the abolition of slavery in 1865, African Americans took their place in a new system of racially segregated schools. In 1896, in the case of *Plessy* v. *Ferguson,* the U.S. Supreme Court affirmed the principle of racial segregation as long as the facilities for blacks and whites were "separate but equal." In reality, black and white schools were separate but far from equal. Most white children attended schools with modern buildings, well-trained teachers, and up-to-date textbooks. By contrast, most African American children attended rundown schools with poorly trained teachers and outdated, hand-me-down books.

Formal segregation was the norm throughout the post–Civil War South. The North also had racially segregated schools, due primarily to the fact that almost all African Americans were forced to live in mostly black neighborhoods, where schools were underfunded.

Not until the 1950s, when the civil rights movement gained momentum, did activists challenge the system of segregated schools. They rallied around the case of Linda Brown, a nine-year-old girl in Topeka, Kansas. The Defining Moment box tells her story.

Some local governments tried to overcome the segregation that remained long after the Supreme Court ruled that separate schooling for blacks and whites was unconstitutional. But how could a city or town achieve racial balance in schools if most black

SOCIAL PROBLEMS in Everyday Life

Do you see evidence of racial segregation in schools today? Explain.

SOCIAL PROBLEMS in Everyday Life

How did the Brown decision help construct a new social problem for this country?

CONSTRUCTING SOCIAL PROBLEMS

A DEFINING MOMENT

Linda Brown: Fighting to Desegregate the Schools

More than fifty years ago, in Topeka, Kansas, a minister and his nine-year-old daughter walked hand in hand to the public elementary school four blocks from their home. The girl, Linda Brown, wanted to enroll in the fourth grade. But school officials refused, telling Reverend Brown to take his daughter to another school 2 miles away. Why? Topeka's public schools, like those in most of the United States, were segregated by race. Because she was African American, the rules stated, Linda Brown had to go to the school for "colored" children.

Linda Brown's parents thought that this policy was unjust. They were not alone. A civil rights movement was developing across the United States, and the Browns were soon at the center of what turned out to be a defining moment in U.S. schooling. They filed a lawsuit on behalf of Linda and other African Americans challenging laws that mandated "separate but equal" schools for black and white children.

In 1954, the Supreme Court of the United States considered the case, and on May 17 of that year, the justices handed down a historic ruling. In *Brown* v. *Board of Education of Topeka,* the Court concluded that racially segregated schools provided African Americans with inferior schooling and declared the practice unlawful, overturning the doctrine of "separate but equal" schooling by race (which the Court had affirmed in 1896 in the case of *Plessy* v. *Ferguson*).

As noted in the opening to this chapter, the laws may have changed, but the reality of racially segregated schools continues in the United States more than half a century after the *Brown* ruling. Why? The simple reason is that due to differences in income and racial prejudice as well, black and white people typically live in different neighborhoods. The common practice is that children attend schools near their homes. Thus residential segregation places children in schools that are filled almost entirely with students of their own race. But Linda Brown and her father will long be celebrated as trailblazers in the drive for racial justice in U.S. schooling.

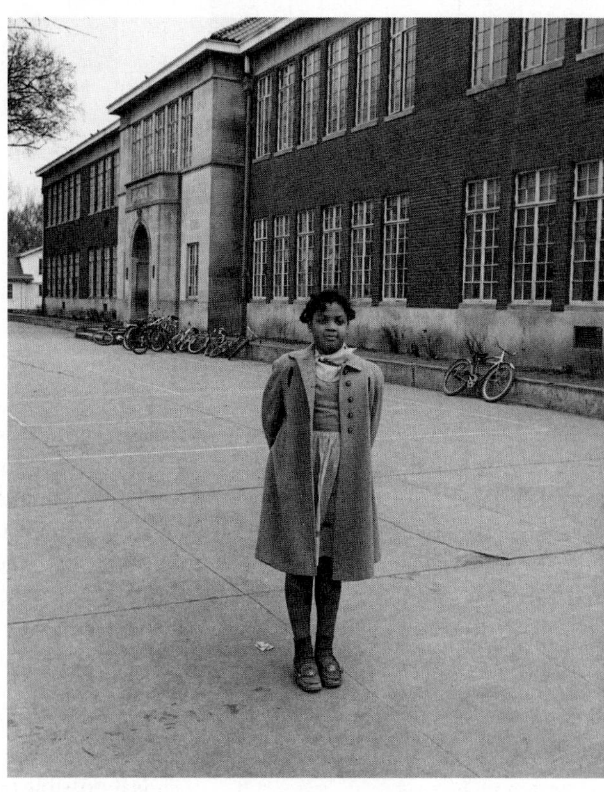

It has been more than half a century since Linda Brown lent her name to a landmark legal effort intended to desegregate U.S. public schools. How much has changed since then?

people and white people live in separate neighborhoods? One answer that emerged in the 1960s was to bus students from one neighborhood to another in order to achieve racially balanced schools. Especially when white children were the ones being bused, white parents strongly opposed the policy, objecting to the time their children had to spend on buses and the poor education the children received at the new schools. Black parents had a mixed reaction to busing: Some hoped the policy would improve their children's educational opportunities, but others objected to the time their children spent traveling to another part of the city.

As the debate continued between supporters of "equal schooling" and supporters of "neighborhood schools," it became clear that the policy of busing would never succeed in integrating urban schools. In the 1960s, many white families moved from the central cities to suburbs—a pattern commonly called *white flight*—to place their children beyond the reach of

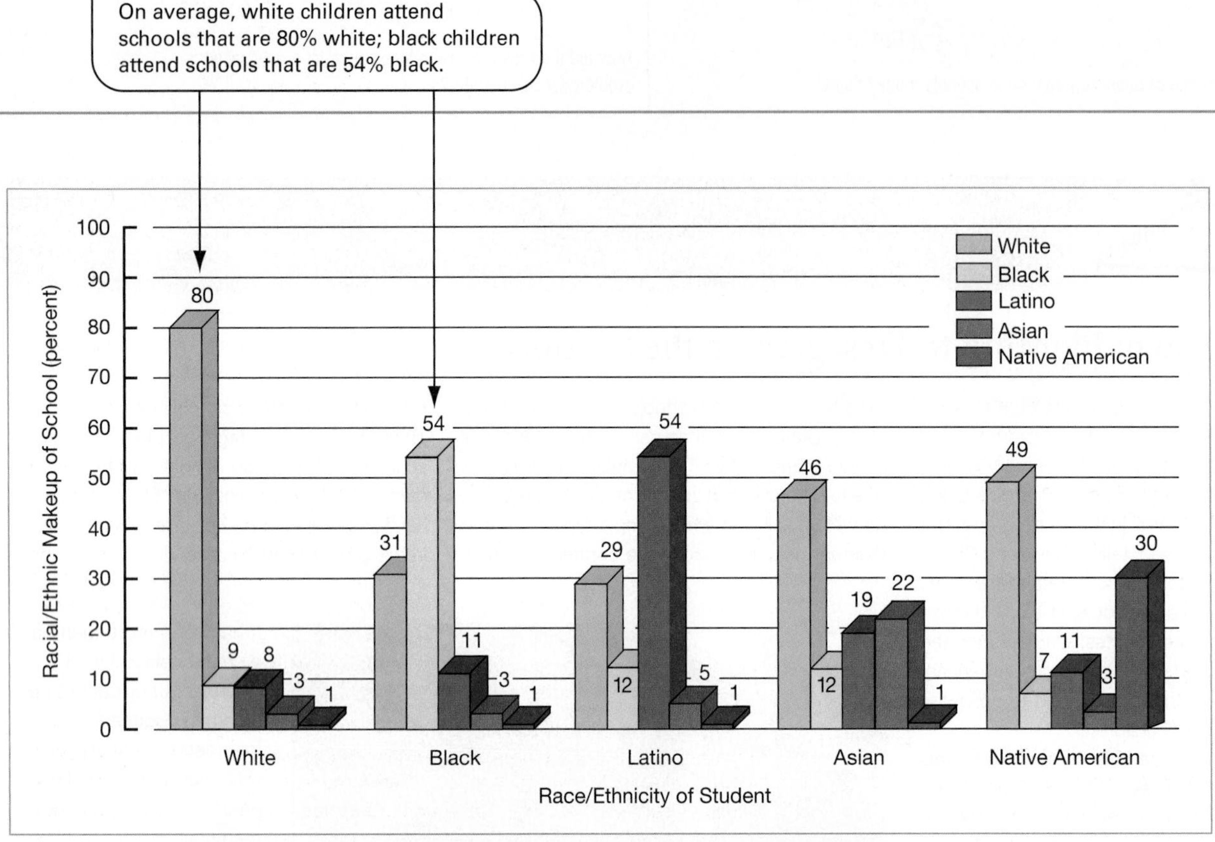

FIGURE 13–3 Racial Makeup of the Average Student's School, by Race and Ethnicity

Research shows that most students in the United States attend schools where most of the other students are of the same race and ethnic background as their own.

Source: Orfield & Lee (2007).

busing plans (S. J. L. Taylor, 1998). As described in Chapter 14 ("Urban Life"), the loss of urban population meant a decline in tax revenues, so schools in central cities actually became worse than before.

During the 1990s, the courts finally called an end to school busing. Because most neighborhoods are still home to mostly people of the same race, schools today are just about as racially segregated as they were in the 1960s. Figure 13–3 provides the results of one study showing that racial and ethnic segregation remains strong in today's schools.

School Funding

Schools throughout the United States differ not only in terms of their racial composition but also in the resources they can offer to students. Why? Typically, a school system is funded by tax money from the people who live in the local community, which is added to funding provided by the state.

But some communities are far richer than others, and differences in tax revenues produce strikingly unequal school budgets. In a classic study, Jonathan Kozol (1991) reported that the school system in affluent Great Neck, New York, was spending five times more money per student than the school system in Camden, New Jersey. On a national scale today, per-student funding differs from about $17,500 per student each year on New York's Long Island, down to around $8,000 in poor areas like Laredo, Texas (Winter, 2004).

Such differences in funding make a vast difference in schooling. The school in a poor neighborhood may be rundown, lack library and science facilities, have crowded classrooms, and be staffed with poorly trained teachers. The Diversity: Race, Class, & Gender box takes a closer look at Jonathan Kozol's account of what he calls the "savage inequalities" in U.S. education.

Is it possible to level the educational playing field? Doing so would require equalizing the school funding in rich and poor communities. In 1998, Vermont enacted a policy called Act 60 to do exactly that. This law combines school taxes all across the state and redistributes funding on an equal per-student basis. This means that students in richer communities, with above-average property taxes, get the same amount in school funds as children in poorer communities. Such "Robin Hood" laws, which take from the rich and give to the poor, do make funding more equal. But they are controversial, finding favor in poor school districts and criticism in wealthier communities (T. M. Edwards, 1998; Shlaes, 1998; Goodman, 1999).

SOCIAL PROBLEMS in Everyday Life

Do you understand the meaning and importance of cultural capital to school performance?

SOCIAL PROBLEMS in Everyday Life

Can you think of several ways parents, regardless of income level, can help their children learn more at school? What are some special challenges low-income parents face?

DIVERSITY: RACE, CLASS, & GENDER

The "Savage Inequalities" of Schooling in the United States

"Excuse me," the sociologist Jonathan Kozol calls out his car window. "Can you tell me where P.S. 261 is?" "Sure," replies one of the two women on the sidewalk drawing shopping baskets behind them. "Just keep going straight ahead another two blocks and look for the mortician's office."

"Mortician's office, indeed," Kozol thinks to himself as he looks for a parking spot across from the school. There seems to be something deadly about this whole neighborhood: rundown buildings, trash strewn across empty lots, graffiti all over the walls, and the whole scene punctuated by the deafening sound of an elevated train thundering past along the overhead tracks.

In the center of this setting stands New York's Public School 261, although one may not realize it because the school has no sign. Kozol introduces himself to a teacher as he steps through the door. The teacher mentions that the building used to be a roller-skating rink.

Kozol makes his way to the principal's office. The principal explains that in this minority community of the North Bronx, 90 percent of the students in P.S. 261 are African American or Latino. Officially, she continues, the school is supposed to have 900 students, but actual enrollment is about 1,300. City education guidelines state that class size should not exceed thirty-two students, but Kozol soon observes classes with as many as forty. The cafeteria is small, forcing the school to feed the children in three shifts. There is no playground, so after lunch, teachers try to keep children in their seats until it is time to return to the classrooms. Moving about the school, Kozol finds only one classroom with a window.

An interview with a teacher sums up the state of this school. "I had an awful room last year," she explains, shaking her head. "In the winter, it was 56 degrees. In the summer, it was up to 90." Kozol asks, "Do the children ever comment on the building?" "They don't say much," she responds, "but they know. All these kids see TV. They know what suburban schools are like. Then they look around them at their school. They don't comment on it, but you see it in their eyes. They understand."

A few months later, Kozol visits a second school across town. Public School 24 is in New York's affluent Riverdale section of the Bronx. Like the other buildings in this upscale neighborhood, the school stands in good repair and is set back from the road by a green lawn with flowering trees. To the left, Kozol notes a playground for the youngest children; farther behind the school are playing fields where the older kids engage in team sports.

"It is no surprise," explains the principal, "that many people are willing to pay the high prices of Riverdale homes to be able to send their children to a school like this." "What is the enrollment?" Kozol asks. "Eight hundred and twenty-five children," comes the reply, "almost all in classes under thirty." Looking up and down the halls reveals that most students are white, with a handful of Asian, Latino, and African American children. The building is a wonderful learning facility, featuring bright and attractive classrooms, a large library, and even a planetarium.

During his visit, Kozol joins a group of children in one of the many classes for gifted students. "What are you learning today?" he asks. A well-dressed young girl answers, "My name is Laurie; today, we're doing problem solving." A tall, good-natured boy continues, "I'm David. The point is to develop our ability to do logical thinking. Some problems, we find, have more than one good answer." "Let me ask your opinion," says Kozol. "Do you think this kind of reasoning is innate, or is it something a child learns?" Susan smiles, revealing shiny braces, and responds, "You know some things to start with when you enter school. But we learn some things that other children don't. We learn certain things that other children don't know because we're *taught* them."

WHAT DO YOU THINK?

1. Some people claim that local communities have the right to spend whatever they want to educate their children, even though some school systems will be better funded than others. How do you respond to this argument?
2. If you were in a position to create an education funding policy, what would you do?
3. If all children could attend schools that were exactly equal, do you think educational performance would be the same? Why or why not?

Source: Based on Kozol (1991:85–88, 92–96).

Cultural Capital

Funding is not the only way in which schools differ. Even if all schools were able to spend the same amount of money per child, the educational experiences of richer and poorer children would still be unequal. This is because, as noted earlier, the quality of children's home life affects their learning. Parents with higher incomes are able to give their children greater *cultural capital*, the experiences and opportunities that shape a student's ability to learn and to succeed at school and elsewhere.

High-income parents are more likely to have a home that is spacious, quiet, and equipped with a personal computer. Having more education themselves, well-off parents are more likely to teach young children language skills by, say, reading with them regularly. Low-income parents are more likely to have a smaller, more crowded home and are less likely to own a computer, books,

MAKING THE GRADE

How can tracking be a form of institutional discrimination?

tracking the policy of assigning students to different educational programs

self-fulfilling prophecy a situation in which people who are defined in a certain way eventually think and act as if the definition were true

and other learning materials. With less schooling (and a higher likelihood of speaking a language other than English in the home), they can provide less help to children doing schoolwork (Coleman, 1966, 1988; McNeal, 1999).

The cultural capital a family gives its children has a lot to do with the family's income level, a point that is often made by political liberals. But cultural capital is also a matter of the importance people attach to schooling and to doing well in school, a point often made by political conservatives. For example, Abigail and Stephan Thernstrom (2003) argue that parents (as well as schools) must foster a "culture of success" in order for children to do well. Their research suggests that on average, black parents have lower expectations of their children than white parents do and that Asian parents are the most demanding of all. These cultural differences explain the fact, according to the Thernstroms, that white children from families with $25,000 in annual income outperform African American children from families with $90,000 in annual income.

Tracking

Schooling can be unequal not only from one school or community to another but also within a single school as a result of **tracking,** *the policy of assigning students to different educational programs.*

The idea behind tracking is to place students in classes based on their performance on achievement tests. In this way, schools can better address the abilities and interests of each child. Supporters of tracking point out that if all students were to take the same curriculum, the brightest and most motivated would succeed but the less intelligent and the less motivated students would quickly fall behind (Brantlinger, 1993; Loveless, 1999).

Critics of tracking counter that this policy amounts to a form of institutional discrimination: In practice, tracking provides affluent children with the best a school has to offer, leaving children from lower-income families with a second-class education. The testing used to assign students to tracks is likely to be culturally biased, asking for information that well-off children are more likely to have. In short, because family background affects how well a child performs in school, tracking transforms a *social* advantage into an *educational* advantage (Bowles & Gintis, 1976; Oakes, 1985; Cloud, 2003).

Typically, students in higher tracks attend classes that move them along quickly, with emphasis on critical thinking and creativity. Those in lower tracks are likely to progress more slowly, with a focus on basic skills and the importance of following directions.

To illustrate, imagine that children in two different tracks were studying the civil rights movement. Teachers in the advanced track might ask students to identify the strategies used by activists to bring about change and to identify strengths and weaknesses of each. Then they might ask the class to apply lessons to the struggle of today's immigrants to gain more economic security and a greater political voice. Teachers in a lower track might ask children only to identify the movement's leaders and highlight key events.

We now know that tracking can set in motion a **self-fulfilling prophecy**—*a situation in which people who are defined in a certain way eventually think and act as if the definition were true.* In this case, how the school defines children affects how the children see themselves. Children in higher tracks learn to see themselves as bright and able, which encourages them to work hard and to do well. Children in lower tracks develop lower self-esteem, question their own abilities, and end up doing less well. In light of the controversy over tracking, schools across the country are now more careful about assigning children to different programs and allow more mobility from one track to another (Kozol, 1991; Gamoran, 1992; Loveless, 1999; Olin, 2003).

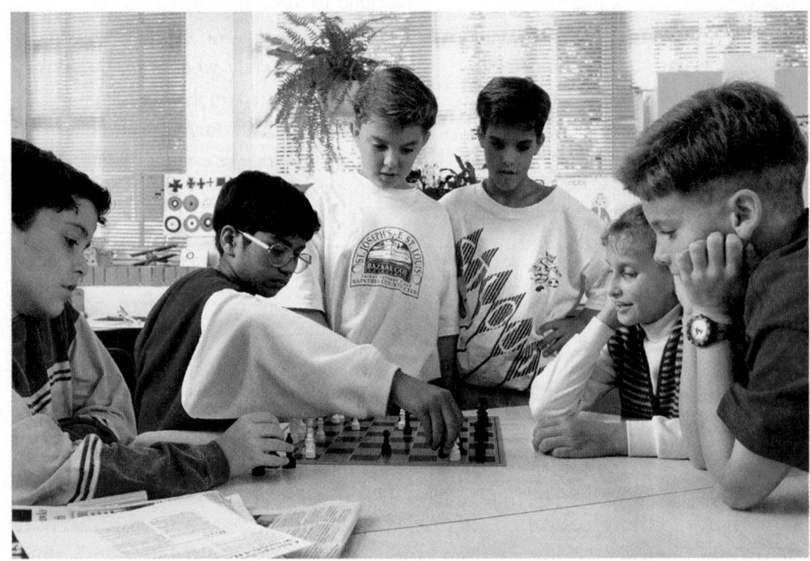

One example of tracking is placing "gifted" students together in "enriched" classes. What effect might the label "gifted" have on the way teachers treat students?

Gender Inequality

Gender also shapes the quality of education in the United States. For generations, the two sexes followed different programs of study. Schools steered boys into courses such as woodworking

GETTING INVOLVED

Do you see gender inequality on your campus? In what areas?

English immersion the policy of teaching non–English speakers in English

bilingual education the policy of offering most classes in students' native language while also teaching them English

and mechanical shop that would prepare them for industrial jobs in factories. Girls were tracked into courses such as home economics, typing, and shorthand that prepared them to be homemakers or to perform clerical work in offices. In college, men were encouraged to study the sciences, including physics, chemistry, biology, and mathematics. College women mainly majored in English, elementary education, foreign languages, and the social sciences.

School textbooks also reflected the two sexes in stereotypical roles. Books portrayed women working in the home and men in the paid workforce (Spender, 1989; Basow, 1992; Wood & Chesser, 1993). Even the organization of the school itself provided lessons concerning gender. Generations of students observed that most teachers (especially in the lower grades) were women, and most of the people in charge—principals and senior administrators—were men (Richardson, 1988; U.S. Department of Labor, 2006).

This nation's high rate of immigration creates challenges for schools. In this ESL (English as a Second Language) classroom, students who speak a wide range of languages at home come together to learn English.

Over the course of the twentieth century, girls and women gradually gained more equal standing in schools. One important step occurred in 1972 when Congress passed Title IX of the Education Amendments to the Civil Rights Act. Title IX bans sex discrimination in education and requires schools receiving federal funding to provide equal programs for male and female students. Today, as a result of such efforts, girls are as likely as boys to be placed in classes for gifted students, and more young women than young men qualify for high school advanced placement courses, which provide better preparation for college. For more than a decade, women have outnumbered men on this country's college and university campuses and now represent 57 percent of all undergraduates. In 2006, women also became a majority of students in graduate and professional degree programs (U.S. Department of Education, 2009).

Not all doors are fully open to women, however. Women are still concentrated in many traditionally feminine majors, such as the health professions (including nursing and physical therapy), teaching, graphic arts, office technology, languages, drama, and dance (U.S. Department of Education, 2009).

Immigration: Increasing Diversity

Another challenge facing U.S. schools involves the more than 1 million immigrants who enter this country every year. As Chapter 3 ("Race and Ethnic Inequality") describes in detail, these immigrants represent more than 100 cultures and languages. Most newcomers, today as in the past, look to public schools to provide their children with the knowledge and skills needed to get good jobs.

English Immersion versus Bilingualism

Many young immigrants and children of immigrants do well in school. But one in five people under the age of eighteen speaks a language other than English at home. How should schools respond to the challenge of teaching students who know little English? Two opposing policies are being hotly debated. The first policy is **English immersion,** *the policy of teaching non–English speakers in English.* In many cases, a single class, English as a Second Language, is taught in the student's native language with a native language teacher.

The second approach is **bilingual education,** *the policy of offering most classes in students' native language while also teaching them English.* In this case, schools must hire many teachers skilled not only in a particular subject matter but also in a non-English language. In school districts where students may speak dozens of different languages—common in California and other states—providing bilingual education is a tremendous challenge.

The debate over English immersion versus bilingual education is partly about how well students learn. Supporters of English immersion claim that students do learn more quickly in

mainstreaming integrating students with special needs into the overall educational program

special education schooling children with physical or mental disabilities in separate classes with specially trained teachers

SOCIAL POLICY

More than Talk: The Politics of Bilingual Education

Schooling is not just about teaching children to read and write. Schooling is also a way to socialize children—including those from diverse social backgrounds—to find a place within U.S. society. A century ago, as immigration to the United States surged, our country expanded schooling to teach newcomers the ways of their new land and to teach them the English language.

So important was the goal of teaching English that many states (Nebraska was the first in 1919) passed a law requiring all teachers in public schools to teach in English until at least the ninth grade. Public support for these laws was high because in the wake of World War I, people feared that immigrants who kept their native language might be disloyal to the United States should war break out again. But others opposed these laws as narrow-minded and intolerant of cultural diversity. The issue ended up in court, and in 1923, the U.S. Supreme Court, in the case of *Meyer* v. *State of Nebraska,* declared that all English-only laws were unconstitutional.

Fast-forward to 1971, when the San Francisco school system offered no classes in Chinese to its 2,800 Chinese students. A group of parents came together, defined this situation as a problem, and decided to file a lawsuit against the school district. The suit claimed that the lack of Chinese-language classes violated the Civil Rights Act of 1964, which bans any program receiving federal funds from discriminating on the basis of race, color, or national origin. This case made its way to the U.S. Supreme Court, which ruled in *Lau* v. *Nichols* (1974) that all students have a right to be taught in a language they can understand. School administrators took this decision to mean that public schools had to create programs to give all children instruction in their native language, whether it is English or some other tongue. At that point, the policy of English immersion was replaced with the policy of bilingual education.

Supporters of bilingual education applaud treating all languages equally and respectfully. Critics of bilingualism claim that bilingual education encourages cultural division instead of emphasizing the cultural patterns most people share.

In 1998, the policy of English immersion gained ground in California when voters there passed Proposition 227, which bans bilingual programs in favor of the English immersion approach. The debate over how to respond to the millions of recent immigrants to the United States—both legal and illegal—will keep this issue in the headlines for years to come.

WHAT DO YOU THINK?

1. Have any members of your sociology class had experience with either English immersion or bilingual education? If so, discuss advantages and disadvantages of each policy.
2. In your opinion, is the debate surrounding language instruction in schools really about what's good for students or more about whether people favor cultural unity or cultural diversity?
3. As preparation for working in a global economy, does it make sense for everyone to become skilled in more than one language? Explain.

Sources: Portes (2002) and Winerip (2007).

the short term when taught in their native language, but focusing on English helps students' long-term learning.

But supporters of bilingualism point to evidence that becoming bilingual at a young age helps overall cognitive development. That is, young children who develop language skills in their native language and also in English go on to outperform one-language students on achievement tests. In addition, there can be little doubt of the value of gaining bilingual skills in today's global economy (Portes, 2002).

But there is even more at stake. The two policies have different political and cultural objectives. English immersion seeks to "Americanize" students by making English the central language and teaching them the dominant culture. By teaching in a student's native language, bilingual education places all cultural backgrounds on an equal footing and encourages acceptance of all ways of life. The Social Policy box takes a closer look at the politics underlying this debate.

Schooling People with Disabilities

The debate over whether schools meet the needs of students extends to people of all classes, colors, and cultures and people with mental or physical disabilities. In 2008, almost 7 million students with disabilities were enrolled in special-education programs in public schools, at a cost exceeding $20 billion (U.S. Department of Education, 2009).

Throughout most of U.S. history, few children with disabilities received any schooling at all. This changed in 1975, when Congress passed the Education for All Handicapped Children Act, which requires states to educate all children with disabilities. This law also directs schools to place students with disabilities in the "least restrictive environment," meaning that schools should try to treat them like anyone else while meeting their special needs.

This requirement to include students with disabilities in regular school programs led to the policy of **mainstreaming,** *integrating students with special needs into the overall educational*

Now in his tenth year of middle school teaching, Tom Samuels lives near Butte, Montana, and earns $42,400 a year.

Fresh out of college, J. P. Saunders just landed a teaching job in Albany, New York, with a starting salary of $42,000 a year.

GETTING INVOLVED

Have you considered a career in teaching?

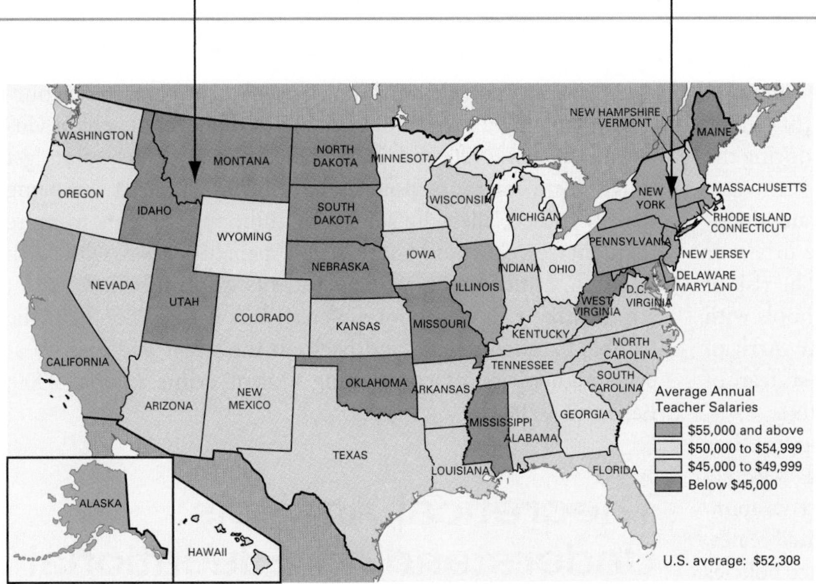

A Nation of Diversity

NATIONAL MAP 13–1

Public School Teachers' Pay across the United States

Over the last decade, teachers' salaries have increased only about 0.3 percent per year, not keeping up with the rate of inflation. Average pay in some states is far higher than in others. Looking at the state-by-state averages, what pattern can you see?

Source: National Education Association (2008).

program. Supporters of mainstreaming argue that taking part in regular classes gives students with disabilities a better education. In addition, students without disabilities learn to interact with people who differ from themselves.

Critics of mainstreaming point out that there is little solid research showing that this policy improves anyone's academic performance. On the contrary, they argue, many students with disabilities find it difficult or even impossible to participate in regular classes. The alternative to mainstreaming is **special education,** *schooling children with physical or mental disabilities in separate classes with specially trained teachers.*

In general, which policy is best depends on the students. People with physical or mental disabilities that do not greatly restrict their activities can easily be mainstreamed. Those who are more severely challenged typically require more costly special classes. In the United States, about half of students with disabilities are mainstreamed, and the other half spend some or all of their time in special classes (U.S. Department of Education, 2008).

The Teacher Shortage

Another problem for U.S. public schools is hiring enough teachers to fill the classrooms. Across the country, about 300,000 jobs remain unfilled each year. Looking ahead, some 4 million new teachers will be needed in the coming decade (Projections of Education Statistics to 2018. U.S. Department of Education, 2008). In practical terms, a shortage of teachers means larger class sizes and a greater burden on the nation's current teaching staff.

Why are teachers in short supply? Low salaries are one factor: Many districts simply pay too little to attract many well-qualified teachers. National Map 13–1 shows teacher salaries across the United States.

But more than money is involved. Many people have left teaching due to frustration over extensive bureaucracy that makes the hiring process long and then imposes rigid rules on how classes are to be taught. Some holders of an education degree have had trouble passing state certification tests in specific fields, such as mathematics, biology, or English. An even greater number are turning away from teaching because of problems of discipline and violence in the schools.

The problem comes down to being sure good teachers are in the classroom. One solution is to force less qualified teachers to get the training they need in order to keep their jobs. A second part of the solution is to attract new and highly qualified people into our schools. In recent years, school systems have devised new recruitment strategies. Some are using incentives such as higher salaries and signing bonuses to draw into teaching people who have already established successful careers in other fields. Others are encouraging community colleges to provide more programs that will prepare people to become teachers. Finally, many school districts are going global, actively recruiting in countries such as Spain, India, and the Philippines, where talented educators are eager to be invited to work in U.S. classrooms (Lord, 2001; Evelyn, 2002; Ripley, 2008).

School Violence

Recent years have witnessed deadly violence at schools across the United States. Between 1996 and 2009, more than thirty incidents involving students armed with guns in school took the lives of forty students and eleven teachers and left another forty-three students and six teachers wounded.

The most serious form of school violence is, of course, homicide. Serious violence also includes offenses such as aggra-

GETTING INVOLVED

How much of a problem was violence in your high school? What policies did the school use to control violent crime?

MAKING THE GRADE

School has both manifest (intended and obvious) functions and latent (less widely recognized) functions. Be sure you can give examples of each type.

vated assault and forcible rape, which are even more common. According to the federal government, 86 percent of public schools reported at least one serious crime at school during the 2005–2006 academic year (Dinkes et al., 2009).

In general, the larger the school, the higher the rate of violence. The risk of serious violence is greater in large urban or suburban schools than it is in small, rural schools. The risk of violence is also higher in poor areas, especially in schools with mostly minority students. Research shows that African American and Latino students express the greatest fear of school violence (Thernstrom, 1999; Dinkes et al., 2009).

What can schools do to fight back? One recent approach is a *zero-tolerance policy* under which school officials severely punish or perhaps expel any student who brings a weapon, alcohol, or some other drug to school. Across the United States, 95 percent of schools now have adopted zero-tolerance policies for firearms, and about half employ security guards, security cameras, and metal detectors to screen all students as they enter the building (Dinkes et al., 2009).

Another policy is enacting a dress code to prevent students from wearing gang colors and insignia, which are symbols that can spark violence. School uniforms also appear to discourage students from attacking others to steal shoes, jackets, or other clothing.

A final strategy used by many schools is a program in conflict resolution. In such programs, teachers instruct children in ways to resolve conflict peacefully (U.S. Bureau of Justice Statistics and National Center for Education Statistics, 2006).

In recent years, schools across the United States have tried to safeguard students by installing security systems on buildings. To assess how effective this policy may be, consider first what are the sources of school violence?

Are these policies working? Government data are encouraging, showing a substantial decline in the level of school violence between 1990 and 2006 (Dinkes et al., 2009). But "get tough" zero-tolerance policies have been criticized for being racially biased, allegedly subjecting minority students to more frequent searches and more severe penalties than whites. In addition, critics claim, kicking students who misbehave out of school may reduce school violence, but it does not help the troubled students who land back on the street and end up at even higher risk of committing violent crime (Skiba, 2000; Ballantine, 2001).

Theoretical Analysis: Understanding Educational Problems

Each of sociology's major theoretical approaches offers insights into the purposes and the problems of schooling. We begin with structural-functional analysis.

Structural-Functional Analysis: The Functions of Schooling

Structural-functional analysis points out that the smooth operation of modern societies depends on schooling. Teaching a wide range of knowledge and skills to young people enables them to take their place as productive adults. As the foundation of the U.S. economy moved from farming to industry, responsibility for training the young moved from parents to specially trained teachers.

Schooling also functions as an important system of social placement. Our society looks to schools to help people develop their talents and abilities so they can find an appropriate job. For just about anyone, schooling increases employment opportunities. Throughout our nation's history, schooling has been a major avenue of upward social mobility for people in search of a better life.

Given the cultural diversity of the U.S. population, schools also have the function of teaching widely shared cultural beliefs and values. For example, U.S. schools teach young people about the importance of achievement and the rules of fair play. In addition, U.S. society relies on schools to prepare people to participate in this country's political and economic systems. In short, schools help integrate individuals from many different cultural traditions into a single national community (Fine, 1993; Ballantine, 2001).

Schooling also performs many latent, or less widely recognized, functions. For example, schools provide child care for

hidden curriculum explicit and subtle presentations of political or cultural ideas in the classroom that support the status quo

working parents. They also occupy young people who might otherwise have trouble finding jobs or might turn to crime. Given the great importance of schooling to the operation of modern societies, it is easy to understand why many people view issues such as poor teaching, dropping out, and classroom violence as serious social problems (Fuller, Elmore, & Orfield, 1996; C. N. Stone, 1998).

CRITICAL REVIEW The structural-functional approach points out the many important contributions schools make to the operation of our society. It treats schooling in a general way, as a major social institution. But critics of this approach point out that the reality of schooling is different for different people, and some people find the experience much more positive than others. To understand how people experience schools, we turn to the symbolic-interaction approach, which highlights the interaction between students and school personnel.

Symbolic-Interaction Analysis: Labels in the Schools

The symbolic-interaction approach provides a micro-level look at how individuals experience the school system. At this level, we see how school officials define the academic ability of each student.

On the basis of grades and performance on standardized tests, students are labeled by their schools as, say, "gifted," "average," or "deficient." These labels reflect the work students have done, although, as noted earlier, other factors, including social class and race, may play a part in the label attached to each child's performance.

Just as important, labels influence each student's future. The individuals that school officials label as exceptionally bright or as slow learners are likely, over time, to think of themselves in this way and perform accordingly. Thus symbolic-interaction analysis suggests that tracking and other forms of labeling can create a self-fulfilling prophecy. This means that students labeled as slow learners are likely to perform poorly. It is not surprising that they are also at higher risk for leaving school altogether.

The spoken and more subtle messages conveyed to a student by teachers, coaches, and counselors can also shape the student's future. For example, if school personnel consider some areas of study suitable for girls and others suitable for boys or if they believe that certain majors or honors courses are expected of students in some racial and ethnic categories and not others, we can see how students end up segregated into different areas of study (Sadker & Sadker, 1994; Sadker, 1999; Ballantine, 2001).

CRITICAL REVIEW The strength of the symbolic-interaction approach lies in providing a "street-level" view of how interacting individuals generate reality. At the same time, however, the participants in any social situation are not all equal. For example, teachers have more power to shape the reality of the classroom than students do. In the same way, larger social forces—such as social class—influence what different students may experience in the same school and generate different realities from school to school. These disparities bring us to the social-conflict approach.

Social-Conflict Analysis: Schooling and Inequality

The social-conflict approach highlights how schooling is linked to social inequality in U.S. society. As already explained, schooling in this country is very unequal, to the benefit of some categories of students and to the disadvantage of others. Some students do very well in U.S. schools; others are left behind by our educational system through no fault of their own.

One important dimension of differences, noted earlier, is school funding, with some schools receiving far more money per student than others. The predictable result, following this approach, is that some schools are well equipped and beautifully maintained and are staffed by highly trained and motivated teachers. Others are rundown and lacking in basic facilities, with teachers who are poorly trained and ineffective in the classroom.

In addition, within any single school, the policy of tracking mandates that the best the school has to offer goes to the students who already have a lot going for them—those from higher-class backgrounds. On the other hand, children who are socially disadvantaged at the outset find that school only reaffirms their second-class standing (Oakes, 1985; Kozol, 1991, 2005, 2007).

Social-conflict theory claims that schooling in the United States amounts to a system of social control. Our system of schooling socializes all students—regardless of race, class, and gender—to be docile, obedient workers and patriotic citizens. We might describe these messages as schooling's **hidden curriculum,** *explicit and subtle presentations of political or cultural ideas in the classroom that support the status quo.* Examples of these ideas include teaching students that social problems reflect the personal failings of individuals, that the existing economic and political systems are "right" or "natural," and that the United States is a better nation than any other. In short, rather than learning to think critically and creatively—especially about social justice—most students learn only to follow directions, to respect authority figures, and to fit into the system (Bowles & Gintis, 1976; Kozol, 1991; McLaren & Giarelli, 1995).

MAKING THE GRADE

Use the table below to review the three theoretical approaches to education.

APPLYING THEORY

Education

	What is the level of analysis?	What is the importance of schooling to society?	What are important educational problems?
Structural-functional approach	Macro-level	The structural-functional approach reveals that schooling helps our society operate by performing numerous functions, including transmitting knowledge and skills to young people, preparing them for the world of work according to their talents and interests, and uniting the population by teaching common values and beliefs. Schooling also performs many latent functions such as supervising young people during the day while parents are working.	Because of the importance of schooling to the operation of society, anything that threatens the effectiveness of our schools—including poor teaching, classroom violence, and students dropping out of school—is likely to be defined as a social problem.
Symbolic-interaction approach	Micro-level	The symbolic-interaction approach focuses on the meanings and understandings that people construct in their everyday social interactions. Using this approach, the experience of schooling is likely to be different in some ways for every individual. How a school labels a particular child—as, say, "gifted" or a "slow learner"—is likely to shape that child's experience of schooling.	How we label children can create problems. Because labels can become real to us and have real consequences, a school's decision to label a child in a certain way can create a self-fulfilling prophecy. Children may come to think of themselves in terms of the labels used by school officials and perform accordingly.
Social-conflict approach	Macro-level	The social-conflict approach links schooling to social inequality. Rather than showing how schooling helps the entire society operate, this approach highlights how schooling reflects existing divisions in society based on class, race, and gender and how it helps perpetuate this inequality by passing these differences from one generation to the next.	Educational problems include the inequality in funding that sets some schools well above others and also the system of tracking that often places young people from well-to-do families in the best classes and programs and those from disadvantaged families in the worst classes and programs.

CRITICAL REVIEW A strength of the social-conflict approach is that it shows the many ways in which schooling reflects and perpetuates social inequality. But this approach, too, has its critics. One issue is that a social-conflict approach overlooks how far our society has gone over the course of the last century in schooling its people and especially in sending so many to college. In addition, schooling has opened the door to upward social mobility for generations of people of all social backgrounds, including immigrants. Finally, although schools teach beliefs and values that support the status quo, the fact that schools mix people of different cultures and class positions suggests that schooling is also a force for change.

The Applying Theory table summarizes what we learn from each theoretical approach.

charter schools public schools that are given more freedom to try out new policies and programs

magnet schools public schools that offer special facilities and programs in pursuit of educational excellence

school voucher program a program that provides parents with funds they can use at a public school or private school of their choice

POLITICS AND EDUCATION

Constructing Problems and Defining Solutions

As we have found in earlier chapters, politics plays an important part in what people define as social problems and what policies they support as solutions. Here we examine conservative, liberal, and radical-left perspectives on the state of education in the United States.

Conservatives: Increase Competition

Schooling is one area in which conservatives do not support the status quo. On the contrary, they are outspoken in their criticism of public education in the United States. As they see it, the poor performance of many public schools has become a scandal, and they point to the failure of many big-city public school systems to graduate even half their students. Some school systems, of course, do better. But conservatives claim that throughout the United States, educational standards haven fallen.

The reason for the crisis, as conservatives see it, is that the government has monopoly control over the system of public education, and as a result, the nation's public schools do not have to compete for students. Schools receive tax money regardless of how schools perform, and parents living in districts with poor schools have few choices. This lack of competition has fostered rigid bureaucracy that prevents innovation and policies that discourage excellence, such as linking teachers' salary to seniority rather than how well they perform in the classroom (Thernstrom & Thernstrom, 2003).

No business operating as a monopoly feels competitive pressure to provide consumers with high value. Therefore, conservatives argue, we should expect this one-provider system to perform poorly. The solution to the problem of poor schools is to make schooling more competitive. If public schools had to compete for students, they would have to do a good job or go out of business.

Increased competition is the heart of the strategy of school choice. One policy designed to increase choice is the creation of **charter schools,** *public schools that are given more freedom to try out new policies and programs.* Charter schools are subject to less regulation than regular public schools as long as their students perform above the average. About 4,000 charter schools have been established in forty states, Washington, D.C., and Puerto Rico, and these schools enroll about 1.2 million students. Many of these schools have established records of high academic achievement (U.S. Department of Education, 2009).

Adopting a similar strategy, some districts have developed **magnet schools,** *public schools that offer special facilities and programs in pursuit of educational excellence.* There are now some 2,700 magnet schools in the United States offering special instruction in areas including the sciences and foreign languages. Magnet schools enroll only about 1 percent of public school students but have been able to improve learning for their students (U.S. Department of Education, 2009).

Conservatives also support increased competition by allowing private companies to engage in *schooling for profit.* Private schools are nothing new, of course: More than 35,000 private schools now operate in the United States. The point here is to let for-profit companies take over the operation of inefficient public schools, based on the claim that they can operate the school system more efficiently than government bureaucrats. A number of U.S. cities, including Baltimore, Miami, Hartford, and Boston, have experimented with for-profit schooling but decided to go back to conventional public school systems. More recently, when Philadelphia's school system failed to graduate one-third of its students, the state took over the school system and brought in private companies to run most of the schools, resulting in some improvements in learning. Emotions on both sides of the schooling-for-profit issue run high as everyone seeks to help those who are caught in a troubled system—the schoolchildren themselves (Sanchez, 2003; Garland, 2007; Richburg, 2008).

A final conservative policy is the **school voucher program,** *a program that provides parents with funds they can use at a public school or private school of their choice.* A voucher program says, in effect, "You are entitled to use your tax money to school your children wherever you want." Vouchers are especially popular among low-income families, who seek alternatives to the poor public schools in their neighborhoods. Many who have this option choose to send their children to parochial schools, which are run by a church (most are operated by the Roman Catholic Church), where there is greater discipline, less disruption, more learning, and fewer students dropping out. Many U.S. cities, including Cleveland, Indianapolis, Minneapolis, Milwaukee, Chicago, and Washington, D.C., have experimented with choice plans in recent years, and in 2002, the U.S. Supreme Court upheld Cleveland's voucher programs as lawful (Lord, 2002; Morse, 2002). The Personal Stories box on page 360 takes a closer look at one family's experiences with vouchers.

Conservatives support school choice and the certification or testing of teachers as means to force all schools, both public and private, to show greater *accountability.* In 2002, President Bush signed an education bill, popularly called "No Child Left Behind," that required the testing of all public school students in grades three through eight in language arts, mathematics,

GETTING INVOLVED

What two or three specific policy changes would you suggest to improve public education?

PERSONAL STORIES  "I Want a Better School for My Sons"

Every morning, Delvoland Shakespeare walks out of his house in Cleveland, Ohio, buckles his two sons into the back seat of his gray Ford, and drives them to a Catholic school called Our Lady of Peace. Shakespeare thinks the school is the best opportunity his sons have ever had. Eight-year-old Landel has learned to use a computer; five-year-old Isaiah is learning to read. After dropping off the boys, Shakespeare parks the car and watches his sons line up to enter the building. "Seeing them going to a good school," he says with a wide grin, "gives me the best feeling."

When Landel was ready to begin kindergarten, Shakespeare and his wife, Charlynn, decided to do some investigating. They knew that Cleveland's public schools, like other inner-city schools across the United States, have serious problems, including the failure to graduate more than half of their students. So they planned a visit to the public school in their neighborhood. On several corners around the school, they noticed drug dealers and prostitutes. Inside, they found the books to be in terrible shape—some without covers, many replaced by photocopies. Shakespeare's worst fears were confirmed when he entered the boys' restroom and a young man tried to sell him marijuana.

One visit was enough to convince the Shakespeares that they had to do whatever it took to find a better school for their children. They cut back on their spending, trying to save enough to afford a private school. But the cost of private schooling is high, and the tuition for two children was simply out of their reach. Then they heard about a new, experimental "choice" program: Low-income families could enter a lottery in the hope of winning a voucher worth $2,500 that could be used for tuition at a school of their choice. They signed up and were delighted when Landel won a school voucher. Three years later, when Isaiah was ready to start kindergarten, he also won a voucher.

Like most low-income families in the inner city, the Shakespeares are strong supporters of school choice, which they believe has greatly benefited their children. But not everyone agrees that a voucher program is a good idea. Some people object to giving tax dollars to religious schools on the grounds that doing so violates the constitutional separation of church and state. Others claim that voucher programs are drawing the best students from public schools, leaving the weakest students behind. Finally, some oppose vouchers simply because, as they see it, the real solution should be fixing public schools, not abandoning them.

WHAT DO YOU THINK?

1. Older students have long used government grants and loans to attend colleges and universities affiliated with religious organizations. Should younger students be able to use vouchers to attend parochial schools? Why or why not?
2. Do families such as the Shakespeares who apply for vouchers differ, on balance, from families who don't? How? Might a voucher system penalize children of less involved parents?
3. On balance, do you think a voucher program improves public schooling or not? Why?

Source: Based on Shlaes (1998).

and science; the law received wide support from conservatives. Schools in which students perform poorly are required to show improvement in coming years; if they do not, parents will get the option of moving their children to another school. At this point, "No Child Left Behind" has succeeded in identifying schools that are doing well and those that are not. In addition, there have been some increases in overall school performance. However, there has been little change in many of the worst-performing schools (Wallis & Steptoe, 2007).

Liberals: Increase the Investment

Liberals consider public schools a vital part of U.S. society. Schooling is a necessary task for all, and for this reason, the job should be the responsibility of government.

Although liberals concede that some schools are not doing their job very well, they view struggling schools as a symptom of broader social problems, including racial discrimination and economic inequality. Recall the great differences in school funding, for example: With some schools receiving much less than others, year after year, should we be surprised that some students are left behind? Furthermore, given the striking class differences in U.S. society, some students benefit from greater cultural capital at home, just as others have the odds stacked against them long before they reach their first year in school. In addition, as already noted, millions of young people face the challenge of speaking a first language other than English. Government-funded programs such as Head Start are designed to help the children who need it most.

Some liberals support the idea of school choice (particularly charter schools and magnet schools, because they are still *public* schools), but the liberal policy for improving schools is greater investment of tax money in *all* schools so that they can better meet the needs of all students. Polls reveal solid majori-

Looking ahead, do you expect to see changes in public schooling? Consider learning technology, funding, and student performance.

ties—not only among minorities but among whites as well—supporting the policy of poor minority children having the same educational resources as rich whites (Close, 2004).

At all levels of schooling, liberals voice strong support for bilingual programs, which conservatives oppose. Liberals claim that bilingual education not only allows students to progress in other subjects at the same time that they are learning English but also helps everyone recognize and value the full range of cultural diversity found in the United States (Ochoa, 1999; Portes, 2002).

Finally, liberals argue in favor of investing in outside-the-classroom programs, both during and after school, that help involve students more deeply with their school. An additional benefit of these programs involving music, science, or athletics is that they decrease the likelihood of problems such as drug use and violence (Hawkins, Farrington, & Catalano, 1998; Samples & Abner, 1998).

Liberals support expanding the national investment in education to fund all these strategies. They claim that it is far less costly to pay for good schools today than to pay the costs of dealing with the problems that result from poor schools—including crime, drug abuse, and functional illiteracy—later on.

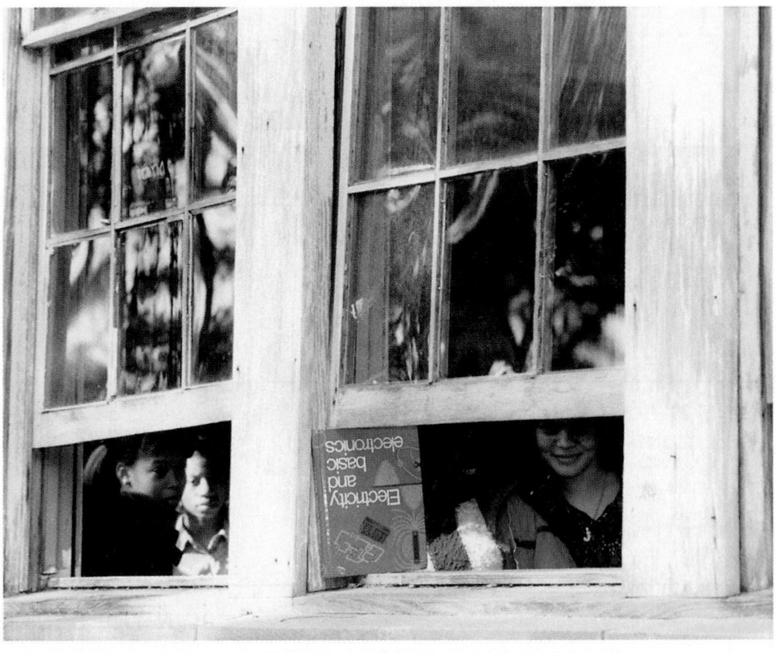

Most people agree that inner-city schools have problems. Conservatives blame the government monopoly and teachers' unions that resist competition. Liberals call for greater spending on schools and more equal funding from district to district. Radicals claim that as long as striking inequality exists in society, schools will serve some students and fail to teach others.

The Radical Left: Attack Structural Inequality

Radicals on the left argue that many social problems, including problems of our schools, arise from basic flaws in the economic and political structure of society. As long as wealth and power are highly concentrated, this nation can never provide good schooling to all. From a radical-left point of view, schools are not the cause of the problem; the capitalist economy is. But schools do make the problem worse by defining the cause of poor academic performance as a shortcoming of *individuals* rather than as the result of *structural inequality.*

Radicals on the left agree with liberals that public schools deserve more funding. At the very least, they argue, we need to eliminate the disparity of funding between wealthy schools and those in less affluent districts. A step in that direction is the action taken by the state of Vermont in 1998 to equalize funding to school districts statewide on an even per-student basis. By ensuring that all schools receive the same amount of funding per student, the Vermont program should increase educational equality.

Yet the Vermont program goes only so far. Even if schools were all exactly the same, some students would still have great advantages over others based on their social background. Radicals on the left conclude that the only way to make good education available to everyone is to eliminate the striking inequality found throughout society as a whole. This revolutionary idea would require basic changes to both the capitalist economy and the existing political system.

The Left to Right table on page 362 summarizes the conservative, liberal, and radical-left perspectives on the state of U.S. schools.

Going On from Here

Most people in the United States believe that schooling is the key that opens the door to economic opportunity: A high school diploma and a college degree (perhaps also a graduate degree) ensure both better jobs and higher income (NORC, 2007). For this reason, we like to say that our schools provide every student not only with basic learning but also with the chance to develop personal abilities and interests.

In recent decades, as the Information Revolution has raised the importance of literacy skills, schooling has become more

MAKING THE GRADE

Use the table below to review the three political approaches to education.

LEFT TO RIGHT

The Politics of Education

	RADICAL-LEFT VIEW	LIBERAL VIEW	CONSERVATIVE VIEW
WHAT IS THE PROBLEM?	Because schools operate within a social system marked by striking inequality of wealth and power, they fail much of the U.S. population and perpetuate class differences.	Although schools are educating more young people than ever before, they lack the funds and programs to meet the needs of some categories of the population.	Schools are a government monopoly that does not operate efficiently and is not accountable. Schools fail to educate a significant share of young people.
WHAT IS THE SOLUTION?	Equalize funding for all schools; ultimately, the solution lies in making radical changes in the economic and political systems to create a more egalitarian society.	Increase government funding for schools, especially in disadvantaged areas; expand Head Start and bilingual programs to improve schooling for minorities and low-income children.	Various strategies such as schooling for profit and the use of school vouchers will force public schools to become more competitive; all schools must be made accountable for their performance.

JOIN THE DEBATE

1. All political perspectives agree on one thing: Schools in the United States are not doing the job they should be doing. In light of this fact, why do you think there has been little change in schools over recent decades?
2. Using each of the three political perspectives, respond to the following assertion: "Schooling in the United States advances the goal of equal opportunity by providing a learning program that matches a student's abilities and interests."
3. Which of the three political analyses of U.S. schooling included here do you find most convincing? Why?

important than ever. Yet as this chapter has shown, U.S. public schools are plagued by shortcomings: Measures of student performance are not what they used to be, and almost 20 percent of young people (more than one-third in some large cities) drop out before finishing high school.

What are the prospects for change? People across the political spectrum agree that changes must be made. But there is far less agreement as to exactly what the problems and solutions are.

Conservatives focus on the school system itself. They argue that it will have to provide more choice and competition before student performance will improve.

Liberals focus on government action to increase school funding. Liberals offer strong support for the idea that government should run high-quality schools and the public should bear the cost. They counter that school choice policies are likely to help some students—especially those with involved parents—but will leave others students behind. Liberals also note that in decades to come, this country's schoolchildren will become ever more culturally diverse, highlighting the importance of bilingual and multicultural programs.

Radicals on the left are also likely to shape the future of schooling. Vermont has already enacted a bold and controversial program to ensure that all school systems receive equal per-student funding. So far, governments in other states have not enacted similar legislation. Will they in the years to come? Because the idea of equal funding challenges the long-established practice of local control of schools, change in this direction is likely to be slow and hotly contested. Yet given the extent of funding inequality noted in this chapter, public support for a more equal policy may well grow.

When it comes to schools in the United States, almost everyone is in favor of change. But precisely what changes are to come is a political decision that will be made as today's students take their places as adults.

DEFINING SOLUTIONS

What can we do to improve the state of public schools in our large cities?

As this chapter has explained, the public is split on whether our urban schools are doing their job. The fact that in many large cities about one-third of public school students never graduate from high school is certainly cause for concern. Look at the two photos below to see two approaches to solving this problem.

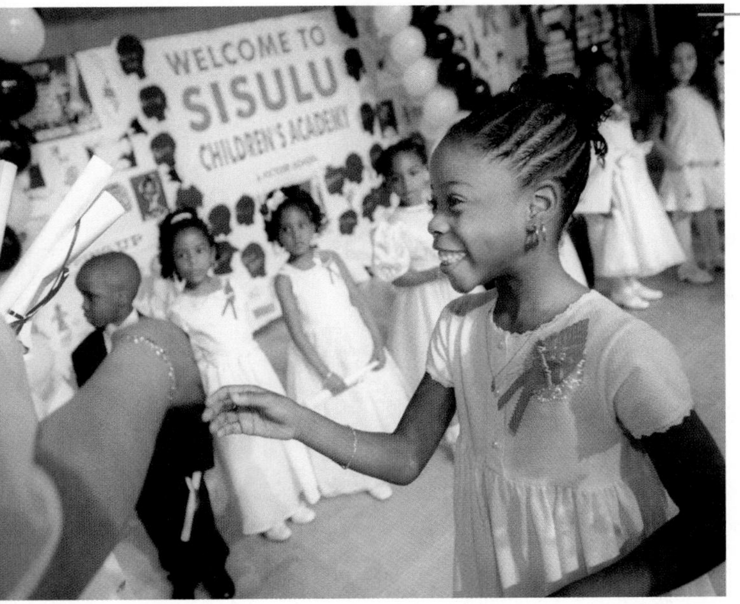

In general, liberals link poor performance to inadequate school funding. But an increasing number of liberals also see stifling bureaucracy as part of the problem and support the expansion of charter schools. Operating as public schools but not subject to the rigid rules and regulations of the larger public school system, charter schools are free to be creative in terms of organization, scheduling, and instruction. Because it is vital to liberals that excellence be created in public education, they see charter schools as one promising approach. How much do you support the concept of charter schools?

From a conservative point of view, the main reason that public schools do not function well is that they lack competition. In short, conservatives would like to see an educational marketplace, where parents and their children can choose the school that offers the greatest value. The policy that maximizes such choice is vouchers, which means that parents use public funds to pay for whatever school they wish, whether public or private. What do you see as strengths and weaknesses of a voucher system?

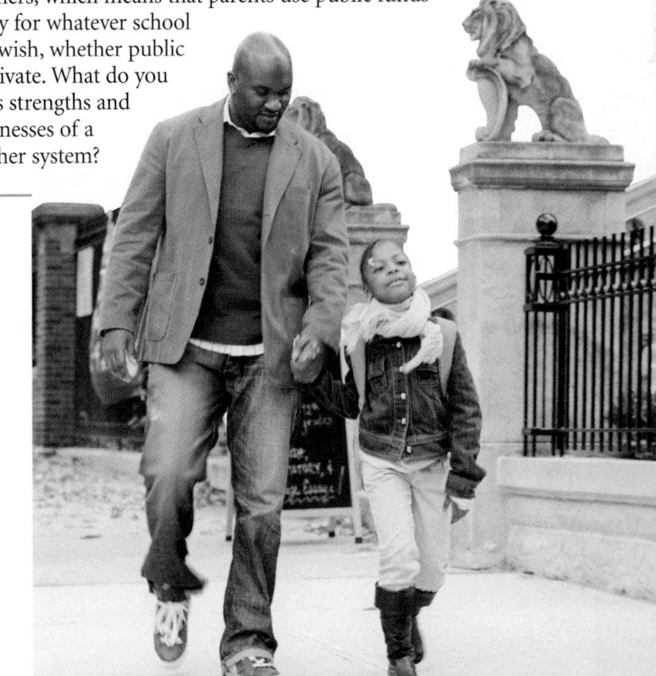

HINT

In the end, where you stand on the issue of our urban schools depends on how committed you are to the idea of public education. Vouchers, which would allow tax money to go to any school, public or private, would create the most choice but might well end up creating a bigger gap between the best and worst performing schools. For that reason, urban governments (almost all of which are overwhelmingly Democratic) have permitted only very limited voucher programs. Charter schools may represent a chance for political compromise, because they offer some choice while also preserving the idea of keeping tax money in public education. Radicals on the left would be unlikely to sign on, however, because they look for greater change—toward a system of equally funded public education.

Getting Involved: Applications & Exercises

1. Most communities offer programs that train volunteers to teach adults to read. To find one in your area, ask about literacy programs at a local school or library, or call a social services agency. See how you can help others learn to read.
2. Head Start is a government program that helps disadvantaged children succeed in school. Contact your county government and ask about volunteer opportunities with a Head Start program in your area.
3. Talk to your campus office that assists students with special needs. How does your campus deal with students with learning disabilities? What about access for people with physical disabilities?
4. On your campus or one nearby, you probably can find an education department with faculty who are preparing tomorrow's teachers. Arrange to visit several such faculty, and ask what they see as the prospects for U.S. public schools in the decade ahead.

MAKING THE GRADE

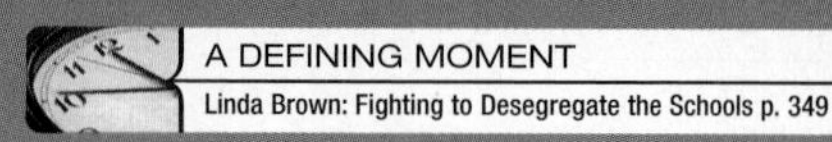

A DEFINING MOMENT

Linda Brown: Fighting to Desegregate the Schools p. 349

CHAPTER 13 Education

Problems of Education: A Global Perspective

- **EDUCATION** is the social institution by which a society transmits knowledge—including basic facts, job skills, and cultural norms and values—to its members.
- As societies industrialize, they require young people to attend schools, where students receive instruction by specially trained teachers.

pp. 342–44

- In high-income countries, most people complete secondary school, and a significant share complete college.
- In low-income countries, many young people, especially girls, receive little or no schooling; about one-fourth of adults in the world are illiterate.

pp. 342–44

education (p. 342) the social institution by which a society transmits knowledge—including basic facts and job skills, as well as cultural norms and values—to its members

schooling (p. 342) formal instruction carried out by specially trained teachers

EDUCATION IN U.S. HISTORY

- Only after the abolition of slavery did large numbers of African Americans attend school.
- With industrialization and the rise in immigration, all states passed mandatory education laws by 1918.
- As women moved into the labor force over the course of the twentieth century, they also joined men at colleges and universities.

pp. 344–45

Problems with U.S. Education

ACADEMIC PERFORMANCE

- Of all industrialized nations, the United States has the second highest percentage of adults (about 30%) with college degrees. But on tests of literacy and science skills, U.S. students lag behind their counterparts in many other high-income nations.
- Socially disadvantaged categories of students score lower than students from affluent families on standardized tests.

pp. 345–46

DROPPING OUT

- In 2008, 8.7% of young people (3 million) had dropped out before completing high school.
- African Americans (8.4%), Hispanics (21.4%), and Native Americans (14%) have higher dropout rates compared with whites (5.3%).
- Dropping out of school raises the risk of drug abuse, arrest, unemployment, and poverty as adults.

p. 347

FUNCTIONAL ILLITERACY

- Functional illiteracy is a serious problem in the United States, where about 15% of adults cannot read or write well enough to carry out their daily tasks.

pp. 347–48

literacy (p. 342) the ability to read and write

functional illiteracy (p. 348) the inability to read and write or do basic arithmetic well enough to carry out daily responsibilities

tracking (p. 352) the policy of assigning students to different educational programs

self-fulfilling prophecy (p. 352) a situation in which people who are defined in one way eventually think and act as if the definition were true

English immersion (p. 353) the policy of teaching non–English speakers in English

bilingual education (p. 353) the policy of offering most classes in students' native language while also teaching them English

mainstreaming (p. 354) integrating students with special needs into the overall educational program

special education (p. 355) schooling students with physical or mental disabilities in separate classes with specially trained teachers

SCHOOL SEGREGATION AND BUSING

- The concept of "separate but equal" schools was established by the Supreme Court in 1896 (*Plessy* v. *Ferguson*).
- In 1954, the Court reversed itself and declared laws that racially segregate schools to be unconstitutional (*Brown* v. *Board of Education of Topeka*).
- When busing was used to integrate schools, "white flight" took many white families to the suburbs. As a result, public schools today remain about as racially segregated as they were in the 1960s.

pp. 348–50

SCHOOL FUNDING

- Because U.S. public schools are funded by state and local taxes, the richest school districts spend several times more as much per student as the poorest school districts.
- In addition to attending better schools, children from affluent families also benefit from greater *cultural capital*: experiences and opportunities at home that enhance learning.

pp. 350–52

TRACKING

- Tracking is a school policy that assigns children to various academic programs.
- Supporters claim that tracking provides students with schooling consistent with their interests and abilities.
- Critics claim that tracking assignments often are made according to social background, so that affluent students benefit and disadvantaged students are harmed.

p. 352

GENDER INEQUALITY

- Today, a majority (57%) of college students are women.
- However, gender still operates as a form of tracking that guides women and men into different majors.

pp. 352–53

IMMIGRATION AND CULTURAL DIVERSITY

- Cultural diversity is another challenge to U.S. schools. A debate centers on whether it is better to place non–English speakers in English immersion courses or to use a policy of bilingual education.

pp. 353–54

STUDENTS WITH DISABILITIES

- Some 7 million people with disabilities are enrolled in U.S. schools. Whether it is better to mainstream these students or to provide them with separate specialized programs is an ongoing issue.

pp. 354–55

SCHOOL VIOLENCE

- Violent crime is a serious problem in U.S. schools. In response, most schools have adopted a zero-tolerance policy toward both violence and bringing weapons and drugs to school.

pp. 355–56

Theoretical Analysis: Understanding Educational Problems

Structural-Functional Analysis: The Functions of Schooling

The **STRUCTURAL-FUNCTIONAL APPROACH** highlights the importance of schools to the operation of society as a whole.

- Schooling prepares young people for the workforce and serves as a means of upward social mobility as students gain the knowledge and skills to perform jobs.
- Schooling teaches the dominant cultural values of a society.
- A latent function of schooling is providing child care for working parents.

pp. 356–57

Symbolic-Interaction Analysis: Labels in the Schools

The **SYMBOLIC-INTERACTION APPROACH** focuses on how the interaction of students and school personnel constructs reality, including how students come to see themselves.

- Schools' labeling of students as gifted or deficient can be a **SELF-FULFILLING PROPHECY** with important consequences for what students expect of themselves.

p. 357

Social-Conflict Analysis: Schooling and Inequality

The **SOCIAL-CONFLICT APPROACH** highlights the links between schooling and social inequality.

- Unequal funding from school to school and tracking within any single school perpetuate class differences from one generation to the next.
- Schooling's **HIDDEN CURRICULUM** socializes students to respect authority and not to challenge the status quo.

pp. 357–58

hidden curriculum (p. 357) explicit and subtle presentations of political or cultural ideas in the classroom that support the status quo

See the **Applying Theory** table on page 358.

Politics and Education: Constructing Problems and Defining Solutions

The Radical Left: Attack Structural Inequality

- **RADICALS ON THE LEFT** argue that the shortcomings of U.S. schools are symptoms of the structural inequalities of U.S. society.
- Radicals on the left call for equalizing student funding in all schools. Ultimately, the radical goal is to bring about basic change in the direction of economic and political equality in the United States.

p. 361

Liberals: Increase Special Programs

- **LIBERALS** believe that the problems of schools are rooted in the larger society.
- Liberals support greater investment in schools, especially in programs such as Head Start and bilingual education to enhance the cultural capital of disadvantaged students.

pp. 360–61

Conservatives: Increase Competition

- **CONSERVATIVES** criticize U.S. public schools as inefficient and not accountable to the people they are supposed to serve.
- Conservatives propose making education competitive by giving parents choices about where to send their children through the use of charter schools, magnet schools, for-profit schools, and voucher programs.

pp. 359–60

charter schools (p. 359) public schools that are given more freedom to try out new policies and programs

magnet schools (p. 359) public schools that offer special facilities and programs in pursuit of educational excellence

school voucher program (p. 359) a program that provides parents with funds they can use at a public school or private school of their choice

See the **Left to Right** table on page 362.

CONSTRUCTING THE PROBLEM

What is urban sprawl?

Urban sprawl is the rapid outward growth of cities. Atlanta, among our fastest-growing urban areas, has been gobbling up 500 acres of open ground each week.

Don't cities have plenty of jobs?

Yes, but in the inner-city neighborhoods of many large U.S. cities, a majority of adults can find no work in their local communities.

How big a problem is homelessness in the United States?

More than 3 million people are homeless for at least some time during the course of a year.

CHAPTER 14

Urban Life

CHAPTER OVERVIEW

CAN YOU IMAGINE the United States without its great cities? This chapter explores urban life, explaining how cities developed over our nation's history. You will learn about many urban issues, including cities in financial crisis, urban areas sprawling outward, substandard housing, racial segregation, and homelessness. You will carry out theoretical analysis of urban issues and learn how "problems" and "solutions" involving cities reflect people's political attitudes.

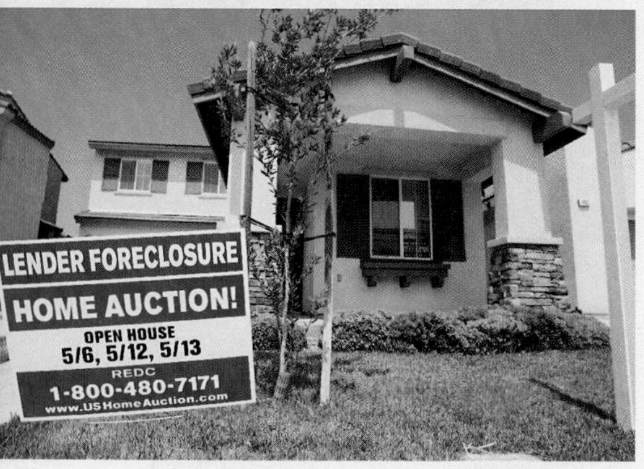

Mary Saccacio walked slowly into the living room carrying the envelope in her right hand, her morning coffee in her left. Her husband, Vernon, looked up from the couch where he had been watching the news on television. "Here's the letter from the bank." Mary spoke softly, a tremor in her voice.

When Mary and Vernon bought their modest house in southern Florida, they knew it was a stretch. But at first, the monthly mortgage payments were low enough for the two retired teachers to afford. With housing prices in Florida going up so rapidly each year, they thought they would end up way ahead.

But then the housing bubble popped. They were soon "underwater," meaning that the value of their home was now much less than what they paid for it. To make matters worse—much worse—the mortgage agreement they signed jumped to a higher rate after thirty-six months. This raised the payment to more than they could afford. Now that they have fallen several months behind in their payments, the bank has written to announce the start of foreclosure proceedings.

As Mary read the letter, Vernon looked down at the floor. There was to be a court hearing. If they could not come up with the money they owe the bank or negotiate some settlement, they would be evicted. The house would then be sold to the highest bidder at a sheriff's sale (Saporito, 2008; El Boghdady & Cohen, 2009; Von Drehle, 2009).

As the economic recession intensified in 2008 and 2009, a housing crisis spread across the United States. As many as 6 million homes may be lost to foreclosure by 2012. National Map 14–1 shows the rate of foreclosure filings in recent years.

The loss of homes and the disappearance of jobs are clear evidence that all is not well in the cities of the United States. U.S. cities are home to beautiful architecture, brightly lit shopping districts, and universities, museums, and other cultural centers. But cities also are centers of much of this country's poverty, inadequate housing, homelessness, and crime.

The United States is a nation of cities; 80 percent of our population lives in an urban area (U.S. Census Bureau, 2010). This means that many of the problems we face as a society are problems of cities and urban life. This chapter examines cities in the United States and offers a brief look at the state of cities around the world. To understand the state of our cities today, we begin with a brief look at how cities have grown and changed during our history.

Cities: Then and Now

It is not easy to imagine this country without great cities such as New York, Atlanta, Chicago, or Los Angeles. Four centuries ago—before we became the United States—this continent was home to several million native people who made few permanent settlements. From coast to coast, there was not one tall structure or a single paved road.

Colonial Villages: 1565–1800

The first cities were created by Europeans who colonized what they called the "New World." The Spanish settled Saint Augustine, Florida, in 1565. In 1607, the English founded Jamestown, Virginia. In 1624, the Dutch founded New Amsterdam—later renamed New York—at the southern tip of Manhattan Island. In 1630, the English settled Boston.

These settlements began as tiny villages, with narrow streets, small houses, and just a few hundred residents. They

SOCIAL PROBLEMS in Everyday Life

How many people do you know who are concerned about holding on to their homes as a result of the recent recession?

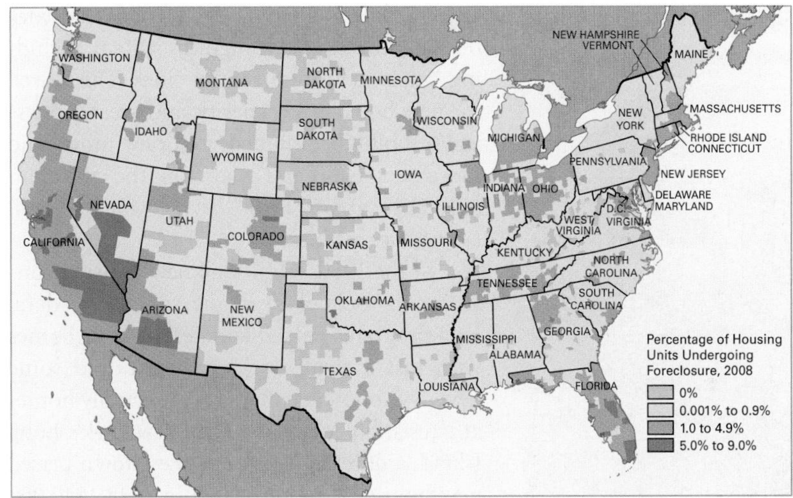

Seeing Ourselves

NATIONAL MAP 14–1

Foreclosures across the United States, 2008

The recession beginning in 2008 resulted in millions of people struggling to make payments on their home loans. For many unable to pay, foreclosure was the result. The map shows the rate of housing foreclosure for counties across the United States. What pattern do you see?

Source: RealtyTrac (2009).

were all the shelter there was for a few settlers in a new and unfamiliar world. People living in these settlements worked hard, and most managed to survive.

By the time the United States declared independence in 1776, about 5 percent of the population lived in cities. The largest city in the new nation was Philadelphia, with 42,000 people—a far cry from the roughly 6 million in the Philadelphia metropolitan area today.

Westward Expansion: 1800–1860

After 1800, people began pushing westward, following new transportation routes, including the National Road (1818), the Baltimore & Ohio Railroad (1825), and the Erie Canal (1825). Along these routes, migrants settled what became the great cities of the Midwest, including Buffalo, Cleveland, Detroit, and Chicago. During this time, *urbanization,* the movement of people from the countryside to the cities, steadily increased. By the time of the Civil War in 1860, some 20 percent of the nation's people were urbanites.

The Industrial Metropolis: 1860–1950

The outbreak of the Civil War gave rise to many new factories to build weapons, which drew even more people from rural counties to the cities. In addition, about a million immigrants, mostly from Europe, were entering the United States each year, and almost all of them settled in cities. This mix of factories and surging population created the industrial *metropolis* (from Greek words meaning "mother city"). By 1900, Chicago boasted 2 million residents, and New York City had 4 million people, more than the entire colonial population in 1790.

Cities grew not just in number of people but also outward and upward. New train and trolley routes allowed city boundaries to move into the surrounding countryside. Steel beams replaced bricks and wood and ushered in the age of skyscrapers—tall buildings with elevators to move people up and down. By 1930, New York had expanded well beyond Manhattan Island and had a striking skyline, with the Empire State Building towering 102 stories above the streets.

Social Problems in Cities

Cities were changing, and not all for the better. By 1900, most people in the United States were coming to think of cities as a source of social problems. One reason for the bad image was a flood of immigrants. At that time, two-thirds of the people living in the ten largest cities had been born abroad or were the children of immigrants (Glaab, 1963). This cultural diversity fueled ethnic prejudice, which became an antiurban bias. Especially among the majority of people who had lived for generations in rural communities, "city folk" were not considered "real Americans."

Most city residents were well aware of this prejudice. But their immediate problems centered on needs such as housing. In 1900, more than one-third of New Yorkers lived in *tenements,* buildings full of small apartments with few windows and shared bathrooms. Tenements were the home to most recent immigrants, who were very poor.

To make matters worse, in industrial cities, the air was fouled by factory smoke, and sewage flowed freely into the streets, eventually reaching the same rivers and lakes used for drinking water. Children ran around dirty and unsupervised, epidemics raged in poor neighborhoods, and violent crime was

MAKING THE GRADE

The image below shows how the mass media in the mid-nineteenth century constructed "urbanism" as a "problem."

suburbs urban areas beyond the political boundaries of cities

City life was widely defined as a social problem by rural people in the nineteenth century. This drawing, depicting city streets as chaotic and dangerous, appeared in several rural newspapers in 1858.

rampant. The greatest suffering was experienced by the thousands of people—including children—who had no place to live at all except under a bridge or a stairway.

In these industrial cities, there were plenty of jobs, but most demanded hard labor for ten or more hours a day for very low wages. Things got even worse with the onset of the Great Depression in 1929; at its worst point, one-fourth of all U.S. workers were thrown out of work and lost all their income. Homelessness, breadlines, and begging on the streets were widespread. Not until the start of World War II (1939–1945) did the United States rise out of the depression. By the end of the war, a new era of prosperity was about to begin. But as you will see, these "good times" were a mixed blessing for cities.

Postindustrial Cities and Suburbs: 1950–Present

The industrial metropolis reached its peak population by the end of the 1940s. After World War II ended in 1945, soldiers returned home, and many couples wasted little time before they began having children. This pattern was to change the face of our cities.

The postwar baby boom sent the U.S. birth rate soaring and pushed many families to look for new housing. Economic prosperity allowed many households to own at least one car, and the federal government was hard at work building the interstate highway system, including beltways around central cities. The search for new housing, prosperity, and greater physical mobility combined to draw more and more people out and away from the cities into **suburbs,** *urban areas beyond the political boundaries of cities.*

In the 1950s, almost all new housing construction took place in the suburbs. Federal loan programs helped families buy new homes with just a small down payment, and some new developments offered single-family homes at irresistibly low prices. On New York's Long Island, a development called Levittown priced new houses at about $8,000 in 1948 ($40,000 in today's dollars). Many people made fun of Levittown's small (720 square feet), identical "cookie-cutter" houses. But Abraham Levitt quickly sold all 17,447 of his houses in the first Levittown and then went on to build two more large developments in suburban Philadelphia (Wattel, 1958). Across the country, developers had little trouble selling new homes to families eager to own their own piece of leafy suburban real estate.

In the 1960s and 1970s, suburbs grew even more as a result of economic change. The great metropolis was the result of industrial production that had centralized the population in cities where factories and transportation links were located. But the postindustrial economy that emerged after the 1960s, marked by service work and computer technology, changed all that because work was now mostly in office buildings, most of which were not downtown but out in the suburbs. In other words, the postindustrial economy *decentralized* the population. By 1970, most of the "urban" population of the United States lived not in central cities but in suburbs; by 2000, a majority of the *entire* country's population were suburbanites (U.S. Census Bureau, 2010).

Problems of Today's Cities

The population shift away from central cities toward the suburbs created a number of urban problems, including bankruptcy, sprawl, and high rates of inner-city poverty.

Fiscal Problems

Is it possible for a city to go broke? A number of U.S. cities flirted with bankruptcy in the 1970s. One was New York—the

SOCIAL PROBLEMS in Everyday Life

Have you ever thought about urban sprawl as a social problem? Why or why not?

megalopolis a vast urban region containing a number of cities and their surrounding suburbs

country's largest city, with a population exceeding 8 million. The trouble was that New York stood at the center of an urban region that was expanding outward as people steadily crossed the city limits to live in outlying suburbs. Between 1970 and 1980, New York actually lost 860,000 in population, which is more than the entire city of Boston. The movement of industry from downtown factory districts to suburban industrial parks cost the city not only lots of residents but jobs as well. Corporate mergers and downsizing further reduced the demand for both industrial and office workers. By 1980, New York had lost more than half a million jobs.

Urban sprawl is sure to remain a matter of controversy for decades to come. Should we define a suburban development like this one in Las Vegas as a problem, or is it a solution for people who seek affordable housing in a residential area? Explain your position.

These trends set the stage for a fiscal crisis. Fewer people and fewer businesses in the city meant a smaller tax base. To make matters worse, those who moved from the city were, on average, richer and better educated than those who remained behind, who were more likely to be poor and unemployed, including many who relied on social service programs. By the mid-1970s, the costs of social service programs as well as the rising payroll for city employees was simply too much for New York to handle, and the city stood on the brink of bankruptcy. The picture was much the same in many other cities in the industrial regions of the Northeast and Midwest (Johnson & Lueck, 1996; U.S. Census Bureau, 2011).

The Postindustrial Revival

New York and other industrial metropolises such as Cleveland and Detroit did not collapse. New sources of financing, revised union contracts, and reductions in welfare payments helped them carry on.

But the biggest boost to the old industrial cities turned out to be adapting to the new postindustrial economy. Many jobs were lost when older, industrial factories closed their doors. But new types of work have added millions of new jobs, especially in the service sector, including entertainment, sales, financial services, law, consulting, publishing, and computer-based businesses. New York's midtown and downtown are now not industrial regions but postindustrial business centers.

A second factor that has helped cities recover is rising immigration. After 1980, New York once again began gaining population as immigrants, many from Latin America and Asia, arrived in search of the same economic opportunities that drew people from Europe a century before. Most of these immigrants hold service jobs in restaurants, hotels, and hospitals, working long hours for low wages and adding billions of dollars to U.S. economic output (Martin & Midgley, 2003).

The last several years have been difficult for most major cities as the economic recession has cut jobs, devalued property, and brought down tax revenues. In addition, both factory and office jobs continue to move overseas, where costs are lower. The economy will eventually recover. But many cities—such as Detroit, with an unemployment rate of 22 percent and which has lost most of the industrial jobs it had a decade ago—are unlikely to ever be the same (Sullivan, 2009).

Urban Sprawl

Because inner cities have had a tough time does not mean that the larger urban regions have not continued to expand. Beginning in the 1950s, as cities began to spread outward, vast urban regions were taking shape. The French geographer Jean Gottman (1961) coined the term **megalopolis** to refer to *a vast urban region containing a number of cities and their surrounding suburbs.*

Flying south from Boston on a clear night, you can look down on an unbroken carpet of lights all the way through New England down to northern Virginia, some 700 miles away. The same supercity pattern extends from Cleveland westward to Chicago, along the entire east coast of Florida, and up and down most of the nation's West Coast.

urban sprawl unplanned, low-density development at the edge of expanding urban areas

SOCIAL PROBLEMS in Everyday Life

Do you think the suburban living that causes urban sprawl is a problem or a solution? Why?

This pattern is the result of people moving from central cities to suburbs and also the increasing share of jobs being found in outlying office parks. Urban expansion has also resulted from several specific government policies. One is the interstate highway system, built by the federal government after World War II. These new highways, coupled with economic prosperity and the increasing popularity of automobiles, created booming growth in outer suburbs served by urban "outerbelts." With the government offering low-cost housing loans as well, millions of people were quick to leave central cities for the expanding suburbs.

This decentralization of the urban population has led to **urban sprawl,** *unplanned, low-density development at the edge of expanding urban areas.* Urban sprawl is a mixed pattern of new construction, including roads, homes, schools, and shopping areas.

There is no doubt that many people are eager to buy into these developments. But most analysts consider urban sprawl a serious problem. Why? One reason is the numbing sameness of much of this cityscape (Kunstler, 1996). Across North America, mass-produced housing developments and strip malls have no regional distinctiveness and often provide little that is pleasing to the eye. Driving through the urban sprawl around Atlanta, for example, you will see many of the same housing styles and stores that you would see outside of Columbus, Ohio; Portland, Oregon; Denver, Colorado; or any other large city.

A more serious problem is that sprawling urban developments have low densities (relatively few residents per acre) so that they consume land at a dizzying rate. The population of the New York metropolitan area increased by 5 percent between 1980 and 2008. But in the same twenty years, the people in this area were living on 60 percent more land. Atlanta, among the fasting-growing urban areas in the United States, is about 150 square miles, more than twice its size just twenty years ago. The Atlanta sprawl gobbles up 500 acres of fields and farmland every week. Phoenix now covers 600 square miles and is larger than the state of Delaware.

Although the rate of sprawl has slowed with the economic downturn, over the next fifty years, California is expected to lose 3.5 million acres of its Great Central Valley, its agricultural heartland, to development. Nationwide, the building of housing developments, malls, parking lots, golf courses, and highways is likely to continue to consume as much as 1 million acres of open land annually (Cheslow, 2006; Davis, 2009).

Another problem with urban sprawl is that the only way to get around these vast urban regions is by automobile, and commuting is slow and expensive. Most suburban households need several cars and spend a lot of their income on cars, insurance, and gasoline. In addition, today's suburbanites spend a great deal of their time on the road. The typical worker in the Los Angeles metropolitan area drives 21 miles round-trip to the job; in the Dallas area, 30 miles; and in Atlanta, 37 miles (Florian, 1999:25). Because much of this driving is in stop-and-go traffic, travel time to and from work often exceeds one or even two hours a day. The full consequences of sprawl, then, include the high costs of commuting, loss of personal time, stress from dealing with traffic congestion, and increased air pollution.

Finally, from a rural family's point of view, sprawl threatens this country's farmland. According to the American Farmland Trust (2009), 85 percent of the fruits and vegetables produced in this country are grown near urban areas. This puts vital farm production right in the path of urban sprawl.

Many people say the answer to the many problems associated with sprawl lies in more and bigger highways to help people move farther and faster. But is that likely to solve the problem or to make it worse? The more roads we build, the more we encourage people to rely on their cars, and the more our urban areas are likely to expand outward.

Edge Cities

The movement of businesses away from the central city has created *edge cities,* business centers some distance from the old downtowns. Unlike suburbs, which are made up mostly of homes, edge cities are mostly commercial developments, including corporate office buildings, shopping malls, hotels, and entertainment complexes. In suburbs, the population peaks at night; in edge cities, the population is greatest during the working day.

Most major urban areas in the United States now contain one or more edge cities. Examples include Tyson's Corner (in Virginia, near Washington, D.C.), King of Prussia (northwest of Philadelphia), and Las Colinas (near the Dallas–Fort Worth airport). Many edge cities do not have clear boundaries, and in some cases they even lack names and are known by the major highways that flow through them. Examples include Route 1 near Princeton, New Jersey, and Route 128 near Boston (Davis, 2009; Macionis & Parrillo, 2010).

Poverty

The high costs of suburban, automobile-based living keeps out most of the poor. With urban decentralization, richer people move away from the central cities, leaving the poor behind. As more jobs relocate to outlying areas, economic opportunities for inner-city residents decrease. This is one reason that the highest concentrations of poverty are found in central cities.

After the 1950s, businesses in downtown Camden, New Jersey, began to move out to the suburbs. Some people—particularly those who were younger, more educated, and bet-

MAKING THE GRADE

Poverty rates are higher in central cities than in suburbs or in rural areas. Overall, however, urban areas have a lower poverty rate than rural areas.

SOCIAL PROBLEMS in Everyday Life

Some people say poverty is more visible in cities than in rural ares. Do you agree? Why or why not?

SOCIAL POLICY

When Work Disappears: Can We Rescue the Inner City?

William Julius Wilson, one of the nation's most influential social scientists, points out that most of the problems of the inner city can be traced to one major factor: a lack of jobs. Over recent decades, as jobs have disappeared from the inner city, few of our national political leaders have paid much attention. In 1996, when Congress enacted welfare reform intended to move poor people from welfare to work, little was said about where people were to find jobs.

In 1950, when industrial cities were at their peak populations, Wilson explains, most adults in the African American community of Washington Park in Chicago were working and supporting their families. By the 1990s, however, two-thirds were unemployed, a pattern Wilson found was true of poor, inner-city communities from New York to Los Angeles. One elderly woman, who moved to Washington Park in 1953, explains:

> When I moved in, the neighborhood was intact. It was intact with homes, beautiful homes, mini-mansions, with stores, Laundromats, with Chinese cleaners. We had drugstores. We had hotels. We had doctors over on 39th Street. . . . We had the middle class and the upper middle class. It has gone from affluent to where it is today. (1996b:28)

Why has this neighborhood declined? Based on eight years of research in the area, Wilson points to a stark reality: There is almost no work to be found. The loss of jobs pushed residents into desperate poverty, weakened families, and forced people to turn to welfare. In Woodlawn, another Chicago community near Washington Park, more than 800 businesses operated in 1950; today, there are just 100. A number of big employers, including Western Electric and International Harvester, closed their plants in the late 1960s. The inner cities collapsed as companies closed, downsized, moved to the suburbs, or relocated factories abroad.

Wilson believes we can rescue the inner cities by creating jobs. But how? As a first step, the government can hire people to do all kinds of needed work, starting with clearing slums and building low-income housing. This strategy, modeled on the Works Progress Administration (WPA) enacted in 1935 during the Great Depression, can move people from welfare to work and, in the process, create much-needed hope.

A second step is to improve city schools. Doing this will require raising the necessary financing, attracting good teachers, and expecting students to meet challenging academic standards and learn the language and computer skills needed to succeed in today's postindustrial economy.

A third step involves improved regional public transportation. Workers without cars need train and subway links to get to job sites in suburban areas.

Finally, workers need affordable child care programs. Child care must be made available to help parents meet the responsibilities of parenting while also holding down a job.

Why have these steps not been taken already? Wilson explains that many people incorrectly think cities already have plenty of jobs, and therefore they conclude that poor people simply don't want to work. Another concern is that Wilson's proposals, at least in the short term, are more expensive than continuing to funnel welfare assistance to jobless communities.

In the long run, however, what are the costs of letting parts of our cities decay? Can we afford to let generation after generation of our children grow up in hopeless and often violent surroundings where they join the ranks of the restless and often angry people who have no work?

WHAT DO YOU THINK?

1. Do you support Wilson's proposals for change? Why or why not?
2. Do you expect that conditions in cities such as Chicago and Detroit will change under the Obama administration? If so, how?
3. If the United States is willing to spend hundreds of billion of dollars bailing out big financial companies, should we also spend the money it takes to bail out our cities? Explain your position.

Source: W. J. Wilson (1996a, 1996b).

ter off financially—followed the flow away from the central city. Camden saw its population fall from 125,000 in 1950 to about 79,000 today. More than one-third of the remaining families are poor (U.S. Census Bureau, 2011). The future is bleak for Camden's children, who are half the city's population, as once busy streets stand empty and thousands of houses have been boarded up or torn down.

Camden is not alone in facing these problems. Across the United States, every large city contains such neighborhoods. Typically, the residents of these so-called ghetto communities are African Americans, Latinos, or other disadvantaged minorities. Many of these communities were once thriving industrial areas, with many retail stores, professional offices, and middle-class as well as working-class residents. Today, many inner-city communities contain only the poor, who live cut off from economic opportunity, as the Social Policy box explains.

In 2009, the poverty rate for central cities in the United States stood at 18.7 percent. In the suburbs, the rate was 11.0 percent.

GETTING INVOLVED

Have you ever taken a stand on a housing issue? If so, explain what you did and why you did it.

public housing high-density apartment buildings constructed to house poor people

For the urban region as a whole, the poverty rate was 13.9 percent. The poverty rate was even higher—16.6 percent—in rural areas, which have even fewer jobs (U.S. Census Bureau, 2010). Although cities do contain high concentrations of poverty, urban areas generally provide more economic opportunity than rural areas do.

Housing Problems

Like work, housing is a basic human need. Because our society defines housing as a product to be bought and sold, a family's income determines its housing. The economic inequality of U.S. society creates enormous disparities in the quality of housing.

Tenement Housing

Most people today can only imagine the housing problems in the early industrial metropolis. In the final decades of the nineteenth century, developers built tenements to house the greatest number of families in the smallest amount of space. Not only were tenement apartments very small, but most had few windows and little ventilation. As many as six families shared a single bathroom. Insulation was poor, and in the winter, there was not much heat.

Most tenement residents were far from comfortable. But some were much worse off. The historian James D. McCabe describes the conditions in the cellars of the tenement buildings:

> If the people [in the tenements] suffered, at least they lived upon the surface of the earth. But what shall we say about those who pass their lives in the cellars of these wretched buildings?
>
> Most have but one entrance and that furnishes the only means of ventilation . . . [and] the filth of the streets comes washing down the walls of the rooms within. The air is always foul. The drains of the houses above pass within a few feet of the floor, and as they are generally in bad condition, the filth frequently comes oozing up and poisons the air with foul odors. . . . The poor wretches who seek shelter here are half stupefied by it. (1970, orig. 1872: 405, 406, 409)

Because most of the 1 million immigrants entering the United States each year were poor, the public accepted the tenements as a necessary evil. But some people had the courage to speak out against the horror. The leading opponent of tenement housing a century ago was Jacob Riis, who managed single-handedly to sway public opinion. The Defining Moment box tells his story.

As millions of people lived out their lives in tenements and cellar rooms, the elite few who owned the industries and controlled the financial life of our nation enjoyed lives of luxury. These families, with names most people still recognize today—including Vanderbilt (railroads), Morgan (finance), and Rockefeller (oil) in New York, Ford (automobiles) in Detroit, and Armour and Swift (meatpacking) in Chicago—lived in spacious mansions staffed by dozens of servants.

This pattern of mansions for the few and inadequate housing for the many continued for decades even as public opposition to tenements grew. Not until the 1930s did housing quality begin to improve. As part of President Franklin Roosevelt's New Deal, the federal government raised taxes to fund the construction of new housing and began to provide loans to help people buy homes. In addition, cities across the United States enacted housing codes with the goal of eliminating the worst conditions of the tenements. Despite these efforts, in 1940 the government reported that 40 percent of houses in urban areas had some serious defect, such as inadequate plumbing or a lack of running water.

Urban Renewal

After World War II, as people migrated from the older neighborhoods in central cities out to the new suburbs, many central-city neighborhoods fell into disrepair. In response, the federal government passed the Urban Housing Act of 1949, which marked the beginning of *urban renewal.* Urban renewal gave local city governments the right to seize a decaying neighborhood, forcing out the families who lived there with only nominal compensation for their homes. The city then sold the properties to a developer, who tore down the remaining houses and rebuilt the area. Because developers were interested in profits, they built not low-income housing but town houses and apartments for people with more money. Rarely was the housing produced by urban renewal within reach of the people who had lived there before. As this policy went into effect in cities across the United States, many so-called slum areas were rebuilt to look nice and attract some higher-income people back to the city. But urban renewal failed to provide housing for those who needed it the most. In practice, urban renewal has operated as a form of "urban cleansing," pushing out poor people without providing housing alternatives. Many of the poor who were evicted by urban renewal crowded into the remaining low-cost housing, creating more slums in the process (Macionis & Parrillo, 2010).

Public Housing

With urban renewal clearing away block after block, city officials gradually realized that many of the poor people displaced from their homes had nowhere to go. The need to house these people led to the creation of **public housing**, *high-density apartment buildings constructed to house poor people.*

MAKING THE GRADE

The photojournalist Jacob Riis helped to define tenement housing as a serious problem.

CONSTRUCTING SOCIAL PROBLEMS

A DEFINING MOMENT

Jacob Riis: Revealing the Misery of the Tenements

In 1870, a young man of twenty-one set sail from his native Denmark for the United States, hoping to find a better life. Jacob Riis (1849–1914), who shared the dreams of millions of other men and women, settled in the Richmond Hill district of New York City, a neighborhood almost entirely populated by immigrants living in tenements.

Riis made his career as one of the earliest photojournalists. On countless evenings, Riis walked around the poorest neighborhoods of New York collecting stories, which became the basis for his writing, and photographing scenes of urban life. He used his essays and especially his photos to call public attention to the suffering of families in New York's tenements and other slum housing. To people who never ventured into these areas, the photographs were eye-opening, shocking, even revolting.

Riis gave hundred of public lectures and wrote many books featuring thousands of photographs, many of which are still widely viewed today. His lifetime of effort made a difference in defining tenement housing as a serious problem of urban life.

Baxter Street Court, circa 1889. Courtesy of the Museum of the City of New York/The Jacob A. Riis Collection.

Jacob A. Riis, *In Poverty Gap: An English Coal-Heaver's Home.* Courtesy of the Museum of the City of New York.

MAKING THE GRADE

During the 1970s, our society began moving away from high-rise public housing projects. Do you understand why?

GETTING INVOLVED

Have you ever lived in a high-rise dorm or apartment? What type of social climate does this architecture encourage? Did your experience agree with Newman's findings?

High-rise "superblocks" can be hazardous to your health. This claim became widespread by the 1970s, leading many cities to dynamite huge public housing projects. This demolition took place in 2001 in New Brunswick, New Jersey. What were some of the reasons cities took such drastic action?

From the outset, public housing was met with criticism from just about everybody. Liberals viewed it as a Band-Aid approach to the problem of a lack of affordable housing. As they saw it, much public housing was worse than the neighborhoods that had been knocked down by the urban renewal bulldozers. Conservatives objected to government getting into the housing business in the first place, claiming that government-run housing would be no better than government-run schools. But perhaps the most vocal critics of public housing were poor people themselves. For one thing, given how important owning a home is to our society's definition of success, few people are proud to live in a government-owned apartment, and many said they were stigmatized by living in "the projects." For another, public housing was simply bad housing. Public housing projects in almost every major city were badly constructed, rundown, and plagued with illegal drug use, crime, and violence.

A final concern, especially among architects and city planners, was the physical design of public housing. At the outset, because city officials wanted to house poor people in as little space as possible, they favored building high-rise towers. Soon, however, crime in these high-rise structures became rampant. Was there something about this type of design that encouraged crime?

In 1972, Oscar Newman provided an answer. In a study of New York public housing projects, Newman compared buildings that housed the same types of residents but used different architectural designs. Newman reported that crime rates in high-rise buildings (those with more than six stories) were much greater than in low-rise buildings (with six or fewer stories). In general, he concluded, the taller the building, the higher the crime rate. Newman also discovered that most crimes took place not in people's apartments but in public spaces of the buildings, including parking lots, entrances, hallways, stairways, and elevators.

What accounted for the difference in crime rates? High-rise buildings have higher crime rates, Newman reasoned, because they breed anonymity. Placed far above the ground, residents are likely to feel detached from their surroundings. Lower buildings, by contrast, encourage a greater sense of community and allow people to know their neighbors and to keep an eye on public spaces, informally "defending" their community.

In light of such findings and the generally dismal record of early public housing projects, by the 1970s many of these projects were becoming defined as a social problem. In 1972, the city of Saint Louis dynamited several high-rise towers of the Pruitt-Igoe public housing complex, a stark indication that this type of public housing was simply not healthy for people. Decades later, the city of Chicago began demolition of Cabrini-Green, another project with lots of crime.

In many cities, "projects" still exist. But social policy in recent decades has shifted from large-scale housing developments to providing financial assistance to families to rent in the private housing market. Established in 1974, the Section 8 program directs federal government subsidies to developers who rehabilitate existing rental housing or build new apartments. In exchange for this subsidy, developers agree to allocate a share of the housing to low-income families. When low-income families move in, they pay 30 to 40 percent of their adjusted gross income for rent, with the government paying the rest. The advantages of this program include giving low-income families some choice about where to live and avoiding the past practice of creating housing in which all the residents are poor.

The Section 8 program did increase the availability of low-income housing. But funding has not been sufficient to meet the demand. A number of large cities in the United States have

SOCIAL PROBLEMS in Everyday Life

Do you think most people in this country see racial segregation as a problem? Do some see it as a solution? Explain.

SOCIAL PROBLEMS in Everyday Life

What policies do you think might reduce the number of homeless people? Do you think of homelessness more as a housing problem or as a poverty problem? Explain.

had tens of thousands of people on the waiting list for Section 8 vouchers, indicating that much more needs to be done (Thigpen, 2002).

Racial Segregation

In cities across the United States, the poor—especially poor people of color—are isolated from the mainstream of society. In a classic study, Douglas Massey and Nancy Denton (1988, 1989) examined large cities across the United States and documented the existence of what they called *hypersegregation:* Entire districts of cities (commonly called ghettos) contain only poor African Americans, and these people are cut off from the larger society in several ways. Not only are poor minority urbanites isolated *spatially,* meaning that they are highly concentrated in certain neighborhoods, typically near the city's central business district, but they are also isolated *socially;* they live almost entirely in these neighborhoods, rarely venturing out into the larger city. Similarly, richer people living elsewhere rarely enter these communities.

How prevalent is hypersegregation? Massey and Denton estimate that about one in five African Americans lives cut off from the larger society. By contrast, hypersegregation characterizes just a few percent of Latinos and whites with the same income levels (Jagarowsky & Bane, 1990).

The fact that a large share of the African American population but few people of other categories experience hypersegregation shows that racial inequality is a key element in the problems of U.S. cities. Our cities remain racially divided; in fact, the urban decentralization of the past fifty or sixty years was prompted to a significant extent by a desire by whites to distance themselves from people of color. The trend continues: The white share of the population of the 100 largest U.S. cities fell from 52 percent in 1990 to 48 percent in 2005 (U.S. Census Bureau, 2007). The pattern of largely white suburbs and largely African American inner cities persists throughout the United States.

Homelessness

A century ago, every large city in the United States had tens of thousands of homeless people. In fact, the homeless were so much a part of the urban landscape that many people at that time considered homelessness a normal part of city life rather than a serious social problem.

Although the number of homeless people is lower than it was a century ago, homelessness remains a social problem in the United States. One might also say that homelessness is a greater tragedy today because our nation is now much richer than it was back then.

There is no precise count of the homeless population. In 2007, the Department of Housing and Urban Development surveyed cities and towns across the country to estimate the number of people who were homeless for some period of time during that year. They counted about 750,000 people, including people living on the streets, in shelters, and in transitional housing. Based on that finding, they estimate that as many as 3.5 million people may be homeless for some period of time over the course of a year, and activist organizations suggest that the number may be higher (National Coalition for the Homeless, 2007; Ohlemacher, 2007).

Homelessness is primarily an urban problem. In a study by the U.S. Department of Housing and Urban Development (HUD, 1999), researchers interviewed more than 4,000 poor people across the country—most of them homeless at the time—and reported that 92 percent are urban: 71 percent reside in central cities, and 21 percent live in suburbs. Just 8 percent live in rural areas.

This HUD study documented that homeless people are the poorest of the poor. In the survey, homeless people reported income averaging $348 per month (barely $10 a day). For homeless families, the figure was $475. With so little income, it is easy to understand why people cannot afford housing. In addition, 40 percent of homeless people said they went without food for at least one day in the previous month.

Everyone agrees that homeless people are poor. We also know that a substantial share of homeless people suffer from mental illness, just as many abuse alcohol or other drugs. But are these behaviors the "cause" of homelessness (as conservatives sometimes claim) or are they the "consequences" of homelessness (as liberals typically claim)?

GETTING INVOLVED

Have you ever walked around in Los Angeles, Phoenix, or another Sunbelt city? How does the experience differ from walking around in Chicago, Boston, or New York?

supportive housing a program that combines low-income housing with on-site social services

Table 14–1 The Ten Largest Cities in the United States, 1950 and 2010

1950			2010		
Rank	**City**	**Population**	**Rank**	**City**	**Population**
1	New York	7,892,000	1	New York	8,175,133
2	Chicago	3,621,000	2	Los Angeles	3,792,621
3	Philadelphia	2,072,000	3	Chicago	2,695,598
4	Los Angeles	1,970,000	4	Houston	2,099,451
5	Detroit	1,850,000	5	Philadelphia	1,526,006
6	Baltimore	950,000	6	Phoenix	1,445,632
7	Cleveland	915,000	7	San Antonio	1,327,407
8	Saint Louis	857,000	8	San Diego	1,307,402
9	Boston	801,000	9	Dallas	1,197,816
10	San Francisco	775,000	10	San Jose	945,942

Note: Cities shaded in blue are located in the Snowbelt; those shaded in yellow are in the Sunbelt.

Source: U.S. Census Bureau (2011).

Research also shows that most homeless people do not work, although about 20 percent report having at least a part-time job (U.S. Conference of Mayors, 2007). Some (more conservative) people point to this lack of work and say that homeless people are themselves responsible for their situation. In addition, one-third of homeless people are substance abusers, and one-fourth are mentally ill (U.S. Conference of Mayors, 2007; U.S. Department of Housing and Urban Development, 2007).

Other (more liberal) people see homelessness as caused mostly by our society. From this point of view, the main causes of homelessness are low wages and a lack of affordable housing (Kozol, 1988; L. Kaufman, 2004). Supporters of this position note that as the economy has turned downward in recent years, the number of people who have become homeless—through no fault of their own—has gone up.

However we define the problem, it is clear that the homeless need more income. But more than that, many homeless people also need social support and help with personal issues. Some of these problems—including depression and substance abuse—may be the result of being homeless. But in other cases, the problems began in childhood. Of homeless people interviewed in the HUD study, 25 percent said they were physically or sexually abused as children, one-third reported running away from home, and 27 percent claimed to have lived for some time in foster care. Half of the adult homeless reported significant problems of physical health, 40 percent had mental health problems, 40 percent abused alcohol, and 25 percent had some other drug problem.

The homeless, then, face many challenges. Yet the HUD study also provided some good news. After receiving physical and mental health care services and substance abuse treatment, 75 percent of homeless people living in families and 60 percent of homeless individuals living alone were able to move to what the report called "an improved living situation."

In some cases, the key to a more secure life is **supportive housing,** *a program that combines low-income housing with on-site social services.* People with substance abuse problems, mental disabilities, or simply the scars of living poor and alone on the streets find they can live independently and hold a job with the help of such programs.

Keep in mind that these programs, although costly, may actually end up saving money. The cost of supporting one person with affordable housing and social services might cost $15,000 a year; the cost of supporting a prison inmate is about three times that.

But our society's policy for dealing with the homeless has not always been guided by a desire to help. Especially in the 1990s, public opinion was critical of the homeless. Dozens of cities across the United States enacted antivagrancy laws and issued tickets to homeless people for a range of behaviors, including sleeping in doorways, asking for money in public, or carrying open containers of alcohol. Many cities also conducted nightly "police sweeps" to get homeless people off the streets. In the tough economic times our society has faced during the past few years, it seems likely that attitudes toward the homeless—which include thousands of people who have lost their homes through foreclosure—have softened.

Snowbelt and Sunbelt Cities

Every city contends with poverty and homelessness. But the way these problems play out across the United States is part of a trend: Take a look at the changing list of the ten largest cities in the United States, shown in Table 14–1. In 1950, eight of the

Cheryl Richardson, age 36, has just moved to Las Vegas to work in the expanding tourism industry, which has boosted the region's population.

Tom and Ellen Posten, in their sixties, live in Wichita County, Kansas; like many other families in the area, their children have all moved out of the county in search of better jobs.

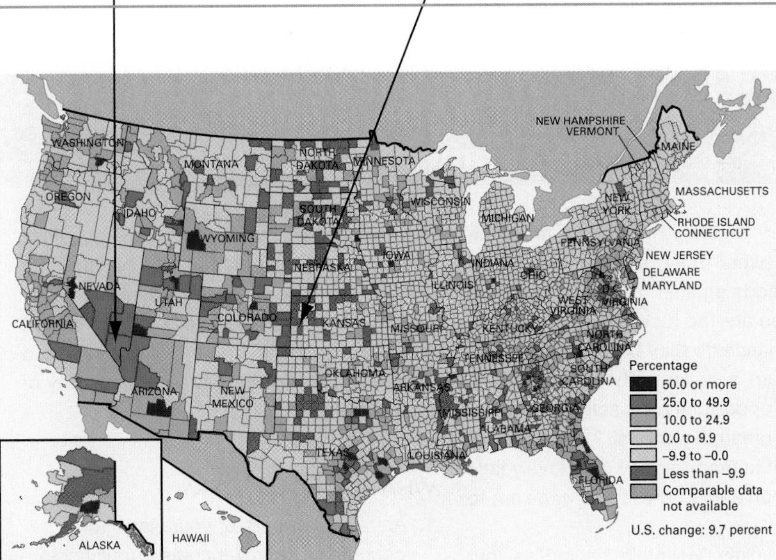

A Nation of Diversity

NATIONAL MAP 14–2

Population Change across the United States, 2000–2010

The map shows areas of the country where population density went up or down between 2000 and 2010. What is the general pattern to this change? What problems does rapid population increase bring to a county? What about rapid population loss?

Source: U.S. Census Bureau (2011).

top ten cities were in the Northeast and Midwest, often called the Snowbelt; by 2010, however, seven of ten were in the South and West, often called the Sunbelt (U.S. Census Bureau, 2011).

Snowbelt cities have lost population in the postindustrial era as people and businesses have decentralized across the city limits to suburbs. Not so in the Sunbelt, where cities are rapidly gaining population. In part, this is because our national population is shifting south and west. In 1940, the Snowbelt was home to 60 percent of the U.S. population; today, it is the Sunbelt that holds 60 percent of the people. National Map 14–2 shows recent population shifts that have occurred in the United States between 2000 and 2010.

Why hasn't decentralization hurt Sunbelt cities? The answer is a difference in their political geography. A century ago, Snowbelt cities were locked within a ring of politically independent suburbs. As the urban area decentralized, the cities lost population. But Sunbelt cities don't have this ring of independent suburbs; as population has grown, they have simply sprawled outward, annexing land as they expand. For this reason, Sunbelt cities are much larger physically than the older, industrial metropolises. Jacksonville, Florida, for example, now covers more than 750 square miles, more than three times the size of Columbus, Ohio, even though both cities have about 750,000 people. Sunbelt cities have expanded their city limits to maintain their tax base as people and jobs move outward.

Cities in Poor Countries

As we have seen again and again in this book, many of the social problems found in the United States are far worse in the world's poor nations. The same is true of urban problems such as poverty, inadequate housing, and poor sanitation. The Social Problems in Global Perspective box on page 380 offers a look at the striking poverty in one of the world's major cities, Manila, capital of the Philippines.

Global Map 14–1 on page 381 shows the level of urbanization for all regions of the world. More than 75 percent of the populations of rich nations live in and around cities. In the poorest countries, by contrast, just one-third are urbanites. But everywhere in the world, the number of city dwellers is increasing. By 2008, for the first time in history, most of the world's people were living in urban places (World Bank, 2008; Population Reference Bureau, 2009).

As explained in Chapter 15, "Population and Global Inequality," world population was 6.8 billion in 2009 and is increasing by about 82 million people each year. The urban population of the world is increasing twice as fast; in Latin America, Africa, and Asia, people are migrating from rural areas to cities in search of economic opportunity, more schooling, and a better quality of life. As Table 14–2 on page 382 shows, eight of the ten largest cities in the world are now in economically developing nations. Only one of these cities—New York—is in the United States. By 2025, according to current projections, most of the world's ten largest urban areas will be much bigger still.

Mumbai (Bombay), Shanghai, Mexico City, and others on the list are becoming true megacities, with populations greater than at any time in history. Even a rich nation such as the United States faces serious challenges in meeting the housing, transportation, and sanitation needs of the 19 million people in the sprawling New York urban region. How, then, will nations where incomes are much lower—such as Bangladesh,

MAKING THE GRADE

Be sure you understand Tönnies's concepts of *Gemeinschaft* and *Gesellschaft.* (They correspond to two terms used by Durkheim.)

Gemeinschaft a type of social organization in which people are closely bound by kinship and tradition

Gesellschaft a type of social organization in which people interact on the basis of self-interest

SOCIAL PROBLEMS IN GLOBAL PERSPECTIVE

World-Class Poverty: A Visit to Manila's Smokey Mountain

What caught my eye was how clean she was—a girl no more than seven or eight years old, hair carefully combed and wearing a freshly laundered dress. Her eyes followed us as we walked past; camera-toting Americans stand out here, in one of the poorest neighborhoods in the entire world.

Fed by methane from the decomposing garbage, the fires never go out on Smokey Mountain, Manila's vast garbage dump. The smoke envelops the hills of refuse like a thick fog. But Smokey Mountain is more than a dump. It is a neighborhood, a place that thousands of people call home.

The residents of Smokey Mountain are the poorest of the poor, and one is hard pressed to imagine a setting more hostile to human life. Surrounded by smoke and squalor, men and women do what they can to survive, picking plastic bags from the city's garbage and washing them in the river, salvaging cardboard boxes that pile up alongside a family's plywood shack.

All over Smokey Mountain are children—kids who must already sense the enormous odds against them. The girls and boys we see are the lucky ones, of course. But what chance do they have, living in families that earn a dollar or two a day? With barely any opportunity for schooling? Year after year, breathing this air? Against this backdrop of human tragedy, one lovely little girl has put on a fresh dress and gone out to play. . . .

With Smokey Mountain behind us, our taxi driver threads his way through heavy traffic as we head for the other side of Manila. The contrast is amazing: The forbidding smoke and smells of the dump give way to polished neighborhoods one might find in Miami or Los Angeles. On the bay in the distance, a cluster of yachts floats silently at anchor. No more rutted streets; now we glide quietly along wide boulevards lined with trees and filled with expensive Japanese cars. On each side, we pass shopping plazas, upscale hotels, and high-rise office buildings. Every block or so stands the entrance to an exclusive residential enclave set off by gates and protected by armed guards. Here, in large, air-conditioned homes, the rich of Manila live—and many of the poor work.

WHAT DO YOU THINK?

1. Are any members of your class from countries with low-income populations? If so, invite them to share their experiences.
2. How would you feel as a traveler from the United States witnessing such intense poverty? Why?
3. See photographs of Smokey Mountain at http://www.jkfoto.nl/manilla/manilla.html.

Source: Personal visit to Manila, October 1994.

and Mexico—be able to support their soaring urban populations?

Throughout history, cities have offered the promise of a better life. But cities provide no sure solution to social problems. We can see this in the ever-present shantytowns, settlements where people have built makeshift homes from whatever materials they can find and where most people do not have clean water and sewerage. A pressing question is whether cities that so far have failed to meet the needs of so many millions of people will be able to meet the needs of many millions more.

Theoretical Analysis: Understanding Urban Problems

Let us now apply sociological theory to the problems of cities. Each of the major theoretical approaches provides insights into how urbanization is changing people's lives.

Structural-Functional Analysis: A Theory of Urbanism

The main contribution of the structural-functional approach to our understanding of cities is the theory of urbanism. The theory emerged in the writings of two European sociologists, Ferdinand Tönnies and Emile Durkheim, and Louis Wirth of the United States.

Ferdinand Tönnies: *Gemeinschaft* and *Gesellschaft*

Tönnies (1855–1937), who lived during the Industrial Revolution, tried to explain how social life changed as rural living gave way to life in the industrial metropolis. His built his answer on the two terms *Gemeinschaft* and *Gesellschaft.*

Gemeinschaft is a German word (roughly translated as "community") meaning *a type of social organization in which people are closely bound by kinship and tradition.* Living in small rural villages, people have a strong sense of community based

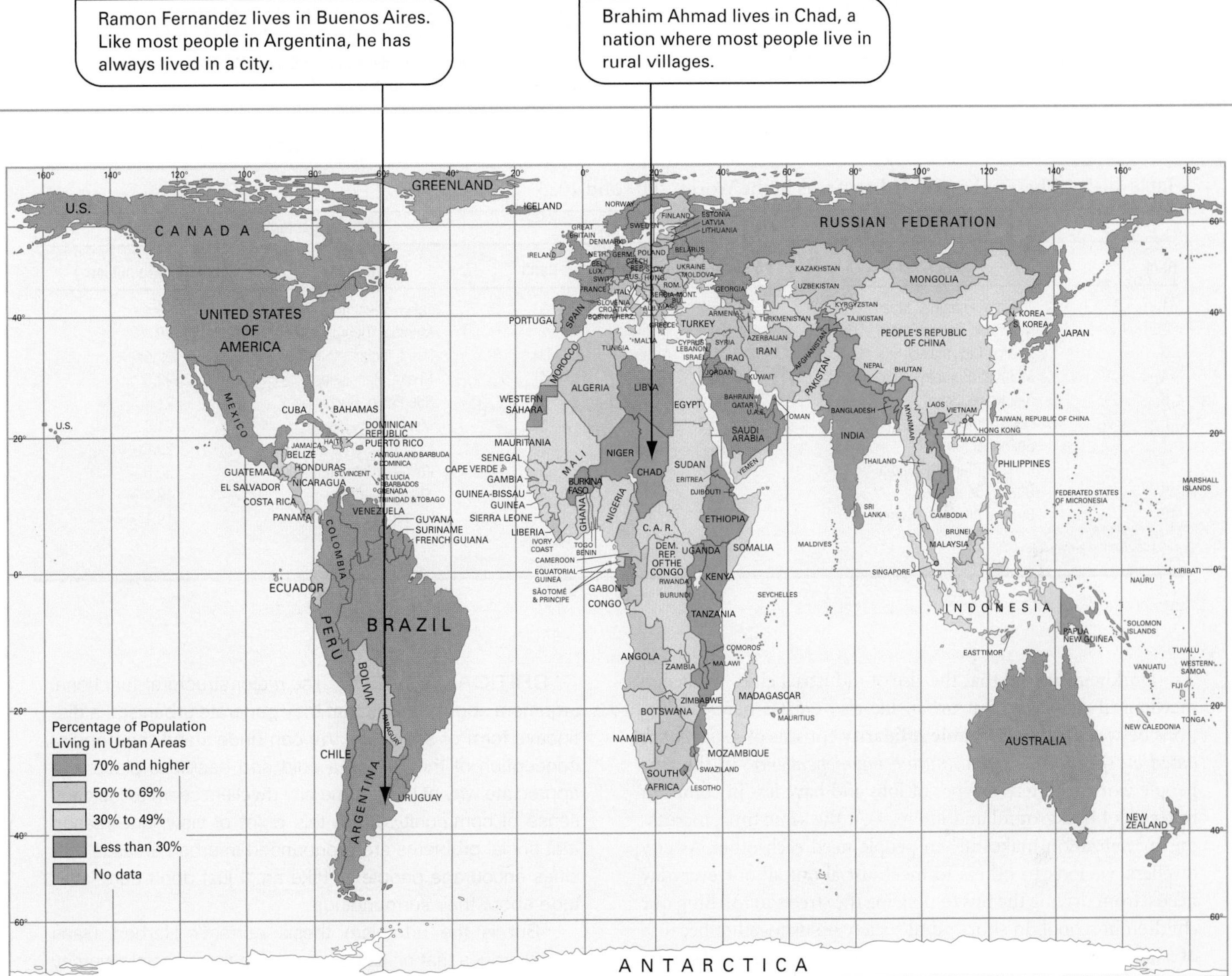

A World of Differences

GLOBAL MAP 14–1 Urbanization around the World

Half the world's people now live in cities. A nation's share of city dwellers depends on its level of economic development. In high-income nations such as the United States and Canada, more than three-fourths of the people live in urban places. By contrast, in low-income nations in Africa and Asia, only one-third of the population lives in cities. Even so, the largest cities in these countries are growing very rapidly.

Source: Population Reference Bureau (2009).

on kinship and shared traditions. At its best, explained Tönnies, rural living is guided by a concern for the needs of all rather than people pursuing their self-interest.

In the industrial city, however, traditional community is lost and life approximates ***Gesellschaft*** (roughly translated as "association"), *a type of social organization in which people interact on the basis of self-interest.* In the city, Tönnies explained, a person typically pays only passing attention to the welfare of the community and mostly "looks out for number one."

Emile Durkheim: Mechanical and Organic Solidarity

The French sociologist Emile Durkheim (1858–1917) agreed with Tönnies that the rise of cities brought changes to the organization of society. Durkheim characterized social ties in rural areas as **mechanical solidarity,** *social bonds based on common sentiments and shared moral values.* Durkheim's concept of mechanical solidarity is similar to Tönnies's concept of *Gemeinschaft.*

mechanical solidarity (p. 381) social bonds based on common sentiments and shared moral values

organic solidarity social bonds based on specialization and mutual interdependence

GETTING INVOLVED

Would you rather live in the city or in a rural area? Why? Use ideas from Tönnies and Durkheim in your answer.

Table 14–2 The Ten Largest Urban Areas in the World, 2007 and 2025

2007			2025 (Projected)		
Rank	**Urban Area**	**Population (in millions)**	**Rank**	**Urban Area**	**Population (in millions)**
1	Tokyo-Yokohama, Japan	35.7	1	Tokyo-Yokohama, Japan	36.4
2	New York, United States	19.1	2	Mumbai (Bombay), India	26.4
3	Mexico City, Mexico	19.0	3	Delhi, India	22.5
4	Mumbai (Bombay), India	19.0	4	Dhaka, Bangladesh	22.0
5	São Paulo, Brazil	18.8	5	São Paulo, Brazil	21.4
6	Delhi, India	15.9	6	Mexico City, Mexico	21.0
7	Shanghai, China	15.0	7	New York, United States	20.6
8	Kolkata (Calcutta), India	14.8	8	Kolkata (Calcutta), India	20.6
9	Dhaka, Bangladesh	13.5	9	Shanghai, China	19.4
10	Buenos Aires, Argentina	12.8	10	Karachi, Pakistan	19.1

Source: United Nations (2008).

Durkheim agreed that the rise of industrial cities weakened mechanical solidarity. But urban life also creates new connections between people. **Organic solidarity** consists of *social bonds based on specialization and mutual interdependence.* In the city, people work at different types of jobs and have less in common in terms of background and interests. At the same time, increasing specialization makes urban people need each other. As city dwellers, we look to others to meet just about all our everyday needs, from driving the bus to policing the streets to teaching our children in school. In short, rural society holds together because of *likeness,* and urban society holds together because of *difference.*

Durkheim's view of urban life is more positive than that of Tönnies. Although something may be lost in the process of urbanization, Durkheim concluded, people gain more individual choice, moral tolerance, and personal privacy.

Louis Wirth: Urbanism as a Way of Life

From the ideas of Tönnies and Durkheim, Louis Wirth (1897–1952) developed a formal theory of urban life. Wirth (1938) began by defining the city as a settlement with a large, dense, socially diverse population. These traits, he continued, make social ties within the city fleeting and impersonal. Because urbanites live with millions of others around them, they never get to know even most people they see every day.

When urbanites can identify others, it is usually not in terms of *who they are* in any personal sense but simply *what they do.* In other words, we recognize but know little about the bus driver, the school principal, the police officer on the beat, or the grocery store owner. This limited knowledge of others, coupled to the social diversity of the city, makes urbanites more tolerant than rural villagers.

CRITICAL REVIEW The major structural-functional argument about cities is that they generate urbanism, a distinctive form of social life. We can understand the popular conception of the city as a cold and heartless place and appreciate why at least some city dwellers seem to lack any sense of community. From this point of view, one reason that social problems are pronounced in urban areas is that cities encourage people to take an "I just don't care" attitude about their surroundings.

But is the urbanism thesis correct? Herbert Gans (1968) argues that cities contain much more social diversity than Wirth's theory suggests. Gans agrees that some people do have the detached, cosmopolitan attitude that Wirth describes. But what about "ethnic villagers" who live in traditional neighborhoods where almost everyone else is like them? The Italian and Polish communities that existed on New York's Lower East Side early in the twentieth century, as well as Korean and Vietnamese neighborhoods in Philadelphia and Los Angeles today, have many of the traditions we link to rural living. Gans's research reminds us that class, race, ethnicity, and age create an urban mix far more complex than any single profile of "urbanites" will allow.

Claude Fischer (1975) points out that cities also create new social groups because their size allows a critical mass of individuals of almost every kind. Although every small town has some gay men and lesbians, for example, only large cities such as New York and San Francisco have gay communities, with thousands of residents and a distinctive subculture supported by gay newspapers, gay bars, gay theater, and other amenities.

SOCIAL PROBLEMS in Everyday Life

How much truth do you see in the stereotype of city people as "cold" and "detached"? Explain.

Symbolic-Interaction Analysis: Experiencing the City

On a micro-level, the reality of city living is a matter of personal experiences. How do people construct reality in the city?

Georg Simmel: Urban Stimulation and Selectivity

The German sociologist Georg Simmel (1858–1918) explained that people living in cities experience intense stimulation. The sights, sounds, and smells of city life—not to mention the vast number of people—all combine to overwhelm the senses. In other words, so much takes place around you in the city that you couldn't respond to most of it even if you wanted to. The result, claimed Simmel, is that urbanites develop a *blasé attitude* as they "tune out" much of what is around them.

Simmel explained that in the midst of urban overstimulation, a blasé attitude can be a strategy for survival. It does not mean that people lack concern for others. On the contrary, by responding to only certain others, urban people focus their time and energy on those who really matter.

A common theme in the writings of Tönnies, Durkheim, and Simmel is the impersonality of cities. Urban living, it seems, makes people indifferent to those around them. Do you agree with this assessment? What evidence can you point to in support of your position?

Leo Srole: Mental Health in the Metropolis

If people have to tune out most of what goes on around them to survive in the city, are cities an unhealthy environment? Over the years, a number of researchers have tackled this issue, and their general conclusion is that cities pose no harm to people's mental health. In one of the largest studies, Leo Srole (1972) monitored the mental health of New Yorkers in the 1950s and again in the early 1970s. Srole found that overall, mental health in New York was actually a little better than in rural areas, especially for women.

Later research confirmed these results (Fischer, 1973; Hackler, 1979; Weisner, 1981; Kadushin, 1983). City living may involve more stimulation, but this does not contribute to problems of mental illness. On the contrary, many people thrive in an environment where they have access to many other people and activities and lots of choice about how to live.

CRITICAL REVIEW On a micro-level, we find that cities do differ from rural areas in the level of stimulation that people commonly experience. Yet contrary to the impression we get from Simmel's theory (and also that of Tönnies), cities turn out to be relatively healthful places.

But this upbeat conclusion has a major limitation: Some urbanites live far better than others. Any general conclusions about the quality of life in the city must take into account social inequality, which brings us to the social-conflict approach.

Social-Conflict Analysis: Cities and Inequality

As in earlier chapters, the social-conflict approach focuses on social inequality. In this case, the issue is how social stratification in the United States shapes the city and urban life.

Urban Political Economy

The application of social-conflict theory to cities—urban political economy—differs from the approaches of Tönnies and Wirth, who treated the city as defined simply by its size, density, and social diversity. Rather than treating the city as self-defining, this approach asks how the economic and political structures of the larger society shape the city and its problems.

Following the lead of Karl Marx, this approach asserts that social class plays an important part in defining urbanism. Consider, in any city, how much the lives of the rich differ from those of working-class people and, even more, from those of the poor and the homeless. On another level, this approach seeks to

MAKING THE GRADE

Use the table below to review the three theoretical approaches to urban life.

APPLYING THEORY

Urban Life

	What is the level of analysis?	How do we understand urban life?	Is urban life a problem?
Structural-functional approach	Macro-level	Using a structural-functional approach, Tönnies, Durkheim, and Wirth developed a theory of urbanism that contrasted social life in urban and rural places. Wirth explained that a large, dense, and socially diverse population generated a distinctive way of life marked by impersonal relationships and tolerance.	As Tönnies saw it, urban life was something of a problem because *Gesellschaft* was based on self-interest and lacked the broader social bonds of *Gemeinschaft.* Durkheim was more optimistic, noting that cities give people more privacy and personal choice.
Symbolic-interaction approach	Micro-level	The symbolic-interaction approach focuses on the way we experience urban life. Simmel explained that urban life exposes us to intense stimulation, causing urbanites to develop a blasé attitude. Urbanites effectively tune out much of what goes on around them. Srole and others, however, found that urban living does not harm people's mental health.	The common view of the city dweller as cold and heartless is based on a bit of truth, as urban people are selective about what they respond to. At the same time, however, nothing in the nature of modern cities inevitably causes problems for people in everyday life.
Social-conflict approach	Macro-level	The social-conflict approach claims that cities are not self-defining based on large, dense, and diverse population but are actually shaped by the larger political economy. Marx pointed to capitalism and the social class differences it creates as defining modern, urban life. Harvey explained how the search for profit guides the actions of government and banks to the benefit of the rich and the disadvantage of the poor.	The social-conflict approach supports a radical view that urban problems are caused by the larger political economy. Solving problems like social inequality requires changes to the capitalist economic system.

explain how the physical development of the city reflects the private property and profit seeking central to a capitalist economy.

David Harvey: A Study of Baltimore

David Harvey's study of Baltimore shows that the growth and decline of an urban area have much to do with the process of capital investment. Harvey (1973) found that banks had little interest in lending money to people in inner-city Baltimore for housing or other development. As a result, poor people had to finance their housing through their own funds, through private loans, or through government programs. Under such conditions, this section of the city remained poor and rundown.

By contrast, banks favored the affluent sections of Baltimore. Middle-class and upper-middle-class people had lit-

SOCIAL PROBLEMS in Everyday Life

Do you think the special character of cities comes more from their size and diversity, as Wirth claimed, or more from our capitalist economy? Why?

enterprise zones areas in the inner city that attract new businesses with the promise of tax relief

tle trouble obtaining home mortgages, which banks viewed as good investments.

Harvey reports that even government programs end up serving the interests of investors. In Baltimore and elsewhere, urban renewal turned out to be slum clearance programs that forced out the poor, who often ended up in projects that were worse than the housing they had lived in before. The city turned over their old neighborhoods to profit-seeking developers who built housing and shopping centers that would attract residents with more money. In short, patterns of investment—who makes money available to whom—go a long way toward explaining the differing fortunes of people across the urban area.

CRITICAL REVIEW The older structural-functional theories point to factors such as population size and density as defining urban life. The newer political-economy theory points to capitalism and its drive for profit as the defining factor. The power of money is at work not only in the rise and fall of neighborhoods in the central city but also in the decentralization of population as investment shifts from industrial production to newer information companies.

However, social patterns do differ in cities and in rural areas. Another issue is that the effects of capital investment on urban life are not always clear. Too little investment may cause a community to decline. But too much investment can result in overbuilt areas and urban sprawl. In the final sections of this chapter, we examine how politics guides the ways in which people construct urban problems and define solutions.

The Applying Theory table summarizes what we learn from each theoretical approach to urban life.

POLITICS AND URBAN LIFE

Constructing Problems and Defining Solutions

To hear some people tell it, our large cities are enjoying a rebirth; others see our cities in crisis. To better understand how people define urban problems—and what they see as solutions—we must look at today's urban issues from different political viewpoints.

Conservatives: The Market and Morality

In assessing the state of our cities, conservatives would have us consider where we have been and how far we have come. A century ago, when Jacob Riis walked the streets and alleyways of New York's Lower East Side, one-third of New Yorkers lived in desperate circumstances, with many families crowded together in dark tenement rooms. Sanitation was minimal. Two of every ten children born in the tenements did not live even one year. This level of infant mortality is 2½ times higher than the rate today across Africa, the poorest region of the world (Population Reference Bureau, 2009).

Today's urbanites live far longer, and most take for granted safe housing, dependable plumbing, electricity to operate lights and appliances, and far better medical care. What has brought about this improvement? Conservatives would credit economic forces. As the United States became an industrial society, the economy generated ever more products and services, so that cities grew and living standards rose for everyone.

More recently, the ups and downs in cities have also reflected economic trends. The rise of a service economy helped push population outward from the old central cities to the expanding suburbs. These same trends caused economic decline in the central cities, especially in the nation's Snowbelt. Today, in fact, this region is sometimes called the Rustbelt because of all the obsolete factories that now stand empty and rusting.

Conservatives accept the operation of the market economy, and they view the decline of the inner cities as unfortunate but not permanent. As noted, the expansion of the postindustrial economy has already transformed many old industrial areas into business centers or arts and entertainment districts. Examples of this inner-city comeback can be found in the lakefront of Cleveland, the Baltimore harbor area, and the riverfront of New Orleans. In time, even a city like Detroit, which is still reeling from the loss of industrial production, will be remade.

If economic forces shape cities, what can government do? Conservatives have supported the creation of **enterprise zones,** *areas in the inner city that attract new businesses with the promise of tax relief.* Under such programs, government reduces or eliminates taxes on businesses that relocate to an economically depressed area where jobs are needed. This incentive should attract business to areas of the cities where a large share of people do not have work (Kemp, 1994).

Beyond such limited policies, however, conservatives oppose the growth of government social welfare programs, which expanded in the 1960s. Consider, for example, this account by Senator Daniel P. Moynihan of New York City in 1943, the year he graduated from one of the city's high schools:

> By 1943, [the number of New Yorkers on welfare] was down to 73,000 persons, of which the city reported that only 93 were employable.... In 1943, there were exactly forty-four

SOCIAL PROBLEMS in Everyday Life

Has a city you know experienced a "revival" the way Cleveland did (see photo below)?

MAKING THE GRADE

As we have seen before, conservatives see the market economy as good; liberals see government action as good.

> homicides by gunshot in all of the City of New York. . . . In 1943, the illegitimacy rate was 3 percent. Last year, it was 45 percent. Ours was a much poorer city fifty years ago, but a much more stable one. (1993:119–20)

Fifty years later, when Moynihan wrote his account, New York's population had actually declined, but many urban problems had become much worse. Almost 1 million people (one in seven New Yorkers) were on welfare, and the number of murders had risen to almost 2,000 a year. By 2010, the number of households receiving food stamps was greater than 500,000, the number of murders was 471, and 35 percent of babies were born to unwed mothers.

As conservatives see it, the expansion of the welfare state caused the long-term rise in public assistance and even violence. Everyone agrees that the intention of expanding government social programs is to help people. But as Charles Krauthammer (1995:15) puts it, "The growth in the size and power of the welfare state is the primary cause of the decline of society's . . . institutions—voluntary associations, local government, church, and, above all, the family." Conservatives link problems such as street violence and poverty to family breakdown; they blame the breakdown of the family on decades of welfare policies that gave money to people who could but did not work and that provided child support for mothers without jobs or husbands.

Conservatives also direct criticism to the rest of the population as well. The recent economic downturn is in large measure "payback" for years of too much greed on Wall Street and in the nation's corporate boardrooms, as well as too much spending and too little saving among households at all income levels.

In short, a conservative approach claims that the strength of a city—and of an entire society—lies partly in its economic prosperity but mostly in the moral character of its people. From a conservative point of view, we've had decades of positive economic indicators, but the moral indicators are way down (D. G. Myers, 2000; Andersen, 2009).

Liberals: Government Reform

From a liberal point of view, U.S. cities are beset with a number of serious social problems. As explained in Chapter 2 ("Poverty and Wealth"), economic inequality in the United States is increasing as some people are becoming richer while most people experience a lack of economic security. In big cities—from New York to Los Angeles and from Detroit to Houston—we find tens of millions of poor people, many neighborhoods of low-quality housing, and urban schools that do not teach students effectively.

A generation ago, this downtown area of Cleveland was little more than abandoned factories—a place to avoid. Today, it is a thriving entertainment district, home to the Rock and Roll Hall of Fame. Conservatives claim that market forces are the key to reviving inner cities; liberals look to government intervention; radicals claim that capitalism can never save our cities. Which view do you find most convincing? Why?

Liberals believe that all of these problems stem from social inequality, and they look to the government to take action. Enforcing antidiscrimination laws is one part of the liberal solution to urban problems. The law must ensure that racial prejudice does not prevent people of any color or ethnicity from living where they choose, within the limits of their housing budget.

More broadly, liberals look to stabilize an economy that has become unbalanced by decades of anything-goes policies. In part, the liberal solution to economic insecurity is greater government regulation of the economy. In addition, liberals look to government to reduce the income and wealth gaps between different categories of people. At the top, as the Obama administration has said it will do, this involves raising taxes, especially on the rich, who benefit the most

GETTING INVOLVED

Has an urban issue ever led you to become politically active? Explain.

from our cities. At the bottom, reform involves a host of social supports and programs to increase economic opportunity, especially for people living in inner-city areas. The private sector has done little for our inner cities, liberals claim, so the government must step in to create needed jobs and provide transportation to suburbs and other outlying areas where jobs are more readily available.

In sum, liberals reject the conservative idea that our cities should rise and fall as the result of changing economic forces. As a counterpoint to the conservative view that government programs are the heart of the problem, liberals see government as the solution to the problems affecting our cities.

The Radical Left: The Need for Basic Change

Like liberals, radicals on the left believe that the cities of the United States are in crisis. So great is the economic inequality, so deep is the racism, and so limited are government efforts to improve matters, radicals argue, that only a basic change in our economic and political systems will solve urban problems. Left radicals flatly reject the conservative reliance on the market system to guide the development of our cities. They claim that by giving free rein to market forces, the United States is simply making urban problems such as poverty, crime, and urban sprawl worse. At the same time, the reforms proposed by liberals cannot be effective because, as radicals see it, they rest on the same capitalist economic foundation.

To apply the radical approach, recall the history of urban renewal in the United States. Government devised the policy of urban renewal with the goal of reversing the physical decline of the central cities. But rather than providing better housing for the poor, who by definition have the greatest need, the program turned poor neighborhoods over to private developers who used the land for their own profit by building shopping centers and housing for more affluent people. This process points to the conclusion that under a capitalist system, the government operates to serve the private sector. Furthermore, because the private sector is concerned not with people but with profits, it will not meet the need for low-income housing.

Following Marxist theory, the capitalist economy operates in the interest of the capitalist class, not the majority. Today, as a century ago, it operates to the benefit of those who own productive property. Most of our country's elite now live in suburbs and work there or in edge cities, leaving the poor to struggle for survival in the central cities. Districts of striking poverty remain in New York, Detroit, Saint Louis, Houston, Los Angeles, and just about every other major city in the country.

John Logan and Harvey Molotch (1987) argue that the new global economy benefits major corporations and their stockholders, but ordinary people in U.S. cities face declining prospects. As multinational corporations export industrial jobs to poor countries, for example, the urban poor are left with less and less. Social welfare programs may have grown over the course of the past century, but they have not altered the basic patterns of inequality. On the contrary, as Manuel Castells (1977, 1983, 1989) argues, they only "extend" capitalism—that is, they keep a bad system from collapsing entirely.

Thus radicals claim that under the present system, solutions will never be found. The radical perspective seeks more basic change in the economic foundation of U.S. society. Until the basic institutions of the United States operate to the benefit of the many rather than the few, urban problems will remain with us.

The Left to Right table on page 388 sums up the state of U.S. cities from each of the three political perspectives.

Going On from Here

Cities seem to generate controversy. This is because so many of us live in cities and so much social change involves the growth or decline of cities. More than a century ago, the Industrial Revolution occurred mostly in cities. Then, as now, most immigrants to the United States settled in cities.

Just as important, cities have a way of intensifying both the good and the bad in any society. On the one hand, the best hospitals and universities, the most celebrated museums, and the most popular newspapers and other mass media are all city-based. Cities also offer the most jobs and the greatest economic opportunity.

But cities also reveal the failings of U.S. society. Poverty exists almost everywhere, but the greatest concentration of poor people is found in central cities. Much the same can be said for crime, low-quality housing, and bad schools.

For almost a century, the United States has been an urban nation, and no one doubts that cities will stand at the center of our way of life far into the future. From a conservative point of view, the major force shaping future cities should be a market economy. Today, the postindustrial economy is causing sprawling urban regions to spread across the United States. A liberal perspective suggests that the market-based economy alone will not solve many of the problems—such as increasing inequality and racial and ethnic conflict—that continue to plague us. As

MAKING THE GRADE

Use the table below to review the three political approaches to urban life.

LEFT TO RIGHT

The Politics of Urban Life

	RADICAL-LEFT VIEW	LIBERAL VIEW	CONSERVATIVE VIEW
WHAT IS THE PROBLEM?	Cities are in crisis: Under capitalism, cities operate to support and benefit the few who own productive property, ignoring the needs of the majority; urban poverty, crime, and sprawl are all out of control.	Cities suffer from the effects of social inequality; poor people and minorities fare the worst with regard to housing, schools, and other resources.	Urban life is far better than it was a century ago because living standards have risen. Inner cities declined as economic forces relocated and replaced industry after 1950, but the postindustrial economy is reviving them.
WHAT IS THE SOLUTION?	Neither the economy operating on its own nor government programs can bring about needed changes; capitalism itself must be transformed into a system that meets the needs of the many rather than the few.	Government must attack racial segregation by enforcing antidiscrimination laws, reduce income inequality, and bring more economic opportunity to the inner cities, where poverty is greatest.	The improvements in urban life result from this nation's productive market economy. Where needed, government can stimulate economic development with enterprise zones.

JOIN THE DEBATE

1. To what degree, from each of the political perspectives, are cities in the United States in serious trouble?
2. From the point of view of each political perspective, what is the proper role of the marketplace in meeting the needs of urbanites? What about the proper role of the government?
3. Which of the three political analyses of urban life included here do you find most convincing? Why?

radicals on the left claim, the capitalist economy will never be a solution; it is actually the heart of the problem. From this point of view, as long as we let the economy shape cities, we rule out any meaningful solution.

The main question for the future, then, is this: Should government take a larger role in shaping cities and urban life? With ever-increasing sprawl, mounting problems of pollution, and social inequality on the rise, perhaps the time is at hand to consider what kinds of cities we want our children and grandchildren to inherit. The debate will place those (typically conservatives) who want to limit government power in favor of letting market forces shape urban life against those who favor giving government the power to reform (liberals) or completely redefine (radicals on the left) the urban landscape. How this debate is resolved holds the key to the cities of tomorrow.

DEFINING SOLUTIONS

Have our nation's efforts to improve the quality of life in our large cities worked?

Who has benefited the most? Look at the photos below to learn more about the policy of urban renewal, which led to redevelopment in many inner-city neighborhoods in the years after World War II.

In the 1950s, the policy of "urban renewal" was enacted in large, industrial cities, including Baltimore. The "problem" (for which urban renewal was to be a solution), was described by some as "slums" or "urban blight," which referred to low-income neighborhoods where dilapidated housing was thought to breed high levels of violent crime, drug trafficking, and other problems associated with poverty. To many liberals, however, the problem was not just substandard housing but the deeper issue of poverty. Can you see why?

Baltimore tore down blocks and blocks of "slums" and turned the land into the Inner Harbor development, a popular combination of trendy stores, upscale restaurants, and pricey residences. Redevelopment of this kind, also found in Philadelphia, Boston, and most other cities in the Rustbelt, attracted wealthy people back to the city, raised tax revenues, and won a great deal of public support. Why would conservatives support this policy? Why were liberals critical of it?

HINT

By constructing the problem of "urban blight" in terms of housing, politicians (with the enthusiastic help of developers) defined the solution as building new, more expensive commercial and residential developments. Projects like Baltimore's Inner Harbor have certainly been popular and they have made money for cities and developers alike. Therefore, conservatives praise this policy as showing the power of market forces to improve the city. At the same time, liberals counter that urban renewal simply pushed poor people away, often to high-rise "projects," and did little to address the more basic problem of poverty.

Getting Involved: Applications & Exercises

1. What is the extent of the homeless problem in your city? Contact a local social services agency or office of the city government, and ask for available information or an interview. What programs are in place to assist homeless people? What can others do to help?
2. To appreciate the plight of millions of New Yorkers a century ago, go to the local library and obtain a copy of Jacob A. Riis: Photographer and Citizen, by Alexander Alland Sr. (New York: Aperture Books, 1974). Not only does this book provide instructive text, but also you can see hundreds of Riis's own photographs, taken in the tenements of that time.
3. A tour on foot or by bicycle or car in your local area can be enlightening when you bring along a sociological perspective. Travel around your community, making a sociological map as you go. Note the commercial, industrial, and residential areas. From the size and quality of housing, note the rich and poor neighborhoods. Where do people of different class positions live in relation to commercial and industrial areas? Do rich people live on high ground or low ground? How far from the rich do poor people live?
4. Is there a homeless shelter or food pantry in your community? If so, get in touch with someone there, and offer your assistance. This is an excellent way to learn about problems of housing and hunger as you help others.

MAKING THE GRADE

A DEFINING MOMENT
Jacob Riis: Revealing the Misery of the Tenements p. 375

CHAPTER 14 Urban Life

Cities: Then and Now

1700 ← 1900 → 2010

U.S. cities evolved from small villages along the eastern seaboard. New cities sprang up as the nation pushed westward after 1800. The Civil War marked the rise of the industrial metropolis. p. 368

An antiurban bias grew stronger in the late nineteenth century as industrial cities swelled with immigrants. By 1920, a majority of the U.S. population lived in cities. pp. 369–70

After 1950, urban decentralization rapidly expanded suburbs, which now contain more than half the U.S. population. One consequence of the outward flow of people was fiscal crisis for central cities, especially in the Snowbelt. p. 370

suburbs (p. 370) urban areas beyond the political boundaries of cities

Problems of Today's Cities

FISCAL PROBLEMS

- A declining tax base, coupled with a rising need for social services, led some cities to the brink of bankruptcy in the 1970s.
- Cities have rebounded since the 1970s, along with the growth of the postindustrial economy. But millions of urbanites—especially immigrants from Latin America and Asia—work in low-paying service jobs.

pp. 370–71

URBAN SPRAWL

The decentralization of cities has led to urban sprawl. This rapid, unplanned development has caused three problems:

- A boring sameness in the urban landscape
- A rapid loss of open spaces and loss of farmland
- Increasing reliance on automobiles, which consumes resources, pollutes the air, and causes personal stress

pp. 371–72

POVERTY

As more businesses move outward toward *edge cities,* the urban poor who remain in central cities find that their communities have fewer jobs.

- This loss of jobs is the key reason the poverty rate is almost twice as high in the central cities as in the suburbs.

pp. 372–74

megalopolis (p. 371) a vast urban region containing a number of cities and their surrounding suburbs

urban sprawl (p. 372) unplanned, low-density development at the edge of expanding urban areas

public housing (p. 374) high-density apartment buildings constructed to house poor people

supportive housing (p. 378) a program that combines low-income housing with on-site social services

HOUSING PROBLEMS

Inadequate housing has always been a problem for some people in U.S. cities.

- At least one-third of people in the early industrial metropolis lived in overcrowded tenements.
- Not until the New Deal of the 1930s did the federal government act to improve urban housing.
- Urban renewal began in 1949 as an effort to improve declining central-city neighborhoods. In practice, cities claimed poor and working-class neighborhoods and sold the land to developers, who built profitable commercial districts and housing for more well-to-do people.
- Urban public housing—often called "projects"—was constructed to house poor people displaced by urban renewal. Problems with drugs and crime were widespread in projects, especially those containing high-rise buildings that discouraged neighborhood ties.

pp. 374–77

RACIAL SEGREGATION

- *Hypersegregation* affects one in five African Americans, who live in urban ghettos socially isolated from the larger society.

p. 377

HOMELESSNESS

- Estimates suggest that about 750,000 people are homeless on any given night; 3.5 million people in the United States are homeless for at least some time during any year.
- Research shows that homelessness is an urban problem, with 71% of homeless people living in central cities and another 21% residing in suburbs.

pp. 377–78

SNOWBELT AND SUNBELT CITIES

The U.S. population is now less concentrated in the *Snowbelt* (the North and Midwest) and more concentrated in the *Sunbelt* (the South and West).

- Snowbelt cities have fixed borders where they meet politically independent suburbs.
- Sunbelt cities have annexed surrounding territory to grow larger.

pp. 378–79

CITIES IN POOR COUNTRIES

Half the planet's people live in urban areas. Most of the world's largest cities are in poor nations, and their populations are soaring. These cities cannot meet the needs of this surging population.

pp. 379–80

Theoretical Analysis: Understanding Urban Problems

Structural-Functional Analysis: A Theory of Urbanism

The **STRUCTURAL-FUNCTIONAL APPROACH** contrasts rural and urban living.

- In Europe, Tönnies used the concepts of ***GEMEINSCHAFT*** and ***GESELLSCHAFT*** to contrast these settings.
- Durkheim developed similar concepts of **MECHANICAL SOLIDARITY** and **ORGANIC SOLIDARITY**.
- In the United States, Wirth set out a theory of urbanism stating that population size, density, and diversity generate impersonality and tolerance.

pp. 380–82

Symbolic-Interaction Analysis: Experiencing the City

The **SYMBOLIC-INTERACTION APPROACH** takes a micro-level look at the reality of city living.

- Georg Simmel explained that cities expose people to intense stimulation. To cope, urbanites develop a blasé attitude, tuning out much of what goes on around them.
- Despite the widespread idea that cities threaten mental health, research reveals that urbanites have better mental health than people living in rural areas.

p. 383

Social-Conflict Analysis: Cities and Inequality

The **SOCIAL-CONFLICT APPROACH** focuses on how social inequality shapes the city and urban life.

- Economic inequality generates very different neighborhoods in cities across the United States.
- Both government policies and economic investment favor affluent people while ignoring the needs of low-income people.

pp. 383–85

Gemeinschaft (p. 380) a type of social organization in which people are closely bound by kinship and tradition

Gesellschaft (p. 381) a type of social organization in which people interact on the basis of self-interest

mechanical solidarity (p. 381) social bonds based on common sentiments and shared moral values

organic solidarity (p. 382) social bonds based on specialization and mutual interdependence

enterprise zones (p. 385) areas in the inner city that attract new businesses with the promise of tax relief

See the **Applying Theory** table on page 384.

Politics and Urban Life: Constructing Problems and Defining Solutions

The Radical Left: The Need for Basic Change

- **RADICALS ON THE LEFT** blame the market economy for creating urban problems such as poverty, crime, and urban sprawl. They cite the history of urban renewal as an example of the harmful results of putting profits over people.
- Radicals on the left claim that only a basic change in the capitalist economy is likely to result in a better life for the majority.

p. 387

Liberals: Government Reform

- **LIBERALS** point to the increasing economic inequality in U.S. cities that results in millions of people having to live in low-quality housing and attend inferior schools.
- Liberals praise government efforts to improve city life by reducing income inequality, making jobs available, and combating discrimination.

pp. 386–87

Conservatives: The Market and Morality

- **CONSERVATIVES** link the expansion of the welfare state with the rise of problems such as violence and the breakdown of the traditional family, which in turn have caused the deterioration of cities.
- Conservatives claim that most government programs to improve city life are ineffective or counter-productive. They look to the operation of the market economy to transform rundown cities into prosperous urban centers.

pp. 385–86

See the **Left to Right** table on page 388.

CONSTRUCTING THE PROBLEM

Is population increase a problem?

In 2009, Earth's population was 6.8 billion people, four times what it was a century ago.

In a rich world, do people really go hungry?

Around the world, 1 billion people—about one in six—experience daily hunger.

How does gender figure into the issue of global poverty?

Around the world, 70 percent of adults facing life-threatening poverty are women.

CHAPTER 15

Population and Global Inequality

CHAPTER OVERVIEW

WHY IS THE PLANET'S POPULATION a matter of serious concern? This chapter introduces demography, the study of population, and explains important concepts such as fertility, mortality, and immigration. You will learn where in the world population is increasing fastest and how population trends are linked to global inequality. You will carry out theoretical analysis of global inequality and learn two political approaches to constructing "problems" and defining "solutions."

Fatma Mint Mamadou looks out over the stretch of sand and grass that surrounds her. Night is coming, and she is counting camels, as she does every day at this time.

Mamadou is a young woman living in North Africa's Islamic Republic of Mauritania. She has never been to school and cannot read or write. If you ask her age, she smiles and shakes her head. She doesn't know when she was born.

She has spent her life tending camels, herding sheep, hauling bags of water, sweeping the floor, and serving tea and food. For this work, she is paid nothing. She is a slave, one human being owned by another. This young woman is one of about 90,000 slaves in Mauritania.

Mamadou accepts her situation, mostly because she has never known anything else. She explains without anger that she is a slave just like her mother before her and her grandmother before that. "Just as God created a camel to be a camel," she shrugs, "he created me to be a slave."

This young woman lives with her two children, her mother, and her brothers and sisters in a squatter settlement on the edge of Nouakchott, Mauritania's capital city. Their home is a 9-by-12-foot hut they built from wood scraps and other building materials they found at a construction site. The roof is a piece of cloth; there is no plumbing or furniture. The nearest water comes from a well a mile down the road.

A final question is more personal: "Are you and other girls ever raped?" Mamadou hesitates. With no hint of emotion, she responds, "Of course, in the night the men come to breed us. Is that what you mean by rape?" (Burkett, 1997).

The life of this young woman is powerful evidence of the extent of social inequality in the world. Living in a rich society, we take for granted going to school, having enough to eat, and making choices about how to live. But in much of the world, people struggle to survive, and the exploitation of some by others is both stunning and routine.

This chapter begins our look at problems on a global scale, with an eye to the contrasts between rich and poor countries. We begin with the issue of population, which in most low-income regions of the world is increasing rapidly. Then the focus turns to the causes of population increase and why too many people on the planet is widely seen as a problem.

The chapter then turns to global inequality. After exploring more about the problems of global poverty and hunger, we examine explanations of the striking inequalities found around the world and possible solutions to these problems.

Global Population Increase

Global population has not always been a cause for concern. For most of human history, the world's population was low and fairly steady. Only after the Industrial Revolution did the world's population begin to rise. But when it did, it skyrocketed.

Population by the Numbers

Some 12,000 years ago, when our distant ancestors were first forming permanent settlements, the population of the entire world was just 5 million, which is less than the population of New York City today. Population increased very slowly, so that about 1 C.E., global population was about 300 million, or roughly the number of people living in the United States today.

Around 1750, just as the Industrial Revolution was starting in Europe and the American colonies were preparing for independence from Great Britain, the world's population began to rise sharply. Figure 15–1 shows that the world's population reached 1 billion by 1800. By 1930, not much more than a century later, it was 2 billion. At this point, not only was the population going up, but also it was rising faster and faster. The world passed the 3 billion mark in 1962, just thirty-two years later, and 4 billion people crowded the planet by 1974, after only another twelve years. No wonder that about this time, people began to talk about "overpopulation" as a serious problem.

By 1970, although the *rate* of increase began to slow, global population kept pushing upward. The world passed the 5 billion mark in 1987 and the 6 billion mark in 1999. This means that in the course of the twentieth century, global population

demography the study of human population

fertility the incidence of childbearing in a country's population

crude birth rate the number of live births in a given year for every 1,000 people in a population

mortality the incidence of death in a country's population

crude death rate the number of deaths in a given year for every 1,000 people in a population

quadrupled. In 2009, there were 6.8 billion people in the world (Population Reference Bureau, 2009).

Most of the 82 million people being added to the world every year live in poor countries where the problem of poverty is already serious. Looking ahead, the United Nations projects that global population will surpass 7 billion in 2012 and climb to between 8 and 9 billion by 2050 (United Nations, 2009). Whether Earth can support 9 billion people or more—and at what standard of living—is one of the most serious questions we face today (Smail, 2007).

Causes of Population Increase

Tracking these trends is the focus of **demography,** *the study of human population.* Demography (from Greek words meaning "writing about people") is one branch of sociology that not only measures population levels but also tries to explain why they rise and fall. Demographers point to two basic reasons for the current population increase: high fertility and falling mortality.

High Fertility

Fertility is *the incidence of childbearing in a country's population.* Demographers measure a society's fertility using the **crude birth rate,** *the number of live births in a given year for every 1,000 people in a population.* The crude birth rate is calculated by dividing the number of live births in a year by the society's total population and multiplying the result by 1,000. In the United States in 2009, there were 4.1 million live births in a population of 307 million, yielding a crude birth rate of 13.5 (Hamilton, Martin, & Ventura, 2010).

Demographers describe this measure as "crude" because it is based on the entire population, not just women in their childbearing years. But the crude birth rate is a good, easy-to-figure measure of a society's fertility. Figure 15–2 on page 396 shows the crude birth rate for the major regions of the world.

All other factors being equal, the higher a nation's fertility, the faster its population increases. For the world as a whole, the crude birth rate is 21. Against this global average, the birth rate in the United States is low. Birth rates are higher in poor countries such as the Philippines (26) and higher still in many of the world's poorest nations, including Afghanistan (47) in Asia, Angola (47) in Central Africa, the Palestinian Territory in the Middle East (37), and Nicaragua (26) in Latin America (Population Reference Bureau, 2009). The Diversity: Race, Class, & Gender box on page 397 explains how the lack of effective birth control contributes to high birth rates in poor countries.

Falling Mortality

An even more important factor in the upward surge in global population is falling **mortality,** *the incidence of death in a country's population.* Demographers track mortality using the **crude death rate,** *the number of deaths in a given year for every 1,000 people in a population.* The number of deaths in a year is divided by the total population, and the result is multiplied by 1,000. In 2009, there were 2.4 million deaths in the U.S. population of 307 million, yielding a crude death rate of 7.9 (Kochanek et al., 2011).

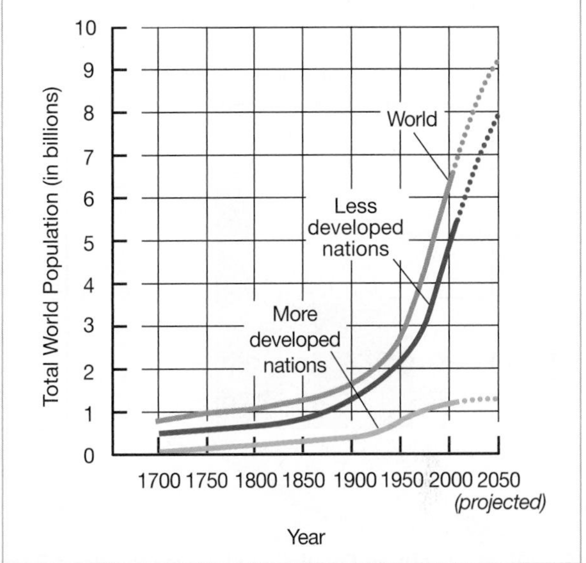

FIGURE 15–1 World Population, 1700–2050

Global population began to increase rapidly after about 1800. Although the *rate* of increase is now declining, the world is likely to have about 9 billion people by 2050.

Source: United Nations (2009).

Other factors being equal, the lower a nation's mortality, the faster its population increases. For the world as a whole, the crude death rate is 8, which makes the U.S. rate about average.

To understand why the U.S. mortality rate is not well below the world average, you need to keep in mind that the global pattern of death rates is more complex than the pattern for birth rates. At first glance, it makes sense that the lower the crude death rate, the healthier the society. This is true to a point. Some very poor nations such as Laos (10) and Mali (15) have high crude death rates. But poor nations also have populations that are, on average, very young because of the high birth rates we have already discussed. Rich nations such as the United States have populations that are, on average, much older. For this reason, the death rate for the United States is higher than you might at first expect. This also explains why the death rates in some poor countries, such as Vietnam (5) and Nicaragua (5), are lower than expected (Population Reference Bureau, 2009). The middle graph in Figure 15–2 shows the crude death rates for the major world regions.

infant mortality rate the number of deaths among infants under one year of age for every 1,000 live births in a given year

SOCIAL PROBLEMS in Everyday Life

Would you expect low-fertility countries (such as the United States) to differ from high-fertility countries (most low-income nations) with respect to attitudes toward women and gender equality? Why or why not?

Dimensions of Difference

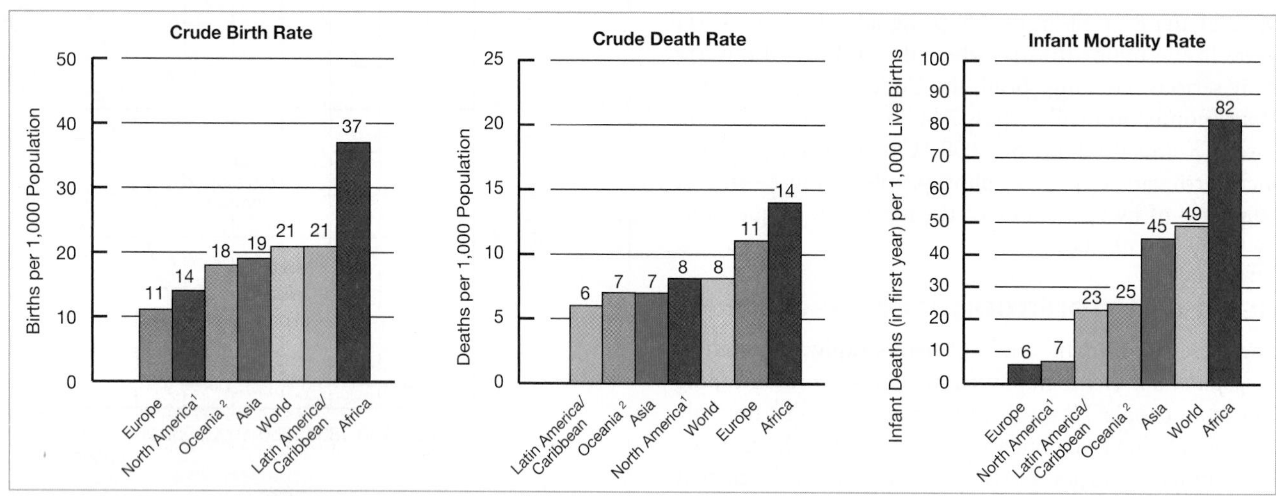

FIGURE 15–2 Three Population Statistics for World Regions

These figures provide a comparative look at the birth rates, death rates, and infant mortality rates for major regions of the world.

¹ United States and Canada

² Australia, New Zealand, and South Pacific islands

Source: Population Reference Bureau (2009).

A better measure of a nation's quality of life is the **infant mortality rate,** *the number of deaths among infants under one year of age for every 1,000 live births in a given year.* In this case, the number of deaths of children under one year of age in a given year is divided by the number of live births during that year, and the result is multiplied by 1,000. In 2009, there were 26,531 infant deaths and 4.1 million live births in the United States. Dividing the first number by the second and multiplying the result by 1,000 yields an infant mortality rate of 6.4 (Kochanek et al., 2011).

For the world as a whole, the infant mortality rate is 49, so quality of life in the United States is quite good. However, the U.S. infant mortality rate is still higher than that of most other rich countries, including Great Britain (5), Australia (5), Japan (3), and Sweden (2) (Population Reference Bureau, 2009). What explains the lower standing of the United States? For one thing, social inequality is greater here than in most other industrial nations. For another, ours is the only high-income country without universal access to health care.

In poor countries, infant mortality is dramatically higher. The rates for Nicaragua (29), Angola (132), Cambodia (67), and Afghanistan (163) reflect the fact that the people of these nations lack adequate nutrition and safe water and have little or no access to high-quality medical care (Population Reference Bureau, 2009).

Measuring Population Increase

Demographers can calculate a society's *natural growth rate* (or rate of natural increase) by combining fertility and mortality rates. To do this, simply subtract the crude death rate from the crude birth rate. In the case of the United States, a crude birth rate of 13.5 minus the crude death rate of 7.9 yields a natural growth rate of 5.6 per 1,000, or 0.56 percent annual growth.

For the world as a whole, population is increasing at the rate of 1.2 percent each year. Global Map 15–1 on page 399 shows that population growth is slow in North America (0.6 percent annually), Europe (–0.1 percent), and Oceania (1.1 percent), rich regions of the planet.

To calculate the *doubling time* for a nation's population, simply divide the number 70 by the growth rate. The population of Central America, with an annual growth rate of 1.7 percent, will double in about thirty-seven years. The population of Central Africa, with a 2.8 percent growth rate, will double in twenty-five years. Clearly, a country that has trouble feeding the population it has now can hardly afford to let population double within little more than one generation.

One other factor that plays a part in a nation's overall population growth but is not included in measures of natural growth rate is immigration. As explained in Chapter 3 ("Racial and Ethnic Inequality"), at least 1 million people enter the United States each year, both legally and illegally. The United

MAKING THE GRADE

Be sure you know how to use an annual rate of population increase to calculate a doubling time.

zero population growth the level of reproduction that maintains population at a steady state

DIVERSITY: RACE, CLASS, & GENDER

Women, Power, and Contraception: The Key to Controlling Population

As recently as 1960, family planning was almost unknown in poor countries and not all that common even in the United States. Today, as women have gained greater control over their lives, birth rates are down, and about three-fourths of U.S. couples in their childbearing years use some form of contraception. Worldwide, however, patriarchy remains strong, and only about half of all women have access to effective birth control.

There are many reasons for not using contraception, including religious beliefs and women's lack of social power in many poor societies. Another important factor is poverty: Women who live in poor societies cannot pay for contraception—and some have not even heard about this technology.

The figure clearly shows the difference contraception makes in lowering fertility. The vertical axis shows the percentage of women using contraception; the horizontal axis shows the average number of children a women bears during her lifetime. Each of the 159 dots represents a country in the world. The dots show a strong *correlation,* or association, between the two variables; the *regression line* is a statistical way of summarizing this linear relationship. In countries where contraception is widespread, women have about two children; in countries where it is not, women have five or more children. It is easy to imagine the consequences of each pattern for population increase.

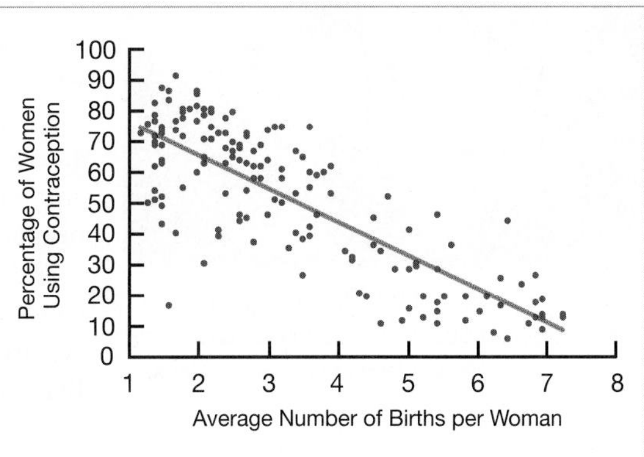

Contraceptive Use and Fertility in 159 Countries

This pattern shows a negative correlation represented by the regression line: As the share of women using contraception goes up, a woman's average number of children goes down.

WHAT DO YOU THINK?

1. In 1900, the average woman in the United States had about five children. What factors do you think brought that number down to about one today?
2. Looking around the world, women are more likely to use contraception in countries where they have more choices about their lives. What does this suggest about the need to raise the social standing of women?
3. If women everywhere in the world were to have five children, what consequences would there be for the planet as a whole?

Source: Data from Population Reference Bureau (2009).

States and other high-income nations grow as much or more from immigration as from natural increase. Low-income nations such as Afghanistan, on the other hand, grow almost entirely from natural increase, with births exceeding deaths.

We now turn to a survey of population patterns around the world. Generally speaking, population growth is slowest in the Northern Hemisphere, where we find most of the high-income countries. But population growth is very high in the Southern Hemisphere, which contains most of the world's low-income countries.

The Low-Growth North

When the Industrial Revolution began, population growth in Western Europe spiked upward to about 3 percent annually. Since then, the growth rate has fallen steadily. Now the birth rate in Europe, the United States, and Canada is below the replacement level of 2.1 children per woman. Demographers call this point **zero population growth,** *the level of reproduction that maintains population at a steady state.* More than seventy-five nations, almost all high-income, have dropped below the point of zero population growth (Population Reference Bureau, 2009).

What explains the great decline in population increase? Important factors include the high cost of raising children, widespread use of contraceptives and abortion, the trend toward later marriage and singlehood, and the fact that the typical family now has both partners in the labor force.

In sum, in high-income nations such as the United States, population increase is not a serious problem. In fact, almost twenty-five European nations are projected to *lose* population between now and 2050. Some analysts suggest that these nations may face the problem of underpopulation in the future because the rising number of elderly people will have fewer and fewer young people to care for them and support them financially (United Nations, 2009). In this country, our high immi-

GETTING INVOLVED

In the past, have you considered global population to be a social problem? What about now? Explain.

MAKING THE GRADE

Why do some analysts claim a key part of controlling population increase is expanding economic and educational opportunities for women?

The birth rate in Cambodia, a low-income nation, is twice that of the United States. Because agrarian societies depend on human labor, large families make economic sense. This explains why almost all of the world's population increase is taking place in poorer countries.

The Social Standing of Women

Most population experts agree that a key element in controlling world population growth is raising the standing of women. Making birth control technology more widely available is important, but the population will continue to increase as long as a culture defines women's primary responsibility as raising children.

Dr. Nafis Sadik, an Egyptian woman who heads the United Nations' efforts at population control, sums up the new approach: Give a woman more choices about how to live, and she will have fewer children. A woman who has access to schooling and jobs can decide when and whether she wants to marry, and she will bear children as a matter of choice, not because it is the only option open to her. Under these conditions, evidence shows, women have fewer children (Axinn & Barber, 2001; Population Reference Bureau, 2009).

gration rate probably ensures that population will continue to increase in the decades to come.

The High-Growth South

Rising population is already a serious problem for many poor nations that lie in the Southern Hemisphere. The problem would certainly be worse were it not for programs to limit births that have been successful in many low-income countries. As a result of these efforts, the number of children born to the average woman in the world has fallen from six children in 1950 to about three children today.

But bringing down the birth rate goes only so far in controlling population increase. In the twentieth century, advances in medical technology sharply reduced death rates. In fact, most of the population increase in recent decades has resulted not from high fertility but from falling mortality. Most poor nations today have high birth rates coupled with declining death rates. Although it is certainly good news that fewer children and adults are dying, the result is rising populations that may end up threatening everyone's ability to survive.

Worldwide, lower-income nations now account for 80 percent of the planet's people. In addition, almost all of the increase in global population is taking place in the low-income nations of the Southern Hemisphere (United Nations, 2009).

Explaining the Population Problem: Malthusian Theory

Thomas Robert Malthus (1766–1834) was an English economist, priest, and pioneering demographer who lived at just the time when global population began heading sharply upward. Malthus (1926, orig. 1798) offered a simple mathematical analysis of population increase that led to a troubling conclusion. Population, he predicted, would increase according to what mathematicians call a *geometric progression,* illustrated by the series of numbers 2, 4, 8, 16, 32, and so on. At such a rate, world population would soon soar out of control.

Food production would also increase, Malthus predicted, but only in *arithmetic progression* (as in the series 2, 3, 4, 5, 6). This is because no matter what new technology people invent, there is only so much farmland.

Putting the two patterns together, Malthus concluded that people would soon reproduce beyond what the planet could feed, leading to starvation and social chaos. The Defining Moment box on page 400 takes a closer look at the warning sounded by Malthus.

CRITICAL REVIEW If Malthus had been right in his conclusion, we might not be here to think about his ideas. But Malthus failed to realize that as the Industrial Revolution took hold, birth rates would drop. The decline in fertility occurred because once children were no longer needed to farm the land, they became very costly to raise.

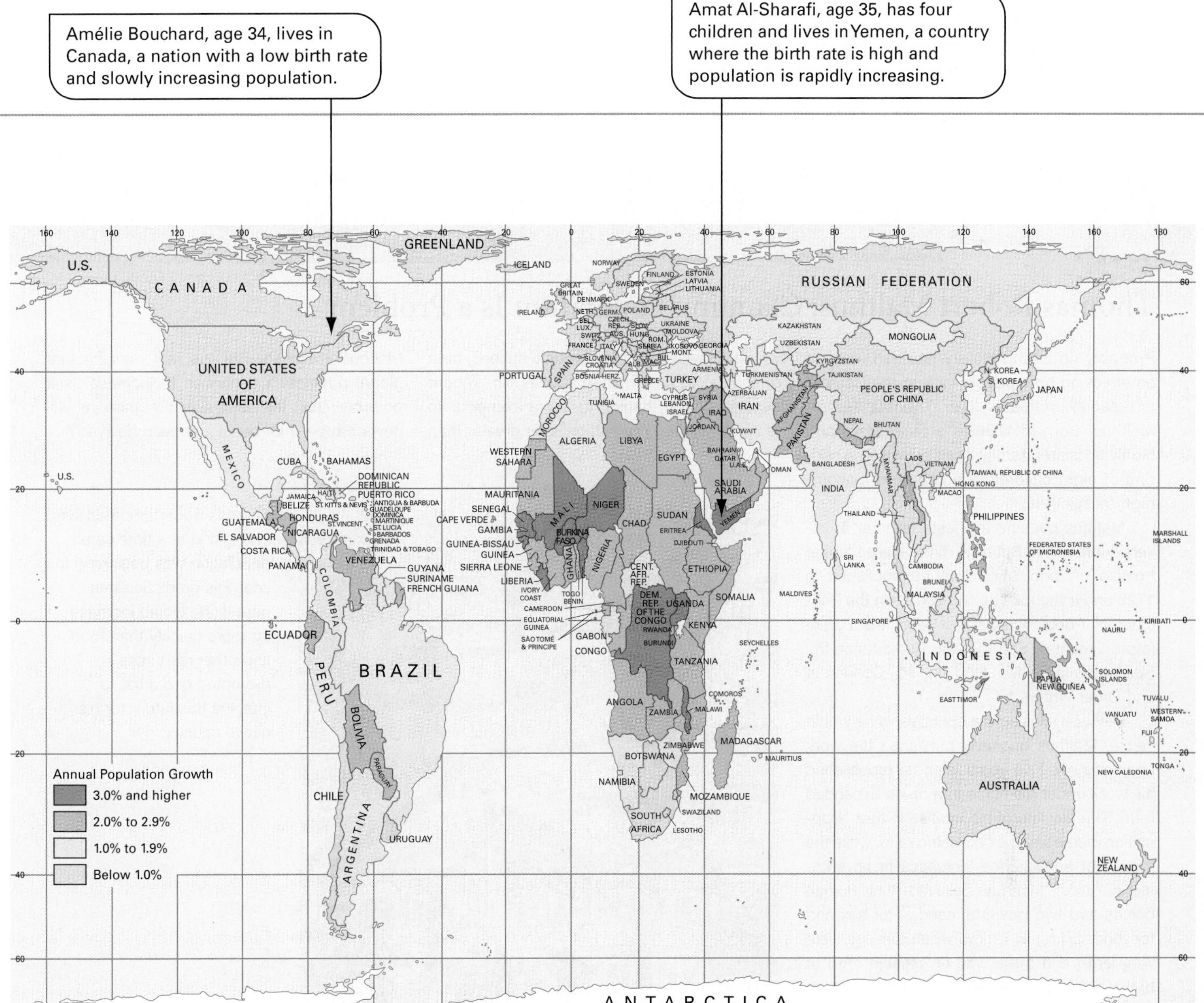

A World of Differences

GLOBAL MAP 15–1 Population Growth around the World

The richest countries of the world—including the United States, Canada, and the nations of Europe—have growth rates below 1 percent. The nations of Latin America and Asia typically have growth rates around 1.5 percent, which double a population in forty-seven years. Africa has an overall growth rate of 2.4 percent (despite only small increases in countries with a high rate of AIDS), which cuts the doubling time to thirty years. In global perspective, we see that a society's standard of living is closely related to its rate of population growth: Population is rising fastest in the world regions that can least afford to support more people.

Source: Population Reference Bureau (2009).

In addition, many people began using artificial birth control. Finally, Malthus underestimated how much food humanity would eventually produce. New technology in the form of irrigation, fertilizers, and pesticides has increased farm output far beyond what he imagined.

But was Malthus entirely wrong? Good land, clean water, and fresh air are all limited resources, so population cannot continue to expand indefinitely. In short, no level of population growth can go on forever. To avoid Malthus's dire prediction, humanity must work out ways to control its own numbers.

MAKING THE GRADE

Malthus claimed population increase was a threat to all of humanity. He lived at a time when European birth rates were rising and death rates were falling.

GETTING INVOLVED

Do you share the pessimism expressed by Malthus? Explain.

CONSTRUCTING SOCIAL PROBLEMS

A DEFINING MOMENT

Thomas Robert Malthus: Claiming Population Is a Problem

Probably no one in history has had more of an effect on how people look at the issue of population increase than Thomas Robert Malthus. Born in 1766 to a prosperous and highly educated family, Malthus was the second of eight children, a number not uncommon for his time.

Malthus became a priest and later a university professor. But he is remembered for the treatise on population that he published in 1798 under the full title "An Essay on the Principle of Population as It Affects the Future Improvement of Society, with Remarks on the Speculations of Mr. Godwin, M. Condorcet and Other Writers."

Perhaps sensing the controversy he would cause, Malthus originally published the work anonymously. Five years later, he republished his work under his name in a much expanded form. The key line of his treatise is this: "Population increases in a geometric ratio, while the means of subsistence increases in an arithmetic ratio." Malthus believed that human beings had two powerful needs—for sex and for food. Living at a time when families were very large and there was no reliable form of birth control, he reasoned that "the number of mouths to be fed will have no limit" so that "the food that is to supply them cannot keep pace."

Was there any hope? Malthus pointed out that "crime, disease, war, and vice" might well slow population increase. But he rejected birth control on religious grounds and thought it highly unlikely that people would give up sex (Malthus himself had just three children). In the end, Malthus could imagine no escape from a future of "famine, distress, havoc, and dismay."

More than two centuries later, we can be thankful that Malthus was at least partly wrong. Especially in high-income nations, birth rates have fallen dramatically in recent decades, and thanks to advancements in technology, food production is far greater than Malthus imagined. But the fact remains that global population continues to increase. Is it possible that the Malthusian nightmare will never happen? Or has it just been delayed?

Thomas Robert Malthus lived in England at a time when population was beginning to soar. His prediction that population would increase far more quickly than food and other resources prompted one artist to imagine this future for his native country.

demographic transition theory a thesis linking demographic changes to a society's level of technological development

SOCIAL PROBLEMS in Everyday Life

Do you think global population will continue to increase throughout this century? If so, will that throw the world into chaos, or will we manage the greater numbers? Explain your prediction.

A More Recent Approach: Demographic Transition Theory

A more recent analysis of population change is **demographic transition theory,** *a thesis linking demographic changes to a society's level of technological development.* Figure 15–3 shows population dynamics at four levels of technological development. Preindustrial, agrarian societies—that is, almost the entire world before 1750—fall into Stage 1. These societies have high birth rates because families depend on the labor of children and because there is little effective birth control. But death rates are also high because poor people have little understanding of health and disease. Periodic outbreaks of plague and other infectious diseases balance out any rise in births, so population bobs up and down but remains fairly steady over long periods of time.

Stage 2, the onset of industrialization, begins the demographic transition. Death rates fall because of higher living standards, including better nutrition and the benefits of scientific medicine. Because birth rates remain high, population begins increasing rapidly. Malthus lived during Europe's Stage 2, which helps explain his pessimistic view of the world's future. The poorest countries on the planet are in this high-growth stage today.

In Stage 3, a mature industrial economy, the birth rate falls into line with the death rate, and population growth slows down. Fertility falls partly because families no longer have to bear many children to ensure that a few will survive to adulthood. Also, mature industrial societies transform children from economic assets (who work to contribute to their families' income) to economic liabilities (instead, children's schooling and other expenses strain family finances). Effective birth control becomes widely available, and limiting family size is important to women who want to work outside the home.

Stage 4 corresponds to a postindustrial economy, which promotes stable population size once again. Both the birth rate and the death rate are low, so there is little or no natural increase in population size. As noted earlier, this is now the case in much of Western Europe and Japan (Population Reference Bureau, 2009).

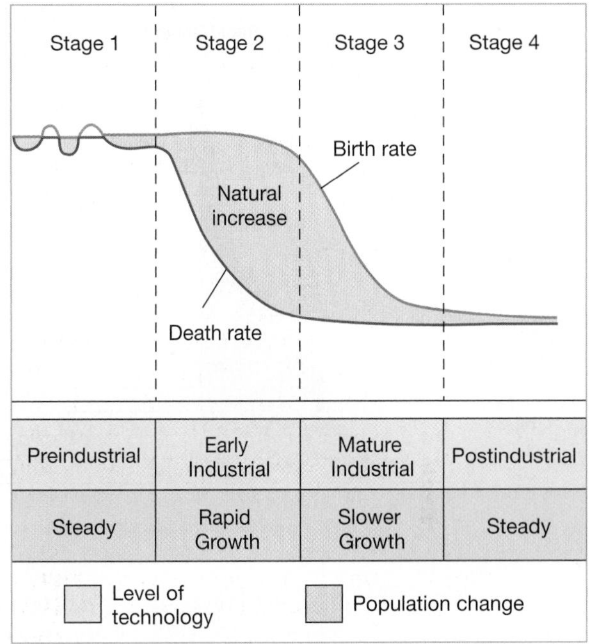

FIGURE 15–3 The Stages of Demographic Transition

Demographic transition theory shows the process by which societies move from high birth rates and high death rates (Stage 1) to low birth rates and low death rates (Stage 4).

CRITICAL REVIEW Compared with Malthus's alarming prediction, demographic transition theory offers a more hopeful view of our demographic future. In this analysis, advancing technology first sparks population increase but then brings it under control, all the while lifting living standards.

But will poor societies develop economically to the point that their birth rates drop? If they remain poor, there is little chance that the world will ever bring rising population under control. As shown in Figure 15–4 on page 402, even if birth rates fall, the very young population of poor nations (such as Kenya) means that most people have yet to bear children. So at least some population increase is inevitable, at least for decades to come.

Global Inequality

You have seen that population problems are far greater in some parts of the world than in others. The same is true in terms of poverty and hunger. As you might guess, the most serious problems of population increase and hunger are found in the same parts of the world.

Chapter 2 ("Poverty and Wealth") explained that people in the United States are divided into classes, with some having far more wealth, income, prestige, and power than others. Social stratification is even greater if we broaden our view to include not just people in the United States but people all around the world.

Figure 15–5 on page 403 divides the world's total income by fifths of humanity. For comparison, recall (from Figure 2–1 on page 29) that the richest 20 percent of the U.S. population earns about 47 percent of the national income. The richest 20 percent of the world's people, however, receives about 74 per-

SOCIAL PROBLEMS in Everyday Life

Based on the population profiles of these countries, how might you expect everyday life on the street to differ in Kenya, the United States, and Italy?

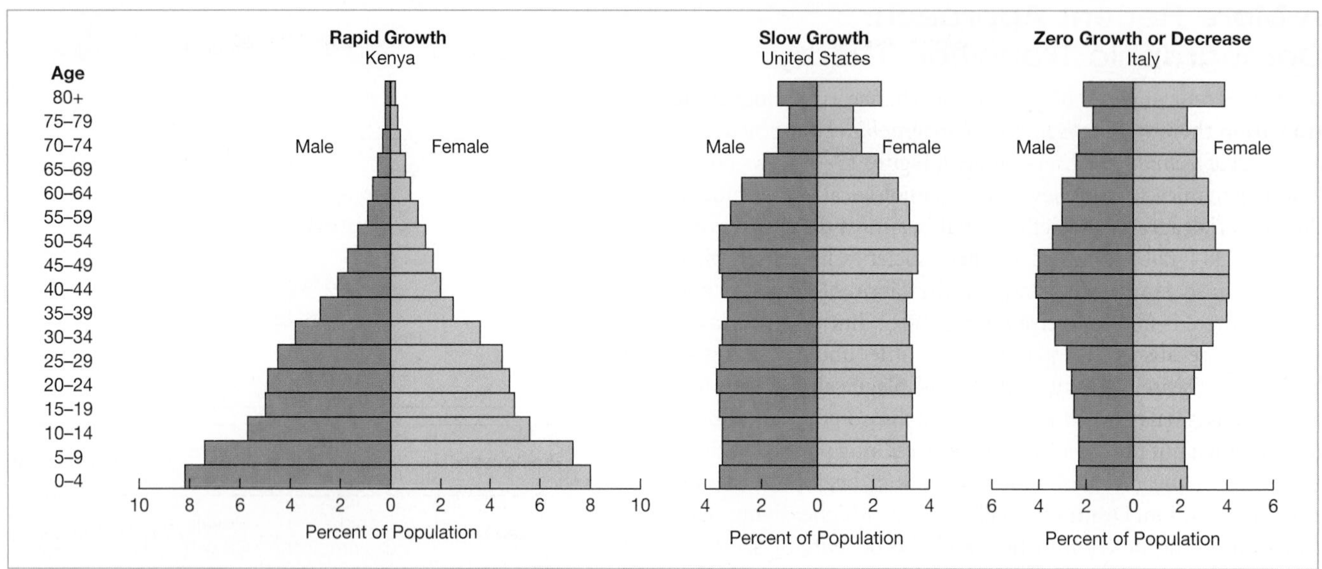

Dimensions of Difference

FIGURE 15–4 Population Pyramids: Kenya, United States, and Italy, 2011

Population pyramids are graphic representations of the population according to sex (male and female) and age (from birth to eighty years and over). In a very poor nation such as Kenya, the youngest people make up the largest share of the society, guaranteeing that population increase will continue as children enter their childbearing years. The United States' pyramid has a more boxlike shape because we are, on average, a much older population. (The average age in the United States is about thirty-seven, compared with about eighteen in Kenya.) Italy is one of the nations that is recording a slight population decrease. There are proportionately fewer young people in Italy, and a larger share are elderly. There the average age is forty-three and rising.

Source: United Nations (2010); U.S. Census Bureau (2011).

cent of all income. In the United States, the poorest 20 percent of the population earns 4 percent of all income; globally, the same proportion struggles to survive on just 1 percent of all income.

The global distribution of wealth, as the second half of Figure 15–5 shows, is even more unequal. The richest 20 percent of the world's adults own at least 90 percent of the planet's wealth. About half of all wealth is owned by just 2 percent of the world's adult population; about 40 percent by the richest 1 percent. At the same time, the poorest half of the world's adults own barely 1 percent of all global wealth. In terms of dollars, about half the world's families have less than $2,500 in total wealth, far less than the $100,000 in wealth for the typical family in the United States (Bucks, Kennickle, & Moore, 2006; Porter, 2006; Davies et al., 2008).

With the world's income and wealth so unevenly distributed, even people who are counted among the poor in the United States live much better than most of the world's people. Well-off men and women in rich countries live so well that many have trouble understanding just how serious the plight of others in the world really is. Each of the world's three richest people—Bill Gates and Warren Buffett in the United States and Carlos Slim Helú in Mexico—is worth more than $35 billion, which roughly equals the combined wealth of all the people in the world's thirty-four poorest *countries* (Kroll, Miller & Serafin, 2009).

High-Income Nations

Just as a single society places individuals at various class levels, the global system of inequality contains high-income, middle-income, and low-income nations. Global Map 15–2 shows which of the world's 194 nations fall in each category. There are now sixty-six high-income nations in the world, including the United States and Canada, Mexico, Argentina, and Chile, the countries of Western Europe, the Russian Federation, Israel, Saudi Arabia, South Africa, Japan, South Korea, Australia, and New Zealand.

MAKING THE GRADE

Comparing the figure below to Figures 2–1 and 2–2, you can see that both income and wealth are more unequally distributed on a global scale than they are in the United States.

GETTING INVOLVED

Have you ever been in any of the low-income nations shown in the global map on page 404? If so, what were some of the differences you noticed in social life there?

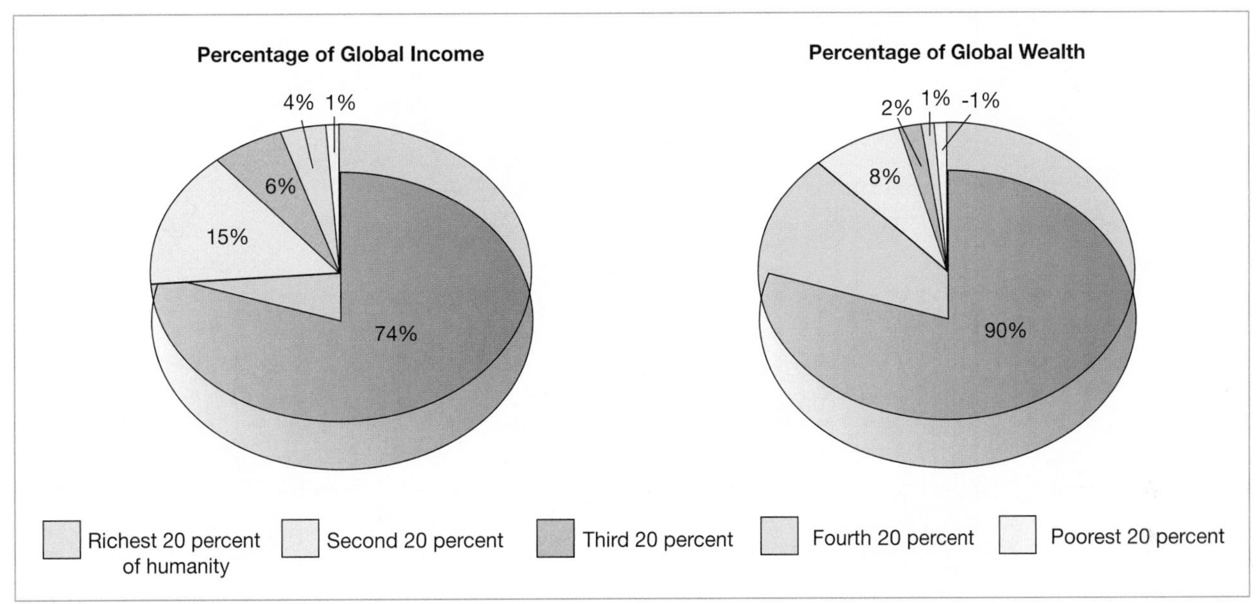

FIGURE 15–5 Distribution of World Income and Wealth

The total income earned by all the people of the world is distributed very unevenly, with the richest 20 percent of people receiving 74 percent of all income and owning 90 percent of all wealth.

Sources: Calculations based on United Nations Development Programme (2008) and World Bank (2008).

The world's rich nations benefit from the productivity of advanced technology. It was in these nations that the Industrial Revolution steadily boosted productivity beginning more than two centuries ago. How much of a difference does advanced technology make? The high-income nation of the Netherlands produces more than the mostly agrarian continent of Africa below the Sahara. Tiny South Korea outproduces all of India (United Nations Development Programme, 2008).

In 2008, high-income nations were home to about 1.5 billion people, or 22 percent of Earth's population. Even at the bottom of this favored category (for instance, the Russian Federation), annual income is at least $10,000; the figure is more than three times that much in the world's richest countries, such as the United States and Switzerland. Taken together, the people in the sixty-six high-income countries earn 80 percent of the world's total income.

Middle-Income Nations

People living in middle-income countries have incomes ranging from $2,500 (in, say, Bolivia in Latin America, Lesotho in Africa, and Vietnam in Asia) to almost $10,000 (in Uruguay in Latin America, Bulgaria in Europe, and Thailand in Asia). These nations—seventy-two in all—have significant industrialization, but more than 40 percent of the people still live in rural areas and work in agriculture. In general, people in rural areas have less access to schooling, medical care, good housing, and safe water than those who live in cities.

In recent years, both India and China have entered the ranks of middle-income nations. In all, this category includes some 3.9 billion people, or about 58 percent of humanity. Overall, they earn about 18 percent of the world's income.

Low-Income Nations

The world's fifty-six low-income nations have populations that are, on average, agrarian and very poor. Most of these nations are found in Central Africa or Asia. In poor countries, about 65 percent of the people live in rural areas and farm as their ancestors have done for centuries. The remainder live in or near cities, where many work in factories. With limited industrial technology, low-income nations are not very productive, which is one reason that hunger, disease, poor schooling, and unsafe housing are so common.

In 2008, some 19 percent of the planet's population, or almost 1 billion people, lived in low-income nations earning only 2 percent of the world's income. For every dollar earned by people living in a rich nation, these people earn just pennies. We now take a closer look at the problems of global poverty and hunger.

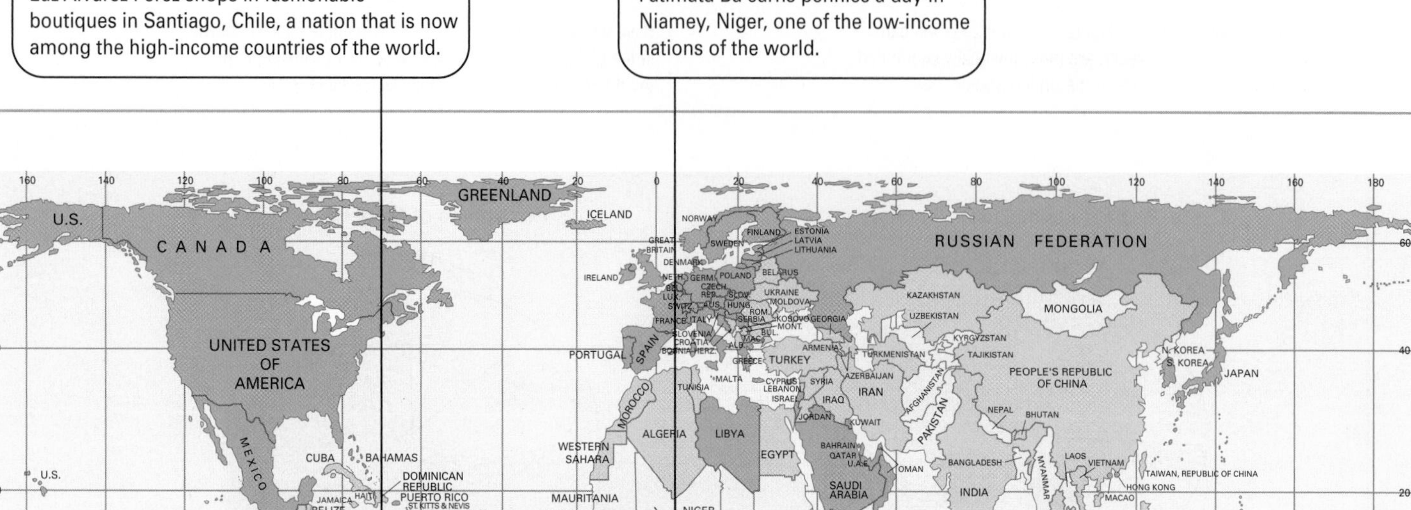

A World of Differences

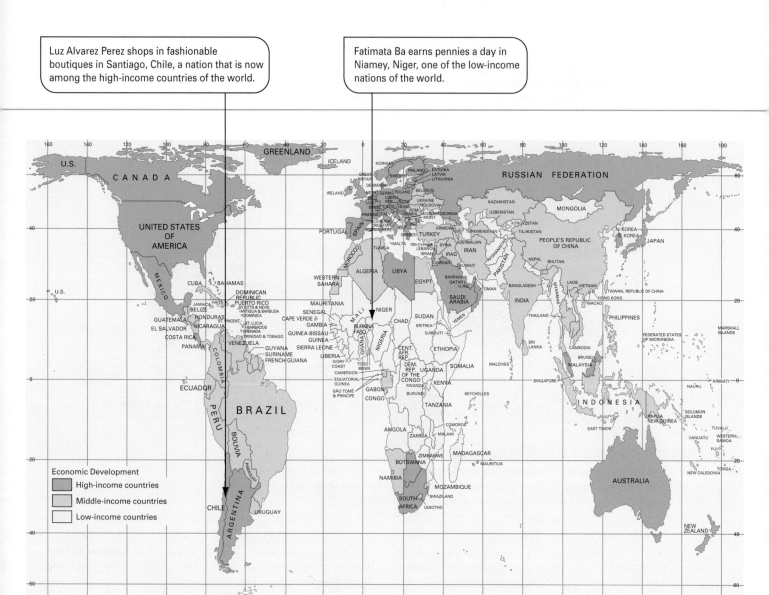

GLOBAL MAP 15–2 Economic Development around the World

In high-income countries—including the United States, Canada, Chile, Argentina, the nations of Western Europe, South Africa, Israel, Saudi Arabia, Australia, and Japan—a highly productive economy provides people, on average, with material plenty. Middle-income countries—including most of Latin America and Asia—are less economically productive, with a standard of living about average for the world as a whole but far below that of the United States. These nations also have a significant share of poor people who are barely able to feed and house themselves. In the low-income countries of the world, poverty is severe and widespread. Although small numbers of elites live very well in the poorest nations, most people struggle to survive on a small fraction of the income common in the United States.

Note: Data for this map are provided by the United Nations. Each country's economic productivity is measured in terms of its gross domestic product (GDP), which is the total value of all the goods and services produced by a country's economy within its borders in a given year. Dividing each country's GDP by the country's population gives us the per capita (per-person) GDP and allows us to compare the economic performance of countries of different population sizes. High-income countries have a per capita GDP of more than $10,000. Many are far richer than this, however; the figure for the United States exceeds $41,000. Middle-income countries have a per capita GDP ranging from $2,500 to $10,000. Low-income countries have a per capita GDP of less than $2,500. Figures used here reflect the United Nations' "purchasing power parities" system, which is an estimate of what people can buy using their income in the local economy.

Source: Data from United Nations Development Programme (2008).

GETTING INVOLVED

Have you ever had any direct experience with absolute poverty, either in the United States or elsewhere? Explain.

MAKING THE GRADE

Both children and women experience greater inequality in a global perspective compared to the United States.

The World's Poverty Problem

Poverty is far more widespread in the world as a whole than it is in the United States. Around the world, about 1 billion people do not have enough to eat. Over time, hunger leads to malnutrition and makes it hard to work; it also raises the risk of disease (United Nations Development Programme, 2008).

In more scientific terms, the typical adult in a rich nation, such as the United States, consumes about 3,500 calories a day, which is too much for good health. The result of this high level of consumption is that about two-thirds of the people in this country are overweight. The typical adult in a low-income country, who performs a great deal of physical labor, consumes just 2,000 calories a day. This is too little for good health, especially among people who do lots of physical labor, and the result is hunger and undernourishment.

The long-term effects of poverty are deadly. In the ten minutes it takes to read through this section of the chapter, about 100 people in the world, sick and weakened from hunger, will die. This amounts to about 25,000 people each day, or 9 million people each year. Global hunger is among the most serious social problems facing the world today (United Nations Development Programme, 2008).

Relative versus Absolute Poverty

Most of the poverty that we have in the United States is *relative poverty,* referring to a lack of the resources that most people take for granted. In global perspective, however, we face the problem of *absolute poverty,* a lack of resources that is life-threatening.

Human beings in absolute poverty lack the nutrition necessary for health and long-term survival. There is no denying that some absolute poverty exists in the United States. But such immediately life-threatening poverty strikes only a tiny percentage of the U.S. population. By contrast, one-third or more of the people in low-income countries are in desperate need. When absolute poverty becomes widespread, death comes early. In rich countries, death typically occurs after age seventy-five. But in the poorest regions of Central Africa, half of all children do not live to age ten.

For every dollar earned by the average person in the United States, people in India earn about 25 cents. Even though India is now a middle-income country, widespread poverty is evident on the streets of Chennai and other Indian cities as families beg for money. If you were a visitor from the United States, what degree of responsibility would you feel for the welfare of a family like this one?

Poverty and Children

Poverty distorts the lives of young people, even those lucky enough to survive. Perhaps 100 million children in the cities of poor countries beg, steal, sell sex, or work for drug gangs to provide needed income for their families. Such children miss out on schooling and are likely to fall victim to disease and violence. Many young girls become pregnant, truly a matter of children having children.

As many as 100 million of the world's children are orphaned or have left their families and are living on the streets doing whatever they must to get by. Latin America faces the greatest problem of poor, homeless children: Brazil reports that millions of children are living on their own, underfed and unschooled, often sniffing glue or using other cheap drugs to numb their suffering (UNICEF, 2006; Leopold, 2007; Levinson & Bassett, 2007).

Poverty and Women

As Chapter 4 ("Gender Inequality") explains, rich societies give men power over women in a number of ways. One consequence is that women are at much higher risk of poverty than men.

In poor countries, gender stratification is even more pronounced. Because traditional societies often are strongly patriarchal, women have few choices, limited schooling, and little economic opportunity. As a result, 70 percent of the adults facing absolute poverty are women (Moghadam, 2005).

SOCIAL PROBLEMS in Everyday Life

Are you surprised to learn that slavery continues to exist in the modern world?

modernization theory a model of economic and social development that explains global inequality in terms of technological and cultural differences between societies

Slavery

Surely the greatest horror linked to poverty in the world is slavery. Many people assume slavery to be an evil of the past. The British Empire banned slavery in 1833; the United States did the same in 1865. But according to Anti-Slavery International (2008), some 140 million men, women, and children (about 2 percent of the world's people) are currently living in conditions that amount to slavery. The chapter-opening story gives a picture of slavery in today's world.

The case of Fatma Mint Mamadou represents *chattel slavery,* in which one person owns another. No one knows exactly how many chattel slaves exist because the practice of buying and selling human beings is against the law around the globe. But the practice has been documented in many countries in Asia, the Middle East, and especially Africa and involves hundreds of thousands of people. Trading in people is one of the most profitable forms of crime (next to selling guns and drugs) to organized crime syndicates around the world (Orhant, 2002).

A second type of bondage is *child slavery,* in which desperately poor families send their children out to hustle on the streets to bring in income. Millions of children, many in poor countries of Latin America, fall into this category.

A third type of bondage is *debt slavery,* in which employers enslave workers of all ages by paying them too little to cover the costs of their debts. In sweatshops throughout the world, workers do receive a wage, but not enough to pay for the food and housing their employers provide. For practical purposes, then, they are slaves who are not free to leave.

A fourth type of slavery is a *servile form of marriage.* In India, Thailand, and some African nations, families marry off women against their will. Many end up as slaves performing work for their husband's family; in other cases, women are forced into prostitution.

In 1948, the United Nations issued the Universal Declaration of Human Rights, which states, "No one shall be held in slavery or servitude; slavery and the slave trade shall be prohibited in all their forms." Even though slavery is both morally wrong and against the law, it persists as part of the sad story of global poverty.

Theoretical Analysis: Understanding Global Inequality

Both of sociology's macro-level approaches provide explanations for global poverty and insights into the problem of population increase.

Structural-Functional Analysis: The Process of Modernization

Modernization theory is *a model of economic and social development that explains global inequality in terms of technological and cultural differences between societies.* Modernization theory begins by pointing out that as recently as two centuries ago, every nation in the world was very poor. As the Industrial Revolution took hold in Europe and later in North America and elsewhere, an increasing number of societies gradually became affluent. At first, new industrial wealth benefited just a few. But industrial technology was so productive that gradually the living standard of even the poorest people began to rise.

In the past century, living standards in high-income countries, including the United States, have jumped fivefold. This means that housing quality, nutrition, and health have all improved dramatically, not to mention having the benefits of household appliances, automobiles, and computers. Industrialization has also transformed most of today's middle-income nations in Asia and Latin America, and there too, living standards have risen. But in low-income countries, where there is less industrial technology, people remain poor.

A general rule is that the poorer a nation is, the greater the domination of women by men. In a country like Afghanistan, how is this fact reflected in the number of children a woman has, as well as her opportunities for schooling and for paid work?

MAKING THE GRADE

Modernization theory claims that both cultural values and technology explain why some nations are richer than others.

At this point, you might be wondering why every society hasn't adopted industrial technology. Modernization theory's answer is this: Not every society is eager to sacrifice tradition in favor of change toward higher living standards. In this analysis, then, tradition, perhaps in the form of fundamentalist religious beliefs, is the greatest barrier to economic development. In societies that have strong families and whose people are taught to respect the past, culture acts as an anchor that prevents people from exploring new ways of life. Held in place by their traditions, people do not adopt new technologies or get the schooling that might improve their lives.

In today's world, there are many examples of societies that reject modernization, including the Amish of North America, the Semai of Malaysia, and fundamentalist Muslims in Iran, Afghanistan, and elsewhere. Typically, these societies reject industrial technology and other elements of modern culture as a threat to their family relationships, customs, and religious beliefs.

Near the end of the Middle Ages, as the sociologist Max Weber (1958, orig. 1904–05) explained, the cultural environment of Western Europe favored change. As Protestant religious beliefs (especially those of John Calvin) took hold in parts of Europe, a progress-oriented way of life emerged. People came to view getting rich—which the Catholic tradition regarded with suspicion—as a sign of personal virtue and ultimate salvation. A new ethic of individualism gradually replaced the traditional emphasis on kinship and community. Such cultural beliefs led people to adopt new technology and helped bring about the Industrial Revolution. Before long, culture and technology had succeeded in lifting Western Europeans from poverty and creating widespread prosperity.

W. W. Rostow: The Stages of Modernization

Modernization theory draws on the work of Max Weber, as well as that of Ferdinand Tönnies and Emile Durkheim, whose ideas were discussed in Chapter 14 ("Urban Life"). But it was Walt Whitman Rostow (1960, 1978) who expressed modernization theory as an easy-to-understand series of stages.

1. **Traditional stage.** People living in traditional, agrarian societies raise their children to look to the past, respecting old ways. Such people do not easily imagine how life can be very different from what they have always known. Therefore, they build their lives around their families and local communities, following the ways of their ancestors with little personal choice or individual freedom. Such societies provide a life that is spiritually rich but poor in a material sense.

   Several centuries ago, most of the world was in this first stage of economic development. Today, nations such as Bangladesh, Niger, and Somalia are still stuck in the traditional stage and remain just as poor as they were then.

2. **Take-off stage.** As societies begin to break free of cultural tradition, they allow people to use their talents and imagination, and the economy begins to grow. As people produce goods not just for their own consumption but also to trade with others for profit, a market takes form. Greater individualism, a willingness to take risks, and a desire for material goods are all forces for change toward material prosperity, although they also weaken family ties and time-honored norms and values.

   Great Britain and the United States reached take-off in the early 1800s. Thailand, a middle-income country in eastern Asia, is now in this stage. Reaching take-off sometimes depends on progressive influences from richer nations, which provide foreign aid, export advanced technology and investment capital, and invite foreign students to take advantage of advanced schooling.

3. **Drive to technological maturity.** As this stage begins, people come to define poverty as a problem, and they see progress and economic growth as solutions. Industrialization is well under way; the economy grows and diversifies as new products are invented and markets expand. People realize that their new way of life is weakening traditional family and local community life, but they soon abandon the ways of the past, which they come to see as "old-fashioned." Great Britain reached this point by about 1840; the United States, by 1860. Today, Mexico, the U.S. territory of Puerto Rico, and South Korea are among the nations driving toward technological maturity.

   Once a society reaches Stage 3, there is much less absolute poverty. Cities swell with people who have left their rural villages in search of better jobs and schooling. Occupational specialization makes relationships less personal. The rising importance of individual freedom and social equality sparks social movements demanding greater political rights for all, including women. Governments pass laws requiring everyone to attend school, and a large share of people go on to college or other advanced training.

4. **High mass consumption.** At this point, industrial technology is widespread, and the economy is growing rapidly with steadily rising living standards. Mass production of an endless assortment of new goods and services fuels mass consumption. People take affluence for granted and learn to "need" things their ancestors never imagined.

   The United States, Japan, and other rich nations moved into this stage of development by about 1900. Recently entering this level of economic development are two former British colonies that are now prosperous small societies of eastern Asia: Hong Kong (part of the People's Republic of China) and Singapore (independent since 1965).

SOCIAL PROBLEMS in Everyday Life

If modernization were to take place as this theory says it can, what do you think will happen to global cultural diversity?

world system theory a model of economic development that explains global inequality in terms of the historical exploitation of poor societies by rich ones

Modernization theory claims that as rich nations colonized much of the world, they spread progressive culture and new technology. World system theory challenges this claim, charging that colonization did little more than make some nations rich while making others poor. Which approach do you find more convincing? Why?

Rostow explains that rich nations play an important part in helping poor countries move through the four stages. Rich nations can export high-tech farming methods to poor nations to help raise agricultural yields. Such techniques—part of what is commonly called the Green Revolution—include hybrid seeds, modern irrigation methods, chemical fertilizers, and pesticides for insect control. Poor countries also look to rich nations for industrial technology as well as computers and other new information technology.

Even an expanding economy will not lift living standards if poor societies do not control their population growth. Rich nations can help poor nations limit population growth by giving them birth control technology and educational programs to promote its use. Also, according to modernization theory, once economic development is under way, birth rates should decline as they have in industrialized nations because children are no longer an economic asset but become an economic liability (Lino, 2008).

CRITICAL REVIEW Since it first emerged in the 1950s, modernization theory has shaped the foreign policy of the United States and other rich nations. Supporters point to rapid economic development in much of the world—especially the Asian nations of South Korea, Taiwan, Singapore, and Hong Kong—as evidence that the affluence created in Western Europe and North America is within reach of all countries (Parsons, 1966; Moore, 1977, 1979; Bauer, 1981; Berger, 1986; Firebaugh & Beck, 1994; Firebaugh, 1996; Firebaugh & Sandu, 1998).

But critics see modernization theory as simply a defense of capitalism. If modernization theory is correct, they ask, why is there still so much poverty in much of the world? Why are living standards in a number of nations, including Haiti and Nicaragua in Latin America and Sudan, Ghana, and Rwanda in Africa, no better, and in some cases worse, than they were in 1960? (United Nations Development Programme, 2008).

Second, critics point out that modernization theory says little about how rich nations often try to prevent poor countries from developing. Centuries ago, European nations began a system of colonial control over much of the world that benefited the European conquerors at the expense of most of the world's people. Such exploitation continues to the present day, as you will soon see.

Third, modernization theory sets up the world's most developed countries as the standard for the rest of the world, as if we have nothing to learn from others. This ethnocentric (culturally self-serving) bias can have harmful consequences. The Western idea of progress encourages the exploitation of other nations and also fuels wasteful consumption, causing harm to the physical environment of the planet, the focus of Chapter 16 ("Technology and the Environment").

Fourth and finally, critics reject modernization theory's implication that poor societies are responsible for their own poverty. Instead of blaming the victims, critics want to shift the focus to the behavior of rich nations.

Such concerns point to a second major approach to understanding global inequality, called world system theory.

Social-Conflict Analysis: The Global Economic System

The social-conflict approach to global inequality centers on **world system theory,** *a model of economic development that explains global inequality in terms of the historical exploitation of poor societies by rich ones.* For centuries, rich nations have used the capitalist global economy to benefit themselves as they exploit poor nations.

This approach rejects the idea that poor nations are simply lagging behind other nations in the race for economic develop-

colonialism the process by which some nations enrich themselves through political and economic control of other nations

neocolonialism a new form of economic exploitation that involves the operation of multinational corporations rather than direct control by foreign governments

MAKING THE GRADE

World system theory claims that the global capitalist system causes some nations to be richer than others.

ment. In this analysis, some nations have become rich only *because* others have become poor.

The origins of the capitalist world economy go back five centuries to the time when Europeans began establishing colonies, which eventually included the Americas to the west, Africa to the south, and Asia to the east. **Colonialism** is *the process by which some nations enrich themselves through political and economic control of other nations.* Great Britain established so many colonies around the world that in 1900 it controlled about one-fourth of the world's land and could boast, "The sun never sets on the British Empire." The United States, which was itself one of the early British colonies, eventually pushed westward across the continent, purchased Alaska, and gained control of Haiti, Puerto Rico, Guam, the Philippines, the Hawaiian Islands, and parts of Panama and Cuba.

Formal colonialism began to decline in the mid-nineteenth century. Today, colonialism has almost disappeared from the world. According to world system theory, however, exploitation continues in the form of **neocolonialism** (*neo* means "new"), *a new form of economic exploitation that involves the operation of multinational corporations rather than direct control by foreign governments.* In the past, colonial powers directly ruled their colonies. Today, rich nations continue to exploit poor nations as multinational corporations operate throughout the world (Bonanno, Constance, & Lorenz, 2000).

Immanuel Wallerstein: The Capitalist World Economy

Immanuel Wallerstein (1974, 1979, 1983, 1984) explains that the "capitalist world economy," in operation for more than 500 years, is centered in today's rich nations. These high-income countries (see Global Map 15–2) are the *core* of the world economy. These nations became rich as they established colonies and systematically collected gold, silver, and other raw materials from countries around the world. The resulting wealth helped them begin the Industrial Revolution. Today, multinational corporations dominate the global economy and continue to draw wealth from around the world to North America, Western Europe, Australia, and Japan.

Low-income countries form the *periphery* of the world economy. Brought into the world economy by colonial exploitation, poor nations continue to support rich ones in two ways. First, they provide inexpensive labor; recall from earlier chapters that multinational corporations have "exported" jobs from the United States to the Philippines, Taiwan, China, and other countries. Second, lower-income nations provide a vast market for industrial products.

The remaining countries fall in between the "haves" and "have-nots" and are called the *semiperiphery* of the world economy. They include middle-income countries such as Brazil, Honduras, and Indonesia that have close ties to the global economic core.

According to Wallerstein and others who use this approach (Frank, 1981; Delacroix & Ragin, 1981; Bergesen, 1983; Dixon & Boswell, 1996; Kentor, 1998, 2001), the world economy not only exploits poor nations but also places them in a position of dependency on rich nations. For this reason, this approach is also called *dependency theory.* This dependency occurs in three ways:

1. **Poor countries have only narrow, export-oriented economies.** Poor nations produce only a few crops, which they sell to rich countries. For example, coffee and fruits from Latin American nations, petroleum from Nigeria, hardwoods from the Philippines, and palm oil from Malaysia are all consumed by affluent people in rich nations. With production under the control of multinational corporations, low-income countries develop little of their own industrial production.
2. **Poor countries lack industrial production.** Having little industrial base, poor nations depend on rich nations to buy their inexpensive raw materials. At the same time, they turn to rich countries for more expensive manufactured goods. For example, British colonialists encouraged the people of India to raise cotton but prevented them from weaving their own cloth. The British shipped Indian cotton to English textile mills in Birmingham and Manchester. The finished goods were then shipped back to India for sale.

   The same pattern applies today to agricultural products. What modernization theorists call the Green Revolution involves poor countries selling cheap raw materials to rich nations and in turn buying expensive fertilizers, pesticides, and mechanical equipment from those same rich nations. Rich countries gain much more than poor nations from such trading.
3. **Poor countries are deeply in debt.** Given such unequal trade patterns, it is little wonder that poor countries have fallen into debt to rich nations. Altogether, the poor nations of the world owe rich countries $3 trillion. Such staggering debt leaves poor countries with little money to build economically; the result is high unemployment and high inflation (World Bank, 2008).

As Wallerstein and other social-conflict theorists see it, the causes of global poverty are the capitalist economy and the policies of rich nations. Modernization theorists claim that rich nations produce wealth through capital investment and technological innovation. As poor nations do business with rich nations and adopt progrowth policies and more productive technology, they too will produce more wealth and prosper. World system theorists, by contrast, highlight how the global economy distributes wealth. They argue that the world's economic system only makes rich countries richer, leaving

MAKING THE GRADE

Use the table below to review the two theoretical approaches to global inequality.

APPLYING THEORY

Global Inequality

	How has the world changed over the centuries?	Why is there global inequality?	What is the political character of the approach?
Structural-functional approach: Modernization theory	People everywhere were very poor until industrial technology started to raise living standards; although some nations are more productive than others, all nations today are better off compared to centuries ago.	Differences in culture and technology are the major reasons: While some countries have shown eagerness to change, others remain more traditional. The United States and other rich countries are part of the solution because they help lower-income countries develop economically.	Although liberals support the way modernization theory attacks traditions, this approach finds greatest support among conservatives who support the capitalist economy.
Social-conflict approach: World system theory	People around the world were roughly equal until the beginning of colonialism, which made some nations rich and other nations poor.	Colonialism created inequality, and the world capitalist system, dominated by multinational corporations, continues to enrich some nations at the expense of others. The United States and other rich countries are part of the problem because they benefit from the capitalist world economy while other nations become poor.	This approach is favored by Marxists and others on the political left: It calls for radical change to the world capitalist system in favor of a more egalitarian economic system.

poor nations little or no opportunity to improve their living standards. In short, the global economy has *overdeveloped* rich nations and *underdeveloped* the rest of the world.

From this point of view, the problem of global population increase is likely to continue. As long as many of the world's nations remain poor, their fertility rates will remain high. Not until the world moves toward a more equal distribution of wealth and resources will there be a real chance for controlling population and ensuring the economic security of all.

CRITICAL REVIEW The central point of world system theory (dependency theory) is that no nation develops or fails to develop in isolation: The global economic system shapes the destiny of all nations. Citing Latin America, Africa, and other poor regions of the world, dependency theorists claim that there can be no development under the current market system dominated by rich countries and their capitalist multinational corporations.

But critics claim that this approach is incorrect in implying that no one gets richer without someone else getting poorer. They point out that corporations, small business owners, and farmers can and do create new wealth through their hard work, imagination, and use of new technology. This is precisely why the wealth of the world has increased sixfold since 1950.

Second, critics challenge the argument that rich nations are to blame for global poverty by pointing to many of the world's poorest countries (such as Ethiopia) that have had little contact with rich countries. On the positive side, many nations with long histories as colonies, including Sri Lanka, Singapore, Hong Kong, and, more recently, India, have prospered (E. F. Vogel, 1991; Firebaugh, 1992; Zakaria, 2004).

MAKING THE GRADE

Conservatives are optimistic, claiming that living standards around the world have risen dramatically.

Third, critics say that by citing a single factor—world capitalism—as the cause of global inequality, world system theory treats poor societies as victims with no responsibility for their own situation (Worsley, 1990). They note that while the Taliban enforced fundamentalist Islam in Afghanistan, that nation had few economic ties with other countries. Similarly, many nations, including Panama, Haiti, the Democratic Republic of Congo, the Philippines, and Iraq, have suffered as dictators looted their wealth. Capitalist societies, then, cannot be blamed for economic stagnation in these nations.

Fourth, critics say that world system theory is wrong to claim that global trade always makes rich nations richer and poor nations poorer. In 2010, the United States had a trade deficit of $647 billion, meaning that this nation imports two-thirds of a trillion dollars more than it sells abroad. The single greatest debt was to China, whose profitable trade with rich nations such as the United States has now pushed that country into the ranks of middle-income nations (United Nations, 2008; U.S. Census Bureau, 2011).

Conservatives praise the power of the marketplace and see world trade as benefiting all nations, rich and poor alike. Liberals argue that markets alone cannot ensure the well-being of a billion desperately poor people around the world—world governments, too, must take action. Radicals contend that global capitalism is incapable of lifting the living standards of the world as a whole; they call for a new, more equitable economic and political system. In your opinion, which viewpoint offers the greatest promise to people like these women, who work for a few dollars a day in sweatshops?

The Applying Theory table summarizes what we learn from both of these theoretical approaches.

POLITICS AND GLOBAL INEQUALITY

Constructing Problems and Defining Solutions

Politics guides what people see as problems and what they support as solutions. This chapter concludes with three political perspectives on global poverty and the solutions each offers.

Conservatives: The Power of the Market

In his study of industrial capitalism, Peter Berger (1986:36) concludes, "Industrial capitalism has generated the greatest productive power in human history. To date, no other socio-economic system has been able to generate comparable productive power." This statement provides a strong foundation for the conservative view of global inequality.

Conservatives believe that poverty is a serious problem throughout the world. But they remind us that the problem is much smaller today than in centuries past. For tens of thousands of generations, most people were poorly nourished, had primitive shelter, received little schooling, and had almost no medical care. Today, on average, people live longer and better than ever before. Some 3 billion—nearly half—of the world's people enjoy long, healthy, and comfortable lives well beyond the imagination of their ancestors. Another 2 billion people are better off than the average person living before the Industrial Revolution.

That leaves about 1.4 billion people whose lives are in serious danger. Consistent with modernization theory, conservatives believe that the solution to global poverty lies in allowing the productive power of industrial capitalism to spread. They point to United Nations studies (United Nations Development Programme, 1994, 1996, 1998, 2003, 2005, 2008) that show that progress is being made toward a better life: Daily calorie intake and average life expectancy are both up, and access to safe water and adult literacy are more widespread than ever before. Worldwide, infant mortality is half what it was in 1960. Many formerly poor nations of the world have made great progress in recent years, including Mexico, South Korea, Taiwan, Hong Kong, Singapore, India, and China.

GETTING INVOLVED

Do you ever wonder if clothing or other products you buy have been made in a sweatshop? Explain.

SOCIAL PROBLEMS IN GLOBAL PERSPECTIVE

Sweatshop Safety: How Much Is a Life Worth?

Poor people have few choices about what to eat, where to live, or where to work. Sweatshops exist because millions of poor people in the world have little choice but to take whatever jobs they can find. The worst sweatshops pay workers as little as 20 cents an hour. Yet they have no trouble finding people willing to work ten hours a day, seven days a week, all year long, to earn perhaps $750 a year. Forget about any paid vacation or other benefits. As the following incident suggests, many sweatshops lack even basic safety protections.

On April 12, 2002, more than 1,000 people were at their jobs in a garment factory in Narsingdi, a small town near Dhaka, the capital city of Bangladesh. Crowded together on the fourth floor of the large building, the women and men worked at sewing machines making T-shirts, creating a steady roar that went on for ten hours a day, every day of the week.

April 12 ended in tragedy. A worker who was shooting spot remover on stained fabric watched in horror as a spark from her machine flew into an open can of flammable cleaning fluid. In a flash, the entire table burst into flames. A dozen fellow workers rushed to the scene, trying to smother the fire with shirts, but it spread quickly. In a matter of minutes, the room, filled with highly combustible materials, was engulfed in flames.

Trying to escape the smoke and fire, workers poured down the steep, narrow staircase that led to the street. But as the human wave reached the bottom, it crashed up against a folding metal gate that was kept locked during working hours to keep employees from leaving. The first people to reach the gate turned in panic, only to be crushed by hundreds behind them. In less than a minute, fifty-two people were trampled to death.

Sweatshop factories such as this one are big business in Bangladesh, where garment making represents 75 percent of the country's total economic exports. Approximately half of the garments shipped from Bangladesh end up in clothing stores in the United States. People who look for bargains on store clothing racks rarely stop to think that the reason for the low price may well be that the workers halfway around the world who made the garments are paid only pennies a day.

This particular factory is owned by the family of Tanveer Chowdhury, who complained bitterly to reporters after the fire. "This fire has cost me $586,373, and that does not include $70,000 for machinery and $20,000 for furniture. I made commitments to meet deadlines and I still have the deadlines. I am now paying for air freight at $10 a dozen when I should be shipping by sea at 87 cents a dozen."

Chowdhury had one other expense as a result of the fire. To settle claims by families for the loss of their loved ones, he eventually agreed to pay $1,952 per person. In Bangladesh, life—like labor—is cheap.

WHAT DO YOU THINK?

1. Some people view the wages paid by textile factories abroad as the "going rate" in low-income nations. Others see them as exploitation of poor people. Which is closer to your view? Why?
2. Are consumers in high-income nations such as the United States partly responsible for situations such as that described in this box? Why or why not?
3. Apply modernization theory and dependency theory to factories such as this one. How do the two approaches lead to different conclusions?

Sources: Bearak (2001) and Amin & Karim (2008).

Liberals: Governments Must Act

Liberals accept the fact that the capitalist market system is highly productive. Yet they reject the position that the capitalist market *by itself* is the solution to global poverty. In addition, they look to government to help the poor.

One reason government help is needed is that modernizing influences, such as the use of high technology, have yet to reach many nations, especially their rural regions. Liberals claim that governments of rich nations—the countries that benefit most from global economic production—have a moral obligation to provide foreign aid to poor nations, especially in the areas of health care and education.

A second issue is that global corporations and smaller businesses in low-income nations try to build their profits on low wages paid to workers in sweatshop factories. It is up to governments in both rich and poor countries to eliminate the exploitation that occurs in such businesses. Most sweatshops are in countries where average wages are quite low. The typical U.S. worker in manufacturing earns about $24 per hour; across our southern border in Mexico, the comparable figure is about $3 (U.S. Department of Labor, 2009). Sweatshops not only pay workers very little, but they are also extremely dangerous workplaces. The Social Problems in Global Perspective box describes one deadly example.

Finally, around the world, most peasants do not own the land they work. In Brazil, for example, three-fourths of all farmland is owned by wealthy landowners who make up less than 5 percent of the population (Galano, 1998). For this reason, as a

MAKING THE GRADE

Radicals on the left are pessimistic, believing that global inequality will get worse until basic changes to the global economy are made.

MAKING THE GRADE

Use the table below to review the three political approaches to global inequality.

LEFT TO RIGHT

The Politics of Global Inequality

	RADICAL-LEFT VIEW	LIBERAL VIEW	CONSERVATIVE VIEW
WHAT IS THE PROBLEM?	Some of the world is overdeveloped, and much of the world is underdeveloped. The world's wealth is concentrated in a handful of very rich nations.	Most people in rich nations have more than they need, but nearly 2 billion people around the world contend with a poor diet, inadequate housing, and little education.	Although 5 billion people in the world live far better than our ancestors several centuries ago, nearly 2 billion of the world's people remain poor.
WHAT IS THE SOLUTION?	Replace the capitalist world economy with a system that values people above profits, eliminate multinational corporations, use land to grow food for local consumption, and cancel foreign debt.	The rich of the world must share their wealth in the form of foreign aid that will improve health, schooling, and housing; oppose sweatshops; and support land reform.	Allow the productive power of the market to raise the living standards of poor nations today as it has done in the past; encourage capital investment and technology transfers to poor nations.

JOIN THE DEBATE

1. From each of the three political perspectives, what role do rich nations such as the United States have in addressing global poverty and hunger?
2. What importance does each perspective assign to government? To a free market?
3. Which of the three political analyses of global inequality included here do you find most convincing? Why?

step toward reducing global poverty, liberals support government action to give working families the opportunity to own land.

The Radical Left: End Global Capitalism

Radicals on the left view global poverty following world system theory. Hunger activists Frances Moore Lappé and Joseph Collins (Lappé, Collins, & Kinley, 1981; Lappé & Collins, 1986) claim that many people in the United States have been raised to think of global poverty as the inevitable result of "natural" events: periodic natural disasters such as droughts and floods and lack of population control on the part of "backward" societies.

From the radical-left point of view, however, global poverty is tragic because it is *not* inevitable. Lappé and Collins point out that the world already produces plenty of food for everyone. In fact, if all the world's food were distributed and consumed equally, every person on the planet would soon be getting fat. Even poor regions of the world such as southern Africa actually *export* food, even though many people in these regions go hungry.

How, then, can we explain the existence of poverty amid plenty? Lappé and Collins see the problem as policies by which rich nations direct the production of food for profits, not people. Corporations in poor nations prefer to produce export crops such as coffee, which bring high profits when sold in the United States and other rich nations. But growing export crops produces fewer staples such as beans and corn that would feed local families. Government officials in poor countries also favor growing for export because they need the money to pay foreign debt. At the core of this vicious circle is the capitalist global economy.

From this point of view, the problem of global poverty is likely to get worse. Some of the world's poorest nations are sinking ever deeper in debt to rich nations. The solution, from the radical-left perspective, is the transformation of global capitalism toward a more socially conscious economic system. At the very least, poor nations should demand a cancellation of existing debt and end economic relations with multinational corporations; in addition, they should nationalize (that is, take control of) foreign-owned industries within their borders. In recent years, leftist leaders in a number of nations in South America have done just that. Of course, such action strikes at

GETTING INVOLVED

How do you feel about the world's future? Looking ahead fifty years, will the world be better off or worse off? How? Why?

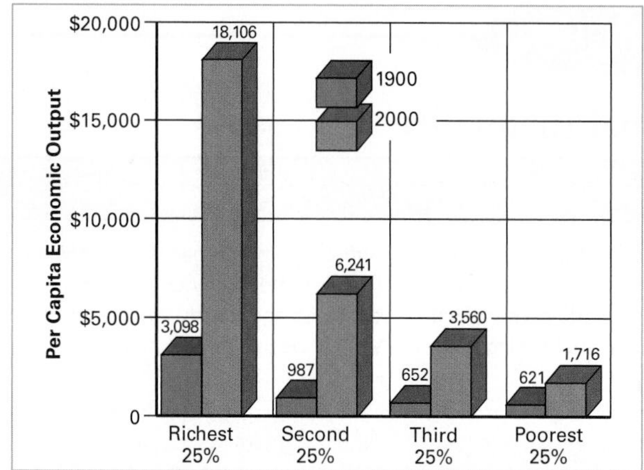

FIGURE 15–6 The World's Increasing Economic Inequality

Although both rich and poor have higher income, the gap between the richest and poorest people in the world is twice as big as it was a century ago.

Source: International Monetary Fund (2000, 2009).

the very root of our global power structure. But from the radical-left point of view, nothing less is likely to work.

The Left to Right table on page 413 summarizes the three approaches to global poverty.

Going On from Here

The increase in world population remains one of the most serious problems facing humanity. Population soared in the twentieth century, and projections call for continued increases—although the *rate* of increase will slow—in the current century.

Because half of the people in high-growth nations have yet to reach childbearing age, there is little doubt that global population will continue to rise for decades to come. This increase will place greater demands on the limited resources in low-income nations, making the task of raising living standards more difficult. For this reason, the United Nations and other organizations are working to bring a halt to global population increase. Some analysts even argue that we need to *reduce* global population to perhaps half of what we have now if everyone in the world is to have a safe and secure life (Smail, 2007).

An even larger problem is global inequality. Currently, the world's wealth is very unequally distributed, with a small share of humanity (including people in the United States and Canada) producing most of the goods and services and consuming most of the planet's resources.

As this chapter has explained, although almost everyone agrees that the situation is serious, there is disagreement about what to do about it. The official policy of the United States has been fairly close to modernization theory: Government leaders have long claimed that poor nations can develop economically as rich nations did in the past. To help poor nations make economic progress, the United States provides roughly $34 billion in foreign aid annually (not counting money for rebuilding Iraq or Afghanistan) to nations in every region of the world.

There is some good news. Over the past century, living standards rose in most of the world. Even the economic output of the poorest 25 percent of the world's people almost tripled. This means that the number of people in the world living on less than $1.25 a day fell from about 1.9 billion in 1981 to about 1.4 billion in 2005 (Chen & Ravallion, 2008). Most people in the world are better off than ever before in *absolute* terms.

At the same time, however, the level of *relative* economic inequality in the world today is about twice as great as it was a century ago (International Monetary Fund, 2000, 2009). As Figure 15–6 shows, the poorest of the world's people are being left behind.

The greatest reduction in poverty has taken place in Asia. In 1980, almost 80 percent of global $1.25-per-day poverty was found in Asia, but by 2005, that figure had fallen to 17 percent. Also important is the fact that both India and China have joined the ranks of the middle-income nations. In recent decades, the economic growth of India and China has actually been great enough to reduce global economic inequality as wealth has shifted from North America and Europe to Asia (Sala-i-Martin, 2002; Chen & Ravallion, 2008; Davies et al., 2008).

In Latin America, the story is mixed. During the 1970s, this world region enjoyed significant economic growth; during the 1980s and 1990s, however, there was little overall improvement. The share of global $1.25-per-day poverty was slightly higher in 2005 (3 percent) than it was in 1981 (2 percent) (Sala-i-Martin, 2002; Chen & Ravallion, 2008).

About half of African nations have reported economic growth. At the same time, in many countries—especially south of the Sahara—poverty is getting worse. In 1981, sub-Saharan Africa accounted for 11 percent of $1.25-per-day poverty; by 2005, this share had risen to 28 percent (Sala-i-Martin, 2002; Chen & Ravallion, 2008).

The plight of the poorest billion people in the world is reason enough for the world to take action. But something even bigger is at stake: Unless the world changes so that all people have a secure existence, can any of us expect the nations of the world to find peace?

DEFINING SOLUTIONS

What should we do about the rapidly increasing population of our planet?

As this chapter has explained, Earth's population has increased sevenfold over the last 200 years, to the point that many analysts are pointing to a population crisis. Look at the two photos below to see two different approaches to solving this problem.

From the left side of the political spectrum, the solution to social problems typically is action by the government. In China, a nation that was facing rapid population increase, the government enacted a one-child policy back in 1979. The government views this policy as a solution to the population problem, claiming that the nation's population is now about 250 million lower than it would have been without this policy. What do you see as advantages and disadvantages of such a policy?

From the right side of the political spectrum, conservatives claim that the market system will encourage economic development and, in time, put the brakes on population increase. As economies develop, children become more and more expensive to raise and more women join the labor force. As a result, birth rates fall—without heavy-handed government mandates.

HINT

China's government mandate has certainly reduced that nation's population increase. But critics point to increases in abortion and also female infanticide as unfortunate consequences. In addition, there is the question as to whether government or parents themselves should make decisions about having children. As for the conservative solution, economic development can take decades, allowing population to climb in the meantime. In addition, a free-market solution allows richer families to have more children than poor families can afford, raising questions of equity. On the population question, which approach to a solution do you support?

Getting Involved: Applications & Exercises

1. Keep a log of mass media advertising mentioning low-income countries (ads selling, say, coffee from Colombia or exotic vacations to India). What images of life in low-income countries does the advertising present? In light of the facts presented in this chapter, do you think these images are accurate?
2. Millions of students from abroad study on U.S. campuses. Identify a woman and a man on your campus raised in a poor country. Approach them, explain that you have been studying global inequality, and ask whether they would be willing to talk with you about what life is like in their country. Also ask them about their impressions of inequality in the United States.
3. Looking over the various global maps in this text, identify social traits associated with the world's richest and poorest nations. Make use of both modernization theory and world system theory to explain the patterns you find.
4. Do some research in the library and on the Internet to explore the status of women in a number of low-income nations. One good source is the Human Development Report, published annually by the United Nations (http://www.undp.org). In poor countries, are women and men more unequal than they are in high-income nations such as the United States? In what ways are they unequal? Why are they unequal?

CHAPTER 15 Population and Global Inequality

Global Population Increase

Factors Affecting Population Growth

High **FERTILITY**, as measured by the **CRUDE BIRTH RATE**
- Birth rates are highest in low-income nations, where access to birth control is limited and women have few choices about how many children to bear.

p. 395

Low **MORTALITY**, as measured by the **CRUDE DEATH RATE**
- The lower a nation's mortality, the faster its population increases.
- Infant mortality is highest in poor nations, where people lack adequate nutrition and safe water and have little access to high-quality medical care.

pp. 395–96

✓ In global terms, U.S. population growth is low. (p. 397)

- Historically, world population grew slowly because high birth rates were mostly offset by high death rates.
- About 1750, a demographic transition began as world population rose sharply, mostly because of falling death rates.

pp. 397–98

- In 1798, Thomas Robert Malthus warned that population growth would outpace food production, resulting in starvation and social chaos.
- More recent **DEMOGRAPHIC TRANSITION THEORY** holds that technological advances gradually slow population increase.

pp. 398–400

✓ World population is expected to reach between 8 and 9 billion by 2050. Such an increase threatens to overwhelm many poor societies, where almost all of the increase will take place.

demography (p. 395) the study of human population

fertility (p. 395) the incidence of childbearing in a country's population

crude birth rate (p. 395) the number of live births in a given year for every 1,000 people in a population

mortality (p. 395) the incidence of death in a country's population

crude death rate (p. 395) the number of deaths in a given year for every 1,000 people in a population

infant mortality rate (p. 396) the number of deaths among infants under one year of age for every 1,000 live births in a given year

zero population growth (p. 397) the level of reproduction that maintains population at a steady state

demographic transition theory (p. 401) a thesis linking demographic changes to a society's level of technological development

Global Inequality

Social inequality in the world as a whole is greater than in the United States.
- About 22% of the world's people live in high-income countries such as the United States and receive 80% of all income.
- Another 58% live in middle-income countries, receiving about 18% of all income.
- The remaining 19% of the world's population live in low-income countries that have yet to industrialize and earn only 2% of global income.

pp. 402–3

Relative poverty is found everywhere, but poor nations contain widespread *absolute poverty* that is life-threatening.
- Worldwide, the lives of nearly 1 billion people are at risk because of poor nutrition.
- About 9 million people, most of them children, die annually from various causes brought on by hunger and lack of adequate nutrition.

p. 405

Nearly everywhere in the world, women are more likely than men to be poor. About 70% of adults facing absolute poverty are women.
- Gender stratification is most pronounced in poor societies, which tend to be strongly patriarchal.

p. 405

- As many as 140 million men, women, and children (about 2% of humanity) live in conditions that can be described as slavery.

p. 406

Theoretical Analysis: Understanding Global Inequality

Structural-Functional Analysis: The Process of Modernization

The **STRUCTURAL-FUNCTIONAL APPROACH** is seen in **MODERNIZATION THEORY**'s model of economic development, which explains global inequality in terms of technological and cultural differences between societies.

- Modernization theory maintains that economic development hinges on breaking free of traditional cultural patterns to seek material prosperity and adopt advanced technology.
- The modernization theorist W. W. Rostow identifies four stages of development: traditional, take-off, drive to technological maturity, and high mass consumption.

pp. 406–8

- Critics of modernization theory say that rich nations do not encourage but actually prevent economic development around the world. Therefore, they claim, poor nations cannot follow the path to development taken by rich nations centuries ago.

p. 408

Social-Conflict Analysis: The Global Economic System

The **SOCIAL-CONFLICT APPROACH** centers on **WORLD SYSTEM THEORY**, a model of economic development that explains global inequality in terms of the historical exploitation of poor societies by rich ones.

- World system theory (dependency theory) claims that global wealth and poverty are the historical products of the capitalist world economy beginning with colonialism and continuing, more recently, with the operation of multinational corporations.
- Immanuel Wallerstein views the high-income countries as the advantaged core of the capitalist world economy, middle-income nations as the semiperiphery, and poor societies as the global periphery. Economic relations make poor nations dependent on rich ones.

pp. 408–10

Critics of world system theory argue that this approach overlooks the sixfold increase in the world's wealth since 1950. Furthermore, the world's poorest societies are not those with the strongest ties to rich countries.

pp. 410–11

modernization theory (p. 406) a model of economic and social development that explains global inequality in terms of technological and cultural differences between societies

world system theory (dependency theory) (p. 408) a model of economic development that explains global inequality in terms of the historical exploitation of poor societies by rich ones

colonialism (p. 409) the process by which some nations enrich themselves through political and economic control of other nations

neocolonialism (p. 409) a new form of economic exploitation that involves the operation of multinational corporations rather than direct political control by foreign governments

See the **Applying Theory** table on page 410.

Politics and Global Inequality: Constructing Problems and Defining Solutions

The Radical Left: End Global Capitalism

- **RADICALS ON THE LEFT** blame the policies of rich nations for creating poverty in poor nations and keeping them in debt.
- Radicals on the left believe that poor nations should nationalize foreign-owned industries within their borders and demand a cancellation of their existing debt to rich nations.

pp. 413–14

Liberals: Government Must Act

- **LIBERALS** claim that the governments of rich nations have a moral responsibility to provide aid to poor nations, especially in the areas of health and education.
- Liberals want governments in both rich and poor countries to eliminate sweatshop exploitation.

pp. 412–13

Conservatives: The Power of the Market

- **CONSERVATIVES** believe that poverty is a problem around the world, but they focus on the improvements that have been made in recent centuries.
- Conservatives believe that the productive power of industrial capitalism will eventually solve the problem of global poverty.

p. 411

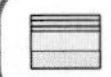
See the Left to Right table on page 413.

CONSTRUCTING THE PROBLEM

Is trash a problem?

Every day, people in the United States generate 1.4 billion pounds of solid waste. What should we do with it?

Does living well hurt the environment?

The average person in the United States uses hundreds of times more gasoline and plastic each year than the typical person in Bangladesh.

Should we protect the planet's rain forests?

The world's rain forests are shrinking by some 58,000 square miles each year.

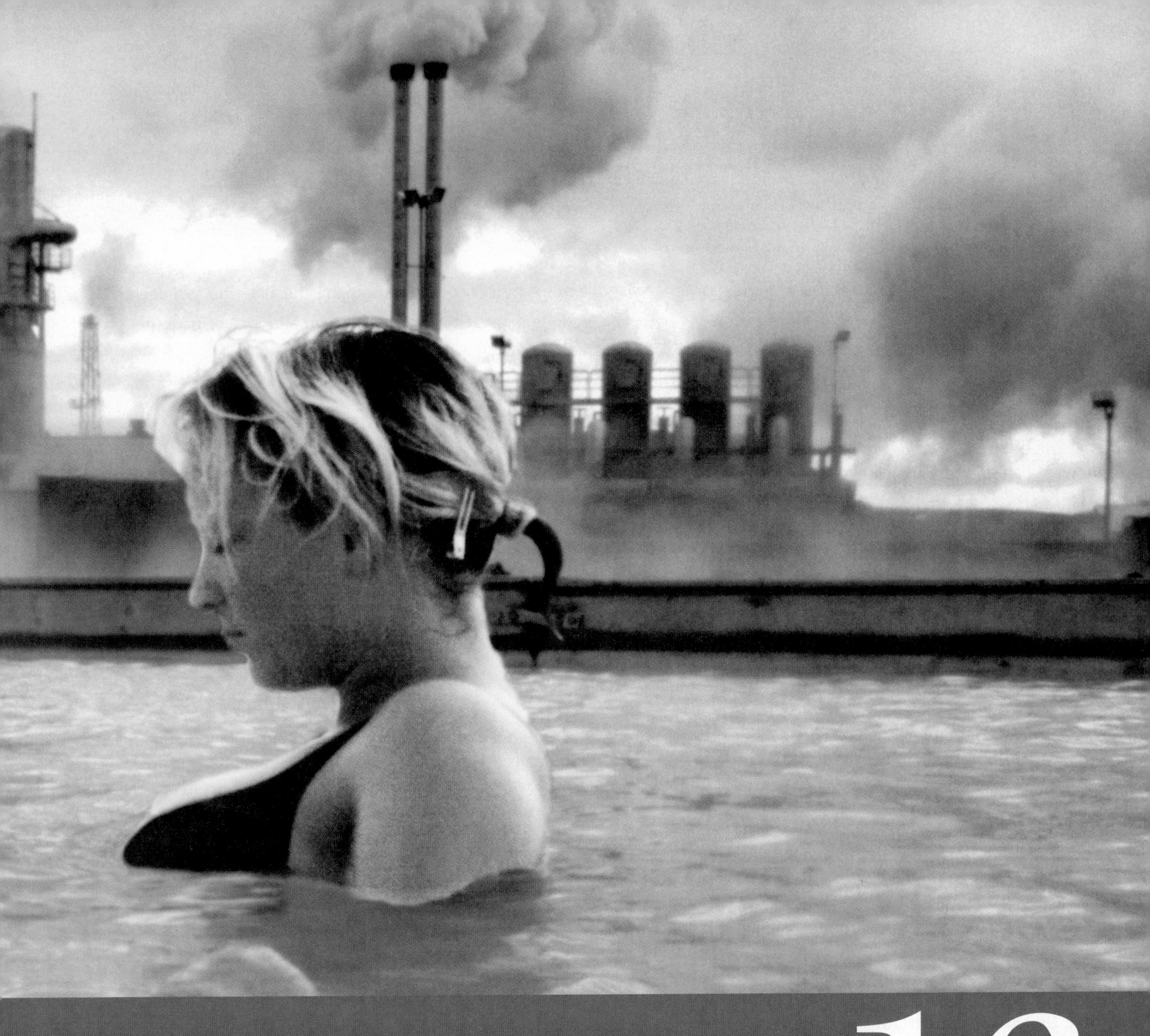

CHAPTER 16

Technology and the Environment

CHAPTER OVERVIEW

HOW IS THE STATE OF THE NATURAL ENVIRONMENT a social issue? This chapter explains that the biggest factor affecting the environment is how we organize social life and looks at specific factors such as population increase, material affluence, technology, and cultural patterns. You will learn about environmental issues involving solid waste, water supply, air and water pollution, and global warming. You will carry out theoretical analysis of environmental issues and learn how "problems" and "solutions" involving technology and the environment reflect people's political attitudes.

Grandma Macionis never threw anything away. Born in Lithuania—the "old country"—she grew up in a poor village, in a world that shaped her entire life even after she came to the United States as a young woman.

Her birthday was an amusing occasion for the rest of the family. After opening a present, she would carefully put aside the box, refold the wrapping paper, and roll up the ribbon so that they could all be used again. The packaging meant as much to her as the gift itself—possibly even more, because Grandma never wore the new clothes she was given. To her, there was nothing wrong with what she already had, so anything new seemed unnecessary and wasteful.

Grandma's kitchen knives were worn down from decades of sharpening, and every piece of furniture she ever owned stayed with her to the end of her life. (Carrying on the family tradition, I still eat at the same round oak table she first placed in her kitchen more than seventy-five years ago.)

As curious as Grandma Macionis often seemed to her grandchildren, she was a product of her culture. A century ago, when she was growing up, there was little "trash." If socks wore thin, they got mended, again and again. When clothes became worn beyond repair, they were used as cleaning rags or sewn together with other old clothing into a quilt. For people like Grandma, everything had value, if not in one way, then in another.

Grandma Macionis never thought of herself as an environmentalist. But she was: She lived a simple life, using few resources and creating almost no solid waste. Living this way may seem strange or hopelessly old-fashioned to most people in the United States today. After all, most of us seem to measure social standing by how much we consume. And our modern way of life also places a high value on "convenience," which leads us to buy our morning coffee in throw-away cups and to rely on private automobiles rather than public transit. As this chapter explains, our society supports a materialistic, fast-paced culture that we view as the "good life" but that places a great strain on our natural environment.

Ecology: Studying the Natural Environment

Ecology, *the study of how living organisms interact with the natural environment,* is a field that connects the social and natural sciences. In this chapter, we focus on the aspects of ecology related to sociological concepts and issues.

The term **natural environment** refers to *Earth's surface and atmosphere, including air, water, soil, and other resources necessary to sustain living organisms.* Like every other living species, humans depend on the natural environment to survive.

Yet humans stand apart from other species in our capacity for culture. This means that we alone take deliberate action to remake the world according to our interests and desires. To do this, we rely on **technology,** *knowledge that people apply to the task of living in a physical environment.* As technology has become more complex and powerful, humans have gained the ability to transform the world, for better or for worse.

The Role of Sociology

Problems related to the environment include solid waste, pollution, acid rain, global warming, and the declining number of living species. None of these problems results from the natural world operating on its own. They are all products of the way humans organize social life. For this reason, environmental issues are *social* problems.

Sociologists examine how people waste or conserve natural resources. They track public opinion on issues such as global warming and identify what categories of people support one side or the other of environmental issues. But the most important contribution sociologists make is in demonstrating how our society's technology, cultural patterns, and specific political and economic arrangements affect the natural environment.

The Global Dimension

Like the problems of rising population and world hunger (discussed in Chapter 15, "Population and Global Inequality"),

ecology the study of how living organisms interact with the natural environment

natural environment Earth's surface and atmosphere, including air, water, soil, and other resources necessary to sustain living organisms

technology knowledge that people apply to the task of living in a physical environment

ecosystem the interaction of all living organisms and their natural environment

environmental problems are global in scope. Why? Because regardless of national divisions, our planet is a single **ecosystem,** *the interaction of all living organisms and their natural environment.*

The Greek meaning of *eco* is "house," which reminds us that our planet is our home, a place where all living things and their natural environment are interconnected. Changes to any part of the natural environment ripple throughout the entire global ecosystem.

These connections can be illustrated by humans' use of chlorofluorocarbons (CFCs, marketed under the brand name Freon), once common as propellents in aerosol spray cans and as gas in refrigerators and air conditioners. CFCs are cheap, easy to use, nontoxic, and effective. But once released into the environment, they accumulate in the upper atmosphere, where they react with sunlight to form chlorine atoms. Chlorine destroys ozone, the layer of the atmosphere that filters out harmful ultraviolet radiation. This process caused a huge hole to open in the atmospheric ozone layer over Antarctica that led to an increase in the incidence of human skin cancers and harm to plants and animals. To protect the ozone layer, the United States and many other nations have banned the use of CFCs in favor of environmentally safer alternatives.

The most important lesson sociology offers about environmental issues is that the state of our planet reflects how societies operate. What facts about U.S. society can you "read" in this photograph?

Population Increase

Sociologists point to a simple formula: $I = PAT$, where environmental impact (I) reflects a society's population (P), its level of affluence (A), and its level of technology (T). In short, the more people in a society, the richer the society, and the more complex the technology, the bigger the environmental impact the society has.

Let's look first at population. As Chapter 15 explained, 2,000 years ago, the world had about 300 million people—roughly the same as the population of the United States today (Population Reference Bureau, 2009).

Once humans developed industrial technology and the medical science that goes along with it, higher living standards sharply reduced death rates in Western Europe. The predictable result was a sharp upward spike in world population. By 1800, global population had soared to 1 billion.

In the decades that followed, growth became even faster, with global population reaching 2 billion by 1930, 3 billion by 1962, 4 billion by 1974, 5 billion by 1987, and 6 billion by 1999. In 2009, the world's population was 6.8 billion. Although the rate of increase is slowing, we are adding 82 million people to the world's total each year (more than 200,000 every day) (Population Reference Bureau, 2009).

A well-known riddle illustrates how runaway growth can wreak havoc with the natural environment (Milbrath, 1989:10):

> A pond has a single water lily growing on it. The lily doubles in size each day. In thirty days, it covers the entire pond. On which day did the lily cover half the pond?

The answer that comes readily to mind—the fifteenth day—is wrong. The lily was not increasing in size by the same amount every day; it was *doubling.* The correct answer is that the lily covered half the pond on the twenty-ninth day, just one day earlier. The point is that for a long time, the size of the growing lily seems manageable. Only on the twenty-ninth day, when the lily covers half the pond, do people finally see the problem, but it is too late to do anything about it because the very next day, the lily chokes the life out of the entire pond.

Most experts predict that the world population will increase to between 8 and 9 billion people by 2050 (United Nations Population Reference Division, 2009). The most rapid population growth is occurring in the poorest regions of the world. A glance back at Global Map 15–1 on page 399 shows the growth rates for nations around the world. Taken together, the nations of Africa are adding to their population at an annual rate of 2.4 percent, which will double Africa's population by 2050 (Population Reference Bureau, 2009).

environmental deficit serious, long-term harm to the environment caused by humanity's focus on short-term material affluence

Poverty and Affluence

Rapid population growth makes the problem of poverty worse. This is because a surging population offsets any increase in productivity so that living standards stay the same. If a society's population doubles, doubling its productivity amounts to no gain at all.

But poverty also makes environmental problems worse. Preoccupied with survival, poor people have little choice but to consume the resources they have, without thinking about long-term environmental consequences.

But the long-term trend for the world is toward greater affluence. What are the environmental consequences of rising population and greater affluence taking place *together*? One way to answer this question is to consider what is happening as India and China, which together contain more than 2.5 billion people, become more affluent. In the decades to come, we are likely to see well over 1 billion new automobiles on city streets in these ever-richer countries. What effect will this trend have on the world's oil reserves? What about global air quality?

Simply put, if people all around the world were to live at the level of material abundance that we in the United States take for granted, the natural environment would rapidly collapse. From an environmentalist point of view, our planet may suffer from economic underdevelopment in some places, but it also suffers from economic overdevelopment in others.

Technology

Finally, consider the historical development of technology. Our earliest ancestors lived by hunting animals and gathering plants. With this simple technology, they had little effect on the environment. They adapted their lives to the rhythms of nature, moving along with the migration of animals and the changing of the seasons and in response to natural events such as fires, floods, and droughts.

Societies that gain the use of horticulture (small-scale farming), pastoralism (the herding of animals), or agriculture (with animal-drawn plows) have a greater capacity to affect the environment. But relying on muscle power for their energy, the environmental impact of these technologies is still quite limited.

The Industrial Revolution changed everything by replacing muscle power with combustion engines that burn fossil fuels such as coal and oil. With this technology, humans are capable of bending nature to their will, tunneling through mountains, damming rivers, irrigating deserts, and drilling for oil beneath the ocean floor. In the process, we consume more energy resources and also release more pollutants into the atmosphere. The overall result of new technology is that humans have brought more change to this planet in the last two centuries than our ancestors did in all of human history before that.

Global Map 16–1 shows that high-income, high-technology countries consume a great deal of the world's energy. Although these nations account for just 22 percent of humanity, they represent about half of the world's energy consumption. Put another way, the typical adult in the United States uses about 200 times more energy each year than the average person in the world's poorest nations (York, Rosa, & Deitz, 2002; International Energy Agency, 2008).

Equally important, members of industrial and postindustrial societies produce 100 times more goods than agrarian societies. Much of what we produce (such as packaging) is never consumed at all and is simply thrown away, creating vast amounts of solid waste.

The Environmental Deficit

This short look at human history teaches an important lesson: The increase in human population, the rising level of affluence around the globe, and the use of more powerful technology have positive consequences, but they also put the lives of future generations at risk. The evidence is mounting that we are running up an **environmental deficit,** *serious, long-term harm to the environment caused by humanity's focus on short-term material affluence* (Bormann, 1990).

Facing up to the environmental deficit is important for three reasons. First, it reminds us that environmental quality is a *social issue,* reflecting choices people make about how many children to have, how much to consume, and what technology to use. Second, it suggests that environmental damage often is *unintended.* By focusing on the short-term benefits of, say, cutting down forests or using throwaway packaging, we satisfy our desire for material goods and convenience. At the same time, however, we fail to see that such behavior has long-term, harmful environmental effects. Third, in some respects the environmental deficit is *reversible.* Societies can undo many of the environmental problems they have created.

Cultural Patterns: Growth and Limits

How we live is guided by culture. Our cultural outlook, especially how we think about "the good life," has important environmental consequences.

The Logic of Growth

Why does our society designate specific areas as parks or wildlife preserves? The unspoken message is that except for these special areas, people may freely use the planet and its resources for their own purposes (N. Myers, 1991). Most members of our society have an aggressive approach to the natural environment. Where does this thinking come from?

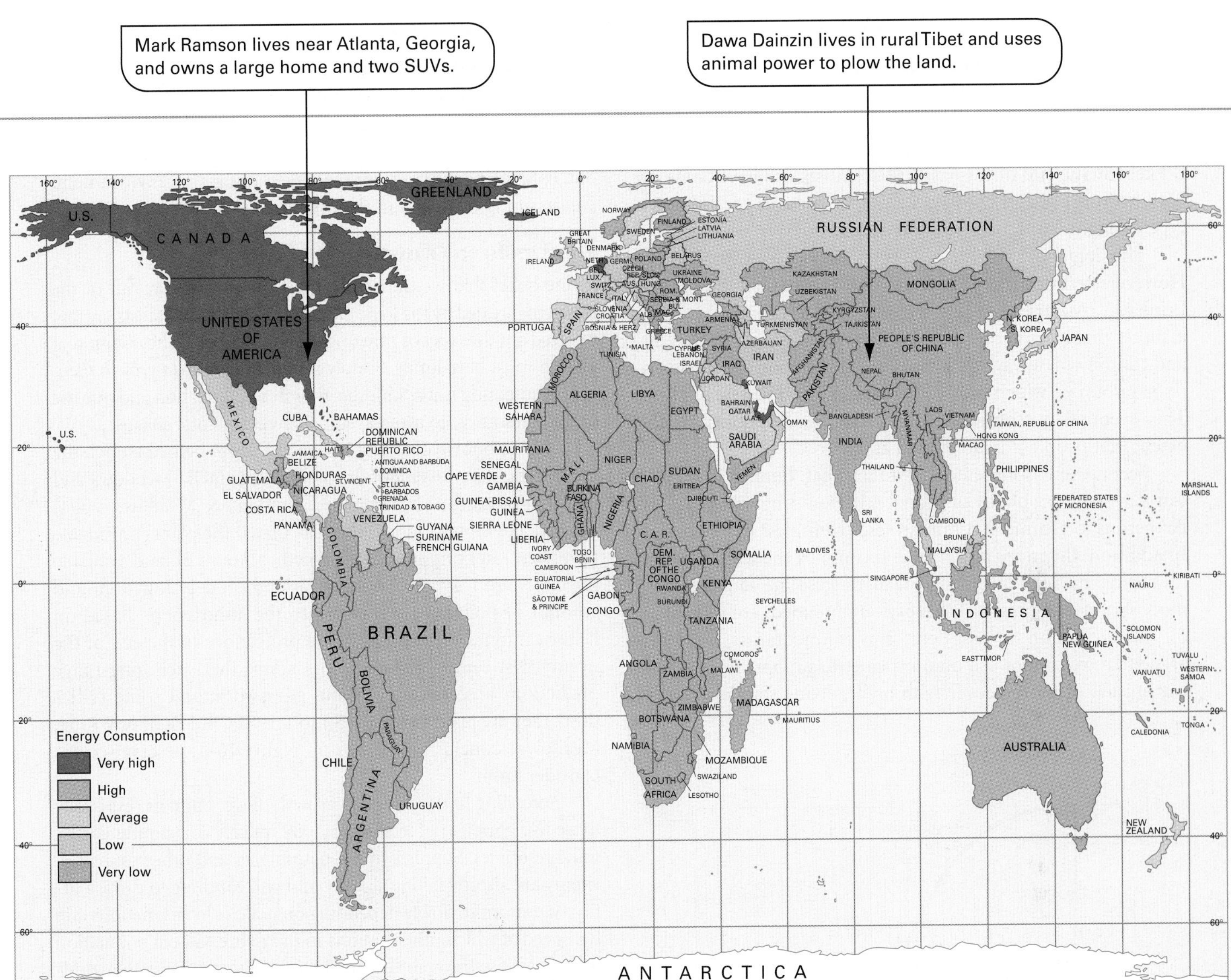

A World of Differences

GLOBAL MAP 16–1 Energy Consumption around the World

People in high-income nations consume far more energy than those living in poor countries. The typical U.S. resident uses the same amount of energy in a year as 200 people in Ethiopia or the Central African Republic. This means that the most economically productive nations also put the greatest burden on the natural environment. In fact, in recent years, the demand for energy in the United States has exceeded the available supply.

Source: Central Intelligence Agency (2009).

In the United States, our way of life is based on a quest for *material comfort.* Most people believe that money and the things it buys enrich our lives. Most of us also believe in *progress,* thinking that the future will be better than the present, and *science,* looking to experts and new technology to improve our lives. Taken together, these cultural values form an outlook that environmentalists call the *logic of growth.*

The logic of growth is rooted in an optimistic view of the world. In simple terms, this way of thinking amounts to believing that material things are "good," "people are clever," and "life will improve."

Of course, even optimists realize that progress can sometimes lead to unexpected problems. For example, the rising number of motor vehicles in the world may make life better in many ways, but it also threatens to drain the planet's oil reserves. The logic of growth argues that people—especially scientists and other experts—are inventive and will find a way around any problems. By the time oil supplies run short, which

SOCIAL PROBLEMS in Everyday Life

Do you think hybrid cars will have a positive effect on the environment? Why or why not?

MAKING THE GRADE

Be sure you understand the difference between the "logic of growth" and the "limits to growth."

is likely by the end of this century, scientists will have come up with hydrogen, electric, solar, nuclear, or some as yet unknown type of engine to free us from oil dependence.

The logic of growth is deeply linked to U.S. culture. However, environmentalists point to several flaws in this line of thinking (Milbrath, 1989). First, this approach wrongly assumes that natural resources such as oil, clean air, fresh water, and topsoil will always be plentiful. On the contrary, these are *finite* resources, which means that they can and will be used up. This eventual outcome will occur that much sooner to the extent that people pursue growth at any cost.

Second, environmentalists doubt that human ingenuity can solve any problems of scarcity. It would be arrogant and dangerous to assume that human resourcefulness has no limits. In addition, the more powerful and complex the technology—say, using nuclear reactors instead of gasoline engines—the more serious the potential (perhaps unintended) consequences of miscalculation or accident. Environmentalists therefore argue that we cannot call on our planet to support the increasing burden of more people with higher living standards without exhausting finite resources, degrading the environment, and harming ourselves in the process.

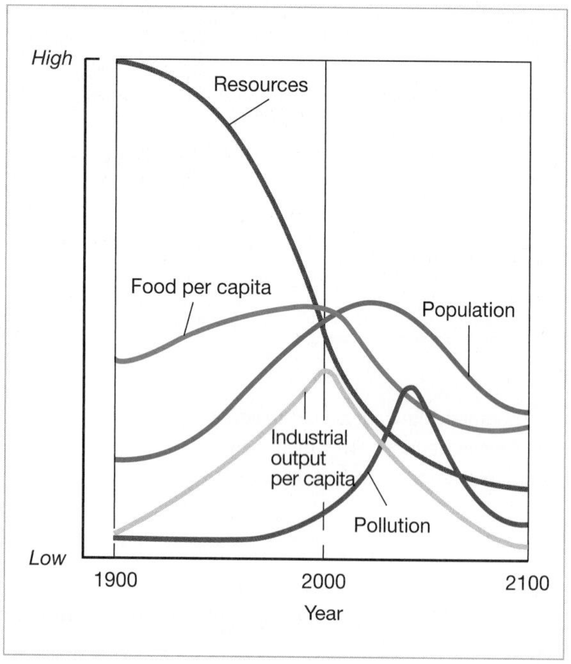

FIGURE 16–1 The Limits to Growth: Projections

This computer model predicts that humanity will deplete most of Earth's resources within a century. Although people disagree over the specifics of such predictions, most agree that significant change is needed to avoid environmental catastrophe.

Source: Based on Meadows et al. (1972).

The Limits to Growth

In the belief that we humans cannot invent our way out of the problems created by the logic of growth, environmentalists say that we need another way of thinking about the world. They claim that growth must have limits. Simply stated, the *limits-to-growth thesis* is that humanity must limit the growth of population and our use of finite resources to avoid eventual environmental collapse.

A 1972 book called *The Limits to Growth* helped launch the environmental movement. In the book, Donella Meadows and her colleagues (1972; Meadows, Randers, & Meadows, 2004) devised a computer model that calculated the planet's available resources, rates of population growth, amount of land available for cultivation, levels of industrial and food production, and amount of pollutants released into the atmosphere. Based on historical trends, the model made projections to the end of the twenty-first century. The authors admit that such long-range predictions are, to some extent, guesswork, and some critics think they are plain wrong (J. Simon, 1981). But right or wrong, Meadows's conclusions, shown in Figure 16–1, deserve serious consideration.

According to the limits-to-growth thesis, humans (especially those using industrial technology) are quickly consuming Earth's finite resources. Supplies of oil, natural gas, and other sources of energy are already falling sharply and will continue to drop, a little faster or more slowly depending on policies in rich nations and the speed at which other nations industrialize. Global population is likely to rise through the first half of this century, with a gradual decline after that. At this point, world hunger—caused by too many people and unequal distribution of food—will increase and may well reach a crisis level. And before long, the world will begin running out of vital resources, reducing industrial output.

Environmentalists who support the limits-to-growth thesis are sometimes called neo-Malthusians because, like Thomas Robert Malthus (discussed in Chapter 15, "Population and Global Inequality"), they are pessimistic about the future of humanity. Believing that current patterns of life are not sustainable through this century, they conclude that we face a basic choice: Either we make deliberate changes in how we live, or calamity will force change on us.

Environmental Problems

Environmentalists express serious worries about our future. A majority of U.S. adults say they share a concern about the environment; most define pollution and other related issues as "dangerous" problems (Kluger, 2001; NORC, 2007). This represents a

GETTING INVOLVED

Are you concerned about chemicals in the food you eat? What do you do to ensure a safe and healthful diet?

GETTING INVOLVED

Try to measure how much solid waste you create in a single day.

CONSTRUCTING SOCIAL PROBLEMS

A DEFINING MOMENT

Rachel Carson: Sounding an Environmental Wake-Up Call

In the United States, the 1950s was a decade of rising prosperity. During these "good times," most people considered "growth" to be good for everyone. Few people viewed the environment as a problem.

Rachel Carson saw things differently. Carson (1907–1964) grew up in a western Pennsylvania farm community, where she developed a lifelong passion for nature. After finishing college, she earned a master's degree in zoology. Then she went to work for the U.S. Bureau of Fisheries, preparing pamphlets on conservation. Carson also wrote books about nature, gaining a national reputation as a naturalist. In 1952, she left her government post to write full time.

During the years that followed, Carson's attention turned to the rapidly increasing use of pesticides. After World War II, many new chemical pesticides came on the market, and most people saw them as a solution to the problem of damage to crops caused by insects. As the use of pesticides in the United States skyrocketed, no one gave much thought to the harm these chemicals posed to the environment.

In 1962, Carson published the book *Silent Spring,* which was truly a wake-up call. The book explained how the use of pesticides such as dichlorodiphenyltrichloroethane (DDT) was poisoning the streams, rivers, and lakes of the United States. Carson's book brought about a firestorm of controversy led by chemical companies, which tried to have the book banned from libraries and stores. But Carson's words went a long way to defining chemical pesticides not as a solution but as a problem. She pulled no punches, asking, "Can anyone believe it is possible to lay down such a barrage of poisons on the surface of the earth without making it unfit for all life?" (1995:409).

In making such statements, she challenged the common view that science was always a force for good. In the process, she created a defining moment that helped launch the modern environmental movement.

Rachel Carson is credited with turning public attention to the environment. Her 1962 book *Silent Spring* documented the health and environmental hazards of pesticides (such as DDT) that were being widely used on farms and lawns. Rather than seeing chemicals as a solution, Carson defined them as a problem and helped spark the modern environmental movement.

shift in public opinion from fifty years ago, when only a handful of people defined environmental issues as problems. The Defining Moment box takes a closer look at one of the first people who did.

What is the state of the natural environment today? The following sections briefly examine several environmental issues, with particular attention to problems in the United States.

Solid Waste: The Disposable Society

One environmental problem is waste—or more precisely, too much of it. The average person in the United States discards about 5 pounds of paper, metal, plastic, and other disposable materials daily; over a lifetime, that comes to 65 tons. The country as a whole generates 1.4 billion pounds of solid waste *each and every day* (U.S. Environmental Protection Agency, 2008). Figure 16–2 on page 426 shows the composition of our national trash.

The problem of solid waste stems from a simple fact about our culture: We live in a *disposable society.* Not only is the United States materially rich, but we value convenience. As a result, we consume more products than any nation on Earth, and many of these products come with lots of extra packaging.

GETTING INVOLVED

Do you recycle? Could you recycle more?

GETTING INVOLVED

See how many products you can think of that are made to have a limited life—that is, to break or wear out so you have to buy another.

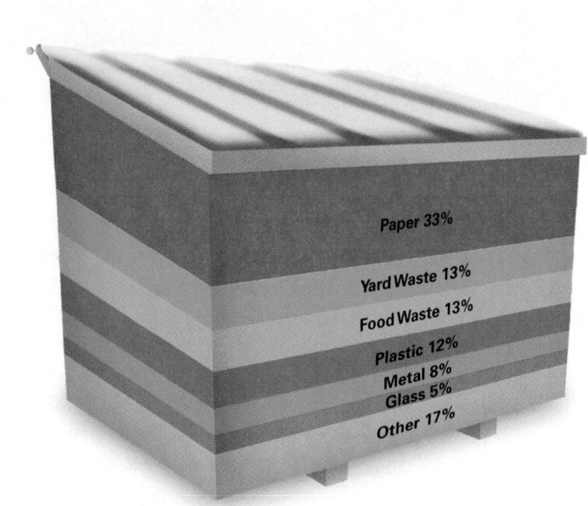

FIGURE 16–2 **Composition of Household Trash**

Here is a rough breakdown of the trash that U.S. society generates—a total of 1.4 billion pounds each day.

Source: U.S. Environmental Protection Agency (2009).

The most familiar case is the cardboard, plastic, and Styrofoam containers that we buy with our fast food and throw away as soon as we finish the meal. Countless other products—from film to fishhooks, cosmetics to CD-ROMs—are elaborately packaged to appeal to the customer and to discourage tampering and theft. Manufacturers market soft drinks, beer, and fruit juices in aluminum cans, glass jars, and plastic containers, and all this packaging not only uses up finite resources but also generates mountains of solid waste. In addition, our corporations intentionally develop and market countless items that are disposable: pens, razors, flashlights, batteries, and even cameras. Other products, from computers to automobiles, are designed to have a short useful life. Much of what we create eventually becomes unwanted junk.

Living in a rich society, the average person in the United States consumes hundreds of times more energy, plastics, lumber, and other resources than someone living in a low-income nation such as Bangladesh or Tanzania. On average, we also consume about 20 percent more than someone living in other high-income countries such as Japan or Sweden. This high level of consumption means that we in the United States not only use a disproportionate share of the planet's natural resources but also generate most of the world's solid waste (World Resources Institute, 2007).

We are quick to say that we "throw things away." But only half of our solid waste is burned or recycled, leaving half (about 140 million tons in 2007) that never does "go away." Rather, it ends up in landfills (U.S. Environmental Protection Agency, 2008).

These dumping grounds pose several threats to the natural environment. First, landfills across the country are filling up. Already the United States is shipping trash to other countries to be discarded. Second, the material in landfills contributes to water pollution. Although most localities have enacted laws that regulate what can go in a landfill, the U.S. Environmental Protection Agency has identified thousands of dump sites across the United States containing hazardous materials that are polluting water both above and below the ground. Third, what goes into landfills may end up being there for centuries. Tires, diapers, and plastic utensils do not readily decompose, and tens of millions of them will become an unwelcome environmental burden for generations to come.

Environmentalists argue that we should address the problem of solid waste by doing what Grandma Macionis and many of our ancestors did: turn "waste" into a resource. This is the basic idea behind *recycling,* reusing resources we would otherwise throw away. Recycling is a common practice in Japan and many other nations, and it is becoming more widespread in the United States, where we now recycle about one-third of waste materials. The share is increasing as more and more states pass laws requiring monetary deposits on glass bottles and aluminum cans or requiring that people recycle these materials. In addition, as more people recycle, the business of recycling is becoming more profitable. The Social Problems in Global Perspective box provides a look at one recycling success story in Egypt.

Preserving Clean Water

Oceans, lakes, and streams are the lifeblood of the global ecosystem. Humans depend on water for drinking, bathing, cooling, cooking, recreation, and a host of other activities.

According to what scientists call the *hydrologic cycle,* Earth naturally recycles water and refreshes the land. The process begins as heat from the sun causes water, 97 percent of which is in the oceans, to evaporate and form clouds. Next, the clouds return water to Earth as rain, which drains into streams and rivers and rushes toward the seas. The hydrologic cycle not only renews the supply of water but also cleans it. Because water evaporates at lower temperatures than most pollutants, the water vapor that rises from the seas is pure, leaving contaminants behind. The hydrologic cycle generates clean water in the form of rain, and pollutants steadily build up in the oceans.

There are two major problems associated with water: inadequate water supply and water pollution.

SOCIAL PROBLEMS in Everyday Life

Don't most of us take water for granted? Is it realistic to assume this resource will always be available?

SOCIAL PROBLEMS IN GLOBAL PERSPECTIVE

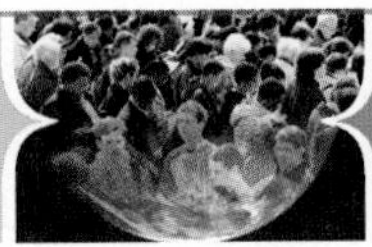

Turning the Tide: Reclaiming Solid Waste in Egypt

Half an hour from the center of Cairo, Egypt's capital city, the bus loaded with students from the United States bumped along a dirt road and then jerked to a stop. It was not quite dawn on that November morning, and the muezzins were soon to climb the minarets of Cairo's many mosques to call the Islamic faithful to morning prayers. The driver turned, genuinely bewildered, to face us. "Why," he asked, in labored English, "do you want to be here? And in the middle of the night?"

It was a good question. No sooner had we left the bus than smoke and stench, the likes of which we had never before encountered, swirled around us. Eyes squinting, handkerchiefs pressed against noses and mouths, we slowly moved up the mountain of trash that extended for miles.

This is the Cairo dump, the final resting place for the trash generated by 20 million people in one of the world's largest cities. Bent over and walking with great care, we were guided by flickers of light from small fires that burned around us. Up ahead, through clouds of smoke, we saw blazing piles of trash where local people were warming themselves and talking.

As we approached, the fires cast a strange light on the people's faces. We stopped some distance from them, separated by a vast chasm of culture and circumstances. But smiles pulled the two groups closer, and soon we all shared the comfort of the fire. At that moment, the call to prayer sounded across the city.

The Zebaleen ("rubbish people"), as they are called, number about 25,000 and are a religious minority—Coptic Christians—in a mostly Muslim society. Barred by religious discrimination from many jobs, the Zebaleen use donkey carts and small trucks to pick up Cairo's trash and haul it here. At dawn, hundreds of Zebaleen gather at the dump, swarming over the new piles in search of anything of value.

During this visit, we observed men, women, and children picking through Cairo's refuse and filling baskets with bits of metal, strips of ribbon, and even scraps of food. Every now and then, someone gleefully displayed a precious find that would bring the equivalent of a few dollars in the city. Watching in silence, we became keenly aware of our sturdy shoes and warm clothing and self-conscious that our watches and cameras represented more money than most of the Zebaleen earn in a whole year.

Two decades later, the Cairo Zebaleen still work the city's streets collecting trash. But much has changed, and they are now one of the world's environmental success stories. The Zebaleen have a legal contract to perform their work and have built a large recycling center near the dump. Dozens of the workers operate huge shredders that turn discarded cloth into stuffing to fill furniture, car seats, and pillows. Other workers separate plastic and metal into large bins for cleaning and sale. Using start-up loans from the World Bank and their own ingenuity, the Zebaleen have become businesspeople.

The Zebaleen are still poor by U.S. standards. But they are prospering and now own the land on which they live and work. They have even built an apartment complex with electricity and running water. Many international environmental organizations hope their example will inspire others elsewhere.

WHAT DO YOU THINK?

1. Why is the amount of recycling so limited in most societies?
2. Will recycling ever become big business in the United States? Why or why not?
3. How much recycling takes place on your campus? What can you do to get involved?

Sources: Personal visit to the Cairo dump, Garwood (2003), and news reports.

Inadequate Water Supply

As early as the ancient civilizations of China, Egypt, and Rome, water rights were an important part of the law, reflecting how vital water is to any society. Some regions of the world, especially the tropics, enjoy a plentiful supply of water. However, in much of North America and Asia, people look to rivers rather than rainfall for their water, making supply a problem. In some regions of the United States, the main source is groundwater, water underground that supplies wells and springs. In many regions, the supply is running low. For example, the Ogallala aquifer runs belowground across seven states, from South Dakota to Texas. It is now being pumped so rapidly that some experts fear it could run dry within several decades.

In China, deep aquifers are dropping rapidly. In the Middle East, water supply is reaching a critical level. Iran is rationing water in its capital city. In Egypt, people can consume just one-sixth as much water from the Nile today as they could in 1900. Analysts project that by 2030, half of the world's people will be living in water-stressed areas (United Nations Environmental Programme, 2008; United Nations Water Assessment Programme, 2009).

Soaring populations are only part of the problem. Complex technology, especially in manufacturing and power-generating facilities, has made the water problem worse. Why? Modern high technology itself uses water, especially for cooling, which greatly increases water consumption. The global use of water (estimated at 1 quadrillion gallons per year) is increasing even faster than the world's population. Underground water

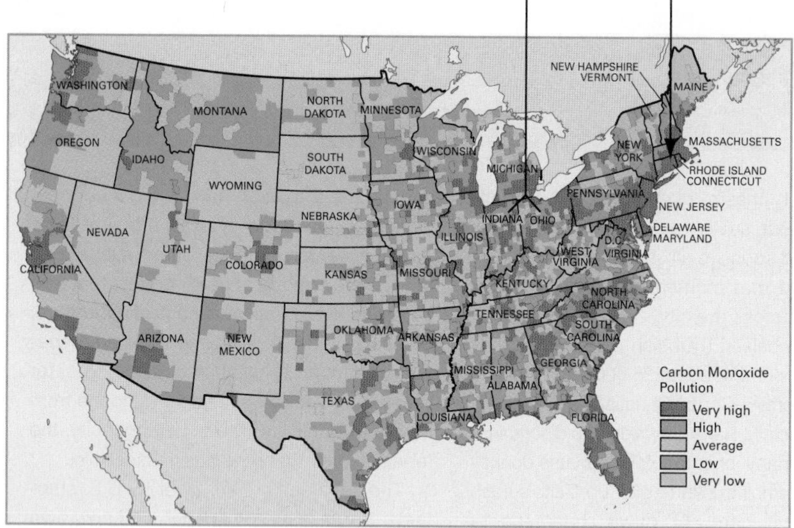

A Nation of Diversity

NATIONAL MAP 16–1

Air Pollution across the United States

The Environmental Protection Agency monitors air quality throughout the United States. This map of the continental United States shows the level of carbon monoxide pollution in the air of all counties. Carbon monoxide pollution is commonly generated by cars and trucks as well as factories. In general, what is the national pattern of air pollution? Can you explain this pattern?

Source: U.S. Environmental Protection Agency (2008).

tables are rapidly dropping in countries all over the world (Rosegrant, Cai, & Cline, 2002; United Nations Environmental Programme, 2008).

In light of these trends, we must face the reality that water is a finite resource. Greater conservation of water by individuals can make a difference—currently, the average person in this country consumes 350,000 gallons in a lifetime. Around the world, however, individuals account for just 5 to 10 percent of all water use. Even more important is limiting water use by industry, which is responsible for 20 percent of global water use, and by farm irrigation, which consumes more than 70 percent of the total.

More efficient irrigation technology may reduce this demand in the future. But here again, we see how population increase, advancing technology, and economic expansion combine to strain Earth's resources (World Health Organization, 2001; United Nations Environmental Programme, 2008).

Water Pollution

In large cities from Mexico City to Cairo to Shanghai, people drink contaminated water every day. As a result, waterborne microorganisms cause infectious diseases, including diarrhea, intestinal worms, typhoid, cholera, and dysentery, which spread rapidly through these populations. The result is millions of deaths each year. This makes water *quality* just as serious a problem as *supply.*

By global standards, water quality in the United States is generally good. However, even here the problem of water pollution is growing steadily. According to the Sierra Club (2009), an environmental activist organization, this country produces 500 million pounds of toxic substances (including farm fertilizer, lawn treatments, and other chemicals) each year, and much of it ends up in rivers and streams.

Air Pollution

One result of the spread of industrial technology—especially of factories and motor vehicles—has been a decline in air quality. A century ago, the thick, black smoke belching from factory smokestacks, often twenty-four hours a day, alarmed residents of industrial cities. By 1950, exhaust fumes from automobiles hung over cities such as Los Angeles that had escaped the earlier rush of industrial development.

In London, factory discharge, automobile emissions, and smoke from coal fires used to heat homes combined to create a deadly haze that the British jokingly called "pea soup." But during five days in 1952, an especially thick cloud of smoke covered the city of London and killed 4,000 people (Clarke, 1984).

In the years since then, great strides have been made in combating air pollution. Laws now forbid high-pollution heating methods, including the coal fires that literally choked Londoners to death. Smokestack "scrubbers" have decreased the noxious output of factories. The switch to unleaded gasoline in the early 1970s, coupled with changes in engine design and exhaust systems, has greatly reduced harmful emissions from automobiles. Still, with more than 250 million vehicles in the United States alone, keeping the air clean remains a challenge. National Map 16–1 shows the level of carbon monoxide pollution for counties throughout the continental United States.

As Chapter 11 ("Work and the Workplace") explained, the world's rich societies have entered a postindustrial era in which computer technology is replacing industrial technology. Because this type of production is cleaner, air quality in these

acid rain precipitation, made acidic by air pollution, that destroys plant and animal life

rain forests regions of dense forestation, most of which circle the globe close to the equator

GETTING INVOLVED

What can you do to turn the tide in terms of issues discussed on this page? Suggest one specific step you can take.

countries has been improving. The benefit of cleaner air is very real: Experts estimate that improvement in U.S. air quality over the past several decades has added almost half a year to the average lifespan (Chang, 2009).

We may be breathing easier, but as factory production overseas increases, the problem of air pollution in poor societies is getting worse. In addition, many people in low-income countries still rely on wood, coal, peat, or other "dirty" fuels for heat. Today, many low-income nations are so eager for short-term industrial development that they ignore the longer-term dangers of air pollution. As a result, many cities in Latin America, Eastern Europe, and Asia have air pollution as bad as London's was fifty or sixty years ago.

Acid Rain

Across the 6 million acres of Adirondack Park in upstate New York, 400 lakes and ponds have been declared "dead" because they are too acidic to support fish or plant life. This deadly trend could claim another 1,000 lakes and ponds by 2050.

The cause of this problem is **acid rain,** *precipitation, made acidic by air pollution, that destroys plant and animal life.* The complex reaction that creates acid rain and acid snow begins with power plants burning fossil fuels such as oil and coal to generate electricity. This burning releases sulfur and nitrogen oxides into the air. Carried into the atmosphere by winds, these gases react with the air to form sulfuric and nitric acid, which makes atmospheric water acidic. Figure 16–3 illustrates this process.

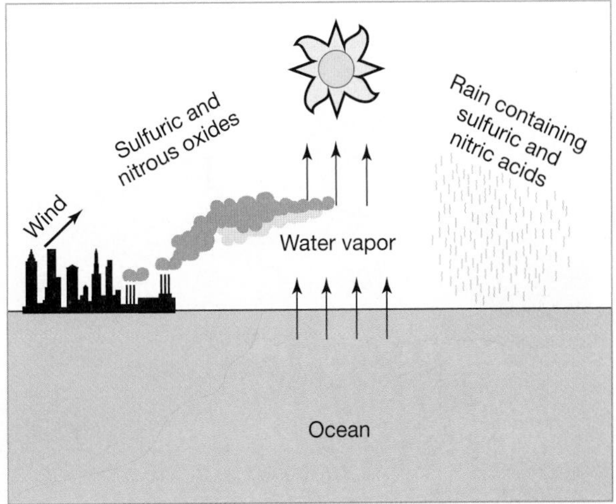

FIGURE 16–3 The Formation of Acid Rain

This figure illustrates the process of creating acid rain, which threatens plant and animal life in many parts of the world.

The process that causes acid rain is a case of one type of pollution causing another. In this case, air pollution from smokestacks ends up contaminating the rain that falls and collects in lakes and streams far away. Acid rain is a global phenomenon because many of the regions that suffer the harmful effects are thousands of miles from the original pollution. Here at home, power-generating facilities in the South and Midwest threaten all of New England. Abroad, tall chimneys of British power plants produce acid rain that has devastated forests and fish as far away as Norway and Sweden.

The Disappearing Rain Forests

Rain forests are *regions of dense forestation, most of which circle the globe close to the equator*. The largest rain forests are in South America, Central Africa, and Southeast Asia. In all, the world's rain forests cover some 1.5 billion acres, or 5 percent of the planet's total land surface.

Like other global resources, the rain forests are falling victim to the increasing needs and appetites of the human population. For example, to meet the demand for beef in North America, ranchers in Latin America burn down forests to gain more grazing land for cattle. Timber companies are also cutting down forests to produce hardwood that ends up being used in high-income countries for furniture, wood floors and paneling, luxury yachts, and even high-grade coffins. Under this economic pressure, the world's rain forests are now just half their original size, and they continue to shrink by about 1 percent (58,000 square miles) annually. If this rate of destruction remains unchecked, these forests will vanish by about 2100, taking with them much of the plant and animal biodiversity of this planet (Rainforest Foundation, 2009).

Global Warming

Scientists have documented the fact that average temperatures throughout the world are rising, a trend called *global warming.* Over the last two centuries, as societies have developed industrial technology, the amount of carbon dioxide (CO_2) released by factories and automobiles into the atmosphere has soared. Experts estimate that the current atmospheric concentration of carbon dioxide is 40 percent higher than it was 150 years ago. As some see it, this change has pushed the planet to a dangerous point where the future of our species is threatened (Gore, 2006; Kluger, 2006; Adam, 2008).

How does carbon dioxide in the atmosphere threaten us? The oceans absorb a certain amount of this CO_2. So do plants, which remove carbon dioxide from the air and expel oxygen. This process is one reason the rain forests are so important to our planet's future.

SOCIAL PROBLEMS in Everyday Life

Because the United States is a rich country, our society produces about one-fourth of all greenhouse gases that cause global warming. Do we have a special responsibility to address this problem? How should we respond?

More and more scientists are now convinced that global warming is a real threat to the environment. They note, for example, that polar ice is melting, which will raise the levels of the oceans. If the average temperature of the planet rises just a few degrees during this century, much of the coastal United States will be underwater. What are strategies to limit global warming? *(© 1999 Daniel Beltra/Greenpeace)*

But the production of carbon dioxide has gone up while the amount of plant life on Earth has gone down. The net result is that the concentration of CO_2 in the atmosphere is steadily rising. As carbon dioxide builds up in the atmosphere, it behaves much like the glass roof of a greenhouse, letting heat from the sun pass to Earth's surface while preventing much of it from radiating back away from the planet. This process is known as the *greenhouse effect.* Holding in some of the sun's heat is necessary to keep Earth warm, especially at night. But as the level of carbon dioxide in the atmosphere keeps going up, so does the amount of heat that the planet retains. This is the source of global warming.

Scientists report that over the past century, Earth's average temperature rose 1.5 degrees to an average of 58.5 degrees Fahrenheit. Before the end of this century, they expect the planet's average temperature to rise by 2 degrees or more (U.S. Global Change Research Program, 2009).

Such a warming trend would melt vast portions of the polar ice caps. Ice is very reflective, sending much of the sun's heat back into space. As the ice caps melt, Earth will become warmer still. In addition, melting ice caps will raise the sea level, flooding low-lying land around the world. Low-lying nations such as Bangladesh would be completely covered with water; much of the coastal United States would be flooded, with the Atlantic Ocean rising right up to the steps of the White House in Washington, D.C.

Weather patterns would also change. The Great Plains, in the midwestern United States, currently one of the most productive agricultural regions in the world, would probably lose so much rain that little would grow there.

Some experts remind us that global temperature changes have been taking place throughout history, with no link to the status of the rain forests. But scientists are moving closer to consensus that global warming is a real threat to the planet (Gore, 2006; Kluger, 2006; International Panel on Climate Change, 2007; S. F. Singer, 2007).

Declining Biodiversity

Another reason to worry about the planet's loss of rain forests is loss of Earth's *biodiversity.* There are about 30 million different living species on the planet, counting all forms of bacteria, plants, and animals. Several dozen species of plants and animals cease to exist each day. But given such a vast number of living species, why is declining biodiversity a problem?

There are three reasons. First, Earth's biodiversity plays a major role in feeding the world's people. By cross-breeding familiar crops with more exotic plants, agricultural scientists make crops more plentiful and increase their resistance to insects and disease.

Second, Earth's biodiversity is a vital genetic resource. Medical and pharmaceutical researchers study the entire range of animal and plant life, which is where they find compounds that will cure disease and improve the quality of our lives. As examples, the oral birth control pill is a product of plant research involving the Mexican forest yam, and from the Pacific yew tree, we produce a drug that is widely used to treat breast cancer.

Third, with the loss of any species of life—from a tiny black ant to the magnificent California condor to the adorable Chinese panda—we lose part of the beauty and complexity of our natural environment. The warning signs are already posted: Three-fourths of the world's 10,000 bird species are declining in number, and more than 1,000 will disappear during this century (Youth, 2003). Protecting the rain forests is vital to maintaining the planet's biodiversity because they are home to half of all living species.

Finally, the extinction of species is irreversible and final. Do we have the right to impoverish the world for those who live tomorrow? (E. O. Wilson, 1991; Brown et al., 1993; Stevens, 2003; Kluger, 2006).

MAKING THE GRADE

List three reasons that protecting biodiversity is an important goal.

SOCIAL PROBLEMS in Everyday Life

Looking to the future, are you optimistic or pessimistic about the state of the environment? Why?

Theoretical Analysis: Understanding Environmental Problems

Sociology's two macro-level approaches can help us gain a deeper understanding of environmental issues.

Structural-Functional Analysis: Highlighting Connections

The structural-functional approach links environmental issues to the overall operation of society. This approach offers three important lessons.

First, technology has a powerful effect on the environment. As noted earlier, the more powerful a society's technology, the greater the society's capacity to alter the natural world.

Second, culture affects the state of the environment. A structural-functional analysis points out how values and beliefs guide human actions. Thus the state of the environment reflects our attitudes about the natural world. Members of industrial societies generally view nature as a resource to serve our needs (a point of view described earlier as the "logic of growth"). It was this vision that pushed our ancestors to clear forests for farmland, dam rivers for irrigation and water power, cover vast areas with asphalt and concrete, and erect buildings to make cities. In addition, our culture is materialistic, so that we look to *things* (as often or perhaps more often than, say, family or spiritual beliefs) as a source of comfort and happiness. Our tendency toward what sociologists call "conspicuous consumption" leads us to purchase and display things not because we really need them but simply as a way to show off our social position (Veblen, 1953, orig. 1899). Such values set the stage for environmental stress.

Third, structural-functional theory points up the interconnectedness of all social patterns. Our ideas about fast, private travel, for example, go a long way toward explaining the U.S. fascination with automobiles. Building and operating hundreds of millions of vehicles has in turn put great stress on resources such as oil and polluted the atmosphere.

Given the connection between the natural environment and the operation of society, the solutions to environmental problems are complex. Is it possible to control the rate at which humanity consumes Earth's resources, for example, while we add more than 200,000 people to the global population each day? Limiting population growth, in turn, depends partly on expanding the range of occupational and educational opportunities open to women so they have alternatives to staying home and having more children.

Solving environmental problems is surely a difficult task. But structural-functional analysis provides grounds for optimism because of its view that systems adapt to changing conditions. Take the case of air pollution. Air quality declined sharply as nations developed industrial technology. But gradually, societies in Europe and North America recognized the problem, enacted new laws, and developed more new technology to clean the air. In short, as long as we are vigilant and creative, we can make the changes needed to ensure a livable environment.

CRITICAL REVIEW Structural-functional analysis shows that problems of the natural environment are created by the operation of society itself. But as noted before, critics charge that structural-functional analysis pays little attention to social inequality. This means that using this approach, we may recognize environmental problems but overlook the fact that burdens of pollution and scarcity fall disproportionately on people with less social power: the poor and minorities.

Critics also question structural-functionalism's optimistic view that society can resolve most environmental problems. For one thing, many people—particularly those operating large corporations—have vested interests in continuing past ways, even if they threaten the well-being of the general public. For another, many environmental problems, especially rapid population growth, are simply too far out of control to justify an optimistic outlook.

Social-Conflict Analysis: Highlighting Inequality

Social-conflict theory highlights exactly the issues that structural-functionalism tends to overlook: power and inequality. Far from being inevitable, conflict theorists claim, problems of the natural environment result from social inequality. In other words, elites directly or indirectly make environmental problems worse as they advance their self-interest.

From a social-conflict point of view, the hierarchical organization of U.S. society gives a small number of people control over our society. As Chapter 10 ("Economy and Politics") describes, a bias in our economic and political systems generates a power elite who set the national agenda.

As the Industrial Revolution began, early capitalists gained huge profits by eagerly consuming Earth's resources to feed their factories. Just as they showed little regard for the social consequences of their actions, they paid little attention to the effects on the natural environment. In addition, capitalists and their managers are protected by laws that treat corporate pollution as a white-collar crime (as discussed in Chapter 6, "Crime, Violence, and Criminal Justice"), so that any legal action usually

MAKING THE GRADE

Environmental racism is an example of institutional discrimination (see chapter 3).

environmental racism a pattern of discrimination in which environmental hazards are greatest for poor people, especially minorities

No one wants to live near a toxic dump. But because poor people have less power, they are the ones who usually end up living in hazardous areas. What effects has living near dangerous chemicals had on people in the past?

results in fines paid by the company rather than jail time served by individuals. For this reason, it is rare that corporate executives who order the dumping of toxic waste are held personally accountable for their actions.

Conflict theorists taking a Marxist view of society see capitalism itself as a threat to the environment. For one thing, capitalism demands the pursuit of profit, which in practice means continuous economic expansion—precisely the pattern that underlies the logic of growth. For another, strategies to maximize profits may include designing products with a limited useful life, a concept called *planned obsolescence.* Such policies may increase profits in the short term, but over the long haul they use up natural resources and produce mountains of solid waste.

A second issue raised by social-conflict theory involves global inequality. It is the people in rich countries who consume most of Earth's resources and who generate most air, water, and land pollution. In other words, not only do we maintain our affluent way of life by exploiting the poor in low-income countries, but we poison the world's air and water in the process.

In sum, this approach condemns rich nations as *overdeveloped* and consuming too much. As Chapter 15 ("Population and Global Inequality") explains, social-conflict analysis suggests that the majority of the planet's people, who live in poor societies, will never raise their living standards under the current capitalist world economy. But from an environmental point of view, this would not even be desirable. What is needed is a more equitable distribution of the world's existing wealth among all its people, which would achieve greater social justice and better preserve the natural environment.

Environmental Racism

One important issue that emerges from social-conflict theory is **environmental racism,** *a pattern of discrimination in which environmental hazards are greatest for poor people, especially minorities.* Historically, factories that create pollution have been located in or near neighborhoods of the poor and people of color. Why? In part because factories draw the poor, who are in search of work. Then, once hired, people with low incomes often find that the only housing they can afford stands in the very shadow of the plants and mills where they work.

Nobody wants to live next to a factory or a garbage dump, of course, but what choice do poor people have? Through the years, the most serious environmental hazards have been found around Newark, New Jersey, rather than in upscale Bergen County; on Chicago's South Side rather than in wealthy Lake Forest; and on or near Native American reservations in the West rather than in affluent suburbs of Denver or Phoenix (Commission for Racial Justice, 1994; Bohon & Humphrey, 2000).

CRITICAL REVIEW The social-conflict approach raises important questions about who sets a society's agenda and who benefits—and who suffers—from the way society operates. From this point of view, environmental problems result from the class structure within a society and, globally, from the world's hierarchy of nations.

Critics of this approach point out that our history shows a steady trend toward legal protection of the natural environment. Over the past half century, this country has achieved significant improvements in air and water quality. Some analysts also claim that the evidence of a systematic pattern of environmental racism is far from convincing (Boerner & Lambert, 1995; Yandle & Burton, 1996).

What of the charge that capitalism itself is particularly hostile to the natural world? There is no doubt that capitalism supports the logic of growth, and this way of thinking does place stress on the environment. But capitalist societies in North America and Europe have shown that they

MAKING THE GRADE

Use the table below to review two macro-level theoretical approaches to technology and the environment.

APPLYING THEORY

Technology and the Environment

	What is the level of analysis?	How do we understand technology and the environment?	What is the approach to environmental problems?
Structural-functional approach	Macro-level	The structural-functional approach highlights links between the operation of society and the stress it puts on the natural environment. Complex technology raises the threat of damage to the environment, as do cultural values that encourage technological development, materialism, and economic growth.	Because a society's technology and culture affect its environmental impact, these forces can adapt, thereby reducing environmental problems. In short, technology and culture can cause problems, but they can also provide solutions.
Social-conflict approach	Macro-level	The social-conflict approach links technology and the environment to social inequality. Capitalism places industrial technology under the control of a small elite who exploit natural resources as they exploit human labor.	Capitalism's demand for economic growth and profit is the key source of environmental problems, which are most serious for minorities and the poor. The solution to these problems lies in greater equality at home and redistribution of resources from the overdeveloped nations to underdeveloped nations.

are able to make strides toward environmental protection. Just as important, the environmental record of socialist societies has been strikingly poor. Back when Europe was divided between capitalist countries to the west and socialist countries to the east, the strongest complaints about the poor quality of the local environment came from the socialist nations of Eastern Europe, such as Poland and the Soviet Union (Dunlap, Gallup, & Gallup, 1992).

The Applying Theory table summarizes what we can learn from each of these theoretical approaches to environmental issues.

POLITICS AND THE ENVIRONMENT

Constructing Problems and Defining Solutions

How do politics shape the way people see environmental problems and define solutions? The conservative approach offers grounds for optimism that environmental problems are improving. The liberal approach emphasizes the need for greater government action to protect the environment. Radicals argue that the only way to head off environmental collapse is to make fundamental changes to the capitalist system.

Conservatives: Grounds for Optimism

Like just about everyone else, conservatives are concerned about environmental issues. But they take an optimistic view that society is able to recognize environmental problems and take action to solve them.

Conservatives point to the trend of increasing environmental awareness in all postindustrial societies (Pakulski, 1993; Jenkins & Wallace, 1996). Especially as production shifts from smoky factories to clean information technology, society awakes to environmental problems and takes action to address them.

As to the warnings of environmental collapse in the near future, Julian Simon (1995) asks, "Why the doom and gloom?" He explains that ever since Malthus predicted social chaos, based on his belief that a rising population would consume all the world's resources, people have forecast society's collapse. But the planet supports six times as many people as when Malthus lived, and on average, they live better and longer than ever before. As Simon sees it, these facts are cause not for gloom but for celebration.

MAKING THE GRADE

Conservatives are sometimes called "anti-Malthusians" because they reject Malthus's pessimism about the future.

MAKING THE GRADE

Liberals are sometimes called "neo-Malthusians" because they share the concern Malthus had about the future.

What is our environmental future? Conservatives base their optimism on the power of technology. Liberals, by contrast, look to government to mandate reforms. Radicals doubt that anything short of fundamental change will turn the tide. Which viewpoint do you support? Why?

Why has the world done so well? Simon points to human ingenuity. It is true that more powerful technology increases a society's potential impact on the natural environment. But the development of new forms of energy and new productive technologies can be good news for the environment. The newest automobiles and factories are far cleaner than older examples. More broadly, today's information technology is far cleaner than the industrial production it is replacing. Looking ahead, there is good reason to be optimistic that high technology will continue to reduce pollution from cars and smokestacks, which is good news for the environment (Dunlop, 2006).

Because this optimistic position opposes the pessimistic view of Malthus, it is often described as *anti-Malthusian.* This viewpoint, which is similar to the logic-of-growth viewpoint described earlier, is conservative because it expresses support for the current system, in the belief that problems people create are problems people can solve.

Liberals: Grounds for Concern

Not everyone shares the optimism of people like Julian Simon. Most environmentalists are deeply concerned about problems such as population increase, resource consumption, and various types of pollution. Many openly predict catastrophe if humanity does not change its ways (Bright, 2003; Gore, 2006; Kluger, 2006). Given this prediction, it is easy to see why such activists are sometimes called *neo-Malthusians.* They are present-day analysts who agree with the warnings sounded two centuries ago by Malthus and who support the limits-to-growth position described earlier in the chapter.

Neo-Malthusians realize that humans have been able to devise new, more productive technologies, even those that Malthus himself could not have imagined. Using these technologies, the world now produces more food and other goods. But the unequal distribution of these resources means that some people benefit far more than others, and as both production and population rise, we are steadily consuming the planet's finite resources. In many poor countries, there is little firewood for cooking or heating. Water supplies are already inadequate in much of the Middle East. Rich nations are rapidly consuming Earth's supplies of oil and natural gas. When these supplies will give out is uncertain, but there is no doubt that some day they will be gone.

In the same way, there is a limit to Earth's ability to absorb pollution. As both population and production rise, we can expect environmental quality to decline. Many analysts suggest that we have already passed the planet's carrying capacity, the number of people that it can support in the long term. In fact, some argue that our natural environment may only be able to support half of the world's present population (Smail, 2007).

In the face of such predictions, liberals call for reform on a number of fronts. Important steps include conservation efforts such as mandatory recycling programs as well as limits on the consumption of natural resources, such as clean water. These programs are especially important in rich countries because this is where most consumption takes place.

In practice, liberals are asking people in rich nations to make some sacrifices in their living standards for the interest of a better natural environment. The final piece of the solution lies in expanded efforts to reduce pollution. These include development of cleaner-burning fuels and engines for cars, power plants, and factories; lighter and more efficient motor vehicles; and the development of strategies to reduce solid waste. In short, liberals look to government to enact new policies and laws that will protect the environment.

The Radical Left: Grounds for Fundamental Change

Radicals on the left do not share conservatives' optimism about humanity's present course on this planet. Although radicals support the liberal agenda, they doubt that liberal reforms will solve the problem.

MAKING THE GRADE

Use the table below to review three political approaches to the environment.

GETTING INVOLVED

Has this chapter sparked any changes in how you think about the environment? Explain.

LEFT TO RIGHT

The Politics of the Environment

	RADICAL-LEFT VIEW	LIBERAL VIEW	CONSERVATIVE VIEW
WHAT IS THE PROBLEM?	The natural environment is in serious danger due to capitalism's ever-increasing appetite for growth and profits. Under the current economic and political system, our society is unlikely to face up to the extent of the problem.	The natural environment is in danger. Both pollution and the rapid use of natural resources including fresh water threaten people now and will threaten future generations even more.	There is no serious problem that can't be solved. Although humanity has created problems of pollution and has taxed natural resources, it has shown itself capable of devising new, "clean" technologies as well as alternative forms of energy.
WHAT IS THE SOLUTION?	A healthy environment requires a socially conscious economic system that will ensure the well-being of today's and tomorrow's people. Overconsumption in high-income nations must end, and global wealth must be distributed more equally.	Government must enact new policies and enforce laws to prevent further environmental damage in the United States. Individuals must conserve, recycle, and support global efforts to protect the remaining rain forests.	Allow the market system to develop new technology. Human ingenuity and an economic system that encourages innovation will extend the human record of living longer, healthier, and richer lives.

JOIN THE DEBATE

1. Looking over the three political perspectives on the environment, do you see any areas of agreement? If so, what are they?
2. From the point of view of each of the three political perspectives, what changes should take place in the United States to protect the future of the planet?
3. Which of the three political analyses of the natural environment included here do you find most convincing? Why?

Those who follow a Marxist approach charge that significant environmental change is impossible under a capitalist system that places profits above all other concerns. This does not mean that we have to give up advanced technology. Most left radicals see technology as a useful tool if it is directed by economic and political systems that represent the interests of the people as a whole.

For radicals on the left, the key to solving environmental problems is replacing the capitalist economy. This must be a worldwide process because as many radicals on the left see it, a key goal for our planet is reducing the extent of global stratification. Rich nations, they say, are simply too overdeveloped already. In the interests of social justice and environmental safety, wealth must be redistributed more equitably around the world.

None of the political positions argues that things should stay the way they are right now. Everyone recognizes environmental problems, with the differences lying mainly in the degree of change people think is necessary to solve them. The Left to Right table summarizes the arguments that follow these three political positions.

Going On from Here

India's great leader Mahatma Gandhi once declared that societies must provide "for people's need but not for their greed." From an environmental point of view, this means that Earth will be able to sustain future generations only if people today slow their consumption of finite resources such as oil, hardwoods, and water. Nor can we go on polluting the air, water, and soil at anything close to current levels. We must stop cutting down our rain forests if we are to preserve the global climate. Finally, we cannot risk the future of the planet by adding people to the world at the rate of 82 million each year (Population Reference Bureau, 2009).

Recall the formula $I = PAT$, which tells us that a society's impact on the environment is a function of its level of population, its level of affluence, and its level of technology.

ecologically sustainable culture a way of life that meets the needs of the present generation without threatening the environment for future generations

SOCIAL PROBLEMS in Everyday Life

Do you think developing a sustainable way of life is a matter of reform? Or will it require radical changes to our way of life?

The main lesson of this chapter is that the state of the natural environment reflects the policies, cultural priorities, and level of technology of human society. As nations such as China become richer, how will the lives of their people change? What effects will these changes have on the use of energy and the world's other natural resources? What changes to our own society would you like to see during this century in the interest of protecting the natural environment?

Worldwide, population is increasing, living standards are rising, and technology is advancing. The predictable result is a larger environmental impact. Our planet's environmental deficit is increasing. In effect, our present way of life is borrowing against the future well-being of our children and their children. From a global perspective, members of rich societies who currently consume so much of Earth's resources are endangering the entire planet.

However the politics play out, the solution to the entire range of environmental problems described in this chapter must be for humanity to live in a way that does not make the environmental deficit any bigger. We need to develop an **ecologically sustainable culture,** *a way of life that meets the needs of the present generation without threatening the environment for future generations.*

To develop a sustainable way of life, we must adopt three basic strategies. First, the world must *conserve finite resources* by meeting present needs with a responsible eye to the future. Conservation involves using resources more efficiently, seeking alternative resources, and in some cases, learning to live with less. The second strategy is to *reduce waste.* The best way to reduce waste is to use less in the first place. In addition, societies around the world need to expand recycling programs through education and legislation. The third key element in any plan for a sustainable ecosystem is to *bring world population growth under control.* Our current population of 6.8 billion is already straining the natural environment. The higher world population climbs, the greater environmental problems will become. Controlling population growth requires immediate action in poor regions of the world where growth rates are highest.

In the end, perhaps, solving environmental problems depends on developing a new outlook. An *egocentric* outlook, common in rich nations today, is all about meeting an ever-expanding set of personal needs. But a sustainable environment demands an *ecocentric* outlook, one that highlights the environmental consequences of the choices we make. Such a way of thinking, which is especially important to those of us lucky enough to live in rich societies, reminds us that today's actions shape tomorrow's world.

In addition, instead of viewing humans as superior to other life forms and assuming that we have the right to dominate the planet, we must remember that all forms of life are interdependent. Ignoring this truth not only threatens the diversity of animal and plant life on the planet but will also eventually harm our own well-being.

Finally, achieving a sustainable ecosystem will require global cooperation. The planet's rich and poor nations differ greatly in terms of interests, cultures, and living standards. Policies such as conservation and reducing waste have little impact among people who are desperately poor. The most difficult part of any effort to solve the world's environmental problems will be coming to terms with global inequality. Most environmentalists argue that the high-income countries of the world are already overdeveloped, using more resources than Earth can sustain over the long term. At the same time, low-income nations are underdeveloped, unable to meet the basic needs of many of their people. Establishing a sustainable ecosystem will depend on bold new programs of global cooperation. Although the challenge is enormous, it is nothing compared with the eventual consequences of not responding to the growing environmental deficit. One certainty is that the state of tomorrow's world depends on choices we make today (Brown et al., 1993; Bright, 2003).

DEFINING SOLUTIONS

What's the best way to address problems of the natural environment?

Look at the two photos below to understand two different approaches to finding a solution to environmental problems.

HINT

The conservative claim that our present system can "invent" us out of our current problems is at least partly true. As conservatives point out, over time, our society has made the air cleaner as cars use less fuel and generate fewer pollutants. At the same time, conservatives' confidence in the future may be optimistic. After all, liberals remind us, it is our current system that got us into this situation. What can government do better? Perhaps it takes government to make decisions—like encouraging us to drive smaller cars and otherwise use less energy—that we as consumers are unlikely to make on our own. Where do you stand on this issue?

From a liberal point of view, business as usual within the market system is unlikely to lead the country to an environmentally sustainable way of life. The solution, from this political perspective, is government legislation mandating changes in how we live. People sharing this viewpoint recently gathered near the U.S. Capitol to urge the federal government to take bold action limiting air pollution and consumption of energy. How much do you support this approach to a solution? Why?

The conservative approach is based on the belief that the market system is, indeed, capable of responding to the environmental challenge. Conservatives expect that by unleashing human ingenuity, and with the advantages of new technology, our current system will generate new solutions to many environmental problems. As one example, in 2009, General Motors unveiled the new Chevrolet Volt, an electric car the company claims is capable of going 230 miles on a gallon of gasoline in city driving. How confident are you that our market system and innovative technology will bring about solutions to environmental problems?

Getting Involved: Applications & Exercises

1. Carry a plastic trash bag around for an entire day, and fill it with everything you throw away. What is the weight of one day's trash? Are you surprised by how much you discard?
2. In Genesis 1; 28–29, God instructs humanity to "fill the earth and subdue it; rule over the fish of the sea and the birds of the air and over every living creature that moves on the ground.... I give you every seed-bearing plant on the face of the whole earth and every tree that has fruit with seed in it. They will be yours for food." Do you think this statement gives humans the right to exploit the environment as they see fit or the responsibility to care for it? Why?
3. Do some research on our society's consumption of gasoline and, despite recent price increases, the relatively low cost of gas in the United States compared with other countries. In light of the dangers of depleting the world's oil reserves, do you think taxes should be even higher on gasoline?
4. On your campus, identify faculty in the social sciences and the natural sciences who are concerned about the natural environment. Visit them during office hours, and ask what they think are the most critical environmental issues. What do they propose as solutions to environmental problems?

MAKING THE GRADE

A DEFINING MOMENT
Rachel Carson: Sounding an Environmental Wake-Up Call p. 425

CHAPTER 16 Technology and the Environment

Ecology: Studying the Natural Environment

The state of the **NATURAL ENVIRONMENT** reflects how human beings organize social life.

- Ecologists therefore study how living organisms interact with their environment.

p. 420

Analyzing environmental problems demands a global perspective.

- All parts of the **ECOSYSTEM**, including the air, soil, and water, are linked. Changes in one part of the world affect the natural environment elsewhere.

pp. 420–21

ecology (p. 420) the study of how living organisms interact with the natural environment

natural environment (p. 420) Earth's surface and atmosphere, including air, water, soil, and other resources necessary to sustain living organisms

technology (p. 420) knowledge that people apply to the task of living in a physical environment

ecosystem (p. 421) the interaction of all living organisms and their natural environment

environmental deficit (p. 422) serious, long-term harm to the environment caused by humanity's focus on short-term material affluence

Factors Affecting the Environment

GLOBAL AFFLUENCE and its emphasis on material abundance leads to pollution and rapid use of energy and other resources.

- **TECHNOLOGY** development gives societies greater control over the natural environment, for better or for worse.

p. 422

GLOBAL POVERTY also results in depletion of natural resources.

- Preoccupied with survival, poor people have little choice but to consume scarce resources.

p. 422

✓ *By focusing on short-term benefits and ignoring the long-term consequences brought on by their way of life, societies build up an* ***ENVIRONMENTAL DEFICIT.*** *(p. 422)*

POPULATION INCREASE affects the natural environment.

- Even though the rate of growth is slowing, world population threatens to overwhelm available resources.

p. 421

CULTURAL PATTERNS—how we as a society live and what we value—affect the environment.

- The *logic-of-growth* thesis supports economic development and asserts that people can solve whatever environmental problems may arise.
- The *limits-to-growth* thesis states that societies have little choice but to curb development in order to avoid environmental collapse.

pp. 422–24

Environmental Problems

SOLID WASTE

- As a "disposable society," the United States generates 1.4 billion pounds of solid waste each day, one-half of which ends up in landfills.

pp. 425–26

LACK OF CLEAN WATER

- Water consumption is rapidly increasing everywhere. Much of the world, notably Africa and the Middle East, is reaching a water supply crisis.

pp. 426–28

acid rain (p. 429) precipitation, made acidic by air pollution, that destroys plant and animal life

rain forests (p. 429) regions of dense forestation, most of which circle the globe close to the equator

AIR POLLUTION

- Since 1950, high-income countries have made significant progress in reducing air pollution. In poor nations, especially in cities, air pollution remains a serious problem because homes and factories burn "dirty" fuels.

pp. 428–29

ACID RAIN

- Acid rain, the product of pollutants entering the atmosphere mostly from industrial smokestacks, contaminates land and water thousands of miles away.

p. 429

DISAPPEARING RAIN FORESTS

- Rain forests serve the planet by removing carbon dioxide from the atmosphere and maintaining Earth's biodiversity. With millions of trees being cut down each year by logging companies and ranchers in search of grazing land for their livestock, global rain forests are now half their original size and are shrinking by about 1% annually.

pp. 429–30

GLOBAL WARMING

- Global warming is the rise in the average temperature of the planet, caused by increasing levels of carbon dioxide released into the atmosphere by factories and automobile engines. Destroying the rain forests makes the problem worse because plant life consumes carbon dioxide.

pp. 429–30

Theoretical Analysis: Understanding Environmental Problems

Structural-Functional Analysis: Highlighting Connections

The **STRUCTURAL-FUNCTIONAL APPROACH** looks at the connection between environmental issues, technology, and culture.

- In the same way that the problems of the environment are created by the operation of society, society also has the ability to adapt to change or to correct environmental problems.

p. 431

Social-Conflict Analysis: Highlighting Inequality

The **SOCIAL-CONFLICT APPROACH** highlights the role of inequality in environmental problems.

- Environmental decay is caused by elites acting in their own self-interest rather than in the interests of society.
- The poor, especially minorities, suffer most from environmental hazards, a pattern known as **ENVIRONMENTAL RACISM.**

pp. 431–33

environmental racism (p. 432) a pattern of discrimination in which environmental hazards are greatest for poor people, especially minorities

ecologically sustainable culture (p. 436) a way of life that meets the needs of the present generation without threatening the environment for future generations

See the **Applying Theory** table on page 433.

Politics and the Environment: Constructing Problems and Defining Solutions

The Radical Left: Grounds for Fundamental Change

- **RADICALS ON THE LEFT** doubt that liberal reforms will be sufficient to solve the world's environmental problems.
- Radicals on the left believe that the capitalist economy, which places profits above all other concerns, must be replaced with a system that will safeguard the environment in the interest of all people.

pp. 434–35

Liberals: Grounds for Concern

- **LIBERALS** believe that government reforms such as mandatory recycling and strategies to reduce solid waste and develop cleaner-burning fuels are necessary to avoid eventual environmental collapse.
- Because of their pessimistic view of the future, liberal environmentalists are sometimes called *neo-Malthusians.*

p. 434

Conservatives: Grounds for Optimism

- **CONSERVATIVES** acknowledge the reality of environmental problems, but they argue that human beings will use their ingenuity and technology to solve them, with little need for government regulation.
- Because conservatives take an optimistic view of the future, their position is described as *anti-Malthusian.*

p. 433–34

See the **Left to Right** table on page 435.

CONSTRUCTING THE PROBLEM

What are the financial costs of war?

Every year, the world's nations spend $1.5 trillion for military purposes.

Is it only soldiers who die in war?

Most of the casualties of war are civilians.

Do the world's armies include children?

Around the world, about 300,000 children—many as young as six years of age—are soldiers, and many take part in armed combat.

CHAPTER 17

War and Terrorism

CHAPTER OVERVIEW

HOW IS TERRORISM A NEW FORM OF WAR? This chapter explains the meaning of war, peace, and terrorism. You will learn several reasons that wars happen, and also why war has become more and more destructive. You will understand the economic and human costs of war. You will be able to explain how terrorism differs from conventional war and why war in the nuclear age poses unimaginable dangers. You will also be able to outline several strategies for peace. You will carry out theoretical analysis of war and terrorism and learn how "problems" and "solutions" involving global conflict reflect people's political attitudes.

It was one of those late-night "discussions" that sometimes happen in the dorms—the kind that use up a lot of energy but end up generating more heat than light. As Brandon (passionate Democrat) saw it, the Bush administration had made the nation and its people much less safe. "Thanks to Bush and Cheney," he thundered, "the world hates us! What could be worse than that? How does that make us safer? Thank goodness we've got Obama to fix things."

But Emma and Zach (passionate Republicans) would hear none of it. "Since September 11," Emma replies, "you know what has happened? Nothing! That's the point. Not another terrorist attack. That's what 'safe' means!"

We've all been there, arguing back and forth about whether the country is safer or not, whether the United States is doing the right thing or making things worse. These are difficult questions that reflect people's political values and attitudes. At the same time, such discussions raise important questions about war—why nations get into wars and whether armed conflict solves anything. In addition, everyone recognizes that terrorism has become common enough that it is often described as a new type of war.

In 2009, the United States was engaged in two wars—in Iraq and in Afghanistan—and our political leaders were trying to resolve a dozen other conflicts that threatened to break out into war in various regions of the world. In addition, the United States had military personnel stationed in about twenty nations in an effort to keep the peace.

Given the importance of war and how controversial war can be, we might well wonder why people go to war in the first place. Some analysts suggest that humans, especially men, are naturally aggressive (Chagnon, 1997). If this is so, there seems to be little that we can do to prevent war. But after decades of research on the causes of armed conflict, most social scientists hold the view that the roots of war lie in society itself. If that is the case, then understanding more about the causes of war should help our leaders develop effective strategies to promote peace.

War and Peace: Basic Definitions

War is *violent conflict between nations or organized groups.* **Peace**, an opposing concept, is *the absence of violent conflict.* Many people think of peace as the normal state of affairs. Yet wars have always been a part of human history. The United States has been involved in many large-scale wars, shown in Figure 17–1, as well as a larger number of minor conflicts played out in Grenada, Panama, Haiti, Somalia, and Bosnia. In the twentieth century, there was no time at which there was not an armed conflict occurring somewhere around the world. In recent decades, civil wars within one nation have been the most common type of war, with the warring parties aided by other countries. Global Map 17–1 on page 444 shows the fourteen countries that experienced at least one armed conflict in 2008.

The Increasing Destruction of War

Over the centuries, the level of war-related violence has increased sharply. Much of this change is due to societies gaining more powerful technology that is applied to warfare. A thousand years ago, the most a human could do in battle was to kill one other person at a time by swinging a sword, throwing a spear, or launching an arrow. Around the twelfth century, the development of guns using black powder made killing far more efficient but still ended one life at a time. By the early sixteenth century, black powder was fed into large cannons that had the power to launch heavy balls that would knock down stone walls. Soon cannonballs were replaced by exploding shells that were able to kill war violent conflict between nations or organized groups

peace is the absence of violent conflict

weapons of mass destruction weapons with the capacity to kill many thousands of people at one time

many people at once. The U.S. Civil War, fought between 1861 and 1865, was this country's bloodiest conflict, in part because soldiers stood near each other firing guns and cannons that were far more deadly than weapons had ever been before.

This trend toward more deadly weapons continued into the twentieth century. Single-shot rifles were replaced by automatic weapons that came to be known as machine guns. In addition, armies were equipped with chemical weapons as well as more powerful explosive bombs. World War I introduced aircraft into military combat, and the role of aircraft—as well as missiles—expanded in World War II, when such technology allowed soldiers to rain death and destruction down on entire cities from miles above.

In short, the last century saw the invention of **weapons of mass destruction,** *weapons with the capacity to kill many thousands of people at one time.* Such weapons increase the destruction of war in two ways: They have far greater destructive power, and they target civilian populations. As the deadly potential of weapons increases and as military technology spreads to more and more nations, the dangers of war become ever greater.

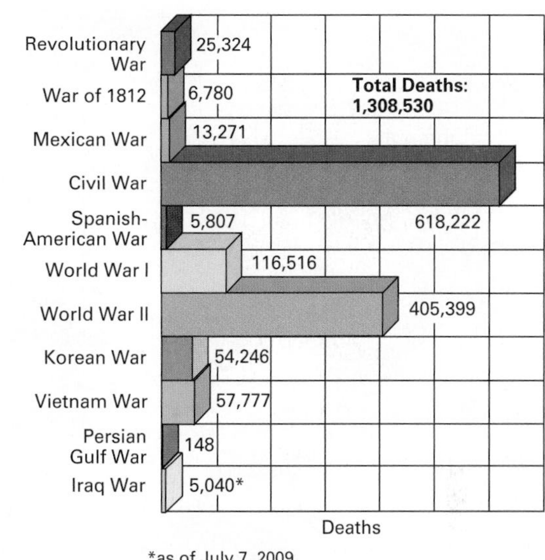

FIGURE 17–1 **Deaths of Americans in Eleven U.S. Wars**

Almost half of all U.S. deaths in war occurred during the Civil War (1861–65).

Sources: Compiled from various sources by Maris A. Vinovskis and the author.

The Causes of War

Why do wars happen? Sociologists have identified seven factors that encourage the outbreak of war (Q. Wright, 1987; Kaldor, 1999; Van Evera, 1999):

1. **Perceived threats.** Societies mobilize their military resources in response to perceived threats. In 1962, the United States prepared for war against the Soviet Union after learning that Soviet nuclear missiles had been set up on the island of Cuba, a nation just 90 miles south of Florida. Only after the Soviets agreed to remove the missiles did the two nations step back from the brink of war. In recent years, Israel has invaded southern Lebanon after rocket attacks across their common border killed a number of Israeli civilians.
2. **Cultural and religious differences.** Another cause of war is cultural or religious differences. Often these differences become exaggerated as societies teach their members to "demonize" those in some other country or group—that is, to see some category not only as "the other" but as evil. At the extreme, one category of people may try to eliminate another from an entire geographic area. In the Balkan conflict of the 1990s, ethnic Serbs rounded up hundreds of thousands of Croats, Muslims, and ethnic Albanians, deported them, placed them in prison camps, or simply killed them in a process called "ethnic cleansing."
3. **Political objectives.** Political objectives can be an underlying factor in war. A periodic show of force can be one way for a nation to assert a leadership position in the world. Examples include the United States' invasion of Grenada in 1982, the deployment of troops in the Persian Gulf War in 1991–92, the bombing of Serbia in 1999, the invasion of Afghanistan in 2001, and the invasion of Iraq in 2003.
4. **Moral objectives.** Nations may go to war to achieve a moral objective. Leaders in the United States justified the Korean War and the war in Vietnam as efforts to make the world safe from communism. The war in Iraq was justified by U.S. leaders in part by the moral goal of ending the rule of Iraq's brutal dictator, Saddam Hussein, and encouraging the development of democracy in the Islamic world.
5. **Wealth, power, and global standing.** Nations may go to war to increase their wealth and power. This was why the Iraqi leader Saddam Hussein invaded the neighboring oil-rich nation of Kuwait in 1990, sparking the Persian Gulf War. Even making the threat of going to war may provide gains for a country. In recent years, for example, tiny North Korea's claims of having developed a nuclear weapon and long-range missiles have attracted the world's attention.

SOCIAL PROBLEMS in Everyday Life

Can you apply the seven causes of war to conflicts that have taken place in the world in recent decades?

SOCIAL PROBLEMS in Everyday Life

Over the course of the last century, only for a few months has the world not had any military conflict.

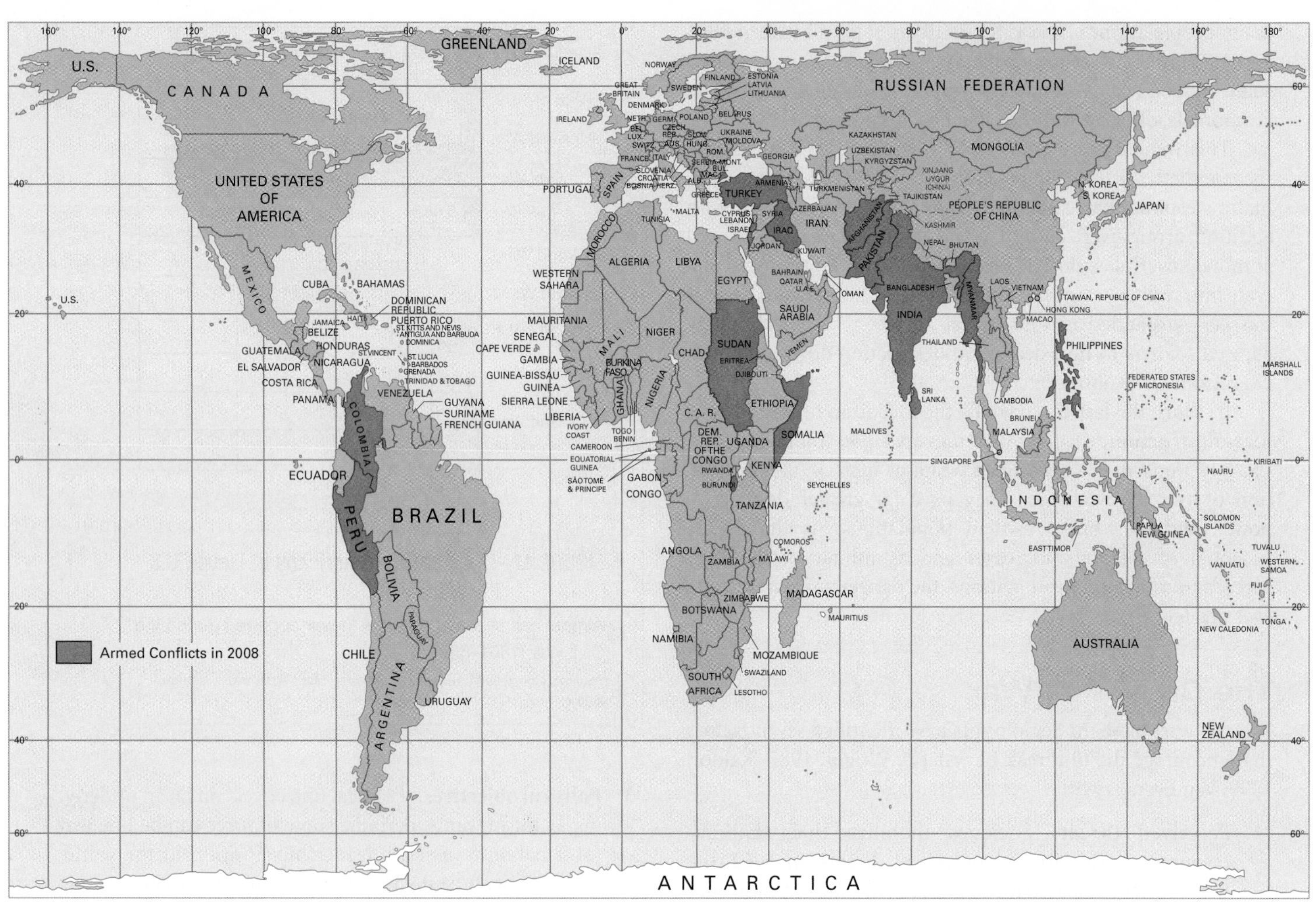

A World of Differences

GLOBAL MAP 17–1 Armed Conflicts around the World, 2008

In 2008, there were armed conflicts in fourteen nations, most of them in Africa and Asia. The United States was directly involved in a military conflict in Afghanistan and Iraq.

Source: Stockholm International Peace Research Institute (2009).

6. **Social problems.** Leaders sometimes use armed conflicts to divert attention from domestic social problems. For example, the People's Republic of China managed to turn attention away from great economic hardship by supporting military conflicts in Korea, Vietnam, and Tibet. Focusing national attention on an external threat encourages people to unify against a common enemy rather than blame the government for their problems.
7. **Absence of alternatives.** Finally, nations go to war because of an absence of alternatives. A nation may simply have no diplomatic means to end a threat or to accomplish its political or moral objectives.

Leaders may draw on many of these factors in making claims about the need for military action. In addition, leaders who use military action usually defend it in one way, say, as a response to a perceived threat or in pursuit of a moral objective. Critics, however, may define the military action quite differently, say, as a political strategy or an effort to gain wealth and power.

The Economic Costs of Militarism

Every year, the nations of the world spend almost $1.5 trillion for military purposes, which amounts to more than $215 for every man, woman, and child on a planet where a billion people are desperately poor (Central Intelligence Agency, 2009).

military-industrial complex a political alliance involving the federal government, the military, and the defense industries

MAKING THE GRADE

Over the last 150 years, wars have become more deadly, taking a larger human toll.

The U.S. defense budget was almost $675 billion in 2009, about $2,200 for each citizen. Overall, military spending accounted for about 22 percent of the federal budget. Militarily, the United States is by far the most powerful nation in the world, spending more on its armed forces than the next twenty countries combined (Stockholm International Peace Research Institute, 2009; U.S. Office of Management and Budget, 2009).

Over past decades, the U.S. economy has grown so that military spending represents a smaller share of all economic activity (now about 5 percent) than was the case during World War II (when it reached 40 percent). But in terms of dollars, the level of military spending has remained quite high. For decades after the end of World War II, a tense relationship between the United States and the Soviet Union was known as the Cold War. During this time, these two world superpowers engaged in an *arms race,* pushing military spending ever higher out of fear that the other might gain a military advantage. Yet the collapse of the Soviet Union in 1991 brought only a slight decline in military spending. The war on terrorism that began with the attacks on September 11, 2001, as well as the U.S. military engagement in Afghanistan and Iraq make it clear that this country's military spending will remain high for years to come.

Some analysts claim that the United States—or more specifically, a powerful group within this country—benefits from high levels of military spending. They see the United States as dominated by a **military-industrial complex,** *a political alliance involving the federal government, the military, and the defense industries* (Marullo, 1987). From this point of view, militarism in the United States is not only a matter of defense and national security but also a matter of profit and influence for the country's power elite (see Chapter 10, "Economy and Politics").

The Economic Costs of War

The economic costs of war involve more than military spending. War also destroys the *infrastructure* of a society: its homes and workplaces, water systems, electrical and communication networks, roads, bridges, railways, harbors, and airports. By the end of World War II, much of Europe lay in ruins and had to be rebuilt at the cost of hundreds of billions of dollars. In the wake of the war in Iraq, the United States has already spent more than $100 billion in efforts to rebuild that country.

Especially in tough economic times, many people wonder if this country can afford to spend so much on military objectives. After all, money spent on war takes economic resources away from programs that improve people's health care, nutrition, and education. Looking globally, if all nations were able to use the funds currently spent on militarism and rebuilding after wars to assist the poor, this planet could go a long way toward ending the global problems of hunger and disease.

The Human Costs of War

As huge as the economic costs of war are, the greatest loss is measured in human terms. As noted earlier, the history of warfare shows that armed conflicts have become ever more deadly. For example, the death toll in the U.S. Civil War was about 600,000. Fifty years later, World War I claimed almost 10 million lives. Thirty years after that, the death toll from World War II was more than 50 million.

The main reason for this increase is the development of weapons of mass destruction. Such weapons kill not only more soldiers but also civilians. Until the end of the nineteenth century, war was armed conflict involving professional soldiers.

The most dramatic example of total war was the use of two atomic bombs by the United States against Japan at the end of World War II. The first bomb almost completely destroyed the industrial city of Hiroshima. The second wiped out Nagasaki (shown here). In each case, the death toll exceeded 100,000 people.

total war deadly conflict that targets both population centers and military targets

concentration camps centers where prisoners are confined for purposes of state security, exploitation, punishment, or execution

war crime an offense against the law of war as established by international agreements and international law

SOCIAL PROBLEMS in Everyday Life

Do the men and women who have served this country in combat deserve more assistance in dealing with their problems? Why or why not?

From time to time, civilians were killed, but for the most part, this was unintended.

The Strategy of Total War

The twentieth century witnessed the development of a much more deadly level of warfare, with the development of a new strategy of **total war,** *deadly conflict that targets both population centers and military targets.* With airplanes and bombs at their command, military leaders had the power not just to kill enemy soldiers but also to level entire cities. To reduce the production of weapons, military leaders try to demolish the enemy's factories, also killing the civilians who worked in the factories and those who lived nearby. During World War II, for example, both the Germans and the Allied forces repeatedly bombed one another's cities in attacks that weakened the enemy's ability and will to fight. For this reason, most of the people who died in World War II were not soldiers but civilians. Analysts conclude that the strategy of total war blurs the lines between soldiers and civilians, putting all people at risk (Renner, 1993; Ehrenreich, 1997).

Concentration Camps

Beginning during World War II, some nations set up **concentration camps,** *centers where prisoners are confined for purposes of state security, exploitation, punishment, or execution.* The United States imprisoned about 100,000 people of Japanese ancestry between 1942 and 1944. These camps, set up within a year of the Japanese attack on Pearl Harbor, were an effort to control a segment of the U.S. population thought to represent a threat to national security.

In Europe, concentration camps took on a deadly mission. Both the Soviet leader Josef Stalin and the German leader Adolf Hitler operated camps that forced prisoners to work so hard, with so little food, that most eventually died of disease brought on by starvation and sheer exhaustion. During World War II, Hitler's Nazis systematically exterminated some 6 million Jews, along with additional millions of political prisoners, Catholics, Gypsies, homosexuals, and anyone else defined as undesirable, in numerous death camps, including those at Auschwitz and Buchenwald. The death toll under Stalin was greater still, reaching as high as 30 million.

War Crimes

Strange as it may seem, there are rules of war. These include individual nations' own standards for fighting and also a series of formal agreements negotiated in Geneva, Switzerland, between 1864 and 1949, called the Geneva Conventions. Violation of these standards is a **war crime,** *an offense against the law of war as established by international agreements and international law.* In the wake of World War II, the Geneva Conventions recognized three categories of war crimes. *Crimes against peace* include preparing for or starting an unjust war against another nation. *Conventional war crimes* include the murder, rape, torture, deportation, or other ill treatment of a population in any occupied territory. And *crimes against humanity* include political, racial, or religious persecution—including systematic killing—of any civilian population during war.

After World War II, an international war crimes tribunal tried twenty-four Nazi leaders at Nuremberg, Germany, convicting nineteen of war crimes. A separate tribunal tried and convicted twenty-five Japanese leaders. The sentences in each case ranged from lengthy prison terms to execution.

More recently, the United Nations International Criminal Tribunal has prosecuted a few officers for war crimes in Rwanda and the former Yugoslavia. However, because this tribunal's power depends on the political cooperation of individual nations and their willingness to aid in apprehending alleged criminals, many military leaders manage to escape prosecution (R. J. Newman, 2002).

War-Related Disabilities

Many war survivors suffer from mental and physical disabilities. Soldiers have long talked about "battle fatigue" or "shell shock." After the Vietnam War, about 15 percent of soldiers experienced *posttraumatic stress disorder* (PTSD), a war-related disability resulting from trauma or stress in battle. Symptoms of PTSD include nightmares, difficulty with concentration and sleeping, flashbacks to traumatic events, jumpiness and hyperalertness, guilt about surviving, and feelings of detachment from other people (American Psychiatric Association, 2002). An everyday event such as hearing an engine backfiring or seeing a helicopter flying overhead can trigger a PTSD episode, causing the person to relive the terror of combat.

As medical technology available to seriously wounded soldiers has advanced, more men and women who would have died from their injuries are now surviving, but many are left with serious disabilities. In all, some 2.9 million U.S. veterans have some disability resulting from an injury during active duty in the military. Of these, about 263,000 are totally disabled. To provide care for disabled veterans, the Department of Veterans Affairs (VA) operates 153 hospitals, 135 nursing homes, and 800 outpatient clinics across the country. Care is provided free of charge to former prisoners of war, individuals with service-related injuries or disabilities, and veterans with income below the poverty line. Thousands of other veterans are treated on a space-available basis (Moakley, 1999; U.S. Department of Veterans Affairs, 2009).

Veterans who are ill or disabled have trouble holding a job. This is one reason that 1.4 million veterans earn incomes below the poverty line. One veterans' organization claims that 130,000 are homeless at any given time and about 250,000 are homeless for some time during any given year (National Coalition for Homeless Veterans, 2009; U.S. Census Bureau, 2010).

War and Children

Finally, the human toll of war falls heavily on children. All major wars during the last century left vast numbers of orphans. Hundreds of thousands of children also died in bombings and other attacks. More recently, children are actually taking part in combat. The Personal Stories box on page 448 takes a closer look.

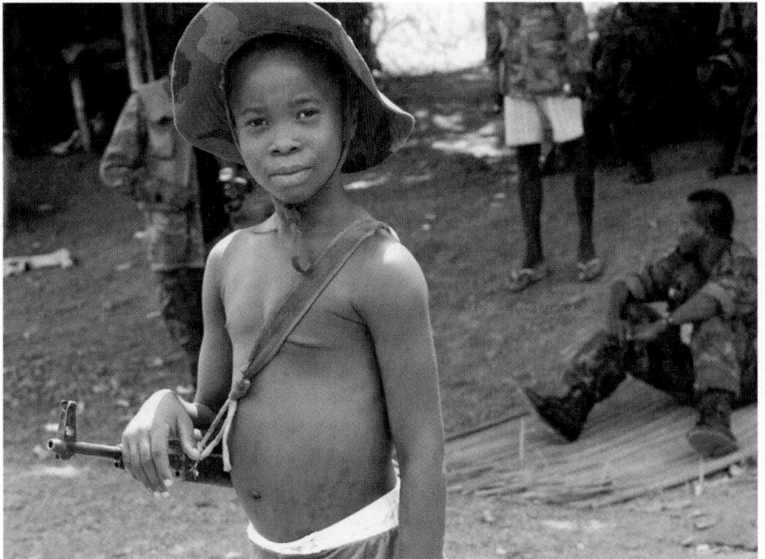

A chilling fact is that around the world, hundreds of thousands of children work as soldiers. This eleven-year-old boy is on duty defending an army checkpoint near the capital of Sierra Leone. What factors, especially in poor societies, lead children to become involved in war?

Social Class and the Military

In World War II, which was a global conflict, three-fourths of the men in the United States in their late teens and twenties served in the military. These men became soldiers either voluntarily or by being *drafted*—called by the government to service. Every male was expected to serve. Only those who had some physical or mental impairment were freed from this obligation.

Today, there is no draft; that policy ended in 1973 and was replaced by the concept of an all-volunteer military. But not every member of our society is equally likely to volunteer. One recent study concluded that the military has few young people who are rich and also few who are very poor. Rather, it is primarily working-class people who look to the military for a job, to earn some money to go to college, or simply to get out of the small town where they grew up. Regionally, the largest number of young enlistees comes from the South, where local culture is more supportive of the military and where most military bases are located. As two analysts put it, "America's military seems to resemble the makeup of a two-year commuter or trade school outside Birmingham or Biloxi far more than that of a ghetto or barrio or four-year university in Boston" (Halbfinger & Holmes, 2003:1).

In today's uncertain economy, the military has found that an increasing number of young men and women are interested in signing up. For some, the attraction lies in training and money to use later on for college. For others, there are few alternative jobs to be found. In any case, our nation now has a "working-class army" (Glater, 2005).

Mass Media and War

We view the world through stories and images provided by the mass media. Reporting war news is, of course, nothing new. But the Iraq War was the first war in which television crews actually traveled with U.S. troops, reporting as the military operations unfolded. Cable television channels made available live coverage of the war twenty-four hours a day, seven days a week.

The mass media not only *report* the events, but also *frame* them, guiding how viewers understand and interpret them. Media outlets critical of the Iraqi war—especially the Arab news channel Al-Jazeera—tended to report the slow pace of the conflict, played up the casualties on the part of the U.S. and allied forces, and presented detailed accounts of the deaths and injuries suffered by Iraqi civilians. All this information and the accompanying "spin" was intended to increase pressure to end the war. Media outlets supportive of the war—including most news organizations in the United States—tended to report the rapid pace of the war, to focus on the casualties to Saddam Hussein's forces, and to downplay harm to Iraqi civilians as minimal and unintended. Obviously, such "spin" was intended to encourage support for the war.

For any point of view, the mass media now operate to provide selective information on armed conflicts to a worldwide audience. The power to shape the reality we perceive means that television and other media are almost as important to the outcome of a conflict as the military forces who are doing the actual fighting.

nuclear weapons bombs that use atomic reactions to generate enormous destructive force

nuclear proliferation the acquisition of nuclear weapon technology by more and more nations

PERSONAL STORIES 

Children in Combat: Not Too Young to Kill

People call him "TS." To some, he may look like a boy of twelve. But the look on his face shows that he is old beyond his years. TS is a soldier with six years of combat experience. He fights on the front lines of Sierra Leone, a war-torn nation in western Africa. In raids of villages along the border of his country, TS has killed people, many people. He has seen so much violence that he finds it difficult to sleep and often wets his bed.

The story of this boy soldier began when rebels invaded TS's village. Soldiers killed his parents and kidnapped the boy, who was only six at the time, telling him he was now a freedom fighter. TS joined the ranks of thousands of child soldiers in Sierra Leone.

Military units that abduct children typically try to turn them against their own relatives and neighbors, a strategy that leaves the children with nowhere else to go. Children are easily molded into fighters, and many develop an intense loyalty to the military. Many children readily obey orders to shoot to kill and even serve as suicide bombers.

According to the Coalition to Stop the Use of Child Soldiers, a Swiss organization, as many as 300,000 children work as soldiers in some thirty lower-income countries in South America, Africa, and Asia. Should people this young be in uniform? It is true that in many lower-income nations, adulthood begins much earlier than is typical in the United States. Many six- or seven-year-olds work for income; by thirteen or fourteen, many marry and take on other adult roles. But most children who become soldiers have little choice in the matter. After as little as one year working as soldiers, they may become socialized to accept violence as a way of life and may find it very hard to live any other way.

And what about rich countries? Some critics say they, too, exploit children. In Great Britain, for example, the navy recruits sixteen-year-olds, and people as young as seventeen join the army. The U.S. military also allows people as young as seventeen to sign up, with parental consent. The Coalition estimates that as many as 3,000 seventeen-year-olds are currently on active duty with the United States' armed forces.

WHAT DO YOU THINK?

1. In poor countries, most young children work for income. In light of this fact, is joining the military so different? Explain your position.
2. Most high-income countries have laws that prohibit children from serving as soldiers, but many low-income countries either do not have such laws or do not enforce them. What should other nations do to assist children forced into military service?
3. U.S. soldiers currently serving in Iraq are as young as eighteen. Is that too young to be asked to perform such service? Why or why not?

Sources: Schlumpf (1999), Hermes (2005), and Coalition to Stop the Use of Child Soldiers (2006).

War in the Nuclear Age

In the 1940s, warfare became far more deadly with the development of **nuclear weapons,** *bombs that use atomic reactions to generate enormous destructive force.* Only twice have nuclear weapons been used in war. In 1945, at the conclusion of World War II, the United States dropped two atomic bombs on Japan. The first exploded over the city of Hiroshima; the second, dropped three days later, fell on Nagasaki. Each explosion instantly killed 100,000 people and leveled the city. Today, estimates suggest that there are some 23,000 nuclear weapons worldwide, and 8,400 of them are operational. Most of these weapons are thousands of times more powerful than the bombs used against Japan (Stockholm International Peace Research Institute, 2009).

The Increase and Spread of Nuclear Weapons

The arms race that followed World War II led the United States and the Soviet Union to build large arsenals of nuclear weapons. At the peak of the Cold War during the 1960s, the two superpowers had built vast stockpiles that totaled about 60,000 nuclear weapons—many times the number needed to wipe out all life on this planet.

After the collapse of the Soviet Union in 1991, the Russian Federation and the United States gradually reduced their nuclear arsenals, cutting them back by 75 percent as of 2006. But these superpowers are not the only nations that have nuclear weapons. Global Map 17–2 identifies the United States, Great Britain, France, Russia, Israel, India, Pakistan, and the People's Republic of China as nations with a substantial nuclear capability.

Recent decades have witnessed a pattern of **nuclear proliferation,** *the acquisition of nuclear weapon technology by more and more nations.* Nuclear proliferation increases the likelihood that regional conflicts, such as the tensions between India and Pakistan in 2002 or the war between Israel and Hezbollah militants in Lebanon in 2006, could trigger the use of nuclear weapons. The use of such weapons would not only cause a huge

MAKING THE GRADE

Check the map below to see how many nations in the world possess nuclear weapons.

GETTING INVOLVED

Have you ever taken a public stand on the issue of nuclear weapons?

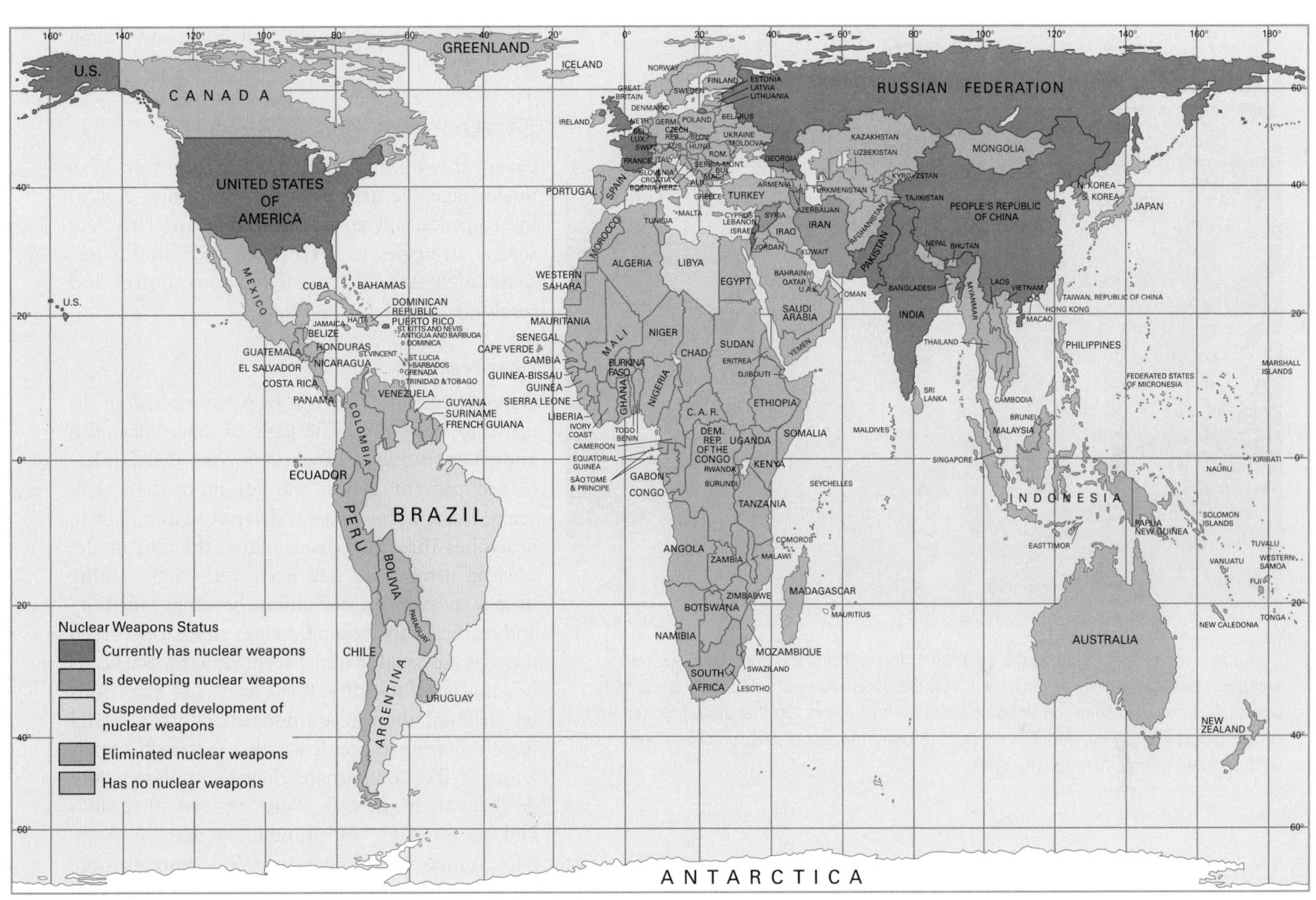

A World of Differences

GLOBAL MAP 17–2 Nuclear Weapons around the World

In 2009, eight countries possessed nuclear weapons. Many more, especially high-income nations, could build these weapons but have chosen not to. How many countries do you think will have nuclear weapons in the year 2050?

Source: Stockholm International Peace Research Institute (2009).

number of casualties but also could very well draw other nations into the conflict.

Today, Israel and North Korea are believed to possess nuclear weapons. In 2009, the world also debates whether Iran might be on its way to developing "a bomb." A few nations—Argentina, Brazil, South Africa, and Libya—have decided to stop their development of nuclear weapons. Even so, it is possible that within the next several decades, as many as fifty of the world's nations may possess at least some nuclear weapons, a fact that places the entire world in increasing danger (Hilsman, 1999; Stockholm International Peace Research Institute, 2009).

The Effects of Nuclear War

The power of nuclear weapons is beyond what anyone can imagine. The bomb that the United States dropped on Hiroshima was a "primitive" 15-kiloton device, with an explosive power of 15,000 tons of TNT, which was enough to destroy a major city. Many of the warheads in the world's nuclear arsenals are rated at 50 megatons, equivalent to 50 million tons of

deterrence a strategy to keep peace based on the threat of retaliation

arms control international agreements on the development, testing, production, and deployment of weapons

Perhaps the greatest threat to the security of the world is the spread of nuclear weapons to more and more countries. In 2006, North Korea tested its first atomic bomb, and several other countries may not be far behind. Do the United States and other "older" nuclear powers have a right to deny the same weapons to nations who wish to have them? Why or why not?

TNT, which is 3,000 times more powerful than the Hiroshima bomb.

Even a small nuclear weapon rated at a single megaton can produce temperatures that exceed the heat on the surface of the sun. Instantly, such heat will vaporize anything nearby and will unleash a firestorm that will consume everything for 10 miles in every direction. The bomb also generates a shockwave that extends outward, destroying everything in its path and drawing debris upward into a giant mushroom cloud. In the days that follow, radioactive debris rains down over a vast area (Sagan & Turco, 1990).

Some scientists claim that exploding even a few nuclear bombs at one time would draw enough debris and dust into the atmosphere to block the sun's rays from reaching the planet's surface for months or even years. This event would trigger a *nuclear winter,* a cooling of Earth's atmosphere by as much as 50 degrees Fahrenheit. The resulting semidarkness and subfreezing temperatures, together with radiation from nuclear fallout, might kill most of the planet's vegetation and animal life. Should multiple nuclear bombs ever be used in war, all life on Earth might come to an end (Sagan & Turco, 1990).

Strategies for Peace

Given the unimaginable horrors of war in a nuclear age, the nations of the world must seek to live in peace. But how can this happen? There are several strategies to keep peace, including deterrence, high-technology defense, arms control, and resolving underlying conflicts.

Deterrence

Deterrence is *a strategy to keep peace based on the threat of retaliation.* The logic of deterrence, also known as *mutual assured destruction* (MAD), has helped prevent all-out war for more than sixty years. Despite this success, deterrence as a path to peace has three drawbacks. First, the cost of the nuclear arms race has been very high, taking money away from education, housing, nutrition, and medical care. Second, today's submarine-based missiles are capable of delivering nuclear warheads in a matter of minutes. If the leaders of one country believed they were under attack, they would have little time to decide whether to launch a retaliatory strike—or perhaps their computers would do it for them. In such a case, the risk of error—and of entering an unintended war—is high. Third, deterrence cannot control nuclear proliferation. As more nations develop nuclear weapons, the risk that they will be used in war increases (Kugler & Organski, 1989).

High-Technology Defense

A second strategy to keep the peace is the use of new technology, including satellites, to defend against a nuclear attack. The Strategic Defense Initiative (SDI), first proposed by the Reagan administration in 1981, is just such a program. In principle, such a system would detect enemy missiles soon after launch and destroy them with lasers and particle beams before they reenter the atmosphere.

But there are problems with this approach. First, preliminary tests of SDI have not shown much success. Second, more than $100 billion has already been spent on this technology, and the cost will rise far higher (Hsin, 2003). Third, if one nation develops such a system, other countries may see this effort as a sign of preparing for war. As of 2009, the Obama administration has said little about whether it will or will not continue this policy toward peace.

GETTING INVOLVED

What actions, policies, or attitudes can you suggest that would promote peace in the world? Explain what you think is needed.

terrorism unlawful, typically random acts of violence or the threat of violence by an individual, group, or government to achieve a political goal

state-sponsored terrorism the practice by one government of providing money, weapons, and training to terrorists who engage in violence in another nation

repressive state terrorism government use of violence within its own national borders to suppress political opposition

Arms Control

A third strategy to keep the peace is **arms control,** *international agreements on the development, testing, production, and deployment of weapons.* Since World War II, the focus of arms control efforts has been on limiting the nuclear stockpiles held by the United States and the Soviet Union. In the 1970s, the two nations entered into the Strategic Arms Limitation Talks (SALT), which led to agreements freezing the number of nuclear weapons held by each side and limiting the development of antimissile defense systems. In the 1980s and 1990s, the United States and the Soviet Union (after 1991, the Russian Federation) entered into the Strategic Arms Reduction Talks (START), which led both nations to reduce the number of their operational nuclear weapons to the present level of about 8,400.

Arms control has limitations. First, treaties focused on existing weapons may do little to slow the development of newer weapons. Second, it is difficult to verify whether nations are living up to arms control agreements. Third, despite recent progress toward arms control, enough nuclear weapons still remain to destroy the entire planet. The more important issue, therefore, is resolving the underlying conflicts that might end up causing their use.

Resolving Underlying Conflict

The most effective path to peace is to resolve conflicts, the strategy of *diplomacy.* Peace depends on the efforts of national leaders and ambassadors posted in various countries as well as the work of international agencies such as the United Nations. In recent years, diplomats have used the term *peace process* to refer to the back-and-forth negotiations between parties in conflict, including the steps each side will take to end hostilities in exchange for a desired objective. Negotiating peace is always difficult, and not every participant in a conflict may want peace, at least not on terms agreeable to all. For example, the Middle East peace process has been going on for decades, but violent confrontations between Israelis and Palestinians continue.

Throughout the world today, there are hundreds of conflicts between nations and groups based on territorial disputes, ethnicity, religion, ideology, and inequality. To suppose that humankind can resolve all these conflicts may seem like wishful thinking. But the fact remains that the world spends far more money on weapons of war than on strategies for peace (Dedrick & Yinger, 1990; Kaplan & Schaffer, 2001).

There are individuals who have shown a lifetime commitment to the pursuit of peace. One of the most influential was the Indian leader Mohandas Gandhi (1869–1948), whose lessons are described in the Defining Moment box on page 453.

Terrorism

Terrorism involves *unlawful, typically random acts of violence or the threat of violence by an individual, group, or government to achieve a political goal.* Every day, several significant acts of terrorism take place somewhere in the world (U.S. Department of State, 2006).

War involves an ongoing conflict that usually follows international law and conventions. But terrorism involves sporadic and unpredictable acts of violence that cause widespread fear. Acts of terror, which include bombings, hijackings, and assassinations, are typically used by individuals or groups against a more powerful enemy.

Some terrorists are individual activists, but others have substantial government support. **State-sponsored terrorism** is *the practice by one government of providing money, weapons, and training to terrorists who engage in violence in another nation.* For example, the Taliban regime in Afghanistan provided military training and other support to members of al-Qaeda, who later engaged in terrorist attacks against the United States and other countries. After the attacks of September 11, 2001, the United States began military action in Afghanistan to drive the Taliban from power and weaken the al-Qaeda network. The U.S. government claims that Iran, Syria, and certain other nations have also sponsored terrorism (U.S. Department of State, 2006).

Any discussion of terrorism involves claims and counterclaims. Organizations may use terrorism to focus world attention on their issues and demands, which they claim to be fair and good. They define violent acts as a legitimate political response to some injustice. For this reason, whether people condemn or celebrate an act of violence depends on which side of a dispute they are on. For example, the U.S. government condemns al-Qaeda for engaging in terrorism, and leaders of al-Qaeda say much the same thing about the United States. The United States also claims that Iran engages in state-sponsored terrorism for supporting Hezbollah fighters in Lebanon who are frequently at war with Israel; Iran counters that Israel, with the support of the United States, engages in terrorism against its neighbors. In short, whether we label actors as "terrorists" or "freedom fighters" is a matter of politics (Sheehan, 2000; J. C. Jenkins, 2003; U.S. Department of State, 2006).

Governments also use terrorism against their own people. **Repressive state terrorism** is *government use of violence within its own national borders to suppress political opposition.* Many governments have used kidnapping, torture, rape, and mass murder to stay in power. The Soviet dictator Josef Stalin used secret police and a system of concentration camps to control or kill anyone he considered a threat. Adolf Hitler used similar

MAKING THE GRADE

The discussion below explains where most of the 11,700 terrorist attacks in 2008 took place.

SOCIAL PROBLEMS in Everyday Life

Notice that our nation's history reveals considerable "home-grown" terrorism.

In 2009, an attack on an Israeli army patrol by Palestinian militants prompted Israel to launch a military offensive in Gaza, destroying many Palestinians' homes. In today's Middle East, it is difficult to separate terrorism and conventional warfare. To make matters more complex, who the "terrorists" are depends on which side of the conflict you are on.

brutal methods to rule Germany during the Nazi era. In the 1970s, Pol Pot conducted a campaign of repressive state terrorism against the people of Cambodia. And until his overthrow by U.S. forces, Saddam Hussein used a brutal campaign of terror to maintain an iron grip on the people of Iraq.

The Extent of Terrorism

In 2008, there were more than 11,700 terrorist attacks worldwide, which claimed 15,765 civilian lives, including 33 Americans. Terrorism caused serious injury to more than 34,000 people. Most of these attacks were in Iraq, but major terrorist attacks occurred in other countries, including Afghanistan, India, and Somalia (U.S. Department of State, 2009).

Terrorism: A Global Perspective

For at least a century, terrorism has played a part in efforts to end colonial rule in many nations of the world. In 1916, for example, Irish people opposed to British rule formed the Irish Republican Army (IRA) with the goal of forcing the British from Ireland. In 1922, the British gave up claim to most of Ireland but kept control of the three counties that make up Northern Ireland. For decades after that, the IRA used terrorism as part of its efforts to end British control there as well.

Many other terrorist campaigns took place around the world. After World War II, a militant faction of the Zionist movement that sought to establish a Jewish state in the Middle East used terrorism to drive the British from Palestine. In 1954, a group called the Mau Mau used terror in its efforts to force British colonialists from the African nation of Kenya. That same year, Algerian terrorists began a campaign of violence against French citizens in their country, which played a part in ending French colonial rule of Algeria in 1962. In recent decades, organizations committed to establishing a Palestinian state on land controlled by Israel have made Israelis the targets of terrorism (U.S. Department of State, 2000, 2003, 2008).

In recent years, a considerable amount of terrorism in the world has been carried out by radical Muslims who have directed their violence against the United States. In 1993, al-Qaeda members exploded a truck full of dynamite at the World Trade Center in New York's downtown business district, killing 6 people and injuring more than 1,000 (Hughes, 1998). In 1998, the same organization exploded bombs at the U.S. embassies in Tanzania and Kenya, killing 257 people and injuring more than 5,000. In 2001, the most deadly attack on the United States in history took almost 3,000 lives when al-Qaeda terrorists seized and crashed airliners loaded with passengers and fuel into the twin towers of the World Trade Center in New York and the Pentagon outside Washington, D.C. Another hijacked plane, in which passengers fought the terrorists, crashed in rural Pennsylvania.

The targeting of the United States reflects this nation's substantial military, economic, and political presence around the world. In addition, some radical organizations, including al-Qaeda, define the United States as an evil influence in the world (Reeve, 1999; Thomas & Hirsh, 2000; U.S. Department of State, 2006).

Terrorism in U.S. History

Although many people here in the United States think of terrorists as people from other countries, the United States has a long history of home-grown terrorism. After the abolition of slavery, the Ku Klux Klan and other organizations used cross burnings,

MAKING THE GRADE

In a sentence, state the contribution of Mohandas Gandhi to the world.

CONSTRUCTING SOCIAL PROBLEMS

A DEFINING MOMENT

Mohandas Gandhi: Spreading a Message of Peace

Mohandas K. Gandhi was a small man who carried a mighty message. He built his life around the idea that the most effective path to peace and justice is to practice not war but nonviolence.

Gandhi's primary goal was the liberation of his native country, India, from the colonial control of the British. Rather than attacking the British militarily or resorting to suicide bombers or other forms of terror common in today's world, he advocated a strategy of *nonviolent resistance*—politely but firmly refusing to cooperate with a system people believe to be wrong.

In one of his most effective tactics, Gandhi urged the people of India to make their own clothes rather than buy garments manufactured in England as part of the exploitative colonial economic system. The spinning wheel became his symbol of resistance, and the Indian people admiringly nicknamed him "Mahatma" ("great soul").

Gandhi faced many challenges and was arrested many times during his life. But in 1947, the movement he founded succeeded in ending British colonial rule. Tragically, just one year later, this man of peace was shot and killed by a crazed opponent. But his message lives on, and it has been embraced by many others, including the U.S. civil rights leader Martin Luther King Jr.

Mohandas Gandhi taught the world that it is possible to pursue justice using nonviolent means rather than war. In the years since Gandhi's death, how well has this lesson been learned?

beatings, lynchings, and bombings to prevent African Americans from exercising their new political rights. In the century after the Civil War, historians estimate, more than 5,000 black men were lynched by white supremacist mobs (Williams, 2000).

Early in the twentieth century, many businesses used violence to prevent union organizing, and some labor groups fought back. The Industrial Workers of the World (IWW), a radical-left labor union, began a war against capitalism that included violent strikes, bombings, and assassinations (Lukas, 1997). In the 1960s, some students on the radical left formed the Weather Underground, a group committed to forming a classless society by destroying the nation's economic and military institutions. This group carried out a number of violent attacks, including a bombing of the Pentagon in 1975 (Finlayson, 1998).

On April 19, 1995, Timothy McVeigh, a military veteran, parked a truck full of explosives in front of the Murrah Federal Building in Oklahoma City. McVeigh, on the radical right, was

MAKING THE GRADE

Note the three defining characteristics of terrorism on this page.

GETTING INVOLVED

How important do you think the current war on terror is to our country's national security? Why?

seeking revenge on the federal government for actions taken against Randy Weaver at Ruby Ridge, Idaho, and against the Branch Davidian compound in Waco, Texas (events discussed in Chapter 6, "Crime, Violence, and Criminal Justice"). The explosion killed 169 people—many of them children—and injured hundreds more (Perlstein, 1998).

The Costs of Terrorism

One great cost of terrorism is loss of life and physical injury: In recent years tens of thousands of people worldwide have been killed or injured by terrorism (U.S. Department of State, 2008). Hostages and other survivors of terror attacks, like soldiers who suffer from battlefield trauma, may well experience posttraumatic stress disorder. Just as important, such acts cause widespread fear. Everyone living in the United States at the time of the attacks on September 11, 2001, can recall the fear and anxiety caused by the events of that day. For people living in Iraq, where the pace of terrorism is far greater, fear and anxiety have been an almost daily occurrence.

The economic costs of terrorist attacks are impossible to measure, but they reach into the hundreds of billions of dollars. There is the immediate loss of property as well as the effects on the entire economy. In the area near where New York's World Trade Center stood before the September 11 attacks, the entire economy collapsed for several years. Similarly, in the aftermath of those plane hijackings, air travel fell dramatically, forcing several airlines into bankruptcy.

After winning the military campaign in Afghanistan, the United States faced a much tougher job—winning the hearts and minds of the Afghan people. How might you react to a foreign army occupying your country?

If we were to calculate the full costs of this country's "war on terrorism," including all the military spending that supports it, the total would surely be trillions of dollars. Such vast sums are hard to imagine, but they easily represent enough money to end poverty not only in this country but everywhere in the world.

Terrorism as a Type of War

Terrorism has emerged as a new type of war. Like war, terrorism is a form of armed conflict, but it differs from conventional war in three major ways.

1. **The parties in conflict are not clearly known.** War is fought between nations known to one another. Terrorism is carried out by organized groups whose identity, leadership, membership, and location may or may not be known. Years after the United States launched its war on terrorism, there is still much to learn about the al-Qaeda organization.
2. **The objectives of the terrorist groups are not clearly stated.** Wars are usually fought with clear objectives, such as gaining territory. The goals of terrorist groups, by contrast, may not be clear. Although al-Qaeda clearly has the intention of harming the United States, the precise goals of the September 11 attacks and other terrorist acts have never been clearly stated.
3. **Terrorism is asymmetrical**. Conventional warfare is symmetrical, with two opposing powers sending their armies into battle. By contrast, terrorism is an asymmetrical or uneven conflict in which a small number of attackers use terror and their own willingness to die in order to take on a far more powerful enemy (Ratnesar, 2003).

Strategies for Dealing with Terrorism

Five strategies for dealing with terrorism are part of official U.S. policy and have widespread support elsewhere in the world: Make no concessions, prosecute terrorists, apply economic sanctions, use military force if necessary, and defend against terrorism. In addition to these responses, nations must address the root causes in order to counter terrorism (Tucker, 1998).

Make No Concessions

Many national leaders say that they will never give in to terrorist groups. This policy is based on the logic that giving terrorists what they want by, say, paying ransom, surrendering land, or freeing prisoners only encourages further violence. Some nations say they will not even negotiate with terrorists.

MAKING THE GRADE

Be sure you can explain the six strategies for dealing with terrorism noted below.

SOCIAL PROBLEMS in Everyday Life

On balance, do you think the war in Iraq has hurt the efforts of terrorists, or has it harmed this country's image and helped the terrorists recruit new members? Explain your view.

But critics claim that a no-concessions policy has little impact on terrorism. They point out that terrorists, such as members of al-Qaeda led by Osama bin Laden, are not looking for concessions but simply want to inflict as much damage as possible. In addition, research suggests that the number of terrorist attacks following a refusal to make concessions is about the same as that after concessions took place.

Prosecute or Kill Terrorists

A second strategy to deal with terrorists is criminal prosecution. The federal government successfully prosecuted Timothy McVeigh for the Oklahoma City bombing; he was executed in 1999. In 2006, Zacarias Moussaoui, the alleged "twentieth hijacker" in the September 11, 2001, attacks, was sentenced to life in prison. In some cases, the U.S. military tries to kill terrorist leaders. Also in 2006, the U.S. military was successful in the effort to hunt down and kill Abu Musab al-Zarqawi, leader of al-Qaeda in Iraq.

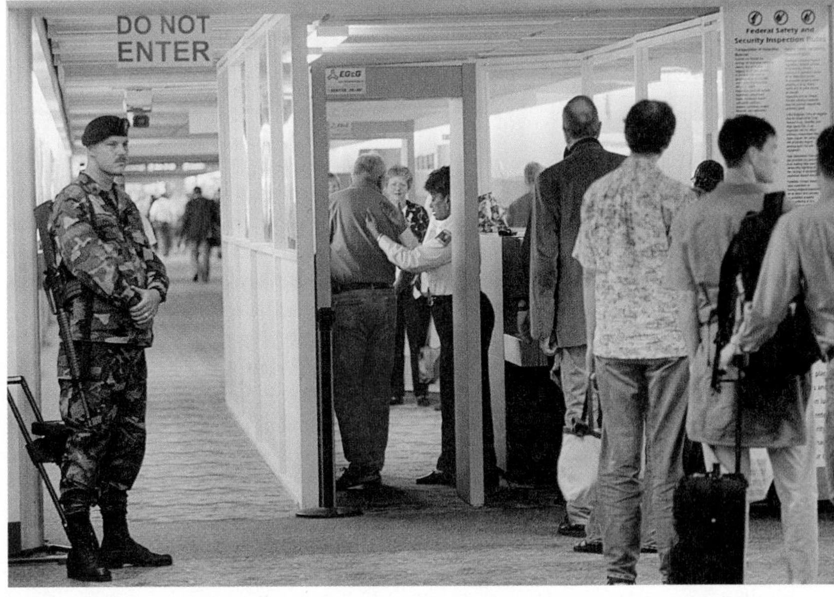

High security, including the presence of armed soldiers, has long been a fact of life in airports around the world. The same is now true of the United States. How has today's heightened security affected you or members of your family?

Apply Economic Sanctions

The United States has applied *economic sanctions* or trade restrictions against a number of nations believed to be supporting terrorism, including Libya, Syria, Iraq, and North Korea. Economic sanctions may harm another country, but bringing about a desired change of behavior may take years, if it occurs at all. In addition, economic sanctions may harm the civilian population of a country while having little effect on leaders. Sanctions against Cuba, for example, have probably hurt the living standards of ordinary people and done little to threaten the power of that country's leaders, Fidel and Raul Castro.

Use Military Force

A fourth strategy to punish terrorists and their supporters is direct use of military force. In 1986, the United States bombed Libya following terrorist attacks on United States citizens in Europe. After the Persian Gulf War, the United States bombed Iraq for attacking its own Kurdish population. After the September 11, 2001, attacks, the United States went to war in Afghanistan. In 2003, the United States invaded Iraq and ousted its leaders, claiming they were planning to engage in terrorism against this country.

Of course, any use of military force is risky because it may provoke further terrorist attacks. In addition, going to war is almost always controversial, as the largely negative response both among the U.S. public and among world leaders to the use of force by the United States in Iraq clearly shows.

Defend against Terrorism

A fifth strategy is to make terrorism harder to accomplish. For more than twenty-five years, the U.S. government has used various security measures to protect airports, buildings, and personnel. In addition, the government gathers intelligence data in an effort to identify terrorist groups, monitor their activities, and prevent their attacks. Shortly after the September 11, 2001, attacks, the U.S. Congress passed the USA PATRIOT Act, which greatly expanded the power of government officials to monitor the behavior of people in the United States. It was renewed in 2006.

Government leaders claim the USA PATRIOT Act has worked, helping prevent new attacks. Critics reply that giving such broad powers to government threatens people's civil liberties, which may be more harmful to the country than terrorism itself. The Social Policy box on page 456 takes a closer look at this controversy.

Address the Root Causes of Terrorism

A final issue, which often gets little attention, may be the most important of all. It points to the need to examine the underlying conflicts and conditions that cause people to engage in terrorism in the first place.

GETTING INVOLVED

Do you support the USA PATRIOT Act? Why or why not?

SOCIAL POLICY

The USA PATRIOT Act: Are We More Secure? Less Free?

The USA PATRIOT Act (the acronym stands for Uniting and Strengthening America by Providing Appropriate Tools Required to Intercept and Obstruct Terrorism) was passed by Congress and signed into law by President George W. Bush at the end of October 2001, less than two months after the September 11 terrorist attacks. Congress reauthorized the act in 2005, and it was signed by the president the following year.

Congress passed this law based on the belief that the United States was likely to be the target of future terrorist attacks and that the country needed to do a better job of defending itself. In practice, the law gives expanded powers to law enforcement officials here and intelligence agencies working abroad so that they can more effectively battle terrorists.

Under this act, law enforcement can track suspected terrorists by monitoring e-mail, checking visits to suspicious Web sites, tapping phone lines, and closely inspecting bank accounts. Supporters of the act—and polls show that a majority, but declining share, of U.S. adults are behind the measure—believe that it has made the country more secure and point to the fact that in the years since the act was originally passed, no major terrorist attack has taken place on U.S. soil.

Critics disagree. First, they doubt that these new powers are necessary to fight terrorism. Second, they claim that expanding government powers has a serious consequence: reducing freedom. "We all want to fight and win the war against terrorism," says one former Republican congressman, "but there is absolutely no need to sacrifice civil liberties." The thought of the government monitoring the telephone calls, e-mails, Web surfing, and bank accounts of people across the country raises great concern among many liberals and also some conservatives. Many fear that the law gives the government too much power over our lives and can be used to silence legitimate dissent.

Perhaps both supporters and opponents of the USA PATRIOT Act are partly right. The law may well help officials defend the country against terrorism. But any law that gives the government greater powers over us also reduces our personal freedoms.

WHAT DO YOU THINK?

1. Does defending national security require giving up some personal freedoms? Why or why not?
2. Would you mind if government officials read your e-mail or checked your bank accounts to look for evidence that you might be planning to engage in terrorism? Explain your position.
3. Support for the USA PATRIOT Act is lower than it once was. Do you think this trend reflects the fact that no additional attack on the United States has taken place? Does it reflect a shift in political attitudes? Explain your view.

Sources: Center for Constitutional Rights (2003), Electronic Frontier Foundation (2003), and Stolberg (2006).

This approach does not assume that the claims made by terrorists are valid, nor does it condone terrorists' use of violence against innocent people. But it does help us see that terrorism is a symptom of the passionate belief on the part of less powerful people that they are being treated unfairly. If there were greater opportunity for such people to express their grievances, and if the powerful nations of the world took greater interest in global inequality and showed greater respect for the cultures of less powerful people, perhaps fewer terrorist acts would occur.

Theoretical Analysis: Understanding War and Terrorism

Theory involves organizing facts to gain understanding. The sections that follow first consider the value of biological theories and then apply sociology's various theoretical approaches to war and terrorism.

Biological Theories of Conflict

Is a tendency toward war and violence a natural part of being human? Some biological scientists claim that it is. Konrad Lorenz (1966, 1981) claims that just as some animals will defend a nest, den, or burrow, humans turn to war to defend their homeland.

Edward Wilson (1975) claims that certain types of human behavior, including war and aggression, result from competition among males in the process of reproduction. In the case of most animals, males fight with each other for sexual access to females. In the case of humans, however, the process is more complex. Wilson argues that more aggressive men typically achieve higher social standing, which in turn attracts females. On average, Wilson continues, more aggressive men are more likely than less aggressive men to reproduce. Over hundreds of generations, this process ensures that genetic traits favoring aggression will become more common in the human species.

CRITICAL REVIEW Most sociologists tend to dismiss claims that humans are naturally aggressive. They

MAKING THE GRADE

Can you point out both positive and negative consequences of terrorism?

point out that we make choices about our behavior and that humans are not guided by biological instincts the way other animals are. Not surprisingly, sociologists point to culture and social structure as the greatest influences on human behavior. These factors, rather than biology, make some societies more warlike than others. If war is natural to humans, why do nations have to go to such great lengths to convince their people to go to war? (Montagu, 1976).

Structural-Functional Analysis: The Functions of Conflict

The structural-functional approach highlights the functions that war and other conflict have for society. Although war has obvious costs in terms of the loss of lives and property, it may accomplish important goals.

Two centuries ago, the Prussian military theorist Carl von Clausewitz (1780–1831) studied the functions of warfare. War, he concluded, is simply politics carried on by other means. Nations go to war to achieve political goals, such as gaining land or increasing their international prestige. War may be a good strategy, Clausewitz (1968, orig. 1832) concluded, if nations expect that the gains of fighting will outweigh the likely costs—and of course, if the country's leaders are sure of winning.

History tells us that war is often not a winning strategy. For one thing, many countries that start wars end up in defeat. But today's sociologists point out that war continues to have important political consequences. Most of the world's territorial boundaries have been established by wars. Similarly, war and even terrorism have played a major part in creating new nations, including the United States. Throughout the twentieth century, war and terrorism have been strategies used by ethnic and religious minorities seeking their own nation-states. As already noted, terrorism can be an effective strategy for a group or nation to use in opposition to a much stronger enemy.

An important function of both war and terrorism is uniting the population of a nation to rally around a patriotic cause. Conflict with a nation or group with a differing way of life also helps clarify and strengthen a society's cultural values. Military efforts also create tens of thousands of jobs, greatly expanding the economy. In addition, many of the technological developments we take for granted today, including the interstate highways, high-speed jet travel, cellular telephones, and the Internet, were the results of military research.

Finally, war has played a part in improving the social standing of women and other minorities. It was during World War II, for example, that African Americans and women of all colors first gained access to good jobs in factories turning out war equipment (Flexner, 1975; Chafe, 1977; Galbraith, 1985). The Diversity: Race, Class, & Gender box on page 458 takes a look at the place of women in today's armed forces.

CRITICAL REVIEW Critics of the structural-functional approach ask, first of all, how we can even think about war as having positive consequences when the weapons of war now threaten to destroy whole nations and possibly the entire planet. Second, by pointing out the positive functions of war and other violent conflict, this approach downplays the tremendous costs of war, including loss of life and property and damage to the environment. Third, the costs and benefits of war are not the same for everyone. Average people who enlist to fight in wars pay a high price; leaders and the people who manufacture and sell the weapons used in war often make out much better. Finally, the reality of conflict is always a matter of how people define it, which brings us to the symbolic-interaction approach.

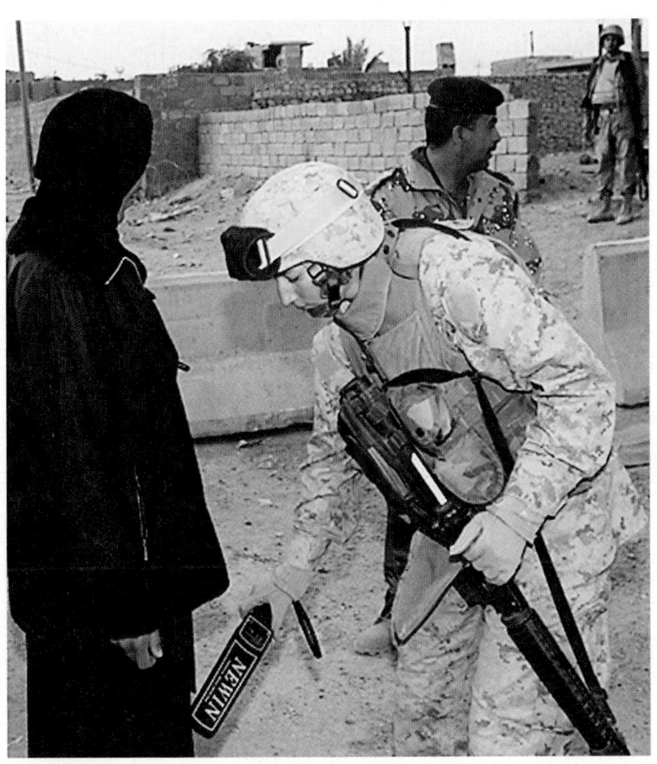

Fourteen percent of the military personnel now deployed by the United States are women. Do you support women moving into combat roles in the military? Why or why not?

SOCIAL PROBLEMS in Everyday Life

Point to specific ways leaders "construct" war as good.

SOCIAL PROBLEMS in Everyday Life

Can you point to specific examples of how our society defines our own way of life in very positive terms and defines some enemy in very negative terms? Are such claims justified? Why or why not?

DIVERSITY: RACE, CLASS, & GENDER

Women in the Military: An Equal Right to Kill?

Although most people think of the military as a man's world, women have served in the U.S. armed forces since colonial times. At the beginning of World War II, women represented 2 percent of the U.S. military forces. Today, women make up about 14 percent of the U.S. military, and they represent about 2 percent of more than 4,000 soldiers killed in the Iraq War (U.S. Department of Defense, 2009).

Nevertheless, some uneasiness remains regarding women serving in combat roles. Some people who oppose women in combat point to the fact that on average, women have less physical strength than men. Others counter that in today's high-technology wars, physical strength plays a smaller and smaller role in armed conflict. Mental strength may matter more to today's soldiers, and data show that women in uniform are better educated and more intelligent than their male counterparts.

Just as important, in this age of high technology, it is hard to draw a line between combat and noncombat personnel. For example, a combat soldier who fires a missile at an enemy position may be miles away from the actual explosion. At the same time, a noncombatant team operating a helicopter may come under fire carrying the wounded from a battlefield.

Perhaps the greatest resistance to having more women in combat is the traditional view of women as nurturers who give life and help to others. As long as U.S. culture defines women in this way (and as long as we engage in wars), it is likely that the military will resist putting women in harm's way.

WHAT DO YOU THINK?

1. Is the fact that women generally have less physical strength than men important in today's military?
2. Do you think that having more women in uniform changes the culture of the military in any important ways? If so, how and why?
3. What about the fact that women in combat may be taken as prisoners of war? Do you think enemy soldiers will treat women POWs differently from men who are POWs? Explain.

Symbolic-Interaction Analysis: The Meanings of Conflict

The symbolic-interaction approach focuses attention on the meanings people attach to war and other types of violent conflict. The importance of meanings was noted earlier when pointing out that one side's "terrorists" may well be the other side's "freedom fighters."

In general, national leaders use symbols and meanings to "spin" the reality of war in a particular way. People tend to define their own country's cause as just, making claims that their soldiers march "with God on their side." In addition, people use various symbols and meanings to demonize the enemy. A generation ago, President Ronald Reagan justified greater military spending by painting the Soviet Union as an "evil empire" that was a danger to the entire world. A few years back, President George W. Bush characterized Iran, Iraq, and North Korea as an "axis of evil." The Iranian president returned the favor, characterizing the United States as "the great Satan."

Within the military, recruits are trained to define the enemy as less than human. In the Vietnam War, for example, many U.S. soldiers learned to regard their Vietnamese counterparts as "gooks." Dehumanizing people in this way, of course, makes killing them that much easier (Said, 1981; Aditjondro, 2000).

CRITICAL REVIEW The symbolic-interaction approach shows us that war is a battle waged not only using guns but also using words and other symbols as people define themselves as just and their opponents as unjust. But this approach says little about the role of power in international conflict. The side that turns out to be "right" typically is the side that is militarily stronger. In addition, within a society's population, some categories of people declare wars, and others fight them. Some categories make money from military campaigns, and some lose everything. To learn more about how inequality shapes war, we turn to the social-conflict approach.

Social-Conflict Analysis: Inequality and Conflict

Social-conflict theory highlights the link between war and social inequality. Karl Marx, who helped develop the social-conflict approach, considered political leaders the servants of the capitalist class, the people who own the means of production. Capitalists want ever-increasing profits, which they get from finding new sources of raw materials, manufacturing new products, and selling them in new markets. In Marx's day, capitalists did all these things through colonizing the world, which led rich nations in Europe to conquer and control other countries.

Formal colonialism is now mostly a thing of the past, but the pattern of foreign control remains. Rich nations, including the United States, use their military power to protect and expand

MAKING THE GRADE

Use the table below to review the three theoretical approaches to war and terrorism.

APPLYING THEORY

War and Terrorism

	What is the level of analysis?	How do we understand war and terrorism?	What does the approach say about war and terrorism as problems?
Structural-functional approach	Macro-level	The structural-functional approach suggests that war is a strategy that a society may use to establish its independence, defend its way of life, or reach other objectives. Terrorism is a strategy used by groups or nations to oppose a much stronger enemy. Conflict helps unite a society and strengthen its core values. Militarism helps expand the economy. Many technological advances that improve our lives, including the Internet, were developed through military research.	Like all social patterns, war has benefits and costs. Whether a particular conflict ends up being thought of as a problem or not has much to do with the outcomes, all of which may not be evident for some time.
Symbolic-interaction approach	Micro-level	The symbolic-interaction approach focuses on the meanings and understandings that people attach to conflict. National leaders use symbols to convince a population that their cause is just. Leaders also use symbols to demonize an enemy.	Reality is socially constructed. Therefore, whether any military effort is celebrated as heroic or condemned as unjust depends on the definitions that are applied. Two parties in conflict may see the same situation in very different terms so that one party's "problem" is the other's "solution."
Social-conflict approach	Macro-level	The social-conflict approach links war to social inequality. Marx explained militarism as efforts by the capitalist elite to gain ever-increasing profits through colonialism; today, the goal is to defend and expand the capitalist global economy. Strong nations use war to dominate the globe; the powerless use terrorism to fight back.	The question becomes, Problems for whom? Elites often benefit from militarism and the wars that are fought by ordinary people who bear most of the suffering and loss.

the global capitalist economy (Wallerstein, 1979; M. C. Hudson, 1992; Tabb, 1992). From this point of view, the war in Iraq is less about helping that country and other nations in the Middle East secure freedom and justice than it is about ensuring the flow of oil and opening more of the world to multinational corporations. Here at home, the rich are the primary beneficiaries of war, and ordinary people make up most of the soldiers and sailors who do the fighting (Halbfinger & Holmes, 2003).

As noted earlier in this chapter, the production of weapons and other military goods helps speed the growth of the capitalist economy, pushing up corporate profits. The arms race a generation ago or the war on terror today may or may not make the nation safer, but developing and producing new weapons and military technology is certainly highly profitable for those who control the U.S. economy (Mills, 1956).

And what of terrorism? Historically, poor nations have been no match for the military might of the colonial powers. For that reason, groups opposing colonial rule often act outside the established political system. As noted earlier, terrorism can be an effective way for less powerful people to focus the world's

MAKING THE GRADE

Why do conservatives support a policy of "peace through strength"?

MAKING THE GRADE

Why do liberals express caution about our nation's use of military power?

attention on what they consider to be injustice. In short, war is the means by which powerful nations dominate the globe; terrorism is the means by which the powerless fight back (B. Hoffman, 1998; Kaldor, 1999; Stern, 1999; Zanini, 1999).

CRITICAL REVIEW By linking war and terrorism to social inequality, the social-conflict approach helps explain ongoing support for militarism in the United States even during times of peace. One limitation of the claim that capitalism is the major cause of war is that socialist nations also engage in war. For example, the Soviet Union used military force to gain and maintain control of Eastern Europe following World War II, just as China has directed its military power against Vietnam, Cambodia, and Tibet. In addition, a broad view of history shows that wars break out not only because of economic concerns but also as the result of religious beliefs and ethnic pride.

The Applying Theory table on page 459 summarizes what we can learn about war and terrorism from each of sociology's three major theoretical approaches.

 POLITICS AND WAR

Constructing Problems and Defining Solutions

Theory provides useful insights about war and terrorism, but the positions people take on problems and their solutions reflect their values and politics. The following sections examine the conservative, liberal, and radical-left views of war and terrorism.

Conservatives: Peace through Strength

Believing that this country represents good in the world and recognizing that the United States has enemies abroad, most conservatives favor military strength as the best way to keep the peace. Similar to their law-and-order view that a strong police force is needed to fight crime at home, conservatives believe that a strong military protects the nation's interests against hostile forces beyond its borders. For this reason, most conservatives support U.S. military actions abroad—at least when our national interests are truly at stake—and this helps explain why this country currently stations troops in some twenty nations.

During the Cold War, which lasted from the end of World War II until the collapse of the Soviet Union in 1991, conservatives supported increased military expenditures in the belief that in facing an enemy that opposed our core value of human liberty, nothing less than the freedom of the United States was at stake. During the past decade, as a result of the Iraq War and the war against terror, President George W. Bush pushed military expenditures higher, claiming that a strong U.S. military presence in the world is vital both for ensuring the security of people here in the United States and for extending freedom to people living in countries that lack democracy. Since his election, President Barack Obama has sought to decrease this country's involvement in Iraq but at the same time increase our military commitment in Afghanistan.

Conservatives also take a hard line against terrorism. In general, they paint those who use violence against innocent people as criminals opposed to freedom and economic development. People to the right of center think the United States should do whatever is necessary to identify those responsible for terrorism and bring them to justice, applauding the effort that led to the death of Abu Musab al-Zarqawi in 2006.

President Bush made the war on terrorism the defining mission of his administration. He and other conservatives believe that the most effective path to peace is using military strength to prevent terrorism and to encourage the spread of democracy abroad.

Liberals: The Dangers of Militarism

Liberals agree with conservatives that the United States needs to be able to defend itself from attack. For this reason, liberals also support our military. However, liberals typically favor a somewhat lower level of military spending than conservatives. One reason is that as liberals see it, the United States has not always used its military wisely. The Democratic victory in the 2006 congressional elections and the election of President Obama in 2008 were driven, in large part, by the voters' view that the Iraq War has turned world opinion against the United States and encouraged even greater terrorism.

A second disagreement centers on how a society should use its limited resources. Conservatives tend to make military spending a top priority, but liberals are keenly aware that military spending takes money away from education, health care, and other important programs. In short, liberals see militarism as draining resources that could be used to provide universal health insurance, reduce poverty, and improve rundown schools. Therefore, liberals typically offer strong support for arms reduction.

When it comes to international tensions as well as terrorism, liberals believe that our country's first response should be diplomacy and negotiation rather than the deployment of troops. For this reason, liberals emphasize the importance of

MAKING THE GRADE

From a radical-left point of view, what is the solution to the problem of war?

international efforts at building peace, including the work of the United Nations.

The Radical Left: Peace through Equality

Radicals on the political left believe that the root cause of war, terrorism, and militarism is inequality. Given the enormous gulf between the rich and the poor around the world, they ask, why should anyone expect people to live in peace? Radicals claim that the United States pours money into militarism not for national defense but so that it can operate as a global police force, expanding U.S. influence and extending the global reach of capitalism throughout the world.

In practice, then, the United States engages in military action when any other nation threatens the operation of the world's capitalist economy. Radicals point to the economic boycott of Cuba after that country's socialist revolution in 1959; hostility toward the socialist Sandinistas in Nicaragua during the 1980s; the onset of the Gulf War in 1991, when the Iraqi army threatened our oil supply in Kuwait; and the 2003 Iraq War and the larger war on terrorism, both seen as efforts to stabilize the world and allow the expansion of corporate influence. Our leaders may justify wars on moral grounds, but radicals claim that the real motive amounts to little more than greed. Left radicals were as likely to see the United States as part of the problem (at least under the Bush administration) as they were to see our country as part of the solution to the world's problems. How the left views the Obama presidency will largely depend on how much he breaks from the past.

Given their critical view of how U.S. society operates, it is not surprising that radicals on the left often express sympathy for the efforts of forces around the world that are seeking change. From this point of view, terrorism is a political response to powerlessness. As long as a handful of powerful nations rule the world, we should expect some oppressed groups to strike back.

In sum, radicals believe that war and terrorism will continue until the world moves toward greater social equality. Radicals therefore call for a national and international redistribution of wealth in favor of the poor majority. The Left to Right table on page 462 summarizes the conservative, liberal, and radical-left views of war and terrorism.

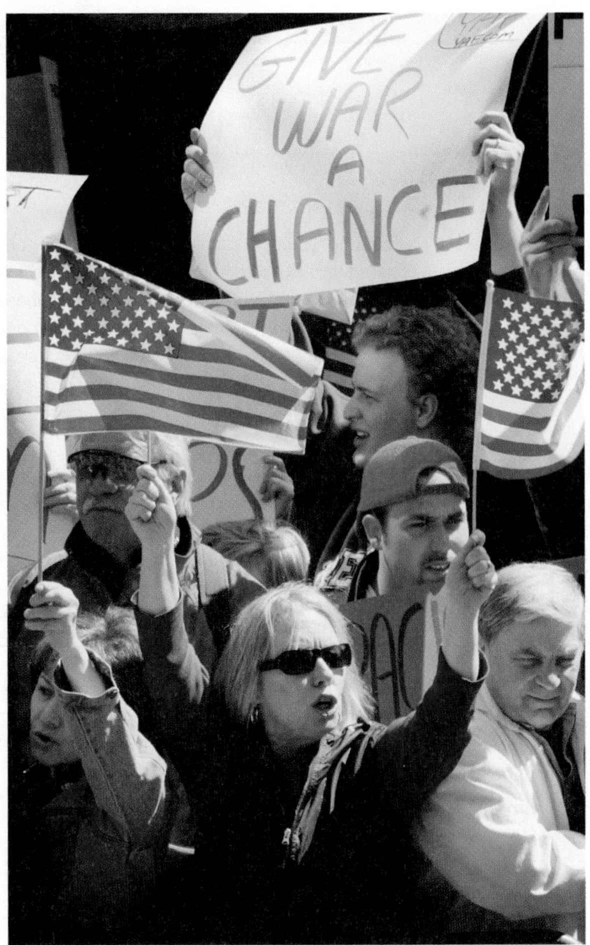

Conservatives regard the United States as a force for good in the world; from this perspective, the war in Iraq is an effort to spread democracy. Liberals are more cautious in this regard; they voice greater support for multinational efforts led by the United Nations. Radicals see militarism as a strategy to extend capitalism; they typically oppose the use of U.S. military power.

Going On from Here

Albert Einstein, whose discoveries in physics led to the development of nuclear weapons, once observed, "The unleashed power of the atom has changed everything save our modes of thinking, and we thus drift toward unparalleled catastrophe." Given humanity's history of warfare and the stockpiles of nuclear weapons on the planet today, what are the odds that we'll get through the twenty-first century without a nuclear war? No one can say for sure, but this chapter seems to support the conclusion that the world has learned a lot more about making war than about making peace. As we look to the future, the fact that more and more nations will have nuclear weapons and other weapons of mass destruction means that even local conflicts could threaten the entire planet.

As we move ahead, winning peace may well depend on implementing three strategies. First, the nations of the world

MAKING THE GRADE

Use the table below to review the three political approaches to war and terrorism.

LEFT TO RIGHT

The Politics of War and Terrorism

	RADICAL-LEFT VIEW	LIBERAL VIEW	CONSERVATIVE VIEW
WHAT IS THE PROBLEM?	The basic problem is capitalism, which encourages militarism in order to expand corporate profits at home and to defend the capitalist economy around the world.	There is a need for defense, but militarism itself can be a problem because an arms buildup provokes conflict; nuclear proliferation raises the risk of nuclear war; terrorism poses dangers to the United States.	The problem is that some nations and groups are hostile to the values and achievements of the United States; nuclear arms development by these nations threatens the security of the United States; terrorists engage in periodic attacks against the United States.
WHAT IS THE SOLUTION?	The solution to militarism is ending the domination of the world by rich nations; eliminating capitalism will end the need for ongoing militarism as well as terrorism.	Reasonable military strength is necessary, but the United States should seek arms reductions and rely on diplomacy as much as possible. Addressing the grievances of less powerful people will reduce terrorism.	Maintaining military strength and strong counterterrorism measures will defeat enemies who are set on our destruction, encourage peace, and ensure the security of the United States.

JOIN THE DEBATE

1. Looking over the three political perspectives on war and terrorism, do you see any areas of agreement? If so, what are they?
2. From the point of view of each of the three political perspectives, what would be the proper role of the U.S. military around the world?
3. Which of the three political analyses of war and terrorism do you find most convincing? Why?

must make significant efforts at arms control, with the goal of greatly reducing the number of weapons of mass destruction. The United States and the Russian Federation have made good progress already. A challenge to this goal is that some nations such as North Korea, which almost certainly has one or more nuclear weapons, permits no inspections of their arms production facilities.

Second, controlling the spread of nuclear technology is equally important. No nation can be secure as long as nuclear weapons continue to spread around the world. It seems likely that Iran is in the process of developing nuclear technology that may lead to nuclear weapons. What country will be next? How can we ensure that all nuclear weapons remain out of reach of terrorist organizations?

The third and final strategy—clearly the most difficult of all—is to address the underlying causes of war and terrorism. In part, this requires the leaders of all nations, rich and poor alike, to demonstrate genuine concern for the well-being of people everywhere, especially the poor. In addition, all world nations must be willing to participate in some forum, whether it be the United Nations or some other organization, in which national leaders can gather to present and discuss their goals and their grievances, with the overall purpose of replacing violence with negotiation and diplomacy. Idealistic? Of course. But in the end, necessary.

Finally, the planet's prospects for peace may hinge on real change that reduces the exploitation of poor people by the well-off. The greatest challenge on the road to peace may be confronting the tremendous problem of poverty and hunger (the focus of Chapter 15, "Population and Global Inequality"). The goal must be to bring about economic development in regions of the world where at present widespread suffering prevents political stability. There is every reason to think that given the will to succeed, world leaders can accomplish this goal. How the world responds to this challenge will shape the lives of us all.

DEFINING SOLUTIONS

What is your view of the U.S. military? What about the extent of militarism in the world?

Militarism has long been a controversial part of our society, sparking spirited critics as well as passionate defenders. Look at the two photos below, which suggest two approaches to this country's military.

The further you move to the political left, the greater your criticism of the U.S. military. Liberals would support the idea of defending the nation against aggressors, but are cautious and often critical about using the nation's military power. Radicals on the left oppose almost all use of U.S. military power, which they see as supporting capitalism. On the sixth anniversary of the U.S. invasion of Iraq, thousands of demonstrators gathered behind the Lincoln Memorial in the nation's capital to call for an end to the country's military presence in Iraq. Judging from the signs they are holding, what would these people rather do with some of the money that supports our military?

HINT

For some, the military is a problem; for others, it is a solution. On the left, there is support for our men and women in uniform, but support for militarism in general is usually limited to defending this country against attack. Beyond that, most liberals would prefer to see much of the billions spent on weapons channeled instead to schools, job creation programs, and other social services. On the right, patriotism is a more popular concept, and there is wide support for most U.S. military deployments. Then, too, for many young people—regardless of their political views—the armed forces is a solution, in that signing up is a way to get a steady paycheck and perhaps save some money to eventually go to college.

From the political right, the U.S. military is necessary to defend this nation against other nations or organized groups that threaten our way of life. In addition, some conservatives believe U.S. military power should be used to bring political freedom to countries around the globe. From this point of view, the military is worth supporting—even by joining up. These young people in Florida are completing their swearing-in ceremony making them part of the United States Marine Corps. Would you consider doing the same?

Getting Involved: Applications & Exercises

1. Speak to several people you know about their military experiences. For those who were in combat, ask whether the experience changed them and changed their attitudes toward war.
2. Contact a military recruiter in your area. See what you can learn about the categories of people (consider gender, age, race, ethnicity, and social class) who are most likely to join the military.
3. Watch two films of the Cold War era, *Fail-Safe* and *On the Beach,* to gain a better understanding of the height of the arms race between the United States and the Soviet Union. For a humorous yet insightful take on the arms race and the dangers of nuclear war, watch *Dr. Strangelove or: How I Learned to Stop Worrying and Love the Bomb.*
4. What student or community organizations on or near campus oppose war? Identify one or two, and try to learn what these organizations do. What are their positions regarding terrorism?

MAKING THE GRADE

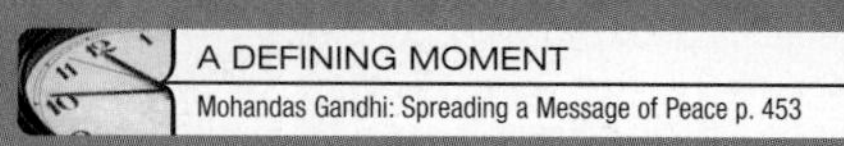

A DEFINING MOMENT
Mohandas Gandhi: Spreading a Message of Peace p. 453

CHAPTER 17 War and Terrorism

War and Peace: Basic Definitions

WAR has occurred throughout human history.
- During the twentieth century, the development of weapons of mass destruction made war far more deadly than ever before.

pp. 442–43

CAUSES OF WAR include
- perceived threats
- cultural or religious differences
- political objectives
- moral objectives
- the desire to gain wealth and power
- the desire to turn a population's attention away from domestic social problems
- the absence of alternatives for resolving disputes

pp. 443–44

ECONOMIC COSTS OF WAR
- Each year the world spends $1.5 trillion on militarism; in 2009, the U.S. military budget was about $675 billion.
- The arms race and now the war on terrorism have pushed U.S. military spending upward.
- War destroys a society's entire infrastructure—its roads, bridges, airports, water systems, and electrical and communications networks.
- Money spent on war is taken away from health care, education, and other programs that benefit a population.

pp. 444–45

HUMAN COSTS OF WAR
- The development of more deadly weapons and the strategy of total war greatly increase the number of civilian casualties.
- Suffering from war continues after the end of hostilities in the form of posttraumatic stress disorder. In all, 2.9 million U.S. veterans suffer from war-related disabilities; of these, 263,000 are totally disabled.
- Wars leave vast numbers of children orphaned. Children today are often forced into combat in wars around the world.

pp. 445–47

WAR IN THE NUCLEAR AGE
The danger posed by war increased dramatically with the development of nuclear weapons at the end of World War II.
- A single nuclear bomb can destroy an entire city.
- Even with recent arms reductions, there are still more than 8,000 nuclear weapons, more than enough destructive power to end life on the planet.

pp. 448–50

STRATEGIES FOR PEACE
Given the horrors of all-out war, humanity must use strategies for peace. These include
- deterrence
- high-technology defense
- arms control
- resolving underlying conflicts

pp. 450–51

war (p. 442) violent conflict between nations or organized groups

peace (p. 442) the absence of violent conflict

weapons of mass destruction (p. 443) weapons with the capacity to kill many thousands of people at one time

military-industrial complex (p. 445) a political alliance involving the federal government, the military, and the defense industries

total war (p. 446) deadly conflict that targets both population centers and military targets

concentration camps (p. 446) centers where prisoners are confined for purposes of state security, exploitation, punishment, or execution

war crime (p. 446) an offense against the law of war as established by international agreements and international law

nuclear weapons (p. 448) bombs that use atomic reactions to generate enormous destructive force

nuclear proliferation (p. 448) the acquisition of nuclear weapon technology by more and more nations

deterrence (p. 450) a strategy to keep peace based on the threat of retaliation; also known as *mutual assured destruction* (MAD)

arms control (p. 451) international agreements on the development, testing, production, and deployment of weapons

Terrorism

TERRORISM involves unlawful and typically random acts of violence in the pursuit of political goals.
- In 2008, there were 11,700 terrorist attacks worldwide, killing 15,765 people and injuring 34,000 more.
- In addition to the economic costs of defending against terrorism, such efforts may reduce our personal freedoms.

pp. 451–54

TERRORISM AS A NEW TYPE OF WAR
Terrorism involves armed conflict but differs from conventional war in that
- the parties in conflict are not clearly known
- the objectives of the terrorist groups are not clearly stated
- terrorism is asymmetrical

p. 454

STRATEGIES FOR DEALING WITH TERRORISM include
- prosecution
- a policy of making no concessions
- the application of economic sanctions to nations that support terrorism
- the use of military force
- defense against terrorism
- addressing the underlying causes of terrorism

pp. 454–56

terrorism (p. 451) unlawful, typically random acts of violence or the threat of violence by an individual, group, or government to achieve a political goal

state-sponsored terrorism (p. 451) the practice by one government of providing money, weapons, and training to terrorists who engage in violence in another nation

repressive state terrorism (p. 451) government use of violence within its own borders to suppress political opposition

Theoretical Analysis: Understanding War and Terrorism

Structural-Functional Analysis: The Functions of Conflict

The **STRUCTURAL-FUNCTIONAL APPROACH** looks at the functions that war and other types of conflict have for society.

- War is a strategy for pursuing political goals.
- War typically unifies a population and encourages economic growth and technological innovation.

p. 457

Symbolic-Interaction Analysis: The Meanings of Conflict

The **SYMBOLIC-INTERACTION APPROACH** focuses on the meaings that people attach to war.

- Societies use symbols and meanings to define their cause as just and to demonize the enemy.
- At the individual level, learning to dehumanize the enemy makes killing easier.

p. 458

Social-Conflict Analysis: Inequality and Conflict

The **SOCIAL-CONFLICT APPROACH** highlights how both war and terrorism are linked to social inequality.

- Karl Marx saw militarism as fueling the capitalist economy at home and expanding the reach of capitalism abroad.
- It is the rich elites of a nation who benefit from wars; the troops who do the fighting typically come from the lower classes.

pp. 458–60

See the **Applying Theory** table on page 459.

✓ *Although some biological theories argue that aggression is natural in human beings, most sociologists are skeptical of such claims, pointing to the greater importance of culture and social structure. (pp. 456–57)*

Politics and War: Constructing Problems and Defining Solutions

The Radical Left: Peace through Equality

- **RADICALS ON THE LEFT** link war and militarism to social inequality.
- Radicals on the left believe that the United States and other rich nations use their military power to defend their economic interests and to support the global capitalist economy.
- Radicals on the left see terrorism as a form of rebellion, one way poor and powerless people can make their suffering known and force change.

p. 461

Liberals: The Dangers of Militarism

- **LIBERALS** support military defense of the United States but caution that a military buildup can provoke the very conflict it is intended to prevent.
- Liberals point out that spending on militarism takes money away from social programs that benefit the population.
- Liberals generally support diplomacy as a way to address the problems that lead to terrorism.

pp. 460–61

Conservatives: Peace through Strength

- **CONSERVATIVES** favor a strong defense against forces in the world hostile to the United States.
- Conservatives supported the arms race and favor achieving peace through strength.
- Conservatives see terrorism as criminal acts opposing freedom.

p. 460

See the **Left to Right** table on page 462.

MAKING THE GRADE

Sample Test Questions

These questions are similar to those found in the test bank that accompanies this text.

Chapter 1 Sociology: Studying Social Problems

Multiple-Choice Questions

1. **The sociological imagination helps us see that social problems**
   a. result from the fact that some people make poor decisions.
   b. result from the operation of society.
   c. are conditions that harm only a small number of people.
   d. are the same issues today as they were several generations ago.

2. **The social-constructionist approach states that**
   a. what people define as problems are always, objectively speaking, very harmful to everyone.
   b. people suffer from problems of their own making.
   c. social problems arise as people define conditions as undesirable and in need of change.
   d. what most people see as serious problems actually harm very few people.

3. **The process of trying to convince the public to define some condition as a social problem is called**
   a. claims making.
   b. propaganda.
   c. emergence.
   d. coalescence.

4. **The reason to take a global perspective on social problems is that**
   a. many problems threaten the entire planet.
   b. many problems are more serious in other countries than they are in the United States.
   c. many problems are global in scope, involving many nations.
   d. All of the above are correct.

5. **Marxist theory of capitalism is an example of which theoretical approach?**
   a. the structural-functional approach
   b. the social-conflict approach
   c. the symbolic-interaction approach
   d. All of the above are correct.

6. **The method of sociological research that is most likely to reveal cause and effect is**
   a. a survey.
   b. secondary analysis.
   c. an experiment.
   d. field research.

7. **If you were trying to evaluate a crime control policy, which of the following questions would you likely ask?**
   a. How do we define success?
   b. What are the costs of this program?
   c. Which people should this program target?
   d. All of the above are correct.

8. **Referring to the political spectrum, where does the largest share of U.S. adults place themselves?**
   a. in the middle
   b. to the left of center
   c. to the right of center
   d. at one extreme or the other

9. **Which of the following is true of people who are social conservatives?**
   a. They support high taxes.
   b. They support feminism.
   c. They are "pro-life" in the abortion controversy.
   d. They support a higher minimum wage.

10. **In general, which of the following categories of people would be most likely to include economic liberals?**
   a. high-income people
   b. low-income people
   c. people with professional degrees, such as doctors and lawyers
   d. All of the above are correct.

ANSWERS: 1(b); 2(c); 3(a); 4(d); 5(b); 6(c); 7(d); 8(a); 9(c); 10(b).

Essay Questions

1. Explain the statement that social problems are socially constructed. Include in your response a discussion of the process of claims making.
2. What is the political spectrum? Describe how U.S. adults are distributed along the political spectrum. What distinguishes social issues and economic issues? What can you say about the people who tend to be liberal and conservative on each type of issue?

Chapter 2 Poverty and Wealth

Multiple-Choice Questions

1. **The richest 20 percent of U.S. families earn about what share of all income?**
   a. 15 percent
   b. 20 percent
   c. almost 50 percent
   d. more than 85 percent

2. **Progressive taxation is a policy that means**
   a. low-income people pay a larger share of their income in taxes than high-income people.
   b. low-income people pay no taxes.
   c. everyone pays taxes at the same rate.
   d. the higher the income, the larger the share of income paid in taxes.

3. **In 2007, the government defined what share of the U.S. population as poor?**
   a. 12.5 percent
   b. 22.5 percent
   c. 32.5 percent
   d. 42.5 percent

4. **Of the following age categories, which has the highest rate of poverty?**
   a. elderly people
   b. children
   c. middle-aged people
   d. people in their twenties

5. **Being poor in the United States means you are likely to experience which of the following?**
   a. poor health
   b. inadequate housing
   c. limited schooling
   d. All of the above are correct.

6. **The 1996 welfare reforms**
   a. just about ended poverty in the United States.
   b. made the poverty level go up.
   c. reduced the number of people on welfare but did little to reduce poverty.
   d. created a pattern of welfare dependency.

7. **Feminist theory focuses on which of the following issues?**
   a. how people define the poor
   b. the fact that U.S. society gives men power over women
   c. the fact that poverty involves cultural capital as well as money
   d. the fact that racial and ethnic minorities are at high risk of poverty

8. **The argument that individuals should have most of the responsibility for their social position is typically made by**
   a. conservatives.
   b. liberals.
   c. radicals on the left.
   d. All of the above are correct.

9. **Support for government assistance programs that form a "social safety net" is typically given by**
   a. conservatives.
   b. liberals.
   c. radicals.
   d. All of the above are correct.

10. **Which of the following would be a radical-left solution to the problem of poverty?**
   a. replace the capitalist economic system
   b. provide a "social safety net" to help needy people
   c. encourage people to take responsibility for their own well-being
   d. raise the minimum wage

ANSWERS: 1(c); 2(d); 3(a); 4(b); 5(d); 6(c); 7(b); 8(a); 9(b); 10(a).

Essay Questions

1. Based on the information presented in this chapter, to what degree are poor people in the United States responsible for their poverty? Present specific evidence to support your claim.
2. Discuss the distinctive ways in which conservatives, liberals, and radicals construct the problem of poverty. In each case, what are the causes of the problem? In each case, what are the solutions to the problem?

Chapter 3 Racial and Ethnic Inequality

Multiple-Choice Questions

1. **Race involves certain _____ considered important by a society, and ethnicity refers to certain _____.**
   a. biological traits; cultural traits
   b. cultural traits; biological traits
   c. differences in social standing; beliefs and attitudes
   d. lifestyles; religions

2. **Which of the following categories represents the largest share of the U.S. population?**
   a. Arab Americans
   b. Hispanic Americans (Latinos)
   c. Asian Americans
   d. African Americans

3. **A minority is defined as a category of people who**
   a. have physical traits that make them different from other people.
   b. are less than half of any society's population.
   c. are defined as being different and subject to disadvantages.
   d. are below average in terms of income.

4. **Sociologists claim that race is**
   a. just a matter of skin color.
   b. the same as ethnicity.
   c. a misleading concept that does not fit reality very well.
   d. not related to social stratification.

5. **The United States is not truly pluralistic because**
   a. most of our population lives in "ethnic enclaves."
   b. different racial and ethnic categories are unequal in social standing.
   c. this country has a history of slavery.
   d. All of the above are correct.

6. Which of the following terms correctly describes immigrants from Guatemala coming to the United States and learning to speak the English language?
   a. assimilation
   b. segregation
   c. genocide
   d. pluralism

7. Most but not all Arab Americans have cultural ties to which regions of the world?
   a. South and Central America
   b. southern Africa
   c. Asia
   d. the Middle East and North Africa

8. Which of the following is an example of institutional discrimination?
   a. A student does not wish to have a roommate of a certain ethnic background.
   b. Police are more likely to stop motorists of a particular race.
   c. A manager refuses to promote a worker because of her race.
   d. All of the above are correct.

9. Both Marx's class theory and multicultural theory are examples of which theoretical approach?
   a. the structural-functional approach
   b. the symbolic-interaction approach
   c. the social-conflict approach
   d. None of the above is correct.

10. In general, people in which political category would show the strongest support for the policy of affirmative action?
   a. people in all political categories
   b. radicals
   c. conservatives
   d. liberals

ANSWERS: 1(a); 2(b); 3(c); 4(c); 5(b); 6(a); 7(d); 8(b); 9(c); 10(d).

Essay Questions

1. Explain the following statement: "Race is not a simple matter of skin color but a socially constructed category."
2. Define prejudice and discrimination. How do prejudice and discrimination reinforce each other? How do assertions of biological inferiority and social inferiority reinforce each other?

Chapter 4 Gender Inequality

Multiple-Choice Questions

1. Gender is not just a matter of difference in the lives of women and men but also a matter of
   a. power.
   b. wealth.
   c. prestige.
   d. All of the above are correct.

2. In global perspective, women have the lowest social standing relative to men in which region of the world?
   a. North America
   b. Latin America
   c. Africa
   d. Asia

3. The problem of sexism is important mostly because
   a. the idea of male superiority is built into all our social institutions.
   b. some men are prejudiced against women.
   c. some people discriminate against women; some discriminate against men.
   d. All of the above are correct.

4. In the United States, about what share of women work for income?
   a. 80 percent
   b. 60 percent
   c. 40 percent
   d. 20 percent

5. In the U.S. labor force,
   a. men and women do the same type of work.
   b. men and women earn the same pay.
   c. women are still concentrated in several types of jobs.
   d. women now earn more than men do.

6. Which of the following terms refers to subtle discrimination that is not easy to prove but often keeps women out of the higher levels in the workplace?
   a. gender stratification
   b. glass ceiling
   c. comparable advancement
   d. gender segregation

7. In the United States, women in the labor force working full time earn about how much for every dollar earned by men working full time?
   a. 78 cents
   b. 86 cents

c. 97 cents
d. 99 cents

8. **In 2009, women held about what share of seats in Congress?**
   a. 17 percent
   b. 25 percent
   c. 44 percent
   d. 66 percent

9. **Which of the following is a key part of feminist thinking?**
   a. the importance of change
   b. eliminating patriarchy
   c. ending violence against women
   d. All of the above are correct.

10. **The argument that gender equality weakens families would be made by someone in which of the following political categories?**
    a. radical
    b. liberal
    c. conservative
    d. All of the above are correct.

ANSWERS: 1(d); 2(c); 3(a); 4(b); 5(c); 6(b); 7(a); 8(a); 9(d); 10(c).

Essay Questions

1. How do the concepts "sex" and "gender" differ? In what ways is gender a dimension of social stratification?
2. What are the problems involving gender found in the claims made by conservatives, liberals, and radicals? What are the solutions to their problems?

Chapter 5 Aging and Inequality

Multiple-Choice Questions

1. **Which of the following concepts refers to the study of aging and the elderly?**
   a. sociology
   b. gerontology
   c. demography
   d. gerontocracy

2. **What effect does industrialization have on the social standing of the oldest members of a society?**
   a. Their social standing goes down.
   b. There is little or no effect.
   c. Their social standing goes up.
   d. Social standing goes up for men and down for women.

3. **The "graying of the United States" refers to which of the following trends?**
   a. The number of women, but not men, over age sixty-five is increasing.
   b. The number of women over age sixty-five is decreasing.
   c. The share of the U.S. population over age sixty-five is increasing.
   d. The fact is that all of us are getting older.

4. **Social isolation is the most serious problem for which of the following categories of people?**
   a. people nearing retirement
   b. people in urban areas
   c. elderly men
   d. elderly women

5. **Most complaints of age discrimination come from people who are**
   a. in their forties.
   b. over age sixty-five.
   c. in their twenties.
   d. successful in their jobs.

6. **Which of the following categories of people in the United States provides most of the caregiving to elderly people?**
   a. nursing home workers
   b. hospital health workers
   c. other elderly people
   d. women

7. **Average income is lowest for people who are about the age of**
   a. forty.
   b. fifty.
   c. sixty.
   d. sixty-five and older.

8. **The structural-functional approach to aging involves**
   a. disengagement theory.
   b. activity theory.
   c. social inequality.
   d. All of the above are correct.

9. **Which of the following statements about the "right to die" debate is correct?**
   a. Most people today in this country die with the help of a physician.
   b. Active euthanasia, but not passive euthanasia, is legal throughout the United States.
   c. Physician-assisted suicide is legal only in Oregon and Washington.
   d. Federal law permits physician-assisted suicide.

10. **People of which political position support the idea of substantially increasing government assistance to elderly people within the existing political system?**
    a. conservatives
    b. liberals
    c. radicals
    d. All of the above are correct.

ANSWERS: 1(b); 2(a); 3(c); 4(d); 5(a); 6(d); 7(d); 8(a); 9(c); 10(b).

Essay Questions

1. Everyone knows that aging is a biological fact of life. How is aging also a cultural issue?
2. A minority is a category of people who have a distinctive appearance and who are socially disadvantaged. Based on the information presented in this chapter, should the elderly be considered a minority in the United States? Why or why not?

Chapter 6 Crime, Violence, and Criminal Justice

Multiple-Choice Questions

1. **Crime is defined as**
    a. violations of laws enacted by federal, state, or local governments.
    b. any rule breaking that involves punishment.
    c. offenses that involve violence or the threat of violence.
    d. norms formally created through a society's political system.
2. **Which of the following serious crimes is most common?**
    a. robbery
    b. forcible rape
    c. larceny-theft
    d. motor vehicle theft
3. **The FBI collects crime data that are based on**
    a. offenses resulting in a criminal conviction.
    b. offenses that the police clear by making an arrest.
    c. offenses the police find about.
    d. all crimes that occur.
4. **Dr. C. Henry Kempe is important in the history of family violence because he was responsible for defining which of the following as a social problem?**
    a. violence against women
    b. child abuse
    c. elder abuse
    d. parental neglect
5. **A majority of the people arrested for a violent crime in the United States are of which racial category?**
    a. Asian
    b. African American
    c. white
    d. Hispanic (Latino)
6. **Which of the following is an example of a victimless crime?**
    a. murder
    b. suicide
    c. stealing a bicycle
    d. gambling
7. **Which of the following is the oldest justification for societies' punishing an offender?**
    a. retribution
    b. societal protection
    c. deterrence
    d. rehabilitation
8. **Emile Durkheim explained that crime is**
    a. defined by the rich and likely to result in arrests for the poor.
    b. harmful not just to victims but to society as a whole.
    c. likely to cause a breakdown in public morality.
    d. found in every society.
9. **When Sasha's friends began calling her a "klepto," she left the group and found new friends who liked to go shoplifting. Before long, Sasha had become very good at stealing and was making most of her living this way. Edwin Lemert would say Sasha's transformation is an example of**
    a. primary deviance.
    b. developing secondary deviance.
    c. the formation of a deviant subculture.
    d. the beginning of retreatism.
10. **A conservative analysis of the crime problem is likely to point to which of the following?**
    a. who does and does not have money and power
    b. how strong the economy is
    c. families not parenting their children enough
    d. the operation of the capitalist economy

ANSWERS: 1(a); 2(b); 3(b); 4(d); 5(c); 6(d); 7(a); 8(d); 9(b); 10(c).

Essay Questions

1. What does each of the three theoretical approaches—structural-functional, symbolic-interaction, and social-conflict—teach us about crime?

2. Write a short essay that explains how conservatives, liberals, and people on the radical left understand the reasons for crime. What does each political position say about solutions to the crime problem?

Chapter 7 Sexuality

Multiple-Choice Questions

1. **The beginning of the sexual revolution changed U.S. society during the**
   a. 1960s.
   b. 1920s.
   c. 1890s.
   d. 1860s.

2. **Which scientist was among the very first to study human sexuality?**
   a. C. Henry Kempe
   b. Alfred Kinsey
   c. Peter Berger
   d. Gloria Steinem

3. **Which of the following concepts refers to experiencing sexual attraction to people of both sexes?**
   a. heterosexuality
   b. homosexuality
   c. bisexuality
   d. asexuality

4. **The first state in the country to permit same-sex marriage was**
   a. Hawaii.
   b. California.
   c. Massachusetts.
   d. Vermont.

5. **In the United States, opposition to pornography is expressed by**
   a. conservatives.
   b. liberals.
   c. neither conservatives nor liberals.
   d. both conservatives and liberals, but for different reasons.

6. **Compared to 1950, the U.S. rate of teenage pregnancy today is**
   a. higher.
   b. the same, but fewer teens become pregnant by choice.
   c. the same, but more pregnant teens are married.
   d. lower.

7. **Which of the following statements about HIV and AIDS is true?**
   a. In the United States, AIDS is becoming a disease of the poor.
   b. Most of the world's cases of AIDS are found in the United States.
   c. The use of a latex condom does not prevent transmission of HIV.
   d. Around the world, most people with HIV were infected through homosexual contact.

8. **Which of the following puts people at high risk for HIVinfection?**
   a. anal sex
   b. sharing needles
   c. using any drug
   d. All of the above are correct.

9. **Queer theory opposes which pattern in our way of life?**
   a. patriarchy
   b. heterosexism
   c. multiculturalism
   d. class inequality

10. **If you were to claim that people ought to be tolerant of how other people express their sexuality, you are supporting which political point of view?**
   a. radical-left
   b. conservative
   c. liberal
   d. All of the above are correct.

ANSWERS: 1(a); 2(b); 3(c); 4(c); 5(d); 6(d); 7(a); 8(d); 9(b); 10(c).

Essay Questions

1. Use the case of sexual harassment to explain the process by which social problems come into being.
2. Explain how conservatives, liberals, and radicals on the left define social problems involving sexuality differently. Provide several specific examples of problems and how they might be solved.

Chapter 8 Alcohol and Other Drugs

Multiple-Choice Questions

1. **The chapter defines a drug as**
   a. anything we eat, drink, or breathe.
   b. any chemical substance other than food or water that affects the mind or body.
   c. any chemical substance that is against the law to use or sell.
   d. any prescription medicine provided by a doctor under the law.

2. **How a society views any drug is affected by which of the following?**
   a. the laws at a given time
   b. which racial or ethnic category the public links with the drug
   c. cultural attitudes and practices involving the drug
   d. All of the above are correct.

3. **Which of the following drugs is most widely used in the United States?**
   a. heroin
   b. marijuana
   c. alcohol
   d. LSD or other hallucinogens

4. **It is correct to say that someone is abusing (as opposed to simply using) a drug if**
   a. the person suffers physical, mental, or social harm.
   b. the drug is illegal.
   c. the drug has been used regularly for a year or longer.
   d. the person cannot afford the cost of the drug.

5. **Which of the following substances is correctly categorized as a stimulant?**
   a. an antipsychotic drug
   b. an analgesic drug
   c. caffeine
   d. cannabis

6. **The concept of "codependency" refers to the fact that**
   a. most people use drugs in a group setting.
   b. other people help a substance abuser continue the abusive behavior.
   c. drug abuse is linked to many other social problems.
   d. the mass media often present drug use in a positive light.

7. **In the United States, which of the following is the most widely supported policy to control illegal drugs?**
   a. prosecution
   b. treatment
   c. education
   d. interdiction

8. **About what share of people in prison in the United States has been convicted of violating drug laws?**
   a. 10 percent
   b. 25 percent
   c. 33 percent
   d. 50 percent

9. **The social-conflict approach shows us that**
   a. which drugs are legal and which are not has a lot to do with social power.
   b. many drugs help ease social interaction.
   c. drug use is learned, like any other pattern of behavior.
   d. societies establish ways to regulate the use of drugs with harmful medical effects.

10. **If you claim that drug use should be a matter of individual choice and that government should have no say in the matter, you are speaking from which political perspective?**
   a. conservative
   b. libertarian, on the far right
   c. socialist, on the far left
   d. liberal

ANSWERS: 1(b); 2(d); 3(c); 4(a); 5(c); 6(b); 7(a); 8(d); 9(a); 10(b).

Essay Questions

1. Provide at least three examples of how race and ethnicity have shaped the society's definition of drugs as legal or illegal.
2. Does the use of illegal drugs make other social problems worse? Provide relevant and specific facts in support of your answer.

Chapter 9 Physical and Mental Health

Multiple-Choice Questions

1. **The chapter defines health as**
   a. a country's rate of infant mortality.
   b. the absence of serious illness.
   c. a state of complete physical, mental, and social well-being.
   d. the absence of chronic disease.

2. **Which of the following is an example of a chronic disease?**
   a. heart disease
   b. cancer
   c. stroke
   d. All of the above are correct.

3. **People living in low-income nations are likely to die from**
   a. acute diseases such as malaria at any time in life.
   b. chronic diseases in old age.
   c. the effects of an overly rich diet.
   d. disease brought on by too little exercise.

4. **In which region of the world is the AIDS epidemic most severe?**
   a. North America
   b. Africa
   c. Asia
   d. Europe

5. **Countries with a socialist economic system provide health care to their people through**
   a. the operation of government.
   b. a free-market system.
   c. privately purchased health insurance.
   d. employer benefits.

6. **Which of the following is a factor that has pushed up the cost of medical care in the United States?**
   a. more doctors specializing
   b. more use of high technology
   c. an aging population
   d. All of the above are correct.

7. **Which of the following countries does not guarantee health care to all its people?**
   a. Sweden
   b. China
   c. United States
   d. All of the above are correct.

8. **The Americans with Disabilities Act, passed in 1990, did what?**
   a. It guaranteed a job for every person with a disability.
   b. It outlawed discrimination against people with disabilities in employment and public accommodations.
   c. It guaranteed health care at government hospitals to all persons with certain disabilities.
   d. All of the above are correct.

9. **The deinstitutionalization movement, which released people with mental illnesses from mental hospitals into local communities, was prompted by**
   a. new thinking that claimed mental illness is a myth.
   b. the demands of people with mental illnesses.
   c. the development of psychoactive drugs.
   d. passage of the Americans with Disabilities Act.

10. **If you claim that health is largely a reflection of the personal choices that people make about how to live, you are speaking from which political perspective?**
   a. conservative
   b. liberal
   c. radical left
   d. None of the above is correct.

ANSWERS: 1(c); 2(d); 3(a); 4(b); 5(a); 6(d); 7(c); 8(b); 9(c); 10(a).

Essay Questions

1. Provide evidence in support of the claim that health is not simply a matter of biological or medical facts but also reflects the operation of society.
2. How do people in the United States pay for medical care? Why do you think this country has not enacted any government program guaranteeing health care to everyone?

Chapter 10 Economy and Politics

Multiple-Choice Questions

1. **Which institution guides a society's decisions about how to live?**
   a. the family
   b. the economy
   c. politics
   d. government

2. **According to Adam Smith, a capitalist economic system operates based on**
   a. self-interest.
   b. tradition.
   c. the collective well-being of society.
   d. government.

3. **Typically, the economic system that creates the least amount of economic inequality is**
   a. capitalism.
   b. socialism.
   c. a mixed system.
   d. None of the above is correct.

4. **Which term refers to a market dominated by a few companies?**
   a. interlocking directorate
   b. monopoly
   c. conglomerate
   d. oligopoly

5. **About what share of U.S. voters turned out to cast a ballot in the 2008 presidential election?**
   a. 13 percent
   b. 43 percent
   c. 63 percent
   d. 93 percent

6. **Which of the following categories of people in the United States is least likely to vote?**
   a. seniors
   b. middle-income people
   c. college-age people
   d. white people

7. **Which model claims that power is widely dispersed throughout the U.S. population?**
   a. the pluralist model
   b. the power-elite model
   c. the Marxist political-economy model
   d. the military-industrial complex model

8. **Which model claims that solving the political and economic problems of our society requires not reform but fundamental change?**
   a. the pluralist model
   b. the power-elite model
   c. the Marxist political-economy model
   d. the military-industrial complex model

9. **Support for the welfare state as a way to deal with economic problems such as poverty comes mostly from**
   a. conservatives.
   b. liberals.
   c. radicals on the left.
   d. All of the above are correct.

10. **If you claim that a market system does a good job of providing for the greatest number of people, you are speaking from which political perspective?**
   a. conservative
   b. liberal
   c. radical-left
   d. None of the above is correct.

ANSWERS: 1(c); 2(a); 3(b); 4(d); 5(c); 6(c); 7(a); 8(c); 9(b); 10(a).

Essay Questions

1. In what ways are politics and the economy related? Consider this question from various political points of view.
2. Why is it correct to claim that in principle, liberals favor bigger government than conservatives? Why is it correct to say that in practice, both conservatives and liberals favor big government?

Chapter 11 Work and the Workplace

Multiple-Choice Questions

1. **Work is important to people as a source of**
   a. self-esteem.
   b. income.
   c. social identity.
   d. All of the above are correct.

2. **The Industrial Revolution caused a sharp drop in the population of**
   a. cities in the Northeast.
   b. cities across the South.
   c. cities in the Midwest.
   d. rural areas across the country.

3. **Today, which of the following types of work has the smallest share of the U.S. labor force?**
   a. farming
   b. industrial work
   c. service work
   d. None of the above is correct.

4. **The most important reason that the number of workers killed and injured in the workplace has gone down is**
   a. higher penalties for workplace violations.
   b. changes in the types of jobs people do.
   c. fewer people in the labor force.
   d. All of the above are correct.

5. **Which of the following results in greater harm to women than to men?**
   a. mining accidents
   b. farming accidents
   c. workplace violence
   d. construction site violence

6. **According to Karl Marx, workplace alienation results from**
   a. powerlessness.
   b. rationality.
   c. competition.
   d. the high number of immigrants looking for jobs.

7. **Which of the following categories of people has the highest unemployment rate?**
   a. women
   b. college graduates
   c. high school dropouts
   d. teenagers

8. **Compared to 1950, today we find that the share of workers who are members of a labor union has**
   a. gone up.
   b. gone down.
   c. gone up among men but gone down among women.
   d. changed little.

9. **Following a social-conflict analysis of work, we would expect, over time, to see**
   a. more workers replaced by machines.
   b. workers receive more and more schooling.
   c. more workers become part owners of their companies.
   d. All of the above are correct.

10. **If you claim that the market provides "rough justice" but government is needed "to smooth the rough edges," you are speaking from which political perspective?**

a. conservative
b. liberal
c. radical-left
d. None of the above is correct.

ANSWERS: 1(d); 2(d); 3(a); 4(b); 5(c); 6(a); 7(d); 8(b); 9(a); 10(b).

Essay Questions

1. In what ways has computer technology changed the nature of work? Include discussion of both the type of work people do and where they do it.
2. What type of work is likely to be characterized as "McJobs"? What changes in the U.S. economy underlie the rise of this type of work?

Chapter 12 Family Life

Multiple-Choice Questions

1. When most people in high-income countries such as the United States think of "family," what they have in mind is
a. the nuclear family.
b. an extended family.
c. families of affinity.
d. cohabitation.

2. The chances of children living with both biological parents until age eighteen is greatest if the parents
a. cohabit.
b. cohabit and then marry after the children are born.
c. marry before any children are born.
d. do not marry at all.

3. Over recent decades, the chances that a twenty-three-year-old person in the United States is married have
a. gone up.
b. gone down.
c. stayed the same.
d. virtually disappeared.

4. The most common pattern of care for U.S. children is
a. being left to fend for themselves.
b. sending children to a child care center.
c. having a nanny or babysitter come to the child's home.
d. having a parent, a grandparent, or other relative providing care in the home.

5. Since about 1980, the U.S. divorce rate has been
a. going down.
b. going up.
c. steady.
d. among the lowest in the world.

6. The concept of the "blended family" refers to a family in which
a. husband and wife have different social backgrounds.
b. one or both parents have a substance abuse problem.
c. children have some combination of biological parents and stepparents.
d. both parents have been divorced at least once.

7. The first state to legalize same-sex marriage in the United States was
a. Vermont.
b. Massachusetts.
c. California.
d. Hawaii.

8. Which theoretical approach describes the family as the "backbone of society"?
a. the structural-functional approach
b. the symbolic-interaction approach
c. the social-conflict approach
d. the feminist approach

9. Friedrich Engels claimed that marriage developed as a strategy to
a. prevent "illegitimate" birth.
b. keep the government from raising people's children.
c. share wealth more equally within a population.
d. allow rich men to pass wealth to their sons.

10. If you accept the family as a social institution but want to encourage tolerance for all the various family forms, you are speaking from which political perspective?
a. conservative
b. liberal
c. radical-left
d. None of the above is correct.

ANSWERS: 1(a); 2(c); 3(b); 4(d); 5(a); 6(c); 7(b); 8(a); 9(d); 10(b).

Essay Questions

1. Highlight changes in family life in the United States over the past century. What factors have caused families to change?
2. Sketch out an understanding of what each of the three political positions—conservative, liberal, and radical left—defines as problems of the family. What solutions do they propose?

Chapter 13 Education

Multiple-Choice Questions

1. **A global perspective of schooling shows that**
   a. boys receive more schooling than girls.
   b. girls receive more schooling than boys.
   c. most schooling goes to adults, not children.
   d. almost 90 percent of the world's children have never attended school.

2. **In which of the following countries does the largest share of people have a college degree?**
   a. Portugal
   b. Sweden
   c. United States
   d. Canada

3. **Students from high-income families typically**
   a. perform below the national average on the Scholastic Assessment Test (SAT).
   b. perform at the national average on the SAT.
   c. perform above the national average on the SAT.
   d. do not take the SAT.

4. **The dropout rate is highest for which of the following categories of the U.S. population?**
   a. Asian Americans
   b. Hispanic Americans
   c. non-Hispanic whites
   d. native speakers of English

5. **A good definition of functional illiteracy is**
   a. the inability to hold a job.
   b. lacking the latest computer skills.
   c. not having completed a college degree.
   d. not having the ability to read, write, or do arithmetic well enough to do everyday tasks.

6. **On campuses across the United States, women represent what share of all undergraduate students?**
   a. 57 percent
   b. 46 percent
   c. 36 percent
   d. 26 percent

7. **Teaching students mostly in their native language rather than English is the policy called**
   a. English immersion.
   b. mainstreaming.
   c. special education.
   d. bilingual education.

8. **Which theoretical approach points out how schools help unite our ethnically diverse society by teaching common values and beliefs?**
   a. the structural-functional approach
   b. the symbolic-interaction approach
   c. the social-conflict approach
   d. the feminist approach

9. **The self-fulfilling prophecy in education refers to the fact that**
   a. our national goal of schooling for all has just about been achieved.
   b. rich families usually give their children the best schooling.
   c. the labels schools attach to people can affect the way they actually perform.
   d. schools teach values that support the status quo.

10. **If you claim that making meaningful change in schooling in this country depends on changing the economic and political structures, you are speaking from which political perspective?**
    a. conservative
    b. liberal
    c. radical-left
    d. progressive

ANSWERS: 1(a); 2(c); 3(c); 4(b); 5(d); 6(a); 7(d); 8(a); 9(c); 10(c).

Essay Questions

1. How do schools help our society function? In what ways do schools perpetuate social inequality?
2. Sketch out an understanding of how each of the three political positions—conservative, liberal, and radical left—defines the cause of poor schooling in much of the United States. What solutions does each propose?

Chapter 14 Urban Life

Multiple-Choice Questions

1. **The industrial metropolis emerged along with**
   a. the founding of the new nation in the late 1700s.
   b. the Industrial Revolution after about 1860.
   c. the Great Depression during the 1930s.
   d. the rise of the postindustrial economy after 1960.

2. **Many large U.S. cities faced fiscal problems and even bankruptcy due to**
   a. the swelling population of the central cities.
   b. the decline of suburbs.

c. the decentralization of population from the central cities to the suburbs.
d. All of the above are correct.

3. Critics claim that as a result of urban sprawl,
a. whole regions have buildings that look much the same.
b. development is consuming open land and farmland rapidly.
c. people are spending more and more time commuting in cars.
d. All of the above are correct.

4. Which of the following areas has the highest poverty rate?
a. central cities
b. suburbs
c. rural areas
d. edge cities

5. Which of the following statements about urban renewal is correct?
a. Urban renewal moved many poor people out of public housing.
b. Urban renewal greatly increased the amount of low-income housing in the United States.
c. Urban renewal transformed many low-income neighborhoods into housing and shopping areas for richer people.
d. Urban renewal caused a rapid increase in inner-city slums.

6. Hypersegregation is a problem mostly for
a. rich people.
b. poor African Americans.
c. suburbanites in exclusive communities.
d. poor white people.

7. The problem of homelessness exists mainly in
a. urban areas.
b. rural areas.
c. Sunbelt cities.
d. Snowbelt cities.

8. In low-income nations, cities are
a. much smaller than they are in the United States.
b. not facing many of the problems that cities in this country are.
c. growing rapidly and becoming much bigger than cities in this country.
d. almost nonexistent.

9. The term that Ferdinand Tönnies used to refer to modern urban life is
a. *Gemeinschaft.*
b. *Gesellschaft.*
c. mechanical solidarity.
d. organic solidarity.

10. If you claim that economic growth in this country has improved urban life in the United States and will continue to do so, you are speaking from which political perspective?
a. conservative
b. liberal
c. radical-left
d. None of the above is correct.

ANSWERS: 1(b); 2(c); 3(d); 4(a); 5(c); 6(b); 7(a); 8(c); 9(b); 10(a).

Essay Questions

1. How did the Industrial Revolution change U.S. cities? Consider the size and shape of cities as well as quality of life.
2. Sketch out an understanding of how each of the three political positions—conservative, liberal, and radical left—defines the cause of urban problems in the United States. What solutions do they propose?

Chapter 15 Population and Global Inequality

Multiple-Choice Questions

1. World population started to increase very rapidly about when?
a. 1500
b. 1700
c. 1900
d. 2000

2. Which region of the world has *both* the highest birth rate and the highest infant mortality rate?
a. Latin America
b. Europe
c. Asia
d. Africa

3. Global studies show that the more access women have to contraception,
a. the fewer children the average woman has.
b. the fewer women attend school.
c. the fewer children grow to adulthood.
d. the fewer women work for income.

4. The highest rate of population increase is found in
a. the Northern Hemisphere.
b. the Southern Hemisphere.
c. the United States and other rich nations.
d. Japan and other countries where the average age of the population is increasing.

5. **Thomas Robert Malthus stated that**
   a. population increases in geometric progression.
   b. food production increases in arithmetic progression.
   c. the world will eventually run out of food and other resources.
   d. All of the above are correct.

6. **In global perspective, the richest 20 percent of all people earn about what percent of the entire world's income?**
   a. 20
   b. 40
   c. 60
   d. 80

7. **In the poorest countries of Central Africa, half of all children die before reaching the age of**
   a. ten.
   b. twenty-five.
   c. fifty.
   d. sixty-five.

8. **At which of Rostow's stages of modernization have countries greatly reduced absolute poverty and are now requiring all children to attend school?**
   a. traditional
   b. take-off
   c. drive to technological maturity
   d. high mass consumption

9. **According to Wallerstein's theory, the main cause of global inequality is**
   a. a lack of modern technology.
   b. the capitalist global economy.
   c. traditional culture that holds back some nations.
   d. inefficient government control of the economy.

10. **Moving to the right on the political spectrum means looking more to which of the following as the solution to global inequality?**
    a. government action
    b. the market economy
    c. nationalizing local industries
    d. the United Nations and other global organizations

ANSWERS: 1(c); 2(d); 3(a); 4(b); 5(d); 6(d); 7(a); 8(c); 9(b); 10(b).

Essay Questions

1. What is Malthus's theory of population? How does demographic transition theory lead to a different conclusion about the world's future?
2. Contrast modernization theory and world system theory in terms of both the causes of global inequality and the solution to this problem.

Chapter 16 Technology and the Environment

Multiple-Choice Questions

1. **Which of the following problems is the result of the natural world operating on its own, with no effect from how society operates?**
   a. pollution
   b. acid rain
   c. global warming
   d. None of the above is correct.

2. **In general, the more complex a society's technology,**
   a. the more it can affect the natural environment.
   b. the less likely it is to cause environmental problems.
   c. the less its people express concern about the environment.
   d. the less the amount of resources its people consume.

3. **The environmental deficit refers to**
   a. the amount of money we will have to spend to clean up the environment.
   b. the population that the world can support at any given time.
   c. long-term harm to the environment caused by our short-term focus on affluence and convenience.
   d. a way of thinking that encourages more and more economic growth.

4. **The limits-to-growth thesis states that**
   a. human ingenuity will allow more and more people to live both better and longer.
   b. humanity must control population increase and limit consumption of resources to avoid environmental collapse.
   c. rich nations must let poor nations catch up in terms of economic development.
   d. the discovery of new resources must keep up with our use of known resources.

5. **The region of the world facing the greatest crisis of too little fresh water supply is**
   a. North America
   b. the tropical rain forest.
   c. Europe
   d. the Middle East.

6. **Which of the following statements about acid rain is true?**
   a. It harms both plant and animal life.
   b. It can harm regions thousands of miles from the source of the pollution.
   c. It is caused by the burning of fossil fuels.
   d. All of the above are correct.

7. **The number of living species on Earth**
   a. is increasing.
   b. has remained about the same for several centuries.
   c. is decreasing.
   d. is expected to go up as the planet warms.

8. **The structural-functional approach states that which of the following has a major impact on the natural environment?**
   a. a society's level of technology
   b. a society's degree of social inequality
   c. the racial composition of a country's population
   d. All of the above are correct.

9. **In general, which political analysis presents the most optimistic view of the future state of the natural environment?**
   a. radical-left
   b. liberal
   c. conservative
   d. All of the political approaches are optimistic.

10. **Most neo-Malthusians support which political approach?**
   a. radical-left
   b. liberal
   c. conservative
   d. None of the above is correct.

ANSWERS: 1(d); 2(a); 3(c); 4(b); 5(d); 6(d); 7(c); 8(a); 9(c); 10(b).

Essay Questions

1. In what ways does technology affect the state of the natural environment? What about cultural values? How would an ecologically sustainable culture differ from our own way of life?
2. What is the problem of environmental racism? What might be some strategies or policies that would address this problem?

Chapter 17 War and Technology

Multiple-Choice Questions

1. **Over the centuries, the destruction caused by war has**
   a. increased dramatically.
   b. changed little.
   c. gone down because war is now rare.
   d. gone down because of advances in technology.

2. **Which of the following is a common reason for going to war?**
   a. responding to perceived threats
   b. conflict caused by cultural and religious differences
   c. to divert public attention from social problems
   d. All of the above are correct.

3. **The twentieth century saw the development of total war, in which**
   a. every country on Earth was drawn into a single war.
   b. weapons of mass destruction destroyed entire cities.
   c. nations decided to avoid targeting any population centers.
   d. there were no longer any rules about how to conduct war.

4. **Only one country has suffered an atomic attack on a major city? Which is it?**
   a. the Soviet Union
   b. China
   c. Japan
   d. India

5. **The country that spends more on militarism than any other by far is**
   a. China.
   b. the United States.
   c. the Russian Federation.
   d. North Korea.

6. **Which of the following best describes the use of terrorism?**
   a. weak organizations attacking powerful nations
   b. powerful organizations attacking weak nations
   c. weak nations attacking weak nations
   d. powerful nations attacking powerful nations

7. **Which of the following statements about terrorism is correct?**
   a. There is a long history of terrorism being carried out by members of U.S. society.
   b. Terrorism against people in the United States has always been carried out by foreigners.
   c. The first case of terrorism taking place in the United States was in 1995 in Oklahoma City.
   d. The United States has never experienced terrorism on its own soil.

8. **The fact that one nation's "terrorists" might well be another's "freedom fighters" is an insight drawn from which theoretical approach?**
   a. the biological approach
   b. the structural-functional approach
   c. the symbolic-interaction approach
   d. the social-conflict approach

9. **The statement that war is a way powerful nations dominate the globe and terrorism is a way for powerless people to fight back is linked to which theoretical approach?**
   a. the biological approach
   b. the structural-functional approach
   c. the symbolic-interaction approach
   d. the social-conflict approach

10. **If you think that the United States is no longer a force for good in the world, you would be speaking from which political perspective?**
   a. conservative
   b. liberal
   c. radical-left
   d. None of the above is correct.

ANSWERS: 1(a); 2(d); 3(b); 4(c); 5(b); 6(a); 7(a); 8(c); 9(d); 10(c).

Essay Questions

1. Use sociology's three theoretical approaches to provide an analysis of militarism and warfare. Give examples of specific insights drawn from each approach.
2. How is terrorism a special type of war? That is, in what specific ways does terrorism differ from conventional warfare?

GLOSSARY

abortion the deliberate termination of a pregnancy
acid rain precipitation, made acidic by air pollution, that destroys plant and animal life
activity theory the idea that people enhance personal satisfaction in old age by keeping up a high level of social activity
acute disease an illness that strikes suddenly
addiction a physical or psychological craving for a drug
affirmative action policies intended to improve the social standing of minorities subject to past prejudice and discrimination
ageism prejudice and discrimination against older people
age stratification social inequality among various age categories within a society
alcoholism addiction to alcohol
alienation (Marx) powerlessness in the workplace resulting in the experience of isolation and misery
alienation (Weber) a rational focus on efficiency, which causes depersonalization throughout society, including the workplace
anti-institutional violence violence directed against the government in violation of the law
arms control international agreements on the development, testing, production, and deployment of weapons
asexuality the absence of sexual attraction to people of either sex
assimilation the process by which minorities gradually adopt cultural patterns from the dominant majority population
authoritarianism a political system that denies popular participation in government
bilingual education the policy of offering most classes in students' native language while also teaching them English
bisexuality sexual attraction to people of both sexes
blaming the victim finding the cause of a social problem in the behavior of people who suffer from it
blended families families in which children have some combination of biological parents and stepparents
capitalism an economic system in which natural resources and the means of producing goods and services are privately owned
caregiving informal and unpaid care provided to a dependent person by family members, other relatives, or friends
charter schools public schools that are given the freedom to try out new policies and programs
chronic disease an illness that has a long-term development
claims making the process of convincing the public and important public officials that a particular issue or situation should be defined as a social problem
codependency behavior on the part of others that helps a substance abuser continue the abuse
cohabitation the sharing of a household by an unmarried couple
colonialism the process by which some nations enrich themselves through political and economic control of other nations
community-based corrections correctional programs that take place in society at large rather than behind prison walls
concentration camps centers where prisoners are confined for purposes of state security, exploitation, punishment, or execution
conglomerate a giant corporation composed of many smaller corporations
corporate crime an illegal act committed by a corporation or by persons acting on its behalf
corporation a business with a legal existence, including rights and liabilities, apart from that of its members
crime the violation of a criminal law enacted by the federal, state, or local government
crime against the person crime that involves violence or the threat of violence against others
crime against property crime that involves theft of property belonging to others
criminal justice system society's use of due process, police, courts, and punishment to enforce the law
criminal recidivism later offenses by people previously convicted of crimes
crude birth rate the number of live births in a given year for every 1,000 people in a population
crude death rate the number of deaths in a given year for every 1,000 people in a population
cultural capital skills, values, attitudes, and schooling that increase a person's chances of success
culture a way of life including widespread values (about what is good and bad), beliefs (about what is true), and behavior (what people do every day)
culture of poverty cultural patterns that make poverty a way of life
decriminalization removing the current criminal penalties that punish the manufacturing, sale, and personal use of drugs
deindustrialization the decline of industrial production that occurred in the United States after about 1950
deinstitutionalization the release of people from mental hospitals into local communities
democracy a political system in which power is exercised by the people as a whole
demographic transition theory a thesis linking demographic changes to a society's level of technological development
demography the study of human population
dependency a state in which a person's body has adjusted to the regular use of a drug
dependency theory *see* world system theory
depressants drugs that slow the operation of the central nervous system
deterrence using punishment to discourage further crime; internationally, a strategy to keep peace based on the threat of retaliation, also known as *mutual assured destruction* (MAD).
direct-fee system a medical care system in which patients or their insurers pay directly for the services of physicians and hospitals
disability a physical or mental condition that limits everyday activities
discrimination the unequal treatment of various categories of people
disengagement theory the idea that modern societies operate in an orderly way by removing people from positions of responsibility as they reach old age
drug any chemical substance other than food or water that affects the mind or body
ecologically sustainable culture a way of life that meets the needs of the present generation without threatening the environment for future generations
ecology the study of how living organisms interact with the natural environment
economic issues political debates about how a society should distribute material resources
economy the social institution that organizes the production, distribution, and consumption of goods and services

ecosystem a system composed of the interaction of all living organisms and their natural environment

education the social institution by which a society transmits knowledge—including basic facts and job skills, as well as cultural norms and values—to its members

English immersion the policy of teaching non–English speakers in English

enterprise zones areas in the inner city that attract new business with the promise of tax relief

environmental deficit serious, long-term harm to the natural environment caused by humanity's focus on short-term material affluence

environmental racism a pattern of discrimination in which environmental hazards are greatest for poor people, especially minorities

epidemic a disease that spreads rapidly through a population

ethnicity a shared cultural heritage, which typically involves common ancestors, language, and religion

Eurocentrism the practice of using European (particularly English) cultural standards to judge everyone

euthanasia assisting in the death of a person suffering from an incurable disease

experiment a research method for investigating cause-and-effect relationships under tightly controlled conditions

extended family parents and children and also grandparents, aunts, uncles, and cousins who often live close to one another and operate as a family

families of affinity people with or without legal or blood ties who feel they belong together and define themselves as a family

family a social institution that unites individuals into cooperative groups to care for one another, including any children

felony a more serious crime punishable by at least one year in prison

feminism a political movement that seeks the social equality of women and men; also, the study of gender with the goal of changing society to make women and men equal

feminization of poverty the trend of women making up an increasing share of the poor

fertility the incidence of childbearing in a country's population

field research a research method for observing people while joining them in their everyday activities; also known as *participant observation*

functional illiteracy the inability to read and write or do basic arithmetic well enough to carry out daily responsibilities

Gemeinschaft a type of social organization in which people are closely bound by kinship and tradition

gender the personal traits and social positions that members of a society attach to being female or male

gender gap the tendency for women and men to hold different opinions about certain issues and to support different candidates

gender stratification the unequal distribution of wealth, power, and privilege between men and women

genocide the systematic killing of one category of people by another

gerontocracy a social system that gives a society's oldest members the most wealth, power, and prestige

gerontology the study of aging and the elderly

Gesellschaft a type of social organization in which people interact on the basis of self-interest

globalization the expansion of economic activity around the world with little regard for national borders

government a formal organization that directs the political life of a society

hate crime a criminal offense against a person, property, or society motivated by the offender's bias against a race, religion, disability, sexual orientation, ethnicity, or national origin

health a state of complete physical, mental, and social well-being

health maintenance organizations (HMOs) private insurance organizations that provide medical care to subscribers for a fixed fee

heterosexism bias that treats heterosexuality as the norm while stigmatizing anyone who differs from this norm as "queer"

heterosexuality sexual attraction to someone of the other sex

hidden curriculum explicit and subtle presentations of political or cultural ideas in the classroom that support the status quo

homelessness the plight of poor people who lack shelter and live primarily on the streets

homophobia an aversion to or hostility toward people thought to be gay, lesbian, or bisexual

homosexuality sexual attraction to someone of the same sex

hospice homelike care that provides physical and emotional comfort to dying people and their families

income salary or wages from a job plus earnings from investments and other sources

infant mortality rate the number of deaths among infants under one year of age for each 1,000 live births in a given year

institutional discrimination discrimination that is built into the operation of social institutions, including the economy, schools, and the legal system

institutional racism racism at work in the operation of social institutions, including the economy, schools, hospitals, the military, and the criminal justice system

institutional violence violence carried out by government representatives under the law

interlocking directorates social networks made up of people who serve as directors of several corporations at the same time

intersection theory analysis of how race, class, and gender interact, often creating multiple disadvantages for some categories of people

in vitro fertilization uniting eggs and sperm in a laboratory

juvenile delinquency violation of the law by young people

kinship a social bond, based on common ancestry, marriage, or adoption, that joins individuals into families

labeling theory the idea that crime and all other forms of rule breaking result not so much from what people do as from how others respond to those actions

labor unions worker organizations that seek to improve wages and working conditions through various strategies, including negotiations and strikes

law a norm formally created through a society's political system

libertarians people who favor the greatest individual freedom possible

life course the socially constructed stages that people pass through as they live out their lives

life expectancy the average life span of a country's population

life expectancy at birth the number of years, on average, people in a society can expect to live

literacy the ability to read and write

lobbying the efforts of special-interest groups and their representatives to influence government officials

magnet schools public schools that offer special facilities and programs in pursuit of educational excellence

mainstreaming integrating students with special needs into the overall educational program

marriage a lawful relationship usually involving economic cooperation, sexual activity, and childbearing

Marxist political-economy model an analysis that sees the concentration of wealth and power in society as resulting from capitalism

mass murder the intentional, unlawful killing of four or more people at one time and place

matriarchy a social pattern in which females dominate males

McDonaldization defining work in terms of the principles of efficiency, predictability, uniformity, and automation

mechanical solidarity social bonds based on common sentiments and shared moral values

megalopolis a vast urban region containing a number of cities and their surrounding suburbs

mental disorder a condition involving thinking, mood, or behavior that causes distress and reduces a person's ability to function in everyday life

meritocracy a system of social inequality in which social standing corresponds to personal ability and effort

military-industrial complex the close association of the federal government, the military, and defense industries

minority any category of people, identified by physical or cultural traits, that a society subjects to disadvantages
misdemeanor a less serious crime punishable by less than one year in prison
modernization theory a model of economic and social development that explains global inequality in terms of technological and cultural differences between societies
monarchy a political system in which a single family rules from generation to generation
monopoly the domination of an entire market by a single producer
mortality the incidence of death in a country's population
multiculturalism educational programs designed to recognize cultural diversity in the United States and to promote respect for all cultural traditions
natural environment Earth's surface and atmosphere, including air, water, soil, and other resources necessary to sustain living organisms
neocolonialism a new form of economic exploitation that involves the operation of multinational corporations rather than direct control by foreign governments
norms rules and expectations by which a society guides the behavior of its members
nuclear family a family composed of one or two parents and their children
nuclear proliferation the acquisition of nuclear weapons technology by more and more nations
nuclear weapons bombs that use atomic reactions to generate enormous destructive force
oligopoly the domination of a market by a few companies
organic solidarity social bonds based on specialization and interdependence
organized crime a business operation that supplies illegal goods or services
participant observation see *field research*
patriarchy a social pattern in which males dominate females
peace the absence of violent conflict
plea bargaining a negotiation in which the state reduces a defendant's charge in exchange for a guilty plea
pluralism a state in which people of all races and ethnicities have about the same overall social standing
pluralist model an analysis of the political system that sees power widely distributed among various groups and organizations in a society
political action committees (PACs) organizations formed by special-interest groups to raise and spend money in support of political goals
political economy the economic and political life of a nation or world region
political spectrum a continuum representing a range of political attitudes from "left" to "right"
politics the social institution that guides a society's decision making about how to live
pornography words or images intended to cause sexual arousal
poverty gap the difference between the actual income of the typical poor household and the official poverty line
poverty line a standard set by the U.S. government for the purpose of counting the poor
power-elite model an analysis of the political system that sees power as concentrated among a small elite
prejudice any rigid and unfounded generalization about an entire category of people
prenatal care health care for women during pregnancy
primary labor market jobs that provide good pay and extensive benefits to workers
progressive taxation a policy that raises tax rates as income increases
prostitution the selling of sexual services
psychotherapy an approach to mental health in which patients talk with trained professionals to gain insight into the cause of their problems
public housing high-density apartment buildings constructed to house poor people
queer theory a body of theory and research that challenges the heterosexual bias in U.S. society
race a socially constructed category of people who share biologically transmitted traits that a society defines as important
racism the assertion that people of one race are less worthy or even biologically inferior to others
rain forests regions of dense forestation, most of which circle the globe close to the equator
rationalization of society (Weber) the historical change from tradition to rationality and efficiency as the typical way people think about the world
rehabilitation reforming an offender to prevent future offenses
repressive state terrorism government use of violence within its own borders to suppress political opposition
retribution moral vengeance by which society inflicts suffering on an offender comparable to that caused by the offense
schooling formal instruction carried out by specially trained teachers
school voucher program a program that provides parents with funds they can use at a public school or private school of their choice
secondary analysis a research method that makes use of data originally collected by others
secondary labor market jobs that provide low pay and few benefits to workers
segregation the physical and social separation of categories of people
self-fulfilling prophecy a situation in which people who are defined in a certain way eventually think and act as if the definition were true
serial murder the killing of several people by one offender over a period of time
sex the biological distinction between females and males; also, activity that leads to physical gratification and possibly reproduction
sexism the belief that one sex is innately superior to the other
sexual harassment unwanted comments, gestures, or physical contacts of a sexual nature
sexually transmitted diseases (STDs) diseases spread by sexual contact
sexual orientation a person's romantic and emotional attraction to another person
sick role a pattern of behavior expected of people defined as ill
social classes categories of people who have similar access to resources and opportunities
social-conflict approach a theoretical framework that sees society as divided by inequality and conflict
social-constructionist approach the assertion that social problems arise as people define conditions as undesirable and in need of change
social disorganization a breakdown in social order caused by rapid social change
social epidemiology the study of how health and disease are distributed throughout a society's population
social institution a major sphere of social life, or a societal subsystem, organized to meet a basic human need
socialism an economic system in which natural resources and the means of producing goods and services are collectively owned
socialized medicine a medical care system in which the government owns and operates most medical facilities and employs most physicians
social movement an organized effort at claims making that tries to shape the way people think about an issue in order to encourage or discourage social change
social policy formal strategies that affect how society operates
social problem a condition that undermines the well-being of some or all members of a society and is usually a matter of public controversy
social stratification society's system of ranking categories of people in a hierarchy
social welfare programs organized efforts by government, private organizations, or individuals to assist needy people considered worthy of assistance
societal protection protecting the public by rendering an offender incapable of further offenses through incarceration or execution

society people who live within some territory and share many patterns of behavior

sociological imagination a point of view that highlights how society affects the experiences we have and the choices we make

sociology the systematic study of human societies

special education schooling students with physical or mental disabilities in separate classes with specially trained teachers

special-interest groups political alliances of people interested in some economic or social issue

stalking repeated efforts by someone to establish or reestablish a relationship against the will of the victim

state-sponsored terrorism the practice by one government of providing money, weapons, and training to terrorists who engage in violence in another nation

stereotype an exaggerated description applied to every person in some category

stigma a powerful negative social label that radically changes a person's self-concept and social identity

stimulants drugs that increase alertness, altering a person's mood by increasing energy

structural-functional approach a theoretical framework that sees society as a system of many interrelated parts

suburbs urban areas beyond the political boundaries of cities

supportive housing a program that combines low-income housing with on-site social services

surrogate motherhood an arrangement by which one woman carries and bears a child for another woman

survey a research method by which subjects respond to items on a questionnaire or in an interview

symbolic-interaction approach a theoretical framework that sees society as the product of individuals interacting with one another

technology knowledge that people apply to the task of living in a physical environment

telecommuting linking employees to the office using information technology, including telephones, computers, and the Internet

terrorism unlawful, typically random acts of violence or the threat of violence by an individual, group, or government to achieve a political goal

theoretical approach a basic image of society that guides theory and research

theory a statement of how and why specific facts are related

total war deadly conflict that targets both population centers and military targets

tracking the policy of assigning students to different educational programs

underclass poor people who live in areas with high concentrations of poverty and limited opportunities for schooling or work

urban sprawl unplanned, low-density development at the edge of expanding urban areas

victimless crimes offenses that directly harm only the person who commits them

violence behavior that causes injury to people or damage to property

violent crimes see *crimes against persons*

war violent conflict between nations or organized groups

war crime an offense against the law of war as established by international agreements and international law

wealth the value of all the economic assets owned by a person or family, minus any debts

weapons of mass destruction weapons with the capacity to kill many thousands of people at one time

welfare state a range of policies and programs that transfer wealth from the rich to the poor and provide benefits to needy members of society

white-collar crime illegal activities conducted by people of high social position during the course of their employment or regular business activities

world system theory a model of economic development that explains global inequality in terms of the historical exploitation of poor societies by rich ones; also called *dependency theory*

zero population growth the level of reproduction that maintains population at a steady state

REFERENCES

*Blue type denotes reference citations new to this fourth edition.

AARP Public Policy Institute. 2005. *Caregiving in the United States.* [Online] Available April 7, 2009, at http://assets.aarp.org/rgcenter/il/fs111_caregiving.pdf

Abadinsky, Howard. 1989. *Drug Abuse: An Introduction.* Chicago: Nelson Hall.

ABC News. 1997. *World News Tonight* (March 15).

ABC News/Washington Post. 2009. "Illegal Drugs." [Online] Available July 23, 2009, at http://www.pollingreport.com/drugs.htm

Abel, E. L. 1990. *Fetal Alcohol Syndrome.* Oradell, N.J.: Medical Economics.

Adam, David. 2008. "World CO_2 Levels at Record High, Scientists Warn." *Guardian* (May 12). [Online] Available July 16, 2008, at http://www.guardian.co.uk/environment/2008/may/12/climatechange.carbonemissions

Adams, P. F., J. W. Lucas, and P. M. Barnes. 2008. *Summary Health Statistics for the U.S. Population: National Health Interview Survey, 2006.* [Online] Available November 11, 2008, at http://www.cdc.gov/nchs/data/series/sr_10/sr10_236.pdf

Aditjondro, George J. 2000. "Ninjas, Nanggalas, Monuments, and Mossad Manuals: An Anthropology of Indonesian State Terror in East Timor." In Jeffrey A. Sluka, ed., *Death Squad: The Anthropology of State Terror* (pp. 158–88). Philadelphia: University of Pennsylvania Press.

Adler, Jerry, and Maggie Malone. 1996. "Toppling Towers." *Newsweek* (November 4): 70–72.

Adorno, T. W., et al. 1950. *The Authoritarian Personality.* New York: Harper.

Akers, Ronald L., Marvin D. Krohn, Lonn Lanza-Kaduce, and Marcia Radosevich. 1979. "Social Learning and Deviant Behavior." *American Sociological Review.* Vol. 44, No. 4 (August): 636–55.

Alan Guttmacher Institute. 2002. "Teen Pregnancy: Trends and Lessons Learned." [Online] Available August 14, 2002, at http://www.agi-usa.org/pubs/ib_1-02.pdf

———. 2004. "U.S. Teenage Pregnancy Statistics: Overall Trends, Trends by Race and Ethnicity, and State-by-State Information." Updated February 19. [Online] Available December 17, 2006, at http://www.guttmacher.org/pubs/state_pregnancy_trends.pdf

Albon, Joan. 1971. "Retention of Cultural Values and Differential Urban Adaptation: Samoans and American Indians in a West Coast City." *Social Forces.* Vol. 49, No. 3 (March): 385–93.

Allen, Mike. 2009. "Card Check Battle Starts Tomorrow." *Politico.* [Online] Available May 8, 2009, at http://www.politico.com/news/stories/0309/19786.html

Al-Shalchi, Hadeel. 2009. "8-Year-Old Girl Divorces 50-Year-Old Husband." *Yahoo News* (April 30). [Online] Available May 9, 2009, at http://news.yahoo.com/s/ap/20090501/ap_on_re_mi_ea/ml_saudi_child_marriage

Alter, Jonathan. 2001. "The War on Addiction." *Newsweek* (February 12): 36–39.

Amato, Paul R., and Juliana M. Sobolewski. 2001. "The Effects of Divorce and Marital Discord on Adult Children's Psychological Well-Being." *American Sociological Review.* Vol. 66, No. 6 (December): 900–21.

American Association of Colleges of Nursing. 2008. "Fact Sheet: Nursing Shortage." [Online] Available February 6, 2009, at http://www.aacn.nche.edu/Media/FactSheets/NursingShortage.htm

American Farmland Trust. 2009. *2009 Report.* [Online] Available June 2, 2009, at http://www.farmland.org/resources/fote/default.asp

American Gaming Association. 2009. *Fact Sheet: States with Gaming.* [Online] Available April 16, 2009, at http://www.americangaming.org/Industry/factsheets/ general_info_detail.cfv?id=15

American Medical Association. 1997. [Online] Available March 4, 1997, at http://www.ama-assn.org

American Psychiatric Association. 2000. *Diagnostic and Statistical Manual of Mental Disorders,* 4th ed. (DSM-IV-TR). Arlington, Va.: American Psychiatric Association.

———. 2002. "Practice Guideline for the Treatment of Patients with Eating Disorders." In *Facts about Eating Disorders and the Search for Solutions.* Arlington, Va.: American Psychiatric Association.

Amin, Aasha, and Elita Karim. 2008. "Nailing the 'If' Factor." *Daily Star* (April 4). [Online] Available December 3, 2008, at http://www.thedailystar.net/magazine/2008/04/01/index.htm

Amnesty International. 2006. "Abolitionist and Retentionist Countries." [Online] Available December 17, 2006, at http://web.amnesty.org/pages/deathpenalty-countries.eng

Andersen, Kurt. 2009a. "Don't Pretend We Didn't See This Coming for a Long, Long, Time." *Time* (April 6): 34–38.

———. 2009b. "That Was Then . . . and This Is Now." *Time* (April 6): 32–33.

Anderson, Elijah. 1994. "The Code of the Streets." *Atlantic Monthly.* Vol. 273 (May): 81–94.

———. 1999. *Code of the Street: Decency, Violence, and the Moral Life of the Inner City.* New York: Norton.

———. 2002. "The Ideologically Driven Critique." *American Journal of Sociology.* Vol. 197, No. 6 (May): 1533–50.

Andrews, Michelle. 2009a. "The State of America's Health." *U.S. News & World Report* (February): 9–12.

———. 2009b. "Weighing In for Love, to Keep a Prenuptual Vow." *U.S. News & World Report* (February): 58.

Aneshensel, Carol S., Carolyn M. Rutter, and Peter A. Lachenbruch. 1991. "Social Structure, Stress, and Mental Health: Competing Conceptual and Analytic Models." *American Sociological Review.* Vol. 56, No. 1 (July): 166–78.

Angelo, Bonnie. 1989. "The Pain of Being Black" (an interview with Toni Morrison). *Time.* Vol. 133, No. 21 (May 22): 120–22.

Angier, Natalie. 1992. "Scientists, Finding Idiosyncrasy in Homosexuals' Brains, Suggest That Orientation Is Physiological." *New York Times.* (August 1): A7.

Anti-Slavery International. 2008. "Slavery Remains Despite Years of Successes." [Online] Available December 2, 2008, at http://www.antislavery.org/archive/press/latestpressrelease.htm

Ariès, Philippe. 1974. *Western Attitudes toward Death: From the Middle Ages to the Present.* Baltimore, Md.: Johns Hopkins University Press.

Armstrong, Elisabeth. 2002. *The Retreat from Organization: U.S. Feminism Reconceptualized.* Albany: State University of New York Press.

Arrighi, Barbara A., ed. 2001. *Understanding Inequality: The Intersection of Race/Ethnicity, Class, and Gender.* Lanham, Md.: Rowman & Littlefield.

Association of American Law Schools. 2008. *2007–2008 AALS Statistical Report of Law Faculty.* [Online] Available April 3, 2009, at http://www.aals.org/statistics/2008dlt/titles.html

Atchley, Robert C. 1982. "Retirement as a Social Institution." *Annual Review of Sociology.* Vol. 8: 263–87.

Attorney General's Commission on Pornography (Meese Commission). 1986. *Final Report.* Washington, D.C.: U.S. Department of Justice.

Axinn, William G., and Jennifer S. Barber. 2001. "Mass Education and Fertility Transition." *American Sociological Review.* Vol. 66, No. 4 (August): 481–505.

Babwin, Dohn. 2003. "Illinois Governor to Commute Death-Row Sentences." *Yahoo News.* [Online] Available January 11, 2003, at http://dailynews.yahoo.com

Ballantine, Jeanne H. 2001. *The Sociology of Education: A Systematic Analysis,* 5th ed. Upper Saddle River, N.J.: Prentice Hall.

Barnett, Ola W., Cindy L. Miller-Perrin, and Robin D. Perrin. 1997. *Family Violence across the Lifespan: An Introduction.* Thousand Oaks, Calif.: Sage.

Barry, Kathleen. 1983. "Feminist Theory: The Meaning of Women's Liberation." In Barbara Haber, ed., *The Women's Annual, 1982–1983* (pp. 35–78). Boston: Hall.

Bartlett, Bruce. 2000. "Death, Wealth, and Taxes." *Public Interest.* Vol. 141 (Fall): 55–67.

Bartlett, Donald L., and James B. Steele. 1998. "Corporate Welfare." *Time.* Vol. 152, No. 19 (November 9): 36–54.

———. 2002. "Wheel of Misfortune." *Time.* Vol. 160, No. 25 (December 16): 44–58.

Basow, Susan A. 1992. *Gender Stereotypes and Roles,* 3rd ed. Pacific Grove, Calif.: Brooks/Cole.

Bass, Frank. 2005. "Katrina's Victims Poorer than U.S. Average." *Yahoo News.* [Online] Available September 24, 2006, at http://news.yahoo.com

Bauer, P. T. 1981. *Equality, the Third World, and Economic Delusion.* Cambridge, Mass.: Harvard University Press.

Baum, Alice S., and Donald W. Burnes. 1993. *A Nation in Denial: The Truth about Homelessness.* Boulder, Colo.: Westview Press.

Baydar, Nazli, and Jeanne Brooks-Gunn. 1991. "Effect of Maternal Employment and Child-Care Arrangements on Preschoolers' Cognitive and Behavioral Outcomes: Evidence from Children from the National Longitudinal Survey of Youth." *Developmental Psychology.* Vol. 27, No. 6 (November): 932–45.

Bearak, Barry. 2001. "Lives Held Cheap in Bangladesh Sweatshops." *New York Times* (April 15): A1, A12.

Bearman, Peter S., and Hannah Brückner. 2002. "Opposite-Sex Twins and Adolescent Same-Sex Attraction." *American Journal of Sociology.* Vol. 107, No. 5 (March): 1179–1205.

Becker, Howard S. 1966. *Outside: Studies in the Sociology of Deviance.* New York: Free Press.

Begley, Sharon. 2001. "How It All Starts inside Your Brain." *Newsweek* (February 12): 40–42.

Bellas, Marcia L., and Barbara Thomas Coventry. 2001. "Salesmen, Saleswomen, or Sales Workers? Determinants of the Sex Composition of Sales Occupations." *Sociological Forum.* Vol. 16, No. 1 (March): 73–98.

Bello, Marisol, and Rick Hampson. 2009. "Classroom of Diverse Dreams Destroyed." *USA Today* (April 6): 4A.

BELLUCK, PAM. 2000. "Indian Schools, Long Failing, Press for Money and Quality." *New York Times.* (May 18): A1.

BENDICK, M. F. 1992. "Reaching the Breaking Point: Dangers of Mistreatment in Elder Caregiving Situations." *Journal of Elder Abuse and Neglect.* Vol. 4, No. 3 (Fall): 39–59.

BENJAMIN, BERNARD, and CHRIS WALLIS. 1963. "The Mortality of Widowers." *Lancet.* Vol. 2 (August): 454–56.

BENJAMIN, LOIS. 1991. *The Black Elite: Facing the Color Line in the Twilight of the Twentieth Century.* Chicago: Nelson-Hall.

BENNETT, WILLIAM J. 1995. "Redeeming Our Time." *Imprimis.* Vol. 24, No. 11 (November). Available January 14, 2007, at http://www.hillsdale.edu/imprimis/1995/11

BENOKRAITIS, NIJOLE V. 1997. *Subtle Sexism: Current Practices and Prospects for Change.* Thousand Oaks, Calif.: Sage.

———. 1999. *Marriages and Families: Changes, Choices, and Constraints,* 3rd ed. Upper Saddle River, N.J.: Prentice Hall.

BENOKRAITIS, NIJOLE V., and JOE R. FEAGIN. 1995. *Modern Sexism: Blatant, Subtle, and Overt Discrimination,* 2nd ed. Upper Saddle River, N.J.: Prentice Hall.

BERGER, PETER L. 1986. *The Capitalist Revolution: Fifty Propositions about Prosperity, Equality, and Liberty.* New York: Basic Books.

BERGESEN, ALBERT, ed. 1983. *Crises in the World-System.* Thousand Oaks, Calif.: Sage.

BERGSTEN, C. FRED, THOMAS HORST, and THEODORE MORAN. 1978. *American Multinationals and American Interests.* Washington, D.C.: Brookings Institution.

BERNARD, JESSIE. 1982. *The Future of Marriage,* 2nd ed. New Haven, Conn.: Yale University Press.

BERNSTEIN, DAVID E. 2001. "Casey Martin Ruling Is Par for the Course." *Wall Street Journal* (May 30). [Online] Available May 18, 2006, at http://www.mason.gmu.edu/~dbernste/caseymartin.htm

BERTRAM, EVA, MORRIS BLACHMAN, KENNETH SHARPE, and PETER ANDREAS. 1996. *Drug War Politics: The Price of Denial.* Berkeley: University of California Press.

BINSTOCK, ROBERT H. 1996. "Shelter and Care for the Elderly Population: Reasons for Cynicism." *Gerontologist.* Vol. 36, No. 3 (June): 410–13.

BIRENBAUM, A. 1995. *Putting Health Care on the National Agenda.* Westport, Conn.: Praeger.

BLACKWOOD, EVELYN, and SASKIA WIERINGA, eds. 1999. *Female Desires: Same-Sex Relations and Transgender Practices across Cultures.* New York: Columbia University Press.

BLANK, ROBERT H. 1997. *The Price of Life: The Future of American Health Care.* New York: Columbia University Press.

BLANKENHORN, DAVID. 1995. *Fatherless America: Confronting Our Most Urgent Social Problem.* New York: HarperCollins.

BLUMENSON, ERIC D. 1998. "The Drug War's Hidden Economic Agenda: Corrupting Effects of Financing Police Departments by Asset Forfeitures in Drug Cases." *Nation.* Vol. 266 (March 9): 1–12.

BLUMER, HERBERT G. 1969. "Collective Behavior." In Alfred McClung Lee, ed., *Principles of Sociology,* 3rd ed. (pp. 65–121). New York: Barnes & Noble Books.

BOERNER, CHRISTOPHER, and THOMAS LAMBERT. 1995. "Environmental Injustice." *Public Interest.* Vol. 118 (Winter): 61–82.

BOGARDUS, EMORY S. 1925. "Social Distance and Its Origins." *Sociology and Social Research.* Vol. 9 (July–August): 216–25.

———. 1967. *A Forty-Year Racial Distance Study.* Los Angeles: University of Southern California Press.

BOHON, STEPHANIE A., and CRAIG R. HUMPHREY. 2000. "Courting LULUs: Characteristics of Suitor and Objector Communities." *Rural Sociology.* Vol. 65, No. 3 (September): 376–95.

BONNANO, ALESSANDRO, DOUGLAS H. CONSTANCE, and HEATHER LORENZ. 2000. "Powers and Limits of Transnational Corporations: The Case of ADM." *Rural Sociology.* Vol. 65, No. 3 (September): 171–90.

BONILLA-SILVA, EDUARDO. 1999. "The Essential Social Fact of Race." *American Sociological Review.* Vol. 64, No. 6 (December): 899–906.

BORK, ROBERT H. 2008. *A Time to Speak.* Wilmington, Del.: Intercollegiate Studies Institute, 2008.

BOSWORTH, BARRY, and GARY BURTLESS. 1998. "Population Aging and American Economic Performance." In Barry Bosworth and Gary Burtless, eds., *Aging Societies: The Global Dimension* (pp. 267–310). Washington, D.C.: Brookings Institution.

BOURDIEU, PIERRE, and JEAN-CLAUDE PASSERON. 1977. *Reproduction in Society, Education, and Culture.* Thousand Oaks, Calif.: Sage.

BOWERSOX, JOHN A. 1995. "Buprenorphine May Soon Be Heroin Treatment Option." *NIDA Notes* (January–February). [Online] Available May 3, 1999, at http://www.nih.gov/NIDANotes/NNVol10N1/Bupren.html

BOWLES, SAMUEL, and HERBERT GINTIS. 1976. *Schooling in Capitalist America: Educational Reform and the Contradictions of Economic Life.* New York: Basic Books.

BOYER, DEBRA. 1989. "Male Prostitution and Homosexual Identity." *Journal of Homosexuality.* Vol. 17, Nos. 1–2 (January–February): 151–84.

BOYLE, ELIZABETH HEGER, FORTUNATA SONGORA, and GAIL FOSS. 2001. "International Discourse and Local Politics: Anti-Female-Genital-Cutting Laws in Egypt, Tanzania, and the United States." *Social Problems.* Vol. 48, No. 4 (November): 524–44.

BOZA, TANYA GOLASH. 2002. "Proposed American Sociological Association Statement on Race." [Online] Available October 24, 2002, at http://www.unc.edu/~tatiana

BP. 2006. *BP Statistical Review of World Energy.* June. [Online] Available January 11, 2007, at http://www.bp.com/statisticalreview

BRADY CAMPAIGN. 2006. "State Gun Laws." [Online] Available December 17, 2006, at http://www.stategunlaws.org

———. 2008. *Brady Campaign to Prevent Gun Violence.* [Online] Available November 13, 2008, at http://www.bradycampaign.org/issues/gvstats/firearmoverview

BRANTLINGER, ELLEN A. 1993. *The Politics of Social Class in Secondary School: Views of Affluent and Impoverished Youth.* New York: Teachers College Press.

BRAULT, MATTHEW. 2008. *Americans with Disabilities, 2005.* [Online] Available May 17, 2009, at http://www.census.gov/prod/2008pubs/p70–117.pdf

BRIGHT, CHRIS. 2003. "A History of Our Future." In Worldwatch Institute, *State of the World, 2003* (pp. 3–13). New York: Norton.

BRINES, JULIE, and KARA JOYNER. 1999. "The Ties That Bind: Principles of Cohesion in Cohabitation and Marriage." *American Sociological Review.* Vol. 64, No. 3 (June): 333–55.

BRODKIN, KAREN B. 2007. "How Did Jews Become White Folks?" In John J. Macionis and Nijole V. Benokraitis, eds., *Seeing Ourselves: Classic, Contemporary, and Cross-Cultural Readings in Sociology,* 7th ed. (pp. 274–83). Upper Saddle River, N.J.: Prentice Hall.

BROUDE, GWEN J. 1996. "The Realities of Day Care." *Public Interest.* No. 125 (Fall): 95–105.

BROWN, LESTER R., et al., eds. 1993. *State of the World, 1993: A Worldwatch Institute Report on Progress toward a Sustainable Society.* New York: Norton.

BRUPPACHER, BALZ. 2008. "Swiss Approve Pioneering Legal Heroin Program." [Online] Available November 30, 2008, at http://news.yahoo.com/s/ap/20081130/ap_on_re_eu/eu_switzerland_heroin_vote

BUCKS, BRIAN K., ARTHUR B. KENNICKELL, and KEVIN B. MOORE. 2006. "Recent Change in U.S. Family Finances: Evidence from the 2001 and 2004 Survey of Consumer Finances." *Federal Reserve Bulletin.* [Online] Available May 11, 2006, at http://www.federalreserve.gov/pubs/bulletin/2006/financesurvey.pdf

BURKETT, ELINOR. 1997. "'God Created Me to Be a Slave.'" *New York Times Magazine* (October 12): 56–60.

BURNS, PETER F., PETER L. FRANCIA, and PAUL S. HERRNSON. 2000. "Labor at Work: Union Campaign Activities and Legislative Payoffs in the U.S. House of Representatives." *Social Science Quarterly.* Vol. 81, No. 2 (June): 507–22.

BUSHAW, WILLIAM J., and ALEC M. GALLUP. 2008. "The 40th Annual Phi Delta Kappa/Gallup Poll." [Online] Available April 19, 2009, at http://www.pdkmembers.org//members_online/publications/e-gallup/kpoll_pdfs/pdkpoll40_2008.pdf

BUTLER, ROBERT N. 1975. *Why Survive? Being Old in America.* New York: Harper & Row, 1975.

———. 1994. "Dispelling Ageism: The Cross-Cutting Intervention." In Dena Shenk and W. Andrew Achenbaum, eds., *Changing Perceptions of Aging and the Aged.* New York: Springer.

CALAVITA, KITTY, and HENRY N. PONTELL. 1993. "'Heads I Win, Tails You Lose': Deregulation, Crime, and Crisis in the Savings and Loan Industry." In Henry N. Pontell, ed., *Social Deviance: Readings in Theory and Research* (pp. 341–63). Upper Saddle River, N.J.: Prentice Hall.

CAMARA, EVANDRO. Personal communication, 2000.

CAMPO-FLORES, ARIAN. 2006. "America's Divide." *Newsweek* (April 10): 28–38.

CARROLL, JAMES R. 1999a. "Three Congressional Panels Probe Uranium Plant." *Louisville Courier-Journal* (September 14): 4B.

———. 1999b. "U.S. Warns of Uranium, Officials Cite Problems Linked to Waste Storage." *Louisville Courier-Journal* (September 15): 1A.

CARSON, RACHEL. 1962. *Silent Spring.* Boston: Houghton Mifflin.

———. 1995 (orig. 1962). "Silent Spring." In John J. Macionis and Nijole V. Benokraitis, eds., *Seeing Ourselves: Classic, Contemporary, and Cross-Cultural Readings in Sociology,* 3rd ed. (pp. 407–10). Upper Saddle River, N.J.: Prentice Hall.

CARTER, STEPHEN. 1991. *Reflections of an Affirmative Action Baby.* New York: Basic Books.

CASTELLS, MANUEL. 1977. *The Urban Question.* Cambridge, Mass.: MIT Press.

———. 1983. *The City and the Grass Roots.* Berkeley: University of California Press.

———. 1989. *The Informational City.* Oxford: Blackwell.

CATALYST. 2009. *Research and Knowledge.* [Online] Available April 3, 2009, at http://www.catalyst.org/publication/271/women-ceos-of-the-fortune-1000

CBS NEWS. 2005. "Poll: Women's Movement Worthwhile." [Online] Available May 6, 2009, at http://www.cbsnews.com/stories/2005/10/22/opinion/polls/main965224.shtml

CENTER FOR AMERICAN WOMEN AND POLITICS. 2006. *Women in Elected Office: Fact Sheets and Summaries.* Eagleton Institute of Politics, Rutgers University. [Online] Available December 17, 2006, at http://www.cawp.rutgers.edu/Facts.html

———. 2008. *Women in Elective Office, 2008.* [Online] Available April 3, 2009, at http://www.cawp.rutgers.edu/fast_facts/levels_of_office/documents/cong.pdf

CENTER FOR CONSTITUTIONAL RIGHTS. 2003. [Online] Available November 19, 2003, at http://www.ccr-ny.org

CENTER FOR MEDIA AND PUBLIC AFFAIRS. 2002. [Online] Available January 24, 2002, at http://www.cmpa.org

CENTER FOR RESPONSIVE POLITICS. 2009. "Lobbying Database." [Online] Available January 23, 2009, at http://www.opensecrets.org/lobbyists/index.php?showyear=2007&txtindextype=i

CENTER FOR THE STUDY OF THE AMERICAN ELECTORATE. 2009. "2008 Election Turnout Data." [Online] Available May 18, 2009, at http://www.american.edu/ia/cdem/csae/pdfs/2008pdfoffinaledited.pdf

CENTER ON HUNGER AND POVERTY. 2000. *Paradox of Our Times: Hunger in a Strong Economy.* Medford, Mass: Tufts University Press.

CENTERS FOR DISEASE CONTROL AND PREVENTION. 1997. 2005. *HIV/AIDS Surveillance Report, 2004.* Vol. 16. [Online] Available December 17, 2006, at http://www.cdc.gov/hiv/topics/surveillance/resources/reports/2004report/default.htm

———. 2006. "Adult Cigarette Smoking in the United States: Current Estimates." Fact sheet. [Online] Available January 8, 2007, at http://www.cdc.gov/tobacco/factsheets/AdultCigaretteSmoking_FactSheet.htm

———. 2008. "Abortion Surveillance: United States, 2005." *Morbidity and Mortality Weekly Reports* (November 28). [Online] Available April 29, 2009, at http://www.cdc.gov/mmwr/preview/mmwrhtml/ss5713a1.htm?s_cid=ss5713a1_e

———. 2008. "Cigarette Smoking Among Adults: United States, 2007." *Morbidity and Mortality Weekly Reports* (November 14). [Online] Available February 5, 2009, at http://www.cdc.gov/mmwr/preview/mmwrhtml/mm5745a2.htm

———. 2008. *HIV/AIDS Statistics and Surveillance.* [Online] Available April 29, 2009, at http://www.cdc.gov/hiv/topics/surveillance/resources/factsheets/pdf/prevalence.pdf

———. 2008. *Trends in the Prevalence of Sexual Behaviors: National Youth Risk Behavior Survey, 1991–2007.* [Online] Available November 7, 2008, at http://www.cdc.gov/HealthyYouth/yrbs/pdf/yrbs07_us_sexual_behaviors_trend.pdf

———. 2009. *Chronic Disease Prevention and Health Promotion: Quick Facts—Economic and Health Burden of Chronic Disease, Obesity.* [Online] Available February 5, 2009, at http://www.cdc.gov/NCCDPHP/press/index.htm

———. 2009. "Fetal Alcohol Spectrum Disorders: Frequently Asked Questions." [Online] Available July 23, 2009, at http://www.cdc.gov/ncbddd/fas/faqs.htm

———. 2009. *HIV/AIDS Surveillance Report, 2007.* [Online] Available February 19, 2009, at http://www.cdc.gov/hiv/topics/surveillance/resources/reports/2007report/default.htm

———. 2009. *Morbidity and Mortality Weekly Reports* (June 20). [Online] Available June 20, 2009, at http://www.cdc.gov/art

Central Intelligence Agency. 2009. *The 2008 World Factbook.* [Online] Available January 26, 2009, at https://www.cia.gov/library/publications/the-world-factbook

Chafe, William. 1977. *Women and Equality: Changing Patterns in American Culture.* New York: Oxford University Press.

Chagnon, Napoleon A. 1997. *Yanomamö.* Fort Worth, Tex.: Harcourt Brace.

Chaker, Anne Marie, and Hilary Stout. 2004. "After Years Off, Women Struggle to Revive Careers." *Wall Street Journal* (May 5): A1, A8.

Chandler, Timothy D., Yoshinori Kamo, and James D. Werbel. 1994. "Do Delays in Marriage and Childbirth Affect Earnings?" *Social Science Quarterly.* Vol. 75, No. 4 (December): 838–53.

Chang, Alicia. 2009. "Study: Cleaner Air Adds 5 Months to U.S. Life Span." *Yahoo News* (January 21). [Online] Available April 10, 2009, at http://www.newsvine.com/_news/2009/01/21/2339450-study-cleaner-air-adds-5-months-to-us-life-span

Chauncey, George. 1994. *Gay New York: Gender, Urban Culture, and the Making of the Gay Male World, 1890–1940.* New York: Basic Books.

Chesler, Phyllis. 1989. *Women and Madness.* New York: Harcourt Brace Jovanovich.

Cheslow, Jerry. 2006. "Loving the Landscape but Not the Sprawl." *New York Times Online.* [Online] Available July 17, 2006, at http://www.researchnavigator.com

Chiricos, Ted, Ranee McEntire, and Marc Gertz. 2001. "Perceived Racial and Ethnic Composition of Neighborhood and Perceived Risk of Crime." *Social Problems.* Vol. 48, No. 3 (August): 322–40.

Christle, Christine A., Kristine Jolivette, and C. Michael Nelson. 2007. "School Characteristics Related to High School Dropout Rates." *Remedial and Special Education.* Vol. 28, No. 6 (June): 325–39.

Chronicle of Higher Education. "A Profile of College Presidents, 1986 and 2006." 2007. [Online] Available May 26, 2009, at http://chronicle.com/stats/acesurvey/data.htm

Chua-Eoan, Howard. 2000. "Profiles in Outrage." *Time.* Vol. 156, No. 13 (September 25): 38–39.

Cisneros, Henry. 2009. "A Fence Can't Stop the Future." *Newsweek* (January 26). [Online] Available January 28, 2009, at http://www.newsweek.com/id/180037/output/print

Clarke, Robin. 1984. "Atmospheric Pollution." In Sir Edmund Hillary, ed., *Ecology 2000: The Changing Face of the Earth* (pp. 130–48). New York: Beaufort.

Clausewitz, Carl von. 1968 (orig. 1832). *On War.* Ed. Anatol Rapaport. Baltimore: Penguin.

Clemetson, Lynette. 2000. "Grandma Knows Best." *Newsweek* (June 12): 60–61.

Close, Ellis. 2004. "A Dream Deferred." *Newsweek* (May 17): 52–59.

Cloud, John. 1998. "Harassed or Hazed? Why the Supreme Court Ruled That Men Can Sue Men for Sex Harassment." *Time.* Vol. 151, No. 10 (March 16): 55.

———. 2003. "Inside the New SAT." *Time.* Vol. 162, No. 17 (October 27): 48–56.

Cloward, Richard A., and Lloyd E. Ohlin. 1966. *Delinquency and Opportunity: A Theory of Delinquent Gangs.* New York: Free Press.

Coalition to Stop the Use of Child Soldiers. 2006. "Child Soldiers." [Online] Available July 27, 2006, at http://www.child-soldiers.org

Cockerham, William C. 2005. *Sociology of Mental Disorders,* 7th ed. Upper Saddle River, N.J.: Prentice Hall.

———. 2007. *Medical Sociology,* 10th ed. Upper Saddle River, N.J.: Prentice Hall.

Cohen, Adam. 2004. "The Supreme Struggle." *New York Times* (January 18): sec. 4A, 22–24, 38.

Cohen, Elias. 2001. "The Complex Nature of Ageism: What Is It? Who Does It? Who Perceives It?" *Gerontologist.* Vol. 41, No. 5 (October): 576–78.

Cohen, Joshua T., and John D. Graham. 2003. "A Revised Economic Analysis of Restrictions on the Use of Cell Phones while Driving." *Risk Analysis.* Vol. 23, No. 1 (February): 5–17.

Cole, George F., and Christopher E. Smith. 2002. *Criminal Justice in America,* 3rd ed. Belmont, Calif.: Wadsworth.

Coleman, James S. 1966. *Equality of Educational Opportunity.* Washington, D.C.: U.S. Government Printing Office.

———. 1988. "Social Capital in the Creation of Human Capital." *American Journal of Sociology.* Vol. 94, No. 1 (July): 95–120.

College Board. 2008a. "Total Group Profile Report." [Online] Available February 2, 2009, at http://professionals.collegeboard.com/profdownload/Total_Group_Report.pdf

———. 2008b. *2008 College-Bound Seniors: Total Group Profile Report.* [Online] Available February 3, 2009, at http://professionals.collegeboard.com/profdownload/Total_Group_Report.pdf

Commission for Racial Justice, United Church of Christ. 1994. *CRJ Reporter.* New York: Commission for Racial Justice, United Church of Christ.

Common Sense for Drug Policy. 1999. "Drug War Facts: The Netherlands and the United States." [Online] Available May 10, 1999, at http://www.csdp.org/factbook/thenethe.htm

Connerly, Ward. 2000. "The Content of Our Children's Character." *Imprimis.* Vol. 29, No. 2 (February): 1–3, 5.

Conrad, Peter, and Joseph W. Schneider. 1980. *Deviance and Medicalization: From Badness to Sickness.* Saint Louis, Mo.: Mosby.

Conway, M. Margaret, and Joanne Connor Green. 1998. "Political Action Committees and Campaign Finance." In Allan J. Cigler and Burdett A. Loomis, eds., *Interest Group Politics,* 5th ed. (pp. 193–214). Washington, D.C.: CQ Press.

Congressional Budget Office. 2008. *Growing Disparity in Life Expectancy.* [Online] Available November 22, 2008, at http://www.cbo.gov/ftpdocs/91xx/doc9104/04-17-LifeExpectancy_Brief.pdf

Corliss, Richard. 2001. "Who's Feeling No Pain?" *Time.* Vol. 157, No. 11 (March 19): 69.

Corliss, Richard, and Michael D. Lemonick. 2004. "How to Live to Be 100." *Time.* Vol. 165, No. 9 (March 3): 40–48.

Cortese, Anthony J. 1999. *Provocateur: Images of Women and Minorities in Advertising.* Lanham, Md.: Rowman & Littlefield.

Cowley, Geoffrey. 1995. "The Prescription That Kills." *Newsweek* (July 17): 54.

———. 2001. "New Ways to Stay Clean." *Newsweek* (February 12): 44–7.

COYOTE L.A./Southern California. 2004. "Who Gets Arrested?" [Online] Available April 28, 2009, at http://www.coyotela.org/what_is.html

Crossette, Barbara. 1995. "Female Genital Mutilation by Immigrants Is Becoming Cause for Concern in the U.S." *New York Times International* (December 10): 11.

Cumming, Elaine, and William E. Henry. 1961. *Growing Old: The Process of Disengagement.* New York: Basic Books.

Currie, Elliott. 1985. *Confronting Crime: An American Challenge.* New York: Pantheon.

Dahl, Robert. 1961. *Who Governs?* New Haven, Conn.: Yale University Press.

———. 1982. *Dilemmas of Pluralist Democracy.* New Haven, Conn.: Yale University Press.

Dalmia, Shikha. 2008. "Obama and Big Labor." *Forbes* (October 29). [Online] Available May 8, 2009, at http://www.forbes.com/2008/10/28/obama-card-check-oped-cx_sd_1029dalmia.html

Daly, Kathleen, and Meda Chesney-Lind. 1988. "Feminism and Criminology." *Justice Quarterly.* Vol. 5, No. 4 (December): 497–583.

Darroch, Jacqueline E., et al. 2001. "Teenage Sexual and Reproductive Behavior in Developed Countries: Can More Progress Be Made?" (November). [Online] Available August 14, 2002, at http://www.agi-usa

Davies, James B., Susanna Sandstrom, Anthony Shorrocks, and Edward N. Wolff. 2008. *The World Distribution of Household Wealth.* Helsinki: United Nations University/World Institute for Development Economics Research.

Davis, Kingsley. 1971. "Sexual Behavior." In Robert K. Merton and Robert Nisbet, eds., *Contemporary Social Problems,* 3rd ed. (pp. 313–60). New York: Harcourt Brace Jovanovich.

Davis, Kingsley, and Wilbert Moore. 1945. "Some Principles of Stratification." *American Sociological Review.* Vol. 10, No. 2 (April): 242–49.

Davis, Lisa Selin. 2009. "A (Radical) Way to Fix Urban Sprawl." *Time* (June 22): 54–57.

Davis, Nanette J. 1980. *Sociological Constructions of Deviance: Perspectives and Issues in the Field,* 2nd ed. Dubuque, Iowa: Brown.

———. 2000. "From Victims to Survivors: Working with Recovering Street Prostitutes." In Ronald Weitzer, ed., *Sex for Sale: Prostitution, Pornography, and the Sex Industry* (pp. 139–55). New York: Routledge.

Dedrick, Dennis K., and Richard E. Yinger. 1990. "MAD, SDI, and the Nuclear Arms Race." Unpublished manuscript. Georgetown, Ky.: Georgetown College.

DeFina, Robert H., and Thomas M. Arvanites. 2002. "The Weak Effect of Imprisonment on Crime, 1971–1998." *Social Science Quarterly.* Vol. 83, No. 3 (September): 635–53.

Delacroix, Jacques, and Charles C. Ragin. 1981. "Structural Blockage: A Cross-National Study of Economic Dependency, State Efficacy, and Underdevelopment." *American Journal of Sociology.* Vol. 86, No. 6 (May): 1311–47.

Della Cava, Marco R. 1997. "For Dutch, It's as Easy as Asking a Doctor." *USA Today* (January 7): 4A.

Deslatte, Melinda. 2003. "Serial Killing Suspect Returns to Louisiana." *San Francisco Examiner* (July 3). [Online] Available July 3, 2003, at http://www.examiner.com

Diller, Lawrence J. 1998. *Running on Ritalin.* New York: Bantam Doubleday Dell.

Dinitz, Simon, F. R. Scarpitti, and Walter C. Reckless. 1962. "Delinquency and Vulnerability: A Cross-Group and Longitudinal Analysis." *American Sociological Review.* Vol. 25, No. 4 (August): 555–58.

DINKES, RACHEL, JANA KEMP, KATRINA BAUM, and THOMAS D. SNYDER. 2009. *Indicators of School Crime and Safety, 2008.* [Online] Available July 23, 2009, at http://nces.ed.gov/pubs2009/2009022.pdf

DIXON, WILLIAM J., and TERRY BOSWELL. 1996. "Dependency, Disarticulation, and Denominator Effects: Another Look at Foreign Capital Penetration." *American Journal of Sociology.* Vol. 102, No. 2 (September): 543–62.

DOBYNS, HENRY F. 1966. "An Appraisal of Techniques with a New Hemispheric Estimate." *Current Anthropology.* Vol. 7, No. 4 (October): 395–446.

DOLLARD, JOHN, et al. 1939. *Frustration and Aggression.* New Haven, Conn.: Yale University Press.

DOMHOFF, G. WILLIAM. 1970. *Higher Circles: The Governing Class in America.* New York: Random House.

DOWNEY, DOUGLAS B., PAUL T. VON HIPPEL, and BECKETT A. BROH. 2004. "Are Schools the Great Equalizer? Cognitive Inequality during the Summer Months and School Year." *American Sociological Review.* Vol. 69, No. 5 (October): 613–35.

DRAWBAUGH, KEVIN. 2009. "U.S. House Approves Crackdown on Financial Bailout." Reuters (January 21). [Online] Available May 6, 2009, at http://uk.reuters.com/article/americasRegulatoryNes/idUKN2150024420090121

DU BOIS, W. E. B. 2001 (orig. 1903). "The Souls of Black Folk." In John J. Macionis and Nijole V. Benokraitis, eds., *Seeing Ourselves: Classic, Contemporary, and Cross-Cultural Readings in Sociology,* 5th ed. (pp. 226–30). Upper Saddle River, N.J.: Prentice Hall.

DUFFY, TOM. 1999. "Campus Crusader: Dartmouth College Nutritionist Gives Students Food for Thought." *People.* Vol. 51, No. 13 (April 12): 71–72.

DUNLAP, RILEY E., GEORGE H. GALLUP JR., and ALEC M. GALLUP. 1992. *The Health of the Planet Survey.* Princeton, N.J.: George H. Gallup International Institute.

DUNLOP, BECKY NORTON. 2006. "Conservation Ethics." *Society.* Vol. 43, No. 3 (March–April): 13–18.

DURKHEIM, EMILE. 1964a (orig. 1895). *The Division of Labor in Society.* New York: Free Press.

———. 1964b (orig. 1893). *The Rules of Sociological Method.* New York: Free Press.

DWORKIN, ANDREA. 1987. *Intercourse.* New York: Free Press.

———. 1991. "Against the Male Flood: Censorship, Pornography, and Equality." In Robert M. Baird and Stuart E. Rosenbaum, eds., *Pornography: Private Right or Public Menace?* (pp. 56–61). Buffalo, N.Y.: Prometheus.

DYE, THOMAS R. 1999. *Politics in America,* 3rd ed. Upper Saddle River, N.J.: Prentice Hall.

EATON, WILLIAM W., JR. 1980. "A Formal Theory of Selection for Schizophrenia." *American Journal of Sociology.* Vol. 86, No. 1 (July): 149–58.

EBY, JOHN. 2009. "Ironies Abound as Obama Called Not Radical Enough." *Niles Daily Star* (March 10) [Online] Available May 6, 2009, at http://www.nilesstar.com/articles/2009/03/10/columnists/ndcolumn03.txt

EDWARDS, TAMALA M. 1998. "Revolt of the Gentry." *Time.* Vol. 151, No. 23 (June 15): 34–35.

EHRENREICH, BARBARA. 1983. *The Hearts of Men: American Dreams and the Flight from Commitment.* Garden City, N.Y.: Anchor Doubleday.

———. 1997. *Blood Rites: Origins and History of the Passions of War.* New York: Holt.

———. 1999. "The Real Truth about the Female Body." *Time.* Vol. 153, No. 9 (March 15): 56–65.

———. 2001. *Nickel and Dimed: On How (Not) to Get By in America.* New York: Holt.

ELBOGHDADY, DINA, and SARAH COHEN. 2009. "The Growing Foreclosure Crisis." *Washington Post* (January 17). [Online] Available May 13, 2009, at http://www.washingtonpost.com/wp-dyn/content/article/2009/01/16/AR2009011604724.html

ELDREDGE, DIRK CHASE. 1998. *Ending the War on Drugs: A Solution for America.* Lanham, Md.: National Book Network.

"Election Results 2008." 2008. *New York Times* (Nov. 5). [Online] Available January 23, 2009, at http://elections.nytimes.com/2008/results/president/exit-polls.html

ELECTRONIC FRONTIER FOUNDATION. 2003. [Online] Available November 19, 2003, at http://www.eff.org

ELMER, VICKIE. 2009. "Age Discrimination Claims by Workers Reach Record High." *AARP Bulletin Today* (March 25). [Online] Available July 23, 2009, at http://bulletin.aarp.org

EMERSON, MICHAEL O., GEORGE YANCEY, and KAREN J. CHAI. 2001. "Does Race Matter in Residential Segregation? Exploring the Preferences of White Americans." *American Sociological Review.* Vol. 66, No. 6 (December): 922–35.

ENGELS, FRIEDRICH. 1902 (orig. 1884). *The Origin of the Family.* Chicago: Kerr.

ENGLAND, PAULA. 1992. *Comparable Worth: Theories and Evidence.* Hawthorne, N.Y.: Aldine de Grutyer.

———. 2001. "Three Reviews on Marriage." *Contemporary Sociology.* Vol. 30, No. 6 (November): 564–65.

ENGLAND, PAULA, JOAN M. HERMSEN, and DAVID A. COTTER. 2000. "The Devaluation of Women's Work: A Comment on Tam." *American Journal of Sociology.* Vol. 105, No. 6 (May): 1741–60.

ESTES, RICHARD J. 2001. "The Commercial Sexual Exploitation of Children in the U.S., Canada, and Mexico." Reported in "Study Explores Sexual Exploitation." *Yahoo News.* [Online] Available September 10, 2001, at http://dailynews.yahoo.com

ETZIONI, AMITAI. 1993. "How to Make Marriage Matter." *Time.* Vol. 142, No. 10 (September 6): 76.

EUROPEAN UNION. 2009. "Eurostat." [Online] Available June 2, 2009, at http://epp.eurostat.ec.europa.eu/portal/page/portal/population/data/main_tables

EVELYN, JAMILAH. 2002. "Community Colleges Play Too Small a Role in Teacher Education, Report Concludes." *Chronicle of Higher Education Online.* [Online] Available October 24, 2002, at http://chronicle.com/daily/2002/10/2002102403n.htm

EWERS, JUSTIN. 2008. "Saving Symbols of Shame." *U.S. News & World Report.* Vol. 144, No. 7 (March 10): 31.

FAGAN, JEFFREY, FRANKLIN E. ZIMRING, and JUNE KIM. 1998. "Declining Homicide in New York City: A Tale of Two Trends." *National Institute of Justice Journal.* No. 237 (October): 12–13.

FALUDI, SUSAN. 1991. *Backlash: The Undeclared War against American Women.* New York: Crown.

FARIS, ROBERT E. L. 1967. *Chicago Sociology, 1920–1932.* Chicago: University of Chicago Press.

FARIS, ROBERT E. L., and H. WARREN DUNHAM. 1939. *Mental Disorders in Urban Areas.* Chicago: University of Chicago Press.

FEAGIN, JOE R., and VERA HERNÁN. 1995. *White Racism: The Basics.* New York: Routledge.

FEAGIN, JOE R., and MELVIN P. SIKES. 1994. *Living with Racism: The Black Middle-Class Experience.* Boston: Beacon Press.

FEDER, JUDY. 2009. "Federal Action Required on Healthcare." *U.S. News & World Report* (January 27, 2009): 6.

FEDERAL BUREAU OF INVESTIGATION. 2006. *Crime in the United States, 2005.* [Online] Available December 27, 2006, at http://www.fbi.gov/ucr/05cius

———. 2008. *Crime in the United States, 2007.* [Online] Available July 23, 2009, at http://www.fbi.gov/ucr/cius2007

FEDERAL COMMUNICATION COMMISSION. 2007. *Violent Television Programming and Its Impact on Children.* [Online] Available April 17, 2009, at http://hraunfoss.fcc.gov/edocs_public/attachmatch/FCC-07-50A1.pdf

FEDERAL ELECTION COMMISSION. 2009. "Growth in PAC Financial Activity Slows." [Online] Available May 20, 2009, at http://www.fec.gov/press/press2009/20090415PAC/documents/4sumhistory2008_000.pdf

FEDERAL INTERAGENCY FORUM ON AGING-RELATED STATISTICS. 2008. *Older Americans, 2008: Key Indicators of Well-Being.* [Online] Available January 18, 2009, at http://www.agingstats.gov/agingstatsdotnet/Main_Site/Data/Data_2008.aspx

FEDERAL RESERVE BOARD. 2009. *2007 Survey of Consumer Finances.* [Online] Available March 23, 2009, at http://www.federalreserve.gov/pubs/oss/oss2/2007/scf2007home.html

FETTO, JOHN. 2003. "Drug Money." *American Demographics.* Vol. 25, No. 2 (March): 48.

FINE, MELINDA. 1993. "'You Can't Just Say That the Only Ones Who Can Speak Are Those Who Agree with Your Position': Political Discourse in the Classroom." *Harvard Educational Review.* Vol. 63, No. 4 (Winter): 421–33.

FINEMAN, HOWARD, and TAMARA LIPPER. 2003. "Spinning Race." *Newsweek* (January 27): 26–29.

FINLAYSON, JOHN. 1998. "Student Terror: The Weathermen." In *Encyclopedia of World Terrorism.* Vol. 3 (pp. 534–35). Armonk, N.Y.: Sharpe.

FIREBAUGH, GLENN. 1992. "Growth Effects of Foreign and Domestic Investment." *American Journal of Sociology.* Vol. 98, No. 1 (July): 105–30.

———. 1996. "Does Foreign Capital Harm Poor Nations? New Estimates Based on Dixon and Boswell's Measures of Capital Penetration." *American Journal of Sociology.* Vol. 102, No. 2 (September): 563–75.

FIREBAUGH, GLENN, and FRANK D. BECK. 1994. "Does Economic Growth Benefit the Masses? Growth, Dependence, and Welfare in the Third World." *American Sociological Review.* Vol. 59, No. 5 (October): 631–53.

FIREBAUGH, GLENN, and DUMITRU SANDU. 1998. "Who Supports Marketization and Democratization in Post-Communist Romania?" *Sociological Forum.* Vol. 13, No. 3 (September): 521–41.

FISCHER, CLAUDE. 1973. "Urban Malaise." *Social Problems.* Vol. 52, No. 2 (May): 221–35.

———. 1975. "Toward a Subcultural Theory of Urbanism." *American Journal of Sociology.* Vol. 80, No. 6 (May): 1319–41.

FLEMING, JILLIAN, PAUL MULLEN, and GABRIELE BAMMER. 1997. "A Study of Potential Risk Factors for Sexual Abuse in Childhood." *Child Abuse and Neglect.* Vol. 21, No. 1 (January): 49–58.

FLEXNER, ELEANOR. 1975. *Century of Struggle: The Women's Rights Movement in the United States,* rev. ed. Cambridge, Mass.: Belknap Press.

FLORIAN, ELLEN. 1999. "Oh, No: It's Spreading." *Newsweek* (July 19): 24–25.

FOLBRE, NANCY, and CENTER FOR POPULAR ECONOMICS. 1995. *The New Field Guide to the U.S. Economy.* New York: New York Press.

FORDHAM, SIGNITHIA, and JOHN U. OGBU. 1992. "Black Students' School Success: Coping with the Burden of 'Acting White.'" In John J. Macionis and Nijole V. Benokraitis, eds., *Seeing Ourselves: Classic, Contemporary, and Cross-Cultural Readings in Sociology,* 2nd ed. (pp. 287–303). Englewood Cliffs, N.J.: Prentice Hall.

FOUCAULT, MICHEL. 1965. *Madness and Civilization: A History of Insanity in the Age of Reason.* New York: Pantheon.

———. 1990. *A History of Sexuality, Part 1.* New York: Vintage Books.

FRANK, ANDRÉ GUNDER. 1981. *Reflections on the World Economic Crisis.* New York: Monthly Review Press.

FRANK, ROBERT. 2008. "Will the Crisis Hit the Rich Like 1990 or 1929?" *Wall Street Journal* (November 19). [Online] Available March 24, 2009, at http://blogs.wsj.com/wealth/2008/11/19/will-the-crisis-hit-the-rich-like-1990-or-1929

FRANKLIN, JOHN HOPE. 1967. *From Slavery to Freedom: A History of Negro Americans,* 3rd ed. New York: Vintage Books.

FREEDMAN, ESTELLE B. 2002. *No Turning Back: The History of Feminism and the Future of Women*. New York: Ballantine.

FREEDMAN, SAMUEL G. 1998. "Is the Drug Racist?" *Rolling Stone*. No. 786 (May 14): 35.

FREEDOM HOUSE. 2000. *Freedom in the World, 1999–2000*. New York: Freedom House.

———. 2006. *Freedom in the World, 2006*. [Online] Available December 17, 2006, at http://www.freedomhouse.org

FREIFELD, KAREN. 2009. "Probes of AIG Bonus Payments Begun by 19 U.S. States." Bloomberg.com (March 20). [Online] Available July 23, 2009, at http://www.bloomberg.com/apps/news?pid=20601087&sid=avJwPOJehjeM&refer=home

FRIAS, SONIA M., and RONALD J. ANGEL. 2007. "Stability and Change in the Experience of Partner Violence among Low-Income Women." *Social Science Quarterly*. Vol. 88, No. 5 (May): 1281–1306.

FUJIURA, GLENN T. 2001. "Emerging Trends in Disability." *Population Today*. Vol. 29, No. 6 (August–September): 10–11.

FULLER, BRUCE, RICHARD F. ELMORE, and GARY ORFIELD. 1996. "Policy-Making in the Dark: Illuminating the School Choice Debate." In Bruce Fuller, Richard F. Elmore, and Gary Orfield, eds., *Who Chooses? Who Loses? Culture, Institutions, and the Unequal Effects of School Choice* (pp. 1–24). New York: Teachers College Press.

FURSTENBERG, FRANK F., JR., and ANDREW CHERLIN. 1991. *Divided Families: What Happens to Children When Parents Part*. Cambridge, Mass.: Harvard University Press.

GAGNÉ, PATRICIA. 1998. *Battered Women's Justice: The Movement for Clemency and the Politics of Self-Defense*. New York: Twayne.

GALANO, ANA MARIA. 1998. "Land Hungry in Brazil." *Courier*. (July/August 1998). [Online] Available December 4, 2008, at http://www.unesco.org/courier/1998_08/uk/somm/intro.htm

GALBRAITH, JOHN KENNETH. 1985. *The New Industrial State*, 4th ed. Boston: Houghton Mifflin.

GALL, TERRY L., DAVID R. EVANS, and JOHN HOWARD. 1997. "The Retirement Adjustment Process: Changes in the Well-Being of Male Retirees across Time." *Journal of Gerontology, Series B: Psychological Sciences*. Vol. 52B, No. 3 (May): 110–17.

GALLAGHER, MAGGIE. 1999. "Does Bradley Know What Poverty Is?" *New York Post* (October 28): 37.

GAMBOA, SUZANNE. 2003. "INS: 7 Million Illegal Immigrants in U.S." *Yahoo News*. [Online] Available January 31, 2003, at http://www.yahoonews.com

GAMORAN, ADAM. 1992. "The Variable Effects of High School Tracking." *American Sociological Review*. Vol. 57, No. 6 (December): 812–28.

GANS, HERBERT J. 1968. *People and Plans: Essays on Urban Problems and Solutions*. New York: Basic Books.

———. 1971. "The Uses of Poverty: The Poor Pay All." *Social Policy*. Vol. 2, No. 4 (July–August): 20–24.

GARFINKEL, HAROLD. 1956. "Conditions of Successful Degradation Ceremonies." *American Journal of Sociology*. Vol. 61, No. 2 (March): 420–24.

GARLAND, SARAH. 2007. "Study Backs Results of For-Profit Schools." *New York Sun Online* (April 11). [Online] Available March 31, 2008, at http://www2.nysun.com/article/52198

GARWOOD, PAUL. 2003. "Garbage Collectors Trash Governor's Plan." *Middle Eastern Times*. [Online] Available November 29, 2003, at http://www.metimes.com/2K1/issue2001-20/eq/garbage_collectors_trash.htm

GATES, GARY J., M. V. LEE BADGETT, JENNIFER EHRLE MACOMBER, and KATE CHAMBERS. 2007. "Adoption and Foster Care by Gay and Lesbian Parents in the United States." [Online] Available July 23, 2009, at http://www.law.ucla.edu/williamsinstitute/publications/FinalAdoptionReport.pdf

GAVE, ELENI N. 2005. "In the Indigenous Muxe Culture of Mexico's Oaxaca State, Alternative Notions of Sexuality Are Not Only Accepted, They're Celebrated." *Travel and Leisure* (November). [Online] Available June 15, 2009, at http://travelandleisure.com/articles/stepping-out/page/2/print

GELLES, RICHARD J. 1997. *Intimate Violence in Families*, 3rd ed. Thousand Oaks, Calif.: Sage.

GELLES, RICHARD J., and CLAIRE PEDRICK CORNELL. 1990. *Intimate Violence in Families*, 2nd ed. Thousand Oaks, Calif.: Sage.

GELLES, RICHARD J., and MURRAY A. STRAUS. 1988. *Intimate Violence: The Causes and Consequences of Abuse in the American Family*. New York: Touchstone.

GELMAN, DAVID. 1992. "Born or Bred?" *Newsweek* (February 24): 46–53.

GENDELL, MURRAY. 2002. "Boomers' Retirement Wave Likely to Begin in Just Six Years." *Population Today*. Vol. 30, No. 3 (April): 1–2.

GIBBS, NANCY, and TIMOTHY ROCHE. 1999. "The Columbine Tapes." *Time*. Vol. 154, No. 25 (December 20): 40–51.

GIELE, JANET Z. 1988. "Gender and Sex Roles." In Neil J. Smelser, ed., *Handbook of Sociology* (pp. 291–323). Thousand Oaks, Calif.: Sage.

GILBERTSON, GRETA A., and DOUGLAS T. GURAK. 1993. "Broadening the Enclave Debate: The Dual Labor Market Experiences of Dominican and Colombian Men in New York City." *Sociological Forum*. Vol. 8, No. 2 (June): 205–20.

GILDER, GEORGE. 1980. "The Myths of Racial and Sexual Discrimination." *National Review*. Vol. 32, No. 23 (November 14): 1381–90.

GILLON, RAANAN. 1999. "Euthanasia in the Netherlands: Down the Slippery Slope?" *Journal of Medical Ethics*. Vol. 25, No. 1 (February): 3–4.

GINGRICH, NEWT. 2009. "The Market Can Fix the Healthcare Problem." *U.S. News & World Report* (January 27): 7.

GLAAB, CHARLES N. 1963. *The American City: A Documentary History*. Homewood, Ill.: Dorsey.

GLAAB, CHARLES N., and A. THEODORE BROWN. 1967. *A History of Urban America*. New York: Macmillan.

GLASS, STEPHEN. 1997. "Don't You D.A.R.E." *New Republic*. Vol. 216, No. 9 (March 3): 18–25.

GLATER, JONATHAN D. 2005. "Blue Collars in Olive Drab." *New York Times* (May 22). [Online] Available June 12, 2009, at http://www.nytimes.com/2005/05/22/national/class/MILITARY-FINAL.html

GLENN, NORVAL, and THOMAS SYLVESTER. 2005. *The Denial: Downplaying the Consequences of Family Structure for Children*. New York: Institute for American Values.

GLUECK, SHELDON, and ELEANOR GLUECK. 1950. *Unraveling Juvenile Delinquency*. New York: Commonwealth Fund.

GOETTING, ANN. 1999. *Getting Out: Life Stories of Women Who Left Abusive Men*. New York: Columbia University Press.

GOFFMAN, ERVING. 1963. *Stigma: Notes on the Management of Spoiled Identity*. Englewood Cliffs, N.J.: Prentice Hall.

———. 1979. *Gender Advertisements*. New York: Harper Colophon.

GOLDBERG, STEVEN. 1974. *The Inevitability of Patriarchy*. New York: Morrow.

GOLDMAN, HENRY. 1991. "The Plight of the Black Child." *Philadelphia Inquirer* (February 10): 5E.

GOLDSTEIN, AVRAM. 1994. *Addiction: From Biology to Drug Policy*. New York: Freeman.

GOMBY, DEANNA S., and PATRICIA H. SHIONO. 1991. "Estimating the Number of Substance-Exposed Infants." *Future of Children*. Vol. 1, No. 1 (Spring): 17–25.

GÓMEZ, LAURA E. 1997. *Misconceiving Mothers: Legislators, Prosecutors, and the Politics of Prenatal Drug Exposure*. Philadelphia: Temple University Press.

GOODE, ERICH. 1993. *Drugs in American Society*, 4th ed. New York: McGraw-Hill.

———. 1997. *Between Politics and Reason: The Drug Legalization Debate*. New York: St. Martin's Press.

GOODMAN, DAVID. 1999. "America's Newest Class War." *Mother Jones*. Vol. 24, No. 5 (September–October): 68–75.

GORE, AL. 2006. *An Inconvenient Truth*. Emmaus, Pa.: Rodale Books.

GOTTMANN, JEAN. 1961. *Megalopolis*. New York: Twentieth Century Fund.

GOVERNORS HIGHWAY SAFETY ASSOCIATION. 2009. "State Cell Phone Laws." [Online] Available February 15, 2009, at http://www.ghsa.org/html/stateinfo/laws/cellphone_laws.html

GRADY, DENISE. 1992. "The Brains of Gay Men." *Discover*. Vol. 13, No. 1 (January): 29.

GREENBERG, JAN R., MARTHA MCKIBBEN, and JANE A. RAYMOND. 1990. "Dependent Adult Children and Elder Abuse." *Journal of Elder Abuse and Neglect*. Vol. 2, Nos. 1–2 (Spring–Summer): 73–86.

GREENHOUSE, STEVEN. 2000. "Despite Defeat on China Bill, Labor Is on the Rise." *New York Times* (May 20): A1, A18.

GRIMM, MATTHEW. 2002. "A Dubious Pitch." *American Demographics*. Vol. 24, No. 5 (May): 44–46.

GROVES, BETSY MCALISTER. 1997. "Growing Up in a Violent World: The Impact of Family and Community Violence on Young Children and Their Families." *Topics in Early Childhood Special Education*. Vol. 17, No. 1 (Spring): 74–101.

GUMBEL, PETER. 2009. "A World of Troubles." *Time* (April 6): 24–25.

GUP, TED. 1991. "The Curse of Coal." *Time*. Vol. 138, No. 18 (November 4): 54–64.

GUPTA, GIRI RAJ. 1993. *Sociology of Mental Health*. Needham Heights, Mass.: Allyn & Bacon.

HACKER, HELEN MAYER. 1951. "Women as a Minority Group." *Social Forces*. Vol. 30, No. 1 (October): 60–69.

HACKLER, TIM. 1979. "The Big City Has No Corners on Mental Illness." *New York Times Magazine* (December 19): A1.

HADLEY, JANET. 1996. *Abortion: Between Freedom and Necessity*. Philadelphia: Temple University Press.

HAFNER-EATON, CHRIS. 1994. "When the Phoenix Rises, Where Will She Go? The Women's Health Agenda." In Pauline Vaillancourt Rosenau, ed., *Health Care Reform in the Nineties* (pp. 236–56). Thousand Oaks, Calif.: Sage.

HALBFINGER, DAVID M., and STEVEN A. HOLMES. 2003. "Military Mirrors Working-Class America." *New York Times on the Web* (March 30). [Online] Available September 8, 2003, at http://www.resrearchnavigator.com/content/nyt/2003/03/30/82.htm

HALLINAN, MAUREEN T., and RICHARD A. WILLIAMS. 1989. "Interracial Friendship Choices in Secondary Schools." *American Sociological Review*. Vol. 54, No. 1 (February): 67–78.

HAMER, DEAN, and PETER COPELAND. 1994. *The Search for the Gay Gene and the Biology of Behavior*. New York: Simon & Schuster.

HAMILTON, BRADLEY E., JOYCE A. MARTIN, and STEPHANIE J. VENTURA. 2007. "Births: Final Data for 2006." *National Vital Statistics Reports*. Vol. 56, No. 7 (January 7). [Online] Available April 16, 2009, at http://www.cdc.gov/nchs/data/nvsr/nvsr56/nvsr56_07.pdf

———. 2009. "Births: Preliminary Data for 2007." *National Vital Statistics Reports*. Vol. 57, No. 12 (March 18). [Online] Available July 23, 2009, at http://www.cdc.gov/nchs/data/nvsr/nvsr57/nvsr57_12.pdf

HANANEL, SAM. 2006. "Meth Still No. 1 Drug Problem, Study Finds." *Yahoo News*. [Online] Available July 18, 2006, at http://news.yahoo.com

HANEY, CRAIG, W. CURTIS BANKS, and PHILIP G. ZIMBARDO. 1973. "Interpersonal Dynamics in a Simulated Prison." *International Journal of Criminology and Penology*. Vol. 1, No. 1: 69–95.

HARRINGTON, MICHAEL. 1962. *The Other America: Poverty in the United States*. Baltimore: Penguin.

HARRIS, DAVID R., and JEREMIAH JOSEPH SIM. 2002. "Who Is Multiracial? Assessing the Complexity of Lived Race." *American Sociological Review*. Vol. 67, No. 4 (August): 614–27.

HARVARD UNIVERSITY. 2006. "The Civil Rights Project." [Online] Available January 11, 2007, at http://www.civilrightsproject.harvard.edu

HARVEY, DAVID. 1973. *Social Justice and the City.* Baltimore: Johns Hopkins University Press.

HAVINGHURST, ROBERT J., BERNICE L. NEUGARTEN, and SHELDON S. TOBIN. 1968. "Disengagement and Patterns of Aging." In Bernice L. Neugarten, ed., *Middle Age and Aging: A Reader in Social Psychology* (pp. 161–72). Chicago: University of Chicago Press.

HAWKINS, J. DAVID, DAVID P. FARRINGTON, and RICHARD F. CATALANO. 1998. "Reducing Violence through the Schools." In Delbert S. Elliott, Beatrix A. Hamburg, and Kirk R. Williams, eds., *Violence in American Schools: A New Perspective* (pp. 180–216). New York: Cambridge University Press.

HENDERSON, DAMIEN. 2003. "Cannabis Cafés Face Ban on Smoking." *Glasgow Herald* (May 29). [Online] Available September 4, 2003, at http://www.theherald.co.uk

HENLEY, NANCY, MYKOL HAMILTON, and BARRIE THORNE. 1992. "Womanspeak and Manspeak: Sex Differences in Communication, Verbal and Nonverbal." In John J. Macionis and Nijole V. Benokraitis, eds., *Seeing Ourselves: Classic, Contemporary, and Cross-Cultural Readings in Sociology,* 2nd ed. (pp. 10–15). Englewood Cliffs, N.J.: Prentice Hall.

HERDT, GILBERT H. 1993. "Semen Transactions in Sambian Culture." In David N. Suggs and Andrew W. Miracle, eds., *Culture and Human Sexuality* (pp. 298–327). Pacific Grove, Calif.: Brooks/Cole.

HEREK, GREGORY M. 1991. "Myths about Sexual Orientation: A Lawyer's Guide to Social Science Research." *Law and Sexuality.* Vol. 1: 133–72.

HERITAGE FOUNDATION. 2009. *Index of Economic Freedom.* [Online] Available June 21, 2009, at http://www.heritage.org/index/default.aspx

HERMAN, DIANNE F. 2001. "The Rape Culture." In John J. Macionis and Nijole V. Benokraitis, eds., *Seeing Ourselves: Classic, Contemporary, and Cross-Cultural Readings in Sociology,* 5th ed. (pp. 38–46). Upper Saddle River, N.J.: Prentice Hall.

HERMES, WILL. 2005. "Straight Out of Sudan: A Child Soldier Raps." *New York Times Online.* [Online] Available July 27, 2006, at http://www.researchnavigator.com

HERON, MELONIE P. 2007. "Deaths: Leading Causes for 2004." *National Vital Statistics Reports* (November 20). [Online] Available July 23, 2009, at http://www.cdc.gov/nchs/data/nvsr/nvsr56/nvsr56_05.pdf

HERON, MELONIE P., et al. 2008. "Deaths: Preliminary Data for 2006." *National Vital Statistics Reports.* Vol. 56, No. 16 (June 11). [Online] Available July 23, 2009, at http://www.cdc.gov/nchs/data/nvsr/nvsr56/nvsr56_16.pdf

———. 2009. "Deaths: Final Data for 2006." *National Vital Statistics Reports.* Vol. 57, No. 14 (April). [Online] Available July 23, 2009, at http://www.cdc.gov/nchs/data/nvsr/nvsr57/nvsr57_14.pdf

HERPERTZ, SABINE C., and HENNING SASS. 2000. "Emotional Deficiency and Psychopathy." *Behavioral Sciences and the Law.* Vol. 18, No. 5 (September–October): 567–80.

HERRNSON, PAUL S. 1998. "Parties and Interest Groups in Postreform Congressional Elections." In Allan J. Cigler and Burdett A. Loomis, eds., *Interest Group Politics,* 5th ed. (pp. 145–68). Washington, D.C.: CQ Press.

HERRNSTEIN, RICHARD J., and CHARLES MURRAY. 1994. *The Bell Curve: Intelligence and Class Structure in American Life.* New York: Free Press.

HEWLETT, SYLVIA ANN, and CORNEL WEST. 1998. *The War against Parents.* Boston: Houghton Mifflin.

HILL, JOHN. "2009. Wong a Regular at Store's Gun Counter." *USA Today* (April 6): 4A.

HILSMAN, ROGER. 1999. *From Nuclear Military Strategy to a World without War: A History and a Proposal.* Westport, Conn.: Praeger.

HIMES, CHRISTINE L. 2001. "Elderly Americans." *Population Bulletin.* Vol. 56, No. 4 (December).

HINGSON, RALPH, TIMOTHY HEEREN, MICHAEL WINTER, and HENRY WECHSLER. 2005. "Magnitude of Alcohol-Related Mortality and Morbidity among U.S. College Students Ages 18–24: Changes from 1998 to 2001." [Online] Available May 5, 2009, at http://www.collegedrinkingprevention.gov/NIAAACollegeMaterials/magandprev.aspx

HINRICHSEN, GREGORY A., N. A. HERNANDEZ, and S. POLLACK. 1992. "Difficulties and Rewards in Family Care of Depressed Older Adults." *Gerontologist.* Vol. 32, No. 4 (August): 486–92.

HIRSCHI, TRAVIS. 1969. *Causes of Delinquency.* Berkeley: University of California Press.

HIXON, ALLEN L. 1999. "Preventing Street Gang Violence." *American Family Physician.* Vol. 59, No. 8 (April 15): 2121–24.

HODKINSON, PAUL, and MARTIN BLOOMER. 2001. "Dropping Out of Further Education: Complex Causes and Simplistic Policy Assumptions." *Research Papers in Education.* Vol. 16, No. 2 (July): 117–41.

HOEFER, MICHAEL, NANCY RYTINA, and BRYAN C. BAKER. 2009. *Estimates of the Unauthorized Immigrant Population Residing in the United States, January 2008.* Washington, D.C.: Department of Homeland Security. [Online] Available March 31, 2009, at http://www.dhs.gov/xlibrary/assets/statistics/publications/ois_ill_pe_2008.pdf

HOFFMAN, BRUCE. 1998. *Inside Terrorism.* New York: Columbia University Press.

HOFFMAN, SAUL D. 2006. "Cost of Teen Childbearing." National Campaign to Prevent Teen and Unplanned Pregnancy. [Online] Available July 23, 2009, at http://www.thenationalcampaign.org/costs/default.aspx

HOGE, WARREN. 2002. "Britain to Stop Arresting Most Private Users of Marijuana." *New York Times* (July 11). [Online] Available September 4, 2003, at http://www.researchnavigator.com

HOLDEN, KAREN C., and PAMELA J. SMOCK. 1991. "The Economic Costs of Marital Dissolution: Why Do Women Bear a Disproportionate Cost?" *Annual Review of Sociology.* Vol. 17: 51–78.

HOLLINGSHEAD, AUGUST B., and FREDERICH C. REDLICH. 1958. *Social Class and Mental Illness: A Community Study.* New York: Wiley.

HOLMES, ELLEN RHOADS, and LOWELL D. HOLMES. 1995. *Other Cultures, Elder Years,* 2nd ed. Thousand Oaks, Calif.: Sage.

HOLMES, RONALD M., and STEPHEN T. HOLMES. 1993. *Murder in America.* Thousand Oaks, Calif.: Sage.

———. 1998. *Serial Murder,* 2nd ed. Thousand Oaks, Calif.: Sage.

HORWITZ, STEVEN. 2008. "Government Regulation, Not Free-Market Greed, Caused This Crisis." *Christian Science Monitor* (October 22). [Online] Available May 8, 2009, at http://www.csmonitor.com/2008/1022/p09s01-coop.html

HOYERT, DONNA L., MELONIE P. HERON, SHERRY L. MURPHY, and HSIANG-CHING KUNG. 2006. "Deaths: Final Data for 2003." *National Vital Statistics Reports.* Vol. 54, No. 13 (April 19). Hyattsville, Md.: National Center for Health Statistics.

HSIN, HONOR. 2003. "Episode II." *Harvard International Review.* Vol. 25, No. 3 (Fall): 15–16.

HUBER, CHRISTIAN. 1994. "Needle Park: What Can We Learn from the Zurich Experience?" *Addiction.* Vol. 89, No. 5 (May): 413–517.

HUDSON, KEN. 1999. *No Shortage of "Nonstandard" Jobs: Nearly 30% of Workers Employed in Part-Time, Temping, and Other Alternative Arrangements.* Economic Policy Institute Briefing Paper. [Online] Available December 10, 2000, at http://www.epinet.org/briefingpapers/hudson/hudson.html

HUDSON, MICHAEL C. 1992. "The Middle East under Pax Americana: How New, How Orderly?" *Third World Quarterly.* Vol. 13, No. 2 (February–March): 301–16.

HUFFMAN, MATT L., STEVEN C. VELASCO, and WILLIAM T. BIELBY. 1996. "Where Sex Composition Matters Most: Comparing the Effects of Job versus Occupational Sex Composition of Earnings." *Sociological Focus.* Vol. 29, No. 3 (August): 189–207.

HUGHES, MATTHEW. 1998. "The World Trade Center Bombing." In *Encyclopedia of World Terrorism.* Vol. 3 (pp. 540–41). Armonk, N.Y.: Sharpe.

HUNT, GEOFFREY, and ANNA XIAO DONG SUN. 1998. "The Drug Treatment System in the United States: A Panacea for the Drug War?" In Harold Klingemann and Geoffrey Hunt, eds., *Drug Treatment Systems in an International Perspective: Drugs, Demons, and Delinquents* (pp. 3–19). Thousand Oaks, Calif.: Sage.

IGNATIEV, NOEL. 1995. *How the Irish Became White.* New York: Routledge.

INCIARDI, JAMES A., ed. 1996. *Drug Control and the Courts.* Thousand Oaks, Calif.: Sage.

———. 2000. *Elements of Criminal Justice,* 2nd ed. New York: Oxford University Press.

INCIARDI, JAMES A., and DUANE C. MCBRIDE. 1991. "The Case against Legalization." In James A. Inciardi, ed., *The Drug Legalization Debate* (pp. 45–79). Thousand Oaks, Calif.: Sage.

INTERNAL REVENUE SERVICE. 2008. "SOI Tax Stats: Individual Statistical Tables by Tax Rate and Income Percentile." [Online] Available March 24, 2009, at http://www.irs.gov/taxstats/indtaxstats/article/0,,id=133521,00.html

INTERNATIONAL MONETARY FUND. 2000. *World Economic Outlook: Asset Prices and the Business Cycle* (May). [Online] Available October 9, 2004, at http://www.imf.org/external/pubs/ft/weo/2000/01/index.htm

———. 2007. *Data and Statistics.* [Online] Available June 21, 2009, at http://www.imf.org/external/data.htm

INTERNATIONAL PANEL ON CLIMATE CHANGE. 2007. *Climate Change, 2007.* New York: United Nations.

INTERNATIONAL TELECOMMUNICATION UNION. 2006. *World Telecommunication Development Report.* Data cited in World Bank, *2006 World Development Indicators.* Washington, D.C.: World Bank.

———. *ICT Database, 2007.* [Online] Available May 26, 2009 at http://www.itu.int/ITU-D/ICTEYE/indicators/indicators.aspx#

INTER-PARLIAMENTARY UNION. 2008. "Women in National Parliaments." [Online] Available December 28, 2008, at http://www.ipu.org/wmn-e/classif.htm and at http://www.ipu.org/wmn-e/world.htm

ISAY, RICHARD A. 1989. *Being Homosexual: Gay Men and Their Development.* New York: Farrar, Straus & Giroux.

JACKSON, SHERI, and SUE SCOTT, eds. 1996. *Feminism and Sexuality: A Reader.* New York: Columbia University Press.

JAGAROWSKY, PAUL A., and MARY JO BANE. 1990. *Neighborhood Poverty: Basic Questions.* Discussion Paper Series H-90-3. John F. Kennedy School of Government. Cambridge, Mass.: Harvard University Press.

JAGGER, ALISON. 1983. "Political Philosophies of Women's Liberation." In Laurel Richardson and Verta Taylor, eds., *Feminist Frontiers: Rethinking Sex, Gender, and Society.* Reading, Mass.: Addison-Wesley.

JANUS, CHRISTOPHER G. 1996. "Slavery Abolished? Only Officially." *Christian Science Monitor* (May 17): 18.

JENKINS, J. CRAIG. 2003. *Images of Terror: What We Can and Can't Know about Terrorism.* Hawthorne, N.Y.: Aldine de Gruyter.

JENKINS, J. CRAIG, and MICHAEL WALLACE. 1996. "The Generalized Action Potential of Protest Movements: The New Class, Social Trends, and Political Exclusion Explanations." *Sociological Forum.* Vol. 11, No. 2 (June): 183–207.

JENKINS, PHILIP. 1994. *Using Murder: The Social Construction of Serial Homicide.* Hawthorne, N.Y.: Aldine de Gruyter.

JENNESS, VALERIE. 1993. *Making It Work: The Prostitutes' Rights Movement in Perspective.* Hawthorne, N.Y.: Aldine de Gruyter.

JENNESS, VALERIE, and RYKEN GRATTET. 2001. *Making a Hate Crime: From Movement to Law Enforcement.* New York: Russell Sage Foundation.

JOHNSON, CATHRYN. 1994. "Gender, Legitimate Authority, and Leader-Subordinate Conversations." *American Sociological Review.* Vol. 59, No. 1 (February): 122–35.

Johnson, Jacqueline, Sharon Rush, and Joe R. Feagin. 2000. "Doing Anti-Racism: Toward an Egalitarian American Society." *Contemporary Sociology.* Vol. 29, No. 1 (January): 95–110.

Johnson, Kevin. 2000. "Serious Crime Down Again: 7% Dip in '99." *USA Today* (May 8): A1.

Johnson, Kirk, and Thomas L. Lueck. 1996. "Region's Economy in Fundamental Shift." *New York Times* (February 19): A1.

Johnston, David Cay. 2005. "Richest Are Leaving Even the Rich Far Behind." *New York Times* (June 5): 1, 27.

Johnston, L. D., P. M. O'Malley, J. G. Bachman, and J. E. Schulenberg. 2008. "Table 1. Trends in Lifetime Prevalence of Using Various Drugs in Grades 8, 10, and 12." *Monitoring the Future Study.* [Online] Available July 23, 2009, at http://www.monitoringthefuture.org/data/08data/pr08t1.pdf

Kadlec, Daniel. 2002. "Everyone, Back in the (Labor) Pool." *Time.* Vol. 160, No. 5 (July 29): 22–31.

Kadushin, Charles. 1983. "Mental Health and the Interpersonal Environment." *American Sociological Review.* Vol. 48, No. 2 (April): 188–98.

Kain, Edward L. 1990. *The Myth of Family Decline: Understanding Families in a World of Rapid Social Change.* Lexington, Mass.: Lexington Books.

Kaiser Family Foundation. 2009. "U.S. Federal Funding for HIV/AIDS: The FY 2010 Budget Request." [Online] Available May 14, 2009, at http://www.kff.org/hivaids/upload/7029-05.pdf

Kaldor, Mary. 1999. *New and Old Wars: Organized Violence in a Global Era.* Stanford, Calif.: Stanford University Press.

Kantor, Glenda Kaufman, and Jana L. Jasinski. 1998. "Dynamics and Risk Factors in Partner Violence." In Jana L. Jasinski and Linda M. Williams, eds., *Partner Violence: A Comprehensive Review of 20 Years of Research* (pp. 1–43). Thousand Oaks, Calif.: Sage.

Kantrowitz, Barbara, and Pat Wingert. 2001. "Unmarried with Children." *Newsweek* (May 28): 46–52.

———. 2003. "What's at Stake." *Newsweek* (January 27): 30–7.

Kaplan, David E., and Michael Schaffer. 2001. "Losing the Psywar." *U.S. News & World Report* (October 8): 46.

Karberg, Jennifer C., and Doris J. James. 2005. "Substance Dependence, Abuse, and Treatment of Jail Inmates, 2002." [Online] Available May 6, 2009, at http://www.ojp.usdoj.gov/bjs/pub/pdf/sdatji02.pdf

Karjane, Heather M., Bonnie S. Fisher, and Francis T. Cullen. 2005. "Sexual Assault on Campus: What Colleges and Universities Are Doing about It." [Online] Available December 8, 2008, at http://www.ncjrs.gov/pdffiles1/nij/205521.pdf

Katz, Michael B. 1990. *The Undeserving Poor: From the War on Poverty to the War on Welfare.* New York: Pantheon.

———. 1996. *In the Shadow of the Poorhouse.* New York: Basic Books.

Kaufman, Leslie. 2004. "Surge in Homeless Families Sets Off Debate on Cause." *New York Times* (June 29).

Kaufman, Walter. 1976. *Religions in Four Dimensions: Existential, Aesthetic, Historical, and Comparative.* Pleasantville, N.Y.: Reader's Digest Press.

Kaukas, Dick. 1999. "The Poor Struggle for Transplants." *Louisville Courier-Journal* (June 6): A1, A14.

Keister, Lisa A. 2000. *Wealth in America: Trends in Wealth Inequality.* Cambridge: Cambridge University Press.

———. 2003. "Religion and Wealth: The Role of Religious Affiliation and Participation in Early Adult Asset Accumulation." *Social Forces.* Vol. 82, No. 1 (September): 173–205.

Keister, Lisa A., and Stephanie Moller. 2000. "Wealth Inequality in the United States." *Annual Review of Sociology.* Vol. 26: 63–81.

Kelly, Kate. 2001. "Lost on the Campus." *Time.* Vol. 157, No. 2 (January 15): 51–53.

Kemp, Jack. 1994. "A Cultural Renaissance." *Imprimis.* Vol. 23, No. 8 (August): 1–5.

Kempe, C. Henry, et al. 1962. "The Battered Child Syndrome." *Journal of the American Medical Association.* Vol. 181 (July 7): 17–24.

Kentor, Jeffrey. 1998. "The Long-Term Effects of Foreign Investment Dependence on Economic Growth, 1940–1990." *American Journal of Sociology.* Vol. 103, No. 4 (January): 1024–46.

———. 2001. "The Long-Term Effects of Globalization on Income Inequality, Population Growth, and Economic Development." *Social Problems.* Vol. 48, No. 4 (November): 435–55.

Kessler, Ronald C., et al. 1994. "Lifetime and 12-Month Prevalence of DSM-III-R Psychiatric Disorders in the United States: Results from the National Comorbidity Survey." *Archives of General Psychiatry.* Vol. 51, No. 1 (January): 8–19.

Kilgore, Sally B. 1991. "The Organizational Context of Tracking in Schools." *American Sociological Review.* Vol. 56, No. 2 (April): 189–203.

Kinkead, Gwen. 1992. *Chinatown: A Portrait of a Closed Society.* New York: HarperCollins.

Kinsey, Alfred, Wardell Baxter Pomeroy, and Clyde E. Martin. 1948. *Sexual Behavior in the Human Male.* Philadelphia: Saunders.

Kinsey, Alfred, Wardell Baxter Pomeroy, Clyde E. Martin, and Paul H. Gebhard. 1953. *Sexual Behavior in the Human Female.* Philadelphia: Saunders.

Kirn, Walter. 1998. "Crank." *Time.* Vol. 153, No. 24 (June 22): 25–32.

Kitman, Jamie. 2003. "Tort Reform for Dummies." *Automobile* (April): 145.

Kivant, Barbara. 2008. "Reassessing Risk." *Time* (November 17): Global 1–4.

Klein, Philip. 2009. "Obama's Big Government Gamble." *American Spectator* (April 15). [Online] Available May 5, 2009, at http://spectator.org/blog/2009/04/15/obamas-big-government-gamble

Kleinman, Arthur. 1997. "Intimations of Solidarity? The Popular Culture Responds to Assisted Suicide." *Hastings Center Report* (September–October): 34–36.

Kluger, Jeffrey. 2001. "A Climate of Despair." *Time.* Vol. 157, No. 14 (April 9): 30–36.

———. 2006. "The Tipping Point." *Time.* Vol. 167, No. 14 (April 3): 34–42.

Knight, Robert H. 1998. "How Domestic Partnerships and 'Gay Marriage' Threaten the Family." In Robert T. Francoeur and William J. Taverner, eds., *Taking Sides: Clashing Views on Controversial Issues in Human Sexuality,* 6th ed. (pp. 196–206). New York: Dushkin/McGraw-Hill.

Kohut, Andrew. 2008. "Post-Election Perspectives." Pew Research Center for the People and the Press (November 13). [Online] Available July 23, 2009, at http://pewresearch.org/pubs/1039/post-election-perspectives

Kontos, Pia C. 1998. "Resisting Institutionalization: Constructing Old Age and Negotiating Home." *Journal of Aging Studies.* Vol. 12, No. 2 (Summer): 167–84.

Koontz, Stephanie. 1992. *The Way We Never Were: American Families and the Nostalgia Trap.* New York: Basic Books.

Kosterlitz, Julie. 1997. "When We're 64." *National Journal.* Vol. 29, No. 39 (September 27): 1882–85.

Kotz, Deborah. 2008. "Sex, Health, and Happiness." *U.S. News & World Report* (September 15): 50–53.

Kozol, Jonathan. 1988. *Rachel and Her Children: Homeless Families in America.* New York: Fawcett Columbine.

———. 1991. *Savage Inequalities: Children in America's Schools.* New York: Crown.

———. 2005. *The Shame of the Nation: The Restoration of Apartheid Schooling in America.* New York: Crown.

———. 2007. *Letters to a Young Teacher.* New York: Crown.

Krauthammer, Charles. 1995. "A Social Conservative Credo." *Public Interest.* Vol. 121 (Fall): 15–22.

Kroll, Luisa, ed. 2008. "Special Report: The World's Billionaires." *Forbes* (March 5). [Online] Available November 21, 2008, at http://www.forbes.com/2008/03/05/richest-people-billionaires-billionaires08-cx_lk_0305billie_land.html

Kroll, Luisa, Matthew Miller, and Tatiana Serafin. 2009. *Forbes Special Report: The World's Billionaires.* [Online] Available March 11, 2009, at http://www.forbes.com/2009/03/11/worlds-richest-people-billionaires-2009-billionaires_land.html

Kromar, Marina, and Patti M. Valkenburg. 1999. "A Scale to Assess Children's Moral Interpretations of Justified and Unjustified Violence and Its Relationship to Television Viewing." *Communication Research.* Vol. 26, No. 5 (October): 608–35.

Krysan, Maria. 2002. "Community Undesirability in Black and White: Examining Racial Residential Preferences through Community Perceptions." *Social Problems.* Vol. 49, No. 4 (November): 521–43.

Kugler, Jacek, and A. F. K. Organski. 1989. "The Power Transition: A Retrospective and Prospective Evaluation." In Manus I. Midlarskky, ed., *Handbook of War Studies* (pp. 171–94). Boston: Unwin Hyman.

Kunstler, James Howard. 1996. "Home from Nowhere." *Atlantic Monthly.* Vol. 278 (September): 43–66.

Kutty, Nandinee K. 1998. "The Scope for Poverty Alleviation among Elderly Home-Owners in the United States through Reverse Mortgages." *Urban Studies.* Vol. 35, No. 1 (January): 113–30.

Labaton, Stephen. 2000. "You Don't Have to Be Old to Sue for Age Discrimination." *New York Times* (February 16): A7.

Lacey, Marc. 2008. "A Distinct Lifestyle: The Muxe of Mexico." *New York Times* (December 7), p. 4.

LaFree, Gary. 1998. *Losing Legitimacy: Street Crime and the Decline of Social Institutions in America.* Boulder, Colo.: Westview Press.

Langbein, Laura, and Roseana Bess. 2002. "Sports in School: Source of Amity or Antipathy?" *Social Science Quarterly.* Vol. 83, No. 2 (June): 436–54.

Lappé, Frances Moore, and Joseph Collins. 1986. *World Hunger: Twelve Myths.* New York: Grove Press/Food First Books.

Lappé, Frances Moore, Joseph Collins, and David Kinley. 1981. *Aid as Obstacle: Twenty Questions about Our Foreign Policy and the Hungry.* San Francisco: Institute for Food and Development Policy.

Laumann, Edward O., John H. Gagnon, Robert T. Michaels, and Stuart Michaels. 1994. *The Social Organization of Sexuality: Sexual Practices in the United States.* Chicago: University of Chicago Press.

Lavella, Marianna. 2002. "Payback Time." *U.S. News & World Report.* Vol. 132, No. 7 (March 11): 36–40.

Leach, Colin Wayne. 2002. "Democracy's Dilemma: Explaining Racial Inequality in Egalitarian Societies." *Sociological Forum.* Vol. 17, No. 4 (December): 681–96.

Lee, Deborah. 2000. "Hegemonic Masculinity and Male Feminisation: The Sexual Harassment of Men at Work." *Journal of Gender Studies.* Vol. 9, No. 2 (July): 141–55.

Lee, Felicia R. 2002. "Long Buried, Death Goes Public Again." *New York Times Online.* [Online] Available November 2, 2002, at http://www.researchnavigator.com

Leff, Lisa. 2008. "California Gay Marriage Vote Still Undecided." *Yahoo News* (November 5). [Online] Available November 5, 2008, at http://news.yahoo.com/s/ap/20081105/ap_on_el_ge/ballot_measures

Leinwand, Donna. 2001. "A Strange New World of Teenage Drug Use." *USA Today* (August 28): 6D, 7D.

Lemert, Edwin M. 1951. *Social Pathology.* New York: McGraw-Hill.

———. 1972. *Human Deviance, Social Problems, and Social Control,* 2nd ed. Englewood Cliffs, N.J.: Prentice Hall.

LEMONICK, MICHAEL D. 2003. "The Search for a Murder Gene." *Time.* Vol. 164, No. 3 (January 20): 100.

LENGERMANN, PATRICIA MADOO, and RUTH A. WALLACE. 1985. *Gender in America: Social Control and Social Change.* Englewood Cliffs, N.J.: Prentice Hall.

LÉONS, MADELINE BARBARA, and HARRY SANABRIA. 1997. "Coca and Cocaine in Bolivia: Reality and Policy Illusion." In Madeline Barbara Léons and Harry Sanabria, eds., *Coca, Cocaine, and the Bolivian Reality* (pp. 1–46). Albany: State University of New York Press.

LEOPOLD, EVELYN. 2007. "Sudan's Young Endure 'Unspeakable' Abuse: Report." [Online] Available April 19, 2007, at http://www.news.yahoo.com

LEPRO, SARA. 2009. "Cuomo Says 15 AIG Execs Agree to Return Bonuses." *Yahoo News* (March 23). [Online] Available March 23, 2009, at http://news.yahoo.com/s/ap/aig_bonuses

LERNER, SHARON. 1999. "Insurers Shortchange Bulimics and Anorexics." *Village Voice.* Vol. 44, No. 15 (April 20): 25.

LEVAY, SIMON. 1993. *The Sexual Brain.* Cambridge, Mass.: MIT Press.

LEVIN, ALAN, THOMAS FRANK, and PAUL OVERBERG. 2006. "Mine Had Hundreds of Violations." *USA Today* (January 4). [Online] Available July 27, 2009, at http://www.usatoday.com/news/nation/2006-01-04-mine-violations_x.htm

LEVINE, SAMANTHA. 2003. "Playing God in Illinois." *U.S. News & World Report.* Vol. 134, No. 1 (January 13): 13.

LEVINSON, F. JAMES, and LUCY BASSETT. 2007. "Malnutrition Is Still a Major Contributor to Child Deaths." [Online] Available December 4, 2008, at http://www.prb.org/pdf07/Nutrition2007.pdf

LEVY, LEO, and LOUIS ROWITZ. 1973. *The Ecology of Mental Disorders.* New York: Behavioral Publications.

LEWIN, TAMAR. 2000. "Now a Majority: Families with Two Parents Who Work." *New York Times* (October 24): A20.

———. 2008. "Girls' Gains Have Not Cost Boys, Report Says." *New York Times* (May 20). [Online] Available December 7, 2008, at http://www.nytimes.com/2008/05/20/education/20girls.html?partner=permalink&exprod=permalink

LEWIS, OSCAR. 1961. *The Children of Sanchez.* New York: Random House.

———. 1966. *La Vida.* New York: Random House.

LIAZOS, ALEXANDER. 1982. *People First: An Introduction to Social Problems.* Needham Heights, Mass.: Allyn & Bacon.

LICHTER, DANIEL T., and MARTHA L. CROWLEY. 2002. "Poverty in America: Beyond Welfare Reform." *Population Bulletin.* Vol. 57, No. 2 (June): 3–34.

LICHTER, DANIEL T., and RUKMALIE JAYAKODY. 2002. "Welfare Reform: How Do We Measure Success?" *Annual Review of Sociology.* Vol. 28: 117–41.

LINDSAY, LINDA. 1994. *Gender Roles,* 2nd ed. Englewood Cliffs, N.J.: Prentice Hall.

LINO, MARK. 2008. *Expenditures on Children by Families, 2007.* U.S. Department of Agriculture, Center for Nutrition Policy and Promotion. Washington, D.C.: U.S. Government Printing Office.

LIPSET, SEYMOUR M. 1994. "The Social Requisites of Democracy Revisited: Presidential Address." *American Sociological Review.* Vol. 59, No. 1 (February): 1–22.

LITTLE, CRAIG, and ANDREA RANKIN. 2001. "Why Do They Start It? Explaining Reported Early-Teen Sexual Activity." *Sociological Forum.* Vol. 16, No. 4 (December): 703–29.

LITTLEJOHN-BLAKE, SHEILA M., and CAROL ANDERSON DARLING. 1993. "Understanding the Strengths of African American Families." *Journal of Black Studies.* Vol. 23, No. 2 (June): 460–71.

LIVINGSTON, KEN. 1999. "Politics and Mental Illness." *Public Interest.* Vol. 143 (Winter): 105–09.

LOFTUS, JENI. 2001. "America's Liberalization in Attitudes toward Homosexuality, 1973 to 1998." *American Sociological Review.* Vol. 66, No. 5 (October): 762–82.

LOGAN, JOHN, and HARVEY MOLOTCH. 1987. *Urban Fortunes: The Political Economy of Place.* Berkeley: University of California Press.

LOMBROSO, CESARE. 1911 (orig. 1876). *Crime: Its Causes and Remedies,* trans. H. P. Horton. Boston: Little, Brown.

LOPEZ, MARK HUGO, and PAUL TAYLOR. 2009. "Dissecting the 2008 Electorate: Most Diverse in U.S. History." Pew Research Center (April 30). [Online] Available May 22, 2009, at http://pewhispanic.org/files/reports/108.pdf

LORD, MARY. 2001. "Good Teachers the Newest Imports." *U.S. News & World Report.* Vol. 130, No. 13 (April 9): 54.

———. 2002. "A Battle for Children's Futures." *U.S. News & World Report.* Vol. 132, No. 6 (March 4): 35–36.

LORENZ, KONRAD. 1966. *On Aggression.* New York: Harcourt Brace.

———. 1981. *The Foundations of Ethology.* New York: Springer-Verlag.

LOSCALZO, JIM. 2006. "A Line in the Sand." *U.S. News & World Report.* Vol. 140, No. 10 (March 20): 40–45.

LOTT, JOHN R., JR. 2000. *More Guns, Less Crime: Understanding Crime and Gun Control Laws,* 2nd ed. Chicago: University of Chicago Press.

LOVELESS, TOM. 1999. "Will Tracking Reform Promote Social Equity?" *Educational Leadership.* Vol. 56, No. 7 (April): 28–32.

LOWNEY, KATHLEEN S., and JOEL BEST. 1995. "Stalking Strangers and Lovers: Changing Media Typifications of a New Crime Problem." In Joel Best, ed., *Images of Issues: Typifying Contemporary Social Problems,* 2nd ed. (pp. 33–57). Hawthorne, N.Y.: Aldine de Gruyter.

LUKAS, J. ANTHONY. 1997. *Big Trouble.* New York: Simon & Schuster.

LUKER, KRISTEN. 1984. *Abortion and the Politics of Motherhood.* Berkeley: University of California Press.

LUND, DALE A. 1989. "Conclusions about Bereavement in Later Life and Implications for Interventions and Future Research." In Dale A. Lund, ed., *Older Bereaved Spouses: Research with Practical Applications* (pp. 217–31). London: Taylor & Francis/Hemisphere.

———. 1993. "Caregiving." In *Encyclopedia of Adult Development* (pp. 57–63). Phoenix, Ariz.: Oryx Press.

MACCOBY, ELEANOR EMMONS, and CAROL NAGY JACKLIN. 1974. *The Psychology of Sex Differences.* Stanford, Calif.: Stanford University Press.

MACCOUN, ROBERT J. 2001. "American Distortion of Dutch Drug Statistics." *Society.* Vol. 38, No. 3 (March-April): 23–26.

MACIONIS, JOHN J. 1978. "Intimacy: Structure and Process in Interpersonal Relationships." *Alternative Lifestyles.* Vol. 1, No. 1 (February): 113–30.

———. 2001. "Welcome to Cyber-Society." In John J. Macionis and Nijole V. Benokraitis, eds., *Seeing Ourselves: Classic, Contemporary, and Cross-Cultural Readings in Sociology,* 5th ed. (pp. 62–67). Upper Saddle River, N.J.: Prentice Hall.

MACIONIS, JOHN J., and LINDA GERBER. 2008. *Sociology.* 6th Canadian ed. Scarborough, Ontario: Prentice Hall Allyn & Bacon Canada.

MACIONIS, JOHN J., and VINCENT J. PARRILLO. 2010. *Cities and Urban Life,* 5th ed. Upper Saddle River, N.J.: Pearson Prentice Hall.

MACKINNON, CATHARINE A. 2001. "Pornography: Not a Moral Issue." In John J. Macionis and Nijole V. Benokraitis, eds., *Seeing Ourselves: Classic, Contemporary, and Cross-Cultural Readings in Sociology,* 5th ed. (pp. 294–301). Upper Saddle River, N.J.: Prentice Hall.

MALTHUS, THOMAS ROBERT. 1926 (orig. 1798). *First Essay on Population 1798.* London: Macmillan.

MANCALL, PETER C. 1995. *Deadly Medicine: Indians and Alcohol in Early America.* Ithaca, N.Y.: Cornell University Press.

MANHEIMER, RONALD J., ed. 1994. *Older Americans Almanac: A Reference Work on Seniors in the United States.* Detroit: Gale Research.

MARQUEZ, LAURA. 2006. "Nursing Shortage: How It May Affect You." *ABC News* (January 21). [Online] Available April 1, 2008, at http://abcnews.go.com/WNT/Health/story?id=1529546

MARSHALL, JIM. 2009. "AIG Bonus Payments $218 million." Reuters (March 21). [Online] Available March 21, 2009, at http://www.reuters.com/article/newsOne/idUSTRE52K19L20090321

MARTIN, DEANNA. 2009. "Mayor to Indiana Governor: Send Stimulus Cash Fast." MSNBC (March 19). [Online] Available March 22, 2009, at http://www.msnbc.msn.com/id/29771876

MARTIN, DOUGLAS. 1997. "The Medicine Woman of the Mohegans." *New York Times* (June 4): B1, B7.

MARTIN, JOYCE A., et al. 2009. "Births: Final Data for 2007." *National Vital Statistics Reports.* Vol. 57, No. 7 (January 7) [Online] Available May 17, 2009, at http://www.cdc.gov/nchs/data/nvsr/nvsr57/nvsr57_07.pdf

MARTIN, PHILIP, and ELIZABETH MIDGLEY. 2003. "Immigration: Shaping and Reshaping America." *Population Bulletin.* Vol. 58, No. 2 (June). Washington, D.C.: Population Reference Bureau.

MARULLO, SAM. 1987. "The Functions and Dysfunctions of Preparations for Fighting Nuclear War." *Sociological Focus.* Vol. 20, No. 2 (April): 135–53.

MARX, KARL. 1964 (orig. 1844). *Economic and Philosophic Manuscripts of 1844.* New York: International Publishers.

———. 1985 (orig. 1847). "The Communist Manifesto." In David McClellan, ed., *Karl Marx: Selected Writings* (pp. 221–47). New York: Oxford University Press.

MARX, KARL, and FRIEDRICH ENGELS. 1959 (orig. 1893). *Marx and Engels: Basic Writings on Politics and Philosophy,* ed. Lewis S. Feurer. Garden City, N.Y.: Anchor.

MASSEY, DOUGLAS S., and NANCY A. DENTON. 1988. "Suburbanization and Segregation in U.S. Metropolitan Areas." *American Journal of Sociology.* Vol. 94, No. 3 (November): 592–626.

———. 1989. "Hypersegregation in U.S. Metropolitan Areas: Black and Hispanic Segregation along Five Dimensions." *Demography.* Vol. 26, No. 3 (August): 373–91.

MATTHIESSEN, PETER. 1984. *Indian Country.* New York: Viking.

MAUER, MARC. 1999. *The Crisis of the Young African American Male and the Criminal Justice System.* Report prepared for U.S. Commission on Civil Rights, Washington, D.C., April 15–16. [Online] Available January 8, 2007, at http://www.sentencingproject.org/Admin/Documents/publications/rd_crisisoftheyoung.pdf

MAURO, TONY. 1997. "Ruling Likely to Add Fuel to Already Divisive Debate." *USA Today* (January 7): 1A, 2A.

MAUSS, ARMAND L. 1975. *Social Problems of Social Movements.* Philadelphia: Lippincott.

MCCABE, JAMES D., JR. 1970 (orig. 1872). *Lights and Shadows of New York Life.* New York: Farrar, Straus & Giroux.

MCCLELLAN, DAVID. 1985. *Karl Marx: Selected Writings.* New York: Oxford University Press.

MCDOWELL, MARGARET A., CHERYL D. FRYAR, CYNTHIA L. OGDEN, and KATHERINE M. FLEGAL. 2008. "Anthropometric Reference Data for Children and Adults: United States, 2003–2006." [Online] Available July 24, 2009, at http://www.cdc.gov/nchs/data/nhsr/nhsr010.pdf

MCGEEHAN, PATRICK. 2009. "Adding to Recession's Pain, Thousands to Lose Job Benefits." *New York Times* (January 11). [Online] Available January 12, 2009, at http://www.nytimes.com/2009/01/12/nyregion/12benefits.html.

MCLANAHAN, SARA. 2002. "Life without Father: What Happens to the Children?" *Contexts.* Vol. 1, No. 1 (Spring): 35–44.

MCLAREN, PETER L., and JAMES M. GIARELLI, eds. 1995. *Critical Theory and Educational Research.* Albany: State University of New York Press.

MCNEAL, RALPH B., JR. 1999. "Parental Involvement as Social Capital: Differential Effectiveness on Science Achievement, Truancy, and Dropping Out." *Social Forces.* Vol. 78, No. 1 (October): 117–44.

MEADOWS, DONELLA H., DENNIS L. MEADOWS, JORGEN RANDERS, and WILLIAM W. BEHRENS III. 1972. *The Limits to Growth: A Report on the Club of Rome's Project on the Predicament of Mankind*. New York: Universe.

MEADOWS, DONELLA H., JORGEN RANDERS, and DENNIS L. MEADOWS. 2004. *Limits to Growth: The 30-Year Update*. White River Junction, Vt.: Chelsea Green.

MEDINA, JOHN J. 1996. *The Clock of Ages: Why We Age, How We Age, Winding Back the Clock*. Cambridge: Cambridge University Press.

MERRITT HAWKINS AND ASSOCIATES. 2009. *2008 Review of Physician and CRNA Recruiting Incentives*. [Online] Available February 6, 2009, at http://www.merrit-thawkins.com/pdf/mha-2008-incentive-survey.pdf

MERTON, ROBERT K. 1938. "Social Structure and Anomie." *American Sociological Review*. Vol. 3, No. 6 (October): 672–82.

———. 1968. *Social Theory and Social Structure*. New York: Free Press.

MEYER, JOSH. 2009. "Obama Administration Urges Equal Penalties for Crack, Powder Cocaine Dealers." *Los Angeles Times* (April 30). [Online] Available May 3, 2009, at http://www.latimes.com/news/nationworld/nation/la-na-crack30-2009 apr30,0,2194990.story

MILBRATH, LESTER W. 1989. *Envisioning a Sustainable Society: Learning Our Way Out*. Albany: State University of New York Press.

MILKMAN, HARVEY, and STANLEY SUNDERWIRTH. 1995. "Doorway to Excess." In James A. Inciardi and Karen McElrath, eds., *The American Drug Scene: An Anthology* (pp. 12–22). Los Angeles: Roxbury.

MILLER, MATTHEW, and DUNCAN GREENBERG. 2008. "The Forbes 400." *Forbes* (September 17). [Online] Available March 24, 2009, at http://www.forbes.com/lists/2008/54/400list08_The-400-Richest-Americans_Rank.html

MILLER, TERRY, and KIM HOLMES, eds. 2009. *15th Annual Index of Economic Freedom*. [Online] Available May 24, 2009, at http://www.heritage.org/index/Default.aspx

MILLER, WILLIAM J., and RICK A. MATTHEWS. 2001. "Youth Employment, Differential Association, and Juvenile Delinquency." *Sociological Focus*. Vol. 34, No. 3 (August): 251–68.

MILLET, KATE. 1970. *Sexual Politics*. Garden City, N.Y.: Doubleday.

MILLS, C. WRIGHT. 1956. *The Power Elite*. New York: Oxford University Press.

———. 1959. *The Sociological Imagination*. New York: Oxford University Press.

MINE SAFETY AND HEALTH ADMINISTRATION. 2006. "Fatality Information." [Online] Available July 21, 2009, at http://www.msha.gov

MINIÑO, ARIALDI M., MELONIE P. HERON, and BETTY L. SMITH. 2006. "Deaths: Preliminary Data for 2004." *National Vital Statistics Reports*. Vol. 54, No. 19 (June 28). Hyattsville, Md.: National Center for Health Statistics.

MINISTRY OF HEALTH, WELFARE AND SPORT. 1998. "Policy on Soft Drugs and Coffee Shops." *Drug Policy in the Netherlands: Continuity and Change*. [Online] Available May 10, 1999, at http://www.thc.nl/Countries/nl/VWSdrugs.htm

MIRACLE, TINA S., ANDREW W. MIRACLE, and ROY F. BAUMEISTER. 2003. *Human Sexuality: Meeting Your Basic Needs*. Upper Saddle River, N.J.: Prentice Hall.

MIROWSKY, JOHN, and CATHERINE ROSS. 1983. "Paranoia and the Structure of Powerlessness." *American Sociological Review*. Vol. 48, No. 2 (April): 228–39.

MOAKLEY, TERRY. 1999. "The Thanks of a Grateful Nation? The Numbers Don't Lie When It Comes to VA Shortfalls." *WE Magazine*. Vol. 3, No. 5 (September–October): 106.

MOGHADAM, VALENTINE M. 2005. "The 'Feminization of Poverty' and Women's Human Rights." [Online] Available December 4, 2008, at http://portal.unesco.org/shs/en/files/8282/11313736811Feminization_of_Poverty.pdf/Feminization%2Bof%2BPoverty.pdf

MONTAGU, ASHLEY. 1976. *The Nature of Human Aggression*. New York: Oxford University Press.

MONTO, MARTIN. 2001. "Prostitution and Fellatio." *Journal of Sex Research*. Vol. 38, No. 2 (May): 140–46.

MOORE, STEPHEN, and LINCOLN ANDERSON. 2005. "Great American Dream Machine." *Wall Street Journal* (December 21): A18.

MOORE, WILBERT E. 1977. "Modernization as Rationalization: Processes and Restraints." In Manning Nash, ed., *Essays on Economic Development and Cultural Change in Honor of Bert F. Hoselitz* (pp. 29–42). Chicago: University of Chicago Press.

———. 1979. *World Modernization: The Limits of Convergence*. New York: Elsevier.

MORRIS, DAVID C. 1997. "Older Adults' Perceptions of Dr. Kevorkian in Middletown, U.S.A." *Omega*. Vol. 35, No. 4: 405–12.

MORSE, JODIE. 2002. "Learning while Black." *Time*. Vol. 159, No. 21 (May 27): 50–52.

MOUW, TED. 2000. "Job Relocation and the Racial Gap in Unemployment in Detroit and Chicago, 1980 to 1990." *American Sociological Review*. Vol. 65, No. 5 (October): 730–53.

MOYNIHAN, DANIEL PATRICK. 1993. "Toward a New Intolerance." *Public Interest*. No. 112 (Summer): 119–22.

MUNSON, MARTHA L., and PAUL D. SUTTON. "Births, Marriages, Divorces, and Deaths: Provisional Data for 2005." *National Vital Statistics Reports*. Vol. 54, No. 20 (July 21). Hyattsville, Md.: National Center for Health Statistics.

MURDOCK, GEORGE PETER. 1949. *Social Structure*. New York: Free Press.

MURRAY, CHARLES. 1984. *Losing Ground: American Social Policy, 1950–1980*. New York: Basic Books.

MURRAY, HARRY. 2000. "Deniable Degradation: The Finger-Imaging of Welfare Recipients." *Sociological Forum*. Vol. 15, No. 1 (March): 39–63.

MYERHOFF, BARBARA. 1979. *Number Our Days*. New York: Dutton.

MYERS, DAVID G. 2000. *The American Paradox: Spiritual Hunger in an Age of Plenty*. New Haven, Conn.: Yale University Press.

———. 2001. *Psychology*, 6th ed. New York: Worth.

MYERS, NORMAN. 1991. "Biological Diversity and Global Security." In F. Herbert Bormann and Stephen R. Kellert, eds., *Ecology, Economics, and Ethics: The Broken Circle* (pp. 11–25). New Haven, Conn.: Yale University Press.

NADELMANN, ETHAN. 1995. "Switzerland's Heroin Experiment." *National Review*. Vol. 47, No. 13 (July 19): 46–47.

NAGEL, JOANE. 1996. *American Indian Ethnic Renewal: Red Power and the Resurgence of Identity and Culture*. New York: Oxford University Press.

NATIONAL CENTER FOR EDUCATION STATISTICS. 2006. "2005 Tables." *Digest of Education Statistics*. [Online] Available December 17, 2006, at http://nces.ed.gov/programs/digest/d05_tf.asp

———.2008. "2007 Tables." *Digest of Education Statistics*. [Online] Available May 12, 2008, at http://nces.ed.gov/programs/digest/d07/tables_1.asp

NATIONAL CENTER FOR HEALTH STATISTICS. 2005a. "Divorce Rates by State, 1990, 1995, and 1999–2004." [Online] Available January 10, 2007, at http://www.cdc.gov/nchs/data/nvss/divorce90_04.pdf

———. 2005b. "Prevalence of Overweight and Obesity among Adults: United States, 2003–2004." [Online] Available January 9, 2007, at http://www.cdc.gov/nchs/products/pubs/pubd/hestats/obese03_04/overwght_adult_03.htm

———. 2007. *Health, United States, 2007, with Chartbook on Trends in the Health of Americans*. [Online] Available January 8, 2009, at http://www.cdc.gov/nchs/data/hus/hus07.pdf

NATIONAL CENTER ON ELDER ABUSE. 2006a. "Elder Abuse Prevalence and Incidence." [Online] Available January 8, 2007, at http://www.elderabusecenter.org/pdf/publication/FinalStatistics050331.pdf

———. 2006b. *Fact Sheet: Abuse of Adults Aged 60+: 2004 Survey of Adult Protective Services*. [Online] Available April 7, 2009, at http://www.ncea.aoa.gov/NCEAroot/Main_Site/pdf/2-14-06%2060FACT%20SHEET.pdf

NATIONAL COALITION FOR HOMELESS VETERANS. 2009. *Background and Statistics*. [Online] Available June 20, 2009, at http://www.nchv.org/background.cfm

NATIONAL COALITION FOR THE HOMELESS. 2007. "How Many People Experience Homelessness?" NCH Fact Sheet No. 2 (August). [Online] Available April 30, 2008, at http://www.nationalhomeless.org/publications/facts/How_Many.pdf

NATIONAL COALITION OF ANTI-VIOLENCE PROGRAMS. *Annual Report, 2007*. 2008. [Online] Available November 12, 2008, at http://www.ncavp.org/issues/Bias.aspx

NATIONAL CONFERENCE OF STATE LEGISLATURES. 2008. "Marriages." [Online] Available January 29, 2009, at http://www.census.gov/compendia/statab/cats/social_insurance_human_services/child_support_head_start_child_care.html

NATIONAL COUNCIL ON ALCOHOLISM AND DRUG DEPENDENCE. 2009. "Alcoholism and Drug Dependence Are America's Number One Health Problem." [Online] Available May 5, 2009, at http://www.ncadd.org/facts/numberoneprob.html

NATIONAL EDUCATION ASSOCIATION. 2008. *Rankings and Estimates: Rankings of the States, 2008, and Estimates of School Statistics, 2009*. [Online] Available June 1, 2009, at http://www.nea.org/assets/docs/09rankings.pdf

NATIONAL HIGHWAY TRAFFIC SAFETY ADMINISTRATION. 2008. *2007 Traffic Safety Annual Assessment: Alcohol-Impaired Driving Fatalities*. [Online] Available February 17, 2009, at http://www-nrd.nhtsa.dot.gov/Pubs/811016.pdf

NATIONAL INSTITUTE OF MENTAL HEALTH. 2007. "Science Update: Global Use of ADHD Medications Rises Dramatically." [Online] Available May 5, 2009, at http://www.nimh.nih.gov/science-news/2007/global-use-of-adhd-medication-srises-dramatically.shtml

———. 2008. "Eating Disorders." [Online] Available February 5, 2009, at http://www.nimh.nih.gov/health/publications/eating-disorders/completepublication.shtml

NAVARRO, MIREYA. 2000. "Puerto Rican Presence Wanes in New York." *New York Times* (February 28): A1, A20.

NEUGARTEN, BERNICE L. 1996. "Retirement in the Life Course." In Dale A. Neugarten, ed., *The Meanings of Age: Selected Papers of Bernice L. Neugarten* (pp. 221–37). Chicago: University of Chicago Press.

NEWMAN, OSCAR. 1972. *Defensible Space: Crime Prevention through Urban Design*. New York: Macmillan.

NEWMAN, RICHARD J. 2002. "Hunters and Hunted." *U.S. News & World Report*. Vol. 132, No. 2 (January 21): 30.

NIGHTENGALE, BOB. 2007. "Some of Sport's Top Stars Implicated." *USA Today* (December 14): 1A.

NOCK, STEVEN L., JAMES D. WRIGHT, and LAURA SANCHEZ. 1999. "America's Divorce Problem." *Society*. Vol. 36, No. 4 (May-June): 43–52.

NORC. 2005. *General Social Surveys, 1972–2004: Cumulative Codebook*. Chicago: National Opinion Research Center.

———. 2007. *General Social Surveys, 1972–2006: Cumulative Codebook*. Chicago: National Opinion Research Center. [Online] Available March 19, 2008, at http://publicdata.norc.org/41000/gss/Documents/Codebook/FINAL%202006%20CODEBOOK.pdf

———. 2008. *General Social Surveys, 1972–2006: Cumulative Codebook* (summer update). [Online] Available November 8, 2008, at http://publicdata.norc.org

NORD, MARK, MARGARET ANDREWS, and STEVEN CARLSON. 2002. *Household Food Security in the United States, 2001*. Washington, D.C.: Economic Research Service, U.S. Department of Agriculture.

NORTON, ELEANOR HOLMES. 1985. "Restoring the Traditional Black Family." *New York Times Magazine* (June 2): 43–98.

NOVAK, VIVECA. 1999. "The Cost of Poor Advice." *Time*. Vol. 154, No. 1 (July 5): 38.

OAKES, JEANNIE. 1985. *Keeping Track: How Schools Structure Inequality*. New Haven, Conn.: Yale University Press.

OCHOA, RACHEL. 1999. "Bilingual Education Challenged Again." *Hispanic*. Vol. 12, No. 10 (October): 12–13.

Ogden, Russel D. 2001. "Nonphysician-Assisted Suicide: The Technological Imperative of the Deathing Counterculture." *Death Studies.* Vol. 25, No. 5 (July): 387–402.

O'Hare, William P. 2002. "Tracking the Trends in Low-Income Working Families." *Population Today.* Vol. 30, No. 6 (August-September): 1–3.

Ohio Department of Education. 2008. *Cleveland Metropolitan School District 2007–2008 School Year Report Card* [Online] Available May 28, 2009, at http://www.ode.state.oh.us/reportcardfiles/2007-2008/DIST/043786.pdf

Ohlemacher, Stephen. 2006. "Study Finds That Marriage Builds Wealth." *Yahoo News.* [Online] Available January 18, 2007, at http://news.yahoo.com

———. 2007. "Official Count: 754,000 People Believed Homeless in U.S." *Seattle Times* (February 28). [Online] Available March 9, 2007, at http://seattletimes.nwsource.com/html/nationworld/2003592874_homeless28.html

Olin, Dirk. 2003. "The Tracking System." *New York Times* (September 28). [Online] Available October 12, 2003, at http://www.researchnavigator.com

Orfield, Gary, and Chungmei Lee. 2007. *Racial Transformation and the Changing Nature of Segregation.* Cambridge, Mass.: Civil Rights Project at Harvard University.

Organisation for Economic Cooperation and Development. 2008. *Stat.Extracts.* [Online] Available February 3, 2009, at http://pisa2006.acer.edu.au

Orhant, Melanie. 2002. "Human Trafficking Exposed." *Population Today.* Vol. 30, No. 1 (January): 1, 4.

Owen, Carolyn A., Howard C. Elsner, and Thomas R. McFaul. 1977. "A Half-Century of Social Distance Research: National Replication of the Bogardus Studies." *Sociology and Social Research.* Vol. 66, No. 1: 80–98.

Padgett, Tim. 2002. "Taking the Side of the Coca Farmer." *Time.* Vol. 160, No. 6 (August 5): 8.

———. 2009. "The Moment." *Time* (April 6): 13.

Padgett, Tim, and Ioan Grillo. 2008. "Cocaine Capital." *Time* (August 25): 37–38.

Pakulski, Jan. 1993. "Mass Social Movements and Social Class." *International Sociology.* Vol. 8, No. 2 (June): 131–58.

Palmore, Erdman B. 1979. "Predictors of Successful Aging." *Gerontologist.* Vol. 19, No. 5 (October): 427–31.

———. 1998. "Ageism." In David E. Redburn and Robert P. McNamara, eds., *Social Gerontology* (pp. 29–41). Westport, Conn.: Auburn House.

Parenti, Michael. 1995. *Democracy by the Few,* 6th ed. New York: St. Martin's Press.

Park, Robert E., and Ernest W. Burgess. 1970 (orig. 1921). *Introduction to the Science of Sociology.* Chicago: University of Chicago Press.

Parkman, Allen M. 1992. *No-Fault Divorce: What Went Wrong?* Boulder, Colo.: Westview Press.

Parler, Karen F., and Matthew V. Pruitt. 2000. "Poverty, Poverty Concentration, and Homicide." *Social Science Quarterly.* Vol. 81, No. 2 (June): 555–70.

Parrillo, Vincent N. 2003. *Strangers to These Shores,* 7th ed. Boston: Allyn & Bacon.

Parrillo, Vincent N., and Christopher Donoghue. 2005. "Updating the Bogardus Social Distance Studies: A New National Survey." *Social Science Journal.* Vol. 42, No. 2 (April): 257–71.

Parsons, Talcott. 1942. "Age and Sex in the Social Structure of the United States." *American Sociological Review.* Vol. 7, No. 4 (August): 604–16.

———.1951. *The Social System.* New York: Free Press.

———. 1954. *Essays in Sociological Theory.* New York: Free Press.

———. 1966. *Societies: Evolutionary and Comparative Perspectives.* Englewood Cliffs, N.J.: Prentice Hall.

Pear, Robert. 2008. "Violations Reported at 94% of Nursing Homes." *New York Times* (September 29). [Online] Available April 7, 2009, at http://www.nytimes.com/2008/09/30/us/30nursing.html

Pear, Robert, and Erik Eckholm. 1991. "When Healers Are Entrepreneurs: A Debate over Costs and Ethics." *New York Times* (June 2): 1, 17.

Pederson, Daniel, Vern E. Smith, and Jerry Adler. 1999. "Sprawling, Sprawling . . ." *Newsweek* (July 19): 23–27.

Perlstein, Gary R. 1998. "The Oklahoma City Bombing and the Militias." In *Encyclopedia of World Terrorism.* Vol. 3 (pp. 545–50). Armonk, N.Y.: Sharpe.

Peters Atlas of the World. 1990. New York: HarperCollins.

Petersilia, Joan. 1997. "Probation in the United States: Practices and Challenges." *National Institute of Justice Journal.* No. 233 (September): 4.

Peterson, J. L. 1992. "Black Men and Their Same-Sex Desires and Behaviors." In Gilbert Herdt, ed., *Gay Culture in America: Essays from the Field.* Boston: Beacon Press.

Pew Research Center on People and the Press. 2006. "Strong Public Support for Right to Die: More Americans Discussing and Planning End-of-Life Treatment." [Online] Available April 9, 2009, at http://people-press.org/report/266/strong-public-support-for-right-to-die

———. 2007. "As Marriage and Parenthood Drift Apart, Public Is Concerned about Social Impact." [Online] Available January 31, 2009, at http://pewsocialtrends.org/pubs/526/marriage-parenthood

———. 2008a. "August 2008 Religion and Public Life Survey." [Online] Available April 29, 2009, at http://people-press.org/report/?pageid=1364

———. 2008b. "Same-Sex Marriage: Redefining Marriage around the World." [Online] Available April 28, 2009, at http://pewforum.org/docs/?DocID=235

Phillips, Anne, ed. 1987. *Feminism and Equality.* New York: New York University Press.

Phillips, Melanie. 2001. "What about the Overclass?" *Public Interest.* No. 145 (Fall): 38–43.

Phillipson, Chris. 1982. *Capitalism and the Construction of Old Age.* London: Macmillan.

Pickler, Nedra, and Liz Sidoti. 2008. "Campaigns Unleash Massive Get-Out-Vote Drives." *Yahoo News* (November 2). [Online] Available November 2, 2008, at http://news.yahoo.com/s/ap/20081102/ap_on_el_pr/campaign_rdp

Pierson, David. 2008. "Americans Want More Regulation of Economy, Poll Finds." *Los Angeles Times* (October 15). [Online] Available May 8, 2009, at http://articles.latimes.com/2008/oct/15/business/fi-econpoll15

Pinker, Steven. 2003. "Are Your Genes to Blame?" *Time.* Vol. 164, No. 3 (January 20): 98–100.

Piquero, Alex R., John M. MacDonald, and Karen F. Parker. 2002. "Race, Local Life Circumstances, and Criminal Activity." *Social Science Quarterly.* Vol. 83, No. 3 (September): 654–70.

Pitt, David. 2009. "Economy Dampens Hope of a Comfortable Retirement." *Yahoo News* (April 14) [Online] Available April 14, 2009, at http://news.yahoo.com/s/ap/20090414/ap_on_bi_ge/retirement_confidence

Pittman, David. 2001. "Memories of Rape." [Online] Available April 13, 2001, at http://www.1gc.apc.org/spr

Piven, Frances Fox, and Richard A. Cloward. 1971. *Regulating the Poor: The Functions of Public Welfare.* New York: Vintage Books.

Pleck, Elizabeth. 1987. *Domestic Tyranny: The Making of Social Policy against Family Violence from Colonial Times to the Present.* New York: Oxford University Press.

Polgreen, Lydia, and Robert F. Worth. 2003. "Children with Foster Parents Found Starving in New Jersey." *International Herald Tribune Online* (October 28). [Online] Available October 28, 2003, at http://www.ith.com/articles/115312.html

PollingReport.com. 2006. "Major Institutions." Gallup poll conducted June 1–4. [Online] Available December 17, 2006, at http://www.pollingreport.com/institut.htm

———. 2009. "Major Institutions." Gallup poll conducted February 10–15, 2009. [Online] Available May 25, 2009, at http://www.pollingreport.com/institut.htm

Polsby, Nelson W. 1959. "Three Problems in the Analysis of Community Power." *American Sociological Review.* Vol. 24, No. 6 (December): 796–803.

Popenoe, David. 1988. *Disturbing the Nest: Family Change and Decline in Modern Societies.* Hawthorne, N.Y.: Aldine de Gruyter.

———. 1993a. "American Family Decline, 1960–1990: A Review and Appraisal." *Journal of Marriage and the Family.* Vol. 55, No. 3 (August): 527–55.

———. 1993b. "Parental Androgyny." *Society.* Vol. 30, No. 6 (September-October): 5–11.

———. 1999. *Life without Father: Compelling New Evidence That Fatherhood and Marriage Are Indispensable for the Good of Children and Society.* Cambridge, Mass.: Harvard University Press.

Popenoe, David, and Barbara Dafoe Whitehead. 1999. *Should We Live Together? What Young Adults Need to Know about Cohabitation before Marriage.* New Brunswick, N.J.: National Marriage Project.

Population Reference Bureau. 2003. *World Population Data Sheet, 2003.* Washington, D.C.: Population Reference Bureau.

———. 2006. *2006 World Population Data Sheet.* Washington, D.C.: Population Reference Bureau.

———. 2008. *2008 World Population Data Sheet.* Washington, D.C.: Population Reference Bureau. [Online] Available May 14, 2009, at http://www.prb.org/Datafinder/Geography/Summary.aspx?region=38®ion_type=2

———. 2009a. *DataFinder.* Washington, D.C.: Population Reference Bureau. [Online] Available July 24, 2009, at http://www.prb.org/DataFinder.aspx

———. 2009b. *2009 World Population Data Sheet.* Washington, D.C.: Population Reference Bureau.

Porter, Eduardo. 2006. "Study Finds Wealth Inequality Is Widening Worldwide." *New York Times* (December 6). [Online] Available April 22, 2009, at http://query.nytimes.com

Portes, Alejandro. 2002. "English Only Triumphs, but the Costs Are High." *Contexts.* Vol. 1 No. 1 (Spring): 10–15.

Powell, Colin L., and Joseph E. Persico. 1995. *My American Journey.* New York: Random House.

Powell, Lawrence Alfred, Kenneth J. Branco, and John B. Williamson. 1996. *The Senior Rights Movement: Framing the Policy Debate in America.* New York: Twayne.

Purcell, Piper, and Lara Stewart. 1990. "Dick and Jane in 1989." *Sex Roles.* Vol. 22, Nos. 3–4 (February): 177–85.

Quillian, Lincoln, and Devah Pager. 2001. "Black Neighbors, Higher Crime? The Role of Racial Stereotypes in Evaluations of Neighborhood Crime." *American Journal of Sociology.* Vol. 107, No. 3 (November): 717–67.

Rainforest Foundation. 2009. "Rainforest Facts and Figures." [Online] Available April 22, 2009, at http://www.rainforestfoundationuk.org/Rainforest_facts

Raley, R. Kelly. 1996. "A Shortage of Marriageable Men? A Note on the Role of Cohabitation in Black-White Differences in Marriage Rates." *American Journal of Sociology.* Vol. 61, No. 6 (December): 973–83.

Ramo, Joshua Cooper. 2001. "America's Shadow Drug War." *Time.* Vol. 157, No. 18 (May 7): 36–44.

Rankin, Susan R. 2003. "Campus Climate for Gay, Lesbian, Bisexual, and Transgender People: A National Perspective." National Gay and Lesbian Task Force. [Online] Available May 6, 2003, at http://www.ngltf.org/ news/release.cfm?releaseID-538

Ratnesar, Romesh. 2003. "Al-Qaeda's New Home." *Time* (September 15). [Online] Available May 23, 2009, at http://www.time.com/time/magazine/article/0,9171,1005665,00.html

Raymond, Joan. 2001. "The Multicultural Report." *American Demographics.* Vol. 23, No. 11 (November): S1–S6.

RECER, PAUL. 1999. "Teenage Smoking Harms Lungs Forever, Study Says." *Louisville Courier-Journal* (April 7): A8.

RECKLESS, WALTER C. 1973. *The Crime Problem.* New York: Appleton-Century-Crofts.

RECKLESS, WALTER C., and SIMON DINITZ. 1972. *The Prevention of Juvenile Delinquency.* Columbus: Ohio State University Press.

RECKLESS, WALTER C., SIMON DINITZ, and E. MURRAY. 1956. "Self Concept as an Insulator against Delinquency." *American Sociological Review.* Vol. 21, No. 5 (October): 744–56.

———. 1957. "The 'Good Boy' in a High-Delinquency Area." *Journal of Criminal Law, Criminology, and Police Science.* Vol. 48, No. 1 (June-July): 18–25.

REEVE, SIMON. 1999. *The New Jackals: Ramzi Yousef, Osama bin Laden, and the Future of Terrorism.* Boston: Northeastern University Press.

REILAND, RALPH. 1998. "Selecting Targets." *Free Market.* Vol. 16, No. 1 (January). [Online] Available May 15, 2006, at http://www.mises.org

REIMAN, JEFFREY. 1998. *The Rich Get Richer and the Poor Get Prison: Ideology, Class, and Criminal Justice.* Boston: Allyn & Bacon.

RENNER, MICHAEL. 1993. *Critical Juncture: The Future of Peacekeeping.* Washington, D.C.: Worldwatch Institute.

RICHARDSON, LAUREL. 1988. *The Dynamics of Sex and Gender: A Sociological Perspective,* 3rd ed. New York: HarperCollins.

RICHBURG, KEITH B. 2008. "School Privatization Plan Sputters." *Washington Post* (June 29). [Online] Available February 3, 2009, at http://www.boston.com/news/education/k_12/articles/2008/06/29/school_privatization_plan_sputters

RICHE, MARTHA FARNSWORTH. 2000. "America's Diversity and Growth: Signposts for the 21st Century." *Population Bulletin.* Vol. 55, No. 2 (June).

RIDEOUT, VICTORIA, DONALD F. ROBERTS, and ULLA G. FOEHR. 2005. *Media in the Lives of 8–18-Year-Olds.* Kaiser Family Foundation (March). [Online] Available October 27, 2008, at http://www.kff.org/entmedia

RIMER, SARA. 1998. "Blacks Carry Load of Care for Their Elderly." *New York Times* (March 15): 1, 22.

RIPLEY, AMANDA. 2008. "Can She Save Our Schools?" *Time* (December 8): 36–44.

RITTER, KARL. 2008. "World Takes Notice of Swedish Prostitute Laws." *Independent* (March 17). [Online] Available April 24, 2009, at http://www.independent.co.uk/news/world/europe/world-takes-notice-of-swedish-prostitute-laws-796793.html

RITTER, MALCOLM. 2003. "Children-TV Violence Link Has Effect." *Yahoo News.* [Online] Available March 9, 2003, at http://www.yahoonews.com

RITZER, GEORGE. 1993. *The McDonaldization of Society: An Investigation into the Changing Character of Contemporary Social Life.* Thousand Oaks, Calif.: Pine Forge Press.

———. 1998. *The McDonaldization Thesis: Explorations and Extensions.* Thousand Oaks, Calif.: Sage.

ROBINSON, JOHN P., PERLA WERNER, and GEOFFREY GODBEY. 1997. "Freeing Up the Golden Years." *American Demographics.* Vol. 19, No. 10 (October): 20–24.

ROCHE, TIMOTHY. 2000. "The Crisis of Foster Care." *Time.* Vol. 156, No. 20 (November 13): 74–82.

ROOSEVELT, MARGOT. 2001. "The War against the War on Drugs." *Time.* Vol. 157, No. 18 (May 7): 46–47.

ROSCIGNO, VINCENT J., and MARTHA L. CROWLEY. 2001. "Rurality, Institutional Disadvantage, and Achievement/Attainment." *Rural Sociology.* Vol. 66, No. 2 (June): 268–92.

ROSEGRANT, MARK W., XIMING CAI, and SARAH A. CLINE. 2002. *World Water and Food to 2025: Dealing with Scarcity.* Washington, D.C.: International Food Policy Research Institute and International Water Management Institute.

ROSENBERG, MICA. 2008. "Mexican Transvestite Fiesta Rocks Indigenous Town." Reuters (November 23). [Online] Available June 15, 2009, at http://www.reuters.com/article/lifestyleMolt/idUSTRE4AM1PB20081123

ROSENBLOOM, STEPHANIE, and MICHAEL BARBARO. 2009. "Green-Light Specials, Now at Wal-Mart." *New York Times* (January 24). [Online] Available May 20, 2009, at http://www.nytimes.com/2009/01/25/business/25walmart.html

ROSENTHAL, ELIZABETH. 1991. "Canada's National Health Plan Gives Care to All, with Limits." *New York Times* (April 30): A1, A16.

ROSS, CATHERINE E., JOHN MIROWSKY, and WILLIAM C. COCKERHAM. 1983. "Social Class, Mexican Culture, and Fatalism: Their Effects on Psychological Distress." *American Journal of Community Psychology.* Vol. 11: 383–99.

ROSTOW, WALT W. 1960. *The Stages of Economic Growth: A Non-Communist Manifesto.* Cambridge: Cambridge University Press.

———. 1978. *The World Economy: History and Prospect.* Austin: University of Texas Press.

ROTHMAN, STANLEY, and AMY E. BLACK. 1998. "Who Rules Now? American Elites in the 1990s." *Society.* Vol. 35, No. 6 (September-October): 17–20.

RUESCHEMEYER, DIETRICH, EVELYN H. STEPHENS, and JOHN D. STEPHENS. 1992. *Capitalist Development and Democracy.* Chicago: University of Chicago Press.

RUSHING, W. 1969. "Two Patterns in the Relationship between Social Class and Mental Hospitalization." *American Sociological Review.* Vol. 34, No. 4 (August): 533–41.

RUSSELL, CHERYL. 1995. "Are We in the Dumps?" *American Demographics.* Vol. 17, No. 1 (January): 6.

RYAN, WILLIAM. 1976. *Blaming the Victim,* rev. ed. New York: Vintage Books.

SACHS, JEFFREY D. 2009. "The Case for Bigger Government." *Time* (January 19): 34–36.

SAAD, LYDIA. 2008. "Economy Entrenched as Nation's Most Important Problem." Gallup (December 10). [Online] Available July 23, 2009, at http://www.gallup.com/poll/113041/Economy-Entrenched-Nations-Most-Important-Problem.aspx

SADKER, DAVID. 1999. "Gender Equity: Still Knocking at the Classroom Door." *Educational Leadership.* Vol. 56, No. 7 (April): 22–26.

SADKER, DAVID, and MYRA SADKER. 1994. *Failing at Fairness: How America's Schools Cheat Girls.* New York: Scribner.

SAGAN, CARL, and RICHARD TURCO. 1990. *A Path Where No Man Thought: Nuclear Winter and the End of the Arms Race.* New York: Random House.

SAID, EDWARD. 1981. *Covering Islam: How the Media and the Experts Determine How We See the Rest of the World.* New York: Pantheon.

SAINT JEAN, YANICK, and JOE R. FEAGIN. 1998. *Double Burden: Black Women and Everyday Racism.* Armonk, N.Y.: Sharpe.

SALA-I-MARTIN, XAVIER. 2002. *The World Distribution of Income.* Working Paper No. 8933. Cambridge, Mass.: National Bureau of Economic Research.

SALE, KIRKPATRICK. 1990. *The Conquest of Paradise: Christopher Columbus and the Columbian Legacy.* New York: Knopf.

SAMPLES, FAITH, and LARRY ABNER. 1998. "Evaluations of School-Based Violence Prevention Programs." In Delbert S. Elliott, Beatrix A. Hamburg, and Kirk R. Williams, eds., *Violence in American Schools: A New Perspective* (pp. 217–52). New York: Cambridge University Press.

SAMUELSON, ROBERT J. 2003. "The Rich and Everyone Else." *Newsweek* (January 27): 57.

SANCHEZ, CLAUDIO. 2003. "Philadelphia Schools." National Public Radio Online (April 16). [Online] Available July 15, 2006, at http://www.npr.org/templates/story/story.php?storyId=1234147

SAPORITO, BILL. 2008. "Is Housing Nearing the Floor?" *Time* (November 10): 56–57.

———. 2009. "How AIG Became Too Big to Fail." *Time* (March 30): 24–30.

SARCHE, JON. 2006. "Colorado Man Says He Committed 48 Murders." *Yahoo News.* [Online] Available July 28, 2006, at http://news.yahoo.com

SCHLUMPF, HEIDI. 1999. "Babes in Arms." *U.S. Catholic.* Vol. 64, No. 12 (December): 34–38.

SCHMALZ, J. 1993. "Poll Finds an Even Split on Homosexuality's Cause." *New York Times* (March 5): A14.

SCHNAIBERG, ALLAN, and KENNETH ALAN GOULD. 1994. *Environment and Society: The Enduring Conflict.* New York: St. Martin's Press.

SCHOEN, ROBERT, et al. 2002. "Women's Employment, Marital Happiness, and Divorce." *Social Forces.* Vol. 81, No. 2 (December): 643–83.

SCHOOFS, MARK. 1999. "The Deadly Gender Gap." *Village Voice.* Vol. 63, No. 53 (January 15): 34–36.

SCHUR, EDWIN M. 1984. *Labeling Women Deviant: Gender, Stigma, and Social Control.* Philadelphia: Temple University Press.

SCOMMEGNA, PAOLA. 2002. "Increased Cohabitation Changing Children's Family Settings." *Population Today.* Vol. 30, No. 7 (July): 3, 6.

SEGE, R., and W. DIETZ. 1994. "Television Viewing and Violence in Children: The Pediatrician as Agent for Change." *Pediatrics.* Vol. 94, pp. 600–07.

SENTENCING PROJECT. 2006. "New Incarceration Figures: Thirty-Three Consecutive Years of Growth." [Online] Available December 17, 2006, at http://www.sentencingproject.org/Admin/Documents/publications/inc_newfigures.pdf

———. 2008. "Felony Disenfranchisement Laws in the United States." [Online] Available January 25, 2009, at http://www.sentencingproject.org/Admin%5CDocuments%5Cpublications%5Cfd_bs_fdlawsinus.pdf

SHEA, RACHEL HARTIGAN. 2002. "The New Insecurity." *U.S. News & World Report.* Vol. 132, No. 9 (March 25): 40.

SHEEHAN, MICHAEL A. 2000. "Post-Millenium Terrorism Review." Speech at the Brookings Institution, Washington, D.C. (February 10). [Online] Available March 13, 2000, at http://www.state.gov/www/policy_remarks/2000/000210_sheehan_brookings.html

SHELDON, WILLIAM H., EMIL M. HARTL, and EUGENE MCDERMOTT. 1949. *Varieties of Delinquent Youth.* New York: Harper.

SHLAES, AMITY. 1998. "A Chance to Equip My Child." *Wall Street Journal* (February 23): A22.

SIERRA CLUB. 2009. "Clean Water." [Online] Available February 11, 2009, at http://www.sierraclub.org/cleanwater/overview

SIMON, JULIAN. 1981. *The Ultimate Resource.* Princeton, N.J.: Princeton University Press.

———. 1995. "More People, Greater Wealth, More Resources, Healthier Environment." In Theodore D. Goldfarb, ed., *Taking Sides: Clashing Views on Controversial Environmental Issues,* 6th ed. Guilford, Conn.: Dushkin.

SIMON, ROGER W. 2002. "Revisiting the Relationship among Gender, Marital Status, and Mental Health." *American Journal of Sociology.* Vol. 107, No. 4 (January): 1065–96.

SIMPSON, SALLY S. 1989. "Feminist Theory, Crime, and Justice." *Criminology.* Vol. 27 (November): 605–31.

SINGER, S. FRED. 2007. "Global Warming: Man-Made or Natural?" *Imprimis.* Vol. 36, No. 8 (August): 1–5.

SINGER, RENA. 2001. "A Sadly Mounting Ritual." *U.S. News & World Report.* Vol. 130, No. 16 (April 23): 34.

SKIBA, RUSSELL. 2000. "No to Zero Tolerance." *Louisville Courier-Journal* (January 16): D3.

SMAIL, J. KENNETH. 2007. "Let's Reduce Global Population!" In John J. Macionis and Nijole V. Benokraitis, eds., *Seeing Ourselves: Classic, Contemporary, and Cross-Cultural Readings in Sociology,* 7th ed. Upper Saddle River, N.J.: Prentice Hall.

SMART, TIM. 2001. "Not Acting Their Age." *U.S. News & World Report.* Vol. 130, No. 22 (June 4): 54–60.

SMITH, ADAM. 1937 (orig. 1776). *An Inquiry into the Nature and Causes of the Wealth of Nations.* New York: Modern Library.

SMITH, DOUGLAS A. 1987. "Police Response to Interpersonal Violence: Defining the Parameters of Legal Control." *Social Forces.* Vol. 65, No. 3 (March): 767–82.

SMITH, DOUGLAS A., and CHRISTY A. VISHER. 1981. "Street-Level Justice: Situational Determinants of Police Arrest Decisions." *Social Problems.* Vol. 29, No. 2 (December): 167–77.

SMITH, RYAN A. 2002. "Race, Gender, and Authority in the Workplace: Theory and Research." *Annual Review of Sociology*. Vol. 28: 509–42.

SMITH-LOVIN, LYNN, and CHARLES BRODY. 1989. "Interruptions in Group Discussions: The Effects of Gender and Group Composition." *American Journal of Sociology.* Vol. 54, No. 3 (June): 424–35.

SMOLOWE, JILL. 1994. "When Violence Hits Home." *Time.* Vol. 144, No. 1 (July 4): 18–25.

SOMMERS, CHRISTINA HOFF. 2003. Lecture at Kenyon College (April 7).

SOWELL, THOMAS. 1981. *Ethnic America.* New York: Basic Books.

———. 1987. "Preferential Treatment," in Thomas Sowell, *Compassion versus Guilt and Other Essays* (pp. 197–99). New York: Morrow.

———. 1990. *Preferential Policies: An International Perspective.* New York: Morrow.

———. 1994. *Race and Culture.* New York: Basic Books.

———. 1995. "Ethnicity and IQ." In Steven Fraser, ed., *The Bell Curve Wars: Race, Intelligence and the Future of America* (pp. 70–79). New York: Basic Books.

SPENDER, DALE. 1989. *Invisible Women: The Schooling Scandal.* London: Women's Press.

SPILLMAN, BRENDA C. 2002. "New Estimates of Lifetime Nursing Home Use: Have Patterns of Use Changed?" *Medical Care.* Vol. 40, No. 10 (October): 965–1006.

SPITZER, STEVEN. 1980. "Toward a Marxian Theory of Deviance." In Delos H. Kelly, ed., *Criminal Behavior: Readings in Criminology* (pp. 175–91). New York: St. Martin's Press.

SROLE, LEO. 1972. "Urbanization and Mental Health: Some Reformulations." *American Scientist.* Vol. 60: 576–83.

———. 1975. "Measurements and Classification in Socio-Psychiatric Epidemiology: Midtown Manhattan Study I (1954) and Midtown Manhattan Study II (1974)." *Journal of Health and Social Behavior.* Vol. 16, No. 4 (December): 347–64.

SROLE, LEO, et al. 1962. *Mental Health in the Metropolis: The Midtown Manhattan Study.* New York: McGraw-Hill.

STACEY, JUDITH. 1990. *Brave New Families: Stories of Domestic Upheaval in Late-Twentieth-Century America.* New York: Basic Books.

———. 1993. "Good Riddance to 'The Family': A Response to David Popenoe." *Journal of Marriage and the Family.* Vol. 55, No. 3 (August): 545–47.

STACK, CAROL B. 1975. *All Our Kin: Strategies for Survival in a Black Community.* New York: Harper & Row.

STANLEY, WILLIAM D., and THOMAS J. DANKO. 1996. *The Millionaire Next Door: The Surprising Secrets of America's Wealthy.* New York: Pocket Books.

STAPINSKI, HELENE. 1998. "Let's Talk Dirty." *American Demographics.* Vol. 20, No. 11 (November): 50–56.

STARES, PAUL B. 1996. *Global Habit: The Drug Problem in a Borderless World.* Washington, D.C.: Brookings Institution.

STARR, ALEXANDRA. 2003. "What McCain-Feingold Really Means." *Business Week Online.* [Online] Available August 15, 2003, at http://www.businessweek.com

STARR, PAUL. 1982. *The Social Transformation of American Medicine.* New York: Basic Books.

STATE OF OREGON. 2009. *Death with Dignity Act Annual Report, 2008.* [Online] Available April 9, 2009, at http://www.oregon.gov/DHS/ph/pas/docs/year11.pdf

STEELE, SHELBY. 1990. *The Content of Our Character: A New Vision of Race in America.* New York: St. Martin's Press.

STEIN, JOEL. 2002. "The New Politics of Pot." *Time.* Vol. 160, No. 19 (November 4): 56–62.

STERN, JESSICA. 1999. *The Ultimate Terrorists.* Cambridge, Mass.: Harvard University Press.

STEVENS, HELEN. 2003. *Declining Biodiversity and Unsustainable Agricultural Production: Common Cause, Common Solution?* Research Paper No. 2, 2001–2002. Department of the Parliamentary Library, Australia. [Online] Available October 31, 2003, at http://www.aph.gov.au/library/pubs/rp/2001-02/02RP02.pdf

STOBBE, MIKE. 2008. "Cancer to Be World's Top Killer by 2010, WHO Says." *Guardian* (December 12). [Online] Available May 4, 2009, at http://www.guardian.co.uk/uslatest/story/0,,-8147108,00.html

STOCKHOLM INTERNATIONAL PEACE RESEARCH INSTITUTE. 2006. *SIPRI Yearbook, 2006: Armaments, Disarmament, and International Security*. [Online] Available December 14, 2006, at http://www.sipri.org/contents/publications/pocket/pocket_yb.html

———. 2007. "SIPRI Data on Military Expenditures." [Online] Available June 25, 2007, at http://www.sipri.org/contents/milap/milex/mex_data_index.html

———. 2009. *SIPRI Yearbook, 2009: Armaments, Disarmament, and International Security.* [Online] Available June 21, 2009, at http://www.sipri.org/yearbook/2009/files/SIPRIYB0900.pdf

STOLBERG, SHERYL GAY. 2006."Patriot Act Revisions Pass House, Sending Measure to President." *New York Times Online* (March 8). [Online] Available July 28, 2006, at http://www.researchnavigator.com

STONE, BRAD LOWELL. 2000. "Robert Nisbet on Conservative Dogmatics." *Society.* Vol. 37, No. 3 (March-April): 68–74.

STONE, CLARENCE N. 1998. "Linking Civic Capacity and Human Capital Formation." In Marilyn J. Gittell, ed., *Strategies for School Equity: Creating Productive Schools in a Just Society* (pp. 163–76). New Haven, Conn.: Yale University Press.

STOUT, DAVID. 2003. "Supreme Court Splits on Diversity Efforts at University of Michigan." *Yahoo News.* [Online] Available June 23, 2003, at http://www.yahoo.com/news

STROM, STEPHANIE. 2000. "In Japan, the Golden Years Have Lost Their Glow." *New York Times* (February 16): A7.

STRONG, BRYAN, and CHRISTINE DEVAULT. 1994. *Human Sexuality.* Mountain View, Calif.: Mayfield.

SULLIVAN, AMY. 2009. "Postcard from Detroit." *Time* (April 30). [Online] Available May 14, 2009, at http://www.time.com/time/magazine/article/0,9171,1894943,00.html

SULLIVAN, ANDREW. 2002. Lecture given at Kenyon College.

SUTHERLAND, EDWIN H. 1940. "White Collar Criminality." *American Sociological Review.* Vol. 5, No. 1 (February): 1–12.

SZASZ, THOMAS S. 1961. *The Manufacturer of Madness: A Comparative Study of the Inquisition and the Mental Health Movement.* New York: Dell.

———. 1970. *The Myth of Mental Illness: Foundations of a Theory of Personal Conduct.* New York: Harper & Row.

———. 1994. "Mental Illness Is Still a Myth." *Society.* Vol. 31, No. 4 (May-June): 34–39.

———. 1995. "Idleness and Lawlessness in the Therapeutic State." *Society.* Vol. 32, No. 4 (May-June): 30–35.

TABB, WILLIAM K. 1992. "Vampire Capitalism." *Socialist Review.* Vol. 22, No. 1 (January): 81–93.

TAGLIABUE, JOHN. 2008. "Woman Who Sought Euthanasia Dies." *New York Times* (March 21). [Online] Available January 18, 2009, at http://query.nytimes.com/gst/fullpage.html?res=9A0DE1D61130F932A15750C0A96E9C8B63&sec=&spon=&partner=permalink&exprod=permalink

TANDY, KAREN P. 2009. "Myth: Legalization of Marijuana in Other Countries Has Been a Success." About.com (March 23). [Online] Available May 3, 2009, at http://alcoholism.about.com/od/pot/a/bldea050426_3.htm

TANNAHILL, REAY. 1992. *Sex in History.* Chelsea, Mich.: Scarborough House.

TANNENBAUM, FRANK. 1946. *Slave and Citizen: The Negro in the Americas.* New York: Vintage Books.

TAVRIS, CAROL, and CAROL WADE. 2001. *Psychology in Perspective,* 3rd ed. Upper Saddle River, N.J.: Prentice Hall.

TAYLOR, FRANK. 2003. "Content Analysis and Gender Stereotypes in Children's Books." *Teaching Sociology,* Vol. 31, No. 3 (July):300–11.

TAYLOR, LAWRENCE. 1984. *Born to Crime: The Genetic Causes of Criminal Behavior.* Westport, Conn.: Greenwood.

TAYLOR, STEVEN J. L. 1998. *Desegregation in Boston and Buffalo: The Influence of Local Leaders.* Albany: State University of New York Press.

TEJADA-VERA, BETZAIDA, and PAUL D. SUTTON. 2008. "Births, Marriages, Divorces, and Deaths: Provisional Data for 2007." [Online] Available February 9, 2009, at http://www.cdc.gov/nchs/data/nvsr/nvsr56/nvsr56_21.htm

TERKEL, STUDS. 1974. *Working.* New York: Pantheon.

"There's Something about Mary." 1998. *Vanity Fair.* Vol. 461 (January): 63.

THERNSTROM, ABIGAIL. 1999. "Courting Disorder in the Schools." *Public Interest.* Vol. 136 (Summer): 18–34.

THERNSTROM, ABIGAIL, and STEPHAN THERNSTROM. 2003. *No Excuses: Closing the Racial Gap in Learning.* New York: Simon & Schuster.

THIGPEN, DAVID E. 2002. "The Long Way Home." *Time.* Vol. 160, No. 6 (August 5): 42–44.

THOMAS, EVAN. 2003. "The War over Gay Marriage." *Newsweek* (July 7): 38–44.

THOMAS, EVAN, and MICHAEL HIRSH. 2000. "The Future of Terror." *Newsweek* (January 10): 34–37.

THOMPSON, MARK. 1997. "Fatal Neglect." *Time.* Vol. 150, No. 17 (October 27): 34–38.

———. 1998. "Shining a Light on Abuse." *Time.* Vol. 152, No. 5 (August 3): 42–43.

THOMPSON, WILLIAM E., and JACKIE L. HARROD. 1999. "Topless Dancers: Managing Stigma in a Deviant Occupation." In Henry N. Pontell, ed., *Social Deviance: Readings in Theory and Research,* 3rd ed. (pp. 277–87). Upper Saddle River, N.J.: Prentice Hall.

THORNBERRY, TERRANCE, and MARGARET FARNSWORTH. 1982. "Social Correlates of Criminal Involvement: Further Evidence on the Relationship between Social Status and Criminal Behavior." *American Sociological Review.* Vol. 47, No. 4 (August): 505–18.

THORNBURGH, NATHAN. 2006. "Dropout Nation." *Time.* Vol. 167, No. 16 (April 17): 30–40.

TIERNEY, JOHN. 2009. "Obama's Drug Policy." *New York Times* (May 3). [Online] Available May 3, 2009, at http://tierneylab.blogs.nytimes.com/2009/03/12/obamas-drug-policy

TILLY, CHARLES. 1978. *From Mobilization to Revolution.* Reading, Mass.: Addison-Wesley.

TJADEN, PATRICIA. 1997. "The Crime of Stalking: How Big Is the Problem?" *National Institute of Justice Research Preview.* Washington, D.C.: U.S. Department of Justice.

TJADEN, PATRICIA, and NANCY THOENNES. 1998. *Stalking in America: Findings from the National Violence against Women Survey.* Washington, D.C.: U.S. Department of Justice.

TRATTNER, WALTER I. 1980. "Social Welfare." In Glenn Porter, ed., *Encyclopedia of American Economic History,* Vol. 3 (pp. 1155–67). New York: Scribner.

TREBACH, ARNOLD S., and JAMES A. INCIARDI. 1993. *Legalize It? Debating American Drug Policy.* Lanham, Md.: University of America Press.

TUCKER, DAVID. 1998. "Responding to Terrorism." *Washington Quarterly.* Vol. 21, No. 1 (Winter): 103–17.

TUMULTY, KAREN. 2006. "Should They Stay or Should They Go?" *Time.* Vol. 167, No. 15 (April 10): 30–40.

Tyler, S. Lyman. 1973. *A History of Indian Policy.* Washington, D.C.: Bureau of Indian Affairs, U.S. Department of the Interior.

Udry, J. Richard. 2000. "Biological Limitations of Gender Construction." *American Sociological Review.* Vol. 65, No. 3 (June): 443–57.

———. 2001. "Feminist Critics Uncover Determinism, Positivism, and Antiquated Theory." *American Sociological Review.* Vol. 66, No. 4 (August): 611–18.

UNAIDS. 2008. *2008 Report on the Global AIDS Epidemic.* [Online] Available February 6, 2009, at http://www.unaids.org/en/KnowledgeCentre/HIVData/GlobalReport/2008/2008_Global_report.asp

UNESCO Institute of Statistics. 2008. "Custom Tables." [Online] Available May 28, 2009, at http://stats.uis.unesco.org/ unesco/TableViewer/document.aspx?ReportId=136&IF_Language=eng&BR_Topic=0

———. 2009. "Data Centre." [Online] Available May 23, 2009, at http://stats.uis.unesco.org/unesco/TableViewer/document.aspx?ReportId=143&F_Language=English

UNICEF. 2006. *Violence against Children in the Community.* New York: United Nations. [Online] Available April 28, 2009, at http://www.unicef.org/media/media_45451.html

United Nations. 2006. "Divorces and Crude Divorce Rates by Urban/Rural Residence, 1998–2002." [Online] Available January 10, 2007, at http://unstats.un.org/unsd/demographic/products/dyb/DYB2002/Table25.pdf

———. 2006. *2006 Report on the Global AIDS Epidemic.* [Online] Available December 17, 2006, at http://www.unaids.org/en/HIV_data/2006GlobalReport/default.asp

———. 2009. *World Population Prospects: The 2008 Revision.* New York: United Nations Population Division.

United Nations Development Programme. 1994. *Human Development Report 1994.* New York: Oxford University Press.

———. 1996. *Human Development Report 1996.* New York: Oxford University Press.

———. 1998. *Human Development Report 1998.* New York: Oxford University Press.

———. 2000. *Human Development Report 2000.* New York: Oxford University Press.

———. 2003. *Human Development Report 2003.* New York: Oxford University Press.

———. 2005. *Human Development Report, 2005.* New York: Oxford University Press.

———. 2007. *Human Development Report 2007/2008.* New York: Palgrave Macmillan. [Online] Available February 26, 2008, at http://hdr.undp.org/en

———. 2008a. "Human Development Indices: A Statistical Update, 2008." [Online] Available January 19, 2009, at http://hdrstats.undp.org/2008/countries/country_fact_sheets/cty_fs_KOR.html

———. 2008b. "The Millennium Development Goals Report, 2008." [Online] Available April 28, 2009, at http://www.undp.org/publications/MDG_Report_2008_ en.pdf

United Nations Environmental Programme. 2008. "Vital Water Graphics: An Overview of the State of the World's Fresh and Marine Waters." 2nd ed. [Online] Available February 9, 2009, at http://www.unep.org/dewa/vitalwater/article186.html

United Nations Population Reference Division. 2009. "World Population Prospects: The 2007 Revision." [Online] Available February 9, 2009, at http://data.un.org/Data.aspx?d=PopDiv&f=variableID%3a46

United Nations Water Assessment Programme. 2009. *World Water Development Report 3: Water in a Changing World.* New York: United Nations. [Online] Available February 11, 2009, at http://www.unesco.org/water/wwap/wwdr/wwdr3/pdf/WWDR3_Facts_and_Figures.pdf

Unrau, William E. 1996. *White Man's Wicked Water: The Alcohol Trade and Prohibition in Indian Country, 1802–1892.* Lawrence: University of Kansas Press.

U.S. Bureau of Justice Statistics. 2002. *Drugs and Crime Facts.* [Online] Available January 8, 2007, at http://www.ojp.usdoj.gov/bjs/dcf/contents.htm

———. 2002. "Reentry Trends in the United States." [Online] Available January 8, 2007, at http://www.ojp.usdoj.gov/bjs/reentry/reentry.htm

———. 2003. *Prison and Jail Inmates at Midyear 2002.* Washington, D.C.: U.S. Government Printing Office.

———. 2005. *Capital Punishment, 2004.* Washington, D.C.: U.S. Government Printing Office.

———. 2005. *Family Violence Statistics: Including Statistics on Strangers and Acquaintances.* Washington, D.C.: U.S. Government Printing Office.

U.S. Bureau of Justice Statistics and National Center for Education Statistics. 2006. *Indicators of School Crime and Safety, 2006.* Washington, D.C.: U.S. Government Printing Office.

U.S. Census Bureau. 2001. *The Black Population, 2000.* Washington, D.C.: U.S. Government Printing Office.

———. 2001. *The Hispanic Population, 2000.* Washington, D.C.: U.S. Government Printing Office.

———. 2001. *Mapping Census 2000: The Geography of U.S. Diversity.* Washington, D.C.: U.S. Government Printing Office.

———. 2001. *The Native Hawaiian and Other Pacific Islander Population, 2000.* Washington, D.C.: U.S. Government Printing Office.

———. 2001. *The Two or More Races Population, 2000.* Washington, D.C.: U.S. Government Printing Office.

———. 2001. *The White Population, 2000.* Washington, D.C.: U.S. Government Printing Office.

———. 2002. *The American Indian and Alaska Native Population, 2000.* Washington, D.C.: U.S. Government Printing Office.

———. 2002. *The Asian Population, 2000.* Washington, D.C.: U.S. Government Printing Office.

———. 2003. *The Arab Population, 2000.* Washington, D.C.: U.S. Government Printing Office.

———. 2003. *Disability Status, 2000.* Washington, D.C.: U.S. Government Printing Office.

———. 2003. *Language Use and English-Speaking Ability, 2000.* Washington, D.C.: U.S. Government Printing Office.

———. 2004. *Ancestry, 2000.* Washington, D.C.: U.S. Government Printing Office.

———. 2004. *Statistical Abstract of the United States, 2004–2005.* Washington, D.C.: U.S. Government Printing Office.

———. 2004. "(Table) MS-2. Estimated Median Age at First Marriage, by Sex, 1890 to Present." September 15. [Online] Available January 10, 2007, at http://www.census.gov/population/socdemo/hh-fam/tabMS-2.pdf

———. 2004. "(Table) 2a. Projected Population of the United States, by Age and Sex, 2000 to 2050." Rev. March 18. [Online] Available December 17, 2006, at http://www.census.gov/ipc/www/usinterimproj/natprojtab02a.pdf

———. 2005. *Fertility of American Women, June 2004.* Washington, D.C.: U.S. Government Printing Office.

———. 2005. *The Hispanic Population of the United States, 2004: Detailed Tables.* Rev. December 14. [Online] Available September 22, 2006, at http://www.census.gov/population/www/socdemo/hispanic/cps2004.html

———. 2005. "Percent Total Population in Poverty, 2003: Small Area Income and Poverty Estimates." Rev. November 29. [Online] Available December 7, 2006, at http://www.census.gov/hhes/www/saipe/maps/maps2003.html

———. 2005. *65+ in the United States, 2005.* Washington, D.C.: U.S. Government Printing Office.

———. 2005. *Statistical Abstract of the United States, 2006.* Washington, D.C.: U.S. Government Printing Office.

———. 2005. "Voting and Registration in the Election of November 2004: (Table) 8." Rev. May 25. [Online] Available December 7, 2006, at http://www.census.gov/population/www/socdemo/voting/cps2004.html

———. 2005. *We the People of Arab Ancestry in the United States.* Washington, D.C.: U.S. Government Printing Office.

———. 2006. "Annual Estimates of the Population by Selected Age Groups and Sex for the United States, April 1, 2000 to July 1, 2005." Rev. May 9. [Online] Available December 17, 2006, at http://www.census.gov/popest/national/asrh/NC-EST2005/NC-EST2005-02.xls

———. 2006. "Annual Estimates of the Population by Sex and Five-Year Age Groups for the United States, April 1, 2000 to July 1, 2005." Rev. May 9. [Online] Available December 17, 2006, at http://www.census.gov/popest/national/asrh/NC-EST2005/NC-EST2005-01.xls

———. 2006. "Census 2000 Demographic Profile Highlights." [Online] Available September 22, 2006, at http://factfinder.census.gov

———. 2006. "Current Population Survey, 2006 Annual Social and Economic Supplement: (Table) FINC-07." Rev. August 29. [Online] Available December 7, 2006, at http://pubdb3.census.gov/macro/032006/faminc/toc.htm

———. 2006. "Current Population Survey, 2006 Annual Social and Economic Supplement: (Table) HI03." Rev. August 29. [Online] Available December 7, 2006, at http://pubdb3.census.gov/macro/032006/health/toc.htm

———. 2006. "Current Population Survey, 2006 Annual Social and Economic Supplement: (Table) HINC-01." Rev. August 29. [Online] Available January 8, 2007, at http://pubdb3.census.gov/macro/032006/hhinc/toc.htm

———. 2006. "Current Population Survey, 2006 Annual Social and Economic Supplement: (Table) PINC-01." Rev. August 29. [Online] Available December 7, 2006, at http://pubdb3.census.gov/macro/032006/perinc/toc.htm

———. 2006. "Current Population Survey, 2006 Annual Social and Economic Supplement: (Tables) POV-01, POV-02, POV-06, POV-14, POV-31, POV-41." Rev. August 29. [Online] Available December 7, 2006, at http://pubdb3.census.gov/macro/032006/pov/toc.htm

———. 2006. *Custodial Mothers and Fathers and Their Child Support, 2003.* Washington, D.C.: U.S. Government Printing Office.

———. 2006. *Educational Attainment in the United States, 2005.* Rev. October 30. [Online] Available January 5, 2007, at http://www.census.gov/population/www/socdemo/education/cps2005.html

———. 2006. "Historical Income Tables—Families: (Table) F-3." Rev. September 15. [Online] Available December 7, 2006, at http://www.census.gov/hhes/www/income/histinc/incfamdet.html

———. 2006. "Historical Income Tables—People: (Tables) P-32, P-35." Rev. January 13. [Online] Available December 7, 2006, at http://www.census.gov/hhes/www/income/histinc/incpertoc.html

———. 2006. "Historical Poverty Tables—People: (Table) 19." Rev. September 6. [Online] Available December 9, 2006, at http://www.census.gov/hhes/www/poverty/histpov/hstpov19.html

———. 2006. *Income, Poverty, and Health Insurance Coverage in the United States, 2005.* Washington, D.C.: U.S. Government Printing Office.

———. 2006. "International Database: IDB Population Pyramids." Rev. August 24. [Online] Available January 11, 2007, at http://www.census.gov/ipc/www/idbpyr.html

———. 2006. "Percent Change in Population, 2000–2005." U.S. Census Bureau Population Estimates Program. [Online] Available January 11, 2007, at http://www.census.gov/popest/gallery/maps/chg0005.html

———. 2006. "(Table) S1601: Language Spoken at Home." 2005 American Community Survey. Rev. August 15. [Online] Available January 5, 2007, at http://factfinder.census.gov

———. 2006. *We the People: American Indians and Alaska Natives in the United States.* Washington, D.C.: U.S. Government Printing Office.

———. 2006. "World Vital Events." [Online] Available January 11, 2007, at http://www.census.gov/cgi-bin/ipc/pcwe

———. 2008. "America's Families and Living Arrangements, 2008." [Online] Available May 27, 2009, at http://www.census.gov/population/www/socdemo/hh-fam/cps2008.html

———. 2008. "Current Population Survey, 2008 Annual Social and Economic Supplement." [Online] Available November 13, 2008, at http://pubdb3.census.gov/macro/032008/pov/new01_100.htm

———. 2008. "Federal Individual Income Tax Returns: Selected Itemized Deductions and the Standard Deduction, 2004 and 2005." [Online] Available March 25, 2009, at http://www.census.gov/compendia/statab/tables/09s0471.pdf

———. 2008. "Historical Health Insurance Tables." [Online] Available February 6, 2009, at http://www.census.gov/hhes/www/hlthins/historic/index.html

———. 2008. "Historical Income Tables: Families." [Online] Available November 21, 2008, at http://www.census.gov/hhes/www/income/histinc/incfamdet.html

———. 2008. "Historical Poverty Tables." [Online] Available April 8, 2009, at http://www.census.gov/hhes/www/poverty/histpov/hstpov1.html

———. 2008. "International Data Base." [Online] Available July 24, 2009, at http://www.census.gov/ipc/www/idb/summaries.html

———. 2008. "Married Couples by Race and Hispanic Origin of Spouses: 1980 to 2007." [Online] Available December 31, 2008, at http://www.census.gov/compendia/statab/tables/09s0059.pdf

———. 2008. "Population Division." [Online] Available June 2, 2009, at http://www.census.gov/popest/estbygeo.htm

———. 2008. "Resident Population by Race, Hispanic Origin, and Age, 2000 and 2007." [Online] Available April 6, 2009, at http://www.census.gov/compendia/statab/tables/09s0008.pdf

———. 2008. "State and County QuickFacts, 2009." [Online] Available June 2, 2009, at http://quickfacts.census.gov/qfd/states/34/3410000.html

———. 2008. *Statistical Abstract of the United States, 2009,* 128th ed. Washington, D.C.: U.S. Government Printing Office.

———. 2008. "2007 American Community Survey." [Online] Available December 30, 2008, at http://factfinder.census.gov

———. 2008. "2008 National Population Projections: Tables and Charts." [Online] Available January 8, 2009, at http://www.census.gov/population/www/projections/tablesandcharts.html

———. 2008. "Voting and Registration in the Election of November 2006." [Online] Available May 22, 2009, at http://www.census.gov/population/www/socdemo/voting/cps2006.html

———. 2009. "Educational Attainment." [Online] Available May 28, 2009, at http://www.census.gov/population/www/socdemo/educ-attn.html

———. 2009. "Families and Living Arrangements." [Online] Available May 27, 2009, at http://www.census.gov/population/www/socdemo/hh-fam.html

———. 2009. "International Database." [Online] Available June 4, 2009, at http://www.census.gov/ipc/www/idb/tables/.html

———. 2009. "Newsroom." [Online] Available June 20, 2009, at http://www.census.gov/Press-Release/www/releases/archives/facts_for_features_special_editions/012781.html

———. 2009. "Population Estimates: Cities and Towns, Places over 100,000, 2000–2007." [Online] Available June 22, 2009, at http://www.census.gov/popest/estbygeo.html

U.S. Charter Schools. 2008. "Charter School Dashboard." [Online] Available July 15, 2008, at http://www.uscharterschools.org/cs/r/query/q/1558?x-title=New+Non-Federal+Research+and+Reports

U.S. Conference of Mayors. 2007. *Hunger and Homelessness Survey.* [Online] Available April 30, 2008, at http://usmayors.org/HHSurvey2007/hhsurvey07.pdf

U.S. Department of Defense. 2009. "Military Personnel Statistics." [Online] Available April 3, 2009, at http://siadapp.dmdc.osd.mil/personnel/MILITARY/Miltop.htm

U.S. Department of Education. 2007. "2003 National Assessment of Adult Literacy." [Online] Available October 12, 2008, at http://nces.ed.gov/naal/kf_demographics.asp

———. 2008. "The Condition of Education." [Online] Available June 1, 2009, at http://nces.ed.gov/programs/coe/2009/section1/indicator09.asp

———. 2008. "Projections of Education Statistics to 2017." [Online] Available June 1, 2009, at http://nces.ed.gov/programs/projections/projections2017/tables/table_32.asp?referrer=report

———. 2009. "Common Core of Data." [Online] Available February 3, 2009, at http://nces.ed.gov/pubs2009/pesschools07/tables/table_02.asp

———. 2009. *Digest of Education Statistics, 2008.* [Online] Available May 28, 2009, at http://nces.ed.gov/programs/digest/2008menu_tables.asp

———. 2009. "Postsecondary Education." *Digest of Education Statistics, 2008.* [Online] Available April 3, 2009, at http://nces.ed.gov/pubs2009/2009020_3a.pdf

U.S. Department of Health and Human Services. 2005. *NIDA InfoFacts: Steroids (Anabolic—Androgenic).* Washington, D.C.: National Institute on Alcohol Abuse and Alcoholism.

———. 2006. *Child Maltreatment, 2004.* Washington, D.C.: U.S. Government Printing Office.

———. 2006. "National Survey of Family Growth." [Online] Available May 27, 2009, at http://www.cdc.gov/nchs/about/major/nsfg/abclist_c.htm-outcomecohab

———. 2006. *Results from the 2005 National Survey on Drug Use and Health: National Findings.* Rockville, Md.: Substance Abuse and Mental Health Services Administration.

———. 2008. *Child Maltreatment, 2006.* [Online] Available January 31, 2009, at http://www.acf.hhs.gov/programs/cb/pubs/cm06

———. 2008. "Mental Disorders Cost Society Billions in Unearned Income." Press release (May 7). [Online] Available May 18, 2009, at http://www.nimh.nih.gov/science-news/2008/mental-disorders-cost-societybillions-in-unearned-income.shtml

———. 2008. *The Numbers Count: Mental Disorders in America.* [Online] Available May 14, 2009, at http://www.nimh.nih.gov/health/publications/the-numbers-count-mentaldisorders-in-america/index.shtml

———. 2008. *Results from the 2007 National Survey on Drug Use and Health: National Findings.* [Online] Available May 4, 2009, at http://www.oas.samhsa.gov/nsduh/2k7nsduh/2k7Results.pdf

———. 2008. "Serious Psychological Distress and Receipt of Mental Health Services." [Online] Available May 18, 2009, at http://oas.samhsa.gov/2k8/SPDtx/SPDtx.htm

———. 2009. "Adoption and Foster Care Statistics." [Online] Available May 27, 2009, at http://www.acf.hhs.gov/programs/cb/stats_research/index.htm

———. 2009. "Drugs of Abuse Information." [Online] Available May 5, 2009, at http://www.drugabuse.gov/infofacts/cocaine.html

U.S. Department of Housing and Urban Development. 1999. "The Forgotten Americans: Homelessness—Programs and the People They Serve." December 8. [Online] Available October 4, 2004, at http://www.huduser.org/publications/homeless/homelessness/contents.html

———. 2000. "A Picture of Subsidized Households, 2000." [Online] Available April 9, 2009, at http://www.huduser.org/picture2000/index.html

———. 2007. *Annual Homeless Assessment Report to Congress.* [Online] Available November 14, 2008, at http://www.huduser.org/Publications/pdf/ahar.pdf

———. 2008. *American Housing Survey for the United States, 2007.* [Online] Available April 9, 2009, at http://www.census.gov/prod/2008pubs/h150-07.pdf

U.S. Department of Justice. 1993. *Drug Enforcement Administration. Briefing Book.* Washington, D.C.: U.S. Government Printing Office.

———. 2000. *Compendium of Federal Justice Statistics, 1998.* Washington, D.C.: U.S. Government Printing Office.

———. 2008. "Crime in the United States, 2007." [Online] Available November 13, 2008, at http://www.fbi.gov/ucr/cius2007/data/table_01.html

———. 2008. "Criminal Victimization in the United States." [Online] Available April 15, 2009, at http://www.ojp.usdoj.gov/bjs/cvictgen.htm

———. 2008. "Hate Crime Statistics, 2007." [Online] Available November 12, 2008, at http://www.fbi.gov/ucr/hc2007/table_01.htm

———. 2008. "Highlights of the 2006 National Youth Gang Survey." [Online] Available April 16, 2009, at http://www.ncjrs.gov/pdffiles1/ojjdp/fs200805.pdf

———. 2009. "Drug Use and Crime." [Online] Available May 8, 2009, at http://www.ojp.usdoj.gov/bjs/dcf/duc.htm

———. 2009. "Stalking Victimization in the United States." Press release (January 13). [Online] Available April 15, 2009, at http://www.ojp.usdoj.gov/bjs/abstract/svus.htm

U.S. Department of Labor, Bureau of Labor Statistics. 2005. "Table 7. Hourly Direct Pay in U.S. Dollars for Production Workers in Manufacturing." [Online] Available November 26, 2006, at ftp://ftp.bls.gov/pub/special.requests/ForeignLabor/ichccsuppt07.txt

———. 2006. *Employment and Earnings.* Vol. 53, No. 1 (January). [Online] Available December 17, 2006, at http://www.bls.gov/cps/#annual

———. 2006. "National Census of Fatal Occupational Injuries in 2005." [Online] Available January 9, 2007, at http://www.bls.gov/news.release/pdf/cfoi.pdf

———. 2006. *2005 Census of Fatal Occupational Industries.* [Online] Available November 26, 2006, at http://www.bls.gov/iif/oshcfoi1.htm#charts

———. 2008. "American Time Use Survey: 2007 Results." [Online] Available April 3, 2009, at http://www.bls.gov/news.release/pdf/atus.pdf

———. 2008. "Census of Fatal Occupational Injuries in 2007." [Online] Available May 26, 2009, at http://www.bls.gov/news.release/pdf/cfoi.pdf

———. 2008. *Labor Force Statistics from the Current Population Survey.* [Online] Available July 24, 2009, at http://www.bls.gov/cps/tables.htm

———. 2008. *Occupational Outlook Handbook, 2008–09 Edition.* [Online] Available February 6, 2009, at http://www.bls.gov/OCO

———. 2009. *A Chartbook of International Labor Comparisons.* [Online] Available July 24, 2009, at http://www.bls.gov/fls/chartbook2009.pdf

———. 2009. "Employment Characteristics of Families in 2008." [Online] Available May 27, 2009, at http://www.bls.gov/news.release/pdf/famee.pdf

———. 2009. "Employment Situation." [Online] Available May 26, 2009, at http://www.bls.gov/news.release/pdf/empsit.pdf

———. 2009. "International Labor Comparisons." [Online] Available May 26, 2009, at http://www.bls.gov/fls/hcaesupptabtoc.htm

———. 2009. "Labor Force Statistics from the Current Population Survey, Annual Average Data, 2008." [Online] Available May 26, 2009, at http://www.bls.gov/cps/tables.htm

———. 2009. "Major Work Stoppages in 2008." [Online] Available May 26, 2009, at http://www.bls.gov/news.release/archives/wkstp_02112009

———. 2009. "Women." *Labor Force Statistics from the Current Population Survey.* [Online] Available April 3, 2009, at http://www.bls.gov/cps/demographics.htm#women

U.S. Department of Labor, Women's Bureau. 2008. "Quick Facts on Registered Nurses (RNs)." [Online] Available February 6, 2008, at http://www.dol.gov/wb/factsheets/Qf-nursing-07.htm

U.S. Department of State. 2000. "Patterns of Global Terrorism, 1998: The Year in Review." [Online] Available January 14, 2007, at http://www.state.gov/www/global/terrorism/1998Report/review.html

———. 2003. *Patterns of Global Terrorism, 2002.* [Online] Available December 26, 2006, at http://www.usis.usemb.se/terror/rpt2002/index.html

———. 2006. *Country Reports on Terrorism, 2005.* April. [Online] Available December 17, 2006, at http://state.gov/s/ct/rls/crt/2005

———. 2009. *2008 Report on Terrorism.* [Online] Available June 21, 2009, at http://wits.nctc.gov/ReportPDF.do?f=crt2008nctcannexfinal.pdf

U.S. Department of Veterans Affairs. 2009. *Annual Benefits Report, Fiscal Year 2008.* [Online] Available June 20, 2009, at http://www.vba.va.gov/REPORTS/abr/2008_abr.pdf

U.S. Environmental Protection Agency. 2006. "Municipal Solid Waste." February 22. [Online] Available January 11, 2007, at http://www.epa.gov/msw/facts.htm

———. 2008a. "Municipal Solid Waste Generation, Recycling, and Disposal in the United States: Facts and Figures for 2007." [Online] Available June 15, 2009, at http://www.epa.gov/osw/nonhaz/municipal/pubs/msw07-fs.pdf

———. 2008b. "National Air Quality: Status and Trends through 2007." [Online] Available June 16, 2009, at http://www.epa.gov/air/airtrends/2008/dl_graph.html

U.S. Equal Employment Opportunity Commission. 2006. "Sexual Harassment Charges." [Online] Available January 8, 2007, at http://www.eeoc.gov/stats/harass.html

———. 2009. "Sexual Harassment." [Online] Available April 28, 2009, at http://www.eeoc.gov/types/sexual_harassment.html

U.S. Global Change Research Program. 2009. "Global Climate Change Impacts in the United States." [Online] Available June 21, 2009, at http://www.globalchange.gov/publications/reports/scientific-assessments/us-impacts

U.S. House of Representatives. Minority Staff, Special Investigations Division, Committee on Government Reform. 2001. *Abuse of Residents Is a Major Problem in U.S. Nursing Homes.* Washington, D.C.: U.S. Government Printing Office.

U.S. Office of Juvenile Justice and Delinquency Prevention. 2006. *Highlights of the 2004 National Youth Gang Survey*. Washington, D.C.: U.S. Government Printing Office.

U.S. Office of Management and Budget. 2008. "The Budget for Fiscal Year 2009." [Online] Available January 23, 2009, at http://www.gpoaccess.gov/usbudget/fy09/pdf/budget/tables.pdf

U.S. Office of National Drug Control Policy. 2009. "National Drug Control Strategy Data Supplement, 2009." [Online] Available May 8, 2009, at http://www.whitehousedrugpolicy.gov/publications/policy/ndcs09/ndcs09_data_supl/09datasupplement.pdf

Urban Institute. 2004. "Nearly 3 out of 4 Young Children with Employed Mothers Are Regularly in Child Care" (April 28). [Online] Available December 17, 2006, at http://www.urban.org/UploadedPDF/900706.pdf

Valdez, A. 1997. "In the Hood: Street Gangs Discover White-Collar Crime." *Police.* Vol. 21, No. 5 (May): 49–50, 56.

Vanden Brook, Tom, and Bill Nichols. 2006. "Tragic Turn Stuns Families." *USA Today* (January 4). [Online] Available July 27, 2009, at http://www.usatoday.com/news/nation/2006-01-04-mine-cover_x.htm

van den Hurk, Arie A. 1999. "Europe: Drugs, Prisons, and Treatment." In *THCi: The Netherlands Law.*

van der Lippe, Tanja, and Liset van Dijk. 2002. "Comparative Research on Women's Employment." *Annual Review of Sociology*. Vol. 28: 221–41.

Van Evera, Stephen. 1999. *Causes of War: Power and the Roots of Conflict.* Ithaca, N.Y.: Cornell University Press.

Veblen, Thorstein. 1953 (orig. 1899). *The Theory of the Leisure Class.* New York: New American Library.

Ventura, Stephanie J., Joyce C. Abma, William D. Mosher, and Stanley K. Henshaw. 2008. "Estimated Pregnancy Rates by Outcome for the United States, 1990–2004." *National Vital Statistics Reports.* Vol. 56, No. 15 (April 14). [Online] Available July 24, 2009, at http://www.cdc.gov/nchs/data/nvsr/nvsr56/nvsr56_15.pdf

Vito, Gennaro F., and Ronald M. Holmes. 1994. *Criminology: Theory, Research, and Policy.* Belmont, Calif.: Wadsworth.

Vogel, Ezra F. 1991. *The Four Little Dragons: The Spread of Industrialization in East Asia.* Cambridge, Mass.: Harvard University Press.

Vogel, Lise. 1983. *Marxism and the Oppression of Women: Toward a Unitary Theory.* New Brunswick, N.J.: Rutgers University Press.

Von Drehle, David. 2009a. "House of Cards." *Time* (March 9): 22–29.

———. 2009b. "The Moment: 4/5/09, New York." *Time* (April 20): 11.

Waite, Linda J., and Maggie Gallagher. 2000. *The Case for Marriage: Why Married People Are Happier, Healthier, and Better Off Financially.* New York: Doubleday.

Wallerstein, Immanuel. 1974. *The Modern World-System: Capitalist Agriculture and the Origins of the European World-Economy in the Sixteenth Century.* New York: Academic Press.

———. 1979. *The Capitalist World-Economy.* New York: Cambridge University Press.

———. 1983. "Crises: The World Economy, the Movements, and the Ideologies." In Albert Bergesen, ed., *Crises in the World-System* (pp. 21–36). Beverly Hills, Calif.: Sage.

———. 1984. *The Politics of the World Economy: The States, the Movements, and the Civilizations.* Cambridge: Cambridge University Press.

Wallis, Claudia. 2005. "A Snapshot of Teen Sex." *Time.* Vol. 166, No. 6 (February 7): 58.

Wallis, Claudia, and Sonja Steptoe. 2007. "How to Fix No Child Left Behind." *Time* (June 4): 34–41.

Wal-Mart. 2008. "Corporate Facts: Wal-Mart by the Numbers." [Online] Available May 20, 2009, at http://walmartstores.com/Investors/7652.aspx

Warf, Barney, and Cynthia Waddell. 2002. "Heinous Spaces, Perfidious Places: The Sinister Landscapes of Serial Killers." *Social and Cultural Geography.* Vol. 3, No. 3 (September): 323–46.

Watkins, T. H. 1993. *The Great Depression: America in the 1930s.* New York: Little, Brown.

Wattel, H. 1958. "Levittown: A Suburban Community." In William Dobriner, ed., *The Suburban Community* (pp. 287–313). New York: Putnam.

Weber, Max. 1958 (orig. 1904–05). *The Protestant Ethic and the Spirit of Capitalism.* New York: Scribner.

Weil, Andrew T., and Winifred Rosen. 1983. *Chocolate to Morphine: Understanding Mind-Active Drugs.* Boston: Houghton Mifflin.

Weinrich, James D. 1987. *Sexual Landscapes: Why We Are What We Are, Why We Love Whom We Love.* New York: Scribner.

Weisner, Thomas S. 1981. "Cities, Stress, and Children." In Ruth H. Moore, Robert I. Monroe, and Beatrice B. Whiting, eds., *Handbook of Cross-Cultural Human Development* (pp. 783–803). New York: Garland.

Weiss, Roger D., Margaret L. Griffin, and Steven M. Mirin. 1992. "Drug Abuse as Self-Medication for Depression: An Empirical Study." *American Journal of Alcohol Abuse.* Vol. 18, No. 1 (February): 121–29.

Weitzman, Lenore J. 1985. *The Divorce Revolution: The Unexpected Social and Economic Consequences for Women and Children in America.* New York: Free Press.

———. 1996. "The Economic Consequences of Divorce Are Still Unequal: Comment on Peterson." *American Sociological Review.* Vol. 61, No. 3 (June): 537–38.

Welch, Sandy, Myrna Dawson, and Annette Nierobisz. 2002. "Legal Factors, Extra-Legal Factors, or Changes in the Law? Using Criminal Justice Research to Understand the Resolution of Sexual Harassment Complaints." *Social Problems.* Vol. 49, No. 4 (November): 605–23.

West, Cornel. 2008. "The Obama Moment." *U.S. News & World Report* (November 17): 29.

Western, Bruce. 2002. "The Impact of Incarceration on Wage Mobility and Inequality." *American Sociological Review.* Vol. 67, No. 4 (August): 526–46.

White, Jack E. 1999. "Prejudice? Perish the Thought." *Time.* Vol. 152, No. 8 (March 8): 36.

White, Jason M. 1991. *Drug Dependence.* Englewood Cliffs, N.J.: Prentice Hall.

White, Joseph B. 2009. "How Detroit's Automakers Went from King of the Hill to Roadkill." *Imprimis.* Vol. 38, No. 2 (February): 1–7.

Whitehead, Barbara Defoe. 1997. *The Divorce Culture.* New York: Knopf.

Whitelaw, Kevin. 2003. "In Death's Shadow." *U.S. News & World Report.* Vol. 135, No. 2 (July 21): 17–20.

"Why Girls in Rural Areas of India Drop Out of School." 1999. *Women's International Network News,* Vol. 25, No. 1 (Winter): 15.

Wiersma, D., R. Giel, A. DeJong, and C. Slooff. 1983. "Social Class and Schizophrenia in a Dutch Cohort." *Psychological Medicine.* Vol. 13, No. 1 (February): 141–50.

Wilkes, Rima, and John Iceland. 2004. "Hypersegregation in the Twenty-First Century." *Demography.* Vol. 41, No. 1 (February 9): 23–36.

Will, George F. 1999. "An Ironic Agony for the Ivory Tower." *New York Post* (April 25): 53.

Williams, David R., David T. Takeuchi, and Russell K. Adair. 1992. "Socioeconomic Status and Psychiatric Disorder among Blacks and Whites." *Journal of Health and Social Behavior.* Vol. 33, No. 2 (June): 140–57.

Williams, Patricia J. 2000. "Without Sanctuary." *Nation.* Vol. 270, No. 6 (February 14): 9.

Williamson, Celia, and Terry Cluse-Tolar. 2002. "Pimp-Controlled Prostitution: Still an Integral Part of Street Life." *Violence against Women.* Vol. 8, No. 9 (September): 1074–93.

Wilson, Edward O. 1975. *Sociobiology: The New Synthesis.* Cambridge, Mass.: Belknap Press.

———. 1991. "Biodiversity, Prosperity, and Value." In F. Herbert Bormann and Stephen R. Kellert, eds., *Ecology, Economics, and Ethics: The Broken Circle* (pp. 3–10). New Haven, Conn.: Yale University Press.

Wilson, William Julius. 1987. *The Truly Disadvantaged: The Inner City, the Underclass, and Public Policy.* Chicago: University of Chicago Press.

———. 1996a. *When Work Disappears: The World of the New Urban Poor.* New York: Knopf.

———. 1996b. "Work." *New York Times Magazine* (August 18): 26–31, 40, 48, 52, 54.

Winerip, Michael. 2007. "Diversity as Normal as Speaking Chinese." *New York Times* (October 7). [Online] Available May 21, 2009, at http://www.nytimes.com/2007/10/07/nyregion/nyregionspecial2/07Rparenting.html?_r=1

Winslow, Ron. 1997. "Long-Term Economic Hardship Can Be Detrimental to Your Health, Study Finds." *Wall Street Journal* (December 26): B11.

Winter, Greg. 2004. "Wider Gap Found between Wealthy and Poor Schools." *New York Times* (October 6). [Online] Available December 17, 2006, at http://www.researchnavigator.com

Wirth, Louis. 1938. "Urbanism as a Way of Life." *American Journal of Sociology.* Vol. 44, No. 1 (July): 1–24.

Wise, David A. 1997. "Retirement against the Demographic Trend: More Older People Living Longer, Working Less, and Saving Less." *Demography.* Vol. 34, No. 1 (February): 83–95.

Wiseman, Jacqueline. 1991. *The Other Half: Wives of Alcoholics and Their Social-Psychological Situation.* Hawthorne, N.Y.: Aldine de Gruyter.

Witkin, Gordon. 1998. "The Crime Bust." *U.S. News & World Report.* Vol. 124, No. 20 (May 25): 28–40.

Wolf, Naomi. 1990. *The Beauty Myth: How Images of Beauty Are Used against Women.* New York: Morrow.

Wolff, Edward N. 2004. *Changes in Household Wealth in the 1980s and 1990s in the U.S.* Working Paper No. 407. Levy Economics Institute of Bard College. [Online] Available May 11, 2006, at http://www.levy.org/default.asp?view=research_distro

———. 2007. "Recent Trends in Household Wealth in the United States: Rising Debt and the Middle-Class Squeeze." Working Paper No. 502. Levy Economics Institute of Bard College. [Online] Available April 28, 2009, at http://www.levy.org/pubs/wp502.pdf

Wolfgang, Marvin E., Terrence P. Thornberry, and Robert M. Figlio. 1987. *From Boy to Man, from Delinquency to Crime.* Chicago: University of Chicago Press.

Women's Justice Center. 2009. "Sweden's Prostitution Solution: Why Hasn't Anyone Tried This Before?" [Online] Available April 23, 2009, at http://www.justicewomen.com/cj_sweden.html

Wood, Peter B., and Michelle Chesser. 1994. "Black Stereotyping in a University Population." *Sociological Focus.* Vol. 27, No. 1 (January): 17–34.

Woodward, C. Vann. 1974. *The Strange Career of Jim Crow.* 3rd rev. ed. New York: Oxford University Press.

World Bank. 1993. *World Development Report, 1993.* New York: Oxford University Press.

———. 2001. *World Development Report, 2000–2001.* Washington, D.C.: World Bank.

———. 2006. *2006 World Development Indicators.* Washington, D.C.: World Bank.

———. 2007. *2007 World Development Indicators.* Washington, D.C.: World Bank.

———. 2008. *Poverty Data.* Washington, D.C.: World Bank.

———. 2008. *2008 World Development Indicators.* Washington, D.C.: World Bank.

———. 2009. *EdStats.* Washington, D.C.: World Bank.

World Health Organization. 1946. *Constitution of the World Health Organization.* New York: World Health Organization Interim Commission.

———. 2001. *Global Water Supply and Sanitation Assessment: 2000 Report.* Washington, D.C.: World Health Organization. [Online] Available October 31, 2003, at http://www.who.int/docstore/water_sanitation_health/globalassessment/GlobalTOC.htm

———. 2008a. "Disease and Injury Regional Estimates for 2004." [Online] Available July 24, 2009, at http://www.who.int/healthinfo/global_burden_disease/estimates_regional/en/index.html

———. 2008b. *WHO Report on the Global Tobacco Epidemic, 2008.* [Online] Available May 15, 2009, at http://www.who.int/tobacco/mpower/mpower_report_full_2008.pdf

World Resources Institute. 2007. *Earth Trends: Environmental Information.* [Online] Available June 11, 2009, at http://earthtrends.wri.org/pdf_library/data_tables/ene5_2005.pdf

Worsley, Peter. 1990. "Models of the World System." In Mike Featherstone, ed., *Global Culture: Nationalism, Globalization, and Modernity* (pp. 83–95). Newbury Park, Calif.: Sage.

Wren, Christopher S. 1996. "Study Poses a Medical Challenge to Disparity in Cocaine Sentences." *New York Times* (November 20): A1.

———. 1997. "Maturity Diminishes Drug Use, a Study Finds." *New York Times* (February 2): sec. 1, p. 27.

Wright, Quincy. 1987. "Causes of War in the Atomic Age." In William M. Evan and Stephen Hilgartner, eds., *The Arms Race and Nuclear War* (pp. 7–10). Englewood Cliffs, N.J.: Prentice Hall.

Wright, Robert. 1995. "Hyperdemocracy." *Time.* Vol. 145, No. 3 (January 23): 15–21.

Wyatt, Edward. 2000. "Tenure Gridlock: When Professors Choose Not to Retire." *New York Times* (February 16): D11.

Yandle, Tracy, and Dudley Burton. 1996. "Reexamining Environmental Justice: A Statistical Analysis of Historical Hazardous Waste Landfill Siting in Metropolitan Texas." *Social Science Quarterly.* Vol. 77, No. 3 (September): 477–92.

York, Richard, Eugene A. Rosa, and Thomas Deitz. 2002. "Bridging Environmental Science with Environmental Policy: Plasticity of Population, Affluence, and Technology." *Social Science Quarterly.* Vol. 83, No. 1 (March): 18–34.

Youth, Howard. 2003. "Watching Birds Disappear." In Worldwatch Institute, *State of the World, 2003* (pp. 14–37). New York: Norton.

Zagorsky, Jay. 2006. "Divorce Drops a Person's Wealth by 77 Percent." Press release (January 18). [Online] Available January 19, 2006, at http://www.eurekalert.org/pub_releases/2006-01/osu-dda011806.php

Zakaria, Fareed. 2004. "Bigger than Both of Them." *Newsweek* (January 19): 39.

Zanini, Michele. 1999. "Middle Eastern Terrorism and Netwar." *Studies in Conflict and Terrorism.* Vol. 22, No. 3 (July–September): 247–56.

Zernike, Kate. 2001. "Antidrug Program Says It Will Adopt a New Program." *New York Times* (February 15): A1, A23.

Zicklin, G. 1992. "Re-Biologizing Sexual Orientation: A Critique." Paper presented at the annual meeting of the Society for the Study of Social Problems, Pittsburgh (August).

Zimbardo, Philip G. 1972. "Pathology of Imprisonment." *Society.* Vol. 9 (April): 4–8.

Zimring, Franklin E. 1998. *American Youth Violence.* New York: Oxford University Press.

Zogby International. 2001. Poll reported in Sandra Yin, "Race and Politics." *American Demographics.* Vol. 23, No. 8 (August): 11–13.

Zuberi, Tukufu. 2001. *Thicker than Blood: How Racial Statistics Lie.* Minneapolis: University of Minnesota Press.

Zuckerman, Mortimer B. 2006. "The Russian Conundrum." *U.S. News & World Report* (March 13): 64.

PHOTO CREDITS

Dedication: Steve McCurry/ Magnum Photos, iv.

CHAPTER 1: ©Richard Mittleman/Alamy, xxxii (*top*); William Thomas Cain/Getty Images, Inc., xxxii (*bottom left*); Damian Dovarganes/AP Wide World Photos, xxxii (*bottom center*); Conor Caffrey/Photo Researchers, Inc. xxxii (*bottom right*); Steve Cole/Getty Images, Inc.- Photodisc./Royalty Free, 2; ©Michael Reynolds / epa / CORBIS All Rights Reserved, 6; The Granger Collection, 8 (*left*); Iraqi Government/AP Wide World Photos, 8 (*right*); ©Dean Conger / CORBIS All Rights Reserved, 12; Eric Grigorian/Polaris Images, 13; Bill Pugliano/Getty Images, 20 (*left*); Mario Anzuoni / Reuters / Landov Media, 20 (*right*); ©Bettmann/CORBIS All Rights Reserved, 22.

CHAPTER 2: Alan S. Weiner/Getty Images, Inc.–Liaison, 26 (*top*); Slim Aarons/Getty Images, Inc., 26 (*bottom left*); ©Design Pics, Inc./Alamy, 26 (*bottom center*); Henny Ray Abrams/Agence France Presse/Getty Images, 26 (*bottom right*); Eric Risberg/AP Wide World Photos, 28; S. Liss/CORBIS- NY, 37; Charles Bertram/Lexington Herald-Leader/AP Wide World Photos. 38; Bill Olmsted/The Gazette/AP Wide World Photos, 40; H. William Tetlow/Getty Images Inc. - Hulton Archive Photos, 42 (*left*); Cecil Stoughton/©CORBIS, 42 (*right*); Esbin-Anderson/The Image Works, 44; Andrew Lambert Photography/Photo Researchers, Inc., 45; David Grossman/The Image Works, 46; 49; Jeff Greenberg/The Image Works, 51 (*lower left*); Tom Olmscheid/AP Wide World Photos, 51 (*upper right*).

CHAPTER 3: AP Wide World Photos, 54 (*top*); Mark Duncan/AP Wide World Photos, 54 (*bottom left*); Corbis RF, 54 (*bottom center*); Stuart Franklin/Magnum Photos, Inc., 54 (*bottom right*); Declan Haun/Getty Images/Time Life Pictures, 56; Getty Images, Inc. – PhotoDisc, 57; AP Wide World Photos, 59; AP Wide World Photos, 62; Kevin Flemming/CORBIS- NY, 64; AP Wide World Photos, 65; ©Bettmann / CORBIS All Rights Reserved, 67; David McNew/Getty Images, 70; Steve Yeater/AP Wide World Photos, 74; Mark Peterson/Redux Pictures, 75; AP Wide World Photos, 76 (*left*), Laub Gillian, 76 (*right*); Jens Krogstad/AFP/Getty Images, 81; Jim West/Alamy Images, 83 (*upper left);* Fred Greaves/Reuters/Landov Media 83 (*lower left*).

CHAPTER 4: David Young-Wolf/Photo Edit, Inc., 86 (*top*); Lawrence Mouton/Getty Images, Inc.-PhotoDisc, 86 (*bottom left*); Krista Greco/Merrill Education, 86 (*bottom center*); Corbis RF, 86 (*bottom right*); Barry Austin Photography/Getty Images, 88; Lynsey Addario/CORBIS- NY, 89; Jason Kempin/WireImage/Getty Images, 91; ©Janet Wishnetsky/CORBIS, 103; The Granger Collection, 106; Monkey Business/Fotolia, LLC - Royalty Free, 108; Mark Wilson/Getty Images, 110; Manny Millan/Sports Illustrated/Getty Images, 111 (*left*); Butch Dill/AP Wide World Photos, 111 (*right*).

CHAPTER 5: Gail Oskin/AP Wide World Photos, 88 (*top*); CORBIS–NY, 88 (*bottom left*); Jean Michel Foujois/Zefa/CORBIS- NY, 114 (*bottom center*); Zoran Milich/Masterfile Corporation, 114 (*bottom right*), Zigy Kaluzny/Stone/Getty Images, 116; ©B.S.P.I. / CORBIS All Rights Reserved, 117; CHRIS O'MEARA/AP Wide World Photos, 121; Lester Sloan/Woodfin Camp & Associates, Inc., 123; Jeff Greenberg/PhotoEdit Inc.,125; Golden Pixels LLC/Alamy Images Royalty Free, 128; AP Wide World Photos, 129; Penny Tweedie/Alamy Images, 131; Eriko Sugita/Reuters Limited, 133; Penny Tweedie/Alamy Images, 135; ©Bettman/CORBIS, 137 (*left*); David Young-Wolff/PhotoEdit Inc., 137 (*right*).

CHAPTER 6: Jeff Greenberg/The Image Works, 140 (*top*); Richard Lord/The Image Works, 140 (*bottom left*); AP Wide World Photos, 140 (*bottom center*); CorbisRF, 140 (*bottom right*); ©Peter Foley / epa / CORBIS All Rights Reserved, 142; Michael Newman/PhotoEdit Inc., 143; Scott Olson/Getty Images, 147; Bill Aron/PhotoEdit Inc., 151; Mike Powell/Getty Images, Inc. – Allsport Photography, 154; Bettmann/CORBIS- NY, 156; Sonja Fleming/CBS/Everett Collection, 157; Hector Mata/ Getty Images, Inc. - Agence France Presse, 158; W. Lynn Seldon Jr./ Omni-Photo Communications, Inc., 161; Steve Lehman/ CORBIS- NY, 165; ©Justin Lane / epa / CORBIS All Rights Reserved, 166; Bill Losh/Taxi/Getty Images, 168; Les Stone / CORBIS All Rights Reserved, 171; Damian Dovarganes/ AP Wide World Photos, 173 (*left*); ©Jim Wright / Star Ledger / CORBIS All Rights Reserved, 173 (*right*).

CHAPTER 7: CorbisRF, 176 (*top*); ©H. Armstrong Roberts/ClassicStock/CORBIS All Rights Reserved, 176 (*bottom left*); Jack Star/Getty Images, Inc. – PhotoDisc, 176 (*bottom center*); Will Hart/PhotoEdit inc., 176 (*bottom right*); Figure 2 from "Chains of Affection" by Peter S. Bearman, James Moody, and Katherine Stovel from *American Journal of Sociology*, 110 (1):44-91, 2004. Copyright © 2004 by The University of Chicago. All rights reserved. Reprinted by permission of the publisher. 178; CORBIS- NY, 179; Reprinted by permission of The Kinsey Institute for Research in Sex, Gender, and Reproduction, Inc., 181; Hannah Johnston/Getty Images-Entertainment, 186; Sergei Supinsky/Agence France Presse/Getty Images, 188; Radhika Chalasani/ CORBIS- NY, 194; Aman Rahman/Agence France Presse/Getty Images, 197; Toby Talbot/ AP Wide World Photos, 201; Wisconsin State Journal, John Maniaci/ AP Wide World Photos, 203 (*left*); Andy Kropa/ Redux Pictures, 203 (*right*).

CHAPTER 8: Uriel Sinai/Getty Images, 206 (*top*); (c) Underwood & Underwood / CORBIS All Rights Reserved , 206 (*bottom left*); Image Source / Getty Images, Inc., 206 (*bottom center*); Getty Images - Stockbyte, Royalty Free, 206 (*bottom right*); Uriel Sinai / Getty Images, Inc., 208; Courtesy of The National Library of Medicine, Bethesda., 209; (c) Jose Luis Pelaez Inc./ Blend Images/ CORBIS RF. All Rights Reserved. 210; Bob Berg/Getty Images – Entertainment, 216; Jeff Greenberg/Rainbow Image Library, 218; Ernesto Benavides/Agence France Presse/Getty Images, 219; Hank Morgan/Photo Researchers, Inc., 223; Nascimento/REA/SABA, 226 (*left*), Michel Porro/AP Wide World Photos, 228 (*right*); Spencer Platt/Getty Images, 229; ©Brooks Kraft / Sygma / CORBIS All Rights Reserved, 231(*left*); Carl J. Single/Syracuse Newspapers/The Image Works, 231(*right*).

CHAPTER 9: Tao Associates/Getty Images Inc. - Stone Allstock, 234(*top*); Juan Silva/ Getty Images, 234 (*bottom left*); ©Kevin Fleming / CORBIS All Rights Reserved, 234(*bottom center*), David Kelly Crow/ PhotoEdit Inc., 234 (*bottom right*); Lucas Allen White/ Shutterstock, 236; (c) Jeremy Horner / CORBIS All Rights Reserved, 238; Hector Mata/STF/Agence France Presse/Getty Images, 243(*left*); Hector Mata/STF/Agence France Presse/Getty Images, 243(*right*); Andreea Angelescu/ CORBIS- NY, 246; Adam G. Sylvester/ Photo Researchers, Inc., 251; Jerry Cooke/ Photo Researchers, Inc., 253; Ferdinando Scianna/ Magnum Photos, Inc., 257; Randy Matusow/ Randy Matusow, 259 (*left*); Getty Images - Digital Vision, 259;

CHAPTER 10: Jason DeCrow/AP Wide World Photos, 262 (*top*); Gu Xinrong / Xinhua / Landov Media, 262 (*bottom left*); ©Najilah Feanny/CORBIS All Rights Reserved, 262 (*bottom center*); Robert Sullivan/Agence France Presse/Getty Images, 262 (*bottom right*); Anthony Jacobs/ Getty Images, 264; Cale Merege/ Polaris Images, 265 (*left*); Jay Directo/Agence France Presse/Getty Images, 265 (*right*); AP Wide World Photos, 269; Alex Brandon/ AP Wide World Photos, 270; James Steidl/ Shutterstock, 273; AP Wide World Photos, 277; AP Wide World Photos, 278; Jonathan Ernst/Reuters/ Landov Media, 279; Mike Groll/ AP Wide World Photos, 281; David De Lossy/Photodisc/Getty Images, 284; Billy E. Barnes/ PhotoEdit Inc., 285 (*left*); Jeff Greenberg/ PhotoEdit Inc., 285 (*right*);

CHAPTER 11: (c) Viviane Moos / CORBIS All Rights Reserved, 288 (*top*); Robert Ghement/epa/ CORBIS- NY, 288 (*bottom left*); ©Andy Rain / epa / CORBIS All Rights Reserved, 288 (*bottom center*); Corbis RF, 288 (*bottom right*); Jim Young/Reuters/ Landov Media, 290; Joel Stettenheim/ CORBIS- NY, 291; J. Patrick Forden/ CORBIS- NY 294; ©Stephen Morrison / epa / CORBIS All Rights Reserved, 297; David Bacon/ The Image Works, 300; Brown Brothers, 302; Shirley Zeiberg/ Pearson Education/PH College, 304; Sonda Dawes/ The Image Works, 306; Jeff Greenberg/ PhotoEdit Inc., 307; Mary Ann Chastain/ AP Wide World Photos, 310; Joe Raedle/ Getty Images, 313 (*left*); Gilles Mingasson/ Getty Images, 313 (*right*);

CHAPTER 12: Corbis RF, 316 (*top*); Bruce Ayers/ Getty Images - WireImage.com, 316 (*bottom left*); Michael Newman/PhotoEdit, Inc., 316 (*bottom center*); (c) David Turnley / CORBIS- NY, 316 (*bottom right*); Arieliona/ Shutterstock, 318; FOX/Andrew MacPherson/ Photofest, 319; Will Hart/ PhotoEdit Inc., 321; Jessica Rinaldi/Reuters/ CORBIS- NY, 329; David Burnett/ Contact Press Images Inc., 330; Richard Levine/ Alamy Images, 331; ©Ellen B. Senisi, 333; (c) Larry Williams / CORBIS All Rights Reserved, 335.

CHAPTER 13: ©Andrew Fox / CORBIS All Rights Reserved, 340 (*top*); Chris Lowe/ Phototake NYC, 340 (*bottom left*); Bob Daemmrich Photography, Inc., 340 (*bottom center*); ©Iris Coppola / CORBIS All Rights Reserved, 340 (*bottom right*); AP Wide World Photos, 342; Mark Richards/ PhotoEdit Inc., 344; Courtesy of the Library of Congress, 345; Carol Iwasaki/ Getty Images/Time Life Pictures, 349; Will Faller/ Will Faller, 352; T. Lindfors/ Lindfors Photography, 353; Thinkstock/ Getty Images Inc. RF, 356; David Martin/ AP Wide World Photos, 361; Chris Hondros/Newsmakers/ Getty Images, 363(*left*); Douglas Todd/DK Stock/ Getty Images, 363(*right*).

CHAPTER 14: Eric Feferberg/ Getty Images, Inc. AFP, 366 (*top*); Benjamin Rondel/ CORBIS- NY, 366 (bottom left); Bill Aron / PhotoEdit, Inc. (*bottom center*); Jacksonville Journal Courier/ The Image Works, 366 (*bottom right*); ©Mark Avery / Reuters Limited, 368; The Granger Collection, New York, 370; ©Lester Lefkowitz/CORBIS, 371; Courtesy of the Library of Congress, 375 (top); Jacob A. Riis, "In Poverty Gap: An English Coal-Heaver's Home". Courtesy of Museum of the City of New York., 375 (*bottom*); Baxter Street Court, circa 1898. Musuem of the City of New York/The Jacob A. Riis Collection. 375 (*right*); Joe McLaughlin/Home News Tribune/ AP Wide World Photos, 376; Robert Yager/ Robert Yager Photography, 377; Robert Brenner/ PhotoEdit Inc., 383; AP Wide World Photos, 386.

CHAPTER 15: Asia Photopress/Alamy Images, 392 (*top*); K.M. Choudary/ AP Wide World Photos, 392 (*bottom left*); David Turnley/ CORBIS- NY, 392 (*bottom center*); Jeremy Horner/ CORBIS- NY 392 (*bottom riqht*); CORBIS- NY, 394; CORBIS- NY, 405; Lemoyne/ Getty Images, Inc – Liaison, 406; Image Works/Mary Evans Picture Library Ltd, 408; Mark Leong/ Redux Pictures, 411; Tim Graham/ Alamy Images, 415 (*right*); dbimages/ Alamy Images, 415 (*right*).

CHAPTER 16: Wilfried Krecichwost/Zefa/CORBIS- NY, 418 (*top*); Science Faction, 418 (*bottom left*); Bonnie Kamin/PhotoEdit Inc., 418 (*bottom center*); Wayne Lawler/CORBIS- NY, 418 (*bottom right*); Getty Images/Digital Vision, 421; AP Wide World Photos, 425; ©1999 Daniel Beltra/Greenpeace, 430; Ben Osborne/Getty Images Inc. - Stone Allstock, 432; ©Ron Chapple / CORBIS All Rights Reserved, 434; ©Redlink Productions / CORBIS All Rights Reserved, 436; Alex Wong/Getty Images, 437 (*top*); Bill Pugliano/Getty Images, 437 (*bottom*),

CHAPTER 17: AP Wide World Photos, 440 (*top*); ©Leif Skoogfors / CORBIS All Rights Reserved, 440 (*bottom left*); AP Wide World Photos, 440 (*bottom center*); Jason Reed/Reuters/CORBIS-NY, 440 (*bottom right*); Gary Conner/PhotoEdit Inc., 442; United States Marine Corps, 445; Brennan Linsley/AP Wide World Photos, 447; Korea News Service/AP Wide World Photos, 450; Kevin Frayer/AP Wide World Photos, 452; AP Wide World Photos, 453; AP Wide World Photos/U.S. Air Force, 454; AP Wide World Photos, 455; Sgt. Stephen M. DeBoard/United States Marine Corps, 457; Reuters/Mike Segar/CORBIS- NY, 461; Saul Loeb/AFP/Getty Images, 463 (*left*); Lynne Sladky/AP Wide World Photos, 463 (*right*);

NAME INDEX

SUBJECT INDEX

ABOUT THE AUTHOR

John J. Macionis (pronounced ma-SHOW-nis) was born and raised in Philadelphia, Pennsylvania. He majored in sociology and earned a bachelor's degree from Cornell University and a doctorate in sociology from the University of Pennsylvania. His publications are wide-ranging, focusing on community life in the United States, interpersonal intimacy in families, effective teaching, humor, new information technology, and the importance of global education.

Macionis is best known for almost thirty years of work as a textbook author, and his books are the most popular in the discipline. *Sociology* and *Society: The Basics* (both from Pearson) are lively introductions to sociology, and Macionis collaborates on various international editions of these texts. He and Nijole V. Benokraitis have edited the anthology *Seeing Ourselves: Classic, Contemporary, and Cross-Cultural Readings in Sociology.* In addition, Macionis and Vincent Parrillo are authors of the urban studies text *Cities and Urban Life* (Pearson). The latest on all the Macionis textbooks, useful information about our discipline, and dozens of Internet links of interest to students and faculty are found at the author's Web site, http://www.macionis.com or http://TheSociologyPage.com. Additional information, instructor resources, and online student study guides are found at the Prentice Hall site, http://www.pearsonhighered.com.

John Macionis is Professor and Distinguished Scholar of Sociology at Kenyon College in Gambier, Ohio. During a career of more than thirty years at Kenyon, he has chaired the Sociology Department, directed the college's multidisciplinary program in humane studies, led the campus senate, and served as chair of the college's faculty. Most important, he has taught sociology to thousands of students.

In 2002, the American Sociological Association named Macionis recipient of the Award for Distinguished Contributions to Teaching, citing his innovative use of global material as well as new technology in the development of his textbooks.

Professor Macionis has been active in academic programs in other countries, having traveled to some fifty nations. Most recently, he has spent time in the Andes Mountains of Peru, studying Q'ero culture and shamanic healing. He writes, "I am an ambitious traveler, eager to learn and, through the texts, to share much of what I discover with students, many of whom know so little about the rest of the world. For me, traveling and writing are all dimensions of teaching. First and foremost, I am a teacher—a passion for teaching animates everything I do."

At Kenyon, Macionis offers a wide range of courses and regularly teaches both introduction to sociology and social problems. In fact, much of the planning and the content of this text was inspired in the classroom. Macionis enjoys extensive contact with students and each term invites members of his classes to enjoy a home-cooked meal.

The Macionis family—John, Amy, and children McLean and Whitney—live on a farm in rural Ohio. In his free time, John enjoys playing tennis, swimming, hiking, and recording oldies rock and roll (he recently released his third CD, available for a charitable donation—visit http://www.macionis.com). Macionis is an environmental activist in the Lake George region of New York's Adirondack Mountains, working with a number of organizations, including the Lake George Land Conservancy (http://www.lglc.org), where he serves as president of the board of directors.

Professor Macionis welcomes and responds to comments and suggestions about this book from faculty and students. Write to the Sociology Department, Ralston House, Kenyon College, Gambier, Ohio 43022, or direct e-mail to macionis@kenyon.edu